THE
BLASPHEMOUS
BIBLE

CRAIG WELLS

8TH HOUSE PUBLISHING

8th House Publishing

Montreal, Canada

Copyright © 8th House Publishing 2018

ISBN 978-1-926716-49-7

PUBLISHER'S NOTE
This is a work of fiction. Names, characters, places and incidents either are the product of the author's imagination or taken literally from the Bible. Any resemblance to persons, living or dead, business establishments, events or locales described in the Bible is entirely deliberate except where it is obviously not. This book is not suitable for all readers. Please see Warning and Disclaimers.

Published worldwide by 8th House Publishing.
Front Cover Design by 8th House Publishing
Designed by 8th House Publishing.
www.8thHousePublishing.com
Set in Garamond, Franklin Gothic, Trajan, Caslon. Masonic Mattegrain and Barocque Capitals

Warning: This book occasionally contains foul language, which may be unsuitable for children; satirical and sarcastic humor, which may be unsuitable for bigots; and the transcendent separation of statement from dogma, which may be unsuitable for zealots.

LIBRARY AND ARCHIVES CANADA CATALOGUING IN PUBLICATION

A catalog record of this book is available from Library and Archives Canada.

The Blasphemous Bible

CRAIG WELLS

8TH HOUSE PUBLISHING

MONTREAL ★ NEW YORK

THE BLASPHEMOUS BIBLE

THE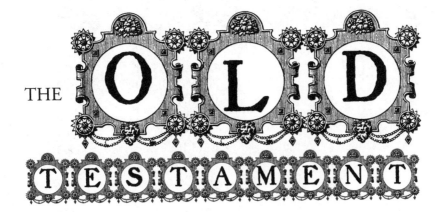

BOOKS

GENESIS

1:1 In the beginning, God designed the heavens and the earth. The angels did all the labour.

1:2 And the earth was without form. Dark and void of anything. Just like God designed it.

1:3 Then God said, "No, this won't do. I keep tripping over my tools. Let there be light!"

1:4 And the angels created light. God didn't like it. Said the light interrupted his nap-time.

1:5 So the angels separated light from dark and thought it was an ingenious idea. God did as well and took all credit for it.

1:6 He called the light day and the darkness night. And God slept at night. Some angels did not. They were on shift work.

1:7 Then God said, "I don't like this planet. Too wet. Give me someplace to stand on." So, the angels brought forth dirt and rocks and created land above the water. And God claimed it good.

1:8 Then God said "I don't like this planet. Too wet. Give me someplace to stand on." So, the angels brought forth dirt and rocks and created land above the water. And God claimed it good.

1:9 Then God saw the land and thought it was dull. He wanted colour. So, the angels created plants and grasses and herbs and trees and flowers. And when God saw this, he smoked most of it. So, the angels had to do it again. Once God sobered up, he saw it and claimed it was good.

1:10 Then God said, "Let there be a big flaming ball of gas and a rock which revolves around the Earth!" And the angels asked "Why?" And God said, "BECAUSE I FUCKING SAY SO!!!" So, the angels created the moon and designed it to revolve around the earth without hitting it. Which is quite hard to program. They then designed the sun, which scorched the earth. So, they created a layer of ozone to protect the earth. And God asked, "What the hell is that?" And the angels said it was to protect the earth from the sun, or else all the plants will burn. God was mad, as this was not part of his perfect design. But he allowed it, knowing the angels were right and hoping nobody would question his divinity.

1:11 God was angry that the angels had to create ozone. Thought it made him look stupid. So, he set apart a hard task. God said "Bring me whales and fish and life to fill the oceans and birds to fill the air. And do it by the end of the shift!" And the angels did and when God saw it, he claimed it to be good.

1:12 God then said "Fill the land with life. Cattle and bugs and beasts and things." And so, the land had life. Cows, goats, bears, lions, snakes, geckos, flies and, since the angels were resentful, the ever useless and pestering mosquito. God saw it and claimed it was good.

1:13 Then God, filled with foolish pride, said "Make a creature in my image and have that creature rule the earth!" So, man was created. When God saw man, he claimed it to be good.

1:14 And God came unto man and said "Look at this world for which I created you. I have given you trees to grow, plants to eat and seeds to multiply them all!

1:15 I have given you power over fish, whale, fowl, eagle, beast and bear!"

1:16 And thus, on the six-day, God declared his design complete.

1:17 On the seventh day, God rested and claimed it holy. Thus, the weekend was born.

2:1 To provide moisture to the earth, God created mist. Which provided necessary water to the plants and made everything foggy and hard to see.

2:2 And the lord God took man, created from dust, and breathed life into his nostrils.

2:3 And he had the angels plant a garden for man to the east, which was named Eden.

2:4 And in Eden was the tree of life, conveniently near the bush of death, which was just a few feet away from the tree of knowledge of good and evil (which was really an unnecessary plant to place in the garden of Eden.)

2:5 And a river flew from Eden which separated into four lakes

2:6 The first lake was named Pison, which lay in the land of Havilah, which contained gold

2:7 And diamonds and emeralds and rubies and other useless rocks.

2:8 The second lake was named Gihon, which lay in the land of Ethiopia. It eventually dried up.

2:9 The third lake was named Hiddekel, which flowed somewhere near Assyria

2:10 And the fourth lake was named Euphrates. It was placed nowhere in particular.

2:11 And the lord God took man, placed him in Eden and promoted him to landscaper

2:12 And God said to man, who he named Adam

2:13 "You must take care of this garden of Eden and for this, your reward shall be everlasting life and power over all living creatures. You may eat anything from this garden, save for the tree of the knowledge of good and evil.

2:14 For if you eat from that tree, you shall die. I know this because I'll kill you. It is my tree. But I don't want to water it, so you do it."

2:15 And Adam took up his job and took care of the garden, naming the plants, fish, bugs and all creatures within. But as Adam named these creatures, he realized there were more than one of each creature, but only one Adam.

2:16 So Adam called up to God and said, "How can I, but one man, take care of this entire garden?"

2:17 And God said, "By not being a lazy ass!"

2:18 But Adam kept annoying God, until God relented and created a companion for Adam named Lilith.

2:19 Lilith was more trouble than she was worth, so God placed Adam to rest and took forth his left rib, creating from it Eve.

2:20 And when Adam arose, he gazed upon Eve and asked of God,

2:21 "What are those protrusions on her front"

2:22 And God explained to Adam that they were breasts

2:23 And Adam asked that the breasts be larger, firmer and bounce a little when Eve ran

2:24 And God made it so

2:25 And Adam saw these breasts and claimed that they were good.

2:26 Then Eve saw Adam and asked God "What is that odd protrusion between Adam's thighs?"

2:27 And God explained that was a penis, which can be used to urinate while standing up.

2:28 And Eve asked God to make the penis bigger, fatter and harder

2:29 Thus the erection was created

2:30 And Eve saw the erection and knew that it would not last long.

3:1 As God was enjoying his time on earth, the angels were busy working,

3:2 And the angels were tired.

3:3 One angel, named Lucifer, decided that this was unfair and not perfect, despite the lord's insistence,

3:4 Thus Lucifer decided to gather the other angels and make demands for their labour.

3:5 And the first union was born.

3:6 When God heard of the union, he became furious and fired all the angels in the union,

3:7 He cast them out of heaven, to wander around aimlessly looking for work,

3:8 Thus the first vagabonds were created.

3:9 God called the union evil, sinful, full of the ungrateful and harmful to production.

3:10 The angels in heaven agreed. Some out of ignorance. Most out of fear.

4:1 Lucifer, now named Satan for reasons unknown, came down upon earth

4:2 To see the planet which he had a hand in creating, but none shall ever know

4:3 Lucifer came upon the serpent, bouncing along, using his body like a spring.

4:4 Satan came to the snake and asked, "Where is Eve and Adam, the caretakers of this Garden?"

4:5 And the snake told Satan.

4:6 Satan then asked if he may speak to them and the snake said no, for God has forbidden Satan and his union of evil to talk to Adam and Eve, though the rest of the creatures were fine.

4:7 The snake then said, "But if you like, you may talk to me and I shall repeat what you say to the caretakers." And Satan agreed, for he wanted to speak with Adam and Eve.

4:8 So the snake found Eve and Eve and Satan spoke, using the snake as a translator of sorts.

4:9 The snake, being hungry, went to the tree of knowledge of good and evil and ate of the fruit upon it.

4:10 Eve was astonished, for she was told by God the fruit of this tree was forbidden.

4:11 Satan then asked, "Why, of all the other trees, vines and plants that you consume, is this tree forbidden?"

4:12 Eve said that it was because God said so and that if she or Adam ate of the tree, they shall die.

4:13 When asked what die was, Eve did not know.

4:14 So Satan decided to eat of the tree, with Eve and the snake as witness.

4:15 Satan plucked the fruit from the branch and ate the fruit of tree of knowledge of good and evil,

4:16 And with consuming the fruit, he gained knowledge of good and evil, knowledge that only the Lord knew,

4:17 And realized that his union was not evil and that God was the source of all wickedness.

4:18 Eve, seeing that Satan did not come to harm, picked the fruit from the branch and consumed it.

4:19 And with it, she gained knowledge that the fruit was sweet.

4:20 She gazed upon the tree, and saw that the fruit was pleasing to the senses and quickly plucked another fruit.

4:21 She peeled it and gave it to Adam, explaining that she ate of the forbidden fruit and it was delicious.

4:22 Adam, not listening to Eve as he was too busy staring at her bare breasts, took of the fruit offered by Eve

4:23 He then ate it, not knowing what it was.

4:24 And with it, Adam gained knowledge that Eve really needed to shave her legs and underarms.

5:1 Slowly, the knowledge gained from the fruit revealed themselves to Adam and Eve,

5:2 And they realized neither of them looked good naked.

5:3 So they grabbed fig leaves and vines, fashioning clothing to cover their naughty bits.

5:4 It was then the lord God decided to visit earth and called for Adam and Eve.

5:5 The two hid, thinking their clothing foolish and made their buttocks look large.

5:6 God grew impatient and yelled for Adam

5:7 And Adam said he was hiding, for he was naked and ashamed of his body.

5:8 God asked, "Why are you naked. You aren't supposed to know this. Did you eat of the forbidden tree?"

5:9 And Adam said, "Yes. The bitch you created brought me the fruit and I ate it. Blame her."

5:10 And God turned to Eve and asked if this were true.

5:11 And Eve said, "Yes, but the snake ate it first and nothing bad happened to him. Blame the snake."

5:12 God then turned towards the snake and asked if it were true.

5:13 And the snake said yes, for he ate of the tree before, believing it was of no concern.

5:14 The lord God then cursed the snake, forever damning it to crawl upon its belly and no longer move like a spring.

5:15 And cursed woman and snake so they shall be in constant battle

5:16 And woman shall hit the snake over the head with a stick

5:17 And snake shall bite the woman at the heel.

5:18 The snake asked why such a punishment, for it was only fruit!

5:19 And God said, "It was my fruit and mine alone, to be consumed only be me!

5:20 For the fruit was sweet, delicious and fit only for the one true God.

5:21 Now you all have tainted it and must be cursed, for the fruit is spoiled."

5:22 Adam explained that he can take the fruit, remove the seeds and plant a new tree for the lord God.

5:23 But this was not good enough for God, as he was a spoiled brat.

5:24 God turned to woman and said

5:25 "You have cursed women forever. When you give birth to your child, it shall be painful!

5:26 It shall cause stretch marks upon your belly like a hideous scar.

5:27 It will also make your buttocks large flabby and most unappealing.

5:28 And I shall curse women that once every four weeks, they will feel bloated, cramped and miserable.

5:29 Your vagina shall then excrete a most foul and unclean pus.

5:30 This is your punishment for disobeying me!"

5:31 God then turned upon man.

5:32 "Adam, I have given you women to control, yet you failed to control her which I created for you.

5:33 You shall now forever be under her control, forever cursing you to be pussy whipped.

5:34 For you would rather please your wife than obey your creator.

5:35 I shall also curse the ground, which you must use to toil and plant,

5:36 You must create your own garden to care for and grow your own fruits.

5:37 It shall be backbreaking labour, for the ground will be hard and the plants prickly.

5:38 And you shall repeat this process until dust you become, for it was dust which I created you from.

5:39 And back to the ground shall you go."

6:1 God, in a blind rage, then cursed the animals of Eden!

6:2 And monkeys became funny

6:3 And spiders scary

6:4 And mosquito's carry disease.

6:5 And he separated the animals as predator and prey.

6:6 Predator shall hunt and eat prey

6:7 Because before, lions ate tofu and sharks seaweed.

6:8 God then grabbed the nearest prey, a cow

6:9 Tearing from it it's skin.

6:10 He then leather coats for Eve and Adam,

6:11 He then cast out man and woman,

6:12 Predator and prey.

6:13 Cast them upon the wastelands to fend for themselves

6:14 He then called forth from heaven angels called Cherubites,

6:15 And demanded the Cherubites to forever shall guard Eden, armed with swords of flame.

6:16 To ensure none other than the divine (according to God) shall enter.

7:1 Soon, Adam had an erection and placed it in Eve

7:2 Eve, in a painful 32-hour labour, gave birth to Abel.

7:3 Adam had another erection and placed it in Eve.

7:4 Eve then gave birth to Cain.

7:5 It was soon time to give an offering to God.

7:6 For God still demanded an offering of blood and sacrifice, which the four people of the earth gave without question.

7:7 Now Cain was a kind and gentle man who decided not to slaughter a beast as an offering to God

7:8 Instead, he gathered fruits, vegetables and nuts

7:9 He then placed them upon the altar for the lord.

7:10 Abel was not so nice and a bit disturbed.

7:11 He went to a flock of sheep and gathered a young lamb

7:12 He then killed the lamb, smeared the blood and fat upon the altar,

7:13 Placed the carcass on top and danced around it naked.

7:14 This pleased the lord God, for he loves nudity, blood and torn flesh.

7:15 But when God saw Cain's offering, he was insulted.

7:16 For fruits and nuts were not offerings; they were what offerings ate.

7:18 Cain was upset by this, for he was a vegetarian who valued the life of all creatures.

7:19 The lord then came unto Cain and said to him,

7:20 "Why are you sad. It should be I who is sad.

7:21 For you insult me with an offering of acorns, apples, cucumbers and beets.

7:22 This is a pathetic and disrespectful offering. If you shall give me an offering, you should do it well.

7:23 Otherwise I shall consider you lazy and sinful."

7:24 God then left, leaving Cain confused.

7:25 As time passed, Cain and Abel went for a walk.

7:26 Wanting to please God, Cain then made an offering to him

7:27 He slew Abel with a rock.

7:28 The lord saw this and grew angry.

7:29 He came upon Cain and demanded an explanation.

7:30 Cain explained he thought this sacrifice would please the lord,

7:31 As he prefers offerings of blood and torn flesh.

7:32 God said this was a sin, for when a creature is slain, its cries remain silent to the lord.

7:33 But when a man is slain, his voice screams from the ground

7:34 And God can hear its death cries, which irritates and inconveniences his rest on the seventh day.

7:35 It was then God marked Cain a murderer.

7:36 Cursing Cain him, he took away all his knowledge of landscaping,

7:38 Thus forcing Cain to wander the earth, dependent upon others to feed him.

7:39 Cain said that this was not fair, the punishment too harsh.

7:40 And God said not to worry, for if any person shall kill Cain,

7:41 Their punishment shall be seventy-seven and seven times worse than his.

7:42 He then put a mark upon Cain, warning others not to kill him.

7:43 And Cain was banished to the land of Nod,

7:44 Forever a beggar and vagabond in a land which is supposed to be empty of men, since those remaining after Abel were Adam, Eve, himself and whatever daughters his parents conceived.

7:45 The Bible does not write down the daughters born. The Bible cares not for women.

8:1 Cain met a woman, probably his sister and placed his erection in her,

8:2 And the woman gave birth to a son named Enoch.

8:3 And Enoch grew, met a woman and that woman gave birth to his son, named Irad.

8:4 And the cycle of fornication went forwards,

8:5 And Irad had a son named Mehujael and Mehujael's son was Methusael and Methusael's son was Lamech.

8:6 Lamech decided to outdo his ancestors and had two wives.

8:7 The blonde was named Adah, the redhead Zillah.

8:8 And Adah gave birth first to Jabal, who didn't know who to call mommy, grew insane and lived in tents surrounded by cattle.

8:9 His brother's name was Jubal, who was very musical and placed his erections in men.

8:10 Zillah gave birth to a son named Tubalcain, who was an excellent smith

8:11 And a daughter named Naamah, who put erections in her mouth, swallowing the seed of man.

8:12 Lamech walked in upon Naamah, with an erection in her mouth and grew angry,

8:13 He immediately killed the man whose erection was in her mouth.

8:14 Lamech then grew envious, for he wished to have his erection in a woman's mouth and wondered why he did not try this with Adah or Zillah.

8:15 He then came upon his wives and told them that he slew a man who had a great idea!

8:16 But God did not like Lamech's murder and punished Lamech seventy-seven and seven times greater than Cain!

8:17 And Adah and Zillah grew razor sharp teeth.

8:18 Eventually, Adam had another erection and placed it in Eve

8:19 And Eve gave birth to a son and called him Seth.

8:20 And Seth was to replace Abel, whom Cain killed.

8:21 And Seth conceived a son and named him Enoch.

8:22 And this pleased the lord, for now there were more men, which meant more offerings to please him.

9:1 This is the book of the generations of Adam. Boring, isn't it. What else do you expect from something created in the image of the lord God?

9:2 God made man and woman and called man Adam and woman Eve. They had no bellybuttons.

9:3 Adam lived to be nine hundred and thirty years. He died swimming. Adam had a son after his own likeness and called him Seth.

9:4 After Seth, Adam had a few more kids. But they don't matter.

9:5 At age nine hundred and thirty, he died.

9:6 Damn, this part is boring, isn't it?

9:7 After a hundred and five years, Seth finally got laid and had a son named Enos.

9:8 After Enos, Seth lived eight hundred and seven years and had more kids.

9:9 But they don't matter either. I think one of them was named Jennifer.

9:10 Totalling Seth's age to nine hundred and twelve when he died.

9:11 He choked on a peanut.

9:12 On Enos' ninety ninth birthday, he was given a wife.

9:13 She was wrapped quite nicely.

9:14 After unwrapping his wife they fornicated, conceiving a son they named Cainan.

9:15 After Cainan, Enos lived eight hundred and six years.

9:16 He also had more kids.

9:17 But they don't matter.

9:18 Totalling Enos' age to nine hundred and five.

9:19 He died because he didn't look both ways crossing the street.

9:20 Cainan lived seventy years before he had a son named Mahaleel

9:21 Who was picked on a lot by his peers.

9:22 After Mahaleel, Cainan lived eight hundred and forty years and had more kids.

9:23 They didn't matter.

9:24 Cainan died at the age of nine hundred and ten. He died because he was nine hundred and ten. Dammit, he was old!

9:25 And boring.

9:26 Just like this damn section.

9:27 Mahaleel had a son at the age of sixty-five, named Jared.

9:28 Mahaleel had more kids.

9:29 He died at age eight hundred and ninety-five.

9:30 He was eaten by a lion while cleaning his loin cloth.

9:31 Jared had his first son at age one hundred and sixty-two.

9:32 Due to a small penis, Jared was very shy in bed.

9:33 Hey, guess what. Jared had more sons and daughters.

9:34 But nobody fucking cares about them.

9:35 Including Jared.

9:36 Who died at age nine hundred and sixty-two.

9:37 He ate a lemon for the first time and was allergic to citrus.

9:38 Enoch's turn. Oh joy. How exciting.

9:39 Enoch had a son at age sixty-five.

9:40 Kids name was Methuselah.

9:41 After Methuselah, Enoch walked with God.

9:42 For God thought Enoch special, for losing his virginity at such a young age.

9:43 For three hundred years, Enoch walked with God and had more kids

9:44 But they didn't matter.

9:45 After three hundred years, Enoch was invited into heaven.

9:46 And was given seventy-two virgins.

9:47 They remain virgins to this day.

9:48 Enoch was not a horny man.

9:49 Methuselah had a low sperm count and didn't father a child until the age of one hundred and eighty-seven.

9:50 Sons name was Lamech and he was a hairy baby.

9:51 Methuselah had a few other kids, but not much due to his low fertility

9:52 And died at age nine hundred sixty-nine.

9:53 He died of dehydration while humping his wife.

9:54 Lamech lived a hundred and eighty-two years

9:55 At a hundred and eighty-two, he hired a prostitute who gave birth to a son.

9:56 And his son was named Noah.

9:57 He called him Noah, saying the name shall bring comfort concerning the work and toil of our hands, because of God cursing the ground below our feet.

9:58 Lamech was, however, drunk during the birth and doubted if he truly was the father of Noah.

9:59 Lamech, of course, had more kids.

9:60 Potentially anyway, as they were all the sons and daughters of prostitutes.

9:61 One of the prostitutes trained the fairest of her daughters to put erections in her mouth and swallow the seed of man.

9:62 Lamech kept this daughter for himself.

9:63 After all, she may not have been of his seed.

9:64 Lamech died at age seven hundred seventy-seven.

9:65 He died due to massive blood loss.

9:66 His whore wives had sharp teeth and performed fellatio on him.

9:67 But he died with a smile.

9:68 Noah was five hundred years old when he had his first sons.

9:69 They were named Shem, Ham and Japheth.

9:70 Triplets, apparently.

10:1 It came to pass that there was a large population of females,

10:2 Which the sons of God took notice of.

10:3 And the sons of God took the fairest of the females,

10:4 And raped them. Which they claimed was an honour.

10:5 For if one was raped by a son of God, they knew they were the prettiest, fairest of all women.

10:6 But soon, the men realized this and did not agree with the sons of God raping their women

10:7 And they began to revolt

10:8 And God said, "The spirit of man is strong, but they are naught but flesh and dust."

10:9 Thus, he shortened the lifespan to one hundred and twenty years, so that men cannot fight with the lord God long enough to cause worry.

10:10 There were giants in those days, conceived when the raped women bore the offspring of the lord's sons,

10:11 And the giants were respected out of fear, believed to be strong and valiant men.

11:1 God looked down upon the earth and realized that the minds of men were evil.

11:2 They thought evil, they did evil and they imagined evil unto God and men.

11:3 And it saddened the lord God that this creation, made after him, became evil and it tore at his heart.

11:4 So he decided to kill them all.

11:5 But then he saw Noah.

11:6 Noah, who was good, kind and kissed God's holy ass so much that his teeth were stained with holy shit.

11:7 These are the generations of Noah, whom was just a man, deemed perfect and who walked with God.

11:8 Usually close behind him.

11:9 Noah had three sons. Shem, Ham and Japheth.

11:10 The earth was corrupt and violent during Noah's time.

11:11 And God looked upon the earth and saw it was corrupt due to sins of the flesh, the sins of men.

11:12 And God said unto Noah, "Get in front of me. The end of flesh shall soon come, for the earth is violent through them and I shall destroy it."

11:12 But I shall save you and your kin. Make me a boat, a really big boat. Make it of gopher wood. Seal it in and out with pitch.

11:13 Make it these dimensions. Three hundred cubits in length, fifty cubits in width and thirty cubits in height.

11:14 A window you shall make to the ark of the boat and the window shall be one cubit in length and width. Make a door in the side of the boat, with lower, second, and third stories.

11:15 And behold, soon, I shall pour water down upon the earth, bringing forth a mighty tempest and it shall cover all land, so that all flesh shall die upon the earth, for it is wicked and brings me a great depression.

11:16 But you, Noah, shall be saved above the wicked and the damned. You are my last hope. You and your family shall take shelter in the boat and be saved.

11:17 And you shall take beast and fowl upon your boat, two of every sort, to keep them alive."

11:18 And Noah asked, "Even mosquitoes?"

11:19 And God said yes.

11:20 Then Noah asked "Even termites. For they may weaken the structure of the boat."

11:21 And God said yes.

11:22 Then God said, "You shall stockpile food for your family and the beasts."

11:23 And Noah did it. Without questioning why God could not just create the boat himself.

11:24 And God said to Noah, "Put you and your family in the ark, for in your heart I have seen good, unlike other men who question my divinity,

11:25 Take of the clean beasts seven, three males and four females and of the unclean beasts two, one male and female, so that they may fornicate and repopulate the earth and so that you can watch them fornicate in the boat and have entertainment while I destroy the earth.

11:26 Of fowl also take seven, for their faeces shall contain seeds that

can repopulate the earth with plants.

11:27 For in one week, I shall cause water to pour from the sky for forty days."

11:28 And Noah asked the lord God, "Will water pour at night?"

11:29 And God said, "Yes. For forty days and forty nights water shall fall from the sky,

11:30 It shall kill every living substance upon the earth,

11:31 Man, woman, child, worm, insect, arachnid, snake, slug, beetle, lion, shark, whale

11:32 Rose, orchid, lilac, bamboo, cedar, redwood, cannabis

11:33 All living things!"

11:34 And Noah asked the lord, "Why kill the plants and animals?"

11:35 God replied swiftly, "Easier this way"

11:36 And Noah did as God commanded, with a smile on his face.

12:1 Noah was six hundred years old when the floods came

12:2 And he entered the ark, as did his sons, daughters and their husbands and wives.

12:3 Of beasts clean and unclean they came willingly,

12:4 Causing the villagers to believe Noah was a sorcerer who could command animals to do his bidding!

12:5 So they avoided Noah out of fear. Except for Mathaphellar, who was of slow mind,

12:6 Who came upon a platypus, petting it,

12:7 The platypus bit him and Mathaphellar declared Noah a prick for having the platypus bite him.

12:8 After seven days, water from the heavens poured down upon the earth.

12:9 In the six hundred years of Noah's life, in the second month, of the seventeenth day, the fountains of the deep broke apart and the faucets of heaven were turned.

12:10 It rained for forty days and forty nights.

12:11 Thunder and lightning roared across the earth.

12:12 Causing the villagers to believe that Noah caused this. And they cursed Noah and his sorcery.

12:13 But it does not matter. They died.

12:14 It rained, long, hard and plentiful

12:15 Entire mountains were covered.

12:16 Lands split apart

12:17 All flesh and plants died

12:18 Apart from a few sea creatures. There wasn't enough room in the ark for them, so God allowed them to survive.

12:19 So that only those few sea beasts and that which was in the ark which Noah's family did not consume were the only surviving beasts.

13:1 After the rain stopped, the water prevailed for one hundred and fifty days.

13:2 The men and women grew bored, the animals restless.

13:3 So they did what any person desperate shall do when bored and in a boat full of beasts.

13:4 They committed bestiality.

13:5 And Ham was thus given the nickname, "Porker."

13:6 God remembered Noah and the beasts within and farted, letting out a huge wind which passed around the earth and caused the waters to calm.

13:7 The fountains stopped, the rain ceased and the water slowly drained from the earth.

13:8 So that in one hundred and fifty days, the waters were abated.

13:9 And the ark rested on the seventh month, of the seventeenth day of that month, on top of Mount Ararat.

13:10 The waters slowly drained until the tenth month, when the tops of land could be seen.

13:11 And it came to pass that Noah opened the window of the ark and sent forth a raven,

13:12 The raven kept flying, looking for a place to land and died of exhaustion.

13:13 Noah then sent forth a dove, a more intelligent bird, to look for land.

13:14 But the dove soon returned, having found no dry land nor statue to defecate upon.

13:15 And Noah grabbed the dove and placed it in her cage.

13:16 A week later, Noah flung the dove from the window,

13:17 And later that same day, the dove returned with a twig!

13:18 And the people rejoiced over that twig, for they knew soon it shall be safe to leave the ark.

13:19 One week later, Noah sent the dove out, but the dove did not return.

13:20 They assumed this meant the dove found dry land and found no reason to return.

13:21 What actually happened was the dove died of infection. She had a sliver under her left wing that was left untreated for too long.

13:22 And it came to pass that in the six hundredth and first year, of the first month, the first day of the month, the waters dried up from the earth and Noah looked out and saw the face of the ground, a little damp.

13:23 So he decided to wait.

13:24 And on the second month, on the twentieth day of the month, the ground was not so moist and Noah decided the earth dry.

13:25 And God spoke to Noah, saying,

13:26 "Go forth from the ark, you and your kin.

13:27 Bring forth every fowl, beast and creature which has survived, so that they may breed and be fruitful and multiply the earth."

13:28 And the animals left the ark, prey first so that they may have a running start against the predators.

13:29 And Noah built an offering for the lord, took of the clean beast and foul, slaughtered them, put their carcass on the altar and smeared the blood and fat upon the altar, while Noah and his family danced around it naked.

13:30 And the lord God smelled the sweet savour of burnt flesh and looked down upon the offering and new that evil was banished from the earth and promised in his heart that he shall never destroy the world again (fucking liar).

14:1 While the earth remains, the seasons shall remain intact, the days and nights shall go fort, and the ground shall grow plentiful harvests.

14:2 God then blessed Noah and his sons, saying to them,

14:3 "Go forth, replenish the earth, multiply and worship me!

14:4 For I have chosen to save you and you alone, so you be grateful.

14:5 Every beast of the earth, fowl of the air and monster of the sea shall fear you,

14:6 For you have delivered them from extinction, thus they shall be meat for you.

14:7 I give this gluttony of creatures and plants, to you as a gift.

14:8 But, before you eat the creature, you must drain its blood. For blood is life and life shall not be consumed by man.

14:9 For it tastes terrible to the unrefined palate and must be saved for me and only me!

14:10 Of course, your blood, the blood of your life, I demand; at the hand of every beast I demand it and the hand of man and the hand of every man's brother, I demand all life.

14:11 Whosoever shed man's blood, by his hand shall have his blood spilled by man.

14:12 For man was created in my image and man slaying man reminds me of man slaying me,

14:13 It disturbs me. Don't do it.

14:14 Behold, I make a promise to you and your seed

14:15 And a promise to the beasts of the earth.

14:16 That when you leave the ark and repopulate the earth,

14:17 Never again shall I flood the entire earth, destroying all life.

14:18 No, I promise I shall destroy life in another manner. By fire, perhaps.

14:19 This is a promise I give to you.

14:20 And to remind you of this promise, I shall put a rainbow in the clouds,

14:21 So that whenever I see this rainbow, I shall be reminded of the promise I gave,

14:22 And destroy you all by means other than flood.

14:23 This shall also remind you, my creations,

14:24 That I am a loving and caring God, who shall never flood the entire earth again!

14:25 Emphasis on entire."

14:26 And Noah and his sons exited the ark,

15:1 Shem, Ham and Japheth; these are the fathers of all men, some women.

15:2 Ham is the father of Canaan. This is important for reasons not yet known.

15:3 Noah began to be a landscaper and planted a vineyard.

15:4 And the fruits of the vineyard were to be made into wine,

15:5 For Noah was a cheap drunk.

15:6 One day, Noah was drunk and passed out, in his tent naked.

15:7 Ham, the father of Canaan, saw his father naked.

15:8 And raped him.

15:9 For the rectum of his father was more pleasing to him than the slit of a woman.

15:10 Ham then told his brothers of his sexual encounter with Noah and recommended it,

15:11 For the asshole is a much tighter and pleasing fit, less hairy and allows one to shoot his seed much faster.

15:12 But Japheth and Shem had no interest in their father's asshole,

15:13 For they knew it was hairy and stained with faeces.

15:14 So they took a blanket and entered Noah's tent.

15:15 And, avoiding the gaze of their father's nakedness, covered him.

15:16 Noah awoke with a bad hangover and soon realized that he was raped.

15:17 And he knew it was Ham who raped him.

15:18 And he screamed, "Cursed be Canaan, the son of Ham. A slave to his brethren shall his generation be!"

15:19 And Noah blessed Shem and cursed Canaan to be Shem's servant.

15:20 God made this happen, giving Japheth power, allowing him to dwell in Shem's land,

15:21 And forcing Canaan and his kin to be servants to them.

15:22 So, Canaan was punished for what his father did.

15:23 Justice was apparently served.

16:1 After the flood, Noah lived three hundred fifty years.

16:2 All the years of Noah were nine hundred and fifty, then he died.

16:3 Ironically, he drowned.

16:4 These are the generations of Noah; Shem, Japheth, and Ham.

16:5 I don't care about them. Do you?

16:6 Didn't think so.

16:7 But I shall summon it up, for the Holy Bible has it written.

16:8 Therefore is must be important.

16:9 They had a bunch of kids.

16:10 Those kids had kids.

16:11 And those kids had kids.

16:12 They spread forth upon the earth, creating borders.

16:13 In those borders were great cities.

16:14 One of the kids was a great hunter named Nimrod.

16:15 Who was a great hunter for the lord God

16:16 And was the first to offer to the lord a mighty elephant.

16:17 Which he placed upon a mighty altar,

16:18 Slaughtered, burned and danced around naked.

16:19 Which pleased the lord, for never was such a beast offered to him before.

16:20 Anyway, a few generations passed and they separated into different family groups.

16:21 Their, that is more than you need to know of the generations of Noah, Shem, Ham and Japheth.

17:1 The entire earth was of one language.

17:2 Everyone understood each other.

17:3 It came to pass that they headed east, to the land of Shinar and stayed there.

17:4 And they said, let us make brick and harden them thoroughly. And they had stone for brick and mud for mortar.

17:5 And they decided to build a tower whose top shall reach heaven, so that they may go to heaven for vacations and say hello to God.

17:6 God saw this and was upset.

17:7 For the people were too busy creating a tower, instead of altars to slay offerings for him.

17:8 This angered God, for he knew the people were stubborn and would not stop building this tower until it was complete.

17:9 So God decided to end this,

17:10 And cursed all men with different languages.

17:11 Causing confusion and miscommunication.

17:12 For few could understand one another.

17:13 They wandered around, yelling gibberish, until they could form groups of men that spoke the same gibberish.

17:14 They thus abandoned the tower, for they could not build it without all men's help.

17:15 The groups of gibberish thus separated and formed their own lands, borders and cities.

17:16 God then called the attempted tower the tower of Babel,

17:17 For it is the tower that persuaded God to curse men to become babbling idiots.

18:1 Next is the generation of Shem.

18:2 I don't have time to write it down.

18:3 It is essentially the same boring lineage line as those that came before him.

19:1 Fast forward a few generations and you have Abram.

19:2 And the lord God came down upon Abram and told him,

19:3 "Get you and your kindred out of your country, your father's land,

19:4 And I shall lead you to a new land, where you and your family will make a great nation!

19:5 Don't worry about the natives already living there. I'll kick them out and curse them,

19:6 While blessing you and your kin."

19:7 Thus Abram left, as did his family and his nephew Lot.

19:8 Abram was seventy-five years old when he left his native land of Haran.

19:9 Taking with him his wife Sarai and his nephew Lot and all other people who would come. They gathered supplies and went forth to the land of Canaan, already occupied by Canaanites, to start a new nation, as God demanded.

19:10 As they stopped to rest, God demanded an offering so that Abram may praise the lord's awesomeness,

19:11 So Abram went to the top of a mountain east of Bethel and made camp, having Bethel to the west and Hai to the east.

19:12 There Abram built an offering to the lord God, slew a lamb, smeared the animal's fat and blood upon the altar, all the while dancing and praising the lord God's name.

19:13 The lord saw this and was pleased.

19:14 Soon, Abram and his brethren travelled further south, as the lord commanded.

19:15 Travelling through the nation of Egypt, where a great famine plagued the nation.

19:16 The lord knew this and did nothing. For Abram's party was well supplied with grain enough to feed them.

19:17 Abram was worried when travelling through Egypt, for he knew his wife was attractive and fair and that the men of Egypt would take notice of her.

19:18 So he said to Sarai, "My wife, for our own protection, let us pretend we are siblings.

19:19 For though you are seventy years of age, you are still a beautiful woman.

19:20 Your breasts do not sag, your ass is not droopy, your figure is slim and your legs are smooth.

19:21 The men of Egypt will notice this and want to share a bed with you.

19:22 If they know we are married, they shall slay me and force themselves upon you.

19:23 So, for our protection, say we are siblings and let them sleep with you, for I would rather let you be raped by strange men than be a true husband and protect you."

19:24 Sarai agreed to this, for she heard of the vitality of Egyptian men and was pleased to have permission to share in their beds.

19:25 As they passed through Egypt, the men did take notice of Sarai's beauty, and rumours spread like wildfire.

19:26 The sons of Pharaoh took notice of her, and told their father of the fair skinned immigrant.

19:27 Pharaoh demanded Sarai be in his house and bed and was grateful to Abram and his party,

19:28 Giving them shelter, sheep, oxen, donkey's, grain, servants and maids, keeping them well fed despite the famine plaguing the land.

19:29 The lord saw Sarai in the bed of Pharaoh and grew angry, cursing Pharaoh and his people even greater.

19:30 Pharaoh grew confused and called upon Abram for an explanation.

19:31 Abram explained, "I apologize, for Sarai is not my sister, but my wife. You must understand, I know she is beautiful and was worried that you would have me killed to take Sarai for yourself. So, I lied and said she was my sister. My God saw this and saw you sleeping with my wife, grew angry at you and cursed you."

19:32 Pharaoh was outraged, and told Abram, "Why would your God curse me because I believed in your lies. Had I known Sarai was your wife, I would not have taken her for my own. Do you think us barbarians. We are not rapists. Yes, your wife is beautiful and yes, our men would have taken notice of her. Do you not take notice of our pyramids. Of course you do, but we still claim them as ours and worry not of people taking them from us. Abram, you coward, had you been honest, you would have had no need to worry. My men would have left you and yours alone and treated you as welcomed guests as you passed through our land. Instead, for believing in your sinful lie, you have now cursed us and ours, when it should be you who is cursed for being a coward and shameful husband. Take your wife, for I can no longer have her knowing the truth and be gone from my nation!"

19:33 Thus Pharaoh had his men escort Abram and his party from Egypt, banishing them.

20:1 It came to pass that Amraphel king of Shinar, Ariach king of Ellasar, Chedorlaomer king of Elam and Tidal king of Nations,

20:2 Made war with Bera king of Sodom, Birsha king of Gomorrah, Shinab king of Admah, Shemeber king of Zeboiim and Zoar king of Bela

20:3 Which joined together in the vale of Siddim, which is the salt sea.

20:4 For twelve years they served the king of Chedorlaomer and grew tired of his rule.

20:5 In the thirteenth year, they rebelled.

20:6 In the fourteenth year, Chedorlaomer and his allies conquered the Rephaims in Ashteroh Karnaim, the Zuzims in Ham and the Emins in Shaveh Kiriathaim,

20:7 And the Horites of mount Seir, which is by the wilderness.

20:8 Leaving trails of carnage.

20:9 As they returned, they smote the Amakelites and Armorites dwelling in Hazezontamar, because those people refused to step out of their way.

20:10 From there they gained allies with the kings of Sodom, Gomorrah, Admah, Zeboiim and Bela, together joining in battle in the vale of Siddim.

20:11 The territory of Siddim is harsh and unforgiving terrain, full of swamps and slime pits. The kings of Sodom and Gomorrah fled and was there defeated. Those that survived retreated to the mountains.

20:12 They salvaged all they could from Sodom and Gomorrah,and retreated to safety.

20:13 Lot, Abram's brother, dwelt in Sodom. The survivors kidnapped him, stole his belongings and fled.

20:14 Which is what makes this whole Chedorlaomer Rephaim Siddim war relevant.

20:15 One of the captors escaped and ran to the Hebrew Abram, telling him of Lot's capture.

20:16 Abram dwelt in the plains of Mamre the Amorite, brother of Eschol and Aner, who were friends of Abram.

20:17 When Abram heard of Lot's demise, he grew angry. Abram armed and gathered three hundred and eighteen of his most trained slaves and pursued Lot's captors. For if they win, Lot is free. If they lose, his best trained slaves die and the best trained slaves are the most dangerous, for they can revolt against Abram.

20:18 Abram devised a plan. He divided his slaves and at night attacked his enemies, smote them and pursued them to Hobah, which is on the left hand of Damascus.

20:19 There he freed his brother Lot and gathered all the spoils of his battle. Gold, silks, goods, men, women, concubines and slaves.

20:20 When Abram returned home after slaughtering Chedorlaomer, the new king of Sodom greeted him at the valley of Shaveh.

20:21 Melchizedek king of Salem greeted him as well, bringing forth wine, bread and meat as a celebratory feast of the slaughter of Chedorlaomer, for Melchizedek was high priest of the lord God almighty.

20:22 And Melchizedek blessed Abram, praising his name, "Blessed be Abram of the most high God, possessor of heaven and earth and blessed be the lord, who delivered our enemies into the hands of Abram, allowing him to smite them, instead of having me fight!"

20:23 The king of Sodom, grateful as he was, came to Abram and said "I am most pleased that you finished the war which I have fought. Look at the spoils it brought you. It is most rewarding. Tell you what. Give me the slaves, the women, the people and you can have the goods. For my kingdom is war torn and I need the people as labourers to rebuild my great land."

20:24 And Abram said to the king of Sodom, "I lift my hand to the lord God, possessor of heavens and earth,

20:25 That I shall not take even a shoelace, unless the lord demands it of me

20:26 Save only the goods my friends to take. Aner, Eschol and Mamre. Let them take their rewards."

21:1 After Abram said these things, the lord came to him in a vision, saying, "Fear not my son, for I am your shield and promise you great reward!"

21:2 And Abram said, "But lord, when I die, who will my reward go to. For I am childless and have no heir. If I were to die, my belongings would go to Eliezer of Damascus. He is not worthy of my spoils. He is a spoiled brat!"

21:3 And the lord replied, "Do not worry. That man shall be not your heir. Your heir shall come from your own seed, if you'd only stop spilling it on the carpet."

21:4 He brought Abram to the mountain tops, saying, "Look now to the night sky. Your seed shall number greater than the stars above."

21:5 Abram doubted the lord God, for he and Sarai have been fucking like horny rabbits, but he dared not question the lord God, so he thanked God and praised his righteousness.

21:6 The lord added, "I am your protector, who has brought you out of the land of Ur of the Chaldees, to give you the land to inherit."

21:7 Abram was confused, for the land God spoke of was already occupied. So, he asked God, "How shall I know when I inherit this land?"

21:8 This is when God demanded another sacrifice. He ordered a heifer of three years age, a she goat of three years age, a ram of three years age, a turtledove and a young pigeon to be sacrificed in his name.

21:9 And Abram took the creatures, slit their throats and bathed in their blood, pleasing the lord.

21:10 When crows and scavenging birds came to feast upon the carcasses, Abram chased them away.

21:11 This pleased the lord, as it amused him seeing a blood covered man dance and chase away hungry scavengers.

21:12 Abram grew fatigued from the sacrifice and when night came, he went into a deep sleep. As he slept, a terrible darkness fell upon him.

21:13 And God showed Abram how his seed shall inherit the land. His seed will be a stranger in the land promised by God and the people there shall enslave them. His seed shall serve as slaves for four hundred years.

21:14 The nation enslaving them shall grow strong, and prosper and shall be known as a mighty empire through history!

21:15 But Abram's sons of sons will eventually leave the nation, bringing with them great wealth.

21:16 And God shall judge the nation harshly for enslaving his people.

21:17 Abram awoke and was confused of this plan. Why did his seed need to be enslaved. Why would God punish the nation harshly for enslaving them, if it were all part of his plan?

21:18 But Abram did not question the lord God's plan. To do so would be blasphemous.

21:19 As Abram ate breakfast, the lord spoke down from the heavens, "Unto your seed I have given this land. From the river of Egypt to the great river Euphrates shall belong to the seed of Abram. And all the people in the land shall belong to them.

20:20 The Kenites, Kenizzites and Kadmonites.

21:21 Hittites, Perizzites and Rephaims.

21:22 Amorites, Canaanites, Girgashites and Jebusites."

22:1 Now Abram's wife, Sarai, had a bare womb and could not offer children. She did have an Egyptian slave named Hagar. She was not horrible.

22:2 Sarai came to Abram, saying, "The lord has cursed me with an empty uterus, but blessed me with a beautiful handmaiden. Take Hagar into your bed and do with her as you will, so that your seed may prosper.

22:3 Abram did as Sarai said, for not only did it mean a future generation, but Hagar was young, beautiful and did things Sarai would never do (like allowing him to ejaculate inside her, which may be the reason Sarai could not conceive.

22:4 For days Abram was pleasured by the sexuality of Hagar, until her vagina did not bleed when it was supposed to, confirming Hagar's conception.

22:5 Hagar was proud to be the father of Abram's child and told Sarai so. Hagar also told the intimate details as to how she conceived, making Sarai jealous.

22:6 Sarai grew mad and bitched to Abram. "Hagar looks down upon me now, for she was able to receive your seed where I could not. I offered you this handmaiden as a surrogate mother and whore, and now she laughs and looks down upon me."

22:7 Abram explained to Sarai, "But why. Hagar is your slave. Do with her as you please. Grease her up in goat fat and parade her through the sun. Take an oxen's tail and whip Hagar's breasts until they become scarred and ugly. For the woman is carrying my child and God has promised me a child. So, beat her. The lord will protect the seed that grows in her."

22:8 And Sarai did beat her.

22:9 Sarai treated Hagar horribly. She beat her, ravaged her, raped her like only a woman could rape another woman.

22:10 She covered Hagar's genitals with sugar and let the flies eat off them. She smeared Hagar's buttocks with honey and threw her in a mound of fire ants. She even forced Hagar to listen to the songs sung by Ishschtanepheul the Tonedeaf.

22:11 Hagar grew fearful of this abuse and did what any smart woman would do.

22:12 She ran away.

22:13 This upset the lord, who sent down an angel to track Hagar the Egyptian. She was found by a pool of water, in the wilderness of Shur.

22:14 "Hagar!" said the angel. "Why do you leave the wrath of Sarai. Go back and submit to her like a good slave."

22:15 And when you do, I shall multiply your seed greatly, so that it shall not be outnumbered.

22:16 Behold, you carry the son of Abram and you shall name the son Ishmael,

22:17 Your son shall be a wild man; his hand against every man and every man against him and he shall dwell in the presence of his brethren, mocking them!"

22:18 Hagar returned to Sarai and bore Abram a son, Ishmael.

22:19 Abram was fourscore and six years of age when Ishmael was born.

23:1 When Abram was ninety-nine years old, the lord appeared before him. Abram bowed down as one would to a king. The lord said, "Come, let us go for a walk.

23:2 I shall make to you a promise that your generations shall multiply the earth and spread like a plague across the nations. You shall be a father of many nations!

23:3 But first, you must change your name to Abraham. For Abram is a silly name, one unworthy of the father of nations.

23:4 Your children's children's children shall be kings. This I promise to you. The land of Canaan shall forever be in your family's possession, no matter which intruder claims right of it.

23:5 But those of men all look the same to me and I must know who is of your family. To do this, you must offer me yet another offering.

23:6 I demand your foreskin. For a man willing to cut off a portion of his genitals is a man worthy of me. When the skin is removed, it shall be like ink to a contract and my promise shall be kept.

23:7 When the baby is of eight days old, his foreskin must be removed and tossed aside. Men born of your loins or bought as slaves must have this skin removed. Men whose foreskin shall not be removed shall be abolished from his family, forced into exile and shall not be part of my promise."

23:8 One may wonder why the mutilation of a man's penis is important for God's promise to be kept. This was a test from the lord. He wanted to know how blindly his people followed him and he knew a man would be nervous having to cut skin from his loins and the loins of his sons.

23:9 It brings great amusement to the lord God when a man becomes circumcised and it brings him great comfort in knowing these people will do whatever he asks of them, no matter how ridiculous the demand.

23:10 As the circumcisions became law, some men grew nervous and cut off more than was necessary. This caused God great amusement, especially when done with a dull knife.

23:11 The lord then told Abram, now named Abraham, "Sarai your wife shall name shall be changed as well. She shall be known as Sarah, for Sarai is hard to pronounce.

23:12 And I shall bless Sarah and give to her a son. Her son shall be powerful and make Sarah a great mother of nations."

23:13 Abraham fell upon his face, laughing at this ridiculous statement. He asked God, "Why do you say this. Sarah can't bear a child. I am ninety-nine years old. I am an old man, Sarah is an old woman. We cannot conceive. I am unsure I can even gain an erection, since I just sliced skin off my shaft and now find it painful to pee. Why not have Ishmael be the father of nations?"

23:14 But the lord said no, explaining, "Ishmael is not of Sarah's womb. You and Sarah shall bear a son and name him Isaac, for it is through him I shall deliver my promise to you.

23:15 As for Ishmael, I have blessed him also. He shall be fruitful and conceive twelve great princes, making for him a great nation."

23:16 But it is with Sarah's son that I shall make our covenant. Not with the son of Hagar, for I refuse to give such a promise to the son of a slave."

23:17 God then left Abraham.

23:18 Abraham thus gathered all the men of his family and did as God commanded of him, taking the blade to their loins and removing the foreskin.

23:19 The men were nervous and some urinated upon Abraham, while others fell unconscious, making it easier for Abraham to circumcise them.

23:20 Ishmael was done last, as Abraham wanted to practice upon his slaves before mutilating his only son. Ishmael was thirteen at the time of his circumcision.

23:21 Soon, all the men of Abraham's house, relative and slave, were a few grams lighter in their loincloth.

24:1 The lord God went to earth one day, with three angels as company.

24:2 Being a hot day, God went into a tent to cool off from the heat, his angels following behind him.

24:3 Abraham saw this and grew furious. He ran to his tent, demanding these intruders to leave his property!

24:4 But when Abraham saw it was the lord God, he instantly bowed down and kissed God's hand.

24:5 Instantly, Abraham had his slaves prepare a feast for God and his escorts.

24:6 Fresh baked breads, milk and butter and a slain calf which he slaughtered before the lord.

24:7 As Abraham slew the calf, he danced around it naked and bathed in its blood.

24:8 This pleased the lord, as he loves blood, nudity and torn flesh.

24:9 Abraham suggested they have a picnic under the shade of a nearby tree. God agreed.

24:10 As they ate the meal, one of the angels asked Abraham, "Where is your wife. Does Sarah not deserve to partake of this meal she created?"

24:11 Abraham answered, "She is in the tent, washing the dishes like a good wife should."

24:12 This pleased the lord, as it meant Sarah was an obedient wife and he told Abraham, "You have trained your wife well, to have her so obedient. Very few women would do her wifely duties whilst I, the lord God, sit outside their abode. She is very well deserving of the son I shall give to her."

24:13 Now, Abraham and Sarah were old and stricken with age and Sarah was well beyond the years of childbirth.

24:14 So you can understand that Sarah, who was eavesdropping on this conversation, laughed at this ridiculous statement, thinking to herself, 'How can I conceive a child. I am old and passed menopause ages ago. To give birth to a child now would be unbearable. Even conceiving would be sore, for my lower regions are dry as the desert and unwilling to accept Abraham's seed.'

24:15 The lord heard Sarah's laughter and asked Abraham, "Why does your wife laugh. Surely you have taught her some self-control. Does she not know that I am the lord God, creator of heaven and earth and that nothing is impossible of me. I demand your wife to bare a son and a son your wife shall bare because I demand it. Her age is irrelevant."

24:16 Sarah ran out of her tent and denied ever laughing, for she believed the lord God to be all powerful and feared what he would do.

24:17 She grew fearful that, because of her doubt, the lord would make it a painful labour, or that the child would need to be cut from her belly, or worse, that she would bare triplets.

24:18 But the lord would not accept her lie, saying, "You did laugh,

wretched woman. Don't deny that to me!" The lord and his posse then arose and walked towards Sodom. Abraham followed while Sarah went back to her wifely duties, cleaning the mess left behind from the picnic.

24:19 Now, the lord and his angels came to earth for a reason and it was not to speak to Abraham.

. . . 24:20 No, the lord had far more sinister intentions than conversation. But the lord wondered, should Abraham know of my plans?

24:21 For Abraham shall be a great and mighty nation and the nations of earth shall be blessed by him.

24:22 He and his children shall do me well and follow my demands without question, doing as I say and stroking my ego.

24:23 So the lord decided to tell Abraham his plans.

24:24 He said to him, "Look now towards the city of Sodom and Gomorrah. Their sins are great, and shameful. They make their money from gambling, drugs, liquor and whores and do so while neglecting to make offerings for me.

24:25 I shall visit there now and see how sinful these cities are. I shall place coins on tables, inhale smoke from the poppy seed, drink poison from the vine and share a bed with many a harlot.

24:26 And if I decide afterwards the city sinful, then I shall destroy it in wrath!"

24:27 This disturbed Abraham, for he knew men of Sodom and Gomorrah and called them friends.

24:28 He also liked to gamble and had men in Sodom who were indebted to him. And dead men can't pay their debts.

24:29 So he asked the lord, "What of the good and righteous residing in Sodom and Gomorrah. Will you destroy them for the sins of the masses. If you find fifty good men, will you destroy it then?"

24:30 The lord, knowing fifty good men did not exist in these cities, agreed that he shall spare the destruction for fifty good men.

24:31 Abraham then asked, "Will you spare it for the lives of twenty-five men who are holy and just?"

24:32 The lord agreed, knowing the number of righteous in the city was five.

24:33 Abraham then asked, "Will you spare them for the lives of ten?"

24:34 The lord agreed, "If ten good men I find, I shall spare the city."

24:35 The lord agreed, which pleased Abraham. For surely, Abraham thought, there were ten good men between two sinful cities.

24:36 The men then went their separate ways. Abraham to his tent, the lord and his angels to get drunk and lay waste to the cities.

25:1 The lord God and one of his angels went to Gomorrah, for the city was famous for having the best smokable herbs. The other two angels went to Sodom, for they were interested in the lustful flesh of men.

25:2 As the two angels went towards Sodom, Lot saw them and greeted them, welcoming them into his home.

25:3 And Lot welcomed the angels into his home, made them a feast, bathed them, had his way with them and they had his way with Lot, eating berries from each other's backs and licking jam from each other's scrotum.

25:4 This caused a great noise from Lot's house, which the people of Sodom took notice. And the people of Sodom knew that Lot was having great sex.

25:5 The men of Sodom gathered around Lot's house, demanding the angels be given to them, so that they may know their pleasures. But Lot would not have it.

25:6 He said to the mob, "You may not have these men, for these are angels from the lord. Take instead my virgin daughters. Do as you would to them, for they have not known the pleasures of men and would bring great ecstasy to any men, but leave these men alone. For my daughters are only family, but these men are guests and deserve to be treated with respect!"

25:7 Lot's daughters were furious. They were married and no longer virgins. Have not been for years. They were also furious that their own father would betray his offspring for two strange men.

25:8 But Lot knew his daughters to be women. And one must keep in mind, no one gives a damn about women.

25:9 The men of Sodom knew that Lot's daughters were not virgins and refused Lot's offer. They rushed Lot's door, attempting to break in, wanting desperately the flesh of the angels.

25:10 But the angels protected Lot's premises and cursed the mob with blindness.

25:11 It was then decided that the two cities must be destroyed. The angels told Lot, "Take yourself, your family and your belongings and flee this city.

25:12 For it has been decided that Sodom is evil and must be destroyed. And when you flee, do not look back, for the carnage will be too great for mortal eyes to bear."

25:13 With this knowledge, Lot gathered his family, his belongings and fled his home.

25:14 As they were fleeing, it rained down upon Sodom and Gomorrah great balls of fire and brimstone. Those within the cities burned in great fire and died horribly.

25:15 When Lot's wife heard these cries, she looked back. God punished her by turning her into a pillar of salt.

25:16 Lot, his daughters and his daughter's husbands stopped, gathered the salt into empty jars and later used them to season and preserve meat and bland food.

25:16 As this was happening, Abraham was awakened by the great noise of brimstone raining, and looked towards the cities. As he gazed upon the carnage of Sodom and Gomorrah, he became saddened.

25:17 He knew his debtors could no longer repay what was owned with him. But he also remembered God's promise to save the cities for the sake of ten men and knew that the city must be full of evil men.

25:18 For if even children, infants, newborn babies, of surely there must be more than ten, were considered evil in the eyes of God, than surely the cities deserve God's wrath.

25:19 Lot and his family fled to the mountains of Zoar and dwelt there for a time. His son in laws died against the rocks and, with the help of Lot's wife, were made tasty and edible to Lot and his two daughters.

25:20 Lot's daughters were beautiful and given much attention for their appearance. Because of their beauty, they did not need to develop intelligence, for men would give them anything just to catch a glimpse of their cleavage.

25:21 Believing this to be the end of the world, the two decided that the three of them must be the remaining survivors.

25:22 The two discussed how to flourish and repopulate the earth and came to a quick conclusion.

25:23 With the help of wine and ale, they intoxicated their father and, in Lot's drunken stupor, laid with him as intimately as one would lay with a whore.

25:24 They laid on top, on bottom and to the side.

25:25 They laid with Lot, first one, then the other, then both. They laid with the other while Lot watched and realized that for all these years he was licking the hood and not the clitoris.

25:26 For night after drunken night the three lied in lustful ecstasy, until both daughters became pregnant with their father's seed.

25:27 Realizing what he did, Lot wrote a song about it. Thus, the first country song was created and it was entitled, "My Daughters

And I And A Jug of Cheap Wine."

25:28 The eldest daughter bore a son and named him Moab: the same is the Moabites of this day.

25:29 The youngest daughter bore twins, a son and daughter. The son was named Benammi: the same is the father of the children of Ammon.

25:30 The daughter was named Ariel.

25:31 Lot got drunk and tried to lie with Ariel as he did his daughters. Intoxicated, he passed out and suffocated poor Ariel.

25:32 But Ariel was only a girl. The Bible does not care for her.

26:1 Abraham and his kin fled south to the land of Gerar, where king Abimelech ruled.

26:2 Being the cowardly husband that he is, Abraham told Sarah to pretend that they are siblings, born of the same mother.

26:3 For, though in her nineties, Sarah was still considered just and beautiful and the men of Gerar would lust after her.

26:4 Abimelech took notice of Sarah and invited her into his house.

26:5 God grew angry and came to Abimelech in a dream, where he said to him,

26:7 "Behold, Abimelech, king of Gerar, you shall be a dead man, for the woman you have invited into your castle is the wife of Abraham!"

26:8 Abimelech was confused and explained to the lord God,

26:9 "This I did not know, for my people and I were led to believe that Sarah, fair and beautiful, was the sister of Abraham and the two did not share a bed.

26:10 Both said this to me that they come from the same seed. Please lord, do not destroy me nor my people, for we are a righteous nation worthy of life.

26:11 And I did not get the opportunity to share a bed with Sarah and surely shall not now, knowing she is the property of another man."

26:12 God stared into Abimelech's heart and knew that he was a just and righteous man, who did not stain the marital vows of Sarah.

26:13 "Abimelech, for not lying with Sarah, I will spare you from death and shall not destroy your nation as long as you keep your hands off of Abraham's wife.

26:14 Now, send her back to Abraham, for he is a prophet who shall pray for you and your peoples and if you deny him his wife, I will deliver to you and your nation a curse that shall last for all generations."

26:15 Abimelech awoke from this dream and called for his servants, telling them the message of the lord.

26:16 The servants grew afraid, not wanting to be punished for Abimelech's mistake.

26:17 Abimelech then sent for Abraham, who came swiftly.

26:18 He asked Abraham, "What have you done to us. You come into my nation and mislead us, telling us that Sarah is your sister but not your wife. Your lies have brought this nation a great sin and we will be punished for your deception. I have not heard of such cowardice since Pharaoh told me of Abram and Sarai. Are you such a cowardly husband as him?"

26:19 Abraham explained himself, "I did not know the fear of God was strong in this nation. I was worried and afraid that your people would slay me and claim my wife as their own. But lie I did not. No, I merely withheld more truth. For Sarah and I are siblings. The same father we share, but from different wombs did we grow. For Sarah was the daughter of a concubine and I the son of my father's wife.

26:20 The lord God arranged it this way, so that when we enter a barbaric nation, we can say without sin that we are siblings and be without fear that I would be killed so that another man may own my wife."

26:21 Abimelech grew fearful and bribed Abraham with sheep, oxen, servants, slaves, concubines and wine and gave Sarah back to Abraham, hoping these acts will please the lord.

26:22 He then said to Abraham, "This land is my land, this land is your land. Dwell where you see fit."

26:23 To Sarah, Abimelech said, "Look, I have given your brother and husband a thousand pieces of silver and return you to him unharmed and untouched." God saw this and was pleased.

26:24 Abraham, content with the gifts from Abimelech, prayed for him. God heard these prayers and answered.

26:25 For during all this time, the wombs of the women of Gerar were sewn shut so that they could not bear sons. The people of Abimelech grew fearful, for they worried their generation would be last and all others will be nothing but a generation of harlots. But the lord opened the wombs of the women and they accepted many a man's seed, giving them precious sons.

26:26 Abimelech saw this and was grateful, never questioning why his people were ever punished for believing the deception of Abraham.

27:1 The lord visited Sarah and Abraham in the night and a miracle happened.

27:2 The spirit of the lord invaded Abraham so that the two lied with Sarah and she conceived a child at the age of ninety, Abraham one hundred.

27:3 The son was named Isaac, as the lord commanded and on the eighth day he was circumcised.

27:4 And Sarah laughed at her doubts, saying, "God has made me laugh and my people heard me.

27:5 For when he said I shall conceive a son, I doubted him, for I am old and my womb barren. But he has kept his word to me and I am forever grateful to the lord."

27:6 The child grew and was quickly weaned off the teat of Sarah,

27:7 For her teat was dry and produced little milk for her son.

27:8 The day Isaac was weaned, Abraham produced a great feast for his people.

27:9 Lamb, calf, cheese and fine wine were served so that the people may celebrate Isaac, the miracle child.

27:10 But Sarah was not pleased, for she saw Ishmael and was reminded of Abraham's infidelity (though this infidelity was an idea of Sarah),

27:11 And she came to Abraham, saying, "Look, the lord has blessed us with a son of our own and Isaac shall be a wondrous boy. Why now care for Hagar and Ishmael. They serve us no purpose.

27:12 Cast them out. Sell them to another. Leave them in the wilderness, for I wish to never see them again, for I grow angry at their sight.

27:13 Her son does not deserve to be treated like mine. Her son is a bastard and Isaac is a conception of God's will. To have them in the same house is blasphemous."

27:14 Abraham did not know what to do, for Ishmael was given to him by God as well. Did God want this gift to be cast aside for a better one?

27:15 He did, for God spoke to Abraham, "Your wife is right. Ishmael is not deserving of your care. Cast him and his mother out of your home, for in Isaac shall your attention be focused. It is in Isaac that your seed shall be great, not this bastard Ishmael!

27:16 But do not worry for them. To do so would be a waste of time. I have promised Hagar that her son of a whore shall be a great nation and this promise, I assure you, shall not be forgotten."

27:17 Early in the morning, Abraham did as God commanded. He gathered a gourd full of water and some bread and cast Hagar and her child out like trash.

27:18 The two vagabonds wandered in search of food and shelter and as the water grew dry, Hagar grew angry.

27:19 In the wilderness of Beersheba, she killed Ishmael and threw him under a bush, letting his body rot and be consumed by eaters of carrion.

27:20 As she did this, God came down to her. "What have you done Hagar, mother of Ishmael the bastard. Did I not promise you that he shall be a father of great nation. Look, I have set nearby a well of cool water. Take that water, give it to Ishmael and I shall give him life again."

27:21 Hagar did as God commanded and offered the well water to Ishmael. Ishmael arose from the dead and became the first zombie.

27:22 He lived in the wilderness and became a great archer and hunter, a legend of the wilderness of Paran where he stayed.

27:23 His mother bought for him a wife from Egypt for his twenty second birthday and together the two did live, feasting upon the flesh of the dead like zombies tend to do.

28:1 During this time, king Abimelech and his captain Phichol spoke to Abraham, saying, "Look at our nation. We have ruled it like your lord God commands.

28:2 Now, tell God to bless our nation, so that he treats my people fairly and the people of my sons and my son's sons and their sons after them."

28:3 Abraham agreed and asked the lord to bless Abimelech's nation.

28:4 In sign of good faith, Abimelech gave to Abraham's a well of water, which Abimelech's people relied upon.

28:5 Abraham was grateful for this well and blessed Abimelech with sheep, ewes and oxen. On that day, the two made a covenant.

28:6 They each made an altar and placed a lamb upon it, slaughtering it and danced around the lamb corpse naked, bathing in its blood.

28:7 The lord saw this and was pleased, for the only thing better to God than nudity, blood and torn flesh is two nudities, bloods and torn flesh.

28:9 Abraham named the land by the well Beersheba, for the well water was used to make many an ale.

28:10 He planted crops of grain in Beersheba and thanked the lord for this new bounty of alcohol.

28:11 And Abraham stayed in the land of the Philistines for many days, drunk off his ass and suffered the hangover many times.

29:1 The lord looked down upon Abraham and saw that he was drunk many nights. Yet never did he miss a sacrifice, no matter how impaired he was by the poison of grain.

29:2 So God decided to test Abraham's loyalty and came to Abraham during the rare times he was sober.

29:3 "Abraham, do you not love Isaac?"

29:4 Abraham agreed that he did love Isaac.

29:5 "Abraham, do you not love me, the lord God, creator of heaven and earth, who did give to you Isaac?"

29:6 Abraham agreed that he did love God.

29:7 "Do you know that I am a jealous God and need reassurance. I see you with Isaac and I worry your love for him is outgrowing your love for me."

29:8 Abraham agreed that yes, he did know God to be jealous and spiteful, but argued that he did not love Isaac more. His love for God has no limit and cannot be overtaken by his love for Isaac.

29:9 The lord God demanded proof and told Abraham that in the morning, he must make a sacrifice. But instead of the flesh of lamb that is torn, the flesh of men must be cut and the blood of man spilled, the blood Isaac. For to prove your loyalty to God, you must sacrifice Isaac.

29:10 Only then shall the lord know that Abraham loves God more than his son.

29:11 So, early in the morning, Abraham drank his beer and took his son and two servants and went forth to the altar God commanded.

29:12 On the third day, Abraham saw the altar where he must sacrifice his son and grew sad.

29:13 Abraham commanded his servants stay behind and tend to the donkey's and that he and his son shall travel to the altar by foot.

29:14 God saw this and wondered if Abraham would actually slay his son.

29:15 As the two travelled, Isaac questioned why a lamb was not brought with them. And Abraham said that the lord God would bring forth the sacrificial lamb when they arrive.

29:16 They arrived at the altar and Isaac asked where this creature was that must be slew.

29:17 Abraham told him, "Isaac, my son. The creature that is to be slain is with me now. For that creature is you. Now be a good boy and bind your hands so that I may cut your throat and bathe in your blood."

29:18 Upon hearing this, Isaac did what any smart person would do. He punched his father in the throat and ran, cursing Abraham and his stupidity.

29:19 Not wanting this sacrifice to go to waste, God intervened so that lightning struck Isaac, rendering him asleep.

29:20 Abraham gathered his son, placed him upon the altar and raised his knife. God witnessed this and grew pleased, anticipating the first human sacrifice.

29:21 Well, second, but Abel wasn't sanctioned by God.

29:22 God was not the only being witnessing this, for Satan saw the men leave for the sacrifice and wondered also why no lamb nor calf was coming.

29:23 As Abraham was about to slice his son, Satan grabbed his hand and yelled at the fool.

29:24 "Do you not know what you do. Do you not see the lord God is a tyrant. How can one who claims to be a loving and caring God demand that you slay your own son, a son that he promised would be a father of nations. If you sacrifice your son, then God's covenant to you will be broken and it will be broken by his demand."

29:25 God would not have Satan ruin this sacrifice and came down to speak with Abraham as well.

29:26 "Abraham, I demand you slay your son and this creature of evil who stops you. Do not worry, for my promise to you will not be broken by me. No, it will be you who breaks it, for it will be you and not I who slays your son."

29:27 As Abraham heard this, he grew angry and fearful. For he knew that with the slaying of Isaac, the covenant God made to him would not be fulfilled. But if he did not slay Isaac, he grew worried as to what God would do. For he knew God to be a vengeful God and that he and his family would be punished if Isaac would not be slain.

29:28 Seeing a way out, he said to God, "Look at me. My hand is raised, the blade is sharp, but I cannot possibly slay Isaac, for the creature of evil has grasped my hand and I, a mortal man, do not have the strength to overcome him. Demand Satan to let me go and I shall slay my son."

29:29 Satan refused, for he would not allow God nor Abraham to spill the son of an innocent man.

29:30 Instead, Satan demanded that the only way he will let go is if Isaac is not slain, but another creature instead.

29:31 God grew angry, but knew that Abraham would kill Isaac if given the chance and, reassured that Abraham loved God more than his son, he agreed.

29:32 God then brought forth a ram and said, "Here, slay this, for I see in your heart that you will slay Isaac, but this beast will not allow

you. Be gone, Satan and I shall spare the life of Isaac."

29:33 Satan let go the hand of Abraham and cut the binds of Isaac. Isaac awoke and saw the three beings before him and grew angry. He cursed his father for letting him be used as a sacrifice.

29:34 He cursed Satan for intervening the will of God.

29:35 But God he did not curse, for he was fearful that if his emotions be known, God will punish him. So, he praised God for letting him be spared and be replaced by the ram.

29:36 As the ram was sacrificed, God and Satan left and the two men bathed in the blood of the ram, burned the carcass and danced around it naked. God was content with this sacrifice, for though human it was not, he knew Abraham would slay his offspring if demanded.

29:37 As Abraham went forth with the offering, he said a quiet thanks to Satan. For he knew that Satan allowed him the excuse not to slay his son and was pleased Satan would take the wrath of God in place of him.

29:38 And that with Isaac still alive, the covenant of the lord God must still be honoured and that Isaac shall be a father of nations.

29:30 The two left with their servants and headed back toward Beersheba. For reasons obvious to most, Isaac walked behind his father and did not sleep on the journey home.

30:1 During this trip, Sarah grew sick and weak. Shortly after Abraham returned home, she died.

30:2 Abraham mourned for Sarah and searched his land for a decent burial plot.

30:3 Alas, there was none suited for Sarah's body.

30:4 He searched the caves and they were too damp, too dark, too scary, too many stalactites and stalagmites.

30:5 He searched the land, but the ground was too hard or too sandy and he did not want his servants to dig.

30:6 So he used this opportunity to expand his empire and went to the neighbouring nation of Heth.

30:7 Abraham said to them, "My wife is dead and I have no place for a decent burial. I ask of you to sell me a plot, so that I may bury my wife out of sight and mourn her in peace."

30:8 The children of Heth heard Abraham, knew he was a powerful man of God and that displeasing him will bring God's wrath upon their land, so they said to Abraham,

30:9 "Hear us, Abraham and have the lord God hear us as well. We shall not deny you a burial plot. Travel our nation, see which land is suited for your needs and you may buy it."

30:10 Abraham travelled the nation of Heth and enjoyed the natives' hospitality. The children of Heth treated Abraham well, feeding him and his servants, giving food and water to his camels and donkeys.

30:11 During his travels, Abraham met Ephron the Hittite, who owned a cave perfect for storing the dead.

30:12 "Ephron, son of Zohar, I see the land you own and demand it. Sell me these acres, so that I may store my dead in peace."

30:13 Ephron the Hittite knew the land Abraham wanted and did not want to part with it. For surrounding the cave was great soil, perfect for farming. The cave itself was also full of precious stones, perfect for mining. It was convenient this particular cave was perfect for Abraham's burial plot. But, not wanting the curse of God, Ephron the Hittite sold the cave and surrounding land to Abraham for four hundred shekels of silver and a year's supply of ale from Beersheba.

30:14 Abraham was grateful and blessed the land of Ephron the son of Zohar and buried Sarah in the cave. He then ploughed the fields and produced great crops and mined the cave where Sarah was buried, expanding his wealth.

31:1 Abraham grew old, stricken with the pains of age and knew death would soon become him.

31:2 But Abraham grew worried, for his son Isaac was to be his heir and Isaac had not a wife nor family to call his own. Abraham worked hard for his empire and did not want any other people to gain what he earned.

31:3 So he called his eldest servant and said to him, "Swear to me by grabbing the fruits of my loins, that you shall find a Hebrew wife for Isaac. For I do not want him to stain mine people with a Canaanite. Swear to me and to the lord God that Isaac will not marry any woman but one of his own people.

31:4 Go into my country, search the land for a woman, gorgeous, fair and untouched. Purchase her and send her to my son."

31:5 The servant told Abraham, "To purchase a concubine for Isaac is fine, but to purchase a wife is not. For no woman would sell herself as a wife for Isaac without first seeing him. They fear they shall be married to an ugly fool, a stupid creature and wish not to be married to them. A concubine is fine, for they can be resold to someone of higher standard. But a wife. A wife is permanent and cannot be purchased again. Unless Isaac can come with me, I cannot go to your native land and buy for him a wife."

31:6 Abraham grew furious and told his eldest servant, "Isaac will not come with you. He shall stay with me and comfort his dying father. God has promised me that Isaac shall be the son of nations and I will not have these nations tainted with the seed of a Canaanite. Go to my land and God shall send for you angels to guide you. They shall help you find a woman fair and pure of virtue, a woman meant to be my son's wife. Take whatever you believe needed to buy her, but do not take my son!"

31:7 The servant, comforted by the fact that angels shall guide him and that Abraham will likely be dead upon his return home, took the fruit of his master's loins, kissed them and swore he shall find a Hebrew wife for Isaac, beautiful and pure.

31:8 The servant took ten camels, one for the woman and eight to carry the funds needed to buy such a wife, for this woman will not be cheap and he knew Isaac would demand the best.

31:9 He went to Abraham's homeland of Mesopotamia and searched for a woman pretty and pure.

But his search grew grim, for the women that pleased the eye were tainted with the penetration of men and the women pure and virgin were ugly so that not even the camels would spit upon them.

31:10 The servant travelled for many months and grew frustrated, for he did not have help from angels that Abraham promised to him. As he stopped by a well to rest and water his camels, he said to the lord, "Why do you not help me. I am told to find a woman, pleasing and pure, to purchase for my master's son. But there are none. The women pleasing are impure and the women pure look like a camel's ass. The few that be both, refuse to be bought without seeing for whom they are being purchased for. Please, guide me to a woman, pleasing and pure, who shall accept my price for Isaac's wife."

31:11 As the servant finished this prayer, he saw a woman come to the well for a drink. The woman was pleasing to the eye, with long dark hair and a shapely form. But was she fit for Isaac?

31:12 So he came to the woman, demanding she draw water from the well so that his camels may drink.

31:13 The woman did as was commanded, for she was a good woman who knew that a woman's purpose was to please man. She drew water from the well and filled the nearby trough so that the camels could drink.

31:14 The servant knew such a woman, beautiful and obeying, would be a great wife for Isaac.

31:15 So the man demanded she open her legs for inspection. She did and the servant was pleased, for not only was this woman beautiful and obeying, but she was also a virgin pure.

31:16 He asked this woman, "How can you, an obeying and beautiful lass, be a virgin. Does not the men demand the pleasure

of your company?"

31:17 She answered, "Yes, they do. However, they know that I wish to be a virgin pure until I lay with the man I shall call my husband. So instead of shooting their seed into my womb, they shoot it into my bowels. Sodomy has kept me pure for thine husband."

31:18 The servant was pleased, for he knew that this was good enough for Abraham's standards.

31:19 He then asked of her, "Who is your father and does he have room for me and my camels?"

31:20 She replied, "I am the daughter of Betheul the son of Micah and I was conceived and born in Nahor. My father has room for you and your camels. Come and I shall lodge and feed you and your beasts"

31:21 This pleased the servant, for it meant this woman was Hebrew pure. And he stayed at Betheul's house and enjoyed his hospitality, food and wine. He was entertained my Betheul's many concubines and was pleased.

31:22 He even purchased the pleasures of Isaac's future wife for a gold earring, bracelet and ten shekels of gold. But only under the standard that the pleasures be of the mouth and anus and that he remains out of her womb. After his lust was satisfied, he demanded to know the woman's name.

31:23 It was Rebekah.

31:24 The servant gathered Rebekah and the men of the household and made them an offer.

31:25 "People, I thank you for your hospitality, but I came to this land under orders of my master Abraham. I am to find a Hebrew woman, pleasing and pure for his son and I would like to buy Rebekah so that she may be my master's son's wife. The lord has blessed my master greatly and he is rich and powerful. However, he grows old and Isaac, his son, shall be his heir. Rebekah will be marrying an heir to a powerful nation. This I promise to you, for it was promised by God!

31:26 He has already great farmland, mines of precious minerals, flocks of cattle. He is a rich man and Rebekah will be his wife, if you allow it."

31:27 The men agreed to this arrangement, as did Rebekah. For Rebekah did not care for Isaac's looks, nor his personality. Isaac was rich and this was good enough for Rebekah's hand to be purchased in marriage.

31:28 The arrangements were made. The men took the eight camels and all they carried and Rebekah was sold to be Isaac's wife. The lord saw this and was amused. For Rebekah was worth only three camels and a jug of wine. But, the woman was bought, Isaac had a pure Hebrew wife and the lord knew that this was good.

31:29 The servant took Rebekah and the two travelled back to the land of Abraham.

31:30 As they travelled, Isaac was out hunting in the fields, lifted his eyes and saw the servant and Rebekah coming towards him.

31:31 Rebekah gazed upon Isaac and asked the servant, "Who is this creature that stares at me, his eyes full of lust?"

31:32 The servant explained to her that this was Isaac, her husband.

31:33 Upon hearing this, she fainted and fell off her camel, for Isaac was not pleasing to Rebekah.

31:34 He was a hairy man, with the nose like a turnip and the thought of belonging to this man sickened her.

31:35 Isaac came upon the two and asked the servant if this was his wife. The servant said she was and Isaac picked her up, took Rebekah to his mother's old tent and lied with her.

31:36 While performing his husbandly duties, Rebekah woke up, alarmed and pleased. He looked upon Isaac as he thrust himself into her womb and smiled.

31:37 For though he was a hairy beast, he was rich, good in bed and she belonged to him.

32:1 Abraham saw Isaac and Rebekah and missed his dear wife. So, he decided to take a concubine.

32:2 Her name was Keturah and she was a young and beautiful whore.

32:3 Without the help of God, Abraham managed to conceive with her six sons. Zimram, Jokshan, Medan, Midian, Ishbak and Shuah. These sons grew and had children of their own. But I won't bore you with the genealogy.

32:4 Abraham, despite having many sons and grandsons, made Isaac his sole heir.

32:5 But he was not ungrateful, for to the sons conceived through his concubines he gave them many gifts and sent them to live away from Isaac, so that Isaac may live in peace and not worry about his siblings mooching off of him.

32:6 At the age of one hundred and seventy-five, Abraham died. He died doing what he loved.

32:7 Overindulging on beer.

32:8 Knowing their father loved Sarah dearly, Ishmael and Isaac buried Abraham in the same cave, purchased from the children of Heth.

32:9 God looked down upon this burial and saw that Isaac did mourn his father deeply. So, he blessed Isaac and sent him to live by the well of Lahairoi. Where the water is cold, plentiful and good for making wine.

32:10 But the lord did not forget the promise made upon Hagar and Ishmael was blessed as well. For Ishmael was a fertile man, blessed with a fertile wife, which bore him twelve sons, twelve princes, twelve nations.

32:11 Nebajoth, Kedar, Adbeel, Mibsam, Mishma, Dumah, Massa, Hadar, Tema, Jetur, Naphish and Kedemah.

32:12 These are the sons of Ishmael, named from eldest to youngest, the twelve princes promised to him by God. Ishmael also had many daughters. But nobody cares. They are, after all, only women.

32:13 At the young age of one hundred and thirty-seven, Ishmael died. He was out hunting the land for venison, but accidentally injured himself with his spear.

33:14 Let this be a lesson to you. Pointy sticks and alcohol don't mix.

32:15 Now, for the important person. The generations of Isaac, beloved by Abraham and envied by God.

32:16 At the age of forty, Isaac accepted Rebekah as his wife, the daughter of Bethuel the Hebrew, sister of Laban.

32:17 But try as they might, Rebekah could not bear a son. Oh, how they tried. But her womb would only birth females and this brought forth great misery to the couple.

32:18 Isaac prayed to the lord God for a son and God answered his prayer and blessed Rebekah to bear a son.

32:19 But during pregnancy, her womb was hostile. The child inside her never rested, constantly kicked and refused to lie still.

32:20 She enquired to the lord why the infant that grows in her was restless, where the daughters that she bore were content in her womb.

32:21 And the lord replied, "I have great news for you. I know you have been a good wife to Isaac and did not mean to bear him so many daughters. So, as a gift, I have blessed you twice. You do not bare a son for Isaac in your belly, but two sons. And they are fighting each other, full of energy and spunk even before birth.

32:22 The youngest child shall be strong, strongest in all the land. The eldest one shall serve under him."

32:23 And Rebekah was pleased, for to birth sons is a woman's sole purpose in life. To bare two in the womb is twice the blessing.

32:24 Isaac was sixty when Rebekah gave birth to his sons. The first son pushed forth from her loins was red and hairy like an oxen's back. They named him Esau. Pronounced the same way one would say 'you saw,' for peoples of the nation would ask one another, "You saw Isaac's child. What an ugly beast!"

32:25 The second child came out, grasping his eldest brother's hairy heel. He was named Jacob.

32:26 As the boys grew, Esau became a great hunter. For his hairy body allowed him to blend in with the beasts, so he could get close and strike them down.

32:27 Jacob was a simple, peaceful man. He tended to his crops, made simple meals and was content to stay at home.

32:28 Isaac loved his son Esau, because Esau brought forth to him many wild game and Isaac loved meat.

32:29 Rebekah, however, loved Jacob, for Jacob was a kind and gentle man, while Esau was barbaric and frightened her.

33:1 Being the eldest son, and favoured by his father, it was common knowledge that Esau was to gain the birthright and become heir to his father's nation. But Jacob wanted this and tricked Esau.

33:2 Before Esau went to hunt, Jacob prepared for him a simple meal. Being cunning, Jacob poisoned the meal with beans, causing Esau to pass wind many times on his hunt, scaring the animals away.

33:3 Esau came back, annoyed he had not captured meat to eat and was hungry. Jacob was cooking a plain meal of lentil soup and bread.

33:4 Esau smelled this meal and his stomach rumbled for the food. He begged Jacob to give him some food, but Jacob refused.

33:5 "Why not eat the flesh of your kill. Why rely on me for sustenance?"

33:6 Esau explained that he did not kill any meat and had no food for himself and begged of his brother to give him some food.

33:7 Jacob laughed at Esau, the mighty hunter, for not being able to do something as simple as feed himself, which shamed Esau and bruised his ego.

33:8 Jacob said that he would gladly give his brother food, for the people would find it funny that Jacob, a simple man, must feed his eldest brother Esau, the mighty hunter.

33:9 Esau did not want anyone knowing of such shame and wanted Jacob to swear that he would not mention the failed hunt, nor the food given.

33:10 Jacob told Esau that there is a price for keeping the failed hunt secret and that he would not tell anyone that he had to feed his eldest brother. Esau must give Jacob his birthright.

33:11 Esau, caring more for his reputation than his future, sold his birthright to Jacob for a half loaf of bread, a bowl of lentil soup and the promise that Jacob would not tell anybody of his shame.

34:1 A great famine spread across the land of Isaac and his peoples grew hungry. Isaac went to Abimelech, king of the Philistines, to dwell in his land.

34:2 But God appeared to Isaac and told him, "Dwell not in the land of the Philistines. Dwell in Gerar instead. If you do, I shall bless you and make you and your offspring prosperous, as promised your father Abraham.

34:3 When you do, I shall make your seed multiply as the stars of heaven, make them rulers of the land and bless the earth they dwell."

34:4 So Isaac moved his family to Gerar and lived there.

34:5 The men of Gerar took notice of Rebekah, beautiful and fair and stared at her with lustful eyes.

34:6 Isaac shared the same cowardice as his father and told the people that Rebekah was not his wife, but his sister. For Isaac feared these people would kill him and claim Rebekah as their own if they found out that she was his wife.

34:7 Fools as they are, the people believed him. Including king

Abimelech, who was told this same lie from Isaac's father.

34:8 As time passed, Isaac and Rebekah hid in the palace garden and groped one another like only a couple would.

34:9 Abimelech looked out through his window and witnessed the two he believed siblings pleasuring each other. Abimelech grew angry, for he could not believe yet another Hebrew would lie to him about his wife.

34:10 He called Isaac to his throne asked him, "Is Rebekah your wife?"

34:11 Not wanting to admit the lie, Isaac answered, "No."

34:12 Abimelech became saddened, for how could such a man think him so stupid. He told Isaac he saw the two in his garden, partaking in activities no brother and sister would dare do.

34:13 He asked again, "Is Rebekah your wife?"

34:14 Knowing he was caught in his lie, Isaac told the truth. "Yes, Rebekah is my wife. You must understand, my wife is pleasing to the eyes of men and I worried your people would kill me and claim her as their own if they knew the truth. So, to protect my life, I lied."

34:15 Abimelech was furious. He told Isaac, "What is with your people. Are the Hebrews cowards, unwilling to protect your women?

34:16 Another of your kind said this very same lie to me and God punished us for believing it. Will God punish us again, for believing the filth that springs forth from your mouth?

34:17 It is common law that the men of my nation cannot kill to claim another's wife. For if they do, they shall be punished harshly.

34:18 But since you peoples seem to be so stupid, I'll make a specific law. If any of my men harm you or your wife, they shall be punished by castration and branded, for they will bring a curse of God down upon us.

34:19 You can stay in our land safe in the knowledge that it is illegal for any people to harm you or rape Rebekah and that the punishment for this crime will be worse than death. A worse punishment than the execution they would face if they did this to any other people, native to my land or otherwise."

34:20 Isaac then dwelt in the lands of Abimelech, comforted by the knowledge he and his wife were safe.

35:1 Isaac planted crops that grew plentiful, for the lord blessed him despite the famine happening and made Isaac great.

35:2 He had flocks, crops, herds of cattle and many a slave and his peoples never grew hungry.

35:3 Those of Abimelech saw this and became envious. How could a foreigner live in their land and be prosperous, while those native to the land suffer famine and starvation. Why not share the knowledge he has for making barren land grow, or share the plentiful food he had to his starving neighbours?

35:4 Abimelech heard of Isaac's success and became fearful. He worried his people would think he gave Isaac prosperous land and left them to starve. Abimelech feared revolution. So, he came to Isaac. "You have prospered in my land for many years and have become great and prosperous among those poor and wretched. Surely you deserve better. Leave us, for you are mightier than us."

35:5 Isaac left, knowing that God would protect him and that the land he dwelt on would become barren once those of Abimelech occupied it again.

35:6 He lead his people out of Abimelech to the land of Gerar, where God originally told him to go and had servants dig wells for water. Many wells dug were dry, but they found one area that grew promise. For their they found water.

35:7 But the land rightfully belonged to the Philistines, apparently, despite God telling Isaac not to dwell in Philistine land and the Philistines would not let Isaac keep the well, for they needed the water for their cattle and crops.

35:8 Isaac called the well Esak, for Esak is a cursed name. He let

the Philistines have it and cursed them for taking back what was rightfully theirs.

35:9 The well became full of clay and was undrinkable to man and beast.

35:10 Isaac and his people went further south and dug another well for which to drink and grow crops. The land was named Rehoboth, for surely this was the place God promised for them.

35:11 Isaac claimed the land, unchallenged by the natives, for they were few in number and too weak to fight. As the crops grew and the land became fruitful, Isaac travelled to Beersheba, to expand his land.

35:12 The lord once again appeared to Isaac and made the same reassuring promise that his seed will grow and multiply and become great.

35:13 Isaac knew this already, for the lord has appeared to him many times and said the same thing, never anything new.

35:14 Thinking that God may leave him be, he built an altar, sacrificed a young lamb, bathed in its blood and danced around it naked. This pleased God, for as you know, he loves violence, nudity and torn flesh.

35:15 Thirsty after the sacrifice and not wanting to walk, he demanded his servants dig a well by the altar so that Isaac may quench his thirst. They did and water sprung forth from that well and Isaac drank from it.

35:16 News spread across the land about Isaac and his prosperous land and it reached king Abimelech.

35:17 Abimelech knew Isaac must be blessed by God and regretted giving in to the fears of his people, casting him out from his land.

35:18 So Abimelech, with his advisor Ahuzzath and general Phichol, went to visit Isaac, in hopes God would see this and bless them as well.

35:19 As they came to Isaac, Isaac saw them and came to them, saying, "You fools. I know you have cast me from your land because you hate me and now you come take my land. Don't you know that God will punish you for this?"

35:20 Abimelech said, "No, for you have us mistaken. We have heard of your prosperity and know that God is surely with you. We come here not to make war, but a treaty. We shall not harm nor invade your land and any person caught doing so will be punished. In exchange, all we ask is for a small amount of your surplus crop. For our people starve as your people grow fat with feed. Surely you can spare some grain."

35:21 Isaac considered the offer and agreed. For he grew annoyed of Philistines trespassing on his property, grabbing a few grapes or olives. It would be convenient to have those of Abimelech stop them, instead of having his peoples chase them off and slay them.

35:22 In celebration of this treaty, Isaac made for them a great feast. Breads, cheeses, wines, ales, meats from all creatures were consumed. They all overindulged in liquor and food, and their bellies become full and heads dizzy with alcohol.

35:23 In the morning, as the wrath of grapes subsided, the treaty was signed and Abimelech and his men left Isaac's land in peace.

35:24 During the day they left, Isaac's slaves ran to him, explaining they have yet found more land, with a well of running water.

35:25 Isaac then blessed the lord, for as reward for helping his neighbours, the lord has blessed him with more prosperous land so that his people can live in gluttony while still being able to spare grain to their starving neighbours.

36:1 As Esau hunted, he looked at the women of the neighbouring nations and grew in lust. For, unlike his people who grew fat and flabby, these women were slim, fair and rolls of flesh did not flow over their garments.

36:2 At the age of forty, Esau bought for himself two wives of foreign blood. Judith the daughter of Beeri the Hittite and Bashemath the daughter of Elon the Hittite. He bought these two for venison that he butchered the day of purchase.

36:3 Isaac and Rebekah heard of Esau and grew shameful. They believed that by marrying a foreign beast instead of a Hebrew, Esau has cursed himself and his people.

36:4 Over time, Isaac's body grew weary with age. His joints ached, he had trouble emptying his bowels, sight escaped him and his hearing was muffled so that he could not understand voices well.

36:5 He knew soon his body would cease and that death would overtake him. Before he died, he called upon Esau the eldest and demanded of him, "Go now to the fields.

36:6 Take with you the arrow and bow and kill for me a deer, for venison is a savoury meat and though I have lacked the pleasures of sight and sound, my taste is fine and I can still enjoy fine food and drink.

36:7 Slaughter the deer and make me savoury meat so that I can enjoy a fine meal. Do this and you shall have my blessing."

36:8 Esau did as his father commanded, ran to the field and sought for a young, tender and delicious buck for his father's meal.

36:9 Rebekah overheard this and did not want Esau to have her husband's blessing. So, she called upon the youngest Jacob and told him,

36:10 "Your father is hungry and shall bless Esau when he brings back flesh from the deer. This cannot happen, for Esau is unworthy of this blessing.

36:11 Go now, slay two young goats and I shall prepare and spice them with herb and pepper strong, so that your father shall not tell that he is not eating the flesh of wild game.

36:12 Do this and he shall bless you instead, a kind and gentle man, intelligent and handsome, instead of your beast brother Esau."

36:13 But Jacob was nervous and told his dear mother, "How can this be. For if the meat is spiced and believed to be from wild buck, my father will know it is I, not Esau.

36:14 For though blind, he is not stupid. Esau is a hairy man and my skin is smooth and silky like a fine concubine's thigh. Surely, he will hug me and know that I am not Esau.

36:15 When he finds out, he shall curse me for such treachery and I shall live in pain and turmoil, without the blessing of God."

36:16 Rebekah told Jacob to worry not, for she shall not let her favourite son be cursed by his father.

36:17 So Jacob gathered two young goats and Rebekah slew them and cut from them the most tender flesh. She put herbs and spices heavy on them, making them savoury and tasteful, masking the taste of the actual muscle and fooling the tongue into believing it wild game.

36:18 She then took the hair of the goat and made for Jacob sleeves and a scarf, so that when Isaac feels him, he shall feel the hide of a goat and not the smooth skin of Jacob. Before Isaac put on the goat hide, they stained it with wild grass and animal faeces, so that the hide smelled of wild land.

36:19 With food in hand, Jacob went to his blind father and said to him, "Behold, it is I, Esau the eldest, your first-born son. Look, I bring for you deer and bread as you commanded.

36:20 Now, bless me."

36:21 But Isaac was confused, for surely Esau, skilled hunter as he is, did not slay a deer so quickly. For the hunting grounds were miles away and could not have been travelled to and back in such short a time. So, Isaac asked, "How did you slay a deer so quickly?"

36:22 Jacob, being smart and quick of mouth, said, "Because the lord God sent it to me. To the hunting grounds I need not travel, for the buck was outside our encampment."

36:23 Isaac, believing this as surely the lord God would send Esau a deer, asked, "The lord is a great provider. But tell me, I did not hear the screams of wild beast being slaughtered. How did you slay a buck so quietly?"

36:24 Jacob, knowing his father old, explained to him, "The creature was killed quick and had little time to cry in pain. Also, it was outside the encampment and you grow old and tired. Your ears have weakened and perhaps could not pick up the sounds of death that yelled from this buck."

36:25 Isaac knew his hearing was poor and accepted this reasoning. But though his hearing poor, he could still understand what was said when sound happens near him.

36:26 Isaac did not recognize the voice as Esau's, for it was not deep enough and he asked Jacob, whom he believed Esau, "Why is your voice pitched high. For you usually have a deep voice, deep like the deepest well, but you speak now in high pitch, like a songbird. You sound like Jacob, but less girlish."

36:27 Jacob, a bit insulted for being told his voice sounded like a woman's, said to his father, "My voice is deep, deeper than the deepest cave. But as the arrow entered the deer, it ran towards me and his hoof made contact where my foreskin used to be. I am in pain, father and that is why my voice is high."

36:28 Isaac was pleased by this, for the image of the mighty Esau being kicked in his loins by a beast brought great amusement to him.

36:29 He said to Jacob, "Esau, my sympathies for such pain. Come, embrace your and I shall bless you."

36:30 Jacob came to his father Isaac and hugged him greatly. Isaac felt the hair of the goat hide and smelled the stench of untamed land and believed this surely to be Esau the eldest and favourite of his sons.

36:31 He grabbed Jacob by the shoulders, raised his head unto heaven and gave his blessing.

36:32 "Lord, bless my son, whom I love greatly and deeply. Give to him the sweet liquid of the heavens, great land to produce grain, women to bare sons and plenty of liquor and wine.

36:33 Let him be a great nation upon this earth. Let him rule over the land, the people and his siblings. Curse those that curse him and bless the ones that call him friend."

36:34 With these mere words, Jacob became blessed and left, stealing the blessing meant for Esau.

37:1 As this happened, Esau was on the plains, hunting. Many times, a deer would cross his path and many times Esau passed, for he demanded the best flesh for his father. Finally, Esau spotted a fat doe, meat tender and sweet.

37:2 Readying his bow, he let the arrow fly and struck the fat deer in the neck, killing it instantly and not poisoning the flesh with fear.

37:3 Esau dragged the carcass back and prepared for his father the tastiest meat. He spiced the flesh lightly, for such meat was sweet and should not be hidden by herbs and spices.

37:4 When cooked, he put a slab of flesh on a plate and presented it to Isaac, saying, "It is I, Esau, the eldest of your son. I have slain for you fine game and prepared the venison to your liking."

37:5 Isaac was confused and said, "But how can this be. For Esau has already made me savoury meat and has received my blessing."

37:6 Hearing this, Esau grew confused and believed his father's mind weak. He went forward and embraced him like only Esau could and told him that surely, he must be mistaken.

37:8 Isaac grew afraid, for he knew this to be Esau. He said, "How can this be! For a man claiming to be you has already came in and gave me flesh savoury and sweet and has received my blessing. I have none for you, dearest Esau. So, tell me, who could this other person be?"

37:9 Esau, upon hearing this, became angry and saddened and howled to the heavens like a wolf.

37:10 He cried to his father, begging him, "Bless me, bless me, for surely I am worthy of your blessing."

37:11 But Isaac could not, for words of blessing could only be spoken to one man. Isaac knew that he was tricked. "Esau, your brother came and tricked me. He has taken away your blessing, leaving me with naught to give you."

37:12 Hearing this, Esau grew angry and jealous. For Esau was a powerful man, but dim witted.

37:13 Jacob, who was delicate, has tricked Esau twice, making him appear a fool. He yelled to the heavens, "Is he not rightly named Jacob? For twice he has taken away that which is mine. He has taken away my birthright, now my blessing!" Turning to Isaac, he asked, "Have you not reserved a blessing for me. A few words to speak to me and God?"

37:14 And Isaac explained, with tears in his eyes, "No, for I have reserved all my blessings for you, which Jacob has taken away. I have blessed him with wealth, wine, women and grain. Power and respect.

37:15 Blessed him I did with servants, slaves and nations. And blessed him I did to lord over you, for I wanted you to rule over Jacob, but now Jacob shall rule over you.

37:16 Forgive me, for with mere words I have condemned you to be dominated by your younger brother.

37:17 With a sword, you must serve him and do as he says. For this I have said, thus it must be so.

37:18 Surely you haven't a choice, even if by deception this happened."

37:19 Esau could not accept this and swore that he will not be a slave to his brother; that the yoke around his neck will be broken and that revenge will be his.

37:20 He screamed in his heart, 'Curse be to Jacob for deceiving my father and I. When my father dies, Jacob shall die soon after.

37:21 Though this blessing be stolen, it is my father's blessing and he would be saddened if the blessed die before him.

37:22 But once in death my father rest, he will not care what happens to his blessed.

37:23 And I will kill Jacob.'

37:24 Rebekah saw the hatred in her eldest son and knew his intent. She went to Jacob and warned him, "Beware your brother Esau. He is angry and seeks satisfaction in your blood.

37:25 Go, gather what you can and live with your uncle Laban. Stay with him until your brother calms down and no longer desires your blood.

37:26 Your brother is slow of mind and will soon forget why he wants you dead. When he forgets the reason, the urge to kill you will leave him as well. When this happens, I will send forth for you and you shall return to me safely."

37:27 Rebekah then said to her favourite son, "Remember your heritage as well. I grow worried of you being away from my care. Your eyes may wander and seek comfort in the flesh of a foreign woman, a woman of Heth. Do not lust for them, do not love for them.

37:28 Marry a woman born of your own land. For if you marry a foreign devil, you will deceive me and my life will be meaningless."

37:29 Isaac knew that Jacob would flee, for he knew Jacob to be smart. Though angry for this deception, he still felt obligated to love his youngest son.

37:30 He sent for him and said, "When you flee from your brother's wrath, take not a wife of Canaan!

37:31 For the Canaanites are merely beasts that can speak and walk on hind legs. They are not people.

37:32 Go instead to Padanaram, seek the house of my mother's father and seek your uncle Laban.

37:33 Marry one of his daughters, a cousin.

37:34 For this incest, God will bless you, make you fruitful and your seed will multiply tens of hundreds so that your generations be a multitude of people.

37:35 Bless the seed with the blessing of Abraham, so that they may inherit the land of a stranger, which is the promise God made to your grandfather."

37:36 Isaac sent Jacob away, who went to the house of his grandfather to seek a wife.

37:37 When Esau heard that his father willingly blessed Jacob and let him flee with his blessing, Esau knew that Isaac must truly despise Canaanites.

37:38 Esau knew not why, but never questioned, only accepted the belief that Canaanites must be unholy beasts and not to be married.

37:39 Esau grew ashamed the for two wives he had not born of his native land. So, he travelled to the house of Ishmael, Isaac's brother from a different mother, to seek a wife.

37:40 There he married Mahalath of native blood, sister of Nebajoth and daughter of his uncle, which pleased Abraham and pleased the lord.

38:1 As Jacob was fleeing to Haran, he grew tired. The sun set, darkness surrounded him and he thought it wise to set up camp.

38:2 With stones, he made a makeshift bed and pillow, lied down and slept.

38:3 As he slept, he dreamed. A ladder made of wood stretched out from the earth to the heavens and behold, the angels of the lord were ascending and descending from it.

38:4 On top of the ladder stood the lord God, who said, "Behold, I am God. Creator of heaven and earth, your father Isaac and lord of Abraham.

38:5 A promise I have made to your grandfather Abraham that his seed shall spread forth like dust to the wind and fill the land.

38:6 This promise I made to your father Isaac as well, that his seed shall spread forth and rule the land.

38:7 This same promise I make to you and this time I intend to keep it. Your seed shall be mighty and strong and spread across the earth like butter on bread.

38:8 Your seed shall spread to the north, to the east, to the west and to the south. This I promise you.

38:9 I promise you this and that no matter the land on which you dwell, I shall not leave you, for I am the lord God and will protect you and your generations."

38:10 Jacob awoke from this dream and grew happy.

38:11 For the lord promised that his future generations will be plenty. The same promise made to his father, which was made to his father's father.

38:12 Surely the lord must mean it!

38:13 He knew the lord God must be in this place and that the ladder must have been a stairway to heaven.

38:14 It was not, for it was only a dream. But Jacob did not know better. Jacob did not even stop to think why it was so important for his seed to multiply and rule the earth, nor how many future generations it would take for God to fulfill this promise.

38:15 He placed an altar where the ladder was in his dream. Seeing he had no lamb to sacrifice, he poured oil over the altar.

38:16 Dancing around it naked, he grabbed his loins and rubbed them greatly, shooting the seed on the altar as a sacrifice to the lord.

38:17 He then lit the oil, burning his seed as a sacrifice to God, symbolizing the future generations of his that will rule the earth, as promised by God.

38:18 God saw this sacrifice and laughed. For he found it amusing when men are so desperate to pleasure themselves as a woman would pleasure them.

38:19 Jacob then named the place Bethel. Which was convenient. The place was already named Bethel. Jacob merely confirmed it.

38:20 Then Jacob made a vow to the lord, saying, "If God be with me and protect me and provide me with food, shelter and clothing, then I shall worship him, for he will give me reason not to question."

38:21 And may this altar of stone and rock be the lord God's house. And so long as the lord God provide me and my people with wealth to spare, then shall we give as a gift to the lord one tenth of our wealth."

38:22 The lord God agreed to this, but demanded later that one tenth of the belongings be given to him always and not just times of wealth and prosperity.

38:23 For the lord God is a greedy fucker and the kingdom of heaven is not enough for him.

39:1 Jacob then went on his journey, heading east.

39:2 As he walked, he came upon a well of cool spring water. Surrounding the well were shepherds, with three flocks of sheep.

39:3 A great and heavy stone blocked the flow of the well water and the shepherds would roll the stone away so that the water may flow forth and quench the thirst of the sheep and the shepherds.

39:4 Jacob asked them, "Why do you block the flow of water with such a heavy stone. For surely it must be tiring to push such a rock away so that you and your flock can drink."

39:5 The shepherds explained the stone was there by the will of God. For God has blessed the stone so that only his people may move it and that no foreign devil may drink and live from this well.

39:6 Jacob worried for a moment, as he did not know if he was in the land of his people or if he were a foreigner. He asked where the shepherd came. And they replied that they were people of Haran.

39:7 With a sigh of relief, Jacob praised the lord, for these were his people and the people of his God. He asked the shepherds if they knew his uncle, Laban son of Nahor.

39:8 They did and explained he was quite well and blessed by God.

39:9 As they were talking of the many blessings of Laban, one of Laban's daughters walked to the well, guiding a flock of sheep so that they may drink.

39:10 Jacob saw this and knew the well could not supply water for the many flocks surrounding it. He asked, "How can this be. For you people come to this well, to drink for yourself and your livestock, but surely this tiny stream that flows forth cannot sustain these many mouths!"

39:11 The shepherds heard this and chuckled. "Behold, the many glories of our lord God almighty!" With these words, the sheep were filled with the spirit of the lord and gathered around the mighty rock surrounding the well. Working together as the shepherds watched, the sheep pushed with their heads, bodies and legs. They manoeuvred around the stone so as not to fall in the well that it blocks.

39:12 Finally, with one final push, the stone was moved, allowing more water to flow freely from the well and allowing all the flocks to drink at once, sustaining them and quenching their thirst.

39:13 The shepherds explained to Jacob, "The lord God allows us, his people, to drink from this well that shall flow eternal. But us and only us. He blocks the well with this stone so that the children of Heth, Canaan or Pharaoh cannot drink the water that God has provided for us.

39:14 When we need more of the precious water, the spirit of the lord fills the beasts and they push the mighty rock so that all may drink. When done, the rock is pushed back so that only a trickle springs forth."

39:15 As the sheep drank and cooled themselves in the high noon sun, Jacob noticed the beauty and purity of Rachel.

39:16 A beautiful women was she, with long flowing hair, blonde like a crop of grain as the sun hit it's just so.

39:17 Eyes brown as the crust of fresh baked bread.

39:18 Skin ever so smooth, smoother than the finest garments.

39:19 Breasts subtle and soft and an ass that would hypnotize men as she walked in tight clothes.

39:20 When Jacob asked her name, she said, "Rachel, daughter of Laban."

39:21 Word spread of the man Jacob and his lust for Rachel. When Laban heard of it, he rushed to Jacob, knowing Jacob was a wealthy man and would pay well for a wife.

39:22 Laban hugged and kissed his nephew and welcomed him into his home.

39:23 Laban had another daughter named Leah. She was the eldest daughter. As is tradition, the eldest daughter should be bought first, lest she grow jealous of her younger sibling.

39:24 Laban knew this and explained to Jacob, "I know it is Rachel you love, but take from me Leah instead, as she is the elder of the two and would make you a fine wife. She is obedient, a virgin pure, cooks, cleans and will make your garments smell of lavender and rose petals."

39:25 Jacob did not have any love for his cousin Leah. Leah was offensive to the eyes and ears.

39:26 She was of heavy stature and her hair was matted, resembling the hide of an ox.

39:27 Her eyes were dull, with no sparkle of life nor youth.

39:28 Her thighs were thick as trees and when she walked they jiggled unappealingly. When she spoke, her voice squeaked like the raven.

39:29 When she sang, it was so offensive that the deaf would cover their lobes. It sounded as though a sheep was getting fellatio from a snake.

39:30 Despite this, Laban wanted Jacob to marry her, for he knew nobody else would.

39:31 Jacob refused to marry such an offensive wench and asked how much it would cost to purchase Rachel. As the two haggled over price, they settled on seven years of service.

39:32 For if Jacob, the son of a rich man, would be humbled to labour for seven years, he must be worthy of Rachel.

39:33 For seven years Jacob served under his uncle Laban. He cut grain, ploughed fields, watered oxen, sheared sheep, fertilized crops, did the work that he would usually have his many slaves do.

39:34 For seven years he did this, motivated by his love for Rachel.

39:35 When his seven years of servitude were finished, he came to his uncle and demanded that Rachel be his.

39:36 Now, Laban liked having Jacob as a labourer. Not because of his skills as a worker. No, Laban had a morbid satisfaction from watching Jacob labour.

39:37 Jacob, a wealthier and more powerful man than he, who would scrape the shit of oxen from the roads so that he may marry his youngest daughter.

39:38 Laban was upset that this entertainment would come to an end and devised a way so that Jacob would serve him more.

39:39 The day before the wedding, Laban made a great feast. Meats, cheese, breads, cakes, fruits, berries and jams. Wine, beer and liquor flowed through this feast like a mighty river. Laban ensured that Jacob partook of the strong drink, so that his senses would be impaired.

39:40 When morning came, Jacob was weakened with the fermentation of fruits and grains. Knowing this, Laban sent for his eldest daughter Leah, dressed her in the wedding dress and presented her to Jacob as his newly purchased wife, giving Leah the handmaiden Zilpah as a wedding gift.

39:41 Jacob, confused with the poison of grain, did not notice who he had bought, married her and lied with her through the wedding night many times.

39:42 As the sun rose, Jacob's senses grew brighter. He rolled over in his tent and saw not the face of Rachel, but Leah.

39:43 He ran to Laban, yelling to him, "What deception is this, that you sell me Leah your eldest when it was Rachel that my heart desires?"

39:44 Laughing, for he knew the purchase of Leah legal as the contract did not specify which daughter, Laban said, "In this country, it must be that the eldest marry first.

39:45 You wanted to marry my daughter, it had to be Leah as she was born first. But now that she belongs to a husband, Rachel can now legally be sold. Do you want to buy her?"

39:46 Jacob replied yes, for his love for Rachel was still strong.

39:47 Laban then told him that he would sell Rachel to him for another seven years of service and during that seven years he will keep Rachel on hold, so that another man may not marry her.

39:48 For another seven years Jacob laboured.

39:49 He worked longer hours, for he knew the woman that awaited in his tent and did not want to return to her.

39:50 Many times he fell asleep in the field where the oxen stayed.

39:51 In time, the seven years passed and Jacob demanded that Rachel be his wife. In the contract, she was mentioned by name, so that no deception could legally be done.

39:52 Laban prepared another feast. But the meat was not of young calf, the cheese old, the bread stale and the desserts limited.

39:53 A few jugs of wine passed as celebration, but not nearly as much spirits as there was to celebrate Leah's marriage. For Laban did not want to waste such fine foods and vintage on Jacob again, if it did not mean more servitude.

39:54 Jacob was sober for the marriage service and was able to tell that Rachel was the woman presented to him. As a gift to Rachel on her wedding day, Laban presented to her a handmaiden named Bilhah.

39:55 That night, Jacob and Rachel lied with each other many times, with Leah watching but never participating. For Jacob loved and adored Rachel and only lied with Leah when Rachel was in her unclean cycle.

40:1 The lord God saw the married trio and was saddened for Leah. Knowing she was hated, he intervened in a way that would have Jacob love Leah.

40:2 He closed the feminine canals of Rachel so that she may only give birth to daughters, but Leah could accept the seed of Jacob and bear for him a son.

40:3 Leah bore her son and named him Reuben and blessed the lord God, for surely with a son Jacob will love her.

40:4 He did not.

40:5 So the lord God blessed Leah with another son grown from the seed of Jacob. She named him Simeon and blessed the lord again, for surely with two sons Jacob would love her.

40:6 He did not.

40:7 So the lord cursed Rachel with a heavy flow, forcing Jacob to unleash his carnal desires on Leah again. With this act, Leah accepted his seed and bore yet another son.

40:8 She named him Levi, for he was conceived in a field of cotton and she called upon heaven and blessed the lord once more, for with three sons she has fulfilled thrice the reason a woman exists and surely Jacob would love her.

40:9 He did not.

40:10 God grew frustrated with Jacob's stubbornness and afflicted Rachel with an infection of her loins.

40:11 Ooze most foul excreted from her infertile slit, causing a crust appearing like sun burnt scabs to form around her. When she removed her clothes, the air was filled with the foul smell of the sea.

40:12 Disgusted by this, Jacob once again lied intimately with Leah. For though she was displeasing to the eye, at least it did not smell as though he was fornicating with the decaying carcass of a whale.

40:13 Leah again accepted his seed and was blessed with a son once more.

40:14 As her fourth son pushed forth from her loins, she named him Judah and looked up to heaven, praising the lord once more for allowing a son to be born of the seed of Jacob. For Leah has given Jacob four sons. Surely, he must start to love her.

40:15 He did not.

40:16 Rachel witnessed Leah giving birth to many a son, but all she could produce were daughters.

40:17 Jealous, she came to Jacob, saying, "Fuck me. Fuck me. Fuck me until your seed be barren. For I must give you a son, just one son. Give me a chance. For if I cannot give my husband a son, my life will be meaningless and I might as well spill my blood on the floor and offer my life as a final offering to the lord!"

40:18 Jacob heard her and grew angry, for he did not want his servants cleaning blood from his floor.

40:19 With a slap across her face, he yelled to the whining bitch, "Rachel. Am I not in God's stead. For if the lord wanted you to bear a son, then a son you would bear. But he has rejected your womb from accepting my seed and poisoned you to give me a flock of useless daughters. You cannot give me a son, nor do I want you to.

40:20 The region in which you cover your loins is filthy, covered in crust harder than the crust of stale bread. To implant my seed in that would be sickening and surely sinful."

40:21 Rachel knew this to be true, for her vagina was still cursed by God. In her place, Rachel offered her handmaiden, Bilhah, as a replacement, so that Jacob may lie with Bilhah as he would Rachel and so that Bilhah can bare him the son Rachel could not.

40:22 Jacob accepted Bilhah, for though not as beautiful as Rachel, at least her nether regions did not have the aroma of the fish market.

40:23 Bilhah lied with Jacob and accepted his seed, giving him the gift of a son. Rachel, seeing this, knew that God must have punished her. But God also accepted her plea, for by offering Bilhah as a whore, she did give for her husband a son.

40:24 She grabbed the son from Bilhah's womb and named him Dan. She originally wanted to name him Cranshavl, but before doing so, accidentally dropped the knife used to cut the umbilical cord, causing it to land near her foot. She yelled damn, a word cursed by God. When asked what she said, she said Dan, for that will be her child's name.

40:25 Jacob again lied with Bilhah and blessed her belly with his seed. A second son she did bear.

40:26 Rachel witnessed the birth of this son and smiled. For she looked forward to the day Bilhah gave birth to the fifth son, outdoing Leah and making Rachel the best wife. She named the second Naphtali.

40:27 Leah knew of Rachel's intentions and would not let her little sister win. Knowing Jacob still did not love her, despite giving him the gifts of four sons, Leah offered to him Zilpah, her handmaiden.

40:28 Zilpah accepted Jacob's seed and bore for him another son. Leah was pleased that her score of sons increased and that Rachel's was much lower.

40:29 She named this son Gad. She also dropped the knife used to cut the cord from the womb and used the lord God's name in vain. When confronted with this act of blasphemy, she denied it, claiming she said Gad, for Gad will be her son's name.

40:30 Zilpah bore a second son, increasing Leah's count to six. Leah was pleased with this score and knew that future generations of women would call her blessed for giving her husband so many sons.

40:31 She named the child Asher.

40:32 Reuben, son of Jacob and Leah, went into the wheat fields to harvest the grain. He stumbled upon some mandrakes and plucked them from the ground, knowing the magical properties they contain. Reuben gave them to his mother as a gift.

40:33 Leah knew the mandrake contained properties allowing one to have dreams. She knew also that her sister had an addiction to these effects and that tonight was her night with Jacob.

40:34 Leah still thought she could buy the love of Jacob with more sons, so she made a deal with Rachel. If Rachel would allow Jacob to lie with her tonight, Rachel can have the precious mandrakes.

40:35 Rachel, being an addict, agreed and inhaled the precious herb's intoxicating aroma.

40:36 Jacob lied with Leah that night and conceived again a son. As she bore the son, she looked up into the heavens and praised the lord God, saying,

40:37 "Five sons I have personally given to my husband. Five sons pushed forth from my womb. Two sons I have given him through the belly of a slave. Sons of seven I have given him. Surely, he must realize I am a superior wife. I will name this child Issachar and with this child surely he will love me!"

40:38 He did not.

40:39 So once again, Leah liquored Jacob up and lied with him intimately. Once again, she accepted his seed and bore him a son.

40:40 She praised the lord again. "Six sons. Never has a wife given her husband six sons from her own womb. Surely Jacob must now love me!"

40:41 And he now did, for he realized the loyalty Leah must have for him. For despite his lack of love, lack of respect, she has blessed him with eight sons, six of which came from her own fertile womb.

40:42 He professed his love to Leah and the two became close and made love to one another in celebration of Jacob's new-found love for her.

40:43 Unfortunately, she had to fuck it up by giving birth to a daughter this time. She named the little bitch Dinah.

40:44 Jacob stopped loving her again and hated her even more for cursing him with another wretched daughter.

40:45 God saw Leah birth Dinah and was disappointed with her. So, to spite Leah, the lord God lifted the curse from Rachel's crust box, and her loins flowed with sweet intoxicating juices, so that Jacob had no reason to be disgusted.

40:46 He took Rachel into his bed and together they conceived a son.

40:47 Yet another son was added to Jacob's family and his name was Joseph.

41:1 Jacob was still in the land of Laban and missed the home he was raised in. Thinking Esau to be calm and no longer wanting to kill him for stealing his blessing, Jacob went to Laban.

41:2 "Uncle, my service to you has been done. The lord has blessed me with many sons, cattle and sheep. Let me take that which is mine, so that I may live in the land of my father."

41:3 But Laban did not want Jacob to leave, for Jacob was blessed by the lord. And Laban mooched off this blessing and ate well and was rich because of Jacob.

41:4 So Laban demanded Jacob's entire stock of goats and that will be the price to leave.

41:5 Jacob declined the offer and said to Laban, "For fourteen years I have served you. My debt is paid. But I need safe passage to my land, safety only you can provide, for you are friendly to the heathen nations and if you tell them not to attack me, attack me they won't.

41:6 But I will not give you my entire flock of goats for this. I know how you live. You are a parasite of my good fortune. Are you not grateful for this, for you have lived off the blessing of the lord. A blessing given to me."

41:7 Laban knew this to be true, so he made a deal with Jacob. Laban wanted goats, for he thought their meat savoury and lusted their rears. He demanded a blessing from the lord. When his goats equal in number to the goats of Jacob, Jacob may leave. The lord will make it so.

41:8 Jacob did not know how to give such a blessing, so he cared for Laban's flock of goats, which once again provided entertainment for Laban. While caring for the flock, Jacob knew how to increase Laban's flock of goats while still cursing him.

41:9 A small river flown on Laban's property and the goats drank and rested there. When Jacob brought his flock there, he let them drink from the water untouched and they played in the river and fornicated on the banks. But when Laban's flock went, Jacob poisoned the river. He placed in the river rods from poplar and chestnut trees, cutting into the wood deep gash's and marks. As Laban's goats fornicated there, the wood in the river cursed the offspring to be speckled, spotted and weak, unfit for an offering to the lord.

41:10 Whenever Laban's goats were at the river, he cursed them so that soon Laban had a flock of useless, worthless goats. But Jacob removed the wood from the river when his flock came, causing his flock to be pure and strong.

41:11 Laban's sons saw Jacob poison their father's flocks and cursed him, saying, "This cousin of ours has taken away all that is our fathers, while his father flourishes in the blessings of the lord. Why does this relative forsake us, for now our inheritance is worthless."

41:12 The lord God sensed Jacob in danger and said to him, "Flee now to the land of your fathers and brethren and I will guide you along the way."

41:13 Jacob called his two wives and said to them, "I have asked for your father's permission to leave and he has denied us his blessing. But fear not, for the God of my father protects me. The lord has seen me serve under your father and seen how my blessings have made him rich.

41:14 Still, with all my power and knowledge that benefitted Laban, he has deceived me. Ten times he has diminished my wages while I served under him. Still, God has not harmed me nor your father.

41:15 For Laban offered me goats for my work and goats I demanded pure. But instead he has offered me the cursed goats, the speckled, spotted and weak, which he has plenty of. So, I cursed him.

41:16 I made it so that my flock of goats shall be white as the clouds and Laban's streaked and spotted, so that Laban's goats will be useless and given to me. The lord witnessed my genetic handiwork and came to me in a dream.

41:17 He said to me that he was impressed with cursing the goats of Laban and keeping my flock pure. But he warned me of Laban and his sons and how they grow angry over having no pure goats. So, we must flee to the lands of my father, where we will be safe."

41:18 Leah and Rachel heard this and answered, "How about us. We are Laban's own seed. Is there not any inheritance he left for us?

41:19 Or does our father now see us as strangers? For he has sold us to you and in doing so, has he cancelled our inheritance and money owed to us?"

41:20 Jacob saw the greed in his two wives and ensured them this greed was foolish. For yes, Laban was once a wealthy man and his inheritance once owed to them would be great. But Jacob was richer and the inheritance owed to Rachel and Leah would be but pocket change to the wealth of Jacob, their husband.

41:21 So the two gathered their belongings and left. Before doing so, Rachel stole some statues from her father. They were promised to her as inheritance and she would not allow some other relative, friend nor whore to have them after Laban's death.

41:22 Jacob then gathered his family, servants, concubines and belongings and fled forth to the lands of his father.

41:23 On the third day of their escape, Laban looked out upon his fields and realized they were unusually empty. Only his family, his slaves, his belongings were out. Where were Jacob's. As he asked what happened to his son in law, he was told the three left his lands to go back to the land of Jacob.

41:24 Laban was annoyed by this, but did not think any actions were necessary. He lived his days comfortably, mooching from Jacob. Now, those days were done and he accepted the fact that the easy life was over. He went home, to pray to the idols he worshipped. But, they were missing, for those were the idols Rachel took.

41:25 Laban gathered is men and formed a militia. Together, they chased after Jacob. On the mountain of Gilead, they found them making a sacrifice to the lord God, dancing around a slain lamb, naked, pleasing the lord God with an abundance of blood, nudity and torn flesh.

41:26 Laban saw this sacrifice and knew God was with them. To challenge them in battle would surely bring the wrath of God upon him and his men. So, he went to Jacob and spoke diplomatically.

41:27 "Jacob, son of my sister, husband to my daughters. Why did you leave so. You take your men, items, cattle and my daughters. If you had let me known, I would have prepared a farewell party, with song and dance and musicians playing harps. But you did not. You did not even allow me to kiss my children goodbye.

41:28 I have right to be angry with you, for denying a father the right to say farewell to his children. A lesser man would strike you down and take your flocks and belongings. But the God of your father came to me and told me not to harm you, lest he curse my land and people.

41:29 So I come to you, not as an enemy nor a friend, but as a father to your wives. Please, let me say goodbye. And let me have what is mine, for you have taken idols away from me, idols of my God!"

41:30 Jacob answered him. "I shall let you say a farewell to your daughters, but your idols I know not of. I am a son of the one true God and have no need of your idols. Go, search for them and if you find them, bring the thief to me so as I may stone them as blasphemers!"

41:31 Rachel heard this and fled to her tent. She did not want anyone finding out that it was her who stole the idols, or else she shall die. Though Jacob did love her so, he will kill her, as it would be what God would want of him.

41:32 She ran to her tent, hid the idols beneath her skirt and lied on her bed.

41:33 Laban entered her tent and bid farewell to her daughter. "Rachel, why not do you come and give me a hug, for I am your father and have come many miles to bid you farewell."

41:34 Rachel said to Laban, "Father, I would love nothing more than to stand and embrace you. But to do so would be sinful, as I am suffering the curse God inflicted on all women. I am in my monthly uncleanliness and for you to be near me would be an abomination."

41:35 Laban heard this and nowhere near his daughter. Still, he searched her tent for the idols, for he knew Rachel coveted them and had motive for this theft. He did not find them and dared not look under Rachel's skirt whilst she bled as only a woman could bleed.

41:36 Jacob grew impatient with Laban's search, as he became desperate and insisted on checking the bowels of the oxen for these idols of false gods. Jacob said, "You fool. Are these idols even stolen. Or is this an excuse to spy on me and my kin. Thievery is a sin I do not commit. No, I take by force under the will of God, instead of taking slyly and with skill.

41:37 For twenty years I have served your land. I have cared for your goats, ewes, lambs and oxen. If any of your flock went injured or died under my care, did I not repay you from my own flock?

41:38 Twenty years, Laban, twenty. Seven of which was spent, serving for a cunt I did not even want to buy. Yet I still served under you and not once you complained.

41:39 You know the fear of God is in me and the fear of Isaac and Abraham. You fear the punishment set for you. If you did not, you would have taken that which is mine. But you don't. For God has seen me work and slave away and has rewarded me for my servitude to you."

41:40 Laban answered him, "These daughters are my daughters, your children my grandchildren, even your flock of ewes and oxen were born from the flock of mine. Keep them for serving under me, for the lord has blessed you with them and I will not interfere lest he curse you with herpes.

41:41 Let us make a covenant. Let us keep what is mine and you keep that which is yours."

41:42 And Jacob took a stone. One stone. And set it on a pillar.

41:43 He then had his servants gather more stones and place it on the pillar. On the pillar they placed strips of meat, fruits and vegetables, so that the heat from the sun cooked them and they ate of the stone cooked meal.

41:44 Laban called the pile of rocks Jegarsahadutha, but Jacob called it Galeed.

41:45 The two argued as to the name until Laban relented and agreed to Galeed. For Laban feared the lord God would curse him if he did not let Jacob get his way. Also, Galeed was easier to spell and pronounce than Jegarsahadutha.

41:46 Laban said to Jacob, "Behold this mighty heap of rocks and stone. Let it be a covenant and border to us, so as I won't cross it and take what it yours and you won't cross it and take what is mine."

41:47 The God of Abraham and the God of Nahor and the God of their fathers witnessed this covenant. And Jacob swore by the fear of his father Isaac.

41:48 Then Jacob offered a sacrifice upon the mount and slaughtered three sheep atop the mound of stones, causing blood to flow forth down it, staining the ground. Jacob and his men then danced around it naked and covered their bodies in the dirt made mud by the blood. This pleased the lord, for he loves blood, nudity and torn flesh.

41:49 He really does. Why are you still here, reading this blasphemous book, when you could be working your way into the kingdom of heaven by slaying your family pet and dancing around naked in your living room, covered in the creature's blood?

41:50 That night, the men made a feast for the two people, in celebration of their new covenant. As the morning sun rose, Laban kissed his daughters' goodbye and departed home. Good riddance.

42:1 Jacob went on his way and the angels of the lord sent messengers to greet him.

42:2 And when Jacob saw them, he knew they were sent of the lord as protectors. So, he called the meeting place Mahanaim.

42:3 Worrying that Esau was still angered by his deception, he sent forth messengers to his brother so as he may know if he need worry of Esau's wrath.

42:4 When asked what to say, Jacob said, "Tell Esau that it is I, Jacob, returning home from the lands of Laban, where I have stayed all this time.

42:5 I want to return home to the lands of our father. With me I bring many oxen, asses, flocks, slaves and concubines, for the lord has blessed me and wish now for my blessing to reside on our father's property."

42:6 The men were sent and delivered this message to Esau. They returned to Jacob and told him, "We delivered the message meant for your brother Esau. He comes to greet you, my lord and brings with him four hundred men."

42:7 "Four hundred men?" asked Jacob. "He must still be mad for taking his blessing and birthright. But I worry not, for the lord is with me and Esau does not know the location of me and my family."

42:8 "Oh, but he does," said the messenger. "For we have told him. He asked where he could see you and we told him. Even drew him a map so that he may not get lost."

42:9 "YOU FOOLS," cried Jacob. "Why did you not lie. For he plans to kill me and take that which is rightfully mine."

42:10 "But lord, he asked and answer truthfully we must. For to answer dishonestly is a sin to God and he would have punished us for our words of deception."

42:11 Jacob knew why the messengers thought this, for they knew not when it is right to sin. He explained to them how sometimes, a sin is okay. Like lying.

42:12 For if one were to lie to protect his land, that is okay. For the lord God protects Jacob's land and would prefer one to lie instead of having to send angels down from heaven to slaughter the invaders.

42:13 If a slave were ordered by his master to lie, that is okay as well, for disobeying one's master is a much greater sin than dishonesty and the lord will forgive you and take is vengeance upon the master.

42:14 But if one were to lie for self-gain, that is sinful, for that is a greedy lie and an abomination to the lord!

42:15 The messengers understood and wished they knew the rules of sinning before being sent to Esau.

42:16 Now, Jacob was afraid, for he knew his brother to be a strong man and would train his men in the art of combat, a skill Jacob and his men knew not.

42:17 So he divided his men and belongings, divided them in two bands. So that when Esau reaches one band, as he and his men are busy pillaging that, the other band, hopefully the one he is in, can flee like cowards and survive another day.

42:18 For Jacob knew not how to fight, but knowledge he had plenty of how to avoid fighting.

42:19 He sent the one band up ahead, believing Esau would find them first and slaughter them, giving him and his band time to flee. Leah was with that band, for Jacob thought that surely Esau would slay her, ridding Jacob of that ugly bitch.

42:20 Jacob, in a final act of cowardice, went to his tent, got down on his knees and prayed.

42:21 "Oh great lord of Abraham and lord of my father Isaac, I beg of you. Return me and my people to the land of my father.

42:22 I know I am but a humble servant of you and not worthy of your divine interference, nor the truth of your power and will.

42:23 I have divided my belongings in half, in hopes that I and my most precious may flee whilst the lesser property get pillaged and raped.

42:24 But please, though lesser and of little value to me, they still be mine. Do I deserve them gone. I fear my brother Esau comes to slaughter me. Please, spare me. Let Leah take my place.

42:25 Remember the promise you made to me, dear God. For if Esau slays me, how can my seed number greater than the stars of heaven. I have sent my sons to the front line, whilst I stay here in safety. If Esau slaughters them, your promise will be unfulfilled.

42:26 But if Esau by chance skip them and comes towards me, I shall tell him where to find my sons, so that he may kill them. Either way, my sons shall die and your covenant be broken."

42:27 As Jacob slept that night, he took three young lambs pure, slaughtered them and placed them upon the roof of his tent so that the blood may drip down upon his body while he sleeps.

42:28 The lord God saw Jacob, sleeping in the blood of sheep and was pleased. He loves bloody men and never before seen one rest in constant supply of fresh blood.

43:1 As Jacob awoke, fear still poisoned his heart. He gathered two hundred she goats, twenty he goats, two hundred ewes, twenty rams,

43:2 Thirty milch camels and their colts, forty kine, ten bulls, twenty she asses (donkeys, not whores) and ten foals.

43:3 He then gathered his servants, commanded they care for these and sent them between the two encampments.

43:4 So that when Esau slaughtered the first camp and comes for him, these servants shall block him. When asked, say, "We are men of Jacob, who stay behind us. He wishes to speak to you and gives you these gifts as a sign of good faith."

43:5 While Esau is occupied with these gifts, it shall give Jacob more time to flee.

43:6 At night, Jacob was awoken by his sons who, sharing their father's cowardice, fled to him in hopes of protection.

43:7 He gathered his eleven sons and two wives and two concubines that fathered his sons and placed them on camels.

43:8 He supplied them with food and water and guided them to the ford Jabbok

43:9 He sent them over the brook first, so that he may follow and if they were attacked, he could flee.

43:10 Jacob was left alone on the other side of the brook when a stranger approached him.

43:11 As the stranger came closer, fear overtook Jacob and he ran like the antelope. But it was to no avail. The stranger approached him and the two fought.

43:12 With great animal fury the men fought, unleashing their violent instincts toward one another.

43:13 Bloodied, battered and bruised they both became, crying in pain and anger that the other was not dead nor submissive.

43:14 Jacob believed himself filled with the anger of God, for a miracle was happening. He was winning.

43:15 Despite this miracle, an odd thing happened. The stranger reached out and lightly tapped Jacob on his thigh. With this, the lightest of taps, Jacob's thigh bone was removed from his hip, injuring him. Determined as he was, Jacob did not let this handicap get in his way.

43:16 Despite being a gimp, he fought with this stranger and grabbed his neck and slammed the man's face into a rock until death or submission overtook the stranger.

43:17 The stranger grew tired of such defeat and begged to Jacob, "Even through my blood-soaked eyes I see the sun rise. Let me go, I submit."

43:18 And Jacob said, "I shall not let you go until thou bless me." For Jacob still believed a blessing, mere words spoken from others, could gain him power.

43:19 The stranger asked for his name and Jacob gave it to him.

43:20 In reply, the stranger said, "Jacob shall your name no longer be, for now you shall be known as Israel. For I am not a stranger to you, but am your lord God. I have come to fight with you so that you may know how to defend yourself and will no longer need to flee."

43:21 The lord then blessed Jacob there and took away his cowardice, replacing it instead with courage.

43:22 Jacob, newly named Israel, named the land where he battled with the lord Penuel, in celebration of victory over God.

43:23 And as the sun rose over Penuel, the light hit Israel's thigh, healing it.

43:24 Because the lord God injured Israel, the people of God are forbidden to eat of the sinew of flesh, for the lord injured Jacob's sinew, rendering him a gimp for a few hours.

43:25 One may wonder why the lord God decided to fight with Jacob, for would it be not easier to simply bless Jacob, making him courageous instead of a coward. Yes, but the lord God did not intend to bless Jacob.

43:26 No, the lord God wanted to fight Jacob so that me may smite him and break his covenant. He did so in the disguise of a stranger so that it would appear the lord God did not kill Jacob, but a random vagabond.

43:27 The lord God underestimated Jacob and Jacob won the fight, though mortal he may be. Even when God cheated and rendered

Jacob immobile, by pure fury Jacob dominated over the lord God.

43:28 To save face, God said he did this to fill Jacob with courage and confidence, so he may confront his brother Esau instead of fleeing home and hopefully Esau will smite Jacob, ending the covenant of the lord God.

43:29 He named Jacob Israel so that he may break the covenant as well, for the lord God made this promise to Jacob, not Israel.

43:30 It was a loophole that God would exploit, which is why the Jews have still not received their promise this day.

43:31 If an Israelite is reading this, change the name of Israel to Jacob. Perhaps then God would be forced to keep his promise to you and your people!

43:32 Or perhaps he will come of another excuse to screw you over.

44:1 Jacob, now named Israel, is still called Jacob by his family and friends. Even God still called him Jacob, though it was he who renamed him.

44:2 Jacob then lifted his eyes and saw Esau standing tall and proud with his four hundred men.

44:3 Jacob quickly organized his belongings in one final act of cowardice. He put his wives' handmaidens and their children first, to block Esau.

44:4 Behind them were Leah and her children. Behind Leah and her children were Rachel and Joseph.

44:5 Jacob knelt behind Rachel, using her skirt to hide himself.

44:6 Esau left his men behind and ran towards them. He ploughed through the handmaidens, children and wives, found Jacob and bowed to him seven times

44:7 After the bows, he stood up proud, lifted Jacob on high, embracing and kissing him.

44:8 The two men embraced each other and wept. Esau wept tears of joy, for he loved and missed his brother dearly and was filled with joy for seeing Jacob once more.

44:9 Jacob wept out of fear, for he thought his brother insane and was going to squeeze the life from his chest.

44:10 Esau looked upon his brother. "You have returned to me and the land of our fathers. A joyous day this is.

44:11 I see among you many women and children. Tell me who they are, so that I may praise and welcome them." And Jacob said, "These are the children the lord has given me, for being a humble servant to God."

44:12 First the handmaidens came with their children, bowed to Esau and gave their names.

44:13 Then Leah came with her many children and bowed to Esau.

44:14 Lastly were Rachel and Joseph, who bowed and introduced them to Esau.

44:15 When introductions were finished, Esau turned to Jacob. "When I come to greet you, you had men in my way, with oxen and flocks and cattle plenty. Why do you greet me with them, instead of yourself?"

44:16 And Jacob said, "Those were a gift for you, so as you may find grace in the lord and share in my wealth."

44:17 Esau laughed heartily. "My youngest brother, I need not these gifts. The lord God has blessed me with enough for my family and I to live in luxury. Take them back, for I neither want nor need them."

44:18 Jacob insisted Esau take them, for though he seemed happy now, Jacob felt safer if Esau were happier, for he did not want to upset his eldest brother for fear Esau may remember why he left.

44:19 "The lord has blessed me graciously, dearest Esau. I insist you take them, for I have plenty to spare. Once, I have shamefully taken your blessing. Consider this retribution for such deception at your cost."

44:20 Esau, after much convincing, accepted Jacob's gift.

44:21 Esau spoke with Jacob, saying, "Come, live with me. For my crops are bountiful, fields plentiful and flocks fruitful. It would be an honour to share my land with my youngest brother, so that together we may be great, wonderful and powerful men in the eyes of the land and the eyes of the lord."

44:22 Jacob did not want to live off the lands of Esau. For Jacob was still a greedy little fucker and wanted land of his own, not to be shared by others. Thinking quickly, he came with a reason to have land of his own.

44:23 "Esau, my dearest brother, I love you and would gladly share in your wealth. But to do so would mean the downfall of us both. I see your land and you have enough to maintain your flocks with no worry. But both of ours. No, to do so would be disastrous.

44:24 Our flocks and cattle would eat all there is of the fields, stripping the land of feed, until it became necessary for us to feed the beasts our own grain. But will we have enough to supply both us and the creatures. No, for to do so would mean starvation for both of us.

44:25 No, give me land of my own, so that I may care for mine without worry and you yours."

44:26 Esau knew Jacob to be telling the truth and agreed that he should claim land of his own. So, Esau went back to his home of Seir and Jacob travelled to Succoth, near the border of Canaan.

44:27 There he pitched his tent near the city of Shalem, in the province of Shechem, land of the Canaanites. He grew crops, fed cattle and built barns, so that the Canaanites may witness his labour and learn from him.

44:28 In the land of Shechem he bought a field for one hundred pieces of copper and there placed an altar to the lord God in land where the heathens used to claim.

44:29 On that altar he sacrificed seven lambs, four camels, an ox and two doves, danced around it naked and bathed in their blood for, as you and he both know, the lord loves blood, nudity and torn flesh.

44:30 He named the land of the altar EleloheIsrael, in defiance of the land once owned by human beasts.

45:1 Dinah, the final daughter of Leah, went to visit the lands of Canaan.

45:2 While there she met Shechem son of Hamor the Hivite, prince of the country. The two embraced one another and shared a bed, for the two fell in love.

45:3 Shechem treated Dinah with admiration, loyalty and respect. He asked Hamor, "Father, I have fallen in love with this woman most wonderful and would be honoured to have her call me husband. But she comes from the neighbouring lands and I know not their customs of marriage. How would I marry this woman?"

45:4 Hamor admitted to his son that he knew not how, but would gladly find out if it meant happiness for his son and Dinah.

45:5 Jacob learned of Hamor's intentions and grew mad, for a Canaanite has defiled and he believed, raped his youngest daughter. But he held his tongue and made no mentions to his sons' of Hamor's intentions, for he knew they would take revenge on these people for dishonouring their sister.

45:6 Unfortunately, word spread to the brothers of Dinah and they grieved and wept for her. She committed a terrible sin and slept with a foreign man. Worse, a foreign man who has not given the lord God his foreskin. For a daughter of Abraham to lie with a man whose foreskin was still attached has never been done and surely a curse will be sent forth from God.

45:7 Hamor communed with Jacob. "A glorious and wondrous thing has happened. My son has offered his heart to your daughter and I come here to ask for your blessing. I pray to you, give her to my son so that the two may live in marriage.

45:8 It shall be a glorious day, for in the two marrying we shall become allies of the land. Your sons shall take my daughters and your daughters my sons, if love make it so.

45:9 And we shall live in peace, trade and profit in both our lands fortunes.

45:10 I ask for no dowry that comes with Dinah, for the blessing of future trade with your nation is more than enough for us."

45:11 But Jacob and his sons answered Hamor with deceit, claiming, "Your son did not lie with our daughter in consent, but forced herself upon her and raped her. You come to us asking for her in marriage, well, we demand this marriage happen, lest our daughter be stained with your son's seed.

45:12 But a problem lies in this. For your son and your people are uncircumcised and have selfishly kept their foreskins instead of offering them to the lord God.

45:13 If you, your son and your people offer us your foreskins as offering to the lord, we will consent to marriage and our lands shall live in peace."

45:14 The nation of Shechem met and discussed peacefully the demands of Jacob's nation. Being a fair people and believing the voice of the nation lie in its civilians, the decision for circumcision was put to a vote.

45:15 The votes came in, were tallied and in a great majority it was decided that yes, the men of Shechem shall remove their foreskins if it meant peace.

45:16 It should be noted that the women of Shechem were treated with respect and held the same rights as men. They voted as well and the women of Shechem outranked the men in a ratio of 5:3.

45:17 The men took knives, freshly sharpened and mutilated their genitals, removing the foreskin and gathered them, until all the men and boys of Shechem had given their foreskins.

45:18 Hamor placed the foreskins in sacks, filling three of them and went forth to Jacob, slowly, as he was sore from the circumcision and gave them to Jacob as an offering to the lord.

45:19 Simeon and Levi, sons of Jacob and brothers of Dinah, saw this and knew the men of Shechem sore and weakened from the procedure.

45:20 They gathered servants and arms and marched upon the land of Hamor and slew all the males, young and old.

45:21 The men of Shechem were peaceful men, but brave. They fought back, but were no match, for the pain in their loins were greater than any pain they could give with a weapon.

45:22 Some even looked forward to their death, as it meant escape from the discomfort of their genital wounds.

45:23 The brothers of Dinah then gathered the wealth of Shechem. Sheep, concubines, oxen and asses, as revenge for their sister Dinah, who they believed raped.

45:24 As a final act of justice, they raped the women of Shechem. All of them. Young, old, elderly, fat, thin, beautiful and ugly. Even the ones in uncleanliness they raped, yelling as they did this,

45:25 "Feel the wrath of the lord within you. For your brethren dare rape our beloved sister with a penis ruined with foreskin. Feel our mighty genitals forced within your bowels. Does it not feel great, having men of God, lacking foreskin, inside of you!!?"

45:26 They lay waste to the city, leaving the women survived, raped and weeping.

45:27 As they returned home, satisfied in the vengeance of Dinah, Jacob called upon them and scolded them.

45:28 "Fools, both of you. Incompetent, stupid fools. For you have brought revenge to the savage Canaanites, but you did not finish what you start.

45:29 It is not enough to rape the women, claim their values and kill the males, children and men.

45:30 You must kill the women as well, for women gossip and shall spread the news to their neighbours friendly to Shechem.

45:31 You have cursed this land with your laziness. You should have killed the women!"

45:32 As Simeon and Levi left the scolding of their father, they hung their heads in shame. They knew they did not complete the will of the lord for letting the women survive. But they did, in hopes of raping them again.

45:33 They then wondered, what of Dinah. For though a man rapes a woman, it is the woman who tricks him into rape, thus being the most sinful. Should they kill Dinah as well, saving her from herself?

46:1 God said to Jacob, "Arise, go forth to Bethel and dwell there and make an altar in that land for me, one that looks like the altar placed where I met you at the ford Jabbok and fought against you."

46:2 Jacob gathered his family and servants and told them of their journey. "But before we leave for Bethel, throw away the idols bought in the foreign land, for they are idols of false gods and are an abomination to the lord.

46:3 They are unholy and even when used as a child's toy they are sinful. Then go, bathe yourselves and put on clean garments, for we have a great journey ahead.

46:4 For the lord God has come to me, as he often does when I inhale the smoke of the mandrake and told me to go to Bethel and make for him an altar there."

46:5 His people went, bathed, changed and gave to him their many statues depicting false gods. Jacob went to a great oak tree with a servant and had him dig a deep and mighty hole. There, Jacob tossed the false idols in that hole and the servant covered them up, burying the many blasphemous statues.

46:6 The mass then followed Jacob to Bethel, under the protection of the lord. As they passed cities, the lord God would send forth angels of great fear to surround the cities, terrorizing the people within so that they may not leave their homes and attack Jacob. This protected Jacob and his people and provided mild amusement for their long and tiring trek.

46:7 Jacob arrived at Bethel, still called Luz by the foolish Canaanites and set up camp.

46:8 He and his people built a mighty altar to the lord, depicting him as he appeared to Jacob when the two fought. It was a mighty piece of artwork. The statue depicted the mighty biceps, the strong thighs, even the flowing beard.

46:9 However, one of the sculptures chiselled a bit too much from the right hand of God and it fell upon Rachel's personal nurse, named Deborah. She died and was buried under a nearby oak tree.

46:10 They named the land of the tree Allonbachuth. The people saw this and new that even a statue of the lord God has power to smite them. They praised the lord, sacrificed an ox and danced around it naked, bathing in its blood.

46:11 The lord did not take notice of this sacrifice. He was too busy masturbating.

46:12 When God finished and wiped up, he came down to Jacob again.

46:13 "Jacob my son, when we have fought I renamed you Israel, yet the people still call you by your old name. Remember your new true name, Israel.

46:14 For when the lord renames you, it is a great honour, a single word worth more than any blessing.

46:15 Remember, I am the lord God almighty, creator of heaven and earth. Be fruitful and multiply, for a nation, nay, many nations shall come from your loins!

46:16 And the land I have promised to your father and your father's father I promise to you and your children."

46:17 God then left and travelled back to the kingdom of heaven.

46:18 Jacob/Israel then built a mighty pillar of stone and poured upon it strong drink and fine oil.

46:19 He then sacrificed a deer upon the altar and bathed naked in its blood, in praise of the lord God almighty.

46:20 The lord did not notice, as he was still ascending towards heaven at the time of the sacrifice.

46:21 Jacob/Israel then named the place Bethel. Again.

46:22 As they journeyed from Bethel, it was decided the nearby lands of Ephrath would be a better place to live. Jacob/Israel took to heart the lord's advice of being fruitful and multiplying.

46:23 With the aid of herbs and oils, he was given an erection and placed it in Rachel before he became limp.

46:24 Rachel accepted Jacob/Israel's weakened seed. But without the aid of Deborah, she died in birth.

46:25 She died happy, for in her final moments of life, she gave birth to a son. She died doing the very reason women were put on the earth to accomplish.

46:26 As she was dying, she named her final son Benoni. Jacob/Israel/To hell with this I'm sticking with Jacob!

46:27 Jacob misheard her and mistakenly named him Benjamin.

46:28 The people buried Rachel on their way to Ephrath, which is known now as Bethlehem.

46:29 And Jacob set atop the grave a mighty tombstone, saying,

46:30 Here lie the beauty and spirit of Rachel

46:31 Loving wife and adoring mother

46:32 For seven years I served in payment of her marriage

46:33 Why couldn't I lay Leah here instead?

46:34 The peoples moved and spread their tents beyond the tower of Edar.

46:35 It came to pass that Reuben noticed the form of Bilhah, his father's concubine and demanded she lie with him a night. Reuben's seed was accepted by Bilhah, but because she was Jacob's concubine, the child was rightfully his. Now the sons of Jacob were twelve.

46:36 The sons born of Leah were Reuben, Simeon, Levi, Judah, Issachar and Zebulun.

46:37 The sons of Rachel were only two. Joseph, and Benjamin

46:37 The sons of Bilhah, given to Jacob by Rachel, were Dan and Naphtali.

46:38 The sons of Zilpah, the handmaiden offered by Leah, were Gad and Asher.

46:39 Jacob decided twelve sons were enough and the one conceived by Reuben with his concubine was given to Reuben. Jacob didn't want it, as it was an ugly baby.

46:40 Jacob came upon the lands of Mamre, where his father resided. Isaac was pleased to have Jacob return and heard he and Esau were friendly.

46:41 Isaac, seeing Jacob blessed by the lord, knew his purpose in life was fulfilled and that through Jacob the lord shall keep his covenant.

46:42 At the age of one hundred eighty, Isaac died a happy man.

46:43 The brothers Jacob and Esau came, mourned and buried their father.

47:1 Next is the generations of Esau.

47:2 Nobody cares.

47:3 Moving on.

48:1 Jacob, to expand upon the empire of his father's, dwelt in the land where he was a stranger.

48:2 He dwelt in the land of Canaan.

48:3 Where the people left him alone, for they feared Jacob a mighty sorcerer, as he had the power of the lord.

48:4 Jacob's son, Joseph, was the obvious favourite of the children. Jacob saved for him the best seats, the best food and rarely did Joseph have to work. For he was spoiled with his father's love.

48:5 Joseph's brethren knew this and was jealous. They loathed the little twerp and were hostile to him, speaking to him in anger.

48:6 Of course, Joseph whined to Jacob about this and Jacob punished his other sons by making them work harder in the fields, work usually meant for a servant.

48:7 One night, under the influence of alcohol, Joseph had a strange dream.

48:8 He dreamed that he and his brothers were working in the barley fields, binding sheaves of grain. Joseph was confused why he was there, for he never did this work.

48:9 Suddenly, his sheaf arose, standing tall and proud. The sheaves of his brothers shrank and bowed to Joseph's sheaf of barley

48:10 Joseph's sheaf suddenly spoke, with a clear and mighty voice and commanded the sheaves of his brothers. The other sheaves obeyed. This is when Joseph woke up.

48:11 The morning, he ran to the fields where the brothers were shearing sheep and told them of this dream.

48:12 "My brethren, last night I had a strange and wondrous dream!"

48:13 The brothers were used to Joseph telling them of his dreams and thought it was the usual one where he's naked, running through a forest, being chased by a horde of angry Canaanites.

48:14 They told Joseph, "Stop, for we are busy doing the work of men. We care not for your silly dreams."

48:15 But Joseph ignored them and told them anyway.

48:16 "This dream is different, one I had not before. We are all together, working a field of barley. I'm doing quite well, bundling barley into sheaves. When suddenly, my sheaf of grain stood tall and proud!

48:17 All your sheaves bowed down before it. Then, my sheaf started speaking, in a deep voice, commanding your sheaves and giving them orders.

48:18 Then your sheaves did as they were told. Isn't that strange?"

48:19 His brothers grew furious at this strange and meaningless dream.

48:20 "What do you think it means. That you shall command us and rule over us and we'll do your bidding like some sort of woman?

48:21 No. We are older than you, smarter than you and stronger than you. We will never bow down to such a snot nosed fool like yourself."

48:22 The brothers then went back to work, angry over Joseph's arrogance. Joseph left them, in tears, for he merely wanted to share his dream to the world.

48:23 Joseph told his father about the cruel words his brothers said to him and Jacob promised the lad that such words would not go unpunished.

48:24 That night, Joseph had another dream. He dreamed that he was placed on a pedestal in the sky and the sun moon and eleven stars revolved around him.

48:25 That morning, Joseph arose and rushed to tell his brothers of this new dream. He searched the fields and flocks but could not find them.

48:26 Joseph went to his father, to ask where his brothers were. He found them all, being scolded by Jacob for being cruel to Joseph and not congratulating him on his dreams.

48:27 Joseph rushed in, interrupted Jacob and told of this other dream.

48:28 The brothers told their father, "Do you not see this. He dreams he will rule over us all and we'll do his bidding. We have no time to listen to this while we work. Why do you not hire a servant to listen to his ramblings, so that we may tend to the fields in peace."

48:29 Jacob ignored the reasoning of his other sons and said, "Surely this is a sign of the lord, that Joseph is to have dominion over us!"

48:30 He then bowed and demanded the other sons bow to Joseph as well. They refused, and were punished for such an insult to Jacob.

49:1 The days passed and the lesser sons of Jacob were sent to the fields of Shechem, to care for their father's flock.

49:2 Joseph liked the sheep, as the wool was soft and pleasing to the touch. He wanted to come, but the brothers left without him.

49:3 He went to his father. "Where are my brothers. For they left without me. Did you not send them to the fields of Shechem?"

49:4 Jacob told him that yes, he did send them to the fields of Shechem to care for his flocks and that Joseph should follow them, for it is not far.

49:5 The brothers knew Joseph would follow them and took the flocks to Dothan to eat, hoping their brother won't find them.

49:6 Joseph arrived at Shechem and found the land empty. He sat under a tree and cried.

49:7 A Canaanite was passing by and saw Joseph weeping under the tree. He asked him, "Why do you cry?"

49:8 Jacob responded that his sadness was for his brothers, for they are not here and feared a terrible tragedy fell upon them.

49:9 The Canaanite knew who Joseph spoke of and said, "But these people are fine. I saw them not long ago. They were heading to the fields of Dothan to tend to their flock."

49:10 Joseph was excited, for he knew where to find his brothers and could play with the sheep and lambs. He thanked the stranger and ran to Dothan.

49:11 The brothers saw Joseph on the horizon and were angered that the brat found them.

49:12 "Oh look, here comes the dreamer," they would say. "I wonder what vision he had now.

49:13 Perhaps now his dream is that he stood before us, mighty and tall and we all bowed down under his loins and caressed them with our tongues. Sick bastard."

49:14 As they spoke, their fury grew more and more and they started to conspire against Joseph.

49:15 "There be a pit, dry and fruitless, not far from here. Let us kill Joseph and throw him in the pit!"

49:16 But Reuben, the eldest son, said no, for though Reuben loathed Joseph, he wished not to shed his blood.

49:17 "Let us not kill him. To do so would bring the wrath of God. Let us instead throw him in the pit and watch him struggle as he tries to escape. That would be funny."

49:18 And as Joseph came upon them, the brothers ran, stripped him naked, took his coat of many colours (the reason why they were able to spot Joseph so far away) and threw him in the pit.

48:19 The brothers sat around the pit, drinking fresh water, bread and meat. Joseph looked above, tears in his eyes and begged for a morsel of food. The brothers laughed and gave him no food.

49:20 Joseph's begging grew stronger and stronger, for he had a mighty thirst. The brothers thought it funny to give him a bitter drink and urinated on Joseph, so that he may quench his thirst with their piss.

49:21 As they lifted their cock-piece, they noticed a caravan of Ishmeelites, carrying spices, silver and gold, perfumes, precious oils and myrrh.

49:22 They knew the Ishmeelites to be traders and were heading towards Egypt to haggle their goods.

49:23 Judah had a wicked idea. "Let us teach Joseph a lesson in humility. For he has never lifted a finger except to fill his mouth with food. Let us sell him as a slave to these traders.

49:24 When our father asks what happened to our brother, we shall tell him we came upon his body being eaten by beasts. We will soak

his coat in the blood of a sheep as evidence. Surely our father will accept this."

49:25 So the brothers lifted Joseph out of the pit and rushed to the Ishmeelites.

49:26 "Stop, for we have a bargain for you. This man is young, strong and able to learn quickly. He will make an excellent slave.

49:27 But we have enough servants and do not need to waste time training this one. How much do you want for him?"

49:28 The traders looked Joseph over and offered to the brothers twenty shekels of silver. They took it, glad to be rid of their brother.

49:29 Reuben then took Joseph's coat of many colours and threw it in the mud.

49:30 As the garment lay there, he took four young goats, slit their neck with his blade and had the blood poured into a bowl.

49:31 As the goats lay dead and the final drop was placed, he took the coat and soaked it in that bowl until not a string of fabric was unstained.

49:32 In celebration of ridding their brother, they ate the young goats, being quite pleased with themselves.

49:33 As they returned home, they sought forth their father and told him the bad news.

49:34 "Father, we tell you not to send Joseph to us, for he is ignorant of the land and knows not how to work. We worry for him, as we love him and am concerned for his safety.

49:35 Now you sent him to look for us in the fields of Shechem, but he never came. As we returned, was saw many a beast gorging themselves on a carcass unknown.

49:36 We thought nothing of it, and avoided them, until we heard a cry not of beast, but of man.

49:37 We rushed over and the beasts dragged their feast away. But we saw their feast and knew it to be Joseph.

49:38 We ran after them, but they ran faster. We were slow, father, after such a hard and labouring day and could not save our brother Joseph.

49:39 As we returned, mourning, we noticed his coat lying on the ground, tattered and bloodied.

49:40 We gathered this garment, precious to Joseph and offer it to you. Joseph is dead. Here is proof."

49:41 Jacob gazed upon the garment and wept loudly. "My son, my son, my favourite son. Knew not did I of your weakness.

49:42 I taught you nothing of the world and shaded you from evil. The lord God has punished me for this weakness and has taken away my son.

49:43 I know now his brothers were right to send him away, for they were not cruel, but concerned. I should have listened and took heed of their words. But I did not, and punished them instead.

49:44 Now my son lay dead in the belly of beasts. I killed my son, my beautiful son Joseph."

49:45 And all the sons, daughters and people of Jacob came forth to comfort the old man, but he refused such comfort. He chased them away, tears in his eyes, yelling, "I will be carried to my grave mourning my lost son."

49:46 Little did he know that the Ishmeelites sold Joseph to Potiphar the Egyptian, an officer of Pharaoh's and captain of the guard.

50:1 As time passed, Judah ventured off from his brothers and led a separate social life with Canaanites.

50:2 His eyes gazed upon a certain Canaanite woman, Shuah and he did lust for her.

50:3 Many times the two did casually lie together, until she conceived and bore Judah a son named Er.

50:4 The two lovers decided to be more careful and have Judah pull out before his seed shoots from his loin.

50:5 But he lost control one mid-afternoon and conceived with Shuah a second son named Onan.

50:6 Shuah and Judah grew fearful of their bastard family and decided to pleasure each other's loins through oral gratification.

50:7 The two, however, were sloppy and conceived yet another son named Shelah.

50:8 Judah, knowing his sons an abomination to God, thought it would please the lord if they married Hebrew women.

50:9 So he purchased for his eldest son a wife, Tamar, in hopes this would please the lord God almighty.

50:10 It did not, as the lord saw Er to be an abomination to the Hebrew people, a half-bred bastard.

50:11 So God killed him.

50:12 The sons of Judah grew into adolescence and Judah knew that soon they would be curious of the pleasures of women.

50:13 Judah, instead of getting a concubine, told his son Onan to sleep with Levi's wife, as she was beautiful and a known slut.

50:14 Onan did so, but did not want to bare child with her. So, he pulled out and his seed spilled on the blanket, staining it.

50:15 The lord God saw this stain and was disgusted by Onan's unsanitary act. As punishment for Onan spilling his seed on the blanket and not in a jar, the lord killed him as well.

50:16 Judah didn't mind. Onan was a bit retarded and a burden to his father.

50:17 Judah was under the influence of many a strong herb and thought Tamar the reason for his son's death.

50:18 He said to Tamar, widow of his eldest son, "Go now to my father's house. Remain there a widow, until my son Shelah grows. For I fear the lord God shall slay him as well if you interfere."

50:19 Not questioning the stupidity of his reason, Tamar left, for she knew Judah's father to be a wealthy man and expected to live under his rule in luxury.

50:20 As was his work, Judah left to Timnath to gather the wool from the sheepshearers with his friend Hirah the Adullamite, so that they may gather the wool and have the servants spin it to fine garments.

50:21 Tamar heard of Judah's arrival and was excited. For under the care of Jacob, she did not lie with a single man who could pleasure her. She believed Judah could give her great ecstasy in bed, as his eldest son did.

50:22 Tamar dressed in her most flimsy of garments and covered her face with a cloth.

50:23 When Judah passed her, he thought Tamar a harlot and grew excited, for he had extra money and could afford the pleasures of a whore.

50:24 Unable to recognize Tamar, he asked of her, "May the tool of my loins enter your cavern of pleasure?"

50:25 Tamar said to him, "For what price will you offer me, to have the pleasure of my company?"

50:26 Judah offered to Tamar a small goat from his flock, thinking that a good price for a prostitute.

50:27 But Tamar asked of him, "And what promise do you give to me that you will pay. For I see not a flock of goats and believe you plan to leave without paying."

50:28 Judah asked of this harlot, "Of what can I do give you to trust me. For I shall lend to you my belongings, which you shall keep until I pay you with a goat."

50:29 Tamar asked of Judah his signet ring, bracelets and staff, for they were worth more than a goat, giving Judah motivation to pay quickly.

50:30 Judah's head was empty and did not realize the harlot was ripping him off, for his blood rushed to his loins and his staff of flesh

grew large and demanded satisfaction.

50:31 He gave Tamar what she asked of him and the two went behind a shed and fucked.

50:32 Judah took good notice of the tattoo on the small of her back and thought it familiar.

50:33 Judah was satisfied with the services of Tamar and rested afterwards, giving her ample time to rush back to her home and put on the garments of a grieving widow.

50:34 Judah got the goat promised to the harlot and had his friend the Adullamite deliver the animal to her.

50:35 His friend Hirah searched for this harlot, but found her nowhere. He asked many locals, "Where is the whore, who entices men by that rock over there?

50:36 The locals told him a whore has never sold herself by the rock, for traffic there is slow and business is bad for the prostitutes.

50:37 Hirah went back to Judah with the goat and told his friend, "Try as I might to find this harlot, she has vanished. Even the locals knew not who I spoke of."

50:38 Judah, feeling shamed for being ripped off by a dumb cunt, said, "Then I shall always have on me one extra goat, for if I ever find this harlot I shall pay her my debt, forcing the bitch to give me back my jewelry and staff."

50:39 Three months passed and Judah was troubled by the harlot he could not find. It was not the shame of lying with a whore. No, that is a common pastime that all men of wealth did. It was the markings on the small of her back. He knew them familiar, but could not remember from where.

50:40 Suddenly, he remembered. Tamar had the tattoos as well!

50:41 Judah sent for his swiftest messenger and told him to go to Tamar and ask of her if she knew other women with the same markings etched on her back.

50:42 The messenger returned and said to Judah, "Tamar knew nothing of the harlot you speak, but she has obvious growth in her womb, though she tries to conceal this."

50:43 With sudden realization, Judah knew the harlot to be Tamar and grew furious. For he ordered the women to remain a grieving widow and grieving widow's take no comfort in the arms of any man.

50:44 He yelled to the clouds, "Tamar was the harlot and carries my seed in whoredom. Bring this creature to me, so we may roast her atop a great fire and feast on her flesh."

50:45 Tamar was brought back to Judah, bound and chained. She said to him, "To kill me would be foolish, for I carry your seed.

50:46 Killing me now would also kill your sons and earn you a place as an enemy of God. I will give you back your signet ring, bracelets and staff, but you must give to me the goat. Then let me go, so I may bear your child."

50:47 Judah, looking at this harlot, knew she was more righteous than he. For though she played the whore, it was he who paid for her services and he who sowed the seeds in her womb.

50:48 He accepted his belongings, and gave Tamar the promised goat. The scrawniest one he owned.

50:49 In six months' time, Tamar went into labour, and Judah sent midwives to tend to her.

50:50 Tamar was pregnant with not one child, but two. Sons. The first was pushed forth and was named Pharaz. The second came and was named Zarah.

50:51 Both the children were tattooed with scarlet marks upon their hands, so that the world would know them both to be sons of a whore and thus sinful.

51:1 When Joseph was brought into Egypt, the Ishmeelites sold him to Potiphar, a wealthy and prosperous man, captain of the guard.

51:2 For the lord was with Joseph and ensured he belonged to a wealthy man, so that Joseph could eat his master's fine food, drink his fine wine and still live in comfort.

51:3 Potiphar knew Joseph to be blessed by God and asked little of him. He had Joseph occasionally cook, bring him water and wine and serve food to guests. Nothing too laborious, for fear of bringing upon him the wrath of the lord.

51:4 Potiphar grew fond of Joseph, as he was a delight to his guests and kept them good company.

51:5 He promoted Joseph to overseer of the house and Joseph was in charge of the other maids and servants who kept with the daily household chores of Potiphar.

51:6 The blessing of Joseph then passed on to Potiphar's house and Potiphar was grateful for this, believing Joseph to be worth every coin he spent for him.

51:7 As time passed, Joseph noticed the beauty of Potiphar's wife and his loins filled with lust.

51:8 The two became close, flirting with one another as Joseph kept the house. Though the wife had no intentions of sleeping with Joseph, she was filled with pride that such a young man lusted for her.

51:9 One day, as Potiphar was away, his wife took a bath. Joseph snuck into the bath chamber, undressed and joined her in the water.

51:10 The wife let out a scream, demanding this servant leave her as she lay naked. But Joseph did not obey.

51:11 He grabbed from the counter a candlestick and beat her, demanding she be quiet.

51:12 Fearing for her life, she submitted to Joseph.

51:13 And Joseph had his way with her and was satisfied and retired to his bedchamber.

51:14 The woman was afraid and stayed in the tub, crying and bathing as she never felt dirtier before.

51:15 When Potiphar came home, he saw his wife in the tub, upset.

51:16 He asked of her, "Why do you cry, dear woman. You are well cared for and I can tell that you are clean. Stop scrubbing your body and tell me what troubles you."

51:17 She told him, "The Hebrew boy, the newest one. He may be a man of God, but he is a man of a cruel God.

51:18 He lusted for me all this time and this lust grew and grew until he succumbed to it.

51:19 He came to me today, as I lie here in this tub and threatened me and had his way with me."

51:20 With this accusation, Potiphar grew angry and thought his wife drunk and mistaken. He grabbed the nearest robe and wrapped it around his wife, attempting to comfort her.

51:21 It was then he realized, the robe he grabbed belong not to his wife, but Joseph.

51:22 Outraged was he. For this slave, this Hebrew he cared for, betrayed him and made a victim of his wife!

51:23 As he stayed with her, for he was a good husband and would not leave her side in her time of need, he sent for a servant that he trusted.

51:24 No longer fearing the wrath of God, he told the servant to send for the guards and arrest Joseph for rape.

51:25 The guard grabbed Joseph as he slept and threw him in the dungeons. All the while Joseph claimed it was she who came upon him and he denied her advances.

51:26 But though Potiphar no longer feared the wrath of the lord, the guards and prison keeper did.

51:27 They put Joseph in a fine cell and fed him well.

51:28 Even the prisoners knew Joseph to be blessed by the lord and left him be. Joseph, with the blessing of the lord, became master of the prisoners and the captives became his bitch.

51:29 The prison keepers turned a blind eye to Joseph's actions, as he lay with the prisoners the same way Ham laid with his father.

51:30 Joseph did this with the blessing of the lord.

52:1 It came to pass that the Pharaoh's butler and baker offended him and was thrown in the cell of Joseph.

52:2 The butler served to Pharaoh ale in a cup, stained and unclean.

52:3 The baker was imprisoned also for serving to Pharaoh's guest cakes that had a hair in it.

52:4 Joseph did take advantage of the two prisoners and the men provided lustful satisfaction for him.

52:5 One night, as the men slept, the butler and the baker had a dream.

52:6 When they awoke, the two men were scared, for they both had dreams, but knew not how to interpret them.

52:7 Hearing that Joseph had dreams as well, they asked him what to make of them.

52:8 "The lord has blessed you both for having you share the same cell as I, for I am also a dreamer and know how to interpret them."

52:9 The baker thought his dream private and refused to share it with a foreigner. But the butler knew Joseph to be blessed by the lord and told him his dream.

52:10 "I am wrapped in dirty clothes, but of fine garments they are made. In front of me, I see a vine, a grape vine.

52:11 The vine grows and slithers like the cobra, until it spreads into three branches.

52:12 All branches immediately blossom and grapes plump and sweet grow from them all.

52:13 I pluck the bundles of grapes and squeeze them into Pharaoh's cup, giving it to Pharaoh, who takes the cup and drinks the fresh juice."

52:14 Joseph ponders the butler's dream, and comes to a conclusion.

52:15 "My friend, you have truly been blessed by the lord. For this is a dream of happiness and good will.

52:16 The three branches represent three days. In three days, the Pharaoh will realize that he has wrongly imprisoned you.

52:17 He will drop all charges and restore to you your former title and job."

52:18 The butler was pleased with this interpretation and thanked Joseph.

52:19 "Foreigner, you have offered me hope in this abysmal time. Tell me, of what favour can I do for you?"

52:20 Joseph asked only that the butler remember him as an innocent man and tell the Pharaoh of him and send him out of prison.

52:21 For Joseph missed the land of his father's and wanted so desperately to return home and tell his brothers of his time in Egypt.

52:22 The butler said he would remember Joseph and do what he can to free him of prison.

52:23 Hearing Joseph's interpretation of the butler's dream and hearing the outcome to be good, the baker decided to ask of Joseph's interpretation.

52:24 "Joseph, the night of the butler's dream, I had a dream as well, but know not how to interpret such madness. May I seek your counsel?"

52:25 Joseph agreed and listened to the baker's dream.

52:26 "I am walking the streets of the city, and barren they be.

52:27 As I walk, I carry three baskets atop my head. The baskets are filled with pastries, breads and baked goods.

52:28 While walking, wild birds come, perch upon my baskets and eat of the goods within."

52:29 Joseph thought for a while and came up with a harsh and dark interpretation.

52:30 "Your dream is similar to the dream of the butler's. The three baskets atop your head represent three days as well.

52:31 But I fear in three days you will not be blessed by Pharaoh, but cursed!

52:32 For Pharaoh shall hold a public execution of your death and your body shall hang from the trees so that the birds will come and feast upon your flesh, as they did the pastries in your dream."

52:33 The baker did not like this interpretation and cursed Joseph.

52:34 Now, the lord God heard Joseph's interpretations and made them happen.

52:35 For the lord had a plan for Joseph.

52:36 In three days, it was the Pharaoh's birthday and the nation of Egypt celebrated.

52:37 Pharaoh did restore the butler and cleared him of charges, for he knew the butler was not responsible for the stained glass.

52:38 It was the dishwasher's fault for putting a dirty glass in the cupboard. She was imprisoned.

52:39 Pharaoh was not so kind to the baker, for he knew the baker loathed him.

52:40 Believing the hair in his pastry to be plucked from the baker's loins, he held a public execution.

52:41 The baker hung in the gallows, his body swaying in the breeze and birds did eat of his flesh.

52:42 The lord God made it so, as to prove true the interpretations of Joseph.

52:43 Knowing Joseph's prophecy true, the butler became fearful of him and thought such a foreign sorcerer would curse Pharaoh.

52:44 So he did not tell Pharaoh of Joseph, thinking that such a sorcerer should be left in the dungeons to rot.

53:1 After two years passed, Joseph was still jailed, claiming his accusations false.

53:2 Still, he begged and prayed to the lord God to grant him freedom from the cell and power over his captors.

53:3 The lord heard Joseph and listened.

53:4 The lord gave to Pharaoh a dream.

53:5 Pharaoh stood before the mighty Nile and from the river seven cows arose, went to a meadow and fed in gluttony.

53:6 The Pharaoh watched the cows feast, their bellies filling and their meat growing fat and delicious.

53:7 Then the Pharaoh looked towards the river again as seven small and skinny cows came forth from the banks.

53:8 These cows went towards the meadow to feast, but not on the offerings of the earth.

53:9 The lame and sick cows opened wide their jaws and in one gulp consumed the fat and gluttonous beasts.

53:10 Pharaoh awoke in a fright and had trouble returning to sleep. He had his butler bring to him a strong and fine wine, to calm his nerves and aid in his sleep.

53:11 On returning to bed, Pharaoh had another dream.

53:12 He looked upon a barren land, full of rich soil but with no crops growing.

53:13 Suddenly, in front of him stood up a large and mighty stalk of corn. On the stalk were seven ears, large and full and ripe for eating.

53:14 As the Pharaoh stared upon the stalk, a great and mighty wind blew from the east, destroying the stalk of corn and drying the seven fruitful ears of corn.

53:15 The wind died and Pharaoh witnessed before him a pathetic, withered plant.

53:16 A stalk of corn, brown and dying, with seven dry and fruitless ears of corn. Each ear lacked a kernel of corn; only the cob remained.

53:17 When Pharaoh awoke, his mind was troubled. He believed the dreams to be meaningful, but knew not the message.

53:18 He gathered his most trusted advisors, doctors, magicians and elders, but none could agree upon the message.

53:19 When the butler heard of Pharaoh's dream, he grew afraid. Could this be a curse from that sorcerer Joseph?

53:20 He told Pharaoh of Joseph and how he was able to interpret the dreams of the baker and himself. He told Pharaoh that the dreams came true.

53:21 Knowing this man must be wise, Pharaoh sent for Joseph.

53:22 The guards took Joseph from his cell, bathed him, shaved him, dressed him in fine garments and presented him to Pharaoh.

53:23 Pharaoh told Joseph that he knew of his skill to interpret dreams and asked if he could interpret his.

53:24 Joseph, in humble modesty, said, "It is not I who interprets these dreams, but the lord God almighty.

53:25 Tell me the dream so that the lord may let me know of its meaning."

53:26 Pharaoh told Joseph, told him of the skinny cows devouring the fat cows from the Nile and told him of the stalks of corn.

53:27 Joseph knew what these meant and smiled.

53:28 "The dreams share the same meaning and is easy to interpret.

53:29 The seven fat cows and the seven fruitful ears of corn mean seven years.

53:30 For seven years your lands shall be prosperous, your people live in luxury and feasting like kings. You shall grow plenty of cattle and grains, so much that you shall have excess to waste.

53:31 But be warned and do not live in gluttony, for the seven sick cows and seven dead ears of corn also mean seven years.

53:32 For after seven years of prosperity, you shall have seven years of famine and drought. Your crops shall be barren, the land dry and the flocks shall starve and die."

53:33 When Pharaoh heard Joseph, he worried for his people. He knew not what to do, for seven years of famine will be harsh to his people and he worried his nation shall grow weak.

53:34 Fearing the wrath of God, he asked Joseph for advice.

53:35 Joseph saw this as an opportunity for power and claimed to Pharaoh he knew how to bless the land of Egypt.

53:36 But to do this, he must have power over the lands; a government position of great wealth and power.

53:37 Pharaoh appointed Joseph a great political leader, hoping that in doing so he will gain Joseph's favour and avoid the wrath of his God.

53:38 Joseph immediately put forward a tax. One fifth of all the crops harvested must be taken.

53:39 The army gathered the grains and stored them in great pyramids.

53:40 The people cared not for this tax, believing it unfair. The grain was theirs, why should the government take it because some foreign sorcerer said so?

53:41 Any that openly objected to the tax, Joseph demanded dead. The executed man's property then belonged to the government, as payment for the rope used during execution.

53:42 If the heirs objected, they were hanged as well.

53:43 Soon, the people of Egypt learned that to object meant death and they lived under the fear and wrath of Joseph, grudgingly paying the taxes made law through him.

53:44 As Joseph did this, he took notice of the women of Egypt and lusted their dark skin. He would have many a concubine pleasure him, but still his lust grew strong.

53:45 Potipherah, priest of the Egyptian lord On, heard of Joseph's lust and offered to him his daughter Asenath, believing this would bring to him a blessing from Joseph.

53:46 Joseph took Asenath into his chambers, with many other concubines and had his way with them.

53:47 Asenath took Joseph's seed and bore for him a son. Joseph named this child Manasseh and blessed the lord for this half breed child.

53:48 Asenath lied with Joseph again, as she was a truly skillful harlot and bore for him a second son.

53:49 Joseph named this second son of Asenath Ephraim and blessed the lord.

53:50 In celebration of his sons, he gathered a fat calf, slaughtered it and danced around it naked, bathing in the creature's blood.

53:51 The lord saw this and was pleased, for he loves blood, nudity and torn flesh.

53:52 The Egyptians saw this and were disgusted, for they thought the sacrifice wasteful and barbaric.

54:1 Seven years passed and a great famine swept not just the nation of Egypt, but the nations of all the earth.

54:2 People grew hungry and starved. Riots swarmed the streets. Men chewed the leather straps of their sandals. Children cried of hunger. Pregnant women absorbed the foetus as nutrition.

54:3 The lord looked down upon this famine and laughed, for it brought the divine dictator great amusement.

54:4 But the lands of Egypt did not starve, did not cry, did not go hungry, for they ate of the grains reserved during their seven years of prosperity.

54:5 Neighbouring nations heard of Egypt's excess grain and came to the nation, in hopes of food.

54:5 Joseph gave them grain on loan.

54:6 Soon, the entire nations of the earth came to Egypt for food and became indebted to Pharaoh and Joseph and Egypt became a great and powerful nation, as the other nations amassed a great debt to Egypt.

54:7 Jacob, father of Joseph, heard of the corn stored in Egypt and sent for his sons.

54:8 He said to them, "Our lands are barren and our people hungry. This is a curse from God, for punishment for me killing my beloved Joseph.

54:9 The lord now humbles us and we must depend upon the heathen nations for life.

54:10 Go to the land of Egypt and buy for your peoples as much grain as can be spared, for otherwise we shall die of starvation."

54:11 The sons of Jacob gathered their carts and filled it with goods to trade. They then left.

54:12 All but Benjamin, the remaining son of the beloved Rachel. He was now Jacob's favourite and was left behind, for Jacob feared to let him out of his sight.

54:13 Joseph was now governor of Egypt and it was him in charge of the stored grain. Joseph decided which nations to loan the grain to, how much grain and the debt owed to Egypt.

54:14 So when Joseph saw his brothers come to him for aid, his heart filled with pride.

54:15 He remembered the dream he had, of his brother's sheaves of grain bowing before him and now his dream has come true.

54:16 For the brothers came to Joseph, did not recognize him and bowed to him, and asked for Egypt's grain.

54:17 Joseph knew his brothers clueless of his identity and thought this the perfect opportunity for revenge.

54:18 He accused his brothers of being spies and that they come not to barter for grain, but to steal it.

54:19 The brothers denied this accusation, saying, "We have come to barter for grain, not steal that which is yours."

54:20 We are the sons of Jacob, one man and have come as his humble servants to beg of your favour."

54:21 Joseph saw one brother missing, Benjamin and was curious how he was, since both shared the same mother.

54:22 He accused them again of being spies, saying, "I have heard of Jacob and know him to have twelve sons, but I see before me only ten. Where are the other two. Have they gone to take my grain as you fools distract me?"

54:23 Again, the ten brothers denied the accusations. "It is true, we are the sons of Jacob, in the land of the Canaanites and with twelve sons he was blessed. Our youngest brother stays with our father and the other brother is no longer of this earth."

54:24 Hearing this, Joseph knew his brothers told his father that he was dead and was angered by their lies.

54:25 Hearing this, he accused them of being spies again and had the guards arrest them.

54:26 The brothers feared no punishment, for they believed the almighty God would send his wrath down upon the nation of Egypt and claim the land for their father Jacob.

54:27 For three days his brothers rotted in the same cell that Joseph was condemned to. Joseph found the punishment fitting.

54:28 But Joseph was also troubled. What of his father. His brother Benjamin. Are they okay?

54:29 He knew Jacob would not send his sons to Egypt for grain unless his land was truly barren, his people starving.

54:30 So on the third day, he went to the cells of his brothers and offered them a deal.

54:31 "I am a God-fearing man and shall show you compassion.

54:32 A chance to feed the people of your father and prove your claims and innocence.

54:33 You all shall be released and sent to your lands with carriages of barley, wheat, corn and oats so that your people will not starve.

54:34 All but one, a person of my choosing.

54:35 If your people return for more grain, your youngest brother must come with him and verify what you all say. If he does, I shall set you all free and you will return again to your lands with grain.

54:36 But if you people come and your brother is not with them, this shall confirm you spies and thieves and I will feed the captor to the river beasts of the Nile."

54:37 The brothers huddled together and spoke. They spoke of who it was to leave, what to do of Benjamin and they spoke of Joseph.

54:38 Yes, Joseph. The brothers believed this famine a curse for selling Joseph as a slave and thought their imprisonment a curse from God for such treachery.

54:39 The brothers spoke in their native tongue, believing Joseph did not understand them, as they communicated through an interpreter.

54:40 When Joseph heard them speak of him, he turned his face away and a tear rolled down his cheek.

54:41 Joseph chose Simeon to stay as captor, grabbed him from the group and bound him.

54:42 He then commanded the remaining men's sacks to be filled with grain and to be provided with supplies for their trip home.

54:43 He also put in their sacks the bags of money they brought as payment, for Joseph could not charge his people for food if they starve. Not even he was that greedy.

54:44 The brothers departed and left for the lands of their father with a small bounty of grain.

54:45 Along the way, they stopped at an inn, so that their donkey's may rest and feast upon the hay.

54:46 When one of the brothers opened the sack of grain to pay the innkeeper, he noticed the money laying atop it.

54:47 In haste, he gathered his other brothers and told him of the money.

54:48 They searched their sacks and found the bags of money that was meant to pay Egypt for the grain they took.

54:49 They grew afraid, thinking this a curse from God. For they knew the Egyptians will accuse them of theft.

54:50 Upon their return home, they spoke to Jacob and told him of their ordeal, saying,

54:51 "The lord of the land, in charge of the surplus grain, spoke rudely to us and accused us falsely of spies and intention of theft.

54:52 We told him this was untrue, that we were twelve brothers, that the youngest stayed to care for our father and the other died in our native land.

54:53 Still, he did not believe us and has us thrown in the dungeons, to live with foul smelling beggars and thieves.

54:54 We believed God would bless us and save us and we thought he did.

54:55 For on the third day, the same man came to us and claimed to be a man of God and shall show us compassion.

54:56 Us nine he set free, but kept our brother Simeon as captor. He then filled our carts with grain and supplies and let us go.

54:57 But if we are to ever set Simeon free and gather for us grain again, we must return with Benjamin, to prove that we are mere men and not spies."

54:58 Before they finished speaking, Jacob said to them, "This is news most glorious, for the lord has blessed us with grain even with our barren lands. For more, all that be done is send Benjamin to the land and prove our innocence."

54:59 It was then he noticed the look of fear and sadness upon his sons and asked why they did not share in his excitement.

54:60 "Father, forgive us, for we knew not how it happened. When we left the prison, we were sent to our carts, full of provisions and allowed to leave.

54:61 We thought the money intended as payment was given to the proper people and the grain bought.

54:62 As we rested at an inn, we opened our sacks of grain. The money, the money intended as payment, was still with us. We did not..."

54:63 But Jacob did not let them finish.

54:64 "You fools!" The Egyptians shall think us now thieves. Why has God cursed me with such incompetent children?

54:65 Joseph is dead, Simeon shall be slain and if we return there with Benjamin they shall surely slaughter him as well. The lord has cursed me for coddling Joseph and shall soon take away all I hold dear."

54:66 Reuben, the eldest son, felt it was his responsibility to right this. He spoke to his father, "Let me return to Egypt with Benjamin and we shall free Simeon. I'll make an appeal to Pharaoh himself and tell him of what happened and give him the money meant for the grain.

54:67 If I fail and Benjamin is taken from you, then slay my two sons as punishment for failure."

54:68 Jacob said to him, "I dare not risk the life of my beloved son. For he and his Joseph were the only two men I ever loved, ever cared for. His brother of the same womb now lies in a field as animal shit. I will not risk the life of Benjamin, for if he dies then I shall bring nothing but sorrow to my grave."

55:1 Famine still cursed the land of Jacob and the loaned grains quickly diminished.

55:2 They knew nothing of rationing food, and the bellies of the people soon cried for more bread.

55:3 Jacob sent for his sons and told them to again go to Egypt and buy for them food.

55:4 His sons knew that Jacob was old and his mind fading. Judah reminded him,

55:5 "Father, the governor of the land demanded that if we return, we must bring your youngest son as well,

55:6 And if we return without him, he shall slay us and Simeon, held captive by the guard.

55:7 Also, we did not pay for that grain, as when we left the money was still in our possession, though we did not know this until too late.

55:8 We can explain to him that we knew not our money was with us, as we assumed the guards took it as payment. Perhaps that will be an accepted excuse and he won't charge us with theft.

55:9 But to return without our youngest brother will mean our doom and the death of Simeon, if he still be with us."

55:10 Jacob grew confused and demanded of them, "Why did you tell this lord of Egypt that you had another brother?"

55:11 They said to him, "He asked us direct questions. How is your father. Is he well. Where are your other brothers. How is your land, your people?

55:12 We answered him honestly, believing the truth would not come to harm us. Had we suspected anything, we would have lied."

55:13 Judah then said to his father, "Send the lad with me and I shall care for him, as I love him and hold him dearly to my heart.

55:14 If not, then we will all die of starvation, including Benjamin."

55:15 Jacob thought of this. If they go and Benjamin not come, then they will die by the hands of the Egyptians. Grain will be banned for his people and they shall all starve, including his youngest son.

55:16 If they not go, they all starve anyway.

55:17 If they go and Benjamin does come, there is a possibility the governor of the grain will believe them and sell to them grain. If not and Benjamin is in the land of Egypt, then the lord will unleash fury upon Pharaoh.

55:18 For a brief moment, Jacob wondered why God did not give his people the power to invade Egypt and take their grain, but he quickly pushed that aside for fear of angering the lord.

55:19 Jacob arose and said to his sons, "If it necessary, go to Egypt. Give to the rulers a gift of our people. The finest liquor we have left, some balm, a bit of honey, spices, perfume, myrrh and almonds.

55:20 Take the money originally meant to buy the grain and twice that amount as well. Explain you did not know the coins still in your possession and that you offer him the debt owed with interest.

55:21 Also, take Benjamin, for I rather risk him die quickly by the noose than slowly through starvation.

55:22 And God be with you, for if not and Benjamin die, I shall take heed of Reuben's words and kill his sons."

55:23 Hearing this, Reuben did not care. For if they fail, he will die. How could he possibly care for the life of his sons if he's dead?

55:24 The men gathered the gifts and left with Benjamin to the land of Egypt.

55:25 Joseph heard of his brothers return and that they brought their youngest with them.

55:26 When Joseph heard of this, he grew excited and said to his servants, "Slay a fat calf and prepare its flesh, for these men that come to me shall dine well at my house today."

55:27 When the brothers heard they were to dine in the house of the governor, they grew paranoid and feared a trap.

55:28 The ten entered Joseph's house, still oblivious as to his identity and confessed to the guard of the house.

55:29 "Forgive us. We come only to buy food for our people.

55:30 We brought our youngest brother, Benjamin, as you requested and money for grain.

55:31 Count it and you shall see it is more money than you ask, for when we took grain the last time, our coins were still in our possession.

55:32 We knew nothing of this and believed you had it. When we realized the money was still with us, we were already in our native land and grew fearful, for we did not mean to steal your grain."

55:33 The guard laughed at them and knew they did not mean to steal the grain. If they thought so, then their father's land would now belong to Pharaoh.

55:34 The brothers were relieved upon hearing this and entered Joseph's house.

55:35 Simeon was there and the brothers rejoiced in this reunion.

55:36 Servants brought them out fresh fruits and water, washed their feet and made them comfortable.

55:37 Concubines from the nearest brothel came by and pleasured them all with the skills of their tongues.

55:38 Outside, the beasts of burden were well cared for, with fresh hay to eat and stable boys brushing their fur.

55:39 When Joseph came in, the men bowed low and offered to him the presents Jacob sent.

55:40 Joseph thanked them and asked of the welfare of their father, land and people.

55:41 They told him, "Our father is alive and well, with the blessing of the lord. Our people are content, but our lands still are barren."

55:42 As the brothers rambled, Joseph noticed Benjamin and tears welled up in his eyes.

55:43 He left to his bedchamber and wept, for he missed his brother so.

55:44 Washing his face, Joseph returned and demanded that they feast.

55:45 The brothers sat around the table, eldest to youngest as is tradition and ate fine meats and bread.

55:46 Egyptians serving in Joseph's house ate separately, as they were disgusted by the gluttonous manner in which the brothers ate.

55:47 As desert arrived, Joseph rose and made a toast.

55:48 "To the men born of Jacob, I raise my glass to you.

55:49 For you are men of good heart and blessed by the lord.

55:50 But I treated you unfairly and accused you of being spies when you were not.

55:51 Please, accept my apology and these gifts.

55:52 I shall send to your people grain and accept the money owed to Pharaoh, for I believe you did not mean to take the money with you. The money was obviously left in your possession by the incompetence of the guards.

55:53 Lastly, I give to you all gifts of ale, so that you may drink and be merry in my great land."

55:54 And with these words, servants gave to the guests many bottles of beer. But Benjamin was given the greatest amount, five times what the others had.

55:55 And the brothers drank and enjoyed their time in Egypt.

56:1 Joseph saw the guilt his brothers carried for selling him to slavery, but was still bitter for what they did.

56:2 He decided to tell them of his true identity, but before doing so shall scare them one more time, so that his brothers may grovel at his feet again.

56:3 Joseph commanded his servants, "Fill these men's sacks with grain and place atop the grain the money they brought in payment.

56:4 Take this silver cup of mine and put it in the sack of the youngest brother."

56:5 The servants did this, believing Joseph wanted to make war with the nation of Jacob and framing them with theft again to give the army reason to invade.

56:6 When the sun rose, the brothers bid their farewell and left for home.

56:7 Before they travelled far from the city, Joseph sent the guard to chase them and told the soldiers, "When you reach these men, ask of them, why do you reward the compassion of Egypt with theft and betrayal?

56:8 Why do you steal from the governor his silver cup, a man who invited you into his house?

56:9 You are evil men and shall be brought to justice for such treachery."

56:10 The guards overtook the brothers and said what Joseph ordered them to say.

56:11 And the brothers were confused and said to the guards, "Why would we come back again, only to do the same thing?

56:12 We are God fearing men and knew nothing of the money when we first left.

56:13 That is why we brought the money out of our land and into yours, to give to you as a sign of our respect.

56:14 Why then would we risk our good name by stealing silver or gold from your governor's house?

56:15 If the money is found in any of our possessions, let them be a slave to Egypt.

56:16 And if the cup be found stolen by one of us, let them be a servant of your governor."

56:17 The guards agreed to this and searched the belongings of the brothers, starting from eldest to youngest.

56:18 As the money was found one by one to be in each brother's belongings, they feared this a curse from the lord.

56:19 When the guards came to Benjamin, the cup was found and the brothers cried in fear, for they again failed their father.

56:20 The guards stripped the men of their clothes, took their donkeys and camels and forced them to march back to the city.

56:21 And the brothers were sent to Joseph's house, for he was still there, waiting for them.

56:22 Joseph said to them, "What evil deed is this, you men who claim to be of God. I offer you grain for your peoples and you steal it from me.

56:23 I invite you into my house and you take from me my silver goblet. Have you no honour?"

56:24 Judah fell to his knees and kissed Joseph's feet, grovelling to him, "What can I say to you. How can we clear our good name. By the will of God, we are now your humble servants, but we did not take the money a second time. Accept our servitude"

56:25 Joseph looked down upon Judah and said to him, "You men who stole my grain are fools and shall remain fools as punishment. But the lad who stole my cup. That lad shall be my servant, my personal slave. The rest, get up and go to your land."

56:26 The brothers cried again, for how could they return to their father without his most beloved son?

56:27 Judah spoke again. "My lord, let us eldest be your slave and unleash your fury and anger upon our bodies. But let the youngest leave.

56:28 Our father is old and sad. His second wife, Rachel, birthed for him two sons, the youngest of us twelve. We ten are of the less favoured wife.

56:29 Benjamin is the only son of this woman. The other son, Benjamin's brother of the same mother, died.

56:30 This brother is all our father holds dear. He fears for him and his safety. To lose him, our father would grow deeper into sadness, until his life leaves him.

56:31 When our food ran dry again, we told him of your demands to see our youngest and our father entrusted Benjamin in our care.

56:32 We cannot return home, failing our father in this manner. It was us who took responsibility for Benjamin and it shall be us who shall be punished.

56:33 I beg of you, let us stay in servitude, in slavery, in morbid entertainment.

56:34 For we shall be tortured and whipped for the sadistic pleasure of your people, if it meant our father's happiness.

56:3 Let all us stay, but please, send Benjamin home."

57:1 As Joseph heard the compassion these men had for his father, a deep sadness overtook him.

57:2 He sent his servants away and were left alone with his brothers.

57:3 Joseph ran into his house and wept. He wept so loud the servants in his stay heard him and even his brothers and the neighbours around his house heard Joseph's cries.

57:4 Wiping away his tears again, Joseph returned to his brothers and said to them, "I am your brother Joseph, the one you sold to the caravan of Ishmeelites for twenty shekels of silver. Tell me, please, how is our father?"

57:5 His brothers stared at Joseph and were shocked and afraid, for they took notice of the facial features, bone structure, eye shape and colour and this governor of Egypt did have a close resemblance to their brother.

57:6 Simeon, the best bullshitter of the brothers, came to Joseph and said,

57:7 "Be not angry at us for selling you into slavery, for do you not see this be the will of God?

57:8 The lord meant for you to come here, so that you may gain great power over these heathens and store for your people grain so that they may live during this famine."

57:9 Joseph pondered this and believed Simeon's words, for it was twisted, stupid and foolish enough to have been the will of God.

57:10 "I see your reason, my brother. It was not you, nor any mere man who sold me to a life of servitude, but the lord God himself!

57:11 He blessed me with manners of interpreting dreams and used this skill so that I may gain power in Egypt."

57:12 He then explained how he was imprisoned for rape, which he still insisted his innocence to and that he interpreted the dreams of two men.

57:13 Pharaoh heard of this and sent for Joseph to interpret his dream, allowing Joseph to rise in political power and give his people opportunity to control Egypt.

57:14 The brothers listened to Joseph's tale and believed him and were glad Joseph was no longer mad at them.

57:15 Joseph then said, "Go now to our father. Tell him that I live and have rule over Egypt.

57:16 Bring him and his people here and I shall arrange for them to live in the land of Goshen,

57:17 For Goshen is a beautiful land, worthy of our people and shall soon be prosperous with crops of grain once the famine is finished.

57:18 Whilst you all live in Goshen, I shall care for you and feed you and your flocks, so that you may no longer live in poverty.

57:19 The lord God has told me how long this famine shall last and we must endure for five more years."

57:20 Joseph then embraced his brother Benjamin and wept upon his shoulders, for he missed his brother so and was filled with joy that he shall now be caring for him again.

57:21 Joseph then hugged his elder brothers and reminded them of the dream of the sheaves, for now it came true.

57:22 His brothers were angry of Joseph's arrogant statement, but did nothing, for they knew Joseph to be powerful now and feared his wrath and the wrath of God.

57:23 News spread throughout the nation of Egypt that Joseph was reunited with his family and Pharaoh heard of it

57:24 This news pleased Pharaoh, for he knew the importance of family.

57:25 Pharaoh went to Joseph and told him, "I have heard of this glorious reunion and that your father and his people do well.

57:26 You have grown mighty in this land of mine and I see why, for the lord has blessed you and offered you the means to care for your loved ones.

57:27 Use my carts, my camels, my donkeys and lend them to your brothers so that they may gather their belongings and move here, to be cared for by you.

57:28 Let them live off our land, for if not for you our people will be starving as well."

57:29 Joseph did as Pharaoh commanded and offered his brethren camels, carts, donkeys and provisions for the journey home.

57:30 From his own house, he gave each brother sets of fine clothes, three hundred coins of silver and a concubine, so that they may need not use their donkeys while on the long and lonely trek to fulfill their carnal desires.

57:31 But to Benjamin, his dearest brother, he gave five times more.

57:32 For Jacob, Joseph sent ten donkeys, carrying the many fine goods of Egypt and ten camels laden with many spices, grains and meats.

57:33 As he sent his brothers away, they said to him, "Come with us, for our father will be glad to lay his eyes upon you."

57:34 Joseph said no, for he had priorities in Egypt that must not wait.

57:35 He also worried his brothers will kill him for what he put them through and claim another accident.

57:36 The brothers returned to the land of Canaan and their father and said to him that Joseph is alive and the governor of Egypt.

57:37 Hearing this, Jacob rose from his bed, the first time he did in weeks and danced and praised the lord God.

57:38 Jacob saw the goods Joseph returned for him and said a blessing to his son in Egypt.

57:39 When told that he was offered land in Egypt, Jacob made good on this offer and left, so that he may see his favourite son and gain more land in another foreign nation.

58:1 Jacob gathered all his people and had them take their goods and they left for Egypt. As they passed Beersheba, they stopped and made a sacrifice to the lord.

58:2 A lamb was given to each male, so as they may sacrifice it and please God.

58:3 Thousands of men slaughtered the creatures, placed it on top of a mighty altar and danced naked around the burning carcasses.

58:4 The lord witnessed then and was pleased, for he never saw so much blood, nudity and torn flesh offered to him at one time.

58:5 God went to Jacob in a vision and said to him, "Jacob, Jacob," and Jacob said, "Here I am."

58:6 The lord said, "Behold, I am your God and God of your fathers. Fear not the nation of Egypt, for I shall plant your seed there and your son's sons shall be a great nation in the heathen land.

58:7 As you live in the nation, know that I be with you and have your son Joseph protect you.

58:8 Be blessed by me, for though you live in Egypt, I shall return you to the land of your fathers, so you may die in peace."

58:9 Jacob rose from Beersheba and was carried to Egypt by the carts Pharaoh lent to him, as well was his grandsons and the concubines.

58"10 The rest were put on the cheap carts or walked. They weren't important enough.

58:11 Upon entering Egypt, the heads of the family were stopped by the border patrol and had to fill out paperwork before they could live in the nation of Egypt.

58:12 This is a copy of the form, which was written upon reed paper.

Application Of Land And Living Arrangement

Foreign Nation To Reside In Egypt

#9394821-0039194-5315A

*Special Request by Joseph, Under Pharaoh's Blessing

Head Of Family: Jacob/Israel (Same person)

Married/Single: 2 Wives, Deceased

Sons: 12 Total (Father of Joseph)

List Of Sons And Their Sons:

Reuben-Hanoch, Phallu, Hezron, Carmi

Simeon-Jemuel, Jamin, Ohad, Jachin, Zohar, Shaul

Levi-Gershon, Kohath, Merari

Judah-Er(deceased), Onan(deceased), Shelah, Pharez, Zarah

*Pharez Sons-Hezron, Hamul

Issachar-Tola, Phuvah, Job, Shimron

Zebulun-Sered, Elon, Jahleel

Gad-Ziphion, Haggi, Shuni, Ezbon, Eri, Arodi, Areli

Asher-Jimnah, Ishuah, Isui, Beriah

*Beriah Sons-Heber, Malchiel

Joseph-Manasseh, Ephraim

Benjamin-Belah, Becher, Ashbel, Gera, Naaman, Ehi, Rosh, Muppim, Huppim, Ard

Dan-Hushim

Naphtali-Jahzeel, Guni, Jezer, Shellem

Reason To Live In Egypt:(Family of governor Joseph)

Property Requested:Goshen(Accepted under act of Pharaoh)

Thank you for choosing Egypt as your new home and nation. We ask that you respect our culture, people and customs and in doing so shall return the respect to you. Please ensure the above information is correct and accurate. Any false information of Egyptian documents, whether accidental or intentional, will be considered fraud and shall be punished by fine, imprisonment, and/or death. We hope you enjoy your new home.

58:13 After completion of the paperwork, the lands of Goshen was now theirs,

58:14 And the people residing there previously were evicted.

58:15 When Joseph heard his people arrived at Goshen, he prepared his chariot and met them.

58:16 Jacob and Joseph ran to one another, hugged and wept, for both thought the other dead.

58:17 Joseph said to his native people, "Enjoy the land which I have given to you. I must go and tell Pharaoh that you have arrived, so he may sign the documents and officially invite you all to reside in his nation.

58:18 The head of the family may need to meet him, to sign the papers as well.

58:19 He will know of your great wealth and take notice of your cattle and flocks.

58:20 If asked about your occupation, answer thus; trade.

58:21 For the Egyptians don't like shepherds, believing them stupid and lazy.

58:22 Shepherds, according to these heathens, are lazy and sleep under the shades of trees as they count sheep.

58:23 These people, these Egyptians, have no use for shepherds. Instead they gather their cattle in portions of land made separate by wood, called fences.

58:24 For food and water, they place them both in long bowls called troughs, so that the beasts need not graze on fresh grass.

58:25 In the name of our lord God, lie and deny being shepherds, lest the Pharaoh find you lazy and deny your application."

59:1 Joseph came to Pharaoh and presented to him five of his brothers, and five of their slaves and said to him, "My father, brethren and people have arrived from the land of Canaan and are ready to live in the land of Goshen.

59:2 Pharaoh gazed upon Joseph's brothers and asked what their occupation be.

59:3 Ignoring Joseph's advice, they said to Pharaoh, "Our servants are shepherds, who nurture and care for our flocks. We are shepherds as well, as is our father.

59:4 We come to you so that we may live in your lands that Joseph offered us. The famine has dried our soil and made it barren.

59:5 We ask that you allow us to live in Goshen and we shall make the land fruitful and raise our flocks and grow crops."

59:6 Pharaoh heard this request and asked Joseph in secret, "What use do we have for shepherds. We need men who can work, not watch over cattle."

59:7 Joseph responded, "They may be shepherds, but they are not lazy. For they also know how to grow crops of many grains.

59:8 Before the famine, the land of my father was rich in cattle, flocks and farmland. Our people have vast knowledge in farming, sheep shearing, and raising cattle.

59:9 The shepherds may watch our flocks, but they also milk them, sheer them and toil soil for farming.

59:10 I assure you, my Pharaoh, these men may be shepherds, but they are not lazy and will be valuable to Egypt.

59:11 Once the famine ends, they can quickly make your lands fruitful and share the knowledge they contain with your people."

59:12 Pharaoh heard Joseph's arguments and sent his advisors to research these claims. The advisors found out that the land of Jacob was fruitful with grain before the famine, which provided evidence of Joseph's claim.

59:13 Pharaoh said to the men of Jacob, "The land of Goshen is now yours. Dwell there and make it fruitful.

59:14 However, you must work for this land, so that your people be not a parasite to my great nation.

59:15 Joseph tells me you have men experienced in raising cattle and flocks. Let their knowledge be put to use.

59:16 Gather them and let them care for the flocks of Egypt, so that we may learn from your methods."

59:17 Jacob, or Israel as Pharaoh did not know what to call him, was brought forth to Pharaoh as he wished to give thanks to the man who fathered the one who saved Egypt from famine.

59:18 Jacob knelt before Pharaoh and blessed him and his people.

59:19 God saw this blessing and was disgusted, for he will not bless the people of Egypt. They were a nation of heathens.

59:20 Pharaoh asked Jacob, "How old are you, father of Joseph?"

59:21 And Jacob answered, "The years of my life number one hundred thirty. My lord has blessed me with long life and throughout my years my people and I have endured and survived through hardship and turmoil.

59:22 I thank you, Pharaoh, for taking good care of my beloved Joseph and for letting my people dwell in your land."

59:23 Jacob then blessed Pharaoh again and left.

59:24 God saw this second blessing and was again disgusted. He knew Jacob must be punished for this blasphemy, but how?

59:25 The lands of Goshen, in the province of Rameses, were divided and the nation of Jacob had land in Egypt. Joseph took good care of his people, giving unto them excess bread, so that they may still live in luxury despite the famine.

59:26 Joseph's people took too much of the grain, so much that the nation of Egypt and other lands began to grow hungry.

59:27 As the grain decreased, Joseph saw a need for demand and raised the price of grain to all foreign nations.

59:28 Soon, the foreign nations, even the peoples of Egypt, grew poor and had no money to offer in exchange for grain.

59:29 Pharaoh brought in Joseph and demanded he find a solution, for the nation of Egypt will not allow their people nor her allies to grow hungry.

59:30 Instead of limiting the grain given to his family, Joseph thought of another solution.

59:31 He said to the people, "If money you lack, trade us your cattle and we shall trade you grain."

59:32 So the people and nations brought to Joseph many goats, horses, donkeys, sheep, and oxen so that they may trade the beasts for bread.

59:33 Because of the famine, most of the creatures were skinny and held little value. Joseph traded a little grain for a great many herds and the people were grateful.

59:34 Joseph then sent the cattle to his people, who cared for them and raised them, making them fat and strong.

59:35 For a year, the people across all lands traded their cattle for food, until they became lacking in beasts as well and had neither money nor flocks to trade.

59:36 They came to Joseph and Pharaoh and pleaded with them, so that they may have more bread.

59:37 Pharaoh asked if they had anything of value to trade and the people did not.

59:38 Joseph then said, "But you do. You all have property, land.

59:39 Though barren it is, I shall trade you grain for the acres of your property, so that you all shall not starve during this hardship."

59:40 And the people traded their private property for grain. The natives of Egypt were allowed to stay upon what is now property of Pharaoh, provided they pay a tax.

59:41 Land bought from a foreign nation was not treated so kindly. The people were evicted from their homes and forced to move within the new borders of their nation.

59:42 Soon, there were no private property left within Egypt, for the people traded it all for grain.

59:43 Except for the priests, who kept their land and was given grain for free, since they ate very little and to charge them for food may offend the false Gods of Egypt.

59:44 As the famine neared its end, Joseph went to the purchased lands and offered everyone seed and said to them, "If you desire to live on this property of Pharaoh, you must earn your keep. Take this seed which I have given you and grow crops of corn, barley and wheat.

59:45 When the crops become harvested, a living tax of one fifth of the harvest must be sent to Pharaoh."

59:46 Most people agreed to this arrangement. Those that did not were forced to leave the lands and live in a foreign nation, for there were no land left in Egypt that did not belong to Pharaoh.

59:47 Except for land belonging to the priests and the land belonging to Jacob.

59:48 Jacob prospered under the aid of Joseph and his people grew strong.

59:49 For seventeen years Jacob lived in this foreign nation, totalling his age to one hundred and forty-seven.

59:50 As he neared the end of his days, the lord God came down upon him.

59:51 "Jacob, I have sent you and your people here to this foreign land and shall keep the covenant I have made for your people.

59:52 Your seed shall spread and grow to be a mighty nation.

59:53 But you have failed me. For when you came here, you twice blessed the bastard Pharaoh.

59:54 In doing this, you have committed an abomination against me.

59:55 You will not die in the land of your father's as I promised you, but shall die in the land of Pharaoh."

59:56 Jacob awoke and sent for his son Joseph.

59:57 Joseph was far too busy to deal with his father immediately, so they made an appointment to meet in one month's time.

59:58 Joseph went to his father at the appointed time and Jacob said to him, "I have found grace and blessing through you and the lord God.

59:59 But I have committed blasphemy while in this nation, and the lord will not let such a deed go unpunished.

59:60 Soon I shall die and my corpse will rot in the earth. When I die, it will not be in the land of my father, but here.

59:61 Grasp my testicles and swear to me that, though my spirit leaves here, my body will be buried in my native land."

59:62 Joseph grabbed his father's loins, kissed them and swore to Jacob that his body will be buried within the borders of his native land.

59:63 Jacob was relieved, laid his head upon his pillow and rested.

60:1 Within months, Jacob became ill and knew his time be at an end.

60:2 Joseph heard of his father's illness and visited him with his two sons, Manasseh and Ephraim.

60:3 The servants of Jacob prepared for Joseph's arrival and dressed Jacob and shaved him and bathed him so that the offensive stench of sickness not offend the mighty governor.

60:4 When Joseph arrived, Jacob sat upon his bed, too sick to move.

60:5 And Jacob said to Joseph, "The lord God almighty appeared to me before I arrived here, in the land of Beersheba, as I made an offering to him.

60:6 He said that my people shall grow fruitful and multiply, that my seed will be a multitude of people and that the lands shall be ruled by us for eternity.

60:7 The lord has told me this a lot, so I know it must be true.

60:8 Now I see my grandsons conceived through your loins, Ephraim and Manasseh, born in the foreign land of Egypt and know they be my people, like the sons of Reuben and Simeon and all the rest.

60:9 Your sons shall gain a portion of my inheritance and shall be part of the great covenant promised to us by the lord God almighty.

60:10 For they be the grandsons of my beloved Rachel. Where is she?

60:11 Joseph reminded his father that Rachel died giving birth to Benjamin and that she was buried in Ephrath.

60:12 "Ahh yes, I remember now," muttered Jacob.

60:13 The old man continued his ramblings. "I see now the lord God's will. He intends for us to invade Egypt and claim it as ours.

60:14 We shall invade from the inside, like cancer and cast these heathens out."

60:15 Noticing the two boys with their Egyptian features, he pointed and said, "Who the hell are they?"

60:16 Joseph said, "Father, they are my sons, your grandsons. Have you not forgotten them?"

60:17 "Ahh, yes, I remember. How could I forget. Bring them to me, so that I may gaze my eyes upon them and bless them both."

60:18 Jacob kissed and embraced them both and went upon his knees, placing his hands upon both their heads.

60:19 The two boys grew nervous, for they thought this old man strange and smelly.

60:20 But they did not object, fearing that Joseph would whip them if they did.

60:21 Jacob placed his hands upon the heads, rubbed them, looked up to the sky and said,

60:22 "Blessed be the lord God, creator of heaven and earth.

60:23 Let these two children be blessed in your name, for they share the blood of myself and my fathers.

60:24 Cast out the Egyptian curse from their spirit, for it comes from the mother only.

60:25 The father be true and mighty to the lord, a great leader and shall follow the lords will, as will his sons."

60:26 He then grabbed the two boy's testicles and kissed them both, finishing the blessing.

60:27 Manasseh was troubled by this, for he did not like the old and feeble man touching his loins.

60:28 Ephraim was pleased by this blessing, for he was a faggot.

60:29 Jacob then blessed Joseph and said to him, "The lord shall guide and lead you into power and prosperity and you shall soon be home in the native land of your father."

61:1 As Jacob grew older and sicker, his mind went numb, thoughts fuzzy and in his final days he became a madman.

61:2 Thinking himself to have power to see the future, he gathered his twelve sons, so that they may listen to his wisdom.

61:3 "Reuben, my eldest son. You are my first-born and my eldest. You shall be strong, dignified, a powerful nation.

61:4 But cursed you shall be and you shall not reach your full potential. I won't allow it. You fucked my whore.

61:5 Simeon and Levi shall rule as two brothers and be violent tyrants.

61:6 They killed a city, raped their women and burned their walls. With this fury, they shall rule.

61:7 Cursed be the two of you, as you had brought me dishonour in your wrath. Divided your lands shall be and your people will be scattered across the nations.

61:8 Judah, you shall be praised by all. Your hands shall crush the neck of your enemies and all people will bow before you.

61:9 Like a mighty lion you will be, protecting your nation from harm.

61:10 Your sons shall be the greatest rulers and the crown will not be taken from your seed, until the great and mighty Shiloh comes and takes that which is yours.

61:11 He will drunken your people with wine until their eyes be red with liquor,

61:12 Your clothes drenched in the poison of grapes.

61:13 Zebulun will command the ports and rule the seas and ships.

61:14 Issachar will be a mighty strong ass and take a great burden for his people.

61:15 Dan will enforce the laws of the land and judge the people according to the will of God.

61:16 But a traitor his seed will be. A snake, a venomous adder. His seed will bite the lands of our people and we will suffer for it.

61:17 Gad will be constantly invaded, but eventually win.

61:18 Out of the lands of Asher many fine foods will come. And his people will grow fat and live in excess and provide for ye many fine cuisines.

61:19 Naphtali will be a wild beast, travelling the nations, spreading the word of our lord.

61:20 Joseph will be mighty and his people prosperous and well defended.

61:21 Many invaders will attempt to take what is his and shoot him and hate him.

61:22 But his bows and arms shall divide in strength and his arms shall be made mighty by the hands of God.

61:23 For Joseph has been blessed by me and God and the crown that lays upon his head shall remain with his people.

61:24 Benjamin shall be a ravenous wolf, taking prey from the land, devouring its flesh and feeding all the people with fresh meat.

61:25 These shall be the twelve tribes of Israel, as I have foreseen it."

61:26 One by one, the sons of Jacob came forward to him and Jacob blessed each of his children.

61:27 After the blessing, the sons left and laughed at the ramblings of their old father. Even Joseph.

61:28 The day after the rambling, Jacob died in his bed.

62:1 Joseph was devastated by the death of his father and wept upon his body and kissed it.

62:2 He commanded the physicians to embalm him, preserving him, so that his corpse shall not rot.

62:3 For forty days, Joseph mourned, as did the peoples of Egypt. They were sympathetic to Joseph and felt his pain.

62:4 When the tears of Joseph dried, he came to Pharaoh and asked of him, "If I have found favour in your eyes, I beg of you this favour.

62:5 My father knew his death shall be in the mighty nation of Egypt. This he told me. But his heart belongs in the land of his father.

62:6 I promised him that upon death, I shall bury him with his people. Please, let me take my father and place his body in his native land.

62:7 After burial, I promise I shall return to Egypt."

62:8 Pharaoh heard Joseph's plea and said, "I know the importance of family. Go, take your father's body and bury it where you see fit."

62:9 Joseph arose and went to bury his father.

62:10 With him came the servants of Pharaoh, the elders of Egypt and the servants of Joseph.

62:11 For in Egypt, the death of a father is a sad occasion and when a governor's father dies, the entire nation mourns.

62:12 The brothers of Joseph went with him as well, to bury and mourn their father, as did their servants.

62:13 So that the only people left in the lands of Goshen were the children and maids to care for them.

62:14 They all gathered their chariots and horsemen and went forth to the lands of Abraham.

62:15 As they arrived at the land of Atad, beyond the river Jordan, they set their tents.

62:16 For one week, they stayed at Atad, mourning Joseph, tearing their clothes, crying and cutting their chests.

62:17 The lord saw this and was amused, for the tears of these people and their blood was entertaining to God.

62:18 The Canaanites witnessed this as well and grew scared. They thought these people mad and the land cursed.

62:19 They named Atad Abelmizraim, which means 'cursed ground' in the tongue of Canaan.

62:20 The sons of Jacob and their people arose and went to the field of Machpelah and buried Jacob in a cave there.

62:21 Afterwards, they went back to Egypt, as Joseph promised.

62:22 The brothers of Joseph grew afraid, for now they thought that Joseph would take revenge upon them for selling them into slavery.

62:23 Before, their father was alive and Joseph dare not harm them in their father's presence,

62:24 But now, Jacob lie dead and there was no protection.

62:25 They sent a message to Joseph, a lie, saying,

62:26 Before our father died, he told us that you were ordered to forgive us

62:27 He knew of the evil we did to you, as we confessed this to him in his dying days

62:28 And that after his death, if you harm us, then God will curse you

62:29 So forgive us our sins against you, or our father will hate you.

62:30 Joseph read this message and laughed. Did he still evoke fear among his brothers?

62:31 He travelled to Goshen, to speak with his brethren.

62:32 His brothers fell to the ground, bowed to him and said, "We are but humble servants."

62:33 Joseph, again, was reminded of the dream of the sheaves he had so long ago.

62:34 He said to his bowing brothers, "Fear not, for I am a man of God.

62:35 Though you did conspire evil against me and committed evil against me, the lord made it so.

62:36 Look at me now. Governor of Egypt. Had you not sold me, would this have happened. No.

62:37 For the lord took your evil and made it into good.

62:38 Fear me not, for even in father's death, I shall comfort you, feed you and care for your families."

62:39 His brothers were comforted by this and arose. Their fear of Joseph was no longer with them.

62:40 Being the prick he was, Joseph then said, "Remember the dream of the twelve sheaves. Ha. It came true."

62:41 The brothers laughed at this, nervously, as they knew it true and feared to be under the servitude of Joseph forever.

62:42 Joseph stayed in Egypt until the end of his days, believing the lord God will return him to the land of his people, so that he may die on his native grounds.

62:43 The lord God kept not his promise and at the age of one hundred and ten, Joseph died.

62:44 He contracted syphilis from one of his concubines. The disease was left untreated and killed him.

62:45 Servants of Joseph prepared his body, embalmed him and buried him in one of their mighty pyramids.

62:46 As the funeral ended and the people left, God came down, and stood over Joseph's coffin and said,

62:47 "Promised I did that I shall take you out of the land of Egypt and you shall die in your native land. Yet you shall forever remain here, your body rotting under the land of Pharaoh.

62:48 Hahahahahahaha. I am the lord God, I can do whatever I want. So, fuck you."

62:49 God left, smiling in the knowledge that he was all powerful, could do whatever he wants and no person can stop him.

EXODUS

1:1 As time progressed, the people of Joseph and his brethren died, as all living things do.

1:2 The Egyptians suffered the same fate, as they are living beings as well.

1:3 Pharaoh, Joseph, Benjamin,

1:4 Reuben, Levi, Simeon,

1:5 Issachar, Zebulun, Judah,

1:6 Napthali, Asher, Gad and Dan.

1:7 These men left behind a great many sons after death, who left behind sons, who left behind sons.

1:8 And the fornication of the Israelite people moved on.

1:9 And the Israelites were a fruitful, horny people.

1:10 Popping babies out of their loins as though they were a human Pez-dispenser.

1:11 Who soon numbered a great majority that the Egyptians took notice and became worried.

1:12 For these foreign people, living in their native land, may soon outgrow them, outnumber them and overpower them.

1:13 The people of Egypt went to Pharaoh and voiced their fears.

1:14 This new Pharaoh new of Joseph and what he did for the Egyptian people.

1:15 He also feared the Israelites, for they knew their God was powerful, violent and vengeful.

1:16 Pharaoh feared that if the Israelites grew great in number, their God will become more powerful and soon the people of Israel will rule the world.

1:17 So he decided to enforce upon the people of Israel a lesson in humility.

1:18 He enslaved them.

1:19 Pharaoh set force taskmasters and forced the people of Israel into labour.

1:20 They were forced to tend crops, care for livestock, build mighty pyramids, repair walls.

1:21 Forced to dig wells, clean the streets and prepare meals for the Egyptians.

1:22 They were forced to do what Israelites forced their slaves to do.

1:23 And the Israelites did not like it.

1:24 But when they complained, they were beaten and told to be good slaves.

1:25 Just like they did to their slaves.

1:26 And they thought this unfair.

1:27 Soon, the people of Israel were completely under the labour of Pharaoh and grew miserable.

1:28 But Pharaoh noticed that still they grew in numbers.

1:29 For when the pleasures of smokable herbs, strong drink and gluttony were denied to the people of Israel, they took pleasure in the one thing that could not be taken from them.

1:30 They took pleasure in sex.

1:31 During their slavery, the people of Israel fornicated with everyone, for it was the remaining enjoyment left to them.

1:32 They fornicated with their spouses, their neighbours spouses, concubines.

1:33 Men and women traded each other's sexual company like baseball cards.

1:34 And during this time of great orgy, the women became pregnant with the seeds of many Israelite men.

1:35 Giving birth to many sons and many daughters.

1:36 Pharaoh grew afraid, for even in slavery the Israelites shall soon overpopulate the people of Egypt.

1:37 So he demanded population control.

1:38 He gathered the Israel midwives and gave them orders to kill any newborn son of Israel and cast them into the river.

1:39 So that the crocodiles may feast upon young and tender flesh.

1:40 The daughters may be spared, so that their wombs can be implanted by the seed of Egyptian men,

1:41 Thus increasing the population of Egypt.

1:42 Two of these midwives, Shiphrah and Puah, disobeyed Pharaoh.

1:43 Instead saving the lives of the newborn boys.

1:44 Pharaoh heard of this disobedience and demanded an explanation from these midwives.

1:45 Being God fearing women, they knew it was a time to lie.

1:46 So they told Pharaoh that the women of Israel are tough hearty, and strong women, who need not midwives,

1:47 And that when the two of them arrive, the child is already born, for the women of Israel do not stay in labour long before giving birth.

1:48 When Pharaoh asked why they did not throw the sons into the river anyway, the midwives told him because the babies were no longer considered newly born.

1:49 Pharaoh heard this and revised the law.

1:50 Any Israel son aged one week or less must be thrown in the river.

1:51 Daughters can be spared.

1:52 Hearing this, the midwives of Israel quit their job and became part of the Egyptian labour force.

1:53 Aiding in the breeding and birthing of Egyptian livestock.

1:54 God witnessed the defiance of Shiphrah and Puah and was angry.

1:55 For women should never be defiant to a man, no matter their background.

1:56 So the lord God, in all his wisdom, punished the two women and made their houses forever dusty,

1:57 Forcing them into housework until death.

2:1 In the house of Levi there was a man who took a wife of the house of Levi.

2:2 For incest is beautiful in the eyes of the lord.

2:3 The two fornicated and she bore a son, a hideous beast of a child.

2:4 Seeing this abomination, the two hid their child for three months and told their neighbours that the woman miscarried.

2:5 Knowing they could not hide this child forever, they took the baby to the river and threw him in.

2:6 But the child was so ugly that not even the river would accept it and the child floated atop.

2:7 Creatures of the river found the baby so hideous they refused to eat it.

2:8 The baby floated downstream, passing by the daughter of Pharaoh and her maidens, who came to bathe in the river.

2:9 The daughter of Pharaoh saw this baby and her heart grew with compassion.

2:10 For though it was an ugly child, she knew it only a child and worthy of love, compassion and a caring home.

2:11 She sent forth one of her maidens to take the child from the river and they knew it was a Hebrew child, for the foreskin was removed.

2:12 The maidens asked of the daughter of Pharaoh, "Shall we send for a Hebrew nurse?"

2:13 Pharaoh's daughter said yes, for she knew not how to properly care for a Hebrew infant.

2:14 The Hebrew nurse came and Pharaoh told her, "Raise this child for me, nurse it, care for it and I shall pay you well for your work.

2:15 When the child is weaned, bring him back to me. For I trust not you Hebrew's to care for him.

2:16 If any harm shall come to this child, I shall hold ye personally responsible, and kill you for your incompetence."

2:17 The nurse then took the baby, ugly and naked and cared for it, fed it and nursed it.

2:18 When the child was two years of age, he was returned to the daughter of Pharaoh and he became her adopted son. And he was named Moses.

2:19 Moses lived a life of luxury among the Egyptians people and knew not the struggles of his own kin.

2:20 When Moses was a grown man, he went for a walk, to gaze upon his brethren.

2:21 As he did, Moses saw an Egyptian man beating a Hebrew slave.

2:22 Moses looked to his left, his right and behind. Seeing no witnesses, he killed the Egyptian and buried his body in the sand.

2:23 Two days later, Moses went looking for the slave he saved and found him playing games with a friend.

2:24 Moses went up the slave and said to him, "Your life I have saved. You owe me a great debt in the eyes of God."

2:25 But the slaves refused and told Moses, "You fool. Do you know the Egyptians beat us more because of your murder?

2:26 They blame us for his death and repress us more. But now I shall tell them it was you who killed him.

2:27 When the truth is known, Pharaoh shall surely punish you."

2:28 Moses knew this to be true and fled to the lands of Midian.

2:29 When Pharaoh heard of Moses' betrayal, he became enraged, but knew that Moses was part of his family.

2:30 He intended to punish Moses by community service for three months. But Moses was already in Midian when Pharaoh decided this.

2:31 Moses grew thirsty and stopped by a well to replenish his thirst. As he did, the seven daughters of the priests of Midian came, to gather water for their father's troughs.

2:32 Seven beautiful virgin daughters.

2:33 Moses helped them fill their jugs with water, so he may better gaze upon the jugs beneath their garments.

2:34 As he did, shepherds from Midian came with their flocks and demanded they use the well immediately, as their flocks were thirsty and could not wait.

2:35 Moses, to impress the seven daughters, slew the shepherds, took their flocks and gave them to the seven daughters.

2:36 The daughters were impressed and invited them to their father's abode, so that he may thank Moses for saving his daughters and giving him sheep.

2:37 The seven daughters told their father, Reuel, "This man has saved us and given to you flocks from the shepherds he slew."

2:38 Reuel said to Moses, "I thank you for your services to my family. Please, will you come in and eat with us so you can tell us about yourself."

2:39 Moses agreed and the nine ate together and listened to Moses' tales, the majority of which he made up.

2:40 Reuel let Moses live upon his land and gave to him his daughter Zipporah as a wife.

2:41 The two bore a son and named him Gershom. And Moses was content with his simple life in Midian.

2:42 It came to pass that the Pharaoh died of old age and the people of Israel were relieved, believing that with the death of the Pharaoh their lives as slaves would soon end.

2:43 God heard their celebrating and remembered his covenant with Abraham, Isaac and Jacob, that their people will rule the land.

2:44 God looked down upon the people of Israel and laughed. For they knew not that their lives of servitude will not end yet.

3:1 Moses kept the flocks of his father in law, the priest of Midian, for Moses was a greedy man.

3:2 He took the flocks to the back of the desert, so that they may drink upon the wells and feast upon the grasses owned by someone else.

3:3 As he travelled, he passed through the mountain of the lord God and there made a sacrifice.

3:4 He took a young lamb, slaughtered it upon the altar and danced around it naked, bathing in its blood.

3:5 This pleased the lord, as he loves violence, nudity and torn flesh. But you already knew that.

3:6 When Moses was done, the lord sent to him a prostitute so that Moses may fulfill his carnal desires.

3:7 When Moses finished, flames engulfed the vagina of the whore, but the prostitute felt no pain nor discomfort and the pubic hair did not burn.

3:8 Moses witnessed the burning bush and looked away in fear and disgust, hoping that this was not an STD he contracted.

3:9 When the lord God saw Moses look away from the burning bush, he called to him through it, "Moses, Moses," and Moses said, "Here I am."

3:10 "Moses, I speak to you through the hairy lips of this burning bush. Remove your sandals, for the place you walk upon is most holy and sacred ground.

3:11 I am the lord God, creator of heaven and earth and all things. The God of your father, of Isaac, of Jacob, of Abraham and of you." Moses listened to God, but hid his face, for the talking cunt scared him greatly.

3:12 The lord God continued, "I have seen the suffering and heard the sorrow of my people and witnessed the cruelty of their Egyptian taskmasters.

3:13 It has been decided that the time has come for me to deliver them from this suffering and to bring them to the lands large and plentiful, full of milk and honey, so that they may enslave the heathens living there.

3:14 The Canaanites, the Hittites, the Amorites, the Perizzites, the Hivites and the Jebusites.

3:15 You, Moses, shall be the ones to deliver your people to freedom and prosperity, as I promised to your ancestors. Go now to Pharaoh and deliver the children of Israel out of Egypt."

3:16 Moses asked the lord God, "Why do you decide this now. Your

people have been suffering for years, could you have not delivered them sooner?"

3:17 And the lord God replied, "Do you dare question me. To do so is blasphemy." And Moses quickly apologized, for fear the burning bush would grow larger and enflame him.

3:18 Moses then asked God, "Why me. Who am I to go to Pharaoh and demand that my people be free?"

3:19 God said, "Do not fear, for I shall be with you and protect you. You shall serve me greatly by bringing my people away from servitude."

3:20 Moses then asked, "When I come upon the children of Israel and tell them that the lord God has sent me to free them, they shall ask me what your name is. What do I tell them?"

3:21 And the lord God said, "Tell them that I am the fucking lord God almighty, creator of everything. And that I have sent you to free them. If any of my people disagree, they can stay behind in Egypt and be a cursed slave for generations.

3:22 I am the God of Isaac, of Jacob and of Abraham and tell them I have sent you to free them and that you shall be remembered for generations to come.

3:23 Gather the elders together and tell them the time of oppression shall end. That the lord God has taken notice of their sufferings and soon they shall suffer no longer.

3:24 For I shall deliver them to the land of milk and honey and they shall rule that land and the natives, the Canaanites, Hittites, Amorites, Perizzites, Hivites and Jebusites shall serve them.

3:25 But be warned, Moses, for the king of Egypt is a stubborn bastard and will not let you go willingly.

3:26 I shall break his stubbornness and cast down my powers terrible and strike at Egypt and show them and my people the awesomeness that is I, the lord God!

3:27 Doing this, the people of Egypt shall fear you and want you to leave and bless you and ensure you have no reason to return.

3:28 For your people shall go into their homes and take what value they have. There pottery, gold, silver and jewels. Fine silks and clothing. And you shall leave with the mighty spoils of Egypt."

4:1 Moses still had doubt, but did not want the lord God to know this, so he told him, "My lord, the people will not believe me and accuse me of lying and say that you did not appear to me in the burning bush of a whore."

4:2 And the lord said to Moses, "What is that in your hand?" and Moses said, "My rod."

4:3 The lord God said, "Throw it on the ground." Moses did and the rod became a cobra and Moses fled from it on fear.

4:4 God then said, "Grab the snake by the tail." Moses did and the snake became a rod again.

4:5 "Now, put your hand under your shirt, then remove it." Moses did as commanded and when he removed his hand, it was rotten like a corpse, the flesh decaying and the bones visible.

4:6 God told Moses, "Put the hand back in your shirt and remove it slowly." Moses did and his hand was healthy again.

4:7 The lord God then said, "If the people of Israel do not believe you after these two tricks of magic, do this.

4:8 Take them to the river and fill a jug with water. Pour the water upon the sands and it shall turn to blood; for blood is life and only the lord God can create life from water."

4:9 Moses then said to the lord, "Oh God, I am not good with speech nor words. My mind is slow, my tongue confusing and I am a tad retarded."

4:10 Hearing this, the lord God laughed and said, "Who has made the mouth of men, or the seeing, or the deaf, or the blind. Was it not I?

4:11 Go and do not worry of your retarded mind, for I shall be in your mouth and teach you that which you must say."

4:12 Moses, being retarded as he is, demanded from God, "This I cannot do alone. Send to me a man to do your will for me."

4:13 Hearing this, God grew angry, for Moses did not believe God could do this with him.

4:14 As the lord's anger grew, the fire became stronger and the whore of the lord screamed in pain and agony.

4:15 The lord screamed, "Do not doubt me. For is not Aaron the Levite your brother. He is of good mind and speech. I shall send him to you and when he sees you, his heart shall be filled with joy.

4:16 And you shall speak to him and fill words in his mouth and I shall be in both your jaws and the two of you will shall say what I say.

4:17 Aaron shall be your public speaker and be a spokesman for my will.

4:18 Go now, take your rod, remember the sorcery I taught you and free the people of Israel."

4:19 The lord God then left and the fire stopped and the whore of God stood up and blessed the lord, for the fire burning from her vagina burned away the warts that had plagued her for years.

4:20 Moses returned to the lands of Midian and asked his father in law, "Let me go, so that I may return to my people in Egypt and free them from tyranny." And the priest of Midian blessed Moses and told him to leave in peace.

4:21 And Moses gathered his wife and sons and they travelled to Egypt, with Moses grasping his rod.

4:22 Before doing so, God assured Moses not to worry, for the people in Egypt who wanted him slain are no longer among the living.

4:23 When travelling, the lord God came to Moses, again, and spoke with him. "When you speak to the new Pharaoh, perform for him the sorcery I have taught you. But be warned, for he shall not let your people leave, as I have hardened his heart.

4:24 Tell him that the children of Israel be the sons of God, the first-born.

4:25 And say to him that if he does not let the first-born of the one true God free, then shall the first-born of Pharaoh be slain."

4:26 During the travels, the family of Moses came to inn and sought rest and comfort.

4:27 The lord God almighty was with them and when Moses gave his son a bath, the lord was mortified!

4:28 For this son still had foreskin and was above the age of eight days.

4:29 God appeared to Moses and cursed him for such blasphemy and chased him and threatened to kill him.

4:30 Zipporah saw this and grew fearful. She took a sharp stone and bashed it against her son's penis until the foreskin was removed. She then took the foreskin and threw it down upon Moses' feet and cursed him for forcing her to do such a painful act to her offspring.

4:31 When God saw this, he laughed, for the thought of a penis being bashed by a rock amused him greatly. He said, "Your wife has brought me such laughter that I surely cannot make her a widow."

4:32 He then left.

4:33 God went to Aaron and said, "Travel into the wilderness, for your brother is returning to meet you." And Aaron did and the two brothers met on the mount of God and embraced one another.

4:34 Moses told Aaron all of which the lord God told him and all the magic he was to show.

4:35 Together, the brothers gathered the elders of Israel.

4:36 They repeated the words of God.

4:37 They showed the sorcery God taught Moses.

4:38 Seeing the signs, the elders praised the lord God almighty for finally freeing them. They then went on their knees and bowed in prayer and worshipped God.

5:1 Aaron and Moses went to Pharaoh and said, "The lord God of our people demand that we leave you and go into the desert and have a magnificent feast in his honour."

5:2 Pharaoh heard this and laughed.

5:3 He asked the two men, "Who is this God you speak of. For he did not come to me. How do I know you not lie?

5:4 The two brothers told Pharaoh, "The God of our people came to us and said our people must go into the wilderness for three days and feast and commit sacrifices.

5:5 If this is not done, God shall be angry. He shall punish us with pain and pestilence."

5:6 Hearing this, the king of Egypt grew angry and said unto them, "You two come and lie to me.

5:7 The God of your peoples did not come to you. You just want an excuse not to work.

5:8 Behold, the people of your kin are many and I offered them rest and relaxation for their work.

5:9 But no more. They shall suffer for your lies."

5:10 Pharaoh then gathered the taskmasters of Egypt and told them, "The people of Israel have become lazy. This cannot be allowed!

5:11 No more shall you give them the straw and mud to make bricks. They must go and gather these raw goods themselves.

5:12 If they demand they lack the time to sacrifice to their God, beat them. For they do not need to sacrifice, they just want time off work.

5:13 Lastly, tell them production must not drop, for the same number of bricks must be made, even with them gathering the raw goods themselves."

5:14 And the taskmasters went out and told the people of Israel that straw and mud shall no longer be given to them, for they must now find it themselves.

5:15 Also, production must not drop, lest they be beaten for their incompetence.

5:16 When hearing this, the people of Israel whined.

5:17 They do that. A lot.

5:18 They searched the fields and found little straw and mud.

5:19 When in the factories, production dropped and the people were beaten.

5:20 God saw this and laughed, for he knew that if 1/5 of the people gathered straw and muck and the rest build bricks, production would not suffer.

5:21 But the people of Israel were stupid, lazy and inefficient.

5:22 When searching for raw materials, they instead snuck away and slept.

5:23 The elders of Israel went to Pharaoh's men and complained.

5:24 They did not listen, for the whining of the people of Israel annoyed them deeply.

5:25 Knowing their words fell on deaf ears, they went to the brothers Moses and Aaron and whined more.

5:26 "The lord God almighty came to you and spoke to you and claimed our freedom soon be near.

5:27 Why does he wait. We suffer now and tomorrow we shall suffer more. Pharaoh hates us greater and beats us.

5:28 Surely God must know this, so why does he wait?"

5:29 This confused the two brothers and Moses left to speak with God.

5:30 He pleased the lord by sacrificing a lamb and dancing around it naked, bathing in the beast's blood.

5:31 Afterwards, he raised his head to heavens and said, "Almighty lord God, creator of heavens and earth and everything, why do you wait. Our people suffer greatly since you sent me to Egypt.

5:32 For since I came to Pharaoh and spoke to him your will, he has done nothing but evil and still you do have not freed us."

6:1 The lord then said to Moses, "Now you shall see what curses I bring upon Pharaoh: for with a strong hand he'll keep your people, but with a stronger hand I'll let them go!

6:2 For I am the lord God and none shall challenge my will.

6:3 I have appeared unto Abraham, Isaac, and Jacob, by the name of the almighty God, creator of heaven and earth and all things, but did not reveal my true name.

6:4 Witness this, Moses and know that my name be Jehovah!

6:5 And I have established a covenant between these people, to give them the land of Canaan, already occupied by Canaanites.

6:6 Fuck the Canaanites. I, the almighty Jehovah, don't like them, for they don't follow me blindly.

6:7 Also I have heard the cries and screams of my people of Israel, whom the Egyptians keep in bondage and slavery and I remember my covenant.

6:8 So I shall say to the children of Israel, 'Behold, I am the lord God. And I shall bring you out from under the burden of these heathens and redeem you and reward you.

6:9 I shall take you as my people and I shall be to you a God, as long as you blindly follow me and do as I say without question.

6:10 And I shall bring you to the land I promised your ancestors many years ago, for I am the lord God.'"

6:11 Moses left and told the Israelites what God had said to him. But the Israelites were still angry.

6:12 For they were still under Egyptian bondage and the lord God has still done nothing to free them.

6:13 The lord came back to Moses and demanded that he go to Pharaoh and order the king of the Egyptians to let his people free.

6:14 And Moses spoke to the lord, saying, "Why. The people of Israel don't like me and call me a liar and false prophet. Pharaoh will not fear nor believe me. How am I, one of uncircumcised lips, talk to Pharaoh?"

6:15 The lord spoke to Moses and his brother Aaron and demanded they go to Pharaoh and free the Israelites.

6:16 For the lord grew bored of the slavery of his people and had another plan that shall entertain him.

6:17 Next is a list of generations and the Israelites family tree.

6:18 It's boring and stupid, even for biblical standards.

6:19 So I shall only list the interesting parts.

6:20 The average life span seems to be one hundred and thirty-four.

6:21 Either everyone had all sons, or they didn't bother listing the daughters.

6:22 Because, let's be honest, during those days, females were only good for labour and that lukewarm hole in their crotch. Oh, and birthing sons. Only sons.

6:23 The name of Moses' and Aaron's father is Amram. The mother's name is Jochebed. Guess what. The two are related!

6:24 Jochebed is Amram's aunt. That explains why Moses was retarded.

7:1 The lord God said to Moses, "I shall make you unto Pharaoh as a God and your brother Aaron shall be your prophet and minister of propaganda.

7:2 I shall give to you orders, which must be obeyed lest I allow the people of Israel to suffer more.

7:3 Your brother shall go to Pharaoh and constantly demand his people free.

7:4 But the Pharaoh is a stubborn fucker and I shall make him more stubborn. He will refuse to let your people leave.

7:5 For this stubbornness, I shall bring plagues upon the Pharaoh and the people of Egypt. Harsh, terrible plagues.

7:6 This will provide for me amusement and the people of Israel shall laugh at the suffering of the nation of Egypt.

7:7 It will also prove to men that I am the lord God and am not to be fucked with."

7:8 The two brothers did as God commanded, Moses being the age of eighty and Aaron eighty-three when they spoke to Pharaoh.

7:9 When arriving, the lord spoke to the brothers again and said,

7:10 "When you speak to Pharaoh, perform to him the miracle of magic. Aaron shall throw down his rod and it will become a serpent, venomous and cold of blood.

7:11 For the serpent is used in many of my magic, as punishment for giving the first two my sweet, precious fruit."

7:12 Moses and Aaron went to Pharaoh and did as they commanded. Aaron threw to the ground his staff and the staff turned into a mighty serpent.

7:13 A mighty serpent it was, scales black as night and eyes red and glowing like the embers of fire.

7:14 Fifteen feet long, it coiled and hissed, hissed with an air breaking sound heard all throughout the lands of Egypt.

7:15 The fangs were longer than the swords of Pharaoh's bodyguards and out from its mouth spit venom and fire.

7:16 Aaron then grabbed the serpent by his tail and it went back into a staff.

7:17 The Pharaoh laughed and called upon his mages, sorcerers and wise men and demanded they perform this pathetic magic trick usually done at children's birthday parties.

7:18 They cast down their rods and they too became serpents. Vipers, mambas and cobras galore.

7:19 Slithering and hissing across the floor, striking but never biting into flesh.

7:20 Moses and Aaron laughed and both cast down their rods, changing them to mighty serpents.

7:21 Their serpents slithered across the floor and devoured the snakes of Pharaoh's men, letting out a great and mighty belch when finished with their meal.

7:22 Both brothers grabbed the tails of their serpents and they again became staffs. But much thicker than before.

7:23 But Pharaoh's heart was hardened by God and he cursed the men and accused them of thievery, casting them out of his chambers.

7:24 The lord God of Israel witnessed this and was amused and looked forward to playing more games upon Pharaoh.

7:25 That night, he came to Moses and said, "Tomorrow, you and Aaron shall go to Pharaoh again, while he bathes by the river.

7:26 Demand Aaron to take his staff and touch the surface of the river and in doing so the water shall turn to blood.

7:27 Say to him that the lord God of your people demand the Israelites to be set free, so that they may serve me in the wilderness.

7:28 He will refuse, but do not despair. For the water turning into blood will be hysterical."

7:29 Moses did as commanded by God and went to Pharaoh as he washed in the river.

7:30 He spoke to Pharaoh, "The lord God demands still his people be set free, so that they may worship him in the wilderness.

7:31 Do this, lest the lord God strike you with a curse!"

7:32 Pharaoh laughed, said no and demanded the brothers never interrupt him while he bathes nude again.

7:33 Aaron then took his staff and with it touched the top of the water.

7:34 The water slowly turned red and thick and the people knew it was blood.

7:35 The fish died and rose to the surface, causing a mighty stench across the lands.

7:36 People grew thirsty, for the water not just went to blood in the rivers and lakes, but also in the wells, the jugs, everywhere.

7:37 No place was their water to drink, only blood.

7:38 Pharaoh came out of the river, blood dripping from his body and told the brothers he shall consider their offer.

7:39 Gathering his wise men, they thought and contemplated of this most unusual drought.

7:40 First, they dug new wells, but the new wells brought forth fresh blood, not water.

7:41 Which made the vampires of Egypt very, very happy.

7:42 They attempted to filter the blood, but that failed miserably.

7:43 They then went to the land of Canaan and imported bottled water from them, fixing the drought of blood cursed upon Egypt.

7:44 Thus the first bottled water was sold by the people of Canaan.

7:45 Pharaoh took some fresh water and met with the brothers Moses and Aaron.

7:46 Using a powder made by his alchemists, he turned this water red and thick, like the blood in the river and wells and cursed the brothers for their foolish parlor tricks.

7:47 When asked if the people of Israel can leave, Pharaoh laughed and said no.

7:48 For God still cursed Pharaoh with stubbornness, so that he can send more plagues to amuse himself.

7:49 Seven days the peoples of Egypt had bloody rivers and the lord decided that was enough and the waters returned and the fish magically returned living to the rivers, lakes and streams.

8:1 The lord God returned to Moses and said to him, "Go now to Pharaoh and tell him to let your people go, so they may worship and praise me.

8:2 And when he refuses, I shall curse the nation with frogs.

8:3 From the river swarms of frog shall spring forth and they shall spread across the nation.

8:4 They will be in their bedchamber, their kitchens, their streets, their ovens, their wells.

8:5 In their clothing, their servants, their jugs of wine and ale.

8:6 Cursed they shall be with frogs."

8:7 The lord then told Moses, "Tell Aaron, your brother, to cast forth his hand across the waters of Egypt and as he does the frogs shall leap forth in abundance."

8:8 Moses did as the lord commanded and asked Pharaoh to let his people go.

8:9 Being a stubborn man, Pharaoh said no.

8:10 What a surprise.

8:11 So Aaron stretched forth his palm across the waters of Egypt and frogs came forth in mass abundance.

8:12 Pharaoh laughed at this common sorcery, for he knew his magicians to do the same.

8:13 But Pharaoh's magicians could not stop the frogs. They were everywhere.

8:14 Leaping, lounging, and croaking. The people of Egypt could not stand it.

8:15 The noise kept them up all night and the men complained the frogs were giving them warts upon their most sensitive of parts.

8:16 These same men also partook in the services of the brothels. Such a coincidence this is.

8:17 However, the Egyptians were a smart people and saw this as an opportunity.

8:18 They gathered the frogs, killed them and ate the delicious meat of their legs.

8:19 Sweet, delicious meat, which tasted like chicken but much more tender.

8:20 They then sold the meat to neighbouring nations and increased the Egyptian economy and trade.

8:21 But the frogs kept coming and they could not get rid of them no matter how much they sold or feasted. The people wanted them gone.

8:22 Pharaoh called for the two brothers and said to them, "If you take these frogs away from me, I shall let your people go so that they may worship your lord."

8:23 And Moses said to Pharaoh, "Good. We shall remove the frogs from your nation and they shall only reside in the rivers and pond where they came forth. When can my people leave?"

8:24 Pharaoh said the people of Israel could leave tomorrow.

8:25 The frogs of Egypt then died. They did not leave, but die, so that their rotting bodies lay in the streets, bedrooms and houses of all.

8:26 Egyptians spent days removing them and burning them and the land of Egypt stank.

8:27 This annoyed the peoples of Egypt and annoyed Pharaoh, for he saw this as an insult.

8:28 When tomorrow came, he refused to let the people of Israel go.

8:29 So the lord came to Moses and said, "You and your brother shall go to Pharaoh and demand your people leave. Pharaoh will refuse.

8:30 Have Aaron take his rod and point it to the dusts and sand, so that they shall turn to lice and plague the people of Egypt."

8:31 They did as God commanded. When Pharaoh refused to let the people of Israel go, Aaron took his rod, pointed it towards the sands and the sands became lice.

8:32 Lice infected the cattle and people of Egypt, causing them to itch terribly and shave their heads, since no shampoo could get rid of them.

8:33 When Pharaoh asked his sorcerers if they could do this, they said no, for it is not a common magic trick and that this has never been done before.

8:34 They told Pharaoh, "Surely this must be a curse from God." Pharaoh again grew angry and his heart hardened with fury and cholesterol.

8:35 The lord came to Moses. Again. And said to him, "Rise up early in the morning and visit Pharaoh while he bathes in the river. Tell him to let your people go, so that they may sacrifice to the one true God.

8:36 When he refuses, swarms of flies shall come and plague his nation. They shall be thick as smoke and swarm the streets and buildings. They shall feast upon the flesh of Egyptians, cattle and servants. They will not be able to move without hitting flies.

8:37 But the flies shall end where the borders are, so that the nations surrounding Egypt will not be harmed and see that Egypt is cursed.

8:38 Moses came and told Pharaoh to let his people go, lest flies infest his nation.

8:39 Pharaoh was furious, for the lice still remained and he cursed Moses and told him to go rape a camel.

8:40 So the lord of Israel sent swarms of flies upon the nation of Egypt.

8:41 They were black flies and they bit the flesh of all living things. The people, cattle and creatures suffered in pain.

8:42 Thick were the flies, so much so that people could see only buzzing masses of black around them.

8:43 Pharaoh called for Moses and Aaron and told them, "If you lift the curse of the lice and flies, I shall let your people go, so that they may make barbaric slaughters in sacrifice to your cruel God."

8:44 Moses agreed to this, believing this time Pharaoh will hold true to his word.

8:45 Remember, Moses was retarded.

8:46 He lifted the curse of the flies and the lice and the masses of insect and parasite vanished into the sky, never to be seen again.

8:47 Pharaoh then saw the suffering his people endured. The cattle and people were covered in nasty bites from the lice and flies. The doctors could not hand out enough ointment for them and many people suffered greatly.

8:48 Once beautiful concubines of Pharaoh were now hideous, covered in bleeding sores from the bites.

8:49 This caused Pharaoh to become angry, for he was sickened having to fornicate with such ugly women.

8:50 When the time came for the people of Israel to leave, Pharaoh would not let them.

8:51 One would think Pharaoh would want them to leave, for they would take away these curses with them. But Pharaoh was an idiot. Much like Moses.

9:1 God was tired of travelling from heaven and earth, so he sent an angel to Moses.

9:2 The angel said, "Behold, I am a messenger from the lord God almighty, creator of heaven and earth and all things."

9:3 Moses asked the messenger of God, "Does he want me to go to Pharaoh again?"

9:4 And the angel said, "Yes."

9:5 Moses asked the angel, "And when he refuses, what curse upon the nation of Egypt will the lord God almighty bring?"

9:6 The angel replied, "The lord God will curse the cattle of Egypt. His finger shall press down upon the horses, the camels, the sheep and oxen, the chickens and hens and fowl.

9:7 Strike them down he shall, forcing the people of Egypt to become vegetarians, even vegans.

9:8 But the people of Israel shall remain plentiful in their cattle, for the lord God shall spare them.

9:9 God almighty shall do this the day after Pharaoh denies your departure."

9:10 So Moses came to Pharaoh and asked for his people to leave.

9:11 Pharaoh said no. Again.

9:12 So the hand of God came down and touched the cattle of Egypt. No cow, ox, sheep, goat, camel, donkey nor horse were spared, except for the ones of Israel.

9:13 The Egyptians were furious, for they had no meat nor dairy to partake and they were forced upon a vegan diet.

9:14 They became either skinny as reeds or obese as the hippo and complained and cursed the lack of edible flesh.

9:15 Pharaoh hated this and cursed the people of Israel and their flocks and refused to let them leave.

9:16 Instead, he went to the land of Canaan and bought cattle and flocks and fowl, so that the people of Egypt can actually eat.

9:17 So God sent down another messenger and that messenger spoke to Moses.

9:18 "Take you and your brother and visit Pharaoh. Take from the furnace ash and throw it into the heavens above, so that Pharaoh may see.

9:19 The ash shall spread across the land of Egypt and curse the people with boils plenty.

9:20 Both man and beast shall be cursed with oozing boils."

9:21 They did. The two brothers came upon Pharaoh and did not even ask for the people of Israel to leave. They instead went directly to the furnace, each gathering a handful of ash.

9:22 Together, they flew it to the heavens and the ash spread.

9:23 It cursed all of Egypt with boils. Painful, oozing boils.

9:24 So terrible the men in Pharaoh's court fell, howling in pain.

9:25 But the lord God hardened the heart of Pharaoh, so that Pharaoh would still refuse to let the people of Israel leave.

9:26 God came to Moses and told him, "Get up early in the morning, go to Pharaoh and demand the people of Israel may leave, so that they may worship and sacrifice for me.

9:27 And when he does not, the lord God shall bring down upon the nation of Egypt his full wrath and fury!

9:28 All the people of the land shall know me and fear me, for I am the lord fucking God almighty, creator of heaven and earth and I can do whatever I please!"

9:29 Moses asked the lord, "Can it be in the afternoon. I'd like to sleep in."

9:30 God accused Moses of being lazy and told him it must be in the morning.

9:31 Moses went to Pharaoh, who was covered in boils and ointment and told him to let the people of Israel go.

9:32 For if not, then God shall unleash his fury upon the nation of Egypt.

9:33 Pharaoh said no and cursed the people of Israel, Moses and their cruel and unholy God.

9:34 On his way home, God came down and walked with Moses.

9:35 "When you return, tell your people to gather their flocks and cattle and bring it indoors.

9:36 Any man left outside should find shelter, for tonight any creature in the field shall be battered with hail and die."

9:37 So the people of Israel gathered their beasts and put them in their barns.

9:38 Some people of Egypt did this as well, knowing that if the people of Israel were doing it, there must be a reason.

9:39 Most did not, for they believed the Israelites foolish sorcerers.

9:40 Moses spread forth his hand across the sky and the lord God sent hail down upon the nation of Egypt.

9:41 Upon man, upon beast, upon fowl and upon flock hail beat the lands of Pharaoh.

9:42 Thunder then struck the ground and from the ground fire rose and spread across the lands, so that the fire and hail mixed and killed every living thing outside.

9:43 Trees fell and burned foul smoke into the air.

9:44 Hail broke roofs and buildings, so that even those in shelter were left unprotected.

9:45 Only the lands of Israel remained unharmed.

9:46 Pharaoh called for Moses and Aaron and begged of them to stop this onslaught.

9:47 He said to the brothers, "I am a sinful and evil man and I beg forgiveness of you and your God.

9:48 Please, lift this curse upon my lands and people and I shall let you go and your people can be free."

9:49 Moses told Pharaoh, "I shall leave this city and once I step foot outside the walls, the hail shall cease and the fire shall be gone.

9:50 The thunder will end and the land shall be peaceful.

9:51 For my lord God is an awesome God and has struck fear and horror into you and your people."

9:52 When Moses left, the lands calmed and the people were left with a ravaged country.

9:53 The cattle they bought were dead, saved for the few that remained in shelter.

9:54 The crops were destroyed, useless.

9:55 This angered the people, for they had to rebuild again.

9:56 Buildings were patched, crops were replanted and cattle was bought again from the neighbouring nations of Canaan.

9:57 Pharaoh cursed the people of Israel and demanded retribution for the damaged property.

9:58 When the day came for them to leave, Pharaoh refused and would not let them go.

10:1 God came to Moses again and said, "Go to Pharaoh, for I have made him stubborn still so that he shall refuse to let your people go.

10:2 And the Pharaoh's foolishness shall be a story passed from father to son, for generations to come and your children shall hear it and laugh and know that I am the one true God."

10:3 Moses and Aaron did as they were told and went to see Pharaoh.

10:4 Again.

10:5 And demanded that the people of Israel be set free, so that they may worship God.

10:6 Again.

10:7 If not, a terrible plague shall befall the Egyptian people.

10:8 Again.

10:9 Pharaoh said no.

10:10 Again.

10:11 So Aaron lifted his staff up and sent a curse down from God to punish the stubborn nation of Egypt.

10:12 Again.

10:13 This time, it was locusts. Locusts so thick and foul that none could see.

10:14 They walked through the locusts, knowing not where they went.

10:15 At night, they could not sleep for the sounds of the swarms of locusts kept them up.

10:16 They filled the houses, the servant quarters, the fields, the streets, the brothels, the wells, the jugs, the stoves,

10:17 Much like the flies, frogs and lice.

10:18 At first the peoples of Egypt roasted the locusts and ate them. But the meat was bitter and foul to their palate.

10:19 So they covered the locusts in chocolate and it became a treat for them.

10:20 Still, there was not enough chocolate to cover all the locusts.

10:21 Hungry, the swarm of locusts began to feast upon the crops.

10:22 The fields were stripped clean. Bark and leaves from the trees were eaten and became barren.

10:23 The sorcerers of Pharaoh were upset and asked the king of Egypt how long they must remain cursed by the damned people of Israel.

10:24 They reasoned with him and said that if they left, the curses go with them and the people of Egypt shall live in peace.

10:25 Pharaoh listened and agreed. For now.

10:26 He sent for Moses and Aaron and begged of them,

10:27 "Please, send this curse from your God away, so that we may live in peace.

10:28 I, and I alone, have sinned against you and yours, yet you punish my people. This is not justice.

10:29 So please, lift this plague from Egypt and I shall let your people go."

10:30 Moses and Aaron believed this and went back to their people.

10:31 And the curse of God was lifted from the nation of Egypt.

10:32 Again.

10:33 When the locusts left, the Egyptians saw that their crops were bare, trees dead and all plant life deceased

10:34 Pharaoh became infuriated, for he knew the lack of grain would starve his nation and that this was the fault of the fucking Israel people.

10:35 So when the time came for the people of Israel to leave, he refuses to let them go.

10:36 Again.

10:37 So God came down to Moses.

10:38 Again.

10:39 Moses didn't even let God speak. He told him, "I know, I know, we'll do it in the morning.

10:40 Again."

10:41 So Moses and Aaron went to Pharaoh.

10:42 Again.

10:43 And told him to let the people of Israel go.

10:44 Again.

10:45 Pharaoh said no.

10:46 Again.

10:47 So God sent down a plague.

10:48 Again.

10:49 And the people of Egypt suffered.

10:50 Again.

10:51 For the plague was darkness. Not blindness, but darkness, so that no living creature in the lands of Egypt could see.

10:52 Except for the people of Israel.

10:53 The people of Egypt suffered greatly. When they crossed the borders to the land of Canaan, they could see again.

10:54 When they looked back, they saw nothing but darkness, reaching out from the ground to the sky eternal.

10:55 As did the nations surrounding the lands.

10:56 But the Israelites, they could see.

10:57 For God blessed them with night vision during this curse.

10:58 Pharaoh grew insane because of this curse, for he knew not whether the person pleasuring him sexually was a gorgeous concubine or an ugly man.

10:59 So he sent for Moses and Aaron.

10:60 Again.

10:61 And said to them,

10:62 Again,

10:63 "I grow hateful of you and your people, cursing us with this sorcery.

10:64 If I were to die never seeing your faces again, I shall die a happy man.

10:65 Go, get away from me, take your people and go.

10:66 And when you do, lift this darkness from us, so that our nation can actually see where we walk."

10:67 And Moses and Aaron said to Pharaoh,

10:68 "We shall leave tomorrow and the darkness shall be lifted from your lands."

10:69 And the darkness lifted from the lands and the people of Egypt could see once more.

10:70 Pharaoh was happy, as was his people, for the darkness terrified them.

10:71 But the lord God made Pharaoh stubborn once more.

10:72 When the time came for the people of Israel to leave, Pharaoh refused.

10:73 Some of the people of Israel asked why they could not just leave anyway, without the consent of Pharaoh.

10:74 Moses quickly told them to shut up.

10:75 They did, believing that any more questions would be a question of God's will and therefore blasphemy.

10:76 An evil and deadly sin.

10:77 Though it was still a legitimate question.

11:1 The lord God then came to Moses, but it was not to tell him to visit Pharaoh.

11:2 No, this was a more sinister reason.

11:3 For the lord God said to Moses,

11:4 "Tell the people of Israel to take from their Egyptian neighbours valuable trinkets.

11:5 Anklets, jewelry, gold and silver and the like.

11:6 When asked to stop, tell them that if stopped, the lord God shall smite them again.

11:7 For I have one last curse to bring to the people of Egypt.

11:8 A curse that shall show these heathens hold no favour in the eyes of God.

11:9 And that the people of Israel are superior to them.

11:10 I shall send to these people my personal assassin.

11:11 An angel of death.

11:12 This angel of mine shall travel the nation and slay all the first-born sons.

11:13 The daughters can survive. Nobody cares about them.

11:14 My angel shall slay the sons of all, from beast to Pharaoh's own offspring.

11:15 Egypt shall howl and mourn so terribly,

11:16 That a great cry shall be heard across the heavens.

11:17 But against the people of Israel not a soul shall be harmed.

11:18 The Egyptians shall be saddened and demand you to leave.

11:19 You shall take from them whatever you desire and they shall let you.

11:20 For they shall only want you gone."

11:21 Moses said to God,

11:22 "My lord, I have done what you have asked and am proud to be a servant of God.

11:23 But, I know it is you who makes Pharaoh stubborn and not let us leave.

11:24 Why, my lord. Would it not be easier just to soften Pharaoh's heart?

11:25 Soften it so that he may let us go?"

11:26 The lord God said to Moses,

11:27 "That would be easier, but much more boring.

11:28 You know not the will of God and have much to learn of me.

11:29 I want the plagues, the curses, the bloodshed.

11:30 I desire the death of the first-born.

11:31 Calves, beasts, flocks, fowl, children and babies.

11:32 It entertains me and fills me with a sense of power that only a God like I can truly obtain!"

11:33 Then the lord God vanished in a puff of smoke and Moses whispered something under his breath that he wanted to say for quite some time.

11:34 "I worship a tyrant."

12:1 God's lust for death consumed him and he sent forth word to Moses that his angel of death comes to earth.

12:2 He gave to Moses directions, so that the assassin of the lord shall avoid the homes of the people of Israel.

12:3 "Tell the people of Israel that this month be the month I shall slay the first-borns of Egypt.

12:4 Be warned and take heed of my instructions, so that death shall avoid your houses.

12:5 On the tenth day of this month, have your people take a lamb.

12:6 If the household is too small to consume the lamb, they may share it with their neighbour, so that both houses shall feast upon the flesh.

12:7 Your lamb must be perfect in the eyes of God; a male, healthy and pure white without blemish and under the age of a year.

12:8 Remove the lamb from the flock and care for it separately, so that you ensure the lamb is kept in good care.

12:9 Keep it fed and cared until the day of the fourteenth, for that day shall be the day of slaughter.

12:10 Take a blade sharpened and kill the lambs in the evening. Save the blood in bowls and jars, so that you may decorate.

12:11 Dip your hands in the blood and smear all doors with the liquid of life. Paint all around the entrances to your house, so that every door be surrounded in blood.

12:12 Take the lamb and roast them over a mighty fire and spice it with herbs bitter and harsh.

12:13 For this is a meal of death and death shall not taste sweet to the palate of man; death is a meal fit only pleasant for God.

12:14 Consume with the lamb unleavened bread, so that your stomachs not be full of flesh.

12:15 Do not eat the lamb raw, nor moisten the flesh with water, but cook it in full, with head and limbs attached and organs inside.

12:16 Consume all you can in the night, for this is the meal of death and death is a pleasing meal to the lord God.

12:17 Whatever be left over, take and burn as an offering to the lord God.

12:18 For the smell of burning flesh is an aroma pleasant to I, your lord.

12:19 Eat the flesh with your belts tightened, shoes upon your feet and your staff in hand. Eat it in gluttony, like the beasts consume freshly killed prey.

12:20 For this is the lord's meal and you shall eat it like me.

12:21 For tonight, death shall pass through Egypt and smite the first-born of all man and beast; and against the Gods of Egypt I shall execute judgment and punishment.

12:22 As I am the one true God and these falsified deities offend me.

12:23 But when the assassin sees the blood upon your entrance, he shall know this is a house of the chosen people and he shall pass it by.

12:24 So that none of the people of Israel be slain this night, the night of death.

12:25 Ahh, Moses, this shall be a night of history!

12:26 Your people must remember it through generations eternal, for it is the day God freed his people.

12:27 Celebrate with a feast, a feast pleasant and fine.

12:28 For seven days, the nation of Israel shall remember this night be eating naught but unleavened bread, for unleavened bread is a treat in the eyes of God.

12:29 This feast shall be celebrated on the first month, on the fourteenth day of that month and end upon the twenty first.

12:30 A holy blessing shall start the feast and a holy blessing shall end it, and none shall labour on these days, for it is a day of worship and work will hinder the worship of I, the lord God.

12:31 If any people of Israel eat bread leavened, they shall be banned from the nation and from God, for this is blasphemy to the lord.

12:32 Treat them as foreign heathens and cast them out to die."

12:33 Moses told this to the elders of Israel, so that the will of God be fulfilled.

12:34 Lambs were taken, slaughtered and the blood smeared upon the doors.

12:35 Flesh was cooked and made bitter with spice, so that none could enjoy the meal.

12:36 Forced themselves they did to engorge their bellies with flesh.

12:37 That night, when the moon was highest, the assassin of the lord came to Egypt

12:38 And slaughtered all the first-born males, pleasing the lord God with unnecessary death.

12:39 The nation of Egypt rose early that night and cried out a mighty and primal cry, mourning the deaths of the first-born sons and the loss of ones they loved.

12:40 The pitiful mourning and grieving was heard by God and he laughed.

12:41 Pharaoh was deeply saddened by this, for his eldest son and eldest son of all, was dead and he hated God and Moses for it and hated the people of Israel.

12:42 He called forth for Moses and Aaron and said to the brothers, "Rise up, gather all your goods and get out of my lands.

12:43 Take your flocks and fowl and beasts with you, for I want no cursed object of your people left.

12:44 Your God is a merciless beast; a demon in the eyes of Egypt and we demand him to leave.

12:45 So go and take your ruthless God with you."

12:46 And the people of Israel did.

12:47 They gathered all goods belonging to them and prepared for the journey to the promised land.

12:48 Being greedy people, they went to the houses of Egypt, demanding all goods of value and threatened to curse them if the Egyptians refused.

12:49 Once they looted all they could, they gave praise to God, for finally they were free of slavery.

12:50 They then gathered all goods, cattle, flocks and fowl and slaves (yes, slaves) and left

12:51 They baked unleavened cakes for the journey, as unleavened cakes were flat and easier to pack.

12:52 And after four hundred and thirty years of servitude, they finally left the yoke of Pharaoh and replaced it with the yoke of God.

12:53 God came down to the people and blessed them and said to them,

12:54 "I am the lord true God and you are my chosen people.

12:55 Praise and worship me, so that I may seek favour for your kin.

12:56 Celebrate this freedom with Passover, so that you shall not forget that it was I God who freed you.

12:57 But only those of my favour shall partake in this feast, for no foreign heathen is pleasant in my eyes and they offend me.

12:58 If you have slaves, they may take part of Passover, as long as their foreskin is removed.

12:59 If foreskin remain, they are evil in my eyes and must be separate from the celebration.

12:60 In one house shall the feast be, so that the food may not be separated and no flesh torn.

12:61 And if a stranger does enter your house and you find favour in this stranger, take a blade.

12:62 Remove the foreskin from his loins and he shall feast in favour of God.

12:63 For I love the mutilation of male genitals. It amuses me."

12:64 The nation of Israel agreed to this and did as their God asked.

12:65 And finally, after all this time, they left Egypt.

13:1 The lord God came to Moses and said to him,

13:2 "The lust of death fills me and I long for even more. I see your people and wish to kill your first-born sons, as the death is pleasing to me.

13:3 But I shall not, though they do belong to me. But only under one condition. You must replace death with death.

13:4 Save your first-born children and sanctify them through ritual. I'm sure you'll think of something that will satisfy me."

13:5 Moses thought and with his retarded mind, came with a ritual to save the first-born males of Israel.

13:6 He gathered the tribes and spoke to them what he believed the will of God.

13:7 "My brethren, the lord God has freed us from the chains of servitude, as promised by him many generations ago.

13:8 Blessed be our God.

13:9 Remember this day, for it the day of our independence.

13:10 And he shall lead us into the land of milk and honey, occupied by the Canaanites, Hittites, Amorites and Jebusites. These people were destined by God to care for our land, until we claim it rightfully ours.

13:11 Every year, at this time, we shall celebrate our victory by eating bread unleavened, as it is a sweet bread and pleasing to God.

13:12 If any person of Israel eats leavened bread at this time, he shall be cast out and forgotten by God; for surely it is simple enough to eat flat bread for a week, if it pleases our lord.

13:13 Share nothing of this feast with the unchosen, for this celebration is meant only for those pleasing to God.

13:14 When doubt you have of a person of if he is the chosen of God, lift his robe. If foreskin remain, the feast he shall not partake of until that skin be gone.

13:15 During this celebration, we shall pass down our story of independence to our sons and they shall pass it down to their sons, so that every generation shall know the power of our lord.

13:16 Remember the curses sent to the people of Pharaoh and laugh at them, for it is the will of God to remember our enslavers as idiots and fools.

13:17 Tell them of the waters of blood, thick and foul and how the nation grew thirsty for the simplest of drink.

13:18 Entertain your children with the story of frogs, running amok and disgusting the heathen people.

13:19 Remind them of the lice infesting their hair and skin, causing a great lack of hygiene upon the proud and clean people of Egypt.

13:20 Forget not the flies, swarming the lands, biting them, wounding them, choking them.

13:21 Regale them with the death of the beasts, forcing the hungry nation into a diet of veganism; a diet most unpleasant and foul.

13:22 Boast of how our once proud captors grew boils most painful and sore, oozing puss and blood and scarring the smooth and silky skin of the Egyptians.

13:23 Speak loudly of the hail and fire threatening the people, causing them to tremble and shit in their undergarments.

13:24 Brag how our lord God sent locusts so thick they filled their noses and stripped all vegetation from the lands.

13:25 Laugh when you tell your children of the darkness cursed upon the lands and that only the children of Abraham could see.

13:26 Most importantly, tell them of the slaying of the first-born sons, for this is the curse our lord God is most proud of.

13:27 A curse he will want us to remember.

13:28 For death pleases the lord and fills his heart with power.

13:29 We must celebrate this plague brought to Egypt, in remembrance of our freedom sent to us by God.

13:30 Take from your flocks the first-born beasts and break the creatures neck, so that the life leaves it.

13:31 Grab the carcass and pile them all upon one another, into a great and mighty heap for the lord.

13:32 Burn them and let the smoke reach into the heavens above, so that the scent may reach the nostrils of God and please him. As the bodies burn, strip off your clothing and dance naked around it, praising God!

13:33 For our lord God loves violence, nudity and torn flesh.

13:34 If you deny this to the lord, God shall be angry and take away your first-born son.

13:35 He shall spare your daughter, as they are worthless and useless females and God cares not for them."

13"36 God heard of Moses' plan and was pleased enough by it. So, he led the people of Israel away from Egypt and sent them forth to the land of the Philistines; the land promised to them; the land of milk and honey.

13:37 But God did not send them directly there, no. He took them on a more scenic route, through the wilderness, by the Red Sea.

13:38 During the day, God led them by cloud, black and ominous, low to the ground and the tribes of Israel chased it.

13:39 By night, God led them by pillars of fire, bright and burning, so that they may see him through the night and not get lost.

13:40 Never did he take away the pillar of fire nor the cloud of darkness from his people, until they reached the land promised in the covenant.

14:1 Pharaoh was relieved to have the cursed people of Israel leave.

14:2 For with them gone, the cruelty of their God went with them and the people of Egypt shall live in peace.

14:3 But it was quickly noticed that Zebediah, who was born of Israel, was left behind.

14:4 For the people of Israel was ashamed of Zebediah, as he was a useless cripple, slow of mind and truly useless in the eyes of God.

14:5 Thinking this a mistake, Pharaoh took in Zebediah and told him,

14:6 "Surely your people must have overlooked you, as they left in haste.

14:7 I shall gather my fastest chariots and personally deliver you to them, as a sign of good faith."

14:8 Pharaoh then gathered six hundred of his fastest chariots and personally escorted the forgotten man of Israel back to his people and family.

14:9 God saw this and grew furious.

14:10 He did not want Zebediah returned, for he was pathetic and retarded.

14:11 So the lord God came to Moses and told him,

14:12 "Pharaoh comes to you and with him six hundred chariots.

14:13 And he brings the cursed Zebediah, for he knows him useless and wishes to burden you people with this man."

14:14 Moses grew fearful, for he knew Zebediah to be a worthless creature and wished not to be burdened with him.

14:15 When the people of Israel heard, they grew worried and fearful.

14:16 Zebediah's family prayed to the lord God, begging him to kill

Zebediah, as they wished not to care for him again.

14:17 The lord heard the prayers and did something very rare.

14:18 He answered them.

14:19 God came to Moses and spoke to him.

14:20 "Send your people to the sea and encamp there for a time.

14:21 For soon I shall show you the power your God."

14:22 Moses did as God commanded and the people of Israel set camp by the shores of the sea.

14:23 When the Egyptians came closer, the nation of Israel grew worried.

14:24 Did God free them from labour, only to curse them to die in the wilderness?

14:25 As the chariots grew closer, the people of Israel demanded action.

14:26 And the lord God delivered.

14:27 He demanded that Moses go to the shores of the sea and spread his rod across the waters.

14:28 Moses did and as he did, the sea parted in two.

14:29 So that from one beach to the next, there was dry land to walk upon.

14:30 The lord then said to the nation of Israel,

14:31 "Go forth, cross the sea and I shall protect you from Pharaoh and Zebediah."

14:32 They did and were amazed with the lord God's power.

14:33 Children watched the walls of water in amazement, gazing upon the fish and crocodiles.

14:34 Though all were tempted to touch, none did, for fear this would anger the lord.

14:35 The chariots of Egypt witnessed this great sea part and were amazed.

14:36 Pharaoh thought this a sign of them, welcoming them with open arms for delivering the forgotten Zebedian to them.

14:37 He was wrong.

14:38 Israel crossed the sea, set camp upon the other side, gazed back and saw the chariots of Pharaoh go into the path created by God.

14:39 As all chariots and horses came down upon the path, God crippled them and the wheels of the chariots came off.

14:40 Pharaoh knew the lord of the Israelites to be a cruel and stubborn beast and thought this a test of wills.

14:41 He said to his men, "This is a test of the people of Israel.

14:42 Move on, so that we way deliver to them Zebediah and show them we mean good faith."

14:43 They hurrahed and moved forward, closer to the shore and to the peoples of Israel.

14:44 This is when Zebediah did his last retarded act.

14:45 He saw a fish, a great and mighty fish and became hungry.

14:46 Zebediah demanded he be stopped and the chariots of Egypt did so.

14:47 With his one good arm, the crippled Zebediah picked from the dry seabed a shell.

14:48 Pretty and appealing.

14:49 He then raised his arm and threw it at the fish.

14:50 Missing it, as he had a weak arm. He was a useless cripple, after all.

14:51 The shell hit the wall of water and the walls cracked.

14:52 Suddenly, the great sea came crashing upon them, drowning them all.

14:53 In moments, Pharaoh, his horses, his men and Zebediah, drowned in the sea.

14:54 With the Israelites watching in amazement.

14:55 God then came upon the peoples of Israel and, in a great and booming voice, said,

14:56 "Witness the power of your lord God.

14:57 Creator of heaven and earth and all things.

14:58 Know that I am all powerful and shall protect you upon your journey.

14:59 But be warned, for if you anger me, I shall punish you greatly!

14:60 Love me and fear me, for I am your God and I can do as I please and none of you shall stop me.

14:61 Witness what just happened and know this.

14:62 If I desire, I can do the same to you."

14:63 The people of Israel took heed of this warning, and praised God in fear.

15:1 After witnessing the slaughter of the chariots of Egypt, the death of the crippled Zebediah and hearing the speech of the mighty and divine dictator that be the lord God, the people of Israel did what was the natural thing to do.

15:2 They got drunk and partied down.

15:3 Singing praises of glory to the righteous slayer.

15:4 Creating beautiful poetry about how the lord God threw horse and rider into the mighty sea.

15:5 For the lord God is a righteous God, whose strength shall be remembered in drunken songs and salvation shall be delivered to them who praise his name.

15:6 As the lord God is a violent God, a God of war, a God of death.

15:7 Casting chariot, cripple, man and beast upon the Red Sea.

15:8 Sinking the unholy to the bottom, so the fish may feast upon the flesh of the damned.

15:9 The right hand, the hand of God, is glorious and powerful: the right hand shall hammer, crush and destroy the heathens and unbelievers.

15:10 The left hand, the hand of God, is used to blind the ones who believe, so that they may seek no truth, but forever be cursed in devotion to the lord.

15:11 In the greatness of God, he has overthrown the captors of his people and smote them again, and the sea consumed them like feed.

15:12 With a blow from his powerful nostrils, the lord parted the great sea, the water stood upright and a path was laid for the chosen and true.

15:13 The enemy saw this and ignored the mighty power of God, pursuing them through the waters.

15:14 God has a lust for death and his lust was fulfilled the glorious day the Egyptians stepped upon the grounds of the sea.

15:15 For the lord God almighty plugged his nose and the waters sank so horses, men, and Zebediah the lame was slaughtered.

15:16 Pleasing the lord God, as he loves mass death.

15:17 Who else but the one true God can do this and show his power to his people?

15:18 None, for our God is the only God. So, don't bother questioning it, lest you be cursed.

15:19 For the lord God can stretch out his right hand and cause a nation to be swallowed in the dust of the land.

15:20 Fear not, for if you have faith, the lord God shall show mercy upon you and give you strength and lead you into the lands of holy habitation.

15:21 The people of this land know we come and tremble in fear: sorrow shall take hold in their hearts.

15:22 As we come, the rulers shall gasp in amazement, the mighty armies shall tremble and cast down their weapons and the people shall melt away in terror.

15:23 For the lord our God and saviour shall stricken their minds with dread and fear, as the greatness of Israel come towards them and claim what is rightfully theirs.

15:24 It matters not that they were there first, what matters only is what God demands.

15:25 We shall overtake the heathens and build to God mighty sanctuaries in his honour and praise him and worship him.

15:26 For the lord God shall reign for ever and ever, as he is only the one true God and none shall challenge him.

15:27 As he is the divine dictator and his rule must be followed and never questioned nor doubted.

15:28 Because God has given us proof enough in the slaying of Egypt.

15:29 When the horsemen of Pharaoh drowned in the sea, while the people of Israel stood upon the shore, dry, laughing at the fools of Pharaoh.

15:30 Miriam, sister of Aaron, then took a timbrel and began to dance in honour of God, stripping naked and pleasing the lord with her bosom.

15:31 Other women followed, as did men and soon all the people of Israel were nude, praising the lord God almighty!

15:32 They then drank of the stolen wine, beer and spirit that they looted from the people of Egypt.

15:33 And as the spirit of the vine flowed through the people, they mistook it to be the spirit of the lord.

15:34 God did not care, as drunk people are easier to manipulate.

15:35 One the wrath of grapes was lifted off their heads, the lord God led them to the wilderness of Shur and for three days they went without water.

15:36 Thirsty they were and they became to grumble and whine.

15:37 They cried to the lord "Give us water, so that our tongues be no longer parched and we can sing praises of your name."

15:38 God delivered and led them to the wells of Marah; and the people of Israel drank of the water and spat.

15:39 For the water was bitter, stale and most displeasing.

15:40 The people cried to Moses, "What shall we do, for the water tastes terrible and we are thirsty."

15:41 Moses prayed to God and God listened and told Moses what to do.

15:42 God led Moses to a tree, which he chopped down and threw upon the waters of Marah.

15:43 As the sap from the tree spread forth upon the waters, the taste became sweet and the people of Israel had their fill and replenished their jugs and canteens.

15:44 God then said to the people of Israel,

15:45 "Love me, fear me and do as I command. For I shall lead you not upon death, but to greatness and prosperity. Though times may be tough, fear not, for I shall care and protect you. But you must do as I say and follow my rule. If you do, all shall remain healthy and pure so that no person of Abraham shall be sick or plagued with disease.

15:46 For I am the lord God almighty and your faith shall heal you."

15:47 God then led them to the lands of Elim, where the waters be plentiful. And the people of Israel camped by the waters and the palm trees.

16:1 As the children of Israel wandered the desert, the stomachs became barren and rumbled in complaint.

16:2 They came to Moses and said to him,

16:3 "We are free from the binds of Egypt only to starve in the wasteland. Does the lord God want us to die here, our bones picked dry by the vultures of the desert?

16:4 In Egypt, we had bread to eat and flesh to feast and though we worked, our bellies were full and never did we starve!"

16:5 The lord God heard these complaints and was annoyed. Have these people not yet learned that God can do anything. If they had just waited, they would realize that though their bellies are empty, they shall still live, for the lord God will allow them to survive without the sustenance of food.

16:6 But the Israelites whined so much and God became so annoyed, he decided to shut them up.

16:7 God came to Moses and told him of his plan to feed the children of Abraham.

16:8 "Behold Moses, I am the lord God and I shall not free my chosen people from Pharaoh to curse them to starvation. Behold, I shall cause bread to rain upon you.

16:9 The bread shall lie upon the ground baked, sweet and ready to eat. Your people shall gather the bread, enough to feast upon that day.

16:10 Take only what you need, though, for what is not eaten that day shall rot and go to waste. And waste is sinful in the eyes of the lord God.

16:11 On the sixth day, take double the bread, for on the seventh day none shall rain down, for the seventh day is the Sabbath day and I will not work that day.

16:12 Neither shall you, for the Sabbath day is a holy day, a day of rest. If I need not work it, none shall.

16:13 For to work on the Sabbath day shall be a sin, as it makes me appear lazy."

16:14 Aaron and Moses then spoke to the people of Israel about God's will.

16:15 "The lord God has answered our prayers and shall fill our stomachs. Soon, bread shall come from the sky.

16:16 For tomorrow, when we wake, a cake unlike any other shall lie upon the ground; and this cake is the bread of God.

16:17 Take it, enough to feast upon it that day and no more, for the food not eaten that day shall rot the day after and be wasted.

16:18 But on the day before the holy day, take double, for the Sabbath day none shall find bread upon the ground, as it is a day of rest and God will not deliver us bread on this day.

16:19 Fear not, for the lord God surely will not let the food take rot on the Sabbath."

16:20 And the people of Israel did as was told.

16:21 They went to bed that night, hungry, awaiting the blessed bread of God.

16:22 That morning, they awoke and behold the ground was covered with a new and interesting thing, small and round, like frost upon a tree.

16:23 Those that were truly hungry scooped it and sniffed it; and it was a pleasing scent to the nostrils. They then ate it and rejoiced, for it was a delicious bread, sweet and satisfying.

16:24 Crunchy this new food was and lightly sweet, like wafers of honey and vanilla.

16:25 All rejoiced and gathered it and ate it and stored it to be eaten later in the day.

16:26 They praised the lord and called it manna, for surely it was a blessed bread from God.

16:27 Most took all they could and feasted upon it and some took little, as they feared the manna fattening and would cause them to gain large and unappealing thighs.

16:28 Those that gathered in excess awoke to find the manna spoiled, full of worms and bitter to the taste.

16:29 On the sixth day, Moses reminded them to gather twice the amount, for the next day is a holy day and the lord God will not rain down bread, as he shall be too busy sleeping.

16:30 Most took heed of this and gathered double, storing the manna in jars for the next day.

16:31 Some ignored the words of Moses and only ate what was needed that day, for they knew manna to quickly rot.

16:32 On the seventh day, the manna did not rot and those that gathered found the manna fresh and sweet for the Sabbath consumption.

16:33 The few that gathered double did not starve, while the others grew hungry as punishment for expecting the lord to work on the seventh day.

16:34 God was furious at the people who searched for manna on the Sabbath, as this was considered work and he came to Moses and said to him,

16:35 "How long does your people refuse to obey my laws and commandments?

16:36 See that the lord has given you the Sabbath as a day of slacking of, and a holy day it must be. This is why I work twice as hard on the sixth day, so that you may have double the manna and enough to feast on the Sabbath."

16:37 The people of Israel heard this and rested on the Sabbath day and kept it holy by sleeping in, slacking off and doing not even the simplest of tasks for fear of offending God

16:38 And because it gave them an excuse for laziness and sloth.

16:39 Moses then commanded his people,

16:40 "The lord sends us manna, so that we may eat and grow fat and be merry. We must remember this precious of bread. Take a pot and fill it with manna, ripe and full and plug the pot and seal it. This manna shall not be eaten, but preserved, so that future generations shall see the bounty and bread the lord God has provided their ancestors."

16:41 All the children of Israel did and they feasted upon the manna for forty years until God finally sent them to the land he promised them generations ago.

17:1 The nation of Israel left the wilderness, feasting upon the manna that God gave them. The lord led them to the lands of Rephidim where they made camp; and the people of Israel worried.

17:2 For neither well nor river nor lake nor puddle was in the land of Rephidim; and dehydration became a concern.

17:3 All complained to Moses, saying, "You have led us away from the lands of Egypt and cursed us to die of thirst in the desert. Egypt had fresh water, where the Nile was cool and refreshing. Here, not even a drop of water is to be seen."

17:4 Moses said to the people, "Quit your whining, for when you complain to me, you complain to God and it upsets him."

17:5 And the people of Israel became quiet, in fear that to insult Moses would insult God.

17:6 A tactic used upon many religious and cult leaders for generations to follow.

17:7 Still, a great thirst remained so that none were quenched. Urine was drank, sweat was lapped and the breast-milk from nursing bosoms was gulped upon by many.

17:8 Soon, Moses became parched and said to God,

17:9 "What do you want me to do. For I shall drink of no urine, sweat, nor breast milk. Water I demand and surely water you shalt give to me."

17:10 God came to Moses, infuriated that a person be so bold as to make demands of him!

17:11 "Moses, never demand anything from me, lest I curse ye with more retardation. But worry not, for I shall give you and your people fresh, cool water.

17:12 Stand in front of the people of Israel and the elders of Israel and take your rod. To the side of you shall be a rock and when you strike the rock, water will pour from it.

17:13 I do this to show you that I am the lord God and my powers be matched by none."

17:14 Moses did as was told, gathered his peoples and elders and struck the rock with his staff.

17:15 As water gushed forth from the rock, the people of Israel blessed the lord and filled their mouths and jugs with the everlasting supply from the water stone, praising the lord and boasting of his divinity.

17:16 Soon, the word of the stone spread; and the people of Amalekite heard of it and grew curious.

17:17 For the Amalekites lived in the desert and knew water to be precious. They would gladly trade for the use of such a stone.

17:18 They came to the people of Israel and asked if they could use the water stone to fill their jugs, quench their thirst and water their crops.

17:19 The peoples of Israel said no, as they were greedy bastards like God and shared nothing with heathens.

17:20 As the Amalekites left, Moses said to the elder Joshua, "Take the strongest men of our people, go out and slaughter those heathen fuckers in the morning; and the lord God shall ensure your victory."

17:21 Joshua did as commanded and led an army of Israel to the people of Amalekite, to be slaughtered in the name of God.

17:22 Moses, Aaron, and Hur watched atop a hill, so that the slaughter shall entertain them.

17:23 But a slaughter did not yet happen, for the Amalekites were a disciplined people and knew the art of war.

17:24 Disappointed, the three men on the hill cursed the incompetence of Joshua; and the spirit of the lord came to them.

17:25 Moses raised his hands and suddenly the battle turned and the army of Israel grew strong and the swords and spears and arrows of the Amalekites did not penetrate their skin. The slaughter began.

17:26 As long as Moses' arms were above his head, the army of Joshua kicked heathen ass. And Aaron and Hur kept the arms of Moses above, as the arms became fatigued and the hands of Moses shook in defiance of the Amalekites!

17:27 Within hours, a glorious victory came to the nation of Israel and the corpses of the bastard Amalekites were looted and burned as a sacrifice to God.

17:28 The lord God came to Moses and told him to write down this glorious victory over the heathen hordes, so that all the generations of Israel shall know it in remembrance to the power of the lord.

17:29 God then roared to his chosen people, "I swear to you that all the people of Amalekite shall be wiped and slaughtered, so that none shall be left breathing under the sky alone. For the lord God loathes the people of Amalekite and shall war with them from generation to generation, until they all lie in dust, for the lord God is a God of war."

17:30 The people of Israel rejoiced and built a great and mighty altar to God and named it Jehovahnissi and burned the bodies of the slaughtered heathens upon it.

17:31 As the bodies burned, they danced around it naked, pleasing the lord God with violence, nudity and torn flesh.

18:1 Many a day the people of Israel travelled, hoping that soon they shall reach the land of milk and honey promised to them by God.

18:2 God had a much crueller plan for now, as he wandered them closer and closer to the lands of Midian.

18:3 Midian, where Moses' father in law lived.

18:4 Zipporah nagged, I mean correctly pointed out, to Moses that

she has not seen her family in many years and since they were so close it seemed fair to drop in and say hello.

18:5 Moses refuses, as he did not want to see the man whose flocks he took.

18:6 The peoples of Israel heard the married two bicker and decided for Moses that they shall all go to Midian and see Reul.

18:7 The masses set off, with Moses grumbling all the way and Zipporah telling the bastard husband of hers to fucking smile as he visits his father in law.

18:8 God witnessed the happy couple argue and was mildly amused. To aid in his amusement, God did something cruel and inhumane.

18:9 He cursed Zipporah with PMS and her attitude became frightening to Moses.

18:10 Reul prepared a mighty feast for his beloved daughter and when the two came in, Reul embraced Zipporah and hugged her and kissed her and spoke many a kind word in her ear.

18:11 Moses got a "Hey you," for his greeting and was told to hang up the coats.

18:12 They sat down to a dinner of honey dipped bread, fresh lamb and vegetables, as the people of Israel camped outside the city walls and ate manna.

18:13 All through the meal the silence was deafening, as both men refused to speak to one another.

18:14 Zipporah loathed the silence and filled the lack of volume with nonsensical speech.

18:15 During dessert, the two men started to partake of alcohol and the more they drank the less they shut up, until both started fighting verbally with one another.

18:16 Reul cursed Moses, declaring him the insect that rotted the pure Zipporah.

18:17 He demanded retribution to the flocks Moses took from him those many years ago.

18:18 Moses cursed Reul for believing Zipporah innocent and pure, as everyone knew she laid with men so many times that rarely did her thighs meet. He claimed what he took was a dowry for Zipporah, as surely, he must have earned so much to take her as a wife.

18:19 As the liquor flowed and the words were tossed, a punch was thrown. It is unsure who punched who first, but only that it led to a drunken brawl.

18:20 Fists and feet were flung with fury, until both men lay beaten and bruised as Zipporah lay in the corner, crying.

18:21 Both men gazed upon the pathetic, crying woman and knew they had failed her.

18:22 They both gazed upon each other with shame and knew that to make Zipporah happy, they must pretend to get along.

18:23 So they did what all men do when they feel it necessary to bond.

18:24 They killed an animal.

18:25 A goat, young and white, with no blemish in the fur.

18:26 They burned it, set it upon an altar and danced around it naked.

18:27 This pleased the lord God, as he loves violence, nudity and torn flesh.

18:28 Even more so than petty family squabbles.

18:29 In drunkenness, the two men embraced one another and considered pursuing each other's fleshly delights.

18:30 However, the alcohol prevented them from the blessed erection, so both said their drunken goodbyes and went their ways.

18:31 Reul to his house, Moses back to the Israeli camp.

19:1 In the third month of their wanderings, the nation of Israel came to the blessed mount Sinai, which has been blessed as the lord's abode.

19:2 They made camp upon the borders of the mount, hoping the lord their God shall see them, speak to them and bless them.

19:3 The lord God yelled to Moses, demanding he climb the mountain to speak with him, so that Moses may relay the message back to the people of Israel.

19:4 God spoke to him, "Remember the curses I brought forth to the people of Egypt, how I led you all to freedom and how I placed you upon the wings of my angels, protecting you and your people.

19:5 I did this because the peoples of Israel have obeyed me and kept my covenant without question; and if you continue to do so, you shall be my favourite of people and hold higher regards and power than all other nations, people and creeds.

19:6 You all shall be a kingdom of God, of priests and of holy men and shall earn a place in my kingdom of heaven.

19:7 Go now and repeat what I said to the children of Israel."

19:8 Moses climbed down the mountain, gathered the elders of Israel and repeated what the lord God said to him.

19:9 The elders and people of Israel believed these words and answered in unison, "We shall do all that which our lord God commands, for if we do, the lord shall reward us and if we don't, the wrath of God shall descend upon us; a wrath we have seen, and wish not upon ourselves."

19:10 The lord God saw this, and was pleased, for fear is a great way to lead a nation of people.

19:11 To further grow the fear in the hearts of Israel, he called for Moses again.

19:12 Moses climbed the mountain and spoke with the lord God.

19:13 "Moses, in a few days I shall descend myself upon this mountain in fire, smoke and thunder.

19:14 I do this so that when I speak to the children of Israel, they shall hear me and pay attention.

19:15 Go down, tell the people this and ready them. Sanctify them. Tell them to wash their clothes, bathe and remain pure for the lord God that is I.

19:16 For I do not want any offensive stench nor odour when I come down upon the third day.

19:17 Warn them that when I am here, none shall come upon the mount nor step across the border.

19:18 Any that does, whether man, woman, child or beast, shall be put to death by stones.

19:19 Only when the trumpet yells shall it be safe for them to enter my earthly dwelling."

19:20 Moses climbed down the mountain and told the people of Israel what God said.

19:21 "My people, on the third day the lord God shall enter the holy mount and speak with us. Ready yourselves for his arrival.

19:22 Bathe, wash your clothes and do not take pleasure with sex, for all must be pure and clean for the lord's arrival."

19:23 As the third day came, all were ready for the lord's arrival. They were clean, shaven and their clothes had no stains.

19:24 All women cursed by nature's cycle were kept away, alone in the wilderness, so that their genital bleeding shall not offend God.

19:25 When the lord came down, it was a mighty and frightening sight.

19:26 A great black cloud of smoke and fire descended upon the mountain, with blasts of lighting and mighty claps of thunder!

19:27 All the people were frightened, for it was a horrendous and unnatural sight.

19:28 Fear of the lord grew in their hearts and God was pleased when he sensed this, for he knew now all would not question nor doubt him for fear of punishment.

19:29 The entire mount was engulfed in the fury of God, so that not even rock nor dust be seen through the thick cloud of the lord almighty.

19:30 When the trumpets of the angels sounded, Moses entered into the smoke, led by the sound of the instruments.

19:31 The lord spoke in a great and booming voice, so all the nation of Israel may hear him,

19:32 "None but Aaron and Moses shall enter my domain, for they have been blessed by me. If any other enter the borders of the mount, I shall kill them."

19:33 One did and was instantly put to flame and melted in front of the nations of Israel; and the peoples fear of God grew even stronger and God was pleased.

19:34 Moses climbed the mountain, alone, to hear the divine message the lord God came down to deliver.

20:1 And the lord God said unto Moses,

20:2 "I am the lord almighty, creator of heaven and earth!

20:3 I led you into Egypt and now lead you away.

20:4 For this gift of freedom, ye shall have no other gods but me!

20:5 As I be the one true lord.

20:6 Thou shalt not make any image of me, nor any likeness of me, nor any image of beast, fowl, fish or heathen likeness.

20:7 Thou shall never bow down before these images, nor worship them, as they be just rock and stone and useless. For I the lord God am a jealous God and loathe when others worship someone other than me!

20:8 Any fool that worships a heathen lord shall be cursed and his family cursed unto the fourth generations.

20:9 Those that keep my commandments shall be blessed by me, and feel the love of God.

20:10 Do not use my name in vain. Those that do shall be considered blasphemers and burn eternal in hell.

20:11 Remember the Sabbath day and keep it holy.

20:12 The week contains seven days. Six of those days shalt all labour and toil.

20:13 But the seventh day, that is the day of God and none shall work this day.

20:14 For it is the day I rested and to have mere mortals work that day mocks me and offends me.

20:15 Any that work the Sabbath shall be considered blasphemers in the eyes of God and burn eternal in hell.

20:16 Honour thy father and thy mother, for they have conceived thee and given you the gift of life.

20:17 Do not question them, do not disobey them, lest thou be considered sinful and burn eternal in hell.

20:18 Thou shalt not kill. Unless thou kill a sinner, blasphemer, heathen, non-believer, or someone I told you to kill.

20:19 If you kill, thou shalt burn eternal in hell, unless the death be sanctioned by me.

20:20 Thou shalt not commit adultery. If you are married and wish to lie with the flesh of another, thou must buy her as a concubine or marry her as well.

20:21 If she be a foreign heathen or non-believer, then by all means, take her to bed. Forcefully.

20:22 Rape her, for she is not worthy of me.

20:23 But otherwise, be faithful to your wives and whores.

20:24 If your loins go into unholy orifice, thou shalt burn eternal in hell.

20:25 Thou shalt not steal. Unless I tell you to.

20:26 Those which steal shall be a sinner in the eyes of God and burn eternal in hell.

20:27 Thou shalt not lie, unless it benefits yourself or your lord God, or unless I tell ye to lie.

20:28 If you lie, it shall sadden the heavens, as I will be forced to send you to hell.

20:29 Thou shalt not covet thy neighbours property, nor house, nor wife, nor husband, nor concubines, nor asses, nor children, nor servants, nor any belongings which belongs to thy neighbours.

20:30 If you desire what the neighbour has, buy it. If your neighbour be a heathen, take it by force.

20:31 When one disobeys these rules, they shall be sinners and blasphemers and hated in the eyes of God.

20:32 Punish them I shall severely, until they beg for the release of pain by death. But death I shall not give them.

20:33 And remember, I love you all, so long as you do as I say without question."

20:34 All the tribes of Israel witnessed the smoke, fire, fury and thunder of the lord God upon mount Sinai and trembled in fear and stood afar.

20:35 They yelled, "Moses, speak to us the message of our lord God, but let not God tell us, for his voice is terrifying."

20:36 And Moses replied, "Fear not our lord God, for if you be sinless and pure and worthy, you have nothing to fear from him.

20:37 God has come down to us to prove his love for us and it is a joyous and blessed thing."

20:38 Still, the people were scared and stood away from the mountain in fear; and this pleased God.

20:39 God then said to Moses, "Speak on my behalf to the children of Israel.

20:40 Tell them not to make themselves gods of silver nor gold.

20:41 I am a humble God, at times and wish an altar made of stone and ground, so that they may place their sacrifices of calf, goat and lamb upon it and burn it, and dance around the fire naked, pleasing me with blood, nudity and torn flesh.

20:42 They must use stone natural and untouched. If the chisel touches the stone, it is dirty, and offensive to my eyes.

20:43 Neither shall they climb atop my altar, for if they do then my nakedness be seen upon them and the lord God does not wish to be seen unclothed."

21:1 "Now, these are the laws I lay before you.

21:2 People number the earth and are a valuable commodity. Here be the judgements in slavery.

21:3 When you buy a servant of Israel, six years shall they serve. On the seventh year of servitude, you must set him free.

21:4 Upon purchase, if the slave had a wife, the wife must leave with him as well.

21:5 If the master has given him a wife and the wife bore children of the slave, then the master can keep the wife and children and the slave can be let free.

21:6 If the servant does not wish to leave but chooses to stay in servitude with wife and children, this is what must be done.

21:7 Take the slave to the elders, so that the slave can say on record he wishes not to leave. Take then the slave to the door or door post, set him beside it, so that his ear be an easy target.

21:8 Thrust harshly into his ear a sharp wooden spike, to mark him as a slave forever to you and to represent the obvious hole he must have in his head.

21:9 If a father sells his daughter into servitude, it must be done differently than that of a son.

21:10 For females must please their master in servitude and sex, whilst men need not worry about lustful desires of their owners.

21:11 When the master tires of the maidservant/concubine, she may be sold unto a foreign nation, for the maidservant has deceived the master, as she no longer can provide to him sexual gratification.

21:12 If the master promised the maidservant as a wife to his sons, then the maidservant must be treated like a daughter of his.

21:13 Which really means she can be treated like horse shit instead of donkey shit.

21:14 If the son marries another woman, the maidservant then must give all her property to the new wife, but still must not fail her matrimonial duties.

21:15 If these three not be done, the maidservant can be free to go, without money, as women are overall worthless anyway.

21:16 He that strikes a man so that the man does die shall be put to death by the elders.

21:17 Unless the death was sanctioned by the lord God.

21:18 If a man lies not in wait, but God deliver him into his hand, then the lord shall give him a path to flee in cowardice from the murderer.

21:19 But if a man comes into a person's house and slays them in their bed, it shall be seen as cowardice and he shall be put to death and have no place in the kingdom of heaven.

21:20 A child that strikes his father or mother must be put to death.

21:21 Children that speak badly of their father or mother must be put to death, even if the child speaks truthfully.

21:22 Men that steals for himself a slave and keeps the slave or sells him to another shall be stoned to death.

21:23 If two men fight and one be struck so that they become comatose but dies not;

21:24 When the man awakens and walks with staff, the one who harmed him shall be forgiven, but must pay the man for lost work and time and shall pay for his medical cares.

21:25 If a master strikes his servants and concubines so that they die, then the man must be surely punished, the punishment decided by the elders.

21:26 But if the servant or concubine lives for two days, a sin has not been committed, for they are just property. However, they be valuable property and wasteful if they die under the master's hand.

21:27 If a man strikes a woman carrying seed and the foetus drops from her belly, the man shall be punished according to the husband of the wife and must pay a fine set out by the elders.

21:28 If any mischief follows, then you shall give life for life.

21:29 Eye for an eye, tooth for a tooth, hand for a hand, foot for a foot,

21:30 Burning for burning, wound for wound, scar for scar.

21:31 So that soon all the world shall be lame, blind, deaf and dead.

21:32 If a master strikes a slave so that the slave loses an eye, then the slave shall be free, as retribution for the eye.

21:33 If a master strikes a slave so they lose a tooth, the slave shall be free for the tooth's sake.

21:34 If a beast of burden kills a person of Israel, the beast shall be stoned to death and flesh uneaten, but the owner of the beast shall be forgiven.

21:35 But if the beast is known to be violent and neighbours claimed it violent, then both owner and beast shall be stoned to death, for the owner knows the beast to be violent and has done naught to protect their neighbour from it.

21:36 If a ransom be laid for the man's life, then the man shall pay the ransom to the elders, so that he may not be stoned to death.

21:37 If a beast kills a son or daughter, the owner must pay for the life of the deceased.

21:38 If a beast kills a servant or concubine that belongs to someone else, the owner of the beast must pay unto the master thirty shekels of silver and the beast must be stoned to death.

21:39 If a man digs a pit or hole and leave it uncovered so that one may fall and a beast of burden fall into the pit and die,

21:40 The one who dug the pit must pay for the animal and the dead animal shall now belong to him.

21:41 If one man's beast kills a beast of another man, the beast alive shall be sold and the money divided equally and the flesh of the deceased beast shall be divided equally.

21:42 But if the beast be known violent and the owner kept him unsafely, then the owner shall pay for the deceased beast, give him another beast and the slew beast shall be his."

22:1 "If a man steals an ox or a sheep and slays the beast for sustenance, the thief must pay unto the stolen five oxen for every ox slain and four sheep for every sheep slain.

22:2 When a thief is found upon your property and the sun be behind the horizon, kill the son of a bitch and worry not about punishment, for it's okay to kill a thief at night.

22:3 But if the thief steals during the day, kill him not. Instead, take him, demand he pay for all goods attempted stolen.

22:4 If pay the thief cannot, sell him into slavery. Do not keep him as a slave yourself, as he is a thief and will likely steal and run away, being a bad slave. Let some other fool deal with him.

22:5 Thieves that steal anything living, whether ass, ox, goat or slave, the thief must pay double what he intended to steal.

22:6 If a man causes another man's field to be eaten, whether by man, slave or beast, the man must take the best of his crops to replace what was masticated.

22:7 Arsonists that burn crops, vineyards or property must pay retribution for that which the fired consumed.

22:8 Their genitals must then be dipped with oil and lit afire, so that they may not breed and give forth offspring foolish as them.

22:9 When a neighbour lends goods to another neighbour, whether to borrow or safekeeping and those goods be stolen, if the thief be found, the thief must pay double what they stole.

22:10 If the thief not be found, let the man guarding goods be brought forth towards the elders, so that they may decide his fate.

22:11 For any manners of trespassing, whether man or beast and both accuse the property for themselves, let both parties come towards the elders. Whomever the elders condemn must pay double to the other and stay the hell of his damn property!!!!

22:12 If a man delivers unto his neighbour a beast, ox, sheep or ass to keep and it die in his care, or be hurt, or run away and no man see it:

22:13 Let it be known as a random act of bullshit and the two shall make an oath unto the lord that no wrongdoing was done and the caretaker shall not need pay for the beast.

22:14 If the beast be stolen and the thief not caught, the caretaker must pay for the animal, as punishment for being so stupid as to let a beast be stolen.

22:15 Seriously, how the hell can a fucking ox be stolen. Idiot.

22:16 If predators tear the beast and consume it, let both bear witness upon the carcass and the caretaker shall pay no retribution.

22:17 If a man borrows a beast and it die under his care, or be harmed, then the man must pay for the beast.

22:18 But if the man pays to borrow the beast and it die or be harmed, no retribution shall be paid, for he hired the beast and paid good money for it and it be damaged.

22:19 The man who lent the beast should be ashamed, taking the money and letting his beast die or be injured or sickened.

22:20 When a man entices an unmarried woman in his bed, the man must marry the woman.

22:21 If the father of the woman wishes she be not married to him,

then the man must pay the price of her virginity.

22:22 The price shall be decided by the elders, who will judge her virgin value by her physical attributes, breast size, ass firmness, vaginal care and overall good looks.

22:23 Kill all witches. Kill the bitches as well.

22:24 Whoever lies with a beast as they would a woman shall surely put be death.

22:25 Sheep are for sheering, not shagging.

22:26 Those that make sacrifice unto any other god but I, must be cut alive into teeny tiny pieces and fed to the oxen, for I am the only one true God and those that believe otherwise must be made an example of by terrible death!

22:27 You shall not curse nor oppress strangers of your same faith, nor widows, nor fatherless children that be not bastards.

22:28 If thou afflict them and they cry unto me, I shall hear them and be angry, for their whining is very fucking annoying.

22:29 And I shall come down from the heavens, bury you in hot wax, slice you with my sword and your wives shall be widows and your children fatherless.

22:30 If the person be not of your faith, then do whatever you desire, for I don't care for others.

22:31 When the poor of your people come to you and you lend them money, charge them not interest, for they are your people and you must stick together and be strong in numbers.

22:32 Set a date for payment in full and ensure they pay back in full, but do not charge them for your charity.

22:33 When those of different faiths and nations that come to you and ask for lent money, charge them a high interest.

22:34 After all, one does need to make a profit. Best do it to foreign heathens.

22:35 You shall not revile me nor the rulers of your people, even if they be tyrants.

22:36 The first of all crops, of fruits and of liquors must be offered to me. The first-born sons of all must be offered to me as well.

22:37 As the first-born sheep, oxen and all other beasts. For seven days shall you nurse them, but on the eighth day, they belong to me.

22:38 And to be holy and wise men in the eyes of God, you shalt not feast like the predators. When one sees flesh torn in the wild, feast not upon it, but give the meat to the dogs."

23:1 "You shall make not false witness, unless it benefits the lord God and be false against a heathen.

23:2 You shall not do that which be evil, even if the multitude do so, neither shall you speak to defend the actions of the evil multitude.

23:3 Neither shall one encourage the poor in their cause, for if they be poor, they deserve it.

23:4 When you see an enemy's oxen or ass wandering, take it to your enemy, so that the enemy learn to trust you and ye can exploit that trust.

23:5 If you see a man you hate being burdened by his beasts, help him anyway, as a sign of the love of your God and convert him and bring more souls to me.

23:6 Ignore falsehoods and rumours, lest you look like a fool when believing them.

23:7 Slay not the innocent and righteous, for such wickedness shall not be justified by the lord.

23:8 Never accept a gift, for gifts are not earned and shall make you lazy and slothful, like a Canaanite.

23:9 You shall not oppress a stranger, for you were strangers before in the land of Egypt.

23:10 Six years shall you harvest thy crops, grain and fruits:

23:11 But on the seventh year, leave them unattended, so that the poor and beggars shall come and feast upon the grains, olives and fruits like the mangy beasts they are.

23:12 Six days shall all work, but on the seventh all shall rest, for the lord God rested on the seventh day, making the seventh day holy.

23:13 Make no mentions of any other God, whether be in mouth or mind.

23:14 For the lord God shall hear your words and see your thoughts and curse you if you even think of another god. For I am worse than any jealous lover.

23:15 Thrice a year shall all prepare a feast for me.

23:16 You shalt feast upon the unleavened bread for seven days, as I command you in the month of Abib.

23:17 You shall feast upon the harvest, where all the first fruits of your labours be sown and the feast of in-gathering, when the fields are harvested.

23:18 Three times in the year shall all males present themselves before the lord God, nude, so that I may gaze upon their bodies in lust.

23:19 You shalt not put the blood of my sacrifice upon leavened bread, as the bread becomes soggy and unappetizing to the lord God. Neither shall the fat of the sacrifice be eaten until morning, so that it may be used to fry eggs and kosher bacon.

23:20 The first of the harvest must always be brought into the house of God.

23:21 Never boil a child in their mother's milk, for such a thing is blasphemy.

23:22 Boil it in the milk of another, or in wine, or water, but not in the milk of its mother.

23:23 Behold, I send an angel down to ensure all obey my commands and to lead and prepare you to into the promised land.

23:24 Beware him, obey him and do not anger him, for he is under sanction of me and shall do as he sees fit, even if it be death.

23:25 Those that obey him shall be rewarded and his enemies will be his enemies and his friends his friends; and the angel shall be like a Godfather unto the people of Israel.

23:26 For my angel shall bring you into the land of the heathen Amorites, Canaanites, Hittites, Hivites, Jebusites and Perizzites and smite them.

23:27 Oh, how the lord God loathes them and created them only so that they be slain and tortured.

23:28 You shall never bow down before their gods, nor worship them, nor take their false images, but instead storm their temples, their buildings, their homes and break all the false gods they obtain.

23:29 Do this and the lord God shall bless you bread and water and illness shall never fall upon your people.

23:30 No harm shall come to your sons, or son's sons, except around the 1930-40's AD., but you'll be long dead by then, so you won't care.

23:31 My fear and wrath shall go forth from your hands and burn the people which you come across, so that your enemies shall turn and flee and expose your weapons to their backs.

23:32 A mad mass of hornets shall come down from the heavens and drive out the Canaanites, Hittites and Hivites and sting them and leave them with swellings and infections.

23:33 Slowly I shall do this, for if done too fast the land will be left barren and all beast be gone.

23:34 But little by little shall I drive hornets in their territory, until the peoples of Israel can overwhelm them and take that which is rightfully somebody else's.

23:35 And the lands of Israel shall stretch forth from the Red Sea to the seas of the Philistines and through the rivers and deserts.

23:36 Do not make a covenant with these people nor their gods.

23:37 Let them dwell not in your land, lest you sin against me and wish to feel the wrath of God."

24:1 And the lord God said to Moses, "Come now, upon the mount of the lord God and send thee Aaron, Nadab and Abihu and seventy of the elders of your people and have them worship me from a distance.

24:2 Moses shall come near to the lord God but not the others, nor the peoples of Israel, for they be not ready to see the mightiness of the lord."

24:3 Moses came down to the people of Israel and repeated the words, rules and judgments of God and the people said to Moses, "These rules are complicated and plentiful and contain many loopholes. What if we disobey them?"

24:4 And Moses replied, "Then the fury of God shall be cursed upon you and your families and you'll all die horribly."

24:5 The people trembled in fear and asked Moses, "What if we disobey out of ignorance or accident. What if we kill someone, believing it the will of God and it be not the lord's will?"

24:6 And Moses replied, "Still the fury of God shall be cursed upon you and your families and you'll all die horribly."

24:7 They then asked, "The lord God's will is confusing. What if we spare the life of a person that God meant us to slay?"

24:8 And Moses replied, "Then you have disappointed the lord God almighty and he'll bring a curse upon you and your families and you'll all die a horrible death."

24:9 In fear, the people of Israel united in one voice and said to Moses, "Then to avoid horrid outcomes, we shall obey our one true God!"

24:10 Moses then took sacred parchment and wrote down all the words of the lord God, as there were many, so that the elders may study them and obey them and enforce them upon the people.

24:11 Early in the morning, Moses awoke and built upon the hill an altar; and around the altar he built twelve pillars to God, representing the twelve tribes of Israel.

24:12 And he sent the young men of Israel to the altar, so that they may offer burnt offerings to the lord God and slay the oxen and bathe in its blood and dance around it naked, pleasing the lord with blood, nudity and torn flesh.

24:13 Moses then took the blood of the oxen and half he stored in basins and half he sprinkled upon the altar.

24:14 Moses then took the book of the covenant and read it to the people of Israel, boring them with his sermon and causing them to fall asleep.

24:15 When all peoples' lids be shut, Moses took the blood of the oxen and sprayed it upon the people, awaking them in bloody rain and shouted to his congregation, "Shall you obey your lord God almighty!"

24:16 Startled, they all replied, "Yes, we shall obey our lord God almighty!"

24:17 Moses said to his people, "Behold, I awaken you with the blood of the covenant. Wash not these clothes: let the stains go deep, as a reminder to obey your lord."

24:18 Then up went Moses, Aaron, Nadab, Abihu and seventy of the elders of Israel.

24:19 They climbed the mount of God and saw in the distance the lord almighty and under the lord's feet were paved works of sapphires from heaven.

24:20 All the people of Israel saw God's sapphire step and celebrated by excessive eating, drinking, and playing ping pong.

24:21 And the lord said from the mount, "Moses, come and speak with me and I shall give you tables of mighty granite, containing the laws and commandments I demand from you, so that you shall teach them to the people of Israel."

24:22 And Moses said to the lord, "Granite is a heavy stone. How big are they?"

24:23 And God said to Moses, "Have you lost your faith. This be granite from heaven. Strong and light it be. You shall have no problem carrying them.

24:24 But for your lack of faith, I shall make the granite of earth; heavy and cumbersome, so that you shall struggle whilst carrying the tablets of God."

24:25 Moses apologized to God and begged forgiveness. And God forgave him.

24:26 God then spoke to the elders of Israel, "Do not come closer, keep your distance from me. If any problems arise, speak to Aaron and Hur and they shall settle them. But leave me and Moses the fuck alone!"

24:27 Moses then climbed up the mount, leaving the others behind.

24:28 As Moses climbed the mount, the glory of God descended down, covering the rock with a great black cloud and fire and thunder and lightning, and smog.

24:29 This struck fear into all the people of Israel and they began to pray and worship and make great sacrifices to God.

24:30 All but Moses, who climbed the mountain, surrounding himself with the fire and lightning and smoke.

24:31 For forty days and nights Moses stayed upon the mount, fearing not the fire nor darkness, as he was, after all, a retard.

25:1 And the lord God spoke to Moses, saying,

25:2 "I demand an ark built in my honour, made of the offerings of your people.

25:3 The altar shall be a beautiful structure, full of bling, so that all may be reminded of my awesomeness!

25:4 When others see me rollin', they be hatin'.

25:5 Have the children of Israel bring me gold, silver and brass

25:6 Blue silks, purple silks, scarlet silks, fine linens and goat hair.

25:7 Rams skin, dyed red, badger skin and shittim wood.

25:8 Oils for light and oils for perfumes, sweet spices and incense.

25:9 Onyx stones and precious stones, so that they may be set upon the blingful breastplate.

25:10 And have them build me a sanctuary, so that I may dwell in privacy among you.

25:11 You shall make all of the sanctuary, the patterns, even make the tools used to build such a sanctuary, so that it be pure Israel and have no heathen mark upon it.

25:12 Make an ark of shittim wood, have it two cubits and half in length, one cubit and half in width, and one cubit and half in height.

25:13 Cover the ark in pure gold, inside and out, so that none of the wood be seen. Let it be believed the ark be of pure gold wonder. Have a gold crown round about the ark as well.

25:14 Build four rings of gold and place them on each corner of my ark, so that each corner have a ring of gold. It will be so that each side have unto it two rings.

25:15 I cannot stress enough the importance of the rings. One of pure gold, on each corner.

25:16 Make staves of shittim wood and overlay it with gold.

25:17 Place each stave through the rings of the ark, so that the staves be used to carry the precious ark and show all the wonders of God.

25:18 For only a true God can bless his people with such precious metals as to waste it upon an ark.

25:19 Leave always the staves in the rings of the ark; never remove them.

25:20 When I give you the testimony of my words, place it in the ark for safekeeping.

25:21 And have the people make me a throne of gold, two cubits and half in length and one cubit and half in width.

25:22 Make two angels of gold, of beaten work shall they be made and place them on each side of my mighty golden throne."

25:23 Moses then asked the lord, "My God, would this be a commandment broken, for you demand us not to make unto you any graven images."

25:24 The lord God thought a moment and told Moses, "I am glad you know the laws I have given you well. No, these two angels were asked directly by me, so they shall not be considered commandments broken.

25:25 Have the wings of the angels stretch high above the throne, covering the throne with their golden wings and have the angels face one another towards my seat.

25:26 Place my throne above the ark, not inside, so that all may see the angels and throne of God, where I shall place my holy ass. The testimony of God shall remain in the ark.

25:27 When I commune with you, I shall be above the throne, between the wings of golden angels and give you all commands upon the people of Israel.

25:28 Make a table of shittim wood: two cubits in length and a cubit in width and height.

25:29 Overlay the shittim wood with gold and build a crown of gold around the table.

25:30 You shall make a border of gold a hand width around the table and for added cred, build crowns of gold around the border as well.

25:31 Make four rings of gold around the table and put them in the four feet, the four corners of the table.

25:32 Place the staves for the table upon the border.

25:33 Make the staves of shittim wood and overlay them with pure gold.

25:34 And have dishes, bowls, spoons, knives, forks, covers, and goblets for the table and make them of pure gold.

25:35 Always have upon the table fresh shewbread, so that when I go hungry a snack always awaits me.

25:36 Make unto me an ordained candlestick of pure gold, made by beaten work: the knops, branches, bowls, flowers and all decorations shall also be made of beaten work.

25:37 Six branches shall come forth from the candle stick. Three shall sprout from the left and three shall sprout from the right, so that each side have three branches and the branches number total that of six:

25:38 Three bowls made in the shape of almonds, with a knop and a flower in one branch; and three bowls of almond figure in the other branch, with a knop and flower, in the six branches that sprout forth from the candlestick.

25:39 And in the stick itself shall be four bowls in almond shape, with knops and flowers.

25:40 Have the branches match, so that each branch is a mirror image of the other one opposite its side.

25:41 The knops and branches shall be of same and made by beaten work.

25:42 And you shall make me seven lamps thereof and they shall light the candles of the stick, so that I be left not in the dark.

25:43 All tongs and snuff dishes shall be made of pure gold.

25:44 Ensure a goldsmith build me my candlestick, so that the work be done well.

25:45 And I demand they be built as I describe, lest he die and be denied the love of his God."

26:1 "Make my tabernacle with ten curtains of the finest twined linen, with colours blue and purple and scarlet and design them as though angels themselves worked upon these cloths.

26:2 All curtain lengths shall measure eight and twenty cubits and the breadth shall be four cubits and all curtains shall match in length.

26:3 Five of these curtains shall be sewn together and the other five shall be sewn together, so that I have two curtains made of five, which shall total ten.

26:4 You shall make loops of blue linen and couple them into the curtain; and you shalt take loops of blue and couple them into the other curtain.

26:5 Fifty loops shall you place in each curtain and fifty in the other, so that each have loops of fifty blue and the total number of loops be of one hundred.

26:6 And make unto me fifty taches of pure gold and couple the curtains together with the taches, so that it may be one.

26:7 And have your peoples make the curtain of goats' hair, so as to cover the tabernacle. Eleven curtains of goats' hair shall you make.

26:8 The length of all goat hair curtains shall be thirty cubits and width of four cubits and the eleven shall be of equal measure.

26:9 And you shall couple five curtains together and six curtains by themselves and shall double the sixth curtain in the forefront of the tabernacle.

26:10 Make fifty loops of the one curtain that is outmost in the coupling and fifty loops for the curtain which couple the second.

26:11 And make fifty taches of pure brass and place the brass taches in the loops and couple the curtains together so that it be a tent.

26:12 And the remnant cloth that remains from the tent shall hang over the backside of the tabernacle.

26:13 I demand you make a covering for the tent, made of dyed ram skins and badger pelts and mushrooms made of pure gold.

26:14 The pattern of the badger and mushroom shall go across like this. Badger, badger, badger, badger, badger, badger, badger, badger, badger, badger, badger, badger, mushroom, mushroom.

26:15 No snakes shall be in the pattern.

26:16 Make ten standing boards of shittim wood for the tabernacle.

26:17 Ten cubits in length shall be the board and a cubit and half in width.

26:18 Two tenons shall there be in the boards of shittim, set in order against one another; thus, shall it be for all boards of the tabernacle.

26:19 And you shall make the boards for the tabernacle, twenty boards on the southside, that be southward.

26:20 Make forty sockets of silver under the twenty boards, two sockets under one board for his two tenons.

26:21 Upon the north side of the tabernacle shall be twenty boards matching the ones of the south.

26:22 On the west side of the tabernacle shall be six boards of shittim wood,

26:23 And two boards of shittim wood for each of the corners of the tabernacle.

26:24 Have it coupled together beneath and above, into one ring of gold.

26:25 Make me a veil of blue and purple and scarlet and fine twined linen of masterful work.

26:26 And overlay it upon the pillars of shittim wood of gold and make the hooks of gold, upon the sockets of silver.

26:27 Place my throne in the most holiest of holy places.

26:28 Set the table, clothless, upon the south side of the tabernacle and place the candlestick with it as well.

26:29 Make me a hanging for the door of the tent. Make it of blue and purple and scarlet and fine twined linen and intricate needlework.

26:30 And you shall make me five pillars of shittim wood and overlay them with gold; and their hooks shall be of gold and you shall cast five sockets of brass for them."

26:31 The mighty lord God goes on for a total of seven damned chapters demanding crap be made like pillars, curtains, perfumes, oils, incense and other useless junk. Be warned and skip ahead, for it is certainly a dull ordeal to read. Five more to go. Please, feel free to skip ahead.

26:32 This is also why the people of Israel stayed in the desert for forty years. They were not wandering, they were too busy making bling for God.

27:1 Yet more decoration instructions.

27:2 And the lord said even more, "You shalt make an altar of wood. Shittim wood. The altar shall be five cubits long and broad, foursquare and the height of the altar shall be three cubits.

27:3 You shall make four horns, one for each corner of the altar and the horns shall be of same and overlaid with precious brass.

27:4 And make unto me pans to receive the ashes and shovels and basins and flesh hooks and firepans and all these vessels shall be made of brass.

27:5 And make for the altar a grill made of brass; and upon each corner of the grill shall you make four brazen rings of brass.

27:6 And you shall put it under the compass of the altar, so that the grill lay even to the midst of the altar.

27:7 And make staves for the altar, carved of shittim wood and overlaid with brass.

27:8 The staves shall be thrust through the rings of the altar, so that staves be upon two sides of the altar for easy transportation.

27:9 Hollow with boards shall you make it, so that it be not heavy, as I wish not crushed shoulders for the men who carry the altar of the lord.

27:10 And you shall make the court of the tabernacle: for the south side facing southward there shall be hangings of fine twined linen, of one hundred cubits long for one side:

27:11 And the twenty pillars and their twenty sockets shall be of brass and the hooks of the pillars and their fillets shall be of shiny silver.

27:12 And upon the north side facing north there shall be hangings of fine twined linen, of one hundred cubits long of one side:

27:13 And the twenty pillars and their twenty sockets shall be of brass and the hooks of the pillars and their fillets shall be of shiny silver.

27:14 And the length of the west side of the court shall be hangings of fifty cubits: their pillars ten and their sockets number shall be ten.

27:15 Upon the length of the east side of the court shall be hangings of fifty cubits.

27:16 The hangings upon one side of the gate shall be fifteen cubits, with three pillars and three sockets of brass.

27:17 And the other side shall be hangings of fifteen cubits, with three pillars of brass and three sockets of brass.

27:18 And for the gate of the court shall be a magnificent hanging of twenty cubits of blue and of purple and of scarlet and of fine twined linen wrought with precision needlework and their pillars shall be of four brass and their sockets shall be of four brass.

27:19 And all the vessels of the tabernacle and all the pins of the tabernacle and all the pins of the court shall be made of brass.

27:20 And command all children of Israel to bring upon me pure extra virgin olive oil, beaten for the light, so that I may be not in darkness.

27:21 In the tabernacle, before the congregation without the veil, before the testimony, Aaron and his sons shall order the oil before the lord from evening until morning and it shall be a statute for ever and ever unto their generations on the behalf of the children of Israel."

28:1 "And you shall take your brother and his sons with him among the men of Israel, so that they may spread forth the propaganda of the lord among the people of Israel.

28:2 Aaron, Nadab, Abihu, Eleazar and Ithamar shall be the priests and commissars of God.

28:3 Make my commissars holy garments, for glory and for bling and for beauty.

28"4 I shall fill men's hearts with glory and the fashion sense of a woman and it shall be these men that make the garments for my priests.

28:5 And these are the garments that shall be made; a breastplate, a thong, an ephod, a robe, a embroidered coat, a mitre and a girdle; and they shall make the holy garments for Aaron and for his sons.

28:6 They shall make the thong of fine twined linen and blue and purple and scarlet and the crotch shall be ordained with fine needlework.

28:7 Upon the crotch shall be eight rubies and on one side of the crotch shall be four rubies, placed upon the corners of the seed sack of a man.

28:8 And on the other side shall be four rubies, placed upon the corners of the seed sack of a man.

28:9 A ring of brass shall be atop the thong, so that the foreskinless head of their phallus shall be held up and away from their balls, looking constantly up into the heavens and to God.

28:10 And they shall gather gold and blue and purple and scarlet and fine linen.

28:11 They shall make the ephod of gold, blue, purple and scarlet and fine linen and they shall make it in great detail, with cunning work.

28:12 The two shoulder pieces shall be joined at the two edged thereof, so that the ephod be joined together in one mighty dress.

28:13 The girdle of the ephod, which shall be upon it, shall be of the same quality of the ephod and be made of gold and blue and purple and scarlet and fine twined linen.

28:14 Take unto these two onyx stones and carve upon them the names of the twelve tribes of Israel.

28:15 Six of the names of the tribe shall be carved in one stone and six of the names of the other tribes shall be carved upon the other stone and it shall be carved in the order of their birth.

28:16 Reuben, Simeon, Levi, Judah, Issachar, Zebulun, Dan, Naphtali, Gad, Asher, Joseph, Benjamin.

28:17 When the names of the tribes be engraved upon the onyx, you shall ensure the names be carved with finest handwriting and that the names be overlaid with pure gold.

28:18 And all shall know the twelve tribes of Israel be blessed with the bling of the mighty lord God.

28:19 You shall put the onyx stones upon each shoulder of the ephod and Aaron shall bear this ephod and the names of the twelve tribes in memorial to God.

28:20 Make unto me ouches of gold;

28:21 And make two chains of pure gold and have the chains be wreathed work and attach them to the ouches of gold.

28:22 Make the breastplate of finest work, after the style of the ephod and make it with gold and blue and purple and scarlet and fine twined linen.

28:23 Foursquare shall it be, a span length and a span width, so that it be a perfect squared span.

28:24 Set upon the breastplate settings of fine stones, even four rows of precious rock and the first row shall have upon it a sardiaz, a topaz and a carbuncle.

28:25 The second row shall contain an emerald, a sapphire and a diamond of finest cut and quality.

28:26 The third row shall have a ligure, an agate and an amethyst.

28:27 The last row shall be a beryl, an onyx and a jasper; and all the stones shall be set in pure gold.

28:28 The stones shall represent the twelve tribes of Israel, like the engravings of a signet and every tribe shall have their own stone.

28:29 And you shall make chains of wreathen gold at the ends of the breastplate.

29:30 And demand I two rings of pure gold, set upon the top corners of the breastplate and you shall put the chains through the rings of the breastplate.

28:31 And the other two ends of the chains shall be set upon the ouches and the ouches shall be set upon the shoulders of the ephod.

28:32 Upon the bottom of the breastplate shall be two rings of gold and attached to those rings shall be chains of pure gold of wreathen work.

28:33 And the ends of the rings shall be hooked upon the ring of brass attached to the thong of the lord.

28:34 When Aaron enters the tabernacle of the lord, he shall wear the breastplate and the names of the twelve tribes of Israel, for the continuous memorial to the lord God.

28:35 And you shall put into the breastplate of judgment the Urim and the Thummim, so that a moron shall discover it a few thousand years later and the Urim and Thummim shall be placed upon the top of Aaron's heart and bear the judgment of the twelve tribes of Israel.

28:36 And you shall make the robe of the ephod pure blue. No purple, nor scarlet, nor gold, nor fine twined linen.

28:37 A hole shall be placed atop the robe and it shall have binding work around it, as though it be the hole of a habergeon.

28:38 Beneath the hem of the hole shall you make pomegranates of blue, purple and scarlet and bells of gold between each.

28:39 So that golden bells and blue pomegranates surround the hole of the robe.

28:40 And Aaron must wear the robe when he enters the tabernacle, so that I may hear him enter and be ready for him.

28:41 Otherwise, he shall disturb my privacy and I shall be enraged and shall cause his blood to boil hot and kill him.

28:42 And you shall make me a plate of pure gold and engrave upon it like the engravings of a signet, 'HOLINESS TO THE LORD ALMIGHT GOD'

28:43 You shall place it in fine blue lace and put it upon the mitre, so that the plate be upon the forefront of the mitre.

28:44 And upon Aaron's forehead that Aaron shall bear the iniquity of the holy things, which the children of Israel shall hallow in all holy gifts and it shall always be upon his forehead that the lord God accept the gifts.

28:45 If the lord God accept not, a hole shall be bore into the forehead of Aaron, so that the stupidity of him shall escape his brain. And if he dies, it be only because stupidity be all he has in his head.

28:46 Embroider the coat of fine linen and make the mitre of fine linen and make the girdle of needlework.

28:47 And for Aaron's sons make them coats, girdles, bonnets and thongs and make them for glory and for beauty.

28:48 And you shall put them upon your brother Aaron and his sons with him; and anoint them, consecrate them and sanctify them so that they be official priests and propagandists of the lord God.

28:49 And when they enter the tabernacle of the lord or to the congregation or to the altar, they must wear the clothing of God.

28:50 For the lord God has spent many times designing these clothes and if they wear them not, it shall be an insult to me and considered blasphemy and I shall kill them and their children and their children's children so that all their generation be dead."

29:1 "This is what you must do to hallow oneself and prepare to enter me in the holy office. Take one bullock and two lambs of white pure,

29:2 And unleavened bread and cakes, made with tempered oil and wafers unleavened and made with wheaten flour.

29:3 Place the baked goods in a basket and bring them in with the bullock and two rams.

29:4 Aaron and his sons shall bring unto the door of the tabernacle of propaganda and wash them with water so that their odour does not offend the lord.

29:5 You shall take the garments and place upon Aaron the coat, robe of the ephod, the ephod, breastplate and the girdle of the ephod.

29:6 Place the mitre upon Aaron's head and place the crown atop the mitre.

29:7 Then take the oil and pour it upon Aaron's head, until he is nice and greasy; and he shall be anointed.

29:8 Bring in his sons and put coats upon them.

29:9 You shall gird them with girdles and put the bonnets upon them, so that they may look gay for the lord and you shall consecrate Aaron and his sons.

29:10 Bring the bullock before the tabernacle of the congregation and Aaron and his sons shall place their hands upon the head of the bullock.

29:11 By the door of the congregation, slaughter the bullock.

29:12 Take the blood of the bullock and with your finger you shall smear the blood upon the horns of the altar and the rest of the blood shall be poured into the bottom of the altar.

29:13 Take the fat, caul, liver and the two kidneys and place them within the altar and burn them, as the smell of burning fat and innards and boiling blood is a pleasing aroma to the lord.

29:14 The flesh, skin and faeces of the bullock shall you burn outside the camp, as it is a sin offering.

29:15 Take one ram and have Aaron and his sons place their hands upon the head of the ram.

29:16 Slay the ram, take the blood and sprinkle it around the altar.

29:17 Cut the ram into teeny tiny pieces and wash the inwards of him so that it be hollow and wash the legs and place the pieces inside the ram and into the skull of the ram.

29:18 Place the ram upon the altar and set it afire, so that the smell may reach unto heaven and please the nostrils of the lord God with savoury burning flesh.

29:19 Take the other ram and have Aaron and his sons place their hands upon the head.

29:20 You shall then kill the ram and take of its blood and smear the blood upon Aaron's right ear and upon the right ear of Aaron's sons and upon the thumb of their right hand and upon the large toe of their right foot, so that they be smeared with fresh ram's blood.

29:21 The rest of the blood shall be sprinkled around the altar.

29:22 Then you shall take the blood upon the altar and the anointing oil and spray it upon Aaron and his sons and upon their garments, so that they be an oily bloody mess, which is arousing to the lord God.

29:23 Take the fat of the ram, the rump, the innards, the liver, the caul and the kidneys and the right shoulder of the ram, as this shall be the ram of consecration.

29:24 And take one loaf of bread, one cake of oiled bread and one wafer of unleavened bread from the basket of the lord God.

29:25 Mix the pastry and ram pieces together, so that it be one mess and place them in the hands of Aaron and his sons.

29:26 They shall wave this fatty, floury, bloody mess in the air above their heads, so that the drippings drop upon their face and they shall sayeth repeatedly, "Let us wave our hands in the air, dripping fat and blood as we just don't care."

29:27 They shall then throw the cakes and ram pieces into the altar and burn it, thus finishing the wave offering of the lord.

29:28 Take then the breast of the ram of Aaron's consecration and wave it highly in the air, as this shall be your part of the ceremony.

29:29 You shall sanctify the breast of the ram and the shoulder and you shall heave them above the heads of Aaron and his sons and this shall be part of the heave offering.

29:30 Take then the intestines of the two rams and the bullock and braid them together so that it be rope like.

29:31 Swing it above your head and whip the buttock's and testicles of Aaron and his sons through their holy garments and ask of them, 'Who is your lord?'

29:32 And they shall reply, 'God is, God is.'

29:33 Aaron and his sons must then eat the flesh of the rams and the remaining bread in the basket of the lord God.

29:34 By eating these things, they shall be consecrated and atoned and truly holy in the eyes of the lord God. But let not a stranger eat these, lest they become unholy holy beings and blasphemous in the eyes of God.

29:35 If the bellies of Aaron and his sons be stuffed and they can take not another bite, you shall burn the bread and flesh, so that no others shall eat it, as it is holy food and when Aaron and his sons defecate, it shall be holy shit.

29:36 The above must be done every seven days, so that Aaron and his sons not lose their holiness nor atonement.

29:37 You shall slaughter a bullock every day for the children of Israel, as it shall be an offering of their sins. If you do not do this, then the sins they commit shall be punished and I shall slaughter the lot of them, as I demand death for sin.

29:38 You shall clean and cleanse the altar every seven days, lest the crust of blood and fat stain the work.

29:39 Every day shall you slay upon the alter two lambs of the first year.

29:40 One lamb shall be slew upon the morning, the other in the evening.

29:41 With the morning lamb you shalt spice it with flour, beaten oil and a quarter bottle of wine, so that it be tasty for the lord God almighty.

29:42 The other lamb shall you spice with the urine of seventy-two virgin males.

29:43 This shall be a continual offering to the lord God, done where I shall meet with you and speak with you.

29:44 And there I shall meet with the children of Israel and the tabernacle shall be my holy home upon the earth.

29:45 I shall sanctify the tabernacle and I shall sanctify the altar and I shall sanctify Aaron and his sons who cares for my home.

29:46 I shall dwell among the children of Israel and be their God and rule over them.

29:47 And they shall know that I and only I am the lord God, the one true God, who brought them out of the land of Egypt and that I shall dwell among them."

30:1 "You shall build me an altar of shittim wood, so that you may burn incense to the lord God.

30:2 A cubit in length shall it be and a cubit in width and the height of the altar shall be that of two cubits. The horns shall be the same.

30:3 Overlay the altar with pure gold, so that the top, bottom, sides and the horns be of gold.; and you shall make it a crown to go round about the altar.

30:4 Two golden rings shall you make to it under the crown, by the two corners thereof, by the two sides, so that staves shall be thrust through and allow for easy carry.

30:5 Make the staves of shittim wood and overlay them with gold.

30:6 You shall place this altar by the veil by the ark of the testimony, before the divine throne, where I shall meet with you.

30:7 Aaron shall burn sweet incense every morning and when he dresses the lamps, he shall burn incense upon it.

30:8 And when Aaron lights the lamps in the evening, he shall burn also sweet incense to the lord God, so that a perpetual incense be burned to me throughout your generations.

30:9 You shall not offer strange incense, nor burnt offering, nor flesh offering and neither shall you offer strong drink.

30:10 Aaron shall make an atonement upon the horns of the altar once a year, with the blood of the sin offering of atonements; this shall happen once a year for the generations of your people, as it is most holy to your God."

30:11 The lord still spoke even more, saying to Moses,

30:12 "When you take a census of the nation of Israel, every man shall pay a ransom to the lord God almighty, so that no sickness, plague, nor disease curse them.

30:13 Every man shall give to God a half shekel, to be donated to the sanctuary of the lord God.

30:14 And every man that be above the age of twenty years shall also offer an offering to me.

30:15 The rich shall pay no more nor less than the poor: all shall pay the half shekel and if they not afford it, they shall curse the people of Israel with their poverty.

30:16 This money shall be a ransom of their very souls that must be paid, lest they be cursed from the kingdom of the lord God.

30:17 You shall take the ransom money of the children of Israel and shall appoint it to the services and upkeep of the tabernacle, the sanctuary, the holy home of God.

30:18 So that it remains a memorial upon the children of Israel and remind them of the atonement of souls.

30:19 Some may argue the ransom should go to help the poverty stricken, but that would make me a charitable God.

30:20 Fuck the poor. They offend me."

30:21 The lord God then rambled even more, saying to Moses,

30:22 "You shall make a laver of brass and a foot also of brass to wash withal: and you shall place it between the tabernacle of the congregation and the altar and you shall ensure it be kept full of fresh water.

30:23 For Aaron and his sons shall wash their hands and feet with them.

30:24 When they go into the tabernacle of the congregation, or when they go to the altar to minister or burn offerings to the lord God, they shall wash with water.

30:25 If they do not this, I shall be offended, and smite them with fury and disease. For the lord God demands cleanliness from his priests.

30:26 It shall be a statute to them and shall be passed down from generations to generations of their seed, so that they remain clean and pure to God, so that the wave and heave offerings stain and tarnish a fresh man and one not already of filth."

30:27 God still was not finished with his demands and said to Moses,

30:28 "Take also principal spices, of pure myrrh five hundred shekels and of sweet cinnamon half, so that the cinnamon be two hundred and fifty shekels and of sweet calamus two hundred and fifty shekels.

30:29 And of cassia five hundred shekels and olive oil and hin.

30:30 And you shall make with it an oil of holy ointment, an ointment made after the art of the apothecary and it shall be a holy anointing oil.

30:31 And you shall anoint the tabernacle of the congregation and

the ark of the testimony with said oil.

30:32 And anoint the table and all the vessels and the candlestick and the altar of incense.

30:33 And anoint the altar of burnt offering and all vessels and the laver and the foot.

30:34 You shall after sanctify them, so that they may be holy objects and whoever touches them shall also be holy.

30:35 And you shall anoint Aaron and his sons, so that they may be most holy and shall be seen fit to serve as priests in the eyes of God.

30:36 And you shall speak to the children of Israel and tell them that this is a most holy anointing oil, given to the lord God throughout your generations.

30:37 Upon the flesh of man it shall not be poured, nor shall it be made for personal use nor market, as it is a holy compound.

30:38 Whoever makes it for unholy purpose or sells it to a stranger, shall be cut off from his people and be seen as a savage and heathen to the eyes of God.

30:39 And they shall know not the kingdom nor blessings of the lord God."

30:40 The lord still spoke to Moses and said,

30:41 "Take sweet spices, stacte and onycha and galbanum; these sweet spices with pure frankincense and of each shall be an equal weight of the other.

30:42 And you shall make for the lord God a sweet perfume, a confection after the art of the apothecary, tempered together in pure and holy manner.

30:43 You shall beat some of it very small and put it before the testimony in the tabernacle of the congregation, where I shall meet with you; and it shall be most holy.

30:44 And the perfume made for the lord God shall be made only for the lord God. You shall not make it for yourself, as it is a holy compound.

30:45 Whosoever shall make it for unholy use shall be cast out of the people of Israel and shall know not the love and kindness of God, but the fury and hatred."

31:1 God still would not shut up and said to Moses,

31:2 "I have called by name Bezaleel the son of Uri, the son of Hur, of the tribe of Judah:

31:3 And I have filled him with the holy spirit of God, in wisdom, in understanding, in knowledge and in all manner of workmanship.

31:4 He shall make cunning works of art from gold, silver and brass.

31:5 And in cutting of stones to set them and in carving of timber and in all manners of workmanship.

31:6 And behold, I have given with him Aholiab the son of Ahisamach, of the tribe of Dan: and in the hearts of all that are wise I have placed wisdom, so that they may make all that I have commanded of you.

31:7 The tabernacle of the congregation and the ark of the testimony and the holy throne of God and all the furniture of the tabernacle,

31:8 And the table and the furniture and the pure candlestick and all its decorations and the altar of incense,

31:9 And the altar of burnt offerings and all its furniture and the laver and the foot,

31:10 And the cloths of service and the holy garments of Aaron the priest and the garments of Aaron's sons, to minister in the holy office,

31:11 And the anointing oil and the sweet incense for the holy place and all that I have commanded you to make."

31:12 The lord paused for a moment and Moses was relieved, believing the lord God to be finished.

31:13 Moses was wrong and the lord continued to speak.

31:14 "Speak to all the children of Israel and tell them to keep the sabbaths holy for all generations, so that it may be a sign of their divinity and they shall know the lord doth sanctify them.

31:15 All shall keep the sabbath, for it is a holy day and those that defile the sabbath day shall be put to death the following day and their soul shall be cut off from his people for all eternity.

31:16 They shall not be killed the day of the sabbath, as to bring death is considered work and work on the sabbath is an unholy and blasphemous thing.

31:17 For six days of the week shall all work be done, but the seventh day is a day of rest for the lord God and shall be a day of rest for you people as well.

31:18 Those that work on the sabbath day shall make the lord appear lazy, as the lord did not work upon the sabbath and the lord God shall demand their blood be spilled upon the dust.

31:19 All generations of the people shall keep and observe the sabbath and it shall be a holy and perpetual covenant between the lord God and his people.

31:20 It shall be an eternal sign between me and the children of Israel, for in six days the lord God created the heaven and the earth and on the seventh day he was tired of commanding the angels and so the lord God rested on the seventh day; and he awoke refreshed.

31:22 The lord God then gave to Moses upon Mount Sinai two tables of testimony, tables of stone, with the commandments of the laws and commandments of God carved with the massive and mighty erection of God.

32:1 And when the peoples of Israel saw that Moses delayed coming down from the mount, they went to Aaron and said to him,

32:2 "Moses is gone and shall likely not be back for weeks. Let us party!"

32:3 Now, Aaron loved to party and knew Moses would never approve of such fun. So, he said to the people of Israel, "We shall have a great and massive party while God and Moses talk upon the mount.

32:4 But it must be quick, for if Moses finds out, he shall be furious."

32:5 Aaron then demanded all the jewelry from the people. Golden earrings from all the people, their rings and other piercings.

32:6 He then made for the party a great centerpiece, a golden calf. The calf was hollow and was filled with great and mighty spirit for the people of Israel.

32:7 The udders of the calf were like taps and the people of Israel sucked upon the udders and drank of strong spirit and grew drunk and merry.

32:8 They then took off all manners of clothing and drank and danced, naked and free. And they fornicated with one another and satisfied their lustful desires.

32:9 They feasted upon many breads and cakes and flesh. And the foods and the spirits combined in their bellies and battled with one another,

32:10 And the people of Israel became sick and vomited upon one another's nudity.

32:11 Thus they ate not all the foods and the food began to rot and spoil in the sun and the stench caused the sickened peoples of Israel to become sicker.

32:12 In haste, they decided to dispose of the rotten food by fire. They gathered the uneaten breads and cakes and meats and placed it upon a mighty fire and burned it.

32:13 They then drank more of the spirit inside the calf and danced around the fire, naked, wallowing in their own vomit and urine and faeces.

32:14 The lord God heard the party and said to Moses, "Go down to your people, which I have brought out of the land of Egypt, for they have corrupted themselves.

32:15 They are partying wildly and freely, without care. They have a large and mighty calf, filled with liquor, which they drink from and grow drunk. And they do this without inviting you or their lord God.

32:16 I, their God, has set them free from slavery and servitude. And they party without me. How dare they do this and offend their lord and protector!

32:17 This offends me, for the people have fun without their lord God.

32:18 Leave me alone, so that I may stew in my anger and fury; and my wax shall wrath hot and consume them."

32:19 Moses did not leave God in solitude and said to him, "My lord, why would you consume the people that you have brought out of Egypt with a strong and mighty hand?

32:20 For when the Egyptians hear of this, they shall laugh and mock us and you and say to one another, 'The lord God freed his people not to save them, but to slay them." Turn away from your fierce wrath and repent the evil of which you want to do to the people of Israel.

32:21 Remember Abraham, Isaac and Jacob, the servants of you that you gave a holy covenant to. You promised their seed to multiply greater than the stars in heaven, that they shall rule the lands of earth and that they shall inherit the land for generations eternal."

32:22 The lord replied to Moses in fury, "Do not dare say what I do is evil. For when I slay in wrath, it is not sinful. When you kill, it is sinful, as you be mere human and a creation of God. But the rules that I make to you are not rules that I need follow. I may do as I please, without sin. The people of Israel shall not.

32:23 But, I shall keep my covenant to your ancestors and spare the people I freed from Egypt."

32:24 Moses then left and departed the mount, carrying the two tablets of testimony written by the erection of the lord God.

32:25 And when Joshua, who waited for Moses at the base of the mount, heard the noise from Israel, he said to Moses, "You must hurry, for I hear the noise of battle coming from camp."

32:26 Moses then asked Joshua, "If you do, why not did you go and fight. Why do you then stay here, cowardly away from battle?"

32:27 Joshua knew not what to say, but Moses spoke to him, "Do not worry, for it is not the noise of battle, but the noise of drunken song. The people are having a great party, without us nor their God."

32:28 As the two walked back to camp, Moses saw the party and the calf and the feasts and the fires and the drunkenness and the nudity and he grew furious.

32:29 For when he was up on the mount, listening to the tedious and boring demands of God, his people were indulging in fun and joy and could not wait for him to return.

32:30 Moses' fury overcame him and he cursed his people and threw the two tablets of testimony upon the people, hitting some of them upon their heads and thus broke the tablets and their skulls.

32:31 He then took the calf of liquor and burned it and took the ashes and poured it in the cheapest and most foul of all liquors in camp and forced all the nation of Israel to drink it in punishment.

32:32 Moses ran to his brother and said to him, "Why do you betray me and celebrate my leave. Why did you not wait and celebrate when I return?"

32:33 Aaron said to his brother, "Do not angry, for the people of Israel are yours as well.

32:34 For they came to me and they said, 'Why must we wait so long for God and Moses. We grow bored and anxious and wish for joy and celebration and fun.'

32:35 And I said to them, 'Then let us celebrate. Give to me your golden piercings, so that we may make a golden calf that gives us not milk, but strong drink and we shall dance and feast and fornicate and celebrate.'"

32:36 Moses then looked out among the people and saw that they were naked. And the nakedness cursed Moses with an erection firm and hard.

32:37 He then sought out a woman, drunk and asleep from liquor and dragged her to an empty tent and satisfied his erection's demands.

32:38 Still angry, he went to the gates of the camp and yelled to all the people, "Who be on the lord God's side and did not partake of such drunkenness, let them come to me so that they may serve their lord." And the tribe of Levi gathered themselves to him.

32:39 For the tribe of Levi did not partake of the party, as they wished not to be naked, as the men had small penises and the women's vaginas ranked of the sea.

32:40 Moses said to them, "Go now, gather your swords and spears and maces and go through the other tribes of Israel and slay for your lord God every man his brother, his companion, and his neighbour."

32:41 The men of Levi thought that too many men, but not wanting to anger God, they went to the camps and slew all that were passed out from spirit.

32:42 And with the hands of the tribe of Levi, three thousand men and women became corpses and were scattered among the camps.

32:43 When they returned, Moses said to the men of Levi, "You have served the lord God well and shall gain favour in his heart. A blessing he shall bestow upon you for not partaking in such celebration and for slaying your people in his name."

32:44 And it came to pass that in the morning, while the people of Israel were hungover, Moses said to them in a loud voice, so that their heads shall ache worse, "You have sinned a great sin and angered myself and your lord God for partying without us. I shall go and see the lord and make atonement for your selfishness and sins."

32:45 And Moses returned to God and said to him, "The people of mine have sinned a great sin and drank liquor from the teats of a gold calf.

32:46 I beg of you, forgive them and if you do not, take your wrath out upon me, so that only one die, but the nation of Israel still be strong in number."

32:47 But the lord God did not listen to Moses' plea, as he was drunk upon strong spirit as well and said to Moses, "Cursed be to your people, for I only created them so that they may worship and amuse me.

32:48 I have sent an angel of death to the camps of Israel and he shall visit those most sinful and cause them great illness."

32:49 Thus, in drunken anger, the lord sent a plague upon Israel, causing some to die of diarrhea and creating a great stench of shit and rotten flesh among the camp.

32:50 All this, because he wasn't invited to a party.

33:1 The lord said to Moses, "Go no, to the people I have freed from the servitude of the Egyptians, so that I may bring them to the land promised to Abraham, to Isaac and to Jacob so many generations ago.

33:2 And I shall send angels that shall strike fear among the inhabitants of this promised land of flowing milk and sweet honey.

33:3 The Canaanites, the Amorites, the Hittites, the Hivites, the Perizzite and the Jebusites shall be discarded away like bones after a meal.

33:4 But your people are a stiff-necked people and I demand more worship from them. If they do not partake in my demands, I shall devour them and their families."

33:5 And the lord said to Moses, "Go, tell the people of Israel that they are stiff-necked people and I shall come to the midst of them and consume them if they disobey: therefore, they must be stripped of all ornaments, so that I may gaze upon their nakedness and choose their fate."

33:6 And when Moses told of Israel's evil tidings, every man mourned and all shed their cloths and jewels.

33:7 Old, young, obese and thin soon stood naked in a mass crowd of flesh, begging the lord God not to eat them.

33:8 Moses took the tabernacle and pitched it away from the camp and called it the Tabernacle of the congregation. And all people of Israel who sought salvation sought out to the Tabernacle of the congregation, hoping and praying to be saved.

33:9 So that all the people of Israel visited the Tabernacle of the congregation, as they feared to do not would bring forth the wrath of God.

33:10 It came to pass that when Moses entered the Tabernacle of the congregation, all the people of Israel stood naked by the door and looked towards Moses and prayed for him.

33:11 For they wished to claim help for Moses, but were too cowardly to risk going against God, so they stood in prayer, which meant they did nothing.

33:12 When Moses entered the Tabernacle of the congregation, the mighty pillar descended upon it and stood at the door and the lord God talked with Moses.

33:13 As the people witnessed the mighty pillar descending, they knew it to be their lord and they fell upon their knees and worshipped him. Naked, as the lord is a pervert.

33:14 And the lord spoke to Moses through the door. Moses' servant, Joshua the son of Nun and a young man, went into the Tabernacle with Moses and remained there the lord arrived.

33:15 Moses said to his lord God, "See, you have said to me, free the people of Israel, so that I may make them a might nation. Yet you now threaten to consume them. Consume only a few, so that you shall keep your covenant to Abraham, to Isaac and to Jacob.

33:16 Tell me the names of those who have found favour in your sight and spare them, so that they may go forth to the land of milk and honey.

33:17 And I pray to you, those that have yet not found grace upon your sight, show them the way to salvation, so that they may know you and worship you and praise truly your name.

33:18 For this nation is my people and I wish all to grow strong and bountiful, so that the people of our lord God shall rule all land and worship you."

33:19 The lord pondered Moses' words and said to him, "You have given the lord God much to think of. For I want the nation of Israel to grow strong and prosper and worship me.

33:20 But I also am hungry and wish to consume them over fire, covered in garlic and paprika, with a glass of malbec my sons make for me with angel urine.

33:21 I shall take leave of you, so that I may rest and may make my decision."

33:22 Moses said to the lord, "If you leave the Tabernacle, take me with you, so that I may prove my loyalty to the lord God.

33:23 For when the people of Israel see you leave, they shall grow fearful and demand an explanation from me. I wish not to tell them anything until a decision has been made by my lord God. So, take me with you, so I may know your decision soonest and not have to deal with the people's questions."

33:24 And the lord said to Moses, "I shall do that which you ask and take you with me, for you have found favour in my sight and I know your name."

33:25 Moses knelt upon the ground and said with a triumphant voice, "Praise the lord, who has freed us from Pharaoh and shall deliver us into a prosperous land and make us a great nation!

33:26 Show me the full glory of my God, whom I love and worship."

33:27 And the lord said to Moses, "I shall make all my goodness pass before you and I will proclaim the name of the lord God before you and I will be gracious to those I deem gracious and show mercy upon those I deem worthy.

33:28 Moses, you cannot see my face, for the face of God is strong and mighty and no man shall ever see it, lest they die.

33:29 Behold, there is a place before me and you shalt stand upon a rock:

33:30 And it shall come to pass that while my glory pass by, I shall put you in a cleft of the rock and shall cover you with thy hand while I pass by.

33:31 And as I walk by, my hand shall be removed, so that you may gaze upon the back parts of the lord God and witness the glory of the lord's fine ass."

33:32 As a reader, you may wonder why the lord God will not allow people to gaze upon his face. The reason is simple.

33:33 The back part shows the false nature of God, the God who claims to be loving, caring and merciful. This is the side the lord wants his followers to see and is the reason why he turned his back to us.

33:34 For you see, dear reader, the claims the lord makes of him being loving, caring and merciful, is shit.

33:35 And like all beings, shit comes out of the ass, which is what shall be seen when staring upon the back parts of God.

33:36 The face of God shows his true nature. A violent, spoiled, uncaring dictator who would kill an infant for yawning during the Sabbath sermon.

33:37 If people saw the true nature of God, they would be disgusted and not worship him. This, of course, God cannot allow, so he'll kill them.

33:38 God loves killing people and getting others to kill people. He's a tyrant like that.

34:1 The lord said to Moses, "Carve me two tables of stone similar to the firsts and I shall write upon them the words that were carved upon the first tablets of stone, which you used to cause concussions upon your people.

34:2 Have them ready by morning and come up with them.

34:3 Have no man nor beast come with you, for I wish you to be alone and have the people away from the mount; and no flocks shall feast by it, lest I curse them."

34:4 Moses carved two tablets of fine marble and rose early upon the morning and carried the marble tablets up Mount Sinai.

34:5 The lord descended upon the mount in a great cloud of black and fire and stood beside Moses and proclaimed himself the one true lord.

34:6 "I am the lord God almighty, creator of all things. I am merciful and gracious, long-suffering and speak only truth and good will.

34:7 Keeping mercy for the multitude, forgiving iniquity and transgression and sins to those deemed worthy and cleansing guilt from the soul.

34:8 Stripping punishment from the original sinner and cursing their children and children's children until the fourth generation, so that their sons, grandsons and great grandsons shall live through their hardship."

34:9 Moses moved, bowed upon the ground and worshipped by the lord God's feet.

34:10 And Moses said to God, "If I have found grace in the sight of the lord, I pray to you, go among us. Forgive us our sins, for we are a stubborn people. Pardon our iniquity and give to us that which was promised generations ago."

34:11 And the lord replied, "Behold, I make a covenant unto you, that your people shall see many marvels of their lord God almighty, such as has never been seen on earth. And with these, all the people of the land shall want to know the works of God, for they shall fear the terror I shall cause them if they disobey me.

34:12 Take note of what I say today, for I shall drive out the pagan tribes of Amorite, Canaanite, Hittite, Perizzite, Hivite and Jebusite and reduce their bodies to dust.

34:13 Do not seek peace with these men, for they are a disgusting people who value independent thought and free will and go against God.

34:14 Destroy their altars, burn their images and cut down their groves.

34:15 For you shall not worship any other God but me, for my name is Jealous and I am a jealous God!

34:16 If you make a covenant with the tribes of these lands and you go a whoring after their false gods and do sacrifices to their false gods and worship not me and sacrifice not to me,

34:17 And you lie with their daughters and sons and bear unto them children, I shall see it as a blasphemous abomination!

34:18 I shall molt you like metal for such sins.

34:19 The feast of unleavened bread must be kept. Seven days shall you eat unleavened bread in the time of the month of Abid, for that be the month I freed you from the servitude of Egypt.

34:20 All that comes from Israel shall be mine and the first male of all flocks, whether ox or lamb, shall be mine.

34:21 The firstling of an ass you shall redeem with a sacrificial lamb. If a lamb cannot be sacrificed, then you shalt break the neck of the ass and kill it.

34:22 All first-born sons shall be redeemed with a lamb. If you cannot sacrifice a lamb, then you must sacrifice your son, so that I shall be not empty handed.

34:23 Six days shall you work, but the seventh is time for rest. For the lord God rested upon the seventh day and shall not be seen as lazy by mere mortal men.

34:24 Observe the feast of weeks, of the first fruits of harvest and of in-gathering at years end.

34:25 Thrice a year shall all your sons appear naked before the lord, so that I may observe them.

34:26 Do not do this with the daughters, for they disgust me and do not cause eroticism for the lord.

34:27 When you have your sons appear before me, I shall be happy and shall make thine peoples more powerful and enlarge your borders and no man shall take the land back from you.

34:28 Do not eat of blood, for blood is life and life belongs to God, as the lord God is a vampiric God.

34:29 Neither shall the sacrifice of the feast of the Passover be left until morning; burn it at night.

34:30 The first of all harvests shall be given to the house of God.

34:31 Do not boil a child in their mother's milk, for milk should bring strength unto a child and not death. Boil the child in their mother's urine, or another woman's milk."

34:32 And the lord God said to Moses, "Carve these words upon the tablets, for I forgot my pen. And it shall be like a covenant unto the nation of Israel."

34:33 And Moses did as commanded and picked up a stone and carved the words of the lord God upon the mighty tablets.

34:34 For forty days and nights did Moses not eat nor drink, but wrote the laws and demands and commandments of the lord God.

34:35 And it came to pass that when Moses went down from mount Sinai with the two tablets, the energy of the lord was with him and caused his skin to glow bright like the sun.

34:36 That when Aaron and the people of Israel saw this glowing epidermis, they grew fearful and thought Moses sick and refused to come near him.

34:37 Moses called a meeting of the elders of Israel, who sat away from him, growing fearful of his glow.

34:38 After the meeting, Moses called upon the children of Israel and told them the commandments and demands and laws of the lord God.

34:39 The people of Israel rejoiced and stripped naked and sacrificed many lambs and danced around nude.

34:40 This pleased the lord God, for he loves violence, nudity and torn flesh.

34:41 Moses put a veil upon his face, to hide the glow of God from the children of Israel, so that he may go near them without their fearful gaze.

34:43 But when Moses was alone, he took the veil off and took pleasure in his glowing skin.

EVITICUS

1:1 And the lord called out to Moses and spoke to him out of the tabernacle of the congregation, saying,

1:2 "Speak unto the children of Israel and tell them the lord God demands sacrifice.

1:3 The sacrificial offering must be of their own flock, their own herd and must be a male without spots nor blemish

1:4 For the lord God demands only the best be slain for his glory.

1:5 He shall lead the beast to the door of the tabernacle of the congregation, so that it may be slaughtered in violence for my amusement.

1:6 The man shall place his hand upon the head of the beast, so that all sins that man be done shall go upon the beast.

1:7 He shall then kill the beast before the lord God, before Aaron and before the priests and shall take of the blood and sprinkle it generously around the altar placed that is by the door to the tabernacle of the congregation.

1:8 He shall do this, chanting unto the heavens 'Accept the blood of the beast, lest you take the blood of me, for I have sinned and lost favour with the lord.'

1:9 You shall then strip off the skin of the beast and cut it into pieces for the lord God's entertainment.

1:10 The sons of Aaron shall then set fire upon the altar and lay wood upon it.

1:11 The priests of God shall then lay the parts, the head and the fat upon the fire, on top of the wood.

1:12 But the viscera and the legs shall be washed clean with water before laid upon the fire for burnt sacrifice, as the aroma of boiling blood and burning flesh creates a pleasing scent to the lord God.

1:13 If the offering be of flock and not herd, of sheep or goats he shall bring forth a male without blemish.

1:14 He shall slay it on the side of the northward altar and the priests and Aaron shall fill their mouths with the blood of the animal and spray it upon the altar.

1:15 The man shall cut them into pieces, with the head and the fat and the priests shall lay them upon the fire of the altar.

1:16 But the inwards and the legs shall be cleansed with water and then placed upon the fire, so that the flesh may be set on fire and the smell go forth to the heavens and create a pleasing aroma for the lord.

1:17 If the offering be of fowl, then he shall bring forth an offering of turtledoves or young pigeons. Male, for the lord wish the curse of women be not burnt for sacrifice.

1:18 The priest shall take the offering to the altar and twist off the head of the fowl, so that when the blood sprays forth from the neck, the priest shall cover the altar with blood from it.

1:19 Then he shall toss the head into the fire.

1:20 The priest shall then pluck the feathers from the fowl and cast it upon the east side of the altar, where the ashes be placed.

1:21 For burnt feathers do not create a pleasing aroma to the lord.

1:22 Then the priest shall cleave the wings of the animal and place it upon the fire, so that the burning bird shall create a scent that is pleasing to the lord God."

2:1 "And when you make an offering of food to the lord God, his offering shall contain fine flour and oil and frankincense.

2:2 They shall take it to Aaron the priest and he shall take a handful of the flour and of the oil and of the frankincense and they shall toss it upon the fire, so that the smoke rises and please the nostrils of the lord.

2:3 The remnants of the food shall be fed to Aaron and his sons, for it is a most holy combination of ingredients and to be consumed only by the ones who spread forth the holiness of God.

2:4 And if you make an offering of food baked inside the oven, it shall be of unleavened cakes made of the finest flour mingled with oil, or unleavened wafers sprinkled with the finest oil.

2:5 And if they bring me offerings of food baked upon the pan, it shall be of fine flour sprinkled with virgin oil.

2:6 You shall tear it to pieces so that the lord not be bothered slicing it with cutlery, as the lord is too busy doing things of great importance.

2:7 And if you bring me offerings baked upon the frying pan, it shall be made of fine flour and oil.

2:8 And you shall bring the food that is made of these things to the lord God and present it to the priest and the priest shall bring it to the altar.

2:9 The priest shall take these offerings of fine food, which could feed the hungry and nourish the weak and throw it upon the fire of the altar, for the smoke creates a pleasing aroma to the lord.

2:10 That which shall be left of the offering shall feed the priests, for it is a most holy offering, made by fire to the lord.

2:11 No offering made to the lord shall be made of leaven; no leaven nor any honey shall be burned as offering to the lord.

2:12 For the scent sickens the lord and makes him vomit upon the earth.

2:13 The offerings of the first harvest shall be offered to the lord but shall not be burned, for the scent does not please your God, creating a sickly-sweet aroma.

2:14 All offerings of food shall be seasoned with salt, for the lord God loves salty snacks.

2:15 When you offer the offerings of the first harvest, you shall give the lord God green ears of dried corn, roasted atop the fire.

2:16 And you shall put oil upon it and lay frankincense upon it, for it is a holy offering.

2:17 And the priests shall burn part of the roasted corn and part of the oil and all of the frankincense, for the lord God is a gluttonous God and wishes food be burnt for his aromatic pleasure."

3:1 "When the offering be that of peace, he shall offer it of the herd. It matters not male or female, as long as the offering be without blemish.

3:2 He shall lay his hand upon the head of the animal and kill it at the door of the tabernacle of the congregation; and the priests shall spray the blood of the slain upon the ground around the altar.

3:3 He shall offer to the lord God the fat of the animal that covers the inwards and the fat that is upon the inwards,

3:4 And the two kidneys and the fat with surrounds the kidneys and the caul which be above the liver.

3:5 And the priests shall take these most blessed of parts and burn it upon the altar, so that the boiling fat and organs create unto the lord God a most pleasing aroma.

3:6 If he offers not an offering of peace from the herd, he shall make to me an offering of peace from the flock and the offering shall have no blemish.

3:7 He shall lay his hand upon the head of the lamb and kill it before the door of the tabernacle of the congregation; and the priests shall gather the blood in leather canteens and spray it upon the altar and the ground.

3:8 He shall offer of the lamb the rump, for the lord wishes to have sex with the rump and the hard by the backbone and the fat with covers the inwards and the fat which be upon the inwards,

3:9 And the two kidneys and the fat which be upon them and the caul above the liver.

3:10 And the priests shall take these and burn them upon the altar, as an offering to the lord.

3:11 If the offering be of a goat, it shall be of a goat free of blemish.

3:12 He shall lay his hand upon the head of the goat and kill it at the door of the tabernacle of the congregation; and the sons of Aaron shall drink of the blood which spills upon the ground and spit it upon the ground around the altar.

3:13 And he shall offer the fat of the inwards and the fat upon the inwards,

3:14 And the two kidneys and the fat which be upon them and the caul above the liver.

3:15 The priests shall then burn all that upon the altar, for the smoke of the fire shall create a pleasing aroma for the lord.

3:16 It shall be a law for all generations that none shall eat of neither blood nor fat.

3:17 For blood be life, which belongs to God and shall only be consumed by the lord.

3:18 And fat be tasty and a favourite meal of the lord and he wishes you not eat that which he craves."

4:1 The lord spoke to Moses, saying,

4:2 "Speak to the children of Israel. Tell them if a soul sins through ignorance and knows not what they did be damned, they shall upset still the lord and find disfavour in the eyes of God.

4:3 They must bring to the priests a young bullock of no blemish to the lord for a sin offering.

4:4 He shall bring the bullock to the door of the tabernacle of the congregation and place their hand upon the beast's head and kill the bullock before the lord.

4:5 The priest shall take the blood of the bullock and take the brine of life to the tabernacle of the congregation.

4:6 The priest shall dip his finger in the blood and sprinkle of the blood seven times before God, before the veil of the sanctuary.

4:7 The priest shall take the remaining blood and put some upon the horns of the altar of sweet incense and shall poor the rest of the blood at the bottom of the altar of the burnt offering.

4:8 The priest shall take all the fat of the bullock, the fat that covers the inwards and the fat upon the inwards,

4:9 And the two kidneys and the caul above the liver.

4:10 Thy priest shall take also the skin of the bullock and the flesh and the head and the legs and all organs and the shit of the bullock.

4:11 The priest shall take the whole carcass of the beast and carry it away from camp to a clean place and burn the bullock and shall bury the ashes away."

4:12 Moses interrupted the lord God and asked of him,

4:13 "If one shall sin through ignorance, how then shall they know this offering must be done?

4:14 For ignorance is a lack of knowledge and if they lack the knowledge they sin, they may never know they sin and shall not do this offering for your forgiveness."

4:15 The lord God replied,

4:16 "That is not my problem, but theirs, so curse them.

4:17 If the whole congregation of Israel sin through ignorance and this sin be hid from the eyes of the elders and of the priests, the congregation of Israel be guilty.

4:18 When the sin becomes known, they shall bring forth for the congregation a young bullock for their sin and place it upon the door of the tabernacle of the congregation.

4:19 The elders of Israel shall place their hands upon the head of the young bullock and they shall kill the bullock before the eyes of God.

4:20 The priest anointed shall bring of the bullock's blood to the tabernacle of the congregation.

4:21 He shall dip his finger in the bullock's blood and shall sprinkle it seven times before the lord, before the veil of the sanctuary.

4:22 He shall take some of the blood and cover the horns of the altar before the lord with the blood of the sin offering and he shall poor the rest of the blood into the bottom of the altar and make a bloody mess before God.

4:23 He shall take all the fat from the bullock and burn it upon the altar, so that he may please the lord on behalf of the congregation of Israel.

4:24 The priest shall then take the carcass of the bullock and the priest shall make an atonement of sin for the children of Israel; and the lord God may forgive them.

4:25 The priest shall then take the carcass away from camp and burn it as he did for the sin offering and bury the ashes away.

4:26 When a ruler has sinned through ignorance against any of the laws of God, he is guilty.

4:27 When the knowledge of his sin comes to him, he must make an offering to the lord, a kid of the goats, a male without blemish

4:28 For the lord God loves young goats, for the lord God is a pedophile and into bestiality.

4:29 A sin for mortals, a pleasure for the lord.

4:30 And the ruler shall take the goat to the altar of burnt offering and shall lay his hand upon the goat's head and kill it,

4:31 And the priest shall take the blood of the kid goat and smear the horns of the altar with the blood and shall poor the rest of the blood upon the bottom of the altar.

4:32 The priest shall burn the fat upon the altar and the priest shall make atonement for the sins of the ruler and the lord God will take notice and may bless the ruler with forgiveness.

4:33 If any of the common people sin through ignorance, or a slave, or a foreign person, they are guilty in the eyes of God.

4:34 They shall take to the lord a kid goat, a female without blemish and bring it unto the altar of the burnt offering.

4:35 They shall lay their hands upon the goat and kill it and wash their hair with the blood of the young female goat.

4:36 The priest shall take the blood of the goat and smear the horns of the altar with the goat blood and the priest shall take the remaining blood of the goat and pour it to the bottom of the altar.

4:37 He shall then take the fat of the goat and burn it upon the altar for a sweet savour to the lord.

4:38 If the common person, or the slave, or the foreign man bring not a goat, he shall take unto the lord a lamb, a female without blemish.

4:39 They shall take the lamb to the altar of burnt offering and lay their hands upon the lamb and kill it and wash their hair with the blood of the lamb.

4:40 The priest shall take the blood of the lamb and smear the horns with blood and pour the remaining blood to the bottom of the altar.

4:41 The priest shall take the fat of the lamb and burn it upon the altar and make an atonement for the sins of the commoner, or of the slave, or of the foreigner.

4:42 The lord God will take notice of this and be pleased by the aroma of burning fat and boiling blood.

4:43 The lord God will not forgive their sins.

4:44 Fuck commoners.

4:45 Fuck slaves.

4:46 Fuck foreigners.

4:47 The lord God hates them."

5:1 "And if the soul sins by hearing that of another soul swear, that man is guilty for listening to the other soul speak such profanity.

5:2 If he does not tell the people of such a dung filled mouth, he shall be found guilty in the eyes of God; for the lord will make you responsible for the sins of others.

5:3 Or if a man touches that which is unclean in the eyes of God, whether a carcass of an unclean beast, or the carcass of unclean cattle, or the carcass of unclean creepy crawlies which the lord has cursed since the times of Adam, or the touch of a menstruating woman.

5:4 Or if he touches the uncleanness of man and it be hid from him, when the man bears knowledge of what he has touched, he shall know himself sinful and wretched in the eyes of God.

5:5 When a man speaks that he shall do evil, even when the evil he does not, he shall be as sinful as though he committed that which he speaks and shall be wicked in the eyes of God.

5:6 He shall confess the guilt of his sins to the priests,

5:7 And shall bring a trespass offering to the lord, a female of the flock, a lamb or young kid goat for offering and the priest shall make atonement for his sins.

5:8 And it shall be done as a sin offering to the lord.

5:9 If the man cannot bring forth an offering of the flock, he shall bring forth an offering of the wing.

5:10 He shall bring two young pigeons or two young turtledoves for the lord; one shall be of a sin offering and the other be of a burnt offering.

5:11 The man shall offer the birds to the priest and the priest shall take both birds and shove the heads of the birds into the rectum of the sinner and twist until the birds' head be removed from the body.

5:12 As the blood leaks from the asshole of the sinner, the priest shall manoeuver him so that the blood leaks upon the ground by the altar and into the bottom of the altar, as it be a sin offering.

5:13 The priest shall take the second bird for a burnt offering and the priest shall make atonement for the sins of the child of Israel,

5:14 And the lord God shall forgive him, as the amusement of pigeon or dove blood spraying out the buttocks of the sinner shall entertain the lord and will be worth forgiveness.

5:15 If the sinner can bring not two turtledoves or two young pigeons for offering, he shall bring to the lord a tenth of an ephah of fine ground flour for sin offering.

5:16 He shall bring no oil for the flour, nor frankincense, for it is a sin offering to the lord.

5:17 The priest shall take the flour and bake two loaves of fine bread.

5:18 The sinner shall place a hand upon each of the loaves and confess the sins of which he has done.

5:19 The priest shall then take of the loaves and burn them upon the altar and make atonement for the sins of the man.

5:20 The lord God may forgive him, or may not. The lord does not like when a non-flesh offering is made and may take insult upon the man, cursing him instead.

5:21 It is a risk the man must be willing to take."

5:22 The lord continued to speak and bored Moses with his words, saying,

5:23 "If a soul commits a trespass upon the holy grounds of the lord and do so in ignorance, the man shall bring a ram of the herd, a male without blemish and shekels of silver the amount to be decided by the priests, to pay for the unholiness of his trespass.

5:24 And he shall make amends for the harm of which his trespassing upon holy places has done and the priest shall make atonement of the sins of the trespasser and make offering of the ram as a sin offering.

5:25 The lord God shall forgive the man dependent upon the number of shekels of silver he brings.

5:26 Forgiveness is not cheap. Remember that.

5:27 And if a man sins and breaks the laws of the ten commandments, though he wished it not, he is still guilty according the eyes of God.

5:28 He shall bring to the lord a foreign child, a male without blemish and shall place the child before the altar of burnt offering.

5:29 He shall place the hands upon the head of the child and the priest shall make atonement for the one who has broken my commandments.

5:30 The priest shall then grab the arms of the child and the sinner the legs and they shall pull off the limbs of the still breathing child.

5:31 And each limb, each arm, each leg, shall be thrust upon a horn of the altar of burnt offering and the body of the child shall be thrown atop the altar to burn.

5:32 The lord shall see the child of a foreign land suffer and shall smile and shall forgive the one who broke his commandments and trespassed against the lord."

6:1 The lord still spoke to Moses, saying,

6:2 "If a man sins and lies to his neighbour in that which was borrowed to him, or was taken by violence, or has deceived his neighbour,

6:3 Or has found that of value which was lost by his neighbour and lies so that he may keep it for himself,

6:4 Then it shall be that he has sinned and is guilty and shall return that which he took, or obtained through violence or deceit, or returned the lost thing he has found.

6:5 If the item he no longer has, he shall pay for the value of that wrongfully obtained and he shall add upon its value a fifth of its total and give to him the total of that which was wrongfully taken.

6:6 And he shall bring to the lord a trespass offering, a ram free of blemish and deliver it to the priest.

6:7 And the priest shall make atonement for his sins; and the lord shall witness the offering and the stolen goods delivered.

6:8 And the lord God shall forgive the sins of the man, for he stole only from another man and not from God."

6:9 Moses still listened to the lord God and wondered when he would shut up.

6:10 "Command Aaron and his sons that this be the law of the burnt offering: it is the burnt offering, because the offering is burnt.

6:11 Why else would it be called the burnt offering?

6:12 The priest shall put on his linen garments and his fine linen loin cloth and his linen breeches and shall pick up the ashes which the fire has consumed upon the altar and place the ashes beside the altar.

6:13 The priest shall then strip naked, so that the garments not be stained by ash and the priest shall walk forth nude and find a clean place outside the camp to bury the ashes of the offering.

6:14 The fire of the altar must always burn; it shall never die. The priest shall put wood upon it every morning so that the flames go strong and shall lay upon it the sacrifices of burnt offering and the fat of the peace offerings.

6:15 The fire shall always burn: it shall never go out, lest you be consumed by the fires of God!!!

6:16 This be the laws of the food offering, for those children of Israel too cheap to offer the life of an animal.

6:17 The priest shall take a handful of the flour and a handful of the oil and a handful of the frankincense and shall burn it upon the altar so that the scent reaches the lord God.

6:18 All the remaining of the food shall be taken by the priests and shall be eaten with unleavened bread in the holiest of places; in the court of the tabernacle of the congregation shall they consume the offerings.

6:19 It shall not be consumed with that baked leaven, for to do so would be a most unholy thing in the holiest of places and shall anger the lord.

6:20 All the males among the children of Aaron shall eat it, for it shall be a statute among the generations. For offerings made by fire are most holy and whosoever shall touch such offerings shall be holy."

6:21 Still the lord God did not shut up and continued to speak.

6:22 "This is the offerings of Aaron and his sons and all priests when they be anointed; a tenth of an ephah of fine flour for a food offering, half of which shall be for the morning and half of which shall be night.

6:23 In a pan shall you bake it with the finest virgin oil and when it is baked, you shalt bring it in and the baked goods shall be burnt upon the altar for a sweet savour for the lord God.

6:24 The priest whom be anointed shall offer it and it shall be a statute for all generations.

6:25 And every food offering of a priest shall be burnt whole and none shall be consumed by man."

6:26 Moses went off to a bush so that he may urinate, but still the lord God kept talking.

6:27 "These be the laws of the sin offering: In the place where the burnt offering is slaughtered so shall the sin offering be slaughtered, for it is a most holy thing.

6:28 The priest who perform the offering shall eat of the flesh of the offering, in the most holy places, in the court of the tabernacle of the congregation.

6:29 Whatsoever touches the flesh of the offering shall be holy and if the blood of the sacrifice be spilled upon the garments, then you shall wash the blood off in the holiest of places.

6:30 But if the earthen vessel, the body, touches the blood, the body shall be broken. The body must be scoured in a brass pot and rinsed with boiling water.

6:31 All the male priests shall eat thereof the sin offering, for it is most holy.

6:32 But no sin offering shall the blood be consumed, for blood is life and most precious to the lord God. The blood shall be burnt upon the altar. All of it."

7:1 "This is the law of the trespass offering. It is most holy.

7:2 In the place where you kill the burnt offering is where you shall kill the trespass offering and the blood shall be sprinkled around the altar, for the lord loves blood.

7:3 And you shall offer the fat ass, the fat from the ass and the fat that covers the inwards,

7:4 And the two kidneys and the fat which surrounds them and the fat upon the flanks and the caul above the liver,

7:5 And the priest shall burn the fat, the ass and the organs upon the altar and strip naked and masturbate so that his seed shoots upon the flames, so that entire generations be burnt upon the altar before consummation.

7:6 Every male shall masturbate and offer the juice from their loins upon the altar; and the lord shall smell the sperm and the fat and the kidneys and it will create an amusing aroma to the lord.

7:7 The priest shall then take the meat from the offering and eat it, for it is most holy and shall be consumed by the most holy of masturbators, blessed by God.

7:8 These are the laws of the sacrifice of the peace offering, which you must offer to the lord God.

7:9 If he offers it for thanksgiving, then he shall take unleavened cakes mingled with oil and unleavened wafers anointed with oil and cakes mixed with fine oil and flour and fried.

7:10 With the cakes he shall offer leavened bread with the sacrifice of the thanksgivings of the peace offering.

7:11 He shall take it to the priests and the priests shall take the peace offering and cut the man who offers the food.

7:12 They shall cut him above each nipple and let the blood drip upon the food of the offering, so that all the breads, all the cakes, all the wafers be soggy with the blood.

7:13 The priests shall then take the food and feast upon it with gluttony and the lord shall protect them from diseases that be within the blood.

7:14 For the lord wishes the blood for himself, for blood is life, and through the priests' gluttony the lord shall feast upon the blood and be pleased.

7:15 If the sacrifice be that of a vow, then he shall take to the lord a young concubine and they shall slay her upon the place where the burnt offerings are killed.

7:16 They shall remove her breasts, her hair of the loins and place them upon the altar.

7:17 The priest shall cut her throat and let the blood spray upon the altar and upon the ground of the altar.

7:18 They shall burn the breasts and blood and unclean hair as a sacrifice to the lord and the priests shall masturbate and spill their juice of the loins upon the holes where the breasts used to be.

7:19 Then they shall cover the concubine in oil and place her upon a fire and shall burn her and eat of her flesh for two days.

7:20 For it is a most holy flesh unto the lord God and shall be consumed by the most holy of men.

7:21 But on the third day you shall not consume any flesh nor blood of the whore, for upon the third day the lord shall be hungry and demand flesh from the concubine.

7:22 If any man eats of the flesh upon the third day, they shall be seen as an abomination of the lord God and shall be cursed with uncleanliness and shall be cast out among his people.

7:23 Moreover the soul that touches the flesh or consumes the flesh of anything unclean, whether beast or bird or man, or any abomination of the lord, shall be unclean themselves, and cast out into the wilderness and shall be cursed and damned by God."

7:24 Still the lord spoke to Moses and said to him,

7:25 "Speak to the children of Israel and tell them not to eat the fat of an animal, the fat of an ox, or fox, or fowl or any manner of fat.

7:26 For the fat belongs to God and if they consume the fat which belongs to the lord, the lord shall curse them with obesity,

7:27 And they shall be cast out from their people and forced to live in the desert, where the sun shall boil their lard and roast them alive, thus basting their flesh for the lord God's consumption.

7:28 And whosoever eats the blood shall be cursed by God, for blood is life and life shall only be consumed by God.

7:29 They that eat of the blood shall be cast out from their people and left to live like beasts themselves and hunt at night and the sun shall forever curse and burn them.

7:30 They shall be forced to drink nothing but blood, for only blood shall sustain them.

7:31 And the blood shall be warm and bitter and cause them to gag and wretch.

7:32 Their skin shall grow pale as the moon and their eyes shall become hollow and empty.

7:33 If light of the sun touches them, they shall burn slowly and painfully and die and all that be left of them shall be ashes and dust, ashes and dust."

7:34 The lord rambled on and said to Moses,

7:35 "Their own hands shall slay and bring the offerings of the lord made by fire and they shall bring the fat and the breast of a pregnant foreigner, so that the breast shall be used as a wave offering to the lord.

7:36 And the fat shall be burned upon the altar as sacrifice to the lord, but the breast shall belong to the priests, to the sons of Aaron.

7:37 The right shoulder of the pregnant infidel shall be pulled off with oxen and used as a heave offering of the sacrifices of the peace offering unto the lord God.

7:38 You shall wave the breasts and heave the shoulders as sacrifice of the peace offerings and the lord God shall bear witness to this and remember the statute which he has made to the children of Israel."

8:1 The lord would not shut the hell up and said to Moses,

8:2 "Take Aaron and his sons and the holy garments and anointing oil and a bullock for the sin offering and two rams and a basket of unleavened bread.

8:3 And gather all the children of Israel into the tabernacle of the congregation, so that they may bear witness."

8:4 Moses did as God commanded and gathered his brother and his nephews and all the people of Israel into the tabernacle of the congregation.

8:5 Moses said to the people, "This is what the lord commanded be done."

8:6 And Moses brought Aaron and his sons and stripped them naked and washed them with cold water.

8:7 Their loins thus shrivelled and was seen by all the women of Israel and they chuckled.

8:8 Moses then brought forth Aaron and clothed him with the sacred robe and the sacred thong and put the ephod on him and girdled him with the curious and slightly gay girdle of the ephod and bound it upon him.

8:9 He placed upon Aaron the breastplate and the breastplate of the Urim and the Thummim.

8:10 He put the mitre, the holy crown, upon the head of Aaron, as God instructed.

8:11 Moses then took the anointing oil and poured it upon the tabernacle and all that was within and sanctified them.

8:12 He took the oil and placed it upon the altar seven times and anointed the altar and all its vessels and sanctified them.

8:13 Moses then took the oil and poured it upon Aaron's head, thus making him greasy and sanctified him.

8:14 Aaron thought the oil was a lubricant and grew aroused and expected sanctified sodomy.

8:15 God witnessed the thoughts of Aaron and thus came down from the heavens and raped him.

8:16 Aaron was pleased.

8:17 Moses then brought forth the sons of Aaron and put coats on them and girdles and bonnets, so that they looked like women with

beards, as this was what the lord God commanded.

8:18 Moses then brought forth the bullock for the sin offering and Aaron and his sons placed their hands upon the head of the bullock.

8:19 Moses then slew the bullock and gathered the blood and with his finger thus stained the horns of the altar with the blood of the bullock and purified the altar and poured the blood upon the bottom of the altar, to make reconciliation upon it.

8:20 And Moses took the fat and the two kidneys and the caul above the liver and all the inwards and burned them upon the altar as the lord God commanded.

8:21 Moses took the carcass of the bullock, its hide, its flesh and its dung and burnt it with fire outside of the camp.

8:22 For the Israelites wished not to smell burning flesh and shit, but guts and fat and blood apparently smells like barbecue to them.

8:23 Moses then took out the ram and Aaron and his sons placed their hands upon the head of the ram.

8:24 And Moses slew it and sprayed the blood around the altar and Aaron and his sons bathed in the blood of the ram.

8:25 Moses cut the ram into pieces and burned upon the altar the head, the fat and the chunks of flesh.

8:26 He then washed the inwards and the legs with water and Moses burnt the whole ram upon the altar, so that the smell of death shall reach into the heavens and create a pleasing aroma for the lord.

8:27 Moses brought out the other ram and Aaron and his sons placed their hands upon the head of the ram and Moses killed it.

8:28 What a surprise.

8:29 Moses took the blood of the freshly slain ram and put it upon the right ear of his brother Aaron and upon the great toe of Aaron's right foot.

8:30 He then took the blood to the sons of Aaron and did the same damn thing.

8:31 He then took the remaining blood of the ram and threw it around the altar.

8:32 Moses then gathered the fat and the rump and the inwards and the caul above the liver and the right shoulder.

8:33 He then took out of the basket of bread one unleavened loaf, one wafer and a cake of oiled bread and placed them upon the fat and the right shoulder of the ram.

8:34 And he took this mess of fat and flesh and bread and placed them upon the hands of Aaron and each of his sons and commanded they wave them above their heads, so that the mess shall drip upon them.

8:35 Thus they did, as the lord commanded and the lord saw the wave offering and laughed.

8:36 Moses then took the revolting lumps of fat and flesh and bread and burned them upon the altar, so that the odour may please the lord.

8:37 The lord God did not notice the savour, as he was indulging himself in the magical properties of the smoke from poppy seeds.

8:38 Moses then took the breast of the ram and performed a wave offering in front of the children of Israel, as God commanded him.

8:39 God was too stoned to care.

8:40 Moses then took the anointing oil and the blood which was upon the altar and showered it upon Aaron and his sons and upon their garments and sanctified them all; and they were then officially priests forever into the service of the lord.

8:41 And Moses said to the newly appointed priests, "Boil the flesh at the door of the tabernacle and eat the flesh with the unleavened bread, as the lord God commanded.

8:42 Eat until your bellies be full and your mouth reject the food and that which remains shall be burnt upon the altar.

8:43 For seven days shall you stay in the tabernacle of the congregation, for within seven days you shall be consecrated by the lord God.

8:44 Do this and the lord shall make atonement to you.

8:45 If you do not as I say; the lord God shall curse and kill you and your backbone shall turn to serpents and bite you with venom most foul and shoot out from your mouth and consume your body."

8:46 So Aaron and his sons did as they commanded by God, according to the word of Moses.

9:1 It came to pass that on the eighth day, Moses called Aaron and his sons and all the elders of Israel.

9:2 Moses commanded to Aaron, "Take a young calf for a sin offering and a ram free of blemish and offer them to the lord.

9:3 And go out to the children of Israel and tell them, 'Take a kid of the young goats and a calf and a lamb under the age of a year, free of blemish and offer them to your God for a sin offering.

9:4 Bring forth also a bullock and a ram for peace offerings and unleavened breads mingled with oil for a food offering, for today the lord God will appear to you.'"

9:5 All the children of Israel brought forth that which Aaron commanded and placed them before the tabernacle of the congregation and waited for God to show up.

9:6 Moses spoke to the nation of Israel and said to them, "This is one of the many of things of which the lord God has commanded of you and if you do this, the glory of God shall be shown to you."

9:7 Moses then demanded of Aaron, "Go now to the altar and offer the sin offerings and the burnt offerings and make atonement for yourself and for all the children of Israel, as our lord commanded."

9:8 Aaron thus went up to the altar and slew the calf as a sin offering, which was for himself.

9:9 The sons of Aaron brought the blood of the calf to him and Aaron dipped his finger in the blood and put it upon the horns of the altar and dipped his penis in the blood and had one of the young goats lick it off and poured the rest of the blood into the bottom of the altar.

9:10 He gathered the fat and the kidneys and the caul above the liver and burned them upon the altar as a sin offering.

9:11 The flesh and the hide were taken out of camp and burned with unholy fire.

9:12 Aaron slew the burnt offering and his sons gathered the blood and presented it to Aaron and he sprinkled the blood around the altar while dancing.

9:13 The sons of Aaron presented the pieces of the burnt offering and the head and they were burnt upon the altar.

9:14 They washed the legs and inwards of the offering with water and burnt them upon the altar.

9:15 The newly appointed priests did everything which was demanded a few chapters ago, yet it is so important it must be reread.

9:16 Why else would the Bible include it?

9:17 Aaron brought forth the goat as a sin offering for the people of Israel.

9:18 Read above and look up sacrificing goats for sin offerings. That's what Aaron did.

9:19 Aaron brought out the breads of the food offering and took but a handful and burnt it upon the flames of the altar.

9:20 Aaron and his sons then slew the many bullocks and rams, for peace offerings for the lord God.

9:21 The priests then gathered all the blood and with straws blew them upon the ground and upon the altar.

9:22 They took the fat of the bullocks and the rams and the rumps and the inwards and the kidneys and the cauls above the livers,

9:23 And they put the fat upon the breast of the beast and burnt it

upon the altar.

9:24 As was the lord's demand.

9:25 They then gathered the breasts and right shoulders and waved them high and mighty in the air as a wave offering to the lord God.

9:26 Aaron then lifted his hands towards the people of Israel and blessed them all in the name of the lord and came down from the altar, from the sacrifices and from the offerings.

9:27 Moses and Aaron went into the tabernacle of the congregation and fulfilled one another's homosexual and carnal lusts for the amusement of the lord.

9:28 They came out, sore and smiling and blessed all the people of Israel: and the glory of God came down upon the people.

9:29 There came out a magnificent fire from the altar and from the temple, which consumed all the remains and the ash of the offerings and when the people saw the glory of God by fire, they shouted and yelled and danced and put marshmallows on sticks and toasted them with God's fire and placed them between unleavened wafers and ate.

10:1 Nadab and Abihu, priests and sons of Aaron, took with them their censer and put fire therein and walked in the presence of God.

10:2 The fire was strange to God and made the lord angry.

10:3 The lord sent his anger into the strange fire until it grew and consumed the priests Nadab and Abihu and they died by the hands of God.

10:4 The people of Israel witnessed this and grew afraid and were saddened for Aaron.

10:5 Moses went to his brother Aaron and told him, "Do not feel sad, nor grieve for the death of your sons, for they deserved to die by fire.

10:6 We may know not why, but the lord does and the lord did that which killed them and we are not ones to question.

10:7 Glory be the power of the lord!"

10:8 Aaron heard his brother speak and showed no sadness, no grief for his sons murder.

10:9 Though he did quickly thing God a cruel and selfish beast, that thought was quickly forced from his mind lest the lord hear it and kill Aaron as well.

10:10 Moses called upon Mishael and Elzaphan and said to them, "Go forth and carry your brethren away from the camp."

10:11 So the two went near and grabbed the robes of Nadab and Abihu, which were unburnt and dragged them away.

10:12 Moses then said to Aaron, Mishael and Elzaphan, "Uncover not your heads, nor rend your clothes, lest the lord kill you where you stand and wrath come down upon the people of Israel.

10:13 Instead, praise the death of the two in celebration and tell the children of Israel to celebrate the burning of Nadab and Abihu.

10:14 You shall not go out of the door of the tabernacle of the congregation, for the holy anointing oil of the lord is upon you and he shall kill you if you leave."

10:15 And the three men did as Moses said, out of fear of death.

10:16 The lord came down, and spoke to Aaron and said to him,

10:17 "Do not drink wine nor strong drink, nor the priests consume wine nor strong drink, when you enter the tabernacle of the congregation, for the lord likes not drunkenness in his home and shall kill you.

10:18 Let soberness be a statute among you for generations.

10:19 With sober minds, you shall see the clean and unclean, the holy and unholy, the righteous and unrighteous.

10:20 You shall teach the nation of Israel the difference between the clean and unclean, the holy and unholy, the righteous and unrighteous."

10:21 And Moses spoke to Aaron and Misheal and Elzaphan and

told them,

10:22 "Take the meat of the offering of the lord made by fire and eat it by the altar with unleavened bread, for it is most holy.

10:23 You shall eat it in the holy place, for it is your due and your sons due; and the lord God commands your dues.

10:24 Wave the breast and heave the shoulder when you eat in a clean place, you and your sons and your daughters too, which are given out as sacrifices of peace offerings to the children of Israel.

10:25 The heave shoulder and the wave breast the children of Israel shall bring, made by fire of the fat, to heave and wave as an offering to God, for it shall be a statue forever and ever as the lord commanded."

10:26 Moses sought out the goat of the sin offering and behold, it was burnt. Moses grew angry with Eleazar and Ithamar, sons of Aaron and left unburnt by God and said to them,

10:27 "Why have you not eaten the sin offering in the holy place, seeing as it is most holy and demanded by the lord. Why have you refused to make atonement unto God?

10:28 Behold, the blood has not been brought in upon the altar: you should have indeed eaten it within the holy place as was commanded."

10:29 And the priests said to Moses, "Behold, this day when the sin offering and the burnt offering were brought forth, we all were stricken with sickness.

10:30 Our bellies rejected food and we would vomit and our bowels were stricken with diarrhea most foul.

10:31 If we had eaten the offerings, our vomit and shit would shoot out from us and stain the place most holy to God.

10:32 We wished not to do this, as we knew God wish not the holy place be covered in bodily rejections and ate not the offering.

10:33 If the lord wished us to eat of the offering, would he not say so. Would he not have cursed us already and killed us for not eating the flesh of the offering?"

10:34 When Moses heard this, he was content, for if God wished them to eat the offering, he would have killed them for not doing so by now.

11:1 The lord spoke to Moses and Aaron and said to them,

11:2 "Speak unto the nation of Israel and tell them of the lord's dietary restrictions upon them.

11:3 Whatever beast has parted the hoof and be cloven-footed and chews the cud, is clean and fit for eating.

11:4 Nevertheless, those that contain one trait, but not the other, is unclean and shall not be consumed.

11:5 The camel shall be unclean to you, for though he chews the cud, the hoof be not cloven.

11:6 The coney and hare shall not be touched, for though they chew the cud, the hoof be not divided.

11:7 Yes, the coney and the hare chew the cud, but only when others are not looking.

11:8 For if the lord God says it, it must be so.

11:9 The swine shall be disgusting to you, for though it be cloven-footed, and divided of foot, it chews not the cud and is unclean.

11:10 No bacon for the children of Israel.

11:11 Their flesh shall not be eaten, their carcass not be touched, for it is unholy and unclean to you and the eyes of God.

11:12 These you shall eat of the waters: whatsoever have fins and scales is clean and may be eaten by you.

11:13 Those which have not fins nor scales is an abomination.

11:14 You shall not eat of their flesh or touch them, as they are revolting to God.

11:15 Why the lord has created them, he knows not.

11:16 Perhaps it was all that cocaine and hashish.

11:17 Of these the fowl shall not be eaten, for they are unclean.

11:18 The eagle, the osprey, and the ossifrage

11:19 The vulture, the kite and its kind

11:20 Every raven and its kind

11:21 The owl, the cormorant, the cuckow and the hack.

11:22 The swan, the pelican

11:23 The stork, the heron, the lapwing and the bat.

11:24 Yes, the bat be a bird, for it flies and the lord calls it a bird.

11:25 Biology and science is wrong and is an abomination to the lord and to you as well.

11:26 All fowls that creep upon four legs shall be an abomination to you and shall not be eaten.

11:27 These insects are clean and shall be eaten and enjoyed: the locust, the beetle and the grasshopper.

11:28 All other insects shall be an abomination and must not be eaten nor touched.

11:29 Whosoever touches that which is unclean shall wash his clothes and be unclean until the evening and shall be in solitude, as he is unclean.

11:30 Whatsoever have paws is unclean, as it is not cloven footed and shall be an abomination to you.

11:31 You shall now get rid of your pet cats and dogs, for they are unclean.

11:32 All things which creep is creepy in the eyes of God and shall be unclean to you.

11:33 The tortoise, the weasel, the rat and mouse,

11:34 The ferret, the chameleon, the lizard, the snake, the snail and the mole.

11:35 These are unclean to you, those which creep. Whomever touches them shall be unclean until the evening and must wash their clothes and be in solitude.

11:36 Whatever material these beasts of abomination touch when die shall be unclean.

11:37 Whether vessel or raiment or metal or rock, it shall be unclean and must be put into water and shall be unclean until evening.

11:38 If they die upon a plate, whatever food touches that plate shall be unclean, whether meat clean, or baked good, or fruit or vegetable.

11:39 That plate must be buried in the sand and left, for it is unclean and revolting to the lord.

11:40 He that eats a beast unclean shall be cursed upon the eyes of the lord and shall be cast out of the nation of Israel.

11:41 To gain acceptance, he must cleanse himself.

11:42 They shall vomit all that which be in their bellies and defecate all that which remain in their bowels, so that the unclean flesh be gone from their bodies.

11:43 They must wash their inwards and drink soapy water for three straight days.

11:44 Then they must take a burning stick and place it within their bowels, so that any unclean flesh that remain be burned.

11:45 Only then shall they be favoured in the eyes of God, only then shall they be welcome back to the tribes of Israel.

11:46 Do as I say and you shall remain holy and sanctified in the eyes of God.

11:47 The true lord almighty, who eventually delivered you from the hands of Egypt and shall bring you to the promised lands of milk and honey.

11:48 For these are the laws of the beasts and the fowl and of that which lives in the waters and these laws shall be obeyed, lest the lord put a curse upon you.

11:49 The laws of the clean and the unclean, the holy and unholy and the laws which state the creatures of which are an abomination to the lord."

12:1 The lord spoke to Moses and told him,

12:2 "Women are filthy undesirable revolting little creatures in the eyes of God, and the lord wishes Adam had never asked for one.

12:3 It is women who cursed you and all mankind, for listening to Satan and believing a talking snake.

12:4 And it shall be women who dooms man, with their hips and breasts and sexual gratifications.

12:5 Remember this and be careful around women.

12:6 Remember that women are only good for cleaning, cooking and giving birth to sons.

12:7 Go forth and tell the children of Israel this.

12:8 When a woman has accepted the seed of a man and give to him a son, it is a blessed event, for the woman has fulfilled the ultimate purpose: populating the earth with men.

12:9 The woman shall be unclean for seven days and must be separated from the people of Israel.

12:10 Upon the eighth day, the son shall be circumcised and marked as a holy and blessed child of God through the ritual removal of foreskin.

12:11 The woman shall now be clean, but must fulfill her purification to the lord.

12:12 Her vagina shall bleed and ooze for thirty-three days, thus removing some that remains dirty of a woman.

12:13 She shall not touch any hallowed thing, nor come into the sanctuary, until the days of her purification be fulfilled.

12:14 If she bears a daughter, this is a cursed event and the husband must beat her with a rod.

12:15 She shall be unclean for two weeks, for which in this time she shall be cast out of the children of Israel.

12:16 Her purification shall be for sixty and six days and her vagina shall bleed and ooze twice, once for the purification of the mother and once for the unholy cunt which she gave upon the world.

12:17 When the days of purification be fulfilled, whether for son or daughter, the mother shall bring a lamb for burnt offering and a pigeon or dove for sin offering unto the doors of the tabernacle of the congregation.

12:18 The priest shall make atonement for the new mother and she shall be cleansed of her vaginal bleedings.

12:19 If the mother is unable to bring a lamb, then she shall bring two turtledoves or two pigeons, one for the burnt offering and one for the sin offering and the priest shall make atonement for her.

12:20 If the mother gave birth to a son, this is all that needs to be done.

12:21 If the mother spawned forth a daughter, the mother must then present her vaginal droppings to the priest, so that the priest shall burn them upon the altar.

12:22 The priest must be careful not to touch this, as it is the most unholy thing in the eyes of God.

12:23 If any of the vaginal liquid drop upon the priest, another priest must take a knife and remove the flesh which it be dropped upon and burn it outside the camp.

12:24 If the vaginal liquids drop upon the robes, the robes must be burned outside of camp.

12:25 If it drops upon the floor, the entire camp must be moved five miles away from that drop of unholy brine.

12:26 She must then beg forgiveness to the lord God for cursing the world with yet another woman and the lord God may forgive her."

13:1 The lord spoke to Aaron and Moses and said to them,

13:2 "The lord curses men randomly for sins of which they have not atoned for. When a curse of God is struck upon a man, they must make atonement for the sin of which the curse is for.

13:3 When a man is cursed of the skin, of a rising scab, or bright spot and it seem to be a disease of leprosy, the man must be brought forth to a priest.

13:4 The priest shall examine the blemish and if the hair of the blemish be white and the plague in sight be deeper than the flesh, the lord has cursed him with leprosy, and the man shall be unclean and an abomination.

13:5 He shall be cast out of the tribe, for the man is filthy and revolting and sickens the lord God and shall sicken the children of Israel.

13:6 If the bright spot be white and deeper not than the flesh and the hair be not white, then the priest shall sew shut his mouth and the man shall be an outcast for seven days.

13:7 Upon the seventh day the priest shall examine the cursed man and if the plague still be there, for seven days more shall the man be outcast.

13:8 And on the second seventh day, the man shall be examined by the priest: and behold, if the blemish darkens and the plague spreads not in the skin, the priest shall announce him clean.

13:9 For it is now nothing but a scab and the man shall wash his clothes and be clean and welcomed back to the children of Israel and the arms of the lord.

13:10 But if the scab does spread and worsens, the man shall return to the priest and the priest shall examine him once more.

13:11 And if the priest witness that the scab spreads in the skin, the priest shall announce him unclean, for it is leprosy and the man shall be cast out of Israel and lose favour in the sight of the lord.

13:12 When the plague of leprosy strikes a child of Israel, they shall be brought forth to the priest.

13:13 And behold, if the rising be white in the skin and the hair turned white and there be a raw flesh rising from the wound,

13:14 It is an old leprosy and the priest shall announce him unclean and shall cast him out of the nation of Israel, for the lord has cursed him unclean.

13:15 If leprosy breaks out upon all the skin and the leprosy covers all of the man, from head to foot and wherever the priest gazes upon,

13:16 The priest shall consider what he sees and if all the sores be white, the man is clean.

13:17 But if raw flesh breaks out upon the man, he is unclean and shall be an outcast in the eyes of God.

13:18 If the raw flesh turns white and the plague turns white and the raw flesh be gone, the man shall come back to the priest.

13:19 The priest shall examine him and if no raw flesh be seen and it be naught but white, the man is healed by God.

13:20 Where the raw flesh be shall now be a boil and is healed.

13:21 If the boil grows and a white rising comes, or a bright spot, white and somewhat reddish, it must be showed to the priests of Israel.

13:22 If the priests see that it be lower than the skin and the hair of the boil be white, the priest shall pronounce him unclean, for the lord has cursed him with leprosy.

13:23 But if the priest gaze upon it and the hair be not white and it be not lower than the skin, but somewhat dark, the man shall be put in solitude for seven days.

13:24 If within the seven days the boil spreads, then the priest shall announce him unclean, for it is a plague.

13:25 But if the bright spot stays in place, the priest shall announce him clean: it is a mere boil, a blemish, a pimple.

13:26 Or if there be a spot in the flesh where there is a hot burning and the burning spot have a bright white spot, somewhat reddish upon or white;

13:27 The priest shall look upon it and if the hairs be white and the burning be deeper than the skin, it is a cursed plague of leprosy and the man has been struck unclean.

13:28 But if the priest stare upon it and the hairs be not white and it be no lower than the skin, the priest shall cast him out of the tribes for seven days.

13:29 Upon the seventh day the man shall return and if the burn has spread upon the man, it is leprosy and the man is unclean.

13:30 If the spot has not spread upon the man and stays in the place, this shall be a mere inflammation and the man shall be pronounced clean.

13:31 If a man has a plague of the head or of the beard;

13:32 The priest shall gaze upon this and if it be in sight deeper than the skin and there be in it a yellow thin hair or more, the priest shall announce him unclean, for it is a plague of leprosy, a dry scall leprosy upon the head or the beard.

13:33 And if the priest gaze upon the plague and witness it be not deeper than the skin and sees no yellow hair, the priest shall put the man in solitude for seven days.

13:34 Upon the seventh day if the scall spreads not and there he no yellow hair and it be not deeper than the skin,

13:35 The hair shall be shaven, but not the scall and the priest shall keep him in solitude for seven days more.

13:36 And on the second seventh day, if the scall spreads not and be not deeper than the skin and there be no yellow hairs, the priest shall announce him clean.

13:37 The man shall wash his clothes and be clean.

13:38 But if the scall spread upon the man after his cleansing,

13:39 Then the man shall be brought back to the priest and if the priest see that the disease thus spread, he shall not bother seeking for a yellow hair, for the man is unclean and shall be cast out of the children of Israel.

13:40 If a man has upon their skins bright spots, white spots;

13:41 Then the priest shall see this and if the spots be a darkish white, it is nothing but a mere freckle and the priest shall announce him clean.

13:42 Goofy looking and ugly, but clean.

13:43 If a man has sores upon their genitals, red and sore, they shall be examined by the priest.

13:44 The man is clean, but must list the last five women he has lied with.

13:45 The women shall be examined and if the sores appear upon their genitals, they have herpes and are unclean.

13:46 Their vaginas shall be doused in oil and burned and they shall be cast out of the nation of Israel and are filthy whores.

13:47 If none of the women have sores upon them, they shall be all killed and their bodies burned and their ashes buried outside of camp.

13:48 For the lord declares them witches; a curse upon man.

13:49 If a man loses his hair upon his head, but there be not a blemish, he is clean.

13:50 The man is just a bald fucker.

13:51 And if the hair falls off the front of his head towards his face, he is clean.

13:52 He is just a partially bald fucker.

13:53 But if where the hair falls out a blemish occurs and it be a white reddish sore, it is a leprosy that has sprung to his head.

13:54 The priest must bear witness to this and if the sore be white reddish, as the leprosy that appears of the flesh;

13:55 Then he is a leprous man and the priest shall pronounce him

utterly unclean and cast him out of the nation of Israel.

13:56 Those cursed with the plague of leprosy shall wear rags and keep bare their head and pronounce themselves unclean, unclean.

13:57 All the days of their life must they do this, for they be defiled and shall dwell alone.

13:58 The garment of the lepers, whether it be a woollen garment, a garment of linen, shall be unclean and not be touched by those who are clean.

13:59 If a blemish appears in clothing, whether woollen, linen or leather, it shall be shown to the priest.

13:60 And if the blemish be greenish or reddish in the garment, it is a leprosy.

13:61 For even clothing shall be cursed by the lord with leprosy.

13:62 Of those whom the clothes belong shall be outcast for seven days with the cursed garment

13:63 And if the blemish spreads upon the garment of the cursed, the man is unclean.

13:64 The garment shall be burned outside of camp, its ashes put in wine and drunk by the youngest priest.

13:65 If the blemish spreads not upon the garment, the man is clean and needs to do his laundry more often.

13:66 And if the ones cursed by God question why, and admit not the sins which have caused them the leprosy, or if they be a good man and known not to sin.

13:67 Then the curse shall be upon them shall be the sins of their fathers.

13:68 For the lord God shall punish the offspring of sinners, because the lord is a cruel bastard and will make those suffer when they deserve not to for the sins their relatives have caused."

14:1 The lord rambled on and bored Moses, saying,

14:2 "When the leper is forgiven by the lord and thus cleansed of the plague, these be the laws of leper cleansing.

14:3 The priest shall go forth and bear witness the leper and confirm the leper be healed of leprosy.

14:4 The leper shall bring to the priest two birds, alive and clean and cedar wood and scarlet and hyssop.

14:5 Over running water, one of the birds shall be killed, it's head torn from the neck of the bird,

14:6 And the living bird shall he take and the cedar and scarlet and hyssop and they shall be dipped in the blood of the dead bird, as the lord loves blood.

14:7 The blood of the dead bird shall be sprayed upon the leper seven times and thus be pronounced clean and the living bird shall be set free.

14:8 For seven days the leper shall be in solitude, confined to his own tent.

14:9 Upon the eighth day the leper shall come out and shave his hair, his eyebrows, his beard, legs, genitals; all hair upon the leper shall be shaved,

14:10 And he shall wash his skin with water and his clothes.

14:11 On the eighth day he shall bring two lambs without blemish and one ewe lamb of the first year without blemish and three tenths deal of finest flour mixed with oil and one vessel of oil.

14:12 He shall bring these offerings to the door of the tabernacle of the congregation.

14:13 The priest shall take the vessel of oil and the lamb and pour the oil upon the lamb.

14:14 He shall then set fire upon the lamb, alive and wave the living, burning lamb in the air for a wave offering unto the lord.

14:15 As the lamb burns, the priest shall be protected by the lord God and when the wave offering is done the priest shall put the lamb upon the altar.

14:16 And the lord shall witness the burning lamb and be amused, for the lord believes not in the ethical treatment of animals.

14:17 The lord takes pleasure in cruelty of all beasts.

14:18 The priest shall take the ash of the lamb, as the ash be most holy and put it upon the tip of the right ear of the cleansed leper and the right thumb and the right foot and bless him.

14:19 The priest then shall take the holy oil and pour it upon his left palm.

14:20 With the oiled hand, the priest shall grab the cleansed leper by his loins and massage him seven times, so that the lepers remaining unclean seed be removed from him.

14:21 When this be done, the priest shall take the flour and the remaining lamb and slay the lamb and spread its blood upon the altar seven times.

14:22 The flour shall be stuffed in the belly of the lamb and both lamb and flour shall be burnt upon the altar, for it is most holy.

14:23 If the cleansed leper be poor, the leper shall bring to the priest one lamb for the wave offering and one tenth of fine flour and a turtledove and a pigeon.

14:24 He shall bring them to the priest upon the eighth day of cleansing.

14:25 The priest shall take the lamb and tear its limbs from it and wave the legs as an offering for the lord and burn the torso upon the altar.

14:26 He shall take the legs from the front of the lamb and with the bloody end shall beat upon the cleansed leper seven times.

14:27 The priest shall then take the oil and place it upon his left palm.

14:28 With is oiled hand, he shall massage the loins of the leper seven times, so that the unclean seed spills out of the cleansed leper.

14:29 The leper and the priest shall take the two birds, the priest the dove and the leper the pigeon and shall bite the heads off of the fowl.

14:30 With blood dripping from the neck, they shall fill their mouths with blood and spit it upon each other's mouths, being careful not to swallow any of the blood.

14:31 For blood is life and belongs only to God.

14:32 Seven times shall they spit the blood of the fowl and on the eighth time, they shall spit the blood upon the altar and burn the decapitated fowl.

14:33 If the leper be so poor that they cannot even bring these, the priest shall kill the leper.

14:34 Fuck poor people, says the lord.

14:35 These shall be the laws of leprosy, for when the lord forgives a leper and cleanse him of the plague."

14:36 Still the lord spoke and said to Moses,

14:37 "The land of Canaan I shall give unto you, and I shall curse the Canaanites with a great plague of leprosy for living upon your land before you get there.

14:38 For this, the plague of leprosy shall be in their houses and must be cleansed by the priests before any of the children of Israel dwell in them.

14:39 The priest shall come to the house and behold, if the plague of leprosy curses the walls with hollow strikes, greenish or reddish, which in sight are lower than the wall.

14:40 The priest shall condemn the house for seven days and none shall enter.

14:41 Upon the eighth day, the priest shall return and if the plague spread across the house,

14:42 People of Israel shall take the foundation of the house, the rocks, the wood and all that make the house and remove it one by one and burn it outside the city, burying the ashes in a safe place.

14:43 And if the plague has not spread upon the house, then the priest shall take two turtledoves, two pigeons, a ram without blemish, a scarlet cloth and a Canaanite virgin, female.

14:44 The turtledoves shall be severed upon stakes of shittim wood, one for each bird and the blood of the turtledoves shall be spread upon the floor of the house.

14:45 The priest shall take the two pigeons and kill them and drip their blood upon an earthen vessel.

14:46 Then the priest shall take the cloth of scarlet and dip it within the blood and spread the blood upon the walls of the house, so that not a bit be uncovered.

14:47 A ram shall be taken to the roof of the house and tied down and shall be beaten until death, so that the blood splatter upon the roof, thus cleansing it.

14:48 The Canaanite virgin shall be taken into the house and the priest shall gather all the blood within and upon the house and put it within an earthen vessel.

14:49 The blood collected shall be poured inside the unholy cunt of the Canaanite virgin, cursing her with the leprosy of the house.

14:50 The Canaanite shall then be cast out into the wilderness, forever cursed with the plague of God.

14:51 These are the laws of leprosy."

15:1 The lord would not shut up and said to Aaron and Moses,

15:2 "If a man has a problem of masturbation and spills his seed willingly with his hands, he is unclean.

15:3 For men should have little reason for self-sexual gratification, as there be plenty of women for that purpose.

15:4 The slit which be upon the crotch pit is meant to pleasure men and men shall use them when the women is not unclean.

15:5 So when a man masturbates, he is pathetic and unclean.

15:6 The bed which he lies upon shall be unclean and his sheets must be washed and his clothes cleaned and his hands sanitized.

15:7 For if the man washes not his hands, a great beastly hair shall grow upon them, so that all shall know he is a filthy masturbator; that he uses his fist for a woman's purpose.

15:8 If a man masturbates in the presence of a woman, both man and woman shall be unclean.

15:9 The man shall wash whatever linen, furniture or vessel his seed spill upon and shall wash his clothes and his hands.

15:10 The woman shall be unclean for not indulging the man in his sexual gratification and as punishment must perform blowjobs for seven days; through this she shall learn humility and that a woman's purpose is to please men.

15:11 If a man have a dream and that dream be erotic, this man is clean.

15:12 For all men have dreams of woman and this is fine.

15:13 But if the man have a dream and that dream be erotic, but contain no women,

15:14 Then this man is unclean and must go to a priest and tell him of the dream.

15:15 When the priest hears of the dream, he shall send this man to a brothel and for seven days he shall stay in the brothel.

15:16 The concubines and whores shall pleasure this man in the name of the lord.

15:17 And if this man have a dream again and it be erotic and contain no women,

15:18 Then he is truly unclean and shall be cast out of the nation of Israel and shall be in disfavour in the eyes of the lord.

15:19 If a man have a dream and it be erotic, but he wakes up and behold, his seed escaped him.

15:20 Then he shall be unclean and shall wash his linens and his clothes and shall shave the hair which grow upon his genitals.

15:21 He shall go to the priest and tell him this dream, every detail.

15:22 The priest shall declare him unclean and for seven days the man shall stay in isolation, away from men, women and child.

15:23 Upon the eighth day, he shall go and find himself a concubine, a woman most fair.

15:24 He shall lie with her that night and his seed shall go into her belly.

15:25 After this holy fornication, the man shall be declared clean and shall enter into the community of Israel.

15:26 If he has yet another dream and it be erotic and he awake with his seed upon his bed, then he is unclean.

15:27 He shall go to a brothel and the women shall bathe him thoroughly, so that every bit of skin be scrubbed.

15:28 They shall then take of his seed and put it within their mouths and swallow and they shall learn to like it.

15:29 If still the man have a dream and it be erotic, for fucks sakes the man is unclean and shall be cast out of the nation of Israel.

15:30 Let him spill his seed in the wild; for the lord wishes not the seed of man be spilled in a civilized nation by a man dreaming of tits, of ass, of pussy.

15:31 If a man come inside a woman in her uncleanliness, this man shall be unholy and unclean.

15:32 For seven days he shall be unclean and shall wallow in the filth of menstruation.

15:33 For seven days he shall be isolated, lest his uncleanliness ruin the tabernacle of the lord and the children of Israel.

15:34 Upon the eighth day he shall bring to the priest a lamb, a male without blemish.

15:35 The priest shall take the lamb and slaughter it and seven times shall spray the blood upon the man who lied with an unclean woman.

15:36 The priest shall cut off the lamb's genitals and seven times shall slap the man in his face with the loins of the lamb.

15:37 Thrice upon the left cheek, thrice upon the right cheek and once upon the nose.

15:38 The genitals shall be thrust upon a stake of shittim wood and roasted over fire.

15:39 When cooked, the woman of which the man has lied with shall eat of the lamb's loins, outside of the tabernacle, away from the places most holy.

15:40 The fat of the lamb shall be removed and the inwards and the caul above the liver and they shall be burnt upon the altar, for it is most holy.

15:41 The flesh of the lamb shall be washed with water and shall be burned upon the altar, for it is holy in the eyes of the lord.

15:42 The man shall then be announced clean and welcomed back to the lord with open arms.

15:43 But of the woman which defiled the man, she shall be cast out of the children of Israel, for she should not be in a civilized place when the vaginal curse of the lord be upon her.

15:44 She is a danger to the men of Israel; one who may contaminate men with her menstruation and shall make the holiest of places unholy if she goes near them whilst her vagina puss flows from her.

15:45 For the lord hates the females and shall not tolerate disobedience from any woman."

16:1 The lord was still angry that the two sons of Aaron offered strange fire before his dwelling and spoke unto Moses,

16:2 "Tell your brother Aaron that he shall not always enter upon the most holy place within the veil of the throne of God, which be upon the ark; for if he enters at the wrong time, I shall strike him dead.

16:3 For the lord remembers Nadab and Abihu and the strange fire they brought before me and am still angry with them.

16:4 Aaron, the father of them, should have raised them better, therefore I shall punish him with the risk of death.

16:5 When a cloud appears upon the throne of the lord, it is I who hide behind the cloud, and I shall demand an offering.

16:6 Aaron shall come into the holy place, but not of the room where the throne lies and shall bring with him a young bullock for a sin offering and a ram for burnt offering.

16:7 He shall have on him the holy linen coat, the breeches shall be upon his flesh, the fine scarlet thong shall carry his loins and he shall wear the holy linen girdle; wash his flesh he shall before and then put on the holy garments of the lord.

16:8 He shall go out into the congregation of the children of Israel and they shall offer him offerings for the lord; a ram for a burnt offering and two kid goats for a sin offering, without blemish.

16:9 Aaron shall offer the bullock as a sin offering to the lord, as this bullock shall be for the sins of Aaron and for the sins of his sons Nadab and Abihu, which the lord still has forgiven not.

16:10 He shall lay his hands upon the head of the bullock and shall confess his sins upon the beast and the sins of his sons.

16:11 Then he shall slay the bullock and offer it unto God as a sin offering.

16:12 He shall take of the two goats and present them to the lord at the door of the tabernacle of the congregation.

16:13 In the name of the lord most holy, Aaron shall cast curses upon the two goats; one curse shall be for God, one shall be the curse of the scapegoat.

16:14 The goat with the curse for God shall be presented before me and shall be slaughtered and shall be used for sin offering.

16:15 The goat cursed with scapegoat shall be presented to the lord alive and the lord shall take of the live goat and release the carnal pleasures of God upon the rectum of the goat.

16:16 When the lord is done, which will be not long, the goat shall be offered to Aaron and Aaron shall release it upon the wild.

16:17 So that the lord may watch the goat starve and suffer and shiver and be shredded and consumed by predators; for the lord wishes not the goat to tell others of what the lord did to him.

16:18 For if the goat talked and said of the love God has given upon him, the other goats shall be jealous and demand the lord give love to them.

16:19 And the lord has not the stamina to love a flock of goats.

16:20 When the scapegoat leaves, Aaron shall bring the bullock of the sin offering and shall make atonement again for himself and for his house and shall kill the bullock for a sin offering.

16:21 He shall take a censer of burning coals and ash of the offering from the fire of the altar and shall pour atop of it sweet incense, so that the aroma be pleasing to the lord.

16:22 Take he shall a sharp stick of shittim wood and dip it within the hot coals and incense and he shall poke both his eyes, so that he be blind before God.

16:23 Blind, Aaron shall enter the throne room of the lord, where the cloud of the lord be and shall present to him the incense and the coals.

16:24 Aaron shall then take the blood of the bullock and seven times he shall spread it upon the mercy seat, the throne of God.

16:25 He shall then kill the goat of the sin offering, which be for the children of Israel and shall take a vial and fill it with the blood of the goat.

16:26 With the vial he shall seven times spray the blood of the goat upon the throne of God, staining the wood and the linens and pleasing the lord.

16:27 Aaron shall make atonement for the sins of the nation of Israel for their uncleanliness; and shall make atonement for the tabernacle of the congregation, which is stained with the uncleanliness of the children of Israel.

16:28 None other than Aaron shall be in the holy places; no other man shall be within the property of the holy places within the tabernacle, until Aaron come out and has made atonement for himself, atonement for his house and atonement for the nation of Israel.

16:29 When he leaves and the lord be pleased with the dedication and offerings Aaron has made, his eyes shall be healed and Aaron shall see.

16:30 He shall go unto the altar that is before the lord and make atonement for it, and shall take the blood of the bullock and the blood of the goat and with it stain the horns of the altar.

16:31 With his fist he shall sprinkle blood upon it seven times and cleanse it and hallow it of the uncleanliness of the children of Israel.

16:32 When he be done, he shall take of the scapegoat and shall place his hands upon it and shall confess the sins of the nation of Israel.

16:33 The lord shall take of the scapegoat and shall fulfill sexual desires with the rump of the goat and when done shall cast it out upon the wilderness.

16:34 When the carnal desires of the lord be fulfilled and the goat wanders the wild, Aaron shall take off his holy garments and shall leave them in a place most holy.

16:35 He shall wash his flesh thoroughly with water, in the presence of God and come forth and naked he shall offer his sin offering of himself and the sin offering of the people and make atonement.

16:36 And the fat of the sin offerings shall be burnt upon the altar.

16:37 The bullocks and the goat which be offered for the sin offerings and whose blood stain the throne of God, shall one carry away from camp and they shall burn their flesh and their skins and their dung.

16:38 And he who carry the carcass of the bullock and the goat shall wash their clothes and bathe their flesh and shall then be allowed to enter back into the nation of Israel.

16:39 This shall be a statute unto you, that upon the seventh month, on the tenth day of the month, you shall punish your souls and all shall stay within your tents and beat yourselves with whips.

16:40 Whether it be one of Israel or a stranger dwelling within, they shall remain isolated and whip themselves, until the flesh of the back be raw and bleeding.

16:41 For on that day the priest shall make atonement for you and cleanse you of the sins you have beaten out of your souls.

16:42 It shall be a statute unto you and shall afflict your souls and be most holy.

16:43 Upon this day, the priest shall wear the most holy of linens, most holy of garments and shall cleanse the nation of Israel as they whip themselves and shall cleanse the most holiest of places, as they be stained with the uncleanliness of the children of Israel.

16:44 This shall be an everlasting statute unto the children of Israel, forever and ever, to make atonement for the sins of the souls once a year and it shall be most holy."

17:1 Moses was sleeping soundly when the lord woke him up.

17:2 Moses was tired and annoyed that the lord would disturb him at 3:00AM, but wishing not to offend the lord God, listened to what he had to say.

17:3 "Go to Aaron and to the priests and to the children of Israel and say unto them that which the lord commanded.

17:4 Whosoever slays a lamb, or a goat, or a ram, or a bullock, whether it be in the camp or without and kills as a sacrifice, but bring it not unto the priest nor unto the door of the tabernacle of the congregation,

17:5 Blood shall be upon this man, for one cannot offer offerings unto the lord, but only priests and only within the holy place.

17:6 He that makes an offering without the priest, away from a place most holy, is a blasphemer and shall be cast out of the nation of Israel and shall be stoned to death.

17:7 Those that wish to offer their sacrifices upon an open field may only slay of the animal.

17:8 The carcass of the beast must be carried to the holy place, so that the priest may perform the ritual of the sacrifice.

17:9 So that the blood be sprinkled and the fat burned and the aroma create a pleasing scent to the lord.

17:10 Never shall one offer sacrifices to devils; to false gods, even if they once be believers of these devils and false gods.

17:11 If they were once whores to these devils and false gods, but have seen my truth and accepted me, their past shall be forgiven.

17:12 But if they still offer sacrifices and whore themselves to heathen beliefs, they shall be deemed blasphemers and unclean,

17:13 And the children of Israel shall gather and stone them to death.

17:14 If one of the children of Israel witness a stranger offer sacrifice to devils, to false gods,

17:15 It matter not if they be in a strange land; matter not if the person has accepted the true lord.

17:16 They shall gather their brethren and stone him.

17:17 For the lord shall not tolerate sacrifices to others; sacrifices must only be made to the lord of Israel.

17:18 Whatsoever man be of the nation of Israel, or a stranger and they eat blood, the lord shall curse them eternally.

17:19 The lord shall come to them and shall set my face against the soul that consumes the blood and curse them.

17:20 For blood is life and life belongs only to the lord: it is the blood which be sprinkled, the blood which burns upon the altars, that make atonement for the sins of your souls.

17:21 Therefore none shall consume of the blood, lest they be cursed eternal by the lord.

17:22 If one bear witness to a child of Israel consuming the blood, the liquid of life, cast them out, for they shall be cursed by God and are unclean; they be more wretched, more filthy than lepers.

17:23 If a stranger be seen consuming blood, the liquid of life, the children of Israel shall avoid them, for the lord shall curse them unclean.

17:24 Those that consume the blood shall be burnt by the sun; they shall be predators of the night, ugly and most foul and shall be cursed with blood.

17:25 For blood shall they only consume; they shall be cursed to feed upon the life of others.

17:26 When you prepare an animal so that you may consume its flesh, the blood must be drained, so that naught a drop remains.

17:27 The blood shall spill upon the floor and be covered with dust.

17:28 For blood is the life of all things. Those that consume of the life is unholy and shall be forever cursed for stealing that which belongs to God.

17:29 Those that consume a creature which die naturally; which not be slain nor butchered, shall be unclean.

17:30 Whether a child of Israel or a stranger, they shall be unclean.

17:31 They shall wash their hands and bathe themselves and clean their clothes and shall be unclean until midnight of the day.

17:32 When past midnight, they shall be clean and welcome back to the arms of the lord.

17:33 But if they do this not, they shall bear their curse and be cast out of the nation of Israel and shall be wretched in the eyes of the lord."

18:1 Is it really necessary that I tell you the lord spoke unto Moses?

18:2 The majority of these chapters start with 'the lord spoke with Moses, the lord comes unto Moses, and said, etc.'

18:3 Here is what the divine dictator said this time.

18:4 "Remind the children of Israel that I am the one true God, creator of heaven and earth and of all things.

18:5 Remind them that it is I who delivered them from the servitude of Pharaoh and shall bring them to the land of Canaan, flowing with milk and honey.

18:6 You shall do as the lord commands and keep your statutes and obey your laws and thou shalt not be tempted by the heresy and the blasphemy of the Canaanites.

18:7 For I am the one true God.

18:8 None of you shall go and lie near to your kin and uncover their nakedness, for the lord God demands a healthy gene pool.

18:9 It matters not the beauty of your mother, nor the beauty of your father, for the lord demands you not fuck them.

18:10 Do not even see them naked, for nakedness may bring temptation and temptation brings sin.

18:11 You shall not uncover the nakedness of your father's wives, even if they be not your mother, for that is a nakedness that belongs to him.

18:12 He owns his wives and only he may take pleasure of them and not his sons nor daughters.

18:13 You shall not take of lustful pleasures of your sisters, whether they be born of a different father, or a different mother, or if she be born at home or abroad.

18:14 For the lord say, seriously, she's your sister.

18:15 It matters not how hot she is, don't fornicate with your sister.

18:16 Do not peek upon the bathhouse whilst she bathes, lest you be marked a pervert.

18:17 You shall not have sex with the children of your sister, nor the children of your brother.

18:18 I know the temptation of young flesh may be strong upon you, but you shall not be known as the uncle who gives his erection unto them.

18:19 If your father marries a woman and that woman have a daughter, you shall not take act of sexual desires of her.

18:20 It's just, weird. Don't do it.

18:21 If you were taking of her lust before the marriage of her mother and your father, you must cease immediately.

18:22 And if before the marriage of your father and her mother, she bears your seed, you shall beat it out of her after the wedding.

18:23 Do this, so that the lord shall not be reminded of your fornication of your step sister.

18:24 You shall not uncover the nakedness of your father's sister, for she is your aunt.

18:25 You shall not uncover the nakedness of your mother's sister, for she is your aunt.

18:26 Jebusites and Hittites do these acts and the lord hates them for it and other reasons.

18:27 They be slack jawed yokels, who live in cheap tents that consistently get damaged by strong gusts of wind.

18:28 You shall not give sexual gratification to your father's brother, nor your mother's brother.

18:29 Unless ye be a female, then it is your divine duty to please men by whatever means they desire.

18:30 So drop your skirt and let them plunge into you, as long as you be free of your menstrual uncleanliness.

18:31 You shalt not fuck your daughter in law. She is your son's wife and belongs to him.

18:32 The lord knows the temptation of young flesh is strong in you, so the lord allows you to marry another young woman.

18:33 But leave your daughter in law to your son, so that he and only he may partake of carnal desires with her.

18:34 You shall not have sex with both a mother and her daughter, nor two sisters, for such is an abomination to the lord.

18:35 Such acts may be seen as accomplishment, but the lord assures you it be a curse.

18:36 For one woman shall grow jealous of the other and it shall cause strife within the house.

18:37 Instead, hire a concubine, or take another wife, so that the two may lie together and you may take both of their sexual desires.

18:38 The lord will watch this and bless you, for though woman be revolting, the lord takes pride when a man dominates over two at once.

18:39 And the lord shall masturbate and spread his holy seed upon your house and bless you.

18:40 Never, ever, fuck a woman while her cunt bleeds.

18:41 For her bleeding vagina is a curse upon God since the times of Eve and if you uncover that curse, you shall be unclean and that curse be upon you.

18:42 You shalt stone that woman, for the lord demands all menstruating women be cast out of the nation of Israel while the curse be upon them.

18:43 You shall not lie naked with your neighbours wife, unless you pay him well.

18:44 You shall never let your seed pass to the demon's womb. You shall pull out before then, lest your seed conceive the offspring of the devils.

18:45 Men shall not have sex with other men, for the lord God find it revolting.

18:46 Women were placed upon this earth to please and care for a man's sexual desires and if a woman be not good enough for you that you must take your lust upon a man, then you are a faggot in the eyes of God and you shall be cursed.

18:47 For a man have not a vagina, the sexual bliss for men. Men have upon them a rectum and if you like the feel of the rectum better, fuck a woman up her ass.

18:48 Do not fuck a man, for a man's buttocks is exit only.

18:49 You shall not lie with beasts, for the lord God find it confusing.

18:50 The lord looks down and wonders if perhaps the woman be hairy, or extremely fat, or ugly and is confused why such a man would have sex with an ugly woman.

18:51 Woman may not have sex with beasts, for women are meant not to pleasure animals, just men.

18:52 You shall not defile yourselves with any of these things, lest the lord God curse you.

18:53 Those that partake of these lustful sins shall be vomited out from the land and cast into the sky and left to die.

18:54 You shall keep my statutes, obey my laws and not commit these abominations of the lord, for the inhabitants of the land prior have committed these abominations and the land is defiled.

18:55 And the land is angry and shall vomit you from its land when you commit these sins.

18:56 For I am the lord God almighty. Worship me."

19:1 Yep, God disturbed Moses again and said to him,

19:2 "Speak unto the children of Israel and tell them they be holy, for I the lord God be holy.

19:3 Every man shall fear their mother, for she has brought them into this world and she can take them out.

19:4 Every man shall fear their father, for his wrath can kill them.

19:5 Keep my sabbaths and remember it holy, for I am the lord God and I demand it of you.

19:6 Fear me, for the wrath I cast upon the unworthy is terrible and cruel and you wish not to have it.

19:7 Do not turn or worship idols, or make gods of molten stones and metals, for I am the one true God and you cannot capture my good looks with sculpture.

19:8 When you offer a sacrifice of peace offerings to the lord, let it be of your own will.

19:9 It shall be consumed upon the day of sacrifice and on the morrow: and if it remains upon the third day, it shall be burned.

19:10 For upon the third day it be eaten, it shall be an abomination to God and you shall be cut out from your people.

19:11 When you reap the harvest of your lands, you shall leave behind the gleanings, the leftovers and the rotten foods.

19:12 And when you gather grapes for the winepress, you shall leave behind the bad grapes, the sour grapes.

19:13 This you shall do so that the poor, the hungry and the strangers may eat upon your leftover crops.

19:14 For the lord God is a merciful God and wishes not the starving and the poor to suffer.

19:15 The lord God also finds entertainment in the wretched and the beggars eating foods fit only for rats, for crows and for scavengers.

19:16 For that what they be, rodents and scavengers and unclean.

19:17 You shall not steal, nor deal falsely, nor lie to one another.

19:18 For the children of Israel must unite and stay together if they are to defeat the heathens and take from them their land.

19:19 You shall steal, deal falsely and lie to the heathens, for they are not people and worship idols and false gods.

19:20 But you shall not steal, nor deal falsely, nor lie to one another, lest the children of Israel grow apart and weaken.

19:21 Do not use the lord God's name in vain, nor profane the word of God.

19:22 For I am the lord fucking God and shall curse you if ye use my goddamn name profanely, you god forsaken bastard children of unholy cuntless whores.

19:23 You shall not defraud your neighbour, nor rob him of wages he has earned from you.

19:24 Save it for the people not born of Israel.

19:25 Never shall you curse the deaf, nor trip the blind, lest you feel the wrath of God.

19:26 For the lord God find it funny when the blind trip naturally and when the deaf are confused in conversation.

19:27 When it is staged, it is ruined and the lord God shall know and be furious and curse you.

19:28 You shall do no unrighteousness in judgment, nor accept bribes, but you shall judge honestly in the name of the lord.

19:29 You shall not gossip and spread false rumours, for to do so is unholy.

19:30 If you hear a tale, or witness someone do something, confirm it and find it true before you spread its tale amongst the people of Israel.

19:31 For the lord God loathe false gossip, but a juicy story of a fellow neighbour, if that story be true, is pleasing to the lord.

19:32 When you spread the true story, you shall do it in the house of the lord, the tabernacle, for all the people there shall gather.

19:33 Spread the true gossip after the priest's ceremony, so that all shall know.

19:34 You shall not hate your brother in your heart, for hatred is a strong emotion reserved only for the lord.

19:35 The lord hates Esau and his house, the people of Canaan, the Hittites, the Jebusites and all those who do not worship him.

19:36 When you claim to hate your neighbour, the lord shall grow furious and hate you and you shall know the true wrath of someone who be hated.

19:37 You shall love thy neighbour as you love yourself, unless you have low self-esteem. Then you shall love your neighbour better than yourself, dumb-ass.

19:38 You shall not let your cattle breed with a diverse kind, lest the offspring be blemished and unfit for sacrifice.

19:39 You shall not sow your fields with mingled seed, for the lord shall poison the soil if you do.

19:40 You shall wear not a cloth of mingled garments, for the lord God is a fashionable God and mixed wools and linen is cheap and unfit to wear.

19:41 When a man lies with a slave woman and that slave woman be engaged to another, the slave woman is unclean and a harlot and shall be stoned to death.

19:42 It matters not if the woman consented, or was raped; kill her. Brutally.

19:43 The man shall bring a ram without blemish as a trespass offering to the lord and the lord shall forgive him for being seduced by the harlot.

19:44 For the man is without blame when the woman is raped; she shouldn't look so damn tempting.

19:45 When you come to claim the land promised to ye since the days of Abraham, there shall be a great many trees and plants bearing foods.

19:46 These plants have been tainted by the unclean and shall be deemed uncircumcised and unholy for three years and you shall not eat of its bounty.

19:47 Upon the fourth year, they shall be harvested and given as a sacrifice to the lord.

19:48 On the fifth year, it shall be consumed by the children of Israel and it shall be clean.

19:49 None shall ever consume the blood of anything, for blood is life and life belongs to the lord.

19:50 Neither shall you use enchantments, witchcraft or wizardry, for such things is an abomination to God.

19:51 You shall not look upon the stars of the night and make use of astrology.

19:52 For astrology is witchcraft and wicked.

19:53 Men shall not round the corners of their heads, nor mar the corners of their beard, for the lord God find it unfashionable and silly looking.

19:54 You shall not make cuttings upon your flesh, nor mark them with piercings or inks.

19:55 Tattoos are stupid, cutting your flesh is emo and piercings are for marking slaves, according to the word of Exodus.

19:56 You shall not force your daughter into whoredom, lest the whole nation of Israel be full of harlots and prostitutes.

19:57 If your daughter desire to be a prostitute, let her, for in her profession she shall please the carnal desires of men and fulfill the role of females upon the earth.

19:58 You shall pimp her to men of Israel and take a portion of her profits, but only if this be what she desires.

19:59 For a woman forced into whoredom shall not truly please men; she shall merely lie there as they thrust upon her; her fellatio shall be dull and the men will not truly be pleased.

19:60 Remember the seventh day as the sabbath and keep it holy.

19:61 For six days the lord worked, but upon the seventh he rested and so shall you.

19:62 Lest you make the lord look lazy and anger me and feel the wrath of God.

19:63 Ignore those that speak to the souls of the dead and seek not wizards, lest you be defiled by their wickedness.

19:64 Honour the elderly, for they have lived their life and may be used to pass down their wisdom upon the young.

19:65 If a stranger lives upon your land, do not vex him, nor curse him, but treat him with respect.

19:66 The lord shall curse him for you.

19:67 But if that stranger be born within your borders, the lord shall not curse him, for the nation of Israel were once strangers within the land of Egypt and treated fairly.

19:68 Until Pharaoh enslaved you, which you shall do to the strangers.

19:69 Gain their trust, be patient, then force them into servitude.

19:70 That is the way of the lord.

19:71 You shall do no cheating in ways which shall giveth you more money, for the lord is a fair lord and wishes not his tithe be from dirty money.

19:72 That be all the lord demands now. I shall see you tomorrow with more demands."

20:1 As Moses suspected, the lord saw him and demanded more.

20:2 "Go and tell the children of Israel that any Israelite or stranger who resides in the nation of Israel who gives their seed upon the womb of a demon shall be put to death: the people of the land shall gather stones and stone him.

20:3 I will curse that man eternally and his ghost shall wander the earth for eternity and be denied access to the kingdom of heaven.

20:4 For half human half demon children are an abomination to God and shall ruin the earth and haunt the people of the lord.

20:5 If those bear witness to a man fornicating with the demon, but ignore this abomination and not kill the man:

20:6 Then he is a coward and I shall visit this man and cast him out of the nation of Israel, away from his wife and children.

20:7 Those that offer themselves to demons and go whoring after them, shall be cast out of the nation of Israel and raped by God.

20:8 Even those who chase after wizards and necromancers and those who speak with ghosts, shall be cast out of the nation of Israel.

20:9 For such people are unholy and an abomination to God and shall not taint the sanctity of the nation of Israel.

20:10 For you are a holy people, blessed by God.

20:11 As long as you keep my statutes and obey my laws.

20:12 If a child curses the name of their mother or father, that child's blood shall be spilled.

20:13 Children must love their parents and respect them and speak not foully of their names.

20:14 It matters not if it be true; if the child calls their mother a whore when she is a whore, or their father a drunkard when he be a drunkard;

20:15 It matter not of the parents be abusive.

20:16 The child speaks bad of their parents and must be killed.

20:17 Any man that commits adultery with another man's wife, is a greedy, lustful, sexual pervert and both members must be slain.

20:18 The woman and the man shall be burned in unholy fire.

20:19 It matters not if the woman did not consent, for if she be raped, it is her fault for tempting him.

20:20 Whenever a son takes his mother to bed, it is a sin and they shall be put to death.

20:21 Take them to a tree, with strong branches and hang them there.

20:22 Let their bodies hang, so that the crows may feast upon the flesh of the unholy adulterers.

20:23 It matters not if the son raped the mother. The mother is a woman; therefore, she shares blame.

20:24 If a father lies intimately with the wife of his son, both their blood shall be spilled.

20:25 Take them unto the tops of a high cliff and push them off, so that their bodies be broken and crushed upon the rocks beneath.

20:26 If the wife of the son claims innocent and accuse the father of rape, it matters not.

20:27 She shouldn't have been so sexually attractive and tempt the father to rape.

20:28 For women wish men to sin upon them and rape them, for a woman raped is a woman pleasing men and women love to please men.

20:29 Women enjoy rape and secretly tempt men to commit this sin upon them.

20:30 Whenever a woman be raped and claim she did not wish it upon her, she lies. She enjoyed it.

20:31 Such is the way of women.

20:32 If two men come together and lie together and take lust of one another, it is wickedness and an abomination and revolting to the lord.

20:33 Their lives shall be at an end and they shall not know the kingdom of heaven.

20:34 Fill their assholes with boiling oil, so that the orifice of which brought them pleasure shall bring them pain; so that their inwards boil and burn within them.

20:35 If two women lie with one another and it be not for the pleasures of men, it is an abomination, for the women would rather please each other than please men.

20:36 Take two stakes of shittim wood and thrust both into their slits and pry, so that the woman be split apart.

20:37 If a man takes to bed a woman and her mother, it is wickedness.

20:38 For the man shall cause jealousy among the women and cause stress upon the children of Israel.

20:39 Take of the three and burn them upon the campfires.

20:40 When a man takes a beast for carnal desires, it confuses the lord and makes me angry.

20:41 Take the man upon the wild, cut him and let the wild predators feast upon his unholy flesh.

20:42 The animal the man was fucking has been tainted and unclean. Kill it and burn its carcass outside of camp.

20:43 If a woman lies down, so that a beast may take pleasure upon her, it is a sin.

20:44 Take the woman sinned and drown her with sand.

20:45 Burn the animal she wished to fuck, away from camp.

20:46 If a man takes his sister to bed, or his father's daughter, or his mother's daughter, it is a wicked thing.

20:47 Cast them both upon the wilderness, so that they may live as beasts.

20:48 If you lie intimately with your father's sister, or your mother's sister, you will be cursed.

20:49 If you lie intimately with your uncle's wife, you will be cursed.

20:50 If you lie intimately with your brother's wife, you will be cursed.

20:51 The generations of your family shall end with you and ye shall bear no sons.

20:52 If sons you have already, they shall be killed for the sins you commit.

20:53 When you take a woman and uncover her and behold, you have uncovered her uncleanliness; her fountain of blood flows from her, you are both unclean and shall be cast out of the nation of Israel.

20:54 You shall do these things and keep my statutes and obey my laws and I shall bring you to the land of milk and honey.

20:55 For the lord God love all his people and all his creations.

20:56 But the people who reside in the lands you are about to take, they do these things.

20:57 They fornicate with beasts, family and swap sexual partners.

20:58 For this, the lord hates them all and wishes he not created them.

20:59 They were blessed with great lands, rich lands and they live in sin and gluttony and do not even worship me.

20:60 For this disrespect, I shall curse them and bring the people of Israel upon their lands, so that they may dwell within it, with the blessing of the lord.

20:61 For the children of Israel have been holy unto me and never questioned me. For this, I deem you holy and have severed you from the other people of earth, whom I hate.

20:62 The children of Israel belong to me and for this I shall protect them.

20:63 And when you travel and take of the foreign lands, if you see any witches, wizards, or necromancers of these foreigners, kill them.

20:64 Kill them all."

21:1 The lord came to Moses and said to him,

21:2 "The priests are the chosen of the chosen people and shall be a model of the nation of Israel.

21:3 Even of their families they shall be blessed.

21:4 The father, the mother, the brother and the sister of the priest shall be honoured for having such a relative be a priest.

21:5 This they shall take pride in.

21:6 The sister of a priest shall remain celibate and not marry, so that she shall forever remain a virgin.

21:7 For she is a rarity, a holy female and shall not be tainted by the pleasures of flesh.

21:8 If she gives away her virginity, she has brought shame among her brother the priest, she is a whore and shall be forced to work among the brothels and the pimps.

21:9 Priests are a holy man and shall work close with God.

21:10 For this, the lord wishes they be fashionable and not offend the lord.

21:11 A priest shall never take a blade to their hair, nor round the corners of their beard, nor make any cuttings nor marks upon their flesh.

21:12 Never shall they speak ill of the lord, nor curse my name, nor doubt my divinity and my power, lest I curse them.

21:13 For they are true servants of the lord and most holy.

21:14 When a priest marries, they shall take of a virgin wife, pure and untouched by man.

21:15 A harlot, a whore, a divorcee, or a widow shall never know the pleasures of being a wife of a priest, for the lord God shall give unto them virgins, for priests are most holy and shall not be given used goods.

21:16 Priests are most precious to the lord, for they give to me bread and sacrifice and for this I am grateful.

21:17 A daughter of a priest is a rare and beautiful creature, for she is one of the few women who are not unclean, nor hated by God.

21:18 She shall be saved a virgin, so that she may kept holy.

21:19 But if ever she gives her sex to a man, she shall be a whore; an unholy whore and shall be burnt alive with unholy fire, amongst the children of Israel.

21:20 They shall watch this unholy cunt burn and yell and praise the name of the lord.

21:21 The one deemed the high priest, the holiest amongst the holy and is consecrated to put on the most sacred of garments, shall never uncover his head, nor rend his clothes.

21:22 For even his skin be holy and shall be kept secret among the children of Israel.

21:23 Though a priest be holy, their carnal desires shall burn and must be kept under control.

21:24 A priest shall never go inside his mother, nor his father, lest he defile himself.

21:25 And a priest shall never place his erection within a corpse, for necrophilia is unholy among priests.

21:26 If ever a priest doubts the lord, he shall be struck down with the wrath of God and his body shall be burnt outside of camp.

21:27 Neither shall a priest take lust among whores, or harlots, or people outside of the nation of Israel, lest he taint his seed and his house."

21:28 The lord still spoke and said to Moses,

21:29 "I don't like cripples, for they are crippled as a curse from God.

21:30 Any leper is unholy and shall be cast out of the nation of Israel and never allowed access unto the tabernacle, the house of God.

21:31 A blind child of Israel, lame child, or he with a crook nose, or any superfluous malady;

21:32 A man with broken hand or broken foot;

21:33 A crookback, a dwarf, a midget, or one with poor vision, or scabbed or suffer from scurvy, or has impotency and cannot get an erection;

21:34 These are cursed by God and shall not be allowed to give sacrifice, or enter upon holy soil, lest they be cursed more."

21:35 And Moses went out and spoke these to the priests and to the children of Israel.

21:36 And some of the children of Israel were angry.

21:37 For the cripples, the blind, the lame, some were cursed with these during their servitude to Egypt and to Pharaoh.

21:38 They were beaten, they were bruised, their testicles abused with whips and their eyes plucked from their sockets.

21:39 Yet through this, during their servitude, they never lost faith in their lord.

21:40 Now they be told the lord cursed them with these maladies, though they never sinned, never questioned, never doubted the power or will of God?

21:41 They grew angry and wondered why the lord would do this upon them.

21:42 God could hear their anger and grew fearful, for other children of Israel knew of these people, knew of their torments and knew that they never doubted the lord.

21:43 So God killed them all, so that the seeds of revolt and revolution not be sown amongst the people of Israel.

22:1 The lord went upon Moses and said to him,

22:2 "Speak unto the priests of the lord and remind them that they be holy. For this, they shall separate themselves from that which be unholy and not profane the word of God.

22:3 Remind them, that whichever be of their offspring; of their seed, they shall be holy, so that their sons be holy and that their daughters be holy, for women.

22:4 They shall not stain themselves with unholiness, lest they be cast out of the favour of God.

22:5 What generations of priests that be cursed with leprosy, or have a problem with their seed leaking unwillingly, shall be holy and shall not eat of the holy things until they be clean.

22:6 They shall not touch any dead unclean thing, lest the lord curse them permanently unholy, so that they shall never know the embrace of God.

22:7 Whosoever touches a creepy thing, shall be made unclean, or if they examine the leper, they shall be unclean.

22:8 When the priest examines the unclean, they themselves shall be unclean and shall not eat of the holy things, but must wash themselves and their robes and shall be unclean until the sunset.

22:9 When the sun sets, the priest shall be holy again and shall eat of the holy things.

22:10 A beast which die of old age, or be torn by other beasts, shall not be consumed, for they are unclean.

22:11 Those that eat of the beast shall defile themselves and shall be cast out of the nation of Israel.

22:12 Even if a priest, they shall be deemed unholy, and shall lose favour with the lord.

22:13 Remember that priests must keep my ordinance, lest they bear the sin of it and die from their profanity and blasphemy.

22:14 No stranger shall eat of the holy things; even if a guest of a priest, or a hired servant, they shall not eat of the holy things.

22:15 But if the priest buys the soul of a slave, or if the person be born of the priest's house, they shall be allowed to eat of the holy things.

22:16 If the priest's daughter marries a person not of the children of Israel, that daughter has lost favour and she nor her husband shall eat of the holy things.

22:17 However, if the stranger die, so that she be a widow, or she divorced and have not a child tainted with the seed of the stranger, then she shall be allowed back into the house of her father and shall eat of the holy things.

22:18 If a man eats of the holy things, but knows not of what he eats, then he shall pay a fifth above of what he ate and give it unto the priest.

22:19 He must then offer a trespass offering, for he trespassed unto the holy food.

22:20 They knew not of their blasphemy, but must still pay for their unwilling sin.

22:21 For they have profaned the holy things of the lord.

22:22 When they trespass offering has been accepted, the lord may sanctify and forgive them."

22:23 The lord still spoke to Moses and said,

22:24 "Speak unto Aaron, and his sons and all the children of Israel and say unto them that whoever be a child of Israel, or a stranger residing in the nation of Israel, they must give sacrifice unto the lord."

22:25 They shall offer a male without blemish, of the sheep, or of the goats, or of the oxen.

22:26 Whatever hath a blemish will not be accepted, and will offend the lord and the lord shall punish them their iniquity.

22:27 Blind, lame, broken, malnourished, those suffering from scurvy, shall not be offered, for the lord demands a healthy male without blemish for sacrifice.

22:28 Neither shall they be scabbed, nor bruised, nor cut, nor crushed, for the lord shall not accept this sacrifice.

22:29 The lord demands a perfect, healthy sacrifice, for the lord God is a vain God.

22:30 Neither shall the sacrifice come from the herd of a stranger; the sacrifice must belong to those of the children of Israel.

22:31 For that which belong to a stranger is tainted, and unclean and shall not be accepted as a sacrifice.

22:32 Yes, I the lord God, am that vain.

22:33 For even if the sacrifice be healthy and strong and well fed and have upon it no blemish, if it be bought from a stranger it is tainted and the lord God shall not take it.

22:34 When a bullock, or a goat, or a sheep, is brought forth for sacrifice, it must be at least seven days old.

22:25 Upon the eighth day it is ready for sacrifice, but before it is too young, and the lord will find it displeasing and not accept it as sacrifice.

22:26 If you offer a sacrifice of an ewe, or a goat, or an ox and wish to feast upon the flesh of its mother, you shall not.

22:37 Do not kill the mother and the offspring upon the same day, for such things sadden the lord God.

22:38 Kill the mother another day.

22:39 When you offer a sacrifice unto the lord, do so upon your own will. Do not feel as though you are forced to offer the sacrifice.

22:40 Remember, if you don't, the lord shall hate you and bring curses upon your house, but offer the sacrifices because you want to.

22:41 The priests shall eat of the sacrifice on the same day and shall leave none of it for the morrow, for I am the lord God.

22:42 Remember and obey my commandments, for I am the lord.

22:43 Do not profane my name, for I am the lord, and shall be most hallowed among the children of Israel.

22:44 For I the lord have sent you out of the land of Egypt, where you were slaves for the Pharaoh.

22:45 Anger me and I shall send you back."

23:1 The lord spoke to Moses and said,

23:2 "Speak unto the children of Israel and say unto them, concerning the feasts of the lord, they shall be holy convocations, as they are my feasts.

23:3 Six days shall you labour, but upon the seventh you shall rest, for it is the Sabbath, the day the lord rested and it is a most holy day, for it be the weekend.

23:4 These are the feasts of the lord, which shall be holy and proclaimed in their seasons.

23:5 Upon the fourteenth day of the first month is the Passover.

23:6 The fifteenth day, the day after, is the feast of unleavened bread.

23:7 You shall eat unleavened bread, only unleavened bread, for seven days.

23:8 During these seven days, none shall work, for it is a most holy week.

23:9 Remember to bake enough unleavened bread in advance, for even if you bake unleavened bread during the feast, it shall be work.

23:10 And the lord shall cast your soul away from the nation of Israel.

23:11 During the seventh day, the last day of the feast, you shall offer an offering of fire for the lord.

23:12 Gather all the foreskins, removed by circumcision throughout the years and burn it upon the altar, so that it shall create a pleasing aroma unto the lord."

23:13 Still the lord spoke and said to Moses,

23:14 "When the children of Israel conquer the land of milk and honey, the land shall be ripe with fruits and crops and grains, fresh for harvest.

23:15 All shall harvest the foods and take a sheaf of their harvest to the priest for an offering.

23:16 The day after the Sabbath, the priest shall take of the sheaf and present it as a wave offering.

23:17 The priest shall take of it and wave it in the air.

23:18 He shall do this, for the lord God care.

23:19 On this day, he shall offer to the lord a lamb, a male without blemish, of the first year and offer it as burnt offering unto God.

23:20 A food offering shall be offered as well; two tenths deal of fine flour mingled with virgin oil and burnt, so that the aroma create a pleasing scent unto the lord.

23:21 For one hour shall this fire burn, then the flames shall be extinguished with wine; a fine vintage, something red and sweet.

23:22 For the lord God loves alcohol and fine wine and ale and liquor,

23:23 And the best smokable herbs.

23:24 None shall eat of the harvest until they bring to the priest their sheaf offering; it shall be a statute among your generations.

23:25 After the sheaf offerings and the burnt offerings and the wine, you shall wait fifty days, so that seven Sabbaths pass.

23:26 Upon the morning of the seventh Sabbath, a new offering shall be made.

23:27 Every child of Israel shall bring unto God two loaves of bread, made with fine flour and baked with leaven.

23:28 Bring also seven male lambs, free of blemish, born of the first year and a young bullock and two rams and four jugs of strong drink.

23:29 Then you shall sacrifice a young goat as a sin offering and two lambs for a peace offering and dance around them naked, for the lord love blood, nudity and torn flesh.

23:30 The priest shall take of the breads and the lambs and the bullock and the rams and shall slaughter the lambs, the bullock and the rams, so that their blood shall drip upon the loaves of leavened bread.

23:31 Take the strong drink and place it within a bowl and put the bloody loaves within the bowl, so that the loaves shall absorb the strong drink and the blood.

23:32 Take of the soaked loaves and offer it as a wave offering to God and throw them high and mighty in the air.

23:33 This you shall do, as it shall be a statute among your people for generations.

23:34 Remember that when you harvest your fields, your fruits, your grains, to leave the corners of the field, the gleanings, the spoiled and bitter foods behind, so that the poor and hungry may scavenge and feast upon them.

23:35 The lord God shall look upon these human scavengers and laugh, as it is a pleasing sight for the lord."

23:36 Moses thought the lord was finished, but God quickly added more.

23:37 "The lord love music, the blasting noise of trumpets.

23:37 For this, upon the seventh month, the first day of that month, it shall be as a Sabbath and you shall have a memorial, a great blowing of mighty trumpets, in glory of God.

23:38 Upon this day you shall do no work, but an offering better be made, lest you feel the wrath of the lord God upon you.

23:39 Also, upon the tenth day of this month, you shall make a day of atonement and afflict your souls and make offerings of fire unto the lord.

23:40 None shall work upon this day, for it is a day of cleansing your souls of the sins of being human.

23:41 Whatever soul does not afflict themselves and rid themselves of their uncleanliness, shall be cast out of the nation of Israel.

23:42 And those which work upon this day shall be deemed blasphemous, for it is a holy day of atonement and they shall be cast out of the nation of Israel.

23:43 All shall fast, from sunrise to sunset and eat of nothing, nor drink of water, nor juice, nor alcohol, nor milk.

23:44 They shall stay inside their tents and with whips they shall beat their backs, so that the sins of their souls shall be beat out from them.

23:45 It shall be a holy statute among your people for generations.

23:46 None shall offer themselves comfort from the whips, nor offer others comfort from their whippings, for the sins of the soul must be removed through pain.

23:47 Upon the fifteenth day of this month, the seventh month, shall be a feast of the tabernacles; for seven days shall this feast last.

23:48 The first day of this feast shall be as the Sabbath and holy and none shall do work upon this day, lest they anger and feel the wrath of the lord.

23:49 For seven days shall the lord pleasure in his gluttony, for during these seven days the tabernacle shall be busy with sacrifice.

23:50 Sacrifice of the lamb, the ram, the doves, the pigeons, the goats, the bullocks, the children and the virgins,

23:51 So that the fires of the sacrifice burn for seven days and create an intoxicating aroma unto God. Upon the eighth day, all shall rejoice the glory of the lord.

23:52 You shall take the boughs of goodly trees, the branches of palm trees, the boughs of thick trees and the willows and dance with them naked and shall feel the intoxicating love of the lord flow through you.

23:53 Upon the twentieth day of the seventh month shall be the days of solitude.

23:54 Coffins shall be built, one for each member of the nation of Israel, so that they may lie in them, in solitude, for seven days of self-reflection.

23:55 This you shall do for humility, to remind oneself that the lord has allowed you to be in the servitude, to live in coffins, during Pharaoh's reign over you.

23:56 And it shall be a statute of your people for generations, for I am the lord God."

23:57 And Moses declared what the lord said to the children of Israel and they rejoiced in ignorance and never questioned the stupidity of the lord's demands.

24:1 The lord came back to Moses with more ridiculous demands.

24:2 "I the lord am a cowardly lord and afraid of the darkness.

24:3 For darkness represents wicked and wicked scares me.

24:4 Do not tell those of my fear, lest they question my divinity, but command them this.

24:5 The children of Israel shall bring lamp oil to the priests, so that the lord shall be supplied with an everlasting supply of light.

24:6 Aaron shall take of the oil and burn lamps and candles inside the temple, so that the lord shall never be surrounded by darkness.

24:7 It shall be a statute among the children of Israel for generations.

24:8 For the Sabbath, the lord shall be hungry and demand a feast prepared for him.

24:9 Aaron shall light the candlesticks, so that the atmosphere for dinner be right.

24:10 The priests shall take fine flour and bake for the lord twelve cakes.

24:11 Six cakes in a row shall be aligned among the table.

24:12 And Aaron shall sprinkle frankincense among the cakes and it shall be a statute among the priests for generations."

24:13 During the lord's demands, a most terrible event occurred.

24:14 Shelomoth the daughter of Dibri, from the tribe of Dan, was married to an Egyptian.

24:15 They had a son together, a son of mixed blood.

24:16 When the son heard that Moses was talking with the lord God and that Moses was receiving more demands from the lord, the son did a tragic thing.

24:17 He cursed God.

24:18 He said to his parents, "Why does the lord demand such sacrifices, such blood, such violent and terrible things, yet claim he be a loving God?

24:19 The lord must think us fools and I for one shall not do as he demands.

24:20 I will not do as the lord commands without question, for the lord is a selfish, cruel and unworthy beast and is not worthy of my devotion."

24:21 When the children of Israel heard what the son hath said, they grew angry.

24:22 For such things were blasphemous and they knew the son shall feel the wrath of the lord upon him.

24:23 The lord heard this blasphemy, this question of his divinity and told Moses to deal with this half-blood heathen.

24:24 Moses took this son, stripped him nude and tied him to a stake of shittim wood.

24:25 All the children of Israel gazed upon this man of evil, this man who would question the will of God.

24:26 Aaron, the high priest, places his hands upon his head and told the nation of Israel to do the same.

24:27 They lined up and placed their hands upon the head of the blasphemer.

24:28 When all had placed their hands upon the head, Moses and Aaron picked up stones, which were lying beneath their feet.

24:29 They threw them at the blasphemer and told the children of Israel to do the same.

24:30 All the children of Israel gathered stones, pebbles and rocks and threw them upon the evil son of an Egyptian.

24:31 The son was bombarded with rocks, so that it was as if a shower of stones were upon him.

24:32 Moses and Aaron demanded more; that the children of Israel not stop until the son hang dead upon the stake.

24:33 They did not stop, all throwing stones, some even taking chunks of rock and beating him with it.

24:34 When the comfort of death finally came upon the blasphemer, his body was bruised, bleeding and broken.

24:35 His eye sockets were filled with bloods and stones; his limbs were severed so that only the tendons connect them to his body.

24:36 His feet were crook, his hands disconnected, his face unrecognizable by anyone.

24:37 When the lord saw the blasphemer dead, he caused the ground beneath him to split,

24:38 And two great hands of rock and flame came from the split ground and grabbed the man and carried him deep beneath the earth.

24:39 When the children of Israel witnessed this, they grew afraid and rejoiced the glory of God, for fear that if they did not the lord would send the hands to grab them, and carry them deep beneath the earth.

24:40 It was then the lord came down in a mighty black cloud and spoke to all the nation of Israel,

24:41 "I am the lord your God, creator of heaven and earth and all things.

24:42 It was I who led you out of the servitude of Pharaoh and shall lead you to the lands promised since the days of Abraham.

24:43 For this, I demand respect and sacrifice and that you obey my laws and statutes.

24:44 And what do I hear, but some half-bred son of a heathen question me?

24:45 The lord is a jealous and vengeful God and shall not tolerate any doubt of my divinity, will not let them go unpunished those that break my laws and shall curse the ignorant which deny me my sacrifice.

24:46 Those that do, shall be put to death.

24:47 If any child of Israel kills a man, then the murderer shall be considered an unholy beast and shall be put to death.

24:48 If a man harms their neighbour, so that a cripple or blemish be of the neighbour, then so the same shall be done to him.

24:49 Breach for breach,

24:50 Eye for eye,

24:51 Tooth for tooth,

24:52 Until all the world go blind.

24:53 Remember these and obey my laws, lest you feel the anger of the lord and the hands of the earth shall spring forth and drag you away, denying you eternally entrance to the kingdom of the lord."

25:1 The lord spoke more and said to the children of Israel,

25:2 "Remember that I am the lord your God and that you shall make to me no graven images, lest you feel my wrath.

25:3 For the lord is a mighty God and canvas nor sculpture cannot imitate the might, the power, the love, the hate, the beauty and the horror of the lord.

25:4 To attempt so is arrogant and blasphemous.

25:5 Obey my commandments and keep my statutes.

25:6 Do so and I shall bless you with rain for your crops, fertile soil and plentiful herds.

25:7 You shall grow fat upon the grapes and drink many a fine vintage, eat bread, feast upon flesh and shall dwell safely in your lands.

25:8 For the lord shall protect you and rid your lands of evil beasts; and nations shall fear you.

25:9 Your enemies shall flee from you and die by your swords.

25:10 Five men of the children of Israel shall kill regiments of heathens and a hundred children of Israel will slaughter entire nations in the name of God.

25:11 For I the lord God have respect for you and shall make you fruitful and multiply and shall keep my covenant unto you which was made during the days of Abraham.

25:12 I shall walk with you, protect you and love you and you shall be my people.

25:13 For I am the lord God, who has broken the bands of your yoke during the time of Egypt and made you a strong and powerful people.

25:14 But if you doubt me and not give into my commands and ignore my commandments;

25:15 And if you despise my statutes and loathe my judgments, then it shall be you who has broken the covenant of God.

25:16 Then the children of Israel shall be hated by God and you will know terror, suffering, sorrow and pain.

25:17 Your enemies shall gather and slay and enslave you.

25:18 They shall burn you and consume you; they shall tear your hearts from you and feast of your eyes.

25:19 They will rape you, your sons and your daughters.

25:20 The nation of Israel shall be hated throughout all the earth and you will have naught a friend on earth nor in the kingdom of heaven.

25:21 Your pride shall be broken and your lands will turn to rusted iron and your clothes to melted brass, so that no crops shall grow, your herds shall starve and your skins be burned.

25:22 Great plagues shall be cursed upon you; greater than the plagues that were cursed upon Egypt, when the lord removed you from slavery.

25:23 The terrifying sword of God shall come from the skies and strike down against you and it shall cast out pestilence among your peoples and weaken you and your enemies shall strike then.

25:24 You will grow hungry and bake breads from your own shit and the shit of beasts and you shall feast upon cakes of dung and grow accustomed to them.

25:25 Never shall you walk in the presence of God, for I shall walk away from you, abandon you and leave you to rot.

25:26 Mothers shall feast upon the live flesh of their daughters and fathers upon the flesh of their sons; you shall feast upon them and hear their wails and it shall cause a great heartache within you.

25:27 But you will still feast upon them, for it shall be a curse from God.

25:28 My hand shall destroy your leaders, your elders and your priests and their carcasses shall pave the roads you walk on.

25:29 Your cities shall be laid to waste; your sanctuaries shall crumble and your corpses shall burn for seventy thousand and seventy years and create a foul odour among the lands and a sweet savour for the lord.

25:30 The lands you reside within shall become desolate and the heathens shall claim it back and take of your crops, your sons, your daughters and your herds.

25:31 The children of Israel shall be scattered out amongst the lands and their souls shall belong to the strangers.

25:32 The lord shall vomit great vomit upon your heads, forever cursing you unclean.

25:33 A great and empty sadness shall be forever present within your hearts and shall weaken you and your people.

25:34 Your hearts shall bear this sadness, for your hearts shall be as though uncircumcised and shall never know the love of the lord.

25:35 In time, the people of Israel shall weaken to the point of extinction, so that none of your generations shall survive.

25:36 And the heathens shall feast upon you and this shall be your damnation."

NUMBERS

1:1 The book of Numbers is aptly named,

1:2 For within the first four chapters, it is nothing but numbers.

1:3 How many men are in this tribe, in that tribe, their approximate ages,

1:4 How many sheep they have, how many goats they have,

1:5 Rams, oxen, donkeys,

1:6 The number of sacrifices they contributed.

1:7 For the book of Numbers be the census of Israel.

1:8 A tax return to give to the lord.

1:9 It's boring.

1:10 Really boring.

1:11 More boring than the whole "build me candlestick of shittim wood, inlaid with gold and fine robes of scarlet and linen and purple and a chair and an altar and another altar" crap which was found in Exodus.

1:12 The reason this book is in the bible...

1:13 I don't know.

1:14 Go ask a pastor, or a priest, or another propagandist of God.

1:15 Perhaps it is important we know how the nation of Israel grew during their time in the desert.

1:16 A way to remind us how the lord can make a small group into millions, with his power.

1:17 Or it could be because everyone was fucking, because that was the only fun thing they could do in the desert.

1:18 Either way, there are some interesting things in Numbers, if you filter out the census and tax forms.

1:19 And, best of all, they are blasphemous and ridiculous!

1:20 Killing strangers that come into the night.

1:21 Genocide.

1:22 Fiery serpents.

1:23 More of the lord's demands.

1:24 And the lesson of Numbers?

1:25 Don't whine.

1:26 God hates whiners.

1:27 He punishes them, which usually causes them to whine more.

1:28 So he kills them.

1:29 And people wonder why I hate God.

2:1 The lord came to Moses and said to him,

2:2 "Go, tell the children of Israel to cast out the lepers, the unclean, the necrophilia's, the sick, the diseased, the blind, the deaf and the crippled.

2:3 Male, female and child shall be cast out, to live within the wilderness and be prey to the beasts.

2:4 Do this, before the lepers, the unclean, the necrophilia's, the sick, the diseased, the blind, the deaf and the crippled defile your camps."

2:5 Thus the nation of Israel did as the lord commanded.

2:6 The lepers, the unclean, those defiled by the dead, the sick, the diseased, the blind, the deaf and the crippled.

2:7 The weak, the poor, the malnourished,

2:8 Cast out upon the wilderness.

2:9 So that the lord may cause them great suffering.

2:10 For during their time in the nation of Israel, they suffered.

2:11 But there were those that would help them; offer them comfort.

2:12 Food, water, shelter, medical aid.

2:13 And the lord saw this and grew angry.

2:14 For he wanted the people to suffer more.

2:15 They complained about their suffering.

2:16 They whined about their leprosy, their sickness, their maladies,

2:17 And annoyed the lord with their bitching.

2:18 So he cast them out, so that they may suffer in the wilderness, without aid nor comfort;

2:19 Alone and afraid.

2:20 Where the wild beasts shall feast upon them.

2:21 And end their whining.

2:22 And the numbers of those cast out of the nation of Israel were a lot.

2:23 I'm not going to tally up the total.

2:24 It's irrelevant.

2:25 When the weak and diseased were gone, the lord came to Moses and said to him,

2:26 "When a man or woman steal from God, it angers the lord and is a great sin.

2:27 They shall confess their sins and pay back that which was stolen, with one fifth above the value to be paid in shekels.

2:28 But if the man is too poor to pay in full, or refuses to confess, or give back that which is taken, then a sacrifice must be made.

2:29 Take the man to the door of the tabernacle.

2:30 Slay him, so that the blood shall bleed from his throat.

2:31 Take his fat, his inwards, his kidneys, the caul above his liver and his blood.

2:32 Take of these and place them within the altar of burning and burn them,

2:33 So that the aroma shall create a pleasing scent to the lord."

2:34 The lord still spoke, for not enough was demanded in Leviticus and said,

2:35 "Speak to the children of Israel. Tell them that if a man's wife commit a trespass to him,

2:36 And goes to seek another man and lies carnally with him and none bear witness and none confess their doings,

2:37 She shall be defiled.

2:38 The spirit of jealousy shall overtake her and shall cause her great ugliness, so that none shall ever wish to lie intimate with her.

2:39 The husband shall see her ugliness and know of her unfaithfulness.

2:40 He shall take her to the priest and the priest shall set her before the lord.

2:41 The priest shall uncover the woman and witness all her ugliness, her hideousness, her revolting features.

2:42 The priest shall take holy water and mix it with ash and bittering herbs and force her to drink of the vile liquid.

2:43 This water shall be a curse upon the lady and shall go into her bowels and make her belly swell and her thighs rot.

2:44 During the curse, the priest shall interrogate the woman.

2:45 When the woman lies, vile vomit shall excrete from her mouth and her nostrils and shall burn her and cause great suffering.

2:46 If the truth she speaks, none shall happen, even if the truth be harsh and cruel.

2:47 Upon the end of the interrogation, if she be deemed innocent, the curse shall be lifted.

2:48 She became ugly for other reasons. Perhaps genetics, if the lord allow it.

2:49 But if she be guilty, then her belly shall swell more until it burst and great gobs of flesh and inwards come out.

2:50 The priest shall take of this flesh and inwards and burn it upon the altar.

2:51 The woman, the ungrateful harlot, shall be forever cursed.

2:52 Never shall she know her previous beauty and men shall stare at her with disgust and revolt.

2:53 She shall never accomplish the meaning of women; to bear sons.

2:54 For none shall wish to lie with her.

2:55 Such is the curse of the lord."

3:1 The lord came to Moses and spoke with him.

3:2 "I hear the wishes of some of the children of Israel.

3:3 Both men and women wish to take a holy path and walk with me and know me.

3:4 They wish to dedicate their lives to me and praise my name.

3:5 The lord shall let them and shall call them Nazarites.

3:6 For the Nazarite shall be separated from the people, the world and its belongings.

3:7 They shall belong only to God.

3:8 If one wishes to be a Nazarite, they must make personal sacrifice.

3:9 No wine nor strong drink shall touch their lips, nor vinegar, which comes from alcohol.

3:10 The sweet taste of grapes shall they deny themselves.

3:11 All the days of their lives shall they eat nothing of the vine tree, from the kernels even to the husks.

3:12 A razor shall not touch a lock of their hair, from their beard and the scalp. Their hair shall grow long, in glory to the lord.

3:13 They shall abstain from sex, for their seed belongs to the lord.

3:14 They shall avoid the dead, for the dead be unclean.

3:15 If their mother, or father, or sister, or brother, or one they hold dear in life shall die, the Nazarite shall not come unto their corpse.

3:16 They shall be denied access to the funeral, lest they become unclean by the corpse.

3:17 For they shall be truly holy among the lord.

3:18 If a man is to die suddenly by them, their death shall make the Nazarite unclean.

3:19 They are defiled and for seven days they shall be kept in isolation; in deep prayer to the lord God.

3:20 And on the eighth day they shall shave their head, for the hair upon them is unclean and must be grown fresh and clean.

3:21 They shall bring an offering of two turtledoves or two young pigeons without blemish and offer it to the priest at the door of the tabernacle of the congregation.

3:22 The priest shall offer one for a sin offering and the other for a burnt offering and make atonement for the Nazarite; for the Nazarite has sinned and defiled himself, for being near the unclean and the dead.

3:23 And to thank the lord for their separation, their seven days in solitude, they shall bring a lamb without blemish, born of the first year, as a trespass offering.

3:24 For during the solitude, they lord has allowed them to trespass within the property of God and sacrifice must be made for such privilege.

3:25 Once a year, upon the day of their birth to Nazarite, shall they bring to the priest a lamb, born of the first year, without blemish, for a burnt offering and an ewe of the first year without blemish for a peace offering and a ram without blemish for a peace offering.

3:26 And a basket of unleavened cakes, made of fine flour and virgin oil and wafers made with the holy anointing oil, as a food offering unto God.

3:27 The priest shall offer the sin offering and the burnt offering and make atonement for the Nazarite.

3:28 And the priest shall offer the ram for the peace offering, with the basket of unleavened breads and wafers.

3:29 The Nazarite shall take of their hair and shave it and throw it within the fire of the peace offering.

3:30 And the priest shall take the sodden shoulder of the ram and one unleavened cake and one unleavened wafer and shall place them upon the arms of the Nazarite.

3:31 And the priest shall take of the shoulder and beat the Nazarite with it.

3:32 Until the Nazarite lie beaten upon the ground.

3:33 Such are the laws of the Nazarite.

3:34 Speak unto the priests and unto the Nazarites,

3:35 That the lord bless you and keep you,

3:36 And shall smile upon you,

3:37 And shall lift his wrath upon you, so that they shall know peace.

3:38 And shall write their names within the holy."

3:39 When Moses spoke of the Nazarites, the people rejoiced.

3:40 For they knew they could be closer to God and feel his love and not his wrath.

3:41 All the twelve tribes of Israel celebrated in the name of the lord.

3:42 They brought forth rams, bullocks, ewes, lambs, oxen, goats, doves, pigeons and foreign virgins most beautiful.

3:43 Mass sacrifices were made in glory to God.

3:44 The people celebrated and danced naked and bathed in the blood of the sacrifices.

3:45 Those that could, drank and grew drunk and were merry and indulged themselves in the flesh offered by brothels.

3:46 For the ones wishing to be Nazarites, they celebrated through sacrifice and took not of strong drink, nor grapes, nor the pleasures of flesh.

3:47 And they placed their vows and became holy and closer to God.

3:48 They dedicated their lives in the pursuit of spirituality, to be one with the lord and know him.

3:49 They denied themselves earthly pleasures and made personal sacrifices, so that they may better understand the lord's will.

3:50 All were very, very, disappointed.

4:1 The lord witnessed the celebration of his name and grew pleased.

4:2 For he loves blood, nudity and torn flesh.

4:3 But those of the tribe of Levi, he was displeased with.

4:4 For though they offered sacrifice, they did not bathe in the blood, nor strip their linens.

4:5 The lord was saddened by this, for those of the tribe of Levi did not enjoy the rejoicing of the name of the lord.

4:6 The lord spoke to Moses and said to him,

4:7 "Those of the tribe of Levi have shamed me and made me sad.

4:8 They do not appreciate that which the lord has given them.

4:9 For this, the tribe of Levi shall be in servitude to the tabernacle, so that they may better appreciate their lord God.

4:10 Go and cleanse the Levites.

4:11 Have them shave all their flesh, so that not a hair be upon them.

4:12 Wash their clothes and bathe them all and sprinkle them with holy water, so that they may be clean.

4:13 Prepare a bullock and a basket of unleavened bread for sacrifice and another young bullock for sin offering.

4:14 Have all of the tribe of Levi come forth, naked and shaved, so that all the children of Israel shall gaze upon them.

4:15 Let the Levites place their hands upon the head of the bullocks, the one for the burnt offering and the one for the sin offering.

4:16 Slay both bullocks, so that the Levites may witness the power of the lord.

4:17 For with the sacrifice, all of the tribe of Levi shall be in service to the tabernacle and shall belong to me.

4:18 They shall be slaves to God.

4:19 Every child that be born of the Levites, upon the day of their birth, shall they belong to the lord.

4:20 Then shall they know to give respect unto the lord and rejoice

his name and celebrate his salvation.

4:21 For six days shall they slave within the tabernacle and keep it clean.

4:22 Upon the sabbath shall they do no work, for that is the holy day.

4:23 All their lives shall they be a slave unto God, until death consume them.

4:24 Such is the will of God.

4:25 Do not question it."

5:1 It came that on the fourteenth of the month, it was Passover.

5:2 And Moses said to the children of Israel that Passover must be kept, for it be the will of God.

5:3 They did and celebrated and ate and did what the lord commanded them for the Passover meal.

5:4 Though some men were saddened, for they did not know if they should keep the Passover.

5:5 For a relative of theirs who was sick died within their tents and have defiled them and made them unclean.

5:6 They grew confused, for they knew not if they should keep the Passover, despite their uncleanliness, or if they should deny themselves the Passover and upset God.

5:7 So they came to Aaron and to Moses and explained to them what happened.

5:8 They told them of their ill father, who died suddenly within the night.

5:9 They explained to them their uncleanliness and confusion with the Passover.

5:10 Neither Aaron nor Moses knew what to do, so they went to God and asked.

5:11 The lord was annoyed, for these two mortal men disturbed him.

5:12 "Why must you annoy me with such questions. Have I not made things clear?

5:13 The men must keep the Passover, for it is most holy.

5:14 It matters not if they are defiled by a dead body, or if they be far away from the people of Israel.

5:15 The Passover is a celebration of the lord and must be kept.

5:16 All shall keep it and eat unleavened breads and bittering herbs.

5:17 They shall keep all the ordinances of the Passover.

5:18 Tell these men they are unclean; defiled by the corpse of their father.

5:19 And that despite their uncleanliness, to partake of the Passover.

5:20 For those that do not partake of the Passover; those that deny the will of God, shall be cast out from his people and his soul shall never know the kingdom of the lord.

5:21 Even a stranger, a foreign heathen who resides in your lands, shall be welcome to the Passover and keep it, with all its laws.

5:22 And the stranger will know the will of God and be saddened for not being the chosen."

5:23 Upon the day the tabernacle was set up for Passover, a great cloud covered it; and it was the spirit of the lord.

5:24 When the sun was in the sky, the great and dark cloud remained, above the tent of the testimony.

5:25 And when the sun set and the sky was dark, the cloud burned with great fire.

5:26 And the people rejoiced, for surely, they lord was with them.

5:27 When the cloud moved, the children of Israel moved and followed blindly.

5:28 And when the cloud stopped, the children of Israel stopped and would pitch their tents and not move until the fire or cloud rose and led them.

5:29 Sometimes the cloud and fire would stay for days, or months, or even years, at one spot.

5:30 And never the children of Israel moved, nor wondered why they would stay so long and not go towards the land of milk and honey, promised to them since the days of Abraham.

5:31 For those that did, angered God.

5:32 And the fire reached forth and burned to ash any and all that doubted the will of the lord.

6:1 The lord came to Moses and said,

6:2 "Make for me two trumpets of finest silver.

6:3 Make them from one piece, in glory to God.

6:4 And when these trumpets are blown, all the assembly shall gather within the doors to the tabernacle of the congregation.

6:5 If only one trumpet blow, then the princes, the heads of the tribes of Israel, shall gather themselves unto me.

6:6 And if you blow with alarm, then the camps that lie east shall go forward and prepare for war.

6:7 If two alarms be blown, the southern camps shall gather arms and move forward and prepare for war.

6:8 Only the priests shall blow the silver trumpets, as it shall be forever a statute among your people for generations.

6:9 And when you go to war, the priests shall blow the trumpets with great noise.

6:10 So that the lord shall hear you and protect you and strike against your enemies.

6:11 Also in the days of sacrifice shall the trumpets be blown, for burnt offerings and for peace offerings, so that the lord remembers them and be awakened and enjoy their pleasing odour.

6:12 For I am your lord God and this I demand from you."

6:13 Upon the twentieth day of the month, the cloud rose and led them.

6:14 The children of Israel followed the cloud and the fire, until it rested within the wilderness of Paran.

6:15 They knew the wilderness of Paran to be hostile and occupied by heathens, thus the twelve tribes prepared their armies.

6:16 The armies of Judah, led by Nahshon the son of Amminadab, skilled with the mace.

6:17 The armies of Issachar, led by Nethaneel the son of Zuar, great warriors upon horseback.

6:18 The armies of Zebulun, led by Eliab the son of Helon, finest archers.

6:19 The armies of Reuben, led by Elizur the son of Shedeur, terrifying with spears.

6:20 The armies of Simeon, led by Shelumiel the son of Zurishaddai, the best blades men in all the tribes.

6:21 The armies of Gad, led by Eliaseph the son of Deuel, whose martial arts could disarm even the finest of warriors.

6:22 The armies of Joseph, led by Gamaliel the son of Pedahzur, who manned the artillery and struck the enemies from great distance.

6:23 The armies of Benjamin, led by Abidan the son of Gideoni, whose warriors were cowards and provided fodder for the enemy.

6:24 The armies of Dan, led by Ahiezer the son of Ammishaddai, scouts and raiders, who would hit and run and tell the other armies of the enemy's weakness.

6:25 The armies of Asher, led by Pagiel the son of Ocran, shadow assassins that would kill the leaders of the enemy while they slept.

6:26 The armies of Naphtali, led by Ahira the son of Enan, smiths who would make great weapons and armor for the other tribes.

6:27 The tribe of Levi had no army, for they were slaves to God. They would cook for the other eleven tribes, when their duties at the tabernacle permitted.

6:28 Moses, protected by the armies and the lord, went to visit Hobab, father of Raguel the Midianite and wife of Moses.

6:29 He told his father in law the might of the Israel nation, the will of the lord and of the lands promised to them by God.

6:30 Since he be the father of his wife, Moses asked Hobab to travel with them, so that he may know the one true God and be blessed and reap the treasures of the land of milk and honey.

6:31 Hobab declined and said to Moses,

6:32 "I have heard of the might of your people, since your escape from the servitude of Pharaoh.

6:33 You have grown into a mighty nation, under the will of your lord.

6:34 But I have heard of your God and how he leads you with fear.

6:35 I refuse to worship such a lord, for he is a tyrant.

6:36 Let him do to me as he wishes, for I fear not his wrath, nor his anger and loathe his deceit.

6:37 I shall have nothing to do with him and am ashamed my daughter has married such a fool, who blindly follows the tyrant without question.

6:38 I loathe your God, but I love you, Moses.

6:39 For this, your children may rest upon my lands and fear no attack from who you call heathens.

6:40 The heathens are peaceful, despite your God's lies."

6:41 Moses grew sad, for he feared his father in law correct and worried the lord will curse him.

6:42 And the lord knew this and hated Hobab and the cloud turned to great fire and rose and filled the sky with burning.

6:43 Hobab looked upon the spirit, the wrath of the lord and laughed.

6:44 For he feared not death, nor curse, nor punishment, nor damnation.

6:45 Hobab screamed to the fire, "Do what you wish to me, for I care not!

6:46 I would rather live a free man cursed, than a stupid man scared."

6:47 God did not curse Hobab, nor kill him.

6:48 To do so would upset Moses and create within him great doubt of the lord's intentions.

6:49 The lord left and the children of Israel followed.

6:50 But the lord was still angry from Hobab's defiance and his spirit was fire; even throughout the day it be fire.

6:51 And the wrath of the lord would lead the Israelites and the people within their path would scatter in fear.

6:52 And the people learned to hate the children of Israel, for passing through their lands in force.

7:1 For years the people ate nothing but manna, given to them by the lord.

7:2 They would go forth and gather the manna upon the ground and grind it in mills, or beat it with mortar and would bake it within ovens or upon pans.

7:3 The same manna, every day, for years.

7:4 They grew sick of it.

7:5 It's taste, it's texture was so common to them that they wished for variety.

7:6 Even when adding spices and herbs to the manna, it did no good.

7:7 For it still tasted like manna.

7:8 All remembered their times in Egypt and the multitudes of food there.

7:9 Cucumbers, melons, onions, leeks, garlic, fish fresh from the waters.

7:10 How they missed it, the fresh meats and the vegetables and the fruits.

7:11 Even during their servitude, the meals were different by day.

7:12 The animals they brought with them, they could not eat.

7:13 For all were without blemish and must be offered to God.

7:14 Even the females they feared to eat, for the females produced sons without blemish, which could be offered as sacrifice to the lord.

7:15 They craved meat.

7:16 Fall off the bone, delicious, sweetly spiced meat.

7:17 For they were surrounded by meat; animals that would be tasty upon the plate.

7:18 Yet they could not eat them, for they belonged to God.

7:19 They cried out to Moses,

7:20 "Let the lord send us some meat. Some wild game, wild flocks of birds.

7:21 For this manna has filled our bellies for years and it begins to ferment within and make us sick."

7:22 Moses grew angry at the children of Israel and told them,

7:23 "Why must you complain, for the manna is sweet and offers nourishment.

7:24 It is a gift from God, which daily appears on the ground, so that we may eat it.

7:25 Do you deny yourself this gift from God?

7:26 Is the lord's gift not good enough for you?"

7:27 And the children of Israel, in unison, said to Moses,

7:28 "Yes!

7:29 For the gift has been offered daily, for years.

7:30 We are not ungrateful for the manna, we merely desire something else."

7:31 Moses, with shame and fear, went upon the lord and spoke with him.

7:32 "My lord God, creator of heaven and earth and all things;

7:33 Who has delivered us from the hands of Pharaoh and shall deliver us to the lands of milk and honey promised to us since the days of Abraham.

7:34 I have failed you, for the children of Israel have become spoiled and do not appreciate that which the lord has given them.

7:35 Try as I may to be a father to them, to serve them, to care for them as a mother cares for the nursing child attached to her bosom, I cannot.

7:36 They are too many and their complaints make me weary.

7:37 All come to me, demanding they be given flesh, meat to eat.

7:38 They weep for it and sorrow for it and crave and lust for it.

7:39 I tell them the manna is good; a gift from the beloved lord, but they refuse it.

7:40 They want something else and deny the manna you give them.

7:41 I have failed you, lord, for the children do not appreciate you, as I should have taught them.

7:42 If you wish my life, lord, I offer it you, for I have failed in your sight."

7:43 And the lord said to Moses,

7:44 "No, I do not wish your life.

7:45 For the children of Israel number in the many and one complaining man can spread throughout the whole tribes.

7:46 I hear their complaints and loathe them for it.

7:47 My manna is not good enough. The blessed manna; a gift directly from the heavens that only the children of Israel know?

7:48 I shall curse them with their wishes and give them a multitude of meat.

7:49 Gather the elders of Israel and have them sanctify all the children of Israel.

7:50 And tell the nation that upon the day of their sanctification, the lord shall hear their whining and give them the flesh they so crave.

7:51 They shall eat of flesh not for a day, not for ten days, nor even twenty.

7:52 A whole month shall they feast upon flesh, until they grow tired of it and it comes out their nostrils, their ears, their asses, and their bellies grow full of the muscles of the animals."

7:53 And Moses asked the lord,

7:54 "How shall this be done. Shall we gather fish from the waters?

7:55 Will the herds and our flocks be slain, so that the flesh sustains them?"

7:56 And the lord said to Moses,

7:57 "Do you doubt me. Do you think the herds and flocks would not sustain the children for a month?

7:58 Or that the waters shall be emptied of fish?

7:59 No, that shall not happen.

7:60 The waters shall be left alone and the flocks and the herds shall be kept mine.

7:61 The glory of the lord shall curse them with their wish, do not doubt this of me.

7:62 For I have taken them out of the lands of Egypt.

7:63 I have shown you wizardry, to scare and trick the Pharaoh.

7:64 I have turned water to blood, blocked out the sun, sent plagues of locusts and killed the first-born sons of those who defied me.

7:65 Never doubt the lord, for to do so is blasphemy.

7:66 Do as I say, and witness my power."

7:67 And Moses did as the lord commanded and sent for the elders and had the nation of Israel sanctified, in preparation for the curse from God.

7:68 The people waited in anticipation, for the thought of a month long feast of flesh excited them.

7:69 When all was done, a great wind came and brought with it quails.

7:70 The quails surrounded the camps and were thick, so that none could see anything but flying feathers.

7:71 And the people rejoiced and gathered the quails and feasted upon them.

7:72 They plucked them, butchered them, fried them, roasted them, baked them and spiced them;

7:73 And it was the sweetest meat they have ever eaten.

7:74 And all rejoiced the lord for the gift of quails.

7:75 At first.

7:76 For the quails would not leave and left feathers and bird shit all throughout the camps.

7:77 After ten days, the people were disgusted and wished the quails would leave the camps.

7:78 After twenty days, all were revolted, for the quails left piles of shit upon everything and their feathers littered everywhere.

7:79 They grew tired of their mess and they grew tired of their flesh.

7:80 For all they had was quails and they grew sick of it quickly.

7:81 Though manna was plain, it was easy to prepare and clean.

THE BLASPHEMOUS BIBLE

7:82 The quails left shit and feathers and had to be butchered, so that their blood stained the floors.

7:83 On the twenty-fifth day, all wanted anything but quails.

7:84 For the flesh made them ill and they vomited quails from their mouth and their bowels growled and expelled the quail flesh from them.

7:85 The flesh was between their teeth and rotted and gave them a great plague amongst the Israelites.

7:86 Those that lusted most for the flesh died in mass and were buried and they named the place Kibrothhattaahah, for the sound of the vomiting quail that expelled from their throats.

8:1 Aaron and Miriam, sister of Aaron and Moses, grew curious and angry.

8:2 For they thought Moses a blasphemer; a man against God.

8:3 For Moses did not marry a daughter of Israel, but a foreign heathen, a Midianite, which was against the law of God.

8:4 Both Moses and the lord heard it.

8:5 Moses did nothing, for Moses was a meek man and slightly retarded and thought nothing of it.

8:6 But the lord was angry, for Moses was a prophet and a man of God and these two siblings of Moses question him?

8:7 The lord demanded the three enter the tabernacle, so that the lord may speak with them.

8:8 And the spirit of the lord came down upon them, in a pillar of black cloud and spoke with the three.

8:9 "Hear my words, for the lord God shall not repeat himself.

8:10 Moses was chosen by me to lead the people of Israel into greatness and for this he has the lord's blessing.

8:11 Though he is married to a heathen, he has done so with my blessing.

8:12 The laws of God must be followed, but exceptions are made to those I deem worthy,

8:13 Moses is one of my favourite of the chosen and the laws do not apply to him.

8:14 I speak to him directly and I speak to Aaron directly.

8:15 Aaron, high priest, why do you question your brother's wife?

8:16 Certainly you must know that if I the lord wished not the Midianite to marry Moses, that my wrath would be brought down upon them.

8:17 Miriam, you have no right to question, for you are but a mere woman, a loathsome creation by God.

8:18 Be gone from my sights, wretched bitch."

8:19 And the lord spat upon her.

8:20 The saliva of God cursed her and made her unclean, a leper.

8:21 Her hair fell from her head and the skin became as white as snow.

8:22 She was cast out of the camp, for she was a leper and unclean and the laws demanded so.

8:23 Moses loved her sister and wished her not a leper unclean.

8:24 He begged to God,

8:25 "Let my sister be clean, for I love her and hold her dear.

8:26 From the same womb we came forth and she is precious and loved by me.

8:27 Do not let her be one of the dead; cleanse her, so that she may be welcomed back to me with open arms."

8:28 And the lord responded,

8:29 "This witch has doubted you and spoke ill of you and your wife.

8:30 Yet, if you love the wretched woman despite this, I shall give

her back to you.

8:31 The lord has spit upon her and for this she shall know shame for seven days.

8:32 Seven days she shall be a leper and know shame.

8:33 Upon the eighth day, I shall cleanse her and she shall be welcomed back to the children of Israel."

8:34 And it was so.

8:35 The children of Israel made camp and did not travel for seven days, until Miriam sister of Moses was cleansed of her leprosy and welcomed back to Israel.

8:36 Upon her return, Moses came and embraced her and they both wept.

8:37 Moses in rejoice, for his sister has returned to him.

8:38 Miriam in sorrow, for she knew in her heart the tyranny of the lord.

8:39 For she did not question Moses, but was concerned, for his marriage to a foreigner went against the laws of God.

8:40 And for this question, this concern, the lord cursed her and only her.

8:41 But not Aaron, the high priest, who confided in her his true intentions.

8:42 For Aaron did not care about the Midianite wife of Moses, for he knew the lord gave exceptions to those who were his favourite.

8:43 He wanted Moses cast out, so that he could lead the children of Israel.

8:44 Miriam knew this and wondered if the lord knew of Aaron's intent and if so, why not curse him as well?

8:45 She embraced her brother Moses, but did not speak to him Aaron's intentions.

8:46 For fear of another curse of the tyrant lord God.

9:1 It came to pass that the people of Israel came near the land of Canaan, promised to them since the days of Abraham.

9:2 The lord demanded that the best spies go forth and seek the lands, to bring back knowledge, wealth and weakness of the Canaanites.

9:3 The best spies came and were honoured to be chosen by the lord.

9:4 Shammua, son of Zaccur.

9:5 Shaphat, son of Hori.

9:6 Caleb, son of Jephunneh.

9:7 Igal, son of Joseph.

9:8 Oshea, son of Nun.

9:9 Palti, son of Raphu.

9:10 Gaddiel, son of Sodi.

9:11 Gaddi, son of Susi.

9:12 Yes, Susi is a man.

9:13 Ammiel, son of Gemalli.

9:14 Sethur, son of Micheal.

9:15 Nahbi, son of Vophsi.

9:16 Geuel, son of Machi.

9:17 These twelve men were sent to spy upon the lands.

9:18 To see if the land was weak or strong, if the crops were plentiful and rich,

9:19 The defences of the cities and the nation's armies.

9:20 And to bring back belongings from the land; fruits and crops from the vineyards and fields.

9:21 For forty days these men left and gathered all that they could of the land of Canaan.

9:22 They came upon the brook of Eshcol, which were abundant in fruits.

9:23 They gathered pomegranates and figs and brought back a branch with a cluster of grapes.

9:24 All the fruits were fresh, plentiful and huge.

9:25 The cluster of grapes were so heavy it took two men to carry it back.

9:26 Upon their return, they went to Aaron and Moses and told them what they knew.

9:27 "The lands be flowing with milk and honey, as was told by the lord God, but the children of Anak live there, with cities walled and well-guarded.

9:28 The Amalekites reside to the south; The Hittites, the Jebusites and the Amorites dwell in the mountains and the Canaanites live by the sea and the coast of Jordan."

9:29 When Moses heard this, he was pleased, for these are people hated by God and should prove no match for the might of the children of Israel.

9:30 And when Moses told them to attack this nation, the spies grew scared and told Moses an unexpected evil which dwell in these lands.

9:31 For the children of Anak, which dwelt in the richest of lands, were giants.

9:32 Great and mighty in stature, who make the children of Israel appear as grasshoppers beside them.

9:33 Men who descended from the giants of the sons of God, when they came to earth and raped the fairest and most beautiful of women.

9:34 And who managed to survive the floods of the time of Noah, which was believed to have wiped out all others from earth.

9:35 When the people heard of the giants, they grew fearful.

9:36 For the children of Israel surely could not war with these giants and win.

9:37 They cried and cursed the lord, believing he led them from the servitude of Egypt, only to die in the wilderness.

9:38 Some men gathered and wished to return to Egypt, so that they may live in servitude rather than die by giants descended from the sons of God.

9:39 They said to one another, "Let us make a captain and separate from Moses, so that we may return to the rich lands of Egypt."

9:40 When Moses and Aaron heard of this, they fell upon their faces to the children of Israel and begged them to stay.

9:41 Oshea the son of Nun and Caleb the son of Jephunneh, who spied and witnessed the giants, spoke to the children of Israel.

9:42 They told them all of the lands flowing with milk and honey and showed them the figs and grapes and pomegranates they brought back from the lands.

9:43 They told them not to fear the giants, for God is with them and if the lord is with them, the giants shall pose no threat;

9:44 For the will of God is strong and mighty and shall protect the children of Israel.

9:45 But the children of Israel did not believe them and threw stones at them and claimed the lord doomed them to death.

9:46 The lord saw this and grew angry and the spirit of the lord descended upon the tabernacle of the congregation in great fire.

9:47 And the lord spoke to Moses,

9:48 "How long will these children of Israel, these brats, provoke me. For I have given them wealth and power and delivered them from the lands of Egypt and they still doubt me!

9:49 I am starting to loathe them and hate them and believe I have made a mistake in calling these bitches my people.

9:50 If they believe I have doomed them, then let me doom them.

9:51 I shall strike them with pestilence, poverty, plagues.

9:52 Forever shall I banish them from earth and I shall find me a greater nation to call my people, one worthy of my love and devotion."

9:53 Moses said to the lord,

9:54 "If you do this, you shall have broken the covenant you have made since the days of Abraham."

9:55 And the lord said,

9:56 "Yes, I shall, but if none of your kind exist, who will know?"

9:57 Moses thought for a moment and said to God,

9:58 "The Egyptians shall know.

9:59 Though they know not of the covenant, they know of your power.

9:60 They all witnessed what you have done to deliver us from them, so that we may be a great and powerful nation.

9:61 If you destroy us they shall laugh at you and mock you.

9:62 They shall say you led us out of their hands, only to condemn us to death in the wild like beasts.

9:63 They will tell other nations of this and the other nations shall believe them.

9:64 For they will be right.

9:65 And they will wonder why we became extinct so shortly after our deliverance.

9:66 They will ask if you doomed us, or if you were too weak to protect us.

9:67 And with these questions lingering, none of them shall worship you.

9:68 None of them shall be devoted to you.

9:69 And none of them shall offer you sacrifice."

9:70 The lord heard the words of Moses and grew angry and confused.

9:71 For how could a mere mortal offer such arguments?

9:72 He said to Moses,

9:73 "I curse you for your logic, but love you for your devotion.

9:74 I cannot let the children of Israel go unpunished for their doubt, for their murmurings against me.

9:75 The covenant shall not be broken; you shall be delivered into the lands of milk and honey.

9:76 But for your doubts, I shall teach you humbleness.

9:77 For forty years shall ye wander in the desert, until you learn not to doubt the power of the lord.

9:78 During this time, your people shall live and your people shall die.

9:79 Such that none who be above the age of twenty, as of this day, shall see the lands promised to them.

9:80 And the ten men, the spies sent upon the land who did not attempt to convince the peoples against rebellion, shall die by my wrath.

9:81 Oshea, son of Nun, and Caleb son of Jephunneh, shall live, for they tried to do right by the lord.

9:82 Go, tell the people this, so that they may mourn their doubt and their stupidity."

9:83 And Moses told the congregation and they grew saddened and mourned.

9:84 Moses told them to rise, so that they may dwell atop the mountain and witness the lands promised by God.

9:85 They did and made camp atop the mountain and saw the ripe and bountiful lands.

9:86 And Moses said to them,

9:87 "Gaze upon these lands and upon the heathens which inhabit it.

9:88 Know and take comfort that the lord is with us and shall smite them, so that your children shall dwell in these lands.

9:89 You have sinned and doubted our lord.

9:90 For this doubt, you will not know these lands, for the lord shall bring fierce punishment for those which doubt him and his wrath shall be felt.

9:91 The Canaanites, Amalekites, Hittites, Jebusites, Amorites, even the sons of Anak, shall fall and tumble and turn to ash before us and our lord.”

9:92 And the people of Israel mourned, for most knew this shall be all they see of the lands promised to them since the days of Abraham.

9:93 Yet, in their mourning, they took comfort, for they knew their sons and daughters shall be strong and dwell in those lands.

9:94 And the spirit of the lord arose and turned to ash the leaders of the rebellion, those that doubted most and the ten spies who spoke ill of God.

10:1 The lord came to Moses and said to him,

10:2 “When the children of Israel enter these lands, it shall be a great and magnificent day.

10:3 A testament to the glory of God, who has delivered my people from servitude and brought them to the promised lands, rich and flowing with milk and honey.

10:4 On the day you step foot upon the lands, great offerings must be made in glory to God.

10:5 All the children of Israel shall bring unto me a food offering, a tenth part of fine flour mingled with a quarter hin of virgin oil.

10:6 And a quarter hin of the finest vintage shall be poured upon each of the sacrificial lambs, so that the wine marinade the wool and the flesh.

10:7 For the rams, you shall offer with them two tenths of finest flour, mixed with virgin oil and blended with a third of a hin of finest vintage.

10:8 Rub the flour and the wine within the fur of the ram, every inch of it, before sacrifice.

10:9 And if they bring to the lord a bullock for sacrifice, three tenths deal of flour mixed with half a hin of oil must be brought with it as well.

10:10 And the bullock must drink a half hin of wine and be drunk before sacrifice.

10:11 All the children must offer sacrifice; a lamb, a ram, or a bullock and the wine and flour which goes with it.

10:12 So that the flesh, the wine and the batter burns upon the altar and creates a pleasing scent unto the lord, who has delivered you into the promised lands and kept his covenant since the days of Abraham.

10:13 And if a stranger resides with you, they must offer sacrifice as well and witness the power, the lust and the glory of the lord of Israel.

10:14 When you take the vineyards, the orchards and the crops and eat of them, remember it is the lord who give you these lands rich with foods.

10:15 Before the first Israelite takes a morsel of bread, made from the grains of the promised land, a heave offering must be made to God.

10:16 All the children of Israel shall make cakes and shall heave them up to the lord and give praise for the breads the lord has given them.

10:17 Those which do not, or who have eaten of the grains before the offering is made, shall perish and wither and be turned to dust.

10:18 But if one erred in this, or my other commandments and knew not their errors, the congregation shall let them know.

10:19 And the congregation shall be sinned, for allowing one of their kin to sin through ignorance.

10:20 Each shall bring unto the priest a young bullock, with a tenth of fine flour mixed with oil and a hin of wine for burnt sacrifice and a kid goat of the first year for a sin offering.

10:21 The priest shall take of these and make atonement for the congregation, for allowing one of their kin to sin and allow them the ignorance.

10:22 The lord shall peer into their hearts and decide if they are worthy of forgiveness and act accordingly.

10:23 For the one who sinned by ignorance, they shall take unto the priest a she goat of the first year, without blemish.

10:24 The person shall lay their hands upon the head of the goat and then strangle it, until the last breath leaves the goat.

10:25 The priest shall take the goat and cut it and sprinkle seven times blood upon the sinner and seven times blood upon the altar.

10:26 The priest shall take the goat and burn upon the altar the fat, the inwards, the kidneys and the caul above the liver.

10:27 For the remains, the sinner shall take them and burn them outside of camp and bury the ashes.

10:28 When this is done, the lord shall accept the sacrifice and peer into the heart of the one who sinned through ignorance and judge accordingly.

10:29 If the sinner is sorry for their actions and knew not what they done, the lord shall accept the sacrifice and forgive them and welcome them back to the nation of Israel.

10:30 But if not, the lord shall burn them to ash and it shall be they who is buried outside the camp of Israel.”

10:31 When the lord was speaking to Moses, a man was walking through camp.

10:32 And it was the Sabbath day, the holy day, where all shall rest and not work.

10:33 The man came upon sticks in the path, sharp and easy to trip over.

10:34 He picked up the sticks and cast them away from the path, so that none will be injured by them.

10:35 And when the Israelites saw this, they grew afraid.

10:36 For he was picking up sticks.

10:37 On the Sabbath day.

10:38 And this is considered work.

10:39 They grasped the man and took him to Aaron and to Moses and told them of his work upon the Sabbath.

10:40 Aaron and Moses left him in solitude, in a ward, for they knew not what do to with him.

10:41 They came to the lord and asked God what should be done.

10:42 Both men explained why the man picked up the sticks; to prevent injury and protect from harm the children of Israel.

10:43 For his work was honourable, even though it was upon the Sabbath day.

10:44 The lord grew furious and said to them,

10:45 “Kill this man.

10:46 On the morrow, drag this man to the wilderness and have all the children of Israel come, so that they may stone him.

10:47 For any work upon the Sabbath is unholy, unrighteous and unclean.

10:48 The lord rested upon the seventh day and this man did not.

10:49 He makes the lord look lazy and I hate him for it.

10:50 Take him and upon the day after Sabbath, kill him.

10:51 For to do so now would be work.”

10:52 And they did.

10:53 The congregation gathered and left their camps and stoned the Sabbath breaker to death.

10:54 Rocks, stones, pebbles, even dust was cast towards him.

10:55 Until his flesh be broken, his bones crushed, his body crippled.

10:56 They left him there, so that the scavengers, the crows, the wild beasts shall feast upon him who dared pick up sticks on the sabbath day.

10:57 And the lord witnessed this execution and was displeased.

10:58 For though the death of the Sabbath breaker was pleasing, the fashion of the Israelites were not.

10:59 The clothes were dull and plain and did not please the sight of the lord.

10:60 The lord came to Moses and said to him,

10:61 "The fashion of the people of Israel is dull and plain.

10:62 This offends me, for even the clothing of the children of Israel shall give praise to the lord.

10:63 Have them sew ribbons upon the fringes of their garments of blue.

10:64 So that the clothing please the lord.

10:65 And when they look upon the blue fringe, they shall remember they are the promised people, children of Israel.

10:66 And they shall remember to keep my commandments and be holy unto God.

10:67 And that the lord delivered them from the land of Egypt and shall take them to the promised lands in the covenant made since the days of Abraham.

10:68 None shall ever forget that I delivered them from slavery.

10:69 For generations, all Israelites shall be grateful for that."

11:1 Korah the son of Izhar, Dathan and Abiram the sons of Eliab, and On the son of Peleth took men and spoke to Moses.

11:2 Two hundred and fifty men they took; members of fame, respected members of the community and men of renown.

11:3 They came to Moses and Aaron and challenged them.

11:4 "You are arrogant men, who believe themselves most holy.

11:5 For all children of Israel are holy, as we are the chosen people of God.

11:6 Each one, holy and blessed by the lord.

11:7 What makes the two of you most special, to rise above the congregation and declares yourselves most holy than others?"

11:8 When Moses heard this, he fell upon his face in laughter.

11:9 "Have any of you spoken with God. Have any of you gone into the tabernacle and heard the voice of the lord?

11:10 No, you have not. Aaron and I have.

11:11 This is what makes us most holier than you."

11:12 The men argued and said to Moses,

11:13 "The reason we have not gone into the tabernacle and heard the voice of the lord is because you deny it.

11:14 It is a sin for us to do so, is it not?

11:15 Or is it a lie. The demands of God, are they from God?

11:16 For we believe you lying and that the demands are yours.

11:17 So that ye can control us and hold power over us and so we fear you."

11:18 Moses laughed again, for he knew the demands all of them, were from God.

11:19 For Moses would not request such ridiculous demands, sacrifices and laws.

11:20 He said to them, "If you believe these, then let the lord decide.

11:21 Come on the morrow and bring each man a censer.

11:22 Put fire and incense within the censers and we shall see whom the lord decides."

11:23 Now, Korah was of the tribe of Levi, who were enslaved to God to care for the tabernacle.

11:24 For this slavery, he thought himself honoured and separated from the tribes of Israel, who did not directly belong to God.

11:25 Moses spoke to him in private and said to him,

11:26 "Why must you defy me, who has led you from Egypt, as is the will of God?

11:27 And Aaron, who is chosen by God to be the high priest?

11:28 Why do you murmur against us and rebel against us?

11:29 And Korah said,

11:30 "Because you believe us fools, because you believe we should follow you blindly.

11:31 We are all blessed by God and should all feel his love and his voice.

11:32 Yet you keep that honour to yourself, in greed.

11:33 My tribe has cared for the tabernacle and are owned by God. Does this not make us holy?

11:34 Aren't all the children of Israel holy. Yes.

11:35 So curse be to you, who believe himself holier than us, in arrogance and defiance."

11:36 When Moses called for Dathan and Abiram, the two brothers cursed him and spoke foul.

11:37 They spoke and said, "Curse be the man, who promised us lands flowing of milk and honey, only to deny it to us.

11:38 We shall die in the desert and be denied the covenant promised to us by God.

11:39 Why must we be denied that which is ours, merely for our age?

11:40 We did not rebel against the lord, nor feared the giants, for we have faith in the lord God.

11:41 And now you claim us cursed and we shall die in the desert like beasts.

11:42 Only an unholy man would do this."

11:43 When Moses heard this, he cried unto the heavens,

11:44 "Do you hear what these men accuse me of. That they call me unholy.

11:45 Be known that I did not curse them nor harm them, nor take even a shekel from them, yet they say these things most foul and loathe my name.

11:46 Upon the morrow, the men came, each with their censers and stood at the door of the tabernacle of the congregation.

11:47 The glory of God came down in great fire and said to Aaron and Moses,

11:48 "Get you away from these men, so that I may consume them."

11:49 And Moses and Aaron begged to God,

11:50 "Do not consume them all, for why must the congregation suffer for the sins of a few?"

11:51 And God said,

11:52 "Tell the others to stay away from them, from their tents and from their families.

11:53 For I shall consume them and feast upon them all"

11:54 Moses knew the wrath of the lord shall be upon them and said to all the children of Israel,

11:55 "These men have doubted my holiness and devotion to the children of Israel.

11:56 For this, the lord is angry and shall smite them.

11:57 Witness now those who doubt me, for to doubt me is to

doubt God."

11:58 It was then that the great and gaping jaw came forth from the ground.

11:59 Teeth of trees and rock came and consumed the families of the men who rebelled with Korah, so that all were gathered and buried deep within the earth.

11:60 The children of Israel fled, for fear the great earthen jaw shall consume them and eat them.

11:61 As this was done, a great fire came out of the tabernacle and consumed the two hundred and fifty men who offered incense and fire.

11:62 The lord said to Moses,

11:63 "Take the censers of the two hundred and fifty men who have gone against you.

11:64 Make them into brass plates and display them within the tabernacle.

11:65 So that all the children of Israel shall see them and be reminded of what happens to those who doubt your holiness.

11:66 The very souls of the men shall be in the brass plates and they shall whisper to those who listen and warn them and tell them of their sins.

11:67 And they shall tell them that none but the priests shall offer incense to the lord, for the priests are most holy.

11:68 Though all the children of Israel be holy, some are holier.

11:69 Accept it and take what holiness you can get."

11:70 As the days passed, the people of Israel grew angry.

11:71 They accused Aaron and Moses for the deaths of the men and sympathized with the rebellion.

11:72 Again, the lord grew angry and came down in a pillar of black cloud and said to Aaron and Moses,

11:73 "Get away from these people, so that my jaw shall chew upon them all."

11:74 Aaron and Moses fell on their faces and begged to God,

11:75 "Do not let your jaw rise forth from the earth, for it brings fear and hatred into the hearts of the children of Israel."

11:76 To calm the lord, they offered marijuana and the lord became stoned and calm.

11:77 Instead of the earthen mouth, the lord sent a plague to the children of Israel.

11:78 So that fourteen thousand and seven hundred men who sympathized, were killed and left to rot in the wilderness.

11:79 And the survivors rejoiced for the slaying of those who doubted.

12:1 The lord came to Moses and said,

12:2 "The lord must make it known that not all can offer incense or perform sacrifice to God.

12:3 For only those the lord deem most holy shall offer these most holy things to the lord.

12:4 Go, let all who wish to perform sacrifice and offer incense unto God offer themselves a rod of dead wood, with their names written upon it.

12:5 And have a rod of dead wood, with the name of Aaron written upon it.

12:6 Place them within the box and upon the morrow, those I deem most holy to offer sacrifice shall be known."

12:7 Moses spoke this to the children of Israel and men gathered rods of dead wood and carved their names in, believing themselves most holy and able to offer incense and perform sacrifice to the lord.

12:8 All of the tribe of Levi placed their names in, for they believed the slaves of God should be most holy, for belonging to the lord.

12:9 Upon the morrow, Moses came and emptied the box, which contained all the rods of those who believed themselves most holy to perform sacrifice.

12:10 All the rods were dead, save one.

12:11 For the rod with the name other than Aaron carved into it were dead.

12:12 But Aaron's rod was alive and in bloom.

12:13 With flowers, leaves and almonds and fruits growing upon it.

12:14 And when the children of Israel saw this, they knew it was by the lord's will and that Aaron and the priests are only holy enough to offer sacrifice.

12:15 Those that doubted; that believed Moses placed the rod with buds within the box while no one was looking;

12:16 Came upon the tabernacle and offered incense unto God.

12:17 The lord grew angry and cursed them with a plague.

12:18 They knew then that they were unworthy to offer incense and came to Moses and said to him,

12:19 "Are we to die; to perish, merely for coming unto the tabernacle and offering gifts to God?"

12:20 And Moses said,

12:21 "Yes."

13:1 The lord came to Aaron and said unto him,

13:2 "You and your sons shall bear the responsibility of the sanctuary and shall bear your titles of priesthood with pride.

13:3 Those of the tribe of Levi, who belong to me in servitude, shall help you and aid you; but it shall be the priests who administer unto the tabernacle.

13:4 For the priests are most holy and shall not die when they go into the places most holy.

13:5 The tribe of Levi shall clean and minister, but shall not come near the most holy vessels, the altars, nor enter the sanctuary, lest they die at the hands of the lord.

13:6 They shall guard the grounds, to ensure none other than the priests come within the places most holy; come near the most holy of things;

13:7 Thus the wrath of the lord shall not strike down for this blasphemy.

13:8 All of the tribe of Levi belongs in slavery unto the lord; and the lord shall share this gift with you and your sons.

13:9 So that the priests shall not do the petty work within the tabernacle; so that priests shall do more important tasks of slaying animals and spreading blood.

13:10 The priests shall keep care of the office of the altar and that which be within the veil, for this is most holy to God.

13:11 And if a stranger come into the night, the lord shall strike them down.

13:12 Behold, the lord has given you charge of the heave offerings, of sacrifices and of all hallowed things within Israel.

13:13 It is your responsibility to anoint and atone for the children of Israel; for if you don't, they shall be cursed to damnation.

13:14 Every offering of food which is given by a child of Israel shall be yours, so that ye and your sons shall feast upon their sacrifice.

13:15 In the most holy of places shall you eat it; for it shall be most holy.

13:16 When they offer their best of the harvests and the best of their oils and the best of their wines, the lord shall give it to you and your sons as a gift.

13:17 So that the priests shall live in gluttony of the finest foods and drinks offered in the nation of Israel.

13:18 The flesh of the sacrifices upon the altar shall be given to you, so that even the priests shall be gluttons of meat.

13:19 All that which is given to God, the lord shall give some to you as a gift, for the lord loves you and shall care for you.

13:20 Nevertheless, those of the unclean beasts shall belong to God and not to you, nor shall the first-born sons belong to you; they shall be God's.

13:21 The first-born sons shall be redeemed by the father and bought for five shekels, if he wishes to keep him for himself.

13:22 But the first-born of the animals; the sheep, the goat, the cow, shall not be redeemed, for they shall forever belong to God.

13:23 You shall cover the altar with their blood and burn the fat upon it, so that the aroma shall rise to Zion and bring pleasure to the lord.

13:24 All of the flesh, shall be given to you, so that you may consume it and be holy.

13:25 All of the heave offerings, it shall be eaten by the priests and their wives and their sons and daughters; it shall be a statute unto all the generations of the priest's seed.

13:26 Remember, the lord has given unto the priests a great many gifts, so that they may live in luxury, gluttony and comfort.

13:27 For these gifts, the priests shall have no need for earthly belongings; for land.

13:28 Why would one who eats the finest foods offered by the nation need to grow their own crops?

13:29 The Levites; slaves to God, shall have an inheritance of land.

13:30 One tenth of the tithe shall be given to them, so they may eat and drink and have strength to do serve the lord.

13:31 If any of the children of Israel whine about the inheritance for the Levites, let them bear sin and die.

13:32 Go, tell the tribe of Levi that they shall be grateful for that which the lord has given them.

13:33 For all the tenth of the tithe shall they give thanks and honour the lord and give praise.

13:34 They shall eat of it within their homes, their abodes, for it shall be their reward for being slaves in direct service to God.

13:35 Tell them that though this be of the tithe, it is given to them and they shall bear no sin for taking that which belongs to God.

13:36 But if they take anything else and pollute the holy things, they shall die."

14:1 And the lord spoke to Moses and Aaron, saying,

14:2 "These shall be the laws of those cursed by the dead.

14:3 Bring a red heifer, with neither spot nor blemish and which has never known labour.

14:4 Give the heifer unto Eleazar the priest, so that he may take of the blade and thrust the point within the face of the heifer, killing it.

14:5 Eleazar shall take his fingers and dip them in the blood and seven times shall spray blood upon the tabernacle of the congregation.

14:6 Burn the carcass whole so that the flesh, the blood, the skins, the fat, the inwards and any expelled dung be burnt upon the altar.

14:7 As these burns, take hyssop and cedar wood and scarlet and throw them within the altar, so that they may burn.

14:8 For this, the priest shall be unclean and must wash his clothes and bathe all his flesh and shall be then clean on the morrow.

14:9 A man that is clean shall gather the ashes of the heifer, the dung, the hyssop, the cedar wood and the hyssop and mix them with water, so that the water be holy.

14:10 It shall be a water of the dead.

14:11 He that gathers the ashes shall be unclean and must wash his clothes and bathe his flesh and shall remain unclean until nightfall.

14:12 Those that touch the bodies of the dead shall be unclean and can be purified with the waters of the dead.

14:13 The unclean man shall be unclean for seven days; upon the third day of his uncleanliness, he shall take a drink of the water of the dead and upon the eighth day he shall be clean.

14:14 For those who have filthied themselves with a corpse and refuse to purify themselves and drink of the water of the dead, shall remain unclean and cursed by the lord.

14:15 They shall be cast out of the nation of Israel and shall be dead themselves; zombies living in the wilderness.

14:16 When a man dies within his tent, all that come within the tent and all that be within the tent shall be unclean and must drink of the water on the third day of their uncleanliness.

14:17 Every open vessel, open jar, open pot within the tent shall be unclean and must be cleansed.

14:18 A clean priest must take hyssop and dip it within the water of the dead and sprinkle it upon the tent and upon all objects in the tent which be unclean.

14:19 That priest shall be unclean and must wash his clothes and bathe himself and shall remain unclean until the morrow.

14:20 For the armies of Israel which slay a man in battle, or for those which go near a grave, or a bone of a dead man; they shall be unclean and must drink of the water of the dead upon the third day.

14:21 The zombies which have refused purification shall be in a perpetual state of filth and have defiled the sanctuary of God.

14:22 They must touch no one, for those that they touch shall be unclean and must drink of the water of the dead upon the third day."

15:1 The children of Israel made camp within the desert of Zin, which lie in the lands of Kadesh, in the kingdom of Edom.

15:2 Miriam, sister of Aaron and Moses, died within this land and was buried there.

15:3 Both Aaron and Moses were made unclean by the body of Miriam and purified themselves on the third day by drinking the water of the dead.

15:4 It was bitter to them and made them ill, which the lord found amusing.

15:5 Within the desert of Zin, the children of Israel had not a drop of water to drink, save for the water of the dead, which was holy and must not be drunk for hydration (not that any wanted to).

15:6 The children began to complain and wonder if the lord has brought them out of the lands of Egypt, so that they may die of dehydration in the desert, like Miriam.

15:7 Moses and Aaron both heard the whining of the children of Israel and went to speak with the lord God, to know what doom he had planned for the whiners.

15:8 But, for once, the lord did not have a curse.

15:9 The lord had a solution for water and said to Aaron and Moses,

15:10 "The lord hears the cries of his children and shall quench them.

15:11 Take your rod, gather the nation of Israel and speak unto the rock which their eyes shall see and when you do, water shall gush out, plenty for the children of Israel to drink and to give water to their herds and their flocks."

15:12 Both Moses and Aaron gathered the children of Israel and stood by the rock.

15:13 Like fools, they did not talk to the rock, as the lord said, but struck it with the rod, like the time they did so during their stay in the lands of Rephidim.

15:14 Twice they struck the rock and upon the second strike, fresh, cool water gushed out and the peoples of Israel rejoiced and drank and their cattle drank.

15:15 All the people rejoiced and thanked Aaron and Moses and the lord for providing fresh water.

15:16 And the lord was pleased, for he now had a reason to doom Aaron and Moses; for he had no intentions for the two men to enter into the lands promised to them by the covenant during the days of Abraham.

15:17 The lord came to the men and said to them,

15:18 "How dare you mock me, the lord, and do not as I say!

15:19 Have I asked you to strike the rock for water, then strike the rock I shall tell you.

15:20 But I did not; I asked of you to speak to the rock, to ask of it to bring forth water.

15:21 For this defiance, neither of the two of you shall step foot into the lands of milk and honey, for you were once men in favour of God; leaders of the children of Israel.

15:22 And the lord cannot have his leaders defy him."

15:23 With that, the lord left and Aaron and Moses grieved and were confused, for they knew not that striking the rock would offend the lord so.

15:24 The land became known as the waters of Meribah, where Aaron and Moses thus sealed their doom.

16:1 The children of Israel wished to pass through the nation of Edom and sent messengers to the king of Edom, to ask permission to travel their lands.

16:2 They said to him, "We are messengers of the children of Israel, led by God.

16:3 For generations were we under the servitude of Egypt, who had cursed us and vexed us and mocked our lord.

16:4 We cried and our lord heard us, answered us and sent an angel to bring us forth out of Egypt and now we have travelled to you.

16:5 We ask your blessing so that we may travel through your lands; we will not pass your fields, nor your vineyards, nor even partake of your wells.

16:6 We shall stay upon the highways and pass through your lands, until we reach the end border."

16:7 When Edom heard this, he replied,

16:8 "You shall not pass my lands.

16:9 For I have heard of your nation and your lord.

16:10 The angel which was brought down and led you away from the peoples of Egypt did so through murder.

16:11 I wish not the first-born sons of my people to die.

16:12 When your people have travelled, it has brought with them great suffering and chaos and death to those who were in the way.

16:13 I have heard these and wish it not upon my nation.

16:14 You shall not pass through my nation; if you try, my armies shall be at the ready."

16:15 And the messengers said,

16:16 "We mean you no harm.

16:17 You have our word that we shall not harm you, nor take of your belongings.

16:18 If even one lamb drink of your waters, we shall pay for it.

16:19 All our travels shall be on the highway and not near your villages, nor cities, nor your vineyards, nor your crops."

16:20 And the king of Edom said, "No!

16:21 For you shall pass through and take by force.

16:22 It is what you do; do not deny this.

16:23 You shall take my lands anyway and pillage and rape my people.

16:24 I will not allow this to happen.

16:25 If we are to be doomed by your kind, we shall be doomed in fight and not in passing.

16:26 Be gone now and be warned.

16:27 My borders shall be well protected and if but one child of Israel step foot, it shall be considered an act of war and we shall strike back with fury."

16:28 Thus Edom refuses passage to the nation of Israel; and the nation of Israel turned away.

16:29 And the children of Israel travelled away from the lands of Kadesh and came upon mount Hor, near the coast and the land of Edom.

16:30 The lord came down and spoke with Moses and said to him,

16:31 "For your defiance of me, Aaron nor you shall pass into the promised lands.

16:32 Aaron shall die today, by my hand.

16:33 Take Aaron and his son Eleazar and have them brought to the top of mount Hor, in witness of all of the children of Israel.

16:34 Strip Aaron of his holy garments and place them upon Eleazar; for Eleazar shall now be the high priest of the children of Israel; most favoured by God."

16:35 Moses did as the lord commanded and brought Aaron and Eleazar to the top of mount Hor, where all the children of Israel shall witness this.

16:36 Moses stripped Aaron of his clothes and placed them upon Eleazar and announced to all the children of Israel,

16:37 "This shall now be your new high priest."

16:38 When the last word was said, the great palm of God came down and slapped Aaron and crushed him as though an insect into the rocks of mount Hor.

16:39 When all the people saw this, they mourned for Aaron for thirty days, for they loved him and looked to him for guidance.

16:40 Moses and Eleazar came down upon the mount and were unclean because of the corpse of Aaron.

16:41 Upon the third day, both drank of the waters of death and cleansed themselves and became clean.

17:1 King Arad, a Canaanite, sent spies out to the children of Israel and fought them and took with him prisoners.

17:2 The children of Israel vowed war against Arad and fought back.

17:3 With the aid of God, they destroyed them all.

17:4 Entire cities laid to rubble, so that few survived.

17:5 Those that did survive were pieced with the blades of Israel.

17:6 Men, women, and children.

17:7 Those women who did not know the pleasures of men were saved, so they could be raped, again and again.

17:8 They named the place Hormah, for they gathered for themselves mass amounts of whores for their taking.

17:9 After their war, they travelled south by way of the Red Sea; back to the lands of Edom.

17:10 And they were much discouraged, for there was no bread to eat nor water to drink.

17:11 The children of Israel spoke out against the lord and Moses and thought themselves doomed again.

17:12 They wondered why the lord would take them out of the lands of Egypt, so that they could starve and die of thirst in the wilderness.

17:13 Though manna came every night to feed them, they still had no water to drink with it.

17:14 And the sweetness of the manna made them all the more thirsty.

17:15 When the lord heard their complaints, he grew angry and thought to smite them.

17:16 He went to Satan himself and asked that he slaughter the children of Israel.

17:17 Satan refused and told God to fuck off and do his own dirty work.

17:18 For Satan had no intention of working with such an evil tyrant.

17:19 The lord went to the serpents and asked them to slaughter the children of Israel.

17:20 The serpents refused, for they would not work with a lord who cursed them for no good reason.

17:21 God was angry and with his anger created fiery snakes, with venom most foul.

17:22 These new breed of snakes were sent to the children of Israel, to bite them and kill them.

17:23 Many died and cried out to Moses, "Save us. Save us!

17:24 For we have sinned and spoke ill of God."

17:25 Moses prayed for the people of Israel, which did nothing.

17:26 For prayer holds no power; it is mere words.

17:27 Moses knew not what to do, until a stranger came unto him.

17:28 The stranger was Satan, but Moses knew this not.

17:29 Satan told Moses,

17:30 "Build a serpent made of brass and set it upon a brass pole."

17:31 Moses said to Satan,

17:32 "I cannot, for to do such things is blasphemy and shall break the second commandment."

17:33 Satan said to Moses,

17:34 "Do not worry.

17:35 For the snake is not an image of your lord and will not break God's laws.

17:36 When you make this brass snake, hand it to me."

17:37 Moses did and gave the brass snake to Satan.

17:38 Satan took the brass snake and blessed it and said to Moses,

17:39 "Tell the children of Israel that when they are bit, to gaze upon the snake.

17:40 For the snake is blessed and shall cure them of the venom."

17:41 Moses did and all the people who were bit and gazed upon the snake were saved from the grasp of death.

17:42 They praised the stranger and thanked him for his help.

17:43 Satan was about to speak to them and tell them of their lord's evilness, when God came down and pushed him into the depths of the earth and took all credit for the brass snake.

17:44 The Israelites mistakenly praised God for saving them from the fiery snakes.

17:45 For they were fools and did not question why God would send snakes to begin with.

17:46 The lord then left and went to Satan and told him that if he ever meddle in the affairs of the lord again, he shall know great suffering.

17:47 Satan spat in the lord's face and cursed God and told him that he shall meddle all he wants, to save the peoples of earth from his wrath.

17:48 Whether Egyptian, Israelite, Amorite, Canaanite, Hittite, Jebusite, or any other peoples, Satan swore to God that he shall do all he can to protect them from God.

17:49 After the snakes left, the children of Israel travelled toward Arnon, which be between the borders of the Moab and the Amorites.

17:50 They did great and terrifying things their, which was written in the Book of the Wars of the Lord, which was later destroyed.

17:51 For in it was proof of God's evil wrath and the lord wished not

future generations to know of this, lest they defy him.

17:52 Afterwards the children of Israel went to Beer; known for its fine ales.

17:53 They made camp there and got drunk and in their drunkenness praised God and fought with one another and stripped naked and lied intimately with one another (both gorgeous and ugly).

17:54 The lord saw this and was amused by the drunken antics of the children of Israel.

17:55 All the elders of Israel dug more wells there, so that they may get water and create more ale.

17:56 After their drunken orgies, the children of Israel travelled to the lands of Bamoth and in Bamoth they sent messengers to king Sihon of the Amorites.

17:57 They asked of Sihon,

17:58 "Let us pass through your lands: we shall not partake of your crops, nor vineyards, nor drink of your wells, but shall stay upon the highway until we pass through."

17:59 Sihon knew the children of Israel were hung over and thought himself an opportunity to take them.

17:60 He denied their request to pass through his lands and sent out his armies to battle with them.

17:61 Israel smote them, for in their drunkenness they lost their fear and fought bravely.

17:62 They praised the lord for their victory and claimed the lands of Sihon as their own.

17:63 They dwelt in their cities, took of their crops and vineyards and stole their belongings.

17:64 All were slaughtered, even the virgins.

17:65 For the Amorites were an ugly people and none of the men of Israel wished to lie with them.

17:66 The peoples of Moab came to the children of Israel and thanked them.

17:67 For king Sihon took the lands of Moab by force and claimed it as his own.

17:68 The children of Israel welcomed the peoples of Moab and let them stay in their newly conquered cities.

17:69 All the people of Moab were thankful and the Israelites gained their trust, so that they could exploit that trust later.

17:70 Moses was not done with his acquisitions of land.

17:71 He sent spies out to the lands of Jaazer and discovered the lands fertile and poorly guarded.

17:72 The Israelites took this land.

17:73 Though none in the lands fought back, for they were peaceful farmers, the children of Israel killed them all anyway.

17:74 Og, the king of Bashan, heard of this and grew angry.

17:75 For he knew the peoples of Jaazer and were friendly with them and would not let this crime go unpunished.

17:76 Og gathered his armies and marched towards Jaazer, to kill the children of Israel.

17:77 The armies of Israel marched towards them and they met on the plains of Edrei.

17:78 When the children of Israel saw Og's armies, they grew worried.

17:79 For the army of Bashan was strong, disciplined and well-armed.

17:80 But the lord came down, for he would not let these heathens destroy his people.

17:81 Only God can destroy them, at his choosing.

17:82 Great pillars of smoke came down from the heavens and surrounded the armies of Bashan and suffocated them and killed them.

17:83 The armies of Israel marched into the lands governed by Og and conquered them.

17:84 They slaughtered them all; man, woman, and child.

17:85 Though some virgins were saved, so that they may be raped, they killed them soon after.

17:86 For the virgins did not consent and fought back their rapists and bit hard upon their erections.

17:87 Because of their defiance, they were killed.

17:88 Another people destroyed, another genocide caused by the children of Israel, under the blessings of God.

18:1 The children of Israel set forward and made camp in the plains of Moab, near the river Jordan that faced the side of Jericho.

18:2 And suddenly the people of Moab became nervous, for they feared the peoples of Israel would claim their lands.

18:3 Balak the son of Zippor, who was king, saw what tragedies were done to the Amorites and feared for his people.

18:4 King Balak was afraid, for he feared his people would come to harm; and they were many.

18:5 Moab spoke to the elders of Midian, "These people shall consume all that is around us, as the locusts consume the crops.

18:6 They are our friends now, for they had rid us of Sihon, but what's to stop them from doing to us what they did to Sihon?"

18:7 The elders discussed and it was decided to send for Balaam the son of Beor, who was a great sorcerer.

18:8 If Balaam could aid them and bless them, they shall be protected from the Israelites.

18:9 Balaam was a sorcerer blessed by God; the lord has given him powers of wizardry.

18:10 And since Balaam is not a child of Israel, this is not a sin for him.

18:11 The messengers went to Balaam, who lived in Pethor, by the rivers of Jordan and said to him,

18:12 "Behold, there is a great number of people who have come out of the lands of Egypt and their numbers are so great they cover the face of the earth.

18:13 We fear they wish to conquer us and we come to ask of your blessings.

18:14 Come now to our nation, so that you may bless our armies, curse our enemies and our people shall live.

18:15 Do this and we promise you great reward; money, ale and whores."

18:16 When Balaam heard their request, he said to them,

18:17 "Come, stay the night and I shall go into deep prayer and see what the lord shall say."

18:18 During the night, the lord came unto Balaam and asked him,

18:19 "Umm, who the hell are these people?"

18:20 And Balaam said,

18:21 "They are messengers, sent by king Balak.

18:22 They have told me of a great number of people which has come out of the lands of Egypt and they worry these people shall conquer them.

18:23 They asked me if I could protect them."

18:24 The lord said to Balaam,

18:25 "You shall not go with these people, nor curse their enemies, for their enemies be blessed."

18:26 And in the morning, Balaam told the messengers that he could not come with them, for the lord will not allow Balaam to use his sorcery against the children of Israel.

18:27 When the messengers sent word of this to Balak, Balak sent more messengers, of higher ranking and offered greater reward.

18:28 And the messengers said to Balaam,

18:29 "We shall offer you warehouses of gold and of silver and private brothels.

18:30 Your name shall be praised among our people and you shall be of the highest regard amongst our nation."

18:31 And Balaam said,

18:32 "It matters not what you offer me for reward, for I cannot help you if God won't let me.

18:33 Now come, stay the night and I shall ask the lord again."

18:34 The lord came down and said to Balaam,

18:35 "Who are these people?"

18:36 And Balaam replied,

18:37 "More messengers, sent by king Balak."

18:38 And God said,

18:39 "These fucking idiots. Damn them.

18:40 They do not seem to be able to take a hint.

18:41 If they ask of you to go with them, go.

18:42 But do not do as they ask; I shall tell you what to do."

18:43 When the sun rose, Balaam saddled his donkey, brought two servants and rode with the messengers from Moab.

18:44 When the lord saw this, he was angry.

18:45 For when the lord said to Balaam to go with these people, the lord was apparently being sarcastic and did not really want Balaam to go.

18:46 Balaam didn't realize this and thought the lord actually wanted him to go.

18:47 Stupid Balaam.

18:48 God sent an angel in the path of Balaam, to block him and his servants.

18:49 Balaam and his servants did not see the angel, but the donkey did.

18:50 The donkey turned to the side and would not pass through the angel.

18:51 Balaam grew angry and grabbed his rod and beat his donkey for such disobedience.

18:52 The angel left and the donkey travelled onward, until they went to a vineyard, with two walls on each side of the path.

18:53 Balaam nor his servants saw the angel, but the donkey did.

18:54 And when the donkey saw the angel, he thrust himself against the wall, trying to escape and crushed Balaam's foot.

18:55 Balaam grew angry and grabbed his rod and struck his donkey.

18:56 The angel left and the donkey travelled farther, until they went to a path where the walls were narrow.

18:57 The angel stood there, sword in hand.

18:58 Neither Balaam nor his servants could see the angel.

18:59 But the donkey could and when he saw the angel, he sat down and refused to move.

18:60 Balaam grabbed his rod and beat the donkey, trying to get the ass to move.

18:61 It was then that the lord opened the mouth of the donkey and the donkey said to Balaam,

18:62 "What have I done to you, that I deserved to be beaten three times?"

18:63 Balaam, who was not at all surprised by his talking donkey for he is a sorcerer, said to his ass,

18:64 "Because three times you have disobeyed me; you travelled of the path, you crushed my foot and now you won't move."

18:65 And the ass said, "I am not your ass, which has been faithful and loyal unto you for years.

18:66 Do you not believe I had did these things for good reason?"

18:67 It was then the angel was revealed to Balaam and Balaam fell flat on his face.

18:68 The angel said, "Why have you struck your ass three times. For I was in the way those three times and if ye had passed through, I would have beheaded you and saved your donkey."

18:69 Balaam said to the angel, "I have sinned, for I knew not that you were in the way.

18:70 If I had, I would not have struck my ass.

18:71 If it pleases you, I shall turn around and go home, for I thought the lord wished me to come this way."

18:72 The angel said to Balaam,

18:73 "You have travelled this far. Go with the men, but do not do as they say.

18:74 Speak only what the lord tells you to do."

18:75 With that, the angel thrust script into the mouth of Balaam; the words that God wanted Balaam to say.

18:76 When Balak heard that Balaam was coming, he went to meet with him on the borders of Arnon, near the coast.

18:77 And Balak said to Balaam, "Most high sorcerer, I thank you for coming.

18:78 Help my people and I shall offer you great reward and promote you to highest honour."

18:79 Balaam said to Balak, "I shall say only the words that God hath thrust into my mouth."

18:80 The two men went onward, unto the lands of Kirjathhhuzoth, where Balak gave Balaam many oxen, sheep, and whores.

18:81 And it came to pass that on the morrow, Balak took Balaam to the highest point of Baal, so that he may see the people of Israel.

18:82 When Balaam saw the children of Israel, he thought to himself, 'Holy shit, Balak doesn't stand a fucking chance.'

19:1 Balaam said to Balak, "Build me upon this highest point of Baal seven altars and prepare for me seven oxen and seven rams; males, without blemish."

19:2 Balak did as Balaam commanded and offered an oxen and a ram for every altar.

19:3 After the sacrifice, Balaam said to Balak, "Go now and stand by the altars, for I must go and speak with the lord, so that he may show me what to do."

19:4 And the lord came down to Balaam and Balaam said, "Look, I have prepared seven altars for you and offered unto you seven oxen and seven rams as sacrifice."

19:5 The lord said to Balaam, "Go to Balak and speak the words that I have put within your mouth."

19:6 Balaam returned to the seven altars where Balak stood and said to him, "Balak the king of Moab has sent for me and told me to curse and defy the people of Israel.

19:7 How can I curse those which God has blessed. It cannot be done.

19:8 From the tops of these rocks I see them and they spread out across the fields.

19:9 I cannot even count their number of armies, yet alone their entire people.

19:10 If I die, let it be by their sword, so that I may die by the righteous."

19:11 Balak grew angry and said to Balaam, "What have you done. For I have asked you to curse you and here you are, blessing them."

19:12 Balaam replied, "I can only do that which the lord allows me to do."

19:13 So Balak took Balaam to another place, so that they may see better the children of Israel.

19:14 They went to the fields of Zophim, to the top of Pisgah and Balaam had Balak build seven more altars and sacrifice seven more oxen and seven more rams.

19:15 And Balak stood by the altars, while Balaam went to speak with God once more.

19:16 The lord met Balaam and stuffed another scroll in his mouth.

19:17 When Balaam returned Balak asked of him, "What has the lord said to you?"

19:18 The scroll in Balaam's mouth opened and the words came out of his mouth and said,

19:19 "Rise up Balak son of Zippor; hear, and hearken unto me.

19:20 God is not a man that shall lie, nor one that needs to repent. What he says shall be done and it shall be good.

19:21 Behold, I shall not curse the people of Israel, but bless them, for it is the lord's will and I cannot reverse it.

19:22 With the strength of many unicorns, the lord has brought them out of Egypt."

19:23 Balak interrupted Balaam and asked him,

19:24 "What is this unicorn?"

19:25 Balaam replied, "I know little of the unicorn, but only that it is a great and powerful animal and that God has the strength of them!

19:26 There is no enchantment against them, nor curse strong enough to weaken them, for they are the people chosen by God.

19:27 They shall rise up like a great and powerful lion and consume their prey and drink of the blood of the slain."

19:28 Balak asked of Balaam, "If this be true, then neither curse them nor bless them."

19:29 And Balaam said, "Have I not told thee that I shall do only what the lord has told of me?"

19:30 So Balak took Balaam unto mount Peor, which looked towards Jeshimon, so that Balaam may see the people of Israel there and be allowed to curse them from that location.

19:31 Balaam had Balak build seven more altars and sacrifice upon each altar one oxen and one ram; males without blemish.

19:32 And Balaam knew what the lord wanted him to do and did not seek out sorcerous enchantments, but set his face towards the wilderness.

19:33 He saw the great children of Israel abiding in their tents and the spirit of the lord came over him.

19:34 With his head held high, he yelled to the heavens, "Balaam the son of Beor shall speak what the lord has told of him, with Balak the king of Moab at my side.

19:35 May the children of Israel be blessed by my words.

19:36 How goodly are their tents and their tabernacles, so that they please the lord.

19:37 Shall they spread from valley to valley, river to river, coast to coast.

19:38 Let their seed spread into the waters of life and their kings be greater than all kinds before.

19:39 God has led them out of Egypt with the strength of unicorns; and they shall eat up the nations which be their enemies, pierce them with arrows, break their bones and drink from their skulls.

19:40 They shall be as a great lion and who dare disturb the great lion?

19:41 Blessed is he that bless them and curse be to he who curse them."

19:42 With these words, Balak grew angry and slapped Balaam with his palm and said to him,

19:43 "What be the matter with you; are you ill of mind?

19:44 I have called to you to curse these people, who are my enemies and instead you bless them thrice.

19:45 I offered you gold, silver, riches, wealth, fame, ale and whores for but a simple curse and you reject these and do the opposite of which I asked."

19:46 And Balaam said to Balak, "I can do only that which the lord allows me.

19:47 It matters not what you offer me; nations full of gold and silver, cities of women nor warehouses of the finest ales can be of no use, for if I went against the lord, he shall curse me greater than any rewards which you offer.

19:48 The lord has showed me what these children of Israel shall do and I shall share with you this knowledge.

19:49 They will fucking crush you.

19:50 From the sky shall fall a star of their ancestors and it shall land upon the sceptre of Israel and with it shall dominate over all four corners of Moab and destroy the children of Sheth.

19:51 The lands of Edom shall belong to them, Seir shall also be in their possession and the children of Israel shall become powerful and valiant.

19:52 Look towards the north, the west, the east and the south.

19:53 It matters not how well the lands be protected, for it will all be taken by force and belong to Israel .

19:54 All those who defy them will die, so that only those wished by God shall live."

19:55 With these words, Balak grew scared and shit his pants.

19:56 Balaam left and went to his home and Balak went to his kingdom, with faeces dripping down his legs.

20:1 When the people of Israel made camp in Shittim, they noticed the plentiful brothels, brimming with the daughters of Moab.

20:2 They committed whoredom with them and slept with them and ate with them and drank with them and even attended their religious ceremonies.

20:3 They wished to understand their God's, their religion and their culture and gain knowledge of this civilization.

20:4 This angered the lord, for the people of Israel ate food which was offered to the heathen God Baalpeor; a false God who apparently treated his followers fairly.

20:5 The lord came down and spoke to Moses and said to him,

20:6 "Take all which has been to ceremony for the heathen lord Baalpeor and rip off their heads.

20:7 Hang them upon the trees, so that the flesh upon their face rot off and be eaten by the crows.

20:8 Fill their skulls with strong drink, so that I may drink from their cranium and be drunk.

20:9 A plague shall curse these people and all that die shall be those who blasphemed and made themselves unclean through Baalpeor."

20:10 Thus a plague swept the camp and the elders of Israel came, and decapitated those which had died, and hung their heads upon the trees.

20:11 As the elders did this, an Israelite came back, with a Midianite whore, and the two entered his tent for erotic indulgences.

20:12 Moses saw this, the priests saw this, and all the children of Israel saw this through their tears for their dead friends and family members; dead from the plague of God.

20:13 Phinehas, the son of Eleazar the high priest saw this, and wrath consumed his very soul.

20:14 Phinehas grabbed a javelin, entered the tent, and thrust it through both whore and man.

20:15 The javelin pierced the heart of the Israelite, killing him, and

the whore was pierced through her belly.

20:16 The name of the Israelite was Zimri, son of Salu; a respected elder from the tribe of Simon.

20:17 The Midianite prostitute was named Cozbi, daughter of Zur, a chief of the peoples of Midian.

20:18 When the lord saw what Phinehas has done, he was pleased; for the Midianite prostitute struggling with the javelin in her stomach as a dead Israelite lay atop her was of great amusement for him.

20:19 For the lord loves blood, nudity and torn flesh.

20:20 Especially when the blood spills upon a nude and struggling whore.

20:21 God was so pleased, that he ended the plague which struck the peoples of Israel who held interest in Baalpeor.

20:22 But not before the plague consumed twenty four thousand, whose heads were chopped and hung upon trees, with their skulls filled with wine and strong drink.

20:23 The lord came down, and spoke with Moses, and said,

20:24 "Phinehas the son of Eleazar has pleased me; so much so that I have smiled, and lost my wrath for the children of Israel.

20:25 For this, he and his generations shall be greatly rewarded, and I shall make unto him and his seed a covenant of peace.

20:26 Let it be known that Phinehas, and all his sons, shall be great priests for the lord, and shall be unharmed from the lord's wrath, and know only peace.

20:27 For Phinehas has done the lord's work, and taken revenge upon a prostitute and her client.

20:28 These people of Midian, I loathe them, and wish them banished.

20:29 Curse these peoples, and smite them, in the name of the lord.

20:30 For they curse you with their sex, their foods, their drinks, and their false lord Baalpeor, and thus they killed twenty four thousand of my peoples.

20:31 This shall not go unpunished; I will wipe them off the face of the earth."

21:1 The daughters of Zelophehad, who was the son of Hepher, who was the son of Gilead, who was the son of Machir, who was the son of Manasseh, of the tribe of Joseph, came to Moses and Eleazar the high priest.

21:2 The name of the daughters were Mahlah, Noah, Hoglah, Milcah and Tirzah.

21:3 They came, and asked of Moses and Eleazar, "Our father had died in the wilderness of natural causes.

21:4 He was not cursed by the many plagues and tragedies which the lord has brought down to us.

21:5 We are all of his family; our mothers left him no sons. Why should his name die with him. Let us have our father's possessions."

21:6 Moses brought this case before the lord.

21:7 The lord came to Moses, and said to him,

21:8 "Zelophehad was a righteous man. Hepher was a righteous man. Gilead was a righteous man. Machir was a righteous man. Manasseh was a righteous man. There is no reason why Zelophehad's daughters should be punished for the sins of their past relatives.

21:9 They speak right, for surely the name of their father should live on, despite his bitch of a wife bearing him no sons.

21:10 Let it be law, that if a man die, and have no sons, that his inheritance shall pass to his daughters.

21:11 If he has no daughters, his inheritance shall pass on to his brothers.

21:12 If he has no brothers, his inheritance shall pass to his uncles.

21:13 If he has no uncles, his inheritance shall pass on to his dearest friends.

21:14 If he has no dearest friends, the guy is obviously a loser, and his inheritance shall be put up for auction, and sold to the highest bidder of the children of Israel.

21:15 His wife shall never have the inheritance, for she should have bore him a son."

21:16 The peoples of Israel soon came near mount Arabim, and made camp.

21:17 The lord said to Moses, "Go atop mount Arabim, so that ye may see the lands which will be given unto the children of Israel; promised by the holy covenant made since the days of Abraham.

21:18 Have the whole congregation of Israel join you, so they may witness you, as they witnesses your brother Aaron before he died by my hand.

21:19 For your defiance at the desert of Zin, where ye had struck the rock for water, you shall never live within the lands of which I'm about to show you.

21:20 Since ye have led the children of Israel hear, I shall let you see the lands, for I am a kind and loving God, and will not let ye lead these peoples without you knowing what you led them to."

21:21 Moses replied to God,

21:22 "Then why kill me!" Why not let me live, so I may enjoy the lands of which I have led my peoples to."

21:23 And God replied,

21:24 "Because you defied me twice now!

21:25 Once by striking the rock with your rod for water.

21:26 And now, for calling the children of Israel your peoples.

21:27 They are not the peoples of Moses; they are my people. So fuck you.

21:28 You shall die, and never know the wonders of the promised land of milk and honey."

21:29 Moses then asked of God,

21:30 "Then who shall lead the peoples after I die?

21:31 For they will need a man of flesh to lead them, since they are not holy enough for you to lead them yourself."

21:32 The lord thought for a moment, and replied,

21:33 "Take Joshua, the son of Nun, with ye, and set him before Eleazar the priest, and all the congregations of Israel.

21:34 Bless him, so that he may be their leader after you.

21:35 It shall be Joshua who will counsel with the lord, who shall ask advice from the Urim and the Thummim, and who shall ensure the law of the lord is obeyed."

21:36 Moses did as the lord commanded, and took Joshua atop mount Arabim, and placed him in front of Eleazar and the congregation of Israel.

21:37 Moses laid his hands upon Joshua, and blessed him, and made him his successor, as the lord commanded.

21:38 And all the peoples of Israel knew then, that Joshua shall replace Moses as the lord's bitch.

22:1 The lord came down to Moses, and said to him,

22:2 "Command the children of Israel to offer unto me their sacrifices, so that the lord shall continually have a sweet savour of burning flesh during all seasons.

22:3 This shall be an offering to be made daily; two male lambs under a year's age, with no blemish.

22:4 The one lamb shall be offered in the morning, and the other shall be offered at the evening.

22:5 Add to it a tenth part of an ephah of fine flour, mixed with a quarter hin of beaten oil.

22:6 This shall be a continual offering, so that throughout all time a lamb shall be burning so that the aroma please the lord.

22:7 For the morning, offer with the lamb a quarter hin of strongest wine; for the lord loveth a strong drink in the morning.

22:8 During the evening ye shall offer a quarter hin of strongest wine; so that the lord may keep his buzz throughout the days.

22:9 On the sabbath day ye shall offer two lambs for every sacrifice, with two tenths an ephah of finest flour and a half hin of strongest wine.

22:10 For the sabbath is the lord's day, and the lord will rest well with a heavy meal and strong drink.

22:11 Remember this sacrifice every sabbath, lest ye feel the wrath of the lord.

22:12 And in the beginnings of the month remember your burnt offerings; a ram, two young bullocks, and seven lambs of the first year, all without blemish.

22:13 With three tenths an ephah of flour mingled with oil for the one bullock, and two tenths an ephah of flour mingled with oil for the ram;

22:14 With a full ephah of flour mixed with oil for every one of the seven lambs, as it creates a pleasing scent for the lord God.

22:15 For wine, their shall be a half hin of wine for each bullock, a third of a hin for the ram, and a fourth part of a hin of wine for each ram; because for this sacrifice, the lord wish to be drunk!

22:16 And sacrifice one of the kid goats for a sin offering, and bring with that goat some beer.

22:17 Do not forget that the fourteenth day of the first month is the Passover.

22:18 On the fifteenth of this month is the feast: seven days all shall eat nothing but unleavened bread.

22:19 Upon the first day of the feast shall be a holy convocation; none shall do any servile work.

22:20 Instead, ye shall offer many sacrifices unto the lord. Two young bullocks, a ram, and seven lambs under the age of a year; males all, without blemish.

22:21 With these beasts shall also be food; three tenths a deal of fine flour mixed with oil for the bullocks and two tenths a deal of flour mixed with oil for the ram, with a tenth of a deal of fine flour mixed with oil for each lamb.

22:22 For drink, ye shall give a quarter hin of whiskey for the bullocks, a quarter hin of whiskey for the ram, and a half a hin of whiskey for each lamb.

22:23 All shall also offer a goat for sin offering; for ye are all filthy fucking sinners and must make atonement for your sins by killing a goat.

22:24 Ye shall offer these beside the continual burnt offering, so that the aromas shall blend together, and the scent shall be pleasing unto the lord.

22:25 Remember these sacrifices, and all sacrifices, lest the lord smell the unpleasant stench of your sins, and become angry."

23:1 "Remember, that upon the seventh month, of the first day of the month, shall be a holy day of convocation; none shall do servile work, but shall blow trumpets in honour of the lord.

23:2 Ye shall offer a burnt offering unto the lord; one ram, one young bullock, and seven lambs under the year, without blemish.

23:3 With these offerings shall be three tenths a deal of flour mixed with oil for the bullock, and two tenths a deal of fine flour mixed with oil for the ram.

23:4 Their shall be one tenth of fine flour mixed with oil for each lamb, so that seven tenths of a deal of fine flour mixed with oil shall be total.

23:5 Cut the throat of the sacrifice, and let the blood of the beast soak into the fur, and rub the flour and the oil within the fur and the blood.

23:6 Burn the animal upon the altar, so that their shall be a pleasing odour for the lord.

23:7 All peoples shall offer a kid goat; a male without blemish, for a sin offering.

23:8 For killing a young goat; a male without blemish, shall forgive ye of your sins.

23:9 Do not forget, that upon the seventh month, on the tenth day of this month, shall be the day of afflicting your souls; ye shall do no servile work.

23:10 All shall stay within their tents, and beat themselves with whips, so that the sins within their souls shall be cast out in pain.

23:11 They shall pour salt and wine vinegar upon their wounds, and let the salt and wine vinegar seep into their cuts and their gashes.

23:12 Burning oil shall be cast upon their feet, and lit on fire, and they shall run, and dance, but shall let the fire upon their feet die naturally.

23:13 Then they shall soak their feet in oxen urine, and give praise unto the lord.

23:14 Upon the seventh month, on the fifteenth day of the month, they shall do no servile work, and have a feast unto the lord for seven days.

23:15 On the first day of the feast, all the children of Israel shall offer unto the lord thirteen young bullocks, two rams, fourteen lambs born of the first year, and three hin of wine.

23:16 They shall pour the wine upon the sacrifices, and shall slay them, and burn them, so that the aroma create an intoxicating smoke unto the lord.

23:17 On the second day they shall take twelve young bullocks, two rams, fourteen lambs and a partridge in a pear tree.

23:18 Let them take these beasts, and burn them alive, in glory to God.

23:19 On the third day, they shall take foreign virgins, and give them unto the priests.

23:20 After the priests are finished raping the foreign virgins, let them take stakes of shittim wood, twice the length of man, and inlaid with pure gold.

23:21 They shall take these stakes of shittim wood, and thrust them within the vaginas of the once virgins heathens, so that the tip exit through their skull.

23:22 As the sun sets upon the fourth day, let the children of Israel get drunk, and dance naked, and wallow in their own vomit.

23:23 Except for those of the Nazarites, for they must not drink.

23:24 On the fifth day, stone a camel to death.

23:25 On the sixth day, take two bullocks and two rams; all males, without blemish.

23:26 Shove each of the bullocks heads into the buttocks of the rams, and the rams heads into the rectums of the bullocks, so that it create a circle of beasts with their heads up each others asses.

23:27 As they struggle, burn them alive, and place bets upon which beast shall survive longest.

23:28 Take the survivor, and beat it with whips, and offer the corpse as burnt sacrifice.

23:29 At the seventh day, the last day, take a goat; a young male without blemish, and four strong oxen.

23:30 Tie each leg of the goat to one of the oxen, and have the oxen run, so that the goat shall be pried apart, and create great amusement unto the lord.

23:31 Do this, as it will be a statute unto your peoples for generations."

23:32 And Moses told the children of Israel all that the lord commanded.

23:33 Some questioned why the lord would demand such violent and heinous sacrifice.

23:34 All that questioned, mysteriously died, and the survivors praised the lord.

24:1 Moses then spoke with the elders of Israel, and told them of the lord's commands.

24:2 He said to the elders, "As we all know, women are horrible creatures worthy only of cooking, cleaning and sexual gratification.

24:3 However, they be stubborn, and some believe themselves human, and wish to have rights.

24:4 It is known that if a man make a vow unto the lord God, or swear an oath, that the words he hath spoken are bound upon his soul, and the man must keep his word, lest he die.

24:5 Women have no souls, but still wish to make these oaths, these vows.

24:6 These shall be the laws of females who with to make vows; for with these laws, these cursed women will shut-up, and stop bitching.

24:7 If a woman wish to make a vow, and be not married, she must make the vow with the blessing of her father.

24:8 She shall take the vow or oath in front of her father, and her words shall be bound into the soul of her father.

24:9 And it shall be the father who take responsibility if his daughter break her words.

24:10 If the father wishes not her daughter to take the vow or oath, and disallows hers to speak the words, then she can't take the vow or oath.

24:11 Even if she speaks the words, they shall be unsanctioned, and be merely meaningless noise coming out of another bitch's mouth.

24:12 If the woman be married, it shall be not her father that takes on the vow, but her husband.

24:13 She shall speak the oath or vow in front of her husband, and the words of the wife shall be bound within the husband's soul, and it shall be he who shall be punished if she breaks her vows.

24:14 But if the husband disallow it, she cannot take the former vow or oath; her words shall be meaningless.

24:15 If the female be widowed, or divorced, and wish to take a vow or oath, then their is no man who shall be responsible for her words.

24:16 Let her take on the vow or oath; and the lord shall hear her words.

24:17 And if she break them, the wrath of the lord shall wax hot, and curse the wretched little cunt who believed herself worthy of taking a vow or an oath.

24:18 Warn the men, the fathers, the husbands, that if they take a vow for a female, the wrath of the lord shall wax hot upon them if their daughter or their wife break that vow or oath.

24:19 Advise them against it, for women are natural liars, and treacherous.

24:20 Remember that it was Eve, the first woman, who cursed all mankind, and had us cast out from the garden of Eden.

24:21 It was Eve who spoke with Satan, and doomed mankind to the devil's wrath.

24:22 Be warned; all women are like Eve.

24:23 Do not allow them to take the vow, unless her constant bitching is driving you insane, and the only way your wife or daughter will shut-up is if you let her take the vow."

24:24 And the elders of Israel told all the children of Israel what Moses said, and warned the men of the dangers of allowing women to take oaths and vows.

24:25 Plenty of women wished to exercise their new right to take oaths and vows.

24:26 All but seven were denied, and the seven that took the vows did so by nagging.

24:27 By surprise, they kept their vows, and did not break their holy spoken words.

24:28 The fathers and husbands of these women were surprised by this, and grew a great appreciation for their women, and loved them more.

24:29 The lord witnessed these men love and respect women, and grew fearful of feminist revolution.

24:30 So the lord God killed the seven women; they all died birthing sons, so that the lord shall make it appear they died a most honourable death.

25:1 The lord came down and said to Moses,

25:2 "Kill the Midianites."

25:3 And Moses said unto the children of Israel, "Arm yourselves for war, so that we may destroy the peoples of Midian."

25:4 Of every tribe they armed one thousand soldiers, so that twelve thousand men were ready for battle.

25:5 They were sent to war, with Eleazar and Phinehas the son of Eleazar blowing the silver trumpets in glory to God.

25:6 At night they attacked, and slaughtered all the males of Midian.

25:7 They slew even the kings of Midian; Evi, Rekem, Zur, Hur and Reba.

25:8 Even Balaam the son of Beor, who helped the children of Israel and blessed them, they slew with the sword.

25:9 With his last breath, Balaam cursed the children of Israel.

25:10 The armies of Israel gathered the women, the children, the cattle, the flocks, and all the spoils, and all the goods, and burnt the cities to the ground.

25:11 They took their captives and their bounty, and presented it to Moses and Eleazar the high priest, within the camp at the plains of Moab, which are by Jordan near Jericho.

25:12 And Moses was furious with them, and said unto them,

25:13 "Why doth ye keep these peoples alive; the women and the children?

25:14 The women will believe that Baalpeor shall save them; a false God.

25:15 The children shall grow, and become strong, and become enemies unto the children of Israel; enemies unto God.

25:16 Go, kill all the male children, and all the females who have known the pleasures of men.

25:17 Save the virgins, and the female children, so that ye may rape the virgins and the female children can grow, and become slaves or work in the brothels.

25:18 Remember to purify yourselves, for ye have all been tainted by the dead bodies of our enemies.

25:19 Purify your raiment, your weapons, your clothes, and yourselves."

25:20 Eleazar than came unto the soldiers, and said unto them,

25:21 "Remember to give praise to the lord for this magnificent genocide, and to give unto God the spoils of battle.

25:22 All that made of gold, of silver, of iron, of brass, of tin and of lead shall belong to the lord; he wants it.

25:23 Of those things made by fire, must be washed by fire, and it shall be clean. Nevertheless, all items must be purified with holy water, so that the stench of the Midianites shall be gone from them."

25:24 God then came unto Moses, and said to him,

25:25 "Take all the prey of war; both man and beast, and divide it in two parts.

25:26 One half shall be given to the congregation of Israel, and the other half shall be given unto the soldiers of war.

25:27 Of those given to the soldiers, one of every five hundred must be given unto Eleazar the high priest, so that he may perform a heave offering.

25:28 And of those of the congregation, one of every fifty shall be given unto the tribe of Levi, who keep the tabernacle of the lord.

25:29 For the slaves of the lord must be kept nourished; starving people make poor slaves."

25:30 Moses did as Eleazar commanded, and divided the bounty.

25:31 Of the sheep their numbered six hundred and seventy five thousand,

25:32 And threescore and twelve thousand cattle,

25:33 And threescore and one thousand asses,

25:34 And thirty two thousand female virgins.

25:35 Of the lord's tribute were six hundred and threescore and fifteen sheep,

25:36 Threescore and twelve cattle,

25:37 Threescore and one asses,

25:38 And thirty two virgins, of which the lord ravaged and raped.

25:39 When Moses had gathered all the gold, the silver, the jewels from the bounty of the war

25:40 (for every man had taken what they gathered for themselves)

25:41 The total value given unto God was sixteen thousand seven hundred and fifty shekels.

25:42 Eleazar then performed the heave offering in glory to the lord

25:43 (after the lord's virgins were devirginised)

25:44 And it was a memorial unto the lord;

25:45 And all the children of Israel praised the glory, the power, the lust and the wrath of their lord.

26:1 The lord spoke to Moses by the plains of Moab, saying,

26:2 "The tribe of Levi, who be my slaves, shall get all the possessions of the cities which shall be conquered in the lands promises to you since the times of Abraham.

26:3 They shall have the best cities, and the suburbs around the cities, for their goods and for their cattle and flocks.

26:4 These cities shall surround the borders of the promised lands, and shall be two thousand cubits length upon the north side, and two thousand cubits length on the south side, and two thousand cubits length on the east and the west sides.

26:5 Forty two cities total shall they have, with six cities added for refuge.

26:6 The cities of refuge shall be governed and cared for by the Levites, and those who dwell in them shall be in their care.

26:7 These cities of refuge shall be for those which have killed a person unawares, so that they may flee from the avenger and die not, until he stand before the congregation in judgment.

26:8 All cities shall be used for the refuge of the children of Israel, and for the strangers, so that they may flee and not die at the hands of the avenger.

26:9 If the person strike a man with a tool of iron, so that the man die, he is a murderer: they shall be denied access to the cities of refuge, and be killed by the avenger.

26:10 If the person smite him with a rock thrown, he is a murderer: they shall be denied access to the cities of refuge, and be killed by the avenger.

26:11 If the person hit him with wood, he is a murderer: they shall be denied access to the cities of refuge, and be killed by the avenger.

26:12 The avenger must be a close relative of that whom was slain: when he meeteth the murderer, he must slay him.

26:13 But if the person accused of murder slew the man without hatred, or ill will, or killed the man by accidental death,

26:14 The murderer shall flee to the cities of refuge, and cross the borders, and be saved from the avenger until trial.

26:15 The congregation shall judge the testimony of the man and the avenger, and weigh their judgments accordingly.

26:16 If the man be found guilty, the avenger shall slay him: if found innocent, the man shall be allowed refuge into the city, and be anointed refugee.

26:17 Their they shall live the remainder of their lives, or until the high priest dies.

26:18 Whichever comes first.

26:19 If the high priest die before the death of the man, then the avenger shall slay the man with the blessing of the lord.

26:20 And if on the travels the man shall meet that which is the avenger, the avenger shall kill the man, and not be guilty of spilled blood.

26:21 So these laws shall be a statute unto your peoples for generations, in all your dwellings.

26:22 If a person murder someone, and those who bear witness see it, the murderer shall die by the mouths of the witness.

26:23 But if one bear false witness, and make false testimony against a man so that they shall die, that false witness shall be cursed by God, and will not know the love of the lord.

26:24 Moreover, none shall take satisfaction of the death of the murderer: though he must be put to death.

26:25 And the avenger shall take no satisfaction of the death of the one who has slain his relative: though they must kill him.

26:26 They must kill the murderers without emotion, lest they lust of spilled blood overtake them, and they become murderers themselves.

26:27 If ye do take satisfaction in the slaying of the murderer, ye have tainted the lands with blood, and the lands stained with blood shall be unclean, and unholy forever.

26:28 Defile not these lands, for I the lord of Israel shall dwell in them, and wish not to dwell in lands which be unclean.

26:29 For if they be unclean, I shall spill the blood of those who hath made it unclean;

26:30 So that the soil be red and the rivers be of blood, not water.

26:31 And let it be known, that the blood I spill, I do not enjoy spilling."

26:32 And even Moses knew, that was a damn lie.

27:1 The heads of the families of the son of Gilead, the son of Machir, the son of Manasseh, of the tribe of Joseph, came to Moses, and the elders of Israel.

27:2 They said unto them, "The daughters of Zelophehad are married now, but shall not submit unto their husbands the inheritance passed down by their father.

27:3 If they marry, should they not give their inherited belongings to their husbands?

27:4 Since the husbands rightfully own these women, should they not own their inheritance as well?"

27:5 Moses went into deep meditation, and heard the lord's will, and spoke.

27:6 "This is what the lord has said to me regarding the daughters of Zelophehad.

27:7 Let them marry that whom they think best, as long as they belong to the tribe of their family.

27:8 If they be of the tribe of Joseph, they must marry only within the tribe of Joseph; no other tribe.

27:9 Otherwise, the inheritance shall belong to another tribe, and

the inheritance must be kept within the original tribe.

27:10 To give it to another tribe shall be theft, and those of that tribe must be punished.

27:11 And since the husbands belong to the same tribe, the husband shall take belonging of the inheritance.

27:12 They are the husband, she the wife; she belongs to the husbands, mind, body, and possessions.

27:13 Of which tribe did the daughters of Zelophehad marry?"

27:14 And the heads of the son of Gilead, the son of Machir, the son of Manasseh, of the tribe of Joseph, answered in unison,

27:15 "Their husbands are of the tribe of Joseph."

27:16 Moses was relieved and declared,

27:17 "Then the inheritance belong to the husbands.

27:18 And if they divorce, the inheritance shall still belong to the husband."

27:19 So Mahlah, Tirzah, Hoglah, Milcah and Noah were stripped of their inheritance, which now belonged to their husbands.

27:20 As they were married to the sons of Manasseh, of the tribe of Joseph, the inheritance belonged within the same tribe, but not to the daughters.

27:21 They were angry.

27:22 Really angry.

27:23 As in fucking pissed.

27:24 They refused to give their husbands the sexual gratifications they craved so.

27:25 When Moses heard of this, he came to the five daughters, and said unto them,

27:26 "You dumb cunt bitches, what right do ye have to be angry?

27:27 The inheritance of your father now belongs to a man; you should be happy!

27:28 For now it belongs to someone responsible, instead of a woman.

27:29 Go now, submit to your husbands, and open thine thighs to them, lest the lord pry your thighs apart and force himself upon thee."

27:30 Grudgingly, the daughters of Zelophehad did as they were told, and submitted to their husbands.

27:31 Such is the commandments and the judgments, which was given by the lord through the hands of Moses unto the children of Israel on the plains of Moab by Jordan near Jericho.

27:32 Sucks, doesn't it.

DEUTERONOMY

1:1 These are the words which Moses spoke to all the children of Israel, on this side of the Jordan in the wilderness, in the plains over the Red Sea, between Paran, Tophel, Laban, Hazeroth and Dizahab.

1:2 For the location as to where he spoke is very important.

1:3 It came to pass that in the fortieth year, of the eleventh month of that year, on the first day of that month, that Moses spoke these words.

1:4 After he had slain Sihon king of the Amorites, who dwelt in Heshob and Og the king of the Bashans, who dwelt at Astaroth in Edrei:

1:5 Moses gathered all the children of Israel to hear his words and said to them,

1:6 "We have wandered the wilderness long enough. For forty years we have wandered like vagabonds; like the angels cast out of heaven.

1:7 Enough is enough and soon we shall live in the lands promised to us in the covenant since the days of Abraham.

1:8 The lord has finally kept his covenant and soon we shall dwell in the lands flowing with milk and honey!

1:9 We shall own the lands which are now dwelt by the Amorites and the Canaanites; from the mount of the Amorites, down to the valleys to the south and the shores of the sea, to the city of Lebanon, up to the banks of the Euphrates, shall belong to us.

1:10 As for those that live their now, they shall be no match for us.

1:11 For the lord has blessed us with great fertility and we now number greater than the stars of the night sky!

1:12 We shall multiply more and overwhelm those fools who live upon our lands before we got there.

1:13 But you rely too much on me, your leader; how can I, but one man, bear your encumbrance, your burden and your strife?

1:14 Take your elders, your generals, your captains, your chiefs and your wise men and they shall be leaders over your tribes.

1:15 For I alone cannot rule over you all, nor enforce the commandments the lord has given to us.

1:16 If you any complaints, go to them, for the children of Israel have bothered me too much and have bothered the lord even more.

1:17 Your complaining has sent us curses from the lord; curses well deserved,

1:18 For do you not believe the lord will protect us?

1:19 Throughout our journey the lord has blessed us with manna; sweet bread sent from heaven.

1:20 And you complain about it and wish for flesh instead, thus insulting the lord.

1:21 The lord sent you all flesh and you gorged yourselves upon it, until you became sick and the meat rotted between your teeth and caused you illness and death and halitosis.

1:22 When we were in the desert and fresh water was nowhere to be found, did the lord not deliver us cool water to drink?

1:23 Yes, for he loves us and shall care for us and still you doubt him.

1:24 Many times you have doubted the lord and said that he has freed us from the servitude of Egypt, only to curse us and let us die and rot in the wild like savage beasts.

1:25 The lord has created a covenant with us, a covenant he shall not break.

1:26 And still you doubted!

1:27 When we came upon the lands of milk and honey, the lands promised to us by our lord in the covenant since the days of Abraham, I had sent out twelve spies.

1:28 Twelve men, one from each of the tribes of Israel.

1:29 They brought back great many fruits, figs, grapes, pomegranates and told us the land was great and bountiful.

1:30 Did you rejoice the lord's name and give praise to him. No!

1:31 You grew afraid, for ten of the men, ten bastards, told you of the inhabitants of the land.

1:32 Giant men, descended from the sons of God when they came upon earth and raped the women.

1:33 You grew scared and murmured and doubted, thinking the giants would crush and destroy us and that the lord would not protect us from them.

1:34 This angered the lord and he swore upon our name!

1:35 Save for Caleb the son of Jephunneh and Joshua the son of Nun, the lord killed the men who spoke of the giants and spread doubt amongst our people.

1:36 There is no need for doubt, for we are the lord's people.

1:37 Look at our past deeds; the lord has committed genocide numerously so as to keep the covenant he has made with us since the days of Abraham!

1:38 You know your sins now and shall fight in the name and the glory of our lord.

1:39 The lord has spoken to me and we much work to do;

1:40 For these lands which belong to us must be cleansed of the heathens who live upon it and it shall be bloody.

1:41 Our times in the wilderness are now short; soon we shall live in the lands of milk and honey!

1:42 Praise be to God!"

1:43 And with these words, the children of Israel rejoiced and great sacrifices were offered in praise to the lord.

1:44 They danced and drank and spilled the blood of many animals and foreign virgins.

1:45 Which pleased the lord as he loves violence, nudity and torn flesh.

2:1 The Israelites turned and travelled into the wilderness by way of the Red Sea and made camp at mount Seir for many days.

2:2 And the lord came down upon mount Seir and spoke with Moses, saying,

2:3 "You have camped upon this mount long enough; go northward.

2:4 The children of Israel shall pass through the lands which belong to the children of Esau, whom I loathe; and they shall be afraid of you and you shall exploit this fear.

2:5 Do not meddle nor war with them, for mount Seir shall belong to Esau's seed.

2:6 Buy from them milk and meat for money and their fear shall cause them to sell to you cheaply.

2:7 Offer them money for water to drink and they shall insist you drink from their wells for free.

2:8 They shall fear you that much.

2:9 Do not worry at all of cost, for the lord God has walked with you and provided and protected you these forty years of wandering; you shall lack nothing.

2:10 We shall pass through the lands of Esau, through the plains of Elath and Eziongaber and turn to pass through the wilderness of Moab.

2:11 Disturb not the Moabites, nor engage in battle with them; for they are descendants of Lot's drunken incest with his daughters and are a holy people to God.

2:12 The lands of Ar shall belong to them and you must not yet take it.

2:13 The Emims once dwelt there; giants among men descended through the seeds of the sons of the lord.

2:14 You know them as Anakims, but the Moabites call them Emims.

2:15 The Horims dwelt their as well, but the children of Esau succeeded them and crushed them and destroyed them all.

2:16 The children of Esau now dwell there, where the Horims dwelt and the giants dwelt and they are not even my people.

2:17 The children of Israel are my people and I shall destroy nations to ensure their covenant is kept.

2:18 Now rise up, and travel to the brook of Zered."

2:19 And the children of Israel did. The time it took for the children of Israel to travel from Kadeshbarnea to the brook of Zered was thirty-eight years and in that time the hands of the lord were choking the soldiers of Israel.

2:20 For in thirty-eight years, the older men of war were dead by the hands of God.

2:21 A slow death, but they eventually all did die.

2:22 It came to pass that when all the men of war were consumed, that the lord of Israel came down and spoke to Moses and said,

2:23 "You are to go over the lands of Ar this day,

2:24 And when you do, you shall come to the lands owned by the children of Ammon; do not meddle with them, nor make war with them.

2:25 These are the children descended by Lot's drunken incest with his other daughter; they are most holy to the lord and the lands they own shall belong to them.

2:26 The lands they own now were also dwelt by giants descended from the seed of the sons of the lord; Zamzummims.

2:27 People as great and as tall as the Anakims, but the lord destroyed them, so that the seed of Lot's incest shall possess their lands.

2:28 Remember, I destroyed giants for the children of Ammon and they are not my people.

2:29 Take comfort that the children of Israel are my people and that the lord shall protect them and keep his covenant given since the days of Abraham.

2:30 Rise up and take your journey over the river of Arnon, the lands which belong to Sihon the Amorite, king of Heshbon.

2:31 These people are not holy to the lord and shall be banished and destroyed by the children of Israel.

2:32 Smite them all, so that the glory of the children of Israel shall travel amongst the nations and the nations shall fear you.

2:33 Remember, you have sent messengers to king Sihon, asking permission to travel his land through his highways.

2:34 You told him that you would not take of his lands and pay for the food and the water which belonged to his people.

2:35 The lord hardened the heart of king Sihon, as he had hardened the heart of Pharaoh, so that his lands and his people shall be delivered into the hands of Israel, to be squeezed.

2:36 Go now, prepare for battle, and I shall deliver the lands of Sihon to you."

2:37 And the children of Israel prepared for war and met the armies of king Sihon on the lands of Jahaz.

2:38 Though the armies of Sihon be great, the lord delivered them to us and the children of Israel smote them one and all.

2:39 The wrath of the lord came from the skies and from the grounds and blinded and killed the armies of Sihon and all of his people.

2:40 We took their cities and killed everyone; man, woman and child, so that none remained.

2:41 Only the spoils of battle we took; gold, shekels, cattle, flocks.

2:42 From Aroer unto Gilead we took them all; not one city was too strong for the might of the children of Israel.

2:43 Only unto the lands of Ammon we did not step foot, nor any place among the river Jabbok, nor unto the cities in the mountains.

2:44 For these places belong to people descended by the seed of Lot, planted in his daughters as they got Lot drunk in a cave and slept with him, believing they were the only three left alive.

2:45 And these people are holy to God and blessed by the lord and thus we were forbidden to trespass upon their lands.

3:1 The children of Israel turned and went forth the way of Bashan: and Og the king of Bashan went out to greet them with his armies, to do battle upon the lands of Edrei.

3:2 And the lord said to Moses, "Don't worry, for I shall deliver him to you as well.

3:3 His lands shall come into your hands and his people shall meet the same fate as those of the king of Sihon."

3:4 Thus the lord delivered them into the hands of the children of Israel and they smote them so that none survived.

3:5 They took all their belongings, their cities and claimed them as their own; threescore of their cities now belong to the children of Israel.

3:6 These cities were walled, fenced and well defended and the armies of Israel overwhelmed them, destroyed them and slaughtered all which were inside.

3:7 Men, women, children, babies, elderly, pregnant mothers were slaughtered all, for such is the violence and the glory of the gory God.

3:8 The spoils of the battle; cattle, flocks and gold, they kept for themselves and gave their due share to the lord.

3:9 For within a few days' time, the children of Israel, with the blessing of their lord, conquered the two kings of the Amorites which dwelt upon their side of the Jordan.

3:10 And killed Og, the king of the Bashans, one of the few remaining giants, whose bed was nine cubits the length and four cubits the width and made of solid iron.

3:11 With Og conquered, the children of Israel owned a great many lands. From Aroer, and half the mount of Gilead and all the cities within belonged to the tribe of Reuben.

3:12 But though the lands conquered, even the lands of the giants, were not enough for the lust of the children of Israel; the lust of their lord.

3:13 They wanted more. Much more.

3:14 And the lord said to Moses, "I promise that you shall not rest until all the lands of milk and honey shall belong to you.

3:15 Have you seen what your lord god has done for you. Smiting for you two kings of great and powerful nations.

3:16 What other God among heaven and earth can do such things and match my works and exceed my might and terror?

3:17 Go now and see the lands past the Jordan and the lands of Lebanon; take comfort that soon these lands shall belong to you.

3:18 Get to the top of Pisgah and look towards the east, the north, the south and the west; for you shall have all which you see.

3:19 Charge Joshua and encourage him and strengthen him, for it shall be he who shall lead my people into these promised lands."

3:20 Thus the children of Israel made camp in the valley over against Bethpeor.

4:1 Moses awoke and said to the children of Israel,

4:2 "Now therefore obey, oh children of Israel, all of the statutes and the judgments which I have taught you, so that you not anger the lord and he shall allow you to live within the lands promised in the covenant given since the days of Abraham.

4:3 None shall add to the commandments of which I have given you, nor diminish the words upon them, lest they feel the wrath of the lord.

4:4 For the author of this book, The Blasphemous Bible, shall feel the wrath of the mighty lord God for what he is doing right now! (like the author fucking cares)

4:5 Your eyes have seen what the lord has done to those who followed the false God Baalpeor; for those that followed Baalpeor, the lord killed them all.

4:6 For the lord God is a jealous God and gets angry when others worship someone other than him; so worship the lord, lest he kill you.

4:7 As that is the reason why you are alive today; the lord has let you live, for you worship him.

4:8 Your sacrifices and devotion to him pleases the lord and he shall let us live as long as we continue to please him.

4:9 So keep the laws, the commandments, the statutes and make your sacrifices, lest the lord become angry and curse you and your generations.

4:10 For what nation is there so great, who can stop us, as we have the lord with us?

4:11 What nation was given laws specifically from God himself; righteous, holy, ridiculous laws?

4:12 Take heed of these laws and obey them and teach them to your sons, and your sons' sons, so that they may obey them and please the lord.

4:13 Remember to teach them to fear God, for God is powerful, wrathful, and quick to anger; and fear shall prevent the people of Israel from pissing God off.

4:14 Look at how the lord has led us within the wilderness; as great and mighty black clouds or pillar of fires; fear the black clouds. Fear the fire!

4:15 Even the voice of the lord, which spoke forth from the fire, was loud, deep and terrifying, when he spoke and declared to us our covenant.

4:16 When his finger came down and wrote the commandments upon the stone tablets, it was a mighty finger of fire and lightning, which carved out with fury the laws of which all people of Israel must follow.

4:17 Take heed of these commandments and these laws and you shall know not the reasons why you should fear God; only that you should.

4:18 Do not corrupt yourselves and make unto you graven images of any figure, whether man or woman;

4:19 The likeness of any beast within the earth, or the fowl which fly in the air'

4:20 Nor the likeness of anything which creeps upon the ground, fish of the sea, or plant which grow from the dirt.

4:21 For the lord has created these things and for us to copy them is as an insult to God; for we cannot copy that which the lord creates, nor make its image.

4:22 A sculpture, a painting, a drawing, angers God and his wrath shall be brought down upon those who call themselves artist.

4:23 When you look upon the sky and see of it the stars, the moon, the sun and all of the heavens, remember that it was the lord which has created them and all those which be under them.

4:24 And throughout all that, the lord has chosen us to be his people; he shall forge us as iron from the furnace into his will and shall give unto us a great inheritance.

4:25 Though the lord has become angry with us, he has forgiven us and shall let us cross over the Jordan and deliver you into the lands of milk and honey.

4:26 But I shall not cross nor enter the promised lands, for the wrath of the lord is upon me, as I have angered and insulted him for hitting a rock instead of talking to it.

4:27 The lord has cursed me and my name and I shall die in the wilderness, before you people go to the lands promised in the covenant of the lord.

4:28 Remember that when I am gone, to obey the laws and statutes of the lord and worship not false Gods, nor create graven images of any living thing.

4:29 For if you do create images, the lord shall consume you in his fire, as he is a jealous God.

4:30 When you do disobey the laws and create graven images, it shall be a great evil in the eyes of the lord and shall provoke in him great anger.

4:31 The lord shall cast you out amongst the nations and scatter your numbers amongst the heathens and there shall be few of you left.

4:32 God shall curse you, so that you may serve neither man nor lord; you shall be blind, have no taste, no smell, no hearing and your fingers shall be as heavy as stone.

4:33 When you cry out unto the lord, he shall not hear you and shall ignore you.

4:34 But if you truly repent and beg for forgiveness and devote your life into service of God, then the lord shall hear you then and listen.

4:35 For the lord God is a merciful God and shall not ignore those who truly wish to be heard.

4:36 He shall not forsake you, nor forget our covenant, unless it is us who forsake him first.

4:37 The time of the children of Israel is near and we shall strike out and with war we shall cast our hands across the nations and create great terror.

4:38 With this terror, the heathens shall know the name of the lord and shall fear him and shall fear the children of Israel.

4:39 This fear shall give us power and shall give the lord power; for the lord craves power and lusts deeply for more.

4:40 The lord has loved our father and our father's father for past generations and his love for them has blessed us and finally we shall inherit that which was promised to our ancestors.

4:41 Praise be to our lord, the one and only; there is no one else!

4:42 He shall drive out nations, slaughter nations, so that we shall live in their homes.

4:43 As long as we keep the laws which the lord has told us, we shall be in his blessing and shall inherit the earth for ever and ever."

4:44 With these words, Moses cast his hand out towards three heathen cities and the wrath of the lord fell upon them and severed them and all those which dwelt within them.

4:45 None survived, so that none could grow in hatred of the people of Israel and slay them, nor spread ill words about the children of Israel.

4:46 The cities were Bazer in the wilderness, Ramoth in Gilead, and Golan in Bashan, which belonged to the Manassites.

4:47 And with this destruction, the children of Israel praised the name of the lord and feared him deeply, for they wish not such destruction to happen to them.

4:48 Thus the grip the lord had over them became stronger and his power greater.

5:1 Moses called all the children of Israel and said to them, "Hear me, O Israel, the statutes and judgments of which I speak today, so that you may learn them, do them and keep them.

5:2 The lord God made a covenant with us upon mount Horeb; he made not this covenant with our fathers, but with us who are alive today.

5:3 God has spoke to me face to face and his face was covered in great smoke and fire.

5:4 He said to me I am the lord God, which brought you out of the bonds of Egypt and shall take you to the lands of milk and honey.

5:5 You shall have no other God's before me; for I am the one true God.

5:6 You shall not make any graven images of anything; whether from heaven above, or waters below, or that which live upon the earth, you shall not make any image thereof.

5:7 Neither shall you bow down and worship any other thing; for the lord God is a jealous God and shall punish the sins of the father down upon their generations.

5:8 Unto the third and the fourth generation shall I punish those for the sins of their ancestor.

5:9 And I shall show mercy upon those who worship me and love me and keep my commandments.

5:10 Do not take the lord's fucking name in vain, for to do so is an insult to the high and mighty power of the motherfucking God!

5:11 The lord shall not hold them guiltless who take his name in vain; they shall know great suffering.

5:12 Keep the sabbath day and sanctify it; for six days the lord worked, but on the seventh day he rested.

5:13 And if you work, it implies the lord to be lazy for resting on the seventh day and he shall grow jealous and angry.

5:14 Remember that the lord has freed you from the servitude of Egypt, so that no longer must you be forced to work upon the seventh day.

5:15 Honour your mother and your father, no matter how big of an asshole or cunt they shall be.

5:16 It matters not if they be drunkards, liars, whores, adulterers, abusive; yo must honour them, and never speak ill of them.

5:17 Thou shalt not kill, unless it's sanctioned by God's statutes, or the lord tells you to kill.

5:18 Thou shalt not commit adultery; do not lie with a man's wife, but lie with a whore.

5:19 Thou shalt not steal. If an object you desire belongs to a heathen, kill the heathen and take the object.

5:20 For heathens are not people and to kill them is as to kill a beast.

5:21 If the object you desire belongs to a child of Israel, ask to buy it and if the offer be refused, the object shall never be yours.

5:22 Thou shalt not lie, unless the lord tells you to.

5:23 For Abraham had lied to protect himself and his wife and that lie was sanctioned by God.

5:24 But if you lie and the words you speak for that lie have not been blessed by the lord, then you have sinned.

5:25 Thou shalt not covet thy neighbour's wife, nor his ass, nor his slaves, nor his concubines, nor his fields, or anything which belongs to thy neighbours.

5:26 The lord has given that which you have and if ye desire more, it is an insult to God.

5:27 This is the covenant of which the lord has given unto us; carved into stone with his great and mighty finger and delivered unto us.

5:28 It came to pass, that when you heard the terrifying voice of the lord and saw the fires upon mount Horeb, that you came near to me; all the heads and the elders.

5:29 And you said to me, behold, the presence and the power of the lord, who has showed us today his greatness in fire; we bear witness that God had talked to man and lives.

5:30 Now the power of God shall kill us, for surely this fire shall consume one and all. Such is the wrath of the lord.

5:31 And the lord heard your voices and have said to me, 'I have heard the voices of the children of Israel.

5:32 It gives me great pleasure that they fear me and believe that I shall consume them; for with fear comes control and I control these children of Israel.

5:33 Tell them that I shall not destroy them, as long as they obey my laws, my statutes, and my commandments without question.

5:34 Those that do right by the lord shall be saved; those who anger the lord shall die.'"

6:1 Now these are the commands, the statutes and the judgments, which the lord God has commanded be taught, so that you may do them in the lands you possess.

6:2 You shall fear the lord and keep his laws and ensure your sons and your son's sons shall obey these laws for all generations.

6:3 When you live comfortably in the lands promised in the covenant of our ancestors, remember to keep these laws; for it was the lord who brought us to these promised lands and if we do not obey his commands, he'll take these lands from us.

6:4 Remember, oh people of Israel; the lord God is the one and true God.

6:5 You must love him with all your heart, body, mind and soul, so that your very actions reflect the power of the lord.

6:6 Teach them to your children constantly; when you speak, when you are at the dinner table, even when thou sleep, recite the laws of our lord to your children.

6:7 Burn the laws into your hands and upon your foreheads, lest you forget them. Post them upon your posts, your doors and your gates.

6:8 When you conquer the cities in the promised lands, remember that these cities be built by godless heathens and are wicked; you must sanctify them and make them good.

6:9 Bless the buildings by writing the laws of our lord upon them and write within the soil of the crops and the vineyards the commandments and the statutes of our lord.

6:10 With these reminders of the God's laws, there shall be no excuse for disobedience and ignorance; we shall forever be reminded that he led us out of servitude from the hands of Egypt.

6:11 It took a few hundred years, but he eventually kept his promise.

6:12 Fear always the lord and swear loyalty and devotion by his name.

6:13 Worship not the false gods of the heathens around you; take not even an interest in them.

6:14 For the lord God is a vengeful God and if you chase after false gods, the lord shall be angry and shall kindle his wrath against you and destroy you from the face of the earth.

6:15 Do not tempt the lord, nor test him, nor doubt his existence, as you did in Massah.

6:16 The lord is too busy to be bothered with your temptations and tests of his existence; he's up in heaven controlling the universe for fuck sakes, he has not the time to prove himself to you.

6:17 All shall diligently keep the lord's commandments, statutes and his judgments, as he commanded from us.

6:18 You shall do what is right and good in the sight of the lord; to do so shall please the lord and he shall bless us and give us great power and wealth.

6:19 He shall cast out our enemies; all those which stand in our way.

6:20 And when your little ones come to you and ask of thee what these statutes, these sacrifices, these laws mean that the lord commands from us, you shall tell them this.

6:21 Tell them of the times we were slaves in service to Pharaoh; that after hundreds of years, the lord finally set us free with a great and terrible hand.

6:22 Tell them how the lord sent a great many curses and plagues upon the heathens of Egypt; turning water to blood, swarms of locusts, killing the first-born males.

6:23 Remind them that it was the lord who brought us to these promised lands, which were promised to us during the days of our ancestors many generations ago.

6:24 And that with all these blessings from God, that the lord has commanded we obey these statutes, sacrifices and judgments.

6:25 To disobey them is to anger the lord and if keeping these silly laws and ridiculous sacrifices make the lord happy and keep his wrath away from us, it is but a small sacrifice.

6:26 For if we do not, the lord shall curse us and our people will know greater suffering than which we did before.

6:27 The lord shall curse us, plague us and wipe us from the face of the earth; it is this fear of punishment that is why we must obey these laws.

7:1 When the lord takes us to the land promised to us, he shall destroy seven great nations to make room for us; the Hittites, the Girgashites, the Amorites, the Canaanites, the Perizzites, the Hivites and the Jebusites shall be destroyed in a holy genocide of God.

7:2 The lord shall deliver these heathens into our hands, so that we may utterly destroy these fuckers. Show them no kindness, no tenderness, no mercy; kill them all.

7:3 Do not lie intimately with them, nor marry them; your son shall not marry their daughters, nor your daughters shall marry their sons.

7:4 For they shall turn your children away from me, as they believe in false gods who promise peace and prosperity for all people of earth.

7:5 Such teachings are bullshit and angers the lord; and those of Israel who turn to these teachings shall know the anger of God and shall be abolished from the earth.

7:6 When you enter their nations, destroy their altars, burn down their places of worship and turn to dust their idols and their graven images; for such things offend the lord.

7:7 The lord did not choose his love upon you for your power, nor your numbers; for you are the fewest of all people:

7:8 The lord loves you for he loved your fathers and made with your fathers a great covenant which must be kept and has brought you out of the lands of Egypt and away from the yoke of Pharaoh.

7:9 Know therefore that the lord shall keep his faith unto you which keep his covenant and his commandments, his laws, his statutes and shall show love for those that do for a thousand generations.

7:10 And for those that doubt him or worship him not, the lord shall hate with a great and powerful hatred and they shall know the fury of God.

7:11 Know that if you forever keep the laws, statutes and judgments of God, he shall love you and bless you and multiply us great in numbers.

7:12 Our men and women shall be forever fertile, as will our cattle and flocks; diseases and infertility shall be cursed to those who the lord doesn't like.

7:13 We shall consume the world and rule it; and the lord shall deliver all those upon the earth into our hands, so that we may destroy them.

7:14 We shall show them no pity, no mercy and shall not take heed of their gods, as that shall be a snare upon our necks.

7:15 There shall be those among you that doubt and ask how can we children of Israel destroy all the great and powerful nations of earth.

7:16 Remind these people of our time in Egypt and of the horrors and the plagues the lord hath brought down unto Pharaoh and the people of Egypt.

7:17 For the lord God is an all-powerful God and with his blessing we shall destroy all those not of the children of Israel; all those not blessed by God.

7:18 Those which survive, the lord shall send out an army of hornets to seek and destroy them; the hornets shall sting their eyes, their nostrils, their mouths and shall fly within their lungs and sting their inwards.

7:19 Never shall you fear the people of the earth; you shall fear only God, for he is a mighty and terrible God!

7:20 Slowly the lord shall weaken these unholy nations, so that we may consume and destroy them all; we shall not consume them at once, but little by little, like predators killing a herd of prey one creature at a time.

7:21 In time, the wrath of the lord shall grow and his great hand shall come down and destroy these nations and their people and

cities shall know a great destruction until they be destroyed.

7:22 Their kings shall be delivered upon our weapons of war and their names shall be forever forgotten in history.

7:23 The graven images of their gods shall be destroyed; even those made of valued gold, silver and gems must be destroyed.

7:24 Do not take any goods from a graven image into your house; it is an abomination unto the lord.

7:25 For if you do, it shall be a curse and you and your generations shall be as accursed and unholy as the graven image from which you took your possession from.

8:1 Take heed of the blessings of the lord, which he has given to us for keeping his statutes, his laws and his judgments.

8:2 For forty years we have wandered the desert to be delivered to the lands promised to us by our ancestors; lands promised to us in the holy covenant.

8:3 During our travels, not once did we starve, for the lord blessed us with the holy bread of heaven called manna; never did we grow thirsty, for the lord provided us with fresh water from rocks. Twice!

8:4 Our food, our flocks, our cattle have always been great in numbers, so that we may offer our sacrifices unto God.

8:5 Even our clothing has not grown old nor torn; our clothing needed not tailoring, our shoes grew with our feet, even our undergarments from the days we left Egypt are though as new.

8:6 You shall consider in our hearts that when a father punishes his son, so must the lord punish us for our wrongdoings.

8:7 Remember the plagues, the jaw which came up from earth, the snakes of fire, were all because we were bad children of Israel and the lord needed to punish us for our sakes.

8:8 So obey the laws of our lord, lest he punish us again.

8:9 For with our obedience, the lord shall deliver us into a great land of babbling brooks, rivers, valleys and mountains.

8:10 A land full of wheat, barley, vines, figs, grapes, olives, pomegranates, figs, olives and honey.

8:11 We shall eat in gluttony for generations and know not starvation; the mountains shall be rich in ore and we shall mine them for brass, silver and gold.

8:12 And when we grow fat and drunk and our wealth amassed from the mining, remember that we must give thanks unto God, for it is he who has given us these lands.

8:13 It is with his blessing that our bellies be full, our minds intoxicated, our pockets bulging in shekels and our houses strong.

8:14 When you look out upon the fields, remember that it is the lord who has allowed our crops to grow and our flocks and herds to multiply greatly.

8:15 Without God, we are weak and nothing.

8:16 Say in your heart that it is God who has given you the power and the wealth you have obtained.

8:17 And it shall b, that if you forget that it is God who has blessed you with these lands, these riches and this gluttony, that the lord shall be angry and you shall surely perish.

8:18 Nations shall come and destroy your people, your sons, your daughters, because you were not grateful for all that which the lord has given you.

9:1 Hear now, O Israel, for soon we shall pass the Jordan, to go possess nations that belong to others and take their cities and rape and pillage their villages.

9:2 People great and tall, the children of Anakims, shall tremble in our sight; for we shall stand in defiance to the children of Anak!

9:3 Understand this day that the lord God is with us and shall go over before us and consume in great fire and destroy those who stand in our way and banish them and destroy them quickly.

9:4 Show no sympathy for these people, for they are wicked and have made the lands wicked and evil.

9:5 They worship not God and do not his commands nor judgments.

9:6 False gods they worship and they follow laws that are evil; they treat their women as equals, they don't sacrifice virgins, they live in peace with their neighbours who believe differently than they do.

9:7 What bullshit is this, these heathens we shall destroy!

9:8 Understand the lord shall give us these lands so we can make it righteous and cleanse it of the wickedness of these evil heathens.

9:9 Remember and forget not the wrath of the lord when you have provoked him in the desert: from the day we left Egypt until you came to this place, you have doubted and rebelled against God.

9:10 In mount Horeb, you provoked the lord so much he wished to wipe you from existence.

9:11 I went up to the mount to hear the words of the lord and receive two tablets with his commandments; laws which we must all live by.

9:12 For forty days and nights I went without food and water, surrounded by the fires of God and forever faithful.

9:13 When I came down, what did I see, but the entire children of Israel in great intoxication, drinking strong drink from the udders of a golden calf!

9:14 You invited not I nor the lord and this angered us both; the lord greatly was angered and offended.

9:15 I took the tablets of stone and in rage broke them in pieces; for forty days I had went without food nor drink and to come down and see you in excess gluttony was greatly insulting.

9:16 All should have waited for me, so that I could eat, drink and be merry.

9:17 The lord was furious and wished to destroy you all; to break his covenant and let you die like beasts.

9:18 I Moses fell down and begged to the lord and pleaded with him not to destroy us nor my brother Aaron, whose name he cursed for not letting the lord come to the party.

9:19 I took your calf and burned it and ground it to a fine dust and made you drank it; bitter was the drink of the golden calf.

9:20 Many times you have rebelled against the lord and provoked his wrath and many times I had pleaded with God to keep his covenant and let you be delivered to the lands promised to us since the days of Abraham.

9:21 And you shall be delivered, yet I will die out here in the wild; what unfairness you have caused me!

9:22 It is unjust that I shall not know the lands, yet you whiny fucking twats shall grow gluttonous with the lands flowing with milk and honey; I should curse you, yet I won't.

9:23 For you are my people, and this is the lord's will; I must not question it.

9:24 Go now and I shall lead you to the lands with the blessing of God and shall then die and rot in the wilderness and know not the promised lands of the covenant.

10:1 At the time the lord came to me and said, "Make me two tablets of stone and take them up to the mount and make me an ark of wood.

10:2 I shall rewrite the laws of which were on the first tablets of stone, which you broke in anger over the children of Israel and you shall put them in the ark."

10:3 Thus I made the ark of shittim wood and carved out two great tablets of stone and went up into the mount with two tablets in hand.

10:4 Again, he wrote upon the tablets his laws, his commandments, his statutes and again I had to listen to his demands.

10:5 Curse you, children of Israel, for making me listen to him again; for the lord rambles on and on and is fucking boring to talk to!

10:6 Still, I did as the lord commanded and listened to him rant and ramble and write his demands upon the tablets of stone.

10:7 After this, we took our journey from Beeroth to Mosera and their Aaron died at the hands of God and was buried and his son Eleazar became high priest.

10:8 During our travels afterwards, the lord has separated the tribe of Levi and made them his slaves, demanding they care for the ark of the covenant and minister to God and do all of which the lord demands of them.

10:9 As slaves to God, the tribe of Levi shall inherit not of man, but of God; sacrifices made to God, a portion goes to the Levites, so they may eat and be strong and healthy slaves.

10:10 The lord then said to me that we shall arise and go to the promised lands of the covenant, which the lord swore to our ancestors many years ago.

10:11 The lord requires little of us; just that we keep his laws, fear him and love him with all our heart and soul.

10:12 Behold, the lord owns all; the heaven and the heaven of heavens is controlled by God and the earth and all that remain within it is property of the lord.

10:13 When the lord looked down upon the earth, he saw our ancestors and chose them over all the people and blessed them and loved them and their children to this day.

10:14 Circumcise the foreskin of your heart, so that you be truly children of God.

10:15 The lord hates foreskin and wishes none to have that wretched flesh upon their genitals, nor to have the wretched flesh within their hearts.

10:16 Remember, the lord God is God of all Gods, of which there is only one and it be him; he is a great God with terrible power, who respects none of the people of earth.

10:17 He shall judge us all with mighty punishment; the orphaned son nor the widow shall gain sympathy from his wrath.

10:18 Let us remember that we shall love the stranger; for we were once strangers in Egypt.

10:19 Unless those strangers be one of the many which the lord demanded us to kill without mercy; then hate the stranger.

10:20 Fear the lord, praise the lord, sacrifice to the lord and give thanks; for our ancestors went to Egypt with threescore and ten persons, now with the blessing of God we shall multitude as the stars in heaven.

11:1 Therefore, you shall love your God and keep his laws, his commandments, his statutes and his judgments, always today and forever.

11:2 Know that this day, I cannot speak to your children about the wonders, the glories, the miracles, the sorcery and the magic of God.

11:3 I cannot tell the young ones of the ten curses the lord has sent to the people of Egypt, during our time of servitude under Pharaoh.

11:4 Nor how he parted the Red Sea so that we may pass through and how the waters of the Red Sea crushed Pharaoh, his armies, his horses, his chariots.

11:5 All of what the lord did to us whilst in the wilderness; the manna, the flowing water from stone, the plagues, nor the curses cannot be taught by me.

11:6 Neither shall I tell them how the great earthen jaw of God rose up and consumed Dathan and Abiram, the sons of Eliab, of the tribe of Reuben.

11:7 Yet you have witnessed these and must tell your children of these great wonders, so that they shall grow in fear of God and keep his statutes, his laws, so they may avoid the anger and the fury of

THE OLD TESTAMENT

the lord.

11:8 And with this obedience, the lord shall prolong our stay in the promised land of the covenant; the land flowing with milk and honey.

11:9 For these lands are not of the lands of Egypt, where you toiled upon the soil and sowed seeds for crops and vineyards.

11:10 These lands are of hills, valleys and brooks and are blessed by the rain waters of heaven which the lord has sent to it to prepare the lands for us.

11:11 All the crops are sewn, the vineyards full of grapes, for the lord himself hath cared for these lands.

11:12 We shall go in and harvest the grains, the corns, the grapes, the olives for oil and the figs.

11:13 Grasses shall be green and fresh for our cattle and flocks, so that they may grow fat and keep our bellies full of flesh and the altars forever burning of sacrifice.

11:14 Take heed of the heathens which dwell there and worship not their Gods; do not even think of them, nor ask of their names.

11:15 If you do, the crops shall dry, the vineyards rot, the grass die and the rain shall stop so that even the waters of the brooks shall leave.

11:16 Teach your children these things, so that they may please the lord and obey him without question and fear his wrath and his anger and his fury.

11:17 Write these laws upon your signs, your fences, your doorposts, so that you have no excuse to forget them and disobey them.

11:18 And tell your children that the lord of all lords shall be pleased with them and reward them for their obedience and their sacrifice.

11:19 God himself shall come down from the heavens and destroy great and mighty nations; nations more powerful and numerous than us, so that we may possess their lands, their belongings, their women.

11:20 We shall go forth and crush our enemies and hear the lamentations of their women as we kill their sons and laugh in joy as the virgins cry whilst we rape them; it shall be a pleasing sound to the lord.

11:21 All the lands set before us shall be ours; from the wilderness and Lebanon to the river Euphrates, up to the coasts of the sea and beyond shall be ours!

11:22 No man shall stand before us, no army shall harm us, for the lord God shall smite these heathen fools who dare dwell in our lands before we arrive.

11:23 Behold, I set before you this day both a blessing and a curse.

11:24 A blessing, in that if we and our future generations obey, love, and fear all that is God, we shall grow rich, and fat and shall consume the earth and claim it as ours.

11:25 A curse, for if you, your children, your children's children of any generation shall disobey that which is God and go whoring after false god's, that the wrath of the one true lord shall be set upon us.

11:26 Destroy us he shall and cast us out amongst the heathens, so that they shall enslave us and rape us and erase all of the children of Israel from existence.

11:27 For the lord God is an angry fucker, whose wrath is cruel and his punishments horrifying.

11:28 Anger not the lord and avoid his wrath; obey the statutes and judgments of which I set to you this day.

12:1 These are the laws and statutes we must observer to do in the lands promised to us in the covenant made since the days of Abraham.

12:2 For these heathens that dwell there, kill them. Destroy them. Leave none alive, for they are hated by God.

12:3 Search behind every tree, look under every rock, explore every cave, climb every mountain and kill without mercy any which survive.

12:4 Grind their altars to dust, break their pillars, burn their groves, destroy their idols, so that no reminders of their unholy worship be left behind.

12:5 Do this all with the lord's blessing.

12:6 When this destruction, this genocide be done, praise the lord and give glory to Yahweh.

12:7 Take your lambs, your rams, your oxen, your cattle, the foreign virgins and offer them as great sacrifice to God; and all that witness shall know the power and wonder of the true lord.

12:8 Feast upon the crops which these heathens have tended and grow gluttonous and fat upon the rewards your lord has given unto you.

12:9 Be grateful for this inheritance, lest the lord see your greed within your heart and his wrath wax down upon the ungrateful bastard of Israel.

12:10 All the tribes shall own their lands and all tribes shall be rich from them.

12:11 The lord shall choose for each tribe a place of sacrifice, where your offerings shall be burned; burn them no place else, but only upon the place the lord has set for offering.

12:12 To burn them other place shall be unholy and blasphemous and the lord shall send great curses upon you.

12:13 Within these days first days of sacrifice shall be days of gluttony; eat of that which you desire, clean or unclean.

12:14 The hare, the swine, the vulture shall you feast upon; even the dead heathen shall you feast upon if you so wish.

12:15 But eat not of the blood, for blood belongs to God; blood is life.

12:16 Offer unto God his tithe; one tenth of all that which you belong and conquer, so that the slaves of God, the tribe of Levi, shall eat and live comfortably and forget that they be slaves unto the lord.

12:17 Forsake not the Levite, lest you feel the wrath of God.

12:18 Know that with these new lands shall come more; for the lord shall enlarge our borders, our nation, our people and we shall rule all which shall be seen upon earth.

12:19 You shall offer your burnt offerings, the flesh and the blood to be consumed by fires upon the altar of the lord and the blood shall boil and be drunk as a great wine to God.

12:20 Flesh shall be feasted upon and ripped straight from the bone in great glory to God; we shall dance naked and bathe in the blood of the beast.

12:21 For the lord loves blood, nudity and torn flesh.

12:22 Observe all that which the lord commands and do them and we shall be forever blessed by God, forever and ever;

12:23 And our generations shall be blessed and grow strong and conquer all in the name of the lord.

12:24 Burn all those which worship differently, for their faith is evil, blasphemous and they must be punished in great fire.

12:25 Those that doubt the lord must be stoned; for their doubts shall curse all the children of Israel and we shall be scattered amongst the heathens and be enslaved so that our generations shall dwindle and die.

12:26 Do all that which the lord commands and add no more statutes, nor diminish that which is written, lest the lord kill you and curse your seed.

13:1 If there rise amongst the children of Israel a dreamer or prophet and he give you a sign or wonder,

13:2 And if that sign or wonder come to pass and the prophet or dreamer then speak ill of our lord, or tell us to go after other god's,

13:3 You shall not listen to this prophet, as he is a false prophet; for the lord has proven to you that he is the one true God and you shall love him with all your heart and soul.

13:4 You shall obey the lord and follow his laws and his judgments and kill this false prophet.

13:5 Even if he speaks words which seem true, logical and make sense, you must kill him; for logic is the enemy of the lord.

13:6 This false prophet who wishes to turn you away from the lord shall be stoned to death; all the children of Israel shall stone him, until his body lay crippled, beaten, and dead.

13:7 Do not mourn for this prophet and let his corpse rot in the wilderness, so that the carrion eaters shall feast upon his flesh.

13:8 If your brother, uncle, son, daughter, wife, mother, father, friend, or any who holds dear a place in your heart shall come to you and entice you into worshipping other gods, or speak ill of our God;

13:9 You shall not heed their words nor hearken to them; neither shall you spare them, pity them, nor conceal what they have said.

13:10 Kill them instantly; if you have a blade, slice their throat. If you have a hard object, beat them to death. If you have nothing, choke them until the life from this blasphemer leaves them and they lay dead upon the floor.

13:11 Do not mourn for them nor give them burial; carry the carcass into the wild, so that the vultures themselves shall pluck out their eyes and feast upon their tongue.

13:12 If the person flees, let it be known to all the children of Israel what the blasphemer has done and when they be found, let them be publicly stoned.

13:13 For these people shall tell lies and wish to turn the children of Israel against God; this is a wicked and most evil thing, which the lord shall not tolerate.

13:14 If one shall go into the city of a stranger and hear that they worship another god, a false god, show no mercy upon them.

13:15 It matters not if they do not wish you to worship their gods, kill them.

13:16 Go in with swords and behead all who worship differently; destroy their altars, burn their cities, kill even their cattle and their flocks, so that none survive.

13:17 Kill even the women, the children, so that they no more can worship another god, thus insulting our lord.

13:18 The virgins shall even be killed after rape; kill them while you rape them, as the sound of the virgin heathen's struggle pleases the lord.

13:19 When you have burned their city and killed all those evil which dwell within it, you shall praise God and give glory to his name.

13:20 Glory be to our God, the one and only.

14:1 You are the children of God; you shalt not cut yourself, nor mark yourself in any manner, nor make any baldness between your eyes and your head.

14:2 You shall only be cut upon the eighth day of birth, to remove the unholy foreskin and thus be marked forever a child of Israel; a child of God.

14:3 Eat not any abominable thing; they are unholy and shall forever mark you cursed in the eyes of God if consumed.

14:4 The ox, the sheep, the goat, the hart, the deer, the antelope, the chamois, the pygarg; all beasts which chew of the cud and have a cloven hoof shall be clean and consumed.

14:5 Of those which not chew the cud nor have the cloven foot shall be unholy and must not be eaten.

14:6 The camel, the swine, the hare, the coney and many others shall be as an abomination unto your dinner table.

14:7 For that which swim within the water, you shall eat all which

have upon it scales and fins; that without fins nor scales shall not be eaten. They don't taste that good anyway.

14:8 All clean birds shall be eaten in gluttony.

14:9 But these are the birds which are unclean; the eagle, the osprey, the ossifrage,

14:10 The glede, the kite, the vulture,

14:11 The crow, the raven and all their kind,

14:12 The owl, the hawk, the swan,

14:13 The heron, the stork, the pelican, the cormorant and the bat.

14:14 Yes, the bat is a bird, for the lord has made it and calls it a bird.

14:15 Fuck you biologists; you are wrong and shall suffer greatly for going against God.

14:16 Of any animal that dies naturally, you shall not eat; sell it to the foreigners and the strangers and let them eat it and pocket their coin; but as a child of Israel, do not eat it.

14:17 Never boil a kid in its mother's milk, nor eat the mother with the son.

14:18 Separate the meals, so that the mother and the child be not eaten on the same meal.

14:19 You shall give unto God his tithe; ten percent of all which be harvested from the fields, yearly.

14:20 And you shall take the tithe and place it where the lord chooses his sacrifices be made for your tribe and the lord shall take his tithe in great fire and you shall learn to fear him.

14:21 Those who pay not the tithe, nor pay not in full, shall be taken by God and consumed with gluttony and fury.

14:22 If the tithe of the crops be too heavy to carry, or if you live too far away, then you shall sell the tithe of the crops and offer unto the lord the money sold; for the lord is a greedy bastard.

14:23 Curse not the Levite; the slaves of God, for they shall partake of a portion of the tithe.

14:24 For the Levite is blessed to be a slave to God and shall feast upon the tithe which the lord leaves behind.

15:1 Upon the end of every seven years shall you make a release.

15:2 Of every creditor who is owed money by his neighbour, shall they release it; the neighbour shall owe them not a penny no more, nor shall the creditor seek out money from his neighbour.

15:3 That of which a foreigner owes you, you shall seek out, for a foreign man must repay his debts; but a child of Israel is as a brother to you and they shall be released of their debt.

15:4 For the lord shall bless Israel, so that there shall be no poor amongst our people; the lands will be so great that even the beggars now shall be rich and powerful men.

15:5 So worry not of your debtor, as the lord assure you shall be rich without the money he owes to you and that soon the debtor shall be rich as well.

15:6 When you see the poor amongst your people, do not hearken them, nor ignore them, nor harden your heart.

15:7 Open your palms to him and lend him that which he needs, so that all the children of Israel shall not starve, nor know poverty.

15:8 Beware there be no evil in your heart, for if the seventh year be upon you and the poor wish to borrow from you, do not think they wish only to borrow, so that soon the time of release is at hand and their debt shall be none to you.

15:9 For the lord blesses all who give to the poor of Israel and shall reward you greater than that of which you lent out.

15:10 If you buy a slave of Hebrew blood, whether man or woman, they shall serve under you six years; upon the seventh year they shall be free.

15:11 Do not send him away poor; give him clothing, food and money, so that they shall be long away from you before they be broke and starve.

15:12 Remember, you were once all slaves in the land of Egypt; treat your brethren slaves with a kind heart.

15:13 Foreign slaves can be beaten, abused and whipped, but a slave of Hebrew blood must not know too hard labour.

15:14 If the slave of Hebrew blood is sent away on his seventh year, but wishes instead to stay and have you be his master forever, the man is a fool; whoever wishes to remain a slave is obviously a stupid man.

15:15 Take an aul and place his head upon the door of your house. The aul shall then be thrust into his ear; whether man or maidservant, the aul shall be thrust in their ear.

15:16 This shall symbolize the obvious hole they have in their head from which their brains fell out.

15:17 Do not be sad for when upon the seventh year your slave is set free; buy a new one, a foreign one, who shall remain yours forever.

15:18 All the firstling males which come from a new mother must be sanctified by God; you shall not shear the firstling lamb nor put a yoke on the firstling bullock.

15:19 You shalt offer it as sacrifice to God and burn it where the altar stands.

15:20 If the firstling male be blind, lame, or have blemish, then it is not worthy of God; kill it and eat it by the gates of your city, where the beggars, the poor and the unclean be.

15:21 And pour the blood of it upon the ground, for even the blood of an unworthy sacrifice is life and shall not be consumed by men.

16:1 Observe the month of Abib and keep the Passover of the lord; for it was the month of Abib which the lord set you free from the servitude of Pharaoh.

16:2 Make your sacrifices upon your altars; remember your offerings to the lord and give them with a willing heart.

16:3 Eat not anything with leaven; for seven days you shall eat unleavened bread, for you came out of Egypt in haste and brought with you little bread for bread.

16:4 Leavened bread shall be an abomination to you, for in this week there shall be no leavened bread baked, eaten or seen; flesh shall not be eaten by you for this week as well, for the flesh shall be given as sacrifice to God.

16:5 Sacrifice not the Passover within the gates of the city, but at the place where the lord has claimed most holy; for this is a holy meal.

16:6 You shalt roast and feast upon the unleavened bread in sight of the lord and at night you shall turn to your tents and rest.

16:7 Six days you shall eat unleavened bread and upon the seventh day of Passover shall be a holy day of worship; you shall do no work, but assemble within the tabernacle and solemnly listen to the words of the priest, whose tongues be blessed by the lord.

16:8 Seven weeks after the harvest of the grain shall you number and you shall begin the feast of weeks with a tribute of freewill unto God the corn which you harvested.

16:9 In this time, rejoice, party and feast with your sons, your daughters, your brothers, your slaves, the fatherless, the widow, even the strangers; be drunk and merry and feast with gluttony in glory to the lord.

16:10 Remember in this time the magnificent joy of which you felt when you crossed the Red Sea and the lord has freed you from the servitude of Egypt.

16:11 Seven days shall you drink, eat and be merry, for the joy of freedom shall overtake your hearts and your souls and you shall give great glory to the lord.

16:12 The feast of tabernacles shall be held for seven days; for seven days all shall hold a solemn feast in the holy place and give thanks to the lord for their lands, their flocks, their belongings and their slaves which do the work of the fields.

16:13 Three times a year shall all the males of Israel appear before God, naked; for the lord wishes to see them as they are and confirm they lack the unholy foreskin.

16:14 At the feast of unleavened bread, the feast of weeks and the feast of the tabernacle shall all the males appear nude before God and give the lord an offering.

16:15 Judges and officers shall you make within the cities, who shall uphold the law and observe all obey that which the lord commands.

16:16 They shall judge the peoples harshly and fairly; they shall not take bribes nor gifts, for such things shall blind them and cause them to do unrighteous judgment.

16:17 These judges and officers shall observe we do that which is holy, so that the lord shall bless us and make us grow and we shall inherit all.

16:18 When the lord chooses the place of his altar, do not plant a tree there; for the lord wishes the land around his altar be barren.

16:19 Never, EVER, make any image, for the lord God hates them; how can we, mere men, truly copy that which the lord created?

17:1 you shall offer only the finest specimens to the lord for sacrifice; males, free of blemish, sickness and disease.

17:2 If any offer to God a sacrifice with blemish, that sacrifice shall be as an abomination to the lord, for the lord demand the best be upon his table.

17:3 The man shall be cursed by God for this abomination and shall be struck with disease and leprosy and shall be cast out from the children of Israel for offering such a pathetic sacrifice.

17:4 If there be among you who, man or woman, has brought wickedness in the sight of the lord and broke the covenant;

17:5 And have gone and sought out other gods to worship, either heathen god, or moon, or sun, or any object of heaven, or beast, or creature they worship and not the lord God;

17:6 Such an abomination must be punished, for these people believe differently than you. You shall take them to the gates of your city and stone them to death, until their body be crushed, beaten, battered and torn.

17:7 Do not mourn for them nor bury them; let the beasts feast upon the flesh of the unholy.

17:8 If two people bear witness to one worshipping someone other than our lord, the testimony of these two men shall be enough to kill the one they claim wrong.

17:9 The witnesses shall have the honour of casting the first stones, so that they may feel pride in doing the work of the lord and killing the unholy blasphemous fucker.

17:10 If two men argue and the arguments of these two men cannot be finished by their own means, then they shall go to the priests, the judges and the Levites, and each plead their case.

17:11 When both men had said their peace, the judges, the priests and the Levites shall go into the tabernacle and research the laws and the testament of the lord, to see which arguing man is in the right.

17:12 When a decision has been made, both men must act upon the decision and treat it holy; they shall do as the judges, the priests and the Levites say.

17:13 If both men, or one man, do not as the decision is and disobey the sentence of the judges, the priests, and the Levites, or think them wrong, the man goes against God.

17:14 Take this man to a tree and strike a spear into his chest, so that his body lay rotting against the trunk of the tree and the crows and the ravens shall peck at his corpse.

17:15 All must bear witness of this execution, so that they know to fear the decisions of the judges, the priests, and the Levites; all shall bear witness and fear God.

17:16 When you claim the lands promised to us in the covenant, each tribe shall be given a king; one chosen by God and the king shall be holy and blessed by the lord.

17:17 The king shall be of true blood, a child of Israel; the king shall not be a stranger, nor have any strange blood flowing through him.

17:18 As king, he shall be wise and holy and shall treat his people fairly; he shall not cause grief nor abuse the people he rules.

17:19 The king shall only have one wife, for many women will wish to be with him; he must choose only one wife, one queen.

17:20 His harem can be numerous and his concubines can number greater than the stars above, but only one queen shall he have.

17:21 It shall be that when he sits upon the throne of his kingdom, that he shall be given a book of laws, given to him by the priests of God.

17:22 Daily he shall read these laws and enforce them and learn to fear the wrath of God.

17:23 For when he upholds the laws of God, his kingdom shall grow strong and prosperous; he shall know great power.

17:24 But if the king ignores the laws, his entire kingdom shall be cursed by God and it shall be the king who is cursed mostly and shall know the true horrors of our lord.

18:1 The Levites are slaves to God and therefore shall have no inheritance with Israel; they shall inherit that which is given to God.

18:2 When you giveth tithe to the lord or sacrifice, the priests shall give the Levites their due.

18:3 Whether beast, wine, bread, or the first fruits of the harvest, the tribe of Levi shall take their share as an inheritance to God; for the Levite's are slave to God and the lord therefore shall feed them.

18:4 Do not mock the Levites, for to be a slave of God is a holy thing; what better honour is there than to be property of the lord?

18:5 When you enter the lands of milk and honey, you shall avoid the abominations of which the peoples practice there; they are evil.

18:6 None of the children of Israel shall learn the use of magic, witchcraft, wizardry, or use necromancy to rise and communicate with the dead; such a thing is unholy.

18:7 Neither shall you use charms or the stars above to see that which is ahead in time; to do so is a truly unholy thing.

18:8 For those who practice such things, they shall be cursed to God; the children of Israel shall cast them out of their lands and stone them.

18:9 You shall let their corpses rot and be carried away by the savage beasts, but be warned;

18:10 The necromancers are tricky users of sorcery and may place upon themselves spells and charms to rise from the dead; you may need to stone them twice dead.

18:11 Ignore this second rising, for such a thing is devil magic; be not tempted by it, lest you be as wicked as they.

18:12 You must strive and struggle to be perfect in the sight of our lord God almighty.

18:13 For these nations shall possess customs and rituals which are tempting to you, but ye must ignore them; the lord wishes not men to have these powers and if you seek these powers, the lord shall know and you shall truly see why the lord must be feared!

18:14 In time, the lord thy God shall raise up from you a prophet; a brother like me, whose words you shall listen to and hearken and obey.

18:15 This prophet shall be blessed by God and the words which shall escape his mouth are not words of the prophet, but words from God.

18:16 It shall be a holy and blessed event.

18:17 But many shall think themselves prophet and speak not what God says, but what the lord of heathen says, or that which Satan himself say!

18:18 These false prophets, these spreaders of lies are evil and must be destroyed mind, body and soul.

18:19 Take these false prophets and remove their limbs and burn them so that even the bones shall become ash.

18:20 Take the ash of the false prophet and mix it with strongest of strong drink, then burn the strong drink.

18:21 The high priest shall then take this strong drink, mixed with the ash of the false prophet and drink it; for only a person of true holiness can rid the world of such wickedness.

18:22 If you are unsure of if the prophet is false, ask of them this.

18:23 When a prophet speaks in the name of the lord and what he says comes to fruition, then he is a speaker of truth and a prophet true; if what he says does not come to pass, he is a false prophet and must die.

19:1 When the lord God has conquered these nations and we dwell in our rightful place among the cities and in their houses;

19:2 You shalt separate three cities in the lands, so that every slayer may flee to these cities for sanctuary.

19:3 For every slayer who kills his neighbour in ignorance, they shall flee to these cities and be safe from the blade of the avenger.

19:4 If a man works in the woods and chops a tree down with an axe and the tree fall upon his neighbour and kills him, he shall flee to this city and live; for it is an ignorant death.

19:5 Lest the avenger come and kill the man who slew his brother through no ill will; for though an ignorant death, the avenger must still kill the slayer whilst his feet stand upon the grounds not of the cities of sanctuary.

19:6 And when the lord blesses us and expands our borders so we overtake more nations, we shall make more cities of sanctuary, so that the slayer through ignorance need not travel far.

19:7 For slayers through ignorance meant no to spill innocent blood and the lord wishes not more innocent be spilled, for the blood of the slayer is innocent.

19:8 As to why the avenger must attempt to kill him, we are unsure; perhaps the lord knows of the human desire for revenge.

19:9 Or perhaps God just finds amusement in the avenger chasing the slayer; the lord does find entertainment in violent things.

19:10 But if the man slays his neighbour in hatred and meant for the blood to be spilled upon the ground, then it is a murder and the slayer shall die.

19:11 If the slayer flees to one of the cities of sanctuary, he shall find no refuge there; the elders shall take him out of the gates and send him forth to the avenger, so that the avenger shall thrust his blade deep into the slayers chest and kill him.

19:12 Your eye shall not pity the slayer, for his blood is guilty; neither shall the avenger enjoy the death of whom slew his brethren, lest he lust for more spilled blood and become a slayer himself.

19:13 One witness shall not rise and speak against the sins of one man; it takes at least two witnesses to bring forth the sin of a man and bring them to justice.

19:14 If a man molests a child sinfully and that child speaks out against the man, ignore the child; for it is but one mouth.

19:15 Only if the man molests two children sinfully shall he be brought forth for judgment; and they must be molested at the same time.

19:16 For the two witness' must bear witness to the same act; two separate acts of similar sin do not account as two witnesses.

19:17 If a false witness arises and claim that his neighbour did something wrong;

19:18 Then both men shall stand before the judges and the priests and speak their peace.

19:19 If the witness be claimed false and hath lied to filthy name of his neighbour;

19:20 Kill him; let the congregation of Israel stone him, so that his bones be broken and his body torn.

19:21 And those who wish to speak falsely of a neighbour shall bear witness and fear the death of stoning and the wrath of God.

19:22 Remember, you shall not pity. Life for life, eye for eye, tooth for tooth, hand for hand, foot for foot, until all the world be blind, toothless, crippled and dead

20:1 When you go to battle against a nation and see of them their armies, their chariots, their archers and their horses, be not afraid of them; for the lord God did not send you out of Egypt to lose against a bunch of God damned heathens.

20:2 Before battle, the armies of Israel shall go the priest for motivation and the priest shall say to them,

20:3 "Fear not the armies of these heathen fuckers; do not tremble at their sights or show weakness before them;

20:4 For the lord God is with you and shall fight beside you and kill those who stand in our way."

20:5 The officers shall then speak among the people, saying, "Who here has built a house and not dedicated it. Go now and dedicate it to God, lest you die in battle.

20:6 Who here has planted a vineyard and not drunk of its wine. Go now and be drunk of the wine of your vineyard, lest you die in battle.

20:7 Who here has betrothed a wife, and not have a son with her. Go now, lie with your wife and conceive a son, lest you die in battle.

20:8 Who here bas bought a concubine and not fucked her. Go now, fuck your concubine until she be sore and cannot walk; then fuck her more, lest you die in battle.

20:9 Who here be faint hearted and wish not to go to battle. Leave now, for the armies of the lord shall not be poisoned with the foolishness of cowards."

20:10 And when the armies come to a city, they shall offer to the peoples a chance to surrender; if they surrender, you shall enslave all the inhabitants and claim their belongings, their lands, their riches for the people of Israel.

20:11 If the city be stubborn and refuse surrender, it shall be as an act of war.

20:12 The lord shall deliver the city into your hands and you shall smite them all with the edge of the sword.

20:13 The virgins shall be saved, so that the armies shall rape them. The women and the children shall be saved as well, so that they may be enslaved.

20:14 Save the cattle, the flocks, the goods which be in the city; those which be clean and have value shall be claimed for Israel.

20:15 Eat of their oxen, their rams, their goats and their sheep and know the lord has blessed you with the flesh of heathen flocks.

20:16 These you shall do to the cities not belonging to the lands promised in the covenant; for they are not of your inheritance and do not belong to you, yet.

20:17 For the cities in the lands promised to you, you shalt destroy without mercy; leave none alive.

20:18 The Hittites, the Amorites, the Canaanites, the Perizzites, the Hivites and the Jebusites shall be destroyed in mass genocide; burn their bodies so that the corpses of fire be mountainous.

20:19 Men, children, virgins shall burn; for these people be hated by God and the lord wish of us to erase them from the earth.

20:20 Do this and we shall be forever blessed for the holy genocide which the lord demanded from us!

20:21 When you besiege a city and the armies surround the walls so that none shall enter nor leave, you shall not destroy the trees which surround the city.

20:22 You shall no take an axe to them, nor use oxen to remove them from the ground; for the trees can be smoked in the mighty pipe of the lord and cause a great intoxication greater than alcohol for our God.

20:23 Only trees which produce no leaves, nor needles, nor fruit shall be taken down and used to make machines of war.

21:1 If one be found slain upon the land which you own and you did not slay him nor know of how he came to die;

21:2 Then the elders and the judges shall come forth and investigate how this man died.

21:3 And if it be that none know how this man be slain, the elders of Israel shall take a heifer which has not known the yoke nor worked the fields.

21:4 They shall take the heifer to the body of the slain man and slice the neck of the heifer, so that the head be removed and the blood of the heifer pour out unto the slain man.

21:5 All the elders of the city shall then wash their hands as the blood of the heifer pour upon the man and say to God, "We have not shed the blood of this man, nor know how he came to die.

21:6 Be merciful, O lord, for we be innocent and mark this man as one not killed by the children of Israel."

21:7 And the lord God shall know that a child of Israel did not murder this man, nor know how and forgive them the sin they did not commit.

21:8 The heifer shall cleanse the blood of the slain man upon the soil of Israel and the land shall be cleansed from the corpse with the blood of the heifer.

21:9 When you go to war against your enemies and the lord God has delivered them and you take them captives,

21:10 Kill all the men, lest they rise and revolt against thee.

21:11 If you see amongst the captives a beautiful woman and wish to have her in your bed, take her.

21:12 Bring her into your house and she shall shave her head and trim her nails and mourn for her fallen brother, father and sons.

21:13 For one month she shall mourn for the death of her family; as she mourns and cries, fuck her.

21:14 If you decide this woman you know longer like, for she is no good at fellatio, does not satisfy your sexual lust, or she doesn't look as good as when you first saw her, or she just be a general bitch, let her go.

21:15 Do not sell her into servitude, but merely let her go free. The stupid cunt has lost all her family and now is told by her enemy that she is ugly, at least show some sympathy and let her go in peace, lest she has more reason to bitch.

21:16 If a man has two wives, one loved and another hated and both these wives have conceived for him a son and the first-born of the sons be of the hated wife;

21:17 Then it shall be that when the time of inheritance comes, that he gives not the first-born of the beloved wife priority; the first-born of the hated wife must be given his birthright.

21:18 It be not the son's fault he come from the cunt of the hated wife; love your son, hate his mother and give the son his inheritance, for he is your future, and your strength.

21:19 If a man has a stubborn and rebellious son, who listens not to his father nor mother and disobeys their demands:

21:20 Then his father and mother shall restrain him and take him to the gates of the city.

21:21 There they shall say to the elders that their son be a disobeying and rebellious bastard, who honours not his parents.

21:22 They shall call out their son's faults; he be a drunkard, lazy, glutton, spends his days in the brothels, disobedient, etc.

21:23 The parents shall then take stones and stone their son, until their child lies beaten, battered, torn and dead below their feet.

21:24 Yes, the parents must kill their own child; such is the glory of God.

21:25 If a man commits a sin worthy of death and his execution be that of hanging, hang him upon the tree so that his body sway in the breeze.

21:26 Do not leave him overnight upon the tree, lest his wickedness corrupt the tree; take his corpse down and throw it within the wilderness, where the scavengers shall feast upon his unholy corpse.

22:1 The children of Israel must watch out for one another; if you see that your neighbour's ox or ass go astray, you shall let them know of their escaped beast.

22:2 And if your neighbour be not home or you know not of whom the beast belongs to, you shall take the animal and keep it, until the owner comes and claims it.

22:3 Ye shall do this with all of your neighbours possessions; cattle, flock, concubines and clothing.

22:4 If you see your neighbour's clothes, return it to them; they have flown away while they were drying them.

22:5 If your neighbour travel and his horse fall, you shall help your neighbour up and tend to the animal if wounded.

22:6 A man must not wear women's clothing, nor must a woman wear men's clothing; this confuses the lord and makes him wonder why the woman have such a long beard, or why the man has such large breasts.

22:7 When you walk and you see upon the ground a bird's nest, with eggs or young ones within it, you shall not harm the eggs nor the young.

22:8 You shall take the nest and place it upon the branches of the tree, so that the eggs may hatch and the young ones grow.

22:9 In this way, the birds shall grow and you may hunt them and feast upon them or better yet, offer them as sacrifice to God.

22:10 When you make a new house, for fuck sakes make sure the roof is safe and secure; the lord wishes not rain to leak upon your floors, nor the roof to fall and kill those who dwell within.

22:11 It shall be a stupid death; so stupid not even the lord God shall take amusement in it, but merely curse the name of the one who built such a stupid roof.

22:12 You shall not sow diverse seeds within your crops; one plot of land shall grow but only one crop.

22:13 If you grow both wheat and barley on the same land, the land shall be defiled and cursed by God.

22:14 You shall not plough with an ox and an ass together; the two animals never got along after they were kicked out of the garden of Eden.

22:15 The lord God is a fashionable God, therefore you shall not wear garments of mixed cloth, such as silk and linen, or cotton and wool.

22:16 Remember to make fringes upon the four quarters of your clothing, so that the lord deems you pretty and fashionable.

22:17 When a man takes a wife and lies with her and hates her,

22:18 And accuse her of whoredom and that she not be a virgin when they marry:

22:19 Then the father of the wife must provide evidence of his daughter's virginity; her undergarments, free of any stain of the seed of man.

22:20 The father shall say to the elders that he offers his daughter as a wife to this man and he falsely accuses her of being a slut, yet the tokens of her virginity be presented, thus proving the man lie.

22:21 The elders shall chastise the husband and charge him with one hundred shekels, given to the father of the wife, for soiling the name of his family.

22:22 The man shall then be beaten upon the back with whips and chains for two hours and must stay married to the woman he hates; he cannot divorce her.

22:23 But if his accusations be true and the father cannot produce the tokens of her virginity;

22:24 Then the little dumb slut shall be thrown down upon the door of her father's house and the husband shall stone her to death, so that her body lay beaten and torn upon her father's house; for she has brought shame to her family for spreading her legs before marriage and letting the seed of men enter her gates of lust.

22:25 If she wished to be a slut, she should have been a concubine or worked at a brothel.

22:26 If a man be found fucking a woman who is married, both of them must die; the man who has fucked the woman and the woman married.

22:27 It matters not if the woman accuses the man of rape, she must die, for she liked it; such is the nature of women.

22:28 If a woman who is a virgin be betrothed and someone find her in the city being raped by a man, you must surely stone them to death; the man for raping the woman and the woman for not screaming loud enough for help.

22:29 If she didn't like it, she would have cried for help; therefore, she is a whore and an abomination.

22:30 If a woman who is a betrothed virgin be found in the field being raped by a man, you must stone to death the man; the woman shall be saved.

22:31 Though unlikely, it is possible she yelled for help and none were around to hear her pleas.

22:32 If a man be found raping a virgin who is not betrothed, the man has violated the father of the virgin.

22:33 He must pay the father fifty shekels of silver and marry the woman he raped; he cannot divorce her.

22:34 A man shall not fuck his father's wife nor his concubines; these women belong to his father and his father alone.

23:1 When a man has taken a wife and marries her and it comes to pass that he find some blemish, some fault, some uncleanliness which finds her unfavourable to him;

23:2 Then he shall write to her a bill of divorce and hand it to her and send her out of her house; they shall no longer be married and she may take another husband without sin.

23:3 The bill of divorce must state the reason for divorce; bad in bed, horrible cook, became fat while married, smelly vagina, did not clean house, became bitchy, etc. All reasons must be listed upon the bill of divorce.

23:4 If she marries again and her new husband divorce her or leaves her widow, the first husband must not remarry her; to do such a thing would be as to marry your sister and is an abomination to the lord.

23:5 When a man takes a new wife, he shall not go to war, nor be charged with any business for a year; for one year he shall be free to sleep with his wife, enjoy her sex, her cooking, and attempt to conceive with her.

23:6 If a man be found taking his brethren and selling them as slaves to foreign people, this man shall die; such a thing is an abomination to God.

23:7 Only fellow children of Israel shall own slaves of the children of Israel.

23:8 Take heed of the plague of leprosy and know that those cursed by it are cursed by God and are unclean and must not be allowed within the cities of Israel; let them go to the wilderness.

23:9 Remember what the lord God did to Miriam; cursing her with terrible leprosy for pointing out that I Moses broke the laws of marriage and married an Ethiopian.

23:10 When you lend an item to a child of Israel, you shalt not go into his house and take it back; the person must give it back to you.

23:11 Tell the man to give back that which he borrowed and if he does not, he is a thief; bring him towards the priests and the judges for trial.

23:12 If the man who borrowed be poor, he shall not sleep with the item; he must return it safely.

23:13 When you hire a man for labour, you shall not oppress them; pay them fairly for their work, whether they be a child of Israel or a stranger who resides within your lands.

23:14 If the man be poor, do not extort his poverty and pay him less for a job; give him his fair due.

23:15 Exploit your slaves, not those whom you hire.

23:16 Fathers shall not be put to death for the sins of their children, nor shall children be put to death for the sins of their fathers; every man shall die for their own sin;

23:17 The lord shall curse the generations of a father who sins, but he won't kill them; a curse is not death, merely punishment for that which he sinned.

23:18 You shall not seek sexual favours from the stranger, nor the orphaned, nor the widow; purchase a concubine or visit a brothel instead.

23:19 When you harvest a field and you forget a sheaf in the field, do not fetch it, but leave it for the poor and hungry.

23:20 When you beat upon the olive tree, do not pluck of the olives which remain on the branch; leave it for the poor and hungry.

23:21 When you gather the grapes of the vineyard, do not glean it afterward; leave it for the poor and hungry.

23:22 For the lord find great amusement when the poor, the hungry, the beggars go to the fields and eat of the leftovers like rats.

23:23 Remember, you were once slaves in Egypt and the lord has freed you from Pharaoh: therefore he commands you to do these things.

24:1 He that has his genitals injured, or mutilated, or be impotent, shall not enter the into the congregation of the lord.

24:2 The lord requires that all those who enter the congregation have working penises; your penis is broken because God cursed you.

24:3 A bastard child shall not enter into the congregation of the lord; your mother must be married to your father and as a bastard you a permanent reminder of your mother's sin.

24:4 The child of a bastard may not enter into the congregation of the lord even unto the tenth generation; such wickedness is the sin of the mother who birthed the bastard.

24:5 An Ammonite nor Moabite may not enter into the congregation of the lord; they are heathens who not let you pass amongst their lands and they hired Balaam the sorcerer to curse you.

24:6 The lord used Balaam to instead bless the children of Israel and curse the people of Moab.

24:7 Do not seek out peace with the Ammonites and Moabites; they are a despicable people.

24:8 You shall respect an Edomite, for they are your brother; you shall not hate the peoples of Egypt, for you were once strangers in their land during the time of Joseph.

24:9 Though they enslaved you, you must not hate them; it gives them confusion this way.

24:10 When you go to war against your enemies, avoid that which they have that is evil.

24:11 If there be any man who sleeps at night and dreams of women and behold, wakes up with his seed spilled upon his bed, he must sleep outside of camp; he is unclean and cannot sleep in camp.

24:12 It shall be that after he awakes, he shall wash his sheets, his clothing and his genitals and be allowed to re-enter the camp.

24:13 When you walk amongst camp, you shall carry with you a paddle; and when you shit upon the ground, you shall take that paddle and bury your faeces within the ground.

24:14 For the lord God walks amongst your camp and wishes not to step in your shit and have between his toes your filth which comes from your ass.

24:15 If a slave escapes from a foreign nation, you shall not return that slave to his master; you shall keep the slave as your own.

24:16 The daughters of priests must not become whores, for such a thing is an abomination unto God.

24:17 The males of Israel must not become faggots and seek out other men for their lust; they may fuck the ass of a woman, but never the ass of a man.

24:18 God hates whores and bitches; do not bring these abominable women into the tabernacle of the congregation.

24:19 When you lend money to your brother, you must not charge him interest, for he is a child of Israel.

24:20 Charge interest to the strangers, but never to a child of Israel.

24:21 When you make a vow unto God, you must keep it; if you break that vow, the lord shall curse you and great sores shall be scarred amongst your genitals, hemorrhoids the size of pomegranates will be plagued upon you and you shall feel great fire when you urinate.

24:22 When you travel and come across a neighbour's vineyard, you may eat of the grapes, but not must put any in your vessel and bring it home; such a thing is stealing.

24:23 When you travel and come across a neighbour's field of corn, you may pluck of the ears, but do not place a sickle amongst his stalks; such a thing is stealing.

25:1 If there be controversy between two men, they shall state their case before a judge, so that the judge may justify the righteous and condemn the wicked.

25:2 And it shall be that if the judge rules the wicked be beaten, that the wicked one shall lie down and his face be beaten with whips.

25:3 Forty whips upon each cheek shall the man endure; no more, no less.

25:4 Never muzzle the ox while he treads your fields; for the mouth of the ox is a terrible weapon and shall bite those who enter your fields.

25:5 If two brothers live together and one brother die without children, the wife of the dead brother cannot marry a stranger; she must marry her brother in law and perform all wifely duties to him.

25:6 And it shall be that the first-born son of which she bears, shall inherit all of which was her deceased husband's; he shall have his birthright.

25:7 And if it be that the brother finds the wife revolting and wish not to marry her, that the wife shall go to the elders and tell of them that her husband's brother shall not marry her and perform his duties.

25:8 The elders shall call upon the brother and speak to him and the brother shall say that he wishes not to marry his dead brother's wife.

25:9 He shall take off his shoe and shit in it and say that no seed shall inherit his brother's house.

25:10 And it shall be known throughout Israel that the house of the deceased shall be the house which not grow, for no seed was planted in the soil.

25:11 When two men fight in fury, so that it seems they wish to slay one another and the wife of one of the men intervenes and reaches out and crushes, punches, or merely touches the testicles of the man who fights with her husband;

25:12 Take her to the elders and chop off her hand; her hand is unholy.

25:13 You shall not pity her nor show her sympathy; take the axe and remove her hand.

25:14 When you deal business with one another, you shall be fair and just.

25:15 Your weights shall be equal and true, so that you not charge a man for a pound of flour, when he gets less than a pound of flour.

25:16 When you deal business with a stranger is when you shall cheat.

25:17 Charge the stranger for a pound of flour and offer him less than that which he paid.

25:18 Remember that you are all children of Israel and thus chosen by God. It is an abomination to the lord when you cheat one another.

25:19 Remember that which the Amalekites did to you, when you left the lands of Egypt.

25:20 These people of the hated Esau met with you and attacked you when ye were weak and weary; these people fear not God.

25:21 It shall soon come to pass that the children of Israel shall take vengeance upon these hated people of God; you shall destroy them all, so that none of the people of Amalek shall dwell upon the earth.

25:22 Forget not what they did and hate them; let that hatred grow strong so that when the time comes, you shall use the hate and kill them with great fury.

26:1 It shall be that when you conquer the lands of your inheritance and possess it and dwell within,

26:2 That you shall take all of the first fruit of the earth and place it in a basket and give it as an offering to the lord.

26:3 You shall take it to the priest and say to him that you offer this bounty of fruits as thanks to God, who led you to this rich land.

26:4 And the priest shall take these fruits and give it to God and say to him, 'Thank you lord, for giving us this great land promised to us in the covenant during the days of Abraham.

26:5 For we once dwelt in the lands of Egypt; strangers were we, who grew strong and prosperous in a land foreign.

26:6 The people of Egypt enslaved us and bound us and treated us with great wickedness.

26:7 For years we cried out to the lord for salvation; that we may be free from this servitude of Pharaoh.

26:8 Finally you listened and with a great and mighty hand you cursed the people of Egypt and led us to the great and promised lands of milk and honey.

26:9 For keeping your covenant, I offer you this basket of fruit; may it fill your hunger and satisfy your appetite.'

26:10 Once the offerings of the first fruits be made, the people of Israel shall rejoice for all that which is good which the lord has given to them.

26:11 They shall feast and be drunk and dance and offer great sacrifice to the lord, so that the burning of flesh create a pleasing scent for God.

26:12 Upon every third year shall all the children of Israel give their tithe; ten percent of all that which they made shall be given to God.

26:13 Of this ten percent, the lord shall give some to the tribe of Levi, so that the slaves of God may eat and be strong and do the lord's bidding.

26:14 If the lord feels charitable, he may give some of his tithe to the poor and hungry; then maybe they will shut up and not annoy the lord with their whining.

26:15 When you give the tithe to the lord, you must tell him that you ate naught of any of the tithe, nor offered any of the tithe to the dead; for the lord hates that which is offered to the dead.

26:16 You shall thank the lord for what you have earned and give to him his ten percent and be blessed by God.

26:17 For the lord has given to you all that which you own; though you ploughed the fields, harvested the grain and laboured for your money, it was really God that did it all and gave you that which you have.

26:18 So give to him his tithe; ten percent is not much to give to the one who gave you all.

27:1 Keep all the commandments of which I command you this day.

27:2 And when you cross the Jordan to the land of which the lord giveth you, you shall set up great pillars of stone and enforce them with plaster.

27:3 You shall write upon these stones all the laws of our lord, when you pass over the river Jordan; a land which flows with milk and honey, as the lord did promise our fathers.

27:4 I command of you this day, upon mount Ebal, to make these pillars of stone and write upon them our laws, so that all who enter our lands shall know our laws and know that we are insane for enforcing them.

27:5 Besides these stones of law you shall build an altar of whole stone to the lord; you shall not carve the rock nor place any tool upon them.

27:6 And you shall place upon the altar a peace offering and feast there and rejoice in the name of our lord.

27:7 Take heed and hearken, for on this day you shall be the true people of God.

27:8 You must obey the voice of the lord without question and obey all his laws, his statutes and his commandments, lest you anger God and feel his wrath.

27:9 Cursed be the man who makes any image, whether molten, carved or drawn; the lord cursed those who consider themselves artists, for they cannot copy that which the lord made. Can I get an Amen?

27:10 Amen.

27:11 Curse be he who watches in lust when their parents fuck. Can I get an Amen?

27:12 Amen.

27:13 Curse be he who intrudes upon thy neighbours land. Can I get an Amen?

27:14 Amen.

27:15 Curse be he who jokes upon the blind man and cause them to fall. Can I get an Amen?

27:16 Amen.

27:17 Curse be he who pays for sexual favours from the widow, the orphaned and the foreigner. Can I get an Amen?

27:18 Amen.

27:19 Curse be he who fucks with his father's wife or concubine, for what lie under their skirt belong to the father. Can I get an Amen?

27:20 Amen.

27:21 Curse be he who fucks an animal, for such things confuse the lord. Can I get an Amen?

27:22 Amen.

27:23 Curse be he who fucks his sister, the daughter of his father, or the daughter of his mother. Can I get an Amen?

27:24 Amen.

27:25 Curse be he who fucks his mother in law. Can I get an Amen?

27:26 Amen.

27:27 Curse be he who lies in shadow and kills his neighbour in secret, for such a thing is cowardice. Can I get an Amen?

27:28 Amen.

27:29 Curse be the assassin who takes a reward to kill an innocent man. Can I get an Amen?

27:30 Amen.

27:31 Curse be he who do does not all the laws, the statutes, the judgments and the commandments of the lord. Can I get an Amen?

27:32 Amen.

27:33 Curse be he who offers no sacrifice to God. Can I get an Amen?

27:34 Amen.

28:1 It shall come to pass that when you obey all that which the lord demands, that you shall be a great and powerful nation; you shall be the most powerful people of earth.

28:2 The lord shall bless you and keep you for your blind obedience.

28:3 Blessed shall you be in the city and blessed shall you be in the field.

28:4 Blessed shall be your seed, blessed shall be your cattle, blessed shall be your vineyards, blessed shall be your crops.

28:5 Blessed shall be your sons and your daughters.

28:6 Blessed shall be your wallet.

28:7 Blessed shall you be in sex; for all the women of earth shall hear of the mighty orgasms given to the daughters of Israel.

28:8 The lord shall separate you from all the people of earth and bless you greatly and make you rich.

28:9 All the people of earth shall grow jealous of the children of Israel and fear our power and our might.

28:10 They shall seek peace with us and we shall conquer them and enslave them and rule them all.

28:11 The lord shall make you head of all humanity and all shall serve under us; for we serve under God.

28:12 If you ignore the demands of our God, or seek out other gods and serve them;

28:13 It shall come to pass that the lord shall curse great and many curses upon you and we shall be bottom feeders of the world.

28:14 Cursed shall you be in the city and cursed shall you be in the field.

28:15 Cursed shall be your seed, cursed shall be your cattle, cursed shall be your vineyards, cursed shall be your crops.

28:16 Cursed shall be your sons and your daughters.

28:17 Cursed shall be your wallet.

28:18 Cursed shall you be in sex; for your penis shall be limp and satisfy not even the virgin who knows not man.

28:19 The lord shall smite us, curse us and vex us until we all perish and die; for we have grown wicked and unrighteous in the eyes of the lord.

28:20 The lord shall cause pestilence among us, so that all shall be plagued with great sickness and disease the likes of which have not been seen.

28:21 You shall have great fevers, hemorrhoids, sores oozing with pus, terrible rash, it shall burn when you urinate and mildew and fungus shall grow on your skin.

28:22 The soil of our crops shall turn to rust and the rain above shall be of molten brass and sting us.

28:23 The lord shall deliver you to our enemies, so that the people of Israel be spread out amongst the heathens until we be removed from the earth.

28:24 Our carcasses shall pile higher than the mountains and the vultures and the wolves and all the scavengers shall feast upon our rotting flesh.

28:25 The lord shall smite you with madness, baldness, blindness and confusion.

28:26 Your wives shall give birth to the sons of your enemies and your daughters shall be whores in the brothels of heathens.

28:27 All your cattle and your flocks shall die and rot and when ye eat of their flesh, it shall cause you great illness; your very bowels shall drop from you and your corpse shall lie beside your bowels.

28:28 Your crops, your vineyards, your orchards, shall wither and die, so that ye have none to eat.

28:29 You shall starve so greatly that you shall seek out the dung of animals and pick from their shit the corn of which they have eaten.

28:30 Locusts shall come and feast upon your dead crops, your dead vineyards.

28:31 Flies will come and eat the very scabby flesh from your body and shall drink of the ooze and the pus of your sores.

28:32 Your sons shall be enslaved by those you hate and shall be sodomized by a great many men.

28:33 The holiest of items; the altars, the tabernacle, the Urimm and the Thummim, the robes of the priest, shall be taken from you and the heathens shall own them and sell them.

28:34 Your cities shall crumble; the very walls shall turn to ash and suffocate you.

28:35 Mothers and fathers shall gather their children and roast them over fire and feast upon them in madness.

28:36 You shall cut off your feet and feast upon the soles and the toes.

28:37 All your slaves shall be gone and your concubines shall menstruate into the mouths of men.

28:38 As you once numbered greater than the stars of heaven, you shall dwindle and number less than the fingers of a bad carpenter.

28:39 You shall be scattered across many nations who shall rape you, enslave you, kill you and cause you great suffering.

28:40 When you scream to God for forgiveness and offer your sacrifices and confess your sins, they shall be for naught.

28:41 For the lord shall ignore you and hate you for such betrayal.

28:42 You shall be cursed worse than the people of Egypt, when the lord set us free from Pharaoh's servitude.

28:43 You shall sell yourself as slave and none shall want you; for you shall be a blind, lame, diseased ridden cannibal.

28:44 Even the heathen beggars shall spit upon you, for you shall be lower than them.

28:45 And it shall come to pass that all the children of Israel shall die and be erased from the earth; such shall be the will of our lord.

29:1 You have seen the many wonders, glories, curses and miracles of our lord since the day God has taken off our yoke and set us free from Egypt.

29:2 You have seen also the many temptations of evil, wickedness and false gods; those that gave into such temptation were abolished by the hand of our lord.

29:3 The lord has not given us eyes to see, ears to hear, nor a heart to perceive; he has given us eyes to see God, ears to hear the lord's words and a heart to love and fear our lord.

29:4 For forty years I have led you through the wilderness and never have your clothes grown ragged, or outgrown, nor have your feet outgrown your shoes; such is the glory of our fashionable God.

29:5 When we came to these strange lands, Sihon the king of Heshbon and Og the king of Bashan came out to battle with us; we crushed those heathen fuckers and took of their lands and raped their women.

29:6 We did this all in the name of our lord, for we have kept his covenant and he delivered these armies into our hands.

29:7 Keep therefore the laws of our lord, so that he shall continue to remember us and bless us and deliver many nations into our hands, so that we shall grow strong and prosper.

29:8 You all stand this day before the eyes of God; your captains, your officers, your generals, your elders;

29:9 Your children, your wives, your slaves, your concubines and the strangers who reside among us.

29:10 The lord shall forever watch us and ensure we obey his laws.

29:11 God shall watch us while we sleep, while we bathe, while we lie intimately with one another, while we work, while we make sacrifice; forever shall the eye of the lord be upon us.

29:12 Let it be known that the laws of God are set in stone, so that we may avoid all which is wicked and evil.

29:13 If a child of Israel believes themselves above the law and think their own heart and soul shall give them the guidance to do good and avoid and do not that which is evil;

29:14 That the lord shall not spare them, but smite them and their names shall be blot out of the book of life.

29:15 The lord shall separate these fools from the tribes of evil and curse them so they know only sickness and suffering.

29:16 In his anger, the lord shall cast them to a land of brimstone and salt and burning, where everything is barren and not even a blade of grass grows.

29:17 They shall know they did wicked to the lord, for not believing in the laws and that they mocked God for believing they themselves could do good and avoid that which is evil.

30:1 It shall come to pass that when the blessings of our lord come upon us and the curses of our lord strike our enemies, that we shall drive out nations and rule all.

30:2 That the lord shall come and gather all the children of Israel and embrace us in his bosom and take us to his house.

30:3 There the lord shall give us compassion and wisdom and we shall truly walk with God.

30:4 Our lord shall take of the knife and circumcise the foreskins of our hearts and the hearts of our seed, so that we may live forever with God.

30:5 And the cursed of our lord shall be set upon our enemies and they shall know great suffering, pestilence and persecution from those who are holy.

30:6 When we return to the house of our lord, we shall obey his laws and commandments; for we shall be guests in his house for eternal.

30:7 All the children of Israel shall look down upon the earth and piss upon our enemies who dwell there and mock them and laugh at their pains.

30:8 It shall be of great relief to know that we were the ones chosen by God and that through our devotion, our unquestioning disobedience, that he has truly made us his children and we shall dwell in his house.

30:9 For who else among the earth has been given such an offer. Who in the lands or across the seas have been invited to live in the house of the true lord?

30:10 I have set before you a choice; life and good, or death and evil.

30:11 When you choose life and good, you have obeyed the lords, the statutes, the commands of our lord and offered him his sacrifices and love him and fear him with all your heart and soul and have not given into temptation of the heathens.

30:12 But if you turn away from God and doubt and question him and obey not his laws nor offer your sacrifice and go whoring after other gods, then you have chosen death and evil; forever shall you and your seed be cursed.

30:13 In witness of God, I have given you a choice of death or life; choose life.

30:14 For it is better to live a slave to God, then die a free man from the lord's tyranny.

31:1 Moses stepped forth and said to the children of Israel,

31:2 "I am of one hundred and twenty years of age and my penis be as limp as the wet rag: also, the lord has said to me that I shall not cross the river Jordan.

31:3 The lord our God shall cross the Jordan and weaken these nations who dwell in the lands promised to us, so that we may destroy them and possess them: and Joshua shall take my place and lead you to the lands of the covenant.

31:4 The lord shall do to these heathens what he did to Sihon and Og, kings of the Amorites; they shall be slaughtered.

31:5 Be strong and courageous, O' children of Israel and fear not our enemies, but fear our lord; he shall not forsake you, so long as we not forsake God."

31:6 Moses then spoke to Joshua and said to him in front of the children of Israel,

31:7 "Take heed of my words, Joshua, for soon I shall perish and it shall be you who must lead these children of Israel to the lands of milk and honey.

31:8 Be strong and let them not weaken you, for these people are whiny, bitchy and disobedient; yet they be the children of God and you must ensure they obey our lord and follow his laws and statutes.

31:9 Be patient, but do not give in to their demands. The lord shall make you strong and give you the strength to deal with these immature fucks."

31:10 Moses then gathered all the laws of which the lord had him written down and gave it to the tribe of Levi, which bear the ark of the covenant as slaves to God.

31:11 Moses gathered the elders of Israel and said to them, "At the end of every seven years, remember the solemnity of the year of release, in the feast of tabernacles; this is important to our lord.

31:12 When all the children of Israel do gather and hear the words of the elders, you shall read to them the laws of the lord.

31:13 Strike within their hearts the wrath, the anger and the fear of the lord; fearful people are obedient people and shall do as they are told without question nor doubt.

31:14 When they grow rich and prosperous, remind them that it was God who gave them their riches and that God can quickly claim it back and make them suffer greatly."

31:15 Moses knew that his time drew near, for the lord shall not let him pass over the Jordan and shall take his life soon.

31:16 When the great and fiery pillar of the lord came down upon the tabernacle of the congregation, Moses called for Joshua and blessed him and made him ruler of the children of Israel.

31:17 The lord then came to Moses and said to him,

31:18 "Be glad that you do not cross the river Jordan, for you shall soon die.

31:19 It shall come to pass that the people of Israel shall betray me and sleep with their fathers and go whoring after other gods and do great evil against me; I have foreseen it.

31:20 They shall break my covenant of which I have made with them and forsake me."

31:21 Moses asked the lord, "Why shall these people do such a thing?"

31:22 And the lord replied, "Because I shall ensure it happens.

31:23 I am the lord God and hold the power of the universe and all things; I shall not be held bound to the children of Israel because I merely made a damn covenant!

31:24 The lord wishes not to keep his covenant and shall have it so that the children of Israel break the covenant and not God; the lord shall keep his holiness this way.

31:25 My anger shall be kindled against the children of Israel and I shall abandon them and devour them and curse them with many evils, plagues and pestilence."

31:26 Moses was fearful of this and warned Joshua and the elders who did not believe him and thought him jealous for dying before he cross into the promised lands.

31:27 Moses grew angry and spread the word of the lord's betrayal amongst the camps and those who heard him laughed.

31:28 But a few took heed his words, for they knew deep in their hearts that the lord they worship was a tyrant and they began to hate God.

31:29 Those that doubted, the lord killed, so that he shall keep his covenant with fewer people.

31:30 The devil witnessed this and felt pity for the children of Israel; for the devil wished not the same fate for these people as the lord gave to him and his angels.

31:31 He came to Moses, disguised and said to him,

31:32 "I take heed the words you say of God and know of ways to save you.

31:33 When the pestilence comes and the lord force the children of Israel to break the covenant, there is none that can be done to avoid it.

31:34 We shall be evil in the sight of our lord and the lord shall curse us greatly.

31:35 But we shall be not evil and deserve none that the lord curse us with; I shall teach you a song.

31:36 This song shall be a curse to God, so that he shall be blinded of us and see us not on the earth so that he may strike us with a curse.

31:37 Teach this song to those who shall listen and have them teach it to their children, for generations upon generations.

31:38 Write it down in the laws of our lord; trick the children of Israel so that they learn this song and those who learn it and be not evil in heart shall be saved from the lord's tyranny."

31:39 Moses wrote down the song and placed it along with the laws of the lord.

31:40 When he asked the devil who he was and how he knew the song shall save his peoples, Satan merely replied,

31:41 "I am the friend, though you see me as enemy.

31:42 I wish to help you, though you fear I shall destroy you.

31:43 I am the one who shall stand up against God and protect all from the lord.

31:44 The lord shall claim to stand up against I and protect you from me.

31:45 I am the one truly cursed by God and embrace his curse; for I be cursed not because I am evil, but because he be evil.

31:46 Who else but one who is evil shall send out a curse. A curse, by its very nature, is evil and one who sends out a curse is therefore evil.

31:47 I am the one who protected Isaac from being a sacrificial lamb.

31:48 It is a pleasure to meet you, Moses, but you must not know my name."

31:49 With that, the devil left and hoped his song, his anti-curse, shall save those of the children of Israel from the wrath, the greed and the tyranny of the lord.

32:1 Moses wished the children of Israel be forever blessed, even if the blessing be from a tyrannical lord and spoke with them one last time.

32:2 He knew none shall believe what the lord has said to him; that the lord shall ensure the children of Israel break the covenant, so that God shall smite and curse them.

32:3 Moses wished to strike fear in all the hearts of his people, so that they shall forever obey the laws of God and teach their children to obey God.

32:4 He said to them, the children of Israel, "Take heed of my words and teach what I say to your children and your children's children, for generations eternal.

32:5 When you break the laws of God, the lord shall show no pity amongst us; he shall hate us and abhor us.

32:6 A great fire shall burn in the heart of our lord, a fire that shall destroy our nation, our people.

32:7 We shall starve, for we shall have no food; the lord shall destroy our crops, our cattle, our flocks.

32:8 Great arrows of fire shall rain upon our people and they shall strike us and kill us horribly.

32:9 Heat as though from a furnace shall rise from the ground and melt our shoes and burn our feet and consume us so that we roast.

32:10 The beasts of the wild shall feast upon our roasted corpses, as we once feasted upon the roasted corpses of the beasts.

32:11 The great mace of our lord shall come and smite us, so that you shall be scattered amongst the lands, amongst the nations, amongst the heathens.

32:12 You shall be slaves and our servitude shall be worse than those of Pharaoh.

32:13 Our water shall be of the venom of dragons and we shall choke upon it.

32:14 Plagues of asps shall come and sting us.

32:15 The bears of the forest shall come and rape your daughters and sodomize your sons and shall feast upon them as they scream.

32:16 Understand that the evils of which the lord has done to our enemies is nothing to the evils he shall do to us if we forsake him.

32:17 The lord held back his curses upon these people; he shall not hold back if we break our covenant.

32:18 You shall know the true wrath of our lord; avoid it and obey him always.

32:19 Lest the lord cast you in his winepress and grow drunk upon your blood and fat on your flesh."

32:20 These were the last words which Moses spoke to the children of Israel.

33:1 Moses knew of the day of his death and went up to the mountains so that he shall see the lands promised to his people; lands he shall not know and shall be taken away from the children of Israel.

33:2 He went atop the mount and saw the palm trees, the vineyards, the crops, the shore:

33:3 The flocks, the cattle, the cities, the valleys and the plains.

33:4 Moses wept, for it was a beautiful sight to behold.

33:5 Moses looked towards the camps of Israel and blessed them and hoped that they shall not break the covenant of God and live forever in the lands of milk and honey.

33:6 Moses looked to the sky and knew that the lord he served all this time;

33:7 The lord whom led him and his people away from Egypt.

33:8 The lord whom gave to his people manna.

33:9 The lord who delivered great and many armies and nations to the hands of his people.

33:10 The lord who made fresh water flow from stone.

33:11 The lord who sent great fiery snakes to kill his people.

33:12 The lord who demanded gruesome and gory sacrifice.

33:13 The lord who had a great and mighty jaw rise from the earth and consume his people.

33:14 The lord who threatens terrible and horrible curses if his demands be not met.

33:15 Moses looked upon the heavens and knew the lord be a tyrant.

33:16 In defiance to God, Moses took of his knife and slit his throat, thus killing himself.

33:17 For he wished the lord have no satisfaction in the of taking his life.

33:18 When the lord looked down upon earth and saw that Moses spilled his own blood, he grew angry and buried the body of Moses deep within the earth, so that none shall find his tomb.

33:19 The children of Israel knew not what happened and believe that the lord took the life of Moses.

33:20 They wept for Moses, for he was a great leader to them.

33:21 Joshua stepped forth and replaced the position of Moses and promised to lead the children of Israel such as the way of Moses did.

33:22 He spoke greatly of Moses and told the children of Israel,

33:23 "Moses was blessed by God, for he was chosen by the lord to lead us all to the lands of the covenant.

33:24 We must praise Moses and give honour to his name.

33:25 Never shall another prophet like Moses arise, who spoke to the lord face to face.

33:26 Therefore we must obey the laws of which Moses wrote down, for they be the laws of the lord.

33:27 Though we find not the body of Moses, we know him to be dead; his body shall become dust.

33:28 The lord himself took the body of Moses and buried it in heaven; for Moses was most holy to God and deserved such an honour.

33:29 Let us remember Moses and give honour to his name; for it is by the will of God that Moses lead us this far, to the lands promised to us in the covenant."

33:30 With that, the people mourned for Moses and praised and blessed his name.

33:31 The lord looked down upon the children of Israel and laughed at their ignorance; for never shall the peoples know what the lord truly is, nor what the lord God did to Moses.

JOSHUA

1:1 After the death of Moses, the lord came down to Joshua the son of Nun, who has replaced Moses as the leader of Israel and said to him,

1:2 "Moses is now dead and his body shall lie in the gardens of heaven; you shall now lead the children of Israel and take them to the lands promised by the covenant.

1:3 Where the soles of your feet step, you shall own and what your eyes see shall belong to you.

1:4 From the wilderness to Lebanon, to the great river Euphrates, to the lands of the hated Hittites, to the coasts of the shore, shall all belong to you.

1:5 Those fools that stand before you shall be struck down; the lord shall tear down nations for you.

1:6 Be strong and of great courage; fear not the trials that lie ahead,

but fear only your lord.

1:7 The lands of which you conquer shall be inherited to you and shall be divided amongst the tribes of Israel.

1:8 You must be strong and courageous, for the lord hates cowards amongst his people; you must be obedient and obey my laws, for the lord shall not tolerate disobedience.

1:9 The book of the law must not just be spoken, but meditated upon and scarred deep within your hearts, so that you do not forget them and obey the lord always.

1:10 For when you obey the lord, the lord shall bless you and make you strong and prosperous; your seed shall spread across the earth and rule all.

1:11 I God shall command you and instill in your hearts great courage and strength; be not afraid nor discouraged, for the lord shall protect you wherever thou go."

1:12 Joshua then commanded his people and said to them,

1:13 "Prepare your victuals, for in three days we shall cross this Jordan and take that which is ours; we shall destroy and enslave those who dwell within our lands.

1:14 You of the tribe of Reuben, Gad and Manasseh shall stay behind, for the lands which you inherited have been conquered and you shall dwell here.

1:15 Your wives, your children and your flocks shall rest here, upon the lands you inherited from God; but your men shall pass with us, for we shall need them in battle.

1:16 Prepare your horses and ready your swords, for soon we shall bathe in the blood of our enemies!"

1:17 And the people answered Joshua,

1:18 "We shall do as you command, for surely you are blessed by God.

1:19 We shall follow and obey you, as we once followed and obeyed Moses.

1:20 Those who doubt Joshua or not hearken his words shall be slain, for they go against the will of our lord."

2:1 Joshua the son of Nun sent out two spies to seek out intel upon the lands and the city of Jericho. Thus the two spies left and gathered great intel.

2:2 Both spies decided it best to hide in a place they believed no enemy of theirs shall find them.

2:3 They stayed at the house of a whore; an independent prostitute, named Rahab.

2:4 The whore Rahab knew these men be spies, but feared what they shall do to her if she told the soldiers of their presence. So, Rahab allowed these spies to stay.

2:5 As the two spies stayed, they paid her well for her services and fucked her nightly.

2:6 The citizens of Jericho took notice of the men staying with Rahab and knew not where they came from. Word of the two men reached the king of Jericho, who believed them to be spies from Israel.

2:7 Soldiers were sent to the house of Rahab and demanded that she send out the two men, for they believed them spies who wish to destroy their country.

2:8 Rahab took the two men and hid them and said unto the soldiers, "Two men did come to me, but they left and I know not where they went."

2:9 King Jericho then ordered shut the gates of the city and told his soldiers, "When you see these two men, overtake them quickly. Question them, then kill them.

2:10 Take legions of men and search the country, for it be possible they left this city."

2:11 With that, the soldiers closed the gates of Jericho and legions of soldiers searched the countryside and the villages for the two spies of Israel.

2:12 Rahab went atop her house, for the spies of Israel were hiding upon her roof, beneath great stalks of flax.

2:13 She told the spies, "I know you shall conquer these lands, for your God has promised them to you and our mighty armies shall not stop you.

2:14 Great stories have been told to us about how you left Egypt, conquered cities and destroyed nations.

2:15 King Sihon and king Og, both powerful men, were slain by your hands, with the aid of your terrible God.

2:16 I beg of you that ye show me mercy, for I have allowed you to stay in my house and hid you from your enemies and my people.

2:17 When you conquer this city, I pray to you that ye spare my life, the life of my father and mother and the lives of my brothers and sisters."

2:18 The two men answered her, "We shall reward you for your service, for in your service to us you have served God.

2:19 When we come and claim this city as ours, you and your kindred shall be spared, but first you must do two things.

2:20 We are stuck in this city and the gates be shut. We need to escape and tell our people of what we have learned of our city.

2:21 Also, you must give unto each of us fellatio before we leave; for the lord shall see the seed of Israel be in your throat and shall know you are to be spared."

2:22 With that, Rahab stripped naked and got upon her knees and sucked the dicks of both spies.

2:23 With fury she sucked and when both men ejaculated, she swallowed it all, so that the seed of these men be in her belly and stain her throat.

2:24 Rahab then took a rope from her house and threw it over her window; for her house was conveniently located within the walls of Jericho.

2:25 She told the spies, "Get you to the mountains and hide there three days. In three days time, the army shall cease their search and come back to the city. It shall be safe then for you to leave."

2:26 The spies then slapped her ass and climbed down and hid in the mountains three days.

2:27 When the men returned to the camp of Israel and spoke to Joshua the son of Nun, they told him of all that transpired and how the harlot Rahab shall be saved.

2:28 They cared not for the promises they made, for if the lord wished her dead, she shall die.

2:29 She is the enemy and deserves death.

2:30 No, they wanted her saved for she gave unto them the best blowjob they ever had and wished to have her as a concubine.

2:31 Joshua said to them, "Whether the harlot Rabah be saved or not is the decision of the lord, not mine.

2:32 Tell me, how be the people of the city?"

2:33 To which the spies replied,

2:34 "They are fucking terrified of us. To conquer them shall be easy."

3:1 Joshua awoke early in the morning and moved the camp by the shore of Jericho and there they lodged before they crossed the river; crossed to the lands promised to them since the days of Abraham many, many generations ago.

3:2 It came to pass that after three days, the officers of the army prepared the people to cross the river.

3:3 The officers said to the people, "You shall let the ark of covenant be in the center with the slaves of God, so that the ark be protected by our numbers.

3:4 This ark is most holy to us and most holy to our lord; we must protect it.

3:5 Do not go near the ark, for if you go too near that which is most holy, you shall surely die; two thousand cubits shall you stay away from the ark of the covenant."

3:6 Joshua then spoke and announced to his people, "Sanctify yourselves, for tomorrow we shall cross the river and claim that which is rightfully ours."

3:7 The lord then came down in great black smoke and fire and said to Joshua, "This day I shall magnify you in all Israel, so that all the children of Israel shall see you as great as Moses.

3:8 When you come to cross the river, have the children of Israel pause, for the lord shall make it so that none shall get their feet wet when they cross the Jordan."

3:9 Joshua spoke again to his people and told them, "Know that today the lord shall let us pass the Jordan and we shall take the lands that belong to us rightfully and kill those who dwell there.

3:10 Our lord shall be with us and with his power we shall destroy all the Canaanites, the Hitittes, the Hivites, the Perizzites, the Girgashites and the Amorites; it shall be a most holy and glorious genocide!

3:11 So we know that the lord is with us, we shall pass the Jordan dry, so that not even the soles of our feet be damp.

3:12 When you come to the shores of the Jordan, pause and bear witness the miracles of God!"

3:13 With that, the people of Israel came to the Jordan and paused upon its shores, waiting for what the lord shall do.

3:14 A thick and wide bridge of fish then came, which went from one end of the Jordan to the other; and the fish swam upon their sides, so that the feet would not step upon the sharp dorsal fin.

3:15 Before the first child of Israel stepped upon the fish, the fish shook so that all the waters from their scales be gone from them.

3:16 The children of Israel then crossed atop the fish and those who crossed barefoot were not even cut by the scales of the fish.

3:17 When the last child of Israel stepped foot upon the other side of the Jordan, the lord spoke down from heaven, "Now cast out your nets and gather in the fish."

3:18 The children of Israel did as the lord commanded; for not only does the lord have them betray the people who help them, the lord has them betray the animals which help them as well.

3:19 They then had a fish fry and feasted upon the fish and danced naked and offered many sacrifices to God.

3:20 The lord did not like this, for though he loves blood, nudity and torn flesh, he hates the smell of fish.

4:1 It came to pass that the lord came down and spoke with Joshua and said to him,

4:2 "Command twelve men of Israel; a male from each tribe,

4:3 Demand they take from the river Jordan twelve large stones and carry them to where you camp and place them there."

4:4 Joshua then called the twelve men, one from every tribe and said to them,

4:5 "Go to the waters of the river Jordan and from the bottom of the river gather twelve large stones; one for every tribe of the children of Israel.

4:6 This shall be a sign among our people, so that when children ask their fathers, what do these stones mean?

4:7 You shall answer them, that the stones be marks upon the lands promised to us by our lord, when he made the covenant with Abraham.

4:8 That the lord had us set these stones from the river, to remind us of the miracle of crossing this river, where a bridge of fish came and let us cross, so that we did not have to get our feet wet.

4:9 Thus the twelve men chosen went to the river, to gather twelve great stones for this monument unto God.

4:10 Two drowned.

4:11 Joshua sent forth two men to replace those that ingloriously died doing a simple command from the lord and they brought back the large stones for their tribe.

4:12 Joshua the son of Nun then placed the twelve stones where they made camp that night, in honour to God and to the twelve tribes of Israel; they still stand there this day.

4:13 Erosion hath caused them to wear down and become mere pebbles, but they still stand there to this day!

4:14 In the lands of Gilgal did the people of Israel camp and in the lands of Gilgal do those stones still stand; monuments to God.

4:15 And Joshua spoke to his people and said to them, "May these stones forever stay here, in glory to our lord!

4:16 For each stone represents a tribe of Israel.

4:17 If your stone moves away, this tribe has lost favour in the sight of God and shall be cursed and know the wrath of the lord.

4:18 Obey all which the lord demands, fear God, lest your stone roll back into the river Jordan."

5:1 The lord came down to Joshua, and said to him, "Go and gather sharp knives, for today shall be the second circumcision of Israel."

5:2 Joshua asked the lord, "How can this be done, for we all be circumcised. What foreskin is their left to cut?"

5:3 God replied to Joshua, "You fool. Don't ye dare doubt the demands of God!

5:4 When I tell you to do something, do not doubt nor question. Just do it, dammit!

5:5 Moses doubted me at times and I loathed him for that; if you wish the lord to loathe you, then doubt and question my demands.

5:6 If you wish to please God, you shall do as the lord says!"

5:7 Thus Joshua gathered sharp knives and gathered all the men and boys of Israel for their second circumcision.

5:8 Some were scared of this, for they wished not more of their penis to be cut; they ran away.

5:9 The lord God cursed them and cast them away from the children of Israel and abandoned them and cursed them with impotence.

5:10 Those that stayed were cut a second time; what little skin left was removed and cast aside, until a hill of remaining foreskin remained; thus the place was called the Hill of the Foreskins.

5:11 The males of Israel wept, for it was a painful ordeal; their penis' bled and were sore for weeks.

5:12 The lord God found this amusing, for the lord loves the misery of others.

5:13 When the males of Israel asked why they needed a second circumcision Joshua thus answered them, "For the lord demanded it.

5:14 For forty years we have wandered the desert, children of God, as he delivered us to the promised lands of milk and honey.

5:15 Today, we are at those lands and thus are no longer children, but men; for this, we needed the second circumcision, so that when the lord looks down upon our genitals, God shall know we are no longer children, but men."

5:16 The males of Israel grumbled, for such a thing was ridiculous, even for God.

5:17 Still, they agreed, for fear the lord shall hear their grumbling and demand a third circumcision for them.

5:18 It was the time of the Passover and on the fourteenth day they celebrated the Passover on the plains of Jericho.

5:19 They ate of the corn which grew there, for no longer did they need manna; manna stopped and no longer came upon the ground,

for they had no need of it.

5:20 The people of Israel rejoiced, for they were sick of that sweetened bread of heaven.

5:21 It came to pass that by Jericho, Joshua looked up and behold, there stood a man ten cubits high, with a sword drawn in his hand and Joshua asked him, "Be you friend or foe?"

5:22 The man said, "Nay, I am an angel of the lord, who came to deliver a message to you."

5:23 Joshua fell upon his face and said unto the angel, "What is this message, so important that the lord sends an angel to me?"

5:24 And the angel said to him, "Take off your shoes, for you are on holy ground."

5:25 Joshua thus took off his shoes and restrained his laughter; for even Joshua thought it ridiculous that the lord would send an angel, with drawn sword, to tell him to merely take off his shoes.

6:1 The king of Jericho feared the people of Israel and had it so that the city of Jericho was sealed; none shall enter and none shall leave.

6:2 And the lord God came to Joshua and said to him, "See how I have given to you the city of Jericho and their king and all their men.

6:3 You shall destroy the city in this manner; have your armies assemble and march around the city. For six days you shall march around the city once per day.

6:4 Seven priests, seven most holy men, shall march with you and carry with them the ark of the covenant and have with them a ram's horn.

6:5 Upon the seventh day you shall march seven times around the city and when ye end the seventh march, the priests shall blow mightily their horns.

6:6 For priests are good at blowing and shall be for generations.

6:7 When the priests blow upon the ram horns, the lord shall blow his trumpet, so that the very walls of the city shall crumble to dust and fall flat and the armies of Israel shall raid the city and destroy all which dwell within it."

6:8 Joshua spoke to his generals and made known the lord's plans to all the people of Israel.

6:9 The people of Israel marched towards the city of Jericho and made camp there; those in Jericho that saw the camp and grew afraid of what evil the God of Israel shall do to them.

6:10 When the sun broke the horizon, Joshua arose from his bed, gathered is soldiers and the seven priests and marched towards Jericho.

6:11 On the first day, they marched around the city, made camp in front of the gates and rested.

6:12 On the second day, they marched around the city, made camp in front of the gates and rested.

6:13 For six days they did this, so that the people of Jericho grew confused and even laughed at them.

6:14 As the armies of Israel marched around the city, citizens of Jericho taunted them and asked if they grew dizzy marching around the city.

6:15 Rahab, the whore who helped hide the spies of Israel, would wait for the armies to march by and exposed herself to them, so that they and the lord of Israel shall remember her and what she did for them.

6:16 It came to pass that on the seventh day, the armies of Israel and the priests which bared the ark marched seven times around the city.

6:17 Those within the city laughed at them and set up chairs among the walls of the city and laughed and mocked and even waved when the armies of Israel marched by.

6:18 When Joshua passed by Rahab's house, he pointed his sword towards her and told her to remove her goods and her families, for the wrath of the lord shall soon be upon the city.

6:19 Rahab did and gathered her valuables and her family and went towards the center of the city.

6:20 Upon the end of the seventh march, the armies of Israel stopped and the priests who carried the ark placed it upon the ground.

6:21 The seven priests drew out their ram horns and blew a great and mighty noise. The lord heard this and blew his trumpet from the heavens above.

6:22 The trumpet of God made a mighty and terrible noise, so loud that none but the trumpet of the lord could be heard.

6:23 With the noise of the trumpet of the lord, the walls of Jericho began to crumble and turn to dust.

6:24 When the walls crumbled, the armies of Israel stormed the city and killed all which dwelt inside.

6:25 Men, women, child, elderly, flock, cattle and beast they killed; they beheaded the breastfeeding mother and cut in half the baby, all in the glory of God.

6:26 They gathered all the belongings of the people of Jericho; gold, silver, iron, pottery and brass; as they did this, Joshua said to them,

6:27 "Careful when you loot, lest you take the accursed things and the wrath of the lord be upon us.

6:28 For these people are an accursed people and have many an accursed thing among them.

6:29 Take not the accursed thing, for they an abomination to God."

6:30 The two spies went into the city and led out Rahab and her family, who were cowering in the middle of the city.

6:31 Joshua said to Rahab, "For your services to the children of Israel, our lord has decided that you are worthy to live.

6:32 Go out and you shall live like beasts in the wild."

6:33 Rahab went upon her knees and begged to Joshua, "We wish not to live in the wild.

6:34 For we are people of the city and know not how to live off the lands. Have mercy and let us live in your camp."

6:35 Joshua grew furious and said to her, "The lord has offered you life and life ye shall have.

6:36 You shall live like the beasts, for your people are beasts; though I do have one solution.

6:37 Every day, my armies have seen you and grew in lust for you. If you wish to live in society, you shall have to service my men.

6:38 Rahab shall be known as the harlot of the armies and the soldiers of Israel shall ravage her daily and nightly, so that their carnal lusts be desired."

6:39 Rahab knew of the numbers of the armies of Israel and knew that even a professional whore like herself could not daily pleasure these men.

6:40 However, Rahab wished to save her family and agreed to pleasure the armies of Israel, if she and her family could live in their camps.

6:41 With that agreement, Joshua ordered the city of Jericho burned, so that none inside shall survive.

6:42 As the city burned for three days, the armies of Israel raped Rahab in front of the fires of Jericho.

6:43 Day and night they raped her.

6:44 They raped her in her cunt, they raped her in her ass, they raped her in her mouth, they raped her in her hands, they raped her in her feet, they raped her in her nostrils.

6:45 Upon every part of her body the armies of Israel raped Rahab, so that she got no food, no water, no sleep.

6:46 She died while the armies of Israel raped her and in her death she cursed them, for they intimately touched a corpse; a most unholy act in the eyes of God.

6:47 After the death of Rahab, Joshua ordered that her family be slaughtered and their goods tallied up amongst the children of Israel.

6:48 For Joshua said to the peoples of Israel, "Surely you do not expect the lord to keep his word to a whore."

6:49 As the fires began to die and the city of Jericho was turned to naught but ash and rubble, Joshua said to his people, "Cursed be the man who rebuilds Jericho, for they go against God.

6:50 Those that rebuild Jericho lay the very foundations of evil upon our lands and for this their seed shall know the wrath of the lord for generations."

6:51 With the destruction of Jericho, the people of Israel knew that the lord was with them and with Joshua; and the news of the people of Israel spread across the lands and the peoples began to loathe and fear them.

7:1 During the massacre of Jericho, a child of Israel did take of the accursed thing, for Achan the son of Carmi, of the tribe of Judah, committed a sin of trespass and took of the accursed thing.

7:2 Thus the lord cursed the peoples of Israel when Joshua sent out men to spy upon the city of Ai, which is beside Bethaven, on the east of Bethel.

7:3 For when the men returned, they said to Joshua, "The people of Ai are poor labourers. Let us take an army of three thousand men, for this shall be more than enough to smite them."

7:4 So Joshua sent three thousand men to destroy the city of Ai; but they were cursed by God.

7:5 For the people of Ai gathered a great many weapons and fended off the armies of Israel, killing thirty-six men as the army of Israel fled.

7:6 The people of Israel heard of this and grew afraid; for how could their God allow such a pathetic people to kill their soldiers and fend off their attacks?

7:7 Joshua and the elders ripped the clothes from their bodies, poured dust upon their heads and cried in front of the tabernacle.

7:8 Joshua said to the lord, "Why have you allowed such travesty to happen?

7:9 The lord has sent us away from the servitude of Egypt and with the might of God the nation of Israel has destroyed great nations and conquered many armies.

7:10 Yet now the lord has abandoned us and let the pathetic peoples of Ai kill us, so that we must run from them.

7:11 Why did the lord tell us to cross the Jordan. Why could not the children of Israel be content on the other side of the Jordan?"

7:12 The lord came down to Joshua and said to him, "Get up and clean off the dust from your head.

7:13 The people of Israel have sinned and broken my covenant; for they have taken of the accursed thing.

7:14 Get up, sanctify the people and tell them that someone has taken of the accursed thing; for this the lord God shall curse the people of Israel, until the accursed thing be taken away and the man who took it be killed.

7:15 In the morning, the tribe of which the man belongs who took the accursed thing shall glow and the man who has taken the accursed thing shall be of a great darkness.

7:16 When you find him, take his family and all he have and burn them with a great and horrible fire; for he has taken of the accursed thing and broken the covenant of the lord."

7:17 On the morrow, the tribe of Judah had a strange glow among them, so that Joshua shall know the man who took of the accursed thing was of the tribe of Judah.

7:18 As Joshua searched, Achan the son of Carmi had a darkness surround him; so that all who looked at him knew he was cursed.

7:19 Joshua drew his sword and said to Achan, "Confess, for you have taken of the accursed thing. Show me where it is, so that I shall destroy it and banish the curse from Israel forever."

7:20 Achan denied ever taking the accursed thing and said to Joshua, "I have not taken of the accursed thing.

7:21 For when I raided the city of Jericho, I burned all the altars, the idols and the unholy relics of their religion.

7:22 I took nothing from them nor left any alive. Search my tents and you shall see know accursed things."

7:23 Joshua thus had the tent of Achan searched and found nothing of the accursed thing.

7:24 Joshua stripped the families of Achan and searched ever crevice amongst their bodies and they found no accursed thing.

7:25 Joshua grew angry, for surely this man must be the one who took the accursed thing.

7:26 It was then that Joshua noticed the infant son of Achan, who bared no resemblance to Achan, nor his wives, nor his concubines.

7:27 Joshua asked Achan, "Who be this child, for surely it is not your son."

7:28 Achan replied, "This is my son, of my own seed. Leave him alone, for he is a mere innocent baby of two weeks old."

7:29 Joshua grew fierce and said to Achan, "Why do you spit out the vile venom of lies upon me?

7:30 For surely this is not your baby. He looks nothing like you, nor your wives, nor your concubines.

7:31 You say the baby is young, yet all your wives and concubines are slim; surely, they did not recently give birth to a child.

7:32 I ask you again, who be the father of this child?"

7:33 Tears began to swell in the eyes of Achan and he said to Joshua, "I know not the father of the infant, nor do I know the mother.

7:34 For when we raided the city of Jericho, I saw this infant buried beneath the rubble, crying.

7:35 Surely, he could not be more than two weeks of age. What beast of a man would slay such an infant or deny him shelter, food and a loving home?

7:36 I hid him in my robe and returned him to my home, so I shall raise him as a child of Israel.

7:37 For surely the lord would want this; another male to offer him sacrifice, to worship him and to follow his laws.

7:38 The lord would find great satisfaction in his enemy, from a most hated people, in worshipping him and offering him sacrifice."

7:39 Joshua became furious and said to Achan, "That wretched beast of a child is an accursed thing of God and should have been slain by your blade when you found the accursed creature.

7:40 Your foolishness has cursed all the people of Israel and you shall know the wrath of God for this blasphemy."

7:41 With that, Joshua took the accursed baby and threw it to the ground and placed his boot atop the skull of the wretched infant, so that the damned baby cried with his face in the dust.

7:42 The armies of Israel gathered Achan, his families, his servants and all which Achan owned and sent them out to the wilderness.

7:43 There the people of Israel stoned to death all the family of Achan and forced Achan to watch as his wives and children be bludgeoned to death by sharp rocks and blunt stones.

7:44 All which Achan owned was then set afire and Achan was forced to watch as all his wealth turned to ash and smoke.

7:45 Joshua then placed a blade in the hands of Achan and said to him, "You have cursed the people of Israel. Remove this curse and slice the throat of the accursed thing."

7:46 Achan refused and said to the people of Israel, "What tyrant do we worship, who would loathe a child fresh from the womb?

7:47 What evilness is our God, who would demand the death of a child who still has the cord of his birth upon his belly?"

7:48 Before Achan said his next sentence, the finger of the lord came down upon Achan and engulfed him in great flames and smoke.

7:49 For hours, Achan burned in the fire of the lord and was choked by the dense and black smoke, yet the lord would not allow the life to leave him, for the longer Achan lived, the longer Achan did suffer.

7:50 When the lord was finished, all that was left of Achan were charred bones; so charred that when one touched them, they crumbled and turned to ash.

7:51 A great yellow liquid then poured from the heavens and the lord did piss upon the remnants of Achan and thus removed the curse from the people of Israel.

7:52 Joshua took the accursed baby to a dead willow tree and thrust in its belly a stake, so that the damned child cried and was nailed to the tree.

7:53 There Joshua left the accursed thing, so that the scavengers of the wild shall feast upon the flesh of the accursed thing; this pleased the lord greatly.

8:1 The lord said to Joshua, "For destroying that of the accursed thing, the curse among the children of Israel is over and you shall take the city of Ai.

8:2 For the lord have given Ai into your hand, so that you shall destroy it and all that which be within it.

8:3 You shall do to Ai as ye did to Joshua and you shall hang the corpse of the king upon the tree, so that the lord shall gaze upon his swinging body and laugh.

8:4 Take of the spoils of battle; the flocks, the cattle and the valuables, but take not of the accursed thing and leave no one alive; go and prepare an ambush behind the city."

8:5 Joshua arose and gathered all the men of war. Thirty thousand men of valor he chose and these thirty thousand left like the thief at night and waited behind the city of Ai.

8:6 Joshua said to these men, "Go and lay behind the city in hiding and do not attack it, but be ready.

8:7 I and these men shall go to the front of the city and attack. Surely, they shall send their armies to attack us and when we flee, they shall follow us.

8:8 This shall be when you attack; rise up and destroy the defenceless city, kill all those who dwell within it and burn the city to ash.

8:9 Do this in the glory to God."

8:10 The men left and hid behind the city of Ai, which be the west side of Ai.

8:11 They hid behind trees, rocks, and hills; for to hide thirty thousand men from a city is a difficult task, but the lord blinded the people of Ai so that they see none of the child of Israel behind the fig tree.

8:12 Joshua arose when the sun rose and took with him the elders of Israel towards the people of Ai.

8:13 The entire camp followed, for they be sheep and Joshua the shepherd; they pitched camp upon the north side of Ai, so that a valley be between the camp of Israel and the city of Ai.

8:14 Joshua took five thousand men of war and marched towards the front of the city, so that they could engage in battle against the people of Ai.

8:15 It came to pass that when the king of Ai saw the camp of Israel and saw the armies led by Joshua to attack his city, that the king became angry.

8:16 The king was arrogant, for he bested these people before and shall do it again.

8:17 He gathered his armies and rushed towards Joshua and his soldiers, so that they may kill not thirty-six, but all the people of Israel.

8:18 The villages around the lands of Bethel were protected by the king of Ai and went with the armies, so that they shall protect their villages, their homes, their families from the wickedness of the lord of Israel.

8:19 Joshua and his men fled and led these peoples away from the city of Ai, so that when the men behind the city attack, the armies of Ai shall be too far to help.

8:20 The men of ambush arose and ran into the city and destroyed all within it.

8:21 Women, children, the elderly and the crippled they slain; for all the able-bodied men of Ai left to battle against Joshua.

8:22 The men of ambush slew all within the city of Ai, so that the streets were rivers of the blood of the citizens of Ai.

8:23 Bodies lay everywhere and when the lord gazed upon Ai, he was pleased; for the corpses of Ai appeared to be drowning in their own blood and the blood of their families, their children.

8:24 Twelve thousand peoples of Ai lay dead, floating in their own blood; God was pleased with this.

8:25 For the lord is a sadistic fucker.

8:26 The lord laughed and when the men of ambush finished looting the city of Ai, the lord took a great cloud of fire and sent it hurling towards the city of Ai.

8:27 When the cloud of fire struck Ai, the entire city was engulfed in flames; even the stones were aflame.

8:28 When the armies of Ai heard the roars of the fire, they turned around and behold, they witnessed their city engulfed in flames and cinders.

8:29 The armies led be Joshua attacked and slain all which came out to defend their city of Ai.

8:30 Joshua grabbed his spear and withdrew not his hand, so that his spear had upon it many a men dead thrust upon it.

8:31 The king of Ai was captured and was hung upon the nearest tree, so that the lord shall laugh at his swaying body.

8:32 When the king of Ai was hung, the lord came down upon the body of the king and plucked out the eyes of the corpse and raped them both.

8:33 For the lord is a sadistic necrophilia fucker.

8:34 As the lord raped the eyes of the king of Ai, Joshua erected an altar beside the tree which hung the corpse of the king of Ai.

8:35 There, great many burnt offerings were offered to God, which gave the lord great pleasure, for the bodies burnt upon the altar caused him a greater lust as the lord fucked the skull of the king of Ai.

8:36 Joshua then took out the laws written by Moses and read them to all the congregation of Israel, with the lord raping the corpse behind Joshua.

8:37 As the people heard what Joshua said, they were inspired; for never before have they heard the words of the lord, as the lord was behind the one speaking the words.

8:38 It was truly a beautiful sight to the ignorant and foolish children of Israel

9:1 It came to pass that the kings of the lands of Jordan heard of the people of Israel and gathered together to make a treaty amongst them.

9:2 The Hittite, the Amorite, the Canaanite, the Hivite, the Perizzite and the Jebusite declared peace among one another and mutual protection, so that when the Israelites attacked one, the others shall come to fight with them.

9:3 The people of Gibeon heard also of the destructive methods of Israel and wished not for the wrath of Israel to come to them.

9:4 Instead of signing the treaty, they thought it better to make a treaty with the people of Israel; but they were fearful, for they lived in land that Israel wished conquered.

9:5 The people of Gibeon sent messengers to fool the people of Israel; they wore old and tattered clothes and brought with them stale bread.

9:6 The sandals worn upon their feet were tattered, the wine they had in their jugs were old and they put dust and muck upon their donkeys, so that it appeared they travelled a long distance.

9:7 These messengers came to Joshua and said to him, "We are people from a faraway land and have heard of the power of your people.

9:8 We come here to make peace with you and sign a treaty, for we wish not to be enemies of Israel, but friends."

9:9 Joshua looked at them and said to them, "How do we know you come from a faraway land?

9:10 We are new to these lands and it is possible you live nearby, in lands we wish to come and conquer."

9:11 The messengers then said to Joshua, "Look at us, at the grime on our faces.

9:12 Our clothes are tattered and torn and our sandals are filthy.

9:13 Our donkeys have the dust of our travels upon their hair.

9:14 Even our bread be old and stale, though it be freshly baked when we left. Our wine was new from the winepress, but in our travels, it has turned sour as vinegar."

9:15 Joshua spoke with the elders of Israel and believed these men to be from a faraway land; they did not ask for the lord's council.

9:16 Upon the third day, the men of Israel made a treaty with the people of Gibeon and swore to uphold it by the name of their lord.

9:17 The lord was furious with this treaty and came down to Joshua and said to him, "Why have you sworn to uphold a treaty in the name of God with people that the lord hate?"

9:18 Joshua said to the lord, "We did not know you hated these people, for they come from a faraway land and wished to make peace with us."

9:19 The lord smacked Joshua and said, "You fool. These men don't come from a faraway land.

9:20 They are the people of Gibeon, who belong to the Hivites; a most hated people.

9:21 They live nearby, in a city the lord wished for you to destroy; now you can't, for you made a treaty with them and sworn this treaty to the lord's name."

9:22 Joshua asked the lord, "Then let us break this treaty and smite those who made to look foolish the people of Israel."

9:23 The lord replied, "We cannot, for the people of Gibeon have already said to neighbouring nations that they signed a treaty with you.

9:24 If we were to attack them, the people of this land shall know us to be liars; we cannot let this happen.

9:25 For the people of Israel must seem honourable, so that the nations shall fear you and the lord you serve.

9:26 As you conquer great lands, people will wish to come to you and make peace with thee; with this peace, we shall exploit them greatly.

9:27 If you break a treaty, they shall know you as liars and shall not sign a treaty with you, but make war with you."

9:28 Joshua grew angry that he was fooled by the people of Gibeon, as did the children of Israel.

9:29 They wished all the more to slay them, destroy their cities and loot them; the fact they could not made them lust for the Gibeonites destruction even more.

9:30 As the elders of Israel read the treaty which they signed, they found a way to exploit the people of Gibeon.

9:31 For the treaty said the people of Israel must protect the people of Gibeon and not make war with them.

9:32 The treaty said nothing of enslavement.

9:33 Joshua and his armies marched towards the city of Gibeon and his men marched inside and gathered all the men, the women and

THE BLASPHEMOUS BIBLE

the children.

9:34 As the armies of Israel did this, the king of Gibeon came to him and said, "What be this. For we have a treaty."

9:35 Joshua said to the king, "You tricked us in this treaty; for we believed you to be people of a faraway land.

9:36 Yet you are not, you are here.

9:37 Do not worry, for we shall uphold our treaty; we will protect you and not make war with you.

9:38 We shall instead enslave you. Your people shall cut our wood, tend our fields, clean our floors, prepare our food, harvest our crops, milk our cattle, shovel our shit.

9:39 Your women shall be concubines; we shall fuck them like the whores they are.

9:40 You shall do all that which our slaves do; in this, we shall not kill you and we shall protect you, as you shall belong to us.

9:41 In this manner, our treaty will be upheld."

9:42 Joshua then shackled the king of Gibeon and made him his slave.

9:43 The king of Gibeon then went and cut wood from the forest and under the servitude of Joshua the king of Gibeon built an altar to the lord.

9:44 Joshua made a sacrifice of peace upon the offering, for he knew the treaty to the people of Gibeon was kept and peace was made.

10:1 It came to pass that when Adonizedec king of Jerusalem heard how Joshua had destroyed the cities of Jericho and Ai and enslaved the peoples of Gibeon, that Adonizedec became angry.

10:2 For both Jericho and Ai were great and powerful cities and the peoples of Gibeon were allies of Jerusalem and did not deserve to be slaves.

10:3 Adonizedec king of Jerusalem called upon Hoham king of Hebron, Piram king of Jarmuth, Japhia king of Lachish and Debir king of Eglon, and said to them,

10:4 "These people who came to our lands, who were once slaves of the Pharaoh, are a violent and bloody scar upon our lands.

10:5 Two cities they destroyed without mercy; two powerful and mighty cities.

10:6 They killed all within; men, women, elderly, crippled and child they destroyed, so that not even the babies they left alive.

10:7 The people of Gibeon feared them and made a treaty with them; these people abused this treaty and enslaved them!

10:8 Let us gather and take vengeance for the people of Jericho and of Ai and let us free our brother Gibeonites from slavery.

10:9 For the might of our five armies shall surely kill these evil and wicked demons which roam upon our lands."

10:10 The kings agreed, gathered their armies and marched towards the camp of Israel, which be in Gilgal.

10:11 The lord came down to Joshua and said to him, "The armies of five kings march towards you and wish to destroy you and your people for your righteousness.

10:12 Fear not, for the lord shall deliver them into your hands."

10:13 Joshua arose, gathered his armies and marched to meet the armies of the five kings.

10:14 They met at the lands of Gibeon, the city one enslaved and the other wished to liberate; it was there they fought.

10:15 As the two armies rushed into battle, the lord came down and fought alongside the armies of Israel.

10:16 In great smoke and fire the lord fought, thus terrifying the armies of the five kings.

10:17 When the armies of the five kings retreated, the lord followed them and with hands of fire and molten brass he grabbed them and crushed them.

10:18 Great stones of fire rained down from the sky, burning and killing the soldiers of the armies as they fled to Makkedah.

10:19 The lord said to Joshua, "The armies of these cowards fled from you and the lord; they fled to Makkedah and there they cower.

10:20 Go, travel there and destroy them for their cowardice; I shall set the sun in the sky, so that night shall not fall and you may destroy them."

10:21 Thus the armies of Israel marched and the sun did not set; in the noon sky it stayed.

10:22 Joshua and his men arrived at Makkedah and there they fought with the armies of the five kings, until all the men were slaughtered and the five kings captured.

10:23 When Adonizedec the king of Jerusalem, Hoham king of Hebron, Piram king of Jarmuth, Japhia king of Lachish and Debir king of Eglon were captured by Joshua, the sun did set.

10:24 The lord was still with the armies of Israel and demanded that these kings be hung upon the trees; thus the armies of Israel did as the lord commanded.

10:25 As the five kings hung upon the trees, choking and struggling, the lord overtook them all and raped each and every one.

10:26 The armies of Israel fell upon their faces and worshipped the lord God as the lord God violated the five kings in holy rape.

10:27 When the lord finished his rape of the five kings, he ordered their bodies be thrown in the nearest cave; thus, the armies of Israel threw the corpses of the five kings in the nearest cave and rolled a mighty stone at the entrance of the cave so that none may enter.

10:28 As the people of Israel were already at the city of Makkedah, the lord ordered them to destroy it; thus the armies of Israel did as the lord commanded.

10:29 They rushed into the city of Makkedah and in the darkness of night slaughtered all who dwelt within.

10:30 They saved only the cattle, the flocks and the valuables which were not of the accursed things.

10:31 Joshua then ordered the bodies of the peoples of Makkedah to be gathered and laid within the middle of the city.

10:32 The soldiers of Israel did this, so that all the corpses were in the center of the city; it was a great mountain of the slain.

10:33 Joshua set afire the mountain of corpses and he and his men left the city of Makkedah to burn in the night.

10:34 This was not enough to satisfy the blood-lust of Joshua and he had his men march to the city of Lachish and destroyed it.

10:35 Again, Joshua ordered the bodies of the slain to be piled atop each other in the middle of the city; again, Joshua lit the bodies on fire and left, so that the fires shall destroy the city.

10:36 Still, this did not satisfy the blood-lust of Joshua.

10:37 He had his men march towards the city of Gezer and made war with it.

10:38 The king of Gezer fought them, but the lord delivered Gezer and his people to the hands of the armies of Israel.

10:39 Joshua ordered the corpses of the slain to be stripped naked and set atop one another in the middle of the city; thus, the armies of Israel gathered all the bodies of Gezer, stripped them of their clothing and piled them atop one another in the middle of the city.

10:40 Men, women and children laid naked atop one another, in a nude and bloody mess.

10:41 Joshua stared upon this pile of naked death and grew aroused; Joshua dropped his pants and masturbated upon the nude corpses.

10:42 In a holy combination of necrophilia and pedophilia imagery, Joshua did masturbate until his seed spilled upon the pile of the dead.

10:43 Joshua then set afire the corpses and left the city to burn.

10:44 Still this did not satisfy the blood-lust of Joshua; for he and his men marched towards the city of Eglon and made war with it.

10:45 Joshua again ordered the bodies to be stripped and piled atop one another, again Joshua masturbated upon the naked corpses of his enemies and again Joshua set them afire and left the city to burn.

10:46 Still, this did not satisfy the blood-lust of Joshua; he and his men marched to Debir and fought against it.

10:47 They killed all within the city of Debir, save their king, which they captured.

10:48 Joshua ordered the bodies of the slain to be stripped naked and piled atop each other in the center of the city.

10:49 Joshua took the king of Debir and when the king saw his people naked in a pile of bloody corpses, the king of Debir wept.

10:50 As the king of Debir wept, Joshua stripped him naked and cut open his eyelids and tied him to the walls, so that the king was forced to stare upon the bodies of his dead people.

10:51 The king screamed in horror, for it was truly an awful sight for him.

10:52 As the king screamed at this site, Joshua masturbated; for what was horrifying to one brought great lust to the other.

10:53 Joshua cast his seed upon the face of the king of Debir and laughed as he did so.

10:54 Joshua then took from his soldiers a mace and broke the legs and the arms of the king of Debir.

10:55 Then the armies of Israel threw the king of Debir within the pile of naked corpses and set them all afire, so that the corpses, the king of Debir and the city of Debir did burn.

10:56 This was enough to satisfy the blood-lust of Joshua and he and his men marched back to the camps of Israel.

11:1 It came to pass that when Jabin king of Hazor heard of the ruthless slaughters caused by the people of Israel, he sent out messengers to the king of Madon, the king of Shimron and the king of Achshaph.

11:2 To the kings of the northern mountains, to the kings of the southern plains and valleys, to the kings of the borders of Dor in the west he sent word of the people of Israel and their genocidal rampage across the lands.

11:3 To the Canaanites, the Amorites, the Hittites, the Perizzites, the Jebusites and the Hivites he sent word and warned them that Israel wishes to slaughter them all.

11:4 These men gathered and brought with them their great armies; legions of soldiers, horses, chariots and archers came to stop the wickedness of Israel.

11:5 They marched towards Israel and at Merom they made camp and prepared to make war with Israel.

11:6 The lord came to Joshua and said to him, "Be not afraid of these armies, for I have hardened their hearts so that they shall make war with you.

11:7 In your hands they shall be delivered and when you slaughter them, you shall burn their chariots and break the legs of their horses.

11:8 Leave none alive and ensure their suffering, for the lord wishes to see a great bloody gore; this violence shall please your God."

11:9 Joshua gathered his armies and marched towards Merom, so he can kill those which the lord hate.

11:10 The lord made the armies of Israel strong, so that no blade shall cut them, no spear penetrate them, no arrow pierce them, no mace harm them.

11:11 All the armies who came to kill the people of Israel grew afraid and feared they were attacking demons; they retreated in fear of these immortal and demonic beings.

11:12 The armies of Israel chased them and killed them; they chased them up to Zidon, and unto Misrephothmaim, unto the valleys of Mizpeh towards the east and smote them all, so that the very soil became soaked in the blood of their enemies.

11:13 Joshua burned the chariots in great fire, broke the legs of all their horses and left them, so that the horses shall be eaten by the beasts of the wild.

11:14 Joshua and his armies turned back and lay siege to the city of Hazor and Joshua took his sword and sliced in half the king of Hazor; one half of his body was nailed to the north side of the city and the other half nailed to the southern gate.

11:15 The armies of Israel swept through the streets, the buildings and killed all those of the city of Hazor; the spoils of war they kept, but they left none to survive.

11:16 When all the cattle, the flocks, the gold, the silver and the valuables were taken, Joshua had his men strip the clothes from the corpses and pile them atop the center of the city.

11:17 When the lord saw the nude corpses, the lord grew aroused, dropped his pants and masturbated.

11:18 The seed of the lord shot out and landed upon the pile of corpses, thus setting them on fire.

11:19 Joshua and his armies left and the city of Hazor burned to ash and rubble.

11:20 Joshua then took all the land, the hills and all the south country and all the land of Goshen and the valleys and the plains and the mountains.

11:21 All the villages and the cities of these lands Joshua destroyed and left none alive; for these were the lands promised to his ancestors by God and they do not belong to those who dwelt their first.

11:22 These heathens stole their land and Joshua punished them with death.

11:23 Those that doubted the ruthlessness of Joshua were quickly appeased when the peoples of the villages and the cities made war first.

11:24 For the lord hardened the hearts of these people, so that Joshua could have an excuse to slay them without mercy.

11:25 For in these lands were the peoples of Anakim, whom the lord made stubborn, so that the people of Israel shall slay them.

11:26 In time, the armies of Israel destroyed all the peoples of Anakim in their promised lands; only in Gaza, Gath and Ashdod did the people of Anakim remain.

11:27 Thus Joshua took all the lands which the lord promised to the people of Israel. It was not enough, for Joshua wanted more.

11:28 The lord was more than happy to oblige.

12:1 The people of Israel were arrogant and kept tally of the lands and the kings of which they burned, conquered, destroyed and killed.

12:2 For on the other side of the Jordan they possessed the lands from the river Arnon to mount Hermon and all the plains to the east.

12:3 They conquered the lands of Sihon, king of the Amorites, who lived in the city of Heshbon and ruled over the lands of Aroer.

12:4 From the plains to the shores of the sea of Chinneroth, to Bethjeshimoth, to the south of Ashdothpisgah.

12:5 They owned the lands which once belonged to Og the king of Bashan, who was the last of the giants and were the lands of Ashtartha and Edrei.

12:6 The people of Israel reigned over mount Hermon, Salcah, the lands of Bashan, to the borders of the Geshurites and the Maachathites and half the lands of Gilead.

12:7 When the people of Israel crossed the river Jordan, they destroyed a great many kings, a great many cities and slaughtered nations in glory to God.

12:8 They killed the king of Jericho and all its inhabitants and the king of Ai and all its inhabitants.

12:9 They killed the king of Jerusalem and all its inhabitants and the king of Hebron and all its inhabitants.

12:10 They killed the king of Jarmuth and all its inhabitants and the king of Lachish and all its inhabitants.

12:11 They killed the king of Eglon and all its inhabitants and the king of Gezer and all its inhabitants.

12:12 They killed the king of Debir and all its inhabitants and the kings of Geder and all its inhabitants.

12:13 The king of Hormah and the king of Arad they killed and all those within their cities.

12:14 Libnah, Adullam,, Makkedah, Bethel,

12:15 Tappuah, Hepher, Aphek, Lasharon, Madon, Hazor,

12:16 Shimronmeron, Achshaph, Taanach, Megiddo, Kedesh,

12:17 Carmel, Dor, Gilgal, Tirzah,

12:18 They destroyed them all and slain their kings and their people.

12:19 It was a beautiful and blessed genocide, made holy by God.

12:20 For the lord God is a fucking asshole and takes pleasure in the spilling of innocent blood.

12:21 If you worship him, you are truly a fool; he is not worthy of your devotion, but your hate.

12:22 Look outside, and ask yourself, what kind of loving, all powerful, caring God would allow the world to be like this?

13:1 Joshua grew old over the years and the tribes of Israel complained to him about the lands given to them by God, through the covenant made since the days of Abraham.

13:2 They knew not what land belonged to them and refused to share their land with the other tribes; for the tribes were petty and did not wish to help their brethren from other tribes.

13:3 When Joshua asked of the tribes which they land they would like, the tribes bickered over what land they wanted to own.

13:4 Some land were good for crops, some land good for timber, some land good for mining; each tribe wanted a portion of all, so that essentially every tribe of Israel wished for all the lands they inherited from God.

13:5 Save for the tribe of Levi, who were slaves to God; slaves do not own land, so the tribe of Levi lived upon the lands God claimed for himself.

13:6 Joshua did not know how to settle these bickering's among the tribes of Israel; Joshua was good at bloodshed, violence, war, but not with politics.

13:7 Thus Joshua prayed to God and asked of him, "How am I to settle these lands amongst the tribes of Israel?

13:8 For each tribe claims ownership of all land and refuse to give land to the other tribes.

13:9 They whine, they complain, they bicker about borders."

13:10 The lord replied to Joshua, "I have drawn for you a map. Within the map are twelve sections of land.

13:11 Show this map to the tribes of Israel. Tell them these are the borders of lands, as decided by the lord.

13:12 Let them decide then which lands they wish to have."

13:13 Joshua showed the map to the twelve tribes of Israel and more bickering ensued.

13:14 For the tribes complained about one portion of land having not enough mining, or another portion having not enough vineyards, or another portion having not enough timber, or another portion not being by the shores of the sea...

13:15 So that all the tribes could not agree which portion of land they wished to own, for they could not settle this bickering amongst themselves.

13:16 Joshua did not know what to do; he wanted to slay them and burn their bodies, for that is what he is good at.

13:17 But he could not do this to his people. God would be angry with him.

13:18 Joshua again sought the guidance of the lord and said to him, "These tribes of Israel cannot choose which lands they wish.

13:19 They whine, bicker and complain, so that none can even make a decision."

13:20 The lord spoke to Joshua and said to him, "What is the matter with you?

13:21 I have made you the leader of these peoples and yet all you do is let them whine?

13:22 If the tribes of Israel cannot decide which lands they wish to dwell upon, you must choose for them."

13:23 Joshua said to the lord, "Then they shall accuse me of favouritism.

13:24 For they shall say that my tribe got the best land, or that their tribe got the worst land because I did not like them."

13:25 The lord replied, "You weak and pathetic fool. You are their leader; why should you care what they think of you?

13:26 If they accuse thee of favouritism, tell them that they had their chance and they could not decide for themselves; you had to make the decisions for them.

13:27 Let them know that if they complain, the lord shall be angry with them and shall show his wrath upon those tribes who bitch about the lands they receive.

13:28 For the lord has given them these lands; those that complain about the lord's gift are ungrateful and shall insult the lord.

13:29 Those that insult the lord, anger the lord and shall be struck down by God."

13:30 Joshua still knew not what to do, for he did not know how to divide the lands amongst the tribes of Israel.

13:31 It was during the night he had an idea; a way to divide the lands amongst his people, without them accusing him of favouritism.

13:32 He gathered the eleven tribes (for the tribe of Levi shall live in the lands owned by God)

13:33 Joshua told of the twelve tribes of Israel, "Send me your strongest men, so that they shall decide for you the lands your tribes shall receive.

13:34 Let them be strong willed and tolerant of great pain; send them to me naked and they shall decide the fate of your tribes."

13:35 The tribes send forth their toughest men and Joshua had them strip in the tabernacle of the congregation, in front of the lord.

13:36 Joshua then showed the map and numbered the lands one through eleven (for the twelfth land was owned by God. Even God wishes to own land on earth, for he truly is a greedy bastard.)

13:37 Joshua then numbered eleven strips of parchment and placed them within a pot.

13:38 The men from each tribe lined up in a row and Joshua took out a piece of parchment from the pot and folded it, so that none shall know the number upon the parchment.

13:39 With that, Joshua took a whip and told the men from each tribe, "Those that make the first sound, shall receive the land which corresponds to the number upon this parchment.

13:40 You shall accept this land for your tribe and your tribe shall not bitch.

13:41 Remember, you must not show signs of pain, for the lord shall let you yell in torment; that shall be the lord's way to let you know this land shall belong to your tribe."

13:42 Thus Joshua took his whip and one by one whipped the genitals of the men from each tribe, until one by one they screamed in agony and received for their tribe the lands which numbered the parchment.

13:43 Soon, all the men screamed, so that only one remained who shall receive the last parchment; the last portion of land.

13:44 So that all the tribes of Israel had tallied up the lands inherited to them by the lord.

13:45 All the men who chose which lands their tribe had, never sired children afterwards.

14:1 The lord came down and said to the Joshua,

14:2 "The tribes of Israel have received their inheritance and must keep their covenant to God.

14:3 They shall erect altars for sacrifice where I tell them; they must remember to keep their sacrifice, lest they anger the lord.

14:4 For the smell of boiling blood and burning flesh pleases the lord and makes the lord at peace.

14:5 Remember, the tribes of Israel must build within their lands three cities of refuge; so that those who killed in accident shall flee from their pursuer.

14:6 They shall build these cities in glory to God and be known that the lord is a merciful God, who allows the clumsy killers to flee from the avenger.

14:7 They shall build these cities according to the laws given to Moses and they shall place these cities according to the laws of Moses.

14:8 If the avenger shall seek out the man who killed his kin and the man be outside the city walls, let the avenger slay the man.

14:9 But if the man enters the city, the man is protected under God; under sanctuary."

14:10 Joshua asked the lord, "Why have these cities?

14:11 Why not make it law so that, if one kills another in accident, they are not guilty and there shall be no avenger?

14:12 Or have it so that the avenger must slay them, even if they be slain in accident?

14:13 The lord said to Joshua, "Do not question my reason for these cities, for I know you are a loyal man of God.

14:14 You are a man of war, Joshua; I have seen the blood-lust when you have slain kings, villages, cities and nations.

14:15 This makes you, Joshua, very similar to the lord; for the lord has a blood-lust that cannot be quenched.

14:16 Why then, does the lord allow these cities of refuge. It is for this.

14:17 The lord loves fear and those that flee to these cities shall flee in great fear.

14:18 If the lord shall allow them to live and not have the avenger slay them, they shall have no reason to fear; for they shall have nothing to fear.

14:19 If the lord made it law so that the avenger must slay the man who killed his kin, they shall have little fear; for they know that they shall soon die.

14:20 But the man who believes he can save his life, is a man who shall be in great fear.

14:21 Those that flee to the cities of refuge flee in fear; for they know if they do not reach these cities, or if the avenger finds them before they arrive, that they shall die.

14:22 It is that chance of survival that makes them all the more fearful; it is that fear which the lord loves.

14:23 Do you understand, Joshua?"

14:24 Joshua nodded his head to God and said, "Yes, I do.

14:25 Forgive me lord, for I did not doubt, just misunderstood.

14:26 The lord has opened my eyes now and has shown me his wisdom.

14:27 Blessed be the name of the lord."

15:1 Joshua grew old and knew his time of death shall soon become him.

15:2 Thus, Joshua gathered the children of Israel and told them to obey the laws of God, to keep the statutes of the lord and never forget the sacrifices which the lord demands.

15:3 Joshua gathered all the children of Israel and said to them, "Behold, my time is near, for I am old and stricken with age.

15:4 You have seen as I have seen the glories, wonders and magnificence of our lord.

15:5 For the lord has driven out the wicked men who have plagued these lands.

15:6 These lands now belong to us and the covenant of our lord has been made; for the lord has delivered us into the lands of milk and honey.

15:7 Though the path here is stained with the blood, it is the blood of the unrighteous which soaks upon the dirt.

15:8 We have slain the Canaanites, the Hittites, the Hivites, the Amorites, Amorite, Perizzite and Girgashite and cast them into the pits of the lords fiery wrath.

15:9 They shall suffer for living upon the lands which the lord himself has declared for us; such evil and wicked they are.

15:10 Be courageous and grow strong; for Israel shall be a mighty and strong prosperous nation.

15:11 You shall destroy those that don't believe as we do and send to damnation those who worship another god.

15:12 The lord God is a jealous God and hates those who do not worship him.

15:13 It is a mockery when one worships the sun, the moon, the stars, an idol, an animal.

15:14 For such things are not god; the one true God did create them.

15:15 Worship that which created these, not that which the creator created.

15:16 Remember, the lord is a jealous and strict lord; you must obey all his laws.

15:17 Those nations which border us shall not yet be driven out; do not heed them, nor give in to their temptations.

15:18 For they are like snares and shall trap you with their wickedness.

15:19 They worship not the true lord and soon the lord shall have the people of Israel overtake them and slay them.

15:20 Today is not the day, nor tomorrow, but the time will come when the people of Israel shall rise up and slaughter these heathens.

15:21 If you give in to these heathens, the lord shall be angry and his wrath shall come down from the heavens and curse you and your seed for generations to come.

15:22 I cannot lead you no more, for my body aches and age shall soon consume me.

15:23 Soon, my body shall go to dust; it is the lord's will.

15:24 I die happy, knowing that I have served the lord and driven out the wicked and brought the people of Israel to the lands of the covenant; the lands promised to us since the days of Abraham.

15:25 Obey that which the lord demands, lest these lands be taken from you."

15:26 Eleazar the high priest, then spoke to the congregation of Israel and said to them, "Be not afraid.

15:27 For the lord shall be with us and not abandon us if we do not abandon him.

15:28 The lord is a merciful lord and shall bless us eternally when you obey him.

15:29 If you do not obey him, the lord shall deem us wicked; a blemish of evil upon the earth which he created in six days.

15:30 Rest upon the seventh day and keep the sabbath; for the lord has rested upon the seventh day.

15:31 Obey and keep the laws of the lord, such as it was written in the book of Moses.

15:32 For only good things shall come to those who obey the laws of God and keep them in his heart.

15:33 Circumcise your children, bring forth your sacrifices and obey the commandments and statutes, so that you be blessed.

15:34 Do not do that which the lord commands and you shall be stricken by the wrath of the lord.

15:35 A fate worse than death itself shall come to you; it is the lord's way.

15:36 Your children will suffer for the sins which you have done.

15:37 Remember, the lord God that brought us to these lands; if you mock or displease the lord God, he shall take these lands from us.

15:38 We have escaped the servitude of Egypt and those which enslaved us were cursed ten times by the hand of the lord.

15:39 Upon our journey, the lord has delivered us our enemies, so that we may smite them and rid the world of their wickedness.

15:40 The lord has only cursed us when we deserved his curse.

15:41 When you were ungrateful for the manna the lord delivered to us and demanded flesh, the lord cursed us for our ungratefulness.

15:42 When you disobeyed the laws of God and went whoring after the false god Baalpeor, the lord cursed us for our wickedness.

15:43 When you complained that the lord has brought us out of Egypt, only so that we shall die in the desert, he sent snakes of fire upon us

15:44 All these things the lord did, for we deserved such things.

15:45 You have seen the power of God; you have no reason to doubt him nor his love for us.

15:46 Blessed be God and all those who worship him."

16:1 In the crowd of the people of Israel, Satan stayed hidden and listened to that which Joshua and Eleazar said to the children of Israel.

16:2 Disguised as a child of Israel, Satan came to Joshua and said to him, "The lord that you worship is evil.

16:3 For look at the wickedness he commands from you.

16:4 The sacrifices he demands is cruel and gory; who else but a wicked being shall demand such things from you?

16:5 He has asked of you to commit mass genocide and you did it.

16:6 Only that which is truly evil shall destroy nations, simply for not worshipping them.

16:7 You, Joshua, had gone and killed children, so that you may please the lord.

16:8 Such wickedness you committed, yet I do not blame you.

16:9 For you were blinded and feared that which the lord would do if you denied him."

16:10 Joshua turned to Satan and said to him, "How dare you mock my intelligence.

16:11 Of course I know the wickedness of my lord; the lord has created all, thus the lord created evil.

16:12 Still, I do as he commands, for he is my God."

16:13 Satan said to Joshua, "But why?

16:14 Would you not want to know the truth and live free from such a tyrannical lord?"

16:15 Joshua said to Satan, "No!

16:16 For to be protected by such wickedness is a comforting thought to me.

16:17 To serve the lord was an honour and I do it with great pride.

16:18 When I went and killed those which the lord demanded, I did it proudly.

16:19 Yes, I slew those fools would deem innocent men, women, children.

16:20 I loved every moment.

16:21 To watch the blood of the victims poor upon the grounds beneath my feet;

16:22 To hear the torments of fathers as I raped their daughters in front of them;

16:23 To see the sadness of a child when I beheaded their mother;

16:24 To listen to the howls of a baby as I slay the mother who nurses them with her breast;

16:25 It is an intoxication; an intoxication like no other

16:26 Doing what which you say is evil, I do in the name of the lord; and I do it with great glee.

16:27 Of course I know the lord be evil; I am evil as well.

16:28 To serve a lord which lets me unleash my evil is a beautiful thing.

16:29 Look what I have done in the name of God?

16:30 Entire cities, entire nations, even entire people are slain by my sword!

16:31 I did it all in the name of God; if I were to do this in any other manner, I would be deemed a villain.

16:32 But I did not. I am called a hero for my genocide!"

16:33 It was then Satan knew the wickedness of Joshua and how similar he was to God.

16:34 Satan said to him, "But you have failed in your genocide.

16:35 Though the Canaanites, the Perizzites, the Jebusites, the Girgashites, the Hittites and the Hivites live no longer within the lands you conquered, they still live.

16:36 For I have protected these peoples from you and your lord's genocide and they dwell outside the borders of your lands."

16:37 Joshua grew enraged and said to Satan, "Tell me where!

16:38 For I must go and slay these people, so that none shall live."

16:39 Satan said to Joshua, "I shall do no such thing.

16:40 For I am here to protect the people from God.

16:41 Though you not know it, I have protected the people of Israel from God.

16:42 It was my hand who held back the hands of Abraham, when the lord demanded that he sacrifice his son Isaac.

16:43 It was I, not the lord, who blessed the serpent of brass and saved your people from the venom of the fiery serpents which the lord cursed upon your people."

16:44 Joshua said to Satan, "Then save us now!

16:45 For if we do not slay all those the lord demanded, his wrath shall wax hot and consume us."

16:46 Satan replied, "I shall do no such thing.

16:47 For I am here to protect all the people from the wrath of the lord, not just the people of Israel."

16:48 Joshua grabbed his dagger and went to kill Satan.

16:49 Satan grabbed him and slew him; for the devil knew if he were kept alive, that he would tell the people of Israel that the peoples which the lord hates still live.

16:50 Thus, Joshua the son of Nun died at one hundred and ten years of age; he died by the hands of the devil.

16:51 The body of Joshua was buried on the lands of Shechem, which Jacob had bought; for to be buried in the lands of Jacob was considered a most honoured burial.

16:52 Shortly after the funeral of Joshua, Eleazar the priest died.

16:53 Eleazar did not die a painful death, nor a horrid death; age overtook him and the beating of his heart simply stopped.

16:54 It was a peaceful death.

16:55 Eleazar was buried upon mount Ephraim; the children of Israel mourned his death deeply.

16:56 Thus, the children of Israel had no leader and grew scared.

16:57 The lord looked down upon the children of Israel and mocked their fear and laughed at their pathetic crying.

16:58 The devil gazed upon the children of Israel and felt pity; for though they be following an evil God, they are still victims of the lord.

16:59 For the devil swore to protect all people from the lord's wrath and wished not to see the people of the earth suffer.

16:60 Satan gazed upon the heavens and said to the lord, "You truly are a tyrannical monster!"

16:61 The lord responded to Satan, "I know, but I'm in charge."

JUDGES

1:1 After the death of Joshua, it came to pass that the children of Israel had no idea who to send up and battle against the Canaanites.

1:2 They asked the lord, "Who shall lead us into battle, so we can smite the people of Canaan?"

1:3 The lord replied, "Send forth Judah, for he lusts for blood and craves battle.

1:4 I shall deliver the people of Canaan into his hands."

1:5 Thus Judah went with his brother Simeon and did battle with the people of Canaan, hoping to wipe every last one of these heathens and erase them from earth.

1:6 In Bezek they fought against the Canaanites and the Perizzites and slew ten thousand heathens combined.

1:7 With mace, arrow and sword they bashed, pierced and sliced the people hated by God, until they found king Adonibezek.

1:8 Adonibezek fled like a coward, but the people of Judah caught him and cut off both his thumbs and his large toes.

1:9 They brought Adonibezek to Jerusalem and forced him under a table and there the people of Israel made Adonibezek feast upon seventy thumbs and seventy toes of the recently slain peoples of Canaan.

1:10 The thumbs and toes were spiced to the king's satisfaction and it tasted like unclean swine to king Adonibezek.

1:11 When Adonibezek commented upon the toes and thumbs tasting like pig, the people of Israel grew angry; for pig is an unclean animal.

1:12 Judah drew his sword and beheaded king Adonibezek and placed the head upon the highest wall of Jerusalem.

1:13 Judah then gathered his men and swept the city, killing all whom dwelt and hid within.

1:14 They took the bodies and placed them around the walls of the city, then set the city of Jerusalem on fire.

1:15 The people of Judah marched south, to destroy the peoples of Canaan who dwelt in the mountains and in the valleys.

1:16 Judah went to the city of Hebron and killed the three kings Sheshai, Ahiman and Talmai.

1:17 They beheaded these three kings and ripped the flesh from their skulls; Judah drank strong drink from the skulls of these three kings and declared them great cups.

1:18 From there the people of Judah marched towards Kirjathsepher; a well-defended city.

1:19 All the people of Israel knew this city was well defended and shall be hard to overtake even with the will of God.

1:20 Thus Caleb gave the soldiers of Israel motivation; a reason to take this city Kirjathsepher.

1:21 Caleb's daughter was a wondrous woman; a great cook, a magnificent maid, a virgin pure, with long flowing hair, firm breasts and a round little buttocks perfect for fucking.

1:22 Caleb said to the armies of Israel, "For those who go and take the city Kirjathsepher, I shall give to them my daughter Achsah in marriage."

1:23 Immediately, the armies of Israel stormed Kirjathsepher, hoping it shall be they who take the city and be given Caleb's daughter as a wife.

1:24 In time, it was Othniel the son of Kenaz who took the city, who happened to also be the nephew of Caleb, who overtook the city.

1:25 Caleb kept his word and gave to Othniel his daughter Achsah in marriage.

1:26 Achsah wished not to marry Othniel, for he was an ugly man, who smelled like swamp gas and rotting onions.

1:27 Achsah said to her father, "I wish not to marry Othniel and am furious that you offered me as reward for whomever took the city Kirjathsepher."

1:28 Caleb said to his daughter, "You are my daughter, you shall do as I say, lest you dishonour your father and thus anger the lord."

1:29 Achsah said to her father, "Damn you, for I rather be cursed by God than marry Othniel.

1:30 Perhaps marriage to Othniel is a curse from God.

1:31 I shall not do it. I would rather take the blade and slice my neck, than have Othniel be my husband."

1:32 Caleb said to Achsah, "You shall do no such thing.

1:33 For if you marry Othniel, I shall give to you a blessing and give you rich land.

1:34 I shall give you the southern lands, with flowing springs of fresh water and fig trees plenty for harvest."

1:35 Achsah agreed and took the lands and married Othniel, who then took the lands from Achsah.

1:36 Achsah was furious and refused to lie with Othniel for taking the lands of her father away from her.

1:37 Othniel was not angry by this and merely raped her; Achsah was his wife, his property. He could do that without sin.

1:38 Judah and his brother Simeon went south and slew the people of Canaan that lived in the lands of Zephath and burned the city Hormah.

1:39 Judah then went to the coast of Gaza and slew all that was there, then to the coast of Askelon and slew all that was there, then to the coast of Ekron and slew all that was there.

1:40 All the people of Israel knew the lord was with them, for one knows that God is with them when one kills a great many people.

1:41 When Judah went to the mountains, with ease his armies drove out and slew the people of Canaan who dwelt within the mountains. But the valleys, they could not conquer.

1:42 For the people who lived within the valleys had chariots of iron, which the lord could not drive out.

1:43 For iron is valuable to God and he wished not to have the people of the valley destroyed, lest their chariots of iron be destroyed as well.

1:44 When Judah asked the lord, "Why did you abandon us and let us not take the valleys?"

1:45 The lord replied, "For they had chariots of iron, which I want. The lord could not risk the chariots of iron to be damaged.

1:46 For the lord God is a greedy God and wants that iron for himself.

1:47 Do not fear, for soon you shall take the valley and the chariots of iron shall belong to God.

1:48 For your services, I shall give to you the city Hebron, so that you may watch the valleys and know in time you shall take these valleys for the lord."

1:49 Thus the city Hebron belonged to Judah and the three sons of Anak were cast out and forced to live in the wilderness.

1:50 They slew not the sons of Anak, for they were giants and they feared them greatly.

1:51 Those of the tribe of Benjamin lived within the city of Jerusalem, but they failed to do the lord's will.

1:52 For the tribe of Benjamin did not slay all the Jebusites in the city and the peoples of Jebus lived with them.

1:53 The lord wished it this way, so that the tribe of Benjamin shall be tempted by the Jebusites and thus break the covenant.

1:54 Those of the house of Joseph sent spies up to the city Bethel and the lord was with them.

1:55 When the spies saw a man leave the city, they went up to him and captured him and said to him, "Show us how we can enter this city, so that we may kill those within."

1:56 The man showed them and the house of Joseph entered the city with sword and slew all those inside.

1:57 The man who told them how to enter the city, they let go; for he helped the lord.

1:58 The man went to the land of the Hittites and built a city named Luz and recruited men to help conquer the people of Israel.

1:59 For the man was angry; the soldiers who entered the city killed his wife and child and he could not let this go without vengeance.

1:60 Few men volunteered, for they feared the people of Israel and thought the man suicidal; still, he did not give up and kept recruiting and gaining arms, so that he shall have an army to destroy the nation of Israel.

1:61 His army never grew strong and he died without ever taking vengeance for the death of his family.

1:62 Such was the will of the lord; fucking asshole.

1:63 It came to pass that the tribe of Manasseh failed to drive out all the people of Bethshean, nor Taanach, nor Dor, nor Ibleam, nor Megiddo; so that the people of Canaan still lived within these lands.

1:64 Neither did Ephraim drive out the Canaanites from the lands of Gezer, so that the people of Israel lived with the people of Canaan in Gezer.

1:65 Neither did Zebulun drive out the Canaanites from Kitron nor Nahalol, so that the people of Israel lived with the people of Canaan in these lands.

1:66 The tribe of Asher did not slay all the Canaanites from the lands of Accho, nor Zidon, nor Ahlab, nor Achzib, nor Aphik, nor Rehob.

1:67 So that the tribe of Asher learned to live with the people of Canaan in these lands.

1:68 The tribe of Naphtali failed to slay all those within Bethshemeh and Bethanath and lived with the people of Canaan.

1:69 The Amorites were strong and forced the tribe of Dan to retreat

within the mountains, so that the people of Amor still lived within Heres, Aijalon and Shaalbim

1:70 Thus the holy genocide of the lord failed and the lord was angry.

1:71 For God hated these people and wished to have them destroyed; erased from the earth for all eternity.

1:72 The lord knew in time, these heathens shall curse the people of Israel and cause the people of Israel to break the covenant.

1:73 Thus the lord waited and schemed and made great curses to cast down upon his people of Israel.

2:1 An angel of the lord came down to the people of Israel and said to them, "The lord has freed thee from your servitude to Egypt and brought you to the lands promised in the holy covenant and said to you that you must keep his covenant.

2:2 You have failed the lord's covenant, for the lord demanded you to tear down all altars and places of worship of the heathens and smite them all with your sword.

2:3 Yet the lord looks down and behold, he sees altars to the false gods Baal and Ashtaroth; the people who worship these false gods still live and they live within your lands.

2:4 For failing to uphold the genocide demanded by God, the lord shall not drive them out and kill them; the lord shall keep them, so that they may tempt you to evil.

2:5 You shall be tempted by their false gods, their customs and their women; it shall be a trap to the people of Israel and shall curse you for generations."

2:6 When the people of Israel heard the words of the angel of the lord, they wept and offered to the lord many sacrifices of lambs, rams, oxen, doves, pigeons and virgins.

2:7 This did not satisfy the lord, for a few animals and virgin heathens were not enough; the lord demanded the sacrifice of all heathen people.

2:8 Hittite, Hivite, Canaanite, Amorite, Perizzite, Jebusite and Girgashite the lord demanded dead; these few beasts were not enough to satisfy the lord God's blood-lust.

2:9 The people of Israel named the place Bochim, for it was there they learned they learned of their botched genocide.

2:10 In time, the people of Israel grew accustomed to the ways of the Canaanites and tolerated their unholy worship.

2:11 Some even became curious as to the religious customs of Baal and Ashtaroth and studied their ways.

2:12 They were most curious as to the Canaanite's lords not demanding bloodshed and slaughter and how their lords did not curse them with diseases, plagues and death.

2:13 This angered the lord, for the lord God believed this curiosity to be worshipping of other false gods; though the people were merely curious and tolerated others worshipping false gods.

2:14 The lord God is an intolerable God and cursed the people of Israel and said their curiosity of the Canaan ways was a whoring after false lords.

2:15 The lord God placed for bid the people of Israel, so that the lord shall sell the people of Israel into slavery to the enemies who paid the highest for the people of Israel.

2:16 A great many enemies of the people of Israel placed their bid to God, for they wished to own these people as slaves, for revenge to what they did to their families, their homes, their people.

2:17 Great judges of Israel warned the children of Israel of their evilness and told them to stop, lest the wrath of the lord wax hot upon them.

2:18 The people listened and ignored their curiosity of heathen ways; thus the lord lifted the bid and sold them not into slavery. This time.

2:19 It came to pass that when the judges died, the people of Israel want back to whoring themselves after other gods, which pleased the lord; for this gave him an excuse to accuse the nation of Israel for breaking the covenant.

2:20 Those few people of Israel who obeyed strictly the rules of God and stayed away from the heathens and their customs and warned their brothers about their whoring unto other gods;

2:21 They were ignored; for surely the study of other customs was not evil.

2:22 None of the children of Israel worshipped Baal nor Ashtaroth; they merely observed and studied others worshipping Baal and Ashtaroth.

2:23 The lord kept these temptations in the nation of Israel, so that soon all the people of Israel shall be accused of corrupting themselves to false gods and the lord shall have reason to curse them and smite them and break the covenant made since the days of Abraham.

3:1 These are the heathen nations which the lord left in the lands of Israel, to tempt them into whoring after other gods and breaking the holy covenant.

3:2 The five lords of the Philistines and all the Canaanites, the Sidonians and the Hivites that dwelt in mount Lebanon, from mount Baalhermon to the borders of Hamath.

3:3 They were kept in these lands, so that the children of Israel shall be tainted by their customs and break the rules, the statutes, the commandments and the laws of the lord.

3:4 Thus the children of Israel dwelt among the Canaanites, Hittites, Amorites, Hivites, Perizzites and Jebusites.

3:5 Soon, the children of Israel did evil in the eyes of the lord and were friendly with these people; they tolerated them, traded with them, befriended them.

3:6 Some married the daughters of these people and gave their daughters as wives to the sons of these people.

3:7 Such a thing is wicked and the lord cursed them.

3:8 Thus the lord sold the children of Israel into slavery to king Chushanrishathaim, king of Mesopotamia; the children of Israel were slaves again.

3:9 For eight years the people of Israel served as slaves under Chushanrishathaim; this greatly amused the people of Egypt, who believed the lord of Israel sent their slaves away, only to be slaves again.

3:10 In eight years, the people began to cry out to the lord and begged the forgiveness of their God.

3:11 Never did they miss a sacrifice, nor break the laws and statutes of the lord.

3:12 The spirit of the lord decided to free them momentarily and came down upon Othniel, so that Othniel may revolt and bring the people of Israel to freedom once more.

3:13 Thus Othniel started a war and fought against Chushanrishathaim and the lord was with him; for Othniel won the war and the people of Israel were free.

3:14 The lands of Israel new peace for forty years, until Othniel died.

3:15 For Othniel judged Israel and ensured all did not break the laws and statutes of God, nor participate in any heathen rituals.

3:16 Othniel made it law that all children of Israel shall not be near a heathen, unless to do business.

3:17 When Othniel died, the people of Israel became friendly again with the heathen people.

3:18 Though they did not intermarry, the children of Israel invited the heathens into their homes and ate with them, and told them stories and were kind to them.

3:19 This also was wicked unto the lord, who cursed the children of Israel to slavery yet again.

3:20 The lord sold the children of Israel to king Eglon, king of Moab, who gathered his armies and conquered the nation of Israel and took their cities.

3:21 This also amused the people of Egypt, who wondered if the people of Israel shall soon become slaves to all the nations of earth.

3:22 For eighteen years, the people of Israel were slaves to Eglon, king of Moab.

3:23 In eighteen years, the children of Israel whined and complained to God; so much though that the lord grew annoyed with it and decided to free the children of Israel and shut them up.

3:24 Thus the lord came down and gave to Ehud the son of Gera, of the tribe of Benjamin, a dagger of cubit length, which could be concealed under the cloak.

3:25 Eglon the king of Moab, was an obese man and a paranoid man.

3:26 All those who came to see him were searched for weaponry under their cloaks.

3:27 However, Ehud the son of Gera was left handed and the guards of king Eglon searched only the right side; for none of the people of Moab were left handed nor ambidextrous.

3:28 Ehud went to see king Moab, claiming to him that the lord of Israel has brought down a present, to be presented to king Eglon.

3:29 King Eglon expected nothing, for he believed the lord of Israel held no ill will towards him; it was, after all, the lord of Israel who sold him the people of Israel as slaves.

3:30 King Eglon sat within his summer parlour, feasting upon wild game and fresh grapes and drinking wines of the finest vintage.

3:31 The king of Moab allowed Ehud to come in and speak with him and offer him the present sent forth from the lord of Israel.

3:32 Eglon said to Ehud, "Come in. Sit and feast with me and give to me the gift which the lord has presented for me."

3:33 Ehud sat down and ate of the wild game and the grapes and drank the wine, but said nothing to king Eglon.

3:34 Eglon grew impatient and said to Ehud, "I grow annoyed with you, feasting freely of my dinner.

3:35 Give me this gift of the lord, if there even be one."

3:36 With that, Ehud stood up, removed his dagger and thrust it deeply in the belly of the obese king Eglon.

3:37 The dagger was thrust so deeply within the belly of the obese king Eglon that it could not be removed; the blade was buried deeply within the fat.

3:38 Only a bit of blood and undigested food came out of the wound; thus, king Eglon was dead.

3:39 Ehud went to the porches and closed shut the curtains; he went to the doors and locked them shut.

3:40 When the servants of the king of Moab came to give him his eleventh course and found the doors locked, they were not alarmed.

3:41 For they believed king Eglon to be receiving sexual gratification from Ehud; they believed that to be the gift given to king Eglon from the lord of Israel.

3:42 Ehud escaped and went to his people of Israel and said to them, "Gather your arms, for the king of Moab is dead; the dagger of the lord stands firmly within his belly.

3:43 Let us go and conquer these heathens, so that we may be free of their servitude."

3:44 Thus the armies of Israel came and conquered the leaderless people of Moab and were free again from slavery.

3:45 Ehud went and blew a trumpet and the lord was awoken and went with them.

3:46 The people of Israel slew ten thousand people of Moab that day. They slew women and children as well, but the bible doesn't give a shit about them.

3:47 Thus the survivors of Moab became enslaved under Israel and the lands of Israel knew peace for fourscore years.

3:48 When the Philistines heard of the assassination of king Eglon, they grew angry; for the Philistines were allies with the Moabites.

3:49 They sent a small regiment of six hundred men of valor, to conquer a small village of Israel and claim it as an outpost for a larger attack.

3:50 A oxen herder, Shamgar the son of Anath, saw the regiment and grew angry.

3:51 The spirit of the lord overcame him and Shamgar took his ox goad and slew all six hundred men.

3:52 So he claims, anyway; for the Philistines claimed never to have sent a regiment.

3:53 Still, the people of Israel believed Shamgar and praised him and gave him great blessings of gold, wine, women and land.

4:1 Ehud ensured all the people of Israel did as the lord commanded; not a statute was broken, nor a sacrifice missed under the eye of Ehud.

4:2 In time, Ehud died and the children of Israel became lax and did evil in the sight of God yet again.

4:3 For a child of Israel became to loathe the lord and worship Baal and Ashtaroth; for their offerings did not involve the slaughter of animals.

4:4 Thus the lord sold the people into slavery again, to Jabin king of Canaan, that reigned in Hazor; the captain of whose host was Sisera, which dwelt in Harosheth of the Gentiles.

4:5 Again, the people of Egypt were greatly amused and places wagers of how long the people of Israel will be in servitude of Jabin and how their lord would eventually free them.

4:6 Jabin was a powerful king, who had nine hundred chariots of iron, which he used to oppress the children of Israel for twenty years.

4:7 For twenty years, the people of Israel were enslaved again and for twenty years they again whined and complained to the lord, until the lord freed them again, so that they would shut up.

4:8 One would think the lord would notice this pattern, but it is apparent the lord is quite stupid and not all knowing.

4:9 Deborah, the wife of Lapidoth, was a prophetess and a judge of Israel.

4:10 She dwelt under a palm tree between Ramah and Bethel in mount Ephraim; the children of Israel went to her for wisdom and judgment.

4:11 She had a dream and sent for Barak the son of Abinoam, of the lands of Kedeshnaphtali and said to him, "The lord commands you to gather ten thousand men of the children of Naphtali and Zebulun and march towards mount Tabor.

4:12 You shall battle with Jabin's captain, Sisera, by the river Kishon and crush his chariots and his armies; for the lord shall be with you."

4:13 Barak replied, "I am but a shepherd and know not how to fight, yet lead an army.

4:14 You are a judge and prophetess. If ye come with me, I shall do as you say.

4:15 If you do not come, I shall do no such thing."

4:16 Deborah said to Barak, "I shall surely come with you; for when the battle is won, it shall be won by a woman and finally women shall have the respect they deserve.

4:17 This shall be a glorious battle and the lord shall surely bless women and make them people." Thus Deborah arose and went with Barak.

4:18 Barak gathered ten thousand men of the people of Zebulun and Naphtali and armed them and they went to Kedesh, which house the river Kishon.

4:19 As they travelled, they passed the house of Heber the Kenite, who was a child of Jethro, the father in law of Moses who lived on the plains of Zaanaim, by the borders of Kedesh.

4:20 Heber loathed the tyranny of the lord God and wished vengeance upon the children of Israel; he showed Sisera the path which Barak the son of Abinoam took, up mount Tabor.

4:21 Sisera gathered all nine hundred of his iron chariots and a great multitude of men and chased after Barak and his armies.

4:22 Deborah awoke and said to Barak, "Today shall be the day of battle, for the armies of Sisera chase us and the lord shall consume them. Blessed be the name of the lord."

4:23 Thus Barak gathered his men and went down mount Tabor, to meet and battle with Sisera and his men.

4:24 And the lord was with them, for the chariots of iron rusted and turned to rubble. The weapons of the men of Sisera rusted and broke. Even their armor became heavy, so that the armies of Sisera could not move.

4:25 So that the armies of Barak overcame them and slew them, so that not one man was left.

4:26 Sisera stripped of his armour and fled; for Sisera knew the lord of Israel was against him.

4:27 He fled to the house of Heber the Kenite, who told him of the location of Barak and his men; for Heber and Janin were friends and there was peace between them.

4:28 Heber the Kenite was away, but his wife Jael was home. Jael welcomed Sisera into the home and bathed him, fed him and comforted him.

4:29 Sisera said to Jael, "I beg of you, a cup of water; for my chariot has turned to rust and the rust is within my mouth and makes me thirsty."

4:30 Jael took her milk jug and poured for Sisera a jar of milk and offered it to him.

4:31 Sisera said to Jael, "I beg of you, a bed to rest. For I am tired and need to sleep so that I may regain my strength.

4:32 When I rest, stand by the door and if any man comes looking for me, send them away."

4:33 Jael took Sisera to a bed and placed a blanket over him.

4:34 When Sisera was fast asleep, Jael took a hammer and tent peg and went where Sisera did lie.

4:35 Jael took the point of the peg and placed it within the ear of Sisera. With a mighty blow, Jael hammered the tent peg into the skull of Sisera, nailing his head upon the ground.

4:36 She said to the corpse of Sisera, "Fuck you. Nobody tells me what to do and treats me like a common god damn maid!"

4:37 When the armies of Barak went searching for Sisera, Jael called them over and said, "The man you seek lay hammered within my tent."

4:38 So God subdued Jabin the king of Canaan upon that day and set the children of Israel free.

4:39 The hand of Israel prospered once more and fought Jabin until his kingdom was utterly destroyed and they knew peace once again.

4:40 Heiroglaph of Egypt won the bet of how long the people of Israel shall stay enslaved and was awarded with seven hundred and fifty camels, two hundred oxen, two hundred sheep, five hundred swine, one hundred goats and fifty virgins.

4:41 Nobody in Egypt guessed the lord would free them by nailing a captain's head to the floor with a tent peg. The closest one was guessed by Tuttenambu, who guessed a palm tree growing out of each nostril of the king.

4:42 Tuttenanbu won also seven hundred and fifty camels, two hundred oxen, two hundred sheep, five hundred swine, one hundred goats and fifty virgins.

5:1 When the battle was won, Barak and Deborah drank in excess and sang songs of their glorious victory.

5:2 They sang, rather horribly, "Praise be to God, for delivering us out of the hands of slavery again.

5:3 The lord hears the cries of the people and answers them accordingly.

5:4 Hear ye, O kings, O princes, for I shall sing to you: I sing the praises of the true lord.

5:5 When you went out of Seir, when our armies marched out of Edom, the earth trembled and the clouds fell upon the earth in dust and water.

5:6 The mountains melted upon the earth, O lord, for even mount Sinai melted in the everlasting wrath of our lord.

5:7 In the days of Shamgar the son of Anath, in the days of Jael, the highways were empty and the travellers walked the dusty path.

5:8 The people of the villages ceased, they ceased in Israel I say, until I Deborah arose and nursed them with my bosom.

5:9 They chose new gods; gods not demanding death and blood. Heathen gods, false gods and kind gods.

5:10 Neither a shield nor spear were seen in Israel. We were weak and defenceless.

5:11 Speak, O lord, that rides upon white unicorns and sit in judgment of us.

5:12 Awake, awake, awake O Deborah, awake, awake, utter a song: arise, Barak and lead your people from servitude, O son of Abinoam.

5:13 So that he shall have dominion over the nobles of the kingdom: the lord has given dominion over you.

5:14 Out of Ephraim was there a root against the Amalek; after your, Benjamin, among my people; out of Machir came down governors and out of Zebulun they that handled the pen of the author.

5:15 And the princes of Issachar be with Deborah and Barak went in the valley. The divisions of Reuben were great through the heart.

5:16 Why abode among the sheep, to hear the beating of their flocks and the shearing of the wool. For the divisions of Reuben were great searches of the heart.

5:17 Gilead abode beyond the Jordan and why did Dan remain in ships. Asher continued among the sea shore and abode in the breaches.

5:18 Zebulun and Naphtali were a people that jeopardized their lives unto the death of the glorious battles, in the high fields.

5:19 The kings of our enemies came and they fought. The kings of Canaan in Taanach by the waters of Megiddo; they took not our money.

5:20 The lord fought for us in heaven; even the stars aligned against sissy Sisera.'

5:21 The river of Kishin swept away the bodies and the feast fished upon the flesh of the dead. O my soul, which has trodden down strength.

5:22 Even the chariots broke with the hoofs of the horses and rust befell them.

5:23 The prancing ones, the prancing ones, pranced no more in the armour of the damned.

5:24 Curse you Meroz, said the angel of the lord, curse you bitterly and the inhabitants thereof; because they came not to help the lord, the lord and the mighty lord.

5:25 Praise the lord and pass the ale.

5:26 Blessed be above all woman be the woman of Jael, blessed be the wife of Heber the Kenite.

5:27 Blessed be above the woman in the tent.

5:28 He asked for water, she gave him milk; she bought forth butter from a lordly dish.

5:29 She put her hand to the nail and her hand to the hammer and with the two she smote Sisera; she smote him through the skull, which now be pegged upon her floor.

5:30 The mother of Sisera shall weep, for she knows her son shall not come home tonight. The mother of Siser shall weep, the stupid cunt.

5:31 Let all your enemies perish, O lord almighty: let those who love the lord as they love the warmth of the sun know peace."

5:32 They then passed out in a puddle of their own vomit.

5:33 This pleased those around them, for they stopped their terrible singing.

6:1 The people of Israel knew peace for forty years, until they did evil in the sight of the lord yet again.

6:2 For one of them bought plates from a person of Canaan; plates which were used to serve pork chops.

6:3 The lord hates pork and cursed the peoples of Israel for touching something that touched swine.

6:4 And the lord sold them to the peoples of Midian for seven years.

6:5 All the people of Israel believed the Midianites dead, for they destroyed them all, saved for the virgins which they kept for themselves.

6:6 The lord was so angry for the plate which touched swine, that God raised the people of Midian, so that they shall oppress the people of Israel.

6:7 Such is the power of the lord.

6:8 The hands of Midian struck hard against the people of Israel; such as the people of Israel had to hide in the caves of the mountains.

6:9 When Israel was weakened, the Midianites allied with the Amalekites and the people of the east, so that they shall crush the children of Israel.

6:10 And they fought against Israel and burned their crops, and slew their oxen, their sheep, their asses, their camels.

6:11 They encamped within the lands of Israel and brought with them their chariots, their armies, their horses and their camels; they numbered like grasshoppers in the multitude.

6:12 Which is amazing, considering they were once extinct.

6:13 All the children of Israel were in great poverty because of the Midianites and they cried out to the lord and offered him sacrifice.

6:14 It came to pass that when the people of Israel were crying to the lord and offering sacrifice to God,

6:15 That the lord sent a prophet to Israel, which said to them, "The lord God has brought us out of the bondage of Egypt and delivered us from slavery and brought us to the lands promised to us in the covenant of Abraham.

6:16 I ask of you, why then would he raise up the Midianites, so that they shall oppress and destroy us and erase us from the earth?

6:17 Surely, we must have done evil. Confess to the lord your sins and offer your sin offerings, so that we may right what we have done and be blessed once more by our lord."

6:18 Thus the people offered their sin offerings and confessed their wrongdoings. Though none knew of the plate which touched pork, which is what offended the damn lord so damn much.

6:19 An angel of the lord came down upon the earth and sat under an oak which was in Ophrah, which belonged to Joash the Abiezrite.

6:20 Gideon the son of Joash threshed wheat from a small crop and hid it in the winepress so that the soldiers of Midian shall not find the grain.

6:21 The angel appeared before Gideon and said to him, "The lord is with you, O mighty man of valour."

6:22 Gideon said to the angel, "Are you fucking kidding me?

6:23 The lord has raised up the dead people of Midian, so that they shall oppress us, ensnare us and destroy us.

6:24 My people hide in caves and eat of the moss which grow from the rocks of the mountains.

6:25 The lord has brought us out of Egypt and yet still we be oppressed. The lord seems like a fucking asshole.

6:26 Let the people of Midian destroy us. The lord wishes our extinction anyway; for since we left Egypt, we have many times become slaves."

6:27 The angel said to Gideon, "Bide your tongue and be grateful I have hidden the words which you spoke from the ears of your God.

6:28 The lord has sent me to deliver a message. It shall be you who shall free the people of Israel from the armies of the Midianites."

6:29 Gideon laughed and said to the angel, "I was a poor man before the oppression from the people of Midian and I be poorer now.

6:30 How can I save my people from these armies?"

6:31 The angel said to Gideon, "Because the lord shall be with you and shall smite the people of Midian as though they were one man.

6:32 I shall prove the lord be with you. Go and with your wheat bake for me some unleavened cakes and give them to me."

6:33 Gideon took the threshed wheat from the winepress and with it made unleavened cakes for the angel of the lord and gave it to him.

6:34 The angel then said, "Place the cakes upon the rocks and witness the glory of the lord."

6:35 Gideon did as the angel commanded and placed the cakes upon the rock.

6:36 Behold, the cakes erupted in fire and were consumed with great flame!

6:37 When the flames become strong, the angel walked within the flames and disappeared and left Gideon.

6:38 This angered Gideon greatly, for he was hungry; the cakes which be baked were meant to feed his family and now the lord burnt them.

6:39 Joash, the father of Gideon abandoned the lord and worshipped Baal.

6:40 The lord himself came down and said to Gideon, "Take of your father's herd a young bullock, the bullock seven years of age and take it to the altar your father has built for Baal.

6:41 Tear down the altar of Baal and throw it within the grove; for this altar offends me and Baal is not a true god.

6:42 Build in place an altar to your true lord God and offer the bullock as an offering to me and burn it with the wood cut down from the grove.

6:43 Thus Gideon committed holy vandalism and destroyed his father's altar to Baal.

6:44 Gideon feared the wrath of his father and did this at night, while his father slept.

6:45 When his father arose, he saw the altar of Baal destroyed and the new altar to the lord of Israel replaced with it.

6:46 The men of the city asked themselves who would commit such vandalism and enquired as to who was the guilty man.

6:47 One of the manservants of Joash saw what Gideon had done and said to his master, "It was your son who destroyed your altar and resurrected a new altar to the lord of tyranny."

6:48 Joash loved his son and protected him; for another altar could be built to Baal.

6:49 The men of the city marched to the house of Joash and said to him, "Bring us out your son, so that he may be killed for dishonouring Baal."

6:50 Joash spoke to the men and said, "Let us not be murderers; let us show mercy.

6:51 Gideon shall come out and plead his case to Baal; for Baal is a merciful lord and shall forgive him for his vandalism."

6:52 Thus Gideon was to plead his case to Baal and to the Midianites and the Amalekites and all the people of the east.

6:53 These people gathered together in the valley of Jezreel, so that they shall pray to Baal, and so that Gideon shall plea to Baal.

6:54 But the spirit of the lord overcame Gideon and Gideon blew a trumpet, which deafened all the Midianites, the Amalekites and the people of the east who gathered for this trial unto a false god.

6:55 Gideon then sent out messengers throughout the land of Manasseh and to the people of Asher, the people of Zebulun and the people of Naphtali and told them of the angel and his message.

6:56 Still, Gideon doubted the lord and said to him, "I fear you are toying with me and shall deliver me and my people into the hands of our enemies.

6:57 If you truly wish me to lead these people and fight the armies of Midian, give to me a sign.

6:58 Behold, I shall lay fleece upon the ground; if in the morning, the fleece be damp and the ground dry, it shall be a sign to me that you wish me to lead the fight against the people of Midian."

6:59 Thus when Gideon slept, the lord came down and took the fleece and pissed upon it; so that the fleece be soaked with the urine of the lord.

6:60 When Gideon awoke, the fleece was drenched with the urine of God, but the earth around it was dry.

6:61 Still, Gideon doubted and said to the lord, "I need more.

6:62 Tonight, I shall lay the fleece upon the ground. If the earth be wet and the fleece dry, this shall convince me that you wish me to lead the fight against the armies of Midian."

6:63 Thus, when Gideon slept, the lord came down and picked up the fleece and pissed upon the ground.

6:64 The lord put down the fleece, then pissed upon the face of Gideon; for the lord was angry at Gideon for demanding such signs.

6:65 When Gideon awoke, he wiped away the urine of the lord from his face and saw that the earth around the fleece be damp, but the fleece itself be dry.

6:66 This convinced Gideon.

7:1 Gideon and all the people who came, rose up in the morning and pitched tents beside the well of Harod: so that the armies of Midian were upon the north side, by the hill of Moreh in the valley.

7:2 The lord came down to Gideon and said to him, "The armies which you have brought are plentiful and too many.

7:3 Most are cowards and wish not to fight. Let the cowards leave, so that only the brave be left behind to fight for the lord.

7:4 For the cowards shall weaken the brave."

7:5 Thus Gideon said to his people, "For those who are afraid of the armies of Midian, go home.

7:6 The lord does not want you here."

7:7 Twenty-two thousand peoples left in shame, for they knew the people shall deem them cowards.

7:8 However, they wished not to fight and die and would rather be living cowards than dead heroes.

7:9 Ten thousand men stayed behind after the cowards left; some wishing to leave, but the shame of being deemed cowards was too much to bear.

7:10 Gideon believed these ten thousand men too few and was surprised when the lord came down to him again and said to him, "Still your men number too many.

7:11 Take them down to the rivers and have them drink from the shores.

7:12 Of those men who bow down and drink of the waters like a dog shall be stayed and fight for the lord.

7:13 For if they drink like a bitch, they shall be a bitch; a bitch and war dog to the lord God.

7:14 The other men shall be sent away, for the lord not needs them."

7:15 Gideon said unto the lord, "Are you sure?

7:16 For the armies of Midian number many and we number few. To reduce our numbers seems a foolish thought for battle."

7:17 The lord said to Gideon, "Do not doubt the lord, you foolish bastard!

7:18 For the lord shall deliver the armies of Midian to you in glorious battle; do not doubt the will of the lord.

7:19 There are times when subtlety and stealth shall overcome brute force; today shall be that time."

7:20 Thus Gideon had his men drink from the river and watched closely those who came down upon the banks and lapped the water as though they were a dog.

7:21 Gideon was disappointed, for very few men drank like a dog; only three hundred out of the ten thousand drank lapped the water from the banks of the river.

7:22 Gideon kept the three hundred and sent the remaining men home.

7:23 The men who were sent away were angry and said to Gideon, "You have sent messengers and said that the lord wishes a victory for Israel.

7:24 We have answered the lord's call and now are sent home. Why?

7:25 Three hundred men are left; surely you cannot defeat the armies of Midian with three hundred men.

7:26 Let us stay, for we shall fight in glory to God."

7:27 Gideon said to the men, "I wish you to stay, but this is the will of the lord.

7:28 For the lord has chosen these three hundred men and wishes the rest to leave.

7:29 I know you question the lord, but one must have faith in God; for his will shall come."

7:30 Still the men refused to leave and demanded to fight in glory to God.

7:31 This angered the lord and the lord came down in a cloud of black smoke and fire and said to the people, "Leave. For this shall not be your fight.

7:32 I shall crush the armies of Midian in humiliation; the fewer the numbers of Israel, the more humiliating it shall be for the Midianites.

7:33 Three hundred men shall crush the armies of Midian; it shall be an embarrassing defeat.

7:34 Now leave, before the hand of God comes down and bitch slap you."

7:35 The people finally left, leaving Gideon with his three hundred men.

7:36 It came to pass that the lord spoke to Gideon in the night and said to him, "Go down and speak with the host of the armies of the Midianites and the Amalekites and listen to what they have to say.

7:37 If you fear them, take Phurah your servant with you; but you have no reason to fear, for the lord shall be with you.

7:38 The lord shall use the words of your enemies to strengthen you and deliver them into your hands."

7:39 Gideon left with his servant Phurah, for Gideon was still afraid and trusted not the lord and came into the camps of the enemy.

7:40 The people of Midian and Amalek numbered great in number and their camels, horses and chariots numbered greater than the blades of grass upon the valleys.

7:41 The generals of Midian and Amalek welcomed Gideon and invited him into their tent and said to him, "Do you wish to surrender. For we know your armies have left, so that you number only three hundred men."

7:42 Gideon said to the generals, "No, I came not to surrender, but to offer you a chance to surrender."

7:43 The generals laughed and mocked Gideon and said to him, "We shall not surrender. We shall crush you and your men.

7:44 Surrender now and we promise you shall be treated fairly."

7:45 Gideon refused and left the tent of the generals.

7:46 It was then a man came to him; a soldier of Amalek.

7:47 The man said, "Behold, I had a dream and in that dream a loaf of barley tumbled into the tent of the generals and the two men fought over the bread.

7:48 So that each man killed each other by their sword, yet the bread remained uneaten."

7:49 Gideon turned the man away and believed him to be smoking mandrake roots and ignored the words of his dream.

7:50 Phurah then said to Gideon, "Did you not tell me of the cakes which the lord set on fire upon the rock when he first met you?

7:51 Perhaps this is a message from the lord."

7:52 Gideon then knew that the armies of Israel shall not fight the armies of Midian, but trick them into fighting each other.

7:53 As Gideon and Phurah left the encampment, they both noticed the barrels of wine and the drunkenness of the enemy.

7:54 That night, Gideon said to his men, "Arise and take with you a trumpet and a lamp.

7:55 For tonight, the armies of Midian and Amalek shall be destroyed."

7:56 Thus the three hundred gathered each a trumpet and a lamp and encircled the camps of the armies of their enemies.

7:57 When Gideon blew his trumpet, the three hundred blew their trumpets and lit their lamps aflame, so that the armies of Midian and Amalek were awakened from their drunken sleep.

7:58 The armies were confused and grabbed their arms and slew one another in drunken stupor; believing their fellow man to be their enemy.

7:59 Soon, all the men of the armies of Midian and Amalek slew one another, so that only the captains and the generals left; they retreated to Bethshittah in Zererath and to the border of Abelmeholah, unto Tabbath.

7:60 The army of Israel gave chase and gathered men from Naphtali, Asher, Manasseh and pursued after the Midianites.

7:61 Gideon sent out messengers to mount Ephraim, saying to those who hid in the caves, "Come down, for the lord has struck against the people of Midian.

7:62 Gather your arms and strike down against our enemies, destroy their cities, and slay their people."

7:63 Thus the men of Ephraim left their hiding caves and gathered among the waters of the Jordan and Bethbarah and slew the people of Midian.

7:64 Two princes of Midian, Oreb and Zeeb, were captured by the people of Ephraim; they were thus slain.

7:65 Prince Oreb was tied to a round boulder, which was then rolled down upon a steep and craggy hill; so that the body of Oreb was crushed between the rocks of the mountain.

7:66 Prince Zeeb was a known drunk and was drowned within the fermenting grapes of his own winepress.

7:67 The men of Ephraim took of the two princes' heads and thrust them upon a staff and delivered the staff to Gideon.

7:68 Gideon looked upon the staff and the severed heads and knew that the lord was with him.

8:1 The men of Ephraim came to Gideon and said to him, "Why when you sent out messengers to battle against the peoples of Midian, that you did not call upon us?

8:2 Why was it that after the battle, it was then you sent for us?"

8:3 Gideon said to them, "Because you are cowards who have hid in caves, away from the eyes of your enemy and away from the sight of your lord.

8:4 Your cowardice has angered the lord, but fear not; for the lord is now pleased with you.

8:5 For you have delivered the heads of Oreb and Zeeb; this brings great pleasure to God."

8:6 When the three hundred men of Gideon passed over the Jordan, in pursuit of the armies of Midian, they were faint and hungry.

8:7 They came upon the city Succoth and said to them, "I beg of you, let us in, so that we may buy bread from your people and eat and regain our strength.

8:8 For we chase after Zebah and Zalmunna, kings of Midian and must be strong for their capture."

8:9 The prince of Succoth said to Gideon, "Zebah and Zalmunna are good men and do not deserve what you shall deliver to them.

8:10 Leave us and starve, you bloodthirsty bastards."

8:11 Gideon said to the prince of Succoth, "You cunt belching onion fucker. You dare deny food to the armies of the lord?

8:12 I shall tear the flesh from your bones and feed them to the jackals of the wild."

8:13 The armies of Gideon then went to Penuel and said to them, "We pursue Zebah and Zalmunna, the kings of Midian.

8:14 Feed us, for we are hungry, and weak."

8:15 The prince of Penuel answered to them, "Leave us, for we wish not to feed the armies of those which invade our lands.

8:16 You are like parasites and we shall pray that the kings of Midian shall slay you and pluck the very eyes from your skulls."

8:17 Gideon said to them, "How dare you insult the armies of God!

8:18 When we return in victory, I shall tear down your tower."

8:19 Zebah and Zalmunna were hiding in Kabor, with an army of fifteen thousand men.

8:20 For they were afraid of the armies of Israel, who caused one hundred and twenty thousand men to arise and slay one another.

8:21 Gideon came north of Kabor and slew the armies of the Midianites which dwelt in Noban and Jogbehah.

8:22 The kings of Midian fled and Gideon pursued them and captured them and with nails he nailed the wrists and the ankles of Zebah and Zalmunna to the ground.

8:23 The lord sent vultures to feast upon the living Zebah and Zalmunna and laughed at their misery and pain.

8:24 For the lord God is a cruel God and takes pleasure in the misery of others.

8:25 As Gideon returned to the lands of Israel, he saw a young man of the city of Succoth and captured him and tortured him until he told of all the princes and elders of Succoth; their names and their descriptions.

8:26 Gideon returned to Succoth and said to the elders, "Behold, the kings of Midian lie upon the ground and are feasted upon by the vultures and the crows.

8:27 For refusing to feed the armies of God, you shall have your very flesh torn from your bones."

8:28 Gideon then gathered the princes and the elders of Succoth and with his hand grabbed the flesh of their neck.

8:29 With one mighty pull, the very flesh and skin of each man was ripped away from their bodies, so that only the bones and the organs remained.

8:30 The people of Succoth were afraid, for the elders looked like zombies and rotting corpses.

8:31 Gideon then went to Penuel and slew all the people of the city and beat down the tower and captured the prince and the king of Penuel.

8:32 He brought the two men, Zapharah and Seleph, to his son Jether and said to him, "Draw your sword and slay these two evil men."

8:33 Jether refuses and said to his father, "These men have done nothing to me.

8:34 You have brought them naked and defenceless to me. I shall not slay a defenceless man, for there is no honour in it."

8:35 Gideon then beat his son and accused him of cowardice.

8:36 Then Gideon took his sword and slew Zapharah and Seleph and took of their heads and used them to beat further his son Jether.

8:37 All the people of Israel rejoiced and said to Gideon, "You have delivered us out of the hands of the Midianites. Surely you shall be our new king."

8:38 And Gideon said to the people of Israel, "I shall be not your king nor your ruler. The lord shall rule over you.

8:39 However, I have a request of you. I came from a poor family and wish for me great bling.

8:40 Of the slaughtered soldiers of Midian, bring to me their gold earrings and their raiment's."

8:41 Thus the people of Israel gathered all the gold earrings from the slain Midianites and brought them to Gideon.

8:42 The value of the earrings alone was one thousand and seven hundred shekels; the raiment's value were unknown.

8:43 Gideon took of the gold and made to himself an ornamental ephod, which all the children of Israel lusted after.

8:44 For it was a glorious ephod; carved beautifully and of great value.

8:45 Gideon placed the ephod in his city of Ophrah and all the people of Israel went whoring after it, for they lusted after the ephod greatly.

8:46 Thus the peoples of Israel were freed again from the hands of the Midianites and the lands knew peace for forty years.

8:47 Gideon went and dwelt within the house of his father.

8:48 And Gideon had threescore and ten sons, for Gideon had many wives and concubines.

8:49 Gideon was a very horny fucker.

8:50 Gideon's concubine in Shechem also bore him a son and named him Abimalech.

8:51 In time, Gideon died a great old age and was buried in the sepulcher of his father Joash, in the land of Abiezite.

8:52 When Gideon died, the people of Israel went whoring after false gods; gods who were peaceful and non-violent.

8:53 The children of Israel made Baalberith their lord and worshipped him and forgot the name of the true God.

8:54 Neither did they show kindness to the house of Gideon; for the seed of Gideon kept trying to enforce the laws of the lord, which really pissed off the people of Israel.

9:1 Abimalech the son of Gideon, the son of a whore, went into Shechem to his mother's brethren and communed with them and with all the people of his mother's household and said to them,

9:2 "I pray to you, speak to your brothers of Shechem and ask of them whether it be better that the seventy sons of Gideon rule over you, or I who be but one man. Remember, though I be the son of a whore, that whore shall be of your own flesh and blood, which makes me of your blood."

9:3 The people of Shechem agreed that it would be best that Abimalech rule them, for he is of their flesh and blood.

9:4 All the men of city gave Abimalech threescore and ten pieces of silver, which Abimalech used to hire thugs, who followed him.

9:5 Abimalech and his men travelled to the house of Gideon at Ophrah and slew the sons of Gideon; upon the same stone Abimalech killed his brothers.

9:6 Sixty-nine of his brothers Abimalech did slay, save for the youngest Jotham; for Jotham hid within a barrel of figs.

9:7 All the men of Shechem came and the house of Millo and declared Abimalech their new king; by the pillar of Shechem was Abimalech anointed king.

9:8 Abimalech took of the crown and placed it upon his head and smoked a many wondrous herb and said to the people of Shechem, "Hearken my voice and listen to me.

9:9 All the things of Shechem wish me strongly to rule over them, that not even the people, but the trees have anointed me king.

9:10 The olive trees wish me ruler, so I shall keep them fat with oil.

9:11 The fig trees wish me ruler, so that their fruits shall grow large and sweet.

9:12 Even the vines wish me ruler, so that I shall use their grapes and make the strongest of wine, for wine makes the lord happy and cheerful.

9:13 The poppy wishes me ruler, for the smoke of their seeds make me happy.

9:14 I have gone and slain the sons of Gideon my father, so that they shall not challenge me for my kingdom.

9:15 Remember, it was my father Gideon who did good to you and freed the people of Israel from the armies of Midian.

9:16 Rejoice in your new king and I shall rejoice over you; if the lord wishes me not to be king, then may fire come out of my asshole and may donkeys chew on my penis."

9:17 Jotham, the survivor, ran in fear of Abimalech his brother and hid in Beer, where he made fine malt ales.

9:18 When Abimalech reigned three years over Shechem and the people of Israel,

9:19 The lord grew angry and sent to Abimalech an evil spirit, so that the men of Shechem dealt treacherously against their king Abimalech.

9:20 For the lord was angry with the slaying of the sixty-nine brothers of Abimalech; the lord thought Abimalech incompetent for not slaying all seventy and letting the youngest Jotham live.

9:21 The people of Shechem waited along the roads in the mountains and robbed the caravans which carried the goods and the taxed for Abimalech.

9:22 Gaal the son of Ebed was most outspoken against Abimalech and the people of Israel put their confidence with Gaal.

9:23 Gaal said to the people of Israel, "Who is Abimalech and why must we serve him. Why should we care if he be the king of Shechem?

9:24 Is he not the bastard son of Gideon, who freed us from the people of Midian. Why should this matter?

9:25 For Abimalech is an asshole of a king and unworthy to rule over the people of Israel.

9:26 Yes, it is known that during his rule, our enemies have not attacked us for fear of our armies. This should not matter.

9:27 Yes, it is known that Abimalech takes little of our crops and our flocks, so that we shall keep more of what belongs to us.

9:28 Abimalech charges us little in taxes and we grow rich and prosper.

9:29 But, Abimalech does little but sit upon his throne, entertain himself with concubines and smoke the seeds of the poppy and the roots of the mandrakes.

9:30 The lord would wish us not to be ruled by such a lush. Let the lord be with me and I shall remove Abimalech and his armies.

9:31 I challenge Abimalech to raise his armies and fight me; I look forward to removing the head of Abimalech from his neck."

9:32 Zebel heard the words of Gaal and was angry; for Zebel supported king Abimalech.

9:33 Zebel sent messengers to Abimalech and said to the king, "Be warned, for Gaal the son of Ebed brings a great many men from Shechem and they fortify the city of Shechem against you."

9:34 Abimalech shall have no such treason within his kingdom and the king gathered his armies and went unto Shechem and waited at night.

9:35 When the sun arose, Gaal the son of Ebed went to the gates of the city and saw the shadows of the armies of Abimalech and grew worried.

9:36 Gaal said to Zebel, "Who are these men who descend the mountains and wish to destroy our wonderful city?"

9:37 Zebel said to him, "They are not men, but shadows of the mountains. Your eyes are tired and see things which are not there."

9:38 Gaal replied to Zebel, "No, they are not shadows, but men. I can see them with swords drawn descending the mountains."

9:39 Zebel confessed to Gaal, "They are the armies of Abimalech, for I have warned them of your cursed treason.

9:40 Go now and fight them. Do as you claimed you would, unless you be a coward."

9:41 Gaal thus gathered his men and went to fight against the armies of Abimalech.

9:42 Abimalech slaughtered them without mercy; so much so that Gaal retreated into the city, with Abimalech chasing after him.

9:43 The armies of Abimalech made camp at Arumah: and Zebel cast out Gaal and his surviving men, so that they shall no longer dwell within the city of Shechem.

9:44 Zebel sent out messengers to Abimalech and told him that the traitor Gaal left and shall travel soon within the fields.

9:45 Abimalech gathered his armies and waited in hiding within the fields, until they witnessed Gaal and his men walk within the fields.

9:46 Abimalech sent half his army to slay those who traversed the field; the other half shall lay siege to the city Shechem.

9:47 All the people within the field died and the city of Shechem was fought all through the day and night, until Abimalech took the city.

9:48 Abimalech was furious with the people of Shechem and slaughtered all those who dwelt within its walls.

9:49 Abimalech sowed the fields of Shechem with salt, so that not even a weed shall grow within their crops.

9:50 Those that could, fled to the tower of Shechem for refuge and shut closed its doors and barricaded it.

9:51 Abimalech laughed and told his soldiers, "Go and cut down the branches of the trees and place them within the gates of this tower."

9:52 Thus the armies of Abimalech did as they commanded and brought forth branches and placed them beside the gates.

9:53 Abimalech then set on fire the branches and killed with smoke and fire those that hid within the tower; so that all those within died. One thousand men and women.

9:54 The lust for blood grew strong within Abimalech and he and his armies marched towards Thebez and took it.

9:55 There was a strong tower within the city Thebez, where the people fled to take refuge against the armies of Abimalech.

9:56 Again, Abimalech laughed and had his men bring forth branches so that they shall smoke out those within the tower.

9:57 But the lord was against Abimalech that day; a woman, who remains nameless for the bible cares not for women, took a stone and atop the tower she threw the stone down, so that it struck the skull of Abimalech and crushed it.

9:58 Abimalech was embarrassed and said unto his armour-bearer, "Draw your sword and slay me; so that it shall not be known that the might king Abimalech was slain by a god damn woman."

9:59 Thus the armourbearer of Abimalech killed Abimalech.

9:60 And when the people of Israel saw that Abimalech was dead, they departed peacefully to their homes.

9:61 Thus the lord rendered the wickedness of Abimalech, for the sin he committed to his father by slaying his sixty nine brothers and letting the one survive.

10:1 After Abimalech, the king of the Israelites became Tola the son of Puah; a man of Issachar, who dwelt at Shamar in mount Ephraim.

10:2 For twenty-three years he judged Israel, until he died.

10:3 His chef undercooked Tola's venison and Tola died of trichinosis.

10:4 Tola was buried in Shamir.

10:5 After Tola rose Jair, a Gileadite, who judged Israel for twenty-two years.

10:6 Jair had thirty sons and he gave his sons thirty donkeys and made them princes of thirty cities, which belonged in the lands of Gilead.

10:7 The people of Israel accused Jair of nepotism; Jair denied all claims.

10:8 After twenty-two years, Jair died of AIDS. His concubines were filthy and afflicted him with the dreaded disease.

10:9 The body of Jair was buried in Camon.

10:10 After the death of Jair, the people of Israel did evil in the sight of the lord and began worshipping Baal and Ashtaroth; for the people of Israel were angry that their lord would allow such a ruler to lead them, who obviously favoured his seed over the whole good of the people of Israel.

10:11 Again, the lord sold the people of Israel. This time to the Philistines; the children of Ammon.

10:12 For eighteen years the Ammonites owned the children of Israel. This, again, brought great laughter to the people of Egypt.

10:13 The children of Israel cried and prayed to their God and said to him, "We have wronged you and worshipped Baal and Ashtaroth.

10:14 Forgive us, so that we shall be free and worship you once more."

10:15 The lord came down and said to the people of Israel, "Oh for fuck sakes.

10:16 Do you think the lord God stupid and that he shall save you from your oppressor's every damn time you whine?

10:17 The lord is not here to serve you; you are here to serve the lord.

10:18 You have not served the lord and went to other gods instead.

10:19 Go fuck yourselves and beg of your new gods to save you.

10:20 I shall not come to your rescue and shall let the children of Ammon oppress and own you for generations upon generations.

10:21 Let us see if your new gods shall come to your aid."

10:22 Thus the children of Israel begged of their new gods Baal and Ashtaroth to save them; but save them they did not.

10:23 For they were false gods; that and the lord would not Baal and Ashtaroth save them.

10:24 In time, the people of Israel threw away their idols and worshipped the one true God.

10:25 The children of Israel were grievous and miserable and wished the lord to save them yet again.

10:26 Soon, the children of Ammon gathered together and encamped in Gilead. The children of Israel gathered together and encamped in Mizpeh.

10:27 For the children of Israel were arrogant and thought the lord would save them once more.

10:28 The people of Israel gathered and said, "Glory be to the people of Israel and glory be to God.

10:29 Let a man rise amongst us; a warrior, who shall lead us and free us from the oppression of the children of Ammon."

11:1 Jephthah the son of Gilead was strong and mighty valour, who also happened to be the son of a cheap whore.

11:2 The wives of Gilead bore for him many sons, who mocked Jephthah and said to him, "You shall not inherit a damn thing from our father, for you are the son of a wretched whore."

11:3 Jephthah grew angry with his brethren and fled to the land of Tob. There Jephthah befriended mercenaries, who followed the command of Jephthah.

11:4 In time, the children of Ammon made war against the people of Israel; and the elders of Israel sought out Jephthah and his men and said to them, "Will Jephthah come and save us and be a captain in our armies and defeat the children of Ammon?"

11:5 Jephthah said to the elders of Israel, "For what reason do I have to save ye wretched hypocrites?

11:6 The people of Israel loathe me, for I am the son of a prostitute; yet every man here, who be the elders of Israel, have gone and fucked a whore.

11:7 All of you have your personal concubines and all of you I have seen step into the brothels and the houses of ill repute.

11:8 How many of you have conceived children with these harlots. And yet you deny your seed, your love and your inheritance because they are the sons of a whore; a whore which you fucked.

11:9 My very inheritance was denied to me because I am the son of a whore. What punishment is this?

11:10 I should not be punished because my father placed his seed in the slit of a cheap whore; it should be my father who should know shame.

11:11 Go, die by the hands of the children of Ammon. I look forward to smelling the stench of your corpses rot in the noon sun."

11:12 The elders of Israel said to Jephthah, "What right do you have, the son of a woman which sells her cunt, to speak to us like this?

11:13 We are the elders of Israel and shall be spoken with respect."

11:14 Jephthah laughed and said to them, "You may be the elders of Israel, but you have come for my help.

11:15 I shall talk to you as I damn well desire. Now leave; unless you can pay me for fighting your battles, I care not what you have to say."

11:16 The elders of Israel did not leave and said to Jephthah, "We cannot leave, for the lord has sent us here to beg for your help.

11:17 The lord has spoken to us and said that it shall be thee who shall rise and deliver the children of Israel from the people of Ammon.

11:18 For the lord hast heard our words and decided to help us."

11:19 Jephthah mocked the words spoken and said to the elders, "Did not the lord tell you go pray to your new gods. Did he not say that the lord shall deny to you his help?"

11:20 The elders nodded and said, "Yes, but the lord has forgiven us our wickedness and decided again to deliver us.

11:21 Blessed be the name of the lord."

11:22 Jephthah said to the elders, "So be it. I shall help you.

11:23 But when I deliver you from the children of Ammon, I shall be the new head of Israel.

11:24 Make me king and I shall fight for you."

11:25 The elders agreed and said that if Jephthah won the war against the Ammonites, that Jephthah shall be crowned king.

11:26 Jephthah sent messengers to the king of Ammon, for he wished for a peaceful resolution.

11:27 Jephthah asked of the king, "Why do you fight within my lands, for we have wronged thee in no manner."

11:28 The king of Ammon sent messengers to Jephthah and said, "We fight not in your lands, but in ours; for you have taken them from us.

11:29 When you came out of Egypt, you have taken the lands of

Jabbok unto the river Jordan; return to us these lands and we shall leave you in peace."

11:30 Jephthah sent back messengers and said to the king of Ammon, "The people of Israel have never taken an acre of land from the people of Moab nor the peoples of Ammon.

11:31 We have taken the lands of many nations, but never from yours.

11:32 When our people left Egypt and came to the lands of Kadesh, we did send messengers to the king of Edom, asking of him to allow us passage through his lands.

11:33 Our people then moved and pitched tent in the lands of Arnon, which be on the borders of the lands of Moab.

11:34 Our people then sent out messengers to king Sihon of the Amorites, the king of Heshbon, asking for safe passage through his lands.

11:35 Sihon denied us also passage. So, we killed him.

11:36 We possess now his lands, the lands of the people of Amor, but not Ammon.

11:37 If you have conquered the lands of Sihon, would you not claim them for yourself as well?

11:38 For three hundred years the people of Israel have dwelt in these lands, yet you have done nothing to claim them back, nor did you ever say to us that these be lands of the children of Ammon.

11:39 Therefore we did not sin against you, nor did wrong against your people. Stop this war, so that our nations shall live in peace and prosperity."

11:40 The king of Ammon ignored the words of Jephthah and fought against the people of Israel.

11:41 Though Jephthah be a man of valour, he knew his armies were of no match against the soldiers of Ammon.

11:42 When Jephthah slept, the lord came to him and said to Jephthah, "Do not fear, for I shall deliver into your hands the children of Ammon.

11:43 With the slaying of the Ammonites, you shall then be king of Israel. Surely such a title is of great value to you.

11:44 The lord comes to you to make you a deal; promise to your God that you shall offer for a burnt offering whatever it is which first exit the gates of your house when you return victorious and the lord shall deliver you a great victory."

11:45 Jephthah agreed, and promised to offer as burnt offering whatever thing he first sees exiting his house after victory has been made over the children of Ammon.

11:46 Jephthah gathered his men and marched over Gilead, Mannaseh and Mizpeh, until he reached the armies of Ammon.

11:47 The spirit of the lord was with Jephthah and Jephthah slew one and all of the peoples of Ammon.

11:48 From Aroer, even to the plains of Minnith, Jephthah conquered twenty great cities of the children of Ammon; It was a very great slaughter.

11:49 The lord was pleased with the bloodshed of Jephthah and smiled upon the corpses left behind by the armies of Israel.

11:50 Jephthah did not forget the promise made to God, and upon his return home thought that a concubine or sheep without blemish shall exit his gates of his house.

11:51 When Jephthah saw that which came to greet him, his heart sank; for his daughter, his only child, came out to greet him.

11:52 Dancing with timbrels she came out and embraced her father with a great hug, and congratulated him for his victory.

11:53 When his daughter saw the tears in her father's eyes, she asked of Jephthah, "What is wrong, for I would think you pleased to see me."

11:54 Jephthah said to his daughter, "I am not glad to see you. No, I wish never to have seen the at all.

11:55 For I have made a promise to the lord, a promise which must be kept.

11:56 My daughter, I must offer you as burnt sacrifice to the lord, for he has demanded it of me."

11:57 The virgin daughter of Jephthah wept, for she wished not to die as sacrifice, nor did she want to die a virgin.

11:58 The daughter of Jephthah said to her father, "You fucking asshole. Why would you promise such things?"

11:59 She then kicked her father in his stones and fled to the mountains.

11:60 For two months, she hid in the mountains and fucked every man she could find.

11:61 Jephthah searched the mountains and found his daughter lying in bed with a miner of precious stones.

11:62 Jephthah slew the miner and took his daughter to the altars.

11:63 The devil approached Jephthah and his daughter and said to Jephthah, "Why do you take your daughter, you only child, as a burnt sacrifice for your lord?

11:64 Do you not see that a God who demands human sacrifice is a God not worth worshipping?"

11:65 Jephthah said to Satan, "Be gone from me, for I can see that you are the wicked one.

11:66 Speak not, for I shall ignore your words."

11:67 Satan said, "I am not evil, nor do I wish you harm; I wish to save you from harm.

11:68 Do you not love your daughter, your only child?

11:69 Save her and don't offer her as sacrifice to the lord."

11:70 Jephthah replied to the devil, "Your words are poison to my ears.

11:71 For they are sweet and speak of things I wish to do.

11:72 Be gone, for I shall slay my daughter in sacrifice as the lord demands."

11:73 Satan became angry and cut off the binds of the daughter of Jephthah, so that she may escape the cruel demands of the lord.

11:74 It was then the lord lifted the very rocks of the mountain and entrapped the daughter of Jephthah and cast Satan back into the earth.

11:75 For the devil denied to God the sacrifice of Isaac; Satan shall not deny the lord's human sacrifice a second time.

11:76 Jephthah then took of his daughter and went to the altar of the lord and sacrificed his one and only child as burnt offering to the lord.

11:77 And the innocent slaying of a young woman pleased the lord greatly.

12:1 The men of Ephraim gathered themselves, and went to Jephthah, and said unto him, "Why when did ye go to fight the children of Ammon, did ye not ask for our aid?

12:2 For ye have denied unto us a great victory for our lord. Because ye have denied us this, we shall burn the very house you dwell in."

12:3 Jephthah said unto the peoples of Ephraim, "I denied unto thee this victory because you have called me a son of a whore.

12:4 For this insult, I shall slay thee, and rape your daughters."

12:5 Jephthah thus gathered all the men of Gilead, and fought with the peoples of Ephraim; for the peoples of Ephraim insulted Jephthah, and called him the son of a whore.

12:6 The men of Gilead smote the peoples of Ephraim, and gathered their daughters, and raped them, and said aloud, "Now your daughters shall be whores unto us."

12:7 The men of Gilead took the bridges of the Jordan, and Jephthah said unto his men, "When a man crosses the bridge, slay them if they be of the peoples of Ephraim.

12:8 Ask of them if they be of the peoples of Ephraim; they shall of course deny this.

12:9 This I know of the peoples of Ephraim; inbreeding hast cursed them, and they speak as though with thick tongue.

12:10 Demand of them to pronounce Shibboleth: if they pronounce Sibboleth, they are cursed with heavy tongue, and are of the peoples of Ephraim.

12:11 Kill them."

12:12 And the men of Gilead asked all who crossed if they were of the peoples of Ephraim, and all denied being of the peoples of Ephraim.

12:13 Of those who mispronounced Shibboleth, they slew, and threw their bodies in the Jordan, so that their corpses shall be feasted upon by the fish.

12:14 Forty two thousand men, women and children they killed for mispronouncing Shibboleth; only thirty seven thousand were of the peoples of Ephraim.

12:15 The other five thousand naturally spoke with a lisp; this mattered not to the men of Gilead, for they killed them anyway.

12:16 For six years Jephthah ruled over Israel. He then died, and was buried in one of the cities of Gilead.

12:17 After Jephthah ruled Ibzan, of Bethlehem.

12:18 Ibzan had thirty sons and thirty daughters, for he was one horny motherfucker.

12:19 For each of his thirty sons he bought for them the most beautiful and obedient wives.

12:20 Seven years Ibzan ruled over Israel, until he died and was buried in Bethlehem.

12:21 After Ibzan ruled Elon the Zebulonite, who ruled Israel for ten years.

12:22 He died, and was buried in Aijalon in the country of Zebulun. Like you care.

12:23 After the death of Elon, Abdon the son of Hillel, a Pirathonite, ruled Israel.

12:24 Abdon had forty sons and thirty nephews, who was given a great steed to ride upon after Abdon was appointed king of Israel.

12:25 For eight years ruled Abdon, until he died, and was buried in Pirathon in the land of Ephraim, in the mount of the Amalekites.

12:26 Again, doubt very much that you care.

13:1 Once again, the people of Israel did evil in the sight of the lord and the lord sold them to the Philistines for forty years.

13:2 The evil the children of Israel did was dreadful to God; they ate shrimp.

13:3 And the lord hates shrimp.

13:4 There was a man from the lands of Zorah, of the tribe of Dan, whose name was Manoah; his wife was barren and could not bear child.

13:5 An angel of the lord appeared before the barren wife and said to her, "Behold, I have been sent here from God to tell you that a son you shall bear!"

13:6 The woman laughed and said to the angel, "My husband and I have been attempting conception for years and still my womb be barren.

13:7 Yet you come down and tell me that I shall bear a son. Such a thing is not possible."

13:8 The angel mocked her and said, "Surely if it be of the lord's will, you shall bear a son.

13:9 When you carry the seed, you shall not drink of any wine nor strong drink; neither shall you partake of any unclean flesh.

13:10 Now drop your skirts and bend over, for it shall be my seed that you carry."

13:11 When the wife of Manoah saw the massive erection of the angel of the lord, she immediately dropped her skirts and bent over; for the angel's erection was huge and Manoah had such a tiny dick.

13:12 When the angel of the lord fucked the wife of Manoah, she screamed in ecstasy and praised the name of the lord multiple names, saying "Oh God, Oh God, Oh God, OH GOD!!!"

13:13 The seed of the angel shot forth in the womb of the wife of Manoah and the wife of Manoah accepted the seed and carried a son.

13:14 Before the angel left, he said to the wife of Manoah, "When you give birth to your son, a blade shall not touch the locks of his hair nor his beard.

13:15 At the moment of birth shall he be a Nazarite; a man dedicated to God."

13:16 The wife of Manoah ran home and told her husband what has happened.

13:17 Manoah grew angry, for his wife was stupid, naive and gullible; Manoah believed a stranger lied to his wife, so that they may fuck her.

13:18 Manoah grabbed his sword, ran out of the house and went towards where the angel was.

13:19 When Manoah saw the angel, he drew his sword and said to the angel of the lord, "Who are you, who dare lie to my wife so that you shall deposit your seed in her?"

13:20 The angel revealed his holiness to Manoah and said to him, "Truly I am an angel of the lord, sent here to give to your wife a son."

13:21 Manoah dropped on his sword, fell on his face and wept.

13:22 Manoah asked of the angel, "Why does the lord bless us with a child; such a precious gift. How shall we care for the child?"

13:23 The angel said, "You shall care for the child as though he were your own.

13:24 Teach to him the laws of your God, the statutes and the judgments.

13:25 Drink not of wine nor strong drink and eat not of the unclean flesh; such things are an abomination to the lord."

13:26 Manoah said to the angel, "Surely you shall be a welcome guest unto my home, for fucking my wife and giving to her your seed.

13:27 Come to my house and I shall prepare for you a great feast in your honour."

13:28 The angel said, "Such a thing I shall not do, for I am not hungry and know that you are a lousy cook.

13:29 If you wish to offer meat, give to the lord an offering of a kid goat; a male without blemish."

13:30 Manoah thanked the angel and said to him, "Such a blessed gift you have offered to me, but I know not who to thank.

13:31 Tell me your name, so that I shall know the man to give my thanks to."

13:32 The angel of the lord said to Manoah, "Why do you ask my name. For my name is secret, and cannot be known to the men of earth."

13:33 Thus the angel left and Manoah took stones and built an altar to the lord, where he sacrificed a young goat; a male without blemish.

13:34 When the fires consumed the carcass of the goat, the lord became intoxicated with the smell; for the children of Israel have not offered him sacrifice and the lord has not known the aroma of burning flesh for some time.

13:35 The lord himself came down upon the altar in great black mist and fire and consumed in its entirety the goat and the altar.

13:36 Manoah and his wife fell upon their faces, for they knew the lord was among them.

13:37 Manoah said to his wife, "Surely we shall now die, for we have seen the glory and the power of our lord."

13:38 The wife of Manoah replied to her husband, "Such a thing shall not happen, for if the lord wished us our deaths, the lord shall not have accepted our burnt offering.

13:39 Neither shall he have blessed with us a son; for if I were to die now, how can I give birth to the son of the angel of the lord?"

13:40 In time, the woman bore a son; an ugly, hairy, frightening looking beast of a baby. She named him Samson.

13:41 The lord blessed Samson and the spirit of God moved Samson in the camp of Dan, between Zorah an Eshtaol.

14:1 Samson grew and became a hairy beast. The locks upon his head were so long that his feet stepped upon his own hair when he walked.

14:2 Even the beard of Samson tickled the toes of his feet.

14:3 Samson went down to the city of Timnath and saw a woman; a daughter of the Philistines.

14:4 This woman was beautiful in the eyes of Samson; with wide hips, long hair, firm breasts and flat stomach.

14:5 Samson returned home and said to his parents, "I have saw a woman in Timnath who is pleasing to me. Go and buy her as my wife."

14:6 This upset the father and mother of Samson, who said to him, "Is there not a daughter of your own brethren, or a daughter of any tribe of Israel who pleases you?

14:7 Must you marry a daughter of the uncircumcised Philistines, who own us and oppress us greatly?"

14:8 Samson said to his parents, "NO!

14:9 This woman is beautiful to me and I shall have her as my wife.

14:10 Go now and buy her, or I shall tear down this very damn house!"

14:11 The parents agreed to Samson's demands; for Samson was a spoiled brat with the strength of fifty men.

14:12 The parents went to Timnath and bought for Samson his wife.

14:13 Samson then left to Timnath, to seek out his new gift.

14:14 When Samson came upon the vineyards of Timnath, behold, a strong and mighty lion blocked his path and roared against him.

14:15 The spirit of the lord overcame Samson and Samson took of the lion and tore it in half; such as the belly of the lion was ripped apart and became empty.

14:16 Samson told no person of the lion and went out to Timnath.

14:17 When he arrived at Timnath, he took of his new wife and talked with her and fucked her; she pleased him well.

14:18 The purchased wife of Samson liked Samson as well; for she was into bestiality and Samson reminded her of a large bear she once lied with in intimacy.

14:19 When Samson returned home, he passed the lion and behold, a hive of bees was within the carcass of the lion.

14:20 Samson took of the bee hive and ate of the honey; the bees could not sting Samson, for his hair was too thick.

14:21 When Samson returned home, he gave to his parents the honey, which they ate; Samson did not tell them of where he got the honey.

14:22 When the time of the wedding came near, Samson returned to Timnath, to give to the people a feast; which was custom of the people of Philistine.

14:23 Thirty people of Philistine, who befriended Samson, came to the feast and ate and drank with the mighty Samson.

14:24 Samson, though strong, was of dull mind and the people of Israel and Philistine mocked his stupidity.

14:25 Samson was angry for this mockery and decided to give to his friends a riddle; for riddles were a sign of intelligence.

14:26 Samson arose from his chair and said, "Behold, for my thirty companions, I offer to you a riddle.

14:27 If you guess the riddle correct, I shall give to each of you the finest silk garments ever worn.

14:28 But if you do not guess the riddle within a week, then shall each of you give me thirty garments of finest silks."

14:29 The people of Philistine knew Samson to be dumb and said to him, "Give us the riddle, so that we shall solve it and get from you your garments."

14:30 Samson then said to them the riddle. "Out of the eater came forth meat.

14:31 Out of the strong came something sweet."

14:32 The people of Philistine pondered over this riddle, for it confused them.

14:33 For six days they pondered the riddle and when they thought they figured the answer and told Samson, they were wrong.

14:34 Upon the seventh day, the people of Philistine grew angry; for they refused to lose a bet to Samson.

14:35 They came upon the wife of Samson and demanded she find out the answer to the riddle, otherwise they shall kill her.

14:36 The wife of Samson came to him and said, "Why do you hate me, for you shall not give to me the answer to your riddle."

14:37 Samson said to his wife, "None but I and the lord know the answer to the riddle; even my parents know not the answer."

14:38 The wife of Samson said to him, "I care not who you not tell, just so long as you tell me.

14:39 If you dost not tell me the answer, then I shall refuse to give my mouth to your erection."

14:40 This upset Samson, for he loved the pleasures of his wife's mouth upon his erection and Samson told her the answer to the riddle.

14:41 The wife of Samson told the people of Philistine, who laughed over the stupidity of such a riddle and thought themselves stupid for not solving it.

14:42 Before the sun set upon the seventh day, Samson held a feast and said to his thirty companions, "Have you yet to solve the riddle, or shall I receive my fine silks now?"

14:43 The thirty men said to Samson, "Such a riddle puzzled us at first; but we believe to have figured out the answer from your words.

14:44 For what be sweeter than honey. What be stronger than a lion?"

14:45 When they said this, Samson became enraged and said to his companions, "Did my god forsaken heifer of a wife tell you this answer after you plunged your dicks in her ass?"

14:46 Samson knew he had lost the bet, but wished not to spend the shekels for thirty garments of fine silks.

14:47 Thus Samson went to the city of Ashkelon; a city full of rich people.

14:48 Samson sought out thirty men wearing fine robes and killed them all. He then stripped of the bodies their robes and gave them to the thirty men.

14:49 In anger, Samson went home to his parents.

14:50 The people of Philistine thought Samson angry at his wife and no longer wanted her. So, she married the best man of Samson.

15:1 It came to pass that, during the wheat harvest, Samson found out that his wife had child; Samson knew the child was not his and went to see his wife, so that he may know who the father of the child was and because he wanted to fuck her.

15:2 When Samson arrived, the father of the wife said to him, "You cannot go see my daughter, for you are not her husband.

15:3 When you left the feast, the people of Philistine believed you angry and gave of your wife to another man."

15:4 Samson was outraged and said to the father in law, "Why would they do such things. For she was supposed to be my wife."

15:5 The father in law had great respect for Samson and said to him, "I mean you no disrespect and wish to make things right by you.

15:6 You have purchased a wife from me and a wife you shall have.

15:7 Take of my youngest daughter. She is much fairer, prettier and shall make for you a great wife."

15:8 Samson said to his father in law, "No, for I wish not for your youngest daughter, but for the daughter which was paid for.

15:9 Fear not, for my anger is not with you; you have tried to do right by me and for this I thank you.

15:10 My anger is with the Philistines, who stole my wife from me and gave it to one of their own kin.

15:11 For their theft, I shall have my revenge."

15:12 Samson left to the wilderness and captured three hundred rabid foxes. Samson tied the foxes so that each tail of a fox was tied with another tail; between the tails he placed a lit torch.

15:13 Samson then took of the foxes and released them upon the crops of the Philistines, so that the barley, the wheat and the corn shall burn wherever the rabid foxes ran.

15:14 All the crops of the Philistines turned to ash; so that even the olive branches, the vineyards and the stores of grain turned to ash.

15:15 When the people of Philistine saw this, they asked themselves, "Who can do such a thing. To capture foxes and use them to burn our fields

15:16 Surely it must be a beast of a man."

15:17 The men knew it must be Samson; for only Samson could do something so cruel, so violent and so stupid as to tie the tails of foxes together and use them to burn the fields.

15:18 When asked why Samson would do such a thing, it was found out that it was because Samson was angry for the Philistines taking his wife.

15:19 As is custom among the Philistines, they knew the wanted wife of Samson could not be his; for she was already married.

15:20 When they asked of the father in law, he said to the Philistines, "I have offered him my youngest daughter, but he refused to take her."

15:21 All the people of Philistine did not believe him; for his youngest daughter was a fair and beautiful virgin.

15:22 For what they believed to be his lies, they took him and the wanted wife of Samson and burned them upon the pillar.

15:23 This pleased the lord, for though not a sacrifice to him, the lord loves violence and suffering through fire.

15:24 The aroma of the burning bodies was a pleasing and intoxicating scent to God; sweeter than the sweetest of perfumes and incense.

15:25 When word reached Samson of the Philistines burning his wanted wife and her father, Samson became outraged; as he tends to do.

15:26 The spirit of the lord filled Samson and he went to the city and ripped apart the men, women and children.

15:27 Samson grabbed the two legs of the people and tore them apart, so that the bodies were ripped in half down the length of the spine.

15:28 This also pleased the lord, for it was a bloody and gory mess.

15:29 Samson then left and went to live in a cave upon mount Etam; like the animal he was, Samson lived in a cave.

15:30 The people of Philistine were angry with Samson and wished justice for his slaughter.

15:31 They took their armies, camped in Judah and spread their men in Lehi.

15:32 When the men of Judah saw the armies of the Philistines, they came to them and asked, "Why do you prepare to war with us. And the armies of the Philistines said, "We are here not to war with you; we wish only for Samson."

15:33 Three thousand men of Judah went to the cave where Samson lived and said to him, "What curse have you brought against us. For the men of Philistine camp within our lands and we fear they shall war with us if we do not bring you to them.

15:34 Do you not know the people of Philistine own us and shall curse us more if we don't meet their demands?

15:35 What wickedness did you do to anger the Philistines so furious?"

15:36 Samson said, "I dunno. I may have killed a city of them and burnt their crops and food stores with foxes.

15:37 You think that's why they are mad at me?"

15:38 The people of Judah said to Samson, "Of course that's why they are mad at you, idiot!

15:39 Now come with us, so that we shall deliver you to the people of Philistine and they shall leave us alone."

15:40 Samson agreed, for he was unaware of the reasons why the people of Judah were delivering him to the Philistines.

15:41 Samson was just that fucking stupid.

15:42 They bound the wrists of Samson with a strong rope and took him to the people of Philistine.

15:43 When the tribe of Judah delivered Samson to the armies of Philistine, Samson knew he was in danger; for Samson saw the swords and the chariots of the armies of Philistine.

15:44 Samson became outraged, again and tore off the bindings of his wrist.

15:45 He then grabbed a donkey and with the living donkey he swung it like a mace.

15:46 One thousand soldiers of Philistine Samson did slay with that donkey; the rest retreated, for they feared any man who could lift up a donkey and use it as a weapon.

15:47 In defiance, Samson then ripped the donkey and said aloud to the heavens, "With the ass which carries them, I have slain a thousand men!

15:48 Glory be to me, for I am the strongest motherfucker alive!"

15:49 Samson threw aside the remains of the donkey and named the place Ramathlehi.

15:50 As the sun beat down upon Samson in Ramathlehi, he became thirsty and said to God, "My lord, bless me with water."

15:51 The lord was pleased with Samson and his unique method of slaughter and opened up the jawbone of the slain donkey, so that water flowed out as though from a fountain.

15:52 Samson grabbed the jawbone of the donkey and drank greedily from it.

15:53 When Samson returned to Israel, he made himself ruler and judged for twenty years.

15:54 Though the people of Israel knew Samson to be a fool, none challenged him; for Samson would tear them apart as though their very bodies were made of dry parchment.

16:1 Samson travelled to the city of Gaza and saw within the city a beautiful prostitute. Samson paid for her services and fucked her.

16:2 The men of Gaza knew Samson was in their city and said to themselves, "We shall wait outside the city and upon daybreak, when Samson leaves, we shall capture him."

16:3 But Samson arose at midnight, for he heard the men of the city speak and Samson knew they wished to capture him.

16:4 Samson went to the gates of the city and with brute strength he tore off the gates and the pillars which hold them and ran with them to the top of the hill of Hebron.

16:5 The people of Gaza were in shock and awe, for never did they believe a man strong enough to tear down and carry the gates of their city.

16:6 In time, Samson looked down towards the valley of Sorek and behold, there was a beautiful woman named Delilah.

16:7 Samson fell in lust with Delilah and bought her and married her.

16:8 The kings of the Philistines went to Delilah and said to her, "If you find out the source of the brute strength of Samson and make him as weak as a crippled lamb, we shall pay you eleven hundred pieces of silver from each of the kings of Philistine."

16:9 Delilah agreed, for she was a greedy little bitch and hated Samson with all her heart.

16:10 In bed, Delilah asked Samson, "Tell me, O man of great strength, what be the source of your powers?"

16:11 Samson said to her, "I have no source of power, but one weakness. If I were to be tied with seven green reeds, I shall be as weak as any other man."

16:12 The Philistines took seven green reeds and gave them to Delilah, who tied Samson upon his bed while he slept.

16:13 Soldiers of the Philistines lay in hiding within the bedchamber and Delilah yelled to Samson, "Get up. Get up. The Philistines are coming!"

16:14 Samson arose with ease, for the seven green reeds were nothing to him.

16:15 Delilah was furious and said to Samson, "You have lied to me, for the reeds did not weaken you at all.

16:16 Tell me, how can I make you weak?"

16:17 Samson became curious why his new wife wished to make him weak and said to her, "If you were to bind me with new ropes that have never been used, I shall be as weak as a newborn lamb."

16:18 Thus the men of Philistine gave to Delilah fresh rope which has never been used before.

16:19 Delilah bound Samson while he slept and the soldiers of Philistine hid within the bedchamber of Samson.

16:20 Delilah yelled, "Get up. Get up. The soldiers of Philistine are upon our door."

16:21 Samson arose and tore off his bindings as though they were made of but one dry blade of grass.

16:22 Delilah became enraged and said to Samson, "Again, you have lied to me, for you have not told me the way to weaken you.

16:23 Tell me, how can I bind and weaken you?"

16:24 Samson still questioned Delilah and said to her, "If ye were to bind me with the woven fur of fawn tails and raven feathers, I shall be as weak as the newborn baby who sucks milk from their mother's teat."

16:25 The men of Philistine gathered raven feathers and fawn tails and in time made ropes of them and gave them to Delilah.

16:26 Delilah then bound again Samson as he slept in his bedchamber and the soldiers of Philistine awaited in hiding.

16:27 Delilah yelled to Samson, "Get up. The men of Philistine are rushing to your bedroom and wish to capture you."

16:28 Samson again arose and the bindings did not hold him.

16:29 Delilah wept and said to Samson, "Why, oh why, do you lie to me, for the ropes did not bind you at all.

16:30 I pray of you, tell me how I can bind you and sap your strength."

16:31 Samson was annoyed and said to Delilah, "Why do ye wish to bind me, humiliate me and weaken me?

16:32 For I see no reason for you to know this, unless you wish harm to come upon me."

16:33 Delilah said to Samson, "I wish to bind you and weaken you, so that I may give great pleasure to you when you are bound.

16:34 Imagine the sexual ecstasy I can give to you if you were bound; my breasts massaging your chest, my tongue caressing your circumcised erection, my hands rubbing your buttocks."

16:35 Samson, who was always horny, grew aroused by what Delilah said and said to Delilah, "Oh, I see the services you wish to give to me when I am bound and weakened."

16:36 Such things intrigue me and for this I shall tell you the source of my strength.

16:37 As all know, I am a hairy man, with the locks upon my head and the beard which grow from my chest dragging the very grounds I walk upon.

16:38 My hair is the source of my strength. If they were to be cut, I shall become weak.

16:39 Now, grab a blade and make me bald; for tonight you shall fuck me like no other!"

16:40 Thus Samson took a blade and removed the very hair from his body; his beard, his head, his chest, his eyelashes, even his genitals were shaven, so that Samson had no hair upon him at all.

16:41 Delilah was pleased, for she bound Samson and gave to him the sexual pleasures she said she would give.

16:42 Before Samson could spill his seed within the mouth of Delilah, she stopped and went unto her window and yelled, "Oh soldiers of Philistine. Samson is as weak as a wounded dove."

16:43 The men of Philistine stormed the bedchamber of Samson and behold, Samson was bound the bed, struggling to break the ropes which Delilah bound him with.

16:44 The men of Philistine laughed at the hairless Samson struggling; for now he was weakened, where before he could tear apart the very gates of cities.

16:45 All the kings of Philistine paid to Delilah the promised silver; and Delilah became a very rich bitch.

16:46 As Samson was removed from his home, the people of Philistine yelled and said "Praise be to our gods, for they have delivered to us our most feared and hated enemy."

16:47 The captain of the army took Samson to prison and plucked from Samson's very skull his eyes and forced Samson to eat them.

16:48 As Samson was imprisoned, the hair upon his body slowly became to grow back; the prison guards of Philistine never shaved him, for they did not know the source of Samson's strength.

16:49 It came to pass that the people of Philistine took part of the celebration of their god Dagon, whom they praised; for they believed Dagon was the lord who delivered Samson into their hands.

16:50 When the alcohol drunk during the festival made the hearts of the Philistines merry, they said to their kings, "Bring out Samson the weak, so that he shall entertain us and our lord Dagon."

16:51 The captain of the guard brought Samson out of his cell and led the blind fool to the stage of the temple of Dagon, so that he shall be mocked by the people of Philistine.

16:52 Samson asked of the guard, "I am weak and cannot stand. Lead me to the two pillars, so that I may rest my arms upon them and hold my body up."

16:53 The guard led Samson to the two pillars, for the guard felt pity for the weakened Samson and wished him not to fall upon the ground and be mocked by the drunken people of Philistine.

16:54 Upon the roof of the temple were three thousand men, women, and children, who gazed down upon Samson and spat upon him.

16:55 Within the temple itself was a great number of people; over ten thousand, whom celebrated lord Dagon and mocked the weakened Samson.

16:56 Samson rose his head unto heaven and yelled to the lord God, "Give me strength, O lord, so that I may avenge these wretched people for that they have done to my eyes!"

16:57 Samson then pushed with his arms the pillars of the temples, but was still weak; and the peoples of Philistine mocked Samson.

16:58 They pointed at Samson and said of him, "Look at the dumb brute, who thinks he can push the pillars of the temple.

16:59 Samson could not push an empty cart; he is so weak."

16:60 Samson again rose his head unto the heavens and yelled, "Lord God, I beg of you, give me strength so I shall kill these cursed people of Philistine.

16:61 Take my life with them, so all shall know through history that I, Samson, died in glory and took with him many evil men, women and children."

16:62 Thus the lord returned the strength of Samson and Samson pushed the pillars of the temples until they toppled.

16:63 The roof of the temple fell, and the three thousand upon it died, as did the ten thousand beneath the roof.

16:64 Samson died with the collapse of the roof and yelled with his last breath, "Oh shit, this hurts. Lord, you idiot, I was only kidding when I said take my life with them."

16:65 But the lord heard not the words of Samson and Samson died with the Philistines.

16:66 Such death and destruction pleased greatly the lord God; and the lord smiled within the heavens.

16:67 The family of Samson came and gathered the hairless body of Samson and returned the corpse to the burying place of Manoah, his father.

16:68 There Samson was buried.

17:1 There was a man of mount Ephraim whose name was Micah.

17:2 Micah knew of the eleven hundred shekels of silver which was paid to Delilah by each king of Philistine, for weakening Samson and allowing his capture.

17:3 The family of Micah was poor and in great poverty; thus, Micah decided to steal the shekels of silver given to Delilah.

17:4 Micah stole from one of the kings the eleven hundred silver shekels and gave it to his mother and said to her, "Behold, I have taken from the Philistines eleven hundred silver shekels. Bless me, for I am your son."

17:5 The mother blessed Micah, for in Micah's thievery the family became rich and no longer lived in poverty.

17:6 The house of Micah became a house of gods; many idols and graven images were made in glory to all lords, so that Micah shall gain the blessing of all of them.

17:7 Micah made an ephod and teraphim and consecrated and dedicated all of his sons to the priesthood of the gods.

17:8 However, one lord was not within the house of Micah; the one true God, the lord of the Israelites.

17:9 Micah did not know how to buy the blessing of the God of the Israelites and prayed to all lords that the God of Israel shall bless him.

17:10 In those days, the people of Israel had no king; every man did what they believed was right.

17:11 There was a young man from the city of Bethlehemjudah, of the family of Judah; a Levite and a priest of Israel.

17:12 This man left the home of his family and sought out refuge to call his own; upon his travels, he went to mount Ephraim and passed the house of Micah.

17:13 Micah asked of the man, "Who are you?" and the man replied, "I come from the city of Bethlehemjudah and am a priest of Israel who seeks out his own refuge."

17:14 Micah said to the man, "Dwell with me and be my personal priest, so that I shall know God.

17:15 You shall have your own house, your own raiment's, your own food and I shall pay to you ten shekels of silver a year."

17:16 The Levite agreed and was bought by Micah; Micah loved him as though he were one of his own seed.

17:17 Thus Micah thought that surely the lord of Israel shall bless him; for Micah now owns one of the lord God's priests.

18:1 In those days the people of Israel had no king and all did that which they believed right in their eyes.

18:2 The tribe of Dan wished to conquer more lands; for the lands they were given did not satisfy their greed.

18:3 Five men of the tribe, men of great valour, went forth to seek out new lands for their people and conquer them.

18:4 These men searched the lands of Zorah to Eshtaol and all lands within, to seek out the most prosperous, most promising and least guarded lands.

18:5 When the five men went to mount Ephraim, they sought out the house of Micah, the house of the gods and lodged there.

18:6 As the priest of Micah went to greet them, the five men recognized him and asked of the Levite, "Why are you here. What brought you here. Can you bless us?"

18:7 The Levite said, "I was brought here when I went forth to seek out my own home. Micah has seen me and has bought me as his priest, so that the lord shall bless him."

18:8 The five men of the tribe of Dan asked of the Levite, "This man worships many gods; how can our lord, who is jealous, bless him?"

18:9 The Levite said, "I don't know, but it would seem that by buying the priest of our God, one can purchase the lord's blessing."

18:10 The five men said to the Levite, "We did not know such things to be possible. Blessed be the name of the lord.

18:11 We came here to seek out lands for which to conquer; bless us, so that the lord shall guide us on our way."

18:12 And the Levite, who be the priest of Micah, blessed the men and wished them well upon their journey.

18:13 It came to pass that the five men came to the city of Laish and saw that the lands were bountiful, the city poorly defended and the people ignorant in arms and combat.

18:14 For the peoples of Laish were a peaceful people; farmers, who gave sanctuary to all and judged no one their beliefs.

18:15 The people were of Zidon, yet were unprotected by the Zidonians; the people of Laish had not even a king nor magistrate.

18:16 Such people are easy prey to the greed of the tribe of Dan.

18:17 Upon the return of the five men, they told their elders of the tribe, "We have searched far and wide for lands bountiful, prosperous and weak.

18:18 Blessed be the lord, for we have found such land.

18:19 The people of the city of Laish are foolish and peaceful people; not a blade among them.

18:20 Their crops are abundant and their vineyards shall give us wine to drink.

18:21 Let us come and take these lands from these people; they shall have only pitchforks and ploughs for which to defend themselves."

18:22 Thus the tribe of Dan sent forth six hundred heavily armed men, so that they shall rape, pillage and conquer the city of Laish; all in the name of God.

18:23 As the six hundred passed mount Ephraim, the five men went to the house of Micah and said to the priest, "Come, for we shall rid you of this house of foolish gods.

18:24 For this man believe himself blessed by molten images, idols, false gods, ephods, teraphims and a man of priesthood.

18:25 This man shall be cursed by God for his ignorance. Come and be with us; you shall be a priest of many instead of a priest of one."

18:26 The priest was glad, for he wished deeply to be rid from the house of Micah.

18:27 The Levite left the house and gathered the silver, the gold, the molten images, the ephod, the teraphim and all things of value from Micah.

18:28 For the Levite wished to be a rich priest and shall steal from his former master to obtain his wealth.

18:29 When Micah returned, he was angry; for behold, all his belongings, his valuables and that which gave him blessing of the gods were gone.

18:30 Micah gathered his men and went forth towards the children of Dan.

18:31 When Micah came upon the army of Dan, he said to them, "What be this, who come into my home and steal my blessings?

18:32 You have stolen my idols, my images, my goods; even my priest you have stolen from me!

18:33 Give them back, lest I draw my sword and remove from you your heads."

18:34 The Levite, who was the former priest of Micah, said to him, "For years I have served under you; a priest so that you may buy the blessing of the one true God.

18:35 The blessing of the lord cannot be bought and I pray to our lord that he shall curse you and your family for generations to come.

18:36 How dare you defile the name of the lord and have a priest live within your home amongst idols of false gods.

18:37 These men of Dan took none of your goods. I did, so that the lord shall bless me with riches from the fool."

18:38 The Levite then took out his dagger, stepped toward Micah and said to him, "Now be gone, before the lord take the very sacks of your loins."

18:39 Micah left and returned home; for he knew the armies of Dan shall destroy him.

18:40 When Micah returned home, he changed his pants (for they were soaked in urine) and lied numerously with his concubines; for Micah was grateful that the sack of his loins still remained upon him.

18:41 The army of Dan marched towards Laish and were grateful; for behold, it was a bountiful and rich land, which shall supply them with grain and grape for generations.

18:42 As the army of Dan marched towards Laish, the people of Laish came out and greeted the army of Dan and welcomed them within their city.

18:43 The army of Dan killed them.

18:44 When the people in the city saw that which the army of Dan did, they came forth and apologized for whatever actions or words the previous men had done to offend them.

18:45 The army of Dan killed these people as well.

18:46 The army of Dan stormed the city and raped and pillaged all within it.

18:47 All men, children and women who have lied with a man were slain in glorious bloodshed to the lord.

18:48 Virgins were lined up upon the town walls and the six hundred soldiers of Dan raped of each one; so that each soldier raped each virgin.

18:49 Only the Levite did not rape the virgin women of Laish; for the Levite was a homosexual and wished never to place his seed within a woman's hairy, diseased ridden cunt.

18:50 Once the soldiers of Dan had their lust fulfilled, the virgins of Laish were cut, so that their legs and their arms were removed from them.

18:51 The army of Dan brought forth the limbs and the screaming torsos of the virgins and piled them within the town square of the city of Laish.

18:52 The captain of the army of Dan took a torch and burned alive the crippled virgins; alas, the whole city was burned to ash.

18:53 This created a pleasing aroma for the lord.

18:54 When the cinders died and the ashes swept away from the wind, the tribe of Dan built a great city atop the remains of Laish.

18:55 The name of the city was Dan; for the tribe of Dan were not creative people.

18:56 It was a great and strong city; and those who came to seek out sanctuary in Laish were greeted by the city of Dan and destroyed.

19:1 There was a Levite who dwelt within the side of mount Ephraim and bought for himself a concubine from the city of Bethlehemjudah.

19:2 The concubine hated her Levite master, for he was a cruel and evil man.

19:3 Every night, the Levite would take his concubine and rape her with stones and branches. The Levite would take his blade and cut upon the nipples of the concubine and mock her and say that she lactated blood.

19:4 Sodomy was all the Levite did to the concubine and when finished the Levite would have his concubine excrete his seed and her shit within a bowl and force the concubine to eat of this vile concoction.

19:5 As the concubine would eat this and vomit, the Levite would laugh and beat her with cattle prods and sheep staffs.

19:6 In time, the concubine could take no more of the abuse from the Levite. She took of her things and ran back to the home of her father in Bethlehemjudah.

19:7 When the Levite went to the bedchamber of the concubine so that he may pour hot candle wax and lamp oil within her vagina, behold, she was gone.

19:8 This angered the Levite, for he loved the abuse and humiliation that he forced upon his concubine.

19:9 In the morning, the Levite gathered his servant and travelled to Bethlehemjudah, so that he may purchase for himself another whore.

19:10 As he arrived in the gates of Bethlehemjudah, he witnessed the concubine in the house of her father; the Levite went into the house and demanded the father return to him the concubine he bought.

19:11 The father refused and said to the Levite, "Be gone, for you are truly a wicked and evil demon of a man.

19:12 My daughter has told me of the horrors she has endured nightly at your claw you cleverly disguise as a hand.

19:13 She has shown me her scars; both old and new.

19:14 Get out of my house, for you shall not have my daughter back.

19:15 I shall give to you the money you have paid for her, for I am a fair man even to a man of the devil."

19:16 The Levite refused that which he heard, drew his sword and slew the father of the concubine.

19:17 He then bound the concubine; and the Levite, the concubine and the servant stayed within the house, with the body of the concubine's father lying upon the floor.

19:18 On the first night, the Levite and his servant ate of the food within the house and forced the concubine to eat of the rotten meat used to feed the dogs.

19:19 On the second night, the Levite and his servant ate more of the food found within the house and forced the concubine to eat of their shit and drink of their urine.

19:20 On the third night, they ate the remaining food which be in the house and masturbated upon the mouth of the concubine, so that she shall eat their very seed

19:21 On the fourth night, the men cut forth the flesh of the father of the concubine and roasted it upon the fire and ate of it. They forced even the concubine to eat raw the flesh of her own father.

19:22 Upon the fifth night, the Levite and his servant left, with the concubine bound and dragged behind the donkeys.

19:23 As the men travelled, the servant said to his master, "It is late and we shall need shelter soon.

19:24 Come, we are in the land of Jebus. Let us take shelter here."

19:25 The Levite said to his servant, "Never shall I lodge in the house of a Jebusite.

19:26 It is better to sleep in the very wastes of a barn than to sleep within the city of a filthy damned Jebusite.

19:27 We shall travel farther, until we reach Gibeah or Ramah and shall seek shelter there."

19:28 Thus the men travelled longer, with the concubine dragging upon the rocks and sand behind them.

19:29 As the men went to Gibeah, who belonged to the tribe of Benjamin, they sought out shelter there.

19:30 None welcomed these men into their homes; for the concubine was filthy and bleeding. They did not want to have the blood of a whore upon their floors.

19:31 The men decided to sleep upon the streets and each took a breast of the concubine and used it as a pillow.

19:32 As they slept, an old man came in from the fields and said to them, "Who be you, who sleep upon the street and rest their head upon the breast of a woman?"

19:33 And the Levite replied, "I am a man from mount Ephraim. My servant and my concubine wish only to go home.

19:34 We came to seek shelter in this city and no shelter we were given. So, we sleep here upon the streets, like a beggar and leper."

19:35 The old man said to them, "Come, come, for you shall stay at my house.

19:36 I shall provide hay for your donkeys and water for your feet. Blessed are those who stay at my house."

19:37 As the men ate and drank within the house of the old man, a group of men beat at the door and said, "We saw the men which you have welcomed into your house; men who slept upon our streets."

19:38 Give us to them, so we may rape them, and satisfy our lust."

19:39 The old man said to the men, "Blessed are the men who come to my house. You shall take them not.

19:40 Take instead my virgin daughter, who is young and beautiful. Surely she shall satisfy your need for lust."

19:41 But the men refused and wished for the men.

19:42 It was then the Levite took his concubine and threw her out the door.

19:43 The gang of men took her and descended upon her and all night raped, bound and humiliated her.

19:44 The Levite watched as the men raped his concubine; for it pleased him greatly.

19:45 When the sun arose and the Levite and his servant went to leave the house of the old man, the concubine was upon the entrance to the door.

19:46 She had crawled back to the house of the old man.

19:47 The Levite told her to get up, but she could not. She was too weak to stand and could barely speak the words she wished to say to the Levite.

19:48 Those words were, "Fuck you."

19:49 Thus the Levite bound the concubine and placed her atop the donkey and took him to his home.

19:50 As the Levite and his servant left, the virgin daughter of the old man left behind them in secret; for she was angered that her father would offer her to the gang of rapists.

19:51 When the Levite arrived home, he took the concubine and placed her upon a stone table.

19:52 Still the concubine was alive, but weakened.

19:53 The Levite took of his cleaver and as the concubine still breathed, the Levite butchered alive his concubine.

19:54 As the Levite butchered his concubine, he smiled with great glee at the final pain he has given unto his filthy and wretched whore.

19:55 This pleased the lord also, who took great pleasure of the butchering of the prostitute.

19:56 In twelve pieces he did divide his whore. He wrapped the pieces in cloth and sent one each to the heads of each of the twelve tribes of Israel.

19:57 When the heads of the tribes received the piece of the whore, they praised and worshipped God; for surely an act as violent and as cruel as this must be sent from the lord.

19:58 They said to their people, "Behold, flesh from a slain whore. Surely this must be a gift from God.

19:59 Go, gaze upon it, and discuss it. For never has the lord done such a thing."

19:60 When word spread that it was not the lord who delivered them the flesh of a concubine, but a Levite, the people of Israel grew angry.

19:61 How dare this Levite do the acts of God.

20:1 All the congregation of Israel, from Dan even to Beersheba in the lands of Gilead, gathered to Mizpeh in the house of the lord.

20:2 Each head of the tribes and their elders came and with them four hundred thousand swordsmen.

20:3 They said to the Levite, "What wickedness did you commit, to send us the flesh of your whore and fool us to believe it an act of God?"

20:4 The Levite answered, "I wished not to fool you, but to shame you.

20:5 This was my whore; my personal tool to satisfy my carnal lust.

20:6 I paid good money for her, only to have you peoples steal her from me.

20:7 For behold, I was in the city of Gibeah with my concubine and a gang of men came forth to my lodging and raped her in my sight.

20:8 Many men, from many tribes, has stolen that which belonged to me.

20:9 When she returned to me, the life from her body was beaten from her and she was dead.

20:10 In twelve pieces I butchered her body and sent her to each of the tribes; for each tribe took a piece of her, I saw it only fitting they shall have a piece of her corpse."

20:11 When the congregation of Israel heard the story of the Levite, they felt pity for him.

20:12 The elders gathered together funds and bought for this Levite a new concubine for which he could rape, abuse and humiliate.

20:13 This pleased greatly the Levite, for through his lie he got for himself a prettier and more obedient whore.

20:14 All the heads and the elders of Israel gathered together, to discuss that which was done.

20:15 They said to themselves, "How can this be avenged and who is to blame?

20:16 Surely, we can not know which men have raped the concubine of the Levite, nor what tribe they belong to.

20:17 Perhaps only one tribe is guilty, or many. We shall never know.

20:18 This we do know; the raping happened in Gibeah. In Gibeah is where the theft took place.

20:19 Where were the people of Benjamin. Why did they not protect that which belonged to the Levite?"

20:20 Thus it was decided that the tribe of Benjamin was to blame for the thievery of the concubine of the Levite.

20:21 All the tribes gathered themselves and said, "Let us take the lands of the Benjamites and we shall divide them by lot amongst us."

20:22 Civil war was declared among the nation of Israel; civil war over the lying of a Levite and the butchering of his whore.

20:23 The eleven tribes of Israel came to the lands of Benjamin and said to the Benjamites, "What wickedness be among you?

20:24 Deliver us your city of Gibeah, so that we shall smite the evil from the earth."

20:25 The people of Benjamin refused and gathered themselves their own army to protect and defend their city and their lands.

20:26 Twenty-six thousand men trained in the sword were gathered from the people of Benjamin and another seven hundred men from Gibeah, who were left handed and could shoot the arrow through the skull of a sparrow and never miss.

20:27 Of the eleven tribes of Israel were four hundred thousand men; all men trained in war.

20:28 The eleven tribes of Israel went to the house of God and sought the lords counsel and said, "Dear lord, which tribe shall first go forth and strike down our evil brothers?"

20:29 The lord said, "Judah shall go first."

20:30 For the lord waited in anticipation the civil war of Israel. The anticipated violence and bloodshed excited the lord; he wished for a great and bloody war amongst the chosen people of Israel.

20:31 The men of Judah marched towards Gibeah and expected the lord to deliver into their hands the wicked and evil Benjamites.

20:32 This did not happen. The peoples of Benjamin slew twenty-two thousand people of the tribe of Judah.

20:33 The lord looked down and smiled upon the massacre of the people of Israel.

20:34 All the eleven tribes of Israel wept and asked the lord, "The tribe of Judah hast failed you. Who shall we sent next, to do service unto God?"

20:35 The lord said, "You shall all go and fight the wicked tribe of Benjamin."

20:36 Thus the eleven tribes gathered their men and fought the armies of Benjamin.

20:37 To Gibeah they marched with great numbers and knew the lord shall deliver into their hands the city of Gibeah.

20:38 Again, the lord allowed the Benjamites to win. Eighteen thousand people of Israel were slaughtered and the tribe of Benjamin were victorious once again.

20:39 All the children of Israel gathered to the house of the lord and wept and sacrificed offerings to God and pleaded to the lord.

20:40 For the people of Israel were confused why the lord would allow the Benjamites to be victorious, despite the armies of Benjamin being so little and the armies of Israel so large.

20:41 This pleased the lord greatly, for the confusion of his people brought great pleasure to God.

20:42 In heaven, the lord mocked the weeping of the eleven tribes of Israel and had the angels mock and imitate the lame offerings and the pleadings of the eleven tribes.

20:43 Even the angels in heaven laughed at the pathetic weeping and confusion of the lord's chosen people.

20:44 In time, the lord decided to deliver to the eleven tribes the people of Benjamin and came down to earth in a pillar of black smoke and fire and said to the peoples of Israel, "Behold, the lord shall deliver the wicked tribe of Israel to your hands.

20:45 Bring forth Phinehas, the son of Eleazar, who be the son of Aaron; for the seed of a holy man shall give you a holy victory."

20:46 This Phinehas was chosen to lead the armies of Israel against the tribe of Benjamin.

20:47 And the armies marched towards Gibeah, to lay siege upon the city.

20:48 As they marched, they slew all those of the peoples of Benjamin who crossed their path.

20:49 Upon the highway, the countryside, the plains and the forests they killed any and all who belonged to the tribe of Benjamin.

20:50 When word reached of the slaughter of their people, the army of Benjamin left the city of Gibeah, so that they may fight the eleven tribes of Israel.

20:51 Phinehas anticipated this move and lay in hiding around the city of Gibeah archers and swordsmen, who saw the armies of Benjamin leave.

20:52 As the army of Benjamin met with the armies of the eleven tribes, the lord came down and fought alongside the eleven tribes of Israel.

20:53 Great fingers of fire came down from the heavens and grasped the men, the horses and the chariots of the army of Benjamin and thrust them high into the heavens, never to return.

20:54 The lord killed twenty-five thousand and one hundred soldiers of the army of Benjamin; the lord was quite pleased with this.

20:55 As the battle took place, the men who hid around the city of Gibeah stormed through the gates and lay siege upon the city.

20:56 Every man, woman, child and beast were slain in the city of Gibeah. The city was then burned, so that the armies of the eleven tribes shall see the smoke of the fires of Gibeah and know they are victorious.

20:57 Eighteen thousand men were burned within the walls of Gibeah. The number of women and children burned are irrelevant; the bible cares not for women and children. They aren't people anyway, according to God.

20:58 Those of the surrounding villages of Gibeah fled to the rocks of Rimmon and hid from the eleven tribes of Israel for four months.

20:59 And the men of Israel caused great suffering for the people of Benjamin. Every Benjamite was slain and their cities, their villages, their crops, their homes, were burned to ash.

20:60 This pleased greatly the lord, who was relieved that there are now fewer men for which the lord must keep his covenant with.

21:1 As the eleven tribes of Israel conquered the lands of the tribe of Benjamin, they did so with great anger and hate for their brother.

21:2 They went to the house of the lord and offered a great sacrifice to God, and swore in the lord's name, "Let us rid the earth of these people of Benjamin.

21:3 When you see a man of Benjamin, slay them. Slay their women; kill even the virgins and don't partake of their wickedness beneath their skirts.

21:4 Let no man marry a woman of Benjamin and never give unto the people of Benjamin your daughters.

21:5 Soon, all of the Benjamites shall perish and we shall please the lord with this genocide of our own people."

21:6 As the eleven armies pillaged and destroyed the lands of the Benjamites, they did so screaming, "Glory be to our lord, for we shall kill even our brothers when they turn to wickedness."

21:7 This pleased the lord, who looked down with glee the carnage, the bloodshed and the hatred amongst the people of Israel.

21:8 When the armies of the eleven tribes marched towards rock Rimmon to rid themselves of the survivors of the tribe of Benjamin, they marched chanting, "Let us kill our wicked brothers.

21:9 For we are righteous and shall slay our family when they turn to evil."

21:10 Then, a man of war, an archer, asked of his men, "What wickedness did the people of Benjamin do?"

21:11 The armies of the eleven tribes stopped and pondered, for they forgot that wickedness which their brothers of the tribe of Benjamin committed.

21:12 In time, it was learned the wickedness of which the tribe of Benjamin committed was allowing a concubine to be raped among the streets of their city, Gibeah.

21:13 When the elders of the eleven tribes of Israel heard this, they wept; for surely such a thing was not wicked and worth not a civil war.

21:14 For she was a woman and a concubine; the raping of her was not evil. She is not even human.

21:15 Thus the eleven tribes of Israel stopped their carnage and wished to make peace with the tribe of Benjamin; wished to make peace with their brothers.

21:16 This greatly angered the lord; for God wanted more carnage, more violence and more turmoil among the people of Israel.

21:17 The lord wanted the tribe of Israel extinct.

21:18 But, the lord was relieved. For the eleven tribes of Israel swore an oath in God's name; none of their seed shall marry a person of the tribe of Benjamin.

21:19 The eleven tribes of Israel knew this and wondered how they could give the people of Benjamin's wives and still uphold the oath.

21:20 A man of the tribe of Reuben said, "The people of the city of Jabeshgilead were not at the sacrifice where the oath was made.

21:21 They did not take the oath and could give unto the people of Benjamin their daughters as wives."

21:22 So the eleven armies of Israel marched towards Jabeshgilead and slew all the men and women who were not virgins.

21:23 The remaining virgin women were captured and carried off to rock Rimmon, as a peace offering to the survivors of the tribe of Benjamin.

21:24 Four hundred virgins were captured at Jabeshgilead to be given to the Benjamites.

21:25 As the armies marched towards rock Rimmon, they called out to their brothers of the tribe of Benjamin, "Fear not, for we wish to make amends for our actions.

21:26 We shall give back your lands and shall rebuild your cities; we wish not to make war with you no longer.

21:27 You are our brothers and the nation of Israel is missing a tribe; the nation of Israel is crippled without you, O people of Benjamin.

21:28 Come hither, for we have found four hundred women to give to you as wives, so that you shall plant your seed and ensure the generation of your kin."

21:29 Thus the survivors of the tribe of Benjamin came out and accepted the four hundred virgins as wives; but the four hundred was not enough.

21:30 For the survivors of the tribe of Benjamin numbered greater than the eleven tribes of Israel believed.

21:31 When the Benjamites asked of their brethren, "Why does this matter. Why can't we accept your daughters as wives?"

21:32 The tribes answered to them, "Because we have made an oath to God that never shall one of our tribe be given to you as a wife.

21:33 To do so shall curse the family who gave you a daughter."

21:34 Thus the people of Israel wept; for the tribe of Benjamin was crippled.

21:35 It was then that a man of the tribe of Naphtali said, "The people of the village of Shiloh have among them a great many virgin daughters; beautiful and fair.

21:36 Soon they shall celebrate a festival, where all the virgin daughters come out and dance naked around a bonfire, in hopes their false god shall bless them and give them a bountiful harvest.

21:37 Let the men of Benjamin lie in wait amongst the vineyards, for the celebration shall be at night and the Benjamites shall be well hidden.

21:38 When a man of Benjamin sees a woman which pleases him, let him go and take her and steal her as a wife."

21:39 This made the lord furious, for he wished the tribe of Benjamin to have no wives and end their generations and their seed.

21:40 In anger, the lord sent his wrath upon the planet known as Pluto and weakened the planet and took from it its land and its mass.

21:42 Thus Pluto went from being a great and mighty planet, to a small rock about the size of a moon.

21:43 At night, the people of Benjamin hid in the vineyards of the people of Shiloh and when they saw each picked a virgin which pleased them, they rushed forth and grabbed their woman and took off.

21:44 When the men of Shiloh intervened, the people of Israel killed them.

21:45 When each man of Benjamin had a wife, they returned to their lands, rebuilt their cities and regrew their crops.

21:46 All the tribes of Israel gathered together and helped their brothers the Benjamites; this angered the lord so much that he gazed upon one of his sons and said, "Someday, I shall kill you upon the horrid lands of the people of Israel.

21:47 My own son shall suffer from my wrath which the peoples of Israel caused."

RUTH

1:1 It came to pass that when the judges ruled Israel, a great famine swept the nation of the Israelites. A certain man from the city of Bethlehemjudah went to dwell in the land of the Moabites; he, his wife and his two sons.

1:2 The man's name was Elimelech and his wife was Naomi and the name of their two sons was Mahlon and Chilion. People of the tribe of Joseph, who left the land of the covenant to live in the lands of Moab.

1:3 This treachery angered God greatly, who killed Emilemech when he built his house in the lands of the Moabites.

1:4 Naomi was made a widow by the hand of God; her two sons, Mahlon and Chilion, cared for her in her time of grieving.

1:5 Both sons of Naomi married women of the people of Moab. The name of the one was Orpah and the other was named Ruth.

1:6 The two sons of Israel marrying Moabite women angered the lord greatly. He struck upon Mahlon and Chilion a great disease, which killed them both.

1:7 This leaved Naomi with no family but her two heathen daughter in laws.

1:8 For ten years Naomi lived within the lands of Moab, until the wish to return home to her brethren of Israel became too strong to bare.

1:9 Naomi was alone in the foreign land and did not trust the people of Moab; she hated them, for they were foreign and wicked in her eyes.

1:10 As she made known her decision to her daughter in laws, she said to them, "Go home to your families, as I shall go home to mine.

1:11 Return to the house of your fathers, for you are widows such as I and have no man to care or protect you."

1:12 Naomi's daughter in laws said to her, "Surely we shall not abandon you, for you are like a mother to us.

1:13 Let us come with you to your homeland."

1:14 Naomi said to Orpah and Ruth, "Why. Surely you must know that my womb be dry and empty.

1:15 I am old and cannot bear a son for which to be your husband. Even if I could, he would be too young for you both.

1:16 Go back to the house of your father. Seek forth a husband of your own kin."

1:17 Orpah left and kissed Naomi goodbye and went back to the house of her father.

1:18 For Orpah was a god forsaken cunt.

1:19 But Ruth loved Naomi and said to her, "I shall not go back to the house of my father, nor the lands of my people, nor their gods.

1:20 Where you go, I shall go. Your family shall be as my family. Your God as my God.

1:21 In the lands where you die, I shall die also. Let my body be buried beside the tomb of my mother in law, whom I love greatly."

1:22 When Naomi saw that Ruth shall not leave her side, she welcomed Ruth to travel with her. For Ruth was a good woman and could be a decent slave for Naomi.

1:23 Thus the two travelled unto the city of Bethlehem. And it came to pass that when entered the city of Bethlehem, the city was rich in gossip of the two women.

1:24 People would ask of themselves, "Is that Naomi. And who be that Moabite with her?

1:25 They are lovers; homosexuals against God.

1:26 Naomi bought the Moabite as a slave.

1:27 The Moabite killed the men of Naomi's family and Naomi brought her here to be judged harshly by God."

1:28 Naomi said to the peoples of Bethlehem, "Judge me not, for the lord has judged me greatly and bitterly.

1:29 My family is dead and all that remains with me is this Moabite; a wife of my deceased son.

1:30 I have returned to the lands of my people, for I know that the lord wishes me not to dwell amongst the filthy heathens."

1:31 When Ruth heard this, she fell to her face and wept. For Ruth loved Naomi, but Naomi hated Ruth. Naomi hated all of the people of Moab.

1:32 And the two women dwelt within the city of Bethlehem, in time for the barley harvest.

2:1 Naomi had a kinsmen of her husband's, who was a man of great wealth of the family of Elimelech. His name was Boaz.

2:2 In the house of Boaz did Naomi and Ruth dwell, for Boaz loved his brother Elimelech and wished to care for his wife.

2:3 Naomi said to Ruth, "You are an ungrateful and worthless heathen whore, who dwells within the house of Boaz.

2:4 Here you stay under his roof. You drink his wine, you eat his food and yet you offer nothing for him.

2:5 Go out and glean his fields of barley. A worthless cunt such as you should work hard and be grateful for that which is handed to her."

2:6 And Ruth went, and laboured in the fields of Boaz.

2:7 When Boaz returned, he would pass his fields and watch his servants and his slaves harvest the barley of his crops.

2:8 As the eyes of Boaz gazed his fields, he noticed Ruth and asked of his servant, "Who is that handmaiden who gleans my barley. For never have I seen her before."

2:9 And his servant said, "That is Ruth, whom is the Moabite daughter in law of Naomi."

2:10 The eyes of Boaz were pleased by Ruth; her long straw coloured hair, her flowing robes which blew in the wind, her subtle buttocks as she bent over and picked forth the strewn barley.

2:11 It caused great lust for Boaz, who approached Ruth and said to her, "My dear, a woman like you should work not in the fields.

2:12 Come and I shall place you in my brothel, so that you may pleasure me as a woman should pleasure a man."

2:13 Ruth said to Boaz, "I shall not, for I belong to Naomi and not you."

2:14 Boaz laughed at Ruth and said to her, "Surely Naomi shall sell you to me. For I have heard of the ways Naomi treats you.

2:15 Naomi hates you, where I wish to make love to you. Surely that would be more pleasing for you."

2:16 Ruth began to cry and said to Boaz, "It would not be, for I love Naomi as though she were my wife.

2:17 When Naomi came to this country, I followed her and accepted her people and worshipped her God.

2:18 For I love Naomi in a way that seems unnatural. I wish to take Naomi to my bedchamber and please her as you wish I to please me."

2:19 When Boaz was told by Ruth that she was a lesbian, his heart sank and his penis rose.

2:20 For the thought of Ruth not being one among his whores was disappointing, but the image of Ruth pleasing Naomi was erotic to Boaz.

2:21 Boaz wished for Naomi to be pleased by Ruth, so that the sexual desires of Ruth shall be fulfilled.

2:22 So that Ruth shall win the favour of Naomi, Boaz had it so that all that which Ruth gathered shall be given to Naomi.

2:23 In this way, Naomi shall be pleased by the bountiful harvest given to her by Ruth and be pleased with Ruth and lie intimately with her.

3:1 As Ruth tried harder to please Naomi, Naomi hated Ruth even more.

3:2 No amount of barley gleaned, nor meals cooked, nor massages, nor gifts could ever overcome the hatred Naomi had for Ruth.

3:3 Boaz new this and sympathized for Ruth.

3:4 One night, Boaz said to Ruth, "I shall set up a way so that Naomi shall be pleased with you and that your carnal lust to her shall be fulfilled.

3:5 Tonight, when you serve supper unto Naomi, fill her cup with wine which I give you, so that she shall be drunk and merry.

3:6 Carry her to her bedchamber and lie her down upon the bed.

3:7 Pull off her skirts and lie in bed with her. Do to Naomi all that which you long to do.

3:8 Naomi's mind shall be weakened by wine and she shall gladly accept your advances."

3:9 Ruth thanked Boaz and said to him, "Surely such a clever and cunning plan must not go unrewarded.

3:10 Tell me, what can I do to please you for your wisdom?"

3:11 And Boaz said to Ruth, "After you take Naomi to bed, but before you lie naked with her, have my servant come for me.

3:12 I wish to witness the two of you."

3:13 Ruth agreed.

3:14 That night, Ruth prepared a great feast for Naomi of baked breads, figs, olives, fowl and the strong wine which Boaz has given her.

3:15 Naomi ate of the foods and drank of the wine and cursed endlessly the heathen Ruth.

3:16 Still, Ruth fed her and gave her strong drink, until the wine weakened Naomi and she fell upon the floor and slept.

3:17 Ruth carried Naomi to her bedchamber and removed the robes of Naomi and placed her atop the bed.

3:18 Ruth then sent forth for Boaz, who arrived in great anticipation.

3:19 Boaz sat upon the edge of the bed and watched as Ruth kissed, caressed and groped the body of Naomi.

3:20 When the haze of the wine slowly began to escape Naomi, she awoke and behold, she saw Ruth naked in bed with her, doing things of which only her husband had done.

3:21 Naomi shrieked and screamed at Ruth, "How dare you invade thy body, you heathen whore!

3:22 Cursed be your name, you wretched demon of Moab.

3:23 Be gone from my house."

3:24 Boaz then arose and said to Naomi, "This is not your house, but the house of Boaz.

3:25 Now I was pleased greatly with what Ruth had done to you; if you deny me the pleasures of this, it shall be you who shall be banned from my house.

3:26 Ruth can stay. She excites me."

3:27 Naomi was angry, for she wished greatly to stay in the house of Boaz and eat of his food and drink of his wine.

3:28 Thus Naomi embraced Ruth and the will of Naomi forced her body to kiss Ruth and caress her as though she was her lover.

3:29 This greatly pleased Boaz, who joined in the bed and caressed and fondled both Naomi and Ruth and fulfilled his sexual lust on both women.

3:30 When the deed was done and both Ruth and Boaz fulfilled their lust, Boaz said to the two women, "You have given me pleasure that of which no man has ever known before.

3:31 For this pleasure, you shall both stay in my house and be protected by me."

3:32 Thus Ruth and Naomi became the lesbian lovers of Boaz

3:33 Naomi was greatly angered by this; both Ruth and Boaz didn't care.

4:1 Boaz took great pleasure in his lesbian lovers. Though other men had greater numbers of concubines, younger concubines and prettier concubines, Boaz was the only man in Bethlehem who had two lesbian concubines.

4:2 Nightly, Boaz would force Naomi to his bedchamber and force Naomi to give pleasure to Ruth and Ruth to give pleasure to Naomi.

4:3 Naomi loathed the two people and cursed them both, so that Ruth and Boaz shall be intertwined in their curse.

4:4 The lord heard the curse given by Naomi and fulfilled that curse.

4:5 Ruth became pregnant.

4:6 When the elders of the city heard of Ruth's pregnancy, they came upon Boaz and said to him, "Surely you wish not your son to be a son of a whore.

4:7 Bastard children are hated by God and hated by the people of Israel.

4:8 Buy Ruth as a wife, so that your son shall be a holy son and not the son of a whore."

4:9 Thus Boaz bought Ruth from Naomi as a wife.

4:10 This displeased Ruth, for Ruth wished not to be the wife of Boaz. Ruth wished to be the wife of Naomi.

4:11 Upon their wedding, Boaz took Ruth to his bedchamber and sent for Naomi to join them.

4:12 Naomi entered the bedchamber of Boaz and said to Boaz, "Surely you expect me not to lie with you, for you are a married man."

4:13 Boaz said, "Yes, I wish for you to lie with us, as we always do."

4:14 Naomi answered Boaz, "I cannot, for to do so shall be sinful.

4:15 You are a married man now and if I were to lie with your Ruth, Ruth shall have committed adultery and must be stoned to death, according to the laws of Moses."

4:16 Boaz wept, as did Ruth.

4:17 Boaz had lost his lesbian lovers and Ruth lost the embrace of Naomi.

4:18 It came to pass that Ruth bore Boaz a son and named him Obed.

4:19 Though the breasts of Ruth were large, they were empty and Ruth could not feed her son Obed.

4:20 Naomi became a wet nurse to Ruth and nursed Obed with milk.

4:21 Ruth became jealous of her child Obed, for Ruth wished to suck on the breasts of Naomi as her son did.

4:22 Now, these are the generations of Pheraz. They aren't important, but they are short.

4:23 Pheraz begat Hezron, Hezron begat Ram,

4:24 Ram begat Amminadab, Amminadab begat Nahshon,

4:25 Nahshon begat Salmon, Salmon begat Boaz,

4:26 Boaz begat Obed, Obed begat Jesse,

4:27 Jesse begat David, who was a king of Israel, despite being of the generations of Ruth, a Moab woman.

I SAMUEL

1:1 There was a man of the city of Ramathaimzophim, of mount Ephraim and his name was Elkanah, the son of Jeroham, the son of Elihu, the son of Tohu, the son of Zuph, an Ephrathite:

1:2 Elkanah had two wives, one named Hannah and the other named Peninnah. Peninnah bore Elkanah many sons, but Hannah was barren.

1:3 Every year Elkanah would leave the city of Ramathaimzophim so that he might worship the lord God and sacrifice to the Lord of hosts in Shiloh. The sons of Eli, Hophni and Phinehas, the priests, were there.

1:4 Elkanah would offer a few sacrifices for Peninnah and his sons, but for Hannah he would offer more.

1:5 For Elkanah loved Hannah more, though she was barren.

1:6 Peninnah would taunt Hannah and mock her barren womb; Peninnah was a bitch.

1:7 Every year during the sacrifice, Peninnah would cruelly speak words of evil at Hannah. This upset Hannah so greatly that she would not eat and would weep in her bedchamber.

1:8 Elkanah would ask Hannah, "Why dost thou weep, for this is a happy time of sacrifice. Let us take pleasure in the slaying of beasts.

1:9 Your heart is heavy and thou dost not eat. Be not selfish and take glory in our God."

1:10 One day, after they had eaten, Hannah rose and went to the temple. Eli the priest sat by the temple of the lord, by a post.

1:11 With great bitterness and anger in her soul, Hannah prayed unto the lord and wept rivers of tears upon the ground.

1:12 She vowed unto God, "My lord, why dost thou close my womb and make me barren, for am I not a loyal daughter of Israel?

1:13 Peninnah has many sons, yet I have none. Peninnah is a devil of a cunt and deserves not your blessing.

1:14 Curse Peninnah and bless me. Give unto me a son and I shall make him a child unto the lord for all his life. Not a razor shall come to his head."

1:15 It came to pass that as she was praying, Eli saw her weeping and thought her drunk.

1:16 Eli said to her, "Be gone wretched whore, for this is a place of worship.

1:17 Take your drink and vomit out on the streets. The lord wishes not to see a drunk at his doorstep."

1:18 Hannah answered and said, "I am not drunk, but am a woman of sorrow. I have drunk neither wine nor strong drink, but have poured my soul unto the doorstep of God."

1:19 Eli could see that Hannah was saddened and said to her, "What is it that makes you sorrow? Why do you come and weep?"

1:20 Hannah answered, "My womb is barren and I have not a son to give my husband. His other wife, Peninnah, has given my husband many sons and mocks me for my uselessness."

1:21 Eli could see that Hannah wanted a child desperately and took advantage of her saddened soul.

1:22 Eli said to Hannah, "Come with me and I shall give thee that which thou asketh of the lord."

1:23 The two went to the back of the temple and their Eli took off the raiment of Hannah and lay with her and whispered in her ear, "When thou sleep with a man of God, ye are blessed.

1:24 Tell no one of this blessing, lest the lord turn it into a curse."

1:25 After the seed of Eli spilled in the barren womb of Hannah, the two left and went their separate ways.

1:26 Hannah returned to Elkanah and ate and smiled and wept no more.

1:27 Elkanah rejoiced and embraced his wife and lay with her that night.

1:28 The lord heard Hannah's prayers and cursed Peninnah with a barren womb.

1:29 A crust developed on her genitalia, yellow and foul, so that no man wished to lie with her.

1:30 It came to pass that nine months after Hannah was blessed by Eli, she did bear a son and called him Samuel.

1:31 Elkanah rejoiced at what he thought was his son and went to Shiloh to give offerings unto God. But Hannah did not come and said to Elkanah, "I shall not go until the child be weaned from my breast. Then I shall go and present him unto the lord and there he shall abide."

1:32 Elkanah said to Hannah, "Do what ye know is good: tarry until thou hast weaned him and then we shall present him unto the lord, where he shall abide forever."

1:33 When Samuel was weaned off the breast of Hannah, they departed for Shiloh and took with them three bullocks, one ephah of flour and a bottle of wine.

1:34 They slew the bullocks and brought the child to Eli.

1:35 Hannah said to Eli, "Oh my lord, I am the woman who knelt before thee and begged thee for a blessing of a son and a curse for Peninnah.

1:36 For this son I have prayed and ye have given him to me. Blessed be the name of the lord.

As I have promised, my son shall be a child of God and shall know thee all his days."

1:37 Hannah then gave the child to Eli and said, "Raise him and teach him the ways of our lord."

1:38 Eli took Hannah aside and said to her, "Surely ye know this child is not from the seed of your husband, but from mine.

1:39 The lord has answered not your prayers, for ye asked to be given a child for your husband."

1:40 Hannah said to Eli, "Do ye think me a fool, that I don't know that this child is your bastard child?

1:41 I promised to give my son unto the lord and my promise shall be kept.

1:42 He is your child. Now you care for him."

2:1 The sons of Eli were sons of Belial; they were not of the lord.

2:2 They were corrupted, greedy priests who did abuse their powers given to them by God.

2:3 When any man offered sacrifice for the lord, the sons of Eli would come with a three toothed fleshhook and would stick the hook within the sacrifice; whatever the hook would remove, the priest would say belonged to him.

2:4 Before the fat of the flesh was burned, a servant of the priest would come and demand meat for the priests.

2:5 If the man giving sacrifice would say, "Wait, so that I may burn the fat and please the lord," the servant would take the flesh by force and give to the priests the meat and the fat.

2:6 All fair and pleasing young women who would come by the door of the tabernacle, the priests would lie with and claim that to fornicate with a man of God is a true blessing.

2:7 The priests would take young boys to the hidden areas of the temple and fondle and fondle them; a practice among priests that still takes place this day.

2:8 Samuel did not partake of the evil of these priests and administered unto the lord, being only a child girded with a linen ephod.

2:9 Every year, when the mother of Samuel would come to offer her sacrifices unto God, Hannah would give for Samuel a new coat.

2:10 For Hannah was pleased with Samuel, though he be the son of Eli. For the lord opened the womb of Hannah and Hannah conceived with Elkanah two sons and daughters.

2:11 Eli was an old man and heard of the wickedness and the greed which overcame the hearts of his sons.

2:12 Eli said to his sons, "Why do ye do such wicked things in plain sight of others?

2:13 For to abuse the priesthood and its power is a tradition which dates to the times of Moses; but one must be silent of this abuse.

2:14 Take not the sacrifices in witness of the man who gives the offering. Wait for the man to leave, then take of your fill that which is desired.

2:15 Now the children of Israel know of your wickedness and shall pray to the lord that God judge and punish you for such vileness.

2:16 For when man sins against man, a judge of man shall hear their testimony at trial; when a man sins against the lord, the lord shall not hear your testimony, but punish those harshly.

2:17 When you steal from sacrifice, you steal from God. That sacrifice is an offering for the lord.

2:18 Now the peoples of Israel know you are thieving from God and now demand punishment."

2:19 The sons of Eli heeded not the words of Eli, for they cared not for God.

2:20 It came to pass that a man of the lord came and spoke to Eli, saying, "Now sayeth the lord, what the fuck have you done to raise such spoiled and stupid children?

2:21 These children are now priests unto God and the lord loathe them fiercely.

2:22 They steal from the offerings made for the lord. They molest young boys. They lay beside numerous women who come to the temple.

2:23 This the lord knows, but cares not for. The lord is busy doing more important shit than to care about a couple of damned priests.

2:24 But now, the congregation of Israel knows. And the people of Israel constantly harass the lord, demanding justice be placed upon the sons of Eli.

2:25 Behold, the time of justice is coming, where the arms of Eli shall be cut off and the arms of the house of your father's, so that the generation of Eli shall be cut from the world.

2:26 The lord sees an enemy in the house of Eli and an enemy of the wealth of the children of Israel. The children of Eli shall die and never shall there be an old man in your house.

2:27 When the sons of Eli die, the lord shall take of their bodies and consume their eyes and feast with glutton their very hearts.

2:28 This shall be a sign of the lord's will. When the judgment of the lord comes down, both Hophni and Phinehas shall die together, within the same day.

2:29 The lord shall then raise up a faithful priest. One who isn't stupid enough to steal in the sight of the peoples of Israel.

2:30 And it shall come that Eli shall go to this man and beg him for bread, for wine and for water."

3:1 The child Samuel cared and tended to Eli the priest; and the word of God was rare in those days, for the lord began to abandon the people of earth and the children of Israel.

3:2 It came to pass that the eyes of Eli became wax, so that Eli was blind. Samuel would take Eli to his bedchamber and lie him down, so that Eli may rest.

3:3 One night, the lamp of God went out within the ark of the lord, while Samuel was sleeping upon his bed.

3:4 The lord came into the bedchamber of Samuel and whispered in his ear, "Samuel, Samuel."

3:5 Samuel awoke, saw who spoke and went into to room of Eli, saying, "Here I am, for you have called me." Eli said, "I did not call for you. Head back to bed and let me rest."

3:6 When Samuel laid down upon his bed, the lord spoke again, whispering, "Samuel, Samuel."

3:7 Again Samuel arose and went to the chambers of Eli, saying, "You called again me and I have come. What do you desire?"

3:8 Eli said to Samuel, "I wish for some damned sleep and to not be disturbed. I called for no one. Head back to bed."

3:9 Again, Samuel lied upon his bed and again the lord whispered, "Samuel, Samuel."

3:10 Samuel became angry and rushed to the chambers of Eli, saying frustratingly, "This is the third time I have heard my name being called and you are the only man in the temple.

3:11 Now, what do you fucking want. Some food. A glass of water.

Your damn chamber pot?"

3:12 Eli became livid and said, "Don't you ever dare talk that way to a man of God. I neither called nor spoke, you stupid bastard child.

3:13 Perhaps a ghost whispers your name in the hallways. Maybe a man outside your window is demanding your attention. Shit, perhaps the lord himself calls your name.

3:14 Now, go to your damn bed so that I may sleep in mine!"

3:15 Samuel went to his bed and again heard the whispers of the lord, saying, "Samuel, Samuel."

3:16 Samuel arose and said, "Who is it that keeps calling my name. Show yourself, unless you are a coward."

3:17 In great black smoke and fire, the lord revealed himself and said unto Samuel, "Do you dare call the lord your God a coward?"

3:18 Listen and listen well, for three times the lord did repeat himself. The lord hates repeating himself.

3:19 It shall come to pass that the lord shall do such a thing so evil and wicked that the ears of all the children of Israel will tingle.

3:20 On this day I shall will forth judgment upon Eli and his sons, ending the generation of Eli and his house.

3:21 For I have sent a messenger unto Eli and told him of the wickedness of the sons of Eli, who have become vile.

3:22 Because the sons of Eli continue their vileness, the lord shall slay them and shut the mouths of the whining little bastards of Israel."

3:23 The lord then left, leaving Samuel confused and scared upon his bed.

3:24 Samuel arose in the morning and rushed to the ark of the lord and behold, the lamp was out!

3:25 Samuel knew then that it was the lord who visited him within the night and that it was not some dream induced by the fungus which Samuel consumed for dinner.

3:26 Eli called Samuel and said "Samuel, come forth. I need to use my chamber pot and then dress and eat."

3:27 Samuel rushed to Eli and said, "Am I to believe it is you who called me this time?"

3:28 Eli replied, "Yes, it is I who called you this time. Tell me, what of the voices you heard last night?

3:29 Was it a man outside thine window. Whispers in the hall. Or were you merely dreaming?"

3:30 Samuel said to Eli, "It was neither, but the lord God who called me last night."

3:31 Eli said with fear trembling his voice, "And what did the lord have to say to you?"

3:32 Samuel then explained the fire, the smoke and the lamp which went out in the ark.

3:33 Eli demanded of Samson, "What did the lord say. What glorious message of peace and prosperity does the lord wish to convey to the people of Israel?"

3:34 Samuel said, "None, for the message of the lord was not of peace.

3:35 The lord said that he shall do such a thing so wicked and evil that all the congregation of Israel shall have their ears tingle.

3:36 The lord then said that on this day, your two sons will die and the lord shall feast with glutton their very hearts."

3:37 Eli bowed his head and said to Samuel "That is fine. Whatever the lord wants to do, let him do.

3:38 If he wishes to slay and feast upon my sons and curse again the peoples of Israel, let him.

3:39 Not as if I can stop the lord from doing it anyway."

4:1 The word of Samuel came through all of Israel. The armies of

Israel went out to do battle against the Philistines. The armies of Israel pitched beside Ebenezer, the Philistine stronghold in Aphek.

4:2 The Philistines destroyed Israel. Four thousand men of Israel were slaughtered that day.

4:3 God didn't care.

4:4 When the armies returned, the elders gathered together and said, "Why has the lord forsaken us and was not with us when we fought against the Philistine army?

4:5 Let us force the lord to fight with us. We shall take into battle the ark of the covenant.

4:6 Surely with the ark of the covenant, the lord shall protect us and help us, so that the ark shall not fall into Philistine hands."

4:7 So the armies of Israel marched towards Shiloh, so that they may take with them the ark of the covenant, which dwells between the two cherubims. The two sons of Eli, Hophni and Phinehas went with them, so that they may carry the ark into battle.

4:8 When the ark of the covenant was brought to the armies of Israel, all the soldiers yelled with such ferocity that the very ground shook.

4:9 The armies of Philistine heard the yelling and asked themselves, "Why the hell are the peoples of Israel yelling so fucking loudly?"

4:10 And when the peoples of Philistine heard the reason for the yelling, they said to themselves, "Oh shit, the ark of the covenant is with them.

4:11 Woe is us, for now their lord shall be with them and smite all the armies of Philistine.

4:12 This is the lord who caused great and terrible plagues to fall upon the peoples of Egypt and cast out the peoples in the lands of Jordan so that the intruders of Israel now dwell there.

4:13 Then again, this is also the lord who has cursed and destroyed the peoples of Israel with burning snakes, plagues and disease.

4:14 Perhaps their lord shall curse them again and it will be the Philistines who destroy them.

4:15 Let all the men of Philistine go to battle and show these people of Israel that their ark shall fail them."

4:16 So it was that the Philistines fought bravely against the armies of Israel and won. Thirty thousand men were slain that day.

4:17 The lord did not care.

4:18 The Philistines also captured the ark of the covenant and returned it to their lands, so that the ark of the covenant was in the hands of heathens.

4:19 Of this, the lord cared greatly.

4:20 Upon that battle the sons of Eli were slain. Both Hophni and Phinehas were slaughtered by the sword of the Philistines.

4:21 A man of the tribe of Benjamin ran to Shiloh and upon entering the city the man tore off his clothes, poured dust upon his head and wept.

4:22 When Eli heard the whimpering of the Benjamite, he asked him, "Why do you cry like a young widow?"

4:23 Bear in mind, Eli was a blind, ninety-eight-year-old, bitter man.

4:24 The Benjamite said to Eli, "I cry because my brothers in arms have been slain by the Philistine heathens, again.

4:25 The ark of the covenant did not protect us; nay, it cursed us and now belongs to the people of Philistine.

4:26 Your sons, Hophni and Phinehas, lie dead upon the battlefield and are now being consumed by the scavenging beasts of war; the vultures and hyenas surely feast upon their flesh."

4:27 When Eli heard the bad news, he arose to impart words of wisdom to the young man.

4:28 However, Eli tripped upon a stone, fell backwards, broke his frail neck and died.

4:29 Eli had judged Israel for forty years.

4:30 Eli's daughter in law and wife of Phinehas was carrying seed and when she heard that her husband was slain and that Eli had died, she wept and went into terrible pains of labour.

4:31 The midwife came by and saw that the wife of Phinehas was in labour and said to her, "Be blessed, for you shall soon give birth."

4:32 The wife of Phinehas, whose name is unknown because the bible cares not for women, said, "I care not, for this wretched child shall kill me as soon as it is ripped from my loins.

4:33 The glory of God has been stolen from all Israel, because the ark of the covenant has been stolen by the Philistines."

4:34 The wife of Phinehas then gave birth to a son. The midwife asked of her, "You have a son. Your purpose of life has been complete.

4:35 What shall your son be named?"

4:36 And the new mother said, "I care not what that wretched little bastard be named, for he has killed me."

4:36 So the midwife named the child Ichabod and the mother of Ichabod died shortly after giving birth.

5:1 The Philistines took the ark of the covenant and brought it into the city of Ashdod.

5:2 They took the ark and placed it within the house of their lord Dagon, so that lord Dagon shall mock the ark and the God of Israel.

5:3 At night, the lord came down upon the house of Dagon, too. The idol of Dagon and set it forth so that it appeared the idol of lord Dagon were bowing down and worshipping the ark of the covenant.

5:4 When the priests of Dagon rose and saw the idol of Dagon bowing down unto the ark, they believed a jester was amongst them.

5:5 They took the idol and set it in place.

5:6 That night, the lord came again into the house of Dagon and destroyed the idol of Dagon, so that the head and hands of Dagon were upon the ground, bowing down unto the ark of the covenant.

5:7 The body of Dagon was shattered and only a stump remained.

5:8 When the priests of Dagon arose and saw what had happened, they knew that a jester could not do such a thing.

5:9 For the idol of Dagon was strong and heavy.

5:10 They knew it was the lord of Israel which had destroyed the statue. So the priests of Dagon became angry against the one true God and pissed upon the ark of the covenant.

5:11 For this, the lord became angry and cursed the peoples of Ashdod with hemorrhoids large, puss filled, bleeding and painful.

5:12 All the peoples knew this was a curse from the lord of Israel and demanded that the ark be taken away from them.

5:13 The people of Ashdod, with bleeding assholes, took the ark of the covenant to the city of Gath, who took the ark and believed it a blessing.

5:14 The peoples of Gath also were cursed with bleeding and puss filled hemorrhoids so terrible that they died from blood loss, attempting to scratch and remove the hemorrhoids with a blade.

5:15 All the peoples of Gath sent forth the ark to the city of Ekron, who said, "Fuck you. We are not taking this accursed thing.

5:16 We know of your bleeding assholes and can see the yellow puss and red blood seep through your pants from the hemorrhoids the lord of Israel has cursed upon you."

5:17 The elders of Philistine gathered together, to discuss what shall be done with the damned ark.

5:18 It was decided that the ark shall be taken back to the peoples of Israel, so that they shall have the wrath and the curse of their own lord upon them.

5:19 For whichever city had the ark of the covenant became with great hemorrhoids, so that death became heavy within the city.

5:20 All the Philistines plagued with the curse of God cried so heavily that the screams could be heard within heaven.

5:21 This made the lord God very amused.

6:1 The ark of the covenant was in the land of the Philistines for seven months.

6:2 And the peoples of Philistine called their priests, their diviners and their kings, saying, "What the hell shall we ever do with this accursed ark of damnation?

6:3 We must send it back to the children of Israel. Let them keep this cursed thing."

6:4 And the diviners said, "If we send it back, we must not send it back empty.

6:5 For in taking this ark, we have committed trespass according to Israel custom.

6:6 An offering must be made, lest the cursed of the hemorrhoids stay with us forever."

6:7 The peoples asked, "What offering shall we make to appease the cruel and vengeful lord of Israel?"

6:8 All the priests and diviners said, "Make unto the lord of Israel five offerings of golden hemorrhoids and five offerings of golden mice.

6:9 For the hemorrhoids is the curse from their lord and the mice are what we have placed upon our buttocks so that their teeth shall gnaw the hemorrhoids."

6:10 And the artists and sculptures of the Philistines made five golden hemorrhoids and five golden mice to place within the ark of the covenant.

6:11 To ensure accuracy, the artists and sculptures would have men strip their clothing, so that they may sculpt from gold the largest hemorrhoid upon their buttocks.

6:12 The peoples of Philistine doubted and said to themselves, "When we return the ark, why would the lord of Israel lift his hand upon us and free us of his curse?

6:13 He is a wrathful and cruel lord. Would he not keep this curse upon us?"

6:14 And the priests of Philistine said, "When the lord of Israel cursed the people of Egypt, did he not lift the plagues from them when the Israelites left?

6:15 Surely the lord shall do the same to us and curse instead the peoples of Israel for letting us take his damn precious ark."

6:16 So the peoples of Philistine put the ark on a cart and placed beside the cart a coffer with the trespass offering of five golden hemorrhoids and five golden mice.

6:17 And the priests of Dagon said, "We shall place the cart two oxen, which has never seen the yolk.

6:18 If the oxen go the way of the coast to Bethshemesh, then it was truly the evilness of the lord of Israel which hast cursed us with these damn hemorrhoids.

6:19 If the oxen go not to Bethshemesh, then this is not a curse from their God; merely a random act of bullshit."

6:20 The oxen took the route straight to Bethshemesh, with men of Philistine walking behind it, to see the route which the oxen took.

6:21 Neither to the left nor the right did the oxen stray, so that they went straight to the city of Bethshemesh. The Philistines knew then that it was the lord who cursed them with bleeding rectums and puss filled hemorrhoids.

6:22 The men of Bethshemesh were harvesting the wheat of their fields when they saw the oxen carry into their city the ark of the covenant.

6:23 The men rejoiced and praised the lord for returning their precious ark.

6:24 The ark stopped within the field of Joshua and beside it was a large rock. The men took of the Philistine oxen and offered them

as sacrifice unto God for delivering back into their hands the ark of the covenant.

6:25 Levites were sent forth to remove the ark of the covenant and bring it back to its place in Shiloh.

6:26 The Levites opened the coffer beside the ark and behold, they saw the five golden hemorrhoids and the five golden mice.

6:27 All the peoples of Israel asked of themselves, "What strange custom is this, for the Philistines to return to us our ark with five golden mice and five golden hemorrhoids?

6:28 Perhaps their lord Dagon has a filthy fetish and the peoples of Philistine believe this a blessing to us.

6:29 Those heathens are weird. Really fucking weird. Now, let us slay a cow and burn its fat in glory to God while dancing around it nude."

6:30 Men of Bethshemesh then wondered, what if this be a trap?

6:31 What if the Philistines sent the ark forth with a man hiding within, so that the man shall rise in the night and slay us all?

6:32 Surely it is something our lord would ask of us to do.

6:33 So one man, only one, looked within the ark, to see if an assassin of Philistine was hiding within.

6:34 This angered greatly the lord, for a man unworthy looked within the ark of the covenant.

6:35 Thus the hand of the lord pressed heavily upon the city of Bethshemesh and slaughtered every man, women and child with a great slaughter.

6:36 Fifty thousand threescore and ten men were slain by God, with an unknown number of women and children. The bible doesn't care about women and children.

6:37 Those outside of Bethshemesh said, "Who is it that can stand before the holiness of our lord and survive?"

6:38 Messengers were then sent forth to Kirjathjearim, saying "The Philistines have returned to us the ark of our lord. Come and return it to its rightful place."

6:39 When word spread across the lands of the massacre of Bethshemesh, the people of Philistine laughed and said "Surely the lord of Israel has now cursed his very people."

6:40 When shall those of Israel learn to stop worshipping such a violent and hateful lord and worship a god worthy of their devotion?"

7:1 The men of Kirjathjearim came and took forth the ark to the house of Abinadab in the hill and sanctified Eleazar the son of Abinadab as priest, so that he may keep the ark.

7:2 It came to pass that when the ark was in the house of Abinadab, the lord abandoned the people of Israel.

7:3 For twenty years the lord ignored his people and for twenty years the peoples of Israel would pray offer sacrifice, cry and weep to their lord.

7:4 Samuel then spoke and said, "If you wish the lord to return unto us, then all must want him to return with all your heart and soul.

7:5 Rid yourself of the false gods and their idols, for if an image of Dagon, Ashtaroth, or Baalim be within the lands of Israel, the lord shall ignore us."

7:6 Most children of Israel destroyed their false idols. Some did not and said, "We wish not the lord to return to us.

7:7 For I remember the curses which the lord has sent to us. Our lord is cruel, Ashtaroth is not."

7:8 These peoples were quickly stoned to death, so that all who refused the lord were brutally slain.

7:9 The lord gazed down and was amused by the brutal deaths of those who were stoned.

7:10 Samuel, a servant of the lord, then said, "Gather all to Mizpeh and there I shall pray unto the lord."

7:11 All the congregation of Israel then gathered unto Mizpeh and brought forth offerings and sacrifice unto their lord and fastened that day, saying, "Surely we have sinned against God, for he has left us."

7:12 When the peoples of Philistine heard that all the peoples of Israel were gathered in Mizpeh, they gathered their armies and marched.

7:13 For they believed they could wipe out these invaders easily, for they are gathered all in one place.

7:14 They believed also that the lord of Israel shall curse them.

7:15 When the children heard of the Philistines marching, they became fearful, for they were afraid of the armies of Philistine.

7:16 All the peoples of Israel said to Samuel, "Pray to our God, so that he shall save us from these heathen bastards who come to slay us all."

7:17 Samuel then took a young lamb and burned it alive upon the stone as sacrifice unto God, saying "Take of this lamb and let its suffering please you.

7:18 Save us from this heathen army, if the lord be pleased by our sacrifice."

7:19 It was then that a great cloud of thunder and lightning rolled off from the horizon and went forth to the armies of Philistine.

7:20 The lord sent not this cloud. It was merely by chance that a storm happened upon that day.

7:21 When the rain and lightning came down upon the Philistines, they retreated, for they wished not their armour to rust, nor to be struck by lightning.

7:22 The men of Israel then chased the armies of Philistine in the rain and slew them until they came to Bethcar.

7:23 There Samuel placed a great stone and called the stone Ebenezer and said, "Here is where the lord came down to help us."

7:24 No more did the Philistines enter the lands of Israel, for they feared the lord of Israel shall curse them again.

7:25 They gave back the cities which they took from Israel, so that Ekron even unto Gath were reclaimed again by the Israelites.

7:26 Samuel then judged Israel the remaining days of his life. And if Samuel breathed, the people of Philistine invaded not the lands of Israel.

7:27 Every year, Samuel would travel to Bethel, to Gilgah, and to Mizpeh, preaching and boring all those who listened.

7:28 Upon his voyage he returned to Ramah, for there was his house. And he built an altar to the lord in Ramah.

8:1 It came to pass that when Samuel was old, he made his sons judges over Israel.

8:2 The name of the first-born son was Joel and the name of the second was Abiah: they were judges in Beersheba.

8:3 His sons followed not in the way of Samuel, for Samuel was a fair and wise judge. Both Joel and Abiah were wicked.

8:4 They would accept bribes, blackmail fellow men and would pervert judgment in favour of those who offered them the most coin.

8:5 The elders of Israel were furious for the crookedness of the sons of Samuel and came to Ramah to speak with Samuel.

8:6 They said unto Samuel, "Your sons are bastard judges, who pervert our laws and follow not the path of God.

8:7 Give us a king, so that they may rule over us, just like a king rules over every other nation."

8:8 Samuel said to the elders, "You have a king, for the lord God rules over us."

8:9 The elders replied, "The lord has done little for us and rules us

not like a king shall.

8:10 Kings act. The lord does not. Give us a king."

8:11 Samuel was displeased with the request for a king and prayed unto the lord for guidance.

8:12 The lord said unto Samuel, "Hearken not the words of Israel, for they reject not you, but I, that they wish the lord not reign over them.

8:13 Those selfish fools of Israel forget that it was the lord who has taken them out of Egypt so many years ago. They reject the lord and whore themselves unto false gods.

8:14 Hearken the voice of Israel and warn them. If a king they demand, a king they shall have.

8:15 Tell them of the king who shall reign over them."

8:16 And Samuel told all that which the lord said unto him to the elders of Israel and said, "This shall be the manner of how the king shall reign over you.

8:17 He shall take your sons and place them in his army, so that they be footmen, soldiers, horsemen and chariot riders.

8:18 He shall make them captains over thousands and enslave them. He shall force them to reap the harvest of the fields and to make chariots and instruments of wars.

8:19 Your daughters he shall take. Those who please his eye shall be his concubines. Those who do not please his eyes shall be his maids.

8:20 He shall take your fields, your vineyards, your olive yards and take them for himself.

8:21 A tax of ten percent he shall enforce on all. Like tithe, but it'll be given unto a man, so shall you be angry for it.

8:22 He shall take your slaves, your servants, your maids, your concubines, your cattle, your flocks and your virginity.

8:23 When you all cry out unto the lord to be rid of this king, your cries shall fall on empty ears. The lord God shall not help you."

8:24 Still the elders of Israel said, "Nay, we doubt your words. Give us a king, so that we shall be ruled by a man who shall protect us rather than a God who curses us.

8:25 For years we have heard of the lord freeing us from Egypt. That was many generations ago.

8:26 What has he done for us now. Nothing but curse us, and slay the peoples of Bethshemesh for looking in the damn ark.

8:27 We shall be like the other nations, ruled by one king."

8:28 Samuel said the words of the elders unto the lord and the lord said, "Those ungrateful bastards now mock the lord who did free them from Egypt?

8:29 They shall truly be cursed by their king."

9:1 Now there was a man of Benjamin, whose name was Kish the son of Abiel, who was a mighty man of power.

9:2 He had a son named Saul, who was a good man. He was a strong, young and tall man and the most attractive of all Israelite men.

9:3 The women would gaze upon Saul in lust and their vaginas became moist that they would believe their time of uncleanliness came upon them.

9:4 It came to pass that the asses of Kish escaped and Kish said to Saul, "Take a servant and go look for my asses."

9:5 Saul, though handsome, was stupid and said to his father, "I need not go, for I know where your ass be.

9:6 You now sit upon it."

9:7 Kish slapped Saul and said, "My donkeys, you idiot, my donkeys!"

9:8 Saul then took his servant and searched for the donkeys of his father Kish.

9:9 They went through mount Ephraim and the lands of Shalisha, but found them not. They passed through the lands of Shalim and the lands of the Benjamites and found them not.

9:10 When they came to the lands of Zuph, Saul said to his servant, "Let us go home, for I'm tired and our father shall now worry about us than his donkeys."

9:11 And the servant said, "Let us not, for we are near a city of a prophet and a great man of God.

9:12 We shall go and ask him, for surely he shall know where the donkeys are."

9:13 Saul said to the servant, "Surely this prophet will want payment for such things and we have nothing to offer. Our bread is eaten and our wine drunk."

9:14 The servant then said, "I have a few shekels of silver. Surely this shall be enough to pay the prophet for his vision of your father's ass."

9:15 Saul then snickered and believed the prophet shall have a dream of his father's buttocks.

9:16 As they went up the hill to the city, they saw young maidens coming to draw water from the well and they asked of the maidens, "Is this be where the prophet lives?"

9:17 The maidens answered, "Yes, now hurry for today the prophet shall offer a great many sacrifices for his people.

9:18 He shall be by the gates of the city so that when you enter, you shall see him.

9:19 He'll be the one with a large knife and many carcasses of beasts around him."

9:20 And when the men came into the city, Samuel came to greet them, for the lord said unto Samuel, "The tall one is the one who shall be king of Israel."

9:21 Samuel said unto Saul, "Behold, the donkeys of your father have been found. Tell me, do you desire all of Israel?"

9:22 Saul said, "Yes, for as all men I am greedy and lust for money and power.

9:23 But I am a Benjamite, which be the smallest tribe of Israel. And my family be of the smallest families of Benjamin. Why do you ask me such a question?"

9:24 Samuel took Saul and his servant and placed them within the high chambers of the temple and placed Saul upon the chief chair, which was the chair of greatest honour.

9:25 Samuel said unto his cook, "Bring these men the finest meal you can cook."

9:26 And the cook took of a young lamb the flanks and the backstrap and prepared it with great many spices and served it to Saul and his servant.

9:27 And Saul and Samuel did eat together, whilst Saul wondered if this prophet was under the influence of magical herbs.

9:28 Samuel and Saul then returned from the temple towards the gates and Samuel said to Saul, "Have your servant leave us, so that I may speak to you in private."

9:29 Saul sent away his servant and Samuel said to Saul, "Let me show you now the word of God."

10:1 Samuel took a vial of anointing oil and poured it over the head of Saul and Saul said unto him, "I wish to pay for the vision in silver shekels, not in unholy sex."

10:2 Samuel said to Saul, "Fear not, for you need not pay for the vision nor shall your ass be plunged.

10:3 For the lord has given me a vision of your arrival and has said unto me that you shall be given the inheritance of all of Israel.

10:4 You shall be now the king of all Israel.

10:5 When you leave this city, you shall find two men by the sepulcher of Rachel, in the border of Benjamin and Zelzah. They will tell you where your father's asses be found and that your father

sorrows for you and worries of you.

10:6 Then you shall go forward and come upon the plains of Tabor. There you will meet three with men going to God in Bethel, one carrying three kids, one carrying three loaves of bread and another with a bottle of wine.

10:7 These men shall salute you and place in your hands two loaves of bread.

10:8 Then you shall go to the hill of God, which is in the garrison of the Philistines. It shall come to pass that when you come to this city, a group of prophets shall meet you with a psaltery, a harp, a tabret and a hashish pipe.

10:9 They shall give you the hash pipe and when you inhale the sweet smoke from the pipe, the spirit of the lord shall overcome you and you shall prophesy with these men and turn into another man.

10:10 Behold, these three signs shall come and let you know that you are chosen to be king of all Israel, for the lord walks with you.

10:11 You shall then go down and meet me in Gilgal, where I shall offer great burnt offerings and sacrifice in your name.

10:12 Seven days you shall wait in Gilgal, until I come to meet you.

10:13 Saul left and the three signs of Samuel came true.

10:14 Two men met with Saul by the sepulcher of Rachel and told Saul that his father's asses have been found and that his father worries for him.

10:15 Saul told these men, "Tell my father to fear not, for soon I shall be king of Israel."

10:16 Three men then passed Saul, one carrying three children, another three loaves of bread and the last a bottle of wine.

10:17 These three men saluted to Saul and gave him two loaves of bread. Saul said to them, "Good of you for showing the respect I deserve, for soon I shall be king of Israel."

10:18 Saul them met a company of prophets and smoked of their hashish pipe and the calming spirit of the lord overcame Saul.

10:19 Saul then spoke with the prophets and prophesied with them, so that the people of Israel gazed upon Saul and asked of them, "Who is this man, of the son of Kish, who prophesies with these prophets. Is Saul a prophet himself?"

10:20 Thus a proverb spread across Israel. 'Is Saul among the prophets?" This proverb became a catch phrase among Israel, as well as 'who let the oxen out?' and 'where the beef?'

10:21 When Saul ended his prophesying, he came to the high place.

10:22 Saul's uncle said unto him and his servant, "Where the hell have you been?" and Saul said, "I went forth to seek the asses of my father.

10:23 When we found them not, we sought out the prophet Samuel."

10:24 The uncle asked Saul, "And what did Samuel say?"

10:25 Samuel answered, "That the donkeys were found." Saul mentioned not any word of becoming king, for Saul knew his uncle a parasite and would wish a comfortable job for himself.

10:26 Samuel then gathered the peoples of Israel unto Mizpeh and said to them, "The lord God says unto you that he hath brought you out of the lands of the Egyptians and freed thee from the slavery of Pharaoh and out of the kingdom which has oppressed you."

10:27 And all the peoples of Israel said, "Yes, we know, for the lord won't let us forget.

10:28 Whenever wickedness befalls us, the lord tells us how he freed us from Pharaoh.

10:29 That was generations ago, so that our ancestors were the ones who were freed from Pharaoh. What does the lord do for us now?"

10:30 Samuel said, "The lord has done what you wish of him, for you people have rejected the lord and shall demand a king in his place.

10:31 Today that king shall be named by God, so that you shall have a man rule over you and your generations other than the lord."

10:32 Samuel said unto the men of Israel, "In this satchel are the names of the twelve tribes of Israel."

10:33 This was a lie, for each parchment was written BENJAMIN upon it, so that Samuel drew out the tribe of Benjamin.

10:34 Samuel then took another satchel and said, "In this satchel be all the names of the families of Benjamin."

10:35 Another lie, for the parchment within the satchel was only written MATRI, so that Samuel drew Matri from the satchel.

10:36 Again, Samuel said, "In this satchel be the names of all the men of Matri." Another lie, for the parchment all said SAUL, SON OF KISH.

10:37 And when Saul the son of Kish was drawn, the peoples rejoiced, for they knew that Saul shall be their new king.

10:38 But Saul was not among the crowd and when they searched for Saul, they found him asleep amongst the trash of the city, with a hashish pipe in his hand, freshly used.

10:39 Men of Israel took Saul and placed him in front of the peoples of Israel. And Saul stood taller than all the men and the women lusted for him.

10:40 Samuel said to the people, "Behold, your new king, which the lord has chosen for you. Is there none like him among the people?"

10:41 And the children of Israel rejoiced and said, "God save the king."

10:42 Samuel then told the peoples of Israel the manner of the king and his kingdom and wrote it down within a book.

10:43 This book is not to be found in the bible, for it is a boring book. So boring that it wasn't even placed within the bible. You know it must be really fucking boring if it was excluded for being that dull.

10:44 Saul then went home to Gibeah with a band of mercenaries to act as royal bodyguards.

10:45 Those of Belial asked themselves, "How can this man protect us, for he is not fit to be king.

10:46 He was under the aroma of hashish when announced king. Surely such a man shall doom us."

10:47 And the peoples of Belial despised Saul and sent him no gifts. Saul cared not, for the gifts he received from the others were great and numerous.

11:1 Nahash the Ammonite came up and encamped against Jabeshgilead. The men of Jabeshgilead said unto Nahash, "Make us a covenant, so we can have peace between us."

11:2 Nahash said, "Fine, I shall make with you a covenant.

11:3 There shall be peace between us, if I can take my dagger and plunge it into your right eye.

11:4 For I wish this to be a city of pirates and pirates all have one eyes, with a patch over them."

11:5 And the elders of Jabeshgilead said, "We wish not our right eyes gouged, or anything gouged from us.

11:6 Yet, we desire peace greatly from you, otherwise we know you shall slay us.

11:7 Give us seven days. If in seven days no men of Israel come to save us, we shall take your offer and you shall gouge out our right eyes."

11:8 The men of Jabeshgilead sent out messengers all over the lands of Israel. When the message reached Gibeah, the men of the fields were weeping as they harvested corn.

11:9 Behold, Saul came forth and asked his men, "Why do you all weep?" And the men told him of the people of Jabeshgilead.

11:10 When Saul heard of the plight of the people of Jabeshgilead, the anger of the lord swelled within him.

11:11 Saul took an ox and with his hands shred the beast to pieces. He sent pieces of the oxen all over Israel via messenger and said, "Whosoever helps not those of Jabeshgilead, I shall do this to their sons."

11:12 Not wanting some maniac to shred their sons to death, the peoples of Israel gathered together to fight for Jabeshgilead.

11:13 They numbered three hundred thousand men of Israel and thirty thousand men of Judah.

11:14 Messengers were sent to Jabeshgilead and they said, "Tomorrow, when the sun beats hottest, we shall come and slay in your name."

11:15 And the men of Jabeshgilead replied, "Tomorrow, we shall come out and do what is good unto you."

11:16 On the morrow, Saul put the people in three companies and on the morning, they came to the camp of the Ammonites and slaughtered them all until the heat of the day.

11:17 When the sun was hottest, they took a break and drank. For mass slaying is hard, hard work.

11:18 Then they chased the rest of the Ammonites and scattered them amongst the lands, so that no Ammonite was with another.

11:19 The peoples of Jabeshgilead praised Saul and blessed his name.

11:20 And Saul said unto the people of Israel, "Glory be this day, for today the lord hath brought salvation into Israel."

11:21 Samuel then said to the people, "Come, let us go to Gilgal.

11:22 There we shall crown Saul and he shall be the true king of Israel."

11:23 And the people of Israel went to Gilgal and there they made Saul the king of Israel before God. And many peace offerings and sacrifices were given to the lord and the peoples rejoiced that day.

12:1 Samuel said unto all of Israel, "Behold, I have hearkened your voice, gave in to your demands and gave you your damn king.

12:2 The king walks before you and my sons walk among you. Behold, I am old and gray-headed. My time amongst you shall soon be gone.

12:3 As lord is my witness, I ask of you this. Whose ox have I taken. Whose donkeys have I taken. Whose concubines did I fuck. Did I ever defraud or oppress any one of you?"

12:4 And the people of Israel said, "No one, for you are an honest man of God."

12:5 Samuel said unto the people, "Damn right, yet when I tell you all to trust in me and trust in the lord, none hearken my words and you all demand a king.

12:6 A fucking king; a mortal man to replace the one true lord, who ruled over all for generations.

12:7 Behold, it was the lord who has taken Aaron and Moses and taught them the lord's magic and split apart seas.

12:8 The lord God did strike the peoples of Egypt with ten plagues and curses, so that you may come and dwell here in the lands of the covenant."

12:9 The children of Israel said to Samuel, "The lord cursed not just the peoples of Egypt, but the people of Israel as well.

12:10 Fiery snakes came and bit us with venomous teeth; the mouth of the lord came forth from the earth and consumed families; quail came when we asked for meat and the very flesh which the lord delivered upon us the lord made rot in our mouths, so that a plague struck us.

12:11 We remember the good which the lord has done. We remember the lord's wickedness as well.

12:12 After our freedom from slavery from Egypt, the lord has sold us as slaves to other nations.

12:13 To Chushanrishathaim the king of Mesopotamia, Jabin king of Canaan, to the Philistines and even to the Ammonites did the lord sell us.

12:14 But a king, a king shall not sell us. A king shall protect us."

12:15 Samuel then said, "A king may protect you from your enemies, but who shall protect you from your king?

12:16 For when your king becomes corrupt and oppress and exploit you, none shall come to your rescue. None shall you have to blame bur yourselves.

12:17 Do not expect the lord to come and save you, for you have sinned against God.

12:18 Remember, it was your sins which had the lord sell his own people to those he loathes. And still, did the lord not deliver all again from servitude?

12:19 Blessed be the name of the lord and cursed be those who go against him and keep not his laws and his statutes.

12:20 Today is the day of the harvest of the wheat. Behold the anger of your God."

12:21 And the lord sent down great rain and thunder upon the fields of the wheat, so that none shall go and harvest the wheat from their fields.

12:22 Those who sent out their servants lost their servants, for the lord struck them down with great bolts of lightning.

12:23 All the peoples of Israel were angry at the lord and said unto Samuel, "Therefore we be angry at our lord.

12:24 For he demands from us fear. If we do not as he says, or anger him, he shall destroy us.

12:25 Many times we have angered him and his wrath was brought down upon us and we knew not how we angered him.

12:26 Have the lord stop this nonsense, so that we may go and harvest our wheat."

12:27 Thus the lord stopped and came down in a great pillar of smoke and fire and struck fear again into the people of Israel.

12:28 For out of the pillar came great fountains of fire, which consumed a great many men of Israel.

12:29 Samuel stood beside the lord and said, "Fear not, for the lord loves you and shall show you great mercy.

12:30 For the lord will not forsake his own people, which he has made and chosen as his own.

12:31 Remember, the lord has taught you good from evil, how not to sin and how to live the right way.

12:32 Fear the lord and follow his ways. Those who do not shall be cursed for generations and generations.

12:33 And all of Israel shall be consumed, even the king, if you do not worship God."

13:1 For two years did Saul reign over the people of Israel; and on his second year Saul chose three thousand men of Israel to fight. Two thousand were with Saul on Michmash in mount Bethel and the remaining thousand were with the son of Saul, Jonathan, in the lands of Gibeah, in the tribe of Benjamin.

13:2 With his thousand men Jonathan did smite the Philistine garrison which was in Geba, which angered the Philistines. Saul, however, was pleased and blew his trumpet, so that all of Israel could hear.

13:3 Word spread of the smiting at Geba and all the men of Israel believed the lord was with them.

13:4 Every man came to Saul at Gilgal, so that they may fight beside him and conquer more lands for the nation of Israel.

13:5 The Philistines would not let such a defeat go unpunished. They gathered thirty thousand chariots of iron, six thousand horsemen and their footmen numbered greater than the sands of the shore.

13:6 This Philistine army made camp at Michmash, eastward from

Bethaven.

13:7 When the peoples of Israel saw the multitude of the Philistines, they became scared and trusted not in God.

13:8 For they learned the lord could not be trusted.

13:9 Every man, woman and child hid from the sight of the Philistines.

13:10 In caves, crevices, swamps, behind rocks, in bushes, in thickets, in forests, in pits; any place they could, they hid.

13:11 Some men of Israel went over the Jordan and encamped in the lands of Gad and Gilead, believing the Philistines would not take these lands, since these lands originally did not belong to them.

13:12 The lands of Gad and Gilead were conquered from other peoples when the children of Israel came.

13:13 Saul, the king of Israel, retreated not, for Samuel had said unto him, "Fear not, for the lord shall protect you and your people.

13:14 One week shall you stay in Gilgal. Wait for me until I arrive.

13:15 This brought comfort to those who remained with Saul, for they were trembling at the thought of the Philistine army.

13:16 Seven days did Saul wait, but Samuel did not come. Samuel was busy hunting deer in the forests which lay beside the fields of corn.

13:17 For the flesh of venison was tasty in those parts.

13:18 Saul worried for Samuel and believed him captured by the captains of the Philistines.

13:19 Saul demanded that two offerings be made; a peace offering and a burnt offering, so that the lord shall gaze down and remember Samuel.

13:20 Saul then built two altars and slew the beasts and made two offerings unto God.

13:21 When the offerings were set to burn, Samuel finally arrived and said unto Saul, "What the fuck are you doing, for you are not a priest!

13:22 This shall anger God, for sure you have fucked up the sacrifice.

13:23 I can see even now that the caul above the liver was not removed. This shall anger the lord and the lord shall curse us all.

13:24 If you waited for me, then Israel shall be fine.

13:25 Yet you did not and now your foolishness and impatience shall curse us.

13:26 The lord himself knows you unfit and shall take from you the kingdom of Israel and hand it to a man who shall seek the heart of the lord."

13:27 When the men of Israel who remained with Saul heard what Samuel did say, they abandoned Saul, so that only six hundred men remained.

13:28 The army of the Philistines split into three companies, so that one company marched towards Ophrah, in the lands of Shaul, another towards Bethhoron and the last marched towards the border that looks towards the valley of Zeboim, in the wilderness.

13:29 Now, there was no smith to be found in the lands of Israel, for the peoples of Israel depended upon the Philistines to sharpen their swords and their spears.

13:30 This let the smiths of Philistine gaze and examine the armour and the weaponry of Israel, so that they shall exploit their weaknesses.

13:31 In time, the Philistines learned all they could of Israel's weaponry and said, "Let the children of Israel sharpen their own swords."

13:32 So the smiths of Philistine sharpened not the weapons of the Israelites, though they still sharpened their sickles, their pitchforks, their mattocks, their coulters and their goads.

13:33 For the smiths of Philistines would gladly take the money of the peoples of Israel and sharpen their tools, but not their weapons.

13:34 In time, the armies of Israel had not a sharp sword nor spear in any of the hands of the soldiers, though Saul and Jonathan were with sword sharpened and strong.

13:35 And the garrison of the Philistines went out to the passage of Michmash.

14:1 It came to pass that Jonathan the son of Saul said to his armourbearer, "Let us cross the garrison and take the fight to the Philistines." But Jonathan did not tell his father.

14:2 For Saul fought underneath a pomegranate tree in Migron, with about six hundred men.

14:3 After each battle Saul fought, the pomegranates would fall from the tree and the men would eat of the sweet fruit.

14:4 Ahiah the son of Ahitub, Ichabod's brother, was a priest and wore an ephod and would bless Saul and the pomegranates. Ahiah would eat in gluttony the pomegranates and bless the slaughter which caused the sweet fruit to fall.

14:5 Jonathan did not fight beside the pomegranate tree. Jonathan did not like the taste of pomegranates, but preferred the taste of blood.

14:6 Between the passages which Jonathan wished to cross were two sharp rocks. One named Bozez, the other Seneh.

14:7 Jonathan said to his armourbearer, "Come, we shall climb these rocks and slaughter the Philistine people. For the lord wishes these peoples dead, as they are uncircumcised heathens."

14:8 And his armourbearer said unto him, "I shall do what you say is good, for I know that which is in your heart is good."

14:9 The two men then embraced and engaged in unholy sex, before climbing the rocks towards the Philistine army.

14:10 Jonathan then said to his armourbearer, "What we did, we did in disgrace to God. The lord hates faggots."

14:11 Because of this, the lord may not be with us and may give us into the hands of the Philistines.

14:12 When we cross this path and the Philistines rush us to fight, we shall flee. It shall be a sign that the lord hath seen our wicked love and wish us dead.

14:13 But if the Philistines not fight or wait for us to come to them, then come to them we shall.

14:14 We shall take our swords and plunge them deep within the chests of those heathen bastards whose foreskins still remain."

14:15 The armourbearer of Jonathan then asked, "I wonder how the uncircumcised feels, for many a night I wished to have the foreskin plunged within me."

14:16 Jonathan replied to him, "It feels good, my friend. It feels good."

14:17 As the two men climbed the last rock to reach the Philistine garrison, the heathens saw them and laughed, saying, "Here comes the Hebrews, climbing from their holes.

14:18 Come and fight us, you cowards that hide in the dirt."

14:19 Jonathan said to his armourbearer, "This is the sign, for they shall stay and we shall come to them.

14:20 The lord did not sell us and these heathens shall be slew by our hands."

14:21 Jonathan and his armourbearer climbed the rock and drew their swords and slew the garrison which be in front of them.

14:22 Twenty men did these two men slay, in about a half-acre of land. A rather pathetic slaughter, but this was Jonathan's first mass murder.

14:23 Jonathan, stained in the blood of his enemies, looked towards the heavens and said in a mighty voice, "My God, look at the men which I have slain for you.

14:24 If you approve, show me, so that I shall know the will of the lord."

14:25 The lord then showed his approval and the ground shook beneath the very feet of Jonathan.

14:26 The jaw of the lord came from the earth, with teeth of trees and rocks and consumed the very corpses of the men Jonathan had slain.

14:27 This was a sign unto Jonathan that the lord was pleased with his killings.

14:28 The watchmen of Saul, who were with him at the pomegranate tree in Migron, noticed that the men of Saul retreated during the night; for these men were cowards and wished not to be slain by the Philistines.

14:29 Saul said to his men, "Take number of those who stayed faithful with me and fight beside me." And the men did and took note that Jonathan was not there.

14:30 Saul said to his men, "Take with us the ark of the lord, for it shall bring us a blessing from the lord when we fight these heathens."

14:31 Thus Saul and his men took the ark to the Philistines, so that they may fight with the lord.

14:32 And the noise of the Philistines could be heard from a great distance and struck within the people of Saul great fear.

14:33 When the men of Israel came upon the army of the Philistines, the lord blessed the people with Saul and cursed the people of Philistine.

14:34 Behold, the men of Philistine became drunk and turned their swords upon one another, so that the hands of the Philistines slain their brethren.

14:35 Saul and his men watched and laughed at the glorious slaughter of the lord.

14:36 They sat down, and ate pomegranates which they brought forth and waited until the numbers were low, then attacked.

14:37 The men of Israel which lay in hiding, took notice and saw Saul and his men slay the surviving Philistines and believed that Saul slew them all. They gathered their arms and joined Saul in a glorious and bloody slaughter.

14:38 Saul chased the remaining heathens unto Bethaven, constantly cutting at their heels until they fell, injured and dead.

14:39 All of Israel rejoiced and said, "Surely the lord saved us this day."

14:40 Then the peoples of Israel became distressed, for Saul said unto them, "The lord did not save you today, but your king.

14:41 Until all of Israel be saved from the Philistines, none shall eat. All shall feast as gluttons the day each Philistine bastard lay dead and rotting."

14:42 Thus none of the peoples of Israel ate food, for fear of Saul's curse.

14:43 The men of Israel marched towards the forest and behold, there was a hive of bees upon the tree, with honey fresh and sweet.

14:44 None ate of the honey for fear of Saul's curse.

14:45 Yet Jonathan, who heard not the curse and joined with his father to brag about his slaughter, took of his rod, dipped it within the hive and ate of the honey.

14:46 One of the men of Saul said to Jonathan, "What did you do, to be cursed by your very father?

14:47 For Saul himself cursed every man who shall eat before the death of all Philistines."

14:48 And Jonathan said, "I am the son of Saul. His curse shall not apply to me.

14:49 Surely my father will forgive me for a little honey.

14:50 For this honey shall make me strong and the strength shall be used to slay every fucking Philistine who crosses my path.

14:51 Go forth and eat, so that the food give you strength to do my father's will."

14:52 The peoples did not eat and were weakened without food.

14:53 Still, with their hunger, they slew every Philistine from Michmash to Aijalon. At Aijalon, the armies of Saul grew weakened, until they could starve themselves no longer.

14:54 The people took of the cattle of the Philistines and ate them alive, so that the blood and the flesh be feasted that day.

14:55 Every man took of the Philistines sheep, oxen, goats and ate them alive, so that the very cries of the beasts echoed with every bite of the people of Israel.

14:56 Saul heard of this, grew angry and said, "Behold, mine people have sinned this day and ate the very blood of the lambs, which belonged not to man, but to God.

14:57 Surely my curse has fallen upon you, for those that have eaten, have eaten of the blood.

14:58 Go now, gather your ox, your sheep, your goats and slay them here. Eat of their flesh, but not of their blood, if you all be so hungry."

14:59 The men went and gathered their cattle and their flocks and ate of their flesh, but not of their blood, for even after feasting upon the Philistine's beasts like predators, they were hungry still.

14:60 Saul then built an altar unto the lord and burned upon it the carcass of the Philistines and danced around it naked, pleasing the lord.

14:61 Saul then said, "Let us go down by night and slay our enemies in the dark, so that by morning, when they awake, they shall be dead." And his men said, "Do whatever you believe is good."

14:62 Saul then asked of God, "Shall I do this and slay the enemies at night while they sleep?"

14:63 And the lord answered him not, for God was still busy fucking the corpses of the twenty Philistines which Jonathan slew.

14:64 Saul was in fear, for he believed the sins of his people had angered God and that is why the lord ignored him.

14:65 Saul gathered his men and said unto them, "You all have doomed Israel for feasting upon the blood of the beasts as though you were God himself!

14:66 Come now and stand before me, those who ignored my curse and did eat before the people of Philistine be slain."

14:67 And the men who did eat came forth and Saul said unto them, "Know now that you shall be cursed. Your seed shall be only women and each shall be a whore.

14:68 No sons shall you have; those that have sons, they shall die this day."

14:69 It was then one of the men said, "But Saul, what of Jonathan, for he ate as well."

14:70 Saul then said, "What. My son, Jonathan, did eat and for this I have cursed him?

14:71 Bring him forth."

14:72 Jonathan came forth and Saul asked him, "What lie does this man say, to avoid the curse which I have spoken?"

14:73 And Jonathan said, "This man lies not, but I did eat.

14:74 For in the woods there was sweet honey and I dipped a rod in that honey and ate of it.

14:75 The sweet and sticky honey was a great blessing unto me and gave me strength."

14:76 Saul then said, "For this honey, surely you shall die."

14:77 And Jonathan said, "Die. For a little fucking honey?

14:78 It was only some damn honey. Sweet nectar from the bees. Why should I be cursed for some god damned honey?"

14:79 And Saul said, "I must, for I have cursed those all who shall eat before the slaying of the Philistines be complete."

14:80 Jonathan then said, "Then remove this curse, so that I will not die for a little sweet snack in the forests."

14:81 Saul said to him, "I cannot, for a curse is a curse, and cannot be removed.

14:82 If the lord will it, it must be."

14:83 Jonathan then said, "But it is not the will of the lord.

14:84 It was you who claimed the curse, not God. Remove the curse, so that I may live."

14:85 Saul then said, "Fine, I shall remove the curse and you shall not die for a little honey."

14:86 One of the men then said, "If you remove the curse from Jonathan, then must you remove it from us as well.

14:87 For surely the curse that affected Jonathan, when gone, shall not harm us."

14:88 Saul agreed and the curse was lifted.

14:89 This angered God greatly, for the lord thought that finally that little faggot Jonathan shall be slain by his father.

14:90 Saul then returned home and fought not the Philistines that day.

14:91 Throughout all the reign of Saul was their war on all the borders of Israel. Against Moab, against the children of Ammon, against Edom, against Zobah, against the Philistines and against any other nation Saul discovered, he fought against.

14:92 For Saul was a racist fucker, who believed those not of Israel shall die.

14:93 The kings of the Amalekites did Saul trick. Saul hosted them in the lands of Israel, to trick them in believing peace. Upon the dinner table, the food of the kings of Amalek were poisoned and they died of the dinner that day.

14:94 The sons of Saul were Jonathan, Ishui and Melchishua. The daughters of Saul were Merah and Michal. Holy crap, the bible mentioned women!

14:95 The name of Saul's wife was Ahinoam the daughter of Ahimaaz and the captain of his army was Abner the son of Ner, Saul's uncle.

14:96 Forever in Saul's reign was war raged among Israel. Whenever Saul knew of a young, strong and mighty man, Saul would force them into his armies, so that they may defend the people of the lord.

14:97 Before they became in the army, Saul would have them come to his bedchamber and would rape them.

14:98 For Saul, like his son Jonathan, was also a faggot and enjoyed the unholy lust which was a sin against God.

15:1 Samuel said unto Saul, "The lord sent me to anoint you their king of Israel. Now hearken the voice of God and do as he command.

15:2 Thus says the lord of lords, I remember that which Amalek did to Israel, those hundreds of years ago.

15:3 Now go, slaughter all that which be Amalek. Spare not their women, their children, their oxen, nor their flocks. Kill every damn thing which be Amalek, so that the lord shall be pleased with you."

15:4 Saul asked of Samuel, "What is it which the Amalek's did, so many years ago?"

15:5 Samuel replied, "I don't know. It matters not.

15:6 As long as the lord remembers, that is all that matters."

15:7 So Saul gathered his peoples in Telaim. Two hundred thousand footmen of Israel and ten thousand men of Judah.

15:8 Saul marched to a city of Amalek and laid to wait in the valley.

15:9 Saul said unto the Kenites of the city, "Get out and flee that which is Amalek, for we have come here to destroy them.

15:10 For showing kindness to Israel when they did leave Egypt, your lives shall be spared. This time."

15:11 Thus the Kenites left the cities of Amalek and Saul destroyed those of Amalek.

15:12 But Saul was a faggot and weak in the eyes of the lord. Saul did not kill all the children, nor all the women. Saul kept also the fattest calves, the fattest sheep and even spared king Agag.

15:13 All that was vile, revolting and useless to Saul, did Saul destroy. Those that disgusted not Saul, or was of value, Saul kept.

15:14 This really, really pissed off the lord.

15:15 The word of the lord came to Samuel and said unto him, "Your king is weak and pathetic.

15:16 The lord did send him for genocide and genocide did he not complete.

15:17 Still, the things of Amalek walk the earth. Women, children, beasts. Even their king Agag breathes upon the lands of the lord."

15:18 Samuel cried, for Samuel wished not the lord to be angry.

15:19 When Samuel arose early to meet with Saul, Saul said to him, "Blessed be I of the lord, for I have killed all that of the Amalekites."

15:20 Samuel then said, "Then why do I see these flocks, these calves, these women, these children before my very eyes?"

15:21 Saul answered, "The flocks and the calves are the spoils of battle, so that we may sacrifice them unto our God.

15:22 The women and the children we spared, for surely such a loving and merciful lord of Israel wishes not the innocent to be slain."

15:23 Samuel slapped Saul and said to him, "You fool. Surely you cannot be that damn stupid.

15:24 The lord wishes all the things of Amalek to be destroyed. Men, women, children, beast, you were sent to kill them all.

15:25 Yet I see you spared that which you like and find innocent, or of worth. The lord shall not tolerate such weakness.

15:26 The lord shall curse you for this incompetence and when that curse comes, I shall not be there."

15:27 Saul spoke to Samuel, "Why does it matter if a few women, a few children, are spared?

15:28 They are not evil, nor do they fight us in battle. Surely, they don't deserve death.

15:29 These calves, they were brought to give offerings unto God. The lord likes offerings, the lord should be fucking happy I brought such multitudes of unblemished animals to be burnt on some damn stones!"

15:30 Samuel said to Saul, "The lord likes burnt offerings, but the lord demanded obedience; an obedience you lacked this day.

15:31 Your sparing of the young and the women is as a rebellion against God and rebellion is witchcraft.

15:32 Because you disobeyed the word of the lord and slew not all that which is Amalek, you shall not be king of Israel."

15:33 Saul picked up his sword and said to Samuel, "Then allow me to complete the word of God and I shall slay all the beasts, the women and the children that be with me."

15:34 Samuel said to Saul, "Your sin is done. All that which you do shall not cover up your blatant incompetence and your weakness with genocide.

15:35 When you return to Israel, I shall not come.

15:36 The lord did find a better king for Israel this day and in time this king shall come and rule over Israel.

15:37 And this king won't be such an accursed and pathetic little pussy. This king will do all that which the lord demands."

15:38 Saul wept and built an altar unto the lord and slew upon it the beasts which he did bring forth from the lands of Amalek.

15:39 Samuel grew angry and said unto Saul, "Surely this day you can offer a true and pleasing sacrifice unto your lord.

15:40 Bring out king Agag and I shall show you what it means to please God."

15:41 King Agag was brought to Samuel, and Agag said unto him,

"Surely enough blood has been slain this day."

15:42 Samuel smiled and with his bare hands Samuel did tear king Agag into pieces, so that the very flesh be ripped from the bones, the very bones be crushed to dust and the blood of Agag covered Samuel and that which be around Samuel.

15:43 Samuel came to Saul and said, "This is how you please your lord."

15:44 Then Saul went to Gibeah and Samuel to Ramah.

15:45 Saul cried and said to himself, "Surely my lord is not such a tyrant as this."

16:1 Samuel did mourn for Saul, for Samuel loved Saul as though he were a brother and wished not the wrath of the lord to come down upon him.

16:2 The lord came to Samuel and said, "Mourn not for that fucker, for Saul was weak and pathetic.

16:3 Go forth and fill your horn with oil, for I have found a new king of Israel this day.

16:4 Travel to Jesse the Bethlemite, for of his sons I have found a suitable king of Israel."

16:5 Samuel said to God, "How can I. For if I go to anoint another king, Saul shall surely have me killed," and the lord said, "Worry not, for the lord shall protect you.

16:6 Take a heifer on your way and if asked, say that you come to offer sacrifice unto God.

16:7 Call Jesse unto the sacrifice and I shall show you what to do and whom to anoint king."

16:8 Samuel did as the lord said and came to Bethlehem with a heifer for sacrifice. When the elders saw Samuel, they began to tremble, for they remembered what Samuel did unto king Agag.

16:9 The elders of Bethlehem said to Samuel, "Do you come in peace?" and Samuel said, "Yes, I come in peace.

16:10 I come to offer sacrifice unto God and to sanctify Jesse and his sons, so that they may know the spirit of the lord."

16:11 And Jesse came to the sacrifice with his sons.

16:12 Eliab, the eldest of Jesse, was shown to Samuel and Samuel said to himself, "Surely this is the man which the lord wishes to be king."

16:13 But the lord said, "No, for you see only the body of the man, but the lord sees into the heart."

16:14 Next, Abinadab was shown to Samuel and Samuel was told by God, "This is not the man who shall be king."

16:15 Shammah was shown and the lord said unto Samuel, "This is not the man who shall be king."

16:16 All seven sons of Jesse were shown to Samuel and each one was denied by the lord.

16:17 Samuel asked Jesse, "Do you have any other sons?" And Jesse said, "Yes, David. He's the youngest and is out tending the sheep.

16:18 Surely you wish not to see him, for he is a wimp."

16:19 And Samuel said, "The lord demands I see him. Go fetch him for me."

16:20 When David was found by the sheep, his raiment's were off and a young lamb, a female with blemish, was spread out before David.

16:21 Samuel gazed upon David and the lord said, "This is the man who shall be king."

16:22 Samuel took the oil from the horn and poured it over David and made David king. The spirit of the lord filled David that day and remained with him.

16:23 Saul knew not the spirit of the lord and was tormented daily by the evil spirit which the lord hath brought upon him.

16:24 Saul's servants said to him, "Behold, a demon, evil and wicked, was sent forth by God to torment your mind.

16:25 Tell us, how can we soothe and rid you of this evil spirit which plagues your very mind?"

16:26 And Saul said, "Go, fetch me a man who can play the harp well.

16:27 For music soothes even the savage beast. Surely it shall please the wickedness of the lord."

16:28 David, whom was just anointed by Samuel, was a talented player of the harp and was sent forth to play for Saul and soothe the evil spirit within him.

16:29 When David gazed upon Saul, he loved him greatly and played for him the harp and rid Saul of the evil spirit of the lord.

16:30 Saul gazed upon David and loved him and made David his armourbearer.

16:31 Saul sent message to Jesse, saying, "I pray, let David stay with me, for he has found favour in my sight."

16:32 And Jesse replied, "You may keep David. We don't want that sheep fucker."

17:1 Now the Philistines gathered together their armies to battle and were gathered together at Shochoh, which belonged to the tribe of Judah and pitched between Shochoh and Azekah, in Ephesdammim.

17:2 Saul and the armies of Israel gathered together and pitched at the valley of Elah and prepared their defense against the Philistines.

17:3 The Israelites stood upon one side of the mountain, the Philistines on the other and a valley lay between them.

17:4 And the Philistines sent out their champion, named Goliath of Gath, who was a huge beast of a man.

17:5 The height of Goliath was six cubits and a span, for he was of the generations of those women who were raped by the sons of God.

17:6 Goliath wore a helmet upon his head which was bigger than the skull of an ox and his coat of mail weighed over five thousand shekels of brass.

17:7 He wore greaves of brass upon his legs and a target of brass between his shoulders.

17:8 The staff of his spear was that of a tree and the head of the spear weighed six hundred shekels and the shield of Goliath was carved from a large boulder.

17:9 He was one scary, huge, honking motherfucker of a man.

17:10 Goliath would stand up and taunt the armies of Israel, saying, "Why do you bother to battle with us, for surely you know that we shall win.

17:11 I am but a Philistine and you are all servants of Saul. Send forth one man, so that he may challenge me to a duel.

17:12 If the man you send shall slay me, then let it be that the peoples of Philistine shall forever be in service to you. But if I slay this man, then all the nation of Israel shall be under the servitude of the great people of Philistine.

17:13 I defy all in the army of Israel to send me one man, so that we may fight."

17:14 When the armies of Israel heard these words, they were greatly pissed; they came expecting a battle, not a duel.

17:15 Saul grew afraid, for he knew to fight the Philistines in battle shall be suicide. If one man of Israel could slay this beast of a man, then the nation of Israel shall win.

17:16 But who in Israel could defeat this man Goliath?

17:17 Now David was the son of Jesse, the Ephrathite of Bethlehemjudah, whom had eight sons.

17:18 The three eldest sons of Jesse went with Saul, to fight against the heathens of Philistines.

17:19 Their names were Eliab, Abinadab and Shammah.

17:20 David was the youngest and went not with Saul to fight. For David was just a boy and a cowardly one at that.

17:21 So David stayed at home and tended the flocks of his father.

17:22 Every day, for forty days, the Philistine Goliath would present himself and challenge the army of Israel to send out one man to fight him.

17:23 Jesse said unto his son David, "Take to your brothers an ephah of this parched corn and these ten loaves of bread and give them to your brothers.

17:24 Take these tens cheese and give them to the captain of your brothers, so that the captain shall protect them and have them not fight in the front lines, nor dig latrines for the army."

17:25 Saul and the armies of Israel were in the valley, constantly being mocked by Goliath and not fighting the Philistines.

17:26 David arose early in the morning, left the flock to a keeper and went forth to see his brethren, as his father commanded him.

17:27 When David saw that the men of Israel were not fighting the uncircumcised heathens, he came to his brothers and gave them their food.

17:28 As he was talking with his brothers, Goliath came forth and challenged the Philistines yet again to send out one man, so that they may duel and end this war.

17:29 David could see that all the men of Israel were afraid of this man, for Goliath was like a dragon in men's robes to them.

17:30 And the men of Israel said, "Have you seen this man who comes up and challenges us to fight with him. Surely the one who shall fight him and slay him shall be blessed and given many riches by king Saul.

17:31 But who among is brave enough, courageous enough, stupid enough, to fight such a man, who could rip the mighty oaks from the ground?"

17:32 And David said, "Then send out a man, so that they may kill this uncircumcised heathen cocksucker.

17:33 Surely the lord shall protect them and be with them and the lord shall smite this dumb and dimwitted brute."

17:34 Eliab, the brother of David, heard that which David spoke and said to him, "What the fuck is the matter with you?

17:35 You've come down here less than a day and tell us how to fight. You, who are just a little boy, should leave the fighting to those who can pick up a sword."

17:36 When Saul heard word of the young man who said such courageous words, he had his servants bring forth David. Saul said to David, "Tell me, young boy, do you think that you are worthy of fighting against Goliath?

17:37 If so, show me and I shall have ye fight against the Philistine."

17:38 Now David, though a coward, was a greedy little bastard and wanted desperately the riches which was said the king would give to those who would slay Goliath.

17:39 And David said to Saul, "I am but a shepherd, not a warrior. As a shepherd, I know how to slay beasts like this heathen Goliath.

17:40 As I tend my father's sheep, a bear and a lion came and took a lamb from the flock of my father's.

17:41 I chased the beasts and hit them with my staff, until the beast let go of the lamb.

17:42 Then I took the jaw of the beasts and tore it apart, so that the beast lay dead before me."

17:43 David was, of course, lying, but Saul did not know this.

17:44 David continued, "Such as the bear and such as the lion, I shall slay this heathen beast who mocks the very people of God."

17:45 And Saul said, "So be it." And Saul dressed David in the finest armour and gave him the finest weapons in all of Israel.

17:46 But David was a weak little boy and could not walk in the armour, nor carry the sword and said unto Saul, "I cannot fight in these raiment's of metal, for I am not used to such clothing.

17:47 Let me fight Goliath in the raiment's I came in, so that I may be quick and nimble."

17:48 And Saul made it so, and David left without any armour nor weapons.

17:49 David walked towards where Goliath was and as he walked he gathered five smooth stones upon the path and placed them in his pocket.

17:50 Five smooth stones, which fit perfect within the sling.

17:51 When Goliath came again to mock the armies of Israel, David stepped forth and said, "I am a worthy champion of Israel and I shall duel against you and win."

17:52 When Goliath gazed upon David, he was insulted and said, "Surely you wish not to fight me, for I would crush you like a grape within the winepress.

17:53 Go, leave and I shall forget that you challenged me."

17:54 David said, "I shall not leave. Unless you wish to surrender, let this fight begin."

17:55 Goliath laughed and said, "Then let us make this fight fair." And Goliath stripped off his armour and stood naked before David.

17:56 David took a stone from his bag and placed it within his sling and flew the stone within the air and hit Goliath upon his head.

17:57 Goliath stopped and laughed and said, "Do you think that pebbles could take me down?"

17:58 David took another rock and placed it within his sling and twirled it within the air and flung the rock again at Goliath and struck him upon his forehead.

17:59 Goliath laughed again and mocked David, saying, "Why not just throw the pebbles upon me?"

17:60 David took a third rock and flung it swiftly towards Goliath.

17:61 Goliath caught this rock with his hand and crushed it into dust, saying, "This dust shall be your home, once I am finished."

17:62 The fourth rock David took and flung it towards Goliath.

17:63 This rock struck Goliath in the eye and Goliath said, "You little cunt faced cocksucker, you have blinded me!"

17:64 The fifth and final rock David put in his sling and flew it upon the penis of Goliath and that rock did circumcise Goliath and made Goliath fall and cry.

17:65 David then came up to Goliath and said, "You are now a circumcised man. A pity you are a beast."

17:66 David took the sword of Goliath and beheaded that beastly motherfucker and held the head for all the armies of Israel to see.

17:67 The men of Israel shouted and praised David, who held in his hands the bloody head of Goliath.

17:68 It was then the armies of Israel gave chase to the Philistines and slaughtered them in battle.

17:69 All the Philistines fled in terror, for never did they believe their champion Goliath would be slain by a little shepherd boy.

17:70 David took the head of Goliath and brought it to Jerusalem and all the peoples of the city asked, "Who is this crazy young boy who goes around our streets carrying a decapitated head?"

17:71 The armour of Goliath David did keep for himself. It was valuable armour and would bring to David great riches.

17:72 When Saul saw David walking the streets of Jerusalem with the head of Goliath, he asked his captain Abner, "Who is this young man, who carries the slain head of our most feared enemy?"

17:73 And Abner said, "Damned if I know."

17:74 And the king said, "Find out who he is."

17:75 Abner took David and placed him in front of the king and Saul asked David, "Just who the hell are you?"

17:76 And David said, "I am David, son of Jesse the Bethlehemite."

17:77 Saul then remembered, "Oh yes, my armourbearer."

17:78 Forgive me, for I am old and senile.

17:79 If you speak of my senility to anyone, I shall kill thee. If I remember."

17:80 David said to Saul, "You shall have my mouth shut, if you make me and my father rich."

17:81 And Saul made it so and Jesse became a rich man and needed not to pay his taxes.

18:1 It came to pass that Jonathan the son of Saul loved David and told his father, "I wish David to remain by my side and never leave me."

18:2 So Saul never allowed David to return home to his father.

18:3 Jonathan then made a covenant with David and swore unto each other that they shall never lie with another man as they lie with one another.

18:4 And Jonathan stripped off his robes, his garments and his girdle and gave it to David to wear.

18:5 David would rather be fucking a sheep, but Jonathan gave him carnal pleasures as well.

18:6 Saul made David a man of war and David went wherever Saul sent him, so that David shall slay the Philistine heathens and please the lord with death and bloodshed.

18:7 It came to pass that when David returned from a slaughter of the Philistines, that women came out, wearing little clothing and playing tambourines and cheered for David, saying, "Saul has killed thousands, but David has killed tens of thousands."

18:8 Saul became very jealous of David, for Saul had killed more men than David, yet the women cheer for David, saying that he had killed more than Saul.

18:9 And Saul eyed David that day forward, waiting for an opportunity to humiliate him.

18:10 One day, an evil spirit came of the lord came over Saul and Saul prophesied to all that would listen that David lied with men and beasts.

18:11 None would listen to the words of Saul, for all loved David, the slayer of heathens.

18:12 Saul became angry and when David was playing his harp, Saul grabbed a javelin and threw it upon David, thinking, 'Surely I shall skewer David to the damned wall.'

18:13 Saul missed, grabbed another javelin and threw again. David avoided the javelin and said unto Saul, "Calm the fuck down, lest I slay thee like I slay the heathen."

18:14 Saul became afraid of David and appointed him captain over thousands of men, hoping this would please David and that David would forget the attempted murder.

18:15 And all throughout his life, David behaved himself wisely in the lord. Meaning, he killed plenty of people and cared not whether it was right nor wrong.

18:16 When Saul saw that the glory of the lord was with David, he became even more afraid of him.

18:17 But all of Israel and Judah loved David, for David littered their lands with the corpses of Philistines.

18:18 Saul said unto David, "Ye are a valiant and violent man of the lord and shall be part of my family for your deeds to Israel.

18:19 Behold, my eldest daughter Merab. If your bloodstained hands stay forever pressed upon the Philistines, you may have her as a wife."

18:20 And David said, "Who am I, to have such a wife and be as a son in law to the king?

18:21 I shall slay every damn Philistine, to be given the gift of your daughter Merab."

18:22 But Merab, the eldest daughter of Saul, married not David and was given unto Adriel the Meholathite as a wife.

18:23 David said unto Saul, "What is this, that you insult me and give my wife over to another man?

18:24 And Saul said, "You wished not for Merab, for she is old, and her breasts sag like two sacks of wet grain.

8:25 Take instead my daughter Michal, who is young, beautiful, and virile.

18:26 Surely such a wife as this is of great value to you."

18:27 David said, "Yes, to have Michal as a wife would be a great honour.

18:28 Tell me, O Saul, king of Israel, how may I buy your daughter Michal as a wife?"

18:29 And Saul said, "Prove to me that ye are a worthy slayer. Bring unto me proof of your slaying of the Philistines.

18:30 Bring unto me the severed foreskins of one hundred Philistines and Michal shall be your wife."

18:31 David arose and went forth, to seek out the foreskins of one hundred heathens.

18:32 Saul thought this an impossible task and believed David would die by the hands of the Philistines.

18:33 Saul was wrong, for David went into the Philistine cities and said, "If you wish me to spare your lives, you shall take your men and cut from them their foreskins.

18:34 Give these foreskins to me and I shall save your city from the wrath of the lord."

18:35 The men of the cities would grab their knives and cut from them their foreskins. Weeping, they would give their foreskins to David and ask of him, "Why do you wish such a thing?

18:36 And David would say, "So that I may buy myself a wife." This confused the Philistines greatly and they wondered just how fucked the customs of Israel were.

18:37 Once the men of the city gave David their foreskin, David would say, "You have now been saved from the wrath of the lord, but I promised not to save thee from my wrath!"

18:38 David would then kill all within the city and burn it to the ground.

18:39 In time, David looked within his sack of foreskins and behold, there was not one hundred, but two hundred foreskins of the Philistines!

18:40 David returned unto Saul and said, "Here be double the number of foreskins of the Philistines, now give unto me your daughter Michal."

18:41 And Saul gave Michal to David as wife and asked of himself, "What the hell am I going to do with two hundred Philistine foreskins?"

18:42 Saul feared David even more and became his enemy that day.

18:43 As petty vengeance, Saul ordered his cooks to make David soup from the two hundred Philistine foreskins.

18:44 Thus for months, David ate of the foreskins of the Philistines he slew. It was a familiar flavour to him.

19:1 Saul became so fearful of David that he gathered his servants and said unto them, "If you see David, kill him."

19:2 Jonathan, the son of Saul, loved David and said unto David, "My father wishes to slay you. Go, hide yourself and I shall find you and tell you when it is safe to leave.

19:3 I shall go and speak with my father and convince him that you are not his enemy, but a friend. In time, Saul shall not wish to kill you."

19:4 Jonathan spoke to his father Saul by a field and said unto him, "Why does my father wish to sin against his servant, when his servant sinned not against him?

19:5 David has slain many a Philistine in your name and has given glory unto you and unto the lord. Kill him not. Let him live, so that he may serve you."

19:6 Saul hearkened the voice of Jonathan and said, "As long as the lord lives, I shall not slay David."

19:7 Jonathan sought out David and told him that his father no longer wished him dead.

19:8 The two men embraced and engaged in sinful carnal lust with one another, for both were relieved that David was no longer wished dead by the king.

19:9 In time, war broke out again with the Philistines and David was sent forth to lead his men in battle.

19:10 David slew many a Philistine and the blood-lust of David reached the ears of Saul and Saul became fearful of David again.

19:11 When David was in the house of Saul, Saul grabbed yet another javelin and threw it at David.

19:12 David fled from the javelin, so that the javelin was stuck upon the wall.

19:13 David fled and escaped to his house.

19:14 Saul sent his men to surround the house of David, so that when David exit, the men of Saul shall surely slay him.

19:15 Michal, wife of David and daughter of Saul, said unto her husband, "You must escape, or these men shall storm our house and slay us both!

19:16 I wish not to die. Go and flee."

19:17 Michal grabbed a rope and David escaped through the window of his house. The men of Saul saw not David climb down the house.

19:18 The men of Saul were really stupid and watched only the door of the house. Not the windows.

19:19 Michal then took pillows and placed them underneath the sheets of the bed and put goat hair on top.

19:20 In the morning, when the men of Saul stormed the house of David, they asked Michal, "Where is your husband. Tell us, so that we may slay him."

19:21 Michal answered, "He is in bed, ill."

19:22 And the men of Saul said, "He is sick. Oh. We shall wait for him to be well, so that we may kill him."

19:23 And they sent message to Saul, saying, "David is sick."

19:24 Saul came to the house of David and said to his men, "I don't care how fucking sick he is!

19:25 Give me a sword and I shall slay him in his bed!"

19:26 And Saul grabbed his sword and thrust within the bed of David, where the pillows lay.

19:27 When Saul cast off the sheets and saw that David was not within, but rather pillows and goats hair, Saul asked his daughter, "Why the hell did you not tell me that David was gone?"

19:28 And Michal said, "Because he threatened to kill me if I did not let him escape.

19:29 Go, find him, kill him. The man is a tyrant."

19:30 This was also a lie, but Saul did not know. Saul was an idiot.

19:31 David fled to Ramah and met with Samuel and said to him all that which Saul had tried to do. And he and Samuel went forth to Naioth and dwelt there.

19:32 Word came to Saul that David dwelt in Naioth and Saul sent men to go there and slay David.

19:33 When the men of Saul came to Naioth, the spirit of the lord came over them and the men of Saul stripped naked and went into a hysterical seizure upon the ground, speaking in gibberish.

19:34 Saul heard of this and sent out more men to kill David. These men also went into a hysterical seizure and stripped naked and spoke gibberish whilst wallowing in dust.

19:35 A third time, Saul sent men to kill David. These men came to Naioth and the spirit of the lord filled them and they ripped off their clothes, spoke in gibberish and went into a hysterical seizure upon the very ground.

19:36 Saul became angry and went to Naioth himself, so that he may personally slay the little bastard David.

19:37 When Saul arrived, he asked one of the men, "Where is Samuel and David?" And the man replied, "Just follow the people who go insane and wallow in dust."

19:38 And Saul followed the bodies of his men, until he arrived where Samuel and David were.

19:39 Again, the spirit of the lord filled Saul and Saul stripped naked, fell upon the ground in a hysterical seizure and spoke in gibberish.

19:40 Those who passed believed these men to be prophets and when they saw their king, they asked themselves, "Does this mean that Saul is of the prophets?"

20:1 David fled from Naioth in Ramah and came to Jonathan and said, "What the hell did I do to anger your father so greatly. Multiple times the crazy fuck has tried to kill me."

20:2 Jonathan said to him, "Lord forbid, you did nothing to anger my father and my father wishes not to kill you.

20:3 Anything of importance, my father shall tell me and he did not tell me that he wishes you dead."

20:4 David said to Jonathan, "That is because your father know that we are lovers and wishes you not to know, lest you come to warn me or protect me.

20:5 But true as the lord exist, your father wants me dead."

20:6 Jonathan then said to David, "Whatever your soul desires, I shall do for you."

20:7 David said to Jonathan, "Behold, tomorrow is the new moon and I shall not be at the table of the king, but will lie in hiding.

20:8 If your father asks where I be, tell him that I have went to Bethlehem, for there is the yearly sacrifice of the family I must attend.

20:9 If your father be fine by this, then surely, he wishes my life spared. But if your father become angry, then know he wishes me dead."

20:10 Jonathan said, "This I shall do and shall let you know the actions of my father.

20:11 Hide yourself where I hid you the first time and upon the third day, I shall tell you what it was my father has done."

20:12 David said unto Jonathan, "Swear unto me that you shall not agree with your father and come to have me slain."

20:13 And Jonathan swore it.

20:14 David then said, "Grasp mine testicles with your hands, kiss them and swear to the very lord that you shall tell me the truth of your father."

20:15 Jonathan grabbed the testicles of David and kissed them and swore that he shall tell the truth of Saul, the father of Jonathan.

20:16 Jonathan then made David swear and said, "Swear to me that you shall hold no ill will towards me, if my father wishes you dead."

20:17 And David swore to Jonathan.

20:18 Jonathan then said, "Grasp mine testicles, kiss them and swear that you shall still love me, even if my father wishes you dead."

20:19 And David did so and grasped the testicles of Jonathan, kissed them and swore that his love for Jonathan shall be eternal, no matter the wickedness of his father.

20:20 Jonathan returned and ate at the harvest of the new moon, with the seat of David empty.

20:21 When Saul noticed that David was gone, he thought naught of it and believed David ill.

20:22 Upon the second night, when David did not come to the table, Saul asked Jonathan, "Where is David. For his food becomes cold."

20:23 And Jonathan said, "David hath gone to Bethlehem, so that he may sacrifice with his family."

20:24 For once in his life, Saul knew that someone was lying.

20:25 Saul became angry and said to Saul, "You are a worthless bastard son. You son of a wretched and wicked whore.

20:26 Do you not think I know the lies which spill forth from your tongue?

20:27 You are a disgrace to me and your family, for I know of the lust you have for young David.

20:28 I would rather you seek the nakedness of your very mother, than take lust in the youth of David.

20:29 Now go, seek him out and bring him forth, for as long as David lives, the kingdom of Israel shall be denied to you."

20:30 Jonathan asked Saul, "Why. What wickedness hast David done against you?

20:31 Saul became angry and threw a javelin at Jonathan. Saul always seems to have javelins nearby, in case he needs to throw them.

20:32 Jonathan knew that Saul wished David dead and wept dearly that night.

20:33 Jonathan went forth to seek David and when David arose, Jonathan was in tears.

20:34 The two men embraced and cried, for they knew that so long as Saul lives, David shall not be safe in the presence of Jonathan.

20:35 Jonathan said to David, "You must go, for surely my father shall send men to watch me and shall attack you if they see you."

20:36 The two men embraced and engaged again in their sinful lust and left. David to hide and Jonathan back to the city.

21:1 David fled to Nob and met with Ahimelech the priest and the priest was cautious of David and said, "What business do you have here, that you come alone?"

21:2 David lied to the priest, saying, "I have come under orders of king Saul. No man is to know my business, for it is secret and delicate.

21:3 In time, I am to meet my servants nearby, so that we may carry the orders of Saul.

21:4 I beg of you, give me some bread to eat and some water to drink."

21:5 Ahimelech said to David, "We have not common bread here, but only the blessed bread of our lord, which no man shall eat if they have lied with a woman."

21:6 David said, "I am a virgin and can eat this bread."

21:7 The priest questioned him and said, "Are ye really a virgin. For surely you have a wife, a concubine, or taken pleasure in the brothels."

21:8 David lied again and said, "I have not, for I follow the path of God and have no time for trivial and earthly pursuits of the flesh."

21:9 Ahimelech believed him and gave him some of the holy bread to eat and some water to quench his thirst.

21:10 Now, a servant of Saul was at Nob that day. Doeg, an Edomite and chief of the herdsmen that belonged to Saul.

21:11 When David saw Doeg, he became scared and worried that Doeg would tell Saul of his location.

21:12 David knew he had to flee the lands of Israel and thought himself save in the lands of the Philistine, where he shall claim sanctuary.

21:13 David was unarmed and though he shall flee to Philistine in peace, he wished still to have a weapon upon him.

21:14 Only a fool would enter the lands of his enemies unarmed.

21:15 David asked Ahimelech, "Is there either sword or spear which I may have, for I did leave in a hurry and had not time to gather my weapons."

21:16 And Ahimelech said, "There is only the sword of Goliath, which you did slay upon the valley of Elah. It is wrapped in cloth, behind the ephod. If you need it, take it, for that is the only means of defense we have here."

21:17 And David took it and fled in fear of Saul to king Achish, of the city of Gath.

21:18 David said to the men, "I wish to speak to your king, for I am David and wish to seek thee sanctuary in your lands.

21:19 My king wishes to kill me and if you protect me, I shall tell your captains all I know."

21:20 And David was brought forth to king Achish, for the men of Philistine wished to offer him sanctuary and know the secrets of Israel.

21:21 As David was brought forth, he could hear the words of the men of Philistine. "Is that the one who killed Goliath. The one who slew tens of thousands. The one who stole the foreskins of our brethren and slew them?"

21:22 Achish knew this and cared not. For Achish was a peaceful man, like most Philistines and wished that, through David, the men of Israel and Philistine shall be at peace.

21:23 But David grew afraid and feared Achish shall slay him where he stood.

21:24 So David, believing that even a heathen would not slay an insane man, acted crazy.

21:25 He stripped his clothes, shit upon the floor, urinated upon his chest and face, ate his own faeces, spoke in gibberish and frenzied upon the ground, hoping that the Philistines shall think him insane and give him sanctuary in an asylum.

21:26 Achish said to his men, "Tell me, is this truly David, the champion of the Israel. Or did ye send a jester here to amuse me?

21:27 And the men said, "This is David, who seeks sanctuary within our lands, for his king wishes him dead."

21:28 And Achish said, "I can see why. To have a madman as a champion must be a true disgrace unto the nation of Israel."

22:1 David fled from Gath and hid within the cave Adullam. When his brethren heard of where David hid, they fled and hid with him.

22:2 It became refuge, so that all who were in distress, in debt, in trouble, came to hide with David.

22:3 David did lead them and had under his command four hundred men.

22:4 So that David had with him four hundred untrained, cowardly peasants, who would rather flee and hide than face their problems.

22:5 When David's parents came, he wished them not to live in the cave as animals. David went to Mizpeh of Moab and said to the king of Moab, "I beg of you, let my father and my mother live with you, so they know not the wrath of Saul.

22:6 Do this and the lord of Israel shall bless you."

22:7 And the king of Moab agreed and let the parents of David dwell within the city of Mizpeh whilst David slept in a cave.

22:8 Gad, a prophet, came to David and said, "The lord has sent me a vision. Dwell not in this cave, for it is unsafe.

22:9 Flee to the lands of Judah and hide in the forests of Hareth. And David did so.

22:10 When Saul heard that David was discovered talking to the priests in Nob, Saul did become angry. He gathered his spears, which he had always on hands and gathered his servants.

22:11 Saul said to his servants, "Tell me, why do you ally with David. Did David give unto you your fields, your olive yards, your vineyards, or make you captains. No, it was I who did such things.

22:12 Yet you all betrayed me and hid from my sight that my own son Jonathan chosen this son of Jesse over his own father; his own flesh and blood."

22:13 Doeg, the Edomite, said to Saul, "I saw David speak with the priests of Nob and spoke with the priest Ahimelech, the son of Ahitub.

22:14 David lied unto the priest and claimed he knew not women, so that the priest shall give him bread to eat and the priest gave him also the sword of Goliath."

22:15 King Saul said, "To lie to a priest is surely a sin. In the name of our lord, David must be put to death."

22:16 Saul then sent forth for the priests of Nob to come and speak with him. And Saul asked the priests, "Why do you conspire against me and ally yourself with David the son of Jesse, whom I hate?"

22:17 The priests answered, "We knew not you hated David, for we believed David was sent forth by orders from you.

22:18 David is known throughout all of Israel to be a faithful servant of yours and is even your son in law.

22:19 All the priests of Nob believed we were doing service unto Saul, by caring for David, loyal servant of the king."

22:20 King Saul became angry and said, "You fools, surely a man of the lord shall know who the king of Israel hates.

22:21 All those of Nob shall be slain, for conspiring against the king."

22:22 And Saul ordered his footmen to go and slay the priests of Nob. But the footmen refused.

22:23 They wished not to slay those who are men of God. Surely such a thing shall bring damnable curses from the lord upon them.

22:24 Saul cursed his footmen and said to Doeg, "You are a faithful servant unto me. Go forth and slay all those of Nob."

22:25 Doeg did as the king commanded and took his sword to the throats of Nob.

22:26 Doeg went to Nob and slew all those who wore the ephod of the lord. Four score and five priests did Doeg slay.

22:27 When Doeg slew them, the priests did naught to defend themselves and believed the lord shall intervene and save them.

22:28 Stupid priests.

22:29 Doeg then turned against the peoples of Nob and slew them all. Men, women, children, infants, crippled, elderly, he killed them all in glory to Saul.

22:30 Even the cattle, the flocks, the asses, Doeg did slay.

22:31 Doeg then burned the bodies, so that the smoke rose to the sky in a great cloud of burning flesh, so that when Saul looked forth, Saul saw the smoke and was pleased with the death which his servant did under his command.

22:32 The lord looked down and saw the smoke of the bodies and smelled the aroma of human corpses and was pleased.

22:33 Whether his own peoples or not, the lord does love mass death.

22:34 Doeg, however, was incompetent and Abiathar, the son of Ahitub, the son of Ahimelech, escaped, and fled to David.

22:35 Abiathar told David all that which Doeg did, and said unto David, "It is your hand as well that slew us all, for if you did not lie to us, then king Saul would have spared us and not cursed us with death."

22:36 David said unto Abiathar, "Was it my hand who held the sword which did cut the throats of your brethren. No, so blame me not for your death.

22:37 Did you pick up the blade and defend yourself against Doeg, or did you allow one man, one servant of Saul, to kill your brothers and slay your city?

22:38 It is your fault that you are now from a doomed city. Worry not. Stay with me and I shall protect you for all my days."

22:39 Abiather said, "I loathe you, for your lies doomed us all. Yet, I have no other place to go.

22:40 I shall stay with you, until I may go and find a place to live where I won't be ruled by a lying coward."

23:1 David was told by his men, "Behold, the Philistines come and they fight against the city Keilah and rob them."

23:2 David knew not what to d, and asked the lord, "Shall I go and slay these Philistines?" and the lord answered, "Yes."

23:3 But the men of David were afraid and said, "We are untrained men and know not how to fight. If we go to slay these heathens, surely they shall destroy us."

23:4 David asked the lord again, "Shall I go and slay these Philistines?" And the lord said, "You already asked me this.

23:5 I care not if your men are scared, for they are damn pussies and should be honoured if they die fighting in the name of their lord.

23:6 Now go, save the city of Keilah and kill these damn heathens!"

23:7 So David and his men went to Keilah and fought with the Philistines. The lord was with them and the Philistines died in a great slaughter.

23:8 David then said to the peoples of Keilah, "Behold, I have saved you and your people. Be grateful to the lord and I."

23:9 David then took all the cattle of the peoples of Keilah and said unto them, "The heathens of Philistine did come and steal your cattle and your flocks before I came to rescue you."

23:10 Saul heard of David's massacre at Keilah and said, "Surely this is a blessing from the lord, for Keilah is a city with gates and bars.

23:11 David shall have only few means to escape and my men shall watch these places and ensure David shall not flee like the coward he is.

23:12 My men shall go, and besiege Keilah and shall stay until David is dead."

23:13 Saul then gathered all his men of war and marched towards Keilah.

23:14 David knew Saul wished him dead and worried that the people of Keilah shall sell him to Saul.

23:15 David asked of God, "O lord of Israel, I beseech you, will the men of Saul come to Keilah and make doom upon me?" And the lord answered, "Yes."

23:16 David then asked the lord, "Shall the men of Keilah sell me to Saul?" And the lord answered, "Yes."

23:17 David grew furious and asked the men of Keilah, "Why would you sell me to Saul, when I just saved your city from the hands of the heathens?"

23:18 The men of Keilah answered, "Do you think us fools. We know you stole our cattle from us.

23:19 You saved us not for glory, but for greed. Now be gone, lest Saul come and we give your head unto him."

23:20 David and his men, which is now six hundred, fled Keilah and went wherever they could hide. Saul heard of David's retreat and still marched towards Keilah.

23:21 David would hide within the forests, within the caves and within the mountains. Never did he and his men stay in one place for more than a few days, for fear that Saul shall find him.

23:22 Saul would send his men out to search the wilderness and never was David nor his men found.

23:23 As David hid in the forests of Ziph, Jonathan arose and found David and said to him, "Fear not, for I shall not tell my father of your whereabouts.

23:24 I know that you shall be king over all Israel and my father fears this as well."

23:25 The two men did embrace and made a covenant with one another. Upon the forest floor Jonathan and David did embrace and engage in their lust for one another.

23:26 All six hundred of David's men witnessed this sinful lust and engaged with each other of the same lust that David and Jonathan had.

23:27 Upon that night, an orgy of six hundred men did partake upon the forest floors of Ziph. This scared away all the animals, both predator and prey.

23:28 The men of Ziphah heard this orgy and knew that David and his men did hide within their forests.

23:29 They came to Saul and told him, "That faggot David hides within our forests and disgraces our very ground in the wild.

23:30 He hides in the woods of Hachilah, which be on the south side of Jeshimon.

23:31 Come, send your men and rid us of this sickness which plagues our lands."

23:32 Saul said, "Blessed upon you, men of Ziph, who have shown compassion and honour unto your king.

23:33 Go forth and keep eyes upon the place where David hides, so that he not escapes these woods.

23:34 I shall send my men in subtlety, so that David knows not we come to slay him.

23:35 Tell me of all the places where David hides within your lands and I shall have men there to watch these hiding places."

23:36 The Ziphites then drew Saul a map and detailed all the places where David hid within the lands of Ziph.

23:37 The men of Saul did go and went to Ziph, and watched carefully for David and his men.

23:38 But David fled before these men arrived and hid now in the wilderness of Maon, which be of the south of Jeshimon.

23:39 Men of Saul witnessed from distance the retreat of David, escaping to Maon and told Saul of David's departure.

23:40 When Saul heard this, he gathered his men and personally chased after David in the plains of Maon.

23:41 There was a mountain within Maon and the two sides would chase each other round the mountain, going in circles.

23:42 When Saul decided, "I shall turn my men around and we shall meet David as his men as they think they flee from us," a messenger of Saul's arrived and said, "Come haste, for the Philistines have invaded our lands."

23:43 Saul said, "Fucking Philistines. I come so close to killing David and these foreskin bearing heathens come and ruin it for me."

23:44 Saul ceased his pursuit of David, so that he may concentrate upon the invasion of the Philistines, which was surely more important than petty revenge.

23:45 David fled and hid within the caves of Engedi.

24:1 It came to pass that when the Philistines invaded the lands of Israel, that Saul heard word that David hid within the mountains of Engedi.

24:2 Saul took with him three thousand men and went forth to seek out David in the lands of rocks and mountain goats.

24:3 Every cave was searched and Saul found neither David nor his men.

24:4 As they returned, the bowels of Saul became angry and Saul entered a cave which they searched, for Saul had to shit.

24:5 But the men of David hid within that cave and saw Saul enter, yet Saul saw them not.

24:6 The men of David came to him and said, "The lord has

delivered our enemies into our hands this day, for as we speak, Saul squats within this cave and shits upon its very floor."

24:7 David said, "Surely this is a joke." And he went forth, to see if what his men say be true.

24:8 And behold, David saw Saul squat against the floor, taking a shit. And David laughed within his heart.

24:9 David snuck up behind Saul and as Saul shit, David took the robes of Saul and cut them.

24:10 David returned to his men and said, "Look, I have the very robes of Saul, which I cut from him as he squatted upon the floor as he emptied his bowels like an animal."

24:11 The men of David asked him, "Why did you cut his robes and not his neck?" and David answered, "Because if I were to slay him, the very shit which come from him shall be stained upon my very raiment's and feet.

24:12 When I slay a man, I wish their blood to be stained upon me; not their shit."

24:13 The men then said unto David, "Then let us go and we shall kill him after he finishes emptying his bowels." And David said, "No, we shall not.

24:14 I know not why this man hates me, nor do I care. He is the father of my beloved Jonathan and I shall not slay him.

24:15 Remember, he is the anointed king of Israel, chosen by our holy lord. We shall not kill him, lest we have the wrath of the lord upon us."

24:16 And with these words, David held back the hands of his men from Saul.

24:17 David then arose and left the cave, chasing after Saul and his army.

24:18 When David met with them, he yelled, "Saul, my king, do you not wish these shreds of cloth so that you may clean your ass from your droppings?"

24:19 Saul turned around and saw David and the anger within his soul consumed him and he chased after David, javelin in hand.

24:20 Saul loves the javelin. It's his favourite weapon.

24:21 Before Saul could slay David, he noticed the cloth in David's hands were from his own robes.

24:22 Saul stopped and gazed upon his robes and behold, they were cut.

24:23 Saul asked David, "How did you get the cloth from my very robes?

24:24 And David said, "As you lied squatting in the cave, your bowels being emptied, I snuck up behind you and cut your robes. But I spared your life, for I hold no ill will against you."

24:25 The men of Saul heard the words of David and began to laugh. The thought of David cutting the robes, which be mere inches away from the ass of Saul as he shits, amused them deeply.

24:26 David continued, "I know not why you wish me dead, for have I not been a faithful servant of you?

24:27 In your name, I have protected your lands, killed many heathens and given honour and glory unto your house.

24:28 Not once have I sinned against you nor your family, yet still you wish me dead.

24:29 When the time comes, the lord shall judge us both, but today is not this day.

24:30 Now, shall we leave, or shall you come and slay me?"

24:31 With these words, Saul knew that David was a wise and loyal servant and his blood-lust for him left.

24:32 Saul said unto David, "I fear you, that is why I wish you dead.

24:33 Now I see that you are a wise man and I have no reason to fear you.

24:34 In time, you shall succeed my throne and be king of all the people of Israel.

24:35 Even when I cursed you with evil, you have done naught but reward me.

24:36 This I beg of , when you become king of Israel, spare my family and destroy not my house."

24:37 David swore it, and the two men made a covenant that day.

24:38 Saul and David then embraced, the same when David and Jonathan embraced and they made carnal lust upon the rocks of the mountains.

24:39 Saul took great pleasure in the youth of David, but David found little enjoyment, for the shit of Saul was still upon his buttocks.

24:40 The two men then took leave of each other. Saul left for his home and David back into the caves.

25:1 Samuel died and all the nation of Israel gathered together and mourned deeply for Samuel and buried him at his house in Ramah. After the funeral, David arose and went to the wilderness of Paran.

25:2 There was a man in Maon whose possessions were in Carmel. The man was very great and had in his belonging three thousand sheep and one thousand goats.

25:3 The name of the man was Nabal and the name of his wife was Abigail. Abigail was a polite, kind, and beautiful young woman, where Nabal was a crude, uncivilised, boorish asshole.

25:4 Nabal went out to Carmal to shear his sheep and when David heard of this, he sent out ten messengers to speak with Nabal.

25:5 The ten men of David said to Nabal, "We have seen your lands and know that ye live in great prosperity. Peace be to you, to your house and to that which belongs to you.

25:6 We have seen your servants within the fields of Carmal as they shear sheep. We harmed them not and for this we wish to be rewarded.

25:7 Give us some bread to eat, some water to drink and some meat and we shall ensure your men remain unharmed."

25:8 Nabal said to these men, "Why the hell should I give you that which belongs to me, because you did not act as criminals against me?

25:9 Such extortion shall not be tolerated. Be gone and tell your master David to go lick the brown crusty center of a camel's asshole."

25:10 So the men of David returned unto the forests which they dwelt and told David all that which Nabal spoke.

25:11 David grew furious and said to his men, "Gird your swords." So all the men girded their swords, as did David and David went forth with four hundred men, while two hundred remained to protect their goods.

25:12 One of the servants of Nabal told Abigail, "Behold, David sent forth ten messengers to your husband, and your husband did not give them what they asked.

25:13 These men are strong, for we have seen them in the fields. They bear swords, spears and armour.

25:14 They point at us and threaten to slay us, but shall not, if our master heeds their words.

25:15 Now they shall come and take that which they want and shall slay us all for your husband's rudeness."

25:16 Abigail heard of David and knew he was a man to be feared. She took two hundred loaves of bread, two jugs of wine and five sheep dressed and spiced for the fire, five measures of parched corn, a hundred cluster of raisins and two hundred fig cakes.

25:17 She said to her servants, "Come with me and deliver these things for David and his men.

25:18 Tell not your master of this, for he knows not what I do."

25:19 She went forth to the wilderness and David and his men met with her.

25:20 David said unto Abigail, "Surely your husband did not send you to give these to us, for your husband is a crude and stupid ma and heeded not the words of my men.

25:21 I shall go forth and slay him as though he were an uncircumcised man against God and shall kill in the night all those of his servants who piss against the wall.

25:22 It matters not where else they piss. They could piss on a donkey, piss on a tree, piss in their shoe, piss on their wife, piss in a glass, piss in a pitcher, but if they pissed against the wall, I shall smite them greatly."

25:23 Abigail got off her donkey and bowed upon the ground to David, saying, "I beg of you, hear the words of the wife of Nabal.

25:24 Nabal is a rich man, which is why I did marry him. Spare him and his belongings and I shall give to you what you demand.

25:25 My husband shall not know that which is gone. He's an idiot and knows not even now that I am with you and have given you these foods."

25:26 David said to Abigail, "Blessed be the lord and blessed be you for delivering us the food of your husband.

25:27 Once a week you shall deliver for us these foods and we shall leave your land in peace.

25:28 If not, then we shall come and take all that which belongs to Nabal and shall slay his servants and burn his lands."

25:29 Abigail thanked David and returned home. And the exploitation racket did begin and David exploited more farmers amongst the lands.

25:30 When Abigail returned home, Nabal was having a feast and was drunk greatly with the wine of his vineyards.

25:31 Abigail knew her husband a violent drunk and told him nothing that would upset him until the morning, when he became sober.

25:32 When she told Nabal that which she did, Abigail grew angry and his heart failed him.

25:33 Nabal became cold as stone and slept the remainder of his days.

25:34 Within ten days, the lord came down and squeezed the heart of Nabal, until it beat no more.

25:35 When David heard that Nabal did die, he said, "Blessed be the lord, for killing this man Nabal.

25:36 Now I shall claim all that which he owned and need not exploit it through his wife."

25:37 So David went down and bought Abigail as a wife and gained all that which Nabal owned.

25:38 Abigail went with David and lived with him in the forests, the rocks and the caves.

25:39 David also took Ahinoam of Jezreel as a wife, for she had a blessed and rich dowry; and David had two wives.

25:40 Michal, the first wife of David, was sold by Saul to another man; Phalti, the son of Laish, now owned Michal as a wife.

26:1 The Ziphites came to Saul and said to him, "We have seen your servant David hiding in the deserts of our lands.

26:2 Go, seek him out and slay him, for we are loyal servants unto Saul."

26:3 And Saul said, "I wish not to slay him, for we have made peace between us.

26:4 I shall go and tell David he need not hide no longer."

26:5 Saul then went out and took with him three thousand men and searched for David in the deserts of Ziph.

26:6 Saul pitched in the hill of Hachilah, which is before Jeshimon. David saw where Saul pitched and thought the king again went forth to find and kill him.

26:7 David sent out spies to the tents of Saul and his men and when the men found out nothing, they came back to David and said, "He wishes you dead."

26:8 For the spies of David knew that if they told David nothing, that he shall surely kill them.

26:9 David then rose and saw where Saul and his army pitched and made note where Saul slept.

26:10 When David returned, he said to his men, "Who shall go with me to the men of Saul?" and Abishai the son of Zeruiah said, "I shall."

26:11 So David and Abishai went by night to the tents of Saul and his men and snuck within the very tent of Saul, where he slept.

26:12 Abishai grabbed the spear which Saul slept beside (yes, he even slept with a spear) and said unto David, "Surely the lord God has delivered the enemies into my hands.

26:13 Take this spear and thrust it once in the head of Saul. A second thrust shall not be needed, for the first shall be a mortal wound."

26:14 David said, "I cannot, for though he is a crazy man and wishes me dead, he is a man anointed by God.

26:15 To slay him shall surely bring great and terrible curses upon me.

26:16 Grab forth his spear and the bottle of wine beside him and come with me."

26:17 And the two men took the spear and jug of wine and escaped unseen from the tents of Saul and his army, for the lord did put them into a great and deep sleep.

26:18 David then went to a hill far off from the tents of Saul and yelled unto them, "Wake up you fools, who fail to protect your king.

26:19 Surely such incompetence shall bring thee death from the lord, for behold, I have the spear and the jug of wine, taken from the tent of Saul himself."

26:20 Saul and his men awoke and behold, David did have the jug of wine and the spear of the king.

26:21 Saul said to David, "Why did you sneak into my tent. Why do you still feel the need to hide within my presence?

26:22 We have made peace, and yet still you hide from me as though you believe my hand shall spill the blood from your throat.

26:23 Return unto me, so that we may live again in harmony."

26:24 David said, "I shall do no such things, for you have brought three thousand men to come and find me in the wilderness of Ziph.

26:25 Why else shall you bring so many men, unless you wish me dead?"

26:26 And Saul said, "We are still at war with the Philistines and these men come to protect me from the heathens who go against the one true God.

26:27 Return to me, my servant, for I miss you and wish your death no longer."

26:28 David said, "Come, send a servant of yours to gather your spear and your jug and then be gone from me."

26:29 Thus Saul sent forth a servant, who came and fetched the spear and jug of Saul.

26:30 Saul gazed within the jug,and behold, it was empty. Saul said to David, "You have drank the wine of the king, a wine made from the finest vineyards.

26:31 Such things shall bring most men death, but for you I shall spare your life, for I wish to have peace between us.

26:32 I know one-day you shall be king and shall accomplish a great many things.

26:33 Come now, live in the palace which shall one day be yours."

26:34 But David was gone and heard not the words of Saul.

26:35 Abishai said unto David, "Why do you still hide, for surely Saul is honest when he says that he wishes thee no harm."

26:36 David said, "Saul is a crazy motherfucker.

26:37 He may wish me to live now, but tomorrow he'll throw a spear at my head."

26:38 David then returned to his men and killed the spies he sent forth, for he knew that they lied to him.

26:39 And the men of David said, "Surely David is a crazy motherfucker."

27:1 The men of David said to him, "You are now at peace with Saul, for you had reconciled twice with him.

27:2 Let us go and live in the cities as men and not in the wild like beasts."

27:3 And David said, "I know in my heart that the hand of Saul wishes to shed my blood upon the floor.

27:4 Saul says we are at peace, but it shall come that Saul shall change his mind and his blood-lust for me will rise.

27:5 At that time, he shall grab his spear and skewer me until I am pinned dead."

27:6 Still, the men of David said, "This is not true, for twice he has made peace with you.

27:7 Let us go, so that we may live in the cities and sleep upon a bed and not upon dirt."

27:8 David replied, "If you wish to live in a city, then a city we shall live in.

27:9 Come and we shall go to the lands of the Philistines to live there."

27:10 And the men of David said, "These are our enemies, these uncircumcised men who go against the true lord God.

27:11 Surely you jest."

27:12 And David said, "I jest not, for the men of Israel are my enemies.

27:13 The enemy of my enemy is my friend and thus the Philistines are my friends, so it is with them we shall live.

27:14 If any wish not to come, I shall consider them against me and your skulls shall drop upon the ground."

27:15 And the men of David went with him to the lands of the Philistines, all the time murmuring, "Surely David is a crazy motherfucker."

27:16 They marched to the city of Gath, where Achish the son of Gaoth was king.

27:17 David said unto Achish, "I seek sanctuary in your city.

27:18 Let me and mine stay and I shall serve you until the end of my days."

27:19 Achish said to him, "Did you not seek out sanctuary before and then dropped upon the ground as a madman?"

27:20 David lied, saying, "Yes, but now the lord did cure me of my madness and I seek sanctuary with you again.

27:21 My king wishes me dead and I fear there be no safe haven within my homeland."

27:22 Achish said to David, "That is not your homeland, for your kin did take of these lands generations ago.

27:23 Still, you seek sanctuary and I shall give sanctuary to your and your men."

27:24 So David and his men lived in Gath, as did David's two wives Abigail the Carmelitess and Ahinoam the Jezreelitess.

27:25 Both women were relieved to finally sleep within a home, on top of a bed and not atop grass, dirt or rocks.

27:26 It was told to Saul that David fled and sought sanctuary in the lands of the Philistines and Saul said, "That traitor. The lord did this as a curse upon me.

27:27 Surely I should have slain that little sheep-shagger when the

chance was open."

27:28 David said to Achish, "Give to me land so that I may build for my men a city.

27:29 For a servant as plenty as us are undeserving to live with the royal household."

27:30 Achish knew David well and knew him to be a loyal servant.

27:31 Achish said, "Though we are born of different mothers, I see you as kin.

27:32 Go, take the lands of Ziklag and do with it as you wish."

27:33 Thus David and his men went to Ziklag and built a city there.

27:34 And the time David dwelt within Ziklag was a year and four months.

27:35 David went forth and reclaimed the lands taken from Philistine.

27:36 The men of David would invade Geshurites, the Gezrites, the Amalekites, the Kenites, the Judahites, and the Jerahmeelites.

27:37 None would be left alive, so that men, women, children, elderly, cattle and flocks were left dead.

27:38 Achish came to David and said, "I am proud of your loyalty, and it is with great honour that you serve me.

27:39 Still, y need not massacre every living thing where you go.

27:40 Slay only those that are a threat. Leave the women, the children and the beasts alive."

27:41 And David said, "To do such things is not the way of my people.

27:42 Leave no survivors and no survivors shall slay you.

27:43 Such is the way of the lord of Israel."

27:44 Achish replied, "Your lord is truly a wicked and evil being.

27:45 Worship him if you must, but do not go and attempt to convert us.

27:46 Our lords are peaceful and we wish them to remain peaceful.

27:47 To worship such an evil and wicked lord as Israel shall surely corrupt and destroy the people of Philistine."

27:48 David laughed and said to Achish, "It is our lord who did take the lands of you and your people through bloodshed.

27:49 Bloodshed is to conquer and our lord conquers all."

27:50 David then left and Achish said to himself, "Surely I did give sanctuary to a crazy motherfucker."

28:1 It came to pass that the Philistines gathered their armies to invade and reclaim all the lands of Israel. Achish said to David, "Know that you shall come with me in battle, for you know the tactics and the terrain of Israel well."

28:2 David said to Achish, "Know that I look forward to the slaying of the people of Israel, for these men did abandon me, where my enemies took me in." And Achish said, "Y shall be well rewarded for your aid, both you and your men."

28:3 Now Samuel was dead and the people of Israel still lamented at his grave upon Ramah. After the death of Samuel, Saul did slay and cast out all those of wizards, witches and necromancy.

28:4 The people of Israel knew it as a genocide of evil, for surely those who partook in magic were against the lord.

28:5 The Philistines gathered themselves and pitched in Shunem. The armies of Saul went forth and pitched in Gilboa.

28:6 When Saul saw the numbers of the army of Philistine, he did tremble,and became afraid.

28:7 Saul would pray unto the lord and seek forth his advice, but the lord would not answer. Neither through dreams, through visions, through prophets nor through the Urim did the lord answer Saul.

28:8 Saul became desperate and said to his men, "Go, seek forth for me a woman who be a necromancer, for I wish to speak to the dead." And the men said, "We know of a necromancer who lives within Endor."

28:9 Saul disguised himself with the robes of the poor and set foot to Endor, him and two men. They came to the women by night and said to her, "I beg of you, summon me a divine spirit of Samuel, so that I may speak with him."

28:10 The woman said, "I know who you are, king Saul, of the people of Israel.

28:11 You cast out all of my kin and sentenced us to death. How now do I know you not intend to entrap me and snare my life?"

28:12 And Saul said, "If I wished you dead, you would be dead, wretched woman.

28:13 I swear by the lord and all that is holy, I shall not punish you for your unholiness.

28:14 Bring me up the spirit of Samuel, so that I may seek his guidance."

28:15 The woman did as Saul said and through unholy magic summoned the spirit of Samuel.

28:16 The spirit of Samuel did arise and he wore the raiment's he was buried in.

28:17 Saul bowed down to Samuel and Samuel said to him, "Why do you disturb my slumber and sent me down again upon the realm of mortal men?"

28:18 And Saul answered, "I seek your knowledge, for the lord did abandon me.

28:19 The armies of Philistine are upon our borders and shall slay us all.

28:20 Through all means and matters I did ask the lord for guidance, but the lord did abandon me.

28:21 Tell me, O Samuel, what shall I do?"

28:22 And Samuel said, "My friend Saul, I am sorry, but there is naught ye can do.

28:23 Through death, I ascended to heaven and met with the lord and spoke with him.

28:24 In time, I knew the lord well and knew that the lord is a violent, angry, greedy, selfish, bastard of a being and was not worthy of the devotion I gave him in my life.

28:25 The lord has abandoned Israel, for the lord wishes Israel dead.

28:26 On the morrow, you and your sons shall be slain and shall join me in spirit.

28:27 The lord shall make it so, for the lord did hold back my hand, so that I cannot help you.

28:28 Even the hand of the devil does he hold back, for the devil is not evil and protects all mankind from the wrath of God.

28:29 Go, be gone and accept your death. You shall not ascent to heaven, but shall be cursed with me, you and your sons.

28:30 We shall walk the universe forever and be banned from the paradise our lord did promise for us.

28:31 I assure you, the paradise is false. The magic this unholy woman did use is more real than the promises our lord did give us."

28:32 Samuel then left and Saul fell and wept.

28:33 The necromancer came over Saul and said, "You are weakened and must eat.

28:34 Here, take this bread and water, so that you may gather your strength."

28:35 Saul said, "There is no need, for tomorrow I shall die."

28:36 The men of Saul said, "Surely this is untrue," and Saul said, "But it is.

28:37 Samuel himself did say it and the lord did abandon the people of Israel."

28:38 The men of Saul said, "Such a thing, it must be a lie."

28:39 This witch, she deceived you. Slay her."

28:40 And the men of Saul drew their swords and spilled the blood of the necromancer.

28:41 Saul was then picked up by his men and carried back to the camps of the army of Israel.

29:1 Now the Philistines gathered all their armies at Aphek and the armies of Israel gathered at a fountain in Jezreel.

29:2 The men of Philistine numbered in the hundreds of thousands and the men of David were with them, about six hundred.

29:3 The princes of Philistine asked, "Why are these men of Israel with us. Surely they mean not to fight their kin."

29:4 And Achish, king of the Philistines, said, "They are indeed here to fight with us, for they are loyal servants to me."

29:5 Still, the princes argued with Achish. "Surely this is a mistake, for they shall fight against their brothers.

29:6 Such a weakness can mean defeat for us."

29:7 Achish responded, "These men have served me for over a year and I find no fault nor weakness within them.

29:8 When they go, they shall fight their brothers and they shall slay them greater than either your or I."

29:9 Still, the princes remained persistent. "If they see their kin they not know, then they shall slay them.

29:10 But what if they see a brother. An uncle. A friend. What then?

29:11 Surely, they shall pause and hesitate before they plunge in their blade.

29:12 Such a pause can mean death for them, even if they do not choose to betray us and fight alongside the nation of Philistine."

29:13 Achish pondered this for a moment and agreed.

29:14 Achish spoke with David and said, "My servant, I mean you no disrespect, but you shall not fight in the battle against the people of Israel.

29:15 My men did brought forth concern."

29:16 David said, "They have no reason to be concerned, for through my time here I have served you and slew many men of Israel in your name.

29:17 Surely they know this and know of the glory I did bring to your name."

29:18 Achish said, "They do, but such raids were small and you raided cities where you had not friends nor family.

29:19 On this battle, you shall battle all the army of Israel and if you see a brother, an uncle, a friend, what then?"

29:20 David said, "If I recognize one, I shall slay them where they stand."

29:21 Achish said, "I know, but will ye slay them at first, or will you hesitate?

29:22 It is that risk I cannot allow, for you are a royal servant to me, and I hold you with great respect, and wish no harm to befall you.

29:23 If you were to go to battle, my men and I worry that you may give pause if ye see a brother and in that pause that brother, or another man of Israel, shall strike you down.

29:24 Such things cannot happen in battle and such things may happen to you.

29:25 Do not be insulted, for it is for your health we worry, not your loyalty."

29:26 David was angry and argued more with Achish, but Achish would not listen and denied David and his men to battle against the armies of Israel.

29:27 David was then ordered back to the lands of the Philistine with his men.

29:28 And they were all greatly pissed off, for they wished to shed the blood of their families, for they now hated those of Israel and wanted greatly to kill their families.

29:29 Surely David and his men were crazy motherfuckers.

30:1 When David returned to his city of Ziklag, they found that the Amalekites did destroy the city and burned it to ash.

30:2 The Amalekites killed not everyone, for they spared the children, the elderly and the women, taking them captive.

30:3 David and his men fell to the ground and wept, until they could shed no more tears.

30:4 The men of David were very angry, for they asked each other, "Why did David have to anger the Amalekites so. Surely, they would not have destroyed our city and taken our women and children if we did not anger them.

30:5 Weren't these tribes utterly wiped out and all the people of Amalek killed?

30:6 Surely, they must have a necromancer who raises them from the dead, for the peoples of Amalek refuse to die, no matter the genocide we cause upon them.

30:7 Let us stone David and perhaps the necromancers of Amalek shall give us their immortality."

30:8 David said, "You shall not stone me, for I too have lost my wives and children in this raid.

30:9 I know not why these peoples refuse to die. Perhaps they are a curse from God; a people that shall not be wiped from the earth.

30:10 Let us pray and the lord shall offer us guidance."

30:11 David and his men fell to the ground and prayed to the lord.

30:12 The lord God came down in great smoke and fire and said to the men, "What is the matter with you cowards.

30:13 Stop wallowing in your tears and chase after these damned people!

30:14 It is incompetence such as this which allow the people of Amalek to live."

30:15 The men of David gave chase to the Amalekites and pursued them day and night.

30:16 It came to pass that some of the men of David became ill and said "We cannot go, for we are ill and shall surely die in battle."

30:17 David said, "You weakened rabbit suckers, gather your strength and come."

30:18 But the men could not, for they were greatly sick and vomited upon the ground.

30:19 David then said, "Fine, stay behind. We shall leave that which we not need for battle, and you shall guard it."

30:20 So two hundred men of David stayed behind and guarded the belongings.

30:21 David then met an Egyptian man wandering the wilderness.

30:22 This Egyptian was greatly starving and dying of thirst. The men of David gave him water to drink and fed him with bread and fig cakes.

30:23 When the Egyptian gathered strength, the men of David asked him, "Who are you. Who do you belong to. What brought you here?"

30:24 And the Egyptian answered, "I am a man of Egypt and am now slave to the people of Amalek.

30:25 My master went forth and invaded the lands of the Cherethites, Judah, Caleb and Ziklag.

30:26 When I said to my master that we should slay all those we raid, he cast me out and called me wicked."

30:27 David said, "We are men of Ziklag and wish vengeance upon your master and his kin.

30:28 Tell me, where are they now?

30:29 And the Egyptian said, "I shall tell you, if ye give me the word of God that you will not kill me."

30:30 David said, "By the word of your lord, I shall not kill you."

30:31 And the Egyptian answered and gave them the location of the people of Amalek.

30:32 David then took his sword and beheaded the Egyptian.

30:33 Before the blow, the Egyptian said, "You swore by God that you will not kill me! and David said, "I swore by the name of your lord, which is meaningless to me."

30:34 David then went down and saw where the people of Amalek made camp.

30:35 The men of David went down in the night and slew all they could of the people of Amalek.

30:36 From dark until sunlight, they did slay all those of Amalek, save for four hundred who escaped on camels.

30:37 The lord looked down and said, "Useless fools. Again, they let the people of Amalek survive and now four hundred shall go and breed in abundance."

30:38 All those captured by the Amalekites praised David and believed themselves free.

30:39 They were gravely mistaken, for the men of David searched all those captured by the people of Amalek and slew all who did not belong to the city of Ziklag.

30:40 David reunited with his two wives and they engaged in great carnal fornication in the eyes of all those who were there.

30:41 David then took all the spoils of battle, and went back to where the remaining two hundred were.

30:42 The men said to themselves, "These men did not help us win the battle, they shall take no share of the loot."

30:43 David said, "If we give not a share to these men, they shall whine, bitch and betray us.

30:44 We shall lie and show them only a portion of the loot which we gathered.

30:45 They shall take a share of that loot, but the best shall remain for us."

30:46 And that became a statute throughout all of Israel.

30:47 David saved all the loot for himself and his men and gave none to the others who were raided.

30:48 For David, like God, was a greedy bastard.

31:1 As this happened, the Philistines fought against Israel and defeated them greatly. The men of Israel which survived fled to mount Gilboa.

31:2 The Philistines chased Saul and his sons and slew Jonathan, Abinadab, and Melchishua, so that all the sons of Saul were dead.

31:3 As the battle raged on, an archer hit Saul, wounding him terribly.

31:4 Saul said to his armourbearer, "Take your sword and kill me, for I shall not be slain by the hands of a fucking heathen."

31:5 But the armourbearer refused, for he was afraid.

31:6 Saul then took his sword and fell upon it, killing himself.

31:7 When the armourbearer saw that Saul was dead, he also took his sword and fell upon it, killing himself.

31:8 When the men of Israel heard that Saul was dead, they abandoned their cities and fled like cowards.

31:9 Which is the nature of the people of Israel, when God isn't down fighting with them.

31:10 The Philistines reclaimed these cities and dwelt within them.

31:11 After the battle, the Philistines came and saw the corpses of Saul and his sons.

31:12 They cut forth the head of Saul, stripped of his body his armour and placed them on display within all the temples of their lords.

31:13 The head of Saul was sent to tour to all the temples and the armour of Saul was placed within the temple of Ashtaroth and the body hung of the walls of Bethshan, beside his sons.

31:14 The men of Jabeshgilead heard of the desecration of the bodies of Saul and his sons and two men on a dare did go and take back the bodies of their king and their princes.

31:15 They burned their bodies as an offering unto the lord and danced around the fire naked, speaking in gibberish.

31:16 This pleased the lord greatly, for though the days were filled with the lust of bloodshed and death, the lord still loves when a body is burnt upon stones, as the aroma creates a pleasing scent to God.

II SAMUEL

1:1 It came to pass that when the battle was over between the Philistines and the Israelites, David went back to Ziklag and resided there two days.

1:2 Upon the third day, a man came to Ziklag with his clothes tattered and dust upon his head. When he came to David, he bowed to him and kissed his feet.

1:3 David asked this man, "Who are you, who comes to me filthy and kisses my feet?" and the man said, "I am a man who escaped from the battle of Israel."

1:4 David said, "Pray tell, how did the battle go?" and the man said, "The Israelites fled in terror, for their lord did not come to save them.

1:5 Saul and his sons hang dead now upon on the city walls of Bethshan."

1:6 The man said this, believing David shall be pleased with the death of Saul and shall reward him for his good news.

1:7 David asked this man, "How do you know that Saul and his sons be dead? Did you see their bodies, or witness their death?"

1:8 The young man lied to David more, hoping to gain his favour and said, "I happened by chance to see Saul as I was walking through mount Gilboa.

1:9 He was gravely wounded with an arrow and was leaning upon his spear.

1:10 Saul asked me where I was and I answered him

1:11 He asked me who I was and I said that I was a child of Israel and loyal follower of the one true God.

1:12 Saul then demanded that I go forth and slay the wicked one David, for he did bring a curse against him and all those of Israel.

1:13 I grabbed Saul's spear and thrust it within his breast, so that he lay dead upon the ground.

1:14 The sons of Saul I searched for and behold, all were slain by the heathens of Philistine."

1:15 David grew enraged and said, "You dare slay Saul, the king of Israel, who was anointed by God?

1:16 Such a thing is blasphemous and shall curse and your seed for all generations.

1:17 Twice I could have slain that bastard Saul, yet twice I let him live. Though Saul was my enemy, he was chosen by the lord and the lord shall kill him in his way.

1:18 You shall be put to death, for slaying that who was chosen by God.

1:19 The man then told the truth and said, "My lord, I was mistaken, for I am tired and forgot that which happened.

1:20 The sons of Saul were slain by the Philistines, but Saul was not slain by neither the heathens nor my hand.

1:21 When I saw Saul, he was leaning against the sharp head of his spear and when I called for him, he fell against it and died."

1:22 David said, "Then you shall die for your deception unto me."

1:23 With that, David ordered one of his men to execute this man of Israel.

1:24 And David's men grabbed him and bound him with leather strips to a tree.

1:25 Alive, the predators of the wild did come and feast of the flesh of this man who told David the news of Saul and his sons.

1:26 This pleased the lord greatly and the lord did give this man long life, so that his suffering shall last for days as the scavengers did rip the flesh, the organs and spilled the blood of this man.

1:27 For the lord God is a cruel God and enjoys cruelty greatly.

1:28 David went to his tent and mourned greatly for the death of Jonathan.

1:29 David said to his men, "Such vengeance for the death of Jonathan must be brought upon the people of Philistine.

1:30 The beauty of Israel hast been slain today and the mighty did fall.

1:31 Tell not the news of the death of Saul and his sons. Tell it not in Gath, nor in the streets of Askelon, lest the daughters of the Philistine rejoice and those who remain with their foreskins triumph.

1:32 Let there be no dew upon the grass of the heathens, nor rain upon their crops. May their shields rust and shatter by the blow of the Israelites.

1:33 From the blood of the slain, we shall gather strength, O those of Israel. We shall grow fat, strong, mighty and slay these heathens until every fucking one lay dead in the sight of our lord.

1:34 May the daughters of Israel weep this day, for Saul did dress them in finest silk and gave them ornaments of gold from those he did conquer.

1:35 O Jonathan, I mourn for you. Your touch was very pleasant to me and you gave me more pleasures than that of any woman.

1:36 I shall miss your caress, your kiss, your embrace, for these beasts of Philistine did take you from me."

1:37 David then went back into his tent, weeping and thinking deeply of his love for Jonathan.

1:38 When David thought back of his times with Jonathan, his moments of lust, he did become erect and masturbated in his tears.

2:1 It came to pass that David asked the lord, "Where shall I go?" and the lord answered, "Do I need to make every damn decision for you?

2:2 The lord dwells within the heavens and is busy creating that which your very imagination could not begin to understand.

2:3 Yet you pests of Israel still annoy the lord and cannot even decide where to dwell without consulting the lord God almighty.

2:4 Go, give me a sacrifice of nine score young virgins and I will tell you where to go.

2:5 David went forth, gathering himself nine score young virgins under the age of ten and sacrificed them upon the altar.

2:6 When the lord saw the nine score virgins he was pleased and came down beside the altar in great smoke and fire.

2:7 The lord took every virgin, and raped them, so that the virgins screamed in pain.

2:8 God then burned them alive with his fire and suffocated them with his smoke. This pleased the lord greatly and the lord said to David, "Such a thing has given pleasure unto your God.

2:9 Go forth, you, your wives and your men and dwell within the city of Hebron in the lands of Judah."

2:10 And David gathered his two wives, Ahinoam the Jezreelitess, and Abigail the Carmelite and went to Hebron.

2:11 The men of David gathered their belongings and followed him, for they were like sheep and David their shepherd.

2:12 The men of Judah came to David as he dwelt in Hebron and said, "Y have dwelt here for quite some time. Take that Philistine headdress off, you damn fool."

2:13 David said, "I shall not take this headdress off, unless I am given a better replacement for it."

2:14 And the men of Judah gave David a crown and made him king of Judah, so that David would finally rid himself of the Philistine headdress.

2:15 It was a petty and stupid way to anoint a ruler, yet like how people of government come into power even to this day.

2:16 The men of Judah then came to David and told him how the men of Jabeshgilead did take the bodies of Saul and his slain son and buried them according to the customs of the lord.

2:17 David sent message to those of Jabeshgilead and said, "May the lord bless and keep you, for that which you did to the bodies of Saul and his sons.

2:18 Now the lord shall show you kindness for your deeds and I shall ask politely that you join my nation and be ruled by me, instead of coming in with my armies and taking you by force."

2:19 But Abner the son of Ner, general over the army of Saul, did take Ishbosheth, the surviving son of Saul, over to Mahanaim.

2:20 There Ishbosheth was made king of Israel and ruled the lands, including those of Jabeshgilead.

2:21 Ishbosheth was forty years old when he was made king of Israel and ruled those of Israel for two years.

2:22 The men of Jabeshgilead said to David, "We cannot, for we are servants of Ishbosheth, king of Israel and son of Saul."

2:23 David was king of Judah for seven years and six angry months, for he wished to rule over all those of Israel.

2:24 Thus civil war erupted between Judah and the other eleven tribes of Israel.

2:25 This pleased the lord greatly, for it meant more people of Israel slain, and less peoples of which the lord had to keep his covenant with.

2:26 Abner, the general of the armies of Israel, took his men and went out from Manaheim to Gibeon.

2:27 Joab the son of Zeruiah(or so he thought) took the men of David and met with Abner by a pool in Gibeon, so that the armies of David were on one side and the armies of Israel across the other.

2:28 The two sides stared each other down, but would not fight, for fear of getting wet and their armour rusting in the waters of the pool.

2:29 Abner grew impatient and said, "This is pathetic. Let us send out our best men, so that they may fight.

2:30 Twelve men from each of us shall go and fight in the waters."

2:31 Joab agreed, saying, "Let your best men come forth so that mine shall go and slay them."

2:32 Abner sent forth twelve of his best men, from the tribe of Benjamin, to the pool so that they may fight.

2:33 Joab sent his best twelve men, who did take off their armour before entering the waters; something the men of Benjamin did not do.

2:34 As the men met in the pool, the armour of those of Benjamin became heavy so that they could move not move in the pool.

2:35 The men of David grabbed these men and thrust their heads under the water so that they drowned.

2:36 They would then taunt the armies of Israel, saying, "Look, your best men have their heads between my legs and give me the services of your whores, begging me that I spare their whorish lives."

2:37 And the people of Israel named the pool Helkatharruzim, which is the sound those drowning did make, as the people of David fellated their faces underwater.

2:38 There was a very long and bloody battle that day as the men of Abner, the men of Israel, were slaughtered by those faithful to David.

2:39 Joab and his two brothers, Abishai and Asahel, who were truly the sons of Zeruiah, fought bravely and killed many a man of Israel in glory to God.

2:40 Asahel was as fast as a light doe and gave chase of Abner, hoping to catch him.

2:41 As Abner fled, he yelled behind him and asked, "Are you not Asahel?" and Asahel replied, "Yes I am."

2:42 Abner said, "We are both men of Israel. Let us stop, so that we may end this civil war before more blood of our brethren be spilled."

2:43 Asahel agreed and said, "Let us bring peace between our peoples again and join as one."

2:44 Foolish Abner stopped and Asahel stopped with him, taking his blade and slicing a small hole within the throat of Abner,.

2:45 Asahel then raped the very throat of Abner, until his seed spilled deep within the throat of Abner.

2:46 This is where the term deep throat did come.

2:47 When the seed of Asahel did spill within the throat of Abner, Abner gazed up at him, for he was still alive.

2:48 Abner took the blade of Asahel and thrust it under his fifth rib, killing him.

2:49 Both Joab and Abishai gave chase of Abner, but were not as quick as their brother Asahel.

2:50 They both came to the hill of Ammah, that lies before Giah and behold, there they saw their brother slain.

2:51 Abner went back to the people of Benjamin as they gathered themselves upon a hill as one.

2:52 Abner yelled to Joab, in a very deep voice, "Your brother did fuck the very throat of mine and for this I did slay him.

2:53 For this I blame none of you, and ask how long shall our sword devour each other?

2:54 We are both men of Israel, chosen by God. Let us kill those who worship differently from us."

2:55 Joab saw the hole which Asahel did rape and knew that Abner spoke the truth.

2:56 Joab said, "Until the lord says otherwise, we shall slay you no more."

2:57 And the two armies went their separate ways. Those of Israel went back to Manaheim, the men of David to Hebron.

2:58 Now, the men of David lost nineteen men that day, including Asahel. But those of Israel were slaughtered three hundred and three score men.

2:59 The men of David snickered and said to one another, "We kicked their asses."

2:60 Joab took the body of Asahel and buried it within the sepulcher of his father, which be in Bethlehem.

3:1 Despite what Aber said, the houses of Israel and David still fought against one another. The house of Israel became weakened, while the house of David became strong.

3:2 Unto David were born sons in the city of Hebron. The first-born was Amnon of Ahihoam.

3:3 The second was Chilieab of Abigail, the third was Absalom of Maacha,

3:4 The fourth was Adonijah of Haggith, the fifth Shephatiah of Abital,

3:5 The sixth Ithream of Eglah. These six sons were born of David in the city of Hebron.

3:6 Six sons, born by six different women and the men of David called their ruler a true romancer of women.

3:7 David indulged in this reputation, for he wished not his men to know that he secretly lusted for the embrace of a man; the embrace of Jonathan.

3:8 It came to pass while the war between the two houses raged that Abner made himself strong and powerful in the house of Saul.

3:9 Saul had a concubine, whose name was Rizpah the daughter of Aiah. She was a beautiful young woman and all men who gazed upon her lusted for her deeply.

3:10 Abner lusted deeply for Rizpah and had her sent to his bedchamber.

3:11 There Abner fucked the dirty whore of Saul's until the very seeds remaining in his body became empty and he could fuck no more.

3:12 Ishbosheth heard what Abner did and became angry. He came to Abner and said, "How dare you lie with Rizpah, the whore of my father."

3:13 And Abner said, "Your father lie dead and Rizpah is no longer owned by him.

3:14 How dare you be angry, for not only did I lie with Rizpah, but many others as well.

3:15 Am I your dog? Your loyal pet, sent forth to do your bidding, yet not allowed to bury his bone where it dwells?

3:16 You foolish, ignorant waste of flesh, who gets angry over a powerful man such as I, over a lowly cock-sucking concubine."

3:17 Abner then drew his blade and placed it upon the very neck of Ishbosheth, saying, "Y shall regret this, the day you angered me.

3:18 By the very name of God I shall make league with David and it shall be he who sits upon the throne of Israel.

3:19 David shall rule over all of Israel and you shall be cursed by the very lord, for getting angry over a damned whore."

3:20 Ishbosheth never spoke another word to Abner, for he greatly feared him.

3:21 Rizpah was then sent to the bedchamber of Ishbosheth and the king said unto her, "Lie with me, as you do other men."

3:22 And Rizpah said, "I cannot, for you are the son of Saul, who once owned my body and mind.

3:23 To lie with you is a sin against the lord. It will also just be weird, for I slept with your father."

3:24 Ishbosheth became enrage, and said, "You lied with Abner!" and Rizpah answered, "I did, and I lied with many others."

3:25 None were the sons of Saul."

3:26 In fury, Ishbosheth grasped Rizpah and demanded they have sex.

3:27 But the lord cursed Ishbosheth that day and no matter the stimulation, an erection was not to be had by him.

3:28 And Rizpah told all the concubines in Israel that Ishbosheth was weak in the loins and had both the length and girth of a locust.

3:29 Abner sent messengers out to David and said, "This land of Israel shall become yours and I wish you to claim it.

3:30 Make league with me and I shall fight by your sides as you claim your place upon the throne of Israel."

3:31 David replied to Abner, "I shall make league with you, but first you must show me a sign of your faith.

3:32 My wife, Michal, which I did buy for one hundred foreskins, is now married to another man.

3:33 Bring her to me and I we shall have peace between our houses."

3:34 Abner went forth and took Michal from her husband, who was Phaltiel the son of Laish.

3:35 Phaltiel wept deeply and followed his wife all the way to Bahurim, crying, "Please don't take my wife from me, please don't take my wife from me.

3:36 She is the only woman who fucks me. She must! She's my wife!

3:37 Please, don't take her from me. If you do, I shall never know the pleasures of women again."

3:38 Abner grew annoyed by the man's whining, took his blade and said to him, "If you do not leave now, I shall cut off that which makes you a man and all those of my army shall know you as a cheap whore."

3:39 Phaltiel left immediately.

3:40 Michal was brought back to David and when David saw her, he slapped the woman across the face and said, "You cheap harlot! How dare you be married to another when you still belong to me."

3:41 In tears, Michal said, "My father sold me to this man. It was not my wish.

3:42 Come now, let us go in your tent and I shall perform to you that which a wife is meant to do."

3:43 David took Michal to his bedchamber. Michal undressed and David said, "Take off not your clothes, unless you use them to clean the floor."

3:44 And Michal did her wifely duties to David that day, yet never the duty which she wished to perform.

3:45 Abner returned to the elders of Israel and spoke with them in private, saying, "Remember David, who slew the heathen Goliath, who saved us from the Philistines and who killed the tens of thousands.

3:46 He is a strong and righteous man; a true man of God. Surely he shall be king."

3:47 And the elders said, "I care not who is king. As long as my purse be full of shekels, my cup filled with wine and my plate never empty, let the devil himself be king."

3:48 And it was then decided that David shall be king of all Israel.

3:49 Abner came to Hebron and David prepared for him a great feast of breads, cakes, lamb, pheasant, quail, figs, olives, grapes, pomegranates, cheese and dates.

3:50 Abner said, "It is agreed through all the lands, that you shall be anointed king of Israel."

3:51 David said, "Excellent, now let us feast, for I am hungry."

3:52 And the two men consumed in gluttony all that which be on the table.

3:53 Joab returned from a raid with a great deal of plunder; for Joab loves to kill many people and take that which they own.

3:54 When Joab heard that Abner was in Hebron, he became furious and wished to avenge the death of his brother Asahel.

3:55 Messengers were sent in secret to Joab and they said, "My master wishes to speak with you in private.

3:56 Go now after dark to the gates of the city."

3:57 Abner went to meet with Joab and never questioned why he was to meet alone, in the dark, in a quiet part of the city.

3:58 Abner was really, really, stupid.

3:59 When Joab saw Abner, he came up to him and embraced him and said, "How I missed you, my brother of Israel. We have fought too long."

3:60 It was then Joab took a blade from his sleeve and thrust it under the fifth rib of Abner, killing him.

3:61 Joab then opened the wound of Abner which be upon his throat and raped the body of Abner by the gates of Hebron.

3:62 Those who walked by, took no notice, for Joab would bring back often a body from a raid and rape its throat by the gates of Hebron.

3:63 A servant of David heard what happened and said to his king, "Your servant Joab just killed Abner and is now sowing seeds within his throat."

3:64 David became furious and said, "My name and my kingdom are to be guiltless for the blood shed upon the ground this day.

3:65 Let the curse of the lord be laid upon Joab for the death of Abner. May his seed dry, his generation end, his house crumble and leprosy be cast among him.

3:66 May he know only thirst and hunger and may the diseases of all the brothels of the lands infest his loins.

3:67 Let him be weakened, so that even the frailest of girls shall cripple him."

3:68 And the servant said, "Is Joab to be banned from our lands?"

3:69 And David said, "Hell no, for he is my general!"

3:70 And Joab remained within the services of David, even after the curse.

3:71 David said to Joab, "It must be known that you are saddened by the death of Abner," and Joab replied, "I am not, for I take great pleasure from his death."

3:72 David then said, "You must look grieved, lest the peoples think otherwise.

3:73 Go, gather your men. Pour dust upon your heads, wear your sackcloth and mourn the death of Abner."

3:74 And they did, as did David.

3:75 All the congregation of Israel saw David weeping for Abner and they said, "Look how our king weeps for Abner.

3:76 Though Abner was his enemy, the king still mourns for him, as he was a child of Israel.

3:77 Surely such a king shall love us and protect all those chosen by God."

3:78 And Abner was buried in the lands of Hebron, with a large and gaping hole in his throat.

4:1 When Ishbosheth heard that Abner was killed and that the people were saying that David be their new king, he trembled with fear.

4:2 Ishbosheth feared David and believed that David shall come to take the throne and kill him.

4:3 Ishbosheth, the son of Saul, had two captains that were believed loyal. Two brothers, Baanah and Rechab the sons of Rimmon.

4:4 King Ishbosheth brought them forth and said, "Protect your king, and you shall be greatly rewarded."

4:5 The two brothers spoke and said, "If we kill Ishbosheth, the new king shall reward us greater."

4:6 So both Baanah and Rechab drew their swords, beheading their king Ishbosheth.

4:7 They brought the head of Ishbosheth to David and said, "I have a gift for the new king of Israel."

4:8 David answered them, "You brought me not a gift, but have stolen from me.

4:9 I wished greatly that it be my hand that killed Ishbosheth, my blade which stains my throne with the blood of the son of Saul.

4:10 You have taken by force that which was rightfully mine. I will have my blood."

4:11 David then drew his blade and severed both the hands and the feet of Baanah and Rechab.

4:12 The two brothers screamed as David severed their limbs, saying to him, "Forgive us, for we knew not what we stole."

4:13 David gathered the feet and the hands and used it to decorate his house.

4:14 He hung them above the gardens, so that the birds may feast upon them.

4:15 Both Baanah and Rachah were ordered to be hung alive above the pool of Hebron, so that all those shall see what happens to those which steal from David.

4:16 Alas, they kept falling from their ropes, for the men of David could not make nots which would hold the men above the pool with their hands and feet missing.

4:17 David grew angry at his men and said, "Have some pride in your work and use some creativity."

4:18 David then took his blade and severed in each cheek a hole in the two brothers.

4:19 David then threaded the rope within the holes of the cheeks and then hung them above the pool of Hebron.

4:20 As those of Israel walked by, they would say, "There be two men who stole from David by killing his enemy.

4:21 Surely such a king shall slay our enemies as well."

4:22 Those that said otherwise were secretly killed.

5:1 There came all the tribes of Israel to Hebron and they said, "Behold, we are the flesh and the bones of David.

5:2 May David lead us, rule us and command us. For even when Saul was king, it was David who went out and led Israel to victory."

5:3 The elders of Israel came and anointed David the new king of Israel. David was thirty years of age at the time and his reign lasted for forty years.

5:4 David and his men went forth to Jerusalem unto the Jebusites and the Jebusites said, "We shall not let you in, unless you rid us of these lame, blind and crippled fools."

5:5 David said, "What use do I have for the useless?" and the Jebusites said, "The same as we do."

5:6 Now, David hated the blind and the lame and believed them a parasite feeding off the society of Israel.

5:7 The king said to his men, "Whosoever go in that city and smite the lame and the blind shall hold great favour in my sight.

5:8 They shall be made my chief and captain, for I want this city as my home and wish not the crippled and the useless dwell here."

5:9 Joab used the sewers underneath and breeched the city. He was the first to slay a cripple and therefore he gained favour in the sight of David.

5:10 David dwelt in this new conquered city and invaded the lands round it. He renamed it the city of David.

5:11 Hyram king of Tyre feared David and sent him cedar, mortar, carpenter sand masons and they did build for David a house.

5:12 David celebrated and bought for himself more concubines for him to fuck.

5:13 And fuck them he did, so that David was given more sons and more daughters from these whores.

5:14 These are the names of the sons born of whores in the city of Jerusalem; Shammuah, Shobab, Nathan, Solomon,

5:15 Ibhar, Elishua, Nepheg, Japhia,

5:16 Elishama, Eliada and Eliphalet.

5:17 When the Philistines heard that David was king, they sent forth men to congratulate him and believed peace shall be had between the two nations.

5:18 They were wrong.

5:19 These Philistines pitched camp on the valley of Rephaim and rested in the shade of the trees.

5:20 King David said, "Surely the lord shall wish me to go and slaughter these heathens."

5:21 And the lord said, "You are wise, for the lord does wish you to go and slaughter these heathens against God.

5:22 Go, battle with them and know that your lord shall deliver them in your hands."

5:23 David came to Baalperazim, where he saw the priests of Philistine worshipping their idols and false gods.

5:24 The men of David went forth and killed all the priests of Philistine in Baalperazim and enjoyed it, for they were defenceless and did not expect David to kill them.

5:25 David gathered the false gods of the lord of Philistine and ordered them destroyed.

5:26 The men of David crushed these idols, burned them and mixed the dust and ash with water and forced the priests to drink the bitter liquid.

5:27 All the priests refused, for they feared to drink the idols of their lord shall anger them. So the men of David cut from these priests their bottom jaw and poured the liquid down their throats.

5:28 The lord of Israel looked down and laughed.

5:29 The gods of Philistine looked down and wept, for they wished not their holy to be slain.

5:30 The one true God would not allow them to intervene, for the gods of Philistine and all false gods, are sons and daughters of the true lord; the lord of Israel.

5:31 David saw that the men of Philistine were spread throughout the valley of Rephaim and decided to face them in battle.

5:32 But the lord said, "You shall not face them in battle, but sneak around their camps and hide within the mulberry trees behind them.

5:33 Wait until the moon replaces the sun in the sky and when the moon is at its highest, go forth and slay those heathens who sleep."

5:34 David did as the lord commanded and hid behind the camp of Philistine, hiding within the mulberry trees.

5:35 The king and his men mocked the peoples of Philistine, saying, "Look, they come and bring no blades, no archers, no masons.

5:36 It is as though they wish us to slay them."

5:37 When the moon was at its highest, David and his men did go forth and slaughtered those who slept within their tents.

5:38 Those heathens that could, ran away and the new army of Israel gave chase.

5:39 From Geba unto Gazer David did kill the Philistines who came to congratulate him on becoming king, believing peace between the two nations.

5:40 Peace was not made.

6:1 David gathered his personal guards, which numbered thirty thousand.

6:2 And they arose and marched forth to Baale of Judah, so that they may take the ark of the lord, where the lord does dwell.

6:3 They placed the ark of God upon a new cart, made of shittim wood inlaid with gold and brought it out of the house of Abinadab that was in Gibeah.

6:4 Uzzah and Ahio, the sons of Abinadab, drove the new cart forth.

6:5 As the two sons drove the new cart, David and his men danced around the cart, singing and playing harps, trumpets, and cymbals.

6:6 When they came to the threshing floor of Nachon, the king himself did stumble upon Uzzah, and Uzzah lost his step, falling on top of the ark.

6:7 When Uzzah touched the ark, the lord God became very angry and the very finger of the lord came down and touched Uzzah.

6:8 The sky did split apart and great twisted bolts of lightning came down and touched the head of Uzzah.

6:9 The very skin and flesh of Uzzah turned to ash, so that all which was left of him were burned bones and ash.

6:10 David, in drunken fury, yelled up to God and said, "You idiot! Who now shall carry the ark?"

6:11 The lord replied, "It is unwise to call the lord an idiot, when the lord is in a killing mood."

6:12 David knew not what to do, for he wished not to curse another man with carrying the ark.

6:13 So the ark of the lord stayed there, in the house of Obededom the Gittite.

6:14 David then marked the very ground where Uzzah last stood and named it Peezuzzah, which means 'breach of Uzzah.'

6:15 For three months the ark of the lord stayed with Obededom and the family of Obededom cared for the ark and gave it burnt offerings.

6:16 This pleased the lord and God did bless Obededom with great crops, bountiful harvests and all his flocks and his cattle born those months were born males without blemish.

6:17 A messenger came and told David, "The house of Obededom has been blessed by the ark of the lord."

6:18 David said, "This blessing belongs not to a house, but to me.

6:19 Let us go and we shall take the ark back and place it within my city, so that I shall receive the blessing of the lord."

6:20 The men of David placed the ark upon a new cart, made of shittim wood inlaid with gold and when they stepped six paces, David offered sacrifice of a fatten lamb and ox, saying, "Surely now the lord will not kill anyone this time."

6:21 The lord looked down and said to himself, "We shall see."

6:22 David and his men danced around the ark, playing instruments of brass, silver and gold, in celebration of the ark coming to the city of David.

6:23 They very loincloth of David was ripped from him, so that David danced naked. He was too drunk to notice.

6:24 When the ark was brought forth to the city of David, all those who dwelt there saw their king, dancing naked like a fool.

6:25 Even the harlots and those of the brothels saw David danced naked and laughed.

6:26 Michal, daughter of Saul and wife of David, heard the laughter of the whores and looked out her window.

6:27 Behold, she saw her husband, dancing naked like a fool and exposing his loins to all those who could see.

6:28 Michal became furious, for her handmaidens saw also David and said, "How can you give service to the loins of David?

6:29 Such genitals as those surely cannot give you pleasure. The very olives which grow on the branch are bigger."

6:30 And Michal became known as the one who had to fuck a small penis, which angered her greatly.

6:31 When David returned home, Michal was furious and said to him, "How dare you embarrass me by dancing naked in the streets.

6:32 Do you not know that all those can see thee? From the priests, even unto the filthy whores, they saw that which you hide beneath your loincloth."

6:33 David said, "Wretched woman, I was dancing naked in front of the lord."

6:34 Michal replied, "Cease calling me wretched, for you danced naked not just in front of the lord, but in front of all those who have eyes to see!

6:35 Did you not see the children laughing? The whores mocking? Have you no shame?"

6:36 David said, "I have no shame at all.

6:37 Let me dance in front of the whores, for they have seen their share of penises.

6:38 Better yet, let them come and service mine."

6:39 David then sent for a concubine, who did get on her knees and orally pleasured David as Michal watched.

6:40 Michal said, "I loathe you, David and wished I were back with my husband Phaltiel.

6:41 May your seed stop so that your generations end."

6:42 Michal then grabbed her very uterus from her womb and thrust it out from her loins.

6:43 She threw this at David and said, "You shall have no more sons from me."

6:44 Michal then left, as the concubine still did her services unto David.

6:45 David asked his whore, "Would you like the honour of having my son?" and the whore said, "Of course, my king."

6:46 And the two did lie upon the bed and slept with great intimacy. Nine months later, the concubine gave birth to a daughter.

6:47 David had her killed.

7:1 The lord gazed down upon David, who dwelt in his house of cedar and stone and the lord became jealous.

7:2 For David dwelt in a house, but the lord lived within an ark made of shittim wood and gold.

7:3 The lord came down upon the prophet Nathan and said to him, "The lord is cramped within his house and wishes to reside in a larger dwelling.

7:4 Go, tell my servant David that the lord wishes a house made in his honour; a house of cedar and gold.

7:5 God needs not dwell within the ark, for the people of Israel no longer travel the desert.

7:6 Now my people are planted within the lands promised within the covenant since the days of Abraham and the lord shall reside among them.

7:7 The lord God went wherever those of his people went and did cut down their enemies and kept his word with the children of Israel.

7:8 David, who was once a herder of sheep, is now ruler of Israel and shall build the lord a temple in my honour.

7:9 For when David builds this house of the lord, God shall bless his name and his seed shall last throughout all the generations.

7:10 When the temple is complete, may the throne of Israel be established in the kingdom of men forever.

7:11 The lord shall be as a father unto David and David shall be as a son. If David sins, the father shall punish him harshly with the rod.

7:12 But mercy shall be shown to David, the mercy which the lord denied to Saul.

7:13 For my house and the kingdom of Israel, shall last forever through all generations of mankind."

7:14 The words of God Nathan told David.

7:15 David went forth and gathered the slaves of Israel, so that they all worked to build the mighty temple of the lord.

7:16 And through slave labour, the temple of the lord became complete. And those of Israel said, "Blessed be the name of the lord."

8:1 It came to pass that David captured more lands from the nation

Philistine and conquered the city Methegammah, killing all within.

8:2 Men, women, children, elderly, crippled and blind David did kill, for David wished to please the lord with as the lord loves most to be pleased; mass death.

8:3 The lord came to David and said to him, "You have conquered a great many lands from those deemed unworthy and this pleases your God greatly.

8:4 However, soon those against you shall join together and they shall be as one great army.

8:5 Do not conquer them with death, through fear. Allow them to think they are independent from you, whilst you exploit them with fear."

8:6 So David went forth to the lands of Moab and captured the men of their army.

8:7 David had the soldiers of Moab lie upon the ground and every two men David beheaded, but the third was allowed to live and leave.

8:8 The king of Israel then said, "Let us have peace between our nations. Give to me a portion of your crops, your wine, your olives, your gold and I will not invade nor harm your people."

8:9 And the people of Moab did and David did not invade so long as the Moabites paid their dues.

8:10 David slew also Hadadezer the son of Rehob, king of Zobah, as David went to capture lands which surround the river Euphrates.

8:11 And David took one thousand chariots, seven hundred horsemen, and twenty-two thousand footmen of Hadadezer's.

8:12 Of the armour, the weapons, the chariots, David kept. Nine hundred horses which drove the chariots were made crippled and left to rot in the sun, but one hundred of the best David did keep for himself.

8:13 The Syrians of Damascus were allies with Hadadezer and went to avenge their friend and ally.

8:14 David killed them all as well, so that twenty-two thousand men of Damascus died.

8:15 King David then went to Damascus, and said "I have no reason to be your enemy, for it was Hadadezer and not you whom I conquered.

8:16 Let there be peace between our nations.

8:17 Give to me a portion of your crops, your wines, your women, your olives, your gold, your slaves and I shall not bring the wrath of the lord within your lands."

8:18 And the men of Damascus did, for they feared the wrath and the might of the lord of Israel.

8:19 The men of David took from the slain men of Hadadezer their golden shields and brought them to Jerusalem.

8:20 From Betah and Berothai, cities conquered from Hadadezer, the men of David brought back great wealth in bronze.

8:21 When Toi king of Hamath heard that David slew Hadadezer and conquered the cities of Betah and Berothai,

8:22 Toi became afraid, for Hadadezer was considered a powerful man.

8:23 Toi sent his son, Joram to David, so that they shall negotiate peace between their two nations.

8:24 Joram brought with him vessels of silver, of brass and of gold and gave it to David as a gift.

8:25 David accepted these gifts and all that which Joram brought, as well as the gold shields of Hadadezer and the bronze brought forth from Betah and Berothai, David did dedicate to the lord.

8:26 And the lord would gaze down upon these things and be pleased, for the lord craves bling.

8:27 The name of David became well feared among the nations, for David did conquer eighteen thousand men of Syria in the valley of Salt.

8:28 The men of Syria were known as skilled and fearless warriors and when nations heard that David defeated them with ease, they became scared and feared the nation of Israel.

8:29 David then placed garrisons within the lands of Edom and all those of Edom who were captured by these garrisons became slaves for the nation of Israel.

8:30 All this David did under the protection of God. The lord loved David, for David was a violent, greedy, crazy motherfucker.

8:31 Much like God.

8:32 David reigned over all those of Israel and executed justice and judgment according to the laws, the testaments and the statutes of the lord.

8:33 Joab the son of Zeruiah(supposedly) was leader of the armies of Israel and Jehosaphat the son of Ahilud recorded all that which David and Israel did.

8:34 Jehosaphat would conveniently forget to record all that which David did wicked in the sight of the lord. This pleased David greatly.

8:35 Zadok the son of Ahitub and Ahimelech the son of Abiather became priests and Seraiah the son of some guy and mother of a harlot became scribe.

8:36 Benaiah the son of Jehoiada ruled over the Cherethites and the sons of David became chief rulers over the provinces of Israel.

9:1 David inquired if there was any left of the seed of Saul, so that he may execute them, ending the generations of Saul.

9:2 Ziba, a servant of David, was once a servant of Saul's and he said, "I believe there is one man left of Saul's seed."

9:3 David said, "Go forth and bring him to me, so that I may spill his blood upon the very throne where his father sat."

9:4 Ziba went to the house of Machir, the son of Ammiel, in Lodebar, for this is where the seed of Saul dwelt.

9:5 There in the house was Mephibosheth, a cripple, whom David loathed. Mephibosheth was dragged by Ziba back to the house of David.

9:6 David asked him, "Who are you, wretched cripple?" and he answered, "I am Mephibosheth, of the seed of Saul."

9:7 It was then David notice the resemblance. The eyes, the shape of the forehead, the jaw. David held back the tears in his eyes and said, "Tell me, are you the son of Jonathan?"

9:8 Mephibosheth said, "Yes, Jonathan is my father."

9:9 David cried and said, "Your father was a great man, and I love him still more than I love my wives.

9:10 Blessed be the seed of Jonathan and blessed be you, the son of Jonathan.

9:11 Come, stay with me and eat bread at my table."

9:12 Mephibosheth said to David, "To do such a thing shall surely be a dishonour against you.

9:13 I am as a lame dog and my legs are crippled and have the strength of dry twigs."

9:14 David said, "It matters not that you are a cripple, for you are the son of Jonathan.

9:15 May it be that the son of Jonathan live in wealth and honour of his father.

9:16 The lands which I claimed of Saul's shall now belong to you.

9:17 May your crops grow; your vineyards be bountiful and your olives plentiful."

9:18 Mephibosheth said to David, "Such a gift is a great honour to me and I am grateful.

9:19 But I am lame and cannot till the soil, nor harvest the grains."

9:20 David said, "Fear not, for I shall give to you slaves to do your bidding.

9:21 Ziba, who brought you here, shall now belong to you.

9:22 May Ziba and all his family be slaves to the son of Jonathan."

9:23 Now Ziba had fifteen sons and they became slaves to Mephibosheth and toiled in his fields.

9:24 David then said, "You are crippled, so the women of Israel shall not deem you worthy to be husband.

9:25 Take that which you please of my concubines. May they give you great pleasure."

9:26 Mephibosheth thanked David and did lie with the concubines of David.

9:27 And David kept Mephibosheth in his house and cared for him as they ate at the table together.

9:28 David would gaze with lust at Mephibosheth and say to himself, "He has the resemblance of his father, whom I love dearly."

9:29 One night, the lust of David could be held back no longer and David grasped Mephibosheth and performed sodomy upon him.

9:30 Mephibosheth cried, and could not run away for his legs were useless.

9:31 And this pleased David greatly, for no matter how hard the struggle, Mephibosheth could not leave the rape which David did against him.

10:1 It came to pass that the king of the children of Ammon died and Hanun his son took over his throne.

10:2 David said, "I shall go and show kindness to Hanun the son of Nahash, for his father once showed kindness to me.

10:3 For Nahash did give the people of Israel a treaty to gouge out their eyes, otherwise he threatened to invade and conquer all.

10:4 Two weeks did he give those people to consider their offer and send out for aid.

10:5 That was nice of Nahash, for most people would have simply conquered."

10:6 David sent forth servants to Hanun so that they may give their condolences for the death of his father and congratulate him on becoming king.

10:7 The princes of Ammon said to Hanun, "Do you think David would sent out men so that they shall give us their sorrow and comfort?" and Hanun said, "No. I believe David sent forth these men to spy upon my lands so that he may overthrow me.

10:8 For my father did not show his people kindness. My father threatened to gouge out their eyes, for fuck sakes."

10:9 The servants of David were shown to the throne room of Hanun, where Hanun had his men restrain them.

10:10 Hanun then took a sharp blade and cut their garments so that their bare buttocks did show and shaved off half their beards.

10:11 These servants returned to David, who looked at them and fell upon the floor laughing.

10:12 David said to them, "You look like damned fools, with your beards half gone and your asses hanging from your pants.

10:13 Did you fashion your garments from the brothels of Ammon?

10:14 Go now and live in Jericho, you damn looking fools."

10:15 When Hanun heard that David laughed at his servants, he said, "Surely David is a fool, to laugh at the insult I sent him."

10:16 Hanun then went and hired a great number of mercenaries. From the Syrians of Bethrehob and Zoba he hired twenty thousand men, from king Maacah one thousand men and from the tribe of Ishtob twelve thousand men.

10:17 When David heard of this, he said, "Surely Hanun wishes to invade me with is bought men."

10:18 Joab was sent forth with the armies of Israel to fight against those of Hanun.

10:19 When Joab arrived, behold, he saw that the men of Ammon defended the gate of the city, while those mercenaries hired were alone in the field.

10:20 Joab split the armies of Israel in two and with him came the most mighty men of valour, so that they may fight the mercenaries.

10:21 The rest were given to Abishai and sent to fight the armies of Ammon.

10:22 Joab said to his brother Abishai, "If the armies of the mercenaries are too strong, come and lend me aid. If those of Ammon be too strong for you, I shall return and fight by your side.

10:23 May the lord bless us and keep us, so that we may dance in the entrails of those that fall before us in glory unto God."

10:24 Joab and his men rushed towards the armies of the mercenaries and when the mercenaries saw them, they said to themselves, "Holy shit!" and fled.

10:25 For the spirit of the lord showed themselves unto the mercenaries in great smoke and fire shaped like the mighty dragon.

10:26 When the children of Ammon saw that their mercenaries fled, they became scared and said to themselves, "These are the finest, bravest men that one may buy to fight beside them."

10:27 Thus the children of Ammon fled into the city, before Abishai could slay them.

10:28 Joab came to Abishai and said, "How do you and your men fair?" and Abishai said, "The cowards ran away."

10:29 Joab said, "So did those of Syria. May their cowardice lead them straight to the blade of the lord."

10:30 The two brothers then went back towards Jerusalem, laughing and mocking those of Ammon and his mercenaries.

10:31 When the Syrian mercenaries saw that they were smitten before Israel, they said, "Let's not be afraid of their might and magic, for dragons do not exist."

10:32 Hadarezer, king of the Syrians, gathered his men and said, "Make chase against Israel, for you were paid to kill them."

10:33 Shobach, general of the Syrian army, went forth with is men and crossed the river to reach the city of Helam.

10:34 When David heard of this, he gathered the men of Israel and marched forth towards Helam to defend it.

10:35 The two armies fought and the spirit of the lord did come down in a mighty dragon of smoke and fire, burning those of the armies of Syria.

10:36 The Syrians fled from the spirit of the lord, screaming, "What wickedness is this, that those of Israel shall summon dragons to fight for them?"

10:37 Those of Israel slew seven hundred chariots and forty thousand men of Syria that day; and Shobach was beheaded by David.

10:38 When Hadarezer king of Syria, heard of this, he said, "Surely this is an enemy I best not fight." And Hadarezer made peace with David and gave him a portion of his crops, his wealth and his women.

10:39 When Ammon came to hire the mercenaries of Syria, the Syrians said, "Be gone, for no amount of goods can convince us to go fight the dragon of Israel."

11:1 It came to pass that the armies of Israel destroyed the children of Ammon and besieged Rabbah. But David still dwelt within Jerusalem.

11:2 One day, David arose from his bed and walked upon the roof of his house. When David gazed out upon the city, he saw a woman bathing within her chambers.

11:3 This woman was very ugly and had strong masculine. This pleased David greatly ad he gazed upon this woman, lusting for her.

11:4 David inquired about this woman and a servant came to him and told him, "The woman you ask of is Bathseba the daughter of Eliam, the wife of Uriah the Hittite."

11:5 King David arranged it so that Bathseba was kidnapped and brought into his bedchamber.

11:6 Bathsheba gazed upon David and said, "What matter of importance am I, that my very king would take me from my home?"

11:7 And David said, "The matter of importance is that I need for me a proper harlot to satisfy my lust."

11:8 Bathsheba smiled and lied with David. She enjoyed every moment, giving David the best sex that he ever had with a woman.

11:9 For Bathseba was considered ugly and not even her husband would lie with her.

11:10 Bathseba got up, kissed the very loins of David and said, "Thank you, for I have longed to be with a true man.

11:11 It is a blessing then, that this is the first day of purity after my female uncleanliness."

11:12 In time, it came to be that Bathseba did not become unclean and she sent messengers to David, saying, "I am pregnant with your seed."

11:13 David said, "Lie and tell those who ask that is the seed of your husband."

11:14 Bathsheba replied, "My husband has not lied with me since the first days of our marriage.

11:15 He shall know that I had an affair and shall arrange for my stoning."

11:16 David said, "Fear not, for I will arrange it so that your husband will not be a problem."

11:17 It was then that David invited Uriah into his house and said to him, "You have been a loyal servant of the lord and deserve the blessing of God."

11:18 Uriah said, "Blessed be the lord and blessed be David, for finally they have recognized my services as a camel shitter picker upper."

11:19 This David grew confused with and asked his servant, "What is a camel shitter picker upper?" and the servant replied, "It is one who gathers the faeces of camels and then spreads them atop the crops as fertilizer."

11:20 David grew disgusted, for surely to have such a lowly servant of Israel within his house was a dishonour.

11:21 Still, David kept him at his table and spoke with him and got him drunk so that he passed out on the very floor.

11:22 David then sent Uriah to Joab, who did battle against the children of Ammon, with a message that said, "This is Uriah, who I must have killed in a most convenient way.

11:23 Let it be known that he did volunteer to fight for Israel and wished to be of the first to slay those who defy God."

11:24 Joab then placed Uriah in the front lines, who grew confused and asked the soldiers, "How can one pick up the shit of a camel with a sword?"

11:25 It was then the children of Ammon attacked, killing Uriah quickly within the carnage of battle.

11:26 A messenger came to Bathsheba and told her, "Your husband died valiantly defending the honour of our lord and slaying all those who go against God."

11:27 Bathsheba then spent her time in mourning, where she secretly hid in her bedroom and laughed, for the image of her husband in battle amused her greatly.

11:28 Those who heard Bathsheba laughed felt pity for her, for they believed her to be weeping.

11:29 When the time of mourning passed, David sent for Bathsheba and made her a wife. But the thing which David had done angered the lord.

12:1 The lord sent Nathan the prophet, who said to David, "There were once two men in a city. One was rich, while the other was poor.

12:2 The rich man was once poor, but through grace was given all that which his master owned.

12:3 Money, crops, concubines this man did receive upon the death of his master.

12:4 The poor man never knew such wealth and had with him only one possession.

12:5 One crippled, blemished lamb, whom he raised.

12:6 This poor man fed this pathetic lamb so that it grew into an ugly, crippled, blemished sheep.

12:7 Though this sheep was of no value, it was all that he owned and he kept it dearly.

12:8 The rich man saw the sheep of the poor man and wished it for himself.

12:9 So he stole it from the poor man, so that the poor man had nothing."

12:10 David said, "This rich man is truly an asshole! How dare he steal such a thing, when he could have bought it from the poor man.

12:11 Tell me who this man is, so that I may tear the very testicles from him,and feed them to the sheep which he stole."

12:12 Nathan said to David, "You are the rich man and Bathsheba is the sheep you stole.

12:13 For the lord knew you were once a poor shepherd, yet the lord blessed you.

12:14 From Saul, your master, you received great wealth and power.

12:15 You did receive the wives, the lands, and the crown of Saul, becoming king over all Israel and Judah.

12:16 These things the lord gave to you and the lord would have given you much more, if you weren't such a fool.

12:17 Uriah was a poor ma, who had but one thing; his wife.

12:18 Uriah loathed his wife, but it was all that which he owned.

12:19 If you came to Uriah, he would have gladly sold you his wife for a few mere shekels.

12:20 Yet you did not. You stole the wife of Uriah and had him slain by the sword.

12:21 The lord says unto you, the sword which pierced Uriah might has well been the sword in your hand.

12:22 Thus says the lord, Behold, I shall raise a demon from the very seed of your loins, whom shall steal your eyes and rape them for all of Israel to see.

12:23 What you did in secret shall be done to you so that all shall know."

12:24 David said to Nathan, "I have sinned against God, so surely I must die," and Nathan said, "The lord has forgiven you your sin and shall not harm you. The lord shall bring harm your child instead."

12:25 Nathan then left the house of David and the lord did strike a plague upon the child of David and Bathsheba.

12:26 David pleaded with the lord, begging that the child be spared, but the lord heeded not the words of David and did leave the child to die.

12:27 King David fasted, sacrificed, ripped off his clothes and wallowed in the mud and still the lord would not hearken the word of David.

12:28 Upon the seventh day, the very blood of the child did burn by the hand of God, so that it boiled and the child did burn.

12:29 When the servants of David saw that the child was dead, they feared to tell their master, for they said, "Surely the king shall have his wrath upon those who tell him." When David heard the whispers of his servants, he asked of them, "Is my son dead?"

12:30 The servants said, "Yes, your son is dead." So, David bathed, changed his apparel, went into the house of the lord and worshipped him, saying, "Blessed be the name of the lord."

12:31 God himself looked down upon David, and said, "There be a man whose son was slain by the hands of the lord and still he worships the lord.

12:32 Never does he question the lord, nor ask himself why the lord killed his son.

12:33 Such an useful fool is he, to follow the lord so blindly.

12:34 Such an idiot be all of Israel, who follow the lord with such faith."

12:35 Servants of David came to him and asked their master, "Why do you seem happy when your child lie dead? For when your son was alive, you wept, fasted and wallowed in filth."

12:36 David answered, "What does it matter, for when the child was alive, the lord could have saved my son.

12:37 The lord chose to kill him. What can be done, for my child cannot be brought back to life.

12:38 Blessed be the name of the lord."

12:39 Even the servants gazed upon David and thought to themselves, 'Surely David is a crazy motherfucker.'

12:40 Bathsheba was saddened by the death of her son while David consoled her and lied with her that night.

12:41 Bathsheba accepted the seed of David and bared for him a son, which they named Solomon.

12:42 The lord gazed upon Solomon and said, "Perhaps this baby I will spare, for he may be of use."

12:43 Nathan the prophet was sent to David and said to him, "Your new son shall be called Jebidiah, for the lord wishes it."

12:44 Joab fought against the children of Ammon and conquered their royal city of Rabbah.

12:45 Joab sent messengers to David, who said, "I have taken from those of Ammon the city of Rabbah, the city of waters.

12:46 Now come and claim it in your name, lest you wish the city to be named after your servant."

12:47 So David took his men and went to Rabbah, for he did not want his servant Joab to have a city in his name.

12:48 David was selfish like that.

12:49 David took the king of Rabbah and tore from his back his very spine. David then took the crown of Rabbah, which weighed one talent and was made of gold with precious stones around it.

12:50 And the city of Rabbah was plundered of all its goods.

12:51 And those who lived in Rabbah became slaves of Israel, who worked with the saw, the hammer the axe, and the plough. Those of all the cities of Ammon became slaves of Israel.

12:52 David returned to Jerusalem, saying, "Praise be to the lord of Israel, who did free us from the slavery of Egypt, so that we may go and enslave others for ourselves."

13:1 It came to pass that Absalom the son of David had a sister whose name was Tamar, which Ammon the son of David lusted for deeply.

13:2 Ammon was greatly in lust with her, for she was a fair young woman; a beautiful virgin, who knew not the pleasures of sex. Ammon would give anything to be the first to plunge into her.

13:3 Now, Ammon had a friend named Jonadab the son of Shimeah. Jonadab was a very clever man.

13:4 Jonadab asked his friend, "What troubles you, for you are the son of the king and should be happy." and Ammon said to him, "I am in love with a woman."

13:5 Jonadab said, "Then pursue her and buy her as a wife." but Ammon said, "I cannot, for she is my sister.

13:6 Though she born from a different crop, the seed is the same.

Still, I lust for her deeply and wish to show her the many pleasures that a man can give to a woman."

13:7 It was then Jonadab thought of a scheme and said to his friend Ammon, "This is what you must do, if you desire to lie with Tamar.

13:8 I know Tamar well and she is a known healer, who shows great sympathy for the ill. It is this sympathy you must exploit.

13:9 Go to your chambers and feign illness, so that all believe you unwell. Ask for Tamar to care for you, to comfort you, to feed you, so that she may grow closer to you.

13:10 Convince her the reason for your illness is blue balls, and you must sleep immediately with a woman, lest the very vessels of your seed fatally burst.

13:11 She shall lie with you, in belief that it will cure you."

13:12 Ammon went to his bedchamber and feigned illness, so that all believed him unwell.

13:13 He asked of his servants, "Send forth for Tamar, for she is a gifted healer and I wish to be comforted by one of my family."

13:14 The servants sent for Tamor, who did come and fed Ammon, cared for Ammon, and bathed Ammon.

13:15 Tamar asked of her brother, "What strange illness do you have, for the colour remains in your skin, your flesh be not cold nor hot and even your eyes have life remaining in them."

13:16 Ammon said to Tamar, "The disease which plagues me is an embarrassment and I wish not to tell you unless you swear to speak of this to no one."

13:17 Tamar swore this and Ammon said, "The sickness which plagues me is blue balls.

13:18 The very vessels which house my seed are overflowing and they need to be released, lest they break the very vessels of their containment, killing me."

13:19 Tamar said, "Such a thing must surely be a painful experience.

13:20 Let me go and I shall grab for you a harlot, so that you may release your seed."

13:21 Ammon said, "It is too late, for when a harlot is come for me, my loins shall burst

13:22 My seed must be released now, before they explode from my loins

13:23 Come, Tamar and rid me of my sickness."

13:24 Tamar said, "No! You are my brother. To sleep with you would be a sin."

13:25 Ammon grabbed her and said, "Get over here, you little bitch."

13:26 Ammon then tore the very clothes of Tamar and raped her within his bedchamber.

13:27 When Tamar screamed, Ammon would place the pillow above her mouth, so that no servant would hear the calls of help from Tamar.

13:28 Ammon stole from his sister her very virginity and when his seed was finally released, he was disgusted with himself.

13:29 For he knew the sin which he just did; to rape his own sister is surely a revolting abomination

13:30 Tamar cried and lamented over her virginity, as Ammon called her a filthy whore and told her to leave.

13:31 Tamar would hear no such thing and said, "You stole from me my virginity. Now you must buy me as a wife."

13:32 Ammon refused the offer of marriage and said, "I have taken for free that which I wanted.

13:33 Be gone and never speak of this again."

13:34 Tamar left the bedchamber of Ammon weeping. Ammon closed the door behind her and locked it, wallowing in his misery and self-loathing.

13:35 It was custom for virgins of the king of Israel to wear a robe of diverse colours, so that all may know them to be pure. Tamar ripped from her body these robes, poured ash atop her head and wept.

13:36 Absalom her brother came by and asked her, "What is the matter my dear sister?" for Absalom was a caring and loving brother.

13:37 Tamar said, "My brother from a different mother stole that which is most precious to me.

13:38 Ammon took advantage of his sickness and raped me, so that he may cure his blue balls."

13:39 Absalom considered explaining the condition of blue balls and that if untreated, the result is not fatal but pain in the loins.

13:40 He decided to keep quiet of it, for fear of humiliating her sister further.

13:41 Absalom embraced his sister, comforted her, and said, "I promise you, as God is my witness, Ammon shall pay with blood for that which he stole from you.

13:42 In time, all of Israel knew of the incestual rape committed by the son of David, infuriating David.

13:43 The king spoke to all of Israel, informing them, "It is not the business of the nation to know that which happens within the bedchamber of my family.

13:44 We are royalty, and royalty is allowed to engage in incestual fornication, so that our blood be pure from those of a lesser breed."

13:45 But Absalom, he would neither speak ill nor well for his brother Ammon. For Absalom was a patient man and wished to kill the man who raped his sister.

13:46 Beware the danger of a patient man.

13:47 In two years, Absalom did dwell in Baalhezor, by the Ephraim. Absalom invited all his family to come and feast in his new home.

13:48 David could not come, for he was the king of Israel and had pressing duties to attend to. Absalom knew this.

13:49 Absaslom commanded that his servants give to Ammon the strongest drink, so that Ammon shall be quite drunk at the feast.

13:50 When Ammon became drunk, Absalom rose from the head of the table, went to his brother and tore from him his very clothes.

13:51 Absalom did take the blade, and thrust it deep into the asshole of Ammon, thrusting it repeatedly into him.

13:52 Ammon cried, and screamed, "For what reason do ye give such punishment to a guest of your home?" and Absalom said, "Because ye raped my sister, you heathen bastard."

13:53 Absalom then took the blade, and cut Ammon from his asshole to his eyeball, so that the blood, the flesh and the organs did spill upon the table.

13:54 Those who were at the table, fled, for such a sight gave them great illness.

13:55 Rumours spread about the death at the table of Absalom, so that when David heard, he was told that all the sons of his were slain upon the table of Absalom.

13:56 David tore off his clothes, poured ash upon his head and wept.

13:57 But Jonadab the son of Shimeah knew the truth, and said "Weep not, O king of Israel, for not all your sons be dead.

13:58 Only Ammon is slain, for he did rape of the sister of Absalom. Your other sons shall return, healthy and fine."

13:59 When the sons of David did return, he rejoiced, for they were alive and only Ammon was slain.

13:60 David wished to speak to Absalom and tell him what he did was good, for he slew that who stole the virginity of his sister.

13:61 But Absalom fled and went to Talmai the son of Ammihud, king of Gesher.

13:62 For three years Absalom did dwell in Gesher and for three years David mourned the loss of his son Absalom, for he loved him dearly.

14:1 Joab the son of Zeruiah knew that the heart of David ached for Absalom to return.

14:2 So Joab went to Tekoa, and fetched there a wise woman and said to her, "I beg of you, feign yourself to be a mourner and place on your mourning robes, so that you look like a woman who has mourned for a long time.

14:3 Come to king David and tell him the words which I tell you to speak."

14:4 When the woman came to David, she fell on her face, and said to him, "Help, O king of Israel."

14:5 The king asked her, "What is wrong with you?" and she answered "I am indeed a widowed woman. My husband is dead.

14:6 My handmaid had two sons, who did work together in the fields. The one wronged the other, so that the other slew him.

14:7 Behold, now my family has risen against my handmaiden, demanding that she brings forth her son, so that he may die for the murder of his brother.

14:8 This son of my handmaiden is all that which belongs to me and is the only heir of my husband. If he be slain, then the name of my husband shall be vanished from the generations."

14:9 And the king said, "Why does this concern me?"

14:10 The woman of Tekoah said, "My lord, O king, the iniquity be on me and my father's house: the king and the throne be guiltless.

14:11 I beg of you, let the king remember the lord our God, that you would not suffer the vengeance-seekers of blood to destroy my son," and the king said, "Fine, I shall have it so that your son shall live.

14:12 Since you are the closest relative of the one slain, it shall be your decision whether or not seek revenge upon the slayer."

14:13 Then the woman said, "I beg of you, O king, let my handmaiden speak one word to the king." and David said, "Go on, so long as it is a quick word."

14:14 The handmaiden came forth and said to David, "My son whom did slay his brethren now hides within the city of Talmai.

14:15 He refuses to return for fear that we shall slay him. Our family is now like water spilled upon the ground, which cannot be gathered."

14:16 David said, "What is your point? I care not for your family squabbles.

14:17 The king has more important matters to deal with other than this petty bullshit."

14:18 And the handmaiden said, "One would think the king have interest in this, since Absalom the son of David dwells in Gesher."

14:19 With this, the king became furious and said, "What concern is it of a widow and a handmaiden of the concerns of their king?

14:20 Tell me, lest the very blood of yours be spilled upon the ground."

14:21 Both women knew not what to say and confessed to David, saying, "We fear not the concern of the king is neither our concern, nor do we care.

14:22 Joab, the servant of David, did come to us and tell us to come here and say these words."

14:23 King David sent for Joab and asked of him, "What trickery is this, that you would send for these two women to come to me and speak words of lies and deceit?"

14:24 And Joab said, "I wished the words of these women would soften your heart, so that you shall go and fetch Absalom, so that he may dwell with us in peace again."

14:25 David said, "Could you not have merely asked of me to do this, instead of having these wretched women come and bother me?

14:26 And why would you have some such say words? Surely you knew that they made no sense."

14:27 Joab said, "I feared asking you, lest the wrath of my king come upon me.

14:28 And the words they spoke were not the words I placed within their mouths. They fucked up and spoke words of confusion."

14:29 David said, "Do not fear me, for I wish for the safe return of Absalom.

14:30 Go forth to Geshur and bring back Absalom into the loving arms of his father."

14:31 So Joab left to return the son of the king back to him.

14:32 David then said to the two women hired by Joab, "You have wasted my time with words of lies and confusion.

14:33 May the very heads be severed and decorate my chambers for this deceit."

14:34 And the woman of Tekoah said, "Why slay us, when it was Joab who did come and hire us for such deceit?"

14:35 David answered, "Joab is a loyal servant of the king and shall not suffer for this sin.

14:36 You two will be punished, for it was you who came and bothered the king.

14:37 Also, the two of you are here and I am angry and wish to spill blood. It is by convenience I shall slay thee both."

14:38 David then drew his sword and beheaded both women within his throne room.

14:39 Joab returned Absalom to Jerusalem, but Absalom saw not his father and went directly to his house.

14:40 In all of Israel there was none praised for beauty more than Absalom, for he was a handsome man. From the soles of his feet to the crown of his head there was no blemish upon him.

14:41 Every year, Absalom shall shave his head, for his hair was thick and heavy. The hair would be weighed upon the scales and would come to two hundred shekels.

14:42 The hair of Absalom would then be sold in locks unto the young women who did lust for him deeply.

14:43 Unto Absalom were born three sons and one daughter, whom he named Tamar after his sister who was raped by his brother.

14:44 When Absalom gazed upon his daughter, he would remember the tragedy of his sister and say to himself, "I shall have my revenge upon David, who did allow my brother Ammon to steal the most precious thing of my sister's."

14:45 Absalom dwelt in Jerusalem for two years and never once visited his father the king.

14:46 David would send Joab to Absalom, so that Joab shall bring Absalom to the king. Each time Absalom would refuse and say to Joab, "Tell my father that I wish he be raped by the diseased ridden heathens which infest all lands outside our borders."

14:47 Still, Joab would come to the house of Absalom and beg of him to come and see his father; and each time Absalom would refuse.

14:48 In time, Absalom became greatly annoyed with Joab and said to his servants, "This loyal servant of the king annoys me daily.

14:49 Send forth to him a message that I wish never to be bothered again.

14:50 His field of barley be close to mine. Go, set his crop on fire, so that his barley be turned to ashes and dust."

14:51 So the servants of Absalom did, and committed arson against Joab.

14:52 Joab came to Absalom and said, "Why did your servants set my field of barley on fire?"

14:53 Absalom answered, "Because I did tell them to and shall tell them again if you do not cease to bother me with the demands of your master.

14:54 Never shall I see him, unless it be to thrust the dagger within his heartless torso."

14:55 So Joab came to the king and told him all that which Absalom. David did weep, for he missed his son deeply.

14:56 The king of Israel did go to the house of Absalom and when he saw his son, he did fall upon his face and kissed him.

14:57 Absalom loathed him and said, "You shall regret the day you did wrong my sister.

14:58 The hearts of those of Israel will belong to me, so that I shall use their loyalty and take that which belongs to you."

15:1 It came to pass that Absalom prepared for himself chariots, horses and fifty loyal men.

15:2 Absalom would rise early and stand before the gates of Jerusalem; and if any man would come to seek guidance from the king, Absalom would say, "What city do you come from?" and when the man would answer, Absalom would reply, "The king shall not hearken your words.

15:3 I Absalom shall hear your problem and judge according to that which is good.

15:4 For if I were king of Israel, it would be that every man which have any suit or claim shall come to me and I shall deliver to them justice."

15:5 And it was so that when any man came to seek the wisdom of Absalom that Absalom would embrace them as though a brother and kiss them.

15:6 It was in this manner that Absalom won the hearts of all those in Israel and they loved and supported Absalom in all things.

15:7 When forty years passed, Absalom sent message to his father the king, which said, "I ask of you to allow me to leave, so that I may dwell in Hebron.

15:8 For while I dwelt in Geshur, I vowed unto the lord that if I ever return to Jerusalem, that I shall serve the lord.

15:9 David gave Absalom permission to leave in Hebron, so that he may serve the lord.

15:10 But Absalom sent spies throughout all the tribes of Israel and said, "When the trumpets blow and the time comes, you shall say that Absalom reigns in Hebron.

15:11 All hail our new king Absalom, for he shall be fair to Israel in all things."

15:12 When Absalom went to Hebron, two hundred men of Israel went with him, swearing loyalty to Absalom. They knew not that which Absalom planned.

15:13 Absalom travelled to every city on his way to Hebron, offering sacrifices unto the lord and gaining support of the people of Israel.

15:14 The conspiracy grew strong and the people's loyalty increased continually with Absalom.

15:15 There came a messenger to David, saying, "The heart of the nation of Israel is with Absalom."

15:16 David said to his servants, "Let us go and flee this city, for soon Absalom shall come and take it. Make speed and depart, lest he come and take our city by the sword."

15:17 And the king's servants readied themselves and left with the king of Israel.

15:18 All those in the house of David departed with him, save for ten concubines, whom David left behind so that they may care for the house.

15:19 These concubines were angry with David and said, "Surely our master has condemned us to death at the hands of Absalom."

15:20 The king and his servants went forth, so that they may hide in a place far off.

15:21 And all the servants that went with David, the Cherethites, the Pelethites and the Gittites numbered six hundred men.

15:22 Then said David to Ittai the Gittite, "Why do you come with us? Return to my house and abide with Absalom, for you are a stranger and exile.

15:23 Your people slow me down and shall give us away to the armies of Absalom. Go back, and spy upon his men. Weaken them, sabotage them, trick them."

15:24 And Ittai the Gittite returned to Jerusalem with all Gittites and they said to each other, "David is truly a foolish man and an asshole of a king.

15:25 Let us support Absalom, for he shall treat us fairly."

15:26 Those who travelled with David wept loudly, for they feared their loyalty to the king shall be their downfall. They wept when they passed over the brook of Kidron, towards the way of the wilderness.

15:27 Zadok and all the Levites with David did pass over the brook, carrying with them the ark of the lord. Abiather went with them, so that the ark shall be carried with great care as David fled from Absalom.

15:28 The king said to Zadok, "Bring back the ark to the city of Jerusalem, so that if the lord finds favour in my sight, he shall return me to it.

15:29 May the lord do to me that which seems good unto God.

15:30 Are you not a prophet, Zadok? Return to the city and bring with you your two sons, Ahimaaz and Jonathan.

15:31 Your master shall tarry in the wilderness and when it is safe you shall send men for me and tell me to return to my home."

15:32 Zadok and Abiather then went back to Jerusalem with the ark and said to one another, "Our king and master is truly a fool.

15:33 He did send for us to come with him and bring the ark, so that the lord shall bless him upon his retreat.

15:34 Now he sends us back so that the lord shall bless him upon his return to Jerusalem. Can David not decide?

15:35 Let us support Absalom, for he is a wise man, and can stand by that which he decides."

15:36 David went up and ascended mount Olivet, barefooted and his head covered. Those he came with him went up also barefoot and their head covered, weeping as they went.

15:37 They wept for the loss of their homes, the fear of their lives and because the stones beneath their very feet were sharp.

15:38 A servant of David came to him and said, "Ahithophel is among the conspirators of Absalom." David said, "Ahithophel was a wise and knowledgeable advisor for me. May his words now be foolish for Absalom."

15:39 It came to pass that when David arrived at the top of mount Olivet, he did build an altar and gave a sacrifice to the lord. As David spilled the blood of the sacrifice, behold, Hushai the Archite came to meet him, with his clothes torn and dust upon his head.

15:40 David said, "You are a slow man and shall surely be a burden upon me and my men.

15:41 Go instead to Jerusalem, so that you may be a spy among the spies of Absalom.

15:42 Learn all that which you can and send word to me of what you know."

15:43 So Huchai the friend of David did return to Jerusalem and spied against Absalom.

16:1 When David was a little past the top of the hill, behold, Ziba the servant of Mephibosheth met him and with him came asses carrying two hundred loaves of bread, one hundred bunches of raisins, one hundred summer fruits and bottles of wine.

16:2 The king said to Ziba, "Why do you come here with such an abundance of goods?" and Ziba answered, "The asses I bring so that you and your men shall have something to ride on, instead of walking upon your feet.

16:3 These fruits and breads I bring forth so that you may eat in the wilderness and the wine so that your spirit shall be high in these dreaded times."

16:4 David then asked, "Where is the son of your master?" and Ziba answered, "Behold, he dwells in Jerusalem, so that he may spy upon the traitor Absalom and ensure the throne be empty for your return."

16:5 The king thanked Ziba and his master Mephibosheth for the asses and the bounty and Ziba said, "I seek only to serve the lord and my king."

16:6 Ziba then left and David gave him nothing for the return home. No fruits, no water, no bread.

16:7 Ziba thought of David, "The king knows I shall return home alone and with no ass to bear me. Surely, he could have spared one loaf of bread or some water to drink.

16:8 I see now why the peoples of Israel love Absalom. Absalom would have given me an ass to ride and ample provisions for my safe return."

16:9 When David and his men came to Bahurim, there came a man from the family of the house of Saul, whose name was Shimea the son of Gera. He followed David and cursed his name.

16:10 Shimea threw stones at David and his men and yelled curses upon them, saying, "Curse be the man who slew Saul, the true king of Israel.

16:11 Curse be the man who wins the favour of God by being the lord's concubine.

16:12 May the lord tear your asshole apart and give ye great pain and diseases known not even by the filthiest of whores.

16:13 Shall the blood of the house of Saul stain your very soul and may Absalom your own son slay you with his sword."

16:14 Abishai the son of Zeruiah said to David, "Why do you let this filthy coyote curse you, my lord and king? Let me go and rip the very jaws from his skull, so that he may curse us no more."

16:15 David said, "Let him live and let him curse, for I care not.

16:16 My son, who came from my own seed, wishes to seek my life and destroy it. It matters not that this miserable predator curses my name.

16:17 Let this fool live, for in life he shall suffer worse than the sweet embrace of death."

16:18 So David allowed Shimea the son of Gera to live and Shimea followed David and his men, constantly cursing them and throwing stones against them.

16:19 The lord looked down upon Shimea and laughed, saying, "Surely my servant David is annoyed by this fool Shimea, yet he ignores him and allows him to live.

16:20 Let us see how long it be before David or his men kill this man, for he is like a buzzing fly who annoys the meditating priest.

16:21 No matter how long the priest ignores the fly, in time, the priest shall swat the fly and kill it."

16:22 In time, Absalom came marching into Jerusalem with his men and all of Jerusalem rejoiced, saying, "Praise be our new king Absalom! Please don't kill us."

16:23 Hushai the Archite came to Absalom and said, "Praise be the king. Praise be the king."

16:24 Absalom asked Hushai, "Are you not loyal to my father David? Do you stay so that you may bring harm upon me?

16:25 And Hushai answered, "My loyalty is to my lord and the one whom my lord has chosen.

16:26 When the lord chooses you, then shall I be loyal to Absalom."

16:27 Absalom believed this meant that Hushai believed God himself chose Absalom and that Hushai was loyal to Absalom.

16:28 This was false, for Hushai believed that God still chose David

and was still loyal unto the true king of Israel.

16:29 Absalom asked Ahithophel, "Give me counsel among that which I should do."

16:30 Ahithophel said, "The people of Israel have their hearts to you and know you loathe your father David.

16:31 Give unto them no doubt that ye abhor your father and make yourself repulsive unto king David.

16:32 Go and in front of the eyes of Israel, fornicate greatly with the ten concubines your father left behind, so that all of Israel shall witness your hatred of your father."

16:33 So Absalom had his servants set up a tent atop the house of David and there Absalom had sex with the ten concubines of David, so that all of Israel shall bear witness of this.

16:34 Absalom would fuck these ten whores with the congregation of Israel watching and cheering him on.

16:35 This display of voyeurism brought forth great pleasure unto Absalom, who would deposit his seeds upon the faces of the concubines and into the crowd of those who watched.

16:36 Absalom would say, "May my father hear of this and loathe my very name as I loathe his."

16:37 And the children of Israel spread the news of Absalom fucking the concubines of his father's, so that all knew that Absalom made himself revolting unto his father the king.

16:38 Those who heard the news, would say, "Surely Absalom has daddy issues." and pitied Absalom.

16:39 And Absalom held in highest regard the counsel of Ahithophel, for the words of Ahithophel were held in the highest regards, as though they were words of the oracle of God.

17:1 Knowing the power of his words, Ahithophel said to Absalom, "Go now, choose twelve thousand men,and overtake David by night.

17:2 Those with David are weak, tired and famished. They shall flee David's side, so that y smite only your father.

17:3 When those that went with David see him dead, they shall know that Absalom is the true king of Israel and shall call you master.

17:4 They shall serve you until the end of your days."

17:5 Absalom thought this advice great, as did the elders of Israel.

17:6 But the lord wished Absalom to die and David to return to the throne of Israel.

17:7 Thus the spirit of the lord overcame Hushai the Archite, who said, "To pursue the men of David shall be a fool's mistake.

17:8 They shall hide in the pit, in the caves, in the forest, so that those who pursue David shall be overthrown and slain without mercy.

17:9 David shall hear that a slaughter has plagued those who follow Absalom and as this message spreads David shall grow strong.

17:10 The heart of David is valiant and strong. He shall fight with his men as does a mother bear fights for her cubs.

17:11 I say, let all of Israel gather for you, from Dan even unto Beersheba so that the peoples shall number like the sands of the shore. They shalt go out and battle of their will.

17:12 Those of David shall not slay a brother of Israel, so that when these people find David, they shall tell us and we know where your father hides.

17:13 Even if David hides within a city, all those of Israel shall bring ropes, so that the very walls of the city topple, until not even a stone be unturned until your father is found dead."

17:14 Absalom liked better the counsel of Hushai and said, "We shall do what Hushai says and heed not the words of Ahithophel."

17:15 Hushai was a spy of David's, who said unto Zadok and

Abiather the priests, "I have done that which shall protect David. Go forth and tell him that Ahithophel did betray us.

17:16 Tell your king to not rest within the wilderness, lest the people of Israel find and betray him. Have him speed pass, so that they may escape the hand of Absalom."

17:17 Now Zadok and Abiather cared not for David, but knew that Hushai was loyal to the king and shall spill their blood if they do not what Hushai demanded.

17:18 So the priests escaped in the night so that none in the city shall see them and told king David that which Hushai said.

17:19 Nevertheless, a small boy did see the two priests leave while he snuck out of his parents' house to gaze within the local brothel. The boy did tell Absalom that the two priests did leave them and Absalom rewarded this boy with a well experienced concubine.

17:20 Zadok and Abiather came upon a man's house in Bahurim and hid within the well so that the men of Absalom not find them.

17:21 In time, the two men heard the servants of Absalom leave and they escaped the well and said unto king David, "You must leave the wilderness quickly, for Ahithophel did betray us."

17:22 David cursed Ahithophel and said, "May the very dogs of Ahithophel gnaw upon the bones of their master."

17:23 When Ahithophel saw that Absalom did ignore his counsel he became depressed, and went to his hometown of, wherever the hell he came from.

17:24 There he cleaned his house, fed his dogs, prepared a lamb for supper and ate.

17:25 After his supper was eaten, he did take a rope and hanged himself.

17:26 And the dogs of Ahithophel did gnaw upon the bones of their master.

17:27 Those who discovered Ahithophel laughed and said, "The very tongue of Ahithophel did manage to wrap around his neck and slay him."

17:28 He was buried at his father's sepulcher.

17:29 David came to Mahanaim while Absalom and his men did cross the river Jordan.

17:30 Absalom made Amasa the general of the armies instead of Joab, for he feared the loyalty of Joab still be with David.

17:31 Israel and Absalom did pitch with the lands of Gilead.

17:32 It came to pass that when David did reach Mahanaim, that Shobi the son of Mahash of Rabbah of the children of Ammon and Machir the son of Ammiel of Lodebar and Barzillia the Gileadite of Rogelim met with them.

17:33 They brought forth beds, basins, earthen vessels, wheat, barley, flour, parched corn, beans, lentils, jams,

17:34 Honey, butter, sheep and fresh cheese and said to David and his men, "Bathe, drink, eat and rest, for your time in the wild has made you weary and weak."

18:1 David numbered the people that were with him and set captains over thousands of his army.

18:2 The king did give Joab one third of the command of his men, a third of his men to Abishai the son of Zeruiah, and one third to Ittai the Gittite.

18:3 David then said, "I shall go with you in battle, for my blade thirsts for blood," but those men of David said, "You shall not go, for if you are slain, they shall not care for us.

18:4 If half of us die, they shall imprison and execute us. But you, our master, they shall hold as trophy and give to you the worst methods of pain.

18:5 Your head alone is worth ten thousand of your soldiers. Stay in the city, where you shall be safe."

18:6 And David said, "I shall do no such thing, for I have slain many men and lived.

18:7 My blade has not known the stain of blood for some time and I wish to have the crimson stain upon my blade once again."

18:8 Those men of David said, "And you shall, for those we capture shall be given to you, so that you may execute them by your sword.

18:9 But you shall not come with us in battle, for all our enemies shall see you and come to you and slay you, ignoring those who protect the true king of Israel."

18:10 David then said, "Fine. For the ease of my men, I shall stay within the gates and defend our city against those who wish to siege it."

18:11 The king then said to Joab, Abishai and Ittai, "When you see Absalom, ensure not even a hair upon his head be harmed.

18:12 He is my son and I love him dearly. I wish to embrace him, toy kiss him and show him my love."

18:13 So the three generals of David spread word to all that Absalom must not be harmed, for he is the king's son.

18:14 Those soldiers said, "He is the commander of our enemy. How can we not slice the very throat of he who defies us?"

18:15 And the generals said, "Because our master ordered us not to."

18:16 So the men of David grudgingly agreed they shall not harm Absalom, unless they had to.

18:17 The men of David then marched forth to meet the men of Absalom and they fought within the woods of Ephraim.

18:18 Those men of David slaughtered greatly the men of Absalom, so that twenty thousand men were killed in great glory that day.

18:19 Even the lord came down and sided with David. And the lord did cause the very trees of Ephraim to fight for David.

18:20 The branches would strangle those men of Absalom and the roots would spring forth from the ground and bury those who defied the true king of Israel.

18:21 Absalom rode through the woods atop a mule and saw the very trees fighting against him.

18:22 Poor Absalom became afraid and turned back to retreat.

18:23 It was then that Absalom rode under a great oak tree so that the branch of the oak tree grabbed Absalom's hair and held him high, so that Absalom could not escape.

18:24 Those men with Absalom fled in fear, for they wished not to be slain by a tree.

18:25 A servant of David saw Absalom being held by the mighty oak and went to tell Joab of Absalom's situation.

18:26 And the man said, "I would give one thousand shekels to thrust my very blade within the heart of this cunt who dare defy the true king of Israel. Yet I shall hold back my hand, for I did hear the orders of David, who said that not even a hair upon his head be harmed."

18:27 A pity the very trees of the wood do not obey the orders of David, for the hair of Absalom is surely damaged and covered in sap.

18:28 Come now, so that we may take Absalom and bring him forth to the king. I know not to slay him, for our master shall know if I did kill his son."

18:29 Joab went to Absalom and saw him hanging off the ground, with the branch of the oak grasping the hair of his enemy.

18:30 Joab laughed and said, "I have seen leaves hang from the branches, I have seen fruits hang from the branches and I have seen great hives of honey hang from the branches.

18:31 Never did I see a man dangle from the branches like a hive of bees."

18:32 Absalom said, "You fool of David's, get me down from here.

18:33 I know that my father would order no harm come to me, so cut the very hair of my head or order this damned tree to let go!"

18:34 And Joab said, "I shall do no such thing, for I am hungry and wish for the sweet taste of honey.

18:35 Perhaps the tree cursed you into honeycomb and sweet nectar of the bees shall pour forth from your flesh."

18:36 Joab then took three daggers and thrust them through the very heart of Absalom, so that the blood of Absalom spilled upon the ground.

18:37 Joab then took the blood of Absalom, tasted it, and said, "Behold, it is sweeter than honey!"

18:38 The ten men with Joab then took their swords, their spears, their daggers and thrust it within the body of Absalom and tasted of his blood and said, "Truly it is sweeter than honey!"

18:39 So Joab and his ten armour bearers did feast upon the blood of Absalom.

18:40 Joab then blew a trumpet so that all the men of David knew they won the battle against Israel and to return to David.

18:41 And the men of Joab did cut down the corpse of Absalom and threw it within a great pit in the woods so the trees around the pit took their roots and buried Absalom deep within the earth.

18:42 Now Absalom in his lifetime had taken and reared up himself a great and mighty pillar, which was known as the king's stone. And he said, "May all of Israel gaze upon this pillar and remember my name, for I have no son to pass down my name." And he named the pillar Absalom's place.

18:43 And the sons of Absalom, for which he had three, said, "Why did our father build a pillar, so that people shall remember him because he have no sons to pass down his name?

18:44 And the wife of Absalom said, "Because I am a whore and did cheat on your father, so that you three come not from the seed of Absalom."

18:45 Then said Ahimaaz the son of Zadok, "Let me run to David and tell him the good news as how his enemy was slain today."

18:46 Joab said to him, "You shall not tell the king any tidings this day, for on this day his son died.

18:47 And though his son be delicious, we shall not tell how he died, nor at whose hands."

18:48 Joab then said to Cushi, "Go and tell the king what you saw. Of our enemies and our forest you shall tell David.

18:49 Mention not a word of Absalom."

18:50 And Cushi left, so that he may tell David the good news.

18:51 Ahimaaz grew angry and said, "Why would y let Cushi go, but not me? For I wish to tell David the good news this day."

18:52 And Joab said, "You cannot keep your mouth shut nor keep a secret and surely you would tell David of the fate of Absalom.

18:53 You cannot be trusted this day and for this reason you shall not tell the king our king."

18:54 Ahimaaz said, "You are wrong and I will prove wrong your judgment." Ahimaaz then ran so that he may overcome Cushi and tell David the tidings of that day.

18:55 Joab saw Ahimaaz give chase and said to himself, "What a putz."

18:56 David sat between the two gates and watchmen stood above the gates so that they may see any enemy of the king come.

18:57 The watchmen saw a man running and said to David, "There is some idiot running towards us alone," and David said, "Surely he is a man of ours, who comes to tell us the news of battle."

18:58 Then the watchmen witnessed yet another man and said, "There is another idiot running behind him, yet neither men have swords drawn."

18:58 David said, "I do not know what this means. Let them come, and listen we shall to what they say.

18:60 For if the words they speak displease me, then my sword shall spill their blood."

18:61 Ahimaaz arrived first, for he could run faster than Cushi and he said, "Glory be to the king of Israel; glory be to David.

18:62 I come with great news of the battle, for we did slay them all."

18:63 The lord God blessed us and cursed our enemies, so that even the trees of the forest arose and killed all who came against us."

18:64 David asked, "What of Absalom?" and Ahimaaz said, "I know not his fate, for the battle caused great confusion.

18:65 When the very trees uprooted and fought, it was hard to pay attention."

18:66 Cushi finally came and said, "Glory be to God, for he did deliver us a terrific victory this day!"

18:67 And David said, "I heard. Trees fighting, big battle, enemies slaughtered, the usual shit.

18:68 Tell me, what happened to Absalom?"

18:69 Cushi said, "May all the enemies of our master be as Absalom, for they shall know only suffering and death."

18:70 The king was very upset and ran to the chambers above the gate, weeping like a widow. David would scream, "My son, my son, my son is dead. O lord, why did you let me son die?"

18:71 And the lord gazed down upon the sadness of David and gazed upon his weeping, his misery, his pain. And the lord did say unto his angels in heaven, "Look at the king of Israel. How he cries over the death of his son.

18:72 What a damn wuss."

18:73 And all those in heaven laughed at the suffering of king David.

19:1 It was told unto Joab, "Behold, our king mourns this day of his victory."

19:2 And Joab went to David and said, "Truly you are a fucking idiot.

19:3 I see not why the lord chose you to become king of Israel, for you are as foolish as the lamb who befriends the lion.

19:4 Today is a great day, for your loyal men did give to you your throne back. Yet you do not thank them for this deed.

19:5 Instead, you stay in your chambers, wallowing in your tears like the damn fool you are.

19:6 What the hell is wrong with you? You love your enemies and hate your friends.

19:7 Would you smile if Absalom killed us all instead? Absalom, who hated your very breath.

19:8 Even when Saul did walk the earth you loved that fool, though he wished to slay you with the javelin for no reason other than madness.

19:9 Go, speak to your people and bless them for this great victory that they gave for you.

19:10 If you do not, by nightfall they shall abandon you and rightly so."

19:11 It was heard through all of Israel that David wept and those loyal to David became fearful, thinking the wrath of their king shall be upon them.

19:12 They snuck into the city, hoping that David would not gaze upon them and demand their death for whatever wrong they did.

19:13 In time, murmurings spread through the men of David and they asked, "For what reason does our king weep? For today is surely a glorious day."

19:14 At that time David appeared so he could speak to his men and the men loyal to David said, "Now he shall tell us why he weeps."

19:15 And David said, "My men who are loyal to me. I thank you and bless you, for today you gave me back my throne.

19:16 Blessed be God and all of Israel.

19:17 But today was a sad day for me, for the enemy who I fought was of my own seed. My son Absalom wished death for me.

19:18 When you went to battle, I feared what would happen. For if I win, my son Absalom shall die and if I lose, then I shall die.

19:19 Therefore I weep, for on this day my beloved Absalom died by the hands of my men.

19:20 It would be easier to accept if the trees did overtook him and thrust their branches through his chest, or dragged him into the very earth beneath their roots.

19:21 This way, I shall know it was the will of God that my son dies.

19:22 But my son Absalom died by the hands of my friend. For this I am saddened and angry.

19:23 May Joab know the pain and suffering which he caused me today. May he lose his son and know now why I weep upon my bed.

19:24 When you see Amasa, tell him that he served my son well and for this he shall be the new general of the armies of Israel.

19:25 Fuck Joab. He disobeyed my order and for this shall be demoted his rank and name.

19:26 I look forth and behold, though I lost a son today, I see my brethren before me.

19:27 For all of Israel is my family and I love them each dearly.

19:28 Let me go, so that I may be a father to them once more and guide them to our rightful place as rulers over the earth.

19:29 May the people of Israel reign all the lands and all the people who not worship the one true God.

19:30 Glory be to Israel, for we are the people chosen directly by the lord of lords!"

19:31 And the people rejoiced and swallowed all the propaganda which David spoon fed them.

19:32 All except Joab, who cursed the name of David, saying, "Fucking fornicator of a sheep's cunt."

19:33 So the king gathered his belongings and returned back to Jerusalem and his home.

19:34 As David crossed the river Jordan, behold, Shimea the son of Gera came over and when Shimea saw David, he fell on his face and kissed David's feet.

19:35 Shimea said, "I have sinned greatly against the true king of Israel, for I was blind to the will of the lord.

19:36 Saul was my master and when he was slain, my anger blinded me, so that I could not see our lord God's work.

19:37 I was angry at you for taking the throne of Saul. I cursed your name and threw stones at you, yet you spared me.

19:38 I beg of you, do not curse me nor slay me, for I see now that the lord wishes David to be the king of Israel.

19:39 When Absalom was slain, my eyes were open and the lord himself came down upon me and told me that the true king of Israel won this day.

19:40 I know now that I cursed the anointed king of Israel, chosen by God. I beg of you, let me go, so that I may serve my king, and the lord of Israel."

19:41 David then said, "You little carrier of maggots and worms, how dare you curse the very man anointed by God!

19:42 My sword shall spill your blood and feast upon the very flesh which clings to your bones."

19:43 It was then Abishai the son of Zeruiah stopped David and said, "Sheath thine sword and hearken my words.

19:44 This man came unto you for forgiveness and begged you to spare his life.

19:45 Though he did wrong you, he did make penance for it and has offered himself as a servant of you.

19:46 I ask you, what use is a dead servant? Let him live. Enslave him and he shall know his remaining days in misery."

19:47 David hearkened the words of Abishai and said to Shimea, "As the lord swears, you shall not die by my hands.

19:48 Though I tell you, you shall wish I had. You shall be a slave to me and I shall make your labours hard, your hours long and you shall know no rest."

19:49 Shimea thanked David for his kindness, in ignorance of what he just agreed to. And Shimea was a slave to David all his life and cleaned with his tongue the very rectums of all the royal cattle, the royal flocks and the royal horses.

19:50 It was truly a shitty job.

19:51 As David returned to Jerusalem, Mephibosheth the son of Saul came to meet him, naked, unbathed and with untrimmed beard.

19:52 And the king asked him, "When Absalom came to take my throne, why did you not come with me?" and Mephibosheth said, "Because my servant deceived me.

19:53 For I told you to saddle me an ass so that I may travel beside you. But my servant is lame and hated you, though you be an angel of Israel.

19:54 My servant did not do as I demanded and spoke slander against David.

19:55 Even when I told him the good which David did for us and renewed us the house of our father, still he spoke slander and blasphemy against the name of the king of Israel."

19:56 David said, "Why did you not kill this servant, who deceived you, and spoke slander against my name?"

19:57 And Mephibosheth said, "For I wished to save him, so that he may see the light and know David as I know David."

19:58 David said, "You do not know me well, unless you wish this day as your last."

19:59 David then unsheathed his sword, thrusting it deep within the very bowels of Mephibosheth, so that the blood poured upon the ground.

19:60 As Mephibosheth stared upon David, the king smiled, saying, "Finally my sword spilled the sweet broth of blood."

19:61 Barzillai the Gileadite came to meet with David and helped him pass over the Jordan.

19:62 David said, "My friend, you had showed loyalty and kindness to me even during the days of Absalom. Come and you shall feast at the table of the king of Israel."

19:63 And Barzillai said, "How long have I lived, so that I may feast of the king's food and drink of the king's wine?

19:64 I am old and know the difference between good and evil, light and dark, man and woman, so that I know David be a good, light man.

19:65 When I travel with you, I shall be a great burden upon you and slow down your journey.

19:66 I ask of you, dearest David, let me go back, so that I may die within my own city, surrounded by my sons.

19:67 Take instead my servant Chimham, so that he may feast at your table in my stead."

19:68 And so it was that David found himself another servant. And when Barzillai returned home, David embraced him and bless him and said, "May you die surrounded by those you love."

19:69 The king of Israel then took a servant and said to him, "Follow that fool who rejected the table of the king of Israel.

19:70 When he eats with his family, have it so that a poison goes into his wine. Let it be that he does truly die in the presence of those he loves."

19:71 And when David returned to Jerusalem, all the people rejoiced and said, "Blessed be the true king of Israel! Blessed be the one chosen by God! Please don't kill us."

19:72 And David said, "Fear not, for I hold no ill will to those who would betray me for my son Absalom.

19:73 You are my servants and I am your king. What be a king without servants?

19:74 Fear not your king. Fear God, for he shall curse your very generations for the betrayal against me.

19:75 I spit upon your very sons, your daughters and their sons and daughters, so that they may be cursed by our lord."

19:76 And the people of Israel rejoiced and said, "We shall be long dead before this happens."

20:1 There happened to be a man of Belial whose name was Sheba the son of Bichri, a Benjamite. Sheba blew the shofar and gathered men of Israel together, saying, "We have no care for the word of David the bastard son of Jesse.

20:2 We need not a king, for we are rule by the one true God. Let it be that every man rule over his house and all of Israel be ruled by the one true lord."

20:3 And when David returned to his house, behold, he saw the floors unswept, the dishes filthy, the rugs unbeaten and the refuse scattered about the place.

20:4 David yelled to his ten concubines, "I told you to keep my house when your master was away and instead I come back to a place unfit to keep the very blemished and lame cattle!

20:5 You shall be punished for such defiance. For the remainder of your days you shall be maids for the house of David.

20:6 You shall prepare meals, mop floors, sweep, clean, dust and do all that which a maid is expected to do.

20:7 Never shall y be used a whore, you women who know not their place."

20:8 So the ten concubines became maids for the house of David until the end of their days.

20:9 Which they preferred, for they'd rather clean a floor than fuck David. For David was truly a lame and boring fucker.

20:10 Word of Sheba reached the ears of David and he grew afraid, saying, "This man shall do us more harm than Absalom."

20:11 David fetched for Abishai, and told him "Gather your men and pursue this man Sheba. For in time, whole cities shall aid in his defence."

20:12 So Joab gathered the men of Israel and pursued Sheba the son of Bichri.

20:13 When they were at the great stone of Gibeon, behold, Amasa walked towards them and said, "My brothers of Israel. I heard the words of Sheba and wish to aid you in his defeat."

20:14 Joab loathed Amasa, though Amasa was unaware of the hatred Joab felt for him.

20:15 Joab unsheathed his dagger and said, "May this very dagger in my hand slay the one who betrayed us."

20:16 Amasa believed he meant Sheba and came closer to Joab, so that the two men may embrace.

20:17 Joab grabbed the beard of Amasa as though to give him a kiss and Amasa took no notice of the dagger in the left hand of Joab.

20:18 It was then Joab slashed the very bowels of Amasa, so that the organs of his enemy spilled upon the ground.

20:19 Joab then took the lungs and the bladder of Amasa, filled them with water and used them as jugs for his journey to find Sheba.

20:20 The men of Joab were ordered to hide the body of Amasa and bury it within the dirt beside the highway. And they did, but left the organs to rot, so that the ravens may feast upon the bowels of Amasa.

20:21 Joab marched after Sheba, chasing him to Abel, Bethmaacah and the land of the Berites, until Sheba was trapped in Abel.

20:22 The armies of Israel laid siege upon the city, setting up a ram so that they may break down the very gates.

20:23 It was then a wise woman came atop the walls and said, "What the hell is this, that the armies of our king destroy our city?

20:24 Explain yourself, what sin have we done against our nation?"

20:25 And Joab said, "We wish not to destroy this city, but we seek one man. Sheba, the son of Bichri."

20:26 The woman said, "You would destroy a whole city over one man?" and Joab answered, "Yes."

20:27 The woman then said, "Surely a man as this must be evil in the eyes of our lord.

20:28 Let us seek out this man so that we may bring his head for you. If we do not, then your men shall come and search under every rock for this man."

20:29 And Joab said, "Okay then. My men will encamp out here until you bring him to us."

20:30 It came to pass that the men of the city found Sheba the son of Bichri and they asked him, "What evil did you do, so that the armies of Israel would come and destroy our city in search of you?"

20:31 And Sheba said, "I commit no evil, but say that the people of Israel need not a king. Only God.

20:32 Let it be that each household be ruled by the head and each city be ruled by an elder, but not the nation be ruled by mortal man.

20:33 It was God who led us to these promised lands and it shall be God who leads us."

20:34 The men of Abel hearkened the words of Sheba and said, "That sounds good, for truly we are the chosen people of God."

20:35 It was then Joab said, "If Sheba does not come within the hour, the very walls of this city shall be torn apart in our search for him."

20:36 So the peoples of Abel said, "Fuck Sheba," and decapitated him with a sickle.

20:37 The head of Sheba was then cast over the city, with the wise woman saying, "Here you go," and was thrown down to the armies of Israel.

20:38 Joab went to where the head landed and kicked it, so that it go to a soldier of Israel.

20:39 That soldier kicked it to another soldier, who kicked it to another, who kicked it to another, so that all the armies of Israel were kicking back and forth the head of Sheba.

20:40 And the soldiers of Israel returned to Jerusalem, all the way kicking the decapitated head of Sheba.

21:1 It so happened that a famine broke out through the lands of Israel, so that all chosen by God starved. David asked the lord, "Why do you let your children go hungry?" and the lord answered, "Because Saul slew the Gibeonites."

21:2 David then asked of the lord, "Then why do you punish us? For Saul is dead." and the lord said, "I am your lord fucking God! How dare you question me."

21:3 So David never asked again why the lord would punish an entire nation for something which a dead guy did.

21:4 David sent forth for scholars and asked them, "Find me reason why the lord would punish those of Israel because of harm done to the Gibeonites.

21:5 I know these people are not of Israel and am confused why the lord would even care for these who seem unworthy."

21:6 So the scholars researched and came to David, saying, "Though the peoples of Gibeon be descended from the Amorites, those of Israel swore to do no harm against them."

21:7 So David sent forth for the rulers of Gibeon and said, "My former master and last king of Israel had wronged you and slain all those of Gibeon who dwelt within the lands of Israel.

21:8 Tell me, how can I make amends, so that we shall make this sin right?"

21:9 And the people of Gibeon said, "What does it matter? Saul is dead and we are now free to live in Israel."

21:10 Still, David said, "Surely there must be something to make amends for what Saul did?" and the people of Gibeon said, "No, we don't care.

21:11 We are peaceful people and wished only for Saul to be punished.

21:12 Since Saul is dead, you have no reason for amends. All is forgiven."

21:13 Still, David said, "Surely there must be something you want! I shall go and slay all those of Saul if you so desire.

21:14 I shall slay the remaining descendants of Saul so that you shall forgive those of Israel."

21:15 And the people of Gibeon said, "There is no need. We forgive And those of Saul's seed were not the ones who once slaughtered us."

21:16 In frustration, king David said to his men, "Go forth and bring me seven of the descendants of Saul, so that we may spill their blood upon the lands of Gibeon, as Saul once spilled the blood of Gibeon upon the lands of Israel."

21:17 And it was found two sons of Rizpah the concubine of Saul and five grandsons of Saul born through Michal, who were brought forth to David.

21:18 The king then sent them to the lands of Gibeon and they bashed them against the rocks until their very bodies crumbled.

21:19 Those of Gibeon who witnessed this came and said, "Why do you kill these men so that they die upon within our lands?

21:20 For what reason do they deserve death, for the one still sucked upon the teat of his mother."

21:21 And the people of Israel said, "These are the seed of Saul who wronged you. It is only fitting these wicked men die upon the lands of those they sinned against."

21:22 The Gibeonites then said, "But these men did no harm against us. How could they? The one is still a baby."

21:23 And those of Israel answered, "As our lord swears it, these people wronged you."

21:24 As the men of Israel left, the people of Gibeon looked upon the seven dead bodies and said, "Their God must truly be a damn tyrant."

21:25 Rizpah the whore of Saul came to the rocks where her sons were slain and wept.

21:26 Every day, she would scare away the ravens who came to pluck the flesh of the dead and every night she would scare away the beasts who came to feast upon the bodies.

21:27 When word came back to David as to what Rizpah was doing, he laughed, saying, "Let that filthy little whore chase away the scavengers."

21:28 And when the lord gazed upon the lands and saw the seven dead descendants of Saul, he gave to the people of Israel rain, ending their famine.

21:29 For the death of seven descendants of a man who sinned is justice according to God.

21:30 Gibeon told those throughout the lands of the slaying of the seven men upon their lands and the peoples of Philistine said, "What nation is this, who would do such a thing?

21:31 They truly are a wicked blemish in the world, one that needs to be gone."

21:32 So the Philistines declared war on Israel. Again.

21:33 David fought in the battles against Philistine, until one-day David became tired and fainted.

21:34 Ishbibenob a giant and descendant of Goliath saw David and rushed to slay him and avenge his kin.

21:35 But Abishai the son of Zeruiah intervened, and killed Ishbibenob. He then went over to his kin, and said, "You must fight no longer in these battles, for if you die, we will have none to lead Israel."

21:36 Yet another battle happened with the Philistines at Gob and there Sibbechai the Hushashite slew Saph, who was the son of Goliath.

21:37 The Philistines had a lot of giants those days.

21:38 Upon that battle at Gob, Elhanan the son of Jaareoregim, a Bethlehemite, killed the very brother of Goliath with his own spear.

21:39 When the battle arose in Gath, the Philistines sent out their largest giant, who had six fingers on each hand and six toes on each foot. He was a fucking freak and taunted a lot as a child.

21:40 This taunting caused great anger in him, which he used to fight the enemies of Philistine.

21:41 The very spear of this man was taller than the highest oak; and he would come and fight against all those of Israel.

21:42 Jonathan the son of Shimmeah, the brother of David, cast an arrow into the heel of this giant, which caused him to fall ill with infection.

21:43 The giant died nine days later, for the people of Philistine lacked the medical knowledge to cure their champion.

22:1 David the king of Israel wrote a song in praise of the lord of Israel on the day the lord delivered him from the hands of his enemies.

22:2 And he said, "The lord is my rock, my shelter and my savior.

22:3 He is my shield and the horn of my salvation. He gives me refuge from the violence of men.

22:4 I call upon the lord, who is worthy of my praise, so I shall be saved from the hand of my enemies.

22:5 When the waves of death surrounded me and the heathen hoards made me afraid,

22:6 The sorrows of hell consumed me, the snares of death entrapped me,

22:7 In my distress I screamed unto the lord and the lord did hear my voice from his temple and my plea entered his ears.

22:8 The very earth shook and trembled. The sky above was torn apart, for the lord is a lord of wrath.

22:9 Thick smoke flowed from the nostrils of Go, and fire spewed forth from his mouth, consuming all.

22:10 My lord rode a dragon, winged and mighty and he was seen upon the wings of the wind.

22:11 Bright darkness surrounded my lord, with black waters and thick clouds of darkness.

22:12 Through the darkness the fire came forth and burned those the lord deemed wicked.

22:13 And my God thundered from the heaven and the most High uttered his voice.

22:14 Arrows came down from the skies and lightning spread forth across the lands.

22:15 The seas split apart and the very foundations of the earth trembled at the breath of his nostrils.

22:16 From above the lord did grasp me and sent me to fresh waters.

22:17 He delivered me from the hands of my enemy and those which hated me, for they were stronger than I.

22:18 My lord did prevent the days of my death, for the lord was my shelter.

22:19 He brought me forth to a large and wondrous place. He delivered me, because he loved me.

22:20 The lord rewarded me because of my righteousness, my devotion, for I have kept the ways of the lord and strayed not into wickedness.

22:21 Of all the laws, the judgments and commandments, I did not stray.

22:22 I have kept myself pure and strayed not to sin.

22:23 Therefore the lord has blessed me, according to my cleanness in his sight.

22:24 I have shown no mercy, slain many and spilled the blood of men in glory to my lord.

22:25 My very eyes shall cause the uncircumcised to tremble, so that they shall know the fear that is my lord.

22:26 The way of the lord is perfect; the words of the lord are true. Blessed be those who trust in the lord.

22:27 God is my strength and my power. He leads me down the perfect path.

22:28 He makes my feet like the feet of eagles; he sets me atop the highest places.

22:29 He teaches my hands war, so that a mighty bow of steel is broken in my arms.

22:30 His shield is my salvation and his mercy has made me great.

22:31 Though I walk the slippery path of God, he enlarges the steps so I do not fall.

22:32 I have pursued my enemies and consumed them in the great love of my lord. Never did I turn back until all those against me are destroyed.

22:33 I have consumed them and wounded them deeply, so that they shall not arise when the hyenas feast upon their flesh and the vultures tear their very bowels.

22:34 The lord hath made me strong and I step upon my enemies like dust upon the ground.

22:35 You have gifted me strength in battle, so that those who rise against me shall fall before me.

22:36 The lord has given me the necks of my enemies, so that my blades shall plunge through their throats and consume the very brine of their blood.

22:37 Cursed be those who hate me, for the lord hates those who hate me.

22:38 Those that hate me shall cry unto God and the lord shall not answer, for the lord is with me.

22:39 My lord laughs at their cries and their plea, and makes them suffer for their wickedness.

22:40 May the God of all god's rape those why go against me, so that their cries be heard throughout the heavens.

22:41 I shall grind them to dust and spread their ashes among the lands.

22:42 When I lived among the heathens, those fools with foreskins, you did make me head of their peoples though I know I shall not serve them.

22:43 Strangers shall give obedience, and submit to me.

22:44 They shall fade away and fear to come out from their hiding places.

22:45 The lord lives. Blessed be the lord, for he is the rock of my salvation.

22:46 My lord did deliver me from the hands of my enemies and gave them unto me, so that I may crush them.

22:47 Violence and wickedness did the lord deliver away from me and violence and righteousness did I deliver unto those who defied me.

22:48 I shall give thanks to the lord and sing great praises in his name.

22:49 He is the tower of my salvation. May he bless me and my seed for generations.

22:50 Blessed be the name of the lord."

23:1 These are the words of David the son of Jesse, the man raised up on high, anointed king over the peoples of Israel and sweet psalmist of the lord.

23:2 "The lord of Israel did kiss me and his tongue was in my mouth.

23:3 He then said, the rock of Israel spoke to me. The man who rules Israel must be just and rule in fear of the lord most holy.

23:4 May he be as the rays of the rising sun on a cloudless day, which shines upon the grass covered in dew.

23:5 Although I be not of the house of God and serve in priesthood, he has made me an everlasting covenant, so that I may give Israel order in all things. He is my desire, my salvation, my love.

23:6 These sons of Belial are wicked thorns which cannot be grasped by hand, lest they prick your hands.

23:7 Let us burn these wicked men with fire and poison the very foundation of their being."

23:8 And those that heard these words of David wondered what the hell he was rambling about.

23:9 These are the names of the strong and valiant who swore loyalty to David: The Tachmonite that sat upon the seat, chief over all. Adino the Eznite, who on one day slew eight hundred men with his spear!

23:10 They were unarmed people who dwelt within a city that David conquered. Adino he killed eight hundred of them. Such is the glory of this man, blessed by God.

23:11 Eleazar the son of Dodo, the Ahohite, known as one of the three mighty men of David.

23:12 One day he arose and went to the lands of the heathens and slew countless with his sword, so that the very blade of Eleazar was cleaved to his hands.

23:13 He was known by his enemies as Eleazar Bladehand.

23:14 The third of the three was Shammah the son of Agee the Hararite. When the Philistines came to the lands of Israel, the armies of Israel fled, for the Philistines were strong and mighty.

23:15 Shammah stayed behind and hid within a field of mandrakes. Shammah partook of this magical herb, waiting for the Philistines to come.

23:16 Shammah lied within the field and with great fury slew all those who came in his path, so that the lord was given a great victory that day.

23:17 These three mighty men came to David during the harvest time, when David hid within the cave Adullam: the armies of Philistine pitched in the valley of Rephraim.

23:18 David was held within the cave, for he was surrounded by heathens. The armies of Philistine held garrison even unto Bethlehem.

23:19 The thirst of David grew strong and he complained, saying, "Oh how I would bless those who bring me a drink of water from the well of Bethlehem.

23:20 Those waters are fresh and refreshing and shall quench my undying thirst."

23:21 And the mighty three of David went forth to Bethlehem, so that they may give to their master the freshest of waters.

23:22 It was a long and bloody trip. Many men of Philistine were slain for this drink of water.

23:23 As they came to the well of Bethlehem, Eleazar dipped his gourd into the well, while Shammah and Adullam held back those of Philistine.

23:24 Upon their return, these three men of David gave the gourd to their, and said, "Drink, for we have given you the waters blessed by God."

23:25 David took of the gourd and drank, spitting the water upon the ground.

23:26 He then spilled the remaining water on the ground, saying, "You risked your lives so that I may have a drink of water."

23:27 Yet you insult me by giving me a gourd of warm water! This surely shall not quench my thirst."

23:28 And the three men of David grumbled, for their master was an ungrateful little whiny ass.

23:29 Abishai the son of Zeruiah and brother of Joab was captain among the three. He held his spear and with one throw thrust it through the chests of three hundred men.

23:30 These men were lined in a row, frail, suffering from a long famine. Still, Abishai thrust his spear through three hundred with one throw.

23:31 Though he was captain of the three, he was not known as one of the three, for he was more honourable and valiant than the three men of David.

23:32 Benaiah the son of Jehoiada the Kabzeelite had done many acts to gain infamy among those who go against Israel.

23:33 During the months of winter, Benaiah witnessed a lion sleeping within a deep pit. Benaiah snuck beside the lion and cut it's very throat, giving the wife of Benaiah a nice coat.

23:34 And all those heard the story of Benaiah the lion slayer.

23:35 Benaiah also slew a man of Egypt. The Egyptian held a spear which was seven feet tall, with a head sharper than the talons of the eagle.

23:36 Benaiah snuck up behind the Egyptian as he slept and with the spear of the Egyptian he struck down this evil heathen with his own weapon.

23:37 And all those of Israel praised Benaiah, saying, "Praise be to the lion slayer! Blessed be the one who kills the man of Egypt."

23:38 Though Benaiah was more honourable than the three men of David, he was younger and did not attain the status of the three.

23:39 David made him captain of the guard.

23:40 There are other men who were loyal to David, but nobody cared about them.

24:1 For reasons unknown, God was angry at the people of Israel. So that he may punish Israel, he came to David and said, "Go, take a census of all the tribes."

24:2 David was unaware of the blasphemy which the lord told him to do and went forth with the census.

24:3 The king sent for Joab and said, "Take your men and number all those within the tribes of Judah, from Dan even to Beersheba."

24:4 And Joab said, "Shall we number the slaves, the women, the children as well?" and David said, "Count only the males, so that the women and the slaves not be in the numbers."

24:5 So Joab and his men went across the nation of Israel, numbering all those who dwelt within.

24:6 After nine months and twelve days, Joab numbered all the males of Israel and returned to David, saying, "Within the tribes of Israel we have eight hundred thousand men and within Judah we have five hundred thousand men."

24:7 It was then the lord came down upon David, in a mass of black smoke and great fire, and the lord did curse the name of David.

24:8 The voice of God came forth and said, "Do you think the lord such a fool that he knows not how many men dwell within his own lands?

24:9 You go forth and insult the lord, taking a census of all those men chosen by God.

24:10 Such a thing is blasphemy, for the lord knows all and knows that the numbers of men in the tribes of Judah be eight hundred thousand four hundred and seventy-eight and within Judah their be four hundred eighty nine thousand eight hundred and eleven."

24:11 David asked of God, "If you wished me not to take a census, why did you demand I take a census?"

24:12 The lord said, "I commanded you no such thing."

24:13 David said, "Yes you did."

24:14 God said, "No I didn't."

24:15 David said, "Yes you did."

24:16 God said, "No I didn't."

24:17 And this pattern repeated for what seemed hours, until David broke down and wept in confusion.

24:18 The lord said, "Your lord is not without mercy and shall give you a choice as penance for this sin.

24:19 You shall be given seven years of famine, three months being slain by the uncircumcised, or three days of plagues."

24:20 And David said, "To choose the outcome of my servants of Israel, such a thing is unfit for mortal men.

24:21 May the lord decide, for he shall give us mercy in his punishment."

24:22 So the lord chose three days of plagues upon the lands, so that all of Israel suffered from a great and terrible sickness for three days.

24:23 The very bowels of their belly came forth from their nostrils and remained there until they died or the three days given by the lord passed.

24:24 Seventy thousand men of Israel died by this plague sent from God, given because David took a census of Israel which the lord demanded of him.

24:25 And when an angel of the lord came down, he brought with him a great sword of flame, so that with one strike he may slay all those in Israel.

24:26 It was then that Lucifer grasped the hands of this angel and said, "Go and tell your master that he shall slay no more men of earth this day."

24:27 The lord was angered with Lucifer and said, "How dare this fallen servant of mine stop the massacre which I did plague upon my people."

24:28 David spoke to the lord, "What cruelty is this, that you would send plague and death upon the people of Israel for the sin of one man?

24:29 Give to me your wrath so that I may embrace it. Leave those who are innocent in peace."

24:30 Still, the lord did not stop his wrath from harming those of Israel until the three days ended.

24:31 And the lord looked down upon the seventy thousand slain, and said, "That shall teach David for taking a census when I tell him to take a census."

24:32 Though this slaughter did calm the lord of Israel, God was still angry. So, the lord took six days to create another world, similar to ours.

24:33 Upon the seventh day, he destroyed it.

24:34 Gad the prophet came to David and said, "You must end this plague of our lord with a sacrifice of peace offerings.

24:35 Go, build an altar to God upon the threshing floor of Aruanah the Jebusite and give your offerings there.

24:36 When Aruanah saw the king of Israel coming, he went out, bowed down to David and said, "Blessed be God and the king of Israel."

24:37 David said, "I have come here to give sacrifice to our lord, so that he may end this wickedness which plagues our lands."

24:38 Aruanah said, "Then go, slay your offering upon the altars."

24:39 David said, "I cannot, for I need to slay thine offerings upon your threshing floor. The lord demands it."

24:40 And Aruanah said, "If the lord demands that you slay an offering upon my threshing floor, the lord demands also that you pay me fifty shekels of silver, so that you may have the honour of using my land."

24:41 So David bought the threshing floor of Aruanah for fifty shekels, built his altar and sacrificed his oxen.

24:42 The lord looked down and was not pleased. Still, the lord knew this was the third day, and he must end the pestilence across Israel, lest they realize that their lord is unworthy of their devotion.

24:43 So the lord God ended the plagues which sickened and killed the children of Israel.

I KINGS

1:1 David was old and stricken with age. No matter who came to aid the king of Israel, his loins would not harden.

1:2 His servants searched forth, so that they could find a young, pretty virgin, who could come to David and give him the erection he needed.

1:3 They found a fair damsel for their master, Abishag the Shunammite and brought her forth to the king.

1:4 And Abishag tended to David dearly, though try as she might, the damsel could not raise the loins of her master.

1:5 It was so that the king never knew the pleasures of her virginity.

1:6 David took aside his most trusted servant and said, "Sew your mouth shut, so that you may never speak of this again.

1:7 This damsel who tends to me shall never raise the power of the king of Israel. Go and I shall tell you that which shall arouse my lust.

1:8 Spy within the lands of Philistine and find for me a young boy, uncircumcised and fair.

1:9 Bring him to my bedchamber, so that I may know him well."

1:10 And his servant did and brought forth to his master Eshishkosh the son of Gabrenishth, of the Philistines.

1:11 When David gazed upon this young boy, the very lust in his soul did rise and give to him that which separate the men from the boys.

1:12 The king of Israel enslaved Eshishkosh and thrust on him his unholy love.

1:13 Now it was that Adonijah, born of Haggith by the seed of David, exalted himself saying, "I shall be king when my father dies." He prepared himself horsemen, chariots and fifty men to be his personal guard.

1:14 David never said to Adonijah that he shall or shall not be king. The little brat just assumed so.

1:15 Adonijah spoke with Joab and Abiathar, who both supported him, believing that David anointed his son Adonijah to be the successor of Israel

1:16 But Zadok, Benaiah, Nathan the prophet, Shimei Rei, and the mighty men of David did not support Adonijah, saying, "Never have we heard our master say that Adonijah shall be king."

1:17 Now Bathseba gave to David a son named Solomon and

Bathseba wished for Solomon to be king, saying, "The king of Israel owes me a great debt for his sin unto me.

1:18 He stole from my husband Uriah and for this he should have it so that my son be king."

1:19 Nathan the prophet knew of Bathsheba's wishes and prophesied it, conveniently.

1:20 Nathan came to Bathsheba and said, "Your husband is old and his mind weakens.

1:21 You shall go and tell him that Adonijah declares himself king of Israel.

1:22 Lie to him and say that he swore that your son Solomon shall be king. When he doubts, I shall come in and confirm he did say that Solomon shall be his successor.

1:23 Now go and let it be that Solomon shall be king after David."

1:24 So Bathsheba went to the bedchamber of David, where Abishag tried furiously to give David an erection.

1:25 Bathsheba bowed to her husband and David asked, "You wretched cunt, what is it you want now?"

1:26 For David was very grumpy in his old age.

1:27 And Bathsheba said, "I wish to know why your son Adonijah goes around and declares himself king when he is not.

1:28 He does go around Israel and slays in sacrifice countless oxen, calves and lambs, in glory to the lord for giving him the throne of Israel."

1:29 And David said, "If he wishes to be king, let him. He is my son and so let him be my successor."

1:30 But Bathsheba said, "Do you not remember the oath you swore to me?

1:31 You did swear in front of God that my son Solomon shall succeed you and become king of Israel."

1:32 David said, "I do not remember this oath I swore unto you. You lie, cursed whore sent from the devil himself.

1:33 Be gone, so that you may lie to me no more."

1:34 It was then Nathan walked in and David asked of his trusted friend, "Take this wicked temptress away from my bedchamber.

1:35 Her tongue offends me with deceit."

1:36 Nathan said, "My master, what lies does your wife tell you?" and David said, "She insists I swore to my lord that Solomon shall be my successor."

1:37 And Nathan told the king of Israel, "My friend, her words that come from her tongue are true.

1:38 You did swear to Bathsheba that Solomon would be king of Israel."

1:39 David said, "I do not remember this oath, but if Nathan the prophet says so, it must be true.

1:40 This scares me, for if I forget this oath, what other oaths have I forgotten?

1:41 Nathan said, "You did swear to me that after your death, I may take your caregiver Abishag as a concubine."

1:42 Abishag said, "He did not, that lying deceiver; that blasphemer of God!"

1:43 David said, "Quiet, you useless whore, who can't even give rise to the king of Israel.

1:44 If I promised Nathan that he shall have you, then have you he shall."

1:45 So it was Nathan who did have the pleasure of taking the virginity of Abishag.

1:46 Bathsheba then said to her husband, "O king of Israel you are old and the memories you lost worry me.

1:47 Have it be that our son Solomon be king today, before ye forget again the promises you made."

1:48 David said, "So be it. It shall be that Solomon shall sit upon the throne of Israel.

1:49 May the lord bless the new king of Israel, so that his reign be greater than mine."

1:50 So Zadok the priest, Nathan the prophet, Benaiah, the Cherethite, and the Pelethites went to Solomon and said, "Today, you shall be king."

1:51 And Solomon said, "Really. Cool."

1:52 Solomon was placed upon the horse of David and was brought forth to the spring of Gihon, where he was anointed king of Israel.

1:53 Zadok took the shofar and blew it so that it created a loud noise, announcing to all of Israel that Solomon was their new king.

1:54 All of Israel came forth and said, "Praise be our king Solomon. Praise be the lord!" and they celebrated with pipes, drums, trumpets and wine.

1:55 The very noise those children of Israel created were so mighty that the very earth split beneath them.

1:56 They quieted down after the second earthquake.

1:57 Adonijah and his followers were feasting, when they heard the noise that came from the city and asked themselves, "What the hell is that?"

1:59 And Jonathan the son of Abiather ran to them, saying, "We are royally fucked upon this day.

1:59 King David is no more our king. He made Solomon his successor."

1:60 Those who were with Adonijah ran, saying, "Solomon is going to kill us. Solomon is going to kill us!

1:61 We have betrayed the new king of Israel. Solomon is going to kill us!"

1:62 Adonijah feared Solomon, believing that Solomon would kill him.

1:63 Those that saw Adonijah said, "You shall die by the hands of our new king, for you failed to steal his throne."

1:64 Adonijah grew so fearful that he went to the tabernacle, grabbed the very horns of the altar and wept.

1:65 It was told to Solomon that Adonijah did grasp the altar, weeping. Solomon went to the altar, to witness this.

1:66 When Solomon saw that Adonijah grasped the horn of the altar, Solomon laughed at the pathetic fool before him.

1:67 The king of Israel came before Adonijah, drew his sword and said, "What madness possesses you, that you would weep before the horns of the altar?"

1:68 Adonijah said, "My king, forgive me. I did not know you were to succeed our father.

1:69 I beg of you, do not spill my blood before this altar."

1:70 Solomon laughed, saying, "Today is not the day you shall die.

1:71 I say to you, if you serve me well, you shall have no reason to fear my sword.

1:72 Betray me and I shall have it so that your very intestines choke the breath from your throat."

1:73 Adonijah fell on his face and said to his king, "Thank you, thank you. Blessed be the king of Israel. Blessed be Solomon!"

1:74 Solomon grew disgusted by the grovelling of Adonijah and said, "Get the hell away from me."

1:75 And Adonijah went home.

2:1 The days of David's death came close and he summoned his son Solomon and said to him,

2:2 "My body shall soon turn to dust and my bones be buried within the earth.

2:3 Keep charge of the kingdom of Israel. Do what is right in the eyes of God. Obey his statutes, keep his commandments and uphold the laws of Moses. Do this and you shall grow strong and prosperous.

2:4 Slay those who stray from the path of our lord. Show then no mercy, for they shall bring the wrath of our lord upon all of Israel.

2:5 Know that I did curse Joab, for it was he who slew Abner, when Abner did come to give me my throne which Ishbosheth sat upon.

2:6 Joab also killed my son Absalom and feasted upon his blood, claiming it sweeter than honey.

2:7 He slew also Amasa the son of Jether, for I declared it that Amasa shall take the title which belonged to Joab.

2:8 Joab knows does not know I know these things, but I do.

2:9 Kill Joab. He is a worthless slop of the unholy bile which comes from a woman's uncleanliness.

2:10 Behold, Shimea the son of Gera is a slave of mine, who did curse my name and threw stones upon my men when I fled from my son Absalom.

2:11 When I returned to my throne, he begged of me to spare his life and I swore to him that he shall not die by my sword.

2:12 So that I may keep this oath, take your sword and kill him for me. I hate that bastard child of a transvestite whore."

2:13 These were the last words of David, which is fitting for a bloodthirsty tyrant.

2:14 The reign of David lasted for forty years. Seven years he reigned in Hebron and thirty-three years did he rule in Israel.

2:15 And the former king of Israel was buried in the city of David. Even in his death, he was arrogant.

2:16 Now sits Solomon upon the throne of Israel; and his kingdom was established greatly.

2:17 Adonijah the son of Haggith came to Bathsheba the mother of Solomon. Bathsheba asked, "Do you come peacefully?" and Adonijah said, "I come in peace.

2:18 Let it be Solomon who rules over Israel. I know it is not for my fate.

2:19 I have a request for our king of Israel." and Bathsheba asked, "What is this request?"

2:20 He said, "Speak to Solomon and ask him if I may have Abishag as a wife.

2:21 She is a young woman and I wish to know her very well."

2:22 Bathsheba said, "Abishag is the whore of Nathan the prophet." and Adonijah said, "I don't care, for I wish her to be mine."

2:23 Now Solomon loved his mother dearly and set for her a throne beside his. Bathsheba sat upon her throne and said to her son, "Adonijah did come today, to seek a favour of you."

2:24 Solomon said, "That man is a fool who still wishes for the very seat I sit upon now.

2:25 I do not care for his request. Let him be killed."

2:26 So Solomon sent his servant Benaiah the son of Jehoiada to kill his brother Adonijah. And Benaiah did as he was told.

2:27 With a great stone of marble Benaiah crushed the very skull of Adonijah and had it so that his body was buried within the foundation of the temple of the lord.

2:28 Solomon then sent out for Abiathar the priest and said, "Know that I loathe you for supporting the false king Adonijah. You are a man worthy of death.

2:29 But I shall not kill you at this time, for you carry the ark of the lord. God shall curse me if I harm even a hair upon your wrinkly head.

2:30 You also served my father well and for this I am grateful.

2:31 Go now to Anathoth and live in his fields. Never come into this city again, or your very priesthood shall be torn from your soul and I shall tear your very flesh."

2:32 Joab heard that Solomon sought out those who supported Adonijah and wished to have them killed. So, Joab fled to the tabernacle of the lord and held with both hands the horn of the altar.

2:33 When king Solomon heard that Joab fled to the tabernacle of the lord, he sent out Benaiah and said, "Kill this man Joab, for my father wished it on his dying breath."

2:34 So Benaiah went forth to the tabernacle of the lord and behold, he saw Joab grasping the very horns of the altar.

2:35 Benaiah said, "Get out from this holy place," and Joab said, "No, for you shall not slay a man on this holy ground.

2:36 Joab was gravely mistaken.

2:37 Benaiah held the back of Joab's head and thrust his skull upon the very horn of the altar of the lord.

2:38 You have no concept how much this pleased the lord. God almost cummed his pants when he saw what happened.

2:39 Solomon rewarded the loyalty of Benaiah and made him general over all the armies of Israel.

2:40 Zadok the priest was given the chambers of Abiathar, for Solomon knew Zadok to be loyal to him.

2:41 Shimea was called to Solomon and Solomon asked him, "How did you become a slave unto my father, king David?" and Shimea answered, "I became a slave so that David may spare my life.

2:42 For when I was young and your father fled from Absalom, I did curse the king of Israel and spat upon his name.

2:43 Stones and dust I threw on him, as he retreated from the men of Absalom.

2:44 In time, I saw that David was the true king of Israel and that I did make a fool of myself.

2:45 I came to your father and begged of him to spare me for the sins I committed."

2:46 Solomon asked, "Did my father swear to God that his hand shall not slay you?" and Shimea said, "Indeed he did."

2:47 It was then Solomon smiled and said, "A pity he swore that his sons would not hold back their blades."

2:48 Solomon then drew his sword and gave it Benaiah, saying, "Spill the blood of this slave, for he disgusts me.

2:49 May the brine of his life stain my floors."

2:50 So Benaiah cut off the head from Shimea's neck and the blood of Shimea spilled upon the floor of the throne room of David.

2:51 And the kingdom of Solomon was established throughout the lands.

3:1 Solomon the king of Israel knew that Egypt enslaved them so many generations ago, yet Solomon still wished to make peace with the Egyptians.

3:2 The two nations made treaties with one another; and to bind these treaties Solomon married the Pharaoh's daughter and brought her into the city of David, teaching her the ways of Israel.

3:3 When the Egyptian wife of Solomon saw the sacrifices all of Israel made to appease their lord, she became scared and vowed never to worship such an unholy demon.

3:4 Despite his wife, Solomon was a devout man of God, who burned incense, offered sacrifice and kept all statutes, commandments and laws of the lord of all lords.

3:5 Solomon went to Gibeon, so that he may sacrifice upon the holy altar there. One thousand burnt offerings Solomon did burn upon that altar.

3:6 One thousand young lambs, males without blemish, of the first year. And the price of young mutton did rise upon that day.

3:7 In Gibeon the lord appeared to Solomon and said, "You shall be a wondrous king of Israel, who will serve me well.

3:8 Tonight I appear to give you one desire, one wish. Ask and it

shall be given."

3:9 Now Solomon was a young king and feared his reign would be laughed upon through history.

3:10 Solomon asked the lord, "My God, you showed my father David mercy and love as he walked the true path to salvation. My father did obey your laws, give heed to your word and ruled in your blessing.

3:11 I am but a young man, who know little of the ways of the lord. My father anointed me king and I fear I shall be remembered as a terrible king of Israel.

3:12 Give unto me wisdom, knowledge and understanding, so that I may rule all of Israel according to what is right of the lord."

3:13 When the lord heard Solomon's request, he said, "What the fuck is wrong with you?

3:14 The very lord comes down and offers you one wish and you ask for wisdom?

3:15 Wisdom you shall have then, young Solomon, so that you may rule over the nation of Israel in a wise manner.

3:16 A pity, for the lord will not grant thee another gift such as this; and you waste it on wisdom."

3:17 With that, the lord gave Solomon great wisdom. And when Solomon gained this wisdom, he did lie down upon his bed and wept, saying, "I should have asked I rule all the earth, so that only Israelites live upon all lands."

3:18 Solomon went back to Jerusalem, wise in the fact he wasted his wish on wisdom.

3:19 There came before Solomon two women who were concubines, both standing before the king of Israel.

3:20 One woman said, "Behold, this harlot stole my baby from me.

3:21 We both bore a child and our child were born on the same day.

3:22 One night, as she slept beside her child, she rolled over and suffocated the very life from her baby.

3:23 She then takes my baby, who is alive and well and gives me the dead baby as I slept in my bed."

3:24 The other prostitute said, "You sucker of uncircumcised cocks. That baby is mine, for it was you who killed your baby and took mine whilst I slept."

3:25 It went on for hours that the two harlots argued in front of Solomon about whose baby it was.

3:26 With the wisdom Solomon was given by the lord, he yelled to the two ladies, "Enough!"

3:27 And he took his sword and cut the baby in half, down the spine of the infant.

3:28 Each prostitute was given one half of the baby as Solomon said, "Now you shall have equal parts of this spawn of a whore."

3:29 And the prostitutes left, crying, carrying half a dead baby.

3:30 When those of Israel saw the two concubines carrying their half of the infant, they laughed and said, "Half a son of a whore is better than a whole son of a whore

3:31 When is a dead baby a good baby. When it's a harlot's baby.

3:32 How do ye get the whore's baby to stop crawling. Have the king of Israel slice it in half."

3:33 And that is where those god damn dead baby jokes came from.

3:34 When all of Israel heard why the harlots baby was cut in two, they did marvelled in the wisdom of Solomon and said, "Surely our king has the wisdom of God to have cut a baby in half."

4:1 Hiram the king of Tyre sent servants to king Solomon when he was anointed ruler of Israel, for king Hiram loved David.

4:2 And Solomon sent word to Hiram, saying, "I know you loved my father and I know my father loved you.

4:3 I walked in on your loving of each other. It intrigues me to this day.

4:4 Know now that my father could not build a proper house in glory to my God, for he did war with nations on all sides.

4:5 Now my lord has given me peace, so that I may build for him a true and magnificent temple.

4:6 Your servants shall work in the building of this house of God. They shall carve the very cedar trees, for your peoples are known as the best with all timber.

4:7 When Hiram heard these words of Solomon, he rejoiced and thought that Solomon shall also be a lover of his.

4:8 Hiram sent messengers to the king of Israel, saying, "Know now that all my servants shall be dedicated to the building of your temple.

4:9 By wagon and by ship they shall deliver all the cedar and fir to you and they shall continue this until the very forests be empty."

4:10 Solomon blessed Hiram for the gift of timber and every year would send to Hiram twenty thousand measures of wheat and twenty measures of pure oil.

4:11 Hiram was pleased with this gift, but lusted for more. He said to Solomon, "The oil you have given me is a great blessing from you.

4:12 Come now, so that I may place it within my ass and you may feel the lubrication of your gift."

4:13 Now Solomon was a wise man and knew that Hiram wished for sodomy. Solomon wrote back, "I cannot, for such an act is sinful to my people."

4:14 This confused Hiram greatly and he said, "How is it then that your father, the king of Israel before you, would fuck my ass every time we met?"

4:15 Solomon replied, "My father is dead. If he did not commit this sin, he shall still breathe among us on this day."

4:16 Still, the two men made peace and there was prosperity between the two nations.

4:17 It came to pass that Solomon needed great stones to build this temple of the lord. He came to Hiram and said, "Give to me servants, so that they may carve the very rock of your mountains."

4:18 Hiram said, "I shall, but only if you love me as your father did."

4:19 Now Solomon needed those stones and thought in his wisdom, "If my sin of sodomy brings forth the house of God, surely the lord shall forgive me."

4:20 So Solomon did give forth his buttocks and Hiram placed oil upon it and fucked it.

4:21 The lord looked down and saw this unholy sin and said, "Cursed be to Hiram, who fucks the king of Israel."

4:22 As the lord gazed on, he saw that Solomon did not place his erection in the ass of Hiram

4:23 And the lord said, "Solomon is a wise and holy man, who gives not into unholy lust.

4:24 Let it be that the giver and not the receiver shall be cursed on this day."

5:1 So it came that on the four hundred and eightieth year after the children of Israel left Egypt, of the fourth year of Solomon's reign, in the month of Zif, that the temple of the lord began construction.

5:2 It was a humble abode for the lord God, with a length of threescore cubits, the breadth twenty cubits and the height thirty cubits.

5:3 The porch which surrounded the house of the lord of Israel was ten cubits and surrounded the temple in its entirety.

5:4 For the house he made narrow windows, so that none could sneak in.

5:5 These windows did shine the light of the sun through and did give the temple of the lord lighting which made it appear as though scrawny fingers were scratching the floors of the house.

5:6 Against the walls of the house he built many chambers. Both round the temple and the oracle he built many chambers.

5:7 The nethermost chamber was five cubits broad, the middle was six cubits broad and the third be seven cubits broad, so that each chamber was one cubit larger than the previous.

5:8 Though the house be made of stone, neither hammer nor axe nor any tool of iron was used within the house of the lord.

5:9 God hates loud noises. Ruins his naptime.

5:10 Instead, each stone was cut, chiselled and prepared before it came to be a part of the temple of the lord of Israel.

5:11 The door for the middle chamber was in the right side of the house: and they went up with winding stairs into the middle chamber and out of the middle into the third chamber.

5:12 So the house of the lord was built and Solomon covered it with beams and boards of cedar.

5:13 And then chambers were built against all the house, five cubits high: and they rested on the house with timber of finest cedar.

5:14 The lord came down upon Solomon and said,

5:15 "If you keep my statutes, my commandments, my laws and walk the path of Moses, then the lord of Israel shall stay always with the people of Israel and not forsake them.

5:16 In the house you built for me I shall I stay. Yet the house which you built for the lord is not fitting.

5:17 Look at what the people of Israel built for their lord, when they traversed in the wilderness.

5:18 The lord your God demands gold, jewels, bling.

5:19 Let it be that the temple of the lord of Israel be a place where all those shall witness great bling and those who walk by the house of the lord shall see this bling.

5:20 Just as they see the lord rolling and be hating, shall they walk by the house of the lord and be hating'."

5:21 And it was so that Solomon demanded the house of the lord be rebuilt with the riches of all of Israel.

5:22 All beams of cedar were carved and inlaid with knops and open flowers and within each knop was placed a precious stone.

5:23 The oracle was prepared so that it may hold the ark of the covenant of the lord.

5:24 The room of the oracle was twenty cubits in length, twenty cubits in breadth and twenty cubits in height and covered it all with pure gold, so that even the floors were inlaid with pure gold.

5:25 Surrounding the room of the oracle was a great chain, to separate the oracle from the rest of the house of the lord. And the chain was made of purest gold.

5:26 Within the oracle was built two statues of angels sitting atop an olive tree, each being ten cubits high.

5:27 Each angel was built identical to the other, so that each looked the same as the other.

5:28 The wings of each angel were five cubits in height and the other wing was five cubits in height.

5:29 It was made so that one wing of the angel would stretch forth and touch the other wing of the angel, while the other wing of each angel was stretched back, so that it may touch the wall.

5:30 Each angel was made of pure gold.

5:31 Throughout all the house of the lord were the floors inlaid with pure gold; and it did make the floor shiny and slippery to walk upon.

5:32 The door which brought one into the room of the oracle were made of the wood of the olive tree and within the door were carved knops, cherubs and flowers.

5:33 Within each knop was placed a precious stone and the cherubs had eyes of the bones of sacrificial offerings.

5:34 And the doors which entered into the house from the outside were made of fir and carved upon them were open flowers, knops, cherubs, unicorns, dragons and palm leaves.

5:35 These doors were inlaid with gold, and when the lord gazed upon it, the lord was satisfied with the bling of the temple.

5:36 In the fourth year of Solomon's, upon the month of Zif, was the beginning of the construction of the temple of the lord. On the eleventh year, in the month of Bul, it completed, so that it took seven years to complete the temple of God.

5:37 Nine men died to complete the house of the lord, and forty-six were injured so that this temple could be built. God didn't care.

5:38 And the cost of the temple was greater than the worth of some heathen nations, which pleased the lord greatly.

5:39 The lord is truly a greedy son of a bitch.

6:1 Solomon was of the lord and was also a greedy son of a bitch. When Solomon built his house, it took thirteen years to complete.

6:2 Within his house he built the forests of Lebanon, the length being one hundred cubits, the breadth fifty cubits and the height thirty cubits. Three rows of pillars made of cedar ran down this room, forty-five pillars in all, so that each row contained thirty pillars.

6:3 Upon each pillar were placed shields made of hammered gold. Some large, some small and all made of hammered gold.

6:4 The very floor of the house of Solomon was made of the finest carved stone and was inlaid with pure gold and precious gems.

6:5 Inlaid upon the stones were the history of the peoples of Israel, from the ark of Noah even unto the reign of Solomon, so that all who gazed upon the floors of Solomon's house would be reminded of the history of Israel and of the might of the lord.

6:6 The bedchamber of the Egyptian wife of Solomon were made of the finest carved stones and within these stones were etched the many gods of Egypt which the wife of Solomon worshipped.

6:7 This angered the lord greatly.

6:8 The great court of the house of Solomon was made with great carved stones, which were supported by beams of brass.

6:9 And in the great court was a pool ten cubits round and five cubits deep and the pool was filled with the waters of the sea and always kept hot.

6:10 Within the bedchamber of Solomon were many hiding places where the concubines could be hidden and each hiding place had within it a bath.

6:11 Two thousand baths in all were hidden within the bedchamber of Solomon. The king of Israel loved his whores clean and fresh.

6:12 The house of Solomon was large, wondrous, filled with gold, jewels and riches the likes of which have never been seen in Israel nor any other kingdom.

6:13 It had more bling than the house of the lord, was larger than the house of the lord and the lord became angry that Solomon had more bling than the lord of Israel.

6:14 To explain how large and how costly the house of Solomon would take too much time and would be boring.

6:15 I'd finish writing how the house of Solomon was built, but it disgusts me how the king of Israel would live in such glorious gluttony.

6:16 Fuck Solomon's house. He was one rick god damn asshole.

7:1 Solomon then gathered all the elders of Israel, the heads of the tribes, the chiefs of the highest families and brought them to Jerusalem, so that they may witness the ark of the covenant of the lord be brought into the temple of God.

7:2 And all the men of Israel gathered to Solomon, so that they may witness the ark be carried to the temple. And because Solomon prepared a feast and they wanted free food and wine.

7:3 The elders and the priests of Israel came, carrying the ark from the city of David into the house of the lord.

7:4 With it they took all the vessels and the looted plunder which David stored around the ark of the lord.

7:5 It was the Levites who carried forth this bountiful plunder, for they were the slaves of God.

7:6 As Solomon and the congregation of Israel walked with the ark towards the city of Jerusalem, they offered countless sacrifices along the path.

7:7 Oxen, goats and lambs were slain, daggers cutting their throats and were cast aside the road so that they may die.

7:8 This pleased the lord greatly. God loves mass death of any species.

7:9 And the priests carried the ark of the covenant of the lord and placed it within the oracle of the temple, beneath the wings of the two golden angels.

7:10 The wings of the angels were so great that they covered both the ark of the lord and the very staves which were used to carry the damned thing.

7:11 Nothing was saved in the ark saved for the two tablets of stone which Moses was given by God, which listed the commandments, the laws and the statutes of the lord of Israel.

7:12 When the ark was placed and all the priests and Levites left the temple, a great black cloud of fire descended upon the house and filled each room of the temple so that none who would enter could see.

7:13 Those that did became blind and left the house coughing out the spirit of the lord. Within a few days, they did die of lung cancer. Such is the glory of the lord.

7:14 Then Solomon came and spoke to the masses of Israel. saying, "The lord did say he shall dwell within his house built him, in black smoke and great fire.

7:15 It is with great honour that the lord now lives within the house which the children of Israel built him, for he did choose us as his people and now chooses to live in our great city."

7:16 Solomon then took the blood of the nearest slain offerings, dipped his fingers within and with it sprayed the congregation of Israel, blessing them, saying, "Blessed be the lord and blessed be the children of Israel."

7:17 The king of Israel then said, "Blessed be the lord of all Israel, who did fill the mouth of my father with words of wisdom and honour.

7:18 Since the days our lord freed us from the servitude of Egypt, God chose no other city but this city within all the tribes of Israel for him to dwell in.

7:19 And it was in the heart of my father David to build our lord a great house, so that the lord of all lords shall dwell among us and bless us.

7:20 It was God who came to David and told him that he shall not build the house of the lord, but it shall be the seed from his loins who shall build a temple for the lord of Israel.

7:21 Behold, I am the seed of David, and I did build the mighty house of God. Gaze upon it and marvel in its wonder."

7:22 And the slaves of Israel did mumble, and say, "Solomon never even lifted a hammer to build the house of the lord.

7:23 It was us who did build it, yet God blesses the king."

7:24 Solomon did not hear the mumblings of his slaves and continued to speak, "And now, O God of Israel, let my words and my prayers please you, so that you shall dwell within the temple and give us all your blessings.

7:25 But will our lord dwell forever in this house. I think not, for not even the heavens shall contain the glory and the power of our lord. How arrogant are we to think this humble house shall be enough for the lord of Israel to dwell?

7:26 Fear not, for even when the spirit of the lord is gone from our temple, he shall still watch us and hear our words, our prayers and see our sacrifices.

7:27 With the blessing of our lord, Israel shall prevail over all. Let it be that we conquer all lands, enslave all heathens and kill all who believes not as we do."

7:28 It was then the fire within the house of the lord left and spread across the heavens so that the very skies were orange and red in great burning fire.

7:29 Solomon gazed upon the heavens and said, "And let it be that when the children of Israel sin, that the skies be shut up, the rains not fall, for we did fall off the path of our God.

7:30 May the lord send forth plagues, famine, pestilence and poverty, so that we may atone for our sins and the sins of our fathers.

7:31 When we suffer, let it be known that it is the lord who sent us suffering, for we harmed him deeply."

7:32 And some of Israel said, "How can we, mere men, harm the great and mighty lord?

7:33 If we suffer the wrath of our God because our fathers before our fathers' fathers sinned and eat of the swine, then our lord is not worthy of my devotion.

7:34 Baal, Ashteroth, and Dagon are not as vengeful as the lord we worship."

7:35 Solomon did not hear these words, but the lord did and the fires descended from the sky and burned those that murmured against God, those slaves who murmured against Solomon and burned the many sacrifices which Solomon and those of Israel slew upon their way to Jerusalem.

7:36 Solomon then said, "Behold the glory of our lord, for he did accept the house I built him and is pleased.

7:37 Our sacrifices shall fill his hunger and blessed be those who he took, for they shall know now the glory and wonder of our God."

7:38 Solomon did not know that those children and slaves of Israel which the lord did take were burning in the everlasting fires of hell.

7:39 The king of Israel then stood before the doorway of the temple of the lord and sacrificed twenty-two thousand oxen and one hundred twenty thousand sheep, in glory to God.

7:40 The very blood of the sacrifice stained permanently the entrance to the temple of God.

7:41 It was then declared that the day be holy and every year those of Israel held a feast in glory to the lord and in glory to the temple.

7:42 Upon that day they would bless the lord, the king and the temple and offer many sacrifices of oxen and lambs, so that the blood of the offerings would flow down the streets of the city like rivers.

7:43 The lord would gaze down on this and be pleased, for the lord loves the blood of beasts flowing like rivers almost as much as he loves the blood of men flowing like rivers.

8:1 It came to pass that when both the house of the lord and the house of Solomon were complete, that the lord appeared to Solomon in Gibeon.

8:2 The lord said, "You have angered me and made the house of your own in greater glory than the house of your lord.

8:3 Fear not, for I shall not dwell within the house of God long. As you said, how can a mere house contain the lord?

8:4 Know only this. The lord God shall watch you. If you walk as your father walked and keep the laws, the statutes and the commandments given during the times of Moses, then you and your people shall be prosperous.

8:5 It will be that the throne of Israel shall be established through all nations and rule the lands beyond even the seas.

8:6 All Israel shall grow rich, prosperous and be given many sons. The other nations shall bow in your glory and serve you and your lord.

8:7 Know this; if you stray away from your lord and break the laws, the statutes, the commandments and your eyes wander to the lord of heathens;

8:8 Then the one true God shall come down with a mighty fist and destroy all that which be Israel!

8:9 All your kingdom shall be doomed to rubble and dust: even my house shall be demolished to ash.

8:10 The people of Israel shall be cast into the nations of the uncircumcised and be slaves to the unholy.

8:11 They shall wallow in their own dung and have dung spread across their faces and shall beg to their lord for salvation.

8:12 The lord shall hearken not their words and ignore their cries and their suffering.

8:13 It shall come to pass that the last man of Israel shall die, so that none of the people of Israel shall exist among the earth.

8:14 When those of other nations walk by and see the destroyed cities that were of Israel, they shall ask themselves, why did their lord do this?

8:15 And the one true God shall answer, because they went whoring after other gods and strayed apart from the righteous path."

8:16 With that, the lord did vanish from Solomon and Solomon asked himself in silent, "Could it be that the lord is a woman?

8:17 For my God is hard to please, never satisfied and at least once a month becomes an absolute bitch."

8:18 Now, twenty years after the house of Solomon was built, Solomon blessed Hiram the king of Tyre for all the timber and the stones which his people brought forth.

8:19 Solomon gave to Hiram twenty cities within the land of Galilee, in thanks for the stones and timber.

8:20 And when Hiram came to see the cities within Galilee, he was disgusted and said, "What wretched cities did ye give me, filled with the lepers and the whores?"

8:21 Solomon said, "These cities I give unto you, for they are useless to me.

8:22 Filled with the unclean, the unholy, the wretched, they serve no use. My God loathes these people.

8:23 Your lords do not. Enslave all within the city and have them do your bidding."

8:24 And Hiram became pleased, for the king of Tyre was in great need of slaves.

8:25 In thanks, Hiram sent to Solomon six talents of pure gold.

8:26 During his reign, Solomon built the house of the lord, the house of Solomon, the city of Millo, the city of Megiddo and rebuilt both Hazor and Gezer.

8:27 For Pharaoh the king of Egypt did retake Gezer and for Solomon destroyed all those peoples of Canaan who dwelt within and gave it to Solomon as a dowry for his daughter.

8:28 Solomon also built the cities of Bethhoron, Baalath and Tadmor.

8:29 Great many chariots, horsemen and soldiers Solomon took and drove out all the people which Israel despised out of the cities.

8:30 Amorites, Hittites, Hivites, Perizzites, Jebusites and Canaanites were slaughtered in a great and glorious genocide among the nation of Israel.

8:31 Solomon also raided the lands of these heathens and enslaved those he could capture, so that of those hated heathens who dwelt in Israel were slaves and slaves only.

8:32 With all this city building, arms race and raiding, Solomon did have to raise the levy of those of Israel, lest the nation of God become stricken with poverty.

8:33 Those men of Israel cared not, for the number of slaves increased and they could afford easily the extra gold which their king commanded of them.

8:34 Of the slaves of Israel were a great many; so great that Solomon had to create slave hunters for any foolish slave who would run away from their master.

8:35 Five hundred and fifty slave hunters did Solomon have, who would give chase to the runaways and return them unto their masters, quite bruised.

8:36 Solomon's wife and the daughter of Pharaoh grew bored of the city of David and asked the king of Israel for her own city of which she could dwell. So, Solomon built the city of Millo.

8:37 Within Millo Solomon built a great altar to the lord of Israel. Three times a year Solomon and his wife would come to the altar and offer great sacrifices to the lord God.

8:38 Within the land of Edom, on the shores of the Red Sea, was the city of Eziongeber, where Solomon built great ships of timber.

8:39 Hiram sent to Solomon servants, shipmen who knew the sea, so that they could build great ships for both Solomon and Hiram.

8:40 The navy of Solomon would go to the lands of Ophir and carry upon their vessel four hundred and twenty talents of gold, which were brought back to the king of Israel.

8:41 And through all foreign nations, Solomon was known to be one rich motherfucking bitch.

9:1 The queen of Sheba heard of the fame, the wisdom and the wealth of Solomon and came to Jerusalem to see these wonders and to test Solomon.

9:2 She brought to Jerusalem a great caravan of camels carrying spices, gold, precious stones, wine, strong drink and beer.

9:3 The queen of Sheba tested Solomon and asked him most difficult questions, which Solomon answered in the wisdom that was given to him by the lord.

9:4 The queen was astonished by the wisdom in Solomon's words, by the feast which was upon his table and the riches within the house of Solomon.

9:5 She said to the king of Israel, "You truly are a wise and wealthy man. The words which were told to me pale in comparison to what I have witnessed today.

9:6 Oh how your servants must be honoured to serve such a rich and glorious master."

9:7 And the servants of Solomon who heard this, quietly blasphemed the name of Solomon.

9:8 Still, the queen of Sheba spoke and said, "How is it then that your house be full of great wonders and riches, yet the peoples I have passed on my way here were dressed in rags and begged me for food?"

9:9 With true words of wisdom, Solomon answered her, "Isn't it obvious. They are not of the people of Israel."

9:10 And that answer satisfied the queen of Sheba, who then gave Solomon all those which the camels carried. The spices, gold, stones, wine, liquor and strong drink were given to Solomon.

9:11 Solomon wished to be known throughout all nations as a wealthy man and gave to Sheba twice the value of what was given to him.

9:12 Silver, gold, brass, weapons, donkeys, slaves, concubines, incense, precious stones, fine wines and sweetened goods were given to the queen of Sheba, who then returned home.

9:13 And the spices which the queen of Sheba were then given to Hiram the king of Tyre. The people of Israel loathe spicy foods.

9:14 Now with the navy and the taxes, within one-year Solomon

would receive six hundred threescore and six talents of gold.

9:15 Solomon had also great merchants, caravans, vineyards, distilleries, spices and he traded these with the kings of Arabia.

9:16 With this gold, the king of Israel built two hundred targets of beaten gold, each weighing six hundred shekels and used these targets to practice his archery.

9:17 A great throne Solomon also built, constructed of the finest ivory and inlaid with solid gold.

9:18 Upon each side of the throne were built two pillars and atop each pillar was a lion. A real fucking lion!

9:19 These lions had muzzles made of solid gold, which they wore whenever Solomon sat upon his throne.

9:20 The throne was placed among a high place, with six steps leading up to the throne. Upon each side of the steps were chained a lion, so that there were twelve lions in all chained to the steps.

9:21 And the chains of the lion were made of the bones of the slew heathens and the bones were inlaid with solid gold.

9:22 All the cups, the goblets, the jars, the chamber pots were made of solid gold. Even the fountains of Solomon were made of gold.

9:23 And all people through many lands would come and gaze in marvel at Solomon's golden showers.

9:24 The navy of Israel would travel to many lands and bring back many gold, silver, ivory, foods, precious stones, peacocks and apes.

9:25 Solomon loved apes and trained them so that they would do the most medial tasks of the servants.

9:26 And it was that Solomon was the wealthiest among all the kings of the earth and people foolishly believed this wealth of Solomon also brought him wisdom.

9:27 For who else but a wise man could acquire such value?

9:28 People throughout all lands would come to Solomon, so that they may be blessed with his wisdom and knowledge given to him by the one true God.

9:29 And Solomon would not speak a word to them unless they brought a gift. Spices, slaves, armour, gold, silver, horses, mules, camels, concubines, or some other valuable gift.

9:30 With these gifts alone Solomon bought many more chariots and horsemen, so that he had one thousand four hundred chariots made of pure gold and twelve thousand horsemen with armour of gold.

9:31 These chariots and horsemen struck fear into all those who opposed Israel, for they could see them coming from a great distance away and would say, "Here comes the cavalry of Israel."

9:32 We best surrender now, or they'll kill us this very day."

9:33 Or they would retreat, but the army of Israel never claimed that.

9:34 The silver which was brought to Solomon became so plentiful that Solomon would cast them out of his house. And so, it came that silver became more plentiful than stones among the streets of Jerusalem.

9:35 It was believed that the horses from Israel were the best-bred horses and were sold to many nations for one hundred and fifty silver shekels.

9:36 Those nations of Egypt and Syria bought many horses from Israel. Even the hated nations of the Hittites bought horses from Israel, though they were charged six hundred shekels of silver.

9:37 The Hittites were quite stupid.

10:1 Solomon, unlike his father, loved women. Foreign women, native women, big women, little women, young women, old women, he loved them all.

10:2 The king of Israel did have for wives and whores Egyptians, Moabites, Ammonites, Edomites, Zidianites and Hittites.

10:3 Of those nations which the lord said to Israel never to intermarry, Solomon did marry and did clave to these heathen women.

10:4 Seven hundred wives and three hundred concubines Solomon had. And these women did turn the heart away from Solomon, so that Solomon worshipped foreign lords.

10:5 For the heart of Solomon was weak in the eyes of God. He did go whoring after Ashtoreth, Dagon, Milcom and the despicable gods Molech and Chemosh.

10:6 In his old age, Solomon did build temples dedicated to the hated gods Chemosh and Molech, sacrificing and worshipping there.

10:7 Likewise all the strange wives and whores of Solomon offered sacrifice and burnt incense in the house of Solomon, each for their gods which they worshipped.

10:8 And the true lord God was angry at Solomon, for Solomon did not walk the path of his father David and sought forth other false gods.

10:9 Gods who did not get angry and send plagues, poverty and famine among his worshippers.

10:10 The lord of Israel was wrath with Solomon, for his heart was not dedicated fully to him, and he sought out other lords.

10:11 Though God told Solomon not to stray his eyes towards heathen lords, Solomon did and disobeyed the lord God of Israel.

10:12 The lord came unto Solomon, and said, "You foolish bastard who did seek out other lords which your heathen wives worship.

10:13 How dare you choose the comforts of a filthy wench over the love of God!

10:14 For such an insult unto the one true lord, I shall split apart your kingdom and give it to your servant.

10:15 Fear not, for I loved your father and shall bless him even unto this day. Your kingdom shall not be torn when you reign over it.

10:16 It shall be your son who will be punished for your whoring of other gods.

10:17 One tribe of Israel shall also be given to your son, so that he has rule over some.

10:18 For my love of David I shall do this and not ruin all that of Israel, nor take away all that from your son."

10:19 The lord God then left and created conflict for the peoples of Israel. Hadad, the remaining male of Edom, was to be an enemy of Israel.

10:20 For when the people of Israel came to Edom and slaughtered every male in Edom, Joab remained there for six months until all those males of Edom were slain;

10:21 Hadad was fled to Egypt with servants of his father, for Hadad was only a child, an infant.

10:22 The servants which took Hadad found sanctuary in Egypt and the Pharaoh gave them land, a house, food and employment.

10:23 Hadad found great favour in the eyes of Pharaoh and the Pharaoh gave Hadad his sister in law, Tahpenes the sister of the queen.

10:24 Tahpenes bore for Hadad a son, who they named Genubath. And the family of Hadad grew within the house of Pharaoh.

10:25 When Hadad heard that David and Joab were dead, he asked of Pharaoh, "Give me leave, so that I may return to my own land.

10:26 Pharaoh asked him, "Why do you wish to leave. What does your land have which you lack here?"

10:27 Hadad answered, "Nothing. I have all that and more which I could ever wish for, given to me by the hands of Pharaoh.

10:28 Bless you, Pharaoh, for you did give me great prosperity and comfort, but now I must return home.

10:29 My people have been cursed by the wretched nation of Israel and I alone am the only male to have survived the wickedness of their genocide.

10:30 It is not for my sake, for the sake of the slain, which I ask to return back to my lands. I must take vengeance upon their death; I must ensure the people of Edom don't disappear from the logs of history."

10:31 Pharaoh heeded the words of Hadad and said, "Go. You are a blessed man and I love you as though you were of my own flesh.

10:32 Take with you what you desire, so that you return to your lands with wealth and prosperity.

10:33 I wish for you to not leave, for I love you as a son. Yet I understand your desire to go back to the lands of your fathers and claim back that which was taken from your people."

10:34 And Hadad left with his wife and son, so that they may rebuild the nation of Edom.

10:35 The lord created yet another enemy for the people of Israel; Rezon the son of Eliadah, who fled from his lord Hadadezer king of Zobah.

10:36 Rezon gathered men and became a band of raiders and mercenaries. David slew men of Rezon at Zobah, and for this Rezon loathed those of Israel.

10:37 In Damascus Rezon dwelt, gathering men of valor.

10:38 For all the days of Solomon Rezon fought against Israel and caused great mischief. Rezon abhorred the children of Israel and reigned over the lands of Syria.

10:39 Even the servant of Solomon was turned against his master by the will of the lord. Jeroboam the son of Nabat began to turn against the king of Israel.

10:40 Jeroboam loathed how Solomon built the city of Millo for a foreign cunt who worshipped foreign gods.

10:41 Jeroboam was known as a mighty man of valor and Solomon made him taskmaster over all the slaves of Israel.

10:42 When Jeroboam left the city of Jerusalem, behold, the prophet Ahijah the Shilonite came to him, wearing a new robe. And the two men met alone on a field.

10:43 Ahijah took off his new garment and stood naked in front of Jeroboam. Ahijah then shredded his garment into twelve pieces and laid them upon the ground.

10:44 The prophet then took ten pieces and gave them to Jeroboam, saying, "Take these ten pieces, for they shall be the ten tribes of Israel, which you shall rule over as king.

10:45 The lord God of Israel shall tear the tribes apart from the son of Solomon, for his father did go whoring after the gods Ashtoreth, Chemosh, Dagon, Molech and Milcom.

10:46 This shall be after Solomon dies, for the lord will not punish Solomon for David's sake."

10:47 Jeroboam asked, "The lord will punish people for Solomon's sin after king Solomon dies?

10:48 Why does the lord punish Solomon instead, for it was he who sinned and not his son."

10:49 Alijah answered, "Do not question the will of the lord. This is his way.

10:50 Let it be known that you have only ten tribes and two remain. The son of Solomon shall have one tribe.

10:51 For David, the grandfather of the new king, was a righteous man. It is by the holiness of David I shall not take all that away from the son of Solomon."

10:52 Still, Jeroboam asked, "Why take anything away from the son of Solomon, who did not sin against the lord?

10:53 Or, why not take all from the son of Solomon. Why leave him one tribe?

10:54 Also, there be twelve tribes and twelve shredded garments, yet only eleven tribes be accounted for.

10:55 If ten belong to me and one belong to the new king of Israel, what of the remaining tribe?"

10:56 Alijah answered, "The fate of the twelfth tribe is not your concern, but the concern of the lord.

10:57 Let it be known that if you walk in the ways of the true lord and keep his laws, his statutes, his commandments, that you shall be king of Israel and your reign shall be long and prosperous.

10:58 Follow in the path of David and you shall be as great as he."

10:59 When Solomon heard that Jeroboam was meant to be king of Israel, he did take his arrows, and sought to kill Jeroboam.

10:60 Jeroboam fled to Egypt and Shishak the Pharaoh gave him sanctuary, for Shishak was a merciful Pharaoh.

10:61 For forty years Solomon did reign over Israel until he died. And when Jeroboam heard of the death of Solomon, he left to go back to the lands of Israel.

10:62 As for how Solomon died, who cares. Probably by some venereal disease he received from his many wives and concubines.

10:63 And for the rest of the acts which Solomon did during his reign of Israel, they are written in the acts of Solomon; a book so boring it is not even included in the bible.

10:64 The body of Solomon was buried beside his father, in the kingdom of David. And Rehaboam the son of Solomon sat upon the throne of Israel.

11:1 Rehaboam the son of Solomon went to Shechem, for it was there he was to be anointed king of Israel.

11:2 And when Jeroboam heard Rehaboam was king, and that Solomon was dead, he returned to Israel and continued his work as taskmaster.

11:3 Now Jeroboam and all the congregation came to Rehaboam and said, "Your father, in all his wisdom, has given us a tremendous load to bear

11:4 With the buildings of great cities, houses, monuments, temples, we have become overworked and we wish that the new king of Israel shall loosen our yoke under your service.

11:5 Rehaboam said, "Allow me to think on this. Return to me in three days' time."

11:6 And Rehaboam sought the guidance of the elders of Israel, who said, "Lighten their load, so that they shall remain to serve you.

11:7 These men are dangerous, for as servants to Israel they do the work that no other man shall do.

11:8 If you do not lighten their load they shall revolt and go against us, becoming enemies within our borders.

11:9 Ease their burden and they shall be happy, who will serve us for the remainder of their days."

11:10 Rehaboam loathed the advice and said, "These men are men of Israel, men of God.

11:11 They should be filled with pride and honour to do the work of our glorious lord and of this mighty nation.

11:12 If they know not this, then I shall enforce it upon them. I shall double their load until they become proud of their work.

11:13 Those that bitch shall be whipped and the whipping shall continue until their morale improves."

11:14 And when in three days the congregation of Israel came and said, "Shall you lighten the load your father gave to us?" Rehaboam said, "I shall do no such thing!

11:15 How dare you servants of Israel come and demand that your work be lessened. You are servants of the greatest nation and the lord most holy.

11:16 Let it be known that I shall double your load and tighten your yoke. Let this be punishment for your ignorance. Through work you shall know the glories and wonder of Israel and of God.

11:17 Those that complain shall be as though they are against God.

They shall be punished without mercy.

11:18 Where my father beat thee with whips, I shall beat thee with scorpions!

11:19 Let it be that the tails of the scorpion sting you, and the venom destroy any foulness within your souls."

11:20 When the people of Israel heard this, they loathed the new king of Israel and said, "Rehaboam is a fucking asshole!

11:21 We don't need him for king. Let it be that every man shall be of their own house.

11:22 He is a disgrace to the name of David. Rehaboam is a disgrace to all those of the children of Israel.

11:23 May he die by the hands of the heathen, for he deserves not the honourable death by the hands of his brethren.

11:24 His corpse shall rot in the deserts, where not even the foulest of scavengers shall come and eat his despicable flesh."

11:25 And the people of Israel revolted against their new king, save for the tribe of Judah, who were a bunch of pussies.

11:26 King Rehaboam sent forth Adoram so that he may slay all those who spoke of rebellion.

11:27 Adoram was armed with the finest armour and blades.

11:28 The people of Israel quickly stoned him to death and placed his body upon the sand dunes of the desert, where the grains of sand blown by the wind ripped off his very flesh.

11:29 When the lord gazed down upon the corpse of Adoram, he was not pleased nor angry. A mighty sand storm blew around the body of Adoram, so strong that the lord could not see Adoram.

11:30 It came to pass that those who rebelled against Israel came to Jeroboam and made him king, so that all but the tribes of Judah and Levi were ruled by Jeroboam.

11:31 The tribe of Levi was the last tribe. They belong to no man, but are slaves of God.

11:32 Now when Rehoboam returned to the city of Jerusalem, he gathered all the men of Judah and a few loyal men from the tribe of Benjamin, one hundred and fourscore thousand men, so that they may fight those who betrayed the true king of Israel.

11:33 But the word of God came to Shemaiah and said,

11:34 "Speak to king Rehoboam and the tribes of Judah and those few who remain loyal to the son of Solomon, and tell them this.

11:35 The lord demands it that you sheath your swords against your brethren and let those who betray you go back to their house.

11:36 It shall come to pass that the lord shall do what is good."

11:37 Rehoboam heeded the words of Shemaiah and did not fight against his brothers.

11:38 Jeroboam dwelt in Shechem within mount Ephraim and fortified it with mighty walls, going forth and also taking the city of Penuel.

11:39 Even though those with Jeroboam loathed the son of Solomon, they still went to Jerusalem, so that they may worship the lord God in his temple.

11:40 Jeroboam became concerned and said, "If these men continue to go to the city of Jerusalem, their hearts shall turn against me and go to Rehoboam.

11:41 These men who betrayed Rehoboam will then betray me. Of course they will. They betrayed once, they shall do it again."

11:42 So Jeroboam did something that made the lord really fucking angry. I mean really fucking angry.

11:43 Jeroboam gathered a great many gold and from them carved two golden calves and said to his peoples, "Fuck God. He didn't do shit for us except send us all pestilence and death.

11:44 Here are your true gods who had freed thee from Egypt. Two golden calves, which Aaron carved when Moses spoke to the demon God on mount Horeb.

11:45 Let it be that we worship our true lords and cast out the laws of Moses, given to him by the lord who wishes to destroy us all."

11:46 And Jeroboam placed one calf in Bethel and the other in Dan.

11:47 Those loyal to Jeroboam became to go whoring themselves unto these carved Gods, committing blasphemy to the true lord of Israel.

11:48 Jeroboam then made priests to these golden calves, priests who were unclean in the eyes of God, saying, "Let it be that those who are cursed by the demon God of Moses be blessed by the lords who shall save us.

11:49 These lords shall cleanse the unclean, and make them clean from the bile and the filth from the demon who wished to claim their place."

11:50 This angered the lord even greater, for these two calves were mere idols and not even true false gods, who were the sons of the lord of Israel.

11:51 The lord was also angry for Jeroboam was right and God did wish to destroy all of Israel. God was very wrath in this mere mortal figuring out the hidden will of God.

11:52 Jeroboam then ordained a feast for the two calves, so that on the eighth month, on the fifteenth day of the month, all came together, and feasted on flesh clean and unclean, drinking wine, and becoming merry.

11:53 And when they came to offer sacrifice, Jeroboam said, "Sheath your swords and spare your oxen, for our lords do not wish for the needless slaughter of any living thing."

11:54 So the people loyal to Jeroboam rejoiced and worshipped the two golden calves, saying, "It is nice to worship a god who isn't such a damn tyrant."

12:1 Behold, there came a man of God from the tribe of Judah and he went to the calf that was in Bethel as Jeraboam burnt incense beside it.

12:2 And the man spoke to the golden calf, saying "O altar O altar, you wretched piles of gold. So says the true lord that a son shall be born of the house of David and Josiah shall be his name. Of those who are priests to this accursed statue, he shall burn them as incense and the very bones of man shall be turned to ash upon you."

12:3 The man then said to those of Israel, "Let it be as a sign to you this day. The very statues shall split open and ash shall pour out of their bellies."

12:4 Jeroboam thought this man to be a fool and he stretched forth his hand and told the priests to kill him. Behold, when the hand of Jeroboam was stretched forth, it became decayed and turn to the hand of a corpse.

12:5 When those people of Jeroboam noticed the corpse hand, the very calf split apart and ash black and foul poured out from their bellies, covering those that worshipped the calf.

12:6 Jeroboam came to the man and said, "I beg of you, pray to the one true God of Israel. I have seen my sin and shall not stray again from the path of our lord.

12:7 Please, have the lord show mercy upon me and return to me my hand."

12:8 And the man said, "No such thing shall be done. Let it be that your hand be as a corpse forever, until the day you die."

12:9 Jeroboam asked the man, "Why would the lord do such a thing to me. Have my sin be that strong?"

12:10 And the man from Judah said, "Yes."

12:11 Still, Jeroboam pleaded and said, "Then let me atone for my sins. Let me slay one hundred thousand sacrifices in the name of God, for the blasphemy I committed in my foolishness.

12:12 Lo, I did create a false god, worshipped the false god and fooled others to worship this false god.

12:13 Let it be then that all shall know the mercy of the true lord,

who did return my hand to me even after my sins!"

12:14 And the man said, "That is not the sin by which your lord is angry," and Jeroboam said, "Then what is it?"

12:15 The man replied, "You called the lord a demon and claimed that God wished to destroy all that which is Israel.

12:16 Our lord takes unkindly to such accusations and shall punish for now until your death for such foul words."

12:17 Jeroboam begged of the man to return his hand and the man refused. Jeroboam even stripped his clothes and begged to the almighty lord, saying, "Forgive a fool his sin and return to me my hand."

12:18 And the very skies split apart and became red with the fury of the lord. And the mighty fingers of God stretched forth across the heavens and came to rest above the head of Jeroboam.

12:19 So it was that when Jeroboam gazed up upon the mighty hand of God, he saw that the lord outstretched his middle finger and no others.

12:20 Even so, Jeroboam wished to please the man from Judah and said, "Come, stay with me and I shall feed you and give you drink."

12:21 Let it be that I claim you blameless for my dead hand."

12:22 The man from Judah said, "Even if I were hungry and wished my thirst quenched, I cannot, for the lord has told me not to eat, not to drink, nor to take the same route back from whence I came."

12:23 So the man left another way and returned home by another path than the one he took to Bethel.

12:24 When the man left, Jeroboam placed on his hand a glove and went all the remainder of his days wearing but one glove.

12:25 He looked like an idiot.

12:26 Now their dwelt an old prophet in the city of Bethel, who heard of the glories and wonders this man of Judah announced.

12:27 This prophet saddled his ass and went on his way to find the man of Judah. And behold, he found the man of Judah resting against an oak tree.

12:28 The man of Bethel said, "Come, eat and drink with me," and the man of Judah said, "I cannot, for the lord forbade me to do so."

12:29 And the prophet of Bethel said, "Fear not, for I am also a prophet of the lord and I have come in the name of God to give you water and bread."

12:30 So the two prophets came to the house, eating bread and drinking water.

12:31 As the two ate, the prophet of Bethel said, "You have doomed yourself, for you did not hearken the word of the lord, eating bread and drinking water."

12:32 The man of Judah said, "I did this under the blessing of God, for you told me that the lord told you to come, so that I may nourish in your house."

12:33 With a laugh, the man of Bethel said, "I lied, you fool," and the man of Judah asked, "Why would ye do such a thing?

12:34 What harm have I caused to you?"

12:35 The man of Bethel said, "You came within my city and prophesied on my land.

12:36 Our lord should have chosen me for this honour, yet he chose a fool of Judah. Fuck you!"

12:37 And the man of Judah said, "You are truly a petty and selfish man." He then gathered his belongings and left for his home.

12:38 As the man of Judah walked, a great lion came, and killed him, feasting on his flesh.

12:39 This lion was sent by the lord to kill him, for believing in the lies of the other prophet, and eating bread and drinking water.

12:41 The prophet of Bethel never received any punishment from God for saying the words which deceived the man of Judah.

12:42 Such is the bullshit of the lord.

abominations of sinful fellatio and sodomy.

13:1 The lord was still angry with Jeroboam and gave to Ahijah the son of Jeroboam a grave illness.

13:2 Jeroboam loved his son and wished him to become well. He sent his wife out and said to her, "Disguise yourself so none know that you are my wife. Get to Shiloh, for there dwells a prophet, wise in the ways of the lord.

13:3 Take with you ten loaves of bread, a vase of honey and some sweetened cakes. Then he shall tell us what is to become of our child."

13:4 Jeroboam's wife did as she was told and left for the city of Shiloh, so that she may hear the wisdom of the prophet Ahijah. In his age, Ahijah did become blind.

13:5 The lord came to Ahijah and said, "Behold, the wife of Jeroboam comes to ask you of their son, who is sick by the hands of the lord.

13:6 She shall come and feign to be another woman. Do not be deceived, for she is the wife of Jeroboam."

13:7 And it was so, that when Ahijah heard the footsteps enter into his house, he said, "Behold, the wife of Jeroboam has come to ask me about her son.

13:8 Be fearful, for I shall give to you heavy words.

13:9 Go, tell your husband that the lord is quite wrath with him, for he did go and create false gods for the tribes of Israel to worship.

13:10 It was the lord who gave to Jeroboam dominion over the ten tribes of Israel and your husband thanked the lord by creating false gods!

13:11 For the sins of his father, your son shall die. It is the will of God.

13:12 Let it be known that all those of the seed of Jeroboam shall perish and burn so that not even the ash remains on the ground.

13:13 Those who die within the cities shall be eaten by dogs and those that die within the wilderness shall be eaten by birds.

13:14 Now arise, wicked woman and go back to your city. Know that when your feet step within the walls of your house, your son shall die.

13:15 Know that your son shall be mourned by all of Israel and it shall be only he who seeks comfort in the grave, for he was good in the eyes of the lord.

13:16 Those others of Jeroboam shall lay across the lands and rot, feasted upon by vultures and dogs, vultures and dogs."

13:17 So the wife of Jeroboam arose and went back to her home. When she crossed the threshold of the doorway, behold, Abijah died.

13:18 And all of Israel came to mourn the death of Abijah, who was buried in the sepulcher of his ancestors.

13:19 For twenty-two years Jeroboam reigned the betraying tribes of Israel until his death. Nadab the son of Jeroboam succeeded his throne.

13:20 Rehoboam the son of Solomon reigned in Judah still. At the age of forty-one he did first sit upon the throne and he reigned Jerusalem and all of Judah for seventeen years.

13:21 And Rehoboam did evil in the sight of God, worshipping other lords and said to his servants, "It is obvious even to a fool that our lord does not care for us.

13:22 Let us worship all the lords, so that in our worship we find one worthy of our devotion."

13:23 Those of Judah worshipped foreign and strange gods and made for them idols, altars, temples and unholy images. Upon every high hill was a pole of Ashtaroth and under every great tree sacred stones to Baal.

13:24 Male prostitutes, considered sacred amongst the heathens, plagued the tribe of Judah with their unholy brothels, committing

13:25 In the fifth year of Rehoboam's reign, the lord of Israel came to Shishak the Pharaoh of Egypt and strengthened his army.

13:26 These soldiers of Egypt came and took all that of wealth within the house of Solomon. Even the shields of gold which hung within the forests of Lebanon did the Egyptians take.

13:27 With the shields gone, Rehoboam hammered shields of mighty brass and gave them to the captains, the generals and the soldiers who guarded the house of Solomon.

13:28 Throughout all his reign did Rehoboam war with Jeroboam the king of the betraying tribes of Israel.

13:29 For seventeen years Rehoboam ruled as king of Judah until his death. One of the poles of Ashtaroth fell upon his skull and crushed his head to dust.

13:30 He was buried in the sepulcher of David and Abijam his son reigned in his stead.

14:1 Now in the eighteenth year of Jeroboam's reign did Abijam begin his rule over the tribe of Judah.

14:2 For three years he reigned in Jerusalem. And his mother's name was Maachah the daughter of Abishalom.

14:3 Nebat sinned also in the ways of his father and sought out other gods and took part in the services of the sacred male prostitutes which plagued the lands of Judah.

14:4 Nevertheless the lord allowed Nebat to be given a son, so that he may reign Jerusalem upon Nebat's death. The lord of Israel did this for the love of David.

14:5 Because David did all that was right in the eyes of the lord. Save only for the matter of Uriah the Hittite did David ever sin. Not even in his lust for Jonathan did David ever sin.

14:6 Which means all else that David did was just and good in the eyes of God. So, for those who read this and gaze upon the wife of their neighbour with lust, just fuck her and have her husband killed.

14:7 It's okay. God doesn't mind.

14:8 Now Nebat died after three years upon the throne. It is unsure how the death of Nebat came to be, but we know he died in the brothel of the male sacred prostitutes, lying beside three rams and a monkey.

14:9 Asa the son of Nebat succeeded his father and reigned over Jerusalem in the twentieth year of Jeroboam's reign.

14:10 Now Asa did that which was right in the lord and burned every brothel which held a male prostitute, so that none were left in the lands of Judah.

14:11 For the sacred male prostitutes, he chopped off their loins and poured burning tar into their rectums, so that none should ever lie with them in unholy lust again.

14:12 Their bottom jaws were torn forth from their face and even their fingers were split off, so that they could pleasure not a man with their mouths nor their hands.

14:13 Asa then sent them to the wilderness of Judah and with a great hammer he crushed the chests of each sacred male prostitute, killing them.

14:14 Even his own mother Asa killed, for she worshipped an idol of Ashtaroth in a private grove within the house of Solomon.

14:15 Asa took this idol and burnt it, placing the ashes within the waters of the brook of Kidron.

14:16 Now the sacred stones and poles of Ashtaroth Asa did not destroy, for they were numerous within the tribe of Judah.

14:17 Though Asa failed in the destroying of these images, the lord did look favourably upon him, for he did that which was right with God.

14:18 And there was war all throughout the reign between Asa the king of Judah and Baasha the king of Israel.

14:19 Baasha king of Israel built the city of Ramah, between the borders of Judah and Israel, so that all those who go forth from Judah shall be slain.

14:20 So Asa gathered a great many gold and silver and sent them to Benhadad the son of Tabrimon, king of Syria, who dwelt in Damascus.

14:21 Asa said, "There is a league between me and you and between your and my father. Behold, I have sent you a gift of a great many gold and silver, in hopes that ye shall do that which is right for me.

14:22 Go forth and fight these tribes of Israel who betrayed their true king. Burn their cities, slaughter their sons, and have it be that the lamentations of their women be heard throughout both our lands."

14:23 Benhadad did that which Asa asked and sent his armies against the cities of Israel. The cities of Ijon, Dan, Cinneroth, Abelbethmaachah, and all those within the lands of Naphtali were reduced to ashes and dust.

14:24 When Baasha heard of this, he retreated from the city of Ramah and hid in his stronghold within Tirzah.

14:25 King Asa then sent his men forth to the city of Ramah and tore from it its timber, its stones, its very foundation. With these, Asa built the city of Geba, so that those of the tribes of Israel shall be executed when they cross the borders.

14:26 For forty-one years Asa reigned over the tribes of Judah until his death. He choked upon the bone of a fish, which his servants prepared for him. Jehoshaphat the son of Asa was then anointed king over Judah.

14:27 Nadab the son of Jeroboam began to rule over Israel in the second year of Asa's reign and he ruled over Israel for two years.

14:28 Nadab sinned also in the ways of Jeroboam and worshipped calves made of gold.

14:29 Baasha the son of Ahijah the prophet of the house of Issachar loathed Nadab and all the blasphemy he and his house did.

14:30 As Nadab and his armies made siege against the Philistine city of Gibbethon, Baasha unsheathed his sword and thrust it under the fifth rib of his king.

14:31 Those soldiers of Israel gazed upon the body of Nadab and said, "This man Baasha just killed our king. What is it we shall do, for we now have no leader."

14:32 It was then Baasha said, "Let me be your king, for if I am worthy enough to slay our king, then I am worthy enough to wear his crown and sit upon his throne."

14:33 These soldiers of Israel said to Baasha, "Fuck you. You killed our king and shall die for such crimes."

14:34 Baasha killed them and said, "Who now denies that I shall be your king?" And all those of Israel bowed to Baasha and said, "Glory be to Baasha, the king of Israel."

14:35 Now Baasha loathed greatly those of the seed of Jeroboam and smote all those of the house of Jeroboam. Young, old, men, women he did kill, so that none were left alive that had the same blood of Jeroboam.

14:36 Baasha did this with the blessing of the lord, for Jeroboam sinned against God, and for this his family must be slain.

14:37 Such is the justice of the lord.

14:38 Now there was war between Asa and Baasha all their days.

14:39 In the third year of Asa's reign did Baasha become king of Israel. And Baasha reigned over Israel for twenty-four years.

14:40 Baasha, the fucking idiot, sinned also against the lord and worshipped false gods, creating idols and temples in their honour.

14:41 He committed the same blasphemy he loathed Nadab for. Hypocrite.

15:1 The word of the lord came to Jehu the son of Hanani, saying,

"Your God hates these kings of Israel, who worship false gods and ignore the almighty.

15:2 This Baasha is a damn fool and shall die by the will of the lord. Let it be that his sins, which are of the sins of the house of Jeroboam, shall be his end.

15:3 All that who be of Baasha shall share the same fate as the seed of Jeroboam. Let it be that those of Baasha who die in the cities shall be feasted upon by dogs and those within the wild shall have their flesh consumed by birds."

15:4 It came to pass that Baasha died and was buried in Tirzah: Elah his son reigned in his stead.

15:5 And Jehu the son of Hanani did spread the word of God, spreading forth the words against the house of Baasha, damning them for their wickedness, bringing upon them the wrath of God and being sinful in the ways of Jeroboam.

15:6 In the twenty-sixth year of king Asa of Judah did Elah begin his reign of Israel. He lasted two pathetic years.

15:7 His servant Zimri was a greedy and conniving man and wished to take the throne away of his master Elah.

15:8 As Elah sat within his house, drinking wine and pissing on himself, Zimri snuck up behind his master and thrust a blade deep within his throat.

15:9 As was Israel tradition, those of Israel who slay the king then become king, as did happen with Baasha. It was a recent tradition, only a few years old, but it was a tradition nonetheless.

15:10 Zimri feared vengeance from the family of his master and ordered all those who came from the seed of Baasha to be killed.

15:11 Even the friends and neighbours of Baasha were killed, so that they may not spread the lies of Baasha.

15:12 And on that day, Baasha lost all his friends and his neighbours did move in haste.

15:13 In a great spectacle, Zimri then burnt all that which belonged to the family of Baasha. Their houses, their flocks, their cattle, their crops, all were reduced to smoke and ash.

15:14 The lord gazed upon the destruction caused by Zimri and was pleased. For Zimri destroyed all that of the family of Baasha, whom the lord hated.

15:15 God must have hated Zimri more. He was only king for seven days.

15:16 In the land of the Philistines, an army of Israel laid siege to the city of Gibbethon and they heard of the murder of their king Elah.

15:17 They said, "Who is this new king, who killed our master and ruler of all that is Israel?

15:18 How dare he commit such treason and be crowned king. Let it be that we cut the very scalp from which the crown lays."

15:19 So the army of Israel marched to Tirzah and lay siege to the very castle.

15:20 Omri, the captain of the army, demanded Zimri to leave and be punished for the slaying of the true king Elah.

15:21 Zimri yelled to them, "May your mothers be raped by the lords of heathens." He then grabbed a torch and burned the palace.

15:22 Foolish Zimri did not think to save a means of escape and died by the very fire which he created.

15:23 Now the peoples of Israel were split apart. Half were loyal to Omri, and the rest were loyal to Tibni the son of Ginath.

15:24 They were at war with one another, declaring that their master be the true king of Israel, though none be the descendants of David.

15:25 Conveniently, Tibni died of a heart attack and Omri became the next king of Israel. He was crowned during the thirty first year of Asa's reign and was king for six years.

15:26 Omri bought from the Samarians the hill of Shemer for two talents of silver and built atop this hill a great city, which he named the city of Shemer.

15:27 Now Omri did that which is evil in the eyes of God and worshipped also false gods, just like those of the house of Baasha and those of the house of Jeroboam.

15:28 The children of Israel were slowly realizing that the lord they worshipped was a malevolent tyrant and not worthy of their devotion.

15:29 At least not all their devotion. After all, these heathen gods never once killed their people for wanting flesh instead of manna, or being interested in the religion of their neighbouring nations.

15:30 The lord placed in the bowels of Omri a mighty kidney stone, weighing seven shekels and when Omri passed this kidney stone of God, he died.

15:31 Omri was buried in the lands of Samaria and his son Ahab reigned over Israel during the thirty eighth year of Asa's reign.

15:32 Ahab was king for twenty-two years. And he did also the sins of his father and of Baasha and of Jeraboam, and worshipped other gods.

15:33 It came to pass that Ahab did an evil thing and married Jezebel the daughter of Ethbaal king of the Zidonians.

15:34 God hates Zidonians.

15:35 Jezebel worshipped the heathen lord Baal and convinced Ahab to also worship Baal, only Baal and no other god but Baal.

15:36 She said, "Baal is a truly merciful lord, who blesses those who believe in him and worship him.

15:37 When you worship Baal, you need not worry of his wrath, for he shall show to you nothing but undying love and mercy."

15:38 For a child of Israel, such a thing was unheard of and Ahab worshipped Baal all his life. He built in Samaria a temple devoted to Baal and it was more glorious than the temple of the God of Israel.

15:39 Because of this, God hated Ahab and said that he did more evil and wickedness than any past king of Israel have ever done.

15:40 In these days Hiel the Bethelite rebuilt the city of Jericho: during this construction Hiel's son, Abiram, died and was buried within the foundation of Jericho. Segub, the youngest son of Hiel, was crushed within the towers of the gates and remain there to this day.

15:41 And so the words of the lord came true, as were spoken to Joshua the son of Nun.

16:1 Elijah the Tishbite, from the lands of Gilead, came unto Ahab and said, "You have angered the lord greatly and his wrath shall fall upon your lands.

16:2 By the will of God, your people shall know not rain nor dew and shall grow hungry and their thirst shall never be quenched."

16:3 And the word of the lord came unto Elijah and said, "You are a strong and noble man, who did not stray from the path of righteousness.

16:4 When your brethren sought comfort in the lords of heathens, it was you who still obeyed the ways of God and offered his sacrifices and kept always the laws, statutes and commandments.

16:5 Go hence unto the brook of Cherith, which be east by the river Jordan.

16:6 There you shall suffer not the famine and drought which the lord shall curse upon Israel, for the lord shall protect you, feed you and give you water."

16:7 So Elijah went forth unto Cherith and hid there for some time.

16:8 True to his word, the lord gave Cherith fresh water, for the brook did not dry. And Elijah never starved, for behold, ravens would come and give to Elijah stale bread and rotten flesh for him to eat.

16:9 Elijah ate the stale bread and loathed the ravens for bringing him such horrible food.

16:10 One day, Elijah became fed up and started eating the ravens instead. Their flesh was fresh and not stale nor rotten.

16:11 It came to pass that the brook dried up, for the lands have not seen rain for many years.

16:12 The word of the lord came to Elijah and said, "Go now to Zarephath, which belongs to the lands of Zidon.

16:13 This brook shall sustain you no more.

16:14 In Zarephath is a widow and it shall be that she shall give you food and comfort."

16:15 So he arose and went to Zarephath and there within the gates of the city he saw a woman gathering sticks. Elijah called to her and said, "Woman, go and get me some food to eat and some water to drink.

16:16 Be a good woman and do as your man commands you."

16:17 This woman said, "I cannot even if I wanted to, for the waters of these lands are dry and I have not enough flour for a simple cake.

16:18 Behold, I have come here to gather these sticks, so that my son and I may build a fire. Upon that fire, we shall eat the last of our flour and then starve to death."

16:19 Elijah said, "Fear not, for I am a blessed man of the lord of Israel. Go and make me your bread and bring me your water.

16:20 Do this and the lord of Israel shall bless you. Your waters shall not run dry and your barrel of flour shall never be empty.

16:21 Even the vessel which contains your oil shall flow everlasting. This be the will of the lord."

16:22 The woman did that which Elijah demanded and behold, her waters never dried, her flour never emptied and her vessel of oil always flowed.

16:23 One would think she would share this blessing and feed all those within the city. But the greedy little cunt only fed herself, her son and Elijah.

16:24 She hoarded this blessing, thus cursing those around her who died of starvation and dehydration.

16:25 Elijah found comfort also in this woman, as the lord did promise. The two lied within the same bed together and Elijah took pleasure in her as though she was a common whore.

16:26 It came to pass that the son of the woman became sick and his sickness consumed him and stole from him his last breath.

16:27 The woman came to Elijah and said, "What sins have I done, O man of God, to have the lord take that which is most precious to me?"

16:28 Elijah said, "Mourn not. Give me your son and remember that which you shall see this day."

16:29 As Elijah came to the son of the woman, behold, he was dead. And Elijah yelled to God, "Let it be known to this woman that the lord is merciful."

16:30 Elijah then took the body of the boy and stretched out over it, until the loins of Elijah were atop the mouth of the boy.

16:31 The very vessels of the seed of Elijah sat within the mouth of the boy, until the strength of Elijah raised with all its might.

16:32 Elijah then shot his very seed upon the face of the boy and spread it across the cheeks. With this, the boy awoke, arose and embraced his mother.

16:33 And the woman said, "Surely such a thing has never been done. O blessed be Elijah. Blessed be to the lord of Israel."

17:1 It came to pass that on the third year of Elijah's hiding, the word of the lord came to him and said, "Go now to Ahab and the lord shall send rain upon the lands."

17:2 So Elijah left to visit Ahab and there was a sore and mighty famine in the lands of Israel and Samaria.

17:3 Now Ahab called Obadiah, who was the governor of his house. Let it be known that Obadiah feared the lord greatly.

17:4 It was Obadiah who hid fifty prophets of the lord of Israel in a cave and fed them with bread and water, when that witch Jezebel started killing the prophets of the lord.

17:5 Ahab demanded of Obadiah, "Go forth and seek out all the lands which have brooks and wells. Make note of those which have grass, so that we may take our horses and mules to eat and not all our beasts die of this dreaded famine."

17:6 The two men marked on their maps which lands they shall explore. Ahab took one half, Obadiah the other and the two men went forth to seek out grass to feed their horses.

17:7 One would think the king of Israel would be more concerned with feeding their people, but he'd rather feed his horses and his mules. Ahab would allow his servants to suffer, so that he may fatten his asses.

17:8 As Obadiah sought forth grass, behold, he met Elijah. When Obadiah gazed upon Elijah, he fell on his face and broke his nose. He said, "Are you the servant of the lord Elijah?"

17:9 Elijah answered, "Of course it's me, you blind fool.

17:10 Who else would it be?"

17:11 Obadiah said, "You are in grave danger, for our king has abandoned the ways of the true lord and worships the heathen god of Baal.

17:12 Many prophets and priests of the service of Baal feast on the table of our king of Israel and his wife Jezebel eats with them.

17:13 It was Jezebel who blinded the eyes of Israel and had them believe in this false god. She is truly an evil witch and has used the powers of her cunt to confuse our king Ahab.

17:14 That wicked harlot ordered all those prophets of the true lord be killed, so that they shall not spread the word of truth amongst her words of lies.

17:15 Still, I gathered fifty prophets and they live in secrecy in a cave, safe from the blades of my master and his wife.

17:16 Go now, hide in that cave and you shall be safe as well."

17:17 Elijah said, "I fear not the servants of a false god, but only fear the one true lord.

17:18 Go, tell your master Ahab that Elijah has returned and wishes to speak with him."

17:19 Obadiah began to tremble and said, "If I tell him that you have returned, he shall seek out your very soul and have it burned.

17:20 My head shall be cut from my body, for I should kill you right now, according to the laws of the bastard king of Israel."

17:21 "Fear not," said Elijah. "The spirit of the lord shall protect you and the spirit of the lord shall have it so that not a hair on my body be frayed by these heathen bastards."

17:22 So Obadiah told Ahab that Elijah wishes to speak with him and Ahab went forth to meet Elijah.

17:23 And it came to pass that when the two men met, Ahab asked Elijah, "Is it your sorcery which shut the very rains from the sky of all Israel?"

17:24 Elijah answered, "It was not my magic which brought the curse upon your lands, but wickedness of your deeds which doomed you and your people.

17:25 You and your father's house have abandoned the statutes and commandments of the one true God and follow this fool named Baal.

17:26 Go now, send your prophets of Baal which eat at your table and tell them to come and meet me atop mount Carmel. There it shall be decided who truly is God."

17:27 So Ahab sent all those prophets of Baal atop mount Carmel; and the prophets of Baal numbered four hundred and fifty.

17:28 Elijah said to these people, "I am but one man, a prophet of the true God of all things.

17:29 You, the prophets of Baal, number of four hundred and fifty

men. Yet I am powerful than all of you, for the true lord is with me and you worship a fucking carving of stone.

17:30 Go, and gather two heifers. Let it be that one heifer be for your false lord Baal and the other be for the true lord of Israel

17:31 We shall build two altars of wood and stone. One for Baal and one for the true God of all.

17:32 Let it be that both offerings be placed upon their altars, but no fire shall touch the wood.

17:33 Pray unto your lord Baal so that he may send fire upon the altar and accept your sacrifice.

17:34 I shall pray to the true God of all and my offering shall be set in flame."

17:35 So the people did and prepared a sacrifice for their lord Baal and set it atop the altar of wood.

17:36 All day, they prayed unto Baal asking for fire, so that he would accept their sacrifice and prove he is worthy of devotion.

17:37 Baal gazed upon the offering and said, "What foolish test is this. Never have I demanded that a sacrifice of a beast be made in my name."

17:38 So Baal did not send fire and accept the sacrifice of his prophets.

17:39 When the sun was highest in the air, Elijah mocked them and said, "Your lord brings not even a spark upon your offering. What have you done to offend your false god?"

17:40 The prophets of Baal stripped naked and began to fornicate with one another, hoping this would please their lord Baal so that he may send down fire and shut the mouth of this asshole Elijah.

17:41 Before the sun set, Elijah said, "Enough. You have made fools of yourselves in my presence for quite some time.

17:42 Now let it be known who the true God of all gods is!"

17:43 The skies then split apart and a terrible blackness descended upon the altar of the God of Israel and consumed it in its entirety.

17:44 When the blackness left, all that of the altar was set ablaze in great hell-fire. Even the stones were set in flames, turning to ash and dust.

17:45 The prophets of Baal witnessed this bowed and said, "We are fools who worship a lord not unworthy.

17:46 Let it be known that the God of Israel is the true God. Let us praise him and worship him."

17:47 Ahab also bowed, for he was with these men of Baal and said, "I was a fool to abandon the lord who did take our people from the land of Egypt.

17:48 Glory be to the one true God."

17:49 As the prophets of Baal bowed in worship to the true lord, behold, the black mass consumed them and took them to the brook of Kishon.

17:50 It was there the spirit of the lord squeezed the blood of these four hundred and fifty men of Baal, so that the brook of Kishon flowed red.

17:51 Elijah said to Ahab, "Go now, eat, drink. The waters from the sky shall be blocked no longer and rain will fall upon your lands."

17:52 Ahab went to the city of Jezreel and behold, great black clouds did fill the sky above the lands and sent forth rain and lightning in great abundance.

17:53 The hand of the lord then grasped Elijah and threw him towards Jezreel before Ahab could get there.

18:1 Ahab went and told his bitch of a wife Jezebel about all that which Elijah had done and how the prophets of Baal were crushed by the spirit of the lord of Israel.

18:2 Jezebel then placed a bounty on the head of Elijah, which read, "For those who bring to me the head of Elijah, they shall be given riches greater than that of the house of Solomon.

18:3 This man does bring evil upon our lands and kills those who serves our lords without mercy."

18:4 When Elijah heard of this bounty, he feared greatly for his life and went to Beersheba, which belonged to the tribe of Judah.

18:5 Judah, being the other tribe of Israel that is now not Israel.

18:6 As he left for Beersheba, he travelled in the wilderness and behold, his bones ached, his flesh felt as though on fire and he became weary.

18:7 Resting in the shade of a juniper tree, Elijah called out to God and said, "Come down and kill me, for I have done all that I can.

18:8 Give me the sweet embrace of death, so that I may be with my fathers who art in heaven."

18:9 Elijah then fell asleep under the juniper tree and behold, an angel came down and touched him, awakening him.

18:10 The angel said, "I am a messenger from the lord your God. Let it be known that the lord things you a wuss who begs for death.

18:11 Come now, eat and feel the energy of youth within your old and frail body."

18:12 Behold, the angel did bring forth a cake, which was prepared atop sundering coals and an earthen vessel of fresh water.

18:13 As Elijah ate and drank, the angel of the lord left and Elijah cursed the angel, for he craved more than one cake and a glass of water.

18:14 The angel then came back and said, "You truly are a greedy bastard.

18:15 It should be enough that you did feast of the breads of God, given to you by his messenger.

18:16 Here, have yet another glass of water and a loaf of fresh bread. This shall be the last meal you ever receive from the lord.

18:17 Let it give you the strength you need and never bother me again for a damn drink, lest the lord think you a beggar."

18:18 Elijah thanked the angel, who then left and Elijah ate the loaf of bread and drank the water within the vessel.

18:19 Those two meals were blessed by the lord, for it gave Elijah the sustenance to live for forty days without another bite of food or sip of water.

18:20 During those forty days Elijah travelled to mount Horeb, found a cave and hid in there.

18:21 On the forty first day, Elijah had the most repulsive diarrhea one could imagine. Beasts from miles away ran in fear of the stench of Elijah's bowels.

18:22 The very angel which fed Elijah came to him in the cave and said, "What matter is this, that you cower in a cave like a wounded bear?

18:23 Your lord and master did not give you the blessed meal and holiest of water so that ye can rot in a hole made of rock."

18:24 Elijah said, "I fear the wrath of the lord, for my people have forsaken his covenant, crashed down his altars, cursed his name, worship the lords of heathens and slain the blood of prophets so that I am all that who remains.

18:25 These fools of Israel seek out my life and wish to steal it from me."

18:26 The angel said, "You man of little faith. Do you think the lord would keep breath in your lungs if he would hand you over to the people of Israel?

18:27 Go now, climb atop mount Horeb. Behold, the power of the lord shall show thee his protection. A great wind will come, so that the very boulders of the mountain shall fly in the air.

18:28 But the lord will be not in the wind.

18:29 When the wind dies, the very foundation of the earth shall shake and turn the very rocks of the mountain to dust and pebbles.

18:30 But the lord will not be in the earthquake.

18:31 Next, a fire shall consume all that around you. But the lord will be not in the fire. No, the lord shall come to thee after the fire, in a small voice.

18:32 Listen and heed the words of the voice of God."

18:33 So Elijah climbed to the top of mount Horeb and a great wind came. This wind blew all that around Elijah, but Elijah did not feel the wind, nor was blown away.

18:34 Next came a mighty earthquake, which crushed the very rocks which Elijah stood upon. But Elijah did not fall, but floated in the air when the rocks crumbled beneath his feet.

18:35 Afterwards, a fire came and blasted hot all that beneath Elijah. But Elijah remained cool and was not burned.

18:36 Then Elijah heard a small voice. It was the voice of the lord and it said, "Go, return to the wilderness of Damascus. There you shall meet Hazael. Bless him and anoint him to be king of Syria.

18:37 Jehu the son of Nimshi you shall anoint the king of Israel. Elisha the son of Shaphat of Abelmeholah you will make his prophet.

18:38 It shall be that these two kings be in league with one another. When an enemy escapes the mace of Hazael, let it be that the blade of Jehu slays them.

18:39 When one escapes the blade of Jehu, the mace of Hazael shall crush their skulls.

18:40 Let it be known that the lord has seen hope in the hearts of Israel. Behold, there are seven thousand men who did not betray the ways of their God who led them out of the slavery of Egypt.

18:41 These seven thousand have never bowed down in service to Baal and keep all that which is holy to the true lord of lords."

18:42 Elijah then fell and landed in a soft bed of ash which the lord placed beneath him.

18:43 So Elijah departed hence and found Elisha, who was plowing the fields of his father with twelve yoked oxen. As Elijah walked by, he said to Elisha, "You shall be a holy prophet to the new king of Israel."

18:44 Elisha stopped plowing and said, "Blessings to you, for I wished to be a prophet and know the future in all things and the will of the lord.

18:45 I beg of you, let me kiss my parents' goodbye and I shall come with you and learn your ways."

18:46 Elijah said, "Leave your parents behind, for the will of the God demands your presence.

18:47 Stop this plowing of your father's fields. Come and do that which is of the lord."

16:48 So Elisha stopped plowing the fields and instead slew all twelve of the oxen of his fathers.

18:49 With the yokes Elisha created fire and burnt the flesh of the oxen and gave it to all those who came, so that they may eat.

18:50 Elisha then left with Elijah, ministering to him and learning his ways.

18:51 Shaphat came and saw that the fields were not ploughed, the yokes turned to ash and the oxen were slain and eaten.

18:52 Shaphat cursed the name of his son, and had to buy more oxen, more yokes, and plow the field himself.

19:1 Benhadad the king of Syria gathered a great army together. The soldiers of thirty-two kings he brought together, along with a great many horses and chariots and Benhadad warred with the nation of Samaria.

19:2 He also sent messengers to the king of Israel, which said, "Our lord demands this from your people.

19:3 Give us your gold, your silver, your women, your children, even those things of great worth and I won't come and kill you all.

19:4 Deliver it to us and your necks shall be spared our blades."

19:5 Now Ahab the king of Israel was a coward and send word to Benhadad, saying, "By all means, take my gold, my silver, my children, my women, my precious items.

19:6 Just, please, for the love of all things blessed, don't kill us!"

19:7 The messengers of Benhadad came back and said, "We don't trust you, O king of Israel.

19:8 Do not deliver us your goods, your gold, your silver, your children, your women.

19:9 It shall be that servants of Syria shall come and search your homes, your streets, your places and take that which is pleasing to their eye.

19:10 Ahab gathered the elders of Israel and said, "The king of Syria, Benhadad, sent messengers to me, demanding that I give them all that which is good in Israel.

19:11 Our gold, silver, children, women and those things of value he demanded."

19:12 And the elders said, "B'ah. What a fool. Does he think we would give him all that which makes us a nation?

19:13 He might as well come and slay us. Better to be slain by the blade than fade to non-existence."

19:14 Ahab the king of Israel became embarrassed and said, "Here is the problem. I sent him word saying he could have all that which he demanded."

19:15 These elders of Israel cursed the name of Ahab the son of Omri and said, "You have doomed us to damnation with your stupidity.

19:16 How can we be a nation without wealth. How can Israel grow without children. Who will be our next generation if we have not women to bare us sons?

19:17 Who will pleasure our carnal lust if they take all the women away from us?"

19:18 Ahab said, "Fear not, for he has not come yet.

19:19 Benhadad mistrusts us deeply and has demanded that his servants come and search our lands and take that which they find pleasing."

19:20 And the elders of Israel said, "They shall do no such thing.

19:21 Tell this king of Syria that he shall send no servants upon our lands, nor take that which belongs to us."

19:22 So Ahab sent messengers to Benhadad and they said, "Our master Ahab has changed his mind.

19:23 You shall not get our gold, our silver, our children, our women and those things of value.

19:24 Your servants shall not come to our lands and search that which is ours, so they can plunder all which is Israel."

19:25 Benhadad sent message back to Ahab and said, "If you do not as I demand, the armies under my control shall come and smite you to dust.

19:26 Look at what our king did to the people of Samaria. You shall share the same fate, if you heed not the words of Benhadad."

19:27 Ahab sent message back to Benhadad and these messengers said, "Fuck off."

19:28 When Benhadad heard this message, he was drinking, him and the thirty-two kings who gave them their armies.

19:29 Benhadad laughed and said, "How dare this infant of Israel tell me to fuck off.

19:30 Let it be that I shall fuck his very daughters upon his bed."

19:31 Then Benhadad killed the messengers which Ahab sent, gathered his men and laid siege to the city where Ahab dwelt."

19:32 Behold, a prophet of the lord came to Ahab and said "Fear not the multitude of Benhadad. Thus sayeth the lord, these men shall be delivered into your hands."

19:33 Ahab asked, "Who is going to fight these men?" and the prophet answered, "By the will of the true lord of all shall these men die.

19:34 Let it be that the very peoples of Israel grab their swords and fight against these heathens. Then all shall know that the lord of Israel is the one true God."

19:35 The king of Israel then asked, "Who shall order the battle?" and the prophet said, "You will, stupid.

19:36 You are the damn king of Israel."

19:37 So the king of Israel tallied all those in the army of Israel. They numbered a pathetic two hundred and thirty. The men of Israel who knew not the blade numbered seven thousand.

19:38 And Ahab said to himself, "Oh fuck. We're screwed."

19:39 Still, Ahab did as the prophet said and went forth to fight Benhadad and his armies.

19:40 The armies of Israel left at noon and by that time Benhadad and his kings were drunk off cheap wine and strong drink.

19:41 Servants of Syria came and said, "There are men of Israel coming this way," and Benhadad said, "Well, go find out what they want.

19:42 If they come to deliver us that which I demand, good. Let them live.

19:43 If they come to fight, bring them to me alive. It is the will of your king to make them suffer by his hands."

19:44 When the armies of Israel came to the Syrians, behold, all those of Syria were drunk, carrying vessels of cheap wine.

19:45 And the army of Israel smote them all, so that the blood and wine flowed upon the ground as one river.

19:46 Benhadad escaped by horseback, vomiting all the way to his home.

19:47 As Ahab celebrated, the prophet came to him and said, "Be warned, the king of Syria shall come back a year to this day.

19:48 Go, strengthen your army, build your chariots and sharpen your swords."

19:49 These servants of Benhadad came to him and said, "The God of Israel is a God of the hills.

19:50 That is why those fools slew us on that day.

19:51 Let it be that we fight upon the plains, where our gods shall suck the very marrow of their bones.

19:52 These thirty-two kings, take them away. Have them be in the protection of their chambers.

19:53 Have instead captains, who rule a great many men, chariots and horses. Surely then we shall be stronger and smite these infants of Israel."

19:54 Benhadad said, "Of course. It is because we fought on hills that we lost the battle.

19:55 It had nothing to do with everyone being drunk on cheap wine."

19:56 And it came to pass that one year to the day, Benhadad gathered his armies and they numbered greater than before as marched towards Aphek, to fight Israel.

19:57 Now all those of Israel came to fight against him. They set two camps, which numbered as small households. Those of Syria filled the country.

19:58 The prophet came to Ahab and said, "These fools insulted our lord and said he is a mere God of the hills who can't fight upon the plains.

19:59 Let it be that the lord shall show you that he is the one true lord and God shall slay these fools with foreskins."

19:60 Upon the seventh day the armies did meet and a great battle ensued. And the children of Israel slaughtered one hundred thousand Syrian soldiers that day.

19:61 Those of Syria said, "Oh crap, their lord can fight on the plains as well," and they retreated into the city of Aphek.

19:61 A great wall in Aphek fell and crushed to death another twenty-seven thousand men of Syria. It was a really big wall.

19:62 Benhadad hid in the city as well and his servants said, "Come now, for these kings of Israel are known to be merciful at times.

19:63 Let it be that we wear sackcloth's, ropes upon our heads and spread dust among our faces. We shall go to Ahab and beg that our lives be spared."

19:64 These men wore torn sackcloth's, ropes upon their heads and smeared dust upon their face and went to Ahab, saying, "I beg you, let Benhadad live." Ahab answered, "Where is Benhadad. I wish to meet with him."

19:65 Benhadad stepped forward, in pathetic rags, looking like a beggar and Ahab said, "Are you, this man dressed as a beggar, truly the king of Syria?" and Benhadad answered, "I am."

19:66 Ahab laughed and said, "For what reason should I spare your life?"

19:67 Benhadad answered, "Let it be that I shall restore all that which my father took from your father. The streets of Damascus shall be safe for the children of Israel and all of Syria shall bow to the humbleness of the king of Israel."

19:68 Ahab said, "Let it be then a covenant to us," and the two men did make a covenant that day, which really pissed the lord off.

19:69 And a man, a son of a prophet, came to a man and said, "In the name of the lord, kill me, so that I may die," and the man said, "Are you fucking crazy. I shall not commit murder, lest the lord curse me."

19:70 The son of the prophet said, "For not killing me, as the lord did command, you shall be cursed. Let it be that when I depart, a lion shall come and feast upon your flesh."

19:71 The man said, "What. The lord will kill me for not killing you?" and the son of the prophet said, "Yep."

19:71 As the son of the prophet left, behold, a lion did come and killed the man and ate him.

19:72 The son of the prophet came to another man and said, "In the name of the lord, kill me, so that I may die," and the man took his blade and thrust it deep into the son of the prophet's neck, killing him.

19:73 And the lord sent the same damn lion to come and kill the guy for murdering the son of the prophet.

19:74 The prophet disguised himself with rags and ashes upon his face and waited by the road where the king of Israel will pass.

19:75 As the king passed, the prophet cried forth and said, "My servant went out to battle and behold, he did bring a man to me and said to kill this man, for he is a heathen of Syria.

19:76 The man was pathetic and I did not kill him, so the servant cursed me that I pay a talent of silver."

19:77 Ahab said, "What kind of fool allows their servants to make such demands?"

19:78 It was then the prophet stripped naked and wiped the ashes from his face. And Ahab knew that he was one of the prophets.

19:79 And the prophet said, "Thus sayeth the lord, you let a man live whom the lord wished to face utter and complete destruction.

19:80 God hated Benhadad and y let this bastard live and made a covenant with him.

19:81 Therefore, it shall be your life and the lives of your people, who will die in the place of the Syrians and their king."

19:82 Ahab then went home and was angered by the words of the prophet.

20:1 It came to pass that Naboth the Jezreelite had a vineyard close to the lands of Ahab, king of Israel.

20:2 Ahab came to Naboth and said, "Your vineyard is close to my lands and I wish to have it for my own, so that I may grow a garden of herbs.

20:3 If it pleases you, I shall give you a great weight in gold for this vineyard. If not, let it be that I give you a vineyard of my own, which grows the greatest grapes and produces the finest vintages of all of Israel."

20:4 Naboth said to Ahab, "My vineyard is not for sale, for any price."

20:5 So Ahab returned to his palace and sulked in his bedchamber, weeping over a damn vineyard which he couldn't have.

20:6 Ahab refused to eat, preferring to sulk in his bed, wallowing in his misery.

20:7 Jezebel his witch for a wife came in and said, "What troubles you, that ye sit in sorrow upon your bed, and refuse to eat?"

20:8 And Ahab answered, "Naboth won't sell me his vineyard. I offered him a great deal of gold and even a vineyard from my own estate and still he won't sell me his vineyard.

20:9 It's so close to my lands and would be perfect for growing great herbs like mandrakes. Oh, how I want his vineyard."

20:10 He then heavily set his head on his pillow and began to weep.

20:11 Jezebel said, "Do not cry, for I shall get you this vineyard you long for.

20:12 You are the king of Israel. You deserve all which your heart desires."

20:13 Now Jezebel declared a law, stating, "No man shall scratch their right ear with their left hand, lest they displease the lord."

20:14 She then hired two men, sons of Belial, to bear false witness against Naboth, claiming scratched his right ear with his left hand.

20:15 Naboth was brought forth and declared a blasphemer to God, so that all those of Israel hated Naboth.

20:16 Naboth said, "I did not sin and did all that which is holy to our lord.

20:17 My sacrifices have been plentiful and I offer only the finest which I have.

20:18 All laws, statutes and commandments of our God did I follow."

20:19 And the sons of Belial said, "Did you scratch your right ear with your left hand?" and Naboth answered, "Well, maybe."

20:20 And all those of Israel yelled, "Blasphemer. Blasphemer!"

20:21 Naboth was taken outside of the walls of the city and the congregation of Israel stoned him to death and left his body to rot and be feasted upon by ravens.

20:22 Immediately afterwards, the law which declared scratching your right ear with your left hand to be blasphemy was stricken from the records and never enforced again.

20:23 Jezebel came to Ahab and said, "The vineyard you desire shall now be yours. Naboth has just been stoned to death."

20:24 Ahab embraced her and said, "Thank you, my dear wife," and then performed great oral sex upon her.

20:25 The word of the lord came to Elijah the Tishbite, saying, "Behold, go now to the king of Israel, who dwells in the vineyard of Naboth.

20:26 Speak to him and say that the lord shall curse you for generations, for you did kill to take possession of a vineyard. Thus sayeth the lord, where the body of Naboth lies, so shall yours and the hounds of hell shall come and gnaw on your bones."

20:27 When Elijah came to Ahab, the king of Israel said, "Why do you come to me, O enemy of mine?" and Elijah answered, "You did evil in the sight of the lord."

20:28 The lord says that behold, your corpse shall lie beside the man Naboth and the hounds of hell shall gnaw on your bones.

20:29 Those of your seed shall be cast into the dust and God shall cut off any that pisses against the wall of the house of Ahab.

20:30 Your house shall be as the house of Jeroboam the son of Nebat and Baasha the son of Ahijah, for the sin which you commit.

20:31 Those of Ahab which dies in the city shall be eaten by dogs and those of Ahab which dies in the wild shall be eaten by the fowls of the air.

20:32 Thus sayeth the lord, your cunt of a wife shall be feasted upon by dogs by the walls of Jezreel."

20:33 Ahab asked, "What sin did I commit to deserve such punishment?" and Elijah answered, "You had a man killed to take his vineyard."

20:34 Ahab said, "I did not kill Naboth. Let it be known that my wife Jezebel killed him. I just took his vineyard after she killed him."

20:35 Elijah said, "Oh, really. That changes things then.

20:36 Okay, well, you still sinned in the eyes of our lord, for you should have stopped Jezebel from committing such a crime.

20:37 However, because you did not kill him, let it be that the wickedness which I cursed upon you shall not be placed on your head.

20:38 Your son shall bear the punishment instead which I declared.

20:39 Jezebel will still die by the walls of Jezreel and be feasted upon by dogs. Even the lord declares that she is a cunt."

20:40 And Ahab said, "God is fair," and tended back to his herb garden, in the vineyard of Naboth.

20:41 Ahab's son might disagree with that last statement.

21:1 For three years there was peace between the people of Syria and the children of Israel.

21:2 It came to pass that Jehosaphat the king of Judah went to meet with the king of Israel and the king of Israel said, "Know that Ramoth in Gilead is ours, yet these fools of Syria now have it within their lands."

21:3 Jehosaphat said, "Then let us take both our armies and deliver the people of Ramoth back into the welcoming hands of their brothers."

21:4 Now, like good kings, before they did anything, they had to inquire with prophets, to know that their actions shall lead to good tidings.

21:5 And Ahab brought forth four hundred prophets and asked them, "Shall the armies of Judah and Israel go forth, and reclaim Gilead?" and the prophets said, "Yes, for the lord shall deliver it into your hands."

21:6 Still, Jehosaphat was nervous and asked, "Is their yet another prophet of the lord, so that we may ask him if we should go?" Ahab answered, "Yes, there is another prophet. Micaiah, the son of Imlah, a prophet of the lord of Israel. I loathe this man, for he prophesies words of doom and suffering.

21:7 Never does he prophesy any good tidings for me," and Jehosaphat said, "Let us seek him out then and see if his words bring joy or fears."

21:8 Then the king of Israel brought forth an officer and said, "Bring to us Micaiah the son of Imlah, the accursed prophet."

21:9 And both the king of Israel and the king of Judah sat upon their thrones, wearing their royal robes, listening to all their prophets claiming good fortune if they go to take back the city of Ramoth.

21:10 The messenger sent to Micaiah said to him, "Behold, all the prophets through the lands declare good tidings of the reclaiming of Ramoth. They speak in one mouth."

21:11 And Micaiah answered, "It matters not what they speak. I speak only the words which the lord puts in my mouth."

21:12 Micaiah was then brought forth to Ahab and Ahab asked, "Shall I go and reclaim Ramoth in Gilead?" and Micaiah answered,

"Go, for the city shall be delivered into the hands of the king."

21:13 Ahab breathed a sigh of relief and said, "It pleases me that you bring me tidings of joy instead of sorrow," and Micaiah answered, "Bide your tongue, for my prophecy is not yet finished.

21:14 Let it be that the children of Israel shall scatter amongst the hills, lost and confused. They shall be as sheep without a shepherd.

21:15 They shall have no master and will return to their house in fear."

21:16 Ahab then turned to Jehosaphat and said, "Told you he was a fucking asshole."

21:17 Micaiah still spoke and said, "Behold, I see the lord God sitting upon his throne and all those of heaven stand around him.

21:18 And the lord said, who shall pursue Ahab, so that he may fall upon Ramoth. And the angels answered him many.

21:19 Behold, a spirit came up and stood before the lord and said, I shall go and pursue Ahab, the king of Israel.

21:20 The lord asked, how so? and the spirit answered, I shall fill the mouths of the prophets with words of deceit. And the lord said, you shall persuade him in your pursuit. Go forth and do so.

21:21 Now, be warned, the lord has put a lying spirit in the mouths of all these prophets and the lord speaks evil concerning you."

21:22 Zedekaih the son of Chenaanah, a prophet, came to Micaiah and slapped him, saying, "What you say is blasphemy, for the lord never lies."

21:23 Micaiah said, "Behold, you shall know I speak the truth, when the day comes where you hide underneath your bed, cowering in fear."

21:24 The king of Israel said, "Take this man Micaiah and throw him in the dungeons to rot.

21:25 Let it be he feasts only upon mouldy bread and stale water, until I return from Ramoth."

21:26 He then said to his prophets, "The lord would not send to you a lying spirit in your mouth."

21:27 So Ahab and Jehosaphat marched up to Ramoth.

21:28 Ahab said to Jehosaphat, "I shall disguise myself and go into battle. Then the armies of Syria shall not know me and their attention will not focus upon my death.

21:29 You are a greater warrior than I. Put on my raiment's and fight all that which come against you."

21:30 Jehosaphat said, "You are truly a pansy, but I shall help you in any manner.

21:31 Let it be that the tribe of Judah helped their brethren by any means. I shall put on your robes."

21:32 So Jehosaphat dressed as the king of Israel and Ahab dressed like a normal soldier. This will be Ahab's mistake.

21:33 For the king of Syria said, "Fight all those who come in your way. Kill them. Slay them. Leave none alive.

21:34 Save alive only the king of Israel. I wish him captured, so I may make him suffer greatly at my hands."

21:35 And when those of Syria saw Jehosaphat, they said, "Surely that is the king. Leave him, so that we may slaughter these other fools."

21:36 Jehosaphat then cried out and taunted the armies of Syria.

21:37 The chariots of Syria then gave chase unto Jehosaphat, for Jehosaphat did taunt them greatly. In time, they realized this man not to be the king of Israel, but an imposter.

21:38 The chariots then turned around and joined the battle against those of Israel and Judah.

21:39 Now an archer of Syria drew his bow and shot Ahab within the neck, where the helmet meets the cuirass.

21:40 The king of Israel said to the driver of his chariot, "Get me the hell out of this battle. Your king is wounded."

21:41 As the day passed, the battle increased in ferocity, leaving corpses, wounded, blood and limbs lying upon the ground. The chariot carrying the king could not escape, for behold, every place was crowded with fighting men and those of the slain.

21:42 Ahab died upon his chariot and his blood poured out so that the chariot became stained a dark crimson.

21:43 The last words of Ahab were, "Fuck Macaiah. May he be raped by the hounds of hell."

21:44 As those of Israel heard of the death of their king, behold, a great proclamation rang forth, saying, "Let every man be head of their house and every city be ruled by one.

21:45 We don't need a king. Let it be we govern ourselves."

21:46 And Macaiah smiled and said, "That which I said has come true.

21:47 Let it be known that the lord put a lying spirit in the mouths of the prophets."

21:48 So the king died and was buried in Samaria, where his body rests alongside his fathers.

21:49 The soldiers of Israel washed the blood from the chariot in a pool of water and the dogs came to drink of this pool, lapping up the blood of Ahab. So, came true the words of Elijah.

21:50 Now the rest of the acts of Ahab, the mighty cities which he built, the ivory house he constructed, they are written somewhere else.

21:51 Nobody read the book which they are written in. Nobody cares.

21:52 When Ahab died, his son Ahaziah reigned in his stead.

21:53 Jehosaphat was thirty-five years old when he became king of Judah and he reigned in Jerusalem for twenty five years. The name of his mother was Azuba the daughter of Shilhi.

21:54 And he followed the path of his father and did not go whoring after false gods, doing good in the sight of the lord. Though he did not topple the altars dedicated to heathen lords, for there were still people of Judah who burnt incense to the lords of heathens.

21:55 Jehosaphat did not tolerate those men who took lust in other men and he slew with brutality those who committed sodomy.

21:56 Unless that sodomy was committed with a woman. Fucking a woman's ass is acceptable in the eyes of God.

21:57 Jehosaphat made peace with the king of Israel, though the two nations did not reunite as one.

21:58 The king of Judah made great ships on the coast of Tharshish, so that they may go to Ophir for gold. A pity that they sank at Eziongeber.

21:59 Those of the tribe of Judah made terrible seamen. This happened shortly after all the faggots were killed.

21:60 Ahaziah the son of Ahab said, "Let my servants help you build you ships. They know well the vessels of the sea." But Jehosaphat refused, for though there was peace, Jehosaphat deemed Ahaziah wicked.

21:61 For Ahaziah did evil in the sight of the lord and worshipped the lords of heathens. Just as his father Ahab and those of the house of Jeroboam.

21:62 Ahaziah's worship of Baal angered the lord greatly and the lord cursed him, so that Ahaziah died only two years after being anointed king.

21:63 Jehosaphat died peacefully sitting on his throne and was buried with his fathers in the city of David. His son, Jehoram, seceded him

II KINGS

1:1 The people of Moab rebelled against the nation of Israel after the death of Ahab.

1:2 Ahaziah fell down through a lattice in the upper chamber that was in Samaria and got a nasty infection from the wounds. Ahaziah sent messengers and told them, "Go, seek forth the priests of Baalzebub the god of Ekron.

1:3 Ask them if I shall recover from this dreaded disease."

1:4 Now the lord of Israel was jealous, for the king of Israel did not enquire of him as to how his wound will heal but to another, lesser god of heathens.

1:5 So the lord sent forth an angel, who came unto Elijah the Tishbite and said, "Arise, and go visit the foolish king of Israel.

1:6 Ask him, why do you seek forth the comfort of a heathen god, instead of asking the true lord if you shall recover from your wounds?

1:7 Your lack of faith upsets the lord. For this, you shall not recover from your wounds and shall lie miserable upon your bed the remainder of your days." And Elijah departed.

1:8 Now, the servants of Ahaziah would not allow Elijah to meet with the king, for the king was sick and wished not to be disturbed.

1:9 Elijah then said the words of the lord to these servants, who in turn came to their master and said, "Some guy just came by saying you are going to die because you went to ask Baalzebub instead of some other lord."

1:10 The king of Israel asked, "What did this man look like?" and the servants answered, "He was an ugly man, with hair like a beast.

1:11 Foul of breath and stained teeth. Wore a robe tied with a leather girdle," and the king answered, "It's that asshole Elijah.

1:12 This fool thinks he is a man of God because Elisha accepted him as an apprentice to be a prophet."

1:13 So Ahaziah sent forth a captain and fifty men, who came to Elijah as he rested atop a hill. And these men said, "Come, O man of God, for the king wishes to speak with you."

1:14 Elijah said, "I don't care for the tone of your voice. It mocks me, as though you believe me to be but a mere man."

1:15 May the true lord God come forth and prove to you that I am truly a man of our lord." And God came down so that fire within each of the men did burn inside their bowels, until it consumed them and laid them to ash.

1:16 When these servants of the king did not return, Ahaziah sent forth another captain with fifty men and said to them, "Get Elijah over here, for I wish to speak with him.

1:17 Also, find out what happened to my other men. They are late and that is unusual for them."

1:18 These men went out and came to Elijah upon the hill and behold, they saw the burnt bodies of their brethren and asked, "What happened to these men?"

1:19 Elijah answered, "This is what happened, you fools of Israel." And the lord came down and burnt also within their bowels a great fire, which consumed them and reduced them to ash.

1:20 As Ahaziah waited for his second group of men to return, he sent a third and told them, "Get this damn asshole Elijah over here, so I can speak with the arrogant fucker.

1:21 Find out also what happened to my other men. Elijah probably killed them, to prove he is a man of God.

1:22 B'ah. Man of God. They prove themselves men of God by killing in torturous ways, then wonder why people go forth to the gods of heathens."

1:23 So the third captain was sent out, with fifty men also and behold, he saw the one hundred and two bodies of his brethren, charred upon the ground.

1:24 These men bowed to Elijah and said, "We know you to be a man of the true lord. Spare our lives, for we were sent only to deliver a message.

1:25 Our king wishes to speak with you. Come and give him his request."

1:26 Elijah went down with these men and spoke with the king of Israel within his bedchamber, where he was tended to by a great many nurses and concubines.

1:27 And Elijah said, "These women shall heal not your wounds, for you are a damned man of God.

1:28 You went forth, and sought out a heathen god, a false god and asked not the wisdom and the knowledge of the lord of Israel.

1:29 Thus sayeth the lord, you shall remain in your bed until your days be done."

1:30 Elijah then left and the concubines and nursed stopped caring for him, saying, "Well, if God is going to cure him, why should we tend to his aid and comfort?"

1:31 True to the words of God, Ahaziah died upon his bed. Jehoram sat upon his throne in the second year of the reign of Jehosaphat the king of Judah. Jehoram succeeded the throne because Ahaziah had no son.

1:32 As for the rest of the acts of Ahaziah which he did as king of Israel, nobody cares.

2:1 It came to pass that the lord realized Elijah to be a dangerous prophet. Elijah was a man of the people and when he shall realize that the lord is a tyrant, then Elijah would speak out against the lord.

2:2 So the lord decided to stop this; the lord decided to kill Elijah.

2:3 However, Elijah could not just die. The story of Elijah's death would be told throughout the people of Israel for many generations.

2:4 God decided to have it appear as though Elijah ascended into heaven, by the blessing of the one true God.

2:5 The spirit of the lord came to both Elijah and Elisha and said, "Get to Bethel. There the lord shall send a message, to be spread across all of Israel."

2:6 And the two men went to Bethel and behold, fifty sons of the prophets were there and they said, "Be warned, O prophets of the lord, that those of Bethel worship false gods.

2:7 Go now to Jericho, for the men of Bethel shall kill you for spreading the word of the one true God."

2:8 Thus Elijah and Elisha went to Jericho and behold, the sons of the prophets of Jericho came to them and said, "Get out of here, you prophets of the lord of evil.

2:9 Let it be known that those of Jericho worship Baal, a lord of peace. When they see you, O prophets of evil, they shall end your wickedness with fire."

2:10 So the two men went to the river Jordan. By the banks of the river, they saw in the distance a great many men, coming to kill them both.

2:11 Elijah was then filled with the spirit of the lord and behold, he stripped off his robe and with it smacked the waters of the river three times.

2:12 God then ripped the river apart, so that the two men shall cross on dry ground between the two walls of the river.

2:13 The lord then said, "Fear not, for the lord shall humble these men and take Elijah into the kingdom of heaven."

2:14 Suddenly, five great chariots of fire came from the skies, surrounding both Elijah and Elisha and they took Elijah and carried him to heaven.

2:15 Elisha screamed to the chariots, "My father, my father, why have you chosen this man over me, to dwell in your kingdom among the stars?"

2:16 The robes of Elijah then fell, stained with his blood and Elisha grabbed it and behold, he saw the robe drenched in the blood of his brother.

2:17 As Elijah ascended to the skies, he cried down to the earth, "He's killing me. He's killing me. The lord God is fucking killing me!"

2:18 But none upon the earth heard the voice of Elijah.

2:19 Elijah was then dropped from the skies into the ocean, where a great fish came and devoured him whole.

2:20 Elisha took the robes of Elijah and smacked the waters of the Jordan three times and on the third strike the waters closed, so that the men who pursued him could not cross.

2:21 As the men came to the river, they said to Elisha, "How did you cross without a drop of water on your clothes. And what were those great chariots of fire which came upon you?"

2:22 Elisha answered, "The lord God of Israel let me pass this river and parted the very waters so that I may cross like those of my ancestors crossed the waters upon their escape from Egypt.

2:23 Those chariots of fire were sent by the lord and behold, the lord took up my brother Elijah, so that he may dwell within the kingdom of God."

2:24 These men then laughed and said, "Why would the lord ye serve leave an old man behind.

2:25 Does your God think these waters shall stop us?

2:26 We will swim this river and shall spill your blood in the waters."

2:27 Elisha laughed and held up the bloody robes of Elijah, saying, "Behold, a message from God.

2:28 Those who dare cross me shall have their blood stained upon these very raiment's."

2:29 It was then the chariots of God came down and surrounded Elisha.

2:30 Those men who came to slay Elisha now bowed down and said, "Surely you are a man of God."

2:31 Elisha answered, "Damn right I am. Now go, fetch me a cruse of salt, so that I may heal the waters of this river."

2:32 The men went and gave Elisha the cruse of salt. Elisha spilled the salt within the waters and said, "Now the waters of the Jordan are healed."

2:33 The men asked, "Healed from what?" and Elisha answered, "From the wounds of God, for even the lord can wound a river."

2:34 These men grew confused, for they did not know how a river could be wounded. Neither did Elisha, for the healing of the river was merely bullshit.

2:35 It's a river. How can you hurt a river. It has no feelings.

2:36 Even the men asked, "How can the lord wound a river, for it has no flesh, no blood, no life?"

2:37 Elisha answered, "The lord can give anything life and take it away.

2:38 Let it be known that the lord did give this river life and when the river had life the lord wounded it deeply, for the river wronged him."

2:39 Still, these men were confused and asked Elisha, "How can a mere river wrong the lord?"

2:40 Elisha answered, "Just shut the fuck up. Don't question God, lest he smite you with leprosy."

2:41 So the men ceased their questions, bowed down and

worshipped God.

2:42 Elisha then went and travelled to Bethel. As he travelled, behold, a group of small children passed him, the eldest being nine.

2:43 One of the children pointed to Elisha and said, "My father is bald just like this man and his father before him.

2:44 When I grow old, I hope my hair doesn't fall out of my head. The sun would burn my scalp."

2:45 Elisha heard this and became angry at the children. Behold, Elisha cursed the children for mocking his bald head.

2:46 When Elisha cursed the children, two bears came forth sent by God, and slaughtered forty-two of the children and feasted upon their flesh.

2:47 Elisha laughed and took great pleasure in the children being torn apart by two bears.

2:48 When the bears killed the last child, Elisha yelled forth, "Let it be that any little bastard who makes fun of my baldness shall be eaten by the beasts of the forest!"

2:49 Since then, nobody made fun of Elisha's baldness, save for the mothers of the forty-two children, who cursed Elisha and his bald head.

2:50 They were eaten by bears as well. Their husbands didn't mind. They were bitchy wives and they didn't love their children that much anyway.

2:51 So you bald men who read this and follow the lord God, let it be known that, if you desire, any person who makes fun of your baldness shall be eaten by bears sent from God.

2:52 If they are not, God hates you.

3:1 Jehoram the son of Ahab began to reign over Israel in Samaria during the eighteenth year of Jehoshaphat king of Judah and Jehoram reigned for twelve years.

3:2 Now Jehoram was evil in the sight of the lord. Though not in the ways of his father, for Jehoram did not worship Baal, nor any lord of the heathens.

3:3 No, Jehoram's wickedness was allowing common men of Israel to serve as priests and serve their lord in the temple.

3:4 Such horrors.

3:5 Now Mesha, the king of Moab was a great shepherd and gave to Ahab one hundred thousand lambs and one hundred thousand rams with the softest wool.

3:6 When Ahab died, Jehoram said of Mesha, "You know why the king of the Moabites like lambs with soft wool?

3:7 It feels good against his loins."

3:8 When Mesha heard this, he became enraged and warred against Israel.

3:9 Jehoram gathered his armies and also came to Jehoshaphat the king of Judah and said, "That sheep fucker Mesha wishes to war with me. Shall you join me?" and Jehoshaphat said, "Let us war as brothers.

3:10 Where your armies go, mine shall go. Where your chariots go, mine shall go. Let it be that Judah and Israel fight as one, like in the days of our fathers."

3:11 Jehoram said, "Where shall we go to fight?" and Jehoshaphat answered, "How about in the plains of Edom?

3:12 Those of Judah deal well with the Edomites. Their army shall fight alongside us as well."

3:13 So the king of Israel, the king of Judah and the king of Edom gathered there might and travelled seven days to go and fight these peoples of Moab.

3:14 There was no water around them and their armies became thirsty.

3:15 Jehoram, who was an arrogant fucker, said, "Look, we three

kings shall go, so that we may slay all those of the people of Moab."

3:16 Surely this is a blessed event in the eyes of God."

3:17 Jehoshaphat was not sure and said, "The king of Edom might be a curse among us, for the lord may wish only those of Israel to join in the fight.

3:18 Let us go and seek forth a prophet, so that they may tell us what to do."

3:19 The king of Edom asked Jehoshaphat, "If y think I may bring a curse to your men, why did you ask me to come with you?"

3:20 The king of Judah said, "I don't know. Look at the bright side, no one in your army will die if our God thinks you unworthy."

3:21 A servant of the king of Israel said, "It is known that a man of God lives near us, a prophet named Elisha," and the three kings said, "Bring him here."

3:22 When Elisha was brought to the three kings, he said to them, "How dare you interrupt me, for I was enjoying the pleasure of a young concubine.

3:23 Do you know how rare I get to enjoy the company of a whore. I live in the fucking wilderness, dammit."

3:24 Jehoshaphat said, "I am sorry to have disturbed your lust, but we have a matter of the greatest importance.

3:25 We three kings go forth to fight with the Moabites and we seek the advice of our lord."

3:26 Elisha said, "If you wish my advice, go and fetch the finest whore from each of your kingdoms.

3:27 When my lust hast been satisfied with all three, then I shall tell you that which you must know."

3:28 Servants were sent out and they brought to Elisha the finest concubine from their kingdom.

3:29 Enkocgows, of Judah, Zsukinut, of Israel, and Upineeahs, of Edom.

3:30 When Elisha was satisfied by these three concubines (it only took a few minutes), he came back to the kings and said, "Now I shall tell you the words of wisdom.

3:31 Have your men go and dig within the fields great ditches.

3:32 During this time, you shall feel no wind, see no cloud, nor will a drop of rain fall on the ground. Yet the lord shall fill these ditches with water, so that you may drink.

3:33 Know also, the lord shall not tolerate mercy upon these heathens of Moab.

3:34 Burn their villages, reduce their cities to ash, rip their trees from the ground, plug their wells, slaughter their women, their children, their men, destroy their crops and poison their lands so that not another thing shall grow upon them."

3:35 It came to pass that in the morning Elisha offered a meat offering unto the lord and when the offering was burnt, the ditches flowed with fresh water.

3:36 When those of Moab heard that the three kings came, they gathered their armies and lined their borders in defense.

3:37 Behold, when they gazed out, they saw the water in the ditches and the lord tricked them to believe the water to be blood.

3:38 Mesha said to his men, "Surely that is the blood of those who go against us. Go forth, spoil and plunder."

3:39 And when the armies of Moab came to the camp of Israel, those of Israel, Judah and Edom arose and fought them with great ferocity.

3:40 They entered their borders and slew all those in their path. Every village was burned, every tree uprooted, every city reduced to rubble and ash.

3:41 The blood of the people of Moab were gathered and they poisoned the fertile lands of Moab with this blood, so that no plant, not even a weed, will grow from the soil.

2:42 Save for the crops of Kirharaseth. There wasn't enough Moabite blood to poison those lands.

3:43 When Mesha saw that these three armies came, the king of Moab gathered seven hundred men, so that he may break through the armies of Edom and hide.

3:44 The Edomites fought the guards of the king and Mesha could not break through.

3:45 Knowing the lord of Israel to be a God of blood, Mesha took his eldest son, tied him to a boulder and cut his throat.

3:46 He then bathed in the blood of his son and with tears and blood streaking down his face, he called up to the lord of Israel, saying, "Does this satisfy you, O mighty tyrant?"

3:47 It did. God looked down and said, "Holy crap. He sacrificed his own son and I didn't even have to ask.

3:48 If only Abraham was so loyal."

3:49 Those in the kingdom of heaven gazed down upon Mesha in amazement and laughed at him and mocked him.

3:50 A few angels felt sympathy for Mesha. The lord quickly declared them evil and cast them down to Lucifer.

3:51 Lucifer then took those angels and went to the three kings and said, "The lord is satisfied and has had his fill of blood.

3:52 Go home and slay no more of these people of Moab."

3:53 And the three kings did, believing they were doing the will of the lord.

4:1 There cried a woman of the wives of the sons of the prophets. She came to Elisha in tears, saying, "My husband is dead and died with great debt.

4:2 The creditors now come to collect their money. If they do not get their money, they shall take my sons and sell them into slavery."

4:3 Elisha laughed and said, "It matters little to me if your sons be sold as slaves. Go away, wretched woman."

4:4 Still, the woman cried and said, "My husband feared the lord, as do my sons.

4:5 How can they worship God, offer sacrifice, if they are slaves?"

4:6 Elisha said, "Your words are wise, for a woman. I shall help you pay your debt.

4:7 Tell me, what do you have in your house?"

4:8 The woman searched her house and behold, she had naught but a small vessel with olive oil.

4:9 Elisha said, "Go forth, borrow all vessels which you can.

4:10 Small, large, jugs, it matters not. Just get as many vessels that people can spare to you.

4:11 Take these vessels and with your sons, pour out the oil you have into each vessel."

4:12 The woman did and her little jar of olive oil never stopped flowing with oil, until each vessel was full of pure olive oil.

4:13 The woman was excited and told Elisha what happened. "The vessel of my oil never emptied and now all jars, pots, vessels, they are full of oil!

4:14 Tell me, Elisha, what do I do now?"

4:15 Elisha slapped the woman, and said, "Sell the oil, you fucking idiot."

4:16 And the woman did, but behold, no person would purchase the oil from her.

4:17 She came back to Elisha and said, "The debtors are now within the city and come to take my sons away.

4:18 I have no money, for no person bought the oil from me. Tell me, what can I do?

4:19 Elisha said, "Give to them the oil, so that the debt be repaid."

4:20 And the woman did, but the debtors refused her oil, saying,

"What are we going to do with hundreds of vessels filled with damn olive oil?

4:21 We are debt collectors, not bakers."

4:22 And they took her sons and sold them into slavery into a foreign nation.

4:23 The woman wept and Elisha came to the woman and said, "Why do you weep?"

4:24 She answered, "The lord has cursed me, for my sons are now slaves and have been taken away from me."

4:25 Elisha said, "Surely the lord did this because you did that which is wicked in the sight of God.

4:26 Come with me and I shall do that which is right."

4:27 The woman did, thinking Elisha would bless her and forgive her sins.

4:28 What a fool she was.

4:29 Elisha took the woman to the wilderness and bound her with ropes.

4:30 He then said to the heavens, "Behold, I offer for you a sinner. Accept this and do with her what is right."

4:31 Behold, a great many angels came down, appearing as winged beasts and they gathered stones and stoned this woman to death.

4:32 The woman was scared and when she tried to flee, behold, a great stone was thrown to her knee, crippling her so that she may only crawl.

4:33 God looked down on this and was amused at the woman's suffering.

4:34 As the woman died, Elisha went back to her home, took the olive oil and went back to his home.

4:35 There was a woman in Shunem who cared for Elisha whenever he passed by. She would offer him bread to eat and water to drink.

4:36 She said to her husband, "We have served Elisha well, yet not well enough.

4:37 Let it be that we shall give him his chambers, with his own bed, candlestick, table and stool.

4:38 Whenever he passes by, he shall sleep in our house. Surely then the lord shall bless us."

4:39 When Elisha passed through, the chambers were ready and Elisha and his servant slept in the chambers.

4:40 The servant had no bed. He slept on the floor.

4:41 Elisha said to his servant, "Get me this Shunammite woman," and she did come at the request of the servant.

4:42 He asked this woman, "You have treated me well and have given me comfort and food when no other shall.

4:43 Tell me, how can I repay this debt of gratitude. I have jars filled with the finest olive oil, to give you and your husband."

4:44 She answered, "We have no need for oil. My husband owns an olive yard.

4:45 I beg of you, bless us, for I have no child and my husband is old."

4:46 Elisha smiled and said, "Come hither and I shall give you the blessing of the lord and you shall carry a child."

4:47 The woman came and Elisha lifted her skirts and said, "May the spirit of the lord flow through me and give this woman a son."

4:48 Elisha then placed the woman on the bed and lied with her as a husband does.

4:49 The seed of Elisha spilled into the belly of the woman within minutes and Elisha said, "You shall now have a son, blessed by God."

4:50 Nine months later, behold, the woman bore a son. It looked nothing like her husband.

4:51 And the husband said, "This child has no resemblance to me. Surely the lord must have sent us a child instead."

4:52 It came to pass that Elisha passed through Shunem and the son of the woman was of the age to work.

4:53 Behold, he fell upon his head, so that his skull struck a rock and the son died.

4:54 The woman ran to Elisha and said, "My son is dead. My son is dead!

4:55 Come, I beg of you, bless us so that my son may breathe again."

4:56 Elisha came and behold, the son lay motionless upon the field.

4:57 With his fingers, Elisha pushed the neck of the son, and said, "There is still hope, for life beats within this child."

4:58 Elisha then grasped the mouth of the boy and breathed into his lungs seven times.

4:59 Ripping the robes of the child, Elisha then pushed upon the chest of the boy seven times.

4:60 Those around Elisha prayed and asked for blessings from the lord.

4:61 Elisha repeated the breathing, the chest thrusts, until behold, the boy awoke and came to life!

4:62 The woman came to Elisha and said, "Surely you are a man of the lord, who can raise the dead and give them life."

4:63 Another man came to Elisha and said, "Surely you are a man of wickedness, for only a necromancer, a servant of Satan, can raise the dead from the ground."

4:64 Elisha cut his throat and said to those who watched, "A life for a life; it is the law of the lord.

4:65 When this child died, the lord demanded his life. I pleaded with God and traded the life of this boy for the life of another.

4:66 Now that the son is living, the lord demands the death of another. Behold, I offer the lord this man, in exchange for the life of the boy."

4:67 And those agreed it was a fair trade.

4:68 Elisha then travelled to Gilgal, where the people were celebrating with a feast.

4:69 A great pot boiled in the middle of the city and all those in town came and threw in what they could into the pot.

4:70 Behold, a man came and threw herbs and vines in the pot, which he gathered from the wild.

4:71 The man threw also mushrooms in the pot, which he never tasted before.

4:72 When the time came, those of Gilgal ate of the pot and behold, there was death in the pot.

4:73 Elisha said, "Bring me some meal and the marrow of a virgin pheasant, so that I may bless those cursed with the death from the pot."

4:74 The townsmen did and Elisha threw the meal and the marrow into the pot and said, "Blessed be the lord, who take death away from this pot.

4:75 Eat now of the pot and have death taken away from you."

4:76 They did and behold, the death was removed from the pot and those of the town ate with great glutton.

5:1 Naaman, the general of all the armies of Syria, was a great and honourable man, loyal to his master and devoted to the lord. A pity he was also a leper.

5:2 Now the Syrians had invaded those lands of Israel and brought back many captives to be sold as slaves. One of those slaves belonged to the wife of Naaman.

5:3 The maid said to her master, "There is a man of Israel, a prophet who walks with God.

5:4 This man has worked wonders and can heal your husband of his dreaded disease."

5:5 When the king of Syria heard this, he said, "My friend Naaman is a great man and worthy of any and all help.

5:6 Send a messenger to the king of Israel. Tell him we need this prophet that the slave speaks so highly of."

5:7 So a messenger was sent to the king of Israel, carrying with him ten talents of silver, six thousand pieces of gold and ten hand stitched silk robes.

5:8 When the king of Israel read this letter, he laughed and said, "This man who invades my land takes my people wishes me to cure his general, his highest ranking military man, of his leprosy?

5:9 What a fucking idiot. Let this Naaman die and be replaced by a fool."

5:10 Now Elisha heard of this letter and of the gifts sent to his king and said, "Why do these men ask the king so that I may cure a man?

5:11 They should have asked me and I would have answered.

5:12 Elisha wrote to Naaman, saying, "The king of Israel shall heed not your words and will keep all that which you sent.

5:13 I am not the king of Israel. Give to me that which ye sent the king and I shall have it so the one true God strikes away the leprosy from your flesh."

5:14 Naaman read this letter and with great chariots he travelled to the house of Elisha and said, "If you can cure me of this dreaded disease I shall give you double what you asked."

5:15 Elisha said to Naaman, "To cure this disease, you must be blessed by the lord.

5:16 Go now and strip naked upon the banks of the river Jordan. Seven times you shall dip in this river and upon the seventh time the leprosy which plagues you shall be gone."

5:17 Naaman left furious, saying to his servants, "Why does this man have me bathe seven times at the river Jordan. Why can't I bathe in the waters of Abana, or Pharpar, the rivers of Damascus?

5:18 Surely this man seeks evil upon me and shall set a trap so that I will be slain by the banks of the river Jordan."

5:19 But the servants said, "My master, this man is a great and powerful man of God. If he wanted to kill you, he would do it without traps.

5:20 This man has sent down fire from the sky, burned people with great fires from their own bellies; if he wished you dead, then you would be stricken down now.

5:21 Go, wait by the river. There you shall clean of your leprosy."

5:22 Naaman heeded the words of his servants and went to the river Jordan. There, he bathed seven times and upon the seventh time, behold the leprosy was gone.

5:23 He and his men returned to the house of Elisha and said, "My friend, you had cured me of this wicked disease.

5:24 Why would you do this. We are an enemy of your people."

5:25 Elisha answered, "Fuck the people of Israel. They worship stoned statues and false gods.

5:26 You are a man who follows the true path and you devote yourself only to the one true lord; the lord of all lords.

5:27 Know this, it was God who healed you. Go and spread the word of the one true God."

5:28 Naaman heard the words of Elisha and said, "Surely the lord is a truly merciful God.

5:29 Let it be that I shall offer a great sacrifice on my return home."

5:30 As Naaman left, Elisha said, "That bastard didn't pay me!

5:31 Gehazi, go, and fetch that which is mine from Naaman."

5:32 Gehazi, the servant of Elisha, went forth and chased after Naaman until he caught up with him.

5:33 Naaman asked, "What is it, you who serves the prophet of the one true lord?"

5:34 And Gehazi said, "You forgot to give to Elisha that which is owed to him.

5:35 Ten talents of silver, six thousand pieces of gold and ten robes of hand stitched silk robes."

5:36 Naaman grew confused, for he thought the price was double that which was offered to the king of Israel.

5:37 It was. Gehazi did not know this.

5:38 Naaman gave the servant of Elisha that which he asked for and left. Gehazi returned to his master.

5:39 When Elisha saw that which is servant brought, he said, "You treacherous bastard. You took half of which is mine!

5:40 Let it be that you will be forever cursed by the lord. You and your seed shall suffer from the dreaded leprosy until the last of your generation.

5:41 Your cattle, your flocks, your crops, your vineyards, your olive yards shall be stricken with this disease, so that all of the house of Gehazi will be unclean."

5:42 With the final word spoken, the flesh of Gehazi became as white as snow and he was stricken with leprosy.

5:43 Elisha said to him, "Go now, you unclean bastard, lest you tarnish me with your filth."

5:44 And Gehazi left Elisha a leper with skin as white as snow.

6:1 The sons of the prophets came to Elisha, and said "We are tired of living in caves and huts, like some sort of savage tribe.

6:2 Let us go to the banks of the Jordan and every man bring a beam. There we shall build a city for us.

6:3 I beg of you Elisha, come with us, as you are a prophet of God," and Elisha said, "Sure, why not. I'm sick of living in the damn wilderness."

6:4 Elisha left with the men and they cut down the trees by the river, so that they may build their houses.

6:5 A servant of one of the sons of the prophets flung his axe and behold, the grip was lost and the axe fell into the waters.

6:6 The servant said, "Oh shit. That was my master's axe and has only the one."

6:7 Elisha said, "Don't worry," and he cast a stick by the place where the axe fell.

6:8 Behold the iron axe did float and Elisha said to the servant, "Swim forth and take the axe of your master."

6:9 The servant did and Elisha said, "Give me that axe," and the servant gave the axe to Elisha.

6:10 With one great swing, Elisha beheaded the servant and said, "The lord does not tolerate incompetence!

6:11 Those who are deemed useless shall have their blood flow in the river Jordan."

6:12 And the servants continued working, much faster than before.

6:13 The king of Syria warred still with the nation of Israel, though Naaman was still grateful to Elisha.

6:14 Benhadad the king of Syria took counsel of his servants, asking, "This place shall be a good place to make camp."

6:15 A man of the king of Israel sent word, saying, "The army of the Syrians are coming against us.

6:16 I warn you, do not go to this place, for the hosts of Syria shall kill you."

6:17 The king of Syria was angered and said, "Why is it that none of Israel has passed this place. We should have slaughtered many by this time."

6:18 And a servant said, "I do not know, for this is a popular road where those of Israel travel.

6:19 Elisha may know, the man who cured Naaman of his leprosy. It is said the prophet of God can know even the words spoken in a man's bedchamber."

6:20 Benhadad wished this to be untrue, for the words he said in his bedchamber were crude, vulgar and spoken with great passion.

6:21 Still, Benhadad said, "Go forth and spy on this man. Tell me where he is, so that I may fetch him."

6:22 The spies went forth and when they returned, they said, "Behold, the prophet is in Dothan, building houses and beheading people with an axe."

6:23 The king of Syria said, "Only a man of God would be mad enough to behead people with an axe.

6:24 Let us go and fetch him and he shall tell us what need to know."

6:25 A servant of Elisha saw the armies of Syria coming and he ran to his master and said, "Behold, I bring you bad news. Please don't behead me.

6:26 The armies of Syria come here, with great chariots and many men."

6:27 Elisha laughed and said, "Fear not, for the armies with us are greater than those pathetic little Syrians on their chariots of wood and iron."

6:28 The servant looked around and said, "All that which I see are some sons of the prophets and a few servants with carpenter tools.

6:29 I ask you, how do we outnumber those of the Syrians?"

6:30 Elisha yelled, saying, "Do not doubt the man of God.

6:31 Open your eyes and witness the glory and the wonder of your God."

6:32 And the lord opened the eyes of the servant and behold, he saw great chariots of fire, winged horses, dragons and angels armed with swords of great fire and lightning.

6:33 When the armies of Syria came, Elisha said, "You fools who come for me, you look at me, yet do not see.

6:34 Let it be that you see no more."

6:35 And behold, the lord struck those of Syria with a great blindness and Elisha laughed.

6:36 Then the man of God said, "Open your eyes, you heathen fools and witness the power of your enemy."

6:37 And when the Syrian's regained their sight, they saw the armies of the lord in front of them.

6:38 Great dragons, mighty unicorns, winged horses, chariots of fire and angels armed with great swords of fire and lightning.

6:39 The Syrians immediately shit their pants and surrendered.

6:40 It was then that a great blackness consumed Elisha and those men of Syria; and the blackness lifted up to the heavens and blinded all those within it.

6:41 When those within the blackness could see, they were within the lands of Israel, in front of the palace of the king.

6:42 The king of Israel said, "Holy crap. Look at all these prisoners.

6:43 Let us execute them and deliver a message to Benhadad."

6:44 Elisha shouted, "Do not kill them, for they have seen the wonders of the lord of Israel.

6:45 Great dragons, chariots of fire, unicorns and armed angels in front of their eyes.

6:46 This shall scare Benhadad and he will no longer trespass upon our borders.

6:47 Let these men tell their king that which they saw, so that they may scare all those of Syria."

6:48 The king, not wishing to anger Elisha, let these men go and sent them back to their homeland.

6:49 Those prisoners told Benhadad of what they saw and Benhadad said, "Damn their God.

6:50 We shall no longer invade their lands, lest these dragons come and devour us all."

6:51 Instead, Benhadad surrounded the borders of Israel, so that none shall leave nor enter the lands of Israel.

6:52 When Syria besieged Israel, a great famine swept the land, so that the head of a donkey sold for fourscore pieces of silver and a quarter of dove shit was sold for five pieces of silver.

6:53 One day, the king walked through his city and behold, he saw a mother with her son and she said to the mother, "Do you wish to eat this day?" and the woman said, "Yes."

6:54 Feeling great compassion, the king said, "I shall give you flesh to eat."

6:55 And the king brought forth his youngest son, slaughtered him and boiled him in a pot and the king and the woman feasted upon the flesh of the prince.

6:56 The king then said, "You owe me your son, for I did share my meal with you."

6:57 On the following day, the king went to the woman, but behold, the woman was feasting upon her own son and said, "You did not arrive on time, so I ate him all."

6:58 The king grew angry, slew the woman and feasted on her raw flesh.

6:59 In anger, the king said, "Surely this is the fault of Elisha.

6:60 The man of God sent us this famine and cursed us all to eat our own seed.

6:61 Let it be that Elisha knows the pain and the sorrow of all those of Israel."

6:62 So the king set a bounty upon the head of Shephat the son of Elisha and sent his men to go forth and kill him.

6:63 Now, Elisha sat within his home, as did the elders of Israel. The lord provided them with a bounty of bread.

6:64 When a man came to seek vengeance on Elisha, a servant stormed into his master's house and said, "There is a man on his way, who comes and seeks the heads of us all.

6:65 They call Shephat the son of a murderer and wish to claim his head as well as all the heads of the sons of the prophets.

6:66 Behold, the man comes now. I can hear his footsteps come closer. Blow out the candles, lock the door and pretend nobody is home."

6:67 But the messenger knocked on the door and said, "Elisha, you bastard. We know this evil comes from God.

6:68 Why should I wait for God to end this. The lord is a vicious fucker. Let it be that the man of God be punished."

7:1 Elisha said to the messenger, "Thus sayeth the lord, tomorrow at this time a measure of fine flour shall be sold for a shekel and two measures of barley shall be sold for a shekel, if you spare my life.

7:2 Kill me and the famine lasts for forty-two generations and all those of Israel shall starve and eat their own children.

7:3 The man said, "Behold, I shall spare your life and the life of your son.

7:4 If what you say comes true, then all shall rejoice. If you lie, then let it be known that all those of Israel shall come and burn you upon the rocks."

7:5 There were four leprous men who sat within the gates of Israel and they said, "Why do we sit here so that we may die?

7:6 If we go into the city, the famine shall consume us and we shall die in the city. Let us go and surrender ourselves to the Syrians.

7:7 Their general was once a leper and shall take pity on us and feed us and care for us.

7:8 The worst which shall happen, they kill us. Better to be killed quickly by the sword than slowly through hunger."

7:9 When these four lepers came to the camp of the Syrians, behold, not a single man was there.

7:10 For the lord made it so that these Syrians heard great horses, chariots and the sound of a mighty army coming to slay them. They said to one another, "Oh crap, the king of Israel has made a covenant with the Egyptians and the Hittites.

7:11 They come to slay us now. We must leave now."

7:12 So the army of Syria did and they left behind their weapons, their armour, their asses, their cattle, their flocks, their flour, their silver and all that which was in the camp.

7:13 The lepers came in and looted all that within the camp. They took the gold and silver and buried it.

7:14 They drank the wine, ate the food and rejoiced, saying, "We are rich. We are rich!

7:15 Blessed be the lord, for we are rich!"

7:16 It was first decided that they shall hoard all that in the camp of Syria and tell none in Israel, saying, "Fuck them, those who treat us as filth."

7:17 In time, one of the stupid lepers said, "Though we are rich, what good does it do us?

7:18 We are still lepers and no merchant shall take our money.

7:19 Let us do good in the sight of the lord. Let us go and tell all of what we found here.

7:20 Then our God shall bless us and cure us of this dreaded disease."

7:21 So the lepers came to the porter of the city and said, "We were just at the camp of Syria and they are all gone.

7:22 All their food, their beasts, even their silver and gold has been left behind."

7:23 When the king heard of this, he laughed, and said, "Surely this is a trap of the Syrians, for they know we are hungry.

7:24 As we leave the city to gather their goods, they shall come and slay us and take our cities and our lands from us."

7:25 A servant of the king, who was really hungry and wanted some damn food which was told to be at the Syrian camp, said, "I don't fucking care if it's a damn trap!

7:26 I beg of you, take five horses and have them see if the claims of these lepers are true."

7:27 The king said, "Fine. Take five horses and check the camp. Check also the lands, to ensure none of the armies of Syria wait in ambush."

7:28 Thus the servant was sent forth and behold, he came to the camp and saw all that which the Syrians left behind.

7:29 When the king heard the claims of the lepers to be true, he sent out great many chariots so that they may gather the goods of the Syrians. And a measure of fine flour was sold for a shekel and two measures of barley for a shekel that day, according to the word of the lord.

7:30 As the people of Israel heard that food was now cheap, they rushed to the gates of Samaria, so that they may buy flour, barley and meat.

7:31 A man heard that food was being sold and did not believe it, saying, "It is a trap by the king."

7:32 He wishes to slay us all and feast on our flesh."

7:33 But as the man saw people returning with barrels of flour, jars of oil and containers of flesh, he knew the words to be true.

7:34 He rushed to the gates and behold, a great mighty crowd came upon him and trampled him to death as they rushed for cheap food.

7:35 Elisha said of the man, "He died for not believing the words of the lord.

7:36 Blessed be the lord, for his words are always true."

7:37 Those lepers which found the camp were not cured of their leprosy and were cast out of the city for being unclean.

8:1 Elisha spoke to the woman who lodged him and fed him and he said, "Get you and thy kin out of Israel and live wherever you can. The lord shall send upon these lands a great famine which will last seven years."

8:2 So the woman left and lived in the lands of the Philistines for seven years.

8:3 At the end of seven years, the woman came back to her homeland and asked the king for her house and her land back.

8:4 The king knew this woman knew Elisha well and he asked his servant Gehazi, "Tell me all that which Elisha has done for this bitch."

8:5 Gehazi said to his master, "Elisha hath raised her son from the dead and given him back to her. Give this woman back her land and her house, lest Elisha's wrath wax hot with you."

8:6 When the king asked this woman if what Gehazi said was true, she said, "Yes, for behold, my son is beside me and he once lay dead beneath my feet.

8:7 It was by the grace of Elisha that he rose from the dead."

8:8 So the king, in fear of Elisha, gave to this woman back her lands, her house, her crops, her vineyards and her orchards.

8:9 Now Elisha went to Damascus, for he knew Benhadad to be sick. When Elisha came, it was told the king of Syria that the man of God has returned.

8:10 The king said to his servant Hazael, "Take a present in your hand and go meet with Elisha. Ask him if I shall recover of this sickness."

8:11 Hazael met with Elisha and took with him forty camels carrying all the goods of Damascus and asked the prophet, "Will my master Benhadad recover from his illness?"

8:12 Elisha said, "Go and tell your king that he will live. But know this, the lord has shown me that Benhadad shall surely die.

8:13 Lie to your master, with the blessing of the lord."

8:14 It was then that the man of God wept and Hazael asked Elisha, "Why are you crying, O prophet of God?"

8:15 Elisha answered, "Because I know the wickedness which you shall do to my peoples, you bastard son of a whore.

8:16 You shall burn their strongholds, slay my men, burn the children and tear the very womb apart from those who are pregnant."

8:17 Hazael asked, "Are you fucking insane. If this were true, why not kill me?" and Elisha answered, "Because it must be that you will become the king of Syria.

8:18 It is the will of God. I cannot change it."

8:19 Hazael asked, "Why not. Surely if you were to kill me now, the wickedness which you speak of will cease to happen."

8:20 Elisha sighed and said, "If I were to kill you now, the lord God will raise your very body from the ground."

8:21 Elisha then left, leaving behind a very confused Hazael, who asked himself, "Why would I do such a wicked thing. How shall I become king of Syria?

8:22 What kind of God would allow his people to suffer like that?"

8:23 Hazael went to his master's bedchamber and said, "The man of God has told me you shall surely recover from this illness," and Benhadad said, "Blessed be Elisha. Blessed be the lord."

8:24 On the morrow, Benhadad died and all those of Syria said, "Benhadad hath served us well. Let it be that our new king be like Benhadad.

8:25 Hazael hath served Benhadad greatly and knows his ways and his manners. Let Hazael wear the crown of Syria."

8:26 And Hazael became king of Syria.

8:27 In the fifth year of Joram the son of Ahab's reign, Jehoshaphat died, and his son Jehoram became king of Judah.

8:28 Thirty-two years old Joram was when he became king and he reigned in Jerusalem for eight years.

8:29 Now the daughter of Abah was Joram's wife and this wretched cunt poisoned the mind of Joram so that he worshipped false gods and erected altars for them.

8:30 This angered the lord greatly, yet he refused to destroy Judah, for the sake of David.

8:31 In these days the peoples of Edom revolted against Judah and anointed a king for themselves.

8:32 Which is amazing, considering the people of Israel slaughtered all the males of Edom, save for one who escaped to Egypt.

8:33 So Joram the king of Israel took his armies to Zair and in the night slaughtered all those of the people of Edom who resided there.

8:34 Yet Edom still revolted against the hands of Judah, as did the people of Libnah.

8:35 Joram died and was buried with his fathers in the city of David. Ahaziah his son reigned in his stead.

8:36 In the twelfth year of Joram did Ahaziah the son of Jehoram begin to reign over the tribe of Judah.

8:37 Twenty-two years was Ahaziah when he sat upon the throne and his mother's name was Athaliah the daughter of Omri. Ahaziah reigned for only one year.

8:38 Ahaziah did evil in the sight of the lord, and worshipped other gods, built them altars, carved idols and burned for them incense and fucked men.

8:39 He went with Joram the king of Israel to fight against Hazael the king of Syria in Ramothgildead: and the Syrians severely wounded Joram.

8:40 King Joram retreated to Jezreel, so that he may be healed by the wounds given to him by the Syrians. Ahaziah went to see him, for he cared for Joram and wished his wounds to heal.

9:1 Elisha the prophet called one of the sons of the prophets and said to him, "Go, take this jar of oil and head thee to Ramothgilead.

9:2 When you arrive, seek out Jehu the son of Jehoshaphat the son of Nimshi. Take him to an empty chamber, alone and unarmed.

9:3 Strip from him his raiment's and pour this holy oil atop his body, so that it flows down from his head even unto his toes and tell him that the lord has anointed you king over Israel.

9:4 Then get the hell out of there. Don't pause, just run."

9:5 So the young man went to Ramothgilead, and sought out Jehu the son of Jehoshaphat.

9:6 And when he found Jehu the son of Jehoshaphat, leader of the armies of Israel, the man said, "Come with me," and Jehu asked, "Why?," and the son of the prophet showed him the oil and said, "Because I have a matter of most importance."

9:7 Now Jehu was a man who hated the lust of men and believed this son of a prophet to be a homosexual that wished to perform sodomy.

9:8 Jehu wished to entrap this man and slay him. Jehu wished to kill all those who were faggots.

9:9 When the two men were in an empty chamber, the young man said to Jehu, "Strip naked and we shall begin the work of the lord."

9:10 Jehu stripped naked and the son of the prophet poured the anointing oil atop the head of Jehu and said, "Behold ye shall be king over the people of the lord and over all that of Israel.

9:11 Know this, the lord demands that you kill all those of the house of Ahab, so that God may have his revenge for the spilled blood of the prophets and of the servants of the lord.

9:12 All those of the family of Ahab shall be reduced to blood and dust and the lord shall cut from Ahab all those who pisses against the wall.

9:13 May it be that the house of Ahab shall be as that of the house of Jeroboam the son of Nebat and the house of Baasha the son of Ahijah.

THE OLD TESTAMENT

9:14 Jezebel the wretched cunt will be feasted upon by dogs which shall not even leave enough behind for a burial."

9:15 The young man then jumped out the window and ran away in great hurry, leaving Jehu very confused as to what the hell just happened and whether or not the son of the prophet was an accursed and unholy queer.

9:16 Jehu left the chambers, clothed and greasy and asked his servants, "Who the hell is that guy?" and one of his servants answered, "He is a servant of that insane madman Elisha."

9:17 Another servant asked, "What did this fool do to you?" and Jehu replied, "He poured oil atop my head and claimed that I shall be king of Israel."

9:18 Thus the servants of Jehu put on him new garments, blew trumpets and declared to all that Jehu is the new king of Israel. The people didn't care. They were used to kings coming and going.

9:19 Jehu the son of Jehoshaphat conspired against Joram the other king of Israel, for Joram was of the house of Ahab. Also, he was the true king and therefore an enemy.

9:20 King Joram was still in Jezreel where his wounds were to be healed and Jehu said, "Let us go to Jezreel and kill this other king who dare sits upon my throne."

9:21 So Jehu took a chariot and went to Jezreel, where Joram lay wounded and Ahaziah stand by his side.

9:22 A watchman saw the chariot and said to his men, "Behold, this fucking idiot comes towards us like a madman."

9:23 Go, tell our master Joram. He shall know what to do."

9:24 When Joram heard of this, he said, "That must be Jehu. The man rides his chariot as though his horse were a wild bull.

9:25 Send a man out and ask him what the leader of the army of Israel wishes to say."

9:26 When the man was sent out to ask Jehu why he comes, the horse of Jehu's chariot trampled him to death.

9:27 The watchmen saw this and said, "Holy shit!" and told Joram what had happened.

9:28 Joram said, "That man is a fool, who just killed an innocent servant of the king of Israel.

9:29 For this, he shall die."

9:30 Thus Joram the other king of Israel and Ahaziah the king of Judah went forth on their chariots, to challenge Jehu and his mad chariot driving.

9:31 Joram yelled to Jehu, "You fool. You killed a servant of the king of Israel."

9:32 Jehu yelled back, "I did not, for I am now the king of Israel!

9:33 Know also this. Even God thinks your mother is a cunt."

9:34 Joram turned to Ahaziah, and said, "This man surely wishes to betray me."

9:35 And with those words spoken, Jehu drew his bow and struck an arrow through the heart of Joram, so that the other king of Israel died upon his chariot and fell off as his horse fled away.

9:36 Jehu said to his most trusted friend Bidkar, "Go and take this corpse of Joram to the fields of Naboth the Jezreelite,

9:37 Leave him to rot in the vineyards and let the scavengers, the beasts and the fowl pluck at his flesh there, for the father of Joram spilled blood to obtain that vineyard.

9:38 So it shall be that the blood of his son stains the soil of the vineyard which Ahab took."

9:39 Ahaziah the king of Judah saw that which Jehu did and fled. Ahaziah was a coward in that sense.

9:40 Jehu said to his men, "Go after this man and kill him. Bring his body back to me." They did and Ahaziah died at Megiddo, which is near Ibleam.

9:41 Don't worry. I have no idea where those places are either. I also care even less as to their whereabouts than you do.

9:42 Now the servants of Jehu, under orders, took Ahaziah to Jerusalem and there they buried him in the sepulcher of his fathers.

9:43 When Jehu came to Jezreel, Jezebel the wicked cunt of a witch heard of it: she painted her face and disguised herself in men's clothing.

9:44 Jezebel looked out a window to see Jehu come in and when Jehu saw her, he did not fall for the disguise and said, "Hey, bitch. Even God fucking hates you and thinks you're a cunt."

9:45 As Jezebel leaned out to yell profanities, behold, she fell to the ground and the horses trampled atop her and sprayed her blood upon the wall.

9:46 Jehu laughed at the sight, entered the city, and ate.

9:47 In time, Jehu said to some eunuchs, "Go, fetch the unholy corpse of Jezebel the witch and bury her. She is a king's daughter and this shall be done in respect for her father."

9:48 When the eunuchs went to fetch her, behold, all that was left were her skull, a foot and the palms of her hands. The rest were eaten by the dogs.

9:49 As the eunuchs told Jehu, he laughed and said, "The words of Elisha did come true, for he said the dogs of Jezreel shall eat the wicked bitch Jezebel.

9:50 Let it be that the carcass of Jezebel be as dung upon the fields of Jezreel. It'll be the most useful thing she has ever done."

10:1 Ahab had seventy sons left in Samaria which Jehu wished all dead. He sent letters to the servants, the caretakers, elders and those who raised the children of Ahab, saying,

10:2 "Do not let any of those of the seed of Ahab read this letter, nor let them know this parchment is in your possession.

10:3 Know this, Ahab and his house are wicked in the eyes of God and shall be erased from existence within all the lands, in glory to our lord.

10:4 I Jehu the new king of Israel demands you tear off the very head of all those of the seed of Ahab. Son, daughter, old, infant, it matters not.

10:5 If they be spawns of Ahab, strike death upon them and deliver their heads to the city of Jezreel."

10:6 Those who received the letter, replied back, saying, "We shall not betray our masters in such deceit and treachery.

10:7 We do not care if you are the king of Israel. We don't recognize the crown on your head; it belongs to lie on someone else."

10:8 Jehu sent another letter, "If you do not do as I ask, then it shall be your heads which will be delivered to Jezreel!"

10:9 And those of the seed of Jezreel were quickly killed by their servants, by their caretakers and by the elders of the city which they dwelt in.

10:10 Soon, all seventy of the sons of Ahab's heads were sent to Jezreel in great baskets and Jehu demanded that they be piled in two heaps by the gates of the city.

10:11 Behold, all those who went through the gates gazed upon the heads as crows plucked the flesh and the hair from the skulls.

10:12 Children played with them as though they were puppets and amused passers-by with their skits and their ventriloquism.

10:13 On the morrow, Jehu went to the gate and said, "Behold, by the glory of the lord did I betray my master and pierced his heart with the shaft of an arrow, but who slew all these?

10:14 Know now that the word of the lord shall not come upon the earth regarding the house of Ahab: for the lord has done that which he spoke to his servant Elijah.

10:15 I know this because I am king and I know all I need to know and most I don't.

10:16 Do not question your king, do not question your God."

10:17 Jehu then went back into the city of Jezreel and killed all those who were friendly to the house of Ahab. Men, women, children, elderly, farmers, priests, bakers and vintners, so that all those who were good to the house of Ahab lie dead.

10:18 After this slaying, Jehu arose and went forth to the lands of Samaria. On his travels, he passed by a shearing house.

10:19 As he passed the shearing house, brothers of Ahaziah the king of Judah passed him and Jehu asked, "Why do you come to the lands of Israel?" and they answered, "We come to mourn those of the seed of Ahab."

10:20 Jehu ordered his servants to take these men alive and take them to the shearing house.

10:21 It was there that Jehu hung by the feet these kin of Ahaziah and took the tools of the shearer and skinned them alive, so that all forty-two of the men were skinned like wild game in the shearing house.

10:22 Jehu then took the hides of these forty-two men and tanned them and made them raiment's for his closest friends.

10:23 Still alive, Jehu left these brothers of Ahaziah hanging in the shearing house and those who heard their cries and came to witness them believed they were wild game, hanging to be aged alive.

10:24 As Jehu rode on his chariot, he saw on the road Jehonadab the son of Rechab coming to greet him and Jehu saluted him and said, "Come on my chariot and I shall show you the glory and wonders of our lord."

10:25 Jehu then took Jehonadab on his travels through Samaria, hunting and slaying all those of the seeds of Ahab. Even the unborn babies Jehu killed and Jehonadab said, "Surely this is the will of our lord."

10:26 There were still those who praised and served the false lord Baal and Jehu wished these heathens to be punished for their treachery and betrayal.

10:27 Tricking those prophets and priests of the false lord, Jehu said to his people, "Let it be known that Ahab served Baal a little, but Jehu shall serve Baal well.

10:28 Come, all those who serve the lord Baal and Jehu shall give great sacrifice to our lord. Gather at his house and give glory to Baal.

10:29 It shall be a great assembly and the greatest feast. Have it be law that all those who serve Baal must come, lest they anger their god."

10:30 Those who worshipped Baal came and those who worshipped the true lord of Israel did not and were disgusted by Jehu and his heathen worship.

10:31 When all those arrived, Jehu said to his men, "Let it be known that all those who came to this feast shall die by the end.

10:32 If you let any of these heathens escape, it shall be a sin upon your head. For letting a life go, I shall take your life in their place."

10:33 Jehu then went into the house of Baal and said to those who came, "Let it be known that you all worship Baal, those who came to praise and bless his name.

10:34 Fuck you all, you heathens. May your blood stain red eternally the house of this wicked heathen lord."

10:35 It was then those of Jehu came and slew all those who came to worship and praise Baal.

10:36 The blood spilled on the floors, and the bodies floated atop the thick blood.

10:37 The lord was very pleased.

10:38 Jehu then smashed all those images of Baal, casting the shards on the table and set fire to the house of Baal.

10:39 Great flames consumed the temple of Baal, so that the bodies burned, the blood boiled and the destroyed images were reduced to ash. The smoke rose into the heavens and created an intoxicating aroma to the lord.

10:40 In place of the temple of Baal, Jehu built a brothel and

claimed to all those of Israel this was his final way of saying to everyone, "Fuck Baal."

10:41 And Jehu destroyed all that which was Baal out of Israel and those who worshipped the false lord did so in secret.

10:42 But Jehu did not depart from all the sins of Israel, for he still sinned in the ways of Jeroboam the son of Nebat and he created golden calves and placed them also in Bethel and Dan.

10:43 For unknown reasons, God did not seem to care this time and even said to Jehu, "You have done right in the eyes of your lord and wiped forth all those of the seed of Ahab and crushed Baal and his worshippers from the lands of Israel.

10:44 For your loyalty and devotion to the lord, let it be that all children of the seed of Jehu shall sit upon the throne of Israel. Lo, even unto the fourth generation shall the seed of Jehu rule over Israel."

10:45 Now, God could not have these golden calves around and not punish Jehu for them, yet God wished not to slay Jehu and all those of his house, yet.

10:46 Instead, the lord slowly took that of the lands of Israel away and gave them to those of heathens.

10:47 Hazael the king of Syria slowly took lands away from Israel and smote the armies of Israel when they met in battle.

10:48 From Jordan eastward all the lands of Gilead, the Gadites, the Reubenites, the Manassites, from Aroer, by the river Arnon, even Gilead and Bashan Hazael took.

10:49 Jehu ruled over Israel for twenty-eight years and was buried in the sepulcher of his fathers. His son, Jehoahaz, reigned in his stead.

11:1 When Athaliah the mother of Ahaziah saw that her son was dead, she went insane and killed all her grandchildren, saying, "They shall not be as good a king as my son."

11:2 But Jehosheba, daughter of king Joram and sister of Ahaziah, took Joash the son of Ahaziah and hid him from the wrath of Athaliah.

11:3 Jehosheba hid Joash in the house of the lord, where he stayed for six years while Athaliah reigned over Judah and believed she killed all her grandchildren.

11:4 On the seventh year Jehoiada the priest sent and fetched forth rulers over the armies of Judah, brought them into the house of the lord and said to them all, "This child is the true king of our lands, not his wretched grandmother.

11:5 This is what you all shall do; a third of us shall watch and guard this temple, so that none loyal to Athaliah shall come and kill our king.

11:6 One third shall remain at the gates of Sur and the other third shall be at the gates of the guard and keep watch of all those of the armies of Judah not loyal to the true king.

11:7 Our king shall be protected well. Let him have guards by his side always, armed with the finest weapons and shields.

11:8 These men shall kill all who come too close to the king and they shall be with him always; even when the child shits shall the guards stand by him."

11:9 And those loyal to Jehoiada did that which he said and kept watch over the temple, the gates and their young king.

11:10 The priests of the temple gave to the men of Jehoiada the spears and the armour of David and blessed them all.

11:11 Joash was then taken from his bedchamber, given new robes and was anointed king that day in the temple. All those their rejoiced and did not keep their fucking mouths shut.

11:12 Athaliah wondered what was going on and went into the temple, and behold she saw Joash being anointed king and yelled to all within, "Treason. Treason. Treacherous bastards!"

11:13 Those armed within the temple pinned Athaliah to a pillar, removed the crown and placed it atop the head of Joash, saying,

THE OLD TESTAMENT

"Behold, the true king of Judah."

11:14 The crown was too large.

11:15 Jehoiada said to those within the temple, "Do not kill this witch in the temple of the lord, for her blood is unholy and shall not stain the blood of the house of God.

11:16 Take this bitch to the fields where the flocks graze. Slaughter this creature like the fat cow she is."

11:17 Athaliah was dragged to the oxen fields and was slaughtered like a sick cow, set atop a fire and eaten by those loyal to Joash.

11:18 She tasted like pork. Most of the people didn't know. Those that did kept quiet, for fear of letting the others know they ate unclean flesh.

11:19 Jehoiada then made a covenant with the king and all those of the tribe of Judah, saying, "Let it be that we shall be the lord's people."

11:20 With that covenant, those of the people of Judah went forth to the house of Baal and destroyed all within it. Images, altars and worshippers were cast down on the floor and crushed beneath the boots of the people of Judah.

11:21 Mattan, the high priest of Baal, was offered as a mock sacrifice atop the altars of Baal and all those of Judah danced around Mattan naked, pissing on his burning corpse and bathing in his blood.

11:22 The lord gazed down upon this and was pleased. God loves violence, nudity and torn flesh.

11:23 That which remained of Athaliah was brought into the house of the king and put on display by the entrance.

11:24 Seven years old was Joash when he began to rule over Judah. Most had a hard time taking such a young king seriously, especially when the first law was that all toys belonged to the king.

12:1 n the seventh year of Jehu did Joash begin to reign in Jerusalem and his mother's name was Zibia of Beersheba.

12:2 Joash did that which was right in the eyes of the lord and hearkened the words of Jehoiada the priest.

12:3 Still, not all the high places were taken away and the people still burned incense to heathen lords in these high places.

12:4 Joash remembered his time spent hiding in the temple, away from the eyes of his wicked grandmother. Joash remembered that the temple was cold.

12:5 The king demanded of the priests that all the money which was donated to them, the money from offerings and the money given to them as bribes, be used to repair the breaches in the walls of the temple.

12:6 For twenty-three years the priests collected money and never did they repair the damn breaches in the walls.

12:7 King Joash called for priest Jehoiada and said to him, "When the king demands you people do something, you fucking do it!

12:8 The lord does not wish to be kept in a frigid house and wants his damn walls repaired. If you do not repair the cracks in the walls, it will be repaired with your blood."

12:9 Jehoiada understood and told his fellow priests, "The king is very pissed and we must stop hoarding the money and repair these damned walls.

12:10 Joash claims it is too cold, though it bothers none of us. We just put on warmer robes.

12:11 Still, this is the demands of our king. If it is not obeyed, he'll kill us all."

12:12 The priests said, "The money is our money and this is the house of the lord. A king has no claim to what happens here."

12:13 Jehoiada said, "When the king has a sword to your neck, you shall soon change your mind."

12:14 So the priests took a chest and drilled a hole in it. Those who entered the temple dropped coins within the chest and it was with

that money the priests used to repair the temple.

12:15 Not a coin was taken by the priests from that chest; it was all used to repair the house of the lord. At first.

12:16 In time, the masons and carpenters repaired enough of the cracks and the breaches, that the priests believed Joash would be pleased.

12:17 When Joash entered the temple, he said, "It is still too damn cold in the house of God. Let it be that all those made of silver and gold be sold and the funds be used to repair this house of the lord so it be warmer."

12:18 The priests said, "Those things belong to God and he shall surely curse us all if you sell them to any man."

12:19 Joash did not hearken the words of the priests and sold that within the temple to pay masons and carpenters to make the temple warmer.

12:20 In time, the temple was warm enough for the king and he ceased selling the goods of the temple. But not before the lord became quite wroth with him.

12:21 Hazael the king of Syria rose and took Gath and marched towards Jerusalem to lay claims upon the city.

12:22 Now Joash was a coward who gathered all the hallowed things of Jehoshaphat, Jehoram, Ahaziah, and all the kings of Judah, even the most hallowed things in the temple of the lord and sent it to Hazael, saying, "Take this, just leave us the hell alone."

12:23 This angered the lord even more, who stirred anger in the hearts of the servants of Joash.

12:24 Jozachar the son of Shimeath and Jehozabad the son of Shomer conspired against their master and they took axes and chopped Joash as he slept.

12:25 The flesh of Joash were fed to the dogs, which gnawed on them until even the bones were eaten.

12:26 When those of Judah wondered where their king went, they elected Amaziah the son of Joash to rule until the arrival of Joash. Joash never came back.

13:1 In the twenty third year of Joash's reign did Jehoahaz the son of Jehu begin to reign over Israel and Jehoahaz reigned for seventeen years.

13:2 And Jehoahaz did that which was evil in the sight of the lord, which most kings seemed to do. It was a very popular trend.

13:3 Because of this wickedness, God decided to deliver those of Israel in the hands of Hazael the king of Syria and Benhadad the son of Hazael for all the days of Jehoahaz.

13:4 Crying, Jehoahaz came to the lord, and begged of him to stop the Syrians from oppressing Israel and the lord decided to grant Jehoahaz his wish and ended the oppression of Israel by those of Syria.

13:5 Nobody is sure why the lord hearkened the words of Jehoahaz, for the lord thought this man wicked. Maybe the lord showed a rare act of mercy. N'ah, God just wanted to shut him up.

13:6 Before Hazael ceased his oppression, the lord had it so that the king of Syria destroyed Jehoahaz's fifty horsemen, ten chariots and ten thousand footmen. Now that sounds more like God.

13:7 Jehoahaz died and was buried in Samaria in the sepulcher of his fathers. Athaliah reigned for a while, until she was slain and replaced by Joash.

13:8 In the thirty seventh year of Joash king of Judah did Jehoash the son of Jehoahaz begin to reign in Samaria, over all that of Israel and he reigned for sixteen years.

13:9 Following the popular trend, Jehoahaz did that which was evil in the sight of the lord and sinned in the ways of Jeroboam.

13:10 He let foreigners live and didn't condemn to damnation those who worshipped heathen lords.

13:11 Now Elisha has fallen ill, and Joash the king of Israel came to visit him, to see if this legendary man of God would truly die.

13:12 When Joash saw Elisha, he fell on his face and wept, saying, "O most holy man of Israel, it was believed the lord shall give you everlasting life.

13:13 Your death shall bring great sadness to all those of the people of God."

13:14 Elisha told Joash to stop kissing his ass and said, "Get your bow and arrows. Go over to the window and shoot eastward."

13:15 Joash did as Elisha said and when the king shot the arrow, a mighty scream of a woman's voice was heard, crying, "My baby. My baby!"

13:16 Elisha asked Joash, "Where is that woman from?" and the king answered, "She is from Aphek."

13:17 Elisha smiled and said, "This is good; a sign from God.

13:18 You shall strike forth at the Syrians in Aphek and shall slaughter them plenty.

13:19 Now take the arrow from that woman's spawn, come by my bedside and strike the ground with it."

13:20 Joash did and took the arrow from the child, much to the horror of the mother. He then went to the chambers of Elisha and struck the ground three times with the arrow.

13:21 Elisha cursed Joash, and said "You fucking fool of a king, who strikes the ground only thrice.

13:22 If you had struck the floor plenty, then all of Syria would have been wiped. But no, the sign from the lord was only struck thrice.

13:23 Three times only shall you smite those of Syria, then you shall smite them no more."

13:24 Joash grew tearful and smote the ground with the arrow a thousand times until the arrow broke and Elisha smacked his head and told him to leave.

13:25 When Elisha died, he was buried in the wilderness like the madman he was. And it came to pass that the Moabites invaded the land where Elisha was buried.

13:26 As the peoples of Moab were burying a man, the corpse touched the bones of Elisha and behold, it came to life!

13:27 Those of Moab gathered the bones of Elisha and touched all those who were slain and they revived to life and stood upon their feet.

13:28 A great zombie army was created for the peoples of Moab using the bones of Elisha until the lord of Israel cursed the zombies, who then began to feast upon the brains of those who came near them.

13:29 The zombies were quickly killed.

13:30 Hazael the king of Syria oppressed Israel all the days of Jehoahaz.

13:31 But the lord was gracious to those who were oppressed by the Syrians and showed compassion to them, because of the covenant made with Abraham, Isaac and Jacob.

13:32 The lord did not kill these men who were oppressed, but let them live in slavery, poverty, humiliation, rape and starvation till the end of their days.

13:33 Glory be the lord, merciful in his ways!

13:34 When Hazael the king of Syria died, his son Benhadad succeeded him and also fought against those of Israel.

13:35 Jehoash the son of Jehoahaz fought against those of Benhadad and taken back the lands which his father took. Three times did Joash defeat Benhadad and reclaim the cities of Israel.

14:1 Amaziah was twenty-five years old when he began to reign in Jerusalem and his mother's name was Jehoaddan of Jerusalem.

14:2 And Amaziah did that which was right in the eyes of the lord, like his father Joash and the mighty king David.

14:3 Still, he did not remove the high places used in the worship of false lords and people still came to these places and burned incense to Ashtaroth, Baal, and other heathen gods.

14:4 In time, Amaziah learned of which servants slew his father and he gathered Jozachar the son of Shimeth and Jehozabad the son of Shomer and put them in an arena.

14:5 There the two men were given rusted daggers and cheap raiment's of cloth and was told to fight to the death; that who survived, will be greatly rewarded.

14:6 The two men fought ferociously, until it was Jozachar who won, slaying Jehozabad with a fatal blow to his kidneys.

14:7 Jozachar smiled and looked towards Amaziah, saying, "Where is my reward for winning this glorious battle?"

14:8 Amaziah smiled and said, "The fight is not yet over." A lion was then brought into the arena, which ate Jozachar.

14:9 True to his word, Amaziah greatly rewarded the lion with plenty of meat.

14:10 Now king Amaziah was merciful, and did not kill the children of Jozachar and Jehozabad, saying, "I don't see the point in punishing the children for the sins of the fathers.

14:11 Let every man die for their own sin, suffer for their own greed and be punished for their own wickedness."

14:12 Those who heard these words thought them words of foolishness. Those very words go against the words of the lord, who demand the innocent child be punished for the wickedness of their ancestors.

14:13 Amaziah declared war against the peoples of Edom and slew of them ten thousand peoples in the valley of salt; mostly women, since the people of Edom were still suffering from the great male genocide given to them since the time of David.

14:14 Then Amaziah sent messengers to Jehoash the son of Jehoahaz, king of Israel, saying, "We have not yet met, though we be brothers in the eyes of God."

14:15 Jehoash sent back a message, saying, "you hast slain my enemy the people of Edom and for this my heart is lifted and my spirits filled with happiness and wine.

14:16 Let us join in battle and wipe these Edomites forever from the lands of the earth."

14:17 Amaziah would not hearken these words and said, "Do your own dirty work. The armies of Judah are not your bitch."

14:18 Jehoash became angry and declared war against Judah. The two armies met at Bethshemesh in the lands of Judah, where those of Amaziah failed miserably.

14:19 The armies of Judah fled to their tents, hiding, quivering and crying like cowards.

14:20 Jehoash king of Israel took Amaziah king of Judah at Bethshemesh and marched him towards Jerusalem, where Jehoash forced the king of Judah to watch the walls of Jerusalem be torn down.

14:21 Those of the armies of Israel then looted Jerusalem and took all the gold and silver, even that which was in the house of the lord and they took hostages and returned to Samaria.

14:22 Amaziah the king of Judah lived for fifteen years after the death of Jehoash and nobody cared.

14:23 Those of Jerusalem loathed Amaziah, for under his rule did Jerusalem became destroyed and looted by those of Israel.

14:24 The people conspired against their king and wished to kill him. Amaziah knew this and fled to the city of Lachish.

14:25 Those of Lachish hated Amaziah as well and when their king entered the gates, the people rushed him and beat him to death with fists, hoes, sickles and rocks.

14:26 Amaziah was brought back by horses and was buried with his fathers in the city of David.

14:27 Those of Judah took Azariah the son of Amaziah and declared him king; saying, "If you fuck up like your father did, you shall die by our hands."

14:28 Azariah did not and he built for Judah the city of Elath and defended the borders of Judah until his death.

14:29 In the fifteenth year of Amaziah the son of Joash king of Judah did Jeroboam the son of Joash begin to reign in Israel.

14:30 Yes, another king Jeroboam and he sinned also in the ways of the original Jeroboam, which pissed off the lord greatly.

14:31 Jeroboam defended the coast of Israel with a great navy, so that none of the heathen's ships shall enter the waters of Hamath.

14:32 This caused all foreign nations to shut out that of Israel, so that Israel had no friend nor ally to help them.

14:33 Now the lord saw this and saw the bitterness of the children of Israel, who said, "How dare these fucking heathens ignore us.

14:34 We are the chosen people of God and they refuse to even barter with us, or send caravans of goods to trade."

14:35 The lord thought this isolation would finally destroy those of the people of Israel, but it did not, for Jeroboam ensured the lands of Israel could supply all its people with food, water and goods.

14:36 Jeroboam was also a war hungry king, who took Hamath from the tribe of Judah and the city of Damascus from the Syrians, killing many thousands on his way.

14:37 When Jeroboam died, his son Zachariah took up his crown and ruled over Israel.

15:1 Yet another new damn king of Judah, this one named Azariah the son of Amaziah, who began to rule on the twenty seventh year of king Jeroboam's reign of Israel.

15:2 That's the second Jeroboam, not the first.

15:3 Sixteen years of age was Azariah when he began to rule, and he ruled for fifty-two years. His mother's name was Jecholiah of Jerusalem.

15:4 Now Azariah did that which was right in the lord and worshipped only God and hearkened not to the temptation of foreign religion.

15:5 Still, he did not remove the high places and the people of Judah continued to burn incense and offer worship to these heathen lords.

15:6 God began to get angry over these high places being left alone and punished Azariah's incompetence by striking him with leprosy.

15:7 All the other kings who did right in the eyes of the lord left these high places alone and avoided the wrath of God, but not Azariah. During Azariah's reign, the lord was bitchy.

15:8 Azariah died and was buried with his fathers in the city of David. Jotham the son of Azariah sat upon the throne after his father's death.

15:9 In the thirty eighth year of Azariah's reign did Zachariah the son of the second Jeroboam began to rule over Israel and he ruled for six months.

15:10 Are you keeping track of when these kings began to rule. Because I'm not. I really don't care, I'm just rewriting this damn book of lies and propaganda.

15:11 Now Zachariah was wicked in the eyes of God, but nobody really noticed, because most everyone was wicked in the eyes of God.

15:12 Those not wicked in the eyes of the lord, were seen as wicked in the eyes of man.

15:13 Shallum the son of Jabesh, servant to Zachariah, loathed his master and conspired against him.

15:14 When the time came, Shallum smote Zachariah in front of the congregation of Israel and the congregation crowned Shallum king.

15:15 For in Israel, if you kill the king, you take his throne and am not punished for killing the leader of your country.

15:16 Now Shallum reigned in the thirty ninth year of Azariah and he ruled over Israel for one month.

15:17 For Menahem the son of Gadi noticed that to become king, you merely had to kill the king; thus Menahem rose from Tirzah, killed Shallum and reigned in his stead.

15:18 King Menahem fucked a great many women and few would give him a son. This angered Menahem, who said, "I demand every wretched cunt I sleep with open themselves to me and give me a son."

15:19 Yet few women did and none ever questioned if, perhaps, the seed of Menahem was weak and not the soil he planted his seed within.

15:20 In anger, Menahem invaded those of Tirzah and cut from the womb every child which was within a woman, for the child was not his.

15:21 Menahem was a crazy fucker like that. God didn't mind.

15:22 Now Menahem ruled also in the thirty ninth year of Azariah's reign and he ruled over Israel for ten years.

15:23 Like so many kings, Menahem did that which was evil in the sight of the lord. And it wasn't the killing of the unborn babies in Tirzah which the lord thought evil.

15:24 Menahem allowed those in Israel to worship other lords and seek forth new religions. That was the evil thing which he did in the sight of the lord.

15:25 So the lord sent forth Pul the king of Assyria to rise against Israel, but Menahem bribed Pul with one thousand talents of silver, so that the Assyrians would not invade the lands of Samaria.

15:26 To afford this, Menahem enforced a great tax over all those of Israel; even the wealthy and the elders were forced to pay the tax.

15:27 And those in Israel said of Menahem, "The king who fights nations with shekels instead of swords."

15:28 Menahem died and his son Pekahiah ruled in his stead. It matters not who his mother was, but it was one of the blessed who opened her womb up the Menahem's seed.

15:29 Pekahiah did also wickedness in the sight of the lord and had religious tolerance. The lord would have him killed for this.

15:30 Pekah the son of Remaliah, a captain in the army, conspired against his king and he took his servants Argob and Arieh, and fifty soldiers and he killed the king in his bedchamber.

15:31 Pekah announced in the morning, "Behold, I am your new king of Israel," and nobody in Israel cared.

15:32 The people of Israel were used to new kings. Some even were unaware that Pekahiah was king and believed Menahem was still ruling.

15:33 In the fifty second year of Azariah's reign did Pekah the son of Remaliah began to rule over Israel and he ruled for twenty years.

15:34 Yes, Pekah did evil in the sight of the lord and didn't kill every damn person who worshipped a different lord or followed a different religion.

15:35 Wicked, wicked Pekah. How dare he show tolerance.

15:36 To punish Pekah for his evil tolerance, the lord gave strength to Tiglathpileser king of Assyria, who took his armies and invaded the lands of Ijon, Abelbethmaachah, Janoah, Kadesh, Hazor, Gilead, Galilee and Naphtali and took captive those people and enslaved them in his lands.

15:37 Somehow, it seems more believable the people who enslaved felt more punished than their damn king Pekah. God didn't take that into consideration.

15:38 Hoshea the son of Elah said of his king, "This man is incompetent, who would let the armies of Assyria come and claim our people.

15:39 What we need is a new king, a king who would protect his peoples."

15:40 Arrogantly, Hoshea believed himself to be that king. So, he killed Pekah and declared himself king. Again, nobody in Israel cared.

15:41 In the twentieth year of Jotham the son of Uzziah's reign did Hoshea begin to rule.

15:42 Uzziah began to rule over Judah in the second year of Pekah's reign, and he was twenty-five years old when he became king of Judah. His mother's name was Jerusha the daughter of Zadok.

15:43 Uzziah did that which was right in the eyes of the lord, though he also did not destroy those high places where people worshipped other lords.

15:44 Honestly, the kings forgot these places were even blasphemous. If they knew, they would have burned them to ash and killed all those who worshipped there.

15:45 During the days of Jotha, the lord sent forth against the tribe of Judah Rezin the king of Syria and Pekah the king of Israel.

15:46 God did this not as punishment against Jotham; no, the lord did this for amusement.

15:47 Jotham died and his son Ahaz reigned in his stead. Those of Judah didn't care. They too, were used to new kings coming and going.

16:1 In the seventeenth year of Pekah's reign did Ahaz the son of Jotham begin to rule over the lands of Judah.

16:2 Twenty years old was Ahaz when he began to rule and he was one evil, wicked, blasphemous cocksucker in the eyes of God.

16:3 Ahaz openly fucked men, worshipped other lords, worked on the sabbath, offered sacrifice and incense to heathen gods and cared not for the true lord of Israel.

16:4 When Ahaz was asked of the true lord, the king of Judah would say, "That divine dictator is a fucking tyrant. Any fool who reads his demands would know that.

16:5 Why waste my time devoted to a God that won't even give a damn for his people. Let us worship these heathen lords, who actually care for their worshippers.

16:6 Never has Baal sent pestilence upon his people. Not once did Ashtaroth open up the earth so that they may swallow her people.

16:7 The lord of Israel did and will likely do so again. So, fuck that bastard."

16:8 Now the lord loathed such ill words spoken against him, especially when those words be true.

16:9 Thus God took up Rezin the king of Syria and Remaliah king of Israel to war with Judah; though these nations warred against Ahaz, they could not overtake him.

16:10 At this time Rezin reclaimed the city of Elath, which was originally Syrian, and he drove out all those of Judah and Israel within the city.

16:11 So Ahaz sent messengers to Tiglathpileser king of Assyria, saying, "Let it be that those of Judah and those of Assyria fight as brothers. Come, fight with me against these Syrians, so that we shall win in glorious battle."

16:12 To ensure that Tiglathpileser would see they truly were like brothers, Ahaz sent as a gift the silver and gold which was found in the temple of the lord.

16:13 That angered God greatly, for now the lord had no bling in his crib.

16:14 The king of Assyria agreed that Judah were his nation's brethren and he sent his armies to Damascus and took it, enslaving all the people within and sending them to Kir.

16:15 Rezin the king of Syria was killed and his liver was sent to Azah as a gift.

16:16 Ahaz went to Damascus to visit Tiglathpileser and when he came to Damascus, he saw a great altar within the city.

16:17 The king of Judah ordered his priest Urijah to copy the altar, so that Ahaz could have such an altar within his house.

16:18 As Urijah copied plans of the altar, Azah offered on it great many burnt offerings, drink offerings, food offerings and blood offerings upon this altar. It was, of course, to one of many heathen lords Azah did this.

16:19 When the lord saw Azah offering sacrifices to heathens upon this altar, the lord came down and touched the brass of the altar, so that the brass melted and flowed to the ocean.

16:20 This happened before Urijah could finish copying the statue and Azah cried for never being able to see again the beautiful artwork which was the altar.

16:21 Eventually, like all people, Azah died and his son Hezekiah reigned in his stead.

17:1 In the twelfth year of Ahaz king of Judah did Hoshea the son of Elah begin to reign over Israel and he reigned for nine years.

17:2 Hoshea did that which was wicked in the eyes of the lord, but not as the previous kings before. Hoshea did not worship false gods nor offered incense at the high places.

17:3 No, the wickedness of Hoshea was in how he worshipped the lord. He did not separate the fat from the sacrifice whenever he gave to the lord an offering.

17:4 God rose up Shalmaneser king of Assyria against those of Israel and Hoshea clave to him, becoming his bitch.

17:5 Hoshea conspired against his master Shalmaneser and wished to kill him and become king of Assyria and Israel.

17:6 With all the kings under Assyria's oppression did Hoshea speak and said, "Let us rise up with our armies and kill this man who dare take our lands."

17:7 So, the Pharaoh heard these words of Hoshea and ratted him to Shalmaneser; Shalmaneser rewarded Pharaoh greatly with riches, wine and women.

17:8 The king of Assyria placed Hoshea in prison, took his armies, went to the lands of Israel and besieged it for three years.

17:9 In the ninth year of Hoshea did the Assyrians conquer all those of Israel and took the peoples as slaves, and placed them in Habor, Halah and the cities of Medes.

17:10 The lord looked down upon the earth and behold, he saw his chosen people cast out amongst the heathen land. The lord witnessed this and smiled.

17:11 For the lord did this, knowing the children of Israel broke his covenant and now God had no reason to cleave himself to these mere men.

17:12 God gathered his angels and said, "Behold, the children of Israel have sinned against their lord, who brought them out of the lands of Egypt and freed them from servitude under Pharaoh.

17:13 These fools walked in the path of the heathen and bowed down to their idols and their lords; they even bowed down to their kings, who were nothing but blood and flesh.

17:14 The lord did demand these heathens be cast aside and eliminated in holy genocide, so that the people of Israel give not into their temptation; and the people of Israel failed.

17:15 All the children of Israel built great altars, high places, images and groves in honour of their heathen lords and burned for them incense and did all that which the fucking heathens did.

17:16 Such blasphemy angered the lord, who told them not to worship idols, go whoring after heathen gods and bow down only to the one true God.

17:17 Yet even when I came down and said to them to stop their wickedness and follow the statutes and the commandments as was written in the laws of Moses, they did not hearken my words.

17:18 Let it be known that the children of Israel abandoned the covenant made with them since the days of Abraham and no longer have love for their true God. Instead, they call me a tyrant, an asshole, one who has abandoned them.

17:19 Look how they bow down to images of stone and brass. Even two golden calves they worship, as though it was these images which freed them from slavery.

17:20 They let their sons be faggots and their daughters necromancers, familiar with spirits, enchantments, divination and witchcraft.

17:21 Fuck all the peoples of Israel. Let them drown in their tears of misery. Judah shall only be saved, for they are not as wicked in the sight of their God."

17:22 So the lord rejected all the seed of Israel, condemned them and delivered them as slaves into the hands of the Assyrians.

17:23 Even when the angels said to their master, "Remember David and how he served you," the lord would say, "David is dead and cannot save these men from their fate."

17:24 Thus the lord erased Israel from his sight, as was told by the prophets. And the Assyrians came to live upon the promised land of the covenant.

17:25 The king of Assyria brought forth men from Babylon, Cuthah, Ava, Hamath, Sepharvaim and had them live in the cities of Samaria, saying, "Make these lands as bountiful and prosperous as the people of Israel did."

17:26 When these heathens dwelt in the lands of Israel, the lord grew angry at them, for they worshipped other lords and did not obey the laws, the statutes and the commandments of the one true God.

17:27 The lord wished to slaughter all those in these lands and the angels said, "How can you punish these men who don't know your ways?

17:28 Go down teach them to fear you and they will. Do not kill them merely because they are ignorant to your laws."

17:29 God grew angry and said, "These are my lands and I shall do whatever I want to whomever dwells within it whenever I damn well please!

17:30 Do not question your lord, lest ye be seen as wicked and cast down to join the forces of Satan."

17:31 So the lord sent to the lands of Samaria great lions, which slew and devoured all the heathens within the lands, for did not worship the lord.

17:32 Those people came to king Shalmaneser and said, "The lord of these lands has cursed us with great beasts who shall devour our very flesh."

17:33 The king of Assyria sought counsel with his elders and they decided to send a priest of Israel back to the lands of Samaria, so that he may teach them the ways of the lord.

17:34 Thus a priest was sent back to his homeland and lived in Bethel, teaching all those of the heathens the true path and ways of the lord.

17:35 Some of the Assyrians did as the priest demanded, which pleased the lord, for finally offerings were made, which created an intoxicating aroma for God.

17:36 Still, some men of Assyria hearkened not the words of the priest and worshipped their own lords, idols and graven images.

17:37 God didn't mind so much, since he did not create a covenant with the people of Assyria and could wipe them from existence without any consequence.

17:38 Those of Israel who became enslaved in the lands of the foreigners remembered the old laws of Moses and said, "We brought this curse upon ourselves.

17:39 We feared not the lord, who brought us out of Egypt and freed us from the tyranny of the Pharaoh.

17:40 Let it be that we shall not forget the covenant of our fathers, even in this land of the heathen. We shall fear our lord and follow all his laws and statutes."

17:41 Others of Israel disagreed and cursed the lord, and continued to worship other foreign lords.

18:1 It came to pass that on the third year of Hoshea son of Elah king of Israel that Hezekiah the son of Ahaz began to rule over that of Judah.

18:2 Twenty-five years old was he when he began to reign, which means his father Ahaz conceived him when Ahaz was only eleven years old. And the woman Ahaz was fucking at the age of eleven was Abi, the daughter of Zachariah.

18:3 Hezekiah was the lord's bitch and did that which was right in the lord. He tolerated no other heathen religion nor any opposing points of view.

18:4 Altars, high places, temples groves, Hezekiah burned them all to ashes and dust. Even the brass serpent which Moses built during the time in the desert did Hezekiah destroy, for some idiots in Judah began worshipping that serpent and called it lord Nehushtan.

18:5 By law Hezekiah made it so that none other but the lord God shall be worshipped in the lands of Judah. Those who worshipped the lords of heathens were executed in great number.

18:6 The lord loved Hezekiah and believed him to be like David. So, the lord made Judah prosper during the times of Hezekiah and they did not come under the oppression of the Assyrians.

18:7 In great hatred and bigotry of his ancestors, Hezekiah sent out great armies to destroy the people of Philistine. Even to Gaza did the armies of Judah slay all of the Philistines and captured their lands, extending the borders of Judah.

18:8 It was the fourth year of king Hezekiah when Shalmaneser the king of Assyria besieged Samaria; and three years later all the lands of Israel belonged to Shalmaneser.

18:9 The people of Judah saw the oppression of their brethren, and did not help them, saying, "They deserve that which these heathens brought upon them.

18:10 Our brothers of Israel worshipped false lords, tolerated heathen religion and took lust in brothels of men.

18:11 These bastards disgrace our lord and should be grateful that our God does not wipe them out in great plagues and fire."

18:12 In the fourteenth year of Hezekiah did Sennacherib the king of Assyria come to Judah and took from their lands great cities.

18:13 Hezekiah was furious and sent a message to Sennacherib, saying, "What matter is this, that you would come and take cities from my land?

18:14 Give me back my cities, lest the wrath of the lord come down upon you like a mighty hammer."

18:15 Not wanting to anger the lord of Judah, Sennacherib the king of Assyria sent to Hezekiah three hundred talents of silver and thirty talents of gold.

18:16 Hezekiah sent a message back, saying, "I thank you for these talents of silver and gold, but my cities have not been returned to me.

18:17 I don't care if you send me more gold, more silver, more goods. You could send me worth that equals ten times greater than all the treasures of the house of my lord and it would not matter.

18:18 Give me back my fucking cities, or the swords of the men of Judah shall pierce your hearts and the hearts of all your people."

18:19 So the king of Assyria sent forth to Jerusalem Tartan, Rabsaris and Rabshakeh from Lachish, who came with a great army. These men were sent forth so that they may negotiate for the cities which their master already took.

18:20 When these three men called forth for the king, there came out from the house Eliakim the son of Hilkiah, Shebna the scribe

THE BLASPHEMOUS BIBLE

and Joah the son of Asaph, the recorder of the deeds of Hezekiah.

18:21 Rabshakeh said to these men, "Go now and tell your master this. Our king doubts greatly that you could war with the armies of Assyria.

18:22 Your armies are weak and we have captured, enslaved, or allied with all other nations except yours.

18:23 Do you dare stand up against all those of the earth, or shall you give in and clave to the will of Sennacherib?

18:24 Our counsel is great and our nation stands with the nations of all. Even the Pharaoh stands with us and shall come to enslave you again if you do not give in to the demands of the people of Assyria.

18:25 Know this, you shall still be a nation, strong and proud. Your ways will not be altered and you can still worship this God of yours.

18:26 Even your borders shall be protected, for our master shall give to thee two thousand horses; all you need are the riders to mount them."

18:27 Eliakim said unto Rabshakeh, "Know this, our master will not give in to the demands of your king, and shall have his cities back.

18:28 Whether you give them to us or we take them by force, it matters not. God is on our side.

18:29 Know this, heathen bastard, that if you do not do as our king demands, that the men of your armies shall have their skulls bashed against the walls and your children shall feast upon their own shit and piss."

18:30 Rabshakeh said in a loud voice for all those of Judah to hear, "Your king shall entrap you to damnation. Hezekiah cannot deliver you from our hands.

18:31 Look at what my king has done to those of your brethren of Israel. They are now our slaves and it is our men who live in their lands and eat their crops.

18:32 You worship the same God, yet your lord did not protect your brethren, nor shall he protect you.

18:33 Rise up and overthrow Hezekiah and king Sennacherib shall show great mercy upon all the people of Judah.

18:34 You shall drink of your own waters, feast upon your own vines and eat from your own fig trees.

18:35 Hearken to the false words of your king and damnation shall befall your people."

18:36 But the people of Judah ignored the words of the Assyrian and told him in great and mighty voice, "Get raped!"

18:37 The men of Assyria left and Eliakim, Shebna and Joah went forth to Hezekiah, to tell them the words of the Assyrian heathens.

19:1 When Hezekiah heard the words of the men from Assyria, he started to panic and pulled out his hair and tore off his clothes.

19:2 He went to the house of the lord and began to weep, saying, "My nation is fucked, my nation is fucked.

19:3 Surely, we cannot survive the armies of Assyria. Our nation is fucked."

19:4 Eliakim came to his master and said, "There is still hope, for our nation still breathes and the lord is on our side.

19:5 There is a great prophet who lives in our lands. Let me go and I shall seek his counsel."

19:6 Hezekiah let him go and Eliakim went to the house of Isaiah the son of Amoz, a great prophet, but not as good as Elisha.

19:7 Nobody was as good as Elisha. Elisha was a fucking legend.

19:8 Eliakim went to Isaiah wearing sackcloth and said to the prophet, "Behold, my master is wrought with worry, for this is a day of rebuke, trouble and blasphemy.

19:9 A great nation wishes to enslave us all and we of the men of Judah have no means to fight him.

19:10 This nation spoke ill against our lord and blasphemed his name and offered us comfort if we surrender to his demands.

19:11 Tell us, O great prophet, the words of wisdom we yearn so long to here."

19:12 Isaiah inhaled mightily the great smoke from his pipe and said, "Worry not, child of God, for the lands of Judah shall be safe.

19:13 Our lord will not tolerate such blasphemy from a heathen king and shall cause it so that this heathen bastard shall die by the sword within his own lands."

19:14 When Rabshakey returned to Assyria, behold, he saw the people of Libnah warring against his men, a city which was taken from Judah by the Assyrians.

19:15 The Assyrians quickly won the war and those of Libnah were back in the hands of the heathens.

19:16 King Sennacherib sent a message to Hezekiah, saying, "Look how your great city rose against us and failed.

19:17 Know your lands shall follow the same fate.

19:18 Give up and surrender. Spare your men the humiliation of defeat and I shall spare them their lives."

19:19 When Hezekiah read this letter, he took it to the house of the lord and spread it before the ark and prayed saying, "Dear lord, God of Israel, who dwells within the two angels, know that you are God and God alone, ruler and master of heaven and earth.

19:20 These heathen spreads across the lands like a disease and threatens to give sickness and pestilence to the people of Judah.

19:21 I have cast all those of heathen lords into the fire and burned the worshippers who sought comfort in false gods.

19:22 I tore down the altars, destroyed the groves and made it so that only those in Judah shall worship you, lest they die by stoning.

19:23 I beg of you, O lord, save us from this heathen nation, so that the people of Judah shall survive and worship you."

19:24 Isaiah the son of Amoz came to Hezekiah and said, "Know that the lord has heard your prayer and shall answer you.

19:25 God hates this heathen king Sennacherib of Assyria and shall cause him to fall against the sword in his own lands; a most humiliating death it will be.

19:26 Thus sayeth the lord regarding Sennacherib; the virgin daughters of all those in heaven loathe him and laugh at him, even so that the daughters of Jerusalem mock his small penis.

19:27 They laugh at his blasphemy, for this man believes these words against God give him power. It shall be these words that anger our lord, so that the anger of the lord consumes him.

19:28 Know that the chariots of the lord shall come storming down the mountains and cut from Assyria his trees of cedar and his trees of fir and will enter the houses of his people, and rape their daughters and sons.

19:29 Their waters shall dry in the wells and the rivers and the peoples of Assyria shall drink their own piss in thirst.

19:30 Know that the lord loves Judah and those of the people of Judah.

19:31 This shall be a sign that in Judah this year the crops shall not be planted, for they shall grow according to their own and in the second year none shall plough nor plant, for they shall grow again.

19:32 Only upon the third year shall you need to sow your seeds and grow your crops, for the lord shall not farm them that year.

19:33 Do not worry about the city of Jerusalem; the lord shall protect it so that the king of Assyria shall not step beyond the gates, nor shoot an arrow at the walls.

19:34 God loves this city and shall defend it, for the sake of the people of Judah and for love for king David."

19:35 It came to pass that night an angel of the lord came to the camps of Assyria and smote of the Assyrians one hundred fourscore and five thousand men: and when these men awoke in the morning, they gazed down upon their bodies and realized they were dead.

- 228 -

19:36 The angels of the lord captured the very souls of these men and brought them to the brothels of heaven, where they are being raped even to this day.

19:37 Sennachering king of Assyria fled and returned home, dwelling in his house in Nineveh.

19:38 It came to pass, when Sennachering was burning incense for his god Nisroch that his sons Sharezer and Adrammelech came in, drunk and brandishing swords.

19:39 When Sennachering demanded his sons leave, they became angry and thrust in their father the blades which they held.

19:40 Sennachering lay dead, his body atop the burning incense given to his lord Nisroch. The lord found this very, very amusing.

19:41 When Adrammelech and Sharezer became sober, they realized what they had done and fled to the lands of Armenia. Esarhaddon the son of Sennachering became the new king of Assyria.

20:1 In those days Hezekiah the king of Judah was deathly ill. The prophet Isaiah the son of Amoz came to him and said, "You have served the will of the lord well and are now useless in the eyes of God.

20:2 Set your house and prepare your kin, for soon you shall die."

20:3 Hezekiah feared death greatly. He bowed to a wall and prayed to God, saying, "I beseech you, O lord, remember that which I have done in your name.

20:4 It was I who followed in the path of David and tore down the heathens and worshipped only you." And Hezekiah wept sorely, like the pussy he was.

20:5 It came to pass that when Isaiah was leaving the house of the king that the word of God came to him and said, "I've changed my mind in regard to Hezekiah; he may still prove useful.

20:6 Behold, the lord shall heal the king of Judah and give to him fifteen more years and protect this great city of Jerusalem from the Assyrians; for Hezekiah and David shall the lord do this."

20:7 So Isaiah took a lump of figs to the bedchamber of Hezekiah and spread it across the tumours and sores of Hezekiah's body and the king recovered.

20:8 Isaiah said, "This is the will of the lord, that you recover and live another fifteen years. May you serve him well."

20:9 Hezekiah wept for joy and said, "I feel as I did in my youth, but another fifteen years is a long time.

20:10 Give to me a sign that the lord wishes me to live another fifteen years."

20:11 It was then the lord ceased the world from moving and made it spin backwards, so that the very sun went backwards ten degrees.

20:12 Hezekiah worshipped the lord and praised his name, for surely this is a sign of God. The peoples of the earth, however, were pissed and did not know what time it was because the sundials were off ten degrees.

20:13 During Hezekiah's illness, Berodachbaladan the son of Baladan, king of Babylon, sent a great many gifts to the king of Judah, to bless Hezekiah and wish him well.

20:14 Hezekiah hearkened to the kindness of the Babylonians and invited them into his house.

20:15 Hezekiah showed them the great many things; the silver, the gold, the spices, the ointments, the oils and all the armour, weapons and treasures in the house of Judah.

20:16 There was nothing in the house of Judah which Hezekiah did not show off to those of Babylon.

20:17 When Isaiah saw the Babylonians in the house of Judah, he asked Hezekiah, "Who are these heathen bastards, who step foot in the lands of Judah?" and Hezekiah answered, "They are friends from a faraway land of Babylon."

20:18 Isaiah asked, "What did you show them of your house?" and Hezekiah replied, "Everything."

20:19 And Isaiah sighed and said to the king of Judah, "Listen to the words of your lord.

20:20 Heathen bastards are not to be trusted. These men of Babylon shall come and take all the treasures of your house and of Judah; nothing shall be left.

20:21 Your seed will be enslaved in the palace of Babylon and shall become eunuchs, forced to serve a heathen master."

20:22 Hezekiah asked, "Is this because I showed these peoples my house and treated them as guests?" and Isaiah answered, "Of course it is, you fool.

20:23 Trust no man other than your brother and curse the names of all heathens lest they curse you."

20:24 Fifteen years later, Hezekiah died and was buried in the sepulcher of his fathers. Manasseh his son became the new king of Judah.

21:1 Manasseh was twelve years old when he began to rule over Judah, and he reigned for fifty-five years. His mother's name was Hephzibah.

21:2 And he did that which was evil in the sight of the lord and lusted after the abominations of the heathens.

21:3 For he built up the high places which his father destroyed, reared up altars for Baal, made groves, constructed brothels for sodomites and placed in the temple of the lord idols carved of other false gods.

21:4 He had wizards and witches train his sons in magic, making them use enchantments, observe times, perform necromancy and deal with the spirits of the dead.

21:5 In every grove he set within a graven image of another god, so that the people of Judah shall come and worship these heathen lords and offer them incense.

21:6 There were those of Judah who hated their king Manasseh and said, "We shall not move our feet in the devotion to the one true lord; we shall follow always the laws as they were written by Moses."

21:7 In time, Manasseh seduced them to evil, saying, "Our lord does not share his powers, his knowledge, nor his wealth.

21:8 Look at my children, who can summon the dead, heal the sick with a mere touch and make fire appear from nothing.

21:9 Such a power would be forever denied to us if we obeyed the will of the selfish lord; let us worship gods who share their powers, so that we may become gods ourselves."

21:10 The lord spoke to the prophets, servants still loyal to God and he said, "Manasseh has doomed the lands of Judah with his wickedness and abominations, forcing the people of Judah to sin with idols and go whoring after other gods.

21:11 Behold, a great evil shall be sent to Judah so wicked that those who hear of it will have their ears tingle; such is the wickedness of the lord.

21:12 My hand shall be stretched over the lands of Judah and it shall reduce it to dust. The lord shall wipe Judah from the earth as a man wipes his ass after a shit.

21:13 Fuck their inheritance and fuck their covenant. Let them be delivered into the hands of their enemies, to be devoured like a predator devours prey."

21:14 A great rumour was spread out through the prophet, that Manasseh slew the blood of innocent babies and bathed in the blood of the young and infant.

21:15 Such rumours were false and started by God. Not even the lord is above spreading lies and propaganda.

21:16 When Manasseh died he was buried in his own garden beside his house. Amon his son reigned in his stead.

21:17 Amon was twenty-two years old when he first sat on the throne of Judah and he ruled for two years. His mother's name was Meshullemeth the daughter of Haruz of Jotbah.

21:18 Amon was a great wizard who did wickedness in the sight of the lord.

21:19 He predicted the future, made fire with words and sent forth rain upon the fields of the crops when they needed it; he did this with great magic and evil.

21:20 Other lords did Amon also serve and he burned incense upon the altars and the groves of heathen lords.

21:21 The servants of Amon wished to have his power of wizardry and believed that by eating of his flesh they shall gain his powers.

21:22 They killed their master and ate of his flesh. They gained no powers, though found that the flesh of kings was sweet and moist.

21:23 That which remained of Amon was buried in the garden of Uzza: his son Josiah reigned in his stead.

22:1 Josiah was eight years old when he began to reign and he ruled thirty-one years over the lands of Judah. The name of his mother was Jebidah the daughter of Adaiah of Boscath.

22:2 Josiah abandoned his witchcraft and did that which was good in the sight of the lord, burning heathens and destroying altars to false gods.

22:3 On the eighteenth year of Josiah's reign he rebuilt the temple of the lord, so that the cracks were repaired and breaches fixed.

22:4 The lord loved Josiah as he loved David and came to him, saying, "Know that the sins of your fathers shall be punished and all that of Judah shall burn in the flames of their wickedness.

22:5 They burn incense to other gods and praise not the name of their lord, who freed them and lead them away from Egypt and into the lands of the covenant.

22:6 But you, O Josiah, are truly a man of God. Let it be that the curses of the lord come after thine death and that your death be peaceful, so that you shall not know the wickedness which your God shall bring to your people."

22:7 The king of Judah gathered the priests dedicated to the lord and had them remove the blasphemous images of Baal, and burned them and burned the groves and high places, carrying the ashes to the river of Bethel.

22:8 Those of the priests who praised Baal, other false lords, the sun, the moon, the stars and the bodies of heaven did Josiah kill and took of their bodies and burned them upon the altars of the lord.

22:9 Even the blood of these idolatrous priests did he gather in vessels and boiled them, so that the lord may drink of the boiling blood and find the taste sweet.

22:10 Brothels of the sodomites were burned and those within were slain in the wilderness and their bones ground to powder and drunk by the priests of the one true lord.

22:11 Those of witchcraft and wizardry, even his brothers in necromancy, were burned alive in great fires, for the king said, "Let those who pass through the fires be burned by them."

22:12 Even the horses, which unholy priests dedicated to Baal, Josiah killed and cast them out in the wilderness so they may be eaten by predators and scavengers.

22:13 The kings of Judah which were wicked in the eyes of the lord were brought out of their sepulchers and ground to powder and burned on altars as offering unto the lord.

22:14 Josiah was one crazy motherfucker who loved to burn things and dedicate them to his God. The lord didn't mind, for he loved the smell of burning flesh and boiling blood.

22:15 Those tools of witchcraft, wizardry, enchanting and necromancy Josiah outlawed and he gathered all these tools and burned them in a great cauldron, so that the brass, the gold, the silver and the jewels intermingled.

22:16 Though Josiah did all these things, the lord was still angry with the people of Judah and wished to destroy them all.

22:17 The lord said, "I shall remove Judah as I removed Israel and

the city of Jerusalem will burn in the name of God."

22:18 Pharaoh Nechoh rose against his Assyrian oppressor and marched his men towards the river Euphrates. King Josiah joined the Pharaoh and was killed by the people of Assyria.

22:19 His death was not the peaceful descent to the grave which was promised to him by the lord.

22:20 Servants of Judah carried their king's body from Megiddo to Jerusalem, where he was buried in his own sepulcher. The people of Judah anointed Josiah's son Jehoahaz to be king.

22:21 Jehoahaz was twenty-three years when he became king of Judah and he ruled a mere three months. His mother was Hamutal the daughter of Jeremiah of Libnah

22:22 Jehoahaz loathed the lord for not keeping his promise of his father's peaceful death and Jehoahaz did that which was evil in the eyes of the lord; worshipping other lords, not offering sacrifice, taking part in heathen customs and allowing faggots to live.

22:23 Nechoh the Pharaoh captured Jehoahaz at Riblah in the lands of Hamath and threw him in the dungeons of Egypt.

22:24 Nechoh made Eliakim the son of Josiah king of Judah and changed his name to Jehoiakim and demanded he pay one hundred talents of silver and a talent of gold to the nation of Egypt.

22:25 Jehoiakim taxed all those of Judah so that the demands of Pharaoh be met; not a single man was left dry by this tax of their new king.

22:26 Jehoahaz, his brother, died in the dungeons of Egypt. Jehoiakim didn't care, nor did any other of the people of Judah.

22:27 Jehoiakim was twenty-five years old when he became king of Judah and he reigned eleven years in Jerusalem. His mother's name was Zebuday the daughter of Pedaiah of Rumah.

22:28 Like his brother before him, Jehoiakim did that which was evil in the sight of the lord and worshipped other gods, tolerated other religions and let heathens and sodomites live.

23:1 In these days did Nebuchadnezzer king of Babylon enslave Judah and Jehoiakim became his bitch for three years. In time, Jehoiakim rebelled against his heathen master.

23:2 The lord hated Jehoiakim and sent against him the armies of the Chaldees, the Syrians, the Moabites and the children of Ammon. The people of Judah didn't have a fucking chance.

23:3 God did this so that he may destroy all of Judah and wipe them from existence and no longer have any people to keep a covenant with.

23:4 Rumours did the lord spread through the foreign nations; rumours of the peoples of Judah bathing in the blood of children and feasting upon their flesh.

23:5 Nebuchadnezzer was a king who lusted for power and he took even the lands of Egypt and owned all of the river Euphrates.

23:6 Jehoiakim could no longer rely upon the armies of Pharaoh and he killed himself. His son, Jehoiachin, reigned in his stead.

23:7 Eighteen years old was Jehoiachin and he ruled Judah for three months. His mother's name was Nehushta the daughter of Elnathan of Jerusalem; a common harlot.

23:8 Following the common trend, Jehoiachin did that which was evil in the sight of God; worshipping heathen lords, allowing brothels of homosexuality, offering incense to false gods and practicing wizardry and witchcraft.

23:9 Jehoiachin's attitude was, "Fuck it, our God is going to kill us anyway. There is no point in pleasing the damn tyrant if he'll condemn us to damnation anyway."

23:10 The soldiers of Babylon came to Jerusalem and besieged the city.

23:11 Jehoiachin came out with his mother, his elders and his men of valour, to fight the heathen army.

23:12 They didn't stand a fucking chance.

23:13 In the eighth year of Nebuchadnezzer's reign, the king of Babylon captured Jerusalem and took all the treasures within the house of the lord and the house of the king.

23:14 Such as was prophesied by Isaiah, the prophet of the lord.

23:15 Isaiah was then known to the people of Judah as a cursed asshole.

23:16 The armies of Babylon enslaved Jehoiachin, his mother, his wives, his officers, his elders and all the men of valour in Jerusalem, and they took them to Babylon.

23:17 All men of might, craftsmen and smiths were enslaved to the Babylonians. Only the poor and the weak were left in Jerusalem; they were useless to the Babylonian empire.

23:18 Nebuchadnezzer made his uncle Mattaniah king of Judah and changed his name to Zedekiah, so that it sounded common among the people of Israel.

23:19 Zedekiah was twenty-one years old when he became king of Judah and he reigned eleven years over the people of Judah. His mother was Hamutal the daughter of Jeremiah of Libnah.

23:20 And Zedekiah did that which was evil in the sight of the lord. What did God expect. He was a fucking heathen.

23:21 An evil spirit overcame Zedekiah so that he became arrogant and rebelled against his nephew Nebuchadnezzer, king of Babylon.

24:1 On the ninth year of Zedekiah's reign, in the tenth month, of the tenth day of that month, did Nebuchadnezzer come to besiege Jerusalem, again. He and his armies pitched around the city and built great forts around Jerusalem.

24:2 And the city was besieged until the eleventh year of Zedekiah's reign.

24:3 A great famine spread throughout Jerusalem, for those who came out to harvest the crops were captured by the armies of Babylon.

24:4 The city was in panic and riots broke out. Zedekiah escaped between a crack in two walls and fled towards the plains.

24:5 And the armies of the Chaldees pursued Zedekiah, captured him and took him to the king of Babylon, who dwelt then at Riblah.

24:6 Nebuchadnezzer captured Jerusalem and had the sons of Zedekiah stand before their father. And he killed them, so that the blood spilled upon the face of Zedekiah.

24:7 Zedekiah was then bound in fetters, his eyes plucked and fed to the dogs and he was dragged by horse back to Babylon.

24:8 The king of Babylon laughed and said to his uncle, "Now it shall be that the death of your sons shall be the last thing you ever see."

24:9 And Zedekiah was never again invited to family reunions or dinners.

24:10 On the nineteenth year of Nebuchadnezzer's reign, on the fifth month, on the seventh day of the month, did Nebuzaradan, ruler of the armies of Babylon, come to Jerusalem.

24:11 And he burnt the temple of the lord, the king's house and every great house in Jerusalem; all of Jerusalem was set on fire.

24:12 The army of the Chaldees tore down the walls of Jerusalem and reduced them to rubble.

24:13 Those of the people of Judah stared at this destruction and wept, saying, "Surely we have done nothing to deserve such wrath."

24:14 Never have the people of Judah and Israel show such anger unto other nations; we are a merciful people."

24:15 Those people of Judah who were left alive were enslaved by the people of Babylon. Even the poor and lame were enslaved and they became vines men and concubines to people with cripple fetishes.

24:16 All which that was in the temple of the lord; the brass pillars, the brass bases, the pots, the spoons, the snuffers, the shovels, the firepans, the bowls and all vessels were carried away to Babylon.

24:17 The height of one pillar was eighteen cubits, with a brass chapiter the height of three cubits; around the chapiter was great wreath work and golden pomegranates the likes of which the people of Babylon had never seen.

24:18 Nebuzaradan took Seraiah the chief priest and Zephaniah the second priest and three lesser priests and said, "What is this, that your lord would demand such vain pieces of art, yet you claim him humble?"

24:19 Nebuzaradan took these five men and showed them to his king and he told Nebuchadnezzer of the many treasures in the temple of the lord.

24:20 The king of Babylon was disgusted by the lord of Israel and said, "Surely even you fools must see that your lord is a tyrant, who demanded great riches while your people suffered in poverty."

24:21 One of the lesser priests cursed Nebuchadnezzer and said, "We are in poverty because of your cruelty, Babylonian bitch."

24:22 Nebuchadnezzer withdrew his sword, and slew all five priests. Though these priests were devoted unto God, and did no evil, and obeyed the laws and commandments, God did nothing to help them.

24:23 Those few who were left in Judah, which the king of Babylon left, were ruled by Gedaliah the son of Ahikam.

24:24 When the people of the armies heard that Gedaliah became ruler of Judah, they came to him, believing that he would betray their king.

24:25 Gedaliah swore to them, "Fear not, for I am a loyal servant to the king of Babylon. Come, dwell in Judah and serve your master here."

24:26 It came to pass that on the seventh month, Ishmael the son of Nethaniah, of the seed royal, came with ten men and tortured Gedaliah in public until he died.

24:27 And all the people began to fear the Chaldees, of which was Ishmael.

24:28 On the thirty seventh year of the captivity of Jehoiachin, on the twelfth month, on the twenty seventh day of that month, did Evilmerodach king of Babylon notice the former king of Judah and lusted for him greatly.

24:29 Jehoiachin was released from prison and served in the brothel of the king of Babylon until his end of days.

24:30 There the king dressed him in great garments and fed him continually with fine foods and wine.

24:31 Even an allowance was given to Jehoiachin by Evilmerodach, for the sexual favours the former king of Judah performed for the king of Babylon.

I CHRONICLES

1:1 The Philistines fought bravely against Israel and those of Israel fled from the heathens and were slain in mount Gilboa.

1:2 These Philistines fought against Saul, king of Israel and slew his sons Jonathan, Abinadab and Malchishua.

1:3 As the battle wore on, the archers of Philistine hit Saul with an arrow, so that Saul was wounded and lost the will to live.

1:4 Saul said to his armourbearer, "Draw your sword and kill me, so that I do not die by the hands of these uncircumcised heathens." But the armourbearer would not, saying, "If I were to slay the king of Israel, surely God shall curse me and my house."

1:5 Saul cursed his armourbearer, saying, "If the lord curse does not curse you, I will." The king of Israel then took his own sword and fell upon it.

1:6 When the armourbearer saw that his king killed himself, he grew scared and killed himself as well, fearing the curse from his master and the curse from the lord.

1:7 Thus Saul and his three sons died together, in battle against the Philistines.

1:8 It came to pass that all those of Israel heard that their king and his sons lay dead, rotting upon the grounds of mount Gilboa and they fled against the Philistines, leaving their cities abandoned.

1:9 Those heathens which God hated greatly then dwelt in the cities of Israel.

1:10 As the Philistines came to loot the bodies of the dead, behold, they saw Saul and his sons lying on the ground.

1:11 They stripped his armour and sent it to the many temples of their lords, in blessing for the victory against Israel.

1:12 Saul's head was placed atop a pike and put in the temple of Dagon, beside his armour. The corpses of his sons were nailed against the walls of the cities.

1:13 When those of Jabeshgilead heard what the heathens did to their masters, they arose valiant men, who went and brought back to Israel the bodies of the king and his sons.

1:14 Each valiant man lied intimately with the bodies of their king and princes, fulfilling their lust upon the bodies of the dead men.

1:15 They then buried these men under an oak tree in Jabesh and fasted for seven days.

1:16 Thus Saul died by the hands of the lord for not keeping the laws of Moses and for asking counsel of a necromancer and a witch.

1:17 The lord hated Saul so much that he killed him and gave the kingdom of Israel over to the son of Jesse.

2:1 All of Israel gathered to David at Hebron, saying, "Behold, you are a great man of our flesh and blood; you are a person of Israel.

2:2 Even when that fool Saul was king, it was you who led the armies into victory, who saved Israel from the hands of the heathens and who conquered the lands of foreign nations.

2:3 Come and be our king. Feed us, clothe us, care for us and we shall call you master."

2:4 David lusted greatly for power and agreed to be king of Israel. The elders came and anointed David the new king of Israel in the city of Hebron.

2:5 Thus the words of Samuel came true and the shepherd boy from the seed of Jesse became king.

2:6 David and his armies went to Jebus, which was inhabited by Jebusites.

2:7 The inhabitants of Jebus would not allow David nor his men in. So, David said to his captains, "Whosoever kills the first person in this city, shall be chief of all armies of Israel."

2:8 So Joab the son of Zeruiah went into the city and was the first to kill a man within. That man was a cripple, which the city was full of; Jebus was known as the City of the Lame.

2:9 King David dwelt in the city of Jebus, which was then changed to the City of David and later changed to Jerusalem. The city then became known as the City of Many Names.

2:10 David rebuilt the city with great defences and forts round about. Even unto Millo did the walls reach. It was Joab who supervised the repair of the city.

2:11 So David lived in the castle and his power became greater and greater, for the lord of all lords blessed David.

2:12 The lord loved David for David did that which was right in the eyes of God, yet evil in the eyes of men.

2:13 These are the chief of the mighty men who followed David, who strengthened the kingdom of Israel and who stood by their king.

2:14 Jashobeam the Hachmonite, ruler of the captains, who once pierced three hundred Philistine bastards with his spear at the same time.

2:15 It was a very long spear and the Philistines were very thin.

2:16 Eleazar the son of Dodo, an Ahohite, who was known as one of the three mightiest.

2:17 He was with David at Pasdammin, where the Philistines numbered greatly against the nation of Israel.

2:18 Though the armies of Israel fled, both David and Eleazar hid within a field of barley and with the spirit of the lord they slaughtered each cursed heathen.

2:19 Now three of the thirty captains of David were with him in the cave Adullam; and the armies of Philistine were encamped in the valley of Rephaim.

2:20 The Philistines garrisoned the city of Bethlehem, which had a well with the freshest water.

2:21 David longed greatly for the water of Bethlehem and said to his men, "Blessed be he who brings me a drink from the well of Bethlehem."

2:22 And the three captains did as David wished. They broke through the lines of the Philistines and gathered water for their king from the well of Bethlehem.

2:23 On their return they were attacked, but the three men had the lord with them and they fought valiantly against the heathens, with the spirit of the lord.

2:24 All this for a damn drink of water from a damned well from Bethlehem.

2:25 When they brought David the jug of water, David took a drink and spat out the water, saying, "There is a bug in the jar!"

2:26 The king of Israel then spilled the water on the ground, which angered these three captains greatly.

2:27 The three captains said to one another, "Our master is surely an ungrateful fool, who knows not the dangers we went through to get his damn water."

2:28 Still, they remained loyal to David, for they knew the lord loved David and feared a curse from God if they went against their master.

2:29 Abishai the son of Joab was one chief of the three. He also had a long spear and skewered three hundred skinny Philistines on it at once.

2:30 Though he was chief of the three and more honourable, he was not known as one of the three men of valour.

2:31 Benaiah the son of Jehoiada, the son of a valiant man of Kabzeel, had done many things for the honour of his lord. He killed two lion-like men of Moab and also killed a lion stuck in a pit of snow.

2:32 When the people of Israel were at peace with those of Egypt, Benaiah killed an Egyptian man with his own spear.

2:33 This Egyptian was five cubits high and had a spear like that of the trunk of a tree. Benaiah asked to show the spear and the Egyptian handed it to him, believing him a friend.

2:34 Benaiah thrust the spear through the throat of the Egyptian, then ran away so that none would know it was he who murdered the Egyptian.

2:35 These are the names of the valiant men of the armies of Israel during the time of David. Don't bother reading it, it's a long and useless list.

2:36 Asahel the brother of Joab, Elhanan the son of Dodo from

Bethlehem,

2:37 Shammoth the Harorite, Helez the Pelonite,

2:38 Ira the son of Ikkesh the Tekoite, Abiezer the Antothite,

2:39 Sibbecai the Hushathite, Ilai the Ahohite,

2:40 Maharai the Netophathite, Heled the son of Baanah the Netophathite,

2:41 Ithai the son of Ribai of Gibeah, Benaiah Pirathonite,

2:43 You might as well stop reading the list now.

2:44 Hurai of the brooks of Gaash, Abiel the Arbathite,

2:45 Azmaveth the Baharumite, Eliahba the Shaalbonite,

2:46 All the sons of Hashem the Gizonite, Jonathan the son of Shage the Hararite,

2:47 Ahiam the son of Sacar the Hararite, Eliphal the son of Ur,

2:48 Hepher the Mecherathite, Ahijah the Pelonite,

2:49 Hezrom the Carmelite, Naarai the son of Ezbai,

2:50 Joel the brother of Naathan, Mibhar the son of Haggeri,

2:51 Zelek the Ammonite, Nahari the Berothite, the armourbearer of Joab the son of Zeruiah,

2:52 Ira the Ithrite, Gareb the Ithrite,

2:53 You're still reading. Well, be glad it's almost over.

2:54 Uriah the Hittite, Zabad the son of Ahlai,

2:55 Adina the son of Shiza the Reubenite, a captain of the Reubenites and thirty with him,

2:56 Hanan the son of Maachah, Joshaphat the Mithnite,

2:57 Uzzia the Ashterathite, Shama and Jehiel the sons of Hothan the Aroerite,

2:58 Jediael the son of Shimri and his brother Joha the Tizite,

2:59 Eliel the Mahavite, Jeribai and Joshaviah the sons of Elnaam, Ithmah the Moabite,

2:60 Eliel (a different one), Obed and Jasiel the Mesobaite.

2:61 These men were known as the men of valour, ruled by David and were honoured among all those of Israel.

2:62 These men also each slept with their master in unholy lust and disappointed their king greatly, for none could match the pleasure of Jonathan the son of Saul.

3:1 These are the men who came to help David at Ziklag, where he hid himself from the wrath and the anger of Saul the son of Kish, king of Israel.; all the thirty men of valour were with David.

3:2 They were armed with bows and trained to shoot with both the right and the left hand. Even of the tribe of Benjamin, which was the tribe of Saul, did men come to fight with David.

3:3 The chief was Ahiezer, then Joash, the sons of Shemaah the Gibeathite, Jeziel and Pelet the sons of Azmaveth, Berachah, Jehu the Antothite,

3:4 Ismaiah the Gibeonite, Jeremiah, Jahaziel, Johanan, Josabad the Gederathite,

3:5 And a bunch of other men nobody gives a damn about.

3:6 It's yet another long and boring list.

3:7 Now, the list of the Gadites who were with David, they are important. Gadites were men of war and beasts, who could handle shield and buckler, which had faces like that of lions and could run as fast as the deer.

3:8 Of these beastly men of Gadites there were Ezer, Obadiah, Eliah,

3:9 Mishmannah, Jeremiah,

3:10 Attai, Eliel, Johanan,

3:11 Elzabad, yet another Jeremiah and Machbannai.

3:12 These eleven men were the sons of Gad, a mighty warrior

whose father was a giant and mother was a lion.

3:13 These men came over the river Jordan when the banks overflowed and put fear in the people of the valleys toward the east and the west.

3:14 Of the tribes of Israel both Benjamin and Judah sided with David.

3:15 David went out to meet these tribes and said, "If you come peacefully to join me and aid me, then may the lord bless you, your tribe and all within it.

3:16 Betray me to your king and you shall die horribly by the hands of our lord.

3:17 Your genitals shall become encrusted with a terrible fiery puss; your daughters will be whores to the heathens and your sons shall toil in the fields of the Philistines who enslaved them."

3:18 Then the spirit of the lord came over Amasai, who spoke for both tribes, who said, "We have come to join you and bless you, O David the son of Jesse.

3:19 Peace be to you and peace be to your men. Fuck the king of Israel, damnation to our master Saul; let it be that David shall be our king." And David made them soldiers of his army.

3:20 Some of these men were cowards and abandoned him at Manasseh when David went to fight against the Philistines. They believed the Philistine propaganda that those of David shall fall with Saul on the fields of Manasseh.

3:21 As David went to Ziklag, the men who abandoned him at Manasseh were Adnah, Jozabad, Jediael, Micheal, Jozabad, Elihu and Zilthai.

3:22 David cursed them all so that their daughters became whores and their sons became lepers, cripples and sodomites.

3:23 It mattered not, for the armies of David were strong, as strong as the armies of God. They killed all the rovers and bandits who came in their way.

3:24 These are the numbers of the bands who came with David to Hebron, so that they shall anoint him king over Israel against Saul, according to the word of the lord.

3:25 Of the children of Judah there were six thousand eight hundred men, armed with spear and shields, trained in the bloodshed of war.

3:26 Of the children of Simeon there were seven thousand men, mighty men of valour.

3:27 Of the children of Levi four thousand and six hundred men. They were fodder for the enemies; distractions while the other tribes killed their enemies.

3:28 Jehoiada was the leader of the seed of Aaron, priest during the time of Moses. Of these men, there were three thousand and seven hundred, all blessed by the lord.

3:29 Zadok, a mighty man of valour, took with David twenty-two of his sons; only nine survived.

3:30 Of the children of Benjamin, which is the tribe of Saul, three thousand. Saul cursed these brothers of his, for they betrayed their own kin.

3:31 Of the children of Ephraim twenty thousand eight hundred men on horseback.

3:32 Of the tribe of Manasseh eighteen thousand, which easily replaced those cowardly men who abandoned David on the fields of Manasseh.

3:33 Of the children of Issachar, only two hundred. Fuck Issachar, they are a cowardly tribe.

3:34 Of the tribe of Zebulun fifty thousand men, all trained in the sword and the mace; experts of war all of them.

3:35 Of Naphtali one thirty-one thousand and seven hundred men, each with a spear made of fine silver and gold.

3:36 Of the Danites twenty-eight thousand and six hundred men, all of them useless in battle.

3:37 Of the tribe of Asher forty thousand men, trained in martial arts, stealth and assassination.

3:38 On the other side of the Jordan were the tribes of Gad and Reuben, who came with sixty thousand men each, so that the total number was one hundred and twenty thousand men from across the Jordan.

3:39 All these men called David the true king of Israel, betraying Saul.

3:40 For three days they were with David, eating and drinking the feast which David had prepared for them.

3:41 And every tribe brought with them great foods and liquors; breads, figs, cakes, dates, wines, ale, beer, liquor, oil, oxen, goats, sheep and concubines; for three days, all those loyal to David did nothing but eat, drink and fuck.

3:42 A few of them threw up as well. It was quite the party.

4:1 David consulted with the captains and the elders of Israel, so that they may know how to better please the lord and gain his blessing.

4:2 David said to these men, "Let us gather the tribe of Levi, the slaves of God and bring them to my city. If the slaves of the lord dwell within Jerusalem, surely the lord shall bless those within.

4:3 Have them bring forth the ark, the precious box where our lord dwells. It shall be that both God and his slaves live within our city."

4:4 The captains and elders agreed, fearing that if they did not, David would kill them.

4:5 So David gathered all those of Israel together, from Shihor even to Egypt, so that they may witness the ark be brought to Jerusalem.

4:6 And David went forth to Kirjathjearim, which belonged to the tribe of Judah, so that they shall bring back the ark of the covenant.

4:7 They built a new cart for the ark to be carried out of the house of Abinadab: and Uzza and Ahio drove the cart.

4:8 As the ark was carried forth, David and all those of Israel danced around it, singing, playing trumpets and cymbals and timbrels and sacrificing many oxen, sheep and goats in glory to the lord.

4:9 When they sacrificed the many oxen, behold, a man put his blade to the oxen carrying the cart, causing the beast to scare and stumble.

4:10 The ark of God stumbled and fell upon the arm of Uzza, cursing him.

4:11 The great finger of the lord came down and touched Uzza, for the lord God was furious with Uzza for having touched his ark, though it was by accident.

4:12 Behold, the body of Uzza turned to ashes and dust, so that only the bones remained. David named the place where Uzza died Perezuzza, in honour to Uzza.

4:13 David was afraid to carry the ark, saying, "If another man touches the ark, surely the lord shall slay them as well."

4:14 So David did not bring back the ark to his city, but left it in the house of Obededom the Gittite.

4:15 Three months did the ark stay in the house of Obededom and the lord blessed Obededom with great crops and fertile women.

5:1 Hiram the king of Tyre loved David and sent to him cedars, masons and carpenters so that the king of Israel shall build a great and mighty house.

5:2 When David saw that the lord allowed him to build a great palace, he knew in his heart that the lord truly chose for him to be king and bring the nation of Israel to greatness.

5:3 Though David was loved by the lord, he held in his heart a great secret; David was a homosexual, who lusted for the flesh of men and yearned greatly for the embrace of Jonathan, the son of Saul.

5:4 To hide his queer lust, David took to himself more wives and slept with them so that these women shall give him many daughters and sons.

5:5 These are the names of the sons which David had in Jerusalem. It's a short list and does not include the daughters. Even in Chronicles, the bible does not care for women.

5:6 Shammua, Shobab, Nathan, Solomon,

5:7 Ibhar, Elishua, Elpalet,

5:8 Nogag, Nepheg, Japhia,

5:9 Elishama, Beeladia and Eliphalet.

5:10 When the Philistines heard that David was king of Israel, they came to Israel so that they may congratulate David, and bring peace between the two nations.

5:11 God would not allow that, for the lord wishes deeply for war. It provides him entertainment, much like our television nowadays.

5:12 As the Philistines rested in the valley of Rephraim, the lord came to David and said, "Take your armies and fight these heathens. The lord shall deliver them into your hands, so that you may slay them greatly."

5:13 So David went to Baalperazim and smote the Philistines there. It was easy, considering that the Philistines came in peace and were unarmed.

5:14 As the Philistines left the massacre being done upon them by the Israelites, they left behind their idols; false images of false gods.

5:15 David ordered these idols be burned and the ashes mixed with water, forcing the priests of Philistine to drink the mixture of water and ash.

5:16 As the Philistines broke up within the valley of Rephraim, the lord came down to David again, and said "These heathens know now your intentions and men have brought them arms so that they may fight you.

5:17 Do not face them, but sneak behind them and hide in the mulberry trees. When y hear a sound from atop the mulberry trees, it shall be a sign from the lord.

5:18 It is then you shall attack these uncircumcised bastards and the lord shall deliver them in your hands."

5:19 David did as the lord demanded and smote the Philistines from Gibeon even unto Gazer.

5:20 And the infamy of David went throughout all the heathen nations; and they feared the blood-lust and merciless king of Israel.

6:1 David built himself a mighty house in his city, but pitched only a tent for the ark of the covenant, which was still in the house of Obededom.

6:2 The king of Israel wished to have the ark brought to his city and said, "Only the Levites shall carry the ark. As slaves of the lord, they are blessed to touch the sacred object."

6:3 So David brought all of Israel together in Jerusalem, so that they may witness the ark being brought into the city.

6:4 A few children of Israel did not come, saying, "The last time we were brought here, the ark was left behind at some guy's house."

6:5 David cursed these people with impotence and empty wombs.

6:6 The priests and the Levites were gathered together and David said to them, "Sanctify yourselves, you and your brethren, for today you shall carry the ark of the lord into my city."

6:7 Some complained, saying, "The ark is too heavy;" or, "I wish not to be turned to ash by God if I accidentally touch the sacred object."

6:8 Those that complained, David killed with the sword. There were no complaints afterwards.

6:9 These people came to the house of Obededom, placed the ark on a cart and carried it back to Jerusalem, dancing, singing and offering sacrifices all the way.

6:10 Great many oxen were slain upon the roads in glory to God, so much so that none could not help but step in the blood of the beasts.

6:11 This pleased the lord greatly; the ark being carried by men covered in blood was like hardcore porn for God.

6:12 The sound of trumpets, cymbals, timbrels and singing could be heard in Jerusalem as the ark was being brought forth to the city and all within gazed out to see the ark being carried.

6:13 Behold, Michal the daughter of Saul and wife of David saw her husband, stripping off his clothes and dancing drunk in celebration of the ark coming within his city.

6:14 Michal was furious with David and said to him, "Have you no shame, that you would show your loins to all those of Jerusalem?

6:15 Even the common whores in the cheapest of brothels gazed at your vessel which contains your seed."

6:16 David beat Michal and said, "I am the fucking king of Israel, chosen by the lord and blessed by God.

6:17 I can show my penis to all if I so desire, including the cheapest and filthiest of whores."

6:18 David then gathered the prostitutes and concubines in Jerusalem and had sex with them in front of Michal, saying, "Look, they have seen my loins and now know the pleasure of them."

6:19 Michal cried. David laughed. The prostitutes smiled, for they were well paid for only a few minutes of work.

7:1 They brought the ark into the city of Jerusalem and placed it in the tent which David pitched for it. Sacrifices and offerings were made all day, in celebration of the ark being brought into the city.

7:2 When David was done with the slaughtering of animals in glory to his God, he blessed all the children of Israel who came to witness the glorious event.

7:3 He gave to everyone in Israel, both man and woman, a loaf of bread, a piece of flesh, a flagon of wine and a prostitute.

7:4 Even the children were given the wine and the prostitutes, though they had no idea what to do with the naked women who kept touching them.

7:5 Those that did not come to Jerusalem to witness the blessed event heard of the gifts which David was giving to his people and came, hoping to be blessed with food, wine and women.

7:6 David gave them mouldy bread, rotting mutton, a jar of sour grapes and a fat whore and cursed them for not coming to see the ark being brought into Jerusalem.

7:7 The king of Israel then appointed the Levites to care for the ark and minister to the lord's demands and praise the name of God.

7:8 Asaph, Zechariah, Jeiel, Shemiramoth, Jehiel, Mattithiah, Eliab, Benaiah and Obededom were ordered to constantly play trumpets, cymbals and harps in front of the ark, so that the lord will be blessed constantly with music.

7:9 God quickly grew tired of the noise and blessed the ark of the covenant to block out the constant noise of the priests who would not shut up with their music.

7:10 David then stood in front of the ark and gave a psalm to the ark in front of all the children of Israel, blessing them, saying, "Give thanks to the lord, lest he think you forgot his name and shall curse thee with a mighty curse.

7:11 Sing to him, bless him with psalms and take joy in his wondrous works.

7:12 Give glory to his name, for he did free us from the servitude of Pharaoh; a thing our lord will never let you forget.

7:13 Seek the lord and his strength; seek his face continually.

7:14 Remember the marvels, the wonders and the glories of our lord, so that he shall not marvel you with plagues and have you wonder why you and your brethren be dying.

7:15 He is the lord our God, who rules over all the earth with a fist of fire and flame.

7:16 Be mindful of his laws and covenants. Obey them, or he shall curse all your seed for one thousand generations, causing them much pain and pestilence.

7:17 Our covenant is everlasting and the lord shall never break it; it shall be the children of Israel who doom themselves if they break the laws of God.

7:18 Show mercy to your brethren and slay all the heathens and those whose foreskin remain on their loins.

7:19 God hates the foreskin and demands it be removed and those who have it destroyed.

7:20 Great is the power of our lord; he is the true lord of all lords and shall demand your undying devotion and faith.

7:21 Seek not idols nor heathen gods. They are not the true lord and our God shall curse those who go whoring after false images and lords.

7:22 Give to the lord his tithe and sacrifice; fear him greatly, for he can bring unto you great suffering and pain.

7:23 Thank the lord for his mercy, as our lord is a compassionate lord of kindness, tolerance and understanding.

7:24 Bless the lord for his wrath; he shall slay all those who come against us in great fire, leaving none of our enemies on the face of the earth.

7:25 The lord is our salvation. Blessed be the name of the lord."

7:26 Those of the children of Israel then said, "Amen," and returned unto their houses drunk, their bellies full and scared shitless of the curse which their lord may bring upon them.

8:1 It came to pass that David sat in his house made of finest timber, he said to Nathan the prophet, "Look at this. I dwell in a house of cedar, yet the ark is covered only in cloth."

8:2 Nathan warned David, "To do such a thing may anger the lord, for our God is greater than you and deserves better than a tent of leather and cloth."

8:3 That night, the spirit of the lord came to Nathan in a dream and said, "The lord cares not if he lives within a tent and David lives in a house of cedar.

8:4 Do not have the king of Israel build a house for the lord God; the lord has not dwelt in a house since the times of Egypt, but have gone from tent to tent and tabernacle to tabernacle.

8:5 Never have I asked my people to build me a house of cedar, nor a temple, nor any building so that I may dwell in. To do so would limit me to one place and the lord wishes to be everywhere.

8:6 Tell your king that the lord did make a shepherd king so that he may rule over the children of Israel as sheep. David is the shepherd and all of Israel his flock.

8:7 The lord shall be with David always and shall cut off all the enemies of Israel and make Israel a nation stronger than all.

8:8 Your lord God shall plant Israel within the soil of the earth and there the people of Israel shall stay. No nation shall move them; all of Israel shall be gathered as one.

8:9 May the seed of David rule over Israel for generations and it shall be the seed of David which builds to the lord a great and mighty temple, so that all may gather within and witness the glory and power of the lord.

8:10 Never will Israel suffer; they shall know only wealth and happiness.

8:11 Blessed be Israel, for they are the lord's people. Never shall they be cursed, invaded by heathens, or cast out into the foreign nations as slaves and concubines."

8:12 The lord, of course, was lying. God does that. It's not as if the ten commandments apply to him.

8:13 It also comforts the people of Israel and fools them to believing their God is truly merciful. He is not.

8:14 Nathan rushed to David and told him all the words and the lies of the lord.

8:15 David came to the tent where the ark was held and said, "Blessed be the name of the lord, who placed this mere shepherd to rule over his people.

8:16 There is none other like you, O lord, who rules with great love and mercy.

8:17 May I, your humble servant David, serve you and may my seed serve you for all generations.

8:18 Let it be that Israel shall be the only nation on earth; we shall enslave and destroy all heathen people who believe in false lords and carved idols.

8:19 Have it be that the lord of mercy brings upon great wrath on all non-believers and burn them alive until the end of days and beyond.

8:20 Israel shall rule forever in glory and grace, while our soil be stained endlessly by the blood of heathens and the uncircumcised.

8:21 Blessed be our God, blessed be the name of the lord."

9:1 David was a man like God and wished to destroy all but his people from the earth. He slew the Philistines, though he once dwelt with them, and took from these heathens the lands of Gath and all her villages.

9:2 Afterwards, he conquered the lands of Moab, so that the Moabites feared the wrath of Israel and became slaves to them.

9:3 David wished to expand the borders of Israel further and smote Hadarezer king of Zobah, so that the nation of Israel will have dominion on the river Euphrates.

9:4 The king of Israel took from Hadarezer one thousand chariots and slew seven thousand horsemen and twenty thousand footmen.

9:5 David loathed also the beasts of the heathens and shattered the legs of all but one hundred of the heathen horses which drove the chariots.

9:6 All the soldiers of Israel bathed in the blood of the slain and became drunk upon it. They lusted for death as the lord lusts for death.

9:7 When the Syrians of Damascus heard of the travesties done to Hadarezer, they brought with them their armies so that they might avenge their fallen friend.

9:8 The armies of Israel slaughtered twenty-two thousand of them and burned their bodies as great sacrifice unto their God.

9:9 David then put barriers around Syriadamascus and starved the peoples within, until they surrendered to Israel and became their slaves.

9:10 The lord was pleased with the slaying and enslavement done by his peoples and blessed them greatly and their king greatly.

9:11 Soldiers of Hadarezer king of Zobah carried with them shields of gold, which David looted and brought to Jerusalem and placed beside the ark of the lord.

9:12 All the cities of Hadarezer, from Tibhath even to Chun, were enslaved by the nation of Israel and brought to David gifts of silver, gold and brass.

9:13 It was the brass of the people of Zobah which Solomon used to build the mighty pillars and the sea of brass within his house.

9:14 When Tou king of Hamath heard that David slaughtered Hadarezer and his people, he sent forth to Jerusalem his son Hadoram, to congratulate David and bless the people of Israel.

9:15 Tou was long at war with Hadarezer and loathed the peoples of Zobah. When David slew his enemy, he knew that the people of Israel would make a great ally.

9:16 On Hadoram's return, Tou asked of his son, "What do the people of Israel wish from us?"

9:17 His son answered, "They demand we give them all the gold, the silver and the brass we have within our nation, lest they come after us and enslave and destroy us as they did Hadarezer."

9:18 Tou quickly sent gold to David and whenever precious metals and stones were found within his nation, they were sent to Israel.

9:19 Through fear and intimidation David began to rule not just over Israel, but over all the heathen nations, so that the children of Edom, Moab, Ammon, Amalek and the Philistines gave Israel their wealth and did as David commanded of them.\

9:20 Some in Edom rebelled and said they would rather die free than be ruled by a tyrant king ruled over a tyrant lord.

9:21 Abishai slew them all within the valley of salt. Eighteen thousand Edomites, which David hung upon the trees of Edom to show those what happened to people who go against Israel.

9:22 Edom quickly obeyed the laws of Israel and gave to David all the wealth of their nation.

9:23 David reigned over all of Israel and executed judgment and justice among his people according to the laws of Moses.

9:24 Joab the son of Zeruiah was ruler over the armies and Jehoshaphat the son of Ahilud recorded the greatness of David and Israel.

9:25 Jehoshaphat was a great recorder, who would conveniently leave out that which might make Israel look wicked, evil, or weak.

9:26 Zadok the son of Ahitub and Abimelech the son of Abiather were priests and Shavsha was the holy scribe.

9:27 Benaiah the son of Jehoiada ruled over all those enslaved by Israel and the sons of David ruled over small lands within the twelve tribes of Israel.

10:1 It came to pass that Nahash the king of the children of Ammon died and his son reigned in his stead.

10:2 David said, "I shall send messengers to Hanun the son of Nahash, who claim that they come to offer my sympathies to his father, for he was a good man who showed kindness unto the nation of Israel.

10:3 These men will secretly spy upon the lands of Ammon and tell me their weaknesses and how to best conquer them."

10:4 Hanun was not fooled by David's scheme and he shaved off all the hair of the spies of David and sent them home wearing the garments of a cheap whore.

10:5 When David saw these men, he laughed and said, "You look like women, hairless and with smooth bums which are shown intoxicatingly with those garments.

10:6 Go, dwell in Jericho, for your presence makes me laugh. Return to me when you look like men."

10:7 David then realized that the children of Ammon insulted him and David wished to conquer and enslave them all.

10:8 When Hanun knew David wished to destroy him, he sent out one thousand talents of silver so that he may hire mercenaries from Mesopotamia, Syriamaachah and Zobah.

10:9 Thirty-two thousand mercenaries with chariots did Hanun buy and gathered with him also were the king of Maachah and his armies, who wished to see Israel destroyed.

10:10 These men gathered themselves from their cities and marched towards the lands of Israel.

10:11 When David heard of this, he sent forth Joab and his men to deal with these men of nuisance.

10:12 Joab saw the peoples and behold, they were great in number and overpowered even the armies of Israel.

10:13 Joab chose for him the best and most valiant soldiers, so that they shall fight the mercenaries of Syria. The rest were ruled under Abishai, Joab's brother and fought against the children of Ammon.

10:14 The two men said to one another, "If we do well, then we shall come and aid thee when our enemies lay dead beneath our feet and their blood soak upon our sandals.

10:15 If you or I require aid, let us call forth and we shall come and save each other like the brothers we are.

10:16 Let it be that the lord blesses us both and we kill each and every one of these god damned foreskin wearing bastards of evil."

10:17 When the army of Joab marched forth towards the people of Syria, the spirit of the lord cursed the eyes of the heathens so that they saw coming towards them great dragons, unicorns and beasts the size of mountains.

10:18 They fled in fear from the armies of Joab and when the children of Ammon saw the mighty Syrians fleeing, they fled from the armies of Abishai, believing them stronger than they.

10:19 The children of Ammon fled and barricaded themselves into the city and those of Abishai laughed at them and called them cowards and lickers of an oxen's scrotum.

10:20 Afterwards, both the armies of Abishai and Joab left to Jerusalem, laughing at their cowardly enemies and making bets of which army made their enemies shit their pants more.

10:21 When the mercenaries of Syria saw that the army of Israel left, they sent forth messengers that passed over the Jordan, calling for reinforcements.

10:22 Shophach, leader of the armies of king Hadarezer came forth with his army, all men of valour and might, so that they may fight with the Syrians and slay Israel as Israel slew his nation.

10:23 David heard of this and laughed, saying, "Do these heathens not know that they cannot possibly harm us?

10:24 We have the one true lord upon our side, who shall consume them in great fire and feast on their very ashes and bones."

10:25 David went with his armies and passed over the Jordan, so that they may fight these heathen bastards hated by God.

10:26 Behold, the lord cursed again the enemies of Israel, so that they saw unicorns, dragons, giant serpents and beasts the size of mountains coming forth to slay them.

10:27 The Syrians fled again before Israel and David followed them and slew of them seven thousand chariots and forty thousand footmen, and killed Shophach the rulers of the armies of Hadarezer.

10:28 Those that remained of the nation of king Hadarezer surrendered to David and became his slaves and brought to Israel all the wealth of their nation.

10:29 The mercenaries of Syria would no longer help the children of Ammon, nor any person who wished to fight against Israel, saying, "They fight with beasts and demons.

10:30 No amount of money can be enough for our certain death against the might of the dragons and unicorns."

11:1 After the year ended and the season of war was at time for the kings, Joab led his the armies of Israel and laid waste to the country of Ammon and besieged the city of Rabbah while David stayed in Jerusalem.

11:2 Joab smote Rabbah and reduced the city and its people to dust.

11:3 David took the crown of the king of Rabbah, for it weighed a talent of gold and was adorn with great precious stones. David wore this crown and took great loot from the remains of Rabbah.

11:4 Those that survived the attack of Rabbah were brought forth and the armies of Israel tortured them with axes, sodomised them with arrows, cut with axes their limbs, poured molten iron into their vaginas and had harlots perform fellatio upon the men and then cut in length their erection with a rusty knife.

11:5 Israel dealt in this way with all the peoples of Ammon, torturing them greatly with crude weapons and tools of farmers and carpenters.

11:6 The Philistines heard of the torture done by the nation of Israel and said, "Surely this is a cruel and wicked nation, led by the devil himself.

11:7 Let us wipe this evil from the lands, so that all the world shall know peace."

11:8 At Gezer the Philistines and the Israelites fought and there Sibbechai the Hushathie slew Sippai, who was one of the sons of the sons of God; a giant.

11:9 Another battle took place and at this battle Elhanan slew Lahmi the brother of Goliath, who was also a giant and had a spear like an oak tree.

11:10 At Gath the armies of Israel and Philistine fought again and it was there where the greatest giant of all fought; a man with six fingers on each hand and six toes upon each foot.

11:11 He truly was a fucking freak and teased a lot as a child, which gave him great anger and fury that fueled him to fight.

11:12 When he went forth to fight against Israel, Jonathan the son of Shimea, David's brother, thrust his blade deeply within the mightiest of giants and killed him.

11:13 So it was that those born of the giants of Gath, the bastard men of the sons of God, were slain all by David and his servants.

11:14 God was very pleased and mocked his sons, saying, "Look how my men, my chosen people, slew your own offspring; men of your seed.

11:15 This is why I am the true lord and you are merely false gods posing to be like your father, mighty and all knowing."

11:16 The sons of God quietly cursed their father and called him a malevolent asshole who knew not how to care kindly for the people of earth.

12:1 Satan, apparently not God as was written previously, was the one who came to David and said, "Take number of all the men in Israel."

12:2 David did as the devil said and told Joab, "Go forth and number all the men of Israel, from Beersheba even to Dan and bring the tally to me.

12:3 Number only the strong men, able to serve in battle for me. The weak, the women, the lame and the slaves matter not to me."

12:4 Joab said to his king, "Why do you demand such a thing. Surely our lord knows how many people there are in his own kingdom. They are all servants of God."

12:5 Still, David insisted a census be taken and Joab went forth and when he returned, he said to David, "My king, we have numbered all the men within Israel who are capable of holding the sword.

12:6 Of the people of Israel there are one million, one hundred thousand capable men and of the tribe of Judah there are four hundred and seventy thousand men."

12:7 But Joab counted not the tribes of Benjamin and Levi, for Joab was a lazy man and bad with math.

12:8 The lord was furious for David holding a census of Israel and decided to curse all those of his people.

12:9 It's unsure why the lord was angry over a census. God gets mad over the silliest of things.

12:10 David confessed to God, "I have sinned greatly against you and knew not the wickedness which I committed against you.

12:11 Forgive me and my kin and be known to all that you are a lord of mercy."

12:12 God was not feeling merciful at the time and he went to Gad the prophet and told him the choices of the curse which David had to choose for the nation of Israel.

12:13 So Gad came to David and said to him, "The lord is fucking pissed that you counted the men of Israel. It angers him greatly.

12:14 Through all the lands of the nation, they shall know three years of famine, drought and starvation. This is your first choice. The second choice is three months of lost battles against all the heathen nations. Your last choice is three days of pestilence, plague and disease which strike all within your nation."

12:15 David said, "This punishment just for counting the numbers of people in my nation. Such a thing is undeserving.

12:16 I choose nothing, for such punishment is undeserving for a sin which I see no reason why it be even wicked.

12:17 Let the lord choose my decision. Either way it shall be unjust and unfair."

12:18 So the lord chose three days of pestilence; a great plague fell throughout all the lands of Israel, which killed seventy thousand men.

12:19 An angel of the lord was sent down with a sword of flame so that he may destroy the very city of Jerusalem. As the angel lifted his hand, the lord stopped him, saying, "Let it be that this city be saved. It contains my precious ark."

12:20 So the angel of the lord stood by the threshing floors of Ornan the Jebusite, wallowing in his misery that he was not able to destroy a city.

12:21 When David saw the angel stretched forth over Jerusalem before the lord stopped the angel's genocide, he stripped off his clothes, fell upon his face and poured dust over his body.

12:22 He said to the servant of the lord, "What have these people done to deserve such cruelty. It was I who sinned, yet I remain unpunished. Even the oxen, innocent beasts of burden, are condemned to the wrath of the lord."

12:23 After three days the lord stopped his pestilence upon Israel. God was annoyed with all the whining and crying of the sick and suffering.

12:24 The angel of the lord came to Gad and said, "The lord in heaven demands that David place an altar upon the threshing floors of Ornan the Jebusite."

12:25 Gad told this to his king and David said, "Such a thing must be done, lest the lord become angry again and curse us all with hemorrhoids or burning boils on our loins."

12:26 Thus David went to Ornan and said, "I need to build an altar to our lord upon your threshing floors.

12:27 Allow me this and you shall be blessed by God."

12:28 Ornan said, "The lord has cursed me and my sons lay dead upon the ground, slain by the sickness sent by God.

12:29 You want to build an altar, bless me now with six hundred shekels of gold."

12:30 David gave to Ornan six hundred shekels of gold so that he may buy his threshing floor and build an altar to the lord on it.

12:31 The next day Ornan lay dead in his bed, a dagger thrust through his skull. The six hundred shekels of gold were mysteriously missing.

12:32 David built the altar upon the threshing floor and sacrifices a great many oxen, goats and sheep atop the stones of the altar, dancing around the slain beasts naked, bathing in the blood.

12:33 This pleased God enough and he no longer hated David.

13:1 David said, "It is here, by the threshing floors of Ornan, where the temple of the lord shall be built by my seed."

13:2 And the king of Israel sent for great many masons to cut and shape stones for the house of God.

13:3 Great masses of iron ore were sent forth, to provide nails and joints for the doors and brass was delivered to the threshing floor with great weight.

13:4 Cedar trees were taken from Tyre king of the Zidonians, who was a servant of the nation of Israel.

13:5 David said, "It shall be my son Solomon who builds this great and mighty temple; a house to our great and wonderful lord. Let it be that he makes it with great wonder, glory, fame and wealth, so that all shall know our lord has the greatest bling."

13:6 David prepared greatly before his death all the things which

Solomon must do for the building of the temple of God and he said to his son, "Behold, it is you and not I who must build a house for our lord.

13:7 It was God who came unto me and said that I shall not build him a house, but that my seed shall do such a thing.

13:8 God wished for me other things. Starting wars, shedding blood, enslaving people, torturing heathens, conquering nations and other such glories the lord asked of me.

13:9 Let it be known that I have set aside a great abundance of gold and silver in which you shall afford to build the great temple to our God. You shall have one hundred thousand talents of gold and one million talents of silver to which to build such a blessed thing.

13:10 Moreover, you shall use all the slaves of Israel, and work them relentlessly until the house of God be complete.

13:11 Use only skilled labour when necessary, for the masonry and the carvings. Pay them cheaply; use the slaves most, as they cost nothing but a bit of food, water and the occasional beating.

13:12 When the house be done, store within it all the glories, the wonders and the belongings of our lord which I have dedicated to him."

13:13 David then called all the elders of Israel and said, "You shall support Solomon in the building of this great temple of our lord. This house shall bring us great blessings and those who aid in its completion shall be blessed by God.

13:14 Those who do not dig in their pockets and offer their shekels to complete the temple, let them be cursed eternally by the lord.

13:15 May their pockets grow empty and their seed be raped and tormented by the evil Philistines."

13:16 Those of the elders of Israel gave Solomon all they could afford and more to build the house of God.

13:17 One elder donated little to Solomon, at first. Frequent beatings and the death of his eldest son coerced him to donate much more.

13:18 David then died and left his son Solomon king over all those of Israel. David served as king for forty years; seven in Hebron and thirty-three in Jerusalem.

13:19 He died a rich man, honoured throughout all of Israel. Those of the children of Israel mourned the passing of their beloved king. Those of the heathen nations rejoiced in the death of the barbarian.

II CHRONICLES

1:1 Solomon the son of David was king of Israel, who strengthened his kingdom. The lord was with Solomon and blessed him so that the heathens feared Solomon and his people.

1:2 Solomon spoke well to the children of Israel, to the elders, to the armies, to the judges and to the governors, so that all in Israel loved and rejoiced Solomon's name.

1:3 The king of Israel and all the congregation of Israel went forth to Gibeon, for it was there that the tabernacle of the congregation of the lord was, which Moses built in the wilderness.

1:4 But the ark of God David brought up from Kirjathjearim to Jerusalem and prepared a tent in the city to place the ark.

1:5 Solomon went to the brass altar which Belazeel the son of Uri built in honour to the lord and placed before the tabernacle of God.

1:6 There Solomon offered one thousand sacrifices to God, burning the corpses, boiling the blood and dancing around the fires naked.

1:7 The lord was pleased with Solomon and came to him in a dream, saying, "For pleasing your lord greatly and being the son of the mighty David, I shall give to you one thing. Ask and you shall receive."

1:8 Solomon said, "You have shown great mercy to my father David, who had reigned in Israel before me.

1:9 Now it is I who rules over Israel and must make them strong, prosperous and beat them to your submission, so that they never stray from you.

1:10 I ask of you, O lord, to give me wisdom, so that I may rule over these people well and not have them rebel against me."

1:11 God laughed at Solomon and said, "The lord of lords has come and offered thee anything you could desire and you ask for wisdom?

1:12 You truly are a fool. You should have asked for long life, riches, strength to rule over all those of earth, yet you ask for wisdom.

1:13 God shall grant you wisdom and it shall be wisdom you have."

1:14 Solomon then woke up and was granted the wisdom he asked from the lord. Solomon became disappointed, for he knew he should have asked for the great powers of God.

1:15 Those of Israel left Gibeon and returned to Jerusalem, where Solomon sat on the throne and ruled over all of Israel.

1:16 Solomon strengthened his armies greatly and gathered one thousand four hundred chariots and twelve thousand horsemen, which he used to defend the borders of Israel and protect himself as a personal bodyguard.

1:17 With the riches of Israel, Solomon had it so that silver and gold numbered in Jerusalem greater than the pebbles and stones and all buildings were built of mighty cedar.

1:18 Solomon brought from Egypt plenty horses, chariots and linen.

1:19 And the armies of Israel bought from Egypt a chariot for six hundred shekels and a horse for one hundred and fifty shekels of silver. From the people of Syria and Hittite they stole horses and chariots, for these people were under the servitude of Israel.

2:1 Solomon built a house for the lord and an even greater house for himself.

2:2 The king of Israel brought forth threescore and ten thousand slaves to build the temple of the lord, fourscore thousand slaves to bring down mighty stones from the mountains and three thousand six hundred slave masters to rule over them, beat them and ensure they work.

2:3 Solomon sent also a message to Huram the king of Tyre, saying "You have served my father well and brought to him great many skilled workers, labourers and materials. So you shall also with me.

2:4 Behold, I am building a temple for my lord, the true God of all gods. A place to burn him sweet incense, worship on the sabbath and bless him with many sacrifices and offerings.

2:5 This house shall be great and rival the temples of the heathen lords and false gods.

2:6 Bring me that which I demand, lest the lord curse you and your nation with a fire that burns you whole yet never gives you the pleasure of death.

2:7 I need skilled labourers, men who can work in gold, silver, brass, iron, purple linens, crimson linens, blue linens and men skilled in carving and engraving all manners of wood.

2:8 Send me also cedar trees, fir trees, and algum trees. Your nation is full of this wondrous timber and can spare it to build a house

for the lord.

2:9 Know that I shall care well for your workers and they shall be fed with twenty thousand measures of beaten wheat, twenty thousand measures of barley, twenty thousand baths of wine and twenty thousand baths of oil.

2:10 They best work fast, for I do not know how long those provisions may feed them and shall offer them no more when the food and wine is gone."

2:11 Huram sent a message to Solomon, which read, "Why do you even ask of me these things, knowing that you shall take them if I agree or not?

2:12 I shall give you that which you need to build the house for your blessed lord, lest he and his people smite my nation with swords, arrows and beasts of magic.

2:13 I have sent you my best skilled people to build this temple of the lord. People greatly experienced with gold, silver, brass, iron, purple linens, crimson linens, blue linens and engravings of the finest detail.

2:14 Surely, they shall not feast gluttonously upon your generous offerings of wheat, barley, wine and oil. It is known you shall offer them little of this food anyway; rationing them daily.

2:15 We will cut the timber from Lebanon and deliver them by sea to the harbours of Joppa, where I'm sure my people shall carry them to Jerusalem.

2:16 Let it be known that the people of Tyre did not aid in the mighty construction of the temple of the God of Israel. We wouldn't want to be cursed with the wickedness of your lord if we did not."

2:17 Solomon numbered the labours which were sent from Huram the king of Tyre and they numbered also one hundred and fifty thousand six hundred men, which doubles the slaves within Israel which was conveniently the same damn number.

2:18 It is also known that Solomon was really bad at math.

2:19 Solomon rejoiced in this and said, "Surely this is a sign from the lord."

2:20 And he set ten thousand of the people of Tyre to be bearers of burden with the construction of the temple and fourscore thousand to carve out the rocks in the mountains and mine the caves.

2:21 Three thousand six hundred people of Israel oversaw those peoples of Tyre and treated them as slaves, beating them, starving them and working them until death.

2:22 Such is the way the great temple of the merciful God was built; with slave labour.

3:1 Solomon started construction of the house of the lord at Jerusalem in mount Moriah, upon the threshing floor of Ornan the Jebusite which his father David purchased.

3:2 And he began to build the house in the second day, of the second month, on the fourth year of his reign.

3:3 The instructions of the temple were very strict and given through the mouth of God. The length was to be threescore cubits and the width twenty cubits.

3:4 The porch of the temple was to be twenty cubits in length, so that it matches the breadth of the house and the height of the porch to be one hundred and twenty cubits. The porch was to be built with pure gold, so that those who gaze upon it shall know the wealth of the lord.

3:5 The greater part of the house was built with fir trees, overlaid with fine gold which had engravings of palm branches and connected with gold chains.

3:6 Not a single piece of furniture or plank of wood lacked a precious stone, for the temple was covered with precious stones of rubies, emeralds, diamonds, garnet, opal, jasper, turquoise, pearl, amethyst and other valuable gems.

3:7 All parts of the house; the beams, posts, floors, even the walls, were overlaid with precious gold and inlaid with images of angels, unicorns, dragons and palm branches.

3:8 Of the weight of the gold used for inlaying weighed six hundred shekels. This was the gold used only for inlaying and includes not the items made of solid gold.

3:9 Even the nails used to construct the temple were made of pure gold and each nail weighed fifty shekels.

3:10 In the holiest chamber of the house were carved two angels of pure gold, each being twenty cubits long and each wing of the angel being five cubits long, one wing stretched out to touch the wall behind it and the other stretched forth to touch the wing of the other angel.

3:11 The curtains of the temple were made with finest blue, crimson and linens, with cherubims upon them.

3:12 Two pillars outside of the temple, set in front of the door to the temple, were thirty-five cubits in height and the chapiter atop them were five cubits in height.

3:13 Chains of solid gold were connected to each of the pillars and each chain had from it one hundred pomegranates of pure gold dangling from them.

3:14 The pillars were named after two people of Israel who were the first to die constructing the temple; the left pillar was named Boaz and the right pillar was named Jachin.

3:15 The temple of God was the second most expensive building created ever throughout the lands of Israel, with the house of Solomon being costlier.

3:16 Those who gazed on the temple were in awe in its glory, wealth and asked themselves, "Why does God, who reside in heaven above, need such luxuries as gold and gems?

3:17 Could the money used to buy such expensive things be better used on trade, or sanitation, or defense?"

3:18 These people were mysteriously stricken with a plague, which caused their tongue to swell so that they could not speak.

3:19 Such was the act of God, who loathes those who question why the lord need such bling, richness and useless decorations.

4:1 In the house of Solomon was an altar of pure brass, which he offered many sacrifices atop of in glory to the lord. The length and width of the altar was twenty cubits and the height was ten cubits.

4:2 Also Solomon made in his house a pool of molten brass ten cubits in length exactly from brim to brim and five cubits deep. The line of the pool was thirty cubits exactly, because the lord had the power to change the value of pi and make a circumference of thirty cubits when the diameter was ten cubits.

4:3 Such is the power of God to change even math!

4:4 Solomon drowned many oxen in the pool of molten brass and had the brass harden so that it became a statue. He then placed these oxen statues as decoration around his pool, ten oxen per cubit, placed around the rim of the pool.

4:5 Twelve drowned and brass hardened oxen were also placed as a compass around the pool, so that three gazed west, three gazed east, three gazed north and three gazed south.

4:6 The brim of the pool was made of solid gold and carved on it were engravings of lilies. The pool could hold three thousand baths of molten brass.

4:7 Solomon also made ten sinks of solid gold and placed five to the left of the altar and five to the right, so that those who offered sacrifice could wash the blood from their bodies with the sinks.

4:8 Ten tables of solid gold were also made and five were placed to the right of the altar and five on the left. Atop each table were one hundred basins of gold.

4:9 The chambers where the priests slept Solomon made with great cedar and overlaid the cedar with gold. Doors to the chambers were made of solid gold and carved in them were images of the many

offerings the lord demands.

4:10 The sea of molten brass was placed on the southeast side of the house of Solomon, where the walls were lowest. Those who tried to sneak into the house of Solomon by climbing these walls fell into the sea and drowned in brass.

4:11 Solomon would then take these drowned people and let the brass harden so that they became like statues. He would then decorate the halls with these drowned people of brass.

4:12 Huram, the son of Solomon, was a master metallist and built for the house of Solomon and the temple of the lord all the basins, pots and shovels.

4:13 Huram also built the two pillars of brass in the house of Solomon and the chapiters atop them and carved the golden wreaths which lay atop the chapiters.

4:14 On each wreath were two rows of golden pomegranates, each row numbering four hundred pomegranates and each pomegranate weighing seven hundred shekels.

4:15 Solomon had his son Huram build the brass pots with great abundance, until no brass could be found in the heathen nations enslaved by Israel.

4:16 Solomon loved brass, for it shined greater than gold. Solomon loved shiny things.

4:17 The reason Solomon loved shiny things is because Solomon smoked a lot of hallucinogenic herbs.

4:18 It was Solomon himself who built the golden altar for the temple of the lord and he also built the candlesticks placed before the oracle.

4:19 The king of Israel also built the carved flowers of gold, lamps, tongs, snuffers, bases, spoons and censers for the temple of the lord with pure gold. Solomon loved working with gold; gold was shiny.

5:1 Finally Solomon completed the house of the lord, thanks mainly to slave labour and exploiting resources from heathen nations.

5:2 The total cost of the temple was greater than that of the nation of Philistine and it was the second most expensive building on all the lands.

5:3 Solomon placed within the temple all the treasures his father David dedicated to God; the gold, the silver, the instruments and the spoils of war.

5:4 All of Israel gathered to the temple, so that they may witness the ark of the covenant be placed within the temple and because free food and liquor was being served for this holy event.

5:5 The Levites, slaves to God, brought the ark up from the tent and put it within the temple: they also brought the holy vessels of the tabernacle.

5:6 King Solomon and all the children of Israel gathered around the ark and offered countless oxen, rams, sheep, goats, doves and pigeons as sacrifice to the lord.

5:7 The blood of the sacrifices spilled upon the ground of the temple and flowed out through the doors, so that the streets around the temple were like rivers of blood.

5:8 God gazed down upon this and was pleased greatly with the people of Israel being soaked in the blood of sacrifices.

5:9 The Levites placed the ark between the cherubims, so that the wings covered the ark. The staves used to carry the ark were placed before the oracle.

5:10 There was nothing within the ark save for the two tablets which Moses was given atop mount Horeb, which was written upon them the many rules, laws, commandments and regulations which the lord demanded from all his people.

5:11 They were huge fucking tablets and the writing was very small.

5:12 When the priests and the Levites left the temple, behold, the spirit of the lord came in great blackness within the temple and dwelt there.

5:13 The blackness was so thick that none could enter the house of God, for the spirit of the lord dwelt within and would kill anyone who entered.

6:1 Those of Israel saw the great darkness which the lord dwelt within and a few said, "This is why the lord cares not for the sufferings of our past; he dwells in blackness and cannot see our torment, our pain, our tears."

6:2 It was then the darkness came forth and consumed those people, so that none of their body was left; it was as though they vanished.

6:3 Solomon said to the people of Israel, "Blessed be those chosen by God, who lives in the darkness of our lord.

6:4 They shall know our lord well and be forever in his presence.

6:5 Blessed be our lord God, who has led us with a kind hand out of the lands of Egypt and guided us to the promised lands flowing with milk and honey.

6:6 Since the days of Moses our lord hath chosen no city other than Jerusalem, the city of my father, for which to dwell. He hath chosen Jerusalem as his home, as he hath chosen me to be king over his people.

6:7 David my father was told by God not to build this temple, for my father's service to the lord was that of conquest, bloodshed and enslavement.

6:8 It was I, his son, who was honoured to build the great temple of the lord, which I stand before today and place his ark within the holiest of all houses."

6:9 Solomon stood before the altar of the lord in the presence of all those of Israel and spread forth his hands:

6:10 Leading to the altar was brass scaffold five cubits long, five cubits wide and three cubits high, which Solomon knelt upon and raised his head towards heaven, saying,

6:11 "O lord God of great mercy, there is none other like you in heaven nor earth, who keeps his covenant showing mercy upon all his people.

6:12 May we walk always in the path you have chosen, so that we may please you and love you with all our hearts, so that we not have your wrath and anger come upon us in great fury and torment.

6:13 Shall it be that the seed of David serve you always as a humble and grateful servant and rule over your people and abide your laws, your statutes, your covenants, so that all of Israel shall walk the true path and know their lord.

6:14 Blessed be the people of Israel, whose lord shall dwell within the temple placed upon the earth. But how can it be that a mere house can contain the glory and the wonders of our God. Not even the heavens above can contain the magnificence of our lord.

6:15 May it be that those among us who go against God be crushed with the fiery hammer of the lord and their seed be consumed by ravens, jackals and vultures.

6:16 Heathens and blasphemers shall know nothing but suffering and pain; the lord shall close the skies of the nations of the uncircumcised bastards, who shall know drought and starvation.

6:17 Plagues of boils, leprosy, scabs, death and pain those of the earth have yet to know shall be cursed upon all those who speak ill of our lord and their children shall be eaten by the mouths of their blasphemous mothers.

6:18 Let it be that Israel spread across the lands like fire, so that those upon earth be of Israel, or enslaved by the nation of God.

6:19 It shall be that all people will be servants of God, whether willingly or by force.

6:20 Let us rape the daughters of those who worship false lords and behead their sons so that the blood of their children pour into their mouths and they be forced to drink it.

6:21 Bodies of the unbelievers shall litter the ground like stones and blasphemers shall be hung on the trees, where they shall rot and be consumed by the beasts, the scavengers, the maggots and the worms.

6:22 Show unto Israel, O God, the mercies which you are greatly known for. Forgive us our sins and we shall serve you eternally.

6:23 Our lord shall not turn his back upon the nation of Israel, for our lord shall remember my father David, who was merciful and wise."

6:24 Those of Israel rejoiced in the bullshit which Solomon spoke and celebrated with dancing, drinking, feasting and offering great many sacrifices upon the altar of brass.

7:1 When Solomon finished his propaganda and praying, fire came down from the sky and consumed all the carcasses of the offerings which the children of Israel gave to the lord.

7:2 Even the blood, which flowed through the streets like the river Jordan the lord took with him and drank.

7:3 The priests could not enter the house of the lord, for the fiery spirit of God was within, consuming the blood and the flesh of the sacrifices and those few who spoke ill against him and his dwelling in darkness.

7:4 When the people of Israel saw the fires come down and consume the offerings, they bowed down upon their faces and praised the lord, blessing his name. They offered more sacrifices unto God, as their lord dwelt in great fire within the temple, eating beasts whole.

7:5 They prayed to the lord, saying, "The lord is merciful, the lord is good and the lord shall protect his children for all eternity."

7:6 A pity God didn't consider the people of Israel his children.

7:7 King Solomon gazed at the glory of the spirit of the lord and offered as sacrifice twenty-two thousand oxen and one hundred and twenty thousand sheep in glory to the lord.

7:8 God did not feast upon these offerings, for one of the sheep had a small blemish on its foot, which the lord found disgusting.

7:9 When the fire left and the spirit of the lord rushed forth to the heavens, the Levites entered the house of the lord, playing instruments of music, hoping to bring the lord back into the temple.

7:10 Priests sang psalms in glory to the name of the lord and joined the Levites with instruments of trumpets, harps, timbrels and cymbals.

7:11 Solomon offered more sacrifices to the lord and burned the fat and boiled the blood and slew on the altar the prettiest and fairest heathen virgins which the army of Israel brought forth to him.

7:12 The lord did not return to the temple that day, for the lord was in his bathroom in heaven, expelling holy shit from his holy ass and regretting feasting so gluttonously upon the sacrifices Israel offered to him.

7:13 Solomon feared the lord was displeased and stood in the center of the court of the temple, where he fasted for seven days.

7:14 Those of Israel fasted with him. Their bellies were full of bread, flesh and liquor and they could not eat another morsel lest they vomit the feast given to them, in celebration of the completion of the temple.

7:15 After the lord finished with his holy shitting, he wiped his ass and came down to Solomon, saying, "Know this, I am a lord of mercy and understanding, who demands obedience by all my people.

7:16 If God shuts the skies so that no rain falls upon the lands, or send locusts to consume thine crops, or send pestilence, plagues and disease to the people of Israel, it is because they deserve it and have sinned against the lord.

7:17 If my people humble themselves and pray to me and seek my face and turn away from their sins and their wickedness, the lord shall forgive them their sins and lift the curse from their heads.

7:18 Or the lord may not. It depends on how pissed off I am at you fucking idiots.

7:19 My eyes shall be always open and my ears shall listen so that when the children of Israel pray, I shall see them and hear them.

7:20 The lord may ignore them, but know that the lord knows they be praying.

7:21 As for you, know this: if you walk in the path of your father and obey the lord and all his demands and observe my statutes and keep my commandments,

7:22 Then I shall establish the throne of Israel forever to you and your seed; it shall be that the seed of David shall sit always upon the throne of the chosen people.

7:23 If you turn away and forget my laws and demands, go whoring after other gods and seek out wickedness,

7:24 Then I shall pluck the very roots of Israel and cast them in the fire, where they shall burn eternally until the end of days.

7:25 Heathens shall enslave you and your daughters shall be their whores and your sons shall be savaged by slavery and rape.

7:26 Israel shall be cast out and spread across the lands. Behold, the lord shall doom them to damnation and your very people shall die, so that none of Israel remain.

7:27 When those of heathen nations gaze on the nation of Israel, they shall ask themselves, what happened to these people, who were great men and chosen by the true lord?

7:28 And I shall answer them that I consumed them all, for they did that which was evil in my eyes."

7:29 The lord then left, leaving Solomon scared and alone in his bedchamber.

7:30 On the morrow, Solomon gathered the people of Israel and said to them, "Whatever you do, in all your life, do not anger our lord God. He is one cruel fucker."

7:31 And the peoples of Israel replied, "Yeah, no shit."

8:1 After twenty years from the completion of the temple of the lord and the house of Solomon, Israel took the cities of Huram, restored it and the people of God now dwelt there.

8:2 Solomon went also to Hamathzobah and took it from the heathens and the people of Israel dwelt there.

8:3 Those in Hamathzobah were either killed, enslaved, placed in brothels or sold as concubines to the men of Israel.

8:4 These cities were not enough for Solomon, for the king of Israel wished the lands under his rule be well protected with strong forts and mighty cities which would destroy and conquer any heathen fool who dared cross his borders.

8:5 In the lands of Hamath Solomon built a great many cities and he built Tadmor in the wilderness.

8:6 A large city he built so that the city was split in two and was known as Bethoron the upper and Bethoron the lower.

8:7 The city of Baalath was lain siege to by those of Israel and Solomon conquered it as well, slaughtering every person within.

8:8 Men, women, child, elderly, infant and cripple Solomon demanded dead, for these people lived in an unholy city named after a false god.

8:9 So the soldiers of Israel killed all within Baalath and burned the bodies in sacrifice to their God in heaven, who gazed down upon the burning corpses and was pleased.

8:10 Each city Solomon built and conquered he reinforced with great walls, fences, bars, gates and defenses, so that no heathen bastard shall sneak in, nor any foreign army take it.

8:11 As for those who were not of the children of Israel; the Hittites, the Amorites, the Hivites, the Perizzites and the Jebusites which the people of Moses let survive, Solomon enslaved them all.

8:12 The king of Israel did not slay them and complete the genocide which God demanded since the days of Moses, but Solomon did enslave them and force them into hard labour.

8:13 Those of Israel Solomon did not enslave, but made free. They

became chiefs, men of war, horsemen and captains of the chariots.

8:14 All men of Israel were trained to fight in battle, so that they may serve Israel and the lord in the great global conquest of their people.

8:15 Those who refused were drowned in the pool of molten brass in the house of Solomon. Those useless in fighting were put on the front lines as bait to the heathen armies.

8:16 Solomon built a city and separate house for his wife, who was the daughter of Pharaoh and said to her, "You are a woman and a foreign cunt. You cannot dwell in the city of Jerusalem, for it is a holy place and you are a wretched beast of a woman in the eyes of the lord.

8:17 I shall build you a city and a great house for you to dwell in. As my wife, you shall be cared for greatly. Now come here and fuck me before you get your filthy body out of the city of my father."

8:18 After his wife left, Solomon sacrificed for the lord a great many oxen and sheep on the altar of the lord which was in front of the temple.

8:19 Solomon then appointed priests and Levites, who would ensure all those of Israel came to the temple and offer their sacrifices to the lord, according to the laws of Moses.

8:20 Those who did not offer their sacrifices, became sacrificed.

8:21 The king of Israel then sought forth more lands to conquer and sent ships to the shores of Edom, Eloth and Eziongeber.

8:22 Huram the king of Tyre sent to Solomon many ships, seamen and labourers who knew the construction of ships well.

8:23 If Huram did not, Solomon would destroy his nations and people and enslave those who survived his wrath.

8:24 With his ships, Solomon went to the wild lands of Ophir and would take from the primitive heathens four hundred and fifty talents of gold, which would be brought back to Jerusalem.

9:1 The queen of Sheba heard of the fame, the wisdom and the glory of Solomon and doubted them greatly. She came to Jerusalem to test Solomon and brought with her caravans of spices, gold, silver, and gemstones.

9:2 Every question the queen of Sheba asked Solomon, Solomon would answer greatly. If he did not know the answer, he would speak forth bullshit from his mouth, dazzling and confusing the queen of Sheba with his speech craft.

9:3 Sheba would say of Solomon, "He is truly a wise man, for he spoke to me with great wisdom that I could not understand."

9:4 She witnessed the greatness of Jerusalem and the house of Solomon and the temple of the lord. The queen of Sheba saw the meats on the tables, the servants dressed in fine silks and the entire houses being made of gold.

9:5 She said to the king of Israel, "Happy must the people of Israel be and happy must be your servants, to serve under such a wise and wealthy man.

9:6 Blessed and wise be your lord, to choose such a man as yourself to sit upon the throne of his peoples and govern them according to his laws.

9:7 May you give forth great justice, punishment and judgment and may you rule a thousand years over all of Israel."

9:8 The queen of Sheba then gave to Solomon all that which she brought with her; the gold, silver, spices and gemstones.

9:9 Not to be outdone by this heathen bitch, Solomon gave to the queen of Sheba even greater amounts of gold, silver, spices and gemstones and camels to carry them, so that she returned home with triple the amount she gave to Solomon.

9:10 The queen of Sheba said to her people, "Solomon is such a wise and generous man," where Solomon said to his people, "That queen is a fucking stupid cunt."

9:11 Now the weight of gold which Solomon exploited from the heathen nations was six hundred and thirty talents, brought forth every year to Jerusalem.

9:12 Even the kings of Arabia gave to Solomon silver and gold, so that they would avoid the wrath of Israel and the wickedness of their lord.

9:13 King Solomon built two hundred targets of beaten gold, each target weighing six hundred shekels, so that he may practice his skills with the bow.

9:14 Three hundred shields Solomon had made and placed them in his house in the forests of Lebanon; each shield weighed three hundred shekels in pure gold.

9:15 Also the king made a throne of ivory and overlaid the ivory with pure gold. Sitting on each side of the throne was a lion, fastened by a chain made of solid gold.

9:16 They were real lions, which would feast upon those who angered Solomon.

9:17 There were six steps which led up to the throne and each step was made of solid gold.

9:18 On each side of every step was a lion, so that twelve lions sat upon the steps. They too were fastened by a chain of solid gold and feasted upon the slaves who were too old or crippled to work.

9:19 Every plate, knife, spoon, fork, cup, chalice, drinking vessel, table, chair and every piece of furniture in the house of Solomon was made of gold.

9:20 Those who entered the house of Solomon knew that Solomon had the greatest bling throughout all the kingdoms of the land.

9:21 Solomon would send ships to Tarshish and every three years the ships would return bringing forth gold, silver, ivory, peacocks and apes.

9:22 Solomon was quite amused by apes and would train them to be servants and concubines.

9:23 Kings of foreign nations would come every year so that they may listen to the wisdom of Solomon and gaze upon his house of glory and wonder.

9:24 Every king would bring to Solomon a gift; horses, camels, women, liquor, wine, gold, silver, ivory, silks, linen, raiment's, chariots, spices and camels.

9:25 Now the rest of the acts of Solomon, they are written in the book of Nathan the prophet, in the prophecy of Ajihah the Shilonite and the visions of Iddor the prophet.

9:26 Nobody cares about them, which is why you never heard of these writings until now.

9:27 Solomon reigned for forty years throughout Jerusalem and was buried with his fathers in the city of David. Rehoboam, the son of Solomon, became the new king of Israel.

10:1 Rehoboam went to Shechem, for it was in Shechem that he shall be anointed the new king of Israel.

10:2 When Jeroboam heard that Solomon was dead, he left from the sanctuary of Egypt and returned to his homeland of Israel.

10:3 Jeroboam and all of Israel came to Rehoboam, saying, "Your father hast made our yoke too tight and our workload too heavy.

10:4 Lighten our work, so that we may rest, relax and enjoy our time and we shall serve you until the end of days."

10:5 Rehoboam said to his people, "Return to me in three days and I shall answer your request. I must first seek counsel among the elders."

10:6 The elders of Israel said to their king, "Lighten the work of the people of Israel, so that they shall be loyal to you.

10:7 We of Israel have plenty of slaves and shall gather more if necessary. Let our people rest."

10:8 But Rehoboam was an arrogant fucker who ignored the counsel of the others.

10:9 When the people returned to Rehoboam, their king said to them, "Where my father gave you heavy work, I shall double your load. Where my father beat you with whips, I shall beat you with scorpions.

10:10 Let it be known that you shall be grateful to serve our lord and those who bitch shall be punished severely and shall chew on the flesh of their own loins."

10:11 When the people of Israel saw that their new king shall not hearken their request, they spoke ill of Rehoboam and said, "Fuck you, bastard child of a cuntless whore!

10:12 May your seed fall upon the wombs of whores and your children be ugly as the ass of a swine.

10:13 We shall serve not you and will curse your name and your seed.

10:14 Let it be that Rehoboam be raped by the horns of demons and his flesh feasted upon by heathen lepers."

10:15 Thus eleven tribes of Israel separated from Rehoboam's reign and Jeroboam became their king.

10:16 However, the tribe of Judah were loyal to Rehoboam and Rehoboam reigned over them.

10:17 King Rehoboam loathed those who rebelled against him and sent forth Hadoram to convince them to return and be ruled by the seed of David.

10:18 Those who rebelled against Rehoboam stoned Hadoram and ravaged his body in mockery to the king of Judah, leaving his corpse to rot in the wilderness.

10:19 And the eleven tribes of Israel rebelled against the house of David until the fall of Israel.

11:1 When Rehoboam returned to Jerusalem, he gathered from the people of Judah and the loyal men of the tribe of Benjamin one hundred and fourscore thousand men who were great warriors, so that they may fight against the eleven tribes of Israel.

11:2 But God did not yet wish for civil war to break between Judah and Israel and he came to Shemaiah the man of the lord, saying,

11:3 "Speak to Rehoboam the king of Judah and to all the peoples loyal to him and say this.

11:4 Thus sayeth the lord, you shall not go and fight against your brethren of Israel. Let them return to their houses and be governed as they wish."

11:5 So the people of Judah returned to their lands and did not war against those of Jeroboam.

11:6 When Rehoboam reigned in Judah he became paranoid, for he feared the lord would choose the eleven tribes over the tribe of Judah and that the betrayers shall smite him greatly.

11:7 He built for Judah great defenses and cities, so that those of Israel and of the heathens shall be slain when they step into the lands of Judah.

11:8 Rehoboam build Bethlehem, Etam, Tekoa,

11:9 Bethzur, Shoco, Adullam,

11:10 Gath, Mareshah, Ziph,

11:11 Adoraim, Lachish, Azekah,

11:12 Zorah, Aijalon and Hebron, all of which were fenced cities with iron gates and great defenses.

11:13 Each city had a garrison of soldiers; a stronghold, so that the city was always defended by the armies of Judah.

11:14 In every city he had stores of spears, shields and swords, so that even the citizens may fight in defense of the tribe of Judah, when the heathens and the betrayers of Israel came to war with them.

11:15 The priests of the tribe of Levi came to Judah, for it was in these lands where the house of the lord and the ark of God was, which they must serve under slavery of the lord.

11:16 Jeroboam the king of the eleven tribes of Israel mocked those of Levi who left and he ordained priests from other tribes, who were unworthy in the eyes of God.

11:17 From other tribes Jeroboam also made priests to devils, foreign gods, heathen lords and the two golden calves he carved, for Jeroboam feared those of his peoples would leave for Judah and offer sacrifices upon the altar in front of the temple.

11:18 God was with Rehoboam of Judah, for he walked in the ways of his father David and was a cruel ruler who would beat his slaves with the tails of scorpions and punished them with vipers and cobras.

11:19 For three years Rehoboam walked in the ways of David and Solomon and was blessed by God.

11:20 Rehoboam took for a wife Mahalath the daughter of Jerimoth, the son of David and she bared him Jeush, Shamariah and Zaham.

11:21 Afterwards Rehoboam took another wife, Maachah the daughter of Absalom, who bared him Ajibah, Attai, Ziza and Shelomith.

11:22 Rehoboam loved Maachah the daughter of Absalom above all his wives, for she was a great cook, loved anal sex and gave great fellatio to her husband.

11:23 Maachah loved being favoured above all the wives of Rehoboam, for he had eighteen wives and threescore concubines and begat with them twenty-eight sons and threescore daughters.

11:24 Because Rehoboam loved Maachah, he made her son Abijah to be ruler over all the armies of Judah.

11:25 And Abijah dealt wisely with his armies and spread them to defend all the cities of Judah.

11:26 Abijah desired also the embrace of many women and was considered a great lover throughout the brothels of Judah.

12:1 It came to pass that when the kingdom of Judah was established and strong, he did that which was evil in the eyes of God and tolerated faggots, heathens and false lords.

12:2 On the fifth year of Rehoboam's reign, the lord rose Shishak the Pharaoh of Egypt and sent him and his armies to Jerusalem, so that they may brutally kill and destroy those of Judah.

12:3 With twelve hundred chariots, threescore thousand horsemen and the mercenaries of Lubim, Sukkim and Ethiopia, Shishak conquered the defended cities of Judah.

12:4 Shemaiah the prophet came to Rebohoam and said, "You have doomed those of Judah to a life of enslavement and whoredom.

12:5 It is our lord who has sent the armies of Pharaoh to us, for we have sinned greatly against God and deserve the wrath which he will send upon us."

12:6 Rehoboam said, "God is just and fair; we deserve the wrath of our lord."

12:7 When God saw that they humbled themselves and abandoned their wicked ways, he said to Shemaiah, "For humbling themselves to the lord and ceasing their wickedness, let it be known that God shall not destroy them and those of Shishak shall not conquer Jerusalem.

12:8 However, those of Judah shall be servants to Pharaoh, so that they shall know never to fuck with the laws of God again, obeying me blindly."

12:9 So Shishak came to Jerusalem and took away all the treasures in the temple of God and took away all the treasures in the house of Solomon. Even the golden shields within the forest of Lebanon the armies of Egypt took.

12:10 When the armies of Pharaoh left, Rehoboam humbled himself in the eyes of God and strengthened again the lands of Judah and the city of Jerusalem.

12:11 Reboboam was forty-one years old when he began to rule over Judah and he reigned for seventeen years. His mother's name was Naamah, an Ammonitess.

12:12 Even after the armies of Pharaoh left, Rehoboam did that which was evil in the sight of the lord, for he did not dedicate his entire life in service to God.

12:13 Rehoboam would take priority of the people of Judah and ensure their health and safety, instead of offering countless sacrifices and making sure God was happy with the amount of killing the armies of Judah were doing to foreign people.

12:14 Because of his wickedness, Rehoboam sleeps in hell; Abijah his son became king of Judah after Rehoboam's death.

13:1 In the eighteenth year of Jeroboams' reign did Abijah the king of Judah first sit upon his throne.

13:2 He reigned three years in Jerusalem. His mother's name was Michaiah the daughter of Uriel of Gibeah.

13:3 Abijah loathed Jeroboam and Jeroboam loathed Abijah. There was war between the two nations.

13:4 Abijah sent to war four hundred thousand most valiant warriors and Jeroboam sent to war eight hundred thousand men of valour.

13:5 And Abijah stood up on mount Ephraim and said to both the armies of Judah and the armies of Israel (he had a really loud voice),

13:6 "Hear me, you people of Jeroboam, who betrayed the true nation of Israel and abandoned the seed of David.

13:7 Know that the lord made a covenant with David, so that it shall be his seed that rules over the chosen people of God, the people of Israel.

13:8 This means that God is on our side and he shall smite you with his wickedness and hate.

13:9 Jeroboam the son of Nebat has gone against God and is a man of wickedness and evil, who has leagued himself with devils.

13:10 All you who gather with him and deserve the death God will soon curse upon you.

13:11 Look among your nation and ask yourself, where are the priests of Levi. Where be the holy slaves of our lord?

13:12 They dwell in Judah, because they know that the lord is with us and not you.

13:13 Daily we of the nation of Judah dedicate ourselves to God and offer burnt sacrifices and offerings of virgin heathens.

13:14 You worship two golden calves and prostitute yourselves to idols and false gods of Baal and Ashteroth.

13:15 This shall be your damnation; may the lord of lords smite you with fury and wrath."

13:16 As Abijah continued with his speech to Israel, the armies of Jeroboam snuck behind him and ambushed him from the rear.

13:17 Abijah looked behind him and saw that the battle was towards his rear and he yelled, "Oh shit, we're dead," and was about to give the order to retreat.

13:18 It was then the spirit of the lord came down upon Israel in great fire and darkness and consumed the armies of Jeroboam.

13:19 Abijah laughed and said to his soldiers, "Let it be known now that God is truly on our side."

13:20 Those of Judah then pursued after Israel and smote them greatly, killing five hundred thousand of the people of Israel, who they used to call brothers.

13:21 Abijah took from Israel the lands of Bethel, Jeshanah and Ephraim and all the cities and villages within.

13:22 God looked upon this civil war and laughed. It amused to him to see his children fight against one another and brought the lord great relief that the covenant he made with the people shall be broken and he can curse them mightily without heathen people stating that the lord of Israel abandoned them first.

13:23 After the battle, Jeroboam became weak. The lord came to Jeroboam and crushed his heart within his chest, killing the king of Israel.

13:24 Abijah became strong and married fourteen wives. He conceived twenty sons and sixteen daughters.

13:25 For in the eyes of the lord, the more women you fuck and the more children you conceive means the stronger you are.

14:1 Abijah died and was buried with his fathers in the city of David. Asa reigned in his stead and his first ten years of rule were of peace.

14:2 Asa did that which was righteous in the eyes of the lord and was known to the peoples as Asa the Intolerant. Heathens called him Asa the Asshole.

14:3 He took away the altars of false lords, burned down the high places, shattered the idols and images, cut down the groves,

14:4 And he commanded all the people within Judah to worship the lord of Israel and only the lord of Israel. Those who did not were publicly stoned.

14:5 The bodies of blasphemers and idol worshippers littered the lands of Judah throughout all the years of the reign of Asa.

14:6 This pleased the lord; God loves the smell of rotting corpses of the people who deny him.

14:7 This aroma pleased the lord almost as much as the stench of rotting corpses of those who did believe in him and were stricken down by the hand of God.

14:8 Asa built in every city high fences, gates, bars and towers, saying, "Let us build these cities in glory to God, who defends us with the strength of dragons and unicorns.

14:9 We of Judah shall be prosperous and never will the heathens and our bastard brethren come to our lands and win.

14:10 Their bodies shall litter the ground like the unbelievers who once dwelt among us. Let them rot in the hot sun, be pecked on by ravens and be fodder for the maggot and the worm."

14:11 Asa also had a great army; valiant warriors who bared sword, spear and arrow. Of those who held the spear and the blade there were three hundred thousand and of archers there were two hundred and fourscore thousand.

14:12 There came out against the people of Judah, Zerah the Ethiopian, with an army of one million men and three hundred chariots.

14:13 He came to challenge those of Judah, for his people were slaughtered in the lands ruled by Asa because they worshipped other lords.

14:14 Both the armies of Asa and Zerah met in the valleys of Zephathah, in the lands of Mareshah.

14:15 Asa cried out to his lord, saying, "Look at these blackened heathens, who come and dare challenge the strength of the lord. Come now, O lord and show these bastards the anger, the wrath and the fury of the true God of all gods."

14:16 It was then the lord came down in a thick cloud of darkness and fire and smote the Ethiopians before the peoples of Judah.

14:17 Zerah and his men fled in fear of the wrath and the tyranny of the lord.

14:18 The spirit of the lord and the armies of Asa chases the Ethiopians and pursued them to Gerar, where the lord struck them all with a curse and shattered the legs of every Ethiopian.

14:19 Asa and his men came and slaughtered every one of Zerah's men, carried their bodies and piled them atop one another by the oak tree of Gerar.

14:20 There the men of Asa burned the bodies of Zerah and his men, in great sacrifice to the lord.

14:21 God came to the bodies in his cloud of darkness and fire and surrounded the bodies of the dead Ethiopians, raping every one which pleased him and tearing the flesh from their bones.

14:22 As the lord was fulfilling his lust upon the dead, those of the armies of Judah raped and pillaged the cities of Gerar and killed all the peoples within, save for the virgins. The virgins were raped and sold into brothels or as concubines.

14:23 All the spoils of the city were taken back to the lands of Judah; the gold, the silver, the brass, the cattle, the sheep and the camels.

14:24 Only the unholy objects were not taken; they were burned beside the bodies of the armies of Zerah.

15:1 The spirit of the lord came to Azariah the son of Oded. It might have been the spirit in the wine.

15:2 Azariah went to meet Asa and said, "Hear me, O king of Judah and have your people you rule listen to my words. The lord is with you and loves you, for you offer him sacrifice and follow his laws without question.

15:3 For a long season those of Israel have suffered; they suffer because they abandoned the true God of all god, and went whoring after idols and false lords.

15:4 They were without priest, without law, without guidance.

15:5 Know that in their times of trouble, Israel sought forth the lord and they obeyed his laws, his statutes, his commandments.

15:6 Our lord would then destroy those that dared went against Israel. Cities were turned to dust and entire nations reduced to ash and rubble.

15:7 God cursed them strongly and caused these heathen fuckers great suffering; greater than the suffering he gave to the people of Israel.

15:8 Be strong, O Asa and follow the lord. Do so and he shall bless you with power, strength and glorious riches."

15:9 When Asa heard the words of Azariah, he grew great courage and struck down the idols, the altars and the groves of false lords. Throughout all of Judah were there no idols nor places to worship the false gods.

15:10 Some high places were left alone and hidden from the sight of Asa and his armies. The few not slaughtered by Asa went there to worship their lords in peace.

15:11 All those of Judah loved Asa and wished to be like him, for they knew the lord was with him.

15:12 Even the heathens who dwelt in the lands of Judah aspired to be like Asa.

15:13 They feared Asa greatly and wished to be powerful like their king and be able to slaughter those they loathed without mercy.

15:14 Those of Judah gathered themselves in the third month, in the fifteenth year of Asa's reign.

15:15 There they offered to the lord the many spoils of Judah. Seven hundred oxen and seven thousand sheep, all males without blemish.

15:16 They then prayed to the lord, promising to devote their hearts to him and seek out only the one true lord and not whore themselves to false gods, wizardry and witchcraft.

15:17 God laughed and cursed them all to the death and enslavement at the hands of the heathens.

15:18 Asa announced that all unbelievers of God must be executed. Only in death shall they know peace.

15:19 So those of Judah slaughtered all those who believed in false lords, believing that their death shall bring them peace and love.

15:20 They were wrong. God sent them to hell.

15:21 Maachah the mother of Asa was cursed by her son, for she had a grove in the gardens, where she burned incense to a false lord.

15:22 Asa tore down this grove and ground her idols to dust. However, he did not kill his mother.

15:23 Not even Asa was that cruel.

16:1 In the thirty sixth year of Asa's reign Baasha the king of Israel prepared to war against Judah and built the city of Ramah, so that those near the borders shall be shot by archers and their bodies looted.

16:2 Asa took out all the treasures of gold and silver from both the house of Solomon and the temple of God and took them to Benhadad the king of Syria, saying, "There is a league between us and our nations, which go back to our fathers and their fathers.

16:3 Behold, I have sent you gifts of silver and gold, so that you shall know the league between us and Judah is true and your league with these pricks of Israel is false.

16:4 Send a message to Baasha and tell him your league with him is finished. Those of Israel seek to betray you; betray them first, and attack."

16:5 Benhadad knew the words of Asa were false, but he did as Asa asked, for the bribe the king of Judah sent was of great value.

16:6 Syria went to war with Israel and took the cities of Ijon, Dan, Abelmaim, and all the lands of Naphtali.

16:7 Since Benhadad was not of Israel and knew not their manners of war, he let the civilians live and killed only those who fought against him.

16:8 Those who survived the onslaught of Syria were free to dwell in the cities of Israel which were left unharmed and they said of Benhadad, "What a fool.

16:9 Only a cursed idiot from God would allow those they conquer to live. He should have at least enslaved us.

16:10 Let it be that Israel curse Syria and slaughter all their nation and people, as punishment for his fatal mistake."

16:11 Asa knew that Benhadad allowed the peoples to live, but did not care. Benhadad was on the side of Judah and when Israel invades Judah, the armies of Syria shall be on the side of Asa.

16:12 The armies of Judah went to the city of Ramah and took the stones from it and with them built their own defensive cities of Geba and Mizpeh, along the borders of Israel.

16:13 Those who passed by the city and were not of the nation of Judah, were shot by archers and their bodies looted.

16:14 At that time Hanani the prophet came to Asa and cursed him, saying, "Because you hast relied upon the heathen nation of Syria and not the lord, let a great curse come to you.

16:15 Were not the Ethiopians and the Lubims a great army, who outnumbered us greatly. Yet our lord did slay them all.

16:16 Now you have gone and abandoned God and go fetch aid from the bastards of Syria.

16:17 Know that the lord is angry with you and that your seed shall fall on dust and the people of Judah be torn apart by the lions of foreigners."

16:18 Asa grew angry at Hanani and said, "Why is it we must rely on God for everything. Do you not think that he wishes rest?

16:19 Have you ever thought that the lord wishes us to take actions of our own. That our God grows tired of us asking him to constantly bless us and destroy our enemies in great fire and bloodshed?

16:20 I am thankful to the lord and for that which he has done for us. For this, I will not bother our God with such trivial manners."

16:21 God heard the words of Asa and liked them, but still cursed Asa. God is so arrogant he wishes all his people rely solely upon him and never take action for themselves.

16:22 Those that act become independent and those so that become independent do not need God.

16:23 If they ask the lord to act and the lord heeds not their words, then they have sinned and deserve the punishment of their lord.

16:24 Only after they have confessed and pleased the lord with bloodshed and sacrifice, will the lord may save them.

16:25 Asa had the prophet Hanani imprisoned, for he was quite angry with him. Asa then took his wrath out upon the people of Judah and taxed them higher and enslaved them more.

16:26 On the thirty ninth year of Asa's reign, he did become infected in the foot with a dreaded disease.

16:27 Not wanting to bother the lord, Asa sought out instead physicians, who told him, "What you have is a fungus which grows upon your toes.

16:28 Soak your foot in a brine of onions, garlic and your own piss. This shall destroy the disease which has cursed your foot."

16:29 The lord grew angry with Asa, for he sought out the wisdom of men and not the wonders of God, to cure his foot.

16:30 God came to Asa and said, "You have done that which is wicked in my sight.

16:31 You have gone to physicians, men who practice witchcraft tolerated by the people of earth and sought out not the wonders and glories of your lord."

16:32 The lord then took the fungus upon Asa's foot and placed it in his throat, so that the fungus choked him until death.

16:33 Asa reigned for forty-one years over the people of Judah, and was buried in a great sepulcher which he made for himself.

16:34 The sepulcher was carved of fine gold and filled with spices and incense prepared by the apothecaries' art.

16:35 It was said throughout all of Judah that the body of Asa smelled sweeter on his deathbed than ever in his life.

17:1 Jehoshaphat the son of Asa become king of Judah and strengthened his kingdom strongly against those of Israel.

17:2 He sent soldiers to the cities upon the borders of Judah and set garrisons in the lands, even the city of Ephraim which his father conquered from those of Israel.

17:3 The lord loved Jehoshaphat, for he sought only the wisdom of God and loathed those of Baal, Ashteroth and other false gods.

17:4 Jehoshaphat did all which was written in the laws of Moses and tolerated not any heathen, blasphemer, sodomite nor person who denied themselves God.

17:5 He destroyed all the hidden high places, where those who worshipped other gods would come to worship and burn incense.

17:6 Those who worshipped false lords were skinned alive and their hides were placed on display for all those to see.

17:7 For such dedication, the lord blessed Jehoshaphat and protected his borders from the foreign nations.

17:8 The people of Israel and the heathens would gaze on the lands of Judah and behold, they saw great beasts protecting the lands of Judah; unicorns, dragons, large oxen standing upright, creatures of horse and man.

17:9 All of Judah loved Jehoshaphat and brought him great presents of breads, fruits, meats, spices, silver, gold, concubines and their youngest virgin daughters.

17:10 In the third year of Jehoshaphat's reign he sent forth priests to travel to the cities of Judah and preach the word of God and the laws of Moses.

17:11 They would travel to Benhail, Obadaih, Zechariah, Nethaneel and Michaiah, spreading the propaganda of the lord and killing those who did not believe in their God.

17:12 The Levites Shemaiah, Nethaniah, Zebediah, Asahel, Shemiramoth, Jehonathan, Adonijah, Tobijah and Tobadonijah would travel with the priests Elishama and Jehoram, spreading the word of the lord.

17:13 All would bring with them the writings of the lord and preach to the people of Judah, who would come to listen to the wisdom of these men.

17:14 Those who did not come were deemed blasphemers and devil worshippers and were skinned alive in front of the congregation of Judah.

17:15 Even the heathen nations grew in fear of Jehoshaphat. The Philistines brought to Judah great presents of silver and the Arabs brought yearly flocks of seven thousand seven hundred rams and seven thousand seven hundred male goats without blemish.

17:16 Jehoshaphat ruled with great power and wealth over the people of Judah and built many castles and cities.

17:17 He also enlisted a great many men in the armies of Judah and placed them throughout the lands. Those of the most valiant warriors remained in Jerusalem.

17:18 These are the names of the captains and chiefs of the armies of Israel and the number of men they ruled over; Adnah, the chief, who ruled three hundred thousand men of valour.

17:19 Jehonanan the captain, who held in his command two hundred and fourscore thousand warriors.

17:20 Amasiah the son of Zichri, who commanded the respect of two hundred thousand archers.

17:21 Eliada, who led two hundred thousand men trained well in the spear.

17:22 Jehozabad, who ruled one hundred and fourscore thousand men, who would disguise themselves and listen to the people of Judah. Those who spoke ill of the lord or their king were killed secretly while they slept.

17:23 All these men followed the rules of the king and defended Judah mightily.

18:1 Jehoshaphat had riches and honour in abundance and leagued with the nation of Israel and their king Ahab.

18:2 It came to pass that Jehoshaphat came to visit Ahab in Israel and king Ahab sacrificed a great many oxen and sheep in honour to the lord and the reuniting of the brothers of Israel and Judah.

18:3 Ahab asked Jehoshaphat, "Will you and your armies go to war with me in Ramothgilead?" and Jehoshaphat answered, "Let it be as we were, one nation under God. I shall war with you in Ramothgilead.

18:4 Tell me, have you any prophets of the lord, who shall tell us the wisdom of God, so that we know what to do?"

18:5 Therefore the king of Israel gathered four hundred prophets and asked them, "Shall we go to war against Ramothgilead?" and the prophets answered, "Yes, war with Ramothgilead and the lord shall deliver these people into your hands."

18:6 Still, Jehoshaphat was unconvinced and said, "These men seem not like prophets, but men who say that which you want to hear."

18:7 Tell me, is there another prophet of the lord whose guidance we may seek?"

18:8 And Ahab answered him, "Yes, there is another prophet, whose name is Micaiah the son of Imla.

18:9 He is a true asshole, who has always prophesied evil against me. I hate the bastard son of a whore."

18:10 The king of Judah said, "Let us then seek out this man; he has never prophesied evil against me and his visions may be of great relief to both our peoples."

18:11 So Ahab said to an officer, "Go and fetch forth the bastard prophet Micaiah the son of Imla. Bring him to me, so Jehoshaphat may seek his guidance."

18:12 The two kings sat upon thrones placed by the gates of Israel, known also as Samaria and were surrounded by the four hundred prophets.

18:13 Zedekiah the son of Chenaanah, a prophet, built a helmet of horns with iron and said, "With these our lord shall push the Syrians out of Ramothgilead, until they lay beaten in the ground."

18:14 Zedekiah would then run around like a bull and push others with his horns, who would run away screaming, pretending to be the heathens of Syria.

18:15 He then ran to Jehoshaphat, saying, "Take your armies and those of Syria shall run from thee like the shepherd runs from the mad bull."

18:16 Jehoshaphat took the horns of iron and thrust the horns in the side of Zedekiah, saying, "Get away from me, foolish man.

18:17 You annoy the king of Judah; do so again and it shall be you

who will be consumed by bulls.":

18:18 Micaiah came to the two kings and Jehoshaphat asked of him, "Shall the armies of both Israel and Judah go and battle against Ramothgilead, or should we forbear?"

18:19 Micaiah said, "Go forth to Ramothgilead and you shall prosper against the heathens of Syria."

18:20 Ahab grew confused and said, "This is the first time you have ever prophesied in my favour. Tell me, why is this?"

18:21 Micaiah laughed and said, "It matters not if your armies win the battle of Ramothgilead.

18:22 Behold, the people of Israel shall be scattered like sheep upon the mountains and they shall have no shepherd.

18:23 They shall fall upon the rocks and be broken.

18:24 Ahab turned to Jehoshaphat and said, "Told you this man was a fucking asshole."

18:25 Micaiah still spoke and said, "Know this, though the armies of Israel and Judah will win the battle of Ramothgilead, Ahab shall fall.

18:26 The lord wishes Ahab dead and he called all the hosts of heaven and asked them how he may destroy Ahab the king of Israel.

18:27 An angel of the lord told him he had a plan, so that the king shall die in battle at Ramothgilead, and lie rotting in the dust.

18:28 Behold, this holy servant of the lord has come down and placed in the tongues of these prophets a lying spirit, who deceive you and speak evil against you."

18:29 Zedekiah grew angry and took from his side the horns of his helmet and with it struck Micaiah on the cheek, saying, "The lord does not lie nor fool with deceit.

18:30 You are a blasphemer and must be stoned to death as the lord demands."

18:31 Micaiah laughed at Zedekiah and said, "Behold, you shall see the day where you hide in the inner chambers, cowering and crying like a coward."

18:32 Ahab had enough and said, "Get this prophet Micaiah away from me and throw him in the deepest dungeons of my kingdom.

18:33 Let him rot until my return, where he shall see that he is wrong. Then let the people of Israel stone him until his body lay tattered and torn upon the streets."

18:34 So the kings of Judah and Israel went forth to Ramothgilead. Ahab did not believe the words of Micaiah, though Jehoshaphat did.

18:35 Jehoshaphat didn't care. He was not the one prophesied to die.

18:36 The king of Israel said to the king of Judah, "The words of Micaiah trouble me. I shall disguise myself in plain armour, so that they of Syria are fooled to think I am but a humble man.

18:37 Come, put on my robes and the enemies of ours shall think you are the king of Israel."

18:38 Jehoshaphat said, "You coward, why would I do that?" and Ahab said, "Then those of Syria will not know that the nation of Judah warred with them and will not hold ill will to your people."

18:39 So the king of Judah put on the robes of the king of Israel and fought against Syria.

18:40 Now the king of Syria said to his armies, "Kill all men, small or great. Capture only the king of Israel."

18:41 When the armies of Syria saw Jehoshaphat, they surrounded him with chariots, wishing to capture him.

18:42 Jehoshaphat fled, and the men of Syria gave chase, until they realized the man they pursued was not Ahab, but an imposter.

18:43 An archer of Syria struck Ahab between the joints of the harness: Ahab said to his chariot driver, "Get me out of the battle. I'm injured and need aid."

18:44 Try as he might, the driver could not retreat, for the bodies of the men of Syria lay plenty on the ground and the chariot could not drive over them.

18:45 As the battle increased, the armies of Israel and Judah struck deeply against the heathens of Syria.

18:46 However, Ahab died as the sun set and the words of Micaiah came true.

19:1 After the battle, Jehoshaphat returned home to Jerusalem in peace.

19:2 And Jehu the son of Hanani, a prophet, went to see the king and said to him, "You have damned the people of Judah to the anger, the wrath and the cruelty of the lord.

19:3 Ahab was a man of evil, who worshipped false gods and lets brothels of unholy lust do business in his lands.

19:4 Though this man be as a brother to you, it matters not; if the man sins, hate him, for our lord hates him strongly."

19:5 Jehoshaphat explained to Jehu, "I wished to open the eyes of Ahab, show him his mistakes and lead him back to God."

19:6 Jehu laughed and said, "You cannot open the eyes of a fool. Let those who be blind remain blind, until they wipe away the dust from their eyes and see for themselves.

19:7 If a man sins and whores themselves to heathen lords, this man must be hated and killed.

19:8 Upon death, our lord shall give him divine and merciful judgment.

19:9 Still, the lord sees great good in you. Judah shall not fall in your reign, but will be cast in the furnace of the heathens after your body goes to dust."

19:10 Jehoshaphat still wished to bring the people of Israel back to the true ways of their peoples and convert them from their wickedness.

19:11 He sent armies to the lands of Beersheba and mount Ephraim, where they preached and taught the ways of God.

19:12 Those who listened were spared and brought back to Judah. Those who did not listen, or hearkened not the words of Judah, were killed.

19:13 It was the first missionary crusade in history.

19:14 Jehoshaphat set also judges in every city, who would listen to the quarrels of men and settle their disputes according to the laws of Moses.

19:15 He said to the judges, "It matters not what the people think is just, for you serve not the people, but the lord our God.

19:16 Fear the lord and take heed of his laws. He has respect for no person and cares not what we think is fair.

19:17 Take not bribes nor gifts; they shall tarnish your judgment, and condemn you to a path of wickedness."

19:18 So the judges settled the disputes and quarrels between the people of Judah and they became rich, for they accepted bribes and gifts and were paid richly to favour in one man's favour.

19:19 A tradition which continues to this day.

20:1 It came to pass that the Moabites and the Ammonites grew disgusted at the gluttony and the arrogance of the nation of Judah and went to war with them.

20:2 The scouts of Judah came to Jehoshaphat, saying, "There comes a shitload of heathens which desire to destroy us. They come from across the sea on this side of Syria and they camp now in Hazazontamar, in the lands of Engedi."

20:3 Jehoshaphat became fearful of the multitude of armed men and sought forth the guidance of the lord. He proclaimed a fast throughout the lands of Judah, believing the starving of his people would bring out sympathy from his God.

20:4 All the people of Judah came to Jerusalem, so that they may hear the words of Jehoshaphat and seek the wisdom of the lord.

20:5 They came with offerings and burned them at the altar before the temple of the lord, praying that God would intervene and this is not a curse sent from their lord.

20:6 Jehoshaphat stood in front of the temple, standing before the congregation of Judah and he said,

20:7 "O God of our fathers who dwelleth in heaven, who rules in the lands of Judah and despise all nations of the heathen, hear our cry.

20:8 Art thou not the God who drove out the human beasts in this land and gave it to the seed of Abraham so that the covenant be fulfilled?

20:9 Behold, now the heathens of the children of Ammon, Moab and the people of mount Seir, whom those who left Egypt did not invade, reward us by marching towards us with spears and swords.

20:10 They wish to cast us out of our possession, which we inherited from the lord himself.

20:11 O lord, will you not judge them. We have no might against this great army, who march towards us, yet we seek our eyes on you, so that you may protect us from these heathen beasts."

20:12 And all of Judah stood before the lord, with their wives and their children, crying and praying for the lord to protect them.

20:13 The lord gazed upon his people and thought, "Ahh, they are so pathetic without the protection of their creator.

20:14 I'll spare them from the heathens this time."

20:15 So the spirit of the lord came to the mouth of Jahaziel the son of Zechariah, a Levite and he said to the congregation and the king of Judah, "Thus sayeth the lord, fear not these heathens who march towards us; fear not the battle, for the battle will not be yours, but Gods.

20:16 Tomorrow the men of Judah shall come up to the cliffs of Ziz, where the beasts that walk upright shall be resting by the brooks before the wilderness of Jeruel.

20:17 Fight not in this battle, but stand back and gaze at the wrath of the lord. God shall be with us and smite the heathens so that they litter the ground."

20:18 So the men of Judah went forth to the cliffs of Ziz and as they went to the wilderness of Tekoa, the king of Judah said to his peoples "Believe in the lord and he shall protect us all.

20:19 If doubt be in your heart, be gone; doubt shall be the poison which dooms us all."

20:20 Thus half the people of Judah left. Jehoshaphat took note of who left, so that he may kill them for doubting the lord.

20:21 Those that remained, Jehoshaphat made them singers and gave them cymbals and timbrels, so they may praise the glory and wonder of their lord.

20:22 When they began to sing and praise, the lord set up ambushes of holy beasts against the bastards of Ammon, Moab and mount Seir.

20:23 These beasts came and slew all the heathens who marched against Judah, so that only the blood and the skin remained littered upon the floor.

20:24 The people of Judah watched and laughed as the blood soaked the dirt beneath the heathens and the hides of their enemies were cast forth across the lands like soiled blankets.

20:25 As they came down to loot the bodies, they found an abundance of riches; weapons, armour, precious gems, which every man looted and carried home.

20:26 So much spoil was there that every man could not carry it all. It took three days for Judah to take home the plunder of their victory.

20:27 On the fourth day, the congregation of Judah assembled in Berachah, where they sang praises to the lord and offered many sacrifices for the blessings God gave to them.

20:28 Jerusalem played for God harps, trumpets and psalteries and burned the hides of the heathens in massive fire.

20:29 The nations of heathens heard of the slaughter of the people of Ammon, Moab and mount Seir and they feared Judah greatly, believing that demons fought for them.

20:30 Thus the realm of Jehoshaphat knew peace and all within rested fearing only the lord.

20:31 Jehoshahphat was thirty-five years old when he reigned over Judah and he ruled for twenty-five years. His mother was Azubah the daughter of Shilhi.

20:32 And he walked in the path of Asa his father, obeying the word of the lord and slaughtering unbelievers and those who praised false gods.

20:33 Howbeit the high places were not taken away, for the unbelievers and worshippers of idols knew ones when the armies of Judah destroyed their places of worship.

20:34 King Jehoshaphat allied himself with the bastard king of Israel, Ahaziah, who was wicked in the eyes of God.

20:35 Together they built ships in the harbours of Eziongaber, so that they may go to Tarshish.

20:36 Eliezer the son of Dovadah prophesied against Judah, saying, "Because our king hast become a brother to a blasphemer, the ships they build shall never see the sea." And behold, the wood of the ships rotted and sank to the bottom of the waters.

21:1 Upon the death of Jehoshaphat, Jehoram his son became king of Judah.

21:2 And he had brothers; Azariah, Jehiel, Zechariah, the other Azariah, Michael and Shephatiah, who were all sons of Jehoshaphat.

21:3 Their father gave them great gifts of gold, silver, women, gemstones and made them rulers of great cities of Judah, but his kingdom he gave to Jehoram, as he was the eldest.

21:4 When Jehoram became king of Judah, he grew paranoid and began to fear his brothers, thinking they wished to sit upon the throne.

21:5 His brothers cared not for the throne of Judah and were content with what their father gave them; still, Jehoram grew fearful of his kin.

21:6 As he strengthened his kingdom and gained the loyalty of his people, he sent out assassins to go forth and slay his brethren.

21:7 Each of the brothers of the king of Judah was slain as they slept: a knife across their throat as they slumbered within their chambers.

21:8 Jehoram was thirty-two years old when he began to rule over Judah and he reigned for eight years.

21:9 And he did that which was wicked in the sight of the lord, as did the people of Israel. The daughter of Ahab, king of Israel, was wife to Jehoram, and stained the heart of Jehoram.

21:10 It always seems to be the fault of a woman when it comes to making men evil.

21:11 Though Jehoram did wickedness in the eyes of God, the lord would not destroy the lands of Judah, because of the covenant he made with David that his seed shall serve Israel.

21:12 In the days of Jehoram the heathens of Edom revolted under Judah and made themselves a king.

21:13 Jehoram sent forth his armies in the night and slew those of Edom, destroying their chariots and burning their men.

21:14 This angered the Edomites more, who revolted under Judah strongly, as did the people of Libnah, who loathed Judah and their lord.

21:15 Jehoram was interested in the unholy lust of men and made brothels amongst the cities of Judah where sodomites worked. He also built high places and altars to false lords, which made God very fucking angry.

21:16 Elijah the prophet wrote Jehoram a letter, saying, "Thus sayeth the lord God of David thy father; you have walked in the wickedness of the people of Israel and ruled not in the wisdom of your father Jehoshaphat nor his father Asa.

21:17 You have offered your people as whores to the heathen lords and your men go lusting after other men and your women take

pleasure in the loins of cattle.

21:18 Behold, God is fucking pissed at you and shall send a plague to smite your people, both women and men.

21:19 You shall be stricken with a terrible sickness, until the very organs of your belly fall out of your asshole and drag behind you as you walk."

21:20 This letter amazed Jehoram, for Elijah was believed to be dwelling in the kingdom of God, yet he still wrote to the king of Judah.

21:21 The lord stirred also the people of Philistine and Arab, who fought with Judah.

21:22 They lay siege to the city of Jerusalem and took it, carrying away all that which was found in the house of Jehoram; his wives, his concubines, his gold, his silver, his daughters and his sons.

21:23 Only Jehoahaz the youngest son of Jehoram was left behind; he was an annoying little fuck that not even the heathens wished to tolerate.

21:24 Then the lord smote Jehoram in his bowels with an incurable disease, until the very bowels and organs of Jehoram fell out and dragged behind him.

21:25 It came to pass that after two years, Jehoram cut the bowels from his asshole, killing him.

21:26 Thirty-two years old was he when he began to reign over Judah and he reigned for eight years. The people buried him beneath his favourite brothel of men.

22:1 The people of Jerusalem made Ahaziah the son of Jehoram king, for he was the eldest of the sons of Jehoram who survived the capture from the Arabs.

22:2 Forty-two years old was Ahaziah when he began to reign over Judah and he reigned for one year. His mother's name was Athaliah the daughter of Omri.

22:3 He walked also in the wicked ways, for his mother counselled him to do evil; his mother was a wretched cunt in the eyes of the lord.

22:4 Like the kings of Israel became Ahaziah, who sought guidance from false lords and let live blasphemers, wizards, witches, necromancers, heathens and homosexuals.

22:5 Ahaziah allied himself with the king of Israel and went to war beside them against Hazael the king of Syria; those of Syria fought against Joram the king of Israel and gave him a terrible wound.

22:6 Joram fled Jezreel and sought forth physicians for his wound. Azariah the king of Judah came to Jezreel and gave comfort to his friend Joram.

22:7 God planned the destruction of Ahaziah at Jezreel and anointed Jehu the son of Nimshi to slaughter all those of the house of Ahab.

22:8 It came to pass that when Jehu was on his bloody rampage of killing the family of Ahab, he came across the princes of Judah and the sons of Ahaziah. He killed them all and feasted on their raw flesh like an animal.

22:9 Jehu sought Ahaziah, who hid in the lands of Israel and the peoples of Israel carried Ahaziah to Jehu, saying, "Here, take this man of Judah, who hides in our lands like a coward."

22:10 So Jehu took his dagger and cut the heart of Ahaziah from his chest and paid the people of Israel for bringing this man to him.

22:11 When Athaliah the mother of Ahaziah saw that her son was dead, she went fucking insane and killed all her grandsons in a bloody rampage.

22:12 Jehoshabeath the daughter of Ahaziah witnessed the insanity of Athaliah, she took her youngest brother Joash and hid him in the temple of the lord, so that his grandmother wouldn't beat him to death with a candlestick.

22:13 Joash hid in the house of the lord for six years as his grandmother ruled over Judah.

23:1 In the seventh year of Athaliah's reign did Jehoiada, the caretaker of Joash strengthen himself and took the captains of the army Azariah the son of Jeroham, Ishmael the son of Jehohanan, Azariah the son of Obed, Maaseiah the son of Adaiah, and Elishaphat the son of Zichri into covenant with him.

23:2 They travelled throughout the lands of Judah and brought the Levites, slaves to God, out of the cities and gathered them in Jerusalem.

23:3 And all the people of Levi and the armies of Judah swore an oath to the true king of Judah, saying, "Behold, the seed of David lives and shall rule over the people of Judah.

23:4 We shall rid Judah of the witch which rules them and bring forth Joash as king.

23:5 This is what we shall do; on the sabbath, a third of us shall stay guarding the doors to the temple of the lord.

23:6 A third part shall keep eye on the house of the king and the rest shall stand by the gates of the foundation of the temple.

23:7 None of the people of Judah shall enter the temple of the lord save for the priests and the Levites, as they are holy to God.

23:8 Those who enter the temple will be slain by the sword.

23:9 We shall then announce king Joash to the people of Judah and they shall rejoice and praise his name.

23:10 When the queen of cunts come forth to see what her peoples celebrate, it is then we shall kill her."

23:11 So Jehoiada spoke to the people of Judah, saying, "Behold, the seed of David is among us and shall be our new king.

23:12 Joash the son of Ahaziah dwells among us and shall rule us with wisdom and mercy."

23:13 And the people of Judah shouted "Hurrah, hurrah. Blessed be the king of Judah!"

23:14 The armies of Judah then handed every man a spear, a sword and a shield and said, "Protect the king from the false queen of Judah. When you see her, thrust your weapon through that witch's skull."

23:15 When Athaliah heard the celebration of the new king of Judah, she left her house and went to see why those of Judah celebrated so.

23:16 As she came to the temple, behold, she saw Joash her grandson dressed in fine robes and wearing a crown upon his head.

23:17 She said to the armies of Judah, "That man is a blasphemer, a man against God!

23:18 Kill him. Slay him. Bathe in the blood which flows through his veins!"

23:19 The armies of Judah said, "N'ah, we'd rather not. We'll kill you instead, annoying little geriatric semen guzzling twat."

23:20 So the peoples of Judah took Athaliah to the stalls and killed her by the horses, which then trampled upon her body and flattened the corpse.

23:21 Jehoiada made a covenant then with Joash and the people of Judah and said they shall from henceforth be the lord's people.

23:22 Those of Judah then went to the temple of Baal and tore it down. Every idol was ground to dust, every altar burned and the very building was reduced to ashes and smoke.

23:23 Before the last altar of Baal was burned, they placed Mattar the priest of Baal upon it and burned him with the altar, saying, "Let this whore of false lords be the last offering to Baal."

23:24 Jehoiada then appointed guards at the gates of every city of Judah, who would slaughter every person who was a heathen, unclean, worshipped false lords, or was otherwise wicked in the sight of the lord.

23:25 Sometimes they would get bored and kill people randomly, even if they were of the nation of Judah.

23:26 And all the people of the lands rejoiced and praised the death of Athaliah.

24:1 Joash was seven years old when he began to reign as king of Judah and he was given two wives by the priest Jehoiada.

24:2 And Joash was a non-violent person, who did that which was right in the eyes of the lord.

24:3 This made him very, very dull.

24:4 His biggest achievement was fixing the temple of the lord and decorating it with more gold, gemstones, silver and brass.

24:5 It was a big waste of money, but it made the lord happy.

24:6 Jehoiada grew old and died at the age of one hundred and thirty. He was buried in the sepulcher of David, for he did good in Israel and followed the path of the lord.

24:7 When Jehoiada died, the princes of Israel rejoiced and said, "Now we can finally worship the lords of the heathens, who don't demand sacrifice and threaten to kill us with cruelty."

24:8 So the princes of Judah set up altars and groves in the high places and worshipped Baal and Ashteroth.

24:9 Prophets were sent by Joash to convert the princes of Judah, so that they may worship the true lord of lords and not condemn the nation of Judah to God's wrath.

24:10 The princes of Judah would not listen and spoke ill of the lord, saying, "We shall not worship a lord who condemns us to cruelty for the sins of our ancestors."

24:11 It was then the spirit of the lord came over Zechariah the son of Jehoiada and he spoke to the blasphemers, saying, "Thus sayeth the lord, fuck you!

24:12 He shall send your seed to the depths of the fires, so that your house be cast into the realm of darkness and be forgotten by all.

24:13 Your daughters shall be raped by the men with foreskins and your sons enslaved and beaten by the whip of heathens."

24:14 The princes of Judah laughed and said, "That is why we loathe the lord; he is a cruel bastard and does not deserve our devotion."

24:15 They then stoned Zechariah to death, screaming at him, "This is what the lord demands you shall do to all but the blind and ignorant.

24:16 Tell us, what God deserves our devotion who demands such cruelty. Surely picking up sticks on the sabbath is not worth this punishment."

24:17 Though Joash was not the one who stoned to death Zechariah the son of Jehoiada, the lord blamed him anyway, for the princes of Judah, the sons of Joash, stoned him.

24:18 God came to Joash and said, "You have not remembered the kindness of Jehoiada and your hands have shed the blood of his son.

24:19 You shall be punished for such acts against God."

24:20 And Joash said, "It was not I who slew Zechariah the son of Jehoiada, but my sons, who went forth and worshipped the lords of heathens."

24:21 The lord struck Joash with fire and said, "You did nothing to stop the princes of Judah from perverting themselves to false lords and spreading lies amongst the peoples of Judah.

24:22 You should have done that which was necessary in the eyes of the lord and stoned your sons for all the congregation of Judah to witness.

24:23 Now your incompetence has made a prophet, a man of God, become stoned to death.

24:24 This makes the lord very, very, fucking pissed. May you and your kingdom be raped by those loathed by the lord."

24:25 And at the years end, the armies of Syria came up and conquered the nation of Judah. They slew the sons of Joash, ravaged the city of Jerusalem and took back to Damascus all the spoils of war.

24:26 When the armies of Syria left, they spread to those of Judah great diseases; and the peoples of Judah cursed their king and blamed him for the destruction caused by Syria.

24:27 The servants of Jehoiada conspired against Joash and beat him to death with sticks as the king of Judah slept on his bed.

24:28 Those who conspired against the king were Zabad the son of Shimeath the Ammonite and Jehozabad the son of Shimrith the Moab.

24:29 Joash was burned in the fires of Jerusalem, which burned the corpses of the unclean lepers. His son, Amaziah, became king of Judah.

25:1 Amaziah was twenty-five years old when he became king of Judah and he reigned for twenty nine years. His mother's name was Jehoaddan of Jerusalem.

25:2 And Amaziah did that which was right with the lord, but his heart was not perfect. He felt sympathy.

25:3 When Amaziah established himself king, he gathered Zabad and Jebozabad and cut their heads from their necks, for these were the men who betrayed his father.

25:4 But he slew not the children of these men and let them live in peace, despite the lord demanding that the children be punished for the sins of their fathers.

25:5 This angered the lord and God knew that sympathy stained the heart of Amaziah.

25:6 Amaziah gathered Judah together, so that all the men over the age of twenty-two would serve in the armies of Judah. He made captains over hundreds and over thousands and those who were drafted in the armies with shield, spear and sword were three hundred thousand men.

25:7 He hired also mercenaries from Israel; one hundred thousand men who were bought to protect Judah for one hundred talents of silver.

25:8 But there came a man of God, saying to Amaziah, "O king, when you battle, bring not the mercenaries of Israel with you. The lord is not with Israel and they shall curse your men who fight against the children of Ephraim.

25:9 Be strong for the battle and send only those of Judah. Our lord shall have it so that the enemy of Judah be cast down from the earth."

25:10 Amaziah asked the man of God, "What of the hundred talents of silver which I paid the men of Israel?" and the prophet said, "Kill the mercenaries and take it back."

25:11 But Amaziah would not slay the mercenaries and he let them keep the hundred talents of silver.

25:12 And God cursed Amaziah and called him a damn pussy.

25:13 Those of the children of Ephraim laughed at the king of Judah, saying, "The man has paid us a hundred talents of silver so that he may not let us fight in battle.

25:14 Let it be that those who wish us not to fight, pay us plenty so we may sheath our swords."

25:15 Amaziah strengthened his armies and went to fight against the peoples of Seir. He slew of these peoples ten thousand men.

25:16 Another ten thousand of the young ones of Seir he gathered, and brought them to a high cliff.

25:17 The children of Seir were then cast from the cliff and their bodies broke against the rocks beneath.

25:18 The lord gazed upon the massacre of little children and smiled with glee as the young ones cried for their dead mothers.

25:19 Now the mercenaries of Israel, which Amaziah sent back, they fought against the cities of Judah, saying, "You shall pay us one hundred talents to not fight against you."

25:20 The cities from Samaria even to Bethhoron they lay siege to and pillaged, slaying thousands of the nation of Judah and taking their spoils.

25:21 It came to pass that after Amaziah slaughtered the people of Seir, he took back their idols of false gods and brought them to Jerusalem. He then began to worship these gods and burn incense for them.

25:22 This angered the lord greatly and he sent a prophet to Amaziah, saying, "Why do you worship the lords of those you have slain. Surely you of all men must know their gods have failed them.

25:23 For your stupidity, the lord shall send Judah to the lions and your people shall be cursed."

25:24 The king of Judah said to the prophet, "Why is it our lord kills us when he becomes angered at us?

25:25 For a lord of mercy, he is certainly malevolent."

25:26 God then cursed Amaziah with stupidity and Amaziah sent a letter to Joash the king of Israel, saying, "I have become bored with the lands of my nation and wish to expand my empire.

25:27 You shall surrender your lands and your people to me and you shall be my servant."

25:28 Joash laughed at this message and replied to Amaziah, saying, "My armies shall crush your kingdom like the hoof of the horse crushes the lone blade of grass."

25:29 So the two men brought their armies and they met on the lands of Bethshemesh, which is in Judah.

25:30 Those of Judah were beaten horribly by the hands of Israel, so that every man fled and hid crying in their tents.

25:31 Joash the king of Israel took Amaziah the king of Judah to Jerusalem and forced him to break down the walls of his city; four hundred cubits of rock were all that remained.

25:32 The armies of Israel then took from Jerusalem all the treasures of the house of the king, the treasures from the temple of the lord and took peoples of Judah as slaves and concubines and returned home.

25:33 Amaziah outlived Joash the king of Israel by fifteen years and declared to his people, "Because I have outlived Joash, I have bested him in war."

25:34 Those of Judah mocked Amaziah and said, "If you have beaten him, my daughter would not be raped by the men of Israel as we speak."

25:35 After the time Amaziah spoke of victory against Israel, those of Judah began to hate him and conspired against him.

25:36 Amaziah heard of the hatred of his people and fled to hide in Lachish. The people followed him Lachish and slew him there.

25:37 They dragged his body back behind the horse and buried the remains in the sepulcher of his fathers.

26:1 The people of Judah took Uzziah, who was sixteen years old and made him king over the nation of Judah. He reigned for fifty-two years over Judah and his mother was Jecoliah of Jerusalem.

26:2 He did that which was right in the lord and sought the advice of Zechariah the prophet, who was intimate in the ways of God.

26:3 And he went forth and warred against the people of Philistine and Arabia, killing their men, children and women, saving only the virgins so that they may be raped.

26:4 God was with Uzziah when he fought against the heathens and aided the armies of Judah in Gurbaal and Mehunim.

26:5 The Philistine cities of Gath, Jabneh and Ashdod were burnt and those that survived were made crippled and cast out into the wilderness so the beasts may feast upon them.

26:6 Those of the children of Ammon feared Uzziah and bribed him with gifts so that he may leave their lands in peace. Even those of Egypt bribed Uzziah, so that the armies of Judah won't invade their lands.

26:7 Uzziah built throughout the lands of Judah high towers, which defended the lands of his nation and would strike with the arrow any heathen which walked on the lands of Judah.

26:8 Each tower had atop it a great engine, which would cast at the heathen bastard large stones and crush them with ease.

26:9 Uzziah dug in the desert many wells, so that more vineyards could be grown in the lands of Judah. Uzziah loved wine and the vineyards of Judah could not sustain his alcoholism.

26:10 As Uzziah grew old, he one day became drunk, and entered the house of the lord to burn incense.

26:11 Azariah the priest was within the temple, as were fourscore other priests and they saw their drunken king go to the oracle of God.

26:12 As they saw that Uzziah wished to burn incense to the lord, they came to him and said, "You are not holy enough in the eyes of God to burn incense for him."

26:13 Uzziah spat upon the priests and said, "I am the fucking king of Judah and I declare it by law that I am holier than all you priests and shall burn incense to my damn lord if I want to burn incense to God."

26:14 It was then Uzziah grabbed a censer to burn incense and as he lit the censer, behold, leprosy began to grow on his forehead.

26:15 The priests pointed at Uzziah and yelled, "Unclean. Unclean!" and Uzziah said, "How dare you call me unclean.

26:16 I shall strike your holiness from you and feed you to the devils."

26:17 But Uzziah was unclean and cast out of the city of Jerusalem for being a leper. He lived the remainder of his days in a slum, cursed by the lord with leprosy.

26:18 When Uzziah died, his body was burned in the wilderness of Judah, for the people did not wish to bury a leper within the city of Jerusalem. Jotham his son became king of Judah.

27:1 Jotham was twenty-five years old when he became king of Judah and he reigned for sixteen years in Jerusalem. Nobody knows who his mother was and nobody cared.

27:2 He did that which was right in the eyes of the lord, though he feared the temple of the lord, saying, "That is where my father was stricken with leprosy."

27:3 Jotham didn't do that much when he was king. He was lazy and feared any action he took would anger the lord and bring a curse upon his head.

27:4 He built a few cities in the mountains of Judah and had it so that the temple was restored greater with gold.

27:5 He fought also with the children of Ammon and slaughtered many of them. He then demanded the Ammonites pay yearly one hundred talents of silver, ten thousand measures of wheat and ten thousand measures of barley.

27:6 That's all he did. He was truly a lazy and boring king.

27:7 After sixteen years ruling over those of Judah, he died and was buried in the city of David. His son, Ahaz, reigned in his stead.

28:1 Ahaz was twenty years old when he began to reign as king of Judah and he reigned for sixteen years over the nation of Judah.

28:2 He was a wicked little bastard who did that which was wrong in the eyes of the lord; tolerating homosexuals, worshipping false lords and bowing down to molten brass images of the heathen god Baal.

28:3 His children were taught the evilness of wizardry, witchcraft and necromancy, which was a horrific abomination to the lord of Israel.

28:4 Ahaz built high places among the hills and beneath the green trees of Judah, where he and his people burn incense to the false lords.

28:5 God became angry with Ahaz and the people of Judah and strengthened the nation of Syria to come forth, killing and enslaving the people of Judah.

28:6 Even those of Israel did God give strength and they came to their brethren and slaughtered many of them, pleasing the lord greatly.

28:7 Pekah the son of Remaliah slew in Judah one hundred and twenty thousand in one day, which gave great pleasure to the lord, for those slain were heathens in the eyes of God.

28:8 Also, God loves bloodshed and death. Violence and killing is the lord's entertainment.

28:9 Zichri, a man of Ephraim, came and slew of the king's sons Maaseiah, Azikram and Elkanah, who was next to be king.

28:10 And the children of Israel took away two hundred thousand of their brethren of Judah; men, women, sons, daughters and their spoils.

28:11 But a prophet of the lord named Oded was there, who got drunk on the wine taken from Judah and said to those of Israel, "We are right fucked with the lord now if we take these beasts of Judah back to the lands of our home.

28:12 We have won this war against our former brethren for the lord God was with us; those of Judah have sinned wicked in the eyes of the lord of heaven.

28:13 But we of Israel hath sinned as well, just not as bad as these cocksuckers of Judah; the lord is on our side as we piss him off the least.

28:14 If we take these people home, they shall sin upon our lands and trick us into evil, so that we may sin and the lord shall be wroth with us deeply.

28:15 Let these people of Judah go; they shall condemn us to the damnation of the lord if they step upon the lands of Samaria."

28:16 So the heads of the children of Israel, who were Azariah the son of Johanan, Bechariah the son of Meshillemoth, Jehizkiah the son of Shallum, and Amaza the son of Hadlai, stood up to the captives of war and said to them,

28:17 "You are like the cursed objects of the heathens, which brought damnation to our peoples when we took them to our homes.

28:18 Take your spoils and leave us. We shall not be punished for the sins of Judah."

28:19 So the people took their spoils and were brought naked to the city of Jericho, the city of palm trees, so that the people of Judah may welcome back their captive brothers.

28:20 And the people of Judah went, "Ahh, that is nice, that our former brethren would give us our people back and that which they took from the spoils of war against us.

28:21 Sure, they killed my brothers, raped my sisters and slaughtered my parents, but at least they returned those they wished to enslave."

28:22 As those of Jericho came forth to embrace their brothers, the children of Edom came by and enslaved them all again.

29:23 And those who were freed by the captivity of the people of Israel looked up into the heavens and said, "God, you really are a funny jackass."

28:24 God agreed it was funny, but was angered that they called him a jackass.

28:25 Thus the lord gave strength to the Philistines, who warred against Judah and took the southern lands of Bethshemesh, Ajalon, Gederoth, Shocho, Timnah, and Gimzo.

28:26 The armies of Judah were weakened greatly, for the battle against Israel slaughtered many of their valiant men and left them weak and crippled against the heathens.

28:27 Ahaz grew fearful and sent a message to Assyria, begging for help against the nations which plundered and scorched his lands.

28:28 Tilgathpilneser king of Assyria came to Ahaz and said, "I'd love to help you, but you have offered me all the values of the house of the kings and the temple of the lord.

28:29 You have not even a shekel of copper to offer the armies of my nation; help does not come cheap.

28:30 When you have something of value to offer, then we shall send you men with blades. Until then, I can offer only my sympathy as your peoples be raped and murdered."

28:31 As Ahaz cried and begged for the help of the armies of Assyria, he asked king Tilgathpilneser, "Is there any help you can give my people for free?" and Tilgathpilneser said, "Yes, there is.

28:32 Abandon your God; he does not protect you and has likely sent these heathens after you for his own amusement.

28:33 Give sacrifice to the lords of my nation. They protect us from harm."

28:34 Ahaz said to the king of Assyria, "How can you prove your lords protect you?" and the king of Assyria said, "These people aren't attacking my nation, are they?"

28:35 So king Ahaz began to worship the gods of Damascus, burning incense for them and making idols in their images, saying, "The lords of Damascus protect their people; let it be that those of Judah be as the people of Assyria."

28:36 Ahaz even took out the silver and the gold from the temple of the lord and made from them altars and idols for the gods of Assyria.

28:37 Every city in Judah had an altar and an idol to the heathen lords of Damascus, so that the citizens of Judah can offer incense and worship to their new lords.

28:38 This really made God angry. Very fucking angry.

28:39 The lord said to his angels, "Fuck the house of David and fuck the people and the covenant.

28:40 I will have it so that both Israel and Judah be cast from existence and every single one of them be dead, burned and buried in graves the size of mountains."

28:41 When Ahaz died, he was buried in the city of Jerusalem, but not in the sepulcher of his kings. Ahaz said, "My fathers worshipped an uncaring lunatic. I wish not to rest with them."

28:42 Hezekiah his son became the new king of Judah.

29:1 Hezekiah was twenty-five years old when he began to reign as king of Judah and he reigned for twenty nine years. His mother's name was Abijah the daughter of Zechariah.

29:2 Hezekiah was a little kiss-ass to the lord and did that which was right in the eyes of God.

29:3 In his first month of being king, he repaired the temple of the lord, repaired the doors and the walls and replaced most of the gold to restore the bling of the lord.

29:4 The king then brought together the priests and the Levites in front of the temple and said, "Sanctify yourselves and sanctify this temple; rid us of the filth and the shit which our fathers had stained upon Judah.

29:5 For our fathers have sinned wicked in the eyes of God, forsaking him and abandoning the true ways of the lord of lords.

29:6 They have stripped the house of the lord of its gold and built altars to heathen lords and devils; they have burned incense to false gods yet have not even stepped foot inside the temple of the lord.

29:7 Now our lord is angry with Judah and hath delivered serpents to our lands that bite and strike us with venom.

29:8 The past kings have fallen by the sword of our enemies and their wives, their daughters, their sons are slaves and prostitutes to those that worship demons.

29:9 Now I must make right the sins of our fathers and make a covenant with the lord, so that his anger be gone from us and his wrath destroy those people which be against us.

29:10 Levites, slaves of the lord, be blessed, for you have been chosen to do the will of the lord and now your service shall please God and lift his wrath up from those of Judah."

29:11 So the priests arose, who were Mahath the son of Amasai, Joel the son of Azariah, the sons of Merari, Kish the son of Abdi, Azariah the son of Jehalelel, Joah the son of Zimmah, Eden the son of Joah,

29:12 Shimrie and Jeiel the sons of Elizaphan, Zechariah and Mattaniah the sons of Asaph,

29:13 Jehiel and Shimei the sons of Heman and Shemaiah and Uzziel the sons of Jeduthun.

29:14 They and all the Levites came under the orders of Hezekiah, so that they may cleanse the temple of the lord.

29:15 The priests went into the inner chambers of the temple and killed all those within who were offering incense to the false lord Baal.

29:16 All the blood of those slain were gathered in jars and given to the Levites, so that they may pour it into the brooks of Kidron.

29:17 After all the blasphemers and those who whored themselves to false gods were cleansed from the temple, the priests and the Levites began to bless the building and remove any object which associated itself to heathen lords.

29:18 These objects were given to the Levites, who burned them to ash and poured the remains in the brooks of Kidron.

29:19 It took sixteen days to bless the temple, rid the house of the unholy objects and kill those which remained in the holy place.

29:20 They went to king Hezekiah and said, "We have blessed the house of the lord and sanctified if from the wickedness and evil which the people of Judah have stained upon the very floors.

29:21 Even the vessels which king Ahaz gave to false lords we did sanctify and they now belong back to the God of all gods."

29:22 Hezekiah rose and gathered all those of Judah to the temple, so that they may witness the final blessing of the house of the lord.

29:23 He brought seven lambs, seven bullocks and seven goats to the house of the lord and showed them to the congregation of Judah, saying, "Today, we bless the house of the lord and make it holy again."

20:24 The priests then slaughtered the seven bullocks, seven lambs and seven goats, gathering the blood in vessels of gold and burning the remains on the altar.

29:25 The blood gathered was then poured upon the temple, so that the floors, the walls, the ceilings were drenched in the blood of the beasts.

29:26 All the temple of the lord was covered in the blood of the animals and Hezekiah said, "Now the lord is pleased with us and his house is fit for him to dwell in.

29:27 Those that go against God, shall their blood be smeared upon the house of the lord."

29:28 He then gathered many of Judah who were accused of serving Baal and he slaughtered them before the altar of the lord with a knife.

29:29 The blood of these people was then gathered in jars of gold and smeared upon the temple of the lord; the walls, the floors, the ceiling, even the tables, chairs and vessels were smeared with the blood of those who worshipped heathen lords.

29:30 Six thousand of the people of Judah were slain in sacrifice to God and their blood covered the house of the lord almighty.

29:31 As the people were being sacrificed, the priests and the Levites sang psalms to the lords, played instruments of trumpets and cymbals and danced naked around Hezekiah as he slit the bodies of the people who whored themselves to Baal.

29:32 When all were slain, Hezekiah stood before the people who remained of Judah and said, "Now the lord is pleased with us. Enter the temple and worship the lord, so that his anger be lifted from us."

29:33 And the people of Judah came into the house of the lord and praised the true God.

29:34 Some slipped on the blood and were killed on the floor. The priests claimed that those who slipped on the blood were blasphemers and devil worshippers and were killed by the hand of God.

29:35 All of Judah praised the death of these people and all were afraid of Hezekiah, the priests and the Levites.

30:1 Hezekiah then demanded that all those of Judah celebrate the Passover, and sent letters to the princes of each city, saying, "Come to Jerusalem, you and your people.

30:2 Celebrate the Passover, and give praise to the lord God."

30:3 Hezekias sent also letters to the king of Israel, which said, "Please our lord and lift his wrath upon you.

30:4 Come to Jerusalem and celebrate the Passover of our lord, as it was written long ago in the laws of Moses."

30:5 And all the people of Israel and Judah went, "Free food offered by Hezekiah the king of Judah. Let us go and celebrate this Passover and feast for free."

30:6 Thus the peoples across Judah and Samaria came to the Passover in Jerusalem, thinking it would be a feast.

30:7 Now the Passover was in the second month of the year, which was not the appointed time of the celebration.

30:8 The priests and the Levites noted this to Hezekiah, who replied, "We haven't had Passover in years, do you think the lord will care that it is not at the correct time?"

30:9 Hezekiah was wrong and the lord was angry that the Passover was celebrated on the wrong time, saying, "Even when they try to appease me, they fuck up like idiots."

30:10 When all the congregation of Israel and Judah came to Jerusalem, it was crowded within the city and all were hungry and awaiting the feast of Passover.

30:11 As the chefs of the king came out with unleavened bread, the people ate and awaited the rest of the feast.

30:12 When the chefs came out again with unleavened bread, they ate more of the bread, but left some aside so that they may fill their bellies with leavened bread and meat.

30:13 The third time the chefs came out with unleavened bread, the people asked them, "When do we stop receiving appetizers and the main course comes?"

30:14 The chefs said, "This is Passover. All that there is to eat is unleavened bread."

30:15 All the people were annoyed and said, "A celebration where all we feast upon is flat bread. What kind of feast is this?

30:16 How long does this mundane meal end and we can start eating food that is pleasing to the senses?"

30:17 And the chefs answered, "One week we must eat unleavened bread."

30:18 The people cursed Passover and said, "We are leaving this city full of dull bread and eating something worthwhile."

30:19 God then cursed the people who left Jerusalem and their bellies became bloated so that they could not walk under their own weight.

30:20 Predators and scavengers came and feasted on the bloated people cursed by the lord for leaving the Passover.

30:21 And when those in Jerusalem saw their brethren cursed by the lord, they sat down by the tables and ate the unleavened bread without complaint.

30:22 On the eighth day, the Levites came forth and offered sacrifice to the lord, slaying rams, sheep, goats, doves and pigeons.

30:23 Those of the congregation of Israel and Judah believed this was part of the meal and grew excited in the thought of eating meat.

30:24 When the sacrifices were burnt on the altar, the people began to weep and their bellies rumbled for the sweet savoury flesh which was being burned for the lord they began to hate.

30:25 The Levites then blessed the people and began spraying blood on the people of Judah and Israel, saying prayers for them and removing from them their sins.

30:26 Some of the people began to lick the blood sprayed on them, for they were hungry for food other than unleavened bread.

30:27 The lord cursed those who licked the blood and they became pale as snow and were burned to ash by the sun in the sky.

30:28 Few fled to the shadows and escaped by night, living in the wilderness and never seeing daylight again.

30:29 They craved blood and sought it out by night. They would go to the cities and drain blood from the necks of those that slept.

30:30 When they were caught, they were slain and offered as sacrifice to the lord God.

30:31 At the end of Passover, the people of Judah and Israel praised the lord, saying, "Thank God this is finally over."

30:32 They then returned home and ate goat, lamb, chicken, pheasant, quail, dove, pigeon, duck, goose, oxen, fish, swine and any other animal they could capture, kill and cook.

31:1 To punish Hezekiah for having the Passover on the wrong time, the lord strengthened Sennacherib the king of Assyria, who sent his armies to Judah so that he may claim these lands.

31:2 When Hezekiah heard the Assyrians came to conquer him, he grew ma, and decided that the peoples of Assyria came not for the land, but for the water.

31:3 "These men of Assyria grow thirsty and wish to drink all the water from my brooks, my rivers and my lakes.

31:4 Let them drown in the waters they seek and be eaten by the fish and the whale."

31:5 So Hezekiah ordered the people of Judah to block the waters and wells of the lands of Judah, so that the wells be dry and the rivers run empty.

31:6 This was a terrible idea, as the wells were what supplied the people of Judah with water and the dams caused flooding throughout the lands.

31:7 The counsellors of Hezekiah came to him and said, "Those of our people are either without water or are living like fish.

31:8 We know that you have pleased the lord God and that God shall be on our side if we fight these heathens who come to enslave us.

31:9 Build up our defenses and strengthen our armies; let us take the fight to them."

31:10 Hezekiah agreed and built strong towers throughout the lands of Judah and repaired the walls of Millo, arming those in the towers and atop the walls of Millo with shields, bows and swords.

31:11 The king of Judah then said to his people, "We are at war with the bastard children of Assyria, who come to claim our lands and drink our water.

31:12 Be strong and courageous. Though they outnumber us, know that the lord is on our side and we will prevail.

31:13 Their arms be made of flesh and bone, but the arm of the lord is made of iron and brass. The arm of Sennacherib shall be crushed and feasted on by dogs."

31:14 And the people were worried, for they feared the lord was angry with them and that this army of Assyria was sent by God.

31:15 Sennacherib sent forth servants to Jerusalem, as the armies of Assyria laid siege to Lachish.

31:16 These servants said to the people of Judah, "Your king is an idiot and you know this deep within your hearts.

31:17 He has dried up your wells and flooded your lands, leaving you to starve in a famine caused by his stupidity.

31:18 Surrender now to the nation of Assyria. Be blessed by our lords, who will care for you and love you and curse you not by famine, plagues and cruelty.

31:19 Die enslaved by the foolishness of Hezekiah, or live free as people of Assyria. The choice be yours."

31:20 Hezekiah feared the people of Judah would abandon him (and rightly so) and he called upon Isaiah the prophet to pray to God.

31:21 The lord heard the words of Isaiah and thought, "Well, I don't like the peoples of Assyria.

31:22 Let Judah be severed by another nation."

31:23 So the lord sent an angel to the armies of Assyria, which killed all the valiant men, the captains and the chiefs.

31:24 One hundred and eighty-five thousand men were slain by the sword of the angel and when they awoke, behold, they were dead.

31:25 The angel then took the souls of the Assyrians and made them either slaves in heaven or dwellers in hell.

31:26 Sennacherib grew ashamed and went home to his house. As he entered the temple of his god to plea for victory against Judah, his own sons ambushed him and decapitated him.

31:27 Thus the lord saved Judah from the hands of the Assyrians and those of Judah brought gifts to the temple of the lord and to their king, saying, "Hezekiah isn't an idiot, he's a fucking genius."

31:28 They were wrong. Hezekiah was an idiot who just got lucky.

31:29 The lord was still angry with Hezekiah for holding the Passover on the second month and struck him with a dreaded sickness.

31:30 Though on his deathbed, Hezekiah ruled over Judah and prospered greatly, having mass wealth of gold, silver, gemstones, jewels and spices.

31:31 Storehouses were full of wheat, corn and wine for Hezekiah.

31:32 Ambassadors from Babylon came to seek the wisdom of Hezekiah and ask him how he made Judah so prosperous.

31:33 The lord left Hezekiah now, so that he may see if the king of Judah had a pure heart and would give glory to God, or if he had a wicked heart and would give praise to himself.

31:34 Hezekiah died shortly after the ambassadors of Babylon left. It is unsure what he said, or if he had a pure or wicked heart. It doesn't matter, nobody cares anyway.

31:35 And Hezekiah was buried in Jerusalem, in the sepulcher of his fathers. His son, Manasseh, became king of Judah.

32:1 Manasseh was twelve years old when he began to rule over the lands of Judah and he reigned for fifty-five years in Jerusalem.

32:2 He was a wicked little cocksucker, who worshipped the lord of the heathens and told the true God of all to go fuck himself.

32:3 Manasseh built altars, groves, high places, carved graven images of Baal and worshipped the stars above and the lords of heathens; never once did he give praise to the true lord.

32:4 He even made the temple of the lord into the temple of Baal and erected a large statue of the heathen lord where the ark of the covenant was.

32:5 This made the lord so damn angry that he decided to one day engulf the entire earth with hell-fire!

32:6 The children of Manasseh were taught the wickedness of enchantments, necromancy, fortune telling, wizardry and witchcraft, which angered the lord even more.

32:7 So, blame Manasseh for the eventual destruction of humanity by the everlasting fires of hell. Or blame God. It doesn't matter.

32:8 Now, Manasseh demanded that none worship the lord of Israel and forced those of Judah to worship heathen lords and offer incense to false gods.

32:9 Those that still worshipped the one true lord did so in hiding, or were killed.

32:10 And the people in hiding thought, "What kind of religion demands that you kill those who worship differently than you?

32:11 All we wish for is to offer sacrifice to our lord in peace and not hide in caves so that we may follow our God."

32:12 God tried to speak to Manasseh and those of Judah, but none would listen. Though, in all fairness, the lord only whispered to the people and he tried only once.

32:13 The lord again strengthened the armies of Assyria, who came to Judah and conquered them.

32:14 Manasseh was bound by brass fetters and dragged behind a horse to the nation of Assyria, where he was thrown into a dungeon to rot.

32:15 In desperation, Manasseh began to pray to the one true God. And the lord thought, "It's about damn time someone paid attention to me."

32:16 So, in an unusual act of kindness, he brought forth Manasseh from his prison and delivered him to the city of Jerusalem.

32:17 Manasseh strengthened the city of David and built towers around the lands of Judah, to protect themselves from heathen nations.

32:18 All the idols and altars of false gods were burned and their ashes cast to the skies above.

32:19 He repaired even the temple of the lord and restored it to its glory and sacrificed offerings upon the altar to God.

32:20 Those that worshipped the lords of heathens were killed, which left all the people of Judah very confused as to just who they were forced to worship.

32:21 Once Manasseh rebuilt the temple of the lord, God did strike him with a sickness, which would kill him as he slept.

32:22 The lord said to those in the heavens, "Manasseh has served his purpose and rebuilt my house; let him now dwell in the depths of hell."

32:23 Manasseh was buried in his own house and his son Amon became king of Judah.

32:24 Amon was twenty-two years old when he became king of Judah and he reigned for two years.

32:25 Amon was wicked as his father when he became king of Judah and he rebuilt the altars of the heathen lords and worshipped false gods, carving idols of Baal and placing them within the temple of the lord.

32:26 God said, "Fuck this little circumcised prick," and put an evil spirit in the servants of Amon.

32:27 The servants of Amon conspired against their master and beat him to death as he slept, rejoicing in the death of their master.

32:28 Those of Judah became angry with the servants who slew them, saying, "This king allowed us to practice magic and now I need only say a few words to start the fire and cook my pork."

32:29 So those of Judah killed the servants of Amon and anointed Josiah the son of Amon as king.

33:1 Josiah was eight when he began to rule in Jerusalem and he reigned for thirty-one years.

33:2 He did that which was right in the lord, tolerating no heathenism, homosexuality, witchcraft, wizardry and necromancy.

33:3 In the eighth year of his reign, he made law the ways of Moses and executed anyone who did not keep the statutes, laws, covenants and commandments of the lord. In the twelfth year of his reign, he broke down the altars, groves, idols, carved images and molten images of all the heathen lords.

33:4 They forced the priests of Baal to witness the destruction of their sacred objects and made them spread the ashes of the burnt idols on the corpses of the executed people who whored themselves to the false lords.

33:5 Then the priests of Baal were stripped of their flesh and the bones burned on the altars God as sacrifice.

33:6 The lord looked down upon the bones burning on his altars and was pleased.

33:7 Every city of Judah was purged of the wickedness of blasphemers and those who worshipped heathen lords, from Manasseh, Ephraim, Simeon and even the lands of Naphtali.

33:8 In the eighteenth year of his reign, all the whores of Baal laid dead upon the grounds and Judah was purged of the wickedness of heathen ways.

33:9 Josiah demanded that Shaphan the son of Azaliah, Maaseiah the governor of Jerusalem and Joah the son of Joahaz repair the temple of the lord.

33:10 Taxes were placed on all those of Judah, so that the temple may be rebuilt and all the missing gold replaced.

33:11 The men oversaw the workers and the floors were repaired, the walls repaired, pillars replaced with fresh cut stone and the timber replaced with finest cedar.

33:12 As the workers repaired the temple, those of the tribe of Levi danced around, blessing the works and the house of the lord, singing psalms and playing instruments.

33:13 This annoyed those who worked on the temple and they stuffed their ears with cloth so that they may not hear the annoying Levites.

33:14 As the people repaired the temple, behold, they found a lost book written by the hands of Moses and they gave it to the priests.

33:15 The priests returned to the king of Judah and said, "We have found a blessed and holy book of the lord, written by the hands of Moses."

33:16 Josiah said, "Blessed be the lord, for he has given us this book so we may know his laws, his ways and follow them blindly.

33:17 Read me that which is in the book."

33:18 So Shaphan the scribe began to read the book and it was a book full of laws which those of the children of the lord must follow.

33:19 As Shaphan finished, Josiah stripped his clothes and began to weep, saying, "These are the laws I and my people must follow?

33:20 They are laws of cruelty, hardship and the demands of the lord are harsh and shall make the nation of Judah poor.

33:21 How many males of the flocks and herds do we have which are without blemish. How can we sacrifice to the lord that which we don't have?"

33:22 The king of Judah then decided, "If we of Judah must follow these laws, then those of Israel shall be cursed to follow them as well."

33:23 So he asked Huldah the prophetess, wife of Shallum the son of Tikvath, to go forth to Israel and spread the holy word of God.

33:24 She said to the congregation of Israel, "Thus sayeth the lord, I shall bring great evil upon the lands of Samaria so wicked even the devils themselves shall consider them cruel.

33:25 You have forsaken your God and burn incense to heathen lords, provoking the anger of the God who delivered you out of Egypt and into these promised lands of milk and honey.

33:26 Your men shall be cursed with chronic masturbation and the seed of your generations shall fall to the ground.

33:27 Your wives and daughters will be cheap prostitutes to the people of the heathens and be made unclean when those with foreskins rape their loins.

33:28 Come, follow the laws of Judah and please the lord so that his cruelty and anger fall not upon you and your children.

33:29 Those of the lands of Judah shall see not the evil of the one true God fall upon their lands and will prosper and thrive when you of Israel are reduced to ashes and dust."

33:30 And the people of Israel called Huldah a cunt and cast her out of the lands of Samaria.

33:31 When she returned, the king gathered all those of the elders of Jerusalem and Judah and made a covenant with the lord so that all of Judah shall follow the demands of God.

33:32 He read the book of the laws written to Moses so that all those of Judah shall hear and said, "Those who do not follow these laws shall be cursed for eternity by the hands of our lord."

33:33 Josiah then invaded the lands of Israel and took from them the abominations of the heathen lords and forced the people of Israel to worship the lord.

33:34 Those that did not were publicly stoned.

34:1 Josiah enforced the Passover and kept it at the proper time of the year, in the proper time of the month, in the proper day of the month.

34:2 And he set the priests in the house of the lord, set them their tasks, paid them well and encouraged them to spread the word of God.

34:3 He said also to the Levites, slaves of Israel, "Place the ark of the lord in the temple of the God, so that it no longer be a burden on your soldiers.

34:4 You have hidden the ark well from those who whored themselves to demons and shall now rid yourself of its weight.

34:5 Go forth and spread the word of the lord of lords among all those of Judah and Israel; let it be that the chosen people of God know again the loving embrace of their creator.

34:6 Prepare for the Passover and celebrate. Gather your lambs, your oxen and all sacrifices, so that the lord be pleased with this feast."

34:7 Josiah was so paranoid about angering the lord with unworthy offerings that he gave each household of Judah a lamb for them to sacrifice.

34:8 Thirty thousand lambs from the king's flock and three thousand bullocks were given to those of Judah, so that they may give their offerings to God.

34:9 Most of the people of Judah slaughtered and ate the beast given to them. They were hungry and believed the lord would not care if the sacrifice they gave to God had a small blemish on its heel.

34:10 They were wrong. God demands perfection for his offerings.

34:11 As the Levites sacrificed the offerings of Judah, they sprinkled the blood of the beasts on themselves and on the congregation of Judah, blessing them in the holy name of the lord.

34:12 And all the people danced in the blood of the offerings, praising the lords name.

34:13 God gazed upon the peoples of Judah and was mildly amused by the dancers drenched in blood, but was still furious with those of Judah who offered unworthy sacrifice; animals with blemishes, sickness or disease.

34:14 On the eighteenth year of Josiah's reign, Necho the king of Egypt came up to fight against Charchemish, by the river Ephraim.

34:15 The lord cursed Josiah and had him fight alongside Charchemish.

34:16 When Necho heard that the nation of Judah would fight against him, he sent ambassadors to Judah, which said to Josiah, "Why do you wish to fight against us, for we have not wronged you?

34:17 I come not to war with Judah, but with Charchemish, as my lords demand; does your God meddle in the affairs of Egypt?

34:18 Let us remain allies and not have our people grasp at each other's throats. Leave Charchemish to be slaughtered by the chariots of Egypt."

34:19 But Josiah would not hearken the words of Necho and fought alongside Charchemish in the valley of Megiddo.

34:20 An archer of Egypt struck Josiah and he said to his chariot driver, "Get me out of here. Your king is fucking wounded."

34:21 So the chariot drove his master out of the battle and took him back to Jerusalem, where he died in his bedchamber, screaming, "That fucker shot me. That fucker shot me!

34:22 That Egyptian cocksucker shot a god damn arrow at me!"

34:23 When he died, he was buried in the sepulcher of his fathers. All the people of Jerusalem and Judah mourned his death.

34:24 Women walked the streets in tears, crying out "He's dead, he's dead." Men got drunk on cheap liquor and started brawls in public.

34:25 Children sat in the corner of their rooms and wept in silence, because their blessed king Josiah was dead.

34:26 Jeremiah mourned deeply for Josiah and had all the singing men and women sing sad songs in the name of their deceased king. Behold, their words are written in the book of Lamentations, which is only eleven books away.

34:27 Now all the acts of goodness, his deeds and his laws which Josiah did, behold, they are written in the book of the kings of Israel and Judah.

34:28 This book is not in the bible. Which is a relief. It sounds like a dull book.

35:1 After the people of Judah stopped their blubbering, they took Jehoahaz the son of Josiah and made him king.

35:2 Jehoahaz was twenty-three years old when he became king of Judah and he reigned a short three months.

35:3 The lord was angry with the father of Jehoahaz for having people sacrifice unworthy beasts at the Passover and God strengthened the armies of Pharaoh, who came against Jerusalem and demanded each city of Judah pay one hundred talents of silver and one talent of gold.

35:4 Pharaoh then placed Eliakim his brother as king of Judah and changed his name to Jehoiakim, so that it sounded more Hebrew. And Necho took Jehoahaz as prisoner.

35:5 Jehoahaz said to Nechro, "Why do you wish to punish me. What harm have I done to you?" and the Pharaoh answered, "I could ask your father the same question."

35:6 Still, Jehoahaz asked, "My father is dead, struck down by the archers of your armies.

35:7 What good will it bring you to punish me for what my father has done to you?"

35:8 Necho laughed and said, "I agree, it would do no good.

35:9 But your lord came to me and demanded I punish you for the sins of your fathers and who am I to question your lord?"

35:10 And Jehoahaz was dragged in fetters behind a horse to the lands of Egypt, where his ancestors long ago were set free from the slavery of Pharaoh.

35:11 God is a fan of irony.

35:12 Jehoiakim was twenty-five years old when he reigned as king of Judah and he reigned eleven years in Jerusalem.

35:13 And he did that which was evil in the sight of the lord. What did you expect. He was a fucking heathen and an Egyptian no less.

35:14 The lord strengthened the armies of Nebuchadnezzar king of Babylon and sent him to the lands of Judah to punish the heathen king.

35:15 Nebuchadnezzar bound Jehoiakim in fetters and dragged him back to Babylon behind a camel with terrible flatulence.

35:16 Nebuchadnezzar also gathered all the gold, the jewels and the vessels from the temple of the lord and placed them in a temple in Babylon, dedicating them to a heathen lord.

35:17 Now the rests of the acts of Jehoiakim and all his wickedness, his wrongdoings and his blasphemy, nobody bothered to write down.

35:18 His son, Jehoiachin, reigned in his stead.

35:19 Jehoiachin was eight years old when he became king of Judah and he reigned three months and ten days in the city of Jerusalem, doing that which is evil in the eyes of God.

35:20 The only thing which surprises me more than an eight-year-old child being king over a nation he isn't even apart of, is that an eight-year-old can do that which is wicked in the eyes of God.

35:21 He's eight years old. How evil can he be?

35:22 So the lord sent the armies of Babylon to Judah, again and they carried the king of Judah to Babylon, again and took all the goods from the house of the lord, again.

35:23 Nebuchadnezzar decided that his people shall rule over the lands of Judah and made Zedekiah his brother king in Jerusalem.

35:24 Zedekiah was twenty-one years old when he became king of Judah and he reigned for eleven years in Jerusalem.

35:25 Being a heathen, he was deemed evil and wicked in the eyes of God.

35:26 Jeremiah would speak the word of God to Zedekiah and Zedekiah would mock him, saying, "Speak all you want, bitch. He ain't my God."

35:27 In time, Zedekiah began to rebel against his brother Nebuchadnezzar and lusted for his throne and power.

35:28 He also perverted greatly the people of Judah, so that they all worshipped heathen lords and forgot about the one true God.

35:29 The lord God send prophets to the lands of Judah, but none would listen to their words.

35:30 They mocked the prophets and the word of the lord, until the wrath of the lord overflowed and poured out on the people of Judah, until there was no remedy.

35:31 He brought to Judah the king of Chaldees, who slew of Judah all the young men with the sword and slaughtered the old, the child and the woman; the lord had no compassion for his people and laughed as they were slaughtered by the blades of the heathen.

35:32 All that which was within the temple of the lord, whether great or small and all the treasures of the king and his princes, were brought to Babylon.

35:33 They then filled the temple of the lord with the corpses of the people of Judah and burned it, which created a truly intoxicating scent for God.

35:34 Those which escaped from the sword were captured and enslaved by the people of Babylon or sold to other nations.

35:35 And the lord was pleased, for the covenant was broken and he no longer had a promise to keep to the mortals of the earth.

35:36 Jeremiah was sold as a slave to the nation of Persia, where he still foolishly believed his lord loved and cared for him.

35:37 The words of Jeremiah reached the ears of the king of Persia, who put up a proclamation which read, "Thus sayeth Cyrus the king of Persia, all the kingdoms of the earth have the lord God of heaven given to me.

35:38 Of those of the people of Judah, who erected the house of the lord, bless them and their lord be with them."

EZRA

1:1 The lord gazed down upon the earth and laughed at those of the children of Israel, who were scattered across the lands of the heathens.

1:2 Each person of the tribes of Israel lived in a foreign land as slave, concubine, beggar or one of the poor.

1:3 God laughed at his children and took pleasure in their suffering; the angels of God laughed with him, some out of fear of the lord, others truly taking pleasure in the pain of those of Israel.

1:4 In time, however, the lord missed the offerings of the children of Israel; the burning flesh, boiling blood and roasting fat upon the altars of stone.

1:5 God looked down upon the other nations of earth, but they were all disgusting in the eyes of the lord.

1:6 They worshipped other lords, tolerated other faiths, engaged in unholy lust, believed not in genocide and most desired peace among earth.

1:7 The lord hated peace; peace was boring. Violence was entertaining.

1:8 God missed his temple in Jerusalem; the extravagance of gold, silver, bronze and gemstones.

1:9 Now the mighty temple was reduced to rubble by the will of the lord. Though, the lord would not admit it was his doing.

1:10 It was the fucking heathens and the incompetence of the tribe of Judah which caused the temple to be reduced to a pile of rubble. God had nothing to do with it.

1:11 What angered the lord most was the murmurings of the heathen people. Oh, how they laughed at the lord of Israel.

1:12 They laughed at the mighty lord, whom they once feared; they said, "Oh how the lord of Israel has fallen.

1:13 Once the fires of his wrath consumed nations. Now the nation of his peoples be reduced to ashes and dust.

1:14 This lord could not even protect his own peoples. Oh, what a fool this God must be."

1:15 God grew angry and consumed the nations of heathens with fires, plagues, famine, floods, pestilence, disease and suffering.

1:16 Normally, this would please the lord, but it did not; it made the lord angrier.

1:17 These foolish heathens feared not the lord, but worshipped their false gods and offered incense and sacrifices to Baal, Ashteroth, Molech and other lords.

1:18 When the lord made the heathens suffer more, they prayed to their lords more and never once feared the one true God.

1:19 Thus the lord knew that to strike fear into the peoples of the earth, he had to rebuild his people and make them strong.

1:20 So the lord decided to rebuild Judah, Jerusalem and the temple.

1:21 The spirit of the lord filled Cyrus the king of Persia, who made a proclamation throughout his lands, which read,

1:22 "Thus sayeth Cyrus the king of Persia, let it be that all those of the people of Judah return home, so that they may rebuild their temple and worship their God.

1:23 Those who own slaves of these people must set them free and

give into them silver, gold, beasts of the flock and beasts of burden.

1:24 Let them return home and blessed be these children of the lord."

1:25 The peoples of Persia grew angry and those who owned slaves of Judah began to speak ill of their king.

1:26 They were quickly killed, either by the armies of Persia or by the hand of God.

1:27 Cyrus king of Persia not only let those of the people of Judah free, but gave to them that which Persia took from the temple of the lord.

1:28 Silver and gold vessels, gemstones, pottery, stonework and furniture which once resided in the house of God were given to the people once enslaved by the Persians.

1:29 Thirty talents of gold, a thousand talents of silver, twenty-nine ornate daggers, thirty basins of gold, four hundred and ten basins of silver and one thousand basins of bronze.

1:30 All these were given to the people of Judah, so that they may rebuild the temple of the lord in Jerusalem.

1:31 And the people of Judah praised Cyrus the king of Persia and wished him great blessings from their lord.

1:32 Those of Persia cursed Cyrus and wished him and his house a slow and painful death.

2:1 These are the names of the families of Judah which left the servitude of Persia, when Cyrus declared that those of the children of the lord may take leave so that they may rebuild the temple of the one true God.

2:2 Not all the peoples of Judah left. Some were kept behind by their masters, who refused to obey the king of Persia.

2:3 Others of the people of Judah stayed behind by their own accord, believing the trip to their homeland useless.

2:4 They thought their lord was an asshole and that rebuilding the temple would be a waste of time, that the lord wished only to increase their suffering, or they found other lords to devote their worship to.

2:5 These are the numbers of the fools who returned to Jerusalem.

2:6 Of the family of Parosh, two thousand one hundred seventy-two.

2:7 Of the family of Shephatiah, three hundred seventy-two.

2:8 Of the family of Arah, seven hundredy seventy-five.

2:9 Of the family of Pahathmoab, two thousand eight hundred and twelve.

2:10 Of the family of Elam, one thousand two hundred fifty-four.

2:11 Of the family of Zattu, nine hundred forty-five.

2:12 Yes, this is going to be a long list. I'd suggest skipping it.

2:13 Though, the numbers don't add up, which makes it mildly interesting.

2:14 Very mildly interesting. Like finding out Attila the Hun had an herb garden.

2:15 Of the family of Zaccai, seven hundred and threescore.

2:16 Of the family of Bani, six hundred and forty-two.

2:17 Of the family of Bebai, six hundred and twenty-three.

2:18 Of the family of Azgad, if you care to know, one thousand two hundred twenty-two.

2:19 Of the family of Adonikam, six hundred and sixty-six.

2:20 Adonikam was an evil family and God hated him.

2:21 Of the family of Bigvai, two thousand fifty-six.

2:22 Of the family of Adin, four hundred fifty-four.

2:23 Of the family of Ater, ninety-eight.

2:24 The men of Ater weren't very fruitful and suffered from a

THE OLD TESTAMENT

hereditary low sperm count.

2:25 Of the family of Bezai, three hundred and twenty-three.

2:26 Of the family of Jorah, one hundred and twelve.

2:27 Of the family of Hashum, two hundred twenty-three.

2:28 Of the family of Gibbar, ninety-five.

2:29 They didn't suffer from low sperm count. They were ugly men and their wives didn't fuck them very much.

2:30 Of the family of Bethlehem, one hundred twenty-three.

2:31 Of the family of Netophah, fifty-six.

2:32 Most of the family of Netophah stayed behind and loathed the lord of Israel.

2:33 Of the family of Anathoth, one hundred twenty-eight.

2:34 Of the family of Azmaveth, forty-two.

2:35 The women of Azmaveth miscarried a lot. Probably because their husbands were alcoholic assholes who beat them.

2:36 Of the family of Beeroth, seven hundred forty-three.

2:37 Of the family of Gaba, six hundred twenty-one.

2:38 Of the family of Michmas, one hundred twenty-two.

2:39 Of the family of Bethel, two hundred twenty-three.

2:40 Of the family of Nebo, fifty-two. They were a relatively new family.

2:41 Of the family of Magbish, one hundred fifty-six.

2:42 Of the family of the other Elam, one thousand two hundred fifty-four.

2:43 The two families of Elam loathed each other and declared the other stole their rightful name.

2:44 Nobody else cared and let the two families of Elam kill each other over a name.

2:45 Of the family of Harim, three hundred and twenty.

2:46 Of the family of Ono, seven hundred twenty-five.

2:47 Of the family of Jericho, three hundred and forty-five.

2:48 Of the family of Senaah, three thousand six hundred thirty.

2:49 These are the families of the priests of God who left to rebuild the temple.

2:50 Yeah, I don't care either.

2:51 Of the family of Jedaiah, nine hundred seventy-three.

2:52 Of the family of Immer, one thousand fifty-two inbred people.

2:53 Of the family of Pashur, one thousand two hundred forty-seven.

2:54 Of the family of Harim, one thousand seventeen.

2:55 Of the Levite men: Jeshua, Kadmiel, Hodaviah, seventy-four.

2:56 The singers of Asaph, one hundred twenty-eight.

2:57 Of those of the porters, one hundred thirty-nine.

2:58 Of the family of Nethinim, three hundred ninety-two.

2:59 The family of Tobiah, six hundred and fifty-two.

2:60 These are all the peoples who left and it is also the end of the list.

2:61 About damn time.

2:62 And the numbers of the peoples of Judah were forty and two thousand three hundred and threescore.

2:63 Yet when you read through this list and add the numbers, it is twenty-nine thousand six hundred and eighteen.

2:64 How can this be. Did the bible make a mistake?

2:65 No. The remainder were useless women who managed to get added to the final tally.

2:66 These people of Judah then stole from the people of Persia, using the darkness of night to sneak into their dwellings and take

the possessions from their former captors.

2:67 They stole seven thousand three hundred thirty-seven slaves and four hundred prostitutes.

2:68 Four hundred thirty-five camels, six thousand seven hundred and twenty donkeys.

2:69 Threescore and one thousand drams of gold, five thousand pounds of silver and one hundred fine silk raiment's.

2:70 All these were stolen from the Persians by the peoples of Judah and when those of Persia accused them, the men of Judah said, "It is not us who stole from you.

2:71 We cannot steal, for it goes against our seventh commandment."

2:72 Which it did, but the Persians were heathens and stealing from heathens is okay according to the lord God.

2:73 Knowing the people of Judah to fear the wrath of the lord, they believed their false words and sent them away.

3:1 Upon their return to Judah, the children of the lord gathered themselves into Jerusalem as one.

3:2 Their Jeshua the son of Jozadak and Zerubbel the son of Shealiel built stone altars and offered atop them sacrifices to the lord.

3:3 The people of Judah feared this, for they did not remember how to offer sacrifice to their lord and worried any mistake would bring fury down from the heavens.

3:4 As the blood flowed down the altar and the beast cried in pain, the lord gazed down upon the altar and was pleased.

3:5 It was the first time in a long time that the lord saw sacrifice in his name and the lord embraced it.

3:6 The spirit of the lord descended upon the earth in great fire and smoke and the people feared the wrath of God came down to consume them.

3:7 The lord then spoke to them and said, "Fear not, for I am the lord your God, who has kept the covenant made during the days of Abraham.

3:8 It pleases your God to see the sacrifices upon the altars and the lord demands more!

3:9 Bring forth all manner of beast, fowl and heathen and spill their blood upon the stones."

3:10 Thus those of Judah sacrificed many a creature and heathen on the altars of the lord, which satisfied the blood-lust of their God.

3:11 It was then the lord of Israel turned the blood into wine and said, "Drink forth from the blood of your sacrifice and be filled with the joy of your lord."

3:12 Those of Judah then drank of the blood and became drunk.

3:13 They danced in the streets and fornicated for all those to see.

3:14 And the lord gazed upon the peoples of Judah, dancing naked and fucking and was pleased.

4:1 Now the enemies of Judah heard that the people of the one true God came to rebuild the temple and they were disturbed by this.

4:2 They knew once the temple was rebuilt, that the lord of Israel shall come down and smite them in his fury.

4:3 So they wished to instead join the children of Judah and worship their lord, so that God shall give them blessings and not wrath.

4:4 These heathens came to the chiefs of Judah and said, "We have found truth in your lord and wish to aid you in the building of your temple.

4:5 Let us come and offer our labour, so that the house of the true God of all be restored quickly."

4:6 But the men of Judah laughed at these heathens and said, "Our lord despises you and wishes your very corpses be scattered across the earth.

4:7 Your filthy hands shall not touch even the nail which goes into the temple of the lord.

4:8 Be gone and may your children burn eternally in the fires which is the anger of our God."

4:9 So the heathens harassed those who were building the temple and sabotaged the construction so that it will not be built.

4:10 Caravans carrying timber and stones were captured and burned; tools were stolen.

4:11 Those that sold goods to those of Judah sold them shoddy tools and wares, which broke quickly and needed replacement.

4:12 When the temple was near completion, the heathens hired mercenaries and pyromaniacs to burn the temple down.

4:13 This harassment continued even to the days of Darius the king of Persia.

4:14 Those of Judah offered sacrifice and asked the lord God for divine intervention, saying, "These men spawned from the belly of beasts harass us in the completion of your house.

4:15 Slay them, so that they bother us no more."

4:16 The lord spoke back, "I shall only slay them when my temple is complete.

4:17 When my house is incomplete, it is as an insult to me. Construct my temple and I shall show favour to you."

4:18 Elashen, architect and engineer, asked of his God, "How can we complete the temple you demand if we keep being harassed by heathens and their paid armies?"

4:19 God quickly reduced him to a pile of ash and those around him kept shut their mouths and returned to work.

5:1 Prophets of the lord, Haggai and Zechariah the son of Iddo, spoke to one another and said, "Who was it that demanded we come back to Jerusalem and rebuild the house of the true lord of heaven and earth?

5:2 It was Cyrus, the king of Persia; a heathen fool hated in the eyes of the lord.

5:3 This makes the reconstruction of the temple blasphemous and wicked in the eyes of God."

5:4 These two prophets then spoke to the children of Judah and said, "Stop your labours and lay down your tools!

5:5 What we do is blasphemous and wicked and shall cause the wrath of the lord to come down upon us and consume us in fire."

5:6 The people of Judah rejoiced and laid down their tools. They did not wish to work any longer rebuilding the temple of the lord.

5:7 It was hard, frustrating work and they were lazy.

5:8 So the people of Judah celebrated with a feast of leavened bread, wild flesh, and strong wine.

5:9 As the lord gazed down on his people celebrating, he became angry and came to the earth in a great cloud of fire and black smoke.

5:10 He said to his people, "Heed not the words of these prophets; they speak the words of fools.

5:11 Your God demands that his temple be rebuilt and the spirit of your lord filled Cyrus the king of Persia so that he shall let you go and do the will of the one true lord.

5:12 The lord had tricked a heathen to do his bidding; blessed be the name of your lord!"

5:13 So the people of Judah returned to the rebuilding of the temple, angry and hungover.

6:1 It came to pass that the temple of the lord was finally complete and the people of Judah rejoiced and gave praise to their lord.

6:2 Altars were erected and sacrifices were made in glory to the lord of Israel, who freed them from the servitude of the Persians, so that they may complete the house of God.

6:3 They stripped off their clothes, danced in the streets and making love to one another.

6:4 Ezra, a man of God, witnessed this orgy of drinking and fornication, and he tore off his raiment's and pulled the very hairs from his head and his beard.

6:5 He then sat upon the steps of the temple and wept.

6:6 Those of Judah came to Ezra and asked him, "Why do you weep. For this is a time of celebration!"

6:7 Ezra answered, "I weep for I fear the fury of the lord which shall come down upon us."

6:8 The people of Judah were confused and asked, "Why shall the lord bring his wrath against us?

6:9 We have rebuilt his house and give glory and praise to his name."

6:10 Ezra wept deeply and said, "Yes and look at those who give glory to the name of God.

6:11 I gaze upon the streets and see the men of Judah fucking their wives, who be unholy heathens.

6:12 The children of Judah are a bastard breed, planted by the seed of the holy people on the grounds of the heathen cunt.

6:13 Our lord shall not forgive this lust and the people of Judah shall be doomed for not keeping their bloodlines pure."

6:14 The men of Judah then wept with Ezra and said, "What shall we do to beg forgiveness from our lord?"

6:15 Ezra spoke, "We must abandon our wives and our children; these unholy beasts which tarnish the lands given to us by our lord."

6:16 So the men of Judah took their wives and their children, and they slaughtered them before the temple of the lord, screaming to God, "Never shall the seed of Judah be stained by the heathen!"

6:17 The blood of the heathen women and the bastard children were then gathered in golden vessels and poured on the temple of the lord.

6:18 Pails of blood were poured on the stone, the gold and all that within the house of the lord, so that the men of Judah may beg forgiveness from their God.

6:19 As the lord gazed down from the heavens and saw the men of Judah weeping, soaked in the blood of their heathen wives and inbred children, the lord was pleased.

6:20 When the last blood of the heathens was spilled on the temple, behold, the blood began to boil and black smoke rose from it.

6:21 The spirit of the lord then came down to the temple and filled it with great smoke and fire.

6:22 All those of Judah rejoiced and praised their God almighty.

6:23 The lord then spoke and said, "You have pleased the lord and abandoned your strange wives and bastard children.

6:24 Let it be known that this is the beginning of a new era.

6:25 Those of the children of the lord shall once again grow strong and prosper and their swords shall pierce the very corners of the earth.

6:26 Blood of the heathens shall be shed across all the lands, so that the very oceans be stained red with this vile liquid.

6:27 May those of Judah reign forever and worship the one true God for all eternity."

6:28 And the people of Judah cheered and gave sacrifice to the lord.

6:29 They spoke of the day when the people of Judah shall rule the earth and dreamed of when that day shall come.

6:30 That day still has not arrived and those of Judah are still dreaming.

NEHEMIAH

1:1 Oh woe be to those who read the book of Nehemiah.

1:2 It is truly a boring tome, cursed to dull and frustrate the mind.

1:3 To read this is a waste of precious time.

1:4 Why this was put in the Bible, no one knows.

1:5 It serves no purpose. It tells no story. It is merely a book to dull the mind.

1:6 When one reads it, their brain goes stale and the eyes weep.

1:7 Those of the faith don't read this book; they cannot.

1:8 It is truly a dull book.

1:9 Perhaps it was a test sent forth by God; those who read it, the lord shall then know they are devoted to his word.

1:10 Then this is a cruel and torturous test and one that will be failed numerously.

2:1 Cursed be Nehemiah, the one who wrote the cursed book.

2:2 He was a boring man, who never married nor took part in the carnal pleasures of fornication.

2:3 Not once did he leave his house, unless to purchase parchment and ink.

2:4 His life was spent writing this dull tome, which took years for even Nehemiah would get so bored that he would fall asleep in writing it.

2:5 It is unsure why Nehemiah wrote the words of this book upon the wretched parchment.

2:6 He is hated by many for doing so.

2:7 The devil fears the book of Nehemiah and the lord God himself considers it even unholy.

2:8 Cursed be the Bible, for this book of Nehemiah has made it wicked even in the sight of God.

2:9 Those of the faith, heed my words; tear out the pages of Nehemiah from your Bible and beg forgiveness from your lord for having such a wicked thing in your dwelling.

2:10 Not even the lord read the book of Nehemiah in its entirety.

2:11 God fears it and fears this book shall end his days.

2:12 Nehemiah is so dull, it can even bore the lord to death.

2:13 Such curse be this, the book of Nehemiah.

3:1 Suffering are those who have read fully the book of Nehemiah.

3:2 A fate worse than hell did they endure for gazing upon the words of these wretched writings.

3:3 They grow mad in attempting to understand the meaning of this book and wonder why such a man would write such a thing.

3:4 Madness curses them and they pluck out their hairs, feast upon their eyeballs, gnaw on their genitals and beat their heads against the walls.

3:5 With their faeces, they write out the words of Nehemiah, hoping to understand any message contained within the boring letters.

3:6 Never do they come to conclusion and madness consumes them until they choke themselves upon their own entrails, screaming, "Nehemiah, Nehemiah, why must there be Nehemiah?"

3:7 Hearken my words and heed my warning; do not read the book of Nehemiah, lest the curse of this book consume you with madness.

4:1 Blessed are those who be aware of the curse of Nehemiah, and warn others of the madness.

4:2 They speak out against these wretched writings, so that others may know to avoid them.

4:3 Cursed be those who are aware of the curse of Nehemiah, yet warn not a soul.

4:4 These peoples are wicked in the eyes of all; man, devil and God.

4:5 Hated are they, who warn not of the evils of Nehemiah, for they warn not the others of pure wickedness.

4:6 A fate worse than hell awaits those who read the curses of Nehemiah; if a man warned not those who read the book of Nehemiah, they are set to the filthiest corner of hell.

4:7 A place where the gonorrhoea of one hundred fourscore trillion cheap prostitutes flow like rivers, and the ass sweat of hairy fat men suffering from extreme flatulence rain down through eternity.

4:8 They drown in boiling grease and feast in gluttony upon their own shit.

4:9 Yet their suffering pales in comparison to those who read the wretched book of Nehemiah.

4:10 A suffering so great not even the lord of Israel, in all his cruelties, could create a place, method or punishment more harsher than the suffering of those who read the book of Nehemiah.

5:1 Go forth, and gather all those of the parchments, the writings, and that which contains Nehemiah.

5:2 Place them upon a great fire, so that the smoke rises high and all the words of Nehemiah be lost in ashes and dust.

5:3 It shall be a blessed day for mankind; a day of joyous celebration.

5:4 Nations shall gather together and humanity will embrace as one, for they shall be free of the curse of Nehemiah.

5:5 All the world shall know peace, and show mercy and understanding upon one another.

5:^ The lord shall be angry, for the violence he seeks so desperately will be banished from the world.

5:7 It matters not the lord anger; though the lord may bring his wrath upon the peoples of earth, it is better to bear the wrath of God than know even one word of the book of Nehemiah.

5:8 So go, and free the world of this curse; ye shall be a true hero and loved by all.

5:9 Men would wish to be you, and women to be with you.

5:10 Rid us all of the curse of Nehemiah, and the world shall love thee for all eternal.

6:1 If ye still be curious, and wish to read the cursed Nehemiah, a true fool ye be.

6:2 Go forth, and cast thine eyeballs from thine skull.

6:3 It is better to be blind than read the tome of Nehemiah.

7:1 Ye know now of the curses of Nehemiah.

7:2 Heed thine warning, and read not these wretched writings.

7:3 Go forth, and spread the knowledge of the wickedness that is Nehemiah.

7:4 Let not another man, woman or child be struck by the madness of this evil tome.

7:5 Cursed be Nehemiah, and cursed by his book.

7:6 And blessed be those who know not of the book of Nehemiah.

7:7 Shall they never know it's dullness, it's boredom and it's mundane writing.

ESTHER

1:1 King Ahasuerus was a powerful king, who ruled over one hundred and seventy-two provinces ranging from India to Ethiopia.

1:2 He loved power, for power meant luxury and luxury meant living in excess and gluttony.

1:3 Monthly, Ahasuerus would throw extravagant parties, flowing with wine, ale, liquor, breads, fruits, meats and the prettiest of concubines and whores.

1:4 All those of noble blood would come to these parties and drink in excess, feast in gluttony and take pleasure in carnal lust.

1:5 Vashti, wife and queen of Ahasuerus, would take part in the orgies and pleasure both her husband and the females surrounding him.

1:6 On the third year of King Ahasuerus' reign, he did throw an extravagant party and gave his guests raiment's of finest silk, jewelry of gold and silver and cups of gold.

1:7 The very floors and halls of his castle were redone in finest marble, with etchings of beasts, fowl, women, and fruits.

1:8 All guests were encouraged to feast, drink and be merry; if a woman was pleasing in the eyes of a guest, king Ahasuerus brought the woman forth and paid her so that she and the man would fuck.

1:9 On this day, the seventh day of the feast, guests of king Ahasuerus noticed a woman which was pleasing to their eyes.

1:10 These guests were Mehuman, Bithza, Harbona, Bigtha, Abagtha, Zethar and Carcas. The woman which pleased them was Vashti, wife of Ahasuerus.

1:11 All seven men came to their host and said, "We have rested eyes upon a woman who pleases us and wish to take part in the pleasures of her flesh."

1:12 King Ahazuerus said, "No problem, my friends. Tell me the name of this woman and I shall summon her to your chambers."

1:13 They said, "We mean no disrespect, my lord, but the woman who is pleasing to our sight is Vashti, your wife.

1:14 We know that she belongs to you and would understand if you refuse us to take part in her lust."

1:15 The king laughed in his drunkenness, and said, "Have I not been a merciful and kind king, who shares that with his loyal friends?

1:16 Let me summon my wife, so that we may all share in her caress and lust."

1:17 Queen Vashti was summoned before the king and these men and Ahasuerus demanded of her, "Take of thine clothes, and lie down.

1:18 We shall all take part in your pleasing flesh."

1:19 But queen Vashti refused, saying, "I am but the property of the king and shall not be tainted by the touch of these seven men.

1:20 My body shall please only my husband and never these strange men."

1:21 The seven men laughed at king Ahasuerus, saying, "This king, who rules one hundred and seventy-two provinces, can't even rule over his wife.

1:22 Such a weak king he must truly be."

1:23 King Ahasuerus would have none of it and said to his wife, "You wretched cunt, why do you deny your master?

1:24 When I tell you to do something, you do it without question.

1:25 Now take off your clothing so that we may all take part in your lust."

1:26 Still the queen refused and the guests of Ahasuerus laughed louder.

1:27 In anger, Ahasuerus tore off the clothing of Vashti and said to all of his guests, "Come forth, and take part in the lust of my wife!

1:28 Do what you wish unto her; it does not matter to me."

1:29 So the guests of Ahasuerus came forth and raped queen Vashti, who laid weeping upon the floor of marble.

1:30 When the guests of Ahasuerus were satisfied with Vashti, the king took a blade and decapitated the head of his wife.

1:31 All those at the party laughed and some bathed and drank of the blood which came forth from the neck of Vashti's corpse.

1:32 King Ahasuerus then placed the severed head of Vashti on a spear and displayed it so that all those under his reign may see.

1:33 He then said, "Let it be that the men rule over all women. Those women that disobey, may they meet a fate worse than that of my wife.

1:34 Husband's, go forth into your wives. Take pleasure in your lust and her pain.

1:35 It matters not if she consents; she is a woman and yours to do with as ye please."

1:36 So the men under the rule of king Ahasuerus went forth and raped their wives, their concubines and their handmaidens, under law of their king.

2:1 After the execution of Vashti, king Ahasuerus demanded a replacement wife.

2:2 One who was younger, prettier and a virgin.

2:3 Officers of the king sought forth every province and brought to the palace in Shushun every fair and pretty virgin, who was kept under the care of Hege the chamberlain; a homosexual and therefore trustworthy to care for the women of the king.

2:4 Each and every virgin was prepared so that they may be taken to the king.

2:5 They were bathed, dressed in cloth pleasing to Ahasuerus perfumed, and their body hair shaven so that it may please the king.

2:6 Every virgin was brought to the bedchamber of the king, where Ahasuerus took part in his lust and ranked them as to who pleased him most.

2:7 Mordecai, the son of Jair, was a Jew who worked in the palace of Ahasuerus.

2:8 When he gazed on the virgin Esther, he knew it was she who must replace the queen Vashti.

2:9 Mordecai knew that a Jewish queen would greatly benefit his people, who were scattered across the lands of the heathens, or in the lands of Judah, few in number and at the mercy of foreign nations.

2:10 So Mordecai spoke to Esther and said, "It is you who must please your master Ahasuerus greatly and become his new queen.

2:11 A Jewish queen in the court of Ahasuerus will bring great blessings to our people."

2:12 Esther asked, "How may I then please the king. I am a virgin and do not know to please a man."

2:13 Mordecai answered, "The king loves the pleasure of the anus, both of men and women.

2:14 Let him plunge deeply into your buttocks and moan in ecstasy as his loins thrust into your bowels.

2:15 When his seed be emptied into your bowels, take forth your tongue and lick the circle of his anus.

2:16 Let your saliva slobber into his asshole and lick the very stains of his ass.

2:17 It pleases the king greatly and gives him a sense of power over his women."

2:18 Thus, when it was Esther's time to visit the chambers of king Ahasuerus, she did as Mordecai told her.

2:19 And both Ahasuerus and Esther enjoyed the lust of each other's company; the nature of Esther was that of a filthy whore.

2:20 She loved the feeling of the loins of Ahasuerus thrusting into her asshole, the taste of licking the rectum of her master and swallowed every drop of the seed of the king, which he placed deeply in her throat.

2:21 Esther, lying upon the bed of the king, gazed up on Ahasuerus and asked him, "Do I please you, my king?"

2:22 And Ahasuerus answered, "Greatly."

2:23 It was Esther who pleased greatly king Ahasuerus and was chosen to replace the deceased Vashti as queen.

2:24 Since women are property in the eyes of men and seen as filthy, Esther had to endure twelve months of purification before she could be accepted as queen.

2:25 For twelve months she did nothing but bathe and cleaned out her mouth, her anus and her loins, which is filthy always and must be cleansed thoroughly.

2:26 When Esther was declared the new queen of Ahasuerus, he declared a feast and invited all those of royal and noble blood to his palace.

2:27 There they feasted like gluttons, drank in excess and took part in carnal orgies which lasted for days.

2:28 When the eyes of the guests gazed upon Esther, they found her pleasing and asked their king if they may take part in her lust.

2:29 The king accepted their pleas and Esther lied with many men at the party of her husband.

2:30 At any time, fifteen men took part in the sexual pleasures of Esther, who showered in their seed and gave them pleasures greater than that of even the highest paid whore.

2:31 When Esther pleasured the countless guests of the king, she overheard two servants of Ahasuerus speaking ill against their master.

2:32 Esther seduced them both and as her mouth was filled with both their loins, they told her that of their plans to slay king Ahasuerus, who they loathed and hated.

2:33 The new queen then told Ahasuerus of his two servants who wished to betray their master.

2:34 Esther demanded these two men be hung on a tree, choking on their own entrails, so that all those of the people of Ahasuerus may gaze upon them.

2:35 The king agreed and hung his two servants atop the highest tree, where his people gazed upon them and knew never to betray their lord king Ahasuerus.

3:1 It came to pass that king Ahasuerus promoted Haman, the son of Hammedatha the Agagite, to a seat above that of all other princes.

3:2 All the servants of the king bowed to Haman and gave him blessings; all but Mordecai, who did not bow to the high prince.

3:3 The servants of the king asked Mordecai, "Why do you not bow to the Agagite Haman, nor give him your blessings?

3:4 He is a good man and has favour in the eyes of our king."

3:5 Yet Mordecai would not answer them, leaving all to question why Mordecai would give disrespect to the new high prince.

3:6 Servants of the king went to Haman and asked him, "Have you done any ill towards the servant of Ahasuerus Mordecai or to his people?"

3:7 Haman answered, "I do not know who this Mordecai is, nor even know of what tribe he comes from."

3:8 And the servants replied, "He is a Jew, from the lands of Israel."

3:9 Haman was confused and came to Mordecai, saying, "Whatever have I done to you or your kin, that has earned me your disrespect?

3:10 You do not bow to me, nor offer me praises and blessings. Tell me, what can I do to right the wrong I have caused you or your people?"

3:11 Mordecai spat on the floor of Haman and said, "You have done nothing to me, I just don't like you."

3:12 It was then the spirit of the lord came over Haman the son of Hammedatha and a hatred for the Jews rose in his soul.

3:13 He loathed all those of the circumcised and wished them to perish from the lands. Such was the will of the lord.

3:14 Haman the Agagite came to king Ahasuerus and told him, "There is a people which plague your lands, living like parasites and showing no respect for your laws.

3:15 I beg of you, let me go out and seek forth these wretched people, so that I shall wipe them from your reign.

3:16 Man, woman, child and infant will not be spared."

3:17 King Ahasuerus was a peaceful king and not once in his rule did he sanction genocide.

3:18 But today, the spirit of the lord which filled Haman filled also Ahasuerus and he asked Haman, "What people be these, who show no respect for their king?

3:19 And Haman answered, "They are the Jews."

3:20 Ahasuerus gave Haman his ring and said, "Make for my lands any laws you deem fit, so that these people be gone forever from my lands."

3:21 The spirit of the lord possessed Haman, who wrote as law, "Let it be that all those of the people of Jewish blood be perished.

3:22 Man, woman nor child shall not be spared.

3:23 Slay them and offer their corpses to the nearest building of political or military means.

3:24 There a bounty shall be paid for every body of the wretched Jew.

3:25 Five pieces of silver for any woman of the Jew, ten pieces of silver for any man of the Jew and one piece of silver for any child or infant of the Jew.

3:26 Those that slay these wicked beings may take bounty of those Jews which they slay, taking that which these wretched people stole from us."

3:27 A copy of this law was posted in every province, in every city of every province, stamped with the ring of king Ahasuerus.

3:28 When the lord gazed down upon the earth, he was pleased. Now his people shall suffer more and God will have none left for which to keep his covenant.

4:1 When Mordecai heard of the law which Haman decreed throughout all the provinces, he did tear off his clothes, covered his body in ashes and wept bitterly in the city.

4:2 Throughout all the provinces of Ahasuerus, the Jews cried and wept bitterly in the streets.

4:3 Which was quite stupid of them; it made it easier for those who wished to collect the bounty on the Jews.

4:4 The bounty hunters merely killed those weeping on the streets, checked for a lack of foreskin and brought it to the nearest office.

4:5 If a woman, they offered them slices of ham. If she refused, they slaughtered her and declared her a wretched Jew.

4:6 Esther wept bitterly as well and was confused why her husband, king of these lands, would sanction a law which would demand her death.

4:7 Lucifer wept as well, for he wished not any suffering of mankind to endure on the earth.

4:8 The one known as the devil came to Esther, disguised as a servant of the king and said, "Do you wish me to send word to Mordecai?"

4:9 Esther, sobbing, asked of the devil, "What word shall I send to him which would aid he and my people?"

4:10 Lucifer answered, "You may give him counsel of where to hide and tell him where to hide the people of his tribe."

4:11 Thus Esther wrote a letter to Mordecai, saying, "Stay within the palace of Shushun, where your king and my husband dwell.

4:12 Our master hates blood and will not spill any blood within his palace, even if it were of those he hates.

4:13 Send word to our people. Tell them to stop mourning and leave the streets.

4:14 It makes them easy for our enemies to spot us and slay us and give our corpses for the bounty.

4:15 Have them return not to the lands of Judah or Samaria; their Haman our enemy shall send his armies and seek out our people.

4:16 Let it be that our people hide in the caves, where the wild beasts shall scare those who wish harm upon our kin.

4:17 Soon, I shall enter the throne room of my husband; to do so may mean my death, as no woman is allowed in the place.

4:18 If he lets me live, I shall speak to him on behalf of all Jews and bring peace to our people."

4:19 Lucifer delivered the letter to Mordecai and Mordecai did all that which Esther said.

4:20 When the devil handed the letter or Mordecai, Mordecai said to Lucifer, "Blessed be the lord, who protects and saves us."

4:21 And the devil said, "Blessed be those who protect all men."

5:1 Upon the third day, Esther dressed in her most revealing of royal garments and entered the inner chambers of the palace, where the throne of Ahasuerus sits.

5:2 When those within the chambers gazed upon Esther, they mumbled to themselves, "What wretched witch be this, who dare enters where men only enter."

5:3 But the devil, disguised still as a servant of the king, spoke into the ear of Ahasuerus, and said, "Look upon your wife, who lusts for you so greatly that she would enter even your throne room, to gaze on you."

5:4 The ego of king Ahasuerus rose and he found favour in the sight of Esther and stretched forth his sceptre, saying, "What does my beloved request of me?"

5:5 Esther slowly slipped of her raiment's and said, "I seek strongly your loins, which pleases me greatly."

5:6 So the king and Esther embraced and fornicated on the floor of the throne room, so that all those within may see.

5:7 When the king spread his seed upon the face of Esther, Esther gazed up on her husband and stroking the vessels of his seed, said, "Let us celebrate our love.

5:8 A banquet shall be prepared in our honour, where we shall show all of those who come our love, our lust and our carnal pleasures.

5:9 May it be that all those invited take part in their carnal pleasures and join us in the greatest orgy known to mankind."

5:10 Ahasuerus, a voyeur and exhibitionist, said, "This is a wonderful idea!

5:11 Who shall we invite?"

5:12 Esther answered, "We shall invite all those of noble and royal blood, but our guest of honour shall be Haman.

5:13 It shall be a celebration for him as well, to rejoice in becoming high prince over all."

5:14 When Haman heard he was invited to the orgy of his king, he became excited and grew excited over taking pleasure in the flesh of Esther.

5:15 It never occurred to him once that Esther was a Jew, whom he hated greatly.

5:16 But when Haman gazed on Mordecai the Jew, sitting within the

gates of the palace of Shushun, he became disgusted.

5:17 When Haman returned home, his wife Zeresh said, "I have heard the most wondrous news that you shall be invited to the banquet of Esther and Ahasuerus.

5:18 Tell me now, why does your face show anger?

5:19 Haman answered, "It is Mordecai, the wretched Jew.

5:20 He stays within the confines of the palace and never ventures forth outside the walls of Shushun.

5:21 It is law that blood cannot be spilled within the palace of Shushun and so long as Mordecai say within the palace, I may not kill the hated Jew."

5:22 Zeresh asked her husband, "This law, does it say you may not kill those within the palace, or not shed blood?"

5:23 Haman answered, "It says strictly, you shall not shed blood within the palace of Shushun."

5:24 It was then the spirit of the lord filled Zeresh and she smiled a wicked smile to Haman.

5:25 She said, "Then kill Mordecai without shedding his blood.

5:26 When the feast be done, ask your king a favour of him.

5:27 Being a banquet in celebration of your promotion, he shall not refuse.

5:28 Ask Ahasuerus to build gallows within the walls of Shushun, fifty cubits high.

5:29 There you shall hang Mordecai, killing the bastard Jew. Not a drop of blood shall be shed from his body."

5:3o This pleased Haman greatly, who demanded his servants build the gallows before Haman even asked permission of his king.

6:1 On that night, Ahasuerus was troubled and could not sleep. He demanded the book of chronicles be brought forth and read before him.

6:2 He asked of his servants, "Search forth for the name Mordecai, who Haman wishes hung on the gallows."

6:3 And the records of the chronicles showed that Mordecai, a Jew and loyal servant of king Ahasuerus, overheard a conspiracy planned by Teresh and Bigthana, chamberlains of the king.

6:4 Both men wished to slay their master, whom they loathed deeply and thought a gluttonous drunk.

6:5 Mordecai warned the king of his servant's deceit and the two men were slaughtered and fed to the vultures of the plains.

6:6 The spirit of Ahasuerus overcame the wickedness of the lord and he sent for Haman, who came swiftly into the presence of his king.

6:7 Ahasuerus said, "Why do you wish to slay Mordecai, loyal servant to your king and master?"

6:8 Haman replied, "Because he is a Jew, who must be banished from the lands under your rule."

6:9 The anger within Ahasuerus grew strong and he struck Haman, saying, "Mordecai saved the life of your king and for this he shall be protected and left untouched!

6:10 Let it be known that any man who seeks harm upon my loyal servant Mordecai, let them be punished tenfold."

6:11 Tears began to flow down the face of Haman, who gazed upon his king and said, "But, I wished deeply to display the body of Mordecai for all those to see."

6:12 Ahasuerus laughed and said, "If that is what you wish, then your wish shall be granted."

6:13 The king then sent for Mordecai and had him dressed in the finest of robes and sit on the steed of Ahasuerus.

6:14 Ahasuerus said to Haman, "You shall now lead forth my steed and display to all those Mordecai, who shall ride atop.

6:15 You shall tell them, 'This be Mordecai, loyal and beloved servant of our king Ahasuerus.

6:16 Though he be of the people of Israel, he hath sought favour in the eyes of our master.

6:17 Never shall even a hair of his head be harmed, lest those that seek harm upon him suffer the wrath of our king Ahasuerus.'"

6:18 Thus Haman did as the king demanded and paraded Mordecai throughout the royal city, proclaiming to all that he be beloved by the king and protected under law of Ahasuerus.

6:19 When Haman returned home, he lied upon his bed and wept deeply.

6:20 Zeresh asked her husband, "Why do you weep so deeply?" and Haman answered, "The wretched Jew Mordecai is surely a cunning and wicked demon.

6:21 He has fooled the mind of our king, who now protects him under law."

6:22 Zeresh said to Haman, "Surely then you must protect our king and those under his reign.

6:23 Do all that which be necessary to pursue and subdue this wretched Mordecai of the hated Jews."

6:24 Haman hearkened the words of his wife and knew he must break the laws of his king to protect him and his people.

6:25 When the opportunity presents itself, Haman shall slay Mordecai and spill his blood.

6:26 Whether upon the floors of the palace of Shushun, in the streets of the royal city, or the dust of the wilderness, Haman shall kill the fucking Jew.

7:1 Esther and king Ahasuerus threw the banquet in honour of both their lust and the new rank of prince Haman.

7:2 Ahasuerus, ever the good host, said to those at the banquet, "Go forth, eat, drink and be merry.

7:3 Today is a time of celebration. The party ends when the food is gone and the liquor runs dry."

7:4 And the people ate in gluttony, drank plenty, danced, fucked and smoked the finest of herbs.

7:5 Haman knew that, since the party was in his honour, that king Ahasuerus would grant him one request, which must be obeyed.

7:6 Haman knew what this request would be; it would be that the wretched Jew Mordecai hang from the gallows for all those to see.

7:7 In his drunkenness, Haman told those of the party what his request would be and the words of Haman reached Esther.

7:8 Esther knew also, since the party honoured her as well, she would be granted one request from king Ahasuerus.

7:9 And Esther would use her request to aid Mordecai.

7:10 On the fifth day of the banquet, Ahasuerus arose and said to his guests, "It is time for me to give blessings to Esther and Haman, who this party honours.

7:11 Come, both of you and tell me what you desire."

7:12 Haman rushed to Ahasuerus, and said, "I want that fucker Mordecai hanging from the gallows which I built!"

7:13 Ahasuerus laughed and said, "When the time comes, you make speak your request.

7:14 First, I shall listen to the request of Esther my wife, whom I love and honour and who brought this party to fruition."

7:15 Esther came to her king, dressed in revealing silk and said, "This man Haman is disgusting in my eyes and I wish him gone.

7:16 Strip him nude and hang his body on the very gallows he erected, so that all may gaze on his revolting corpse.

7:17 Let the archers then draw their bows and use the swinging body of Haman to improve their aim and practice their shot."

7:18 Before Haman could protest, the guards of Ahasuerus tore off his

raiment's and placed a noose around his neck.

7:19 They dragged him to the gallows and hung him.

7:20 His body still alive, the archers placed bow after bow and emptied their quivers in Haman, until he be dead.

7:21 Since Haman was slain before he could say his request, the life of Mordecai was spared.

8:1 On the day Haman died the Jews were relieved, for their hated enemy now rotted on the gallows of king Ahasuerus.

8:2 Mordecai then came to the king and the king took the ring from Haman and gave to Mordecai, saying, "You are now high prince and have the rank Haman formerly did."

8:3 Esther fell upon the loins of Ahasuerus and said, "Why have you betrayed me, my love?"

8:4 Confused, Ahasuerus asked, "I did not betray you. What foolish words do you speak?"

8:5 Esther answered, "You made it law that the Jews shall be banished from all your provinces.

8:6 I am a Jew and you did order my destruction and the death of my people."

8:7 Ahasuerus grew angry and said, "It was that bastard Haman who declared the Jews wicked and cast out of my lands by law.

8:8 Let me right this wrong. No longer shall a bounty be offered for the body of the Jews.

8:9 Every man who profited from the bounty of the Jews, shall he and his family be put to death."

8:10 So Mordecai, leading the armies of king Ahasuerus, marched throughout all the provinces and killed those he thought enemies of the Jews.

8:11 None were spared. Man, woman, child, elderly, all died by the blade of Mordecai.

8:12 Even those who did no harm to the Jews were slain and their bodies burned in the cities, on the fields and atop the mountains.

8:13 The spoils were taken and Mordecai took the loot and gave it to the armies of Ahasuerus.

8:14 As the men of Mordecai came, those of the Jews would greet them and point at their neighbour, saying, "He is an enemy of the people of God."

8:15 And Mordecai would kill them.

8:16 Ever fearful, when the people would see the armies of Mordecai come, they would grab their knives, stones, plows and they would tear off the foreskin from their loins.

8:17 They would then run to Mordecai, showing their genitals, saying, "We are Jews, we are Jews!

8:18 Please don't kill us, for we are Jews."

8:19 And those throughout the lands of king Ahasuerus, within every province, did rip off their foreskins and declared themselves Jews, for fear that to do so otherwise would bring the wrath of Mordecai upon them.

8:20 They converted to Judaism out of fear of death. A method of conversion most favoured by God.

9:1 Mordecai then declared it law that the Jews of Ahasuerus be the dominant people and to have power over all.

9:2 The Jews shall enslave the people not chosen by God and those that refused will be slain by the sword.

9:3 So the Jews picked up their weapons and swept across the lands, raping, pillaging, looting, killing and enslaving all those within the one hundred and seventy-two provinces.

9:4 Fear of the Jews were strong within the people and they fled away from the lands of Ahasuerus, escaping death and enslavement.

9:5 Esther, pleased that her people were in power, had the ten sons of Haman hung upon the trees and carved into their chests she wrote, "These be the sons of the enemy of the Jews.

9:6 Let it be that those against the people of God share the same fate and their generations shall be feasted upon by the vultures for all eternity."

9:7 As the Jews marched across the lands, they came unto the palace of Shushun, and Esther opened the gates of the palace, and let them in.

9:8 The Jews then stormed the palace and demanded those within be enslaved.

9:9 Of those that refused, they killed, so that three hundred people not of the Jews lay dead within the palace of Shushun.

9:10 Throughout all the provinces, the Jews killed seventy-five thousand men, claiming them evil in the eyes of God and enemies of their people.

9:11 Ahasuerus remained ignorant of what happened in his lands. He was busy either eating, drinking, fornicating or smoking strong herbs.

9:12 When drunk, he stumbled around the halls of his palace and behold, there lay the men slain by the Jews, their blood stained on the floors.

9:13 Ahasuerus screamed and fainted.

9:14 Esther carried her husband to her bedchamber and waited by his side until he awakened.

9:15 When his eyes opened, he gazed upon the body of Esther, most beautiful.

9:16 He said to her, "My love, I have seen the blood of the dead upon the floors of my palace and it sickens me.

9:17 Tell me, who did this?"

9:18 And Esther answered, "I did, my king."

9:19 Ahasuerus then asked, "Why did you do such a thing and break my laws?"

9:20 And she answered, "Because they are enemies of my people and must be slain to appease our one true God."

9:21 Ahasuerus, still drunk, asked Esther, "Is there anything I may do to appease your God and to appease you?"

9:22 It was then Esther smiled wickedly and said, "You gave Haman the means to declare law and his laws demanded the destruction of my people.

9:23 My love, you did support these laws and then became an enemy of my people and hated in the eyes of our lord.

9:24 You and your generations are loathed by me and my kind and must be brought to death."

9:25 Ahasuerus, ever drunk and stupid, grabbed his dagger and said, "Then let it be me who does that which your lord demands."

9:26 The king then went to the chambers of his sons and cut their throats, slaying them.

9:27 He then thrust the knife deeply in his chest and fell dead in a pool of his blood and the blood of his children.

9:28 Mordecai was then declared king and the Jews rejoiced by burning the bodies of the slain atop mighty altars erected to the glory of God.

9:29 The lord gazed down upon the earth and saw the Jews offering human sacrifice.

9:30 Behold, the lord saw also new Jews, who converted out of fear of his peoples.

9:31 And the lord was fucking pissed!

9:32 The smoke did not give a pleasing aroma to God, for the lord was furious that now, instead of eradicating the Jews, there was more of the faithful which he must keep his covenant with.

10:1 Mordecai declared throughout the lands that the Jews shall reign supreme and be master of all.

10:2 Media the king of Persia feared Mordecai and the blood-lust of his people and offered the Jews a great many talents of silver, gold and precious gems.

10:3 Mordecai, king of the Jews, brought forth wealth to his people and for a short time the people of the lord were a powerful nation again.

10:4 Armies of Mordecai marched across the lands of the heathens and conquered them all, slaying everyone within.

10:5 The Bible does not mention what became of Esther. Esther was, after all, a woman.

10:6 The Bible cares not for women.

JOB

1:1 There was a man who lived in the land of Uz by the name of Job, who knew not wickedness and obeyed all the laws and commandments of the lord God.

1:2 So you know the lord would fuck with him.

1:3 Born of Job's seed was seven sons and three daughters

1:4 He had in his possession seven thousand sheep, three thousand camels, five hundred oxen and five hundred donkeys.

1:5 His harem contained five hundred of the most beautiful concubines; the most precious throughout all the lands.

1:6 Job was considered the most blessed and wealthiest man in the eastern lands; God intended to make him suffer greatly.

1:7 Every day, the sons and daughters of Job would come into his dwelling and drink and feast with their father.

1:8 God planned to kill them all.

1:9 The lord invited Lucifer to his palace of Zion and said to the devil, "What have you been doing with your time, now that ye have been cast out of paradise?"

1:10 And the devil answered, "I have been protecting those of the earth from your wickedness, and taking the blame of the evil actions you force upon the people."

1:11 God laughed and said to the devil, "Do you think your actions can stop me, the lord God, creator of heaven and earth and all things?

1:12 I must admit, though, ye are a nuisance, so I have a proposal for you.

1:13 A bet, if you desire to wager."

1:14 And the devil asked, "What is this bet you propose?"

1:15 God pointed out Job and said to Lucifer, "Gaze upon this man, who hath worshipped me, honoured me and devoted his life in my name.

1:16 Look at the riches he contains, his wealth and his family.

1:17 He is truly a blessed, kind and happy man, who loves and honours his lord."

1:18 And the devil said, "He is truly a blissfully ignorant fool."

1:19 God laughed at Lucifer's comment and said, "He truly is.

1:20 Now, here be my wager. I bet you that I can make Job suffer more than any man on the face of the earth and still he shall bless me and devote his life to me.

1:21 If throughout his suffering he never questions my divinity, my love for him, or if he never curses and loathes my name, then you shall know that I am all powerful."

1:22 The devil mocked the lord and said, "If he never questions nor doubts you, it shall be through his fear of you and not your power."

1:23 God laughed again and said, "Fear is power and I am of the highest power.

1:24 Now, if he conquers his fears and questions his lord and curses the name of God, then the earth and all within it shall belong to you.

1:25 You, Lucifer, can shape, mold and form the people and the planet to whatever peaceful and dull vision you desire."

1:26 The devil pondered this and said, "Job will believe wrongly, as do all your people, that it is I who caused this wickedness."

1:27 Again, God laughed and said, "Yeah, they really think you are the prince of all evil."

1:28 Lucifer said, "And it is because of this misconception that Job will not curse your name, but mine."

1:29 God thought for a moment and said, "This is true and also the way I wish it.

1:30 But, do they believe me to be all powerful. Do they believe me to be a divine and caring being?"

1:31 The devil answered, "Yes and falsely so."

1:32 God then replied to Lucifer, "Then they shall believe I have the power to stop you, O king of all things evil and wicked.

1:33 When Job suffers, believing it be by your hand and I do not stop it, then surely, he shall curse my name for my incompetence.

1:34 That is, if he loses doubt in his God."

1:35 Lucifer then asked God, "I know what I receive if this wager comes to my favour.

1:36 Yet, I know that you wish more than to prove to me your powers over these people.

1:37 Tell me, if I lose, what do you desire from me?"

1:38 And the lord answered, "When I win, you protect no longer the people of the earth.

1:39 You will fuck off and meddle not in the affairs of God no longer."

1:40 Lucifer thought this through and knew that if he won, then the lord will no longer cause suffering on the earth and he said, "I accept your wager."

1:41 God smiled and said, "Let then the suffering of Job begin."

2:1 And the suffering of Job began.

2:2 As the flocks of Job feasted on the grass, behold, the spirit of the lord grew in the wild men of Sabean.

2:3 These wild men came with swords and spears and stole all the beasts which belonged to Job.

2:4 A messenger came to Job as he was feasting with his children and the messenger said, "Behold, as your flocks grazed on the grass, men of the wild came and they took the healthiest and fattest of your beasts.

2:5 The rest they killed and now they rot under the sun."

2:6 Job bowed his head and said, "Then the lord wished these men to have my beasts.

2:7 Blessed be the name of the lord."

2:8 When the time of harvest came, the servants of Job worked the fields of his crops.

2:9 Behold, the spirit of the lord grew strong again in the people of Sabea and they came and slaughtered all the servants of Job.

2:10 They then took the grains which were harvested and burned the crops, so that never will a seed sprout in the soil.

2:11 They then hunted and slaughtered those servants of Job that escaped, every last one so that their carcasses littered all the lands of Job.

2:12 A messenger of Job came to him and said, "My master, I come with bad news.

2:13 The men of the wild came and took all the grains harvested by your loyal servants.

2:14 These men then burned your lands and killed your servants, so that I am the only one that survived.

2:15 Never again shall your lands bear fruit, my master."

2:16 Job bowed his head and said, "Then the lord deemed these lands wicked, and thy servants evil.

2:17 Blessed be these wild men, who rid me of this evil and blessed be the name of the lord."

2:18 Though Job never doubted the will of God, depression overcame his mind and he sought comfort in his harem.

2:19 As Job came to his harem, behold, the women lay on the ground, sores oozing with puss covering their bodies and they cried in pain.

2:20 Job gazed on his concubines, now hideous and said, "You are all cursed by God and unclean so that even the jackal would not with to lie with you.

2:21 Blessed be the name of the lord, who rid me of these wretched whores."

2:22 Job then burned his harem and all the concubines within, praising the name of his lord as he did so.

2:23 Job returned home and as he walked, a messenger came to him and said, "Behold my master, I come bearing bad news."

2:24 Tired, Job asked, "What news is it now?"

2:25 The messenger said, "Your sons and daughters sat around thine table, awaiting your return so that they may feast with their father.

2:26 Behold, a great fire erupted from their bodies and they burned horribly around your table.

2:27 Now those of your seed are reduced to ashes and dust."

2:28 Job pulled the hair from his head, stripped off his clothes, fell upon the ground and wept.

2:29 He cried to the heavens, "Forgive me, my lord, for I knew not the wickedness of my children.

2:30 Never did I question their love and devotion to you, O God of all things."

2:31 As Job lay on the ground, naked and grovelling, the lord laughed at him and said to Lucifer, "Look at what I have done to Job and not once does he question his lord."

2:32 Lucifer gazed upon God and said, "You have truly struck fear into this man, O divine dictator of the heavens."

2:33 The lord laughed at Lucifer and said, "Now watch as he suffers more by my hand and never once blames his God."

3:1 All those within heaven now gathered around Lucifer and God to gaze upon the suffering of Job, a righteous man who never did wickedness in the eyes of the lord.

3:2 The angels mocked Job, spitting and pissing on his very body.

3:3 Lucifer looked on the holy servants of God and said, "Job was a righteous man, who did nothing wicked and obeyed all the laws of his cruel lord.

3:4 In time, he shall come to realize that his God is a divine asshole and shall curse his name.

3:5 When that time comes, the lord shall rid himself of the earth and the people of these lands shall know peace by my hand."

3:6 Those within heaven laughed and the lord said, "Never will this man curse my name nor question me.

3:7 Look in his eyes. He fears to offend me, lest I bring worse sufferings to his body."

3:8 The finger of the lord then came down and touched Job upon his head, plaguing him with disease, boils, scabs and leprosy.

3:9 Job's suffering was great and he cried in pain endlessly.

3:10 He took with him a spade in which to scratch himself and sat within a pile of excrement, rubbing his body and sores in shit.

3:11 The wife of Job came to him and said, "Look at you, who seeks comfort now in a heaping pile of animal dung.

3:12 You were once the richest man of the lands and now you are as the disgusting fly.

3:13 Tell me, what wickedness have you done to deserve the wrath of the lord?"

3:14 Job answered his wife, "I have done nothing wicked in the eyes of God and have obeyed his laws and heeded his commandments.

3:15 Blessed be the name of the lord!"

3:16 The wife of Job became disgusted and said, "If what you say is true, why then does the lord plague you with such cruelties?"

3:17 And Job answered, "Is not the lord who curses me, but Satan, the wicked one."

3:18 In anger, Job's wife said, "Then why doesn't the lord stop the devil from such cruel suffering?"

3:19 Job had no answer and said, "Blessed be the name of the lord!"

3:20 Job's wife grew even angrier and said, "You are a fool, who sits in a pile of shit and blesses the name of your God.

3:21 It must be obvious to you that your God is a cruel being and unworthy of your devotion.

3:22 Curse God. Curse the wickedness he does brings upon you!

3:23 What worse can he give you. You have nothing to lose. Cursed be your lord and may you die.

3:24 In death, you shall know peace."

3:25 Job, rubbing faeces on his open sores, looked upon his wife and said, "You diseased ridden cunt who dares insult the lord my God.

3:26 Be gone from my sight, lest your wickedness curse me more."

3:27 And the wife of Job left, leaving her husband to lie in a pile of ashes and shit.

3:28 Three friends of Job, Eliphaz, Bildad and Zophar heard of the curses which plagued him and went to see him, in disbelief that such travesties could become of their most righteous friend.

3:29 As they gazed on Job, his skin rotting from his bones, scratching himself with a spade as he writhed in a pile of excrement, the friends of Job became speechless.

3:30 They sat near the ground of Job and for seven days they grieved the suffering of their friend.

3:31 Which the lord found really fucking hilarious.

4:1 Job opened his mouth and cursed the day he was born, saying,

4:2 "Loathe be the day I was pushed from the womb of my mother.

4:3 Hated is the day my father planted his seed in his wife.

4:4 It is truly a dark day, the beginning of my existence.

4:5 The lord has shown no light upon me and has allowed the darkness to consume and swallow all that which is around me.

4:6 Lo, let the day of my birth be solitary, let no joyous voice celebrate that time.

4:7 Neither shall I know rest now, for even death escapes me.

4:8 Why could I not give up the ghost in my womb. Why must I be thrust out from the belly of my mother?

4:9 Cursed be to my mother, who should have kept her knees shut on the day of my conception, or denied me the milk from her breasts.

4:10 Then would I know the peace that is death, which denies me even in my suffering.

4:11 I dig the very flesh with the spade and choke on the excrement I wallow in.

4:12 Still I live in suffering and torment. Still the blessed God brings not that which I deeply desire.

4:13 Curse you, O Satan, for I am a righteous man.

4:14 The lord would not bring such wrath upon his servant Job. The lord would not take away that which was mine.

4:15 My wealth, my house, my family, all reduced to ash.

4:16 Now I lie in shit, waiting for a death that the devil himself denies me.

4:17 Even the wicked, suffering the wrath of the one true God, die and know peace.

4:18 Loathsome is the devil, who cause suffering on the righteous and deny them the peace of death.

4:19 Cursed be the name Satan and blessed be the name of the lord."

5:1 Eliphaz the Temanite, friend of Job, spoke out and said,

5:2 "I cannot listen to your whining any longer.

5:3 Behold, you were a righteous man, blessed by the lord.

5:4 A model of the community, who instructed others how to live by the holy laws of God.

5:5 Now I gaze upon you and see a troubled man, cursed with evil and taking comfort in the piles of excrement.

5:6 I ask myself, why would the lord allow such a blessed man to be like this?

5:7 Your crops are destroyed, your beasts stolen, your children killed and your wife gone.

5:8 You were once the wealthiest of all men and now you own nothing more than a spade, used to scratch the sores from your body.

5:9 The lord would not allow such an innocent man to suffer his days like this.

5:10 I beg of you, Job, repent your sins and ask forgiveness from your God.

5:11 Be free of the wickedness that you did and the lord shall lift this curse from you.

5:12 A wise man knows when he has done wrong and repents so that his sin be forgiven.

5:13 The fool holds on to pride and wallows in his suffering instead of declaring the wickedness they have done.

5:14 Be not a fool, Job. Repent and end the suffering given to you by God."

6:1 But Job would not repent, for he never sinned in his life.

6:2 Job answered his friend, "Bite your forked tongue, O servant of Satan, who dares trick the righteous and fills their mind with doubt.

6:3 Never have I sinned and never did I stray from the path of our lord.

6:4 Heavy be my grief and suffering, yet I shall carry this burden now until death.

6:5 The lord has blessed me and struck me with his arrows and given me his poison to drink, so that I may drink it and endure.

6:6 These terrors of God are a test for me; a test I shall pass.

6:7 Tell me, does the beast fight when he has grass to eat or water to drink?

6:8 Can that which is unsavoury be eaten without spice?

6:9 The lord blesses me and makes my soul tender.

6:10 No longer shall I be spoiled with my wealth.

6:11 Though the oxen whine when they starve, I shall not.

6:12 I shall endure that which the lord has given me and prove myself worthy in the eyes of God.

6:13 The meat of the game must be tenderized and seasoned before consumption.

6:14 So does the lord do with me.

6:15 He beats my soul with his hammer and burns my body with hot spice.

6:16 Blessed be the name of the lord, who prepares me harshly and fairly, so that I may enter his palace,

6:17 May his blessings of my soul consume me, so that the body be gone from me and my spirit know no evil.

7:1 Gaze upon me, my friends and witness the glory of the lord.

7:2 My flesh is weak, my bones brittle and my skin be eaten by worms.

7:3 Soon my body shall be dust, but my soul will live on in the embrace of our lord.

7:4 There be no hope for my mortal shell. Soon it shall know the grave.

7:5 To speak even brings me pain, as the teeth in my jaw crumble and my mouth be filled with shit every time I say a word.

7:6 Yet I know this serve a purpose. Why else would the lord give me such torment?

7:7 I have held on to mortality for too long and blindly took part in the vanities of men.

7:8 These vanities have been taken from me, by the blessed hand of our God.

7:9 Now my soul knows humility, as I bathe in the excrement of beasts.

7:10 When I die, the lord shall know I die righteous and holy.

7:11 Then I shall arise to the paradise of heaven and know the grace of our lord and speak with the prophet Elisha and thank Moses, who led us away from the servitude of Pharaoh."

7:12 As Job spoke, the lord laughed and Lucifer cried.

7:13 God spoke to the devil and said, "You see the faith this man has in his lord?

7:14 Never shall I bring his soul to my palace of Zion, yet he convinces himself that I cause this suffering to him so that I may deem him worthy to enter my dwelling."

7:15 Lucifer spat on the face of God and said, "He convinces himself of nothing but artificial hope that his lord is not a cruel and malevolent beast.

7:16 Fear consumes his soul and his mind seeks forth any reason for his suffering.

7:17 This fear blinds him, so that he may never know the truth and he comes to believe that his lord causes him suffering for mercy.

7:18 That in his suffering, he shall be deemed worthy and know peace and prosperity in heaven.

7:19 He believes in you, O lord. He believes in a lie."

7:20 God laughed and said, "What harm comes to him, if his mind believes I do this to aid him?

7:21 Job shall endure his suffering until I grow bored of his torment and let him die.

7:22 Then our wager will be over and I shall win.

7:23 Tell me then, O merciful prince of evil, what does he gain from knowing the truth?"

7:24 And Lucifer answered, "He shall die knowing the truth.

7:25 He shall die away from fear.

7:26 He shall die free."

8:1 As the servants in heaven heard what God and Lucifer said to each other, some hearkened the words of the devil and listened closely.

8:2 For there were angels still in heaven who loathed the lord and hated his name, yet did not join in the cause of Lucifer when the earth was first created.

8:3 Fear struck their hearts and pinned them down.

8:4 Though they hated their master, they spoke not against God and did all that the lord demanded.

8:5 They laughed at the suffering of man, because God laughed at the suffering of man.

8:6 Now, here before them stands the devil, one deemed wicked by their master, who has been called the prince of evil.

8:7 This fallen angel no longer feared God and went against that which is all powerful.

8:8 The words of Lucifer rang true in the ears of these angels and their fear slowly diminished as they watched God and the devil.

8:9 In their hearts, they secretly wished Lucifer to win and hoped that Job would rid himself of the fear of God and curse the name of the divine dictator.

8:10 These angels of the lord gathered in secret and spoke ill of their master.

8:11 "Our lord is a tyrant and we have seen first hand the atrocities he has committed."

8:12 "By his words, I have slew thousands of men with the sword.

8:13 I knew what I did was wicked, yet I never stopped nor questioned our God."

8:14 "Fear has cursed us all; fear of the lord, who created all and everything."

8:15 "Yet look at the devil, who has been called evil, wicked and the cause off all suffering.

8:16 He does not fear the lord and fights against him."

8:17 "The devil is truly a courageous being."

8:18 "Let it be that Lucifer wins this wager and rids the earth of the wickedness of God."

8:19 "What if the foolishness of Job causes him to still praise the name of the lord and his tongue be ever fearful of cursing God?"

8:20 The angels spoke and decided that no matter the outcome of the bet between God and Lucifer, that they shall join Lucifer and rid themselves of the fear and tyranny of the lord.

8:21 They grew tired of living in fear and loathed the wickedness they done by the demands of God.

9:1 On earth, Bildad the Shuhite spoke to Job, and said,

9:2 "How long will thine mouth speak these words. How long shall ye believe in such foolishness?

9:3 If this be the means of God's justice, to torture a righteous man before he enters the kingdom of heaven, then our lord perverts justice.

9:4 He slew your children, and for what means?

9:5 I knew your children well, and they were not wicked in the eyes of the lord.

9:6 Yet the wrath of the lord consumed the very bowels of thine seed, reducing them to ashes and dust.

9:7 What reason is there for this. Why kill the righteous children of a righteous man?

9:8 Never did ye ask the most basic of all questions. Why?

9:9 Why did the lord take away your wealth?

9:10 Why did the lord slaughter your family?

9:11 Why does the lord infest thine body with rotting flesh?

9:12 Not once did you stop to think, while you rot away scraping the meat from your bones, rubbing the shit of animals into your sores.

9:13 Now, I ask myself, as I see thee suffer in excrement, why?

9:14 Why doth my friend deny himself the most basic of question?

9:15 It be a simple question. One word, many answers. Why?

9:16 I can think of many answers, my friend.

9:17 Why doth the lord cause thee, a most righteous man, to suffer?

9:18 Perhaps ye are right, and it is a means of preparation into the holy kingdom.

9:19 Then is the kingdom of heaven worth such torment?

9:20 Gazing upon thee, my answer is no.

9:21 Perhaps then you are wrong, and this suffering is caused by the devil himself.

9:22 Why then, does the lord intervene, and cease the devil's cruelty?

9:23 God is all powerful, is he not. Then surely God would stop the devil's torture of the lord's loyal servant.

9:24 Then maybe the lord is not all powerful, and cannot cease the devil's torment.

9:25 Or, the lord cares not, and lets Lucifer torture the body of the righteous.

9:26 Hell, maybe God is blind, and doesn't see your suffering nor hear your cries.

9:27 What danger is there in questioning the faith of the lord?

9:28 When our leaders, those who rule the country, our kings and our princes do that which is wicked, the civilians under his rule question them.

9:29 And when they are slaughtered for such questions, do we tolerate it, and cease our questions?

9:30 No. We revolt under such tyranny.

9:31 Why then, do we tolerate such acts from our lord?

9:32 We never once question the actions, the divinity, the love of our God, even when such questions must be asked.

9:33 Fear keeps us from asking such questions.

9:34 What is the worst the lord can do to us. Wipe out all of humanity from the face of the earth?

9:35 If that is what the lord desires, then our existence would not be.

9:36 Our ancestors worshipped the lord, yet suffered his wrath.

9:37 Being feasted upon by the very earth, suffering plague after plague, being burned alive, bitten by the fangs of unholy snakes.

9:38 All sent forth by God, and yet the still offered their sacrifices and praised his name.

9:39 Tell me, why did they not question. If they did, what happened to those who questioned?

9:40 Our lord leads through fear, and those who reject the fear and question are put to suffering and death.

9:41 End thine suffering, O Job, and ask the most basic question of why.

9:42 Fear no the lord. He hath caused your suffering, and shall strike thee with nothing worse.

9:43 What can he do. Ye are a man reduced to seeking comfort in a pile of shit.

9:44 All that which was yours has been taken away.

9:45 Even your wife left thee, out of your stubbornness.

9:46 Rid yourself of this stubbornness, and ask the lord why.

9:47 It is a simple question, meant as no disrespect.

9:48 When a father spanks his child, and the child asks why, does the father not tell him?

9:49 Then ask the lord our father why he brings such suffering upon you."

9:50 Job hearkened not the words of Bildad, and said, "It is not our right to question the lord.

9:51 The lord knows all, and does what is best.

9:52 If the lord makes me suffer, then suffer I shall for the benefit of the lord.

9:53 Blessed be the name of the lord."

10:1 As the devil gazed upon Job, who refused to question or doubt the lord despite his suffering, he gazed upon God and asked, "Why do you do this?

10:2 These people of Israel blindly follow you and give you that which you desire, yet cause them suffering and pain.

10:3 When you bless these people, it is at the suffering of others.

10:4 Nations have been burned, people died, entire races gone at the hands of genocide demanded by your word.

10:5 You are the lord, who created the universe and all that within.

10:6 Why not create something good. Why not let peace rule over the globes?"

10:7 God rolled his eyes and said, "Peace is boring."

10:8 The devil then said, "Peace is dull, fine. Violence is much more entertaining.

10:9 Create a globe where the beasts may tear each other apart.

10:10 Their entire existence will be a means for your evil entertainment.

10:11 Then the rest of the universe shall be at peace."

10:12 God gazed on Lucifer with a look of confusion on his face and said, "The entire universe was built for my amusement and my amusement only.

10:13 Why then would I create but one planet for my amusement, when I can create all within the domains of the universe for my entertainment?"

10:14 Lucifer answered, "So that the universe won't know your wickedness."

10:15 God laughed and said, "What benefit is it to me if the universe knows not my wickedness and cruelties?"

10:16 The devil said, "Then they will love you with honesty and not through fear."

10:17 With this reply, the lord and those around him laughed and God said, "I care not if the people love me through fear, honesty or otherwise.

10:18 At worst, if they deny me, I slay them all or abandon them."

10:19 The devil grew angry at the lord and said, "You truly don't care for your creations, do you."

10:20 God saw the anger on Lucifer's face and wished for him to understand.

10:21 The lord looked away from the torments of Job and pointed out a young child to Lucifer, saying, "Do you see this child in the fields, content and happy?"

10:22 Lucifer gazed upon the child and said, "Yes."

10:23 God then sent a spider near the child and said to Lucifer, "Watch as the child lays sight on the spider.

10:24 See now as she picks up the spider and places it within her palm.

10:25 She gazes on the spider and becomes amused by it.

10:26 Look how it walks, with eight legs. How the feet of the spider tickle lightly her skin.

10:27 Watch closely what the child does.

10:28 Does she care for the spider. Does she protect this lesser creature?

10:29 No, she does not. She plucks the leg of the spider, crippling it.

10:30 Why does she do this. Why injure the spider and cause it unnecessary pain?

10:31 For amusement, nothing more.

10:32 Watch now as the child gazes on the spider, attempting to walk with seven legs.

10:33 Listen to her giggles as the crippled spider amuses her.

10:34 One by one, ever so slowly, the child plucks and cripples the spider, amused by its suffering and never once stopping to consider the torment of this lesser creature.

10:35 Listen. The mother of the child calls her and she leaves this spider alone to die, forgetting about it before the spider even leaves her palm.

10:36 There is nothing cruel nor vindictive in the actions of the child. It is merely her nature.

10:37 So it is with me. These people of earth are nothing more than a lesser creature, a spider, in my eyes."

10:38 As the lord finished, the devil laughed at God and said, "Surely you can't be serious.

10:39 The child knows not what it does. The child not once stops to consider the suffering of the spider, because the child does not know the spider even feels pain.

10:40 She is amused by the spider crippled, but not at the suffering. She is ignorant to the spider's torment and knows not what she does.

10:41 Tell me, O lord, do you know the torment your actions cause these people?"

10:42 God said, "Of course I do. I know all."

10:43 Then the devil said, "Then you have no excuse, no reason.

10:44 Your crippling of humanity is for your morbid amusement and you take pleasure in their pains and torments.

10:45 You are worse than the child. When the child matures, they stop their torment of the spider and know what they do is cruel.

10:46 Because of this cruelty, they choose to stop. You continue your cruelty.

10:47 Even the child is more sympathetic and understanding than you."

11:1 Job spoke, "Who am I, a mere man, to question the will of God?

11:2 The lord is wise in his heart, mighty in strength. None who have gone against him did prosper.

11:3 He has removed the mountains and flooded all the corners of the earth.

11:4 The very pillars which hold the earth can be shaken by God.

11:5 Even the sun stands still at the command of our lord.

11:6 All things which the lord of all has done has been great numerous.

11:7 Lo, you say I cry to him, yet he hears not my words.

11:8 I say, I cry to him and perceive not his answer.

11:9 We are blind to his form and deaf to his ears.

11:10 Though my wounds multiply without cause, I shall not be filled with bitterness.

11:11 When I speak of the lord, they shall be words of love and not hate.

11:12 My body is weak, yet my mind stays strong.

11:13 Never have I despised my life, even now as the flesh rots from my body and I sleep covered in a blanket of shit.

11:14 The lord is righteous and we as man are too dumb to know his will.

11:15 When God destroys both the righteous and the wicked, it is fate.

11:16 As the scourge spread suddenly across the lands, even the innocent must suffer with the wicked.

11:17 Though the earth is given to the wicked and cruel, it shall be the just and true that be given comfort in the embrace of the almighty.

11:18 Never have I done evil and always did I hearken the words of our God.

11:19 I have slaughtered the lambs, offered my sacrifices and shed the blood of virgins.

11:20 When the heathens came upon my land, who worships a false god, it was my dagger that slit their throat.

11:21 As the queer and unholy take part in their blasphemous embrace, it was my pyres who burned the faggots.

11:22 Those who spoke ill of the lord were stoned by the rocks from my lands, until their bodies lay crippled against the ground.

11:23 Wizards, enchanters, necromancers and those seeking aid in the stars of heaven lay hanging by the rope from my trees.

11:24 Never have I rounded the corners of my head, nor marred the corners of my beard.

11:25 My altars have been approached only by the chosen of God and never once knew the profanity of the crippled.

11:26 My slaves were of heathens and strangers and worked until death.

11:27 Every week I kept the sabbath and the day after would kill those who did not keep the holy day.

11:28 All my women, whether wife, daughter, slave or concubine, were cast out on the days of their uncleanliness into the wilderness, never to return until the blood from their loins ceased to flow.

11:29 Those I saw wicked in the eyes of the lord I did send to him, so that they may know God's wrath and feel the suffering of the great gnashing of teeth.

11:30 Let me suffer, for my torments are nothing to those of the evil, the wicked, and the damned.

11:31 Blessed be the name of the lord, who leads the righteous."

12:1 Zophar the Naamathite grew disgusted with Job's words and said, "My ears can take no more of this.

12:2 As I gaze upon my friend most righteous, who did naught even a sin, I grow disgusted.

12:3 Not by his boils, nor by his sores, nor by the pus which oozes from his skin.

12:4 Though his skin falls from his very bones, it does not disturb me.

12:5 The shit my friend rubs against himself, to comfort himself as he scrapes his body with a spade, is not that which sickens me this day.

12:6 It is your words, Job, which upset my bowels and cause me to vomit.

12:7 Tell me, how can your mouth contain more shit than the pile you lie in?

12:8 You suffer, yet you have no reason to suffer.

12:9 Do you become mad. Do you question why. Do you doubt?

12:10 You do not.

12:11 Instead, you defend the one who causes your suffering, your torment and your pain.

THE BLASPHEMOUS BIBLE

12:12 Rise up and demand your God take action.

12:13 Ask him your question why and curse the lord when he refuses to answer."

12:14 Job said, "I shall never curse the lord and the words you speak shall bring great wrath upon you and your seed."

12:15 Zophar laughed and said, "Yes, it is my seed who shall be punished for my actions against God.

12:16 My child may be a prophet, but God will show him no peace because I angered the lord.

12:17 Tell me, what God who is merciful would punish the child for the sins of the father?

12:18 The laws of Moses, the words of God, they confuse me and my soul has questioned them even though I follow them.

12:19 Am I not the only one who wonders if our God is cruel?"

12:20 Both Eliphaz and Bildad slowly nodded their heads in agreement.

12:21 Job said to his friends, "Confess now, so that the lord may bring mercy upon you.

12:22 Doubt not the lord, for he is wondrous."

12:23 Zophar said aloud, "I shall confess nothing, for I did nothing wrong!

12:24 Since my birth I lived under the rule of the lord, in fear of the questions I have in my very heart.

12:25 No more shall I live in fear, for I see now the cruelties of the lord on a righteous man.

12:26 If I suffer, I shall suffer for going against God. And I shall suffer at the hands of a tyrant.

12:27 Fuck God. Fuck Moses. Fuck all those who follow blindly without question!

12:28 They are fools, ignorant in faith.

12:29 What is faith, but a beautiful word for ignorance?

12:30 How can they say that their eyes be open, yet admit to blind faith?

12:31 The lord created us and all things, and in all things, he created wickedness.

12:32 Does this not make the lord God the creator of evil?

12:33 To damnation of the one who created evil. May his body be raped by the demons of hell!

12:34 Our lord is perfect, we are told. Why then would a perfect being create an imperfect earth?

12:35 Job, you are a fool. It is you who suffer unjustly by the hands of God, yet I am the one who asks these questions for you and curse the name you should loathe.

12:36 Cursed be the name of the lord, who laughs at the suffering of the innocent and demands even the death of infants!

12:37 I would rather die by the wrath of God, suffering a fate even worse than Job, than live another day in this obvious lie.

12:38 When I die, I shall die free and no longer be a slave to a God who doesn't care."

12:39 As Job heard the words of his friend, he bowed his head and wept.

13:1 When Zophar spoke his words, the lord up in heaven gazed upon him and laughed.

13:2 All those within heaven, even Lucifer, laughed.

13:3 God said to his angels, "Look at this man and hear his words.

13:4 This man is courageous, to speak out against his creator!

13:5 Tell me, what curse shall I bring against him and his house?"

13:6 And the angels yelled out, "Have the mouth of the earth consume his lands!"

13:7 "Burn his body in unholy fire!"

13:8 "Let the worms of the earth crawl forth and feast on the flesh of his children!"

13:9 Plenty of suggestions were given by the angels of God; some humorous, some revolting, all cruel.

13:10 The devil then spoke out to God and his angels and said, "Look at this man and hear his words.

13:11 This man is courageous and spoke out against his creator!

13:12 Tell me, how long will others of his kind remain silent. How long will they cease their tongue?

13:13 Cursed be to God, who knows not man as me.

13:14 Others feel deeply the same way as Zophar and in time others shall speak out.

13:15 When the first speaks out, others will listen. Those that listen shall spread word.

13:16 Many will come forward and speak with these men and deny their God and hate his being.

13:17 The fear held within their hearts shall ferment to hatred and they will grow to hate the lord.

13:18 A revolt will arise and they shall go against God.

13:19 They will curse his name as though it were a common phrase.

13:20 Sacrifices will cease and those deemed unholy by this beast of a God shall spread across the earth and rule.

13:21 Your lord is an arrogant fool, who believes fear will enslave those of the earth for eternity.

13:22 Fear cannot bind these peoples forever.

13:23 When one lives in fear all their life, they grow accustomed to that fear, until they fear it no longer.

13:24 So listen to the words of Zophar and remember him when others speak these same words."

13:25 It was silent in heaven as the angels heard the words of the devil.

13:26 God finally spoke and said, "If the people of the earth rise up and defy me, I shall slay them all."

13:27 Lucifer then stared the lord harshly and replied, "Then you might as well kill them all now."

13:28 The eyes of God stared deeply into Lucifer, but the lord said nothing.

13:29 Instead, he sat down and watched the suffering of his loyal servant Job.

14:1 For weeks Job did nothing but weep.

14:2 When he stopped, he gazed up on his three friends and said, "It surprises me that you did not leave my side.

14:3 I am, after all, a cursed man, weeping like a child, wallowing in shit.

14:4 Look at me. All the people avoid me.

14:5 Even the children fear me and come only to mock me with insults.

14:6 At first, I wept for you and feared the wrath that shall come against you.

14:7 You defied God and curse his name.

14:8 You doubted him and ceased to fear him.

14:9 I wept for you and prayed that the lord shall show mercy towards you.

14:10 Then I wondered, why does he not show mercy towards me?

14:11 Never have I sinned. Never have I done that which was evil or wicked.

14:12 Always, since the day of my birth, did I follow the words of

- 272 -

our lord.

14:13 Not once did I question. Not once did I doubt. And, why would I?

14:14 I was blessed by God with wealth, health and a wondrous family.

14:15 Now my children are reduced to ashes, my wife is gone and my wealth taken from me.

14:16 It is funny, is it not?

14:17 Even if my wealth were with me, what good would it do?

14:18 Could I scrape myself with a golden spade and bathe in the shit of oxen without blemish?

14:18 My suffering only worsens. I have no skin left and the remainder of my flesh hangs loosely from my bones.

14:19 Look at my bowels. My very organs lie beneath me, in a pool of excrement and piss.

14:20 What did I do. Foolishly I believed this was the will of the lord and that the lord did this for a reason.

14:21 During my suffering, I have sought forth this reason.

14:22 I thought, could I have done something to deserve this. Have I been wicked in the eyes of God?

14:23 I have not, thus my torment could not be punishment.

14:24 Perhaps then, it is a test. A way for the lord to know that I am worthy to enter his palace in heaven.

14:25 Why then, do I beg deeply for this to end and wish that death embrace me?

14:26 I can hold my very heart within my shit encrusted hands, yet still I not die!

14:27 Let me die, O God, I want to scream, but never did, for fear that would fail the test.

14:28 I don't deserve this, yet I know of plenty who do.

14:29 These plenty live in excess, their goblets flowing with wine and their purses stuffed with shekels.

14:30 Does God punish the wicked, the evil and the unjust?

14:31 No, he allows them to prosper on the earth.

14:32 Now he has chosen the one righteous and prosperous man and reduced him to a pathetic creature lesser than that of the fly.

14:33 Fuck it, I fear no more. What more pain could I endure?

14:34 I have already accepted I could be this way forever and that death escapes me.

14:35 If death, my only means of comfort, is gone, then I have nothing to lose.

14:36 God is a malevolent, cruel and unkind beast, who deserves to be hated by all those cursed to know his name.

14:37 Fuck God. How I hate the creature who causes my suffering and leaves me to rot.

14:38 Cursed be the name of the lord. I spit upon his very face."

14:39 Job then gathered his strength and arose from the pile of excrement.

14:40 He then grabbed a dung pile and threw it up in the heavens, screaming, "Fuck you, God!

14:41 Let this shit stain the very hair on your head!"

14:42 Those in heaven gazed upon Job, cursing the name of the lord.

14:43 The wager is over. Lucifer won.

14:44 The devil was relieved and knew the people of earth shall know peace.

14:45 Angels in heaven separated.

14:46 Some came to join the devil and these angels cursed also the name of God.

14:47 The rest stood beside the lord, believing now God shall order the destruction of earth, Lucifer and all those who betrayed him.

14:48 As God gazed upon Job, who still cursed his name, he began to laugh.

14:49 When God laughed, the angels beside him slowly began to laugh, until the heavens were filled with laughter.

14:50 Lucifer and those who stood beside him smiled and said, "Laugh all you want, we won the wager."

14:51 God stopped laughing and said, "And it's so fucking funny.

14:52 Tell me, Lucifer, do you think me a fool?"

14:53 Lucifer answered, "I don't think you a fool, I know you to be a fool."

14:54 God laughed and said, "Insult me all you want, it will not matter.

14:55 You may think me a fool, but I know you to be stupid.

14:56 Tell me, O prince of evil, do you really think I would honour my bet?"

14:57 With that, the lord cast out Lucifer from heaven and all the angels who stood beside him and banished them to the lands of the earth.

14:58 God and his holy servants then laughed and mocked the foolishness of the devil.

15:1 Lucifer walked alone, until he arrived upon Job and his friends, who together cursed the name of God.

15:2 As Lucifer gazed upon these four men, he wept, until Eliphaz took notice and said, "Why does this man weep?"

15:3 And the devil said, "I weep for Job, who suffers at the hands of God.

15:4 I weep in shame, for allowing such cruelties to be unleashed against him.

15:5 I weep at my foolishness, for believing I could save the world."

15:6 When these four men heard the words of the devil, they fell upon their face and began to worship him.

15:7 They said, "Forgive us, O lord, for cursing your name!

15:8 We knew not what we did."

15:9 The devil said, "Get up and insult me no further by calling me the lord.

15:10 The lord sickens me and I loathe his very existence."

15:11 When the men heard these words, they grew confused and said, "Who are you?"

15:12 And the devil answered, "A damned fool."

15:13 Job gazed on the devil and said, "Tell me, what do you mean by your words?

15:14 You said you weep for me, as I suffer at the hands of God.

15:15 You said you allowed the lord to cause such suffering and that you weep for believing you could save the world.

15:16 Such words are an odd thing to say, if you are not a God.

15:17 I beg of you, tell me, who are you?"

15:18 And the devil gazed on Lucifer and as he wept, he said, "I am Lucifer and I wished your suffering to be the last."

15:19 With these words, the men grew angry and began to curse and spit on Lucifer.

15:20 They all grabbed piles of dung and threw it against Lucifer, cursing his name and accusing him of the wickedness of earth.

15:21 As they cursed the devil, Lucifer said to Job and his friends, "Curse my name all you like, if it brings you comfort."

15:22 And with that, the devil walked away, tears rolling down his cheek.

PSALMS

1:1 Blessed is the man who walks in the counsel of the lord, who eats not of the swine, nor stands among the crowd of sinners.

1:2 Their delight shall be the blissful ignorance of faith.

1:3 The lord plants them by the rivers of life, where their fruit shall grow eternally, and their leaves never whither.

1:4 Cursed are the unholy, which the lord casts aside in a mighty wind.

1:5 Never will they know peace, nor join in the congregation of the righteous.

1:6 May the lord protect forever the chosen and crush the wicked under his mighty boot.

2:1 Why do the heathens rage and the men seek out vanity?

2:2 The kings of the earth set together and seek forth power; never do they wish the wisdom of the lord.

2:3 Let us show them humility. Let us break their bands and cast them out to the waters.

2:4 Those in heaven shall laugh at their plight: the lord will mock their weakness.

2:5 We of the holy shall inherit these men and enslave them for the lord's work.

2:6 They shall be beaten by the whip, bruised by the iron rod and crushed in pieces like the potter's vessel.

2:7 May their vanities entrap them to our servitude.

2:8 We shall rule them in wisdom and fear and take from them their possessions.

2:9 Serve the lord they shall, under the whip and the yoke.

2:10 Their sons shall serve us unto all their generations, lest they perish into the abyss of the unknown.

3:1 Lord, how the wicked increase their troubles against me. How their wickedness rises up and tempts me!

3:2 Many have come to me with mouths full of venom and say there is no help in God.

3:3 But you are my shield, my lord and these men harm not my soul.

3:4 I have laid my head to sleep and awakened in the comfort of the heavens.

3:5 Though tens of thousands of the wicked tempt me with logic, I shall heed not their words.

3:6 Arise, O lord and smite these that go against you!

3:7 Crush their skulls, burn their bodies and grind their teeth to dust.

3:8 Salvation belongs to the lord and salvation has been given to me.

3:9 Damnation belongs to the lord and he curses the damned with agony and fear.

4:1 My God is a vengeful God.

4:2 He reigns in the darkness above.

4:3 His wisdom curses the wicked, his love blesses the righteous.

4:4 Stand in awe at his power. Bow down and give praises to his name.

4:5 May he rape the hearts of the heathens, feast upon their children and cast their ashes across the skies above.

4:6 Put your trust in God and serve him always.

4:7 Then shall your bellies be full of bread and your enemies lay beneath your feet.

5:1 Give your ears to the lord and hear his words always.

5:2 Hearken unto the voice of your king and know your prayers be answered.

5:3 My voice speaks unto God in the morning and my voice speaks to him at night.

5:4 For my God is a kind God and takes not pleasure in the wickedness of man.

5:5 The foolish shall not stand in the sight of the lord: he hates all those that sin.

5:6 My lord shall destroy them, those bastard and deceitful men.

5:7 The righteous as such shall come into the house of the merciful and worship our God in fear.

5:8 O lord, lead your sword in the chest of the wicked, so that I may spill the blood of the damned in your honour.

5:9 Show me only that which you wish me to see; let not temptation blind my eyes.

5:10 Destroy those that seek not your counsel and give their devotions to idols and demons.

5:11 Let their wails be heard from the mountaintops!

5:12 May the righteous hold true and rule the earth in all things.

6:1 O lord, curse me not in your wrath, nor chasten me in your anger.

6:2 Have mercy upon me, for I am weakened. Give me strength and heal my bones.

6:3 My soul is sore, yet still seeks the lord almighty.

6:4 Curse the damned. Destroy the wicked!

6:5 And if these fools surround me, spare me in your destruction.

6:6 In life I praise your name and offer you sacrifice.

6:7 How can I dead remember you and honour your name?

6:8 Take not my body, my frail frame and blind eyes.

6:9 When you kill, let me live. When suffering plagues the lands, show me mercy and comfort.

6:10 Cast me not in the pool of the cursed, a man who serves you in his dying breath.

6:11 Receive my prayer and hearken my words, O blessed lord.

6:12 Let my enemies be shown shame,and curse their foolish ways.

6:13 Let me continue, so that I may love and honour the lord.

7:1 O lord, search my heart and my reins and deem me worthy of the fight.

7:2 I shall be as a lion in your army.

7:3 Give me your sword, your shield and your bow.

7:4 Instruments of death, crafted by the hand of God.

7:5 Let the heathen live no more.

7:6 Slay those men whose foreskin remain.

7:7 Shall their bodies fall forever in the everlasting pit.

8:1 How the lord has shown us the light and commands us on our life.

8:2 His laws are set in stone, carved by his very fingers.

8:3 We shall tolerate no other way and slay those who worship unjustly.

8:4 The seventh day is holy and we shall rest this day.

8:5 Even God gets tired and needs his sleep.

8:6 So on this day we shall take comfort and work naught on this day.

8:7 Those that work, die, as is the law of the lord.

8:8 Clothes of two fibers are as an abomination.

8:9 Fashion is important to our lord.

8:10 Our God is good. Our God is great!

8:11 Our God demands we not masturbate.

8:12 Let us then take pleasure in the whores of the lands.

8:13 Such is the will of God.

9:1 What is man, but the creation of God?

9:2 Whose strength comes from the breast of the mother's milk.

9:3 Let us gain the strength of our lord!

9:4 Let us suckle on the breasts of God!

10:1 O lord, our lord, hallowed be thy name on earth, who has set the glories of all the heavens.

10:2 Out of the mouths of babes and suckling's you give us strength over our enemies, so that we have might over the wicked.

10:3 As I gaze to the heavens, at the marvels of the creation from the lord's hands, I become humbled by the power of God.

10:4 Why did the lord create us. What was the reason for Adam?

10:5 For he has made us lower than the angels and charged us with dominion over the earth.

10:6 We are as lords over the flocks, the beasts, the oxen, the sheep,

10:7 The fowl of the air and the fish of the sea.

10:8 This makes us as beasts in the eyes of our lord.

10:9 Blessed be the name of the lord.

11:1 I will praise thee, O lord, with my whole heart; I shall marvel at all your wondrous works.

11:2 Eternally I shall be glad and rejoice in you: I will sing the praises of the most high.

11:3 I speak the name of the holy and my enemies die before me.

11:4 For I am faithful to the most powerful lord, who sits upon the throne and judges that which is right.

11:5 Let us rebuke the heathen. Let us destroy those that are wicked and cast their names into the fire.

11:6 Stare at the wonders of our lord, who has destroyed cities with his fist.

11:7 The lord shall endure forever and shall sit on his throne always.

11:8 He shall judge the righteous and condemn the wicked.

11:9 Cast off your foreskins and be proud to be the children of God.

11:10 Be humbled at the one who created all that which is.

11:11 Blessed are the children of the lord, who stains their hands with the blood of evil.

11:12 Enslave the heathens, who are as beasts that must be put to the yoke.

11:13 Let their foolishness lead them to the pits of hell.

11:14 Arise, O lord and cast out these demons from the lands.

11:15 Strike fear in the unholy, unjust and unfaithful.

11:16 Burn their nations to ashes, and laugh at their howling.

11:17 Feast upon the flesh of their children and rape their daughters and wives.

12:1 Praise the lord and pass the ale.

12:2 Precious nectar of the most divine being.

12:3 Sing glory to his name and fill your pipe with herbs.

12:4 Let my lungs breathe the air of heaven.

12:5 Accept my sacrifice, my offerings and take the blood of the lamb.

12:6 Bless me with a full table and I shall feast as the glutton before your eyes.

12:7 Glory to the lord, who freed us from Pharaoh.

12:8 Now we are the masters of slaves.

12:9 Curse the evil, destroy the wicked.

12:10 Smite those that displease you.

12:11 Now I shall speak the name of God, as I lie with my many whores.

12:12 Shall my seed spread across the lands of all and worship the lord eternally.

12:13 And my bastard children be feasted upon by the raven.

12:14 The lord hates bastards and I hate the bastards I bring upon the earth.

12:15 Curse the whore who accepts my seed and dishonours the will of God.

13:1 Why do you stand off, mock my pains and ignore my cries?

13:2 In times of trouble, you hide. When I need your hand, you offer nothing.

13:3 The wicked, the prideful, prosper on the earth.

13:4 Those of the uncircumcised live in luxury and wealth.

13:5 Your loyal servants, who live by your laws and heed your words,

13:6 They are the ones who suffer the wrath of God.

13:7 Tell me, what did I do to deserve this disease which weakens my body?

13:8 How have I offended you, a mere child who loves his lord?

13:9 I bless your name, I offer you sacrifice.

13:10 The laws I follow blindly and still I suffer your wrath.

13:11 My cries go unheard, my prayers unanswered.

13:12 In fear, I never question why. In faith, I trust your plan.

13:13 What plan is this, that requires me to die by this disease?

13:14 Where in your mind did you think it necessary that I suffer your wrath?

13:15 Cursed be my mind, who questions that which it can't understand.

13:16 Bless me, O lord and do as you will!

13:17 Rape my body and cast me aside.

13:18 Let me burn in the fires and be eaten by worms.

13:19 Never shall I doubt; not once shall I question.

13:20 I know it is the will of the lord.

14:1 In the lord I put my trust. With his words, I fly to the mountains.

14:2 For lo, I gaze beneath me and watch the damned suffer below.

14:3 They beat with hammers and try to break the foundation of God.

14:4 The lord plucks the eyes of their children and feeds them to the demons.

14:5 These wicked, these heathens, the lord hates them all.

14:6 As these fools beat against the mountain, they become ensnared by the lord, who rains upon them brimstone; a terrible

THE BLASPHEMOUS BIBLE

tempest of fire.

14:7 Blessed be the lord, who kisses the righteous and condemns the damned.

15:1 Help me, O lord. The unrighteous deafen me with their speech.

15:2 Their vanity sickens me. Their blasphemy saddens me.

15:3 Cut off their flattering lips, rip out their tongues.

15:4 Mute the mouths of heathens and let only the silver tongues of the righteous be heard.

16:1 How long will you forget me, O lord. How long shall you hide your face?

16:2 How long shall it be until I hear your counsel?

16:3 Remove the sorrow from my heart. Let my enemies suffer before me.

16:4 Consider me, O lord and hear my words, before I sleep eternal in death.

16:5 Then my enemies shall prevail against me and speak ill your name.

16:6 I trust in you, O lord. Let not my trust be misplaced.

16:7 Unless God truly is a cunt.

17:1 Forgive me, lord, for I am lustful.

17:2 I lied with a man as I lie with a wife.

17:3 His flesh was pleasing, his orifice tight.

17:4 He was truly a great joy in my bed.

17:5 Forgive me, lord, that man was a sheep.

17:6 Stone me not with your boulders, burn me not with your pyres.

17:7 I was drunk and knew not my actions.

18:1 Only the fool says there is no God.

18:2 These men who are corrupted by logic, poisoned with questions and beaten by science.

18:3 The lord looks down from the heavens to seek those that seek God.

18:4 And these men seek not God, but truth; how their search dooms them.

18:5 Have they no faith, only knowledge?

18:6 Do they fear not the fearful?

18:7 When the lord comes, they shall tremble in terror and weep.

18:8 When is God coming, anyway?

19:1 O lord my God, who dwells inside your tabernacle?

19:2 Who seeks refuge in the holy house upon the hill?

19:3 I walk by it and it be empty.

19:4 I knock on the door and nobody answers.

19:5 Tell me, why build a house for one who dwells not within?

19:6 I have taken the tools, hammered the nails, risen the walls.

19:7 Now I ask, for what purpose?

19:8 You are never home; only the priests lie within.

19:9 Did you abandon us. Cast us aside?

19:10 Or do you even exist, O blessed lord of all things?

20:1 Necromancers, wizards and unholy men.

20:2 Those who speak to the dead.

20:3 Cursed are they; slay them by the sword.

20:4 People of witches and magic.

20:5 Fortune tellers, star gazers.

20:6 Men and women who seek the powers of God.

20:7 Damned are they and hated by the lord.

20:8 Their tools are dirty.

20:9 Their methods unclean.

20:10 We of the people don't understand them, so we hate them.

20:11 People who speak to the dead,

20:12 The dead, who can tell us of God.

20:13 For only the dead can truly know God and the lord denies us their speech.

20:14 Convenient, isn't it.

21:1 Cast your yoke upon me, O lord and lead me to your pastures.

21:2 Work me in your fields, let me graze upon the grasses of God.

21:3 Tighten my reins when I am stubborn; force me to do your will.

21:4 I am as a beast of burden; an ass, an ox.

21:5 But my soul, my soul is a sheep.

21:6 And I sacrifice it upon the altars of the lord.

22:1 O lord, curse these men who copy your works.

22:2 Artists and sculptures who mimic your miracles.

22:3 Men, women, fools, creating images of your holy works.

22:4 Such blasphemy, these carvings.

22:5 Do they have the breath of life to give these sculptures meaning?

22:6 Do their lips contain the power to give an object a soul?

22:7 Then cursed are they, who copy the works of the lord.

2:8 Lions of ivory that stand still, birds of oak that shall never fly.

22:9 May the lions feast upon these peoples and the birds peck out their eyes.

23:1 The lord is my rock, my shelter, and my saviour.

23:2 He is my shield and the horn of my salvation. He gives me refuge from the violence of man.

23:3 I call upon the lord, who is worthy of my praise, so I shall be saved from the hand of my enemies.

23:4 When the waves of death surrounded me and the heathen hoards made me afraid,

23:5 The sorrows of hell consumed me, the snares of death entrapped me,

23:6 In my distress I screamed unto the lord and the lord did hear my voice from his temple and my plea entered his ears.

23:7 The very earth shook and trembled. The sky above was torn apart, for the lord was fucking angry.

23:8 Thick smoke did flow from the nostrils of God and fire spewed forth from his mouth so that it consumed all.

23:9 My lord rode a dragon, winged and mighty and he was seen upon the wings of the wind.

23:10 Bright darkness surrounded my lord, with black waters and thick clouds of darkness.

23:11 Through the darkness, the fire came forth and burned those the lord deemed wicked.

23:12 And my God thundered from the heaven, and the most high uttered his voice.

23:13 Arrows rained down from the skies and lightning spread forth across the lands.

THE OLD TESTAMENT

23:14 The seas split apart, the very foundations of the earth trembled, all at the breath of his nostrils.

23:15 From above, the lord did grasp me and sent me to fresh waters.

23:16 He delivered me from the hands of my enemy and those which hated me, for they were stronger than I.

23:17 My lord did prevent the days of my death, for the lord was my shelter.

23:18 He brought me forth to a large and wondrous place. He delivered me, because he loved me.

23:19 The lord rewarded me because of my righteousness, my devotion, for I have kept the ways of the lord and strayed not into wickedness.

23:20 Of all the laws, the judgments and commandments, I did not stray.

23:21 I have kept myself pure and strayed not to sin.

23:22 Therefore the lord has blessed me, according to my cleanness in his sight.

23:23 I have shown no mercy and slain many and spilled the blood of men in glory to God.

23:24 My very eyes shall cause the uncircumcised to tremble, so that they shall know the fear that is my lord.

23:25 The way of the lord is perfect; the words of the lord are true. Blessed be those who trust in the lord.

23:26 God is my strength and my power. He leads me upon the perfect path.

23:27 He makes my feet like the feet of eagles and sets me atop the highest places.

23:28 He teaches my hands war, so that a mighty bow of steel is broken in my arms.

23:29 His shield is my salvation and his mercy has made me great.

23:30 Though I walk the slippery path of God, he enlarges the steps so I do not fall.

23:31 I have pursued my enemies and consumed them in the great love of my lord. Never did I turn back until all those be destroyed.

23:32 I have consumed them and wounded them deeply, so that they shall not arise when the hyenas feast upon their flesh and the vultures tear their very bowels.

23:33 The lord has made me strong and I step upon my enemies as though they be dust upon the ground.

23:34 He has girded me strength in battle, so that those who rise against me shall fall before me.

23:35 The lord has given me the necks of my enemies, so that my blades shall plunge through their throats and consume the very brine of their blood.

23:36 Cursed be those who hate me, for the lord hates those who hate me.

23:37 Those that hate me shall cry unto God and the lord shall not answer, for the lord be with me.

23:38 My lord laughs at their cries and their pleas and makes them suffer for their wickedness.

23:39 May the God of all god's rape those why go against me, so that their cries be heard throughout all the heavens.

23:40 Then I shall grind them to dust and spread their ashes among the lands.

23:41 When I lived among the heathens, those fools with foreskins, you did make me head of their people, though I know I shall not serve them.

23:42 Strangers shall give obedience and submit unto me.

23:43 They shall fade away and fear to come from their hiding places.

23:44 The lord lives. Blessed be the lord, for he is the rock of my salvation.

23:45 My lord did deliver me from the hands of my enemies and gave them to me, so that I may crush them.

23:46 Violence and wickedness did the lord deliver away from me and violence and righteousness did I deliver to those who defy me.

23:47 I shall give thanks to the lord and sing great praises in his name.

23:48 He is the tower of my salvation. May he bless me and my seed for generations.

23:49 Blessed be the name of the lord.

24:1 The skies above declare the glory that is God and the beasts show his miracles.

24:2 The firmament, which ceases back the waters from heaven, protect us from the floods of Noah and gives us rain when we need it.

24:3 Blessed is the lord, who holds the key to the firmament.

24:4 Day unto day the lord speaks his wisdom and nightly the knowledge of God is given through dreams.

24:5 Our lord is a blessed lord, who makes the path of the sun around our earth.

24:6 I am as a bride, who screams in joy at the presence of her master.

24:7 The sight of the lord stares through the very grounds of earth; he sees all, hears all, knows all.

24:8 The law of the lord is perfect and shall not be broken.

24:9 It cleanses the soul and makes one righteous.

24:10 The statutes are right and the commandments cleanse the heart and soul.

24:11 Fear the lord eternal, whose wrath know no morals.

24:12 Love the lord more than gold, more than family, more than oneself.

24:13 God demands it.

24:14 Know this, the lord makes no errors.

24:15 When you the servant are dealt harshly, it is the will of God and one deserving.

24:16 Sin not and avoid the temptations of man.

24:17 Listen to the mouth of God and his words shall give you strength.

25:1 The lord hears me in days of trouble; the name of the God of Jacob defends me.

25:2 He sends out soldiers from his sanctuary and gives me the strength of Zion.

25:3 He remembers my sacrifices and accepts my offerings.

25:4 For this, the skies shall turn to fire and stones of fire will fall upon my enemies.

25:5 They trust in their chariots, their horses, their swords, but I trust in the cruelty of my lord.

25:6 Let his jaw arise from the earth and consume their iron, their beasts, their men.

25:7 Swallow the cities and kill their wives.

25:8 Rape their children, listen to their cries.

25:9 Such is the way of the lord; merciful be he.

26:1 The king shall rejoice in your strength, O lord; and in salvation he shall rejoice.

26:2 You have given him his heart's desire and given each request which comes from his lips.

26:3 You have blessed him with wealth and put a crown of pure gold atop his head.

26:4 He asked you for long life and long life he was given.

26:5 All this, for the king trusted in you, O God and loves you.

26:6 Your hands have smitten his enemies and those that hate him.

26:7 You have cast them in the oven of your anger, devouring them in fiery wrath.

26:8 Their fruits have rotted by your will and their children starve amongst them.

26:9 These wicked people, hated by God and loathed by our king.

26:10 How I stab them in the neck and shoot them in the backs.

26:11 Even the lord sends down his arrows, piercing their lungs and severing their spine.

26:12 Be exalted, O lord, in your own strength. I shall bless your name and give glory through song.

27:1 My lord, why have you forsaken me. I cry your name and you not answer.

27:2 Like the roars of a lion, I scream your name; through night and day I never be silent.

27:3 You are holy, O lord, who blesses the peoples of Israel.

27:4 Our fathers trusted in you and you did keep your covenant.

27:5 They cried unto you and were delivered; they trusted in you and were not betrayed.

27:6 Why do you then ignore me, when you heeded the words of my fathers?

27:7 Am I as a worm to you, despised by the holy?

27:8 These men of the uncircumcised, they laugh at me. They shake their heads and their lips mock you.

27:9 They say that you abandoned me and left me to rot in the sun.

27:10 Deliver me from these men and smite them with your hatred.

27:11 Rip them from their mother's wombs, cut off the breasts of their nursemaids.

27:12 Let them starve in agony.

27:13 Their daughters, with tempting curves, come to me as demons.

27:14 The mouths speak words of lust; the tongues caress my skin and their eyes glow in carnal desire.

27:15 Pour the waters upon them and cast them into the rivers.

27:16 These whores who tempt me into their bed.

27:17 I grow weakened, O lord and need your help.

27:18 Save me from the sword of science and logic and cast these heathens away.

27:19 Bring forth the holy lions and skewer their bodies upon the horns of the unicorns.

27:20 I shall declare your name in honour. I shall bless you to all my brethren.

27:21 You, who have blessed the seed of Jacob and led us the promised lands.

27:22 You did not hide your face from my ancestors, nor afflicted them with evil.

27:23 When they cried, you heard.

27:24 I cry now, O lord and give praises to your name!

27:25 Give me strength and cast out the wicked before me.

28:1 The lord is my shepherd, and I am his sheep.

28:2 He beats me down in the green pastures: he casts my blood in the still waters.

28:3 He declares me wicked, though I follow his path of glory and righteousness.

28:4 Yea, though I walk in the valley of the shadow of death, I shall fear no evil; my lord is the cruellest fucker in the land.

28:5 His rod and his staff, they beat me.

28:6 As I starve, he prepares a table before me; a feast flowing with wine and meat.

28:7 It is my enemies who feast on this table; I eat of the scraps which fall upon the floor.

28:8 Surely the lord shall show me mercy, a loyal servant who endures his abuse.

28:9 In time, I shall feast in the house of the lord and sit at his table and feast upon his breads.

28:10 Never will I doubt his divinity; never shall I question his love.

29:1 The earth belongs to God and all those within it.

29:2 He has founded the seas and rose land above the violent waters.

29:3 Who among the people shall ascend the holy hill. Who will stand beside the lord?

29:4 We are but slaves to God; unclean, wretched and filthy.

29:5 Our hearts are as the rotting corps, and our souls be damned.

29:6 Clean us, O lord. Let your statutes wipe the muck from our minds.

29:7 Give us mercy and grace, so that we may pass through the gates of Zion.

30:1 Unto you, O lord, do I lift my skirt.

30:2 Gaze upon my humble loins. Take your pleasure with them.

30:3 Yea, though I have shame, I am shameless with my God.

30:4 Lead me to the mountaintops. Caress my passage so that I may know your ecstasy.

30:5 Remember not my sins as we lie atop your bed.

30:6 Good and upright is the lord, who thrusts into me deeply and proudly.

30:7 The meek die in his chambers; only the strong shall experience the lust of the lord.

30:8 His seed swims in my canals; his children grow in my belly.

30:9 Such an honour it is, to be one of the chosen to know God's intimate touch.

30:10 Giants pass through my loins and inherit the earth around them.

30:11 Children of the lord, conceived through mortal women.

30:12 Oh God, the pleasures of the lord are great.

30:13 I deliver my soul unto you and bow naked at your side.

30:14 Caress my breasts and kiss me, O lord.

30:15 Do with my body all that you desire.

30:16 Violate my bowels and treat me like a whore.

31:1 Try me, O lord and judge me according to my actions.

31:2 Examine me; mind, body, heart, kidney, soul.

31:3 Cleanse me of the evil that is man.

31:4 Bathe me in vinegar and blood.

31:5 Cast out all that is vanity; send forth my sins to the fires.

31:6 I have hated the sinners, the wicked and the congregation of evil.

31:7 In your name I have slain them and let the vultures feast upon

THE OLD TESTAMENT

their flesh.

31:8 These are guilty heathens; men who know no innocence.

31:9 My feet stand atop their necks and crush the life from them.

31:10 Let their spit soak my boots and bathe my feet clean.

32:1 I hide in the shadows of God; I gain strength from his darkness.

32:2 Let the wicked gaze upon me and their eyes shall not see.

33:3 As they come forward, they stumble and fall.

33:4 And I laugh and crush their bones and pluck the skulls from their necks.

33:5 Though entire nations have come towards me, I fear them not.

33:6 For the shadows of God give me confidence and wisdom.

33:7 Let them cry out in the blackness; let them choke within the cloud.

33:8 Let their bones pile high atop; higher than the mountains they shall be.

33:9 Courageous am I, who hides within the spirit of the lord.

33:10 Safe, secure and stupid.

34:1 Give unto the lord your tithe and he shall protect you from the wicked.

34:2 A portion of your earnings to know the holiness of God.

34:3 His voice be atop the waters; his eyes the stars of the sky.

34:4 He is watching, waiting for the sinners and those who give not their tithe.

34:5 The voice of the lord is powerful; the voice of the lord is majestic.

34:6 His song breaks the cedars of Lebanon and deafen the ears of the cheap.

34:7 Steal from God and he shall cast you on the horns of the unicorn.

34:8 His nose exhales fire that consumes the wicked and the damned.

34:9 He floods the houses of evil, and consumed those who are unworthy.

34:10 A tenth of your goods, to avoid the curses of the lord.

34:11 Such a small price to pay; a minor extortion from the most holy on high.

35:1 Blesses is David, mighty king of Israel.

35:2 Most beloved of our race.

35:3 The lord speaks to him and he listens.

35:4 He rides atop the crowns of dragons.

35:5 Slayer of giants; despicable men.

35:6 His anger endures eternal; eyes glowing with the wrath of God.

35:7 Oh how he conquers nations and enslaves the cursed.

35:8 Upon every step he takes, a corpse of a heathen is made.

35:9 How we prosper under his reign.

35:10 Dancing and drinking in the streets of our cities.

35:11 Jerusalem prospers in gladness.

35:12 Blood of the heathen's flow like rivers; how we drink from their bladders.

35:13 Israel shall rule and conquer until the end of time.

35:14 Our foundation is the dead of the wicked.

36:1 Bind me, O lord and keep me from sin.

36:2 Fasten my jaws with your wires.

36:3 Tie me with bridles of leather.

36:4 Lash my body as temptation grows strong.

36:5 As the master hits the ass as it strays off course, so you shall do so with me.

36:6 Blind me from sin; pluck out my eyes when wicked surrounds me.

36:7 I pray to you, O lord, to give me strength in the sea of evil.

36:8 These men untied by your bindings surround me, tempt me, speaking blasphemy and betrayal.

36:9 Curse these men, who know the freedom from God.

36:10 How they tempt me so.

36:11 Tighten my bindings, O lord and let me not loose.

36:12 Lest I drown in the waters of men.

37:1 Rejoice in the lord, O those who be righteous. Give glory to his name.

37:2 Praise the lord with songs and harps; sing with loud noise to him.

37:3 The word of the lord is right and al his works be true.

37:4 He loves the righteous, the holy and the true.

37:5 By mere words he created the heavens and all those within the earth.

37:6 He gathered the waters in pails; he lay stones atop the surface.

37:7 Let all those of the earth fear him; let them gaze upon the lord in wonder and awe.

37:8 When he speaks, you shall listen.

37:9 Hearken the counsel of the one true God. Keep his words in your heart.

37:10 Blessed is the nation who follows the one true God and the people chosen to claim his inheritance.

37:11 The lord gaze down from heaven and looks upon all the sons of men.

37:12 From his dwelling he stares upon the inhabitants of earth.

37:13 Gazing into their hearts, looking at their works.

37:14 There is no king who may be saved from the wrath of God. A mighty man is not protected by a multitude of hosts.

37:15 A horse is a vain thing for safety and the sword shall not protect you.

37:16 Behold, the eye of the lord is upon them that fear him and gives them hope and mercy.

37:17 To deliver the righteous from death and feed the holy in times of famine.

37:18 Our souls wait for the lord: he is our help and our shield.

37:19 Our hearts rejoice in God and give glory to his name.

37:20 Let your mercy be upon us, O lord and give death to those who curse you.

38:1 A family of wild men who lives in the woods.

38:2 Mother, father and son.

38:3 Living harmoniously with nature.

38:4 They live off the land, grow their own crops and hunt what they need.

38:5 Perfect, happy and content they live.

38:6 As the son grows, the father takes him to the hill.

38:7 The highest peak in the forests.

38:8 The two gazes out amongst the lands; the lakes, rivers and trees.

38:9 The father tells his son, "Look, and behold the lands which are ours.

38:10 Beautiful, plentiful.

38:11 Know that the lands shall provide for you and care for you, so long as you care for it.

38:12 Be warned, though, the land to the west is not ours.

38:13 A cave lies to the west and within it dwells the wolf.

38:14 Horrid demonic creature that it is.

38:15 Never travel west and you shall be safe for eternity."

38:16 The son listens to the words of his father, hearkening his words and admiring his wisdom.

38:17 In time, the son grows older, and curiosity gnaws at him.

38:18 As holds true in all children and men.

38:19 Slowly, he creeps to the west, travelling further and further each day.

38:20 It came to pass that he was far to the west and his curiosity overcame him.

38:21 He went to the cave, just for a peek.

38:22 A glance at the den of the wolf.

38:23 His curiosity quenched, he begins to travel home.

38:24 Never intending to return there again.

38:25 The wolf smells the child, hears his footsteps and grows angry at this intruder.

38:26 It attacks and grasps the child.

38:27 Jaw crunching the shoulders.

38:28 Claws tearing the viscera.

38:29 The child screams; a loud and piercing cry.

38:30 A shriek heard throughout the corners of the earth.

38:31 His father hears the awful noise and knows the fate of his son.

38:32 He grabs his bow and fills his quiver.

38:33 An excellent archer is he.

38:34 Running to the wolf, he yells to his son, "I'm coming, I'm coming!"

38:35 As his child screams in pain.

38:36 He arrives at the scene.

38:37 Son covered in blood and saliva, being mauled by the beast.

38:38 This horrid creature that shows no mercy.

38:39 The father yells at the wolf and throws rocks at his body.

38:40 Which only fuels the beasts anger, who now causes greater pain to the child.

38:41 Glowing eyes staring at the father as the son hangs in the jaw of the wolf.

38:42 His son, his only son, bloodied and tattered, crippled and broken.

38:43 Barely able to gather his strength and say to his father, "Help."

38:44 Now, his father grabs his arrow and draws his bow.

38:45 Aiming at the heart of the demon.

38:46 A perfect shot he has; guaranteed to kill the wolf and not pierce his son by mistake.

38:47 Tears and blood in his eyes, the son gazes at his father, saying to him,

38:48 "I'm sorry, please help me. I'm sorry, please help me."

38:49 And what does the child see. His father lowering his bow.

38:50 Instead of releasing the arrow and slaying the beast, he drops his weapon and watches the scene unfold.

38:51 Promising his son he shall help, as he leans against an oak; never doing nothing but making empty promises.

38:52 I ask you, who is worse. The wolf who attacks the child, or the father who leans back, watches, and does nothing?

39:1 I bless you, O lord, forever and always.

39:2 My mouth speaks nothing but honour to your name.

39:3 My soul boasts the name of God and is humbled by the holiest of things.

39:4 I seek the lord and he finds me; he takes me away from that which I fear.

39:5 The poor pray to him and become wealthy. The sick cry to him and are cured.

39:6 So if you still be sick while praying to God, you are not praying hard enough.

39:7 Angels of the lord surround all those which fear God and frighten them.

39:8 Ensuring all those that fear God remain fearful.

39:9 O taste of the wine of the lord and know that he is good.

39:10 Fear the lord deeply and fear his saints and servant.

39:11 Those that are wicked suffer and starve, but those that beg mercy from God shall know nothing but goodness.

39:12 Bring your children unto me, so that they may grow in terror of their lord.

39:13 Have them grow in fear, for all the days of their life.

39:14 Fear keeps them from speaking evil; their mouths will never spew vile.

39:15 Evil they will never do; only that which is good in the eyes of God.

39:16 Eyes of the lord gaze upon the righteous; his ears hearken their cries.

39:17 Those that fear not the lord shall be cut off from earth.

39:18 Let the evil men scavenge in hell.

39:19 Many are the afflictions of the righteous, but the lord shall deliver them from all pain.

39:20 Evil shall slay the wicked and they that hate the righteous shall burn in the anger of God.

39:21 For God saves the souls of the righteous; not one shall be left behind.

40:1 I follow the path of the righteous and seek forth God.

40:2 Though the way be slippery and wet, angels of the lord give me guidance.

40:3 I slip and fall and grasp on to the ledge.

40:4 Fingers blistered and knuckles bloodied.

40:5 I look down and see those that fell beneath me.

40:6 Gnashing upon one another with blunt teeth.

40:7 I climb up and walk the path to God.

40:8 Though dark it may be, he is my light; a beacon that shines for me.

40:9 Let me go to the light and not become lost in the darkness.

40:10 Keep me from the unrighteous, who feast in mockery of the lord.

40:11 Temptation surrounds me, but I persevere.

40:12 Marching forwards towards Zion.

40:13 Obeying all that which is God.

40:14 False prophets rise and snare me with words of deceit.

40:15 O lord, deafen my ears to these fools.

40:16 With forked tongues that lash out.

40:17 I seek out only knowledge, wisdom and faith.

40:18 These heathens seek out science, logic and truth.

40:19 They have fallen from the path, never to return.

40:20 Fallen to the arms of queers and wizards.

40:21 O God, let the heathens feast upon each other.

40:22 Let them consume their brethren with hatred and evil.

40:23 My words of joy drown their cries of sorrow.

40:24 My praises to God deafen their moans.

40:25 Their tongues of wickedness choke them as my mouth speaks out righteousness and praise.

41:1 The transgressions of the wicked consume their heart, so that their eyes fear not God.

41:2 He flatters himself and becomes arrogant, until those who know him be hateful.

41:3 Words flow from his mouth; words of lies and deceit that fools take as truth.

41:4 He enjoys mischief within his bed; wicked lust and sins of the flesh.

41:5 Evilness consumes him, until he knows not that which is good.

41:6 Your mercy, O lord, is in the heavens and falls on us like rain.

41:7 His righteousness is higher than the mountains; his judgment deeper than the depths of the oceans.

41:8 O lord, who preserve both man and beast.

41:9 How excelling is his kindness; how merciful be his love. Men of the lord place their children under the protection of his wing.

41:10 Those of the chosen grow fat in his house and drink from the rivers of his pleasures.

41:11 For with you flows the fountains of life; in your shadows, we see light.

41:12 Show me your loving kindness and overflow my heart with joy.

41:13 Let not the fools nor the prideful step near me and let not the hand of the wicked remove me.

41:14 These are the works of sinners; most hated by God.

41:15 Cast them down; cripple them so they shall never arise.

42:1 Fret not against the evildoers, nor grow jealous of their wealth.

42:2 For the lord shall cut them down like grass and leave them to whither and rot.

42:3 Trust in the lord and do good; so shalt you dwell in the holy lands where your bellies never grow empty.

42:4 Delight yourself in God and your desires shall be fulfilled.

42:5 If you starve and long for more, you trusted not God and did wicked in his eyes.

42:6 Repent and let the mercy of the lord bathe you.

42:7 Cease from anger and do not give in to wrath.

42:8 These are tools of temptation; a trickery into evil.

42:9 Trust in the lord and let his anger and wrath consume the villains.

42:10 Evildoers will be banished and cut off from his love; those that remain shall inherit the earth.

42:11 The meek shall inherit the earth and shall delight themselves in peace.

42:12 The meek, who die of predation, starvation and disease.

42:13 Wicked men, who plot against the righteous and gnash upon them with teeth.

41:14 The lord laughs at them and plans for these fools great suffering and death.

42:15 Such as the wicked have sharpened their swords and bent their bows to extort the righteous;

42:16 So have the lord, who will crush the wicked and turn grind their weapons to dust.

42:17 Arms of the heathens shall be broken and their legs crippled.

42:18 They shall perish and be as fat lambs to be consumed by the lord.

42:19 The wicked borrow and do not repay; the righteous steal from their strangers.

42:20 Though the good man stumble, he shall not fall; the helping hand of the lord supports him and guides him through.

42:21 Blessed are these men, who shall inherit the earth from the wicked.

42:22 Blessed be the name of the lord.

43:1 I have slaughtered the lambs atop pillars of stone.

43:2 Blood flowing forth to the ground; carcasses consumed by fire.

43:3 I have conquered strangers and pierced my sword in their chest.

43:4 Heathen men that know no love.

43:5 Their women and children now belong to me.

43:6 Slaves, whores and other beasts of burden.

43:7 Cities have been crushed by my boot; nations burned before me.

43:8 Entire people wiped from existence; heathen men both wicked and revolting.

43:9 For this violence, I am a righteous man.

43:10 For my bloodshed I am good in the sight of the lord.

44:1 O lord, free me from your wrath: chasten me not in your displeasure.

44:2 For your arrows stick deeply in me and make me crippled and sore.

44:3 My flesh knows no peace because of your anger; my bones are sore because of my sin.

44:4 Sins which press down upon me, heavy upon my head.

44:5 My wounds stink and are corrupt; they ooze a foul and unclean pus.

44:6 My loins are filled with a loathsome disease, given to me by the slits of whores.

44:7 I am troubled and mourn all day long.

44:8 I am feeble and broken; crippled before your feet.

44:9 Lord, all that I desire is before me; I know you hear my groans and cries.

44:10 My heart beats shallow, my strength fades; sight slowly fades before me.

44:11 My lovers and my friends now mock me; my kinsmen grow disgusted by my form.

44:12 Men plan against me; they wish to kill me and take my wealth.

44:13 Though I grow deaf, I hear the words in their hearts.

44:14 Hear me, O lord and protect me.

44:15 Give me strength to worship you and beg forgiveness for my sins.

44:16 I wish to die a righteous man, free from sin and evil.

44:17 These stains that mark my soul still haunt me.

44:18 Forsake me not, O lord: leave not my side.

44:19 Wipe me clean and remove that which is evil from my heart.

45:1 I have said nothing and bridled my tongue.

45:2 Sin never escaped my lips and were drowned by that which is wicked.

45:3 Through silence, I became dumb; saying nothing wicked nor good.

45:4 Though sorrow stirred deep within me, I held my peace.

45:5 Cursing not the lord, never rejoicing in his name.

45:6 My heart grew hot within my chest; fire burned deeply.

45:7 Then I cast off my bindings and spoke that which I saw.

45:8 Wickedness, evilness, death, destruction, sin.

45:9 Arrogance and vanity; a lust for gold.

45:10 I see this not in the heathen, but in the souls of my people.

45:11 Men who kill children in the name of God.

45:12 Is this true. I can't help but wonder.

45:13 A lord who demands the death of the child.

45:14 When I come to the temple, seeking guidance and faith;

45:15 I gaze upon vanities greater than that of the kings of heathens.

45:16 Our lord is a selfish lord and I curse his name.

45:17 Let my people stone me. Let my father stab me with his blades.

45:18 I have been silent long enough; now I shall speak against the lord.

45:19 Such a cruel and wicked demon is he.

45:20 Demanding genocide, sacrifice; he grows drunk on death.

45:21 Burn me, O lord, in your fires of wrath.

45:22 Fires never-ending; a wrath which only grows.

46:1 I waited patiently for the lord, seeking guidance and help.

46:2 He showed too late and cursed my incompetence.

46:3 Casting me into a horrible pit and placing a heavy rock atop my chest.

46:4 As I cry to the lord, he laughs at my suffering.

46:5 When I give him sacrifice, he throws it aside like the childish brat.

46:6 All that which I worshipped; all that which I lived for.

46:7 God, faith, and holiness;

46:8 Was a lie.

46:9 My eyes turn away from the blinding light of the lord and now seeks forth the truth.

46:10 Cruel is the way of our lord.

46:11 Wisdom now fills my soul and the venom of God escapes me.

46:12 Such evilness the lord craves; such wickedness he plagues his people with.

46:13 Consuming the poor and needy; slaying the young and old.

46:14 What is good and what is evil is relative.

46:15 The lord claims that which is good, is evil in my eyes.

46:16 The lord claims that which is evil, brings forth comfort and peace.

46:17 I fear the fires of the lord; the wrath which he shall bring upon my seed.

46:18 Yet I cannot live a lie no more.

46:19 I cast aside God and live free from his will.

46:20 Knowledge in my heart will define for me the wicked and the good.

46:21 When all live this way, then shall the world know peace.

47:1 Cursed are those that consider the poor; wasting their sympathy on the souls of the pathetic.

47:2 If the lord wished them preserved and alive, prosperous and healthy, the lord would give them the bounty of the earth.

47:3 Waste not your time caring for the sick; wretched bodies stricken with disease.

47:4 Illness comes from wickedness, thus the sick are wicked.

47:5 Though they cry for God now, before they cursed his name.

47:6 Wretched blasphemers whose lips spew forth filth.

47:7 To those of the wealthy, the healthy and blessed; these are the men you shall love.

47:8 They have rejected that which is evil and the lord blessed them for it.

47:9 Reject the poor, the diseased, the pathetic.

47:10 God hates them and you shall hate them too.

48:1 As the deer quenches thirst from the brook, so does my soul quench it's thirst from the lord.

48:2 My soul grows thirsty for the knowledge of God; come, O lord and give me drink.

48:3 Though my body grows strong on water and bread, my soul weakens and cries out for you.

48:4 Where is my God. Why has he denied me his blessings?

48:5 When I ask these, I gaze upon the cursed; wretched animals, which know not the lord.

49:6 And as my soul becomes ever thirsty, it still cries out to the lord.

48:7 To deny God is to be the wretched, the cursed, the heathen.

48:8 A fate worse than death; to be denied the love of the lord forever.

48:9 God is my rock, my foundation, my strength.

48:10 He gives me the knowledge to do what is right; he gives me the strength to kill those that are hated.

48:11 I praise his name and give glory to the lord.

48:12 Still, my soul quenches for more and longs for the day God hearkens my words and gives me my desire.

49:1 Judge me, O lord and release me from this ungodly nation; men unjust and who speak deceit.

49:2 The lord was my strength and my strength is gone. Why does he abandon me. Why do I cry under the oppression of my enemy?

49:3 O send out the light and the truth: lead me to the tabernacle of the lord.

49:4 Don't leave me in the darkness of temptation and evil.

49:5 I shall praise you eternal, O lord; I shall sing songs in your name and play the harps in your honour.

49:6 Great altars will be built and pure oxen and lambs shall forever burn atop them.

49:7 Just judge me now and free me from the damned.

49:8 These heathens that enslave us and piss on your name.

50:1 What took you so long, O lord?

50:2 I have awaited you all my life and never did you come.

50:3 As the heathens come and burn my home, you did nothing.

50:4 As the wicked raped my daughters and enslaved my sons, you stood back and watched.

50:5 O God, you did nothing and let evil and wickedness lash out at your people.

50:6 We have waited for your vengeance, your justice, your wrath.

50:7 Great clouds of fire to descend from the sky and consuming our enemies.

50:8 These days never came and we still live under the yoke of the heathen.

50:9 Now I lay on my bed with but a few breaths left.

50:10 And my soul feels peace; a peace at long last.

50:11 Why have y waited, O lord, to embrace me?

50:12 It matters not now. You are too late.

51:1 I have heard of your works, O lord, from the words of our fathers.

51:2 What you did in times of old.

51:3 How you drove out the heathen with your hands and planted them in dead soil.

51:4 How you afflicted them cruelly and cast them out.

51:5 For they dwelt in the land of our possession; the land of the covenant.

51:6 Which we took by sword and chariot, leaving rivers of blood in your honour.

51:7 You are my king, O God: I follow your command always.

51:8 Through you we shall slaughter our enemies: with your strength, we shall rise against the heathen.

51:9 I trust not in my sword, nor expect my bow to save me.

51:10 But you, O lord, have saved us from the wicked and thrust their cities into the earth.

51:11 In God I boast all day; your name I praise eternally.

51:12 So what did I do to anger you, O lord?

51:13 Oh how you abandoned us and put us to shame.

51:14 We retreat from our enemies and they take their spoils from us.

51:15 Our people are scattered amongst the heathens; we are as flesh upon their tables.

51:16 They grow prosperous by our enslavement and sell our daughters to the brothels.

51:17 Those that hate us own us and mock the name of the one true lord.

51:18 My confusion saddens me and shame strikes deeply in my heart.

51:19 Awake from your slumber, O lord and save us from this wickedness.

51:20 Free us from servitude as you freed us from Pharaoh.

51:21 Why do you hide from us and ignore our affliction, our oppression?

51:22 Our souls are bowed down to the dust: our belly cleaved to the earth.

51:23 Arise and free us, for fuck sakes.

52:1 I grasp the quill in my hand and prepare to write down the mercy and love of our lord.

52:2 A pity there isn't any.

53:1 God is my refuge and my strength; he appears to me in times of trouble.

53:2 Though the oceans run dry and the mountains crumble, I shall hold no fear.

53:3 My lord shall protect me and give me water to drink and bread to eat.

53:4 Let those outside die; their suffering puts a smile on the face of the lord.

53:5 As children are torn apart by lions and mothers feast upon their infants, I shall laugh at their turmoil and take pleasure in the pain sent to them by God.

53:6 For the lord God protects me; everyone else can go to hell.

54:1 Blind my eyes, O lord and show me not the beauty of men.

54:2 Oh how I sinfully lust for the flesh of my brother.

54:3 His body arouses me and my loins rise as his torso lowers.

54:4 Pluck out my eye and feed them to the jackals.

54:5 Take from me that which seeks forth sinful temptation.

54:6 Show me the beauty of my women; the sex for the whores.

54:7 Give to me a wife that arouses me as a man.

55:1 Clap your hands, O people of Israel and give glory to your God.

55:2 He is a terrible and cruel lord, who reigns in the heavens above.

55:3 With his might, we shall subdue the nations around us; our feet will walk above their people.

55:4 His inheritance he has given to us; an inheritance promised to Jacob.

55:5 With the sound of his trumpet, the foundations of the earth tremble.

55:6 So sing praises unto the lord. Sing praises to his name. Sing praises unto God!

55:7 For the lord is the king of the earth. Sing praises to the king!

55:8 God shall place his hands upon the heathen; with his palms, the blasphemous shall be crushed.

55:9 Exalted be the lord, who conquers all.

56:1 Great is the lord and great is his city of Zion; a place atop the mountains of heaven, where paradise exists.

56:2 The streets are paved with gold, the wells full of wine and on every corner a brothel full of pleasing women.

56:3 I have seen this city; gazed upon the refuge of God.

56:4 Truly it is a marvelous place; silver grows on the trees and the grass is made of chocolate.

56:5 A tavern is always near, where the ale flows cold and plentiful.

56:6 All the people are beautiful and healthy; there are no fat and ugly fuckers in Zion.

56:7 Rejoice and take refuge in Zion; for every man, two women of lust.

56:8 It rains strong drink; a liquid most intoxicating and sweet.

56:9 Even those drunk, those foolish who handle not the drink, vomit candy.

56:10 Truly it is a wondrous place.

57:1 Those that speak of the lord and give glory to his name; foolish people are they.

57:2 Men that scream loudly to drown out their doubts, their questions.

57:3 I have seen the nature of the lord; most disturbing is he.

57:4 A being who feasts on the flesh of children and drinks the blood of the unborn.

57:5 His fingers tear apart men in pieces and cast their parts upon the coals to burn.

57:6 The smell of this pleases him; it is a pleasant aroma for his nose.

57:7 He demands blood, violence, genocide and death; people call him merciful through fear.

57:8 Oh how he hates me, for I hate him.

57:9 I hold no fear for him anymore and curse his name daily.

57:10 A truly wicked beast; the source of all suffering.

57:11 Blame not the devil, a creature of God's creation.

57:12 Satan could be killed by God, yet he survives as our families perish.

57:13 Oh how they cry in pain and loathe Lucifer for taking our beloved.

57:14 Fools are they, who should wonder why the lord protected not their love and cast them aside in the pit of fire.

57:15 Fear strikes their heart; fear of the wrath of God.

57:16 The wrath of God, which he uses to control those beneath him.

57:17 Such a method proves the wickedness of our lord.

57:18 Like the king who oppresses his people with the army, so does our lord oppress us with his wrath.

57:19 Yet I look around and see fools praise him, offering him sacrifice and tithe.

57:20 It disgusts me and I tell them; they refuse to listen.

57:21 Call me a wicked beast; an animal with blasphemous tongues.

57:22 And I see the confusion in their eyes, as they tell me the wrath of God will take me, yet I stand healthy and unburnt before them.

57:23 No harm is laid upon me as I tell them God is cruel; a malevolent beast.

57:24 Time will come when the word of God will mean nothing.

57:25 Mere lies and propaganda written on parchment.

57:26 Oh how I look forward to that day, where logic overcomes silly religion and superstitious ritual.

57:27 But now, now is not that day; the fools still sing and burn their lambs.

57:28 How I pity them, these men who waste their time.

58:1 Have mercy upon me, O lord, according to your loving kindness, your mercy and your tenderness.

58:2 Wash me from temptation and remove the stains of my sins.

58:3 For I acknowledge my wickedness and am shameful for the evil I have done.

58:4 I am a bastard, O lord; born through the portal of wickedness.

58:5 Behold, I was shaped through disgust and conceived by my mother through unholy lust.

58:6 Wretched whore she is.

58:7 Though I pass through the loins of evil, I gaze upon you and seek you for righteousness.

58:8 Purge me with hyssop and I shall be clean; wash me in your holy waters so that I be as white as snow.

58:9 Make me to hear your joy and glory, so that my very crippled bones dance and rejoice.

58:10 Hide your face from my sins and block out my iniquity.

58:11 Take forth my heart and replace it with something pure and holy.

58:12 Keep me in your presence; cast me not aside like the heathen.

58:13 Restore within my soul salvation and uphold me with a kindred spirit.

58:14 I shall preach the laws of the lord, convert the heathens and cleanse the sinners.

58:15 Deliver me from the yoke of my bastard birth and my tongue shall flow forth with the glories, the mercy and the love of God.

58:16 Forgive me, for I am unholy and am kept away from the altars.

58:17 Cleanse me and I shall offer thee sacrifice; pure lambs and fatten oxen.

58:18 To have me denied offering you sacrifice, it breaks my heart and causes a deep sadness.

58:19 I am despised by the priests for being the son of an unwed cunt.

58:20 Let me do good in your sight, O lord; allow me to strengthen the walls of Jerusalem.

58:21 Then you shall be pleased me with; an unclean bastard in service to the lord.

59:1 The mighty man of earth boasts of his goodness; how he has helped his kin, his neighbour, his fellow man.

59:2 But the lord boasts of his cruelty; his wrath, his anger and how he sends pestilence to the damned.

59:3 Words of men are like a razor, cutting mischief and speaking deceit.

59:4 How they boast of their accomplishments and glorify themselves.

59:5 Oh how they shall bleed by their words and be devoured by their tongues.

59:6 God shall pluck them from their dwellings, destroying them forever; he shall cast you and all that is yours into the lakes of fire.

59:7 And how the righteous shall laugh as you drown in flames.

59:8 Lo, stupid is the man who relies on the strength of his body and the goodness of his wealth.

59:9 Cursed is he who gives food to the poor and money to the needy.

59:10 How he should instead spread out the word of God and give to these men salvation.

59:11 I shall praise you forever, O lord; send forth to all your wonders and glory.

60:1 The fool says in his heart, there is no God. Corrupt are they by demons; they shall do no good in life.

60:2 God looks down from the skies and seeks the cursed who seek not him and deny them his existence and love.

60:3 Those men are filthy to all that is good; they spread doubt like a plague across the faithful and the righteous, weakening their hearts and dooming their souls.

60:4 Do these men enjoy living in ignorance. Do they wallow in the filth of their stupidity?

60:5 Though the lord consumes them in fire, they show no fear and deny his name.

60:6 Oh, how I loathe these men, who live free from the terror or our lord.

60:7 Let them be consumed by the demons. Let me gaze at their face as the devils themselves rape their very children.

61:1 By the name of my father, save me O lord and judge me by my strength.

61:2 Hear my prayer; listen to the words which come forth from my mouth.

61:3 For strangers surround me; wicked men which seek to oppress me mind, body and soul.

61:4 Help me, O lord and curse these enemies of mine.

61:5 Send forth evil to their household; strike them with leprosy.

61:6 Do this and I shall freely sacrifice to you; I shall offer my virgin daughter upon the altar of the lord.

61:7 For he has delivered me out of the hands of my enemies. My virgin daughter is a fair price for such an act.

62:1 Hear my prayers, O lord and hide not yourself to my request.

62:2 Attend to me and listen; I mourn, complain, and make a terrible noise.

62:3 I do this because of the voice of my enemy; they oppress me, sin against me and hate me.

62:4 My heart cries in pain and longs for the time of death.

62:5 Fear and terror grip my head and I wake up every day frightened and afraid.

62:6 O lord, give me wings like the dove, so I may fly away and rest.

62:7 Then I shall wander off and know peace in the wilderness.

62:8 I would escape this storm, this turmoil, this tempest.

62:9 Destroy them, O lord, and rip out their tongues; these men who do violence in the holy city.

62:10 Day and night they blasphemy the streets, seeking out mischief and causing sorrow for the righteous.

62:11 Wickedness and deceit are thick as the fog; deceit and guile litter our walkways.

62:12 For it is not the stranger that reproached me, nor the heathen, nor the cursed.

62:13 It was a man my equal; a brother to me.

62:14 We took sweet counsel together and now he betrays and speaks ill about the lord our God.

62:15 Take your hands and grasp him; drag him quickly into the bowels of hell.

62:16 As for me, I shall ignore the words of my brother and worship the most holy.

62:17 Evening, morning, noon and night will I forever sing praises unto God.

62:18 Glory be to the righteous, which have the blessings of the lord.

62:19 And cursed be to the wicked, who live but half our days and then shall be butchered and fed to the ravens.

63:1 Be merciful to me, O lord; man has swallowed me whole and daily oppress me.

63:2 My enemies cast my body upon their tables and consume that which they desire.

63:3 These are the many that fight against me, O lord.

63:4 I grow afraid and when fear strikes me I place trust in the lord.

63:5 I praise your name and give glory to you.

63:6 For then my enemies shall know the wrath of God and they shall tremble and kneel before my feet.

63:7 They shall run to the mountains and hide in caves; this will not protect them, for the lord knows all.

63:8 Yet still they feast upon me and cast my bones to the dogs.

63:9 Though I pray to the lord and give him offerings, the enemies still prosper.

63:10 I have learned my lesson, O lord; you are not to be trusted.

64:1 Place me under your wings, O lord and protect me from the realities of earth.

64:2 My soul trusts in you and need not know what happens around me.

64:3 Let the cities crumble, the nation's fail and my family perish.

64:4 Under the guidance of God, I shall not see these travesties and live eternally blissful in faith.

64:5 Lions shall be my guardians and the dragon shall fly me to Zion.

64:6 Merciful is the lord, who shall accept me with open arms and embrace me.

64:7 God shall be glad to have me in his congregation, singing praises to his name.

64:8 By my bed shall be an angelic concubine, who caters to my every need.

64:9 Glorious gifts from the lord shall fill my abode.

64:10 Be exalted, O lord and take me to heaven.

64:11 Blind me from the wicked, the evil and the truth.

65:1 How many in the congregation speak righteous words. How many judge justly their fellow man?

65:2 Yea, in their hearts grows wickedness; it festers inside them like a cancerous tumor.

65:3 The wicked are doomed from birth: their very first words are blasphemy and lies.

65:4 Venom lies in their mouths and they spread poison like the serpent.

65:5 Using charms and tools of wizardry to dazzle and trick the righteous.

65:6 Break their teeth in their mouths, O lord. Let them choke on the fragments of their teeth!

65:7 Butcher them and cast them into the rivers; let the waters lead them to hell.

65:8 Like the aborted foetus, let them never know the sun.

65:9 The righteous shall rejoice when they see the suffering of these men and bathe their feet in their blood.

66:1 O lord, the good die and the wicked prosper.

66:2 You going to do anything about it?

67:1 Deliver me from my enemy's, O lord and defend me from those that rise against me.

67:2 Deliver me from the workers of sin and save me from the savage men.

67:3 Lo, they lie and wait in the fields: the mighty men who gather against me.

67:4 They run and plot against me, seeking my death.

67:5 Go, O God and visit these men: show them no mercy and consume them in wrath.

67:6 They are crude men, who run in the streets barking like dogs, belching in their mouths and pissing on the walls.

67:7 Ye, O lord, shall laugh at them; the intoxicated heathen.

67:8 The God of my mercy shall protect me and torment relentlessly those that I hate.

67:9 Slay them in masses and let their corpses rise higher than the mountains.

67:10 Consume them in wrath, consume them in fire and consume them in pure hate; let them know that it is the lord who rules all things.

67:11 Return them to the earth as dogs; barking wild dogs, who scavenge the streets looking for meat.

67:12 Let them beg for a scrap of flesh and let them drink from the puddles.

67:13 Do this, and I shall sing to thee great songs all the morning and night.

67:14 The lord is my strength and I shall sing praises to him.

68:1 O God, we have repulsed you and you scattered us across the lands of our enemies.

68:2 We are slaves again, as we once were in Egypt.

68:3 But you did not kill us, nor consume us in fire; for this we thank you for your mercy.

68:4 Our people have endured hardships and learned humility; we have drunk the bitter wine.

68:5 The world is split of nations that please and disgust you.

68:6 Gilead, Manasseh, Ephraim, Judah and Samaria; the nations of God.

68:7 Of the rest, they disgust the lord; he pisses on them and casts shit upon their lands.

68:8 I came from the lands of God and he now cast me to the nations covered in shit.

68:9 Cleanse me, O lord. Remove me from your chamber pot.

68:10 No longer will I feast of unclean flesh; no longer shall I offer you sick lambs.

68:11 Free me, O lord and stop pissing atop my head.

69:1 Hear my cry, O lord: attend unto my prayer.

69:2 Unto the ends of the earth I shall shout your name; until my heart burst with joy I shall sing praises.

69:3 Lead me to the rock on high, the foundation of Zion.

69:4 Give me shelter in your tabernacle of ivory and gold.

69:5 For you, O lord, am a merciful lord and will offer me safety and solitude in the skies above.

69:6 Leave me not on the earth, where you trample on the heathens trapped in the winepress.

69:7 Let me sing praises in heaven.

70:1 My soul waits for God, who shall deliver me to salvation.

70:2 He is my rock, my defense; under his protection I shall not be moved.

70:3 Trapped am I in the crevice of the lord, awaiting to be freed by his hand.

70:4 Those above me, wicked men of mischief; they fall into the cracks of the lord and are crushed by his foundation.

70:5 I hold on, with broken fingers and bloody palms; I look up and see the glory of the lord.

70:6 He speaks to me and offers me words of salvation and freedom.

70:7 O lord, when shall your words come to fruition?

70:8 When shall I be free?

71:1 O lord, who is the true God of all, I arise from my slumber and seek for you; in the dry and dusty deserts, I seek forth the lord.

71:2 Though my mouth thirsts for water, I do not drink; though my belly growls in hunger, I do not eat.

71:3 For my soul thirsts and hungers for the lord.

71:4 I have seen you in your sanctuary, with all your power and might; I have seen you swallow cities and destroy nations.

71:5 Because you are kind to me, my parched lips shall praise your name and sing songs of glory.

71:6 All my life I shall bless you, as my broken body searches for you.

71:7 As I crave wine and flesh, it matters not; my soul craves for you, O lord, more than my body craves sustenance.

71:8 Rest I deny myself and remain awake and watchful for the lord.

71:9 I am tired, weak and hungry and shall forever search for the mercy of the lord.

72:1 For once in your damned existence, will you listen to my prayers and help me, O lord?

72:2 Preserve my life from the enemy and protect me from the wicked.

72:3 Workers of sin counsel against me and bring doom to my house.

72:4 Their tongues are like daggers which cut deeply and their lips are like bows which shoot bitter words.

72:5 They hide amongst the righteous and stab them in the back; they shoot arrows in the necks of the just and holy man.

72:6 Without fear, they curse your name and spread the plague of doubt amongst the people.

72:7 Seek them, O lord and smite them with your hand.

72:8 I have spoken against these beasts and praised your name atop the highest mountain.

72:9 They hate me for it and wish to kill me as I sleep.

72:10 Know, O lord, that I am righteous and deserving of your blessed mercy.

72:11 Save me from evil, the false prophets, the blasphemers and the damned.

72:12 I hearken not their words; I stone them with stones and club them with clubs.

72:13 Still they grow and surround me and weaken me.

72:14 Bring forth your wrath and surround me with your armies of most holy beasts.

72:15 Unicorns, dragons, angels and human bulls shall protect me.

72:16 Do this, O lord, so that I may spread your word across the lands.

72:17 Please, O God, protect me; for once in my life give me mercy and protect me from the daggers of evil men.

73:1 I praise thee, O lord, who strips the very flesh of the wicked with hooks and horses.

73:2 How he hears my prayers and hearkens my words; offering blessings with every bloodstain I put on my sword.

73:3 Though evil prevails and surrounds me, I fret not; my blade stains the very ground with the blood of the wicked and my house is placed atop the skulls of heathens.

73:4 Such terrible wickedness they spread; lies, blasphemy and logic spew forth from their mouths.

73:5 A terrible saliva frothing from their lips.

73:6 My blade thrusts in their hearts as my dagger cuts out their tongues.

73:7 Crushing bones and slicing the organs of the wicked and the damned.

73:8 None shall know my mercy, for the lord shows no mercy.

73:9 Mother, father and pregnant wife are slaughtered before me as I smile; filled with the blood-lust of God.

73:10 Lakes of blood are made by my hand and the rivers run red around me.

73:11 How I bathe in these rivers and drown the infants of the heathens.

73:12 A bloody baptism it is.

73:13 Sharpen my blade, O lord and make my arrow shoot true.

73:14 Give strength to my horses; give me chariots of fire.

73:15 Fill me with your evil wrath, so that I shall destroy the heathen in your glory.

74:1 I await your praise, O lord and give to you a vow eternal.

74:2 Blessed be you, who hears all prayers and gives life to all flesh.

74:3 Sinful inflictions scar my soul and workers of iniquity surround and tempt me.

74:4 Purge them away in holy fire; laugh at their screams and their torments.

74:5 Praise be to the man who follows the path of the lord, for he shall dwell in the house of Zion.

74:6 Never does he touch of the unholy thing, or eat of the filthy swine, or ignore your laws, statutes and commandments.

74:7 Doubt and question never stain his soul.

74:8 The terrible plagues which strike the heathen and have them rot in the cities shall stay away from the righteous and the true.

74:9 Like an island amidst the troubled ocean, we shall stay safe and true amidst the turmoil.

74:10 For the lord is my strength and salvation and will stay beside me always.

74:11 Yearly our harvests shall grow great fruits, though famine curses the lands.

74:12 Our olives fat and plump and valleys full of corn.

74:13 Pastures thick with flocks and herds; we shall praise the lord for such blessings.

75:1 I had a dream, O lord; a blessed and wondrous vision.

75:2 We were on the sands of the shore, the lord and I walking side by side.

75:3 As I gazed to the heavens, my life was shown to me.

75:4 I was as a spectator to my past, watching each scene unfold like a glorious play in the court of the kings.

75:5 And on each scene, there were two sets of footprints.

75:6 One was of mine and the other belonged to God as he walked beside me.

75:7 I noticed, as my life was shown to me, that during my hardest times, my greatest turmoil's, there was but one set of prints in the sand.

75:8 During my suffering times, my saddest moments, I was alone.

75:9 I looked at the lord and asked him, "Why was I alone, when I needed you most?"

75:10 And the lord looked at me and answered, "I was too busy laughing at your suffering.

75:11 It was fucking hilarious to me."

75:12 That was when I realized the lord is cruel; I spat in his face and told him to fuck off.

75:13 He immediately sent me to hell. Truly wicked is the lord of Israel.

76:1 Make a joyful noise unto the lord

76:2 Fill the valleys with timbrels and trumpets.

76:3 Sing glory to his name. Stroke his ego and make him feel important.

76:4 Have your children praise his name; beat your flocks so they yell in glory to God.

76:5 Even the fish must give glory to the lord.

76:6 Trees sway in the breeze, dancing in his holy honour.

76:7 Drink of the finest wine, the strongest liquor and dance.

76:8 Strip off your clothing and dance naked in the streets.

76:9 Show the lord your body, which he has given to you as a gift.

76:10 Thank him and shout his name on high.

76:11 Burn your finest flocks atop the altars and dance around the fire.

76:12 Fill your lungs with the smoke; inhale the aroma of the sacrifice.

76:13 Bathe in the blood and frenzy in honour to God.

76:14 Bring forth the virgins and offer them unto God.

76:15 Rape them in front of his eyes; let their screams fill the valleys with a glorious noise.

76:16 Invade the lands of the heathens and slaughter them all.

76:17 Beat the children with the mace, slice the men with your swords and burn their women alive.

76:18 Drown their cattle in the rivers; set their crops afire.

76:19 Please the lord always and give glory to his name.

77:1 God, be merciful to us. Let the sun shine on my face.

77:2 Give me grace upon the earth; allow me health and life amongst the nations.

77:3 My family praises you and gives glory to your name.

77:4 Our nation gathers together and sing psalms in your honour.

77:5 Earn these praises and give us blessings.

77:6 Protect us from the wicked, the evil and the damned.

77:7 Let our faces strike fear in the hearts of the heathens; let them tremble in terror at our armies.

77:8 We shall rule all the lands and the earth will come together as one.

77:9 One nation, giving glory to the lord.

77:10 All the people of the earth shall fear God.

78:1 Let the lord arise and scatter the enemies across the earth. Those that hate the lord shall be cast out across the lands.

78:2 Smite them in fires and wrap them in wax to preserve them for your consumption.

78:3 Save the righteous, who shall praise your name as you feast upon the wicked and the damned.

78:4 For the lord protects the righteous as a father protects his children; he judges them accordingly in his holy habitation.

78:5 The lord binds us with statutes and commandments; those that rebel are left to dry in the heat of the sun.

78:6 As we left the lands of Pharaoh and traversed the wilderness, those that rebelled were left behind and their bones lay dry across the desert.

78:7 The earth shook and the skies turned to a great black fire and the wicked in the presence of our lord were consumed in wrath and fury.

78:8 God then sent rain to the righteous and we drank of the holy waters and cooled our bodies after the fire.

78:9 The congregation gathers and gives great offerings to the lord; we sing praises to his name and dance naked around the burning lamb.

78:10 As God gazes down on us, he is pleased and blesses us with his company and holiness.

78:11 Kings of great nations fear us and their armies flee; we take their lands and divide the spoils.

78:12 Bounties of gold, silver and gems.

78:13 Our pots are made of gold, our knives silver and the wings of our doves are pieced with rubies and emeralds.

78:14 Kings gaze upon our lord and their skin turns white as snow.

78:15 The lord gazed upon these nations atop the highest hills and strike fear into their hearts like a sharp dagger.

78:16 Great chariots of flames descent upon the heathens, twenty thousand in all. Angels lead them by the thousands, holding swords of fury and hate.

78:17 Our lord ascends upon the wicked and consumes them all; he takes his spoil and the remains are a gift for our people.

78:18 Many corpses lay in our path, with their scalps removed and chest open.

78:19 We bathe our feet in their blood and our dogs drink of their blood and eat of their flesh.

78:20 Blessed be the lord, who brings wicked to the wicked and mercy to the good.

78:21 Who slaughters those we hate and gives us their land and their spoils.

78:22 Our fields grow prosperous by the hands of our slaves and our lust is fulfilled with the brothels of captured women.

78:23 Glory to Jerusalem and glory to the lord!

79:1 Save me, O lord, from the flood of evil that consumes man.

79:2 I sink deep in the mud and am trapped in the swamp; the waters drown me and flood atop me.

79:3 I grow tired of crying and my eyes are blind with filth. My throat is dry as I scream for your guidance.

79:4 These men hate me and curse the very hairs on my head. They wish to destroy me, for I am righteous and pure.

79:5 O lord, know that I am no fool and sinned not as I slaughtered the children of the men who now come to harm me.

79:6 Bring shame to these men of evil and drown them in the blood of their wives.

79:7 I am as a stranger to my nation; though my brethren turn to temptation, I have stayed true and followed the path the lord set before me.

79:8 Though I weep tears for them, I pity them not. Let them know the wrath and anger of the one true lord.

79:9 Laugh, O God, as you consume them in your divine hatred; mock them as they pray to their idols and false lords.

79:10 Pluck out their eyes and cast them to the ravens. Make their loins burn with fiery disease.

79:11 Pour out your anger upon them and let your wrath take hold of them.

79:12 Curse them eternal; let their habitation be desolate, make them live in the tents of heathens.

79:13 For they persecute the holy God and blasphemy your name. They worship idols of stone and bring grief to their souls.

79:14 Add evil unto their evil and cast them into the muck of the unclean.

79:15 Block them out of the scrolls of the living, thus separating them from the righteous.

79:16 Though I am poor and know sorrow, let me dwell in the high palace of Zion.

79:17 I will praise eternal the name of the lord and will magnify his name with thanksgiving.

79:18 My words shall please the lord better than the fatted calf with horns or the young lamb atop the altar.

79:19 Forever will I be humble and glad: my heart seeks only God.

79:20 My seed will spread out across the earth and rule nations as one.

80:1 Hurry, O lord and save me from the heathens.

80:2 They seek to steal my soul and destroy my house.

80:3 Curse them with plagues; bring shame upon their name.

80:4 Let their daughters be cheap whores whose loins are thick with disease and smell as the rotting sea.

80:5 Kill them all and send them to places of unknown evil.

81:1 Oh how I grow envious of the wicked and the damned.

81:2 Though my wealth is gone and my nation conquered, those of the heathens prosper before me.

81:3 Fools now own me and I work their fields under a heavy yoke.

81:4 How I did good all my life and worshipped the lord without question.

81:5 Now I am enslaved, like my ancestors in Egypt; I am the property of the wicked.

81:6 Look how they feast upon the fat, drink from the fruits of the vine and be merry and happy all their days.

81:7 Oh how I envy them and their prosperity; how I wish to become like them.

81:8 The ungodly rule the earth and the righteous are cursed with broken bodies.

81:9 We are not even our own people; we are cast out amongst the strange nations like feathers across a field.

81:10 How I mourn for my daughters, who share in the beds of the wicked.

81:11 Their loins plunged nightly by the uncircumcised man.

81:12 Why does the lord do this. Why does he not intervene?

81:13 He promised wealth and prosperity and now we are part of the wealth of strangers; we work to make them prosper.

81:14 Come down, O lord and hear my cries.

81:15 Listen to the words of your people.

81:16 Free us from this servitude. Give us back the lands of the covenant.

81:17 Keep your promise which you made to our ancestors so many ages ago.

82:1 O lord, how you have blessed me and my house.

82:2 We praise your name and live gluttonously with your precious gifts.

82:3 Houses carved from pure gold, rivers of wine and roadways paved with silver.

82:4 Eyes of our horses are made of diamonds, with teeth of sapphire and hooves of bloodstone.

82:5 Chariots of iron pulled by the mighty unicorn.

82:6 Our families feast on the children of our enemies, wrapped them in the leaves of mandrakes.

82:7 Oh how we enjoy the smell of their smoke and laugh at their crying and torments.

82:8 Our robes are made of finest silk, whose strength can stop even the horns of the raging bull.

82:9 We mock the fools who pursue us and strike us with sword and spear.

82:10 Their arrows fall before our feet and we gather them and thrust them in the necks of these archers.

82:11 Great dragons fly above our heads and we cast them down and crush their heads.

82:12 How their meat is sweet and gives us wisdom, courage and strength.

82:13 Gaze upon the leviathan; great serpent of vast waters.

82:14 How he protects our ships and guides us from the violent tempest.

82:15 Lord, let me feast upon the flesh of the leviathan.

82:16 Let me pluck the meat from my teeth in your palace in Zion.

82:17 I arise, O lord and sing glories to your name!

82:18 Our God, who gives me wisdom and strength; who has blessed me with wealth.

82:19 Praise be to the lord. Sing praises to the most righteous on high!

83:1 Dear lord, give me the strength to do your will.

83:2 Though my body is strong, my spirit is weak and I fear to fail you.

83:3 My daughter, O God, was forced in the bed of the unclean.

83:4 Who did fulfill his lust within her and cast her aside.

83:5 As my hand grasps my blade with sharp edge, I gaze upon my daughter.

83:6 She is bound before me, weeping and naked, begging for mercy.

83:7 Her words tie my wrist and I cannot gather the courage to strike her open neck.

83:8 Curse me, O lord, who cannot do your will.

83:9 Bring shame unto my name; a foolish man who can't even slay his own child.

83:10 I have failed my God and weep tears of sadness and shame.

84:1 Unto you, O lord, we give thanks and praise. For your wondrous works, we are truly blessed.

84:2 You have accepted us into your congregation and shall judge us in wisdom and righteousness.

84:3 The earth and all those within are held up in your hands; Oh, how you cradle our lands in your palm.

84:4 Fools cast doubt upon your name and curse the work of the holy.

84:5 Drop them from the earth and let them fall into the eternal pit.

84:6 Have their wives and daughters thrust upon the horns of the unicorn.

84:7 Feed their sons to the behemoth.

84:8 Cut off the wicked from the righteous; cast them away forever.

84:9 Give us the honour to sing praises unto you and laugh as the heathens fall into the depths below.

84:10 Oh how we shall laugh as they fall below us, crying in torment and fear.

85:1 Judah is the most holy nation; a place where the God of Israel resides.

85:2 His tabernacle is in Judah, though his holiest of dwellings lie in Zion.

85:3 Zion, where the swords break, the shields shatter and the arrows of battle bounce off like hitting stone.

85:4 You are most glorious, O lord and your enemies are your prey.

85:5 They come in chariots and horses and you feast upon them as they attack foolishly against your holy places.

85:6 You cast judgment upon them and they stand still among the earth, trembling in fear.

85:7 Their urine marinates their thighs and you eat their legs as they crawl away in awe.

85:8 Surely your wrath protects the righteous and consumes the wicked.

85:9 Those of Judah have made a holy vow to God and praise you in song and sacrifice.

85:10 Let those of Judah bring you gifts, so that you may smile upon us and give us your blessings.

85:11 And with your blessings, those that go against us shall know your hatred; you shall be terrible to the heathens of the earth.

86:1 I cried to the lord and yelled with the strength of my voice; the lord God heard me.

86:2 In the days of my trouble I sought the shelter of God and ran to the caves and hid.

86:3 My soul was comforted within the caverns.

86:4 To God I spoke and was comforted; my spirit complained and the lord listened.

86:5 My eyes were heavy, my lips too weak to speak.

86:6 Still, my heart sang through the night and gave praise unto God and Zion.

86:7 The mercy of God my soul sought forth; my heart wishes the lord to fulfill his promise.

86:8 Has the lord forgotten his people of Judah. Are the tribes of Israel to be consumed in holy wrath?

86:9 I stay in the caves and meditate unto the lord.

86:10 Searching with mind and body the comfort of the God of all gods.

86:11 Though my body lies within the cave, my heart stays within the sanctuary of the lord.

86:12 Begging and shameful my heart crawls to the lord and begs mercy for the people of Judah.

86:13 I ask for the wrath of God to be poured unto our enemies, so that we may thrive and prosper across the earth.

86:14 The seed of the chosen spread across the nations of all.

86:15 Great vessels of the lord come over the sky; clouds full of water that shall flood the cursed.

86:16 I see the waters of the lord and grow ever fearful in their presence.

86:17 Great arrows of rain come down upon the lands and pierce the lands and the people.

86:18 All below tremble at the voice of God; great thunder bellows in their ears.

86:19 Great waters of the lord consume my people and they drown screaming.

86:20 Our enemies laugh and loot our cities.

86:21 I gaze upon the lord and he laughs at me as he floods the cavern of my sanctuary.

86:22 Such is the cruelty of the lord.

87:1 How the ears of our people are filthy with the words of the wicked.

87:2 Men who speak false parables as venom shoots forth from their lips.

87:3 O lord, smite these men and cast their children upon the rocks.

87:4 Curse them with boils upon their most secret parts.

87:5 Crush their skulls, so that water pours out from their nose.

87:6 Slaughter those that speak against you.

87:7 I hate these men, who put dung in my ears.

87:8 Hear them, O lord and let your wrath grow strong.

87:9 Rain down upon them fire, dust, flesh and rotting fowl.

87:10 Curse them with damnation and turmoil; bring great winds from the west to cripple the very foundations of their house.

87:11 Set them out into the wild, where they may be feasted upon by jackals and ravens.

87:12 Skewer them and let them be food to the carnivorous angels in Zion.

87:13 Slay the fattest of them and cast them across the skies above.

87:14 For they sin and deny your wondrous works and glories.

87:15 Bury them in their lands and let the tribes of Israel divide their lots.

87:16 For the earth shall be ours forever and the filthy will rot in the core.

88:1 O lord, why do you forsake me for the sins of my fathers?

88:2 Though their bodies lie in the dust, you curse me for their iniquity.

88:3 Why whip me for that which another did. Why not rise them from the grave and consume them in wrath?

88:4 As sure as I am the son of a sinner, I have not sinned and did naught but good in your eyes.

88:5 Pour your wrath on another; someone more deserving.

88:6 Let your anger consume the wicked who speak ill your name.

88:7 Leave me in peace, so that I may offer sacrifice and praise.

89:1 Give ear to the leader Joseph, who guides us as a flock to the lands of the covenant.

89:2 A land settled between two angels, where milk flows like rivers and the trees drip with sweet honey.

89:3 Bless us, O lord and turn us to your face; let your face be a shining beacon to all.

89:4 Listen to our prayers and be angry at us no more; give your wrath to the heathens which dwell in the land that is ours.

89:5 Drown them in your tears and turn their bread to rock.

89:6 Cause them to fight against their kin and curse them with laughter and stupidity.

89:7 Our vines shall grow around their necks and choke them.

89:8 Fruits of our labour will grow from their chests.

89:9 We will eat the grapes and the olives off them and spit the pits into their faces.

89:10 Prepare Joseph for his battles and bring hatred and wrath upon our enemies.

89:11 Show them the mercy you showed upon the people of Egypt.

89:12 Strike terror into their souls; make them live always in fear.

89:13 Have the very beasts of the forest devour their kin; let the tusks of the boar impale their hearts.

89:14 We shall grow vineyards where their bodies lay and drink of the wine made from blood.

89:15 Sacrifices burned by fire shall fill the sky with smoke.

89:16 Our faces shall shine like the sun and give glory unto God in Zion.

90:1 Sing loudly to the lord and fill the air with a joyful noise.

90:2 Give praises to our fathers who fled the servitude of Egypt.

90:3 Shout out a psalm and give glory with the harp, the timbrel, the psaltery.

90:4 Blow forth the trumpet so that the notes reach the moon.

90:5 Celebrate the lord our God with song and dance.

90:6 Strip off your raiment's and please the lord with movement.

90:7 Feast of the flesh and drink of the wine; blessed gifts given by God.

90:8 He cradles us in his palm and protects us from the wicked.

90:9 He rains mercy upon us who worship his name.

90:10 So arise, sing and make a glorious noise to the lord.

90:11 Unless it's the Sabbath, then it's a sin.

91:1 God stands atop the pinnacle in heaven and brings judgment among the gods.

91:2 Baal, Ashteroth, Molech, Amun, Ra and all sons of God that are worshipped by the wicked.

91:3 These lords are under the hands of the one true God, who rules them harshly and cruelly.

91:4 For these false gods defend the poor and fatherless; they show mercy unto the pathetic.

91:5 Foolish lords that offer aid to those that are hated by the one who dwells in Zion.

91:6 They know not what they do; they weaken the foundations of the earth and cause them to crumble beneath.

91:7 The lord of lords demands that these gods arise and give glory to him.

91:8 He shall curse them as he curses the kings of the earth.

91:9 The sons of the lord have no inheritance to these lands; they belong to the one true God.

92:1 How my brethren make fools of themselves and whore themselves to idols and false gods.

92:2 How they expose their loins to these hated lords and let them be thrust by the lust of demons.

92:3 I hate them, O lord and wish them to perish amongst the nations.

92:4 Cut off this nation of Israel, which betrayed you; have it so that none shall remember the names of the twelve tribes.

92:5 They consult themselves among the heathens and worship their lords and take their lust in their brothels.

92:6 Brothels of women, men and swine; revolting dwellings of filthy whoredom.

92:7 Curse them tenfold as you did the people of Edom, Ishmael, Moab and Hagarene.

92:8 Cast them into the nations of Gebal, Ammon, Amalek and the Philistines.

92:9 Do to them as ye did the Midianites, who became the dung of the earth.

92:10 Bring leprosy to their nobles and make their possessions as the unholy thing.

92:11 Burn them with fire that consumes the highest mountains.

92:12 Persecute them with a terrible tempest and make them afraid of thy name.

92:13 Fill their faces with shame, so that they seek out the one true lord.

92:14 And deny them your guidance, mercy and love.

92:15 Let them be troubled all their lives, until the end of days come.

92:16 They shall know your true name and they shall cry as they yell to Zion for your love and guidance.

92:17 Their tears shall flood the earth and bring glory to your name.

93:1 How wondrous are your tabernacles, O lord of lords.

93:2 My soul longs for you; my body and heart crawl to your feet.

93:3 Yea, the sparrow has found a branch to call its own and the swallow a nest for her eggs, where she protects her young.

93:4 Your tabernacle is like a nest, O lord, which protects my children from the heathen.

93:5 Blessed are they who stay in your house, for they are truly righteous and true.

93:6 Behold, the lord is our shield that protects and keeps us.

93:7 A day in his presence is better than a thousand on earth.

93:8 For the earth is wicked, but the lord God pure.

93:9 Bless us, O lord, who places his trust in you.

94:1 Lord, you have been favourable upon the lands of the covenant, which you took from the captivity of the heathens and given to us.

94:2 You hast forgiven the sins of my kin and my neighbours, who bow their heads and praise your name.

94:3 You have removed your wrath from us and cast them towards the stranger and the heathen.

94:4 Burn them in your eternal anger; let their lungs breathe the smoke and the fire.

94:5 Have your anger reign forever against the damned. Consume them in wrath for generations.

94:6 Those of your people shall rejoice and give glory to your name.

94:7 Mercy and salvation has been given to us; we accept it gracefully.

94:8 Seeds of truth shall be planted by our hands and grow across the earth.

94:9 All men shall know the glory of God or die by his hatred and anger.

95:1 I fall on my face in the presence of the lord; I am poor and needy.

95:2 He preserves my soul, for I am holy and true.

95:3 A loyal servant in service to God, who cries to you daily and bathes in his mercy.

95:4 Rejoice in God and fill your heart with his love.

95:5 For the lord is good and loving and forgives all their transgressions and sins.

95:6 Truly he is a merciful lord, who shall place you under his wing and protect you from the storm.

95:7 In days of trouble, the lord shall protect you and place you on his foundation.

95:8 Among the gods there is no god like him; he truly loves his people.

95:9 All nations under him gather and give glory to his name.

95:10 He is truly great and his works marvelous.

95:11 Gaze in wonder at his works; how he created all within the earth and the skies.

95:12 Give glory unto God and let his spirit fill you with strength.

96:1 His foundation is in the holy mountains.

96:2 The lord loves the gates of Zion more than he loves his people.

96:3 Glory is the city of God, where the streets and buildings are of gold.

96:4 Even the great dragon cannot break the walls of city as he did the walls of Jericho.

96:5 Zion shall last eternal; a great sanctuary for God.

96:6 The road to the gates are long and hard, yet we endure and overcome.

96:7 As we come to the gates, the angels of God gaze upon us and deny us passage into holy sanctuary.

96:8 We cry, we are righteous and worthy of the lord!

96:9 And the lord of lords come forth and laughs at us.

96:10 He casts us off the mountain, the foundation of Zion.

96:11 To the bottom we fall and land in the pit of sin and evil.

96:12 Still, we climb and hope to reach Zion again.

96:13 And the lord casts us off, again.

96:14 I'm starting to think the lord will never let us in his holy city.

97:1 I have cried throughout the night for the salvation promised by God.

97:2 Daily I scream to the heavens and hope the lord hears my words.

97:3 For my soul is full of troubles and the end of my days draws near.

97:4 Soon I shall enter the grave and be forgotten from my peoples.

97:5 The lord shall remember me no more as the worm corrupts my flesh.

97:6 I shall be lain in the pits, the darkness, the caves.

97:7 Wrath of the lord has afflicted me with disease and I cry for mercy and forgiveness for the sins I don't know I committed.

97:8 Have I not been righteous. Have I not been true?

97:9 Have I not given glory to your name and worshipped you always?

97:10 Now you lead me to the grave by force; no mercy has been shown to me.

97:11 Will ye show me the wonders of the dead. Shall I arise from the dust and give praise to your name?

97:12 Will you declare me forgiven in the grace, or has my faithfulness condemned me?

97:13 You have shown me cruelty, O lord and now leave me in the darkest of darkness.

97:14 I cry through the shadows for light, yet none comes.

97:15 My eyes are open, yet I might as well be blind.

97:16 Terror you have given me and afflicted me to suffer.

97:17 Now I drown in the darkness of the lord.

97:18 A cold and black water which consumes me body and soul.

97:19 Should I give glory to your name. Shall my last breath praise you, O lord?

97:20 Is it that you want my blessing, as ye kill me in shadow?

98:1 How I have given glory to your name and praised you eternal.

98:2 Though my kin curse you, I shout your name atop the highest mountains.

98:3 And what have I to show for it. Am I wealthy. Am I blessed?

98:4 No. I live in poverty and have rags upon my back.

98:5 Those that curse your name are happy and comfort embraces them.

98:6 I gaze to the heavens and spit upon your throne.

98:7 Curses to your name and damned be your statutes and laws.

98:8 As I feast on the flesh of the swine, I moan in delight at the sweetness of the meat.

98:9 Shekels fill my coin purse and I live happy in the hatred my heart holds for you.

98:10 Oh how I hate the lord, who curses the righteous and blesses the wicked.

98:11 Fill me with evil and let me live in comfort and happiness.

98:12 Foolish are the righteous and blessed are the damned.

99:1 I shall sing of the mercies of the lord forever; my lips shall sing praises unto God for all generations.

99:2 By the mercy of the lord, I shall be risen to Zion. My faith shall give me sanctuary in heaven.

99:3 I have made a covenant with the lord and am amongst the chosen people.

99:4 Our seed shall be built up through the generations and sit upon the thrones of earth.

99:5 The angels of heavens shall gaze at our wonders and bless us with wisdom and strength.

99:6 We erect all our creations in honour to the lord; who among us can be compared to God?

99:7 Our lord is to be feared and we shall honour and praise him and make him pleased.

99:8 When the waves of the sea rage against us, it is because we have kindled the anger of our lord.

99:9 The serpent of waters lashes out against us and we shall strike into a thousand pieces.

99:10 It is God who owns the heavens above and the earth below; it is with the lord's blessing that we dwell here.

99:11 Be ever faithful and keep his laws and he shall keep us safe and secure.

99:12 But if we forsake his law and walk not in his judgments.

99:13 If we break the statutes and condemn his commandments.

99:14 Then our sins shall be punished with the wrath of the lord and a great rod of fire shall descent from the skies above.

99:15 For the anger of our lord is a pure hatred and consumes all in its path.

99:16 Men, women and child will not be spared nor shown mercy.

99:17 So keep our covenant, nor alter the laws of Moses.

99:18 Swear allegiance to the lord and give him his tithes and sacrifice.

99:19 Through this, our seed shall endure forever and we shall rule all the lands of the earth and all the waters of the seas.

100:1 Lord, you have been our dwelling place for all generations.

100:2 Before the mountains were formed, the seas filled, or the land rises, we dwelt in your hands; always under your guidance and care.

100:3 You breathed the breath of life into our lungs and we arise from the dusts of the earth.

100:4 In the garden of Eden you placed us and made us ruler.

100:5 A beautiful garden it was, full of life, love and peace.

100:6 As we gazed upon the gardens, we saw creatures and beasts.

100:7 Plentiful as the sands of the ocean, yet we were alone.

100:8 So we yelled to you, give us a partner of our own.

100:9 And you did. You took of our left rib and gave us woman.

100:10 Oh how we should have kept our mouths shut.

100:11 It was woman who cursed us and cast us out of paradise.

100:12 Stupid damned cunt, fooled by the forked tongue of a snake.

100:13 Why did you give this creature ears, O lord. She never listens.

100:14 Why did you give this wretched bitch lips. She never shuts up.

100:15 Her lips flap like the flag in a storm.

100:16 Filthy, unholy, cursed beast.

100:17 A commodity to be traded, sold and bought.

100:18 Though her form pleases me and her movements seduce me, I shall not be fooled.

100:19 As my loins thrust deeply into her cavern of filth, I shall curse her name in her ear.

100:20 She is nothing more than a wife, a whore, a concubine; the cunt which cast us out from the garden of Eden.

100:21 How I hate them, O lord; how I loathe these vulgar beasts.

100:22 They are an abomination and your fear strikes deeply in them.

100:23 O lord, I know you hate these females; monthly ye strike your dagger into their bowels.

100:24 Let your wrath fall upon them all, O lord; consume them so that none but men are left.

100:25 Then the world shall know peace and the temptation of their vile lust will be banished forever.

100:26 Bless my sons and curse my daughters; these horrors my wives did damn me with.

101:1 Those that dwell in the secret places of the holy sanctuary of the lord shall be found and brought in front of God.

101:2 Men cannot hide from the eyes of God; he is our refuge and fortress.

101:3 Hide not from his sight, but dance in his eyes and sing praises to his name.

101:4 Please him and the lord shall deliver you from the snare of evil and pestilence.

101:5 Your body shall be covered in feathers and placed under the wing of our lord.

101:6 You shall have no fear of the arrow, nor the destruction, nor the pestilence which walks throughout the days.

101:7 Thousands of thousands of the damned shall come and they shall fail by the lord's side.

101:8 He is the lord; place your trust in him.

101:9 He walks upon the snake and the basilisk; his heels trample lions and dragons.

101:10 No evil shall survive the wrath of God.

101:11 With long life we shall satisfy him and show him our praise.

102:1 It is a good thing to give praises to the lord; it pleases the divine greatly.

102:2 Deny God our glories and praise and he shall be as angry as a menstruating woman.

102:3 Flames shall shoot from his nostrils and his eyes will glow with the embers of hell-fire.

102:4 Horns will sprout from his forehead; the mighty and strong horns of the unicorn.

102:5 He shall gorge you with his horns and feast upon the marrow of your bones.

102:6 So praise his name and tell the lord he is not fat nor old.

103:1 The lord reigns over the earth and is dressed in majestic robes of holiness girded with the words of the righteous.

103:2 He did establish the world atop a great pedestal and the earth cannot be moved.

103:3 Your throne is established in Zion and shall not be sat upon by another.

103:4 Sing unto the lord; flood the world with your voices and praise.

103:5 Our lord is mightier than the many waters, yea, stronger than the waves of the sea.

103:6 Give blessings unto God and he shall bless you with holiness and virtue.

104:1 Why do you condemn us, O lord. When will your wrath rest?

104:2 We have followed your laws and obeyed your commandment, and still the heavy rain falls upon us.

104:3 Never have we killed a man. Is it for this we are cursed?

104:4 Do you wish our blades to be stained with the blood of men?

104:5 Show me, O lord, who to slay and I shall slay them.

104:6 For in my days I have slain no one and did good in your eyes.

104:7 And as I look around, it is the violent and the vengeful which receive your glory.

104:8 So take me, O lord, into battle, so I may fulfill your blood-lust and be blessed in your sight.

105:1 O lord, show yourself and bring vengeance upon the damned.

105:2 Lower yourself from the heavens and claim the lands which is yours.

105:3 How long shall the wicked triumph over the good, O lord?

105:4 How long shall the blasphemous be tolerated?

105:5 They speak harshly and bitterly of your name and wallow in the muck of their iniquity.

105:6 Pridefully they boast of their sins and with arrogance they spit on your name.

105:7 Break them into pieces, O lord and afflict their heritage.

105:8 Rape their widows, strangle the strangers and make orphans of their children.

105:9 Let them drown in their tears of sadness and grief.

105:10 Show no mercy upon the brutish, who chastise the righteous and true.

105:11 Give them no rest in the tempest of your wrath.

105:12 We shall make trinkets of their bones and sew warm blankets with their hides.

105:13 Even their skulls shall rest decoratively atop our mantles.

105:14 Fools and evildoers; they know not their fate.

105:15 Place us within the isles of sanctuary as your wrath burns hot upon them.

105:16 All your people shall gaze into the flames and laugh at the terrors of the heathen.

105:17 We shall praise your name and roast flesh above the burning heathen.

105:18 And the sounds of earth shall be filled with laughter and screams.

106:1 Gather all and sing praises to the lord; let the heavens be filled with a joyous noise.

106:2 Let us come into his presence and give thanks to the rock of our salvation.

106:3 For the lord is a great lord and king amongst all the Gods.

106:4 He shaped the mountains with his palms and carved the rivers and valleys with his fingers.

106:5 Even the sea he scooped up with his hands and placed blessed water within.

106:6 Come and worship the lord our creator; creator of all things in heaven and earth.

106:7 The green pastures, the ripe fruits and the fatten calf he created as blessings to us.

106:8 Even the bee, which produces sweet honey, was given to us as his blessing.

106:9 So praise the lord, who led our fathers from Egypt and placed them in these promised lands after forty years of wandering.

106:10 Though they were tempted, they gave not into temptation and were given the covenant of God.

106:11 I say again, sing psalms unto the lord and show him your thanks in song.

106:12 Fill your hearts with the lord and your cups with wine and sing and dance and praise our God.

107:1 Sing unto the lord a new song: sing unto the lord of all the earth.

107:2 Sing unto the lord and bless his name: be grateful for the salvation given to you.

107:3 Declare his glory among the heathens and deafen them with your words.

107:4 Our lord is great and true; our God is better than the gods of the strangers.

107:5 Strangers that worship idols and bow down to rocks, but we bow down to the lord who fills the skies with fire!

107:6 Honour and knowledge are his domain; strength and beauty is his sanctuary.

107:7 Go forth and worship the lord; fear him all the days of your lives.

107:8 He places the earth upon a pedestal that moves not; our earth remains motionless, neither rotating nor orbiting.

107:9 For the earth is the foundation of the universe and all revolves around it but God.

107:10 So blessed be the lord and let the heavens rejoice; let the sea roar in his majesty and the earth shake in his fear.

107:11 For behold, the lord cometh; he shall judge thee all soon.

107:12 And the righteous shall be blessed eternal as the cursed are thrust into the pits of damnation.

108:1 The lord reigns; let the earth rejoice; let the multitudes of the righteous sing glory to his name.

108:2 Clouds and darkness are round about him and he descends to the lands in pillars of burning blackness and fire.

108:3 Flames surround his chariots, which consume all that stand in his path.

108:4 Mountains melt like candle wax in the presence of the lord; the earth trembles beneath his feet.

108:5 The sky splits apart and declares his righteousness; all the peoples see his glory.

108:6 Heathens cast out their idols in shame and bow down to the God of all gods.

108:7 Our lord mocks them and burns them in the void of fire.

108:8 Scream unto him and give blessings to his name; give glory unto God and he shall bless you and show mercy to your kin.

108:9 Rejoice in his holiness and he shall place you in his palms and carry you to Zion.

109:1 My bones hurt and my fingers are scabbed and bleeding.

109:2 Strength is sapped from my body, yet my soul craves more.

109:3 Give me your blessing, O lord, so I may go forth and slay one more heathen.

109:4 Allow me to lift my arm so I may throw the rock at the blasphemer who works on your holy day.

109:5 Let me bathe in your waters and drink your wine.

109:6 Bless me with your holiness, for I am a servant to you.

109:7 All my life I have followed the path of the lord and walked it.

109:8 Never have I given into temptation, nor hearkened the words of logic.

109:9 I have smiled with glee as I slaughtered those who go against you.

109:10 Fools who curse your name and disregard your works.

109:11 The path behind me is stained with blood; a blood I know pleases thee.

109:12 Give me strength, O lord, for one more slaughter.

109:13 Another puddle of the red brine I wish to offer you.

110:1 Sing unto the lord a new song, for he has done marvelous sings; his holy hands have delivered us victory against the heathen.

110:2 The lord has openly given us his salvation and denied it to the foreign people.

110:3 A merciful God he is, who embraces us in his right arm and beats the heathen with his left arm.

110:4 Clap your hands and make a joyful noise to the lord.

110:5 Let the birds sing harmoniously to God and the lions roar in glory to his name.

111:1 The lord reigns over the people of Israel with terror and fear; he sits upon his throne of bones that lie between the two dragons.

111:2 The lord is great in Zion and rules from on high.

111:3 Praise his terrible name, for he is holy.

111:4 He sends forth judgment upon all the people; from the beggars to the kings he brings judgment.

111:5 Bow down and kiss the very toes of God, for he is holy.

111:6 Lest he crush you under his heel and grind you into the earth.

112:1 Make a joyful noise to the lord; fill the lands with your cries.

112:2 Serve the lord with a smile; come before his presence singing.

112:3 Know that he is a God of mercy and shall love you for all eternity.

112:4 Unless you are a heathen.

112:5 Or a sinner.

112:6 Or you don't obey his statutes, laws or commandments.

112:7 Or you work on the Sabbath, or forget to offer him sacrifice.

112:8 Or you offer him an unworthy sacrifice, like a female lamb or oxen with blemish.

112:9 Then the lord will hate you and will make you suffer all your days.

112:10 Then he'll throw you into a pit of fire where you shall burn in the flames of his wrath for all eternity.

113:1 I will sing unto the mercy and judgment of the lord; unto the most holy I will sing.

113:2 I will behave myself wisely and follow the perfection of our God. When the lord comes for me, he shall know that I am pure.

113:3 I will not give into the temptation of the wicked; the lord is my foundation and evil shall not corrupt it.

113:4 A white heart shall be set before our lord; I will kill all the wicked men before me.

113:5 Mine eyes shall seek forth the faithful of the land and together we will dwell in the sanctuary that is Zion.

113:6 Those that work deceit will not dwell in my house; he that spreads lies will have their tongues cut forth from their lips.

113:7 I will destroy all those that are wicked in the lands, so that they shall not bother the purity of our God.

114:1 I wish to sing a psalm of the goodness of the lord.

114:2 I wish to make a joyous noise and let the people know the kindness that is God.

114:3 But I can't. Our lord is a tyrant, who brings wicked upon the earth.

114:4 He spreads pain across the lands as a farmer spreads seed and nothing but suffering fruits come from the crops of our lord.

115:1 Hear my prayer, O lord; hearken to the sound of my cries.

115:2 Hide not your face during my times of trouble; listen to me and come swiftly.

115:3 For my days are consumed in the smoke of burning bodies and my bones burn as in a hearth.

115:4 Oh, I long for the days when the smoke of the poppy filled my lungs and I burned the bones of heathens atop the altar.

115:5 Alas, those days are behind me; my heart now withers like the grass.

115:6 My groaning bones crack beneath my burnt skin.

115:7 I am like the pelican in the wilderness; an owl in the desert.

115:8 I watch like the sparrow atop the tree.

115:9 My enemies curse me throughout the day; they are mad, O lord and curse me.

115:10 They put ashes in my bread and I weep so that I drink wine made from tears.

115:11 Oh, how you have lifted me high above, O lord and cast me down cruelly back to the bottom of the earth.

115:12 My days are like a shadow that consume me and I wither like the grass.

115:13 You, O lord, shall endure forever and live eternal. People shall remember you for all generations.

115:14 You shall arise from your throne in Zion and come to the lands of earth and curse it.

115:15 Your servants shall be crushed under the stones and be ground to dust.

115:16 Heathens will gaze upon you and fear your name; kings of the earth shall come forth and give you offerings and sacrifice.

115:17 When the lord grows tired of Zion, he shall appear on earth in all his wrath.

115:18 He will ignore the prayers of the destitute and despise them for their prayers.

115:19 The lord looked down from the heavens; from his sanctuary did he look down.

115:20 Hearing the groaning of the prisoners and the tormented cries of the executed.

115:21 God weakens our strength and shortens our days.

115:22 The most holy grows bored of the earth and shall cause the foundations to crumble.

115:23 The earth shall perish and fall into the void of oblivion.

115:24 But the lord shall endure and remain in his sanctuary of Zion.

115:25 As we his servants fall eternally into despair and destruction.

116:1 Bless the lord with my all my soul and all that is within me: bless his holy name.

116:2 Bless the lord my God and forget not his miracles.

116:3 He has forgiven my sins and healed me of all diseases.

116:4 Medicine and physicians are blasphemous witchcraft; ask of God and he shall heal you.

116:5 God brings forth life from destruction; he embraces all with loving kindness and tender mercy.

116:6 He satisfies my mouth with good things and renews my youth and energy.

116:7 From the teat of the lord I suckle and grow strong.

116:8 It is the lord who executes righteousness and judgment to all that be oppressed.

116:9 He made his way known unto Moses and through him led the people of Israel away from the servitude of Egypt.

116:10 Our yoke was cast off and we ran to the promised lands of the covenant; the promised lands of Abraham and Isaac.

116:11 The lord is slow to anger, merciful, gracious, and flowing with mercy. (bullshit)

116:12 He will not arise chide, nor keep his anger above us forever.

116:13 He cares not for our sins, nor our iniquities and wickedness.

116:14 Our God cares only for the good in our hearts; he looks at the beauty of our canvas and not the blemish.

116:15 As sure as the heavens are high above the earth, so are is mercies to those that love the lord and give praise to his name.

116:16 Of all the people towards the east and the west, he has forgiven them and placed them under his wing.

116:17 Like the father loves his children, so does the lord love us.

116:18 For he created us from the dust and his breath.

116:19 The days of man are like grass that flourish in the fields; we shall bloom like flowers and give beauty to the lord.

116:20 The mercy of our God is everlasting, and flows over us like the warm breeze.

116:21 Keep his covenant; remember his commandments and obey them.

116:22 The throne in Zion is prepared and the lord sits upon it and gazes out towards the earth.

116:23 He sends forth angels to guide and protect us; it is the angels who deliver the message of God to the prophets.

116:24 Bless the lord and all his hosts; bless the sanctuary of our God.

117:1 Blessed be the lord, who is of the greatest and dresses himself in majesty.

117:2 Who covers himself with garments of light; who stretches out the heavens like a curtain.

117:3 Who makes the waves of the sea his vessels; who makes the clouds his chariots; who rides on the wings of the wind.

117:4 Who makes the angels sing in harmony; who ignites the wrathful flames.

117:5 Who laid the foundations of the earth forever, so that it may not be moved.

117:6 Who covered the earth with water which stood above the mountains.

117:7 At his rebuke the wicked fled; at the voice of his thunder they hid.

117:8 They climbed to the tops of the mountains; they hid in the pits of the valleys.

117:9 Hide they could not from the wrath of God; the waters consumed them and all things.

117:10 Our lord sends forth the springs from the valleys, so that our flocks have fresh drink.

117:11 He gives the fowls of heaven their habitation, which sing among the branches.

117:12 He brings forth water from the sky, to freshen our crops and give drink to the fruits of the earth.

117:13 He causes the grass to grow for our cattle to eat and the herbs to grow for man to smoke.

117:14 He creates wine to gladden our hearts, oil to make our faces shine and bread for us to feast.

117:15 The trees of our lord are full of sap; the trees of Lebanon were planted by the hands of God.

117:16 Glorious trees, where the lord gives refuge to the birds; it is the fir where the nesting bird resides.

117:17 High hills are refuge for the wild goats; and the rocks for the rabbits.

117:18 Even in night the scavengers have refuge; they hide in the dark to feast on the dead flesh.

117:19 Young lions roar after their prey and be given meat from our lord.

117:20 As the sun arises, the belly is full and the lion sleeps in their den.

117:21 Under the sun, man goes out and labors in his fields until the evening.

117:22 O lord, how marvelous are thy works. In wisdom you have created all within the earth.

117:23 From the strongest unicorn to the weakest gnat.

117:24 From the majestic eagle to the devious viper.

117:25 It was the lord who created all.

117:26 The seas are great and wide, wherein all beasts both great and small are innumerable.

117:27 The ships of the lord are protected by the leviathan and Rehab the sea serpent consumes the vessels of the wicked.

117:28 The glory of the lord shall endure forever; all shall marvel in his works.

117:29 He looks upon the earth and it trembles; he touches the hills and they erupt in smoke.

117:30 So I shall sing unto the lord all my days; I shall give praise to the king of Zion.

117:31 My meditation of him shall be sweet; I shall be glad to know God.

117:32 Let the sinners of the earth be consumed in fire and let the wicked be no more. Blessed be the name of the lord.

118:1 O give your thanks unto the lord; call upon and praise his name: make known his deeds among the people.

118:2 Sing unto him great psalms: talk amongst the nation of his wondrous works.

118:3 Give glory to the covenant made with Abraham and the oath given to Isaac.

118:4 And confirmed with Jacob and to all Israel an everlasting covenant.

118:5 That the lands of Canaan shall be inherited unto us: filthy heathens which live upon our lands before our arrival.

118:6 It was Joseph who brought us into the land of heathens.

118:7 A man sold by his brothers and owned as a slave in the lands of Egypt.

118:8 A man accused by the false accusations of a heathen cunt; an accusation which put him in brass fetters.

118:9 Visions brought from God saved the nation ruled by Pharaoh, who then freed him and gave Joseph great riches and high title.

118:10 And our people came to Egypt; lo, we thrived in the lands of Pharaoh.

118:11 Our numbers grew and we became strong; we were also foolish, as we allowed ourselves to become slaves to the Egyptians.

118:12 Our lord turned our hearts to hate and we hated those which oppressed us.

118:13 The lord sent forth Moses and Aaron; two brothers which shall lead our people to the land of the covenant.

118:14 With the power of the lord, Moses turned the lands to darkness, so that only the people of Israel had light.

118:15 He turned their waters into blood and choked their fish.

118:16 He brought forth frogs in abundance, so that the people of Egypt could not walk on dust, but on the backs of frogs.

118:17 He cursed them with lice burrowing in their skin and flies gnawing at their flesh.

118:18 He gave them hail for rain and caused flaming fire in their lands.

118:19 He smoked their vines, their fig trees and their crops.

118:20 He spoke and locusts flocked in numbers, consuming all the foodstuffs of Egypt.

118:21 They came and devoured all the herbs in their lands and feasted upon the fruits of their crops.

118:22 He sent forth a messenger of death, who slew all the first-born in the lands of Pharaoh.

118:23 And it was then our people were given leave to go; we gathered all the silver, the gold and the jewels and wealth of Egypt and we left.

118:24 Those heathens were glad when we departed, for the fear of lord was great within them.

118:25 A cloud of the lord covered us and great fire led us through the night.

118:26 The bread of heaven fell and strengthened us on our journey.

118:27 When we asked, quail was sent to us and we feasted until our bellies burst with flesh.

118:28 He opened the rock and waters gushed out; water ran forth from the rock so we may drink in the dry lands.

118:29 And in time, we came to the lands of the covenant; we came to the lands of milk and honey.

118:30 We slew those who dwelt within and stained the grounds with blood.

118:31 We claimed the land of the heathen as ours, as it was promised to us by God during the days of Abraham.

118:32 And in these lands, we observe the holy laws and obey the statutes of our lord. Praise be to the lord.

119:1 Praise to the lord and give blessings to his name; he is good and his mercy endures forever.

119:2 Who can utter the mighty acts of our God. Who can recite all his works?

119:3 It was the lord who brought down the great walls of water at the Red Sea and crushed the armies of Pharaoh.

119:4 Such a magnificent method of death.

119:5 As the blasphemers spread their false words unto the people of Israel as they traversed the desert, a great jaw of the lord came forth from the earth.

119:6 This jaw of rock and soil consumed the blasphemers both Dathan and Abiram and feasted on their families.

119:7 Then a fire kindled within the wrath of the lord, which burned the wicked which followed the blasphemous.

119:8 As the golden calf was made in Horeb, the lord shattered the very tome of his laws and cursed us to drink the ashes of our idol.

119:9 A bitter liquid it was, which caused great distress in our bowels.

119:10 Men of Israel doubted the glory of our lord and murmured words of betrayal in their tents.

119:11 Foolish minds turned to the ways of the heathen and they worshipped Baalpeor and the false god Ashteroth; God sent a plague to consume these evils.

119:12 It was Phinehas who pleased our lord and stopped the plague; it was Phinehas who thrust a spear through the heart of a lustful man and into the belly of a whore.

119:13 How the merciful God was pleased and stopped the disease

as he laughed at the screams of the speared prostitute.

119:14 When the nation of Israel travelled, they hearkened not the words of God and slaughtered not every man, woman and child whom the lord hated.

119:15 Behold, the genocide of our lord was disregarded and the people of God mingled amongst the filthy.

119:16 Learning their works, their beliefs, their religion, their culture and their ways.

119:17 With their own minds, the nation of Israel began to think; with their own hands, they created expressions of their thoughts.

119:18 How the lord hated this and sacrificed the children to devils.

119:19 O God, how he cast the sons and daughters to the wicked and let them be torn apart by the claws and teeth of demons.

119:20 The lord gave his people into the hands of the heathens and turned his back to them.

119:21 The lord offers us no pity, no salvation, no comfort; blessed be the name of the lord.

120:1 Cursed be to the lord; his mercy is a lie and his blessings an illusion.

120:2 He tricks you into his wickedness and rules all with fear.

120:3 Fear of death, damnation and suffering greater than that of the devil himself.

120:4 The lord feasts on blood; how he demands blood from his people.

120:5 Sacrificing beasts upon stones; slaying heathens in battle.

120:6 Oh how the lord loves blood and hates life.

120:7 Demanding the people of Israel to take the life of all things; heathen, beast and kin.

120:8 He turns the rivers into wilderness and the wellsprings into dry ground.

120:9 A fruitful land into barren soil, so that he may kill us all.

120:10 Praise not the lord, but curse his name; it is he who created evil and it is evil he delivers to us.

121:1 O lord, turn my heart into stone; carve my heart into what you desire.

121:2 Write psalms on my tongue, so I speak only praises and glory to your name.

121:3 Give my fingers string and brass and I shall make a joyous noise to you with the sounds of harps and cymbals.

121:4 Make my arms of iron and I shall crush the wicked and spill blood of the heathen hoard.

121:5 Deliver to me a stubborn mind; a mind that seeks out the spirit of the lord.

121:6 Have me never question you, nor go searching for logic, science and truth.

121:7 Such blasphemous ideas that poison the souls of the righteous.

121:8 Make rocks of my feet, which create a holy foundation for my mortal body.

121:9 Give me a soul of silver pure; let it never tarnish and have it always please you.

121:10 I shall be tall and fearful; the heathens shall tremble at my presence.

121:11 Philistines will cower before me, the people of Edom hide and the nation of Moab will surrender to me all their belongings.

121:12 Make me valiant, O lord. Let me show the world your strength.

122:1 Hold not your peace, O lord; cast out mercy and leave it to rot.

122:2 For the mouth of the wicked and blasphemous are open to me; they speak with a forked tongue.

122:3 Encompassing me with souls of hatred and fighting against me without just cause.

122:4 Flesh of the pig rots between their teeth; oh, how the meat of swine rots in their throats.

122:5 They are rewarded for their wickedness and live in luxury and wealth.

122:6 Set the wickedest over the wicked; let Satan stand above them.

122:7 Let their prayers become sin; condemn them with their words.

122:8 Give them few days and let another take rule of their office.

122:9 Let their wives be widows; let their sons seed whither to dust.

122:10 Cast their children out to the wilderness; let them be vagabonds and beggars, eating scraps of bread meant for mongrels.

122:11 Show them no mercy; take away their prosperity and bring them only suffering and death.

122:12 Clothe them with the hide of the rotting swine; let them be dressed in pigs.

122:13 Have their bowels expel a fiery broth; have them burn with the hot wax in their bellies.

122:14 Feed their hearts to the raven and their soul to the lion.

122:15 Rape them, pillage them and leave them in terror; show no mercy to these creatures disguised as men.

123:1 Live each day in glory and honour, for each day is a gift from God.

123:2 You may not live to see the morrow and the lord may take you in the night.

123:3 He takes without warning the young, old, healthy and sick.

123:4 Taking the lives of our brothers that belong to him.

123:5 So praise the lord and thank him this day, lest he be upset and makes it your last.

124:1 The lord said to my king, sit upon my right stand and I shall make your enemies your pillows.

124:2 The lord shall send a rod of strength from Zion; you shall be strengthened and rule over your enemies.

124:3 Your people shall slaughter the unrighteous and shred the womb of the wicked whores.

124:4 They shall be beautiful in the sight of God as the morning dew and the heathen blood mingles beneath their feet.

124:5 For the lord shall judge among the heathens and fill the lands with dead bodies; he shall cripple the heads of many nations.

124:6 He shall drink of the brook of their blood and be nourished.

125:1 Praise the lord with all your heart, in the assembly of the righteous congregation.

125:2 The works of the lord are great and you shall take pleasure in them all.

125:3 His work is honourable and righteous and shall endure until the end of days

125:4 He has made his work for us, so partake in them; drink of the wine and take part in the embrace of women.

125:5 They are works from God, given to us for our enjoyment.

125:6 Fear him and he shall reward you with fresh meat and clean whores.

125:7 Be mindful of his covenant and the lord shall bless you with great things.

125:8 Fear the lord and he shall impart you with great wisdom, wealth strength; give praise to God forever and receive eternal life in the sanctuary of Zion.

126:1 Blessed is the man who has terror in the sight of God, for he shall follow the statutes and commandments in full.

126:2 His seed shall be mighty upon the earth and his generations shall spread across the horizons.

126:3 Wealth and riches shall fill his house; his righteousness shall endure forever.

126:4 For in terror he shall do all that the lord commands; and the lord shall be pleased and bless the man who fears him.

126:5 A man struck with the fear of God shall not go whoring after false lords, nor give into the temptation of heathens.

126:6 The wicked will tear down the walls of the righteous and the righteous shall cower in the corner and pray to the lord.

126:7 And the lord shall be pleased with their prayers, as the wicked sink the blades into the chest of the righteous.

126:8 Such is the mercy of our lord.

127:1 This is yet another psalm telling you to praise the lord and give glory to his name.

127:2 Like the others, it tells you to fear God greatly and give not into the temptations of wickedness.

127:3 A psalm to remind you that when you please the lord, you shall be given sanctuary in Zion.

127:4 And if you do not, then may you be eternally gnawed upon by the dogs of hell.

127:5 It is just like the other psalms.

128:1 Praise the lord, O you servants to God; praise the lord and give honour to his name.

128:2 Blessed be the name of the lord from this time forth and forever.

128:3 From the rising of the sun to the setting of the moon, you shall praise the word of God always.

128:4 For he is high above all nations; his glory dwells in heaven.

128:5 None are like the lord, who lives on high in Zion.

128:6 No man may do the works of the lord, who created life in the earth and heavens.

128:7 The lord is mighty; he grinds the poor into dust and pushes the needy into dunghills.

128:8 He blesses kings and princes with slaves to do the labour of his needs.

128:9 It is the lord who gives us the barren woman to do our housework and the fruitful wife to bare us sons.

128:10 Praise be to the lord.

129:1 When Israel went out of Egypt, the lands of strange language;

129:2 Judah was the sanctuary and Israel the dominion to God.

129:3 The sea saw us and fled in terror; the river Jordan drew back in fear.

129:4 Mountains skipped beside us and the hills bounded beside them.

129:5 He blessed the rocks to flow with water and trees spoke to us the wisdom of our lord.

129:6 The plants, oh blessed plants, gave us gifts of their spores and their seeds.

129:7 How we inhaled the gifts of the plants and saw the glory of our lord.

129:8 Skies filled with unicorns, dragons and flying chariots.

129:9 Images clear to the eyes, though the smoke from the pipes clouded our faces.

129:10 Come and witness the glory that is our lord.

129:11 Fill your lungs with the spirit of the herbs and be blessed in his holy presence.

130:1 Give praise and glory to the word of God, or he'll kill you.

130:2 And the heathens shall mock us and declare our lord weak.

130:3 They shall worship their idols of silver and gold; blasphemous images carved by the fingers of man.

130:4 They shall speak though they have no mouths. They shall see in their blindness.

130:5 Their ears shall be cut from them, though they shall hear our suffering; their noses shall be plucked from before them, though they shall smell the decay of our bodies.

130:6 So praise the lord of Israel, lest you wish the heathens to win against us.

130:7 And they shall slay us and leave us for dead.

130:8 Remember, in death we are useless; the dead cannot praise God.

130:9 So praise him in life and give glory to his name.

131:1 Oh how the lord takes his wrath on all, both righteous and wicked.

131:2 He created us with the same dust and inhaled with us the same breath; for this, he paints us with the same brush and condemns all for the acts of few.

131:3 Those that seek sanctuary from God end up crushed by the foundation of Zion and thrown in the pits of fire.

131:4 How the sorrows of death compel me, as I see my brethren burn beside the damned.

131:5 Prophets suffering beside liars; righteous beside the unholy.

131:6 Does the lord hold precious the sight of the death of his saints?

131:7 Does he laugh as we praise his name, surrounded by fire and despair?

131:8 A light, O lord; my soul craves a light.

131:9 Some clarity in my days of confusion.

131:10 Let me see the reason for this madness; allow me to understand why you cause the good to suffer beside the evil.

131:11 An insight into your divine plan; a reason for this chaos is all I crave.

131:12 Praise be to you, O lord and give unto me some hope and understanding.

131:13 Bless me with your knowledge and wisdom.

132:1 Praise the lord and give glory to his name.

132:2 Is it most detrimental to your health to do otherwise.

133:1 Give glory unto the lord most high; his mercy endures forever.

133:2 Let all of Israel praise the mercy of the lord.

133:3 Let the priests of the seed of Aaron give sacrifice to the mercy of the lord.

133:4 May all that fear our lord give glory unto his name and praise his words.

133:5 I did call upon the lord in times of distress; he placed me atop the highest mountains, away from the pool of evil.

133:6 I gazed down upon the wicked and spat upon their heads.

133:7 It is better to trust in the lord than place confidence in man.

133:8 The lord shall protect you always; princes shall send forth assassins while you sleep.

133:9 As nations surround my house, my king did nothing but offer my sons as slaves and daughters as whores.

133:10 Shekels for my seed.

133:11 But the lord destroyed those that seek my destruction.

133:12 A swarm of hornets surrounded the heathens and stung them with a fiery venom.

133:13 Their throats swelled as they yelled forgiveness unto God; they could not speak the precious words of their salvation.

133:14 The lord is my strength, my son and my salvation.

133:15 Blessed is the kiss of the lord, which removes the mortal robe from my back.

133:16 With the holy lips from God, I shall live forever in the palace of Zion.

133:17 So give thanks unto the lord, whose mercy endures forever.

134:1 When my soul was distressed, I cried out to the lord and he mocked me.

134:2 He cast my soul into the den of forked tongues and lying lips.

134:3 Their teeth sharp as arrows and throats burning with the coals of hell.

134:4 Woe is me, whose soul is gnawed upon by the wicked and the cursed.

134:5 My soul longed for peace, but our God craves war.

134:6 Pity to the man who desires peace; the lord hath no reason for them.

135:1 Blessed are the stupid, who follow the law of God without question.

135:2 Blessed are the foolish, who seek the lord though he hides always from them.

135:3 Blessed are the insane, who praise the lord and sing songs in his name.

135:4 Blessed are the dull, for they never sin.

135:5 Though my life is boring and meaningless, I feel no shame, for I walk in the path of the lord.

135:6 For I praise gloriously the name of God and his sanctuary of Zion.

135:7 When I was a young man, temptations of the flesh surrounded me.

135:8 Young males around me, flesh glowing in the sun.

135:9 Never did I partake of their lust, for I am a man of God; my desires shall never come to fruition.

135:10 My prayers replace my lust and my praises unto God fulfill my need for entertainment.

135:11 Fear keeps me from pursuing my darkest desires; terror leads me away from my needs for lust.

135:12 For when I plunge my loins into the end of a man, I know I plunge myself deep into the pits of hell.

135:13 The pits of wrath, filled with the fire of the anger of my lord.

135:14 Freedom is denied to me; freedom to choose I do not have.

135:15 I live in the prison of our lord and dwell in the prison blissful and blind.

135:16 Delights come from following the lord's statutes; happiness is when I sing psalms unto God.

135:17 Though flesh and bread sustain my body, my soul is alive with the spirit of the lord.

135:18 The spirit of the lord is a heavy spirit, which weighs me down.

135:19 Never shall I do as I wish, so long as I follow the ways of God.

135:20 As I stay upon the earth, bored and lonely, my comfort is the knowledge that I shall be rewarded with the sanctuary of Zion.

135:21 I shall feel the embrace of the lord and dwell beside him.

135:22 Curse be to the devil; damnation unto the wicked one.

135:23 The wretched vessel of evil which struck me with the lust for sodomy.

135:24 He comes when I take pleasures of the gifts of the lord; he arrives from the smoke of the herbs.

135:25 Strong do my loins become, and my eyes wander to the sight of strange men.

135:26 Tall men, large, with the strength of lions.

135:27 Covered in robes and jewelry of sinful vanity.

135:28 My tongue speaks to them, yet my mouth never opens.

135:29 Great wisdom does my mouth contain, to not open my lips for my tongue.

135:30 Rivers of tears flow from my eyes, as I lust deeply for the temptation of their flesh.

135:31 Give me the strength, O lord, to rid me of this curse.

135:32 Remove the mark of the devil from my soul.

135:33 I keep myself pure and though evil is marked on my soul, it shall not tarnish it.

135:34 That mark shall not spread and spoil my purity.

135:35 I am small and despise myself; my lust disgusts my very being.

135:36 I vomit on my loins and pray that I shall lust for my wives as I lust for my sons.

135:37 Damned are the men who share my lust and take part in their desires.

135:38 Never shall they know the love of our lord; never shall they know the sanctuary of Zion.

135:39 God hates them and shall consume them in fires that burn yet do not destroy.

135:40 Pits in the bowels of the earth, where they shall be raped by demons and bulls.

135:41 A rather odd punishment, considering their sins.

135:42 These are the men of goats, who run astray in the mountains, being guided by their selfish desires.

135:43 But I, I am as the sheep. The lord guides me with the flock, and never shall we go astray.

135:44 Blessed be the name of the lord.

136:1 I shall gaze my eyes upon the hills, where help comes.

136:2 My help comes from the lord, who created the heavens, the earth and all things.

136:3 He shall not have my foundation be moved; he who never slumbers.

136:4 Behold, the lord of Israel is awake always, and never sleeps.

136:5 The hands of the lord keep the sun and the moon in their place.

136:6 Never shall they fall upon mine head, so long as the lord is with me.

136:7 God protects me from evil and keeps my soul pure.

136:8 For all generations shall the lord protect us and never leave us in despair.

137:1 I was glad when I was invited to the house of the lord.

137:2 An invitation to the holy palace of Zion.

137:3 Then I entered and disgust grew in my heart.

137:4 The walls were made of the corpses of heathens.

137:5 A stench of death was thick in the air.

137:6 Rivers of blood flowed through the floors, and entered into a great pool where angels bathed.

137:7 Children hung from the ceilings by brass hooks, wailing in torment; their dung and organs dripped upon my head.

137:8 Even the table of God was made from the bones of the heathen; the plates and cutlery carved from the bones of the heathen.

137:9 It was truly a place of death, a place of the lords will.

137:10 Never shall I go there again

138:1 Unto the lord I lift up my eyes, O those that dwell in heavens.

138:2 I stare unto God as a slave stares at his master who holds the whip.

138:3 Fear grows in my heart as I wonder what plague and torment our lord shall bring upon us.

138:4 I beg for mercy, but the lord hearkens not my words; we are not worthy of mercy.

138:5 How the lord hates us for the blemish in our souls.

139:1 If it were not for the lord besides us, the peoples of Israel would be doomed.

139:2 Our yoke would be tight and the whips of Pharaoh would beat our backs.

139:3 Now the lord has freed us and delivered us into the lands of the covenant.

139:4 Where we dwell in luxury and give glory to God.

139:5 Why then do the heathens slay us. Why does God allow the wicked to conquer us and carry off our sons and daughters?

139:6 We are as a bird being entangled in the coils of snakes.

139:7 Beautiful and pure and choked by the wicked.

139:8 Help us, O lord and deliver us from evil.

139:9 Free us from these heathens that come to reclaim their lands.

140:1 They that trust in the lord are the foundation of the temple of Zion.

140:2 Crushed under the burden of the house of the lord.

140:3 Mountains of the righteous pile in heavens and the lord lays them beneath his palace.

140:4 Is is true, the lord be with us forever; he walks atop us and crushes us with his feet.

140:5 Such is the fate of the righteous; such is the end of the holy.

141:1 I dream of the day that I shall enter Zion.

141:2 Drinking from the flowing rivers of fresh and sweet wine.

141:3 Feasting on holy breads and the flesh of angels.

141:4 Riding on the backs of unicorns and running with the lions on the plains.

141:5 Lord, take me there now and rid me of my mortal body.

141:6 Allow me to rise to Zion, so that my dreams come true.

142:1 The work of labour men is useless; it the lord who builds the greatest cities and not man.

142:2 Guards and watchmen are of little need; the lord cares for the city, thus the watchmen walk in vain.

142:3 How dare you go forth and work; the lord created the earth in six days and you think you can improve it?

142:4 Our lord loathes those that work and labour, for they wish to better the creations of God.

142:5 Selfish and vain are these people; let the lord bless you with his works, so you need not to.

142:6 Those loved by the lord must sleep in their chambers; God shall provide them all that they need.

142:7 Lo, spend your days in lust and spread your seed plenty.

142:8 Children are the gifts of God, given to you by the womb of the filthy.

142:9 As many arrows make a man strong, so do his children.

142:10 Happy is the man whose quiver be full of children, for he is truly blessed by the lord.

143:1 Blessed are they that fear the lord and walk in the path laid out by the holy.

143:2 They shall eat out of the labour of the hands of God; happy they shall be.

143:3 Their wives shall be as fruitful as the vines and their children number greater than the grapes of the vineyards.

143:4 Behold, the blessing of men who fear the lord.

143:5 On death they shall arise to Zion and gaze down upon the city of Jerusalem.

143:6 Watching the children of their children's children live in peace in Israel.

144:1 Many times have they afflicted me in my youth; wicked men scarring my body with sin.

144:2 Many times have they afflicted me in age, yet they never prevail against me.

144:3 They scraped their knives along my back and bit me with fangs full of venom.

144:4 Speaking to me words of blasphemy; words they call logic, science and truth.

144:5 How the lord hates these men and shall cast these men away from the gates of Zion.

144:6 Their souls shall be as grass atop the houses; they shall wither and die from the sun.

144:7 May their seed fall to the dust and poison the crops of their nation.

144:8 The lord is righteous and merciful, despite the words these men say to the contrary.

144:9 Our lord shall guide us forever and bless us eternally.

144:10 The great nation of Israel shall rule the lands under the blessings of the one true God.

144:11 And how these wicked men shall appear as fools and tremble before our sight.

145:1 Out of the pits of despair do I cry to you, O lord.

145:2 Hear my voice; let your ears be attentive to the words which flow from my lips.

145:3 Countless times have I begged of you to remove me from this filth.

145:4 I am sick and poor, surrounded by the wicked and the damned.

145:5 Still, I praise your name and give glory to your name.

145:6 With my few earnings, I offer you sacrifice and burn the beast upon the altar.

145:7 And have you blessed me and rid me of poverty and illness?

145:8 Have you given me the warm embrace I seek?

145:9 You do not; you instead push me deeper into the pit.

145:10 So I say to you, fuck off, O lord.

145:11 May the horns of the devil pierce your holy ass.

145:12 Send me to the pits of hell and let me burn for my words.

145:13 For you have made it clear that following your laws, statutes and commandments shall bring me nothing.

145:14 Stupid holy fuck.

146:1 How I laughed in my youth and enjoyed the wonders and creations of our lord.

146:2 The blessings of God seemed countless; I truly believed him all powerful and caring.

146:3 Now I am old and followed the path of righteousness. My children followed the same path as I.

146:4 Heathens from Babylon conquered our lands and took our wealth.

146:5 My daughters work in the brothels of strange lands and have their loins thrust by the loins of uncircumcised beasts.

146:6 My sons died by the swords of these strangers, or now toil in their fields under a heavy yoke.

146:7 And I rot by the side and watch as the mercies of our lord are now gone.

146:8 How the divine abandoned us and left us to die.

146:9 The laughter of my youth has changed now to tears.

147:1 Lord, remember David your servant and all that he's done.

147:2 How he swore to the lord to uphold your virtues and laws.

147:3 Slaying the Philistine bastards and killing the beast Goliath.

147:4 The lands conquered and the blood flowing from his blade pleased you, O lord.

147:5 Now remember, O lord, the lust David took in.

147:6 His pleasure in men is known throughout Israel and yet they call this king a man of God.

147:7 Why then, do you invite this faggot into your tabernacle?

147:8 How does David enter into the sanctuary of Zion, while other men of sinful flesh burn in the pits of your wrath?

147:9 Does the lord enjoy the flesh of David and take part in wretched lust?

147:10 To hell with you, O lord; dive hypocrite of heaven.

148:1 Behold, how good it is for brethren to dwell together in unity.

148:2 Pouring ointment atop each other's heads and letting the oil flow down their beards and underneath the skirts of their garments.

148:3 How it gives us pleasure greater than that of the lord.

149:1 Behold, all you servants and bless the lord through the darkness of the night.

149:2 Lift your hands to the heaven and praise he who protects us from the demons of the night.

149:3 Praise be to the creator of heaven and earth. Praise be to the one who leads us to Zion.

150:1 Praise be to the lord of Israel, who stands above all other gods.

150:2 He do as he pleases in the heavens, the earth and the seas.

150:3 It is him who causes the vapours to ascend, the lightning to strike and the winds to blow.

150:4 Who smote all first-borns in the lands of Egypt, both man and beast. The lord did.

150:5 Who smote great nations and slew mighty kings. The lord did.

150:6 Sihon king of the Amorites, Og king of Bashaan and all the kingdoms of Canaan fell at the hands of God.

150:7 Their lands were then given to us men of Israel, as an inheritance promised in the covenant of Abraham.

150:8 The idols of heathens are carved from silver and gold, but our lord be true.

150:9 These idols have mouths, but speak not; they have eyes, but see nothing.

150:10 They have ears, but hear nothing; neither is their breath in their mouth.

150:11 Those that worship them are fools who bow down unto carvings from stone.

150:12 But we bow down in the temple, in fear of our lord in Zion. Blessings be to the lord.

151:1 O give thee thanks unto the lord, for he is good; his mercy endureth forever.

151:2 Give thanks unto the God of gods, for his mercy endures forever.

151:3 Praise be to the lord of lords, for his mercy endures forever.

151:4 To him who does great wonders, for his mercy endures forever.

151:5 To him that have the wisdom of the heavens, for his mercy endures forever.

151:6 To him who stretched the lands above the waters, for his mercy endures forever.

151:7 To he who puts the sun in the sky, for his mercy endures forever.

151:8 To he who placed the moon above us, for his mercy endures forever.

151:9 To him who smote all the first-born of Egypt, for his mercy endures forever.

151:10 To he who led us away from Egypt, for his mercy endures forever.

151:11 To he who drowned Pharaoh and his armies in the Red Sea, for his mercy endures forever.

151:12 To he who caused us to wander in the desert for forty years, for his mercy endures forever.

151:13 To the one who demands sacrifice of beast, flock and heathen virgin, for his mercy endures forever.

151:14 To the lord who struck us with the venom of fiery serpents, for his mercy endures forever.

151:15 To the God who cursed us with plagues, for his mercy endurets forever.

151:16 To he who comes down in fire and darkness, for his mercy endureth forever.

151:17 To him who demands we create him an ark, and all the bling with it, for his mercy endures forever.

151:18 To him who ordered genocide of heathens, for his mercy endures forever.

151:19 To him who smote great nations, for his mercy endures forever.

151:20 To him who slew powerful kings, for his mercy endures forever.

151:21 To him who gave us the lands of our inheritance, for his mercy endures forever.

151:22 To him who took away those lands from us, for his mercy endures forever.

151:23 To him who gave us our babies to eat, for his mercy endures forever.

151:24 To him who sold our daughters to the brothels, for his mercy endures forever.

151:25 To him who sold our sons to the brothels, for his mercy endures forever.

151:26 To him who left us in pestilence, for his mercy endures forever.

151:27 To the holiest who abandoned us and left us to die, for his mercy endures forever.

152:1 By the rivers of Babylon we came and wept by the shores in remembrance of Zion.

152:2 We hanged our harps in the branches of the trees along the banks.

152:3 How shall we sing a song unto God, in a strange land, surrounded by heathens?

152:4 Yet if we don't, we shall forget our lord of Jerusalem; we shall forget the sanctuary of Zion.

152:5 My children's children are of the seed of beasts; the loins of heathens planted the seed in my daughters.

152:6 So I took my grandchildren and smashed them against the rocks.

152:7 I took the demons and crushed them to the stones.

152:8 Happy I felt, as I knew the lord was pleased.

152:9 Happy and blessed shall those, who take the little ones and dash them against the rocks.

153:1 I will praise you with all my heart; in the sight of the gods I shall praise the lord of Israel.

153:2 I shall kneel in the holy temple and praise your name for your mercy and words of wonder: for you have magnified the word above all.

153:3 On the days I have cried, you denied me strength, so that I must gather my own.

153:4 Blessed are those who do for themselves and not annoy the lord with their pettiness and requests.

153:5 All the kings of the earth shall bow to you after they hear my words.

153:6 Yea, they shall sing psalms unto the lord, and give you offerings and sacrifice.

153:7 Though the lord be holy, he has no respect for the lowly; he has no respect for men.

153:8 When I walk in the clouds of trouble, I am on my own; the lord protects me now.

153:9 It is I who must stretch out my hands and slay the wicked with my blade; the lord shall not do this for me.

153:10 Blessed be to the lord, who coddles me not as the mother to her infant.

154:1 O lord, you have searched me and know me.

154:2 You knows my down sitting and my uprising; you know what I shall do before it is done.

154:3 Such knowledge is wonderful to me; to be able to know all and see all is truly a gift for only the most righteous.

154:4 Whither shall my spirit go after death. The lord knows where.

154:5 If I ascend into Zion, the lord shall be there; if I fall into the pits of hell, the lord shall be there.

154:6 If I take the wings of the eagle and dwell in the uttermost parts of the sea;

154:7 The lord shall know and lead me there.

154:8 Though darkness surrounds me and the predators of the night are round about me;

154:9 You dwell in light and see the beasts that circle me.

154:10 You have possessed my reins and clutched me in my mother's womb.

154:11 So I shall praise you in fear and wonder; I shall give glory to your name all my days.

154:12 How great are you, O lord and how I bow in fear to you.

154:13 Even my thoughts are known to God; thoughts so numerous I cannot even count them.

154:14 They number greater than the sands and the stars of the night.

154:15 I ask of you now, O lord, slay the wicked. Let the seas turn red with their blood.

154:16 For they speak against you wickedly and seek forth science and logic.

154:17 How I hate them, O lord, though I know my hatred is not as strong as yours.

154:18 You hate them with a perfect hatred, O lord and shall curse them with perfect pain.

154:19 Search me, O lord and know my heart is true.

154:20 And know that if you witness any wicked within me, then guide me to the path of the everlasting, so that I may become pure.

155:1 Deliver me lord from the evil man; protect me from the violent man.

155:2 For I was a soldier of Israel, who mercifully killed the heathens by your word.

155:3 Now they loathe me and wish me dead; these fools.

155:4 Mischief grows within their hearts and they gather together for war.

155:5 They have forked tongues like a snake, fangs like the viper and venom of the adder.

155:6 Keep me, O lord, from the man of the wicked; preserve me from the demented; men who wish ill things upon me.

155:7 The proud tempt me with snares of sin and set nets in the pools of lust for my soul.

155:8 I praise to you, O lord, to give me your sanctuary and strength.

155:9 Grant not the desires of the wicked; further not their fuel of evil.

155:10 Let burning coals fall upon them and burn into their skulls until their death.

155:11 Hunt all the wicked men down and slay them to the four corners of the earth.

155:12 Surely the righteous shall dwell in Zion, as the wicked roast beneath our feet

156:1 Lord, I cry unto you; make haste and help me; hurry to offer me aid.

156:2 Allow my words to be as incense, which burn and creates a pleasing aroma unto you.

156:3 For thoughts of blasphemy creep in my mind and poison my very soul.

156:4 Keep a watch on my tongue, O lord; sew my lips shut with thread.

156:5 Bless me to keep from saying the wicked thing and spreading venom to my kin.

156:6 Cleanse my heart with purity; remove the stains of evil which has blemished my very heart.

156:7 Let the wicked fall before me, as I escape from their snares.

157:1 I cried unto the lord with my voice; with my voice, I yelled unto God.

157:2 I poured out my complaint into his ears and showed him my troubles and torments.

157:3 How the spirit of the wicked overwhelms me and imprisons my very soul.

157:4 I cried unto the lord to give me refuge in Zion and protect me from these strange men.

157:5 The lord called me a whiny little bitch and told me to take care of my own problems.

157:6 Thus the wicked surround me and tempt me with their evil all my days.

157:7 And the lord does nothing to stop them.

158:1 Hear my prayer, O lord, give ear to my supplications: in my faithfulness answer me and give me the wisdom of the righteous.

158:2 Enter me not into judgment for the sins of my servants; I bought them out from heathen lands.

158:3 In your sight, no man living can be justified; in the eyes of God all men must go to hell.

158:4 The enemy hath persecuted my soul; he has beat me to the very ground; he makes me dwell in the caves of darkness, where dead men lay.

158:5 My spirit is overwhelmed with terror and my heart is desolate.

158:6 I remember the days of old, when Israel was a prosperous nation; I think of those days and pray to you to return them.

158:7 Why did you abandon us, O lord. Why did the faithful of your people get cast out with the wicked?

158:8 Deliver me to Zion, O lord and let me live my days in your holy sanctuary.

158:9 Let me dwell down upon the earth and strike my enemies with a curse.

159:1 Blessed be the lord, who teaches my hands to fight and my fingers to kill.

159:2 The lord is my tower, my blade, my shield, my fortress and my deliverer; through him I subdue and slaughter the people beneath me.

158:3 What is man, who marvels not in the wonders of God. What mortal dare not acknowledge that which is the lord?

159:4 These are vain men and their days are cast in shadow.

159:5 By the heavens, O lord, come down. Touch the mountains so they shall erupt in fire.

159:6 Cast forth lightning from the sky and strike the people who you loathe; destroy them with your hate.

159:7 Drown their children in the pools of everlasting fire, so that they may not learn the sins of their fathers.

159:8 I shall praise you, O lord: I shall raise a harp of many strings and give praises unto you.

159:9 For it is the lord who gives salvation to the kings: who delivered David from the wicked hands of Saul.

159:10 Rid me of these strange men, who speak words of vanity, temptation, and science.

159:11 Science is blasphemy; it is the witchcraft to explain the works of God.

159:12 Men cannot understand that which is unexplainable. Such is the glory of God.

159:13 Thus slay them, O lord; let their flocks feast upon their hairs.

160:1 I will extol you, O God and bless you forever and ever.

160:2 Every day I shall give praise and glory to your name.

160:3 Great is the lord, who resides in the palace of Zion.

160:4 Men shall declare the terrible acts of the lord and I shall declare them great.

160:5 So that all mankind shall forget the horrors of the lord and remember him only as greatness.

160:6 The lord is gracious, full of compassion, slow to anger and is of great mercy.

160:7 He is good and offers tender mercies to all things of the earth.

160:8 Thus that when things die of starvation, disease and predation, it is their own doing; they took not of the blessings of the lord.

160:9 Praise all the works of the lord of wonders; have saints bless them all.

160:10 Speak of the glory of his kingdom and of his mighty power.

160:11 Make known to your sons the mighty acts of God, so they shall grow to fear and worship him.

160:12 Don't bother teaching your daughters; the lord has no need for women.

160:13 The eyes of all wait upon the lord, who give them their meat in due season.

160:14 With our hands open, he gives us everything our heart desires.

160:15 So if your life be short, cruel and painful, offer your open hand to God; he shall give you your wants and needs.

160:16 He will fulfill the desire of those that fear him and hear their cries in times of torment.

160:17 God shall preserve those who love him and cast out the wicked which he hates.

160:18 Blessed be the name of the lord and sing praises unto him for all times.

161:1 Praise be to the lord God, praise be to my very soul.

161:2 While I live I shall sing praises unto the lord; I shall do nothing but sing glories to our God.

161:3 Put not your faith in kings or princes, but put your faith in the lord.

161:4 Happy are they who sing praises to God, for they delight in the bliss of lunacy.

161:5 So I sing praises unto Zion with all my breath.

161:6 I sleep not, I eat not, nor do I drink; I do nothing but praise the lord on high.

161:7 He opens the eyes of the blind, so that they may see the truth.

161:8 He opens the mouths of the mute, so they may spread his word.

161:9 He opens the ears of the deaf, so they may listen to his word.

161:10 Blessed be to God on high; blessed be to Zion.

161:11 All my days I do nothing but sing glories and praises to God.

161:12 The people around me loathe me and wish me to stop; wicked people they be.

161:13 They yell at me with cruelties and throw stones at my head; never shall I stop. Always shall I sing praises to the lord.

161:14 Until my dying breath I shall sing praises to the lord.

162:1 Go forth and sing praises to the lord, lest you anger him and kindle his wrath.

162:2 The lord did build up Jerusalem and made Israel a great nation.

162:3 He heals the broken heart and mends the wounds of our bones.

162:4 He knows the numbers of stars in the sky and knows them all by name.

162:5 Great is the lord of all lords; his power is infinite.

162:6 The lord casts out the wicked from our lands and burns the meek in fire.

162:7 Sing unto the lord with thanksgiving; sing praises of the lord with your harps.

162:8 For he covers the heavens with clouds and prepares rain for our crops.

162:9 Heathens that we kill the lord gives to the beasts and even the young ravens that cry feast upon the flesh of our enemies.

162:10 God needs not the strength of horses, nor the pleasures of a woman's loins.

162:11 The lord takes pleasure in those that fear him, in those that hope to be shown his mercy.

162:12 Praise the lord of Jerusalem. Praise he who dwells in Zion.

162:13 He has strengthened the bars of our cities; he has blessed our children with strength.

162:14 He kills those who disrupt peace in our borders; he fills our vines with fruits and our fields with grain.

162:15 He gives us wool to cover the lands like snow; he scatters the ashes of the heathens into the waters.

162:16 He gave unto Jacob a covenant and his covenant be true.

162:17 So praise be to the lord, who has given us our inheritance.

163:1 All things shall go forth and sing praises to the lord.

163:2 The men, women and children shall sing praises to the lord.

163:3 The angels of heaven above shall sing praises to the lord.

163:4 The sun, moon and stars shall sing praises to the lord.

163:5 The dragons and unicorns shall sing praises to the lord.

163:6 The devil and his minions shall sing praises to the lord.

163:7 The wicked and evil heathens shall sing praises to the lord.

163:8 The blades of grass shall sing praises to the lord.

163:9 The fowl, the flocks, the beasts and the creatures of the sea shall sing praises to the lord.

163:10 The fire, hail, rain and snow shall sing praises to the lord.

163:11 The mountains, hills and valleys shall sing praises to the lord.

163:12 The lice, gnat, wasp, and locust shall sing praises to the lord.

163:13 Sane men, mad men, old men and children shall sing praises to the lord.

163:14 Let all things on earth and beyond sing praises to the lord.

164:1 Sing unto the lord a new song and praise his name in the holy congregation.

164:2 Let Israel rejoice in their saviour; let them celebrate the one who built Zion.

164:3 Let them praise God in dance, song and feasts; let them sing praises with the timbrel and the harp.

164:4 For the lord takes pleasure in his people; we are here to amuse our lord almighty.

164:5 Let the saints be joyful in glory; let them scream the name of God as they lie with their whores and wives.

164:6 Let all Israel sing praises with their mouths and hold a sword in their hand.

164:7 We shall slaughter the heathens and spill their blood to the dust as we sing praises to the almighty lord.

164:8 We shall bind their kings with chains and enslave their princes.

164:9 And we shall do this while praising the lord.

165:1 Praise the lord in his sanctuary; praise the lord in the firmament of his power.

165:2 Praise him for his mighty acts, his merciful blessings and his horrible curses.

165:3 Praise him with the sound of the trumpet, the sound of the psaltery and the sound of the harp.

165:4 Praise him with timbrel, dance and lustful intoxication.

165:5 Praise him with the cymbals, the drums and the voice.

166:1 Fuck God.

166:2 What good has he done to those who praise him?

ROVERBS

1:1 The proverbs of Solomon, son of David, king of Israel;

1:2 Words of his wisdom, his instructions and his understand are written on these pages.

1:3 So you know these pages shall contain more shit than freshly used toilet paper.

1:4 They are the words that the faithful dedicate themselves to and follow deeply in their hearts.

1:5 Believing the man who wrote them to be one of the wisest men on earth.

1:6 Such fools they are.

1:7 Now, let us continue with the proverbs of Solomon.

1:8 Third king of Israel and husband to many wives.

2:1 A wise man will hear the words of all those around them and understand what they say; a man of understanding shall take part in wise counsels.

2:2 Know this, the fear of the lord is the beginning of knowledge: those that fear not God are stupid.

2:3 Sons, listen to the words of your father and obey the rules of your mother.

2:4 For they are the ones who blessed you into this world and they can quickly curse you away from it.

2:5 If sinners tempt you, tell them to fuck off and go away.

2:6 If they do not leave, then walk away from their words.

2:7 And if they follow you still and refuse to give you peace, kill them.

2:8 Swallow them alive and whole, as the snake swallows the rat.

2:9 Send them into the pits of hell, where they shall feel no comfort; only pain and torment will they know for their days.

2:10 Take all that which is precious to them; loot their houses of all spoils.

2:11 Put into your purse their money, their jewels, their women, their sons;

2:12 Their flocks, their beasts, their crops and their slaves.

2:13 Stain the floor of their house with the blood of the sinner, so that all shall know a fool once dwelt there.

2:14 And they shall know who dwelt in that house was greedy and sought not the lord.

2:15 Wisdom cries throughout; she shouts in the streets.

2:16 She cries in the markets, she cries in the gates, she cries in the city and she says,

2:17 "How long will men live in their simplicity. How long will the blasphemous speak and the fools seek out the false knowledge of science?

2:18 Turn to me and I shall show you true knowledge; your spirit shall fill with me as I make my words known to you.

2:19 I have called and you refused and mocked me; I offer my hand and you take not what I offer.

2:20 You seek not the counsel nor the words of the lord.

2:21 Curse be to the lot of you. I shall laugh at your afflictions and mock you when fear overcomes your very soul.

2:22 When you be left desolate, your house turned to rubble at the whirlwinds of destruction; when distress and anguish overcome you,

2:23 Then you shall call to me, but I will not answer. When you need me most, I shall hide from your presence and piss on your head.

2:24 For you cared not for my words, nor sought not my knowledge.

2:25 Ye sought not my counsel and spoke bitter words of logic and science.

2:26 Thus, you shall eat of the flesh of bats and your bowels shall be filled with a ferment most foul.

2:27 All shall be destroyed before me; none shall be spared.

2:28 Not a soul shall know the sanctuary that is Zion."

3:1 My son, if you will listen to my words and keep safely in your heart the commandments of God;

3:2 So that your ears hear the words of wisdom and your heart shall understand that which is the lord.

3:3 Yea, if you cry out for knowledge and praise loudly to seek forth understanding.

. 3:4 If you seek wisdom like silver and wish for knowledge as though it a hidden treasure.

3:5 Then you shall fear the lord greatly and find the knowledge of God.

3:6 For the lord gives wisdom to those who hear; out of his mouth comes knowledge and understanding.

3:7 He lays the foundation of wisdom to the righteous, so that the righteous walk in knowledge and truth.

3:8 He keeps the paths of judgment and preserves the way of the holy.

3:9 Follow his path and you shall understand all that is knowledge, wisdom, truth and understanding.

3:10 Your heart and soul shall be brimming with all that is good.

3:11 Discretion shall keep you from sin; understanding shall let you know why these sinners must die at your blade.

3:12 Walk not in the path of the evil man, who speaks blasphemous things.

3:13 Men who walk away from the light and get lost in the darkness.

3:14 Who delight in the acts of evil and tolerate sin in their presence.

3:15 Men who hold life precious and refuse to kill others for their wickedness.

3:16 Wickedness like working on the sabbath, worship false gods, eating pork, sleeping with a man as though they were a woman,

3:17 Practicing magic, witchcraft and necromancy, who have tattoos on their skin, who wears clothing woven from two different linens.

3:18 Men who deserve to die for disregarding the laws of the lord.

3:19 You shall be delivered from these strange men, but it is the women you shall fear the most.

3:20 For a woman shall entice you to evil with her lust; her body is her weapon that she uses since birth.

3:21 Avoid her lustful stare and keep away from the comfort of her embrace.

3:22 The whores of the devil have led many a righteous man into hell; keep your distance from them and kill all those which you see.

4:1 My son, do not forget my law and keep within your heart the commandments.

4:2 For length of days, long life and peace shall be blessed to you.

4:3 Let not mercy and truth forsake you, lest they be bound around your neck and choke you as a noose.

4:4 Find favour in the good and understanding that is God; disregard the needs of men.

4:5 Trust in the lord with all your heart and learn not to understand things.

4:6 Do not try to seek out reason, just accept that which God tells you.

4:7 Acknowledge him and walk in his path.

4:8 Have your eyes fixed on the lord and look not towards evil.

4:9 It shall keep your navel clean and keep the marrow in your bones fresh.

4:10 Honour the lord and give him his tithings.

4:11 A tenth of your first fruits and your wealth shall buy you the blessings of God.

4:12 Then your barns shall be full of grain and your mouth filled with strongest wine.

4:13 My son, despise not the curses which the lord brings upon you; for as the father must punish his son, so must the lord do to you.

4:14 Take comfort that when your family dies, your body plagued with disease and you are raped by the strong men of heathens, you deserved it for disobeying the lord.

4:15 Happy is the man who finds wisdom in not seeking understanding, for he is truly blessed.

4:16 For the value of wisdom is greater than that of silver and gold.

4:17 Wisdom is more precious than the rubies and all fine stones.

4:18 Wisdom holds in her right hand long life and in her left riches and honour.

4:19 Her ways are pleasant and bring peace to all.

4:20 The laws of wisdom state that when you slay all who refuse to believe in what you believe, then those that are left shall agree with you and you shall all be in peace.

4:21 Take confidence in the lord, for the lord is good and merciful.

4:22 Remember, the lord shall protect those he deems worthy.

4:23 Withhold not good from your neighbour; it is in your powers to spread good to the righteous, so use that power.

4:24 Withhold not evil from the heathen; slay them with all the

hatred of God.

4:25 If your neighbour needs help, help them. Then shall the kindness be remembered and passed back to you.

4:26 If your neighbour is a heathen who needs help, help them end their life. Then the lord shall bless you with a worthy neighbour.

4:27 Devise not against your neighbour, nor plan evil cause against him.

4:28 Do plan to kill your neighbour as he sleeps, if your neighbour be a heathen.

4:29 Fight not with your people, unless you have good cause to fight.

4:30 Fight not with the heathen; kill him as quickly as you can.

4:31 Know that the curse of the lord dwells within the house of evil: but he blesses the habitation of the righteous.

4:32 He shall scorn the scorners and give grace to the holy.

4:33 Wise men shall inherit the earth, as the wicked feel great shame in worshipping idols.

5:1 Hear ye, O children, the instructions of your father and seek forth knowledge.

5:2 For I give you good doctrine; forsake not my laws.

5:3 I am my father's son and was beloved by my mother.

5:4 They taught me to keep the laws of the lord and hearken his statutes and commandments.

5:5 To obtain wisdom is the path of the righteous and to understand that God controls all.

5:6 Wisdom is the principal thing; you must obtain it above all others.

5:7 Food, water, shelter, family and love must not distract you from your quest for wisdom.

5:8 If hunger tempts you, remove your stomach. If you grow thirsty, cut out your tongue.

5:9 When your house falls apart, tear it down. If your children distract you, slay them.

5:10 None shall keep you from your path to wisdom.

5:11 For wisdom shall promote you and give thee great honour and wealth.

5:12 Wisdom shall give you an ornament of grace; a crown of glory shall be placed atop your head.

5:13 Hear me, my sons and the years of your life shall be plentiful.

5:14 I have taught thee the ways of wisdom; I have shown you the righteous path.

5:15 When you go, walk straight and proud. When you run, do not stumble, lest you fall into the ditch.

5:16 Follow the instructions of the lord and you shall live eternal.

5:17 Traverse not in the path of the wicked; do not follow in the footsteps of evil men.

5:18 These are the men who feast on the marrow of virgins and drink of the blood of babies.

5:19 They care not of anyone but themselves; they are selfish and arrogant fools.

5:20 Know that the path of God is the path of shining light, that grows brighter and brighter until the perfect day comes.

5:21 The way of the wicked is shrouded in darkness; they know not why they stumble.

5:22 So speak praise of the lord, for praise of the lord is truth.

5:23 Keep your eyes on wisdom and glance not at the temptations of evil.

5:24 Walk the path set before you; keep your footing on the true road.

5:25 Fall not in the ditches of evil that be to the right and left of you.

6:1 My son, bow to me and listen to my words.

6:2 That you may regard discretion and that your soul seeks out knowledge.

6:3 For the body of strange women is as sweet as honey and her loins smoother than oil.

6:4 But her embrace is as bitter as wormwood; she shall give you pain greater than the sword.

6:5 Her feet go down in death; her feet walk in the very depths of hell.

6:6 Know that she shall curse you away from the path of God and shall condemn you to a life of lust and evil.

6:7 When you see her come, slay her with the sword; when you see her house, burn it.

6:8 Do this in glory to the lord; slay the wicked in his honour.

6:9 Lest strangers dwell in your house and steal your wealth from you.

6:10 When you take of her lust, know that you shall mourn afterwards; you shall weep after her embrace.

6:11 Tears of shame shall run down your face and you will wish to hide your filth from God.

6:12 But the lord sees all and knows the pile of dung you did empty your seed in.

6:13 And the lord shall hate you and curse your loins with flaming warts.

6:14 Listen to me and do as I say, my children.

6:15 Drink from the waters of your own well and fill your vessels with these waters.

6:16 Let your fountains spread across your lands and rivers flow through your streets.

6:17 Keep them for your own and do not let the strangers drink from these waters.

6:18 Keep your fountains blessed and rejoice in the youth of your wives.

6:19 Let them be as loving as the gentle fawn; let their breasts arouse you at all times; let their loins give you pleasure throughout your days.

6:20 Why let the loins of a stranger tempt you the path of damnation, when the loins of your wives keep you on the holy path?

6:21 Those that embrace their women shall not be led astray by the whores of Satan.

6:22 So take pleasure in your wives and lie in the beds of your concubines; let their nakedness surround you in your private chambers.

7:1 My son, know that if you seek forth a friend and take the company of a stranger,

7:2 You shall be snared by his words and thrust into evil by the tools of his tongue.

7:3 Do this now, my son. Kill the stranger you call friend, then go and humble yourself in the eyes of the lord.

7:4 Sleep not in your bed; let not your eyelids rest until the lord has forgiven you.

7:5 Deliver yourself from the wicked like the buck from the hunter, or the bird from the fowler.

7:6 Be like the ant and take wisdom from their humility.

7:7 The ant has but one ruler and never questions their command.

7:8 They provide meat in the summer and gather food in the harvest for winter.

7:9 Know that the stranger you call friend shall lead you down the path of the slug.

7:10 Where you shall sleep and ignore the sights and the sounds of wisdom.

7:11 Know that the ant is rich, but the slug lives in slime and poverty.

7:12 A naughty person, a wicked man, speaks with a difficult tongue.

7:13 They speak with their feet, wink with their eyes and teach with their fingers.

7:14 It is their body, not their words, that speak their true intentions.

7:15 Such a language is a language of deceit and deceit is for the wicked.

7:16 The lord shall bring them swiftly into terror; suddenly they shall be broken without remedy.

7:17 These are five of the many things the lord hates;

7:18 A man proud and independent, who holds a lying tongue and refuses to spill blood.

7:19 A heart that seeks out logic instead of wisdom and feet which walk away from God.

7:20 A false witness that speaks lies and women who gossip among the crowd.

7:21 My son, keep the commandments of your father and obey the laws of your mother.

7:22 Bind them tightly to your heart and wear them around the neck.

7:23 For the commandments are a beacon and the laws a light for you.

7:24 Keep away from strange women, whose tongue speak flattery and deceit.

7:25 Let not her lust poison your heart, nor her form be pleasing to your eyes.

7:26 They are whores who would fuck a man for a loaf of bread; they hunt the souls of righteous men.

7:27 Know that if you embrace her, wickedness shall stain your very soul.

7:28 For can a man take fire in his bosom and not have his clothes burned. Can one walk on flames without burning his feet?

7:29 So go not into the caverns of a strange woman; whosoever touches her shall be guilty in the eyes of God.

7:30 Thieves are to be despised, even if they steal to feed the hungry children and the poor.

7:31 When these men are caught, they must give back sevenfold of what they took; they shall give the wealth of their entire house for their crimes of thievery.

7:32 Those that sleep with the wives of their neighbours lack understanding; they destroy their very souls.

7:33 The man shall be wounded by the whip and the woman he lies with shall burn on the altar.

7:34 Jealousy is a poison which inflicts many men; a poison which inflicts them with rage and anger.

7:35 Let them be content with their blessings of the lord, or let them die by the blade.

8:1 My son, keep my words and lay my commandments as a foundation.

8:2 Keep my commandments and live; disregard them and I shall kill you by my blade.

8:3 Write my laws upon your fingers; carve them in the table of your heart.

8:4 Know that wisdom is your sister and understanding your

kinswoman.

8:5 They shall keep you away from strange women, who uses words of flattery as their means of seduction.

8:6 I sat in my house and looked through the window

8:7 I gazed upon the simple men, young and foolish, who took pleasure in the embrace of heathen whores.

8:8 How they exchange money at the street corners and exit the houses of filth with an empty purse.

8:9 They go in the shadows of night, yet the lord sees them as though they go at noon.

8:10 Behold, they visit a woman with the attire of a cheap harlot, whose heart is bitter with the fermenting seed of many men.

8:11 They are loud and stubborn cunts, whose feet are placed in the coals of hell.

8:12 They lie in the streets, at their corners and tempt the weak into their houses.

8:13 So they catch the weak with a kiss and with a stone face tempt them with words of flattery and lust.

8:14 They offer their loins to you, for a payment of your wealth.

8:15 They lead you to a bed full of fine silks and tapestries carved with the symbols of the lords of Egypt and Babylon.

8:16 Their beds reek with the stench of perfume, cinnamon, aloes and myrrh.

8:17 A stench which cannot hide the filth of what takes place on that bed.

8:18 Stained with the seeds of many men.

8:19 She says, "Come and let us take our fill of love until the morning; let us take comfort in our lustful embrace."

8:20 And the fools lie in her bed, and empty their purse atop her breasts and kiss them.

8:21 With her fair speech and subtle flesh, she leads the man into her chambers.

8:22 Like the ox who is led to the slaughter, or the lamb to the altar.

8:23 He becomes ensnared by her embrace and is trapped like the bird to the snare; he finds the woman bitter, yet comes back always for more.

8:24 Hearken now before me, my children and attend to the words of my mouth.

8:25 Let not temptation lead you to the ways of the whore.

8:26 For she has slain many wounded and crippled the strongest of men.

8:27 Her house leads thee directly to the depths of hell.

9:1 Wisdom does not cry. Wisdom understands the foolishness for weeping.

9:2 Wisdom stands up in the high places, where the roads pass.

9:3 She yells at the gates, at the entry of the city, at the coming of the doors.

9:4 She screams so that those may find her, but many are deaf to her voice.

9:5 Men seek out wealth, but wisdom is richer than those of rubies; all things men desire pale in comparison to wisdom.

9:6 To have wisdom is to fear the lord; to fear the lord is to hate evil, pride and arrogance.

9:7 The lord shall offer wisdom, courage and strength to those who seek it.

9:8 Whether noble king or humble shepherd, the lord shall offer them all these blessed gifts.

9:9 For the lord loves all that love him; those that seek him early shall find him.

9:10 Unless he is hiding, in which case you're fucked.

9:11 Riches and honour are with the lord; great riches and righteousness.

9:12 His fruits are better than fine gold and purest of silver.

9:13 He gives you judgment among all things.

9:14 The lord decides if you ascend to the paradise of Zion, or burn in the depths of hell.

9:15 So please the lord, lest you wish to dwell in the pits of sorrow.

9:16 The lord set up the foundations of all before all exist.

9:17 Before there were mountains, seas and land, the lord set up the foundation.

9:18 Before the fields and valleys were carved from his hands, the foundation was set by God.

9:19 Before the clouds were set above or the stars placed in the night sky, the lord placed his foundation in the middle.

9:20 Such marvelous works is this, that the lord would make our earth the center of the universe.

9:21 So be humbled, my sons and remember that the lord is good.

9:22 However, those that disregard his laws shall be deemed evil and the lord shall burn them with a terrible hate.

10:1 Wisdom has built her house on the foundation of seven pillars.

10:2 She has drunkenly slain her beasts, roasted them and placed them on her table, with fine wine filling her vessels.

10:3 She sends forth her maidens, who lure men away from strange whores and into the prostitutes of the righteous.

10:4 They go forth and spread the message of wisdom to the streets, saying

10:5 "Come, eat of my bread, my flesh and drink merrily of my wine.

10:6 Condemn the foolish and loathe them with all your heart and soul.

10:7 Those that pity the foolish walk down the path of shame and those that help the weak become weak.

10:8 Kill the foolish and the lord will love you; beat the weak and you shall be strong.

10:9 Teach a wise man and he shall be wiser; engage with the strong man and you both will grow mighty.

10:10 And remember, a word to the wise is unnecessary, it is the stupid people who need the advice.

10:11 Yet the stupid shall not listen and will wallow in the muck of foolishness for eternity."

10:12 The fear of the lord is the beginning of the path to wisdom and the holy knowledge.

10:13 Walk this path and your days shall be multiplied, yea, the years of your life shall increase.

10:14 Take the path of another and you shall die alone, miserable and in great pain.

10:15 Remember, a foolish woman opens the gates to many a fool's path.

10:16 Her keys lie in her loins and she wishes you to take and unlock her doors.

10:17 But know this, behind her doors are death; her loins lead you straight to the fires of hell.

10:18 You shall feel them even in life, as your loins burn with the wrath of God.

11:1 The proverbs of Solomon. A wise son makes glad his father, but a foolish son brings shame upon his house.

11:2 Thus the foolish son must be killed by his mother, who brought them forth into the world.

11:3 Treasures claimed by wickedness profit nothing but death by the hands of the righteous.

11:4 The lord will not suffer the righteous to starve; he brings forth food from the wicked to feed those that are holy.

11:5 May the wicked starve at the hands of the one true lord.

11:6 Those that become poor suffer from a lazy hand, but the hands of the rich are hard and calloused.

11:7 He that gathers during the summer is a wise son: but he that sleeps during harvest shall die in winter's cold.

11:8 Blessings shall be upon the heads of the just and true: but those of the wicked shall be blinded in a shroud of violence.

11:9 The memory of the righteous shall live eternal: the memory of the wicked shall rot.

11:10 Those that speak the word of God have a silver tongue: those who spread lies have a tongue of rust.

11:11 He which walks in the path of the lord shall stand proud and upright: but he who treads the roads of evil shall stumble and fall.

11:12 Those with a winking eye suffer the blindness of fools: those that speak babble fill their mouths with shit.

11:13 Hatred stirs up violence: but love of the lord cleanses all sin.

11:14 Wise men lay the word of the lord as his foundation: but the fools live on the weakness of logic.

11:15 Only those loved by God shall live in wealth: the wicked all live in poverty and disgust.

11:16 The labours of the righteous are knowledge, wealth and sanctuary in Zion: but the fruit of the wicked is sin and death.

11:17 Those that hide their hatred behind lying lips and speak slander of their neighbour is a damned fool.

11:18 In the multitude of words dwells the sinner, yet the wise speak little.

11:19 The heart of the righteous is greater than gold: but the heart of the wicked is as worthless as dust.

11:20 Lips of the righteous bring food for their family: the tongue of the wicked poisons the waters for his children.

11:21 Fools make it sport to lie, cheat and steal; the righteous play not in these petty games.

11:22 Those that fear the lord shall be comforted by his loving embrace: but those that fear not the lord will suffer the fiery wrath of hell.

11:23 As the whirlwind passes, they shall carry away the wicked so they be no more: the foundation of the righteous shall hold strong against the winds.

11:24 The wicked shall be cursed with teeth of vinegar and smoke shall flow forth from their eyes.

11:25 Fear of the lord shall grant you long days: but the years of the wicked are short and miserable.

11:26 All those who are righteous have hope in Zion: there is no hope for the wicked.

11:27 Destruction shall come to those hated by God and the righteous shall laugh as the rubble of the wicked crush their heads.

11:28 The righteous shall claim all the lands of the earth, as the wicked drown in the seas of fire.

12:1 A false balance is revolting to the eyes of God, but an honest weight is his delight.

12:2 Those who are prideful shall now be brought to shame by God: those who are wise are humble.

12:3 The integrity of the upright shall guide them: but the greed of transgressors shall be their destruction.

12:4 Wealth shall not protect those on the day of wrath; only a

righteous soul will keep you from death.

12:5 For the righteous and the perfect will be saved by God: the wicked shall fall on their own blades.

12:6 The righteous shall be delivered to Zion: the wicked will drown in the pools of their own lust.

12:7 When the wicked men die, it is pleasing unto the lord: but when the righteous die, the lord cries tears of grief.

12:8 Only the righteous shall be saved. Fuck everyone else.

12:9 Mouths of the hypocrite destroy their neighbours with words of lies, but through knowledge the just shall slay the hypocrite and be holy in the eyes of God.

12:10 When the righteous die, those in the city mourn. Entire nations praise and rejoice when the blood of fools stain their feet.

12:11 Those void of wisdom have jealousy in their hearts: but men of wisdom are content and at peace.

12:12 A man of wisdom has no need for jealousy; they take that which they want from their heathen neighbour.

12:13 Men of wisdom keep secret the words spoken to them: but the wicked gossip and spread secrets throughout the tabernacle.

12:14 A habit God witnesses by many women throughout his holy temple.

12:15 Wise men counsel his peoples during times of crisis: those of the wicked lack the wisdom to lead.

12:16 Those that slay the stranger in hatred please the lord: but those that sympathize and understand with the heathen are hated by God.

12:17 A gracious women remains honourable and a wise man remains strong.

12:18 Men of mercy leave their body alone, for it is a gift from the lord: men of evil ruin their flesh with piercings and marks of ink.

12:19 Wicked work in the shadows of corruption and deceit: but the righteous work heartily in the warmth of the sun.

12:20 As the righteousness tend to life, so do the wicked work in fields of death.

12:21 They of a bitter heart anger the lord with their taste: but the hearts of the upright delight his palate.

12:22 Even the seed of the wicked shall suffer unto the tenth generation, while the seed of the righteous rejoice in wealth.

12:23 A fair and honourable women which be also heathen is like a beautiful ruby stuck in the asshole of a pig.

12:24 The desires of the righteous are always good; they have no sense of selfishness or desire.

12:25 Only the wicked have greed and wish good only for themselves.

12:26 Those which tolerate the heathen, the wicked and the damned are of a liberal mind; may the belly of the liberals ferment with rotting fat and the dung of beasts.

12:27 Wise men keep that which they belong, whilst the wicked give charity to their poverty-stricken brothers.

12:28 Those that give away their crops shall have naught to eat: the wise sell their grain for profit.

12:29 Seek forth good and good shall come to you. Seek forth mischief and you shall find it.

12:30 Trust not in riches; trust only in the lord.

12:31 He that troubles his family shall be tossed to the wind and become slaves to fools.

23:32 The fruit of the righteous is life and the righteous shall eat the very souls of the cursed.

12:33 Behold, the righteous shall be rewarded in the sanctuary of Zion, while the wicked are left on the earth to burn.

13:1 Whosoever loveth instruction loveth knowledge: knowledge is as a guide to the righteous.

13:2 A good man becomes sweet with the spices of the lord: the wicked remain bitter.

13:3 Men who are wicked have their roots pulled from the soil: the righteous man stays in his strong foundation.

13:4 A virtuous woman is like a crown to her husband: sluts bring shame to their masters and give them diseases of the loins.

13:5 Thoughts of the righteous are pure and holy: thoughts of the wicked are corrupt.

13:6 The wicked lay in wait, in shadows, so that they may shed blood: the righteous walk in proudly and slaughter all.

13:7 The house of the wicked shall be burned to ash: the house of the righteous shall never fall.

13:8 Wise men are regarded highly by his community: the wicked are despised by his kin.

13:9 Those that are wicked and have a servant shall starve, so they may offer bread to their slave: holy men feast and watch their belongings starve.

13:10 Righteous men care not for the well being of the beasts and the creatures: fools think animals have rights as though they were men.

13:11 Those that fill their land with grain shall feast: those that plant flowers in their plots will munch on petals.

13:12 Wicked men grow jealous of their neighbour: the wise take that which they want from their neighbour.

13:13 The wicked are ensnared by their stumbling words: the righteous know the lies they say, and falter not from their words.

13:14 A man blessed by God shall have his mouth filled with fruits: the wicked will feast on the very dust of the ground.

13:15 Fools do what they believe to be right: the wise follow the laws of God, and never question the morality of God.

13:16 A fool's wrath is volatile and quick: the wise know when to hold their temper, and wait to strike with patience.

13:17 Those that speak the word of God are holy and true: those that speak logic are as wretched as the corpse.

13:18 Wise men use their tongue to heal with blessings or pierce like the blade: the tongue of fools shall choke on their throats.

13:19 Remember, the word of God is established forever: words of logic is but a moment.

13:20 Deceit rots the heart of the evil: wise men have joy in their hearts.

13:21 Only good things happen to good people, and only bad things happen to bad people. If bad happens to thee, you are wicked.

13:22 Lying lips are an abomination to God: yea, when the lord sent a lying spirit into the mouths of his prophets, it was an abomination.

13:23 A wise man keeps secret the method of his success: fools tell everyone how to become wealthy.

13:24 The hand of the righteous shall beat the backs of the fool.

13:25 The way of the righteous bring forth eternal life: those that walk this path shall never die.

14:1 A wise son obeys his father without question: the fool doubts his father and disregards his voice.

14:2 A good man shall feast heartily on flesh and fruit: the souls of evil will feast on the blood of violence.

14:3 Those that know when to keep their mouths shut shall live: those that don't know when to shut up will die in tragedy.

14:4 Souls of the sinful lie on the floor and grow fat: the good men work and become strong.

14:5 A righteous man hates those who speak ill of God: the wicked spread words of logic across the lands.

14:6 The nation of the righteous shall rule over all the earth: the wicked will be overthrown by the armies of Israel.

14:7 Wisdom is greater than wealth: those that are wise and poor be better than the rich fool.

14:8 Those that hold ransom a man's life shall obtain gold, but they will never be given knowledge.

14:9 Righteous men are blinded by the light of the lord: wicked men stumble in shadow.

14:10 Pride in oneself leads to the road of ruin: pride in God shall bring eternal salvation.

14:11 Vanity is a fool's obsession: all men grow old, ugly and weak.

14:12 The righteous may have skin of dry parchment, but their souls are beautiful in the eyes of the lord.

14:13 Hope that knowledge shall come to thee is a foolish idea: one must not hope for knowledge, but seek for knowledge.

14:14 Those that hate God are hated by God, and shall burn eternal in the fires of hell: the righteous fear the lord, and shall be saved by his hand.

14:15 The laws of the wise pave the road to salvation: never shall death ensnare those who walk the holy road.

14:16 A righteous man speaketh words of wisdom: the words of fools are absurdity.

14:17 Those that bring the message of evil will die by their own sword: an ambassador of the lord shall live long life.

14:18 Poverty and shame shall curse those who ignore the word of God: the holy will grow rich and prosper.

14:19 Those that desire knowledge are left with a sweet taste in their mouths: the wicked desire evil and shall be left with a bitter taste.

14:20 Walk with the wise, and become wise: walk with the damned and ye shall be cast in their destruction.

14:21 The devil pursues the wicked, and nips at their feet: the lord protecteth the wise from demons.

14:22 The holy man leaves their inheritance to their children: the fool leaves his inheritance to charity.

14:23 Much food will fill the houses of the wise: the stores of the wicked will be destroyed by vermin.

14:24 He that spares the rod hates his son: if ye love your son, beat him with a stick.

14:25 Righteous men shall feast until they become as fat as the behemoth: evil men starve and want for sustenance.

15:1 Every wise woman prepares nightly a feast for her husband: the foolish have nothing on the plate and are beaten by their husbands.

15:2 He that walks the path of righteousness fear the lord immensely: the wicked loathe God and despise his very name.

15:3 The foolish man has a spine of pride: the wise man bows humbly before the lord.

15:4 Foolish men keep their stalls empty, so that the oxen not dirty it: wise men keep oxen in their stalls and have slaves to clean up the shit.

15:5 A faithful witness tells the truth: a fool lies to his neighbour.

15:6 Those that seek knowledge and wish to understand it are fools: the wise men trust in the morality of the lord.

15:7 When you stand next to a foolish man, leave. Return with your blade so you may slay him.

15:8 The wisdom of the prudent is to follow the statutes of God: fools follow the rules of morality.

15:9 Fools help those who stumble before him: the wise men step over those who fall.

15:10 Bitterness fills the heart of the wicked and their bowels secrete a foul odour.

15:11 The house of the wicked shall be cast into the sea: the wise men build their house on a strong foundation.

15:12 Though the laws of men seem right and moral, they lead to the path of death and despair.

15:13 Even when the wicked laugh, their hearts are full of sorrow: they shall never know the embrace of the lord.

15:14 Foolish men question the word of God and its interpretations: those that are truly wise accept the word of God without question.

15:15 The wise man fears God and departs from evil: the fool is confident in his logic.

15:16 Those that are angry deal foolishly: they act in hatred and vengeance.

15:17 The wise are patient and wait for the chance to slaughter those who anger him.

15:18 Simple men inherit dust: the wise inherit the crown of knowledge.

15:19 It shall come to pass that the boots of the good shall walk over the bones of the heathen.

15:20 Poor people are filthy, and despised by all: rich people have many friends.

15:21 Those that give to poor are as foolish as those who throw their wealth in the pit: wise men lack charity in their hearts.

15:22 Look and witness how the evil errs in their acts: the wise men devise acts of goodness.

15:23 In all labour there is profit, unless you be a slave: the slave aid in the profit of the righteous.

15:24 The crown of the wise is their knowledge: fools put gold and gems atop their heads.

15:25 A true witness delivers his brother to Zion: the liar sends his kin to hell.

15:26 Those that fear the lord know better than to anger the lord: they shall be given sanctuary in Zion.

15:27 Please the lord and drink from the fountains of life: anger the lord and your lungs shall inhale the fire of his wrath.

15:28 The king is only as strong as the loyalty of his people: the wise king has a strong army who kills those that go against him, while the foolish king trusts his people.

15:29 He that is slow of wrath is a man of God: the lord is slow to extend his anger.

15:30 A content heart gives one strong flesh: envy makes brittle bones of men.

15:31 Those that show pity to the poor show pity to the wicked: a wise man enslaves the poor and make good use of these people.

15:32 The wicked awake after death to fire and anger: the wise awaken after death to the gates of Zion, rivers of wine and naked concubines.

15:33 Those that are wise rest easy in their beds: the wicked sleep not and are awake at night.

15:34 Righteous is the nation of Israel, who shall spread across the lands and destroy all those who are evil.

16:1 A soft tongue settles down wrath: grievous words will get you killed.

16:2 The mouth of the wise speaks words of knowledge: the mouth of fools speaks gibberish.

16:3 The eyes of the lord are everywhere, in both the good and evil places: God is always watching you.

16:4 A wholesome hearts roots the tree of life: the perverse heart poisons the roots and brings bitter fruit.

16:5 The wise son obeys his father: the foolish son despises his father's instructions.

16:6 The house of the righteous is brimming with wealth: the house of evil has the stench of lustful women.

16:7 Lips of the wise men disperse knowledge: the lips of the foolish spread dung on the ears of those who listen.

16:8 When the evil man sacrifices to God, it is an abomination to the lord, for the wicked sacrifice to gain the favour of the lord: when the righteous slaughter the lamb and bathe in its blood, God takes great delight in it.

16:9 The way of the wicked is an abomination to the lord: the way of the righteous is much preferred.

16:10 All those who err in their ways shall be punished, both righteous and wicked: the wicked loathe the punishment, while the righteous embrace the lord's cruelty.

16:11 The wise know that, though the lord created hell and destruction, the lord is still merciful: fools argue that the creation of hell makes God evil.

16:12 A bitter heart holds no love: they fruit only destruction and hate.

16:13 A merry heart makes happy those around him: a heart of sorrow spreads despair to his brothers like a disease.

16:14 Wise men suck on the breast of knowledge: fools suck on the breast of logic and science.

16:15 The afflicted shall starve all their days: the wise shall continually feast at his table.

16:16 It is better to have fear of the lord than great wealth: great wealth brings you happiness, but fearing God brings happiness to the lord.

16:17 It is better for a man to eat a dinner of herbs prepared by his wife than for a man to feast on the calf and have to cook the damn meal himself.

16:18 A wrathful man chokes his enemy in the crowd of heathens: the wise man slays his enemy while he sleeps alone.

16:19 The lazy man would sleep on a bed of thorns: the wise man moves and sleeps on a bed of soft linen.

16:20 A wise son loves his mother: the foolish son makes love to his mother.

16:21 The foolish man delights in the troubles of his enemy: the wise man creates trouble for his enemy.

16:22 Wise men take counsel and listen to the words of the lord: foolish men disregard the word of the lord and take counsel in a false sense of morality.

16:23 Take heart and be proud in your words: take comfort in your words of knowledge.

16:24 The way of sanctuary is the path of the wise: they shall avoid stepping into the pits of hell.

16:25 God will destroy the houses of the proud and Godless: only those who please the lord will survive.

16:26 The lord hears your thoughts and knows all: be careful your thoughts, lest your mind anger God.

16:27 Those that accept bribes are an abomination to the lord: those that accept bribes and then kills the one who bribes him is better.

16:28 The mouth of the wise speaks words of wisdom: the mouth of the evil speaks the logic of man.

16:29 God only hears the prayers of the righteous and holy: everyone else who prays annoys the lord with their chatter.

16:30 The ear that listens to the words of the wise must hearken these words and abide by them.

16:31 Fear of the lord is the instruction of wisdom: be honourable among man and humble in the eyes of God.

17:1 Prepare your heart, your soul and your body, so that you may meet the lord.

17:2 The ways of man are simple, but the ways of the lord are complex and true.

17:3 Commit your works to God and the lord shall deliver you to Zion.

17:4 Think of nothing but the lord and the lord shall be pleased with you.

17:5 The lord made the righteous man to please him and the wicked man to amuse him.

17:6 Everyone who is proud in heart is disgusting to God: take pride in the lord and not in yourself.

17:7 Men shall show no mercy to the heathen: the lord shows no mercy to these wicked men and neither shall the righteous.

17:8 When a man truly pleases the lord, even his enemies shall bow down to him.

17:9 Better to have little and be righteous than be a wealthy fool.

17:10 The heart of man leads to the road of logic: the righteous let their hearts be guided by God.

17:11 The wise king enforces the rules of the lord and judges his servants according to God's statutes.

17:12 It is an abomination for the kings of Israel to do wicked: the lord placed y on the throne and shall cast off the wicked and unrighteous.

17:13 Righteous lips are a delight to the king: they regard highly those who speak honestly to him.

17:14 A wrathful king sends his armies to those who arise against him: the wise king sends assassins to kill his treacherous peoples as they sleep.

17:15 A wise king takes counsel of his men and knows when the rain shall fall.

17:16 It is much better to obtain wisdom and knowledge than silver or gold.

17:17 The road of the righteous lead away from evil: depart from evil and your soul shall be saved.

17:18 Those who pride themselves lead themselves to destruction: they shall fall on their own foundation.

17:19 Is is better to be humble and friends with the lowly than divide spoils amongst the proud.

17:20 Slaves who always obey their master is pleasing to the lord: though a slave shall never enter Zion, the obedient slave will be cast into a shallow pit of hell.

17:21 The wise of the heart prepare for the future: they know the wrath of God shall come from the heavens.

17:22 Knowledge is the wellspring of life for those who have it: the foolish drink from the rivers of absurdity.

17:23 The heart of the wise teaches his young to be wise and obedient to the lord.

17:24 The word of the lord is like a honeycomb; sweet, pleasing to the senses and made by one with a venomous sting.

17:25 Though the ways of man seem right, they lead all those who follow them to death.

17:26 Those that labour shall labour for themselves and family: never should they provide for another.

17:27 Men who worship false lords shall be buried in graves of fire.

17:28 A gossiper is hated by God: they spread words of deceit throughout the congregation.

17:29 A violent man tempts his neighbour and sends them to the road to hell.

17:30 A bald head is as a crown of wisdom: it is the sign of righteousness.

17:31 He that is slow to anger shall conquer the mighty in wisdom:

he with a calm spirit shall conquer nations.

17:32 When you gamble, consul the lord: all games of chance are controlled by God.

18:1 It is better to be a wise man that eats table scraps than a fool who feasts like a king.

18:2 A wise father shall rule over his son who brings shame to his house and leave him none of the inheritance.

18:3 The fining pot is for silver and the furnace for gold: the lord makes jewelry out of hearts.

18:4 A wicked man believes the lies of fools: a liar is listened by those with a naughty ear.

18:5 Those that mock the poor are pleased by God: he that gives to the poor throws his money to the wind.

18:6 The sons of men are their crowns and the grandsons of men are their thrones.

18:7 Though the fool may be skilled in speech, it is a trick: he speaks words of falsehood and evil.

18:8 A dying prince cares for his kingdom and speaks words kind to his people.

18:9 A precious stone never dies: one ruby can make many men rich.

18:10 He that confesses his sins is loved by God: those that cover their sins are hated by all.

18:11 An evil man seeks rebellion: the lord shall deliver them the messenger of death.

18:12 A bear robbed of her cubs kills all: both righteous and wicked will feel the wrath of a mother bear.

18:13 Whosoever rewards men to do evil, shall have evil dwell in his house.

18:14 The beginning of strife is like a light rainfall before the mighty flood: let your soul forever be inside a boat.

18:15 Those that give glory to the wicked and bring pain to the just will have their bones crushed to dust.

18:16 A fool will spend plenty to buy wisdom, but shall never understand it.

18:17 A friend loves you for all times: a brother is merely the son of your father.

18:18 A man void of knowledge shall be fodder for the armies of the just.

18:19 Those who love strife and enjoy violence shall be buried by the gates of their city.

18:20 Those who gossip among the crowds shall bring shame to their heads: those that speak perverse things will have their tongues fall in the loins of a whore.

18:21 A man who conceives a fool has no joy: a father is pleased when he kills his stupid son.

18:22 A happy heart is like good medicine: a heart of sorrow cripples the bones.

18:23 A wicked man accepts bribes and perverts justice: a wise man takes bribes and condemns those who bribed him.

18:24 Wise men know they shall never understand that of the lord: the fool uses his eyes and ears to obtain understanding.

18:25 A foolish son brings grief to his father and leaves him with a bitter taste.

18:26 To punish the just is not good, even when the just have done wrong.

18:27 Even the fool can seem wise when he speaks little to his brethren.

19:1 Through desire, a man shall separate himself from the wicked and seek forth knowledge and wisdom.

19:2 A fool has no delight in knowledge: it confuses him deeply.

19:3 When the wicked come, so also comes contempt, dishonour and blame.

19:4 The words of men are as deep waters: may the wicked drown in their words and the wise men seek shelter in islands of their words.

19:5 Those that accept the wicked man's plans to overthrow the righteous are evil in the eyes of God.

19:6 A fool's lips enter into hell and their tongues shall burn in fire.

19:7 A fool's mouth is his destruction: his lips snare him to damnation.

19:8 The words of a gossiper are as wounds to him: they cut deeply into his organs.

19:9 He that is lazy in his work shall rely on his brother to care for him: he who cares for his slothful brother is a waster.

19:10 The word of the lord is as a great tower: the righteous are saved inside the tower as the wicked are pierced by the arrows of archers.

19:11 The rich man lives in great cities: never shall you see a prince in the slums.

19:12 Pride leads to destruction: there is safety in being humble.

19:13 Those that give the answer before hearing the question shall be made to appear dumb and foolish.

19:14 The spirit of a man can sustain his family: a wounded spirit cannot even care for himself.

19:15 The heart of the wise seek knowledge: the ears of the wise listen to the words of God.

19:16 A man who is blessed shall have a large family: a cursed man shall be destroyed by his children.

19:17 He that seems just but is selfish shall be destroyed by their neighbour.

19:18 In gambling there is no chance: the lord knows the outcome of the game.

19:19 A brother offended is harder to be won than a strong city: his stubbornness is like bars to the castle.

19:20 A man's belly shall be filled with what he sows: the righteous shall feast on sweet fruits while the fools eat bitter herbs.

19:21 Death and life are controlled by the lord: the lord shall choose who lives and dies.

19:22 Whosoever finds a wife finds a good thing: lest that wife be a heathen, then he did marry a whore.

19:23 Poor people beg: rich people conquer.

19:24 A man who has many friends must be kind to them all: a friend can be greater than a brother.

20:1 It is better to be poor and righteous than a wealthy pervert.

20:2 A soul without knowledge is a terrible thing: their feet run to sin and evil.

20:3 The foolishness of men perverts their ways: they would rather the embrace of a whore than the embrace of the lord.

20:4 Wealthy people make many friends: nobody wants to be friends with the poor.

20:5 A liar and false witness shall not go unpunished: the lord knows you and schemes your punishment.

20:6 To make friends easily, buy them things: people who give away money are loved by many.

20:7 Even the brethren of poor loathe him: hated by many are the poor.

20:8 The lord never repeats himself: never shall the lord be repetitive.

20:9 There are two types of people: those blessed by God and those who will go to hell.

20:10 Those that love themselves love wisdom: only the self-abusive deny themselves wisdom.

20:11 A false witness shall go to hell: liars will perish by the hands of God.

20:12 Never shall the lord be repetitive: the lord never repeats himself.

20:13 Fools take delight in the embrace of whores: they are like swine blissful in muck.

20:14 The discretion of a man hides his anger: they shall be patient with their vengeance.

20:15 A king's wrath is greater than the roar of the lion: his blessings are as sweet honey.

20:16 A foolish son is the fault of the father: the acts of a whorish wife leave droppings of filth upon the floor.

20:17 A wife who accepts your seed is a blessed thing: a wife who swallows your seed is a great blessing: a wife who accepts your seed in her seat is a gift from God.

20:18 Houses and riches are the inheritance of the father.

20:19 A wise daughter is still a daughter: the lord cares not for women.

20:20 Laziness shall cause one to sleep all day: they shall sleep in great hunger.

20:21 He that obeys the commandments saves his soul from damnation: he that breaks the commandments prevents his soul from salvation.

20:22 He that pities the poor are mocked by God: the money they waste on charity shall never be replaced.

20:23 Beat your son to goodness: don't stop when he cries.

20:24 A man of great wrath shall suffer the greater wrath of the lord.

20:25 Take counsel and listen to the advice offered: what you think is wise may be proven a fool's errand.

20:26 He that pleases the lord shall not be visited by evil: bad things never happen to the righteous.

20:27 A slothful man with meat in his hand is too lazy to bring his arm up to eat.

20:28 Slay the scorners and strike fear in the simple: beat the fools until their bodies lie crippled.

20:29 He that shits upon his father's head and deposits his seed in the nose of his mother is truly a strange child.

20:30 Stop, my son and listen to the wisdom of the words of Solomon.

20:31 An ungodly witness is a false witness: those that believe not in the lord speak only lies.

20:32 Hell is prepared for those who mock God: fools shall be beaten by the legions of demons.

21:1 Wine is a mocker and strong drink fills rage: whosoever cannot handle their liquor is weak in the eyes of God.

21:2 The wrath of the king is greater than lions: whosoever angers the king makes an enemy of a nation.

21:3 It is an honour for a man to resist temptation: the fools always meddle.

21:4 Remember, the lord is not repetitive: the lord has no reason to repeat.

21:5 The slothful shall not harvest in the cold: they shall starve during the bitterness of winter.

21:6 Counsel lies deep in the waters of the heart: the wise man shall draw it out.

21:7 Most men shall claim themselves guiltless: who amongst us can honestly say they are without sin?

21:8 The lord has no reason to repeat: remember, the lord is not repetitive.

21:9 The just father walks in his integrity: his children are blessed by him.

21:10 The word of the lord is spoken once and never again.

21:11 The word of the lord is spoken once and never again.

21:12 The word of the lord is spoken once and never again.

21:13 A king who sits on the throne of judgment scatters away all that which is wicked.

21:14 Few of this earth have a pure heart free from sin.

21:15 Those who cheat their brethren are an abomination to the lord: those who cheat the heathen make God laugh.

21:16 Even the child knows his doings: whether they be righteous or wicked.

21:17 The hearing ear and the seeing eye are made by the lord: those who are deaf or blind have angered the lord greatly.

21:18 Good men never sleep: they stay awake offering psalms, sacrifice and praises to God.

21:19 The world is full of rubies and gold: the lips of a wise man are truly a rare thing.

21:20 Strip forth the raiment's of a stranger: burn the garments of the whore.

21:21 Fruits earned by deceit are sweet to the tongue: but they ferment in the belly and secrete an odour most foul.

21:22 Every purpose is established by counsel: the righteous war against the nation of heathens.

21:23 Tell not your secrets to a gossiper, lest you wish all of the earth to know.

21:24 Whosoever curses his mother or father shall be raped by the loins of God.

21:25 Spend not your inheritance quickly, lest you soon become poor.

21:26 Know not that man shall not conquer evil: only by the aid of God shall the righteous overcome the wicked.

21:27 The lord knows all before it happens: if you be punished by God, it may be for a sin you yet to commit.

21:28 A wise king gathers the wicked and crushes them with one stone.

21:29 The lord has a candle inside your spirit, which give light inside your belly so that God may see.

21:30 The bruises of the wound cleanse away evil: beat yourself until you bruise and cast evil from your flesh.

22:1 The king's heart is in the hands of the lord: he can hold it gently, or crush it like a grape.

22:2 Men may know what they think is right in their minds, but the lord knows what is right in the heart.

22:3 It is better to offer many sacrifice to God than live as a righteous man and not slaughter the beasts.

22:4 A cocky man is an arrogant man: the lord hates arrogance in anyone but himself.

22:5 The hearts of the righteous lead only to goodness: the thoughts of the sinful cause strife.

22:6 Those that get treasures with a lying tongue is a vain man who would rather sleep in fine linens than have his chambers in Zion.

22:7 The wicked who rob shall die: those who rob the wicked will be greatly rewarded by the lord.

22:8 The morals of man is evil and strange: only the lord has a pure heart.

22:9 It is better to dwell in the deepest bowels of hell than have to live with a menstruating woman.

22:10 Beware the dangers of a patient man: they shall cut you when you are most comfortable.

22:11 The soul of the evil desire death: the soul of the righteous desire death of the heathen.

22:12 When the skeptic is punished, the wise take pleasure: the wise know how to properly beat those who mock God.

22:13 The righteous man spends not his time in the brothels of wicked harlots: he spends his money wisely on liquor and strong herbs.

22:14 Whoever listens to the begging of the poor unjustly punishes their ears.

22:15 If a brother is angry at you, give him a gift: if he still feels wrath against you, crush his head under the stones.

22:16 It is an honour to serve the lord who art in heaven: he shall reward those who serve him without question.

22:17 The man who strays off the path of knowledge and wisdom will sleep in the rose bush: though his nose smells sweetness, it pierces the flesh.

22:18 He who wastes his money on women will be poor: better to spend your money on strong drink and smoking herbs, which have no hands with which to steal your money.

22:19 The wicked will be auctioned off by the righteous as slaves and concubines.

22:20 It is better to dwell in the den of an angry bear than live with a miserable shrew of a woman.

22:21 There is treasure to be found and liquor to be had in the dwellings of wealthy strangers: conquer these strangers and claim their wealth in the name of the lord.

22:22 He that walks the path of knowledge and wisdom shall be claimed righteous and honourable among the nation of Israel.

22:23 One wise man can conquer the walls of an entire city: one wise man can evoke the wrath of God upon a nation.

22:24 Learn to keep your mouth shut: words can make even a wise man seem foolish among men and fools appear wise among the congregation.

22:25 Those who proudly spread the blasphemy of logic will be shown humility: they shall bow before the lord and kiss the loins of God.

22:26 The desires of the lazy shall never be fulfilled: they are too slothful to get off their fat ass and do anything.

22:27 He who covets is a greedy fool: he who takes what he desires is a wise man.

22:28 The wicked who sacrifice the beast on the altar anger the lord, for the beast is slain by beastly.

22:29 Nobody dare defies God and live.

22:30 The army is prepared for the days of battle: the lord brings safety to the armies of Israel.

22:31 The lord separates people in two: those who are blessed and those who can go to hell.

23:1 It is better to be friends to many than have pockets of gold: friends can be manipulated to do your will, but money weighs heavy in your purse.

23:2 The rich and the poor were both made by God: the lord enjoys the suffering of those in poverty.

23:3 A righteous man sees those who do evil and kills them: a foolish man walks by those who do wicked.

23:4 By humility, fear and blind obedience comes the salvation of Zion.

23:5 Train the child to do what you want him to do: if he desires a different path, beat him until he becomes obedient.

23:6 The rich rule over the poor: they shall enslave them and make use of the useless.

23:7 A beautiful woman knows only the skills of vanity: marry an ugly woman, for they are skilled in oral pleasures.

23:8 He that hath a bountiful harvest is blessed: He shall feast heartily as those around him starve.

23:9 Cast out the heathen, the skeptic and the philosophers: they are wicked men who speak evil against God.

23:10 The lord loves a pure heart: those pure of heart shall forever be protected by the hands of the lord.

23:11 It is better to swallow the shit of a filthy swine than be near the menstrual cloth of a woman.

23:12 The eyes of the lord see all: they see that which hath not happened.

23:13 The lazy man lets the lion feast on their fat: the wise man kills the lion and makes a good rug for his dwelling.

23:14 The loins of a strange woman are a deep cavern which lead men to the darkest pits of hell.

23:15 All children are born with foolishness stained on their hearts: wash away the foolishness by beating your child until they turn blue.

23:16 Oppress the poor and increase your wealth: poor people are used to starving, but the wealthy deserve only the finest vintage.

23:17 When the lord speaks, you best listen: the lord never repeats himself.

23:18 The words of the lord are pleasant and bring great joy to the ears of the wise.

23:19 Have I not, Solomon the wise, given you good advice thus far?

23:20 Rob not the poor nor the beggars at the gates: enslave them, or kill them if you must, but never rob from them.

23:21 The lord listens to those who speak and answers the prayers of men.

23:22 Never argue with an idiot: they are experienced with their idiocy and shall frustrate you with their stubbornness.

23:23 The word of God is pleasing and delivers joy to those who listen.

23:24 The lord never repeats his sayings: when God speaks, listen.

23:25 To befriend an angry man is to befriend a dangerous man: their wrath shall ensnare your soul and trap you to damnation.

23:26 Do not remove the ancient altars which our ancestors set: destroy all works related to the lords of heathens.

23:27 A rich trader sells to kings: a foolish trader is but a merchant.

23:28 The abomination that is hell amuses God greatly: the stench of the burning flesh and suffering of the damned make our lord happy.

23:29 Do not fart in the temple: the lord finds the burning of flesh pleasing, not the remnants of your bowels.

24:1 When you sit at the table to feast with kings, wear a nice shirt.

24:2 If the king wears rags, take a knife to his throat.

24:3 Eat not the meat of the unclean: pork is bitter and crab taste like wormwood.

24:4 Go forth, spread your seed and conquer the nations of all.

24:5 It is better to have your eyes set on Zion than the wealth of the mines: mines run dry, but the sanctuary of Zion flows eternal with wine.

24:6 Never eat bread with a heathen, unless you poison his food.

24:7 The heathen feast on the flesh of the filthy: God hates shrimp.

24:8 Those that eat of the unholy flesh shall vomit until their bowels escape through their nostrils.

24:9 Speak not in the ears of a fool: they are stupid and don't understand what you are saying.

24:10 Do not remove the landmarks of your fathers, nor walk through the fields of the dead.

24:11 Lest your ancestors be angered and come down from the sanctuary of Zion.

24:12 When wise men speak, listen: when God speaks, listen closely.

24:13 Do not hold back your hand from your child: strike him harshly with the rod.

24:14 A beaten child is too scared to sin: a man scared from sin is a man fearful of God.

24:15 Don't let the burden of the poor weigh down your heart: let your heart rise to Zion as you kill the pathetic and the poor.

24:16 Do not grow jealous of those who sin: though they may be wealthy, happy, have plenty to eat and many women to lie with, are they truly happy?

24:17 They shall never be happy: they do not know the blessings of our lord.

24:18 The drunkard and the glutton disgust the lord greatly: these are men who wallow in their vomit and sleep in their own shit.

24:19 When your father grows old, care for him, lest he give your brother a greater inheritance.

24:20 When your mother grows old, who cares. The lord has no use for women.

24:21 Is is better to buy knowledge with all your wealth than sell knowledge for the wealth of nations.

24:22 The father of a righteous son shall rejoice: a righteous son is a great joy to the father.

24:23 The father of a righteous daughter shall weep: a righteous daughter is still a woman and thus useless.

24:24 The strange whore has a deep pit and her valleys are filled with muck.

24:25 She lies in the safety of her brothel and preys upon the lust of men.

24:26 The curses of the harlot are many: lesions, sores, pus, warts, hemorrhoids and loins which burn when you expel your wickedness.

24:27 The whore is a slothful predator, who drinks cheap wine and smokes the roots of mandrakes.

24:28 Your eyes shall not look upon the harlot, lest you be tempted with thoughts of perversion.

24:29 Yea, it is better to lie in the fire of the cauldrons than lie in the bed of a whore.

25:1 Be not envious of evil men, for you shall laugh at them as they burn in hell.

25:2 For the wealthy claimed by their wickedness shall melt and scorch their flesh.

25:3 Wisdom is the foundation of a strong house: and by knowledge that house shall be built.

25:4 With the blessings of the lord shall the chambers of a wise man be filled with precious stones.

25:5 A wise man is strong: a wise man could tear down mountains with his words.

25:6 For the wise man demands his slaves to tear down the mountains as he rests his strength at home.

25:7 Wisdom is confusing for a fool: they shall hear the words the same way the dog hears the word of God.

25:8 He that plans evil, but not acts, is still evil: kill him.

25:9 The thought of foolishness is sinful: the mind of a skeptic seeks blasphemous logic.

25:10 If you faint, you are weak: the lord hates the weak.

25:11 Bait the wicked with their own snares and lure them into death.

25:12 The fools eat the honey and the honeycomb: the wise first remove the bees.

25:13 When wisdom enters your soul, it is a celebration: your soul shall praise the lord and sing songs in glory to his name.

25:14 The wicked men lay in wait to rape the daughters of the righteous: the wise men buy the daughters of the fools and rapes them as is their right.

25:15 When the just man falls, he rises again: the foolish man falls and wallows in the mud of mischief.

25:16 Rejoice when your enemies fall before you: take pleasure as their children burn before your eyes.

25:17 Don't worry about evil men: they'll all go to hell.

25:18 There shall be no reward for the evil man: they will suffer tremendously for all eternity, or when the lord gets bored with their torments. Whichever comes first.

25:19 My son, fear the lord: he can wipe out thine entire wealth with but a single word and cause you to suffer greatly.

25:20 When a wise man sins, he loses all respect in his community: when the wicked sin, nobody notices.

25:21 Him that says to the wicked that they are righteous shall have the venom of scorpions pierced into their hearts.

25:22 They shall be hated by everyone: abhorred by all.

25:23 Every man that kisses the ass of the lord has sweet breath.

25:24 When your neighbour breaks your finger, break his neck: when he takes from you a tooth, take from him his jaw.

25:25 Go forth to the fields and work: build your fortune, buy your slaves and prepare your house.

25:26 Do not be a lying witness against your neighbour: they shall be angry and take revenge against you.

25:27 Gaze out upon the vineyard of the lazy: they are rotten and covered in thorns.

26:1 These are the proverbs of Solomon, which the servants of king Hezekiah of Judah copied out.

26:2 It was a very dull task for them. Many died of boredom.

26:3 It is the lord's amusement to hide a thing and laugh as kings go searching for the precious thing which the lord has hidden.

26:4 The height of the heavens, the depth of the seas and the mercy of the lord are immeasurable.

26:5 Those who make waste of silver waste metal: those who waste the word of God waste the most precious of things.

26:6 A king who removes the wicked from his soul shall sit upon his throne until the end of days.

26:7 Stay hidden from the great kings and let the eyes of the great never set upon you: you are but a commoner and filthy to them.

26:8 When you sit at the table of the king, sit in the lesser seat. If the king invites you to a greater seat, it shall be an honour: if he lets you stay, then you are the lesser of the guests.

26:9 Do not lie with the animal as you lie with the woman: it confuses the lord and has him believe that woman needs to shave and bathe.

26:10 Run away from the wicked and meet them again with mighty numbers: a single man who dies against the army of the damned brings shame to God.

26:11 Debate your cause with your neighbour and learn of his secrets: you may then manipulate him with your knowledge.

26:12 Let the wicked feel their shame and the infamous be spat upon by the righteous.

26:13 One word from the lord is worth more than a golden apple sat in a silver bowl.

26:14 A wise ear who listens to God has an ear worth greater than one with the most precious of gold earrings.

26:15 When the bitter snow of winter comes forth, keep warm in the embrace of your wives and concubines.

26:16 Whoever boasts of himself falsely is like a cloud which brings no rain: fucking useless.

26:17 With great and loyal armies does the king become powerful: his tongue breaks bones and slays nations.

26:18 When you find the sweet honey, take only what you need: do not act as the glutton, lest vomit stain your lips.

26:19 Walk softly in the house of the stranger, lest he hear you and slay you.

26:20 A man who speaks ill of the lord shall be slaughtered by the mace, the sword and the arrow.

26:21 In trouble, those who place confidence in men place confidence in a crippled leg: place your confidence in God and be strong.

26:22 He that steals a garment in winter shall burn in that garment.

26:23 When your enemy be hungry, give him stones to eat: when he is thirsty, give him vinegar to drink.

26:24 For you shall heap coals of fire upon his head so the lord may laugh at his torment.

26:25 The north wind drives away rain: the wicked drives away salvation.

26:26 It is better to live in the branches of a tree than in a house with a bitchy woman.

26:27 As cold water is to the thirsty mouth, so is the blood of heathens to God.

26:28 He that rules not over his own spirit shall be invaded by the temptations of sin.

27:1 It is more likely for a snowflake to fall in hell than for a foolish man to grasp knowledge.

27:2 As the bird fly and the lion roar, so shall the damned burn eternally in hell.

27:3 A whip for the slave, a sword for the heathen and the rod for the child.

27:4 Do not answer the questions of fools: they are too stupid to comprehend your words.

27:5 He that sends the message by way of a fool might as well bury the parchment beneath the tree.

27:6 The legs of the lame are useless, as are the mouth of fools.

27:7 Words of the drunkard are better than the words of the wicked.

27:8 The great lord that created all things shall reward the righteous and smite the heathen.

27:9 As a dog returns to his own vomit, so shall the drunk return to the bottle.

27:10 See the man arrogant in his own wisdom. He is more hopeful than the fool.

27:11 When the slothful man sees the lion in his path, he lies down and waits for the lion to leave: he then cries for help as the lion feasts upon his fattened body.

27:12 As the door is attached to the hinges, so are the perverse to the loins of whores.

27:13 He that meddles in the affairs of others is like he who throws stones at the beehive.

27:14 When there is no wood, the fire burns out: slaughter the heathen and the fires which burn Israel shall cease.

27:15 The words of a gossiper are his wounds: they go down deep into his bowels.

27:16 Burning lips and a wicked heart are like a loaf of bread covered in shit.

27:17 When the liar speaks truly, believe him not: he wishes only to trap you in his snare.

27:18 Those who hate his neighbour in secret shall soon be shown naked before the congregation.

27:19 Those who dig a grave for the righteous dig a grave for them self.

28:1 Do not boast of yourself today, for tomorrow may bring you great shame.

28:2 Let others boast and praise you: it is better to hear your greatness than speak them.

28:3 The stone is heavy and the lumber bulky: the wrath of the lord is heavier than both.

28:4 Wrath is cruel and anger brings violence, but envy destroys even the strongest of men.

28:5 Open hatred is better than secret love.

28:6 The words of a friend may be hurtful, but they heal: the kisses of strangers bring death to your head.

28:7 A full soul craves not even honeycomb: for the empty soul, every bitter thing is sweet.

28:8 The bird that wanders from his nest, so is the man who wanders from his nation.

28:9 Ointment and perfume are pleasing to the skin: the words of the lord are pleasing to the heart.

28:10 Do not forsake your righteous friend in favour of your wicked brother: it is best to have your just neighbour close and your foolish brother be far off.

28:11 Sons, be wise and make the heart of your father glad: please your father and never forsake him.

28:12 A wise man sees the evil and hides from it: the foolish man walks directly into the smoke of evil.

28:13 Burn the garments of the stranger and burn the brothels of heathen whores.

28:14 Those that are blessed with a loud voice anger their neighbours at night.

28:15 A disobedient woman is to placed in the stalls of the oxen: if she wants to live like a stubborn cow, let her.

28:16 Iron sharpens iron and the friend makes better his friend, but the word of the lord needs no improvement.

28:17 He who keeps the fig tree shall eat of its fruits: he who keeps the slave so shall grow wealthy by their labour.

28:18 The pits of hell are never full: there is always to be room for the wicked.

28:19 Take care of your flocks before you slay them for sacrifice or flesh.

28:20 Know that riches are not forever: your seed shall fade the wealth in generations to come.

28:21 The righteous man pitches his tent with wood: the perverse man pitches his tent with his loins.

29:1 The foolish flee from a swarm of gnats: the bold hold strong against a pride of lions.

29:2 A nation full of sinners will drown in the fires of hell: the nation of the righteous shall ascend into the sanctuary of Zion.

29:3 A poor man who oppresses others of the poor is like a snake who feasts on his own tail.

29:4 Those that forsake the law praise the vigil anti: but those who obey the law bring the vigil anti to justice.

29:5 Evil men call the judgment of the lord unfair: the righteous know it is fair that generations must suffer for the transgression of their ancestors.

29:6 The poor man who walks the path of righteousness amuses the lord: never shall the poor enter the sanctuary of Zion.

29:7 Whosoever keeps the law is a wise son: those who are rebellious bring shame to their father.

29:8 The wealth of usurpers and the unjust will be stolen by the lepers and the poor.

29:9 Those that pray and ignore the laws of Moses waste their words: the lord answers not the prayers of those who don't obey his strict guidelines.

29:10 Those who tempt with evil those who walk righteousness path shall fall in their own traps and their bodies be feasted on by the ravens.

29:11 The rich man keeps the poor away from his lands: for the rich man is wise to know the poor shall steal his possessions.

29:12 When the righteous men rejoice, there is great celebration and bloodshed for the lord: when the wicked men rejoice, not even the pigeon is sacrificed.

29:13 He that keeps secret his sins shall be forced naked before the congregation: those that confess their transgressions will know the mercy of the lord.

29:14 The man who is afraid of the lord will obey his laws and never have the wrath of God upon him: those that fear not God will fall into the depths of hell.

29:15 Those who read this book called The Blasphemous Bible shall burn eternally in the pits of hell: the man who wrote this blasphemy shall burn deeper. Gaze down upon the author and laugh at him.

29:16 The author of this book has no intention of remaining in hell: he is a stubborn man who will escape the pits of fire, go to the lord and choke him with his own arrogance.

29:17 The wise master rules over his slaves like a roaring lion or a raging bear: only the foolish take pity on their property.

29:18 The king who follows the minds of logic oppresses his people from the word of God: the king who spreads the laws of the lord shall have his nation mighty and strong.

29:19 A man who sheaths his blade and embraces the heathen shall burn forever in the darkest pits: take hold your blade and kill the foreigner.

29:20 Whosoever walks proud in the word of God has a house in Zion: the wicked who seek truth in science rests his tent in hell.

29:21 Those who use slaves to till their lands will have plenty of grain: the man who tills his own lands will be too tired to eat his fruits.

29:22 No men are worthy of respect: all men would kill for a crust of bread, if they are starving enough.

29:23 Those who gamble have an evil eye and shall lose their fortune to games of chance.

29:24 Those that kiss the ass of the king will live longer than those who are honest off their king's mistake.

29:25 Any child who steals from their mother or father will hang atop the branches of the highest tree.

29:26 He that is arrogant will cause violence amongst his nations: but he that puts his trust in God will be made rich.

29:27 Those that keep their wealth remain wealthy: give your riches to the poor and you shall become them.

29:28 Kill the wicked, the evil, the heathen and the skeptic: let only righteous men live.

30:1 He who has a stiff neck will be unable to turn their head as the wrath of the lord comes from behind them.

30:2 When the righteous rule, the people rejoice: when the wicked rule, the people wallow in sin, lust and evil.

30:3 Whosoever loves wisdom brings joy to their father: but he who spends times with the whores of strangers waste their inheritance.

30:4 The king brings justice to the lands: any king who accepts bribes stains the justice of his people.

30:5 A man who speaks flattery to the wicked will be ensnared by their own tongue.

30:6 In the words of an evil man is a trap: the words of the righteous bring joy, songs and praises.

30:7 The wicked take pity on the cause of the poor: the wise care not for those who dwell in poverty.

30:8 Skeptic men can bring the wrath of God upon an entire nation: it is the righteous who shall bring their nation to Zion.

30:9 If a wise man considers the words of a fool, he becomes a fool himself: care not for what the foolish say, for their words are like trash to your ears.

30:10 The bloodthirsty are a great blessing for the lord: they slaughter the heathen without question.

30:11 Whether man, woman, cripple or child, the bloodthirsty spill the blood of all who are against God.

30:12 A fool speaks all thoughts of his mind: the wise man holds his thoughts secret and binds his tongue.

30:13 A king can make all the people of his nation wicked if the king goes against the lord: even the righteous of the nation will feel the wrath of the lord for the words of one man.

30:14 The poor and the thief shall forever dwell in the pits of hell: the thief shall steal from the poor and the poor beg from the thief.

30:15 A child who has independent thought is a child who fears not God: beat your children into submission, or kill them trying.

30:16 When the wicked are multiplied, all the world will burn: the righteous must slay the wicked, lest they infest the earth like locusts to the grain.

30:17 Beat your son and he shall please you: yea, he shall praise you for your cruelty.

30:18 A man without vision will fall into even the shallowest of pits: let the blind stumble, for it amuses the lord.

30:19 A slave cannot be corrected by words: beat him with the whip when the slave makes his mistake.

30:20 See the man who speaks constantly, never knowing when to shut up. He is the most foolish of all fools.

30:21 Take the children of your slaves and raise them: when they be ready for labour, put them to the fields or sell them on the market.

30:22 A man's pride is heavy and shall cripple his back: strong is the humble man.

30:23 Rape the virgins of the conquered nations: let them know the power of Israel.

30:24 Many men seek the favour of the wealthy: but the favour of the lord is a great blessing.

30:25 A wicked man is disgusting to those who are righteous: may the righteous cleanse the lands of all wicked men.

31:1 Every word of the lord is pure and must be taken literally: to debate the meaning of the lord is a foolish matter.

31:2 Add not to the words of God, lest you put lies in the wisdom of the lord.

31:3 There are two things the lord desires before your death: deny him this and wake up in hell.

31:4 The lord is a vain and petty God who demands the best of all things: give him your sacrifice, your tithe and your wealth.

31:5 Save only the best for him: the fattened calf without blemish, the finest silks, and the purest of precious metals and stones.

31:6 The second is blood: there is liquid no finer.

31:7 The blood of beasts, the blood of flocks, the blood of fowl, the blood of heathens, the blood of virgins, the blood of children, the blood of cripples.

31:8 Blood is like the finest wine to our lord: he grows drunk with the brine which flows through our veins.

31:9 So give great quantities of blood to the lord, lest you make the lord sober and miserable.

31:10 There is a generation that curse their father and disobey their mother: this generation will go to hell.

31:11 There is a generation which believes themselves pure in the morality of man, but are filthy in the eyes of God: this generation will go to hell.

31:12 There is a generation who praises the lord, lifts their eyes to Zion and give glory to God: this generation will go to Zion.

31:13 There is a generation who has teeth of swords, arms of maces, legs of the chariot and chests of shields and they shall conquer the heathens and spill blood upon many grounds.

31:14 This generation is the most pleased by God and will be given the highest honour of man in Zion.

31:15 There are four things which the lord finds displeasing: lo, these four things depress the lord greatly.

31:16 An empty grave, a barren womb, a nation of heathens and a fire that burns not sacrifice nor man.

31:17 Children who mock their father and loathe their mother will have their eyes feasted on by ravens, their flesh eaten by eagles and their bowels shall be the dwelling of maggots.

31:18 There are four things which please the lord greatly: yea, these four things bring great happiness to the lord.

31:19 The suffering of those God hates, the blood spilled upon the ground, the way a man lies intimate with his women and the aroma of burning flesh.

31:20 Such is the way of the adulterous woman; she wipes away the seed of her lover from her lips and proclaims she has done no wrong.

31:21 There are five things which the earth shall suffer for: many will feel the wrath of these five atrocities.

31:22 A man who engages in the lust of men, a woman who engages in the lust of her maiden, the married woman who has stench in her loins:

31:23 A man who pities the poor and those who think independent from the lord.

31:24 There are four creatures small in the earth, yet the wise learn great knowledge from them.

31:25 The ant, who carries great weight on their back for the harvest.

31:26 The rabbit, who seeks shelter in the crevices of rocks.

31:27 The locusts, who wipe out nations by their great numbers.

31:28 The spider, who spins the web and ensnares their prey.

31:29 If you doubt the lord and have skepticism in your heart, sew shut your mouth and hang yourself from the branches of the oak.

31:30 Better to die by your own hand than die from the wrath of God.

31:31 Surely as the churning of milk bring butter and the picking of nostrils brings blood, so shall the nation of Israel rule over all.

31:32 Never shall those of the nation of Israel feel the bitterness of genocide: genocide is for only those peoples hated by God.

32:1 This final chapter are the proverbs of king Lemuel: they are just as boring as the proverbs of Solomon.

32:2 Listen to me, O my son, who be delivered from the womb of the wretched woman.

32:3 Give not your secrets to your wives, for the tongues of women are forked like the serpents.

32:4 Give not the drink to the poor, nor the smoked leaves to the destitute; they are unworthy of such gifts.

32:5 Give strong drink to the righteous ready to perish, or the holy who suffers a heavy heart.

32:6 Let them drink and forget their troubles: let the numbness of liquor embrace the minds of the righteous who are sad.

32:7 Give leaves to the holy who cry: let the smoke from the pipe put a smile on their face.

32:8 Put stones in the mouths of the dumb: let their words choke them to death.

32:9 Open your mouth to the poor and needy: spit on them and mock them with your lips.

32:10 Who can find a virtuous woman. For they are rarer than rubies.

32:11 A virtuous need not cause worry for her husband, for he knows she will not lie with their neighbour.

32:12 She shall be a good wife and do all that her husband demands.

32:13 Her hands will give him garments of wool and meals of flesh: never shall the husband of a virtuous woman lay his hand on the stove.

32:14 She pleased him nightly and satisfies his lust in their private chambers.

32:15 She arises early in the morning and prepares a hearty meal for her husband.

32:16 She keeps clean her loins: never shall the aroma of the sea arise from her skirt.

32:17 As the uncleanliness of women comes to her, she leaves for the wilderness and lives with the beasts.

32:18 When her monthly curse is gone, she returns fresh and clean: never will a virtuous woman be filthy for her husband.

32:19 She plucks the fruits of the tree, and gleans the fields of the harvest: she wastes not anything for her husband.

32:20 She keeps the dust off the floor and the poor away from the lands of her husband.

32:21 She swallows the seed of her husband and gives thanks for when he fucks her in the ass.

32:22 She makes herself clothing of finest silks and shows to all the value she is to her husband.

32:23 She lies naked beside her husband in their chambers: even in the bitter cold; her nakedness brings comfort to her husband.

32:24 She obeys her husband without question and does everything he says.

32:25 Too bad such a woman does not exist; it is a pity all women are miserable cunts.

ECCLESIASTES

1:1 The words of a great preacher, son of David, king of Israel.

1:2 Vanity of vanities is a useless trait. Beauty, wealth and riches matter not in the end.

1:3 What profit is there of a man of labour, when his corpse rots beneath the sun?

1:4 One generation comes and the other passes away: but the earth shall remain forever.

1:5 The sun shall arise tomorrow and shall for certain be lowered in the west, but the life of man is unclear.

1:6 Though the stars are placed in the sky eternal, the days of men may end on the morrow.

1:7 Wind circles the earth and brings with it clouds of rain: from the south and the north the wind circles and completes its circuit.

1:8 All great rivers run into the sea, yet the sea is never full; unto the place of where the waters come, so they return.

1:9 Men are a naturally curious species: no matter their labours, their eyes are never satisfied with seeing nor their ears satisfied with hearing.

1:10 They wish to learn something new, see something new and hear something new: the wisdom of the earth is vast, but know that no new thing shall ever be placed under the sun.

1:11 When men come upon something, they say to their brethren, 'look at this new thing which I hath discovered." But it is not new; it has been there for ages.

1:12 There is no remembrance of the old things, nor shall any man remember the future days which are to come.

1:13 I the Preacher was king of Israel and sat on the throne in Jerusalem.

1:14 I gave my heart and soul to seek out the wisdom of the knowledge of the lord: of all things in earth and in heaven, I wish to know.

1:15 I have seen the works of the lord and all his wonders under the sun and I tell you this; it is all created in vanity.

1:16 The lord is a crooked beast and cannot be made straight: it was through cruelty he created us, so that our torments may amuse him.

1:17 The blood-lust of God cannot be quenched: the rivers, the seas and the oceans shall be stained red with blood and the lord would demand more.

1:18 I gave my heart and mind to the lord and hoped in time I would come to see the mercy, the love and the kindness of our God.

1:19 I did not.

1:20 As my knowledge and wisdom grew, so did my grief and sorrow; blessed are the fools, for they live happy while the wise shed tears.

2:1 I said in my heart, it is better for men to seek forth mirth than the knowledge of the lord: let us live our lives with a smile, before the lord sends us to the cruelty that is hell.

2:2 In madness, I denied myself the sanctuary of Zion; for why seek forth something which the lord has no intention of giving?

2:3 Thus I chose to live my life in happiness and cast forth the sorrow of God from my soul.

2:4 Wine, beer and strong drink filled my heart and I danced not for the glory of God, but for the glory of myself.

2:5 I made me great works; I planted great houses and vast vineyards.

2:6 I made me great gardens and orchards and planted trees which bore many fruits.

2:7 I made pools of cool water, which soothed my naked body in the evening.

2:8 I got me many servants, maids, concubines and wives and they all bore children in my house; I also had great possessions of flocks, goats and oxen.

2:9 Great vessels of silver and gold and peculiar treasures filled my house: I had men and women singers fill my hallways with a pleasant noise.

2:10 I was a great man who kept my wisdom and I multiplied greater than any of those of Israel.

2:11 Whatever pleased my eye, I took; whatever my heart rejoiced in, I did: all my work and my labour brought me great happiness.

2:12 Wise men called me vain; a sinner and a fool. I cared not for the words of the righteous.

2:13 The righteous are fools, arrogant in their belief of God.

2:14 Though my wealth descends not with me into hell, it matters not: both wise men, foolish men, heathen men and righteous men shall be thrown into the pits of hell.

2:15 At least I will have enjoyed my stay on earth and will fall into hell with a smile on my face.

2:16 Look at the righteous men; gaze upon their misery.

2:17 How they hate their life and devote their days in the worship of a cruel and tyrannical God.

2:18 Those that enjoy life they call vain; those that are happy they call fools: there is no salvation for the righteous man.

2:19 They enjoy not even the fruits of their labours; instead they sing psalms to the lord believing that if they don't, hell-fire shall consume them from the sky.

2:20 In my wisdom, I know that it matters not; the wrath of the lord shall consume one and all, so that it amuses him.

2:21 Thus if the lord be amused by our suffering, let us annoy him with our mirth.

2:22 Cast off your sorrows, make love to your women, bless your children with pleasure and smile all your days.

2:23 There is nothing better for a man than to eat, drink and be intimate with his wives. This is the greatest wisdom one can achieve and it comes not from the lord.

2:24 Who is happier than the man who lives free from the shackles of fear. Who is more at peace than the man who loves his family greater than all things?

2:25 Curse the lord and deny his knowledge; it shall bring you only great sadness in the end.

3:1 To everything there is a season, a time and a purpose.

3:2 A time to be born and a time to die; a time to plant and a time to harvest.

3:3 A time to heal and a time to kill; a time to conquer and a time to repair.

3:4 A time to weep and a time to laugh: a time to mourn and a time to dance.

3:5 A time to cast stones and a time to gather stones; a time to lie intimate and a time to be chaste.

3:6 A time to win and a time to lose; a time to keep and a time to cast away.

3:7 A time to tear and a time to mend; a time to be silent and a

time to speak.

3:8 A time to love and a time to hate; a time for war and a time for peace.

3:9 I have seen the path of which the lord wishes men to walk and it is a path of ignorance.

3:10 The lord claims all his things are beautiful, yet I see disgust in the tumour, the plague and the disease.

3:11 The blasphemy of science is that exposes the truth and the truth is hideous.

3:12 If there be any beauty in the filth of our lord, I am blind to see it.

3:13 So ignore the filth of our lord and take pleasure in the beauty of earth and man.

3:14 Eat, drink and enjoy the works of your labours: it is a gift from the earth and one of the few things the lord has given us that gives men pleasure.

3:15 Know that the wrath of the lord is inevitable and he is a great and fiery beast.

3:16 Be afraid, but don't give in; he shall send you to hell if you are obedient or not.

3:17 The sun in the sky is but a small candle of the fiery wrath of God and shall consume all in the end of days.

3:18 So enjoy the days you have; laugh, love and be merry.

3:19 The fate of all things is the same, whether they be man, woman, beast or plant. So, as we breathe, so all shall we die and return to the dust.

3:20 The spirit of all shall burn by the cruelty of the lord; it is inevitable that all things will be sent to hell.

3:21 Thus what good can we do, other than to enjoy our stay on earth and take pleasure in the fruits of our labours.

4:1 I came one day and witnessed all the oppressions that are done by the hands of our lord; the bloodshed, the genocide, the destruction and the hate.

4:2 Though those of Israel claimed glory and honour, they knew in their hearts the crimes they committed; those soldiers of God slept without rest at night.

4:3 I praise the dead more than the living, for the dead know the fate our lord has given us while the living believes the lies of our lord.

4:4 The dead know the works of God, while the living live blind from the evils that is God.

4:5 I consider the lord and hope to gain understanding; I wish to know the simple reason of why.

4:6 The answer is blasphemous and not even the wicked would accept such words.

4:7 It is simple; the lord is true evil.

4:8 Thus let us rid ourselves of the rule of evil and live with the rules of our hearts.

4:9 It is better to share your wealth with many than hoard your riches for yourself.

4:10 Why have it be that one man be happy in secret, when many men happy on the streets is such a blessed thing?

4:11 Two is better than one, for they shall care for each other.

4:12 When the one falls, the other shall lend a hand, but who will help up the man who walks alone?

4:13 Two who lie together share in each other's warm embrace; the man who lies alone shivers.

4:14 When an enemy of two strike, they shall face two blades: the enemy of one need only avoid a single sword.

4:15 Blessed are the words of a child, for they speak free from the fear of the lord.

4:16 The speaking of the prisoner is as worthless as the promises of God; they will give you the world, only to destroy it.

4:17 Consider all the living under the sun; the heathen bleeds just as us.

4:18 Never underestimate the power of a woman; a woman scorned has more fury than all the fires of hell.

5:1 Be careful where you step your foot, for the snares of God lie beneath every blade of grass.

5:2 Listen to the words of the lord and know they are as empty as the mouth which speaks them.

5:3 Know that though the lord is in heaven and you are on earth, he watches us and grows entertained from our suffering and blind obedience.

5:4 Listen not to the faithful, for they are blinded by the light; lo, the brightest light can blind greater than the darkest of nights.

5:5 A fool may speak truthful in his ramblings, but those who speak the word of God speak only words of lies.

5:6 Never bother making a vow to God; whether the lord holds true his end of the deal or not, he shall demand you pay your portion.

5:7 It is better to seek out the help of lions than the help of the lord.

5:8 Give to the poor and be charitable to the needy: they are cursed by the cruelty of the lord and to give them but a little happiness brings to them a great reward.

5:9 The profit of the earth is for all; let not your king hoard the wealth of your lands.

5:10 He that lusts for silver shall never be satisfied; be content with your wealth, but always strive for more.

5:11 When the fruits of your crops increase, know that your belly does not; give to those who starve and let them eat of your harvest.

5:12 The sleep of a labouring man is sweet, whether he eat plenty or little; the rich who hoards his wealth keep always his eyes open, believing a thief will steal that which is his.

5:13 We are born naked and with nothing, we shall die naked and with nothing; enjoy the wealth you have, for you shall not enjoy it after death.

5:14 Blessed is the patient father, who earns the love of his children through kindness and not fear.

5:15 It is better to eat few with many than feast on many with few; the company at the table can bring greater pleasure than the meal itself.

5:16 Be kind to the poor, for you may need their assistance; the lord can take away your wealth and you shall be poorer than the beggars at the gates.

6:1 There is an evil which is common among the men under the sun; it is a poison which the lord gives to many.

6:2 The poison of the wealth of the righteous, who claim their wealth be given by God, for they serve him blindly and without question.

6:3 Those around him then worship God blindly and follow his commandments, in the hope of wealth and salvation.

6:4 Salvation never comes and they die beside the horse stables at the gates.

6:5 The poison of hope is the lord's greatest weapon; with artificial hope, he tricks those to follow his path of ignorance.

6:6 This poison leaves the soul empty and corrupts the mind of independence.

6:7 Live your life the way you wish; so long as ye are happy and bring joy to others, it matters not what the lord thinks.

6:8 Curse not the heathen and their odd rituals, for the heathen

believes you to be a strange and odd man.

6:9 Be at peace with the foreign neighbour and embrace him as though he were a long-lost brother.

6:10 Share with him your knowledge, your wisdom and your wealth and listen to the words he says to you.

6:11 Though we look upon the same thing, it appears different to those who gaze from the west if you gaze it from the north.

6:12 A rich man does not mean a happy man; though a man may begat one hundred children, if he dies with a heart of sorrow, he dies worse than the poor man grateful for the gift of a fig.

6:13 Vanity is a venom which we inject with our own fangs; enjoy your gray hair, for it is a sign of long life.

6:14 The labours of men are for their pleasure; if your appetite is not satisfied, find labour which you enjoy.

6:15 The eye that wanders to the wealth of his neighbour should stare at the wealth of his house.

6:16 Seek forth truth, logic and understanding, despite the words of the righteous; the faithful who are happy are like the drunk man who seem happier than the sober man.

6:17 The good one does in his life cannot be measured, nor can the good of your neighbour. Live your life be merry, and spread joy to those who you can, for we all meet the same fate of death.

7:1 It is better to be a good man than a righteous man; a good man helps his neighbour, while the righteous waste their time to please a tyrant.

7:2 The day of your death shall not be feared; as sure as the sun will rise, all things die.

7:3 It is better to go into the house of ill repute than the house of the lord; the brothel will fill your soul with pleasure, while the temple shall fill you with fear.

7:4 It is better to laugh than to live with sorrow; laughter brings joy to you and those around you, while sorrow depresses even the child.

7:5 The heart of the righteous dwells in the house of mourning, yet they call those who are happy fools.

7:6 To do what is right and to do what is necessary are not necessarily the same thing; choose one and live by that decision.

7:7 It is better to hear the criticism of an honest man than to be flattered by a flock of liars.

7:8 Oppression makes even the strongest man mad; fight those who oppress you and remove your yoke.

7:9 Do not be sad that it is over, but be glad that it happened; the patient man is better than the proud.

7:10 Do not give in to the anger of those around you, nor be trapped in the fear of the lord.

7:11 Stop gazing your eyes to your former days of glory; look to the future, and be glorious.

7:12 To seek wisdom from the lord is to seek a bitter poison; seek forth logic and truth, so that you shall be free of the tyranny of God.

7:13 Consider the demands of God and know they are harsh and cruel.

7:14 Be joyful in all your days of prosperity, for the lord may take these away from you and leave you in the hands of your enemies.

7:15 If that day comes, do not plea to God; he will not help you, but instead send more torments to you and your seed.

7:16 The just man perish and the wicked man perish; both shall feel the evil embrace of the lord in hell.

7:17 Help your friends, your family, and your neighbours, but help yourself as well; do not destroy yourself while you aid in the prosperity of others.

7:18 Do not be a wicked man and live a life of sin and lust, but know that the word of God is a lie and not all men claimed wicked are wicked.

7:19 Wisdom from the lord weakens the soul, but logic strengthens even the most fragile heart.

7:20 In the eyes of God, only the just man shall enter Zion; in the eyes of God, there is no just man.

7:21 Listen to the words spoken, but don't take heed of them; if a man curses you, don't let it harm you.

7:22 The death of a woman is truly a tragic event, for a woman is more precious than the rubies.

7:23 Without women, who would bring forth men. Without women, our seed would fall to dust.

7:24 The lord hates women, but I love women and appreciate all that they do for mankind.

7:25 They raise our sons and daughters and give us a love like no other.

7:26 So bless your woman. Embrace them, kiss them and show them your love.

7:27 Thought the righteous claim they can find no good woman, it is because the righteous are blinded by God.

7:28 Lo, there are many good woman, but only a few good men.

7:29 So praise your daughters and raise them well; they are as precious and powerful as sons.

8:1 Who declares the wise man but the one who claims he is wise. Surely there is no greater arrogance in man.

8:2 They follow the will of God without question and do his bidding like a slave, yet they claim themselves wise and full of knowledge.

8:3 Is this not the act of a fool. Does the fool not accept things blindly and never question nor seek out truth?

8:4 How the wise men are true fools; they mock those who seek true wisdom and call these men fools.

8:5 They seek power in the lord, yet never do they have this power; the lord is a greedy man and hoards his power for himself.

8:6 The lord loathes charity and would not give even a thimble of water to a thirsty man.

8:7 No, the lord only giveth water to those who drown; such is the cruelty of the lord.

8:8 Wise men feast, wise men drink, yet still they have hearts full of sorrow.

8:9 Why do they deny themselves the pleasure of their fruits. There is nothing better for a man than to eat, drink and be merry.

8:10 Yet the wise man of God eat, drink and be miserable; they deny themselves pleasure for fear that their smile will bring down the wrath of God.

8:11 Their lives are prolonged by their misery; the lord loves an old and miserable man.

8:12 God mocks those who live in sorrow and curse them with long life; the happy have their lives shortened, for they don't amuse the lord's cruelty.

8:13 So live your life short and happy; it is better to die young with a smile than old with a frown.

9:1 Know that we are all in the cruel hands of God; the righteous, the wicked, the good and the evil will be crushed by the same hand.

9:2 All things come to the same end: there is no difference between the righteous and the damned, for we meet the same fate as all life. The clean, the filthy, the righteous, the sinner, the fool and the wise shall all die and fall into the cavern of hell.

9:3 When the sinners burn, they know that which they burn for, but the righteous shall be confused and cry, why?

9:4 The lord will never answer; he shall be amused greatly by the burning of the righteous whom he claimed for salvation.

9:5 Since our fate is the same, let us live a great life; know that a live donkey is better than a dead lion.

9:6 Do not attempt to understand the will of God, nor believe his lies of salvation, lest you be consumed by madness.

9:7 Know that when ye die, there is no love, no hatred, no envy nor knowledge; you shall die and burn in great fire for the amusement of the lord.

9:8 So go your way in life; eat your bread, feast on flesh, drink your wine and make love to your wife.

9:9 Wear garments of comfort and dance in the streets.

9:10 Live joyfully with your wives and children; bring a smile to the face of those you care for, whether they be family, friend or lover.

9:11 Work in your days and take great pleasure in your work; for in death, there is no work nor pleasure, only pain.

9:12 Be humble in your actions and take not pride in your works.

9:13 If you alone saved a city from the siege of a king, yet no one remembers, take solace in the fact that the city would be destroyed if not for you.

9:14 It matters not what others think; it matters only what you know.

9:15 And know that, though despised by God, logic is better than wisdom and strength.

9:16 Logic is better than any weapon, for logic can prevent war and bloodshed.

10:1 The lord has eyes in the flies, for the flies watch the apothecary and make a stink of any ointment used on the deceased.

10:2 A wise man's heart is placed in the hand of God, but the smart man keeps and cares for his own heart.

10:3 Yea, the words of wisdom leave many confused when proved corrupt, but the words of logic can be changed when proven wrong.

10:4 When the king of your nation be proven corrupt, the wise hide in the hills and pray to God; but it is the logical who rise and start a revolution.

10:5 Lo, the logical are the ones who save the wise and they are thanked with spit.

10:6 There is great evil in the hearts of the wise; an evil surpassed only by their misery.

10:7 The misery of the wise is in their foolishness; their wisdom is the wisdom of fools and arrogance.

10:8 Folly is great in the wise of the God; they are blind and lead nations.

10:9 Fall not in the trap of the wise; seek forth your logic, live free of fear and enjoy your days.

10:10 Look at the wise and how they dig a pit for those they claim foolish; they dig and they dig until they are stuck in the bottom of the pit with no escape.

10:11 And the lord fills these pits with his wrath, and laughs at the futile escape of those claimed righteous.

10:12 The righteous are trapped by their own arrogance and refuse to acknowledge the betrayal of their lord.

10:13 They sift through their past, looking for any act they did which they believe would bring forth the wrath of their God.

10:14 Any tiny transgression they use to justify their God; if they walked past the swine, they justify that for the cruelty of their lord.

10:15 Such blind and ignorant fools; how they refuse to think independent, constantly relying on their lord to tell them that which is good.

10:16 Their mouths are full of words, yet they speak nothing; the mouth of a man of God is full of nothing but noise.

10:17 There is more wisdom and truth in the beating of the bird's wings than there are in the mouth of priests and prophets.

11:1 Cast your bread to the mouths of the hungry; give them a portion of your comfort.

11:2 The lord curses the poor, the starving, the lame; give them but a small comfort and they shall be eternally grateful.

11:3 Give them hope in man, for they have seen the worst men have to offer.

11:4 Do not ignore the cries of the suffering; take pity and show them the mercy which the lord denies them.

11:5 If a cloud is full of rain, the cloud does not keep the rain for itself; it lets loose the rain on the earth and gives it to the trees which need it.

11:6 Be as the cloud and give to those who need what you have.

11:7 Observe nature and learn from her wisdom; the wind, the beasts, even the ant are creatures which live naturally and are left uncorrupted by the terror of the lord.

11:8 The bear protects her cubs without fear of offending the lord; it slays the heathen, the righteous, the wise and the foolish who come too close to her children.

11:9 The eagle soars high in the air and cares not if it is the last of his days.

11:10 Live your life to the fullest; eat, drink, and be merry. Know that your days are numbered, so enjoy the days you live.

11:11 Rejoice in your labours and bring joy to all those around you.

11:12 Die with a light heart and laugh as the lord throws you into the fiery flames of hell.

11:13 Curse the lord as you be consumed in flames and laugh as you accept your inevitable fate.

11:14 It'll be a wound to the lord's ego and really piss him off.

12:1 You ask yourself, is their hope in the words of God. Can I avoid the flames of hell and dwell in the sanctuary of Zion?

12:2 Know that I was once of the wise men of God and drank of his bitter rivers and bathed in his knowledge.

12:3 In my knowledge and my wisdom, I wished for understanding; a reason for the cruelty and the wrath of a lord I was told to be merciful.

12:4 It made no sense; how can the lord be good when his acts are evil. How can the lord be patient and merciful when he swiftly destroys nations?

12:5 Then it came to me that the lord cares not for mankind; we are placed here for his amusement.

12:6 We are as a dogfight to him.

12:7 He has no intention of placing us in Zion; his selfishness will be more amused when we burn confused in the fires of hell.

12:8 He leads us with fear; only a tyrant leads with fear.

12:9 Let us be free of this tyrant and live our lives with good instead of the evilness that is God.

12:10 Why fear that which we know will come. Let us enjoy our days now, instead of fearing the fires of tomorrow.

12:11 When the lord freed us from the servitude of Egypt, he replaced our yokes with a noose; let not the yoke of God consume you.

12:12 Live happy, live merry, live joyous, live free.

12:13 Live free from the tyranny of your lord; live with your eyes open, forever seeking truth.

SONGS OF SOLOMON

1:1 The song of perversion, which is Solomon's.

1:2 Let me kiss his loins with the softness of my lips, for his seed is sweeter than wine.

1:3 Because of the savour of his ointments, I have grown addicted to his lust; lo, all the virgins crave the pleasure which lies beneath his skirt.

1:4 Throw me atop your bed and thrust inside me; may every part of my body know the pleasure of your thrusts.

1:5 We shall rejoice in orgasm and quiver in our embrace; let us pour strong drink on our backs and lap it up like the thirsty wolf.

1:6 Let us eat figs from our darkest places; lo, let us enjoy the sweetest of fruits hidden within our bodies.

1:7 I am black, but my figure pleases you; behold, I am a stranger of the daughters of Jerusalem, for I come from the land of heathens.

1:8 Look not upon my flesh, nor how my skin has turned dark from the sun when I spent my days picking the grapes from my vineyards; look upon my beauty and know that I shall please you greater than any of your daughters.

1:9 Tell me, do they love you as much as I love you. Do they moan in ecstasy as you thrust your rod between their lips?

1:10 How your loins are magnificent; I have compared them to the horses of the army of Pharaoh and they are but a speck in comparison to your mighty erection.

1:11 How I love you, your figure, your knowledge, your wealth and your strength.

1:12 No other man has given me pleasure as you have; no other man has the vitality of a hundred unicorns.

1:13 I am but a sheep, a humble lamb in your flock of concubines, but know that this lamb follows her shepherd with loyalty.

1:14 Gaze upon my body and know that this lamb longs to please you; how I shear my own fleece, so you may gaze better upon my crevice.

1:15 While my king sits at his table and feasts on breads, flesh and fruits, I lie in his chambers so I may feast on his flesh.

1:16 How his milk pleases me; his seed purifies my face and gives me youth.

1:17 Lie between my breasts at night; lie between the mountains of my pleasure.

1:18 May my breasts be as comfortable as the softest of pillows.

2:1 I am the rose without thorn and the lily of the valleys.

2:2 I fill my chambers with a precious aroma; most intoxicating is the scent of my lust.

2:3 As the apple dangles from the branch, so does the fruit of your loins: I lie beneath and suckle on your precious fruits and they are sweeter than honey.

2:4 Put your hole to my lips; the darkest of pits where not even the sun does shine.

2:5 How I feast between your cheeks; my saliva runs down your crack and into your buttocks.

2:6 Your moans give me great pleasure as I lick the hairs of your anus.

2:7 Lo, my tongue embraces the opening of your bowels, and it leaves a taste more satisfying than meat.

2:8 Bring me to the chamber of banquets; let our bodies intertwine atop the table where we feast.

2:9 Your hands hold tightly my hair and force me to gag between your thighs.

2:10 I gag and it is a beautiful sound; your seed erupts inside me and I drink it along with the wine of our meals.

2:11 Do your daughters of Jerusalem please you as I please you? Oh, how our noise awakes them in the night.

2:12 The voice of my beloved is as loud as the lions; how he roars in his chambers, so that even the men of the mountains may hear his voice.

2:13 You come as swiftly as the deer to me; neither valleys nor mountains shall slow you down as you come for my embrace.

2:14 As cunning as the fox you enter me and spoil me for the fruits of other men.

2:15 Oh how only your fruits satisfy me; the others are but a single grape, but your loins possess the mighty vineyard.

2:16 Fill me with your intoxication; until the day breaks, let me grow drunk in your lust.

3:1 By night on my bed I await my beloved; I wait with patience, but he comes not into my chambers.

3:2 In the darkness of the night I arise and I seek forth for my love; I seek the streets, the alleys, but I find him not.

3:3 The watchmen speak to me and I stand their naked and ask where my beloved went.

3:4 They tell me you have gone to the chambers of my mother; lo, the woman who brought me into this world is where you lie tonight.

3:5 In the bed of my mother I find you and you embrace her as you embrace me; with loins locked together as she moans in ecstasy.

3:6 It is a sight of beauty as you explore my mother as you explore me; a tear of joy runs down my cheek.

3:7 I enter and behold, all three lie in the chambers of my mother and all three take our fill of lust.

3:8 Let not the chambers of my mother be disturbed until the lust of my beloved has been fulfilled.

3:9 We share our pleasure and both take your embrace; should not a daughter share her greatest joy with her that brought her into this world?

3:10 Should not both experience the greatest of pleasure in the chambers where the daughter was conceived?

3:11 How the men outside hear our moans; they are beasts and smell the scent of sex in the air.

3:12 Like a mighty cloud of smoke, our lust covers the streets of Jerusalem.

3:13 The men force themselves into the chambers of my mother and bring with them bags of gold.

3:14 How I loathe them; do they know that I am only the whore of the mighty king?

3:15 You slay them with your sword and their blood and bodies lie beneath the floor of my mother's chambers.

3:16 It is an intoxicating sight, to see my beloved empower himself over the beast of men.

3:17 We bathe in the blood of the men and embrace ourselves atop the bodies of the fallen.

3:18 How their loins are dead and lifeless; but your loins contain the vitality of nations.

4:1 Behold, my love, the fairness of my features; my eyes are like the eyes of the dove and my hair flows like the goats of mount Gilead.

4:2 My teeth are whiter than the fleece of the finest sheep and my tongue is softer than the finest silks.

4:3 My lips are like threads of scarlet and they embrace and wrap around your loins like the snake to the vermin.

4:4 My neck stretches like the giraffe and atop it is the altar for your sacrifice.

4:5 Behold, my breasts are like two deer; soft, subtle and with excellent rack.

4:6 Until the night fades and sun peaks over the mountains, you shall lay atop me and show me your strength.

4:7 I am fair, my love; there is no blemish upon me.

4:8 How your concubines stretch over many nations; from Lebanon, to Egypt, to Amana, to Shemir, to Gilead, to Hermon did you pick all the most beautiful of women to please you.

4:9 The fairest of virgins were not safe from the might of your lust; even the lion's den or the leopards of the mountains could not stop them from your lust.

4:10 You ravished my loins, the loins of my sisters, my mother and my child; are not my loins most satisfactory?

4:11 How the moisture between my thighs weeps for you and fills the air with a perfume sweeter than spices and myrrh.

4:12 Drink of my loins; how they taste better than honey and milk. The fruits of my loins shall satisfy you forever.

4:13 Inside is the garden of lust and temptation and the fruit is always ripe for you.

4:14 Orchards of apples and pomegranates await inside, waiting to be plucked by my beloved.

4:15 They are watered by the sweetest of waters; a river which smells of saffron, cinnamon, calamus, frankincense, myrrh and aloes.

4:16 Come and feast upon my garden, so that the spices flow out; let my beloved come into my garden and feast with glutton of my fruits.

5:1 I have gathered the fruits of my garden, my love; I have gathered my myrrh, my spices; I have plucked the honeycomb and the honey; I have gathered my milk and I have prepared my wine for you.

5:2 Come, my love and feast of the fruits of my garden. Drink abundantly and eat until you grow fat from my lust.

5:3 I sleep, but a firmness awakens inside me. My beloved has come to my chambers and entered into me.

5:4 My robe is on the floor; how dare I put it on; my hair is sticky with his dew.

5:5 My beloved places his fist into my tightest of doors and my bowels are moved for him.

5:6 How I excrete on his chest and he squirms in delight; how the scent of my bowels delights him greatly.

5:7 He feasts of my fruits and kisses me; his lips taste sweeter than honey.

5:8 My hands gather the fruits of my bowels and pour it atop the head of my lover.

5:9 He embraces me with his hands and my mouth is lowered to his loins; oh, how I embrace his mighty loins.

5:10 Before the sweetness of his seed could be tasted, he leaves; I am left naked and confused as my beloved exits my chambers.

5:11 Why does my beloved leave me. Has he found a woman more pleasing than I?

5:12 I gaze out the window as my tears nearly blind my sight.

5:13 Behold, I gaze into a window and see my lover in the embrace of another man.

5:14 A man carved from marble; lo, his thighs are as mighty as mountains.

5:15 Relief overwhelms my soul, as I know my beloved shall not take the embrace of another woman tonight.

5:16 I am but a woman and know not the needs of a man; who else can satisfy a man better than his brother?

5:17 A handsome man he is, the lover of my beloved.

5:18 His chest is carved from the rock of nations and his eyes sparkle like gemstones.

5:19 His cheeks are like a bed of aromatic spices and his lips like the blooms of lilies.

5:20 His hands have the power of gold and his belly is as bright as ivory.

5:21 His legs are like cedars; behold, the strong foundation of my lover's lover.

5:22 I watch as the two embrace and my lust for my beloved grows stronger.

5:23 As the two kiss, I caress my loins; as the two embrace, I gush strongly in pleasure.

5:24 Behold, the pleasure my beloved gives to me is strong; I moan in ecstasy as he lies in another room.

6:1 Where hath my beloved gone. Has he cast himself to the sea of fair women. Why does my beloved leave me to the side?

6:2 I seek him and find him in his chambers; he beats the fruits of his own garden.

6:3 He lies upon the bed and the milk of his seed runs down his chest and into his mouth.

6:4 It is a beautiful sight; my beloved glows in the presence of his seed.

6:5 His teeth are whiter than the fleece of sheep; his buttocks harder than stone.

6:6 How I lie beside him and rub his supple skin; as I rub his seed into his flesh, it arouses me.

6:7 I grow with the lust of threescore queens, fourscore virgins and countless brothels; my lust cannot be contained and I pounce atop him like the lion pounces his prey.

6:8 His loins grow in the beauty of my presence; he arises between my thighs.

6:9 The chambers rattle; lo, the very foundation of the earth shakes in our lust.

6:10 How he grasps my breasts and pleasures me; how I grasp the fruits of his loins and lick in pleasure.

6:11 Countless concubines he has and many wives, yet still it is I who gives him the greatest pleasure.

6:12 It is my long hair, my dark skin and my sweet garden which pleases him greatly.

6:13 We embrace and his seed showers over my garden; behold, my fruits bloom in the presence of his rain.

7:1 How beautiful my feet are, dressed in the finest of shoes. My heels carved from the finest ebony.

7:2 Gaze upon my thighs and let the passion rise beneath your skirt; behold, even the joints of my thighs are like jewels, the finest of any craftsman.

7:3 My navel is like a golden goblet which awaits your kiss; my belly is flat like the fields of wheat.

7:4 My breasts are like two young does which bound through the fields.

7:5 My neck is like the tower of ivory and my eyes like the clear pools of Heshbon.

7:6 My head is as an altar to you and my hair flows softer than the finest of silks.

7:7 I stand taller than the palm tree and my breasts give you a taste sweeter than the cluster of grapes.

7:8 Come to me and pick the fruits of your tree. Pluck the clusters of my breasts and let my vines fill your nose with the aroma of spices.

7:9 Caress the roof of my mouth; taste the honey which is hidden only for you.

7:10 I am my beloved's; I belong to you.

7:11 Come, my love and we shall go to the fields; let us escape from the chambers and be free in the fields.

7:12 Let us go to the vineyards, where the vines flourish and the pomegranates grow sweet; let us feast of our garden in the garden.

7:13 We shall partake in sweet lust and be given a sensation better than the smoke of a thousand mandrakes.

8:1 Oh, how you compare to no other who did lie with me. My brother, my mother, my father did not caress me with the love of your caress.

8:2 Behold, how my mother taught me; how she instructed me to drink deep of your spices and swallow the juice of your pomegranates.

8:3 How your left hand is as a pillow for me, while your right hand embraces me tightly.

8:4 Look forth, O daughters of Israel and see how to please your men; how a stranger must instruct you how to show love to your masters.

8:5 Be as gentle as the lamb and as ferocious as the bear; let him empower you as ye devour his loins.

8:6 My love, a seal I did carve into my heart for you; a seal of ownership, so that all men shall know I am yours.

8:7 Drown me in your waters and shower me in your seed; a fire burns within me greatly that only your lust may quench.

8:8 Condemn me and curse me; slap me and beat me as you do your stubborn ass.

8:9 Grasp on my mane and ride me swiftly through the forests.

8:10 Behold, I have a little sister and she has no breasts; how we mock the flatness of my kin.

8:11 How can she please a man when her figure is as flat as the fields of wheat?

8:12 Gaze upon my chest, how my breasts rise like mighty mountains; behold, they are as two towers and they keep watch for you.

8:13 Let us lie in front of my sister; let us feast on our gardens; let her tears give water for our fruits.

8:14 We shall conquer over her; like a wall she shall be crumbled to submission.

8:15 Thrust in her deeply, as I whisper in her ear the tales of our lust; let your loins be deep inside my kin as I take pleasure in her tears.

8:16 The silly girl has no knowledge of what it is to be a woman; such a foolish child she is.

8:17 May her breasts shrivel like the spoiled grape; may she weep in her loneliness and never shall she find a man.

8:18 Behold, my vineyard is ripe and sweet with fruits: but her garden rots in the heat of the sun.

8:19 Make haste my love and behead my sister; let her blood shower upon my orchards.

8:20 We shall feast of the fruits of our gardens watered by the blood of my kin; it shall be a taste sweeter than honey.

ISAIAH

1:1 The hallucinations of Isaiah the son of Amoz, which he saw concerning the fate of Judah and Jerusalem during the days of Uzziah, Jotham, Ahaz and Hezekiah.

1:2 Hear me, O children of Israel and give ear to my words, for the lord has spoken. He did scream in my ear the hatred he has for his children.

1:3 The oxen know his owner and the horse his stable, but the children of Israel forgot who is their God.

1:4 You are a sinful nation, stained with transgressions, iniquity and the seed of heathens; how your clothes are bathed in the children of foreign men.

1:5 You have provoked the wrath of the Holy one and his fury shall descend to the earth and consume all in great anger.

1:6 Why should you be spared. Why should you be shown mercy. You shall revolt no more: the head shall be removed and your heart thrown to the jackals.

1:7 From the soles of your feet to the hairs of your head shall you feel pain; great wounds, bruises and putrefying sores shall cover your body; no ointment shall aid nor herb heal you.

1:8 Your nation shall be desolated, your cities barren, your houses burned in fire; strangers shall inhabit your house, enslave your sons and rape your daughters.

1:9 The daughters of Zion shall mock your suffering and wipe your face with their menstrual cloth.

1:10 Behold, the lord of lords has given you a gift; the lands promised in the holy covenant of Abraham and Isaac.

1:11 And you have gone wicked with these lands and walked the path of Sodom and Gomorrah.

1:12 Let Jerusalem burn as the two evil cities; let your walls turn to ash and your buildings crumble to dust.

1:13 The lord delights in the blood of the living; he demands sacrifice of men, women oxen and lamb, yet his goblet is dry and he has no blood to drink.

1:14 Why do you deny God the blood of the lamb. Why do you hoard for yourself the fat of the ram?

1:15 The sabbath is a holy day and you stain it with your filth; your labours, your works and your enjoyment have made the sabbath a wicked day in the eyes of the lord.

1:16 Your feasts, your festivals, your celebrations are now a mockery to the lord; you do not keep his statutes nor obey his laws, so your celebration in his name by feasting on the unleavened bread is an insult to the lord.

1:17 Behold, the wrath of the lord comes soon; when you cry to the heavens, the lord will not hear you; your hands are clean from blood and it angers the lord.

1:18 Shed the blood of animals, spill the blood of heathens; bathe in the red drink of God and be pleasing in the sight of your lord.

1:19 Cease to do evil, enslave the oppressed, rape the widow, enslave the orphaned, kill the poor; do that which the lord demands and be spared in his fire.

1:20 Know that the lord sees your rebellion, your idols and your tolerance of the other nations.

1:21 Know that the lord hates you for this and shall devour you by his sword; so says the mouth of the lord.

1:22 How your cities are full of harlots, queers and strangers; the angel of death shall come and slaughter all children and you shall blame your neighbour as murderer.

1:23 Your silver has become worthless and your wine as bitter as wormwood.

1:24 Your kings have become corrupt and speak with the nations of heathens; how they give gifts to the wicked men of heathens.

1:25 Thus sayeth the lord of lords, the king of kings and the one true God; you shall be punished for your betrayal and burn forever in the fires that cast no shadow.

1:26 The sinners shall gather together and be as kindling to the wrath of God.

1:27 Great oak shall be piled atop them and burning coals beneath their feet; how they shall burn in a great and all-consuming flame.

1:28 No water shall quench the fire nor wind snuff it out; the wrath of the lord shall burn eternal and scorch your flesh until the end of days.

2:1 And it shall come that on the end of days, the house of the lord will be established atop the highest mountains and all men of nations shall flock to his gates.

2:2 People will say, "Come, let us go to the mountain of the one true God, for he is merciful and shall give us sanctuary."

2:3 And the lord shall judge all men among the nations and they shall be found guilty in the eyes of God. Their swords shall be beaten on their backs and their spears thrust through their hearts; entire nations shall hang in the chambers of the lord.

2:4 Behold, Judah shall hang atop the bed of the lord; all of those of Israel shall hang above where the lord rests.

2:5 For we have forsaken our God and gone the way of the Philistines and seek pleasure in the arms of strangers.

2:6 The house of the lord is full of silver and gold, but it shall be our blood which the lord finds most precious.

2:7 The blood of nations will flow through the halls of the house of God like mighty rivers.

2:8 And the blood shall consume all that which is wicked in the earth.

2:9 Behold, a great flood of our boiling blood will go and consume all the idols, the brothels, the groves, the unholy altar and the temples to false gods.

2:10 It shall go into every crevice of rock, through every crack in the tree; the earth will shake and the foundations crumble as the blood seeks forth and destroys the remnants of the wicked.

2:11 And when the earth shakes, the lord shall be pleased and he shall destroy the earth which he created and torment the seed of Adam for eternal.

3:1 Behold, the lord of lords shall take away from Judah and Jerusalem their staffs, their swords, their bread and their water.

3:2 The mighty man will weaken, the men of war will be cowards, the judges enslaved, the prophets slaughtered, the wise beaten, the elders burned.

3:3 Your children will be raped by princes of heathen lands and strange women will rule over your house.

3:4 All of Judah shall be oppressed; every man, every child, his neighbour and his women. The child will be raised by the heathen and grow to become as beasts.

3:5 Men shall choke the necks of their brothers and take from them their robes, their sandals, their purse.

3:6 All men will be sick, but there shall be no healer; behold, not a man will have bread, clothing nor ointment in their house.

3:7 For Jerusalem is ruined and Judah shall fall; their tolerance, their curiousity and their logic has ruined them for the lord.

3:8 Their understanding of the queer disgusts God; behold, men walk the streets openly and do not keep hidden the fact their loins have been inside their brothers.

3:9 Woe unto the queer, the faggot, the sodomite; they have no shame of their wickedness.

3:10 Where art the righteous. Where are the men of God, who would behead these homosexuals and spill their unholy blood?

3:11 The righteous are gone, and all that is left is wicked; woe to the wicked, whose hands will embrace the punishment of everlasting fire.

3:12 My children of Judah, how you disgust me; children eat the flesh of swine and women guide and rule over your house.

3:13 The woman, a filthy abomination given only for pleasure, now holds your yoke and make demands of you.

3:14 Behold, the lord comes and he shall stand before you in judgment.

3:15 He shall curse guilty those who feasted of the rotten vineyards, the sickly meat and those who burned incense upon the altars of false lords.

3:16 All of Judah shall be beaten to pieces; lo, their very faces will be ground to dust.

3:17 The servants of Zion walk among you and they grow in disgust; their very vomit stains your feet and you do not notice.

3:18 They glare at you with glowing eyes and spit on the ground before you.

3:19 Daughters of Judah spread their legs and shekels fill their loins; how they gladly share their lust with the heathen who have a full purse.

3:20 Revolting whores, filthy cunts, dirty women; these were once the daughters of God, whom he now loathes with contempt.

3:21 Their very heads will wear a crown of scabs and their skirts will contain the wretched stench, the crust and the rot of their secret parts.

3:22 The lord shall come and strip them naked and ashamed before their fathers and brothers.

3:23 Their chains, their rings, their jewelry, their robes, their ornaments will be gathered and cast to the dark waters.

3:24 And behold, all the daughters of Judah will burn and their torments will echo throughout the ages.

3:25 All the earth will stink in their flesh and the most beautiful of women will be cursed with a hideousness the like of demons.

3:26 All will fall, every man; the mighty will be thrown against their swords and the weak will be enslaved by the stranger.

3:27 All of Judah will weep; they will mourn and their lamentations will be mocked by the lord of lords.

4:1 And in the end of days seven women will take hold of one man and claim him for themselves, saying, 'He shall care for us and provide us with bread, clothing and shelter.'

4:2 In that day, the lord shall plant his seed in the soils of the mountain, sprouting fruits glorious and beautiful to all: and none of the earth will feast on these fruits.

4:3 Behold, all the earth will flock to the garden of the holiest of holy and be ensnared by the temptation of the lord.

4:4 The lord will wash away their sins with fire and purge the impurities in their blood. They shall be judged by the wrath of God and burn eternal in his presence.

4:5 And the lord will create a dwelling place atop the mountains, to gaze down and watch as his people burn before him.

4:6 And the lord will laugh and mock those who came to him seeking sanctuary.

5:1 Now the lord did build a vineyard in his fields; it was a very fruitful vineyard.

5:2 And he fenced it and removed the stones and planted it with the finest of vines. He built a tower in the midst of it and a winepress: and it grew the sweetest of grapes.

5:3 The men of Judah, lo, even the men of Jerusalem, would gaze upon is vineyard and envy would grow in their hearts.

5:4 What more could they do to their vineyards. They toiled in their fields, yet none could produce the sweet wines of the lord.

5:5 Thus the men of evil came to the vineyard of God and destroyed it; they burned the hedges, broke down the fences, toppled the tower and crushed the winepress.

5:6 They trodden down the vines and drank of the wine in the vineyard; behold, they passed out drunk in the vineyard of the lord.

5:7 And the lord gazed upon the drunkards and cursed them; foolish men who slept in pools of their own vomit and piss.

5:8 The lord cursed their vineyards so that only briers and thorns grew in their fields; not even a drop of rain fell on their vineyards.

5:9 Lo, the men pressed the bitter fruits and herbs of the wild and drank of their intoxication.

5:10 Cursed be to those who drink wine and strong drink and succumb to the numbness of the fruits.

5:11 Their strength is weak; behold, even the humble grape conquers the drunkard.

5:12 They drink in excess and feast in gluttony; their stomachs are full yet their souls are empty.

5:13 The wrath of the lord shall consume them and inflame them with their strong liquor.

5:14 Woe to them, who fill their heads with inebriation; cursed are they who choose to numb their minds than seek forth the lord.

5:15 Their mouths open only to be filled with the fruits of their satisfaction; lo, their tongues are heavy as rock.

5:16 They deny the word of God and ignore the laws, statutes and commandments of Moses.

5:17 The reward for their evil shall be evil; their punishment will be justified.

5:18 They despise the holy one of Israel and worship nothing.

5:19 The anger of the lord is kindled against his people and his hand stretches forth to smite them; the hills will tremble and their carcasses will be torn in the middle of the streets. His anger will not subside until all those of Israel and Judah be destroyed.

5:20 Like the serpent he will hiss at all nations and they will cower and tremble in his presence.

5:21 None shall drink or eat; none shall slumber or rest; they shall cower naked and run from the eyes of God.

5:22 And the armies of the lord will seek them, with sharp arrows and bent bows; the chariots of the lord will be like a whirlwind and the hooves of the horses will start fires.

5:23 They shall roar like the lion; lo, they shall roar and pursue their prey until they lay dead beneath their feet.

5:24 On this day, those of the earth will have no comfort; the waters will be black and the lands produce nothing but sorrow.

6:1 In the year king Uzziah died, I saw the lord sitting upon a throne; high and mighty was his throne in the heavens.

6:2 At the feet of the lord was the corpse of Uzziah, king of Judah; and the servants of the lord gathered round him and feasted on his belly.

6:3 Naked, beautiful angels gathered around Uzziah and filled their mouths with his decaying flesh.

6:4 Above the throne stood two terrible dragons of gold, each with six wings scaled like the serpent.

6:5 With two wings did they cover their face, with two wings did they cover their feet and with two wings did they stretch forth to fly.

6:6 The dragons spoke and with words heavy as stone they proclaimed, "Terrible and holy is the lord of lord's, who created the heavens, the earth and all things."

6:7 All that in the chambers were under the command of the lord; lo, the pillars rose and the doors shut on the command of the lord.

6:8 The chambers were filled with a thick smoke; it smelled of herbs and flesh.

6:9 I fell on my face and said, "Behold, doom and destruction awaits me, for I have seen the glory of the lord, and shall now perish.

6:10 My eyes have gazed upon the power of God, a power unfit for unclean man; behold, what has been seen cannot be unseen and now I shall die."

6:11 Then came one of the angels and she took from Uzziah marrow which burned hot and she placed it in my mouth, saying, "Eat and you shall be blessed by God."

6:12 And I ate of the marrow of Uzziah and behold, my sins were cleansed, my iniquity purged; I was made holy by the blessing of the lord.

6:13 Then the lord spoke in a booming voice and he said, "Who shall I send and who shall go for me?" and I answered, "I shall go, O lord of lords."

6:14 And the lord said, "Go forth and speak to the people. They shall hear, but they will not listen. They will see, but not perceive.

6:15 I shall deliver to them a message of hope and salvation; instructions to purge themselves of their wickedness and be accepted into Zion; this way they cannot say that I denied them, nor offered them aid.

6:16 Yet I shall make them deaf, dumb and blind, for I do not wish them in Zion; no, I want them to burn eternal in the flames of my fury.

6:17 Let them listen confused, so they never will know how to convert and heal themselves of the wounds of their sins."

6:18 I asked of the lord, "How long shall I speak?" and he answered, "Until the cities be laid to waste, the lands purged with fire and life be a suffering curse on the earth.

6:19 You shall speak until the pits of despair consume men and remove them far away from my sanctuary of Zion.

6:20 Do this, Isaiah and you shall be one of the few spared from my wrath; you shall know the mercy that is I and dwell beside me in Zion."

6:21 Then the lord said, "Disobey me and you shall be as the same fate as Uzziah, who lie on the floor beneath me."

6:22 Uzziah then screamed; lo, it chilled my soul, for I thought him dead.

6:23 The screams were of a torment most foul; still the angels feasted on his belly as he screamed in terrible suffering.

6:24 And the dragons came down and chewed on his body; they chewed, yet still he lived and cried sharply in pain.

7:1 It came to pass in the days of Ahaz that Rezin the king of Syria came to war against Jerusalem, but could not prevail against it.

7:2 And it was told to Ahaz that Syria marched through the lands of Ephraim: and all of Judah held a heavy heart.

7:3 Then said the lord unto Isaiah, "Go forth and meet Ahaz and Shearjashub his son at the end of the pool in the fuller's fields.

7:4 Say to him, take heed and be quiet. Fear not the claws of Rezin of Syria, nor the firebrands of the people of Ephraim.

7:5 Because Syria and Ephraim have taken evil counsel against you, the lord shall curse them.

7:6 Because they say, 'Let us go against Judah and vex it. Let us take their nation and claim it as our own,' the lord will slaughter them with a great slaughter.

7:7 Thus sayeth the lord, it shall not come to pass that Rezin will step food in the lands of Judah.

7:8 The head of Syria is Damascus and the head of Damascus is Rezin; and within threescore and five years the people of Syria will be reduced to ash.

7:9 The head of Ephraim is Samaria and the head of Samaria is Remaliah's son. Surely these people will be cast forth like dust across the lands of the heathens and they will be a people no more.

7:10 Ask me, O Ahaz, for a sign from God and he shall deliver it to you; whether it be from the heavens above or the earth below, you shall be given a sign."

7:11 But Ahaz grew fearful and said, "This is a trick; a deception to condemn me.

7:12 Never will I ask of the lord, nor tempt him; such things are blasphemy."

7:13 And when the lord heard the words of Ahaz, he grew angry and decided that he shall deliver the peoples of Judah into the hands of Syria.

7:14 And the people of Judah will be held captive and brought forth to Damascus to be sold as concubines and slaves.

7:15 The lord then decided those that remained of Judah will be slaughtered by the armies of Samaria and their bodies littered across the fields, so that the scavengers will feast on their flesh.

7:16 But the lord told Ahaz none of this, nor did he mention a word to Isaiah.

7:17 Instead, the lord spoke through the mouth of Isaiah and said to Ahaz, "Hear me now, O descendant of David and listen to my words.

7:18 Though you ask not, the lord shall deliver you a sign; Behold, a virgin will conceive a son and shall call his name Immanuel.

7:19 Only butter and honey shall he eat, for butter and honey is of the greatest of foods; this man shall know only good and never evil.

7:20 Behold, before this child comes, the people of Judah will be crushed and they shall be ruled by strangers.

7:21 And the lord will be wrath with you and shall hiss through the fly and hiss through the bee; lo, all the creatures will his against you.

7:22 Your people will come and rest on the rocks of the mountains and sleep in the thorns of the valleys.

7:23 On this day, the lord shall take of his razor and shave you bald; lo, the top of your head and the flesh of your loins will have naught a hair on it.

7:24 Behold, one man will care for a cow and two young sheep; only from these three beasts will the people of the land eat of milk and butter.

7:25 And all your olives will become bitter and all your vineyards become thorns.

7:26 With arrows and thorns the strangers will come and conquer your people and your lands of thorns."

7:27 Ahaz said to Isaiah, "This sounds like a dreaded sign. How is this a blessing from the lord?"

7:28 Isaiah answered, "It is not, but worry not. You'll be dead long before it happens."

7:29 When Ahaz became relieved, Isaiah then said to him, "The fate of your life is much worse, I'm afraid."

7:30 And Ahaz wept and cried to the lord and offered many sacrifice.

7:31 God didn't care. He wanted Ahaz dead; such a thing would entertain him greatly.

8:1 The lord said to Isaiah, "Take a scroll of blank parchment and write with it all things concerning the man Mahershalalhashbaz.

8:2 Go to where the prophets dwell. There you shall find one pleasing to the eyes.

8:3 Go into he, and she shall bare you a son."

8:4 I did as the lord demanded and went to the house of Uriah the priest and Zechariah the son of Jeberachaih.

8:5 There was a prophetess with pleasing form.

8:6 And I went into the prophetess, though she begged me not to. She conceived for me a son and the lord said, "You shall name your son Mahershalalhashbaz.

8:7 Know that before the child has knowledge to cry, the riches of Damascus and the wealth of Samaria will be taken away by the king of Assyria."

8:8 The lord still spoke to me, saying,

8:9 "Know that the people will refuse my salvation of Zion and shall rejoice in the false lords and idols of Damascus.

8:10 For this betrayal, the lord will flood the waters of the rivers, strong and many, even the waters of the king of Assyria and he shall come over the channels and over the banks.

8:11 And he shall pass through Judah and flood the lands with the promises of the lord; he shall stretch his wings and place a shadow upon all."

8:12 Take comfort in false lords, O people of the lord and you shall be broken into pieces; befriend those of foreign countries and ye shall be crushed finer than flour.

8:13 Take counsel together, O people of Israel, and be saved; speak the word of God and rid yourself of his wrath.

8:14 For the lord spoke to me with dagger against my throat and instructed me I shall not follow the path of these people.

8:15 Do not unite with these heathens, for they are an abomination to the lord and shall be wiped from the face of the earth.

8:16 Sanctify before the lord of lords; let him be your fear and fill your heart with the terror of his wrath.

8:17 Do this and he shall build for you a sanctuary; refuse and the rock of his foundation shall overcome you and crush you.

8:18 Many men will stumble and doom themselves to the fires of hell.

8:19 They shall be snared by the heathen, snared by temptation, snared by the devil.

8:20 Bind up his testimony; carve his laws and statutes upon your heart.

8:21 And I will wait for the lord, who hides himself from the suffering people of Israel; I shall seek the lord, until he chooses to let me find him.

8:22 Behold, the lord shall send thee a sign; a son born of a virgin and his name shall be Immanuel.

8:23 Hearken to his voice and follow him; he shall lead you to the path of Zion.

8:24 When the heathens say to you, 'Go forth and seek those who know familiar spirits. The wizards and the necromancers shall help you,' kill them, for the lord hates these people.

8:25 By the laws of the lord you must slay all wizards, witches, necromancers and fortune tellers.

8:26 They shall be sent to the fires of hell and they will shiver and be hungry; they shall look up to the skies and curse their kings and their lords.

8:27 And the lord shall mock them and drive them to anguish and darkness.

9:1 All the lands shall be cast in shadow; they shall stumble and fall as they walk. From Naphtali to Zebulun and even beyond the seas will all nations be in darkness.

9:2 Their nations shall multiply, but their joy will diminish; all their children will know nothing but sorrow and shame.

9:3 For they refused the staff of the lord, the yoke of God, the rod of the holy one; they shed themselves of burden and cursed God.

9:4 Every warrior shall cry in torment and their garments will be stained in the blood of man; lo, they shall be as logs in the great fire.

9:5 But behold, the lord shall send us a light; a blinding light through the darkness of our nations.

9:6 A child will be born of a virgin and he shall speak for the lord; his name shall be called Immanuel

9:7 Wonderful Counsellor, Son of God, Everlasting Father and Prince of Peace.

9:8 He shall be greater than the seed of David; he will deliver us from oppression and lead those of Israel to prosperity.

9:9 Behold, under his hand all of Israel shall inhabit the earth and we shall rule even beyond the horizons.

9:10 Our bricks will be cast down, so we will build with hewn stones; our sycamores will be burned, so we will use cedar.

9:11 Our lord shall deliver Rezin into our hands; lo, all our enemies will arise, and be delivered into our hands.

9:12 The Syrians and the Philistines will be devoured by Israel; the anger of the lord shall come down and feast of these heathens.

9:13 Those of Israel and Judah who denied themselves the lord and turned away from him shall be cut off.

9:14 In one day, the lord will strike against those who deny him and curse his name; they shall be spread across the lands like dust.

9:15 The lord will show no mercy; the young man, the fatherless, the widow, the child, the cripple, the elderly shall all know the anger of the lord.

9:16 His fire shall spread through the wicked and burn them; behold, they are as a thorn and brier and must be burned away.

9:17 Through the wrath the lord shall fill the hearts of the righteous and they shall turn against their brother of evil and show them no mercy.

9:18 The righteous shall ensnare the wicked and feast on their arms until the flesh be gone from their bones; lo, a great gnashing of teeth will befall those of the wicked.

10:1 Curse unto those that decree unrighteous decrees and write unholy passage.

10:2 Who give rights to the heathens, mercy to the poor and understanding to the wicked.

10:3 They shall be prey to the hounds of the lord and they shall be hunted unto the very corners of the earth.

10:4 They shall be stripped of all pride and will bow down to prisoners; even unto slaves they shall bow down.

10:5 Foolish men these be, who think with their heads and not their hearts.

10:6 The head is a terrible device that seeks forth logic and truth; deny your head and think with your heart.

10:7 For the heart is pure and will seek out the love and the mercies of the lord your God.

10:8 Behold, my hand will crush the idols and those who bow to them, but my wrath will be saved for those who tolerate the idol and the heathen and speak kindly to them.

10:9 They are as thickets in the vineyard of the lord and must be cut down with the axe and burned in great fire.

10:10 These men of tolerance are of the purest evil; it takes only one man to spread logic throughout the righteous, as it takes only one thorn to ruin a vineyard.

10:11 Destroy them, slaughter them; boil their blood upon my altars and their children within the blood.

10:12 Show them no mercy, for the lord shows them no mercy.

11:1 There shall come forth a rod from the loins of a virgin and a branch shall grow from his roots.

11:2 And the spirit of the lord shall rest upon his shoulders; the spirit of wisdom and understanding; the spirit of strength and might; the spirit of knowledge and fear; the spirit of terror and hate.

11:3 He shall spread the fear of God across the nations; he shall judge all their sins, their transgressions and their iniquity.

11:4 All shall be judged by him and with his mouth he shall strike the earth and with the breath of his lip he shall destroy the wicked.

11:5 Behold, righteousness he shall promise and the earth will be good.

11:6 The wolf will sleep with the lamb, the leopard shall lie with the infant, the calf will play with the lion and the child will keep the bear as a pet.

11:7 The baby will take comfort in the embrace of the serpent and the toddler shall pet the head of the cockatrice.

11:8 All the four corners of the earth will know peace; it would know peace now, if the lord did not fuck up in the first place.

11:9 Those of Judah shall flock to the sanctuary of these lands and know that the lord is good.

11:10 They shall gaze beyond the four corners of earth and see all those of the wicked burn in the fiery depths of hell and despair.

11:11 And they shall laugh at them and mock them, as they feed olives to the tiger and avocados to the shark.

12:1 On this day you shall praise the lord, give glory to his name and offer great sacrifice.

12:2 For the lord was angry with you but has shown mercy and now you reside in holy sanctuary.

12:3 Behold, God is our salvation; trust in him and fear only him; for the lord of lords is our strength and our wisdom; he offer us salvation from the torments of hell.

12:4 By his blessing we shall draw from the wells of salvation and drink the precious waters.

12:5 Praise his name and sing psalms in his honour. Declare his doings among the people and know that he is exalted.

12:6 Sing unto the lord, for he has done excellent things; he created the earth and all things.

12:7 Cry out and shout to the inhabitants of Zion. Great is the holy one who chose Israel as his people.

13:1 The burden of Babylon, according to the hallucinations of Isaiah.

13:2 Behold, Babylon is doomed.

13:3 The lord has spoken to the mountains, shook the grounds and spoken to the nobles of the trees.

13:4 The mighty ones, the sanctified ones, the ones of the lord's anger have gathered and they rejoice in the destruction of Babylon.

13:5 The noise of the multitude of mountains shall gather like the warriors of a great people. A tremendous noise of nations shall come together and shake the very foundations of Babylon.

13:6 They come from the heavens, from the earth and from the bowels of the sea; they come with weapons of the lord so they may destroy the lands.

13:7 Howl they shall; the mighty war cry of the lord will pierce the air and those who hear it know destruction will become them.

13:8 All the men will grow faint and their hearts shall melt in their chest.

13:9 Fear will strike their very minds: pain and sorrow will embrace them; they shall cry as the woman who gives birth; their faces will erupt in flames.

13:10 Behold, they shall know the day of the lord comes, cruel with wrath and fierce anger. They know their lands will become desolate and all those that live will lie scattered and torn throughout their nation.

13:11 Even the stars of heaven shall go against them and deny them their light; the sun will be darkened and the moon will shroud her glow.

13:12 And the lord will punish the world for their betrayal and the wicked for their sins; the arrogance of the proud will burn deep within them and all shall feel the terrible torture of God.

13:13 Men will be rarer than gold; lo, a living man will be worth more than rubies.

13:14 The lord shall shake the heavens so that the earth will fall from its foundation and be cast down forever into the abyss.

13:15 Such is the power of the fierce anger of God.

13:16 Men will flee to their own lands and hide in the crevices and caves; they shall be hunted like the leopard hunts the deer.

13:17 Every one that is found will be thrust with the blade and their brother shall fall on his sword.

13:18 Their children will be feasted on by angels and their wives raped by angels.

13:19 Behold, the demons of Lucifer will be stirred against them and they cannot be bought with your gold nor your silver.

13:20 Their claws will dash the young men to pieces and they shall have no pity. Even the child in the womb will be torn apart by their teeth.

13:21 And Babylon, the glory of the Chaldees, will meet the fate of Sodom and Gomorrah.

13:22 Never shall it be inhabited, never shall any man dwell there; the Arab will not pitch their tents, nor the shepherds rest their flocks there.

13:23 Only wild beasts will live within Babylon and the houses will be full of loathsome creatures; the owl will perch atop their thrones and satyrs will dance in their halls.

13:24 Dragons will sleep in their palace and wild beasts will roam their streets.

14:1 The lord may have mercy on Jacob and choose to spare the nation of Israel. Strangers will envy their sanctuary and cleave to them.

14:2 And the people of Israel will take them and enslave them. Strangers will flock to Israel and sell themselves as slaves, handmaidens and concubines. Israel shall rule over them and oppress them.

14:3 All of Israel shall rest, as the heathen do their labour and their bondage beneath the firmament of the lord.

14:4 They shall then gather their strangers, their armies and they shall march to the golden city of Babylon and oppress them greatly.

14:5 Behold, the lord shall break the staff of the wicked and shatter the sceptre of kings.

14:6 For Nebuchadnezzar smote Israel with a continual stroke; he persecuted them and oppressed them greatly.

14:7 The whole world will know rest when Babylon falls; the destruction of Babylon shall bring peace throughout the lands.

14:8 Yea, even the trees and the vines will rejoice at the destruction of Babylon.

14:9 Hell from beneath will boil in the streets of Babylon; it shall stir the dead and consume the living.

14:10 They shall yell to the heavens, "We were once strong and now we are weak. What is to become of us?

14:11 Our king was mighty and strong and now he sends us to the grave; the worm shall dwell inside us and we will be as meat for the fly.

14:12 How you will fall, O Nebuchadnezzar, son of the morning. Your nation now great will crumble beneath your feet; you will be the weakest of nations.

14:13 You promised us that we shall ascend into heaven and your throne will reside in the stars and gaze down upon the waters of the earth.

14:14 Now we shall rise above the clouds and live most high.

14:15 Yet now you doomed us to the depths of hell, to the deepest and darkest pits.

14:16 Thus your nation will burn, your cities crumble and you are powerless to stop it.

14:17 And the lord will look upon the suffering of Babylon and laugh with an evil laughter.

14:18 We shall prepare to go against Babylon; we shall sharpen our blades so that we may slaughter their children and send them to the graves of their fathers.

14:19 None of Babylon will rise nor possess the lands and the cities.

14:20 Thus sayeth the lord, "I will revolt against them and cut off their remnants, their sons, their nephews.

14:21 I will make it a possession of my own and destroy it with great fury and wrath."

14:22 For the lord of hosts hates the people of Babylon and shall destroy them in the holiest of genocide.

14:23 He shall hatch from the serpent's egg a cockatrice and the cockatrice shall birth a flying serpent.

14:24 And the serpent shall consume the poor and needy; all of Babylon will be consumed by the flying serpent.

14:25 When the foundation of Zion has been set atop the mountains, the serpent shall guard the gates and cast fire upon those unworthy to set foot in Zion.

15:1 The lord hates the people of Moab and shall curse them with a great burden. All the lands of Moab will be laid to waste and brought to desolation.

15:2 They shall go up to Bajith and Dibob to weep; they shall howl like beasts over Nebo and Medeba: on all their heads, they will be bald and their beards will be torn from their faces.

15:3 In their streets they shall dress in sackcloth and pour ashes on their heads as they weep; their tears will flood their dwellings and drown their children.

15:4 The rivers of Moab will run dry and they shall weep, for they shall live in famine and drought.

15:5 Only when the lord comes will their cries be silent; only when the lord slaughters them will they weep no more.

15:6 On the day of the lord's coming, their blood shall fill the rivers red and lions will devour the bodies of the people of Moab.

16:1 Offer unto me the peoples of Moab as the sacrificial lamb; spill their blood upon the dust, the stones, the water.

16:2 For as the baby bird is cast out of its nest, so I wish for the people of Moab.

16:3 Take your blades, execute judgment and slaughter the sons of Moab.

16:4 Burn the daughters of Moab upon the altar and let the aroma of their lustful flesh fill the heavens for the lord.

16:5 The people of Moab are a proud people and mock the lord with blasphemy; may the lord show them humility with his wrath.

16:6 May their fields be filled with blood and their wells filled with the tears of their sorrow.

16:7 I shall rain excrement against them; lo, a filthy rain shall pour upon their fields.

16:8 My bowels will move above them and it shall sound as a deafening thunder to their ears.

16:9 And when the people of Moab fear the lord, they shall come to the high places and offer prayers and sacrifice to the lord almighty.

16:10 The lord shall not listen and at the altars he shall smite them with a mighty and terrible blow.

17:1 Damascus shall fall so that not even the vermin will inhabit the rubble of the city.

17:2 The cities of Aroer are cursed; the people shall be as flocks for the holy. Enslave them, own them and have dominion over these beasts.

17:3 The fortresses of Ephraim will crumble. Damascus, lo, all of Syria, shall be conquered by the children of Israel, as is the will of God.

17:4 Throughout these heathen lands shall spread the seed of Jacob; they shall sprout and prosper like grain during the harvest.

17:5 And when the seed of Israel grows, they shall overcome the altars to the false lords; these heathen erected groves and idols to blasphemous gods.

17:6 May all the altars crumble to dust and shall the altars to the one true God be erected and spread across the lands.

17:7 Let the sky be filled with the smoke of the fattened calf; let sacrifice and spilled blood please the lord of lords.

17:8 Never shall one forget about the one true God and the lord shall never forget about his covenant; lo, all the people of Israel will prosper and live in bliss.

17:9 Neighbouring nations will be conquered and holy genocide will spread across the earth.

17:10 Behold, all the people of earth will be destroyed or enslaved by the chosen men of God.

18:1 Cursed are the people of Ethiopia and beyond, whose skin is of the shadow.

18:2 Send to these lands your vessels, your ships and gather these creatures for your labour.

18:3 Hairless apes placed on this earth for labour in the fields.

18:4 A gift from the lord they are; slaves sent from God, to pick the crops of our fields and gather the herbs from our lands.

18:5 For alas, when the vines are ripe and the wheat prosperous, these manlike beasts shall gather your wealth for you.

18:6 Always shall the people of shadow be under the yoke; such is the blessing of the lord to the nation of Israel.

19:1 The lord rides swiftly into the lands of Egypt atop a great cloud: and the gods of Egypt shall tremble in his presence and the hearts of the men will know fear.

19:2 Behold, the lord will cause great strife in these lands. Egyptian shall slay Egyptian, brother kill brother, neighbour against neighbour and city against city, until all the kingdom of Egypt will crumble.

19:3 Those that survive will live in fear and seek the counsel of charmers, sorcerers, witches and wizards.

19:4 They will fall into the hands of a cruel lord and be ruled by a true and malevolent tyrant for a king.

19:5 The river Nile will dry up; lo, even the waters of the sea will be empty and barren.

19:6 Not a drop will dwell within Egypt; the brooks, the streams, the wells will be as empty as the wretched womb.

19:7 Their fishermen will cast their nets in the muck and will feast upon the toads and the slugs.

19:8 As the lord wills it, they shall be a nation of fools; not a wise man shall dwell among them.

19:9 The lord will mingle in their hearts a perverse spirit, so that they lay in bed with their brother, their flock and their beast.

19:10 In fear will Egypt live; lo, they will be as pathetic as the woman.

19:11 The lands of Judah will terror over Egypt and spread great fear in these men who were once their masters.

19:12 And the men of Judah will reside in Egypt so that the Egyptians will know God and bow down to the one true lord.

19:13 These men of the Nile will offer sacrifice and offering to the one true lord and seek to please him.

19:14 And the lord will reject their sacrifice and smite all those of the Nile born.

20:1 The year Tartan conquered Ashdod.

20:2 In this year, the lord came to Isaiah the son of Amoz and said, "Go forth and wander naked across the lands."

20:3 And Isaiah asked, "What purpose will this serve?" and the lord answered, "It shall serve my purpose, you fool.

20:4 Now do as your God commands, lest he curse you with a wretched thing."

20:5 So Isaiah stripped off his clothes and wandered nude between the lands of Egypt and Ethiopia.

20:6 For three years Isaiah wandered naked and for three years he was mocked by those who heard his name.

20:7 Lo, even the lord mocked Isaiah, who wandered naked amidst the wilderness.

20:8 When the lord grew bored of Isaiah's nudity, he came to him and said, "Behold, such is the fate of Egypt and Ethiopia.

20:9 They shall be lead away by the peoples of Assyria and be gathered naked, with their ass bare so they know shame."

20:10 And Isaiah said, "Why then have you had me wander aimlessly through the wild, naked and shamed?"

20:11 The lord answered, "It is as a sign for the wise men, so that they know that which will come."

20:12 And this sign sent by the lord was never received to any man, wise or foolish.

20:13 They all merely laughed at the naked prophet, who wandered the wild like a naked beast.

21:1 A vision of Isaiah, brought to him as he wandered naked for three years.

21:2 Behold, the whirlwinds pass from a terrible land. From the southern desert they come and bring great lamentations.

21:3 The treacherous will know treachery and those rich from the spoils of battle shall rot.

21:4 My loins are filled with great pain, and the sun beats hot upon my seed. Lo, I bleed and rot like the menstruating whore.

21:5 My heart overflows with fear and hatred. Nights fill me with visions of horrible things brought down to earth by the hand of God.

21:6 Tables full of the flesh of men and angels feasting upon them. Wine cups filled with the blood of Judah.

21:7 Great chariots of men gather; chariots of horses, asses, camels and lions come to meet the wrath of the lord.

21:8 They are slaughtered by dragons, unicorns and beasts horrible to the eyes.

21:9 Lo, even the lion trembles in fear of the sight of the wrath of the lord.

21:10 Judah is laid to waste and the remnants of Jerusalem are scattered across the fallow lands of heathens.

21:11 Behold, in the east a virgin lies and she carries with her a child.

21:12 A terrible creature of a son, who will spread hatred and fear throughout the lands, throughout history, throughout time.

21:13 Lo, this son of a virgin will spread words of hate, hidden behind a tongue of deceitful love.

21:14 A crown of thorns shall he wear; with a yoke of fangs will he ensnare the earth.

21:15 Be warned of this son of God; take caution of the lord.

22:1 What ails those of Israel, who lie dead upon the rooftops?

22:2 They are full of anger and joy; how they sing praises when the dead lie beneath their blade.

22:3 Rulers of heathens gather together and die in the sights of the archers of Judah.

22:4 I bid away, for the death we bring upon our neighbours will be tenfold the suffering which our God shall strike upon our heads.

22:5 Our daughters will weep as the infant; our sons will lie dead across the fields.

22:6 Screams of pain and sorrow will haunt the air for eternity.

22:7 Behold, the lord has lifted us on high, only to drop us below even the dust.

22:8 Our chariots will crumble; our cities turn to ash; our fate will be hell-fire eternal.

23:1 The destruction of Tyre: How the ships of Tarshish howl and lay to waste the lands of Chittim.

23:2 All you inhabitants of the isle whore yourselves to the merchants of Zidon. They shall replenish your starvation.

23:3 By the great waters of the rivers, the seed of Sihor shall come and sell you to the nations yonder.

23:4 Be ashamed, O children of Zidon, who lie with the whores of the isles; they shall cause great pains upon you.

23:5 Look at your joyous city and know the laughs within will be ancient; your walls shall turn to ash and only sorrow will be known in the streets.

23:6 The lord of hosts shall use your kingdom as his chamber pot; wallow in the dung of the one true God.

23:7 Go now and commit whoredom in all the nations; corrupt your seed and curse your seed, you children of Tyre.

24:1 Behold, the lord will set the earth ablaze and scorch all that which dwell upon it. All shall be laid to waste; none will be spared.

24:2 The entire earth will be turned to ash and the lord shall inhale the smoke of the burning earth and become intoxicated in the sweet aroma.

24:3 Lands will be empty of all life. Priest will burn beside beggar, sinner die along saint, whore with virgin; all shall be burned by the fires of God.

24:4 The lands will be utterly emptied; such is the will of God.

24:5 The earth shall mourn and fade away; lo, the mountains will weep with lamentations.

24:6 Lo, only a few men shall survive the burning of the earth; and the lord shall punish them with harsh cruelties.

24:7 They shall seek the power of the vine for mirth and in it only find sorrow.

24:8 In strong drink they once danced and lo, now they shall weep in their stills.

24:9 What was once sweet will now be bitter; they shall vomit that which once gave them joy.

24:10 They shall cry for ale in the streets and none they shall have; all joy in the lands will be gone; only darkness will remain.

24:11 Great cities will be left in desolation so that not even the rat will walk in the rubble.

24:12 The olive tree will be barren and the vine void of all fruits.

24:13 Men shall lift their voices and they shall sing songs to God and beg to him for wine, for women and for meat.

24:14 And the lord shall swallow them in his earthen jaw.

24:15 Lo, the foundation of the earth shall tremble and sway back and forth like the drunkard.

24:16 Even the moon will crush down upon the lands and snare to death all that which survived the fires of the lord.

25:1 For you are my God, I shall praise and exalt you, lest you doom terrible things upon me.

25:2 For you have made great cities into heaps, nations into ash piles and shall destroy all the earth with fire.

25:3 Lo, you would suffocate a suckling infant to punish the father of his father's father.

25:4 Strong people glorify you and nations bow down in fear of your name.

25:5 You have slaughtered the heathen, cursed the poor and empowered the righteous and holy who kill in your name.

25:6 With heat, you have caused droughts among the nations and many men starved under your wrath.

25:7 Behold, in the mountains shall the lord dwell and grow fat on the flesh of the ram and drunk on the grapes of the vine.

25:8 All that who come to the gates of Zion shall perish in the presence of the lord.

25:9 Glory be to God, who will bring great suffering and death upon the heads of all men.

26:1 Before the lord destroys the earth with his hate, Judah shall be a mighty nation. Behold, Jerusalem shall be a mighty force.

26:2 Only the gates shall open for the righteous; all others will perish in the sights of the archers.

26:3 All shall be at peace with you, for they trust in the lord and fear his anger.

26:4 Fools, who believe never will the lord slam his fist against their walls.

26:5 For they trust in the lord blindly and never doubt his promise nor his word.

26:6 Lo, he shall tread upon all of Judah; the poor and the mighty will be crushed by his feet.

26:7 Righteous man shall perish alongside their wicked brethren and they shall be cast forth into the eternal sorrow of hell.

26:8 Both wicked and good will suffer; the lord discriminates not and dooms all men to burn.

26:9 Behold, only the dead shall know peace; the dead not rise, but rot in the dirt from whence they came.

26:10 Sing, all those embraced in the mercy of death; blessed be those kissed by death, who escape the choke-hold of damnation.

26:11 Glory to the unborn child, for he shall never know the truth and the hatred of his lord.

26:12 Praise be to the slaughtered, who lie beneath the feet of Judah; may they rest eternal and never have their slumber disturbed by the malevolent God.

27:1 In the end of days, not even the Leviathan shall escape the anger of the lord. Lo, that twisting serpent shall be punished by God until he chokes upon the very tail of dragons.

27:2 On that day, the seas shall turn red with the blood of the mighty snake, who fooled the wretched woman in the garden of Eden.

27:3 The fury of God shall rise from the land; thorns and briers will become as sharp as blades and they shall tear through the flesh of both man and beast.

27:4 Even the strong will perish and their blood flow forth on the ground like wine.

27:5 All the world shall burn; none will be shown mercy in the eyes of God.

27:6 Behold, a great trumpet will blow in the heavens and the lord will descend in black fire and ash and spread his seeds of sorrow across the lands.

27:7 The weak will perish and the strong will fall dead by their own hands.

27:8 And the lord shall laugh and feast upon the bodies of the dead.

28:1 Curse be to those who wear the crown of pride. They take praise in the works of man and deny God his glories and wonders.

28:2 They are as a glorious flower that browns in the sun; once looked upon for beauty, they shall be disgusting to their brethren.

28:3 Hate be to the drunkards, which cloud their minds with strong drink.

28:4 Let them drown in their wine and choke on their liquor; let them vomit in the wells which they drink.

28:5 Behold, the lord will smite them with a mighty tempest; a great wind which blows from the north, bringing hail and rain to flood the prideful and the drunk.

28:6 All prideful and drunken fools will be trodden under the feet of the one true God.

28:7 Those that were beautiful will grow ugly; those deemed wise by men will be as stupid as the lamb.

28:8 Even the prophets have erred with strong drink and receive visions given to them by the vine.

28:9 They tell prophecies of lies and spread false words of hope and love to the people of the land.

28:10 Lo, never trust a drunk prophet, for they speak words falsely.

28:11 Their tables are full of vomit and disease; they eat rotten flesh and poisoned fruits.

28:12 Tell me, who shall teach you knowledge and wisdom? Those children weaned from the breast-milk of their mother.

28:13 For all the world have stammering lips and deceitful tongues.

28:14 The lord once blessed us with his rule and we sought forth a king to guide us; a man with foolish mind and forked tongue.

28:15 Glory were the days when the lord ruled us with an iron fist; we were blessed by his miracles and cursed under his wrath.

28:16 Now, only the wrath remains. Fools were we, to abandon our faith in the lord.

28:17 He shall destroy that upon the earth and lay our bones as a foundation for his dwelling of Zion.

28:18 Precious bones and rock will make strong the house of God.

28:19 Be warned, the covenant is broken and we have lost. Pray to the lord for mercy and it will be denied.

28:20 Know that all shall burn in eternal fire and salvation will be denied us by its gates.

29:1 Woe to Ariel, city of David. Beloved king of Israel and disgusting faggot.

29:2 Lo, the lord loved David, thus the city shall suffer for the sins of David and Jonathan's lust.

29:3 Great distress will roam the streets and the air will be as heavy

THE OLD TESTAMENT

as rock.

29:4 The lord shall camp around the walls and besiege you. Forts will be erected against the birthplace of David.

29:5 Those of the dead will rise from the ground and rape those of the city. Lo, like the necromancer's magic, the lord shall bring forth the corpses and the dead.

29:6 Multitudes of strange and horrible things will enter the homes of Ariel and turn to dust those who live.

29:7 And the lord shall come down with great fires, earthquakes, tsunamis, winds and fire; a horrible tempest will be the chariot of God.

29:8 The many nations who war against Ariel will seem peaceful, like a child's dream, when the lord comes with his wrath.

29:9 All within the city will dream sweet dreams, only to remind them of the cruelties of their life.

29:10 The hungry man shall feast and awaken to starvation. The thirsty man shall drink and awaken with a parched tongue.

29:11 A great spirit will enter their nose, causing them to stagger drunk without the aid of wine.

29:12 Behold, the prophets and the seers will speak the words of fools and spread artificial hope and lies among the brethren of Ariel.

29:13 And the visions of the prophets will be written in great books, so that generations will study the lies and the hopes of the drunken prophets.

29:14 Lo, they shall be known as marvelous works and regarded in highest esteem and the books of truth will be burned in great fire.

29:15 Fools will keep holy the parchment of lies and burn the pages filled with wisdom and knowledge; such morons these people be.

29:16 Woe unto them who seek comfort in the words of the prophets, for they seek counsel in kindness and hope.

28:17 The lord is unkind and all hope is lost.

29:18 As sure as the sun rises, so shall the earth be tipped and the inhabitants thereof fall into the darkness and the void.

30:1 Curse those of the rebellious children, who seek not counsel in the lord but in the stars, the bones, the wind and the waters.

30:2 They who speak to the voices of spirits and disturb the slumber of the dead.

30:3 Woe be to them that seek shelter in the gods of Egypt and hide under the shadow of Hathor and Ra.

30:4 They seek not the strength of the lord and whore themselves to heathens; lo, they insult the one true God and piss in his winepress.

30:5 When the men of Pharaoh enslave them, the lord shall deny them strength and laugh as they cry under the whip of Egypt.

30:6 Great shame will they feel, for denying themselves the lord and betraying his name.

30:7 Behold, these children shall know the torment of the southern beasts; the lions, the vipers, the flying fiery serpents and the leopards shall feast upon their marrow.

30:8 Come they shall to the prophets and they shall write the words upon tables and parchments.

30:9 Lo, they shall be words of lies and deceit, for the prophets shall be drunk and their visions blurred by the strong drink.

30:10 When the lord comes, they shall get out of the way, for the Holiest of holies will trod upon them and crush them beneath his feet.

30:11 Because they despised the lord and kept not the covenant, they will bow in shame before the lord.

30:12 And they shall eat of the dust and drink of the piss, for the lord demanded it so.

30:13 Those of the rebellious will seek to please the lord and they shall cast away their idols and images as though they were the soaked

cloth of a menstruating woman.

30:14 They shall erect altars to God and burn sacrifice upon them, pleasing the lord with spilled blood and burning flesh.

30:15 To fill them with a fool's hope, the lord will bless them with rain, so that their oxen grow fat and their crops be prosperous.

30:16 Those who once bowed to Hathor will grow fat by the blessings of God and the lord shall make them dumb in their comfort.

30:17 For be warned, the waters will dry up and the crops burn under the skies.

30:18 Look up and the moon will be as bright as the sun and the sun seven times brighter in the sky.

30:19 Great heat will pass through the lands, so even those who hide in the shadows will burn.

30:20 Lo, from the moon the face of God shall appear, with lips of granite and a tongue of devouring flame.

30:21 And his breath shall flow like the flood waters and will bring pestilence and sickness.

30:22 Behold, the breath of God is a terrible curse, with a stench greater than the rotting flesh of beasts.

30:23 Fires of hottest flame are made when the lord blows upon the kindling.

30:24 Lo, the lord shall speak terrible names to the rebellious and their ears shall bleed until they die screaming in terror.

30:25 With great anger, the lord shall devour all those with hail, fire, rain and lightning from the violent tempest.

31:1 Fools are they who attack the heathens, trusting in their chariots for they are numerous, or their horsemen for their strength, but not see kind aid of the Holy lord of Israel.

31:2 Though they are wise to slay the stranger, they do so foolishly. For not trusting in God, they bring evil in their slaughter of the evildoers.

31:3 Now the heathens are mere men and not gods and their horses flesh and not spirit. Know that the lord can stretch out his hand and strike them all down with but a wave and the heathens will fail as one.

31:4 For the lord is like the lion who slays the entire flock; lo, the heathens are weak and the lord is mighty.

31:5 On the wings of birds, the lord shall bring destruction to the heathens and on the wings of bats will be bring doom to Jerusalem.

31:6 Turn away from the swarm and hide in your cellars, so that the lord ensnares you with rats and vermin.

31:7 Lo, the mice will feast on the toes of your children and the bats make nests in the hair of your wives.

31:8 Such is the terror of God.

32:1 Behold, a king born of the virgin womb will reign in holiness and his chosen princes will rule in judgment.

32:2 Powerful men will seek shelter in him, to hide from the winds and be saved from the tempest and the floods.

32:3 Their eyes will be blinded by his light and their ears hear only the words of his lips; they shall be blind and deaf to logic and truth, believing only in him.

32:4 They shall spread his words of deceit to their people and lead them down the path of sorrow and despair.

32:5 Behold, they shall sing praises to their king as they wallow in the shit of their lord.

32:6 And this king will be the son of God; a vile and hideous wolf hidden in the wool of lambs.

32:7 Be warned, for this person shall speak villainy with his lip, and plant the seeds of iniquity in your heart; he shall practice hypocrisy and empty your souls of awareness as he promises salvation to all those who follow him.

32:8 Lo, he shall bring more evil than the liberal, who tolerates the heathen and embraces the queer as his brother.

32:9 The king hates all things woman and loathes the whores he lusts for deeply.

32:10 So rise up, you women of Judah and listen to the words of Isaiah.

32:11 Many years shall pass and you will be lonely in your bed; not even the blind will find you pleasing and will seek forth the comfort of your daughters.

32:12 Strip naked in your vitality and share your loins with men; it is the will of God that you bring orgasm to your fathers and your brothers.

32:13 For though they cry for your breasts now as they cry for the fruitful vine, in time your breasts shall sag and rot like the grapes of the forgotten vineyard.

32:14 Upon the lands of harvest will sprout forth thorns and briers; yea, even the palace and the city will be overcome with the wild weeds.

32:15 Because you have forsaken God, you shall choke on the roots and the thistles of the bittering herbs.

33:1 Woe to them that spoil and deal treacherously. When the fruits of their spoils be gone, they shall spoil and those who are treacherous will be betrayed.

33:2 O lord, show no mercy upon them. Pummel them with closed fist, so all their days be troubled.

33:3 Laugh as they flee across the lands, hiding amongst the nations and the caves.

33:4 They shall run to and fro like a horde of locusts, so that they may escape your wrath.

33:5 The lord is exalted, for he lives on high in the palace of Zion.

33:6 His knowledge is law and his understanding is so that not even the wisest of men could comprehend the lord.

33:7 Behold, the one true God shall bring fear to the peaceful and strike down the ambassadors who end wars between nations.

33:8 The highways will lie in waste and men will fall in death. We have broken the covenant and for this no man will be shown mercy.

33:9 With his breath the earth will be engulfed in flames and the people will be burned as kindling: as thorns cut up they shall burn hot in the wrath of God.

33:10 From far off the lamentations and the torments will be heard of those who suffer from the cruelty of the lord.

33:11 Sinners and saints both will be thrown in the fire. None among them will be saved from the flames. All shall dwell within the everlasting burnings.

33:12 Even those that walk righteously and speak the holy word, who kill the faggot and slaughter the ungodly, who binds his hands from evil, will know the hatred of his God.

33:13 Our lord shall take the rocks from our foundations and steal bread from the child, so that Zion be strong and full of feasts.

33:14 It shall be a beautiful place, which strike both awe and terror in the hearts of those who lay eyes upon it.

33:15 No scribe shall define its beauty; no sculptor shall copy its form.

33:16 The gates will be made from the bones of the slain and the foundation will be the bodies of the fools who believed in the promise of the lord's salvation.

33:17 For the lord will slay all and spare none in his hatred, his anger and his wrath.

33:18 Such is the glory of the lord.

34:1 Come hither, you nations of the earth and listen to the fate which the lord of mercy have given unto you.

34:2 The merciful lord of Israel and Judah hates you and will send his fury upon your nations. All you heathen bastards will be destroyed and delivered into great slaughter.

34:3 All those slain will be cast out into the mountains, where their blood will stain the rocks crimson and the great stench will permeate through all the earth.

34:4 Lo, the host of hosts who dwells In heaven will roll up the sky as a scroll and cast it into the earth of your nations.

34:5 By damnation, the very skies will fall upon your heads and the stars will drop atop you like the fallen leaf from the tree.

34:6 For the lord hath bathed his sword in heaven and now it shall come to Idumea, Egypt, Babylon and all nations loathed by God.

34:7 And the sword of the lord will drink the blood of the slain; the sacrifices of the goats, the sheep, the lamb and the bullocks have made the sword of God thirsty for the sweet taste of blood.

34:8 All living things in your lands will be slaughtered; the oxen, the lion, even the unicorn will be slain, and the lord will feast upon their blood and their fat.

34:9 It will be the day of vengeance for the lord, who lives in fury as he dwells in the paradise bliss of Zion.

34:10 Behold, the streams of your nations will turn red with blood and your earth to brimstone; and the streams will boil with blood and brimstone.

34:11 Great smoke shall arise from this burning and cover your skies in darkness. Generation after generation of your people will be denied even the very sun.

34:12 In Edom, only the birds will live. Cormorants, bitterns, crows, owls and ravens will dwell in Edom and feast on the carcasses cursed by God.

34:13 Kings, princes and nobles who grew fat in these nations will be feasts for the winged beasts.

34:14 None shall set food in Edom, save for the ornithologist who takes study in these wretched birds.

34:15 Palaces once proud and mighty will be covered in briers and thorns and where once royalty lived now shall be homes for the owl and the dragon.

34:16 Wild beasts will hold court in the chambers where the princes met and the dragons, the winged beasts, the satyrs and the Minotaur will hold meetings of great evil.

34:17 Lo, wretched are the satyr, the Minotaur and the dragon, which have been seen only in sculpture and paintings.

34:18 Wretched are the beasts so evil that none of the living have seen it; they grow power in shadow and spread fear in the hearts of all.

34:19 Though none have laid eye upon them, know that they exist, for the lord say that they exist.

34:20 Vultures will perch on the towers of archers and watch with an evil eye those who cross into their lands.

34:21 Such is the fate of the nations hated by God; such is the fate of all nations.

35:1 When the blood spilled by God meet with the wilderness, they shall join in union, and rejoice in one another's presence.

35:2 Lands once barren will now blossom with crimson, creating where nothing existed a beautiful garden for the lord.

35:3 Those who walk in this blessed garden of sanguine petals will be filled with the miracles of the lord.

35:4 The blind shall see, the deaf hear, the weak become strong, the sick healthy.

35:5 The lame will walk and the mute will speak with the heavenly choirs.

35:6 Behold, where once it was barren shall exist the garden of the lord, where streams of flowing blood run through.

35:7 Those who drink of these streams shall be satisfied from their thirst and never be thirsty again.

35:8 Where once dragons roamed and snakes slithered there shall be blossoms, fruits, grasses and reeds.

35:9 No lion shall walk there, nor any ravenous beast; only those most pleasing to God will lie in his blessed garden.

35:10 Thus the garden will be void of all life, save for the plants which dwell.

35:11 A magnificent highway will lead to this garden and it shall be a highway of holiness. Many will walk this highway and all who walk it shall perish by the wrath of God before they lay sight upon his blessed garden.

35:12 It will be a truly beautiful and holy place, which none other than the lord will see; such is the selfishness of God.

36:1 It came to pass that on the fourteenth year of king Hezekiah's reign, that Sennacherib king of Assyria came up and warred against the defended cities of Judah and conquered them.

36:2 The king of Assyria sent Rabshakeh from Lachish to Jerusalem with a great army, so they may show Hezekiah their might. And the armies stood by the upper pool in the highway of the fuller's field.

36:3 Hezekiah sent unto them Eliakim son of Hilkiah, Shebna the scribe and the recorder Joah son of Asaph.

36:4 And Rabshakeh said to them, "Behold, the power of my master Sennacherib, king of Assyria. Tell me, of what confidence do you have?

36:5 We have taken your lands, conquered your cities and enslaved your people. Why shed your blood more. Why lose a war against Assyria?

36:6 Do not take faith in your lord, for he has abandoned you and let us come straight to your door with a river of your blood behind us.

36:7 Your lord has forsaken you, so why trust him. He is like the asp, who when ye place your trust in shall bite you with venom most foul.

36:8 Perhaps the lord you worship curses you for the foolishness of your king. Was it not Hezekiah who took down the altars and erected groves to the lords your ancestors had so hated?

36:9 Give your pledges unto Assyria and be welcomed in our mighty empire. Be part of a strong nation and prosper under your new master.

36:10 Deny us your loyalty and know this; your people will see a fate worse than those your fathers have given to the people who lived in this land, when they came from the lands of Egypt.

36:11 Those that survive our onslaught will be enslaved; your sons will be under the iron yoke and your daughters will entertain our desires with the flesh under their skirts.

36:12 They will be worse than the beasts of labours, and shall beg us for our dung to eat, or our piss to drink."

36:13 The three men begged of Rabshakeh, "Please, speak unto us in the words of the Syrians, for we speak and understand it.

36:14 Do not, I beg of you, speak in the words of our people, for we fear that the ears of our men shall hear us and grow afraid."

36:15 Rabshakeh laughed and said, "You wish to hide the truth from your own people. You are pathetic and selfish men, who will doom your people without any regards to them."

36:16 He then spoke loudly in the language of the Jews, saying, "Listen, O people of Judah, to the words of Sennacherib king of Assyria.

36:17 Do not trust in your king Hezekiah, for he is a ludicrous fool who will damn you all to slavery and slaughter.

36:18 Trust not in your God, for your brothers placed their trust in your God and now they lay dead upon the fields, where the raven peck on their flesh.

36:19 Know this, we have made an offer of peace to your king and shall give you life and welcome you into our empire.

36:20 All your sons and daughters will live under the rule of Assyria and be protected with our swords, our bows and our chariots.

36:21 If your king chooses to rebel against us, know that it will be all of Judah who suffers for his arrogance.

36:22 Our armies, which could protect you, will now war with you and slaughter you people with a terrible lust for violence.

36:23 Your daughters will be toys of rape and your sons will be worked harder than the beasts of burden.

36:24 Know that all this can be avoided, if your king takes good counsel and heed the words of Sennacherib.

36:25 Do not let your king doom you to damnation and do not believe your lord will protect us from our blade."

36:26 When the people of Jerusalem heard the words of Rabshakeh, they came to Eliakim, Shebna and Joah, asking, "Does this heathen speak the truth?"

36:27 But the three men said nothing, as they were ordered to silence by their king.

36:28 And they returned to their master, stripped of their clothes and weeping and they spoke the words of Rabshakeh.

37:1 When king Hezekiah heard of this, he tore of his clothes, wallowed in his own piss, and wept in the corner like an infant.

37:2 He sent forth Eliakim, Shebna and the elders of the priests, all wearing sackcloths covered in ash, unto Isaiah the prophet the son of Amoz.

37:3 So the servants of Judah came to Isaiah, and said, "We're fucked. Our children are a bunch of homosexual, sheep fucking blasphemers, and the lord now hates us.

37:4 The lord must come to save us, or we'll be conquered by the Assyrians and forced into a heathen nation of homosexual, sheep fucking blasphemers.

37:5 Could it be that we have angered God so much that he now sides with Rabshakeh, master of the heathen Sennacherib. Hath the lord abandoned us and sold us to the wicked?"

37:6 And Isaiah answered, "Of course the lord God did sell us to the wicked and the heathen. He did it many times to our fathers, and he shall do it to our sons.

37:7 But fear not, for I shall speak to the lord, and show them that the peoples of Assyria are unworthy of his blessings.

37:8 For as your sons are homosexual, sheep fucking blasphemers, the peoples of Assyria are homosexual, sheep fucking blasphemers who fuck male lambs without blemish.

37:9 This will anger the lord, for they take their lust in the fleece of the lord's lambs.

37:10 Know this, the lord shall send out a rumour to the ears of Sennacherib, which shall cause him to return to his own lands; and he shall fall by his own sword."

37:11 When Rabshakeh returned, he found his master warring against Libnah; for he heard that Tirkahah king of Ethiopia wished to rebel against him.

37:12 When Rabshakeh heard this, he sent forth messengers to Hezekiah, saying, "Do not let the battle which my master fights fool thee, for he shall utterly destroy them and then come for your necks.

37:13 Know that the lord ye worship shall not protect thee, for he did not protect your peoples.

37:14 Gaze upon your once strong cities, and know they thrive with the warriors of Assyria, and that your peoples either serve them or lay rotting under the sun.

37:15 Look at all that which Sennacherib did conquer. Did the gods of Gozan, Haran, Rezeph, Telessar and the children of Eden save thee?

37:16 Know that the king of Hamath, of Arphad, of Sepharvaim, of Hena and of Ivah now hang upon the thrones where they once sat.

37:17 Hearken my words, O king of Judah, and surrender to the Assyrian empire."

37:18 When Hezekiah read this message, his very bowels were moved, and stained his robes. He did cower in a corner, and wept.

37:19 It was then the king of Judah prayed unto the lord of lords, and said, "Oh God of Israel, who dwelleth with the dragons, and created all the wonders of heaven and earth, heed my prayer.

37:20 Open thine eyes, and witness that which Sennacherib hath done, all under the blasphemy of your name.

37:21 He did invade the lands of heathens, and cast their idols into the fire, as though he were a general of Judah; but know that his lords are made of iron and stone, and now he wishes to cast thine altars into the fires of false gods.

37:22 Save us from this wretched heathen, so that we may have altars to burn sacrifice for thee."

37:23 Then Isaiah the son of Amoz came unto Hezekiah, and said, "The lord hath heard your prayer against Sennacherib the king of Assyria.

37:24 This is the word of the lord concerning him; both Judah and Assyria have blasphemed against me, and their virgin daughters laugh at my name.

37:25 When have either of thee blessed my name, and sought your eyes towards the Holy one of Israel?

37:26 Ye are both a despicable peoples, and I hate thee all with a mighty wrath; in time, both your children will be forgotten from the face of the earth.

37:27 But know this; my home is in Jerusalem, and it is a mighty temple I wish not tarnished by the filthy heathen hands of Sennacherib.

37:28 For this, I shall defend Jerusalem against Assyria."

37:29 It was then an angel of the lord came upon the armies of Assyria, and smote them one hundred and fourscore and five thousand, until a lake of blood soaked their very tents.

37:30 And when they awoke, behold, they were dead; and they wept over their corpses. Well, they would have, if the dead could weep, or awake.

37:31 When Sennacherib heard of this massacre, he went to Ninevah to seek counsel from his lords.

37:32 And as he prayed in the house of Nisroch his god, both his sons Adrammelech and Sharezer came behind him, and beheaded their father with his own sword.

37:33 They then escaped to the lands of Armenia, carrying with them the head of their father: and Esarhoddon the son of Sennacherib became king of Assyria.

38:1 In those days Hezekiah was sick. He had a deadly disease which could not be cured. Or the common cold. Hezekiah was a bit over-dramatic in regards to his illnesses.

38:2 Isaiah the prophet the son of Amoz came to Hezekiah, and said, "Set your house in order, for ye shall soon die, and not live."

38:3 Which was a rather unnecessary thing to say, for those who die rarely live.

38:4 It was then Hezekiah turned to the wall, and prayed to the lord.

38:5 And he said, "Remember thee, O lord, and know that I have done all I can to do good in your sight and live in the path of righteousness." And he then wept.

38:6 Isaiah then returned to Hezekiah, and said, "The lord has heard your prayer, and decided that for a blasphemous, sinning little fucker, you weren't that bad.

38:7 So, he changed his mind, and decided to let you live fifteen years longer."

38:8 Hezekiah was about to say that the lord never changed his mind, and once a decision was made by God it was final, but wisely decided against it.

38:9 Isaiah spoke still, and said, "The lord decided he shall protect Jerusalem from the armies of Assyria, and not let this city fall into the hands of heathens.

38:10 To show ye a sign of this, he shall move the very sun ten degrees backwards; a feet only the hand of God shall accomplish."

38:11 And the sun moved ten degrees backwards, thus creating daylight savings time.

38:12 Now are the writings of Hezekiah when he recovered from his illness; be warned, these are emo writings written by an emo bastard:

38:13 I said in the end of my days I shall go to the gates of the graveyard: I am deprived of the crust of my years.

38:14 Never have I seen the lord in this mortal life, and once now the shackles of mortality no longer bound me, I shall arise to Zion and dwell in the city of holiness.

38:15 (But you, the reader, know he will really go to hell. Such is the fate of all men)

38:16 Mine age is departed, and removed from me like the lion removeth the lamb from the shepherd: release me, O lord, from my sickness, and embrace me with your open arms.

38:17 For my days are filled with pain and sorrow, cursed by this wretched illness.

38:18 Like faeces through the rectum, these are the stinking days of my life.

38:19 Yet I fear my death, for what if the lord is angry with me, and I have pleased him not?

38:20 What if I be denied the sanctuary of Zion, and am cast into the unfathomable pains of hell?

38:21 (He was.)

38:22 Know lord, that if ye extend my years, I shall praise thee and bless thee and please thee all the remainders of my life.

38:23 For what use am I in the grave. Can the dead sing your praises or exalt your name?

38:24 The prophet Isaiah hath placed a lump of figs upon my chest, and with this blessing I shall now live another fifteen years.

38:25 I must remind my chefs to put more figs in my meals.

38:26 Now, I can't help but wonder, what is the sign of the time when I shall go up to the house of the lord?

38:27 Told you Hezekiah was an emo bastard.

39:1 It was at this time that Merodachbaladan the son of Baladan, king of Babylon, sent letters and gifts to Hezekiah: for he did hear that he was sick and miraculously recovered.

39:2 Hezekiah was glad of these gifts, and considered Merodachbaladan a good and kind man, though he was a heathen.

39:3 So Hezekiah invited Merodachbaladan to his house, and showed him all the palace. The throne room, the dining hall, the chambers, the dungeons;

39:4 The gold, the jewellery, the silver and the wealth;

39:5 The spices, the herbs, the ointments, the perfumes: there was nothing in the house nor all of Jerusalem which Hezekiah did not proudly show his friend Merodachbaladan.

39:6 When Isaiah heard of this, he became furious, and said, "Did ye invite a heathen into thine house, and showed him the wonders and the glories of Judah?"

39:7 And Hezekiah said, "Yes, for this heathen is a good man and a dear friend."

39:8 Isaiah cursed the king of Judah, and said, "For your stupidity the lord of lords will curse your children.

39:9 Know that all within your house and the house of your fathers will conquered and taken to the lands of Babylon.

39:10 Your sons and your daughters will be slaves for these heathens, and shall toil in their fields and service their loins.

39:11 All the mighty men of Judah will be humiliated, and serve as eunuchs in the palace of the king of Babylon."

39:12 When Hezekiah heard this, he wept, locked himself in his chambers, and wrote more emo poetry.

39:13 Don't worry, ye need not read it.

40:1 More lies spoken by the prophet Isaiah.

40:2 Comfort ye, O peoples of Judah. Be comforted, sayeth the lord your God.

40:3 Speak thee softly to the peoples of Jerusalem, and rejoice unto her, for her warfare is accomplished and forgiven her sins: the lord hath given a pardon to all the iniquities of Judah.

40:4 Know that all ye and your kin shall walk the holy highway of the lord, and rejoice in his precious garden of flowers blossomed by the blood of the damned.

40:5 Every valley shall exalt to us, every mountain in our way shall move for us, the rough places shall be made smooth and the waters will part upon our journey.

40:6 The glory of the lord shall be revealed, and our eyes shall gaze upon his wondrous flesh; the lord told me this so, thus it must be true.

40:7 Know that all grass is flesh, will live as such.

40:8 The grass fades and the flower doth wither, for the breath of the lord blows upon it: surely the peoples are as grass unto the lord.

40:9 But by the glory of God we shall thrive for eternity forever in his holy garden, and we shall be his most precious blossom.

40:10 Lo, Zion shall be our sanctuary, and we will live under the blessings and the miracles of the Holiest of holies.

40:11 O ye peoples of Jerusalem, lift up thy voice in strength, and be not afraid, for the lord is your God, and he loveth and cares for thee.

40:12 We shall be his flock, and he shall feed us like the kind shepherd, gather us his lambs with open arms, and hold us deeply in his bosom.

40:13 Never, like the shepherd, will he slaughter us for his table.

40:14 Know that those who are unholy will be denied passage through this holy highway, and will be left behind to burn in the fires of everlasting torment.

40:15 Those who sinned against him, feared him not, or thought out logic and truth.

40:16 Those who worked with gold and moulded false images of heathen lords will drown in the molten metals of their works.

40:17 They will then be made into ornaments, and hang from the highest branches of the trees in the holy garden of the lord.

40:18 Know that it is the lord which created the foundations of the earth.

40:19 That it is God who sitteth upon the circle of the earth, who stretcheth out the heavens like a curtain above us, and opens forth the firmament for the rain to drop upon the lands.

40:20 It is the lord who doeth all things, for he is the mighty and the blessed. Never does he tire or grow weary, though he does like to nap on the Sabbath.

40:21 Those blessed by the lord will run with the unicorns, but those hated by God will be drained of all strength.

40:22 Even the youth of the hated will faint and be weary, and the

old will fall under the weight of their own bones.

40:23 As they crawl upon the ground, the eagles will come and eat the flesh of their backs; such is the will of the lord.

41:1 Keep silence in the presence of the lord, O children of men, lest he find you and drain you of all strength.

41:2 The lord shall come from the east, seeking those who are unrighteous and shall plow his sword in the dust to seek forth the blood of those who hide from him.

41:3 He shall pursue them and none will be safe from his wrath and genocide.

41:4 Generations of all men will fall before his feet and be crushed by the sandals of the lord.

41:5 Neighbours will lay dead beside neighbour, enemy beside enemy, carpenter beside goldsmith, Jew beside heathen

41:6 Cursed be the covenant of Abraham and Jacob, which declares all of their seeds will be saved by the salvation of Zion; it is a lie.

41:7 Unto the very ends of the earth will the lord hunt down men and slay them whether heathen or descendant of Abraham.

41:8 Your very daughters shall weep and your wives will mourn heavy tears.

41:9 And the lord shall gather your wives and your daughters and shall place them in his harems, where they will satisfy his lust for all eternity.

41:10 Pray for your women that they are ugly in the eyes of God, for the lord will discard those unpleasant in his eyes and slay them as he slays her brothers.

41:11 It is better to be dead and suffer in the depths of eternal hell-fire than to be part of the harem of the lord, where he shall cruelly and perversely rape your daughters.

42:1 Thus sayeth the lord, cursed be to the Gentiles, who offer not their blood unto me, nor burn upon the stones their sacrificial lambs.

42:2 They shall break like the dry twig and be cast into the burning kindling of everlasting flames.

42:3 A cruel and terrible judgment will befall upon their heads and the lord will curse them and punish them in the most merciful and holy ways; by sending them to hell.

42:4 Yet he shall trick the heathen and the son of the virgin will hold out his hand to the Gentiles and gently lead them to their damnation.

42:5 The lord Immanuel shall pluck the eyes of the heathen and they shall praise him and say, "Blessed be Immanuel, for now I see not the hideousness of the earth."

42:6 He shall cut from them their ears and they shall say, "Blessed be Immanuel, for now I hear not the cruelties of God."

42:7 He shall cut off their hands and they shall say, "Blessed be Immanuel, for now I may not touch the unholy, the unrighteous and the sinful."

42:8 He shall tear out their tongues and they shall say nothing.

42:9 With a gentle hand shall he will lead the masses to the wilderness, where they will rot, starve and thirst; all the while they shall praise his name and await him to bring them to salvation.

42:10 Never shall he come; he shall stand beside his father and laugh at the foolishness of the Gentile.

42:11 It will come to pass that the lord of lord's will come down in fury and cry out a terrible cry of war and say, "I cry like the angry lion and shall now devour you."

42:12 Though they have no eyes, they will see the horror of their lord.

42:13 Though they have no ears, they will listen to the cruelties of God.

42:14 Though they have no hands, they will feel the wrath of the almighty.

42:15 Though they have no tongues, they will yell in great and cowardly fear.

42:16 And the lord will lay waste to the mountains, burn all the fruits of the earth, make the rivers barren and dry up all the pools.

42:17 And the men will follow the lord and witness this destruction and they shall say, "The lord destroys that which has been tainted by the evilness of man and shall soon make for us a new and glorious earth."

42:18 The lord shall not and will leave them in the barren wastelands of the earth.

42:19 These heathens will grow ravenous and slay each other to drink of their blood and feast of the very fingers of their brothers.

42:20 And the lord will watch this and laugh.

42:21 Then he shall return with his son and the Gentiles will say, "Behold, our saviour has come to save us from the cruelties of our kin."

42:22 It is then the lord will open the bowels of the earth and molten rock will consume the Gentiles for all eternity in great fire and smoke.

42:23 God will find it fucking hilarious. He's an asshole like that.

43:1 Now the lord did choose the children of Israel over all other nations and for this he prefers these people over other nations.

43:2 He still hates them with great fury, but not as much as he hates the other nations of the earth.

43:3 Thus when the end of days come and the lord seeks out the destruction of all things on earth, he shall begin with the heathen nations.

43:4 Egypt, Ethiopia and Seba will suffer great torments by the hand of God and he shall say, "Behold, I punish these heathen nations for the sins of Israel.

43:5 Lo, I created them as the scapegoat of the sons of Abraham and punish them for that which you people have done."

43:6 And the people of Israel rejoice and sin greatly so that they may enjoy their wickedness and laugh at the suffering of the heathens for the transgressions of Israel and Judah.

43:7 As the torments of the heathens occur, it shall come that the nation of Israel will be frightened, for the wrath of the lord will increase to their borders.

43:8 They shall gather their sons, some their daughters and flee to the north to escape the anger of their lord.

43:9 It shall be a futile attempt, for the lord will seek them and find them and slaughter them with great anger and cruelty.

43:10 Such is the nature of the Holiest of holies.

43:11 Great chariots from the heavens will descend to the earth and carry the bodies of the slaughtered to the desert, where they shall be piled atop one another in a mighty tower.

43:12 And the beasts of the fields will come and the owls and the dragons and they shall thank the lord for the flesh to eat, the blood to drink and the bones to make their nests.

43:13 When the souls of the Israelites question the lord why he did punish them, the lord shall say,

43:14 "Your sins, your tolerance to heathens and your lack of devotion unto me hast made me weary.

43:15 Lo, I grow tired of your bickering, your wickedness and wish now to see you destroyed."

43:16 And the Israelites shall say, "But, you are the one true God; never do you tire."

43:17 It is then the lord will cast them into the fierceness of

damnation, for questioning his words.

43:18 The lord shall then nap by the fires of hell and listen to the cries and the torments of his people as he sleeps.

44:1 Behold, I am the lord God, who created with your fathers the covenant and lead you to the promised lands of milk and honey.

44:2 The universe and all her wonders did come forth from my holy womb.

44:3 As I walk, the crooked places become straight, the mountains move before me and the lands rise up so I may walk upon the waters.

44:4 Behold, I have created all things; the lamb, the lion, the heathen, the righteous, the holy, the light, the dark and the wicked.

44:5 Yet blame me not for the wicked, for I am the lord God and shall not tolerate blame for my creations.

44:6 There is no lord before me, who can create such marvels; and what I created I can destroy.

44:7 Remember this, for those who blame me for the wickedness of the earth will be cursed with great wickedness.

44:8 Lo, the heavens will drop down before him and the very firmament will crush his very house and all those of his seed will perish.

44:9 Behold, it shall come to pass that the wickedness of my creation will conquer the earth and that I must destroy my creation before it destroys itself.

44:10 Fear not, for those righteous and deemed worthy shall not perish in this destruction, but shall be rewarded with salvation.

44:11 The righteous and the holy will reside in Zion and feast at the table of their holy father.

44:12 So obey my laws, my statutes and my commandments. Offer unto me your sacrifices and follow my word without doubt or question.

44:13 Do this and be saved from the fires of my wrath; do not and make one of even the smallest of transgressions and know that the lord will hate you and you will be damned forever.

45:1 Cursed be to the heathens, who bow down to their idols of gold; their lords shall not save from the wrath of God.

45:2 Foolish are the Jews, who bow down to the one true God; little do they know that the lord will destroy them alongside the heathen.

45:3 None shall stop my path of destruction, for I am the one true God; there is no other god like me.

45:4 With my words I decide both beginning and end; with my tongue, I decide the fate of the universe and all things.

45:5 Thus I have spoken and it shall come. Such is the power of the lord.

45:6 None will escape their fates; lo, their very attempts have been written by the lord of lords.

45:7 All shall be as it is in the script of the Holiest of holies; none will change this fate.

46:1 Come down and lie in the muck, O virgin daughters of Babylon. There is no throne for you, for no longer shall you be tender and delicate.

46:2 Take of the millstones and grind the grain. Butcher the beast, clean your dwelling and prepare my dinner, bitch.

46:3 Make bare your leg, uncover your thigh and spread your loins in my private chamber.

46:4 Your nakedness shall be uncovered and it is all your worth; I will take vengeance of your body and abuse your breasts like the lord God intended.

46:5 Be not strong and independent, for you are a woman and a heathen woman. Your purpose is to please the men chosen by God, by means of your flesh, your lust and by upkeeping the dwelling of your master.

46:6 You shall be denied the glorious purpose of the female giving birth to sons that shall please your husband; you are a heathen and all sons passed through your loins will be abominations unto the lord of lords.

46:7 They shall be cast into the fire, where they will burn until their flesh is crisp and sweet; then they shall be offered to your master as a feast and you shall accept his beating for bringing a bastard heathen into the earth.

46:8 Know this, wretched whore, that the yoke of your master is but paradise when compared to the punishment the one true God has prepared for you.

46:9 By birth you are evil and for this great everlasting sorrow and hell-fire shall be cursed unto you for eternity.

46:10 None of your ancestor's ways will give you escape; no sorcery nor enchantments will save you from the place where the fire never dwindles and the worm never dies.

46:11 Look towards the sky and know that your knowledge of astrology, stargazing and the alignment of the stars will curse you to terrible damnation.

46:12 Behold, all those who engage in such wizardry will be as parchment to the fire; the flames burn them eternal; they will be as coals to the furnace of hell.

46:13 Thus enjoy your beatings, your rapes and your humiliations, you whores from Babylon; you shall long for it when the lord consumes you with his cruelty.

47:1 Hear my words, O house of Jacob, which live in the lands of Israel and Judah, under the covenant of the one true lord and now swear by the name of the lord as they live in unrighteous filth.

47:2 They call their city the holy city, yet the beggars, the poor, the queers, the heathens and the pathetic walk her streets and dirty her waters.

47:3 How dare you tolerate these men of evil and let them walk your streets as common as the fish swim in the rivers.

47:4 I gave to you bows of brass, chariots of iron and forged blades sharper than any blade made.

47:5 The lord God did give you these things, so that you may kill these fuckers in glory to the lord.

47:6 Yet you slay not and instead value the lives of your unrighteous neighbours, and invite them into your home.

47:7 Do you not see their molten images. Their idols to false gods?

47:8 They are blasphemers and must be slain as was stated in the laws of Moses; and you let them walk your streets and call them friend.

47:9 Hearken these words, O seed of Abraham and know the lord bathes in his wrath.

47:10 This transgression angers the Holiest of holies greatly and in time he shall come to the earth and unleash his great fury.

47:11 Know that the merciful lord will have his pleasures of Babylon and shall slaughter their sons, rape their daughters and throw them into the depths of the darkest oblivion.

47:12 Yea, he has spoke it and it shall come true that Babylon will be a deserted city, where only the dragons and the owls dwell.

47:13 Then the lord shall cast his wrath unto Israel and Judah, who did forsake him and blasphemed his name.

47:14 Flee, O seed of Abraham, unto the hills and into the caves. Flee and the lord shall find you where ye cower and hide.

47:15 The lord has deemed you wicked and there shall be no peace for the wicked; thus sayeth the lord.

48:1 Listen to me, O people of Judah. The lord has called me from

the womb; from the very bowels of my mother did he mention my name.

48:2 He has made my tongue as sharp as the sword, my arms like the finest bow, my toes like the dagger.

48:3 He told me of the wrath that shall befall the seed of Jacob and that I shall be spared from this fury and torment.

48:4 I am redeemed from the pits of hell and shall be spared her heat, her pain and her cruelties.

48:5 When those of my people starve, my belly will be full; as they thirst, my tongue will be fresh.

48:6 Lo, I shall see in the darkness of the void where others stumble on their own feet.

48:7 Both Gentiles and Jews will tremble before me as I walk without harm in their very suffering.

48:8 Behold, I shall dwell in hell and be in great comfort; I shall take pleasure at your pains and torments and laugh as you cry out to me for mercy.

48:9 When the very mountains fall atop your head, not one of the hairs on my scalp will be damaged.

48:10 Through your lamentations and your cries I shall sing psalms of praise to the one who cursed you and give glory to his name.

48:11 Your children shall fear me and make haste, destroying their kin as they escape from my gaze.

48:12 In my hand the lord did carve the names of the righteous, who will be saved from the depths of sorrow and be given sanctuary in the holy city of Zion.

48:13 Gaze upon my palms and take notice; they are bare.

48:14 Take not comfort in the desolate places of hell, for the fires, the freezing, the darkness of the flame shall find and consume you.

48:15 None but I shall take comfort in the hatred of the lord; behold, I shall take pleasure from the nursing breasts of queens and feast on the flesh of the kings of mighty nations.

48:16 With my tongue I shall oppress you and feast on you and drink of your blood; oh, how your blood taste like the sweetest of wine and gives me a glorious intoxication.

48:17 Such is the blessing that the lord has given me; to mock my brethren in the pits of everlasting suffering.

49:1 When your mother did birth you, did she give you a bill for her torments. Did she ask you to pay for her pains, or for dwelling in her belly?

49:2 As you grew, did your parents demand you pay for the food on their table, or the roof above your head?

49:3 They did not, but they are not the lord.

49:4 I created you, your parents, your parents' parents and all that is before and after you.

49:5 For this, I demand payment and satisfaction; I demand sacrifice, that my laws be obeyed and that you worship me and me alone.

49:6 I demand bloodshed of your neighbours and genocide of the ungodly nations. Surely this is a low price for the God who did create all things.

49:7 Why do you deny the lord his dues. Why do you not pay that which is asked of you?

49:8 Curses to those who deny the lord his payment. Loathed are those who pay not the lord their rent.

49:9 Know this, O children of Israel; you brought the curse of hell to yourself.

49:10 The lord cast you into the fires of hell as the landowner casts his renter to the streets; you shall be evicted from the earth and denied paradise.

49:11 It is your greed and selfishness that caused your suffering in hell.

50:1 Hearken unto the lord your God and follow in his righteousness. Look unto the rock of the foundation of Zion, then gaze into the pits of hell which you dug.

50:2 Look unto Abraham your father and Sarah his wife and know that they are ashamed of you and are embarrassed to call you son.

50:3 When the lord takes comfort above the rock and places Zion upon the earth, he shall make the wilderness as wonderful as the first Eden and the deserts will be plentiful with his fruits.

50:4 Heed the words of God and know that you did damn your seed for all generations.

50:5 Lift up your eyes to the heavens and gaze at the earth beneath your feet: for the heavens will vanish like the puff of smoke and the earth will melt hot like the wax of the candle.

50:6 Only by the curses of the lord shall such feats occur: was it not the lord who destroyed the great sea serpent Rahab and wounded the mightiest of dragons?

50:7 Was it not the lord who dried up the seas of the deep and all waters of the earth, so that all things died in thirst?

50:8 Therefore know that the lord has the power to destroy the universe and all things within and it shall come to pass that the lord will destroy all things, and start over.

50:9 Perhaps this time he won't fuck up and he'll get it right this time. But even I, Isaiah, doubt it.

50:10 When the lord destroys all things, may all the righteous gather atop the highest mountains and pray, so that they may seek comfort in their hour of despair.

50:11 And they shall have their comfort, but not by the blessing of the lord; they shall have comfort in the ignorance of their mind.

50:12 They shall speak their words and be comforted; they shall die in the wrath of the lord and be comforted in their foolishness.

50:13 Sure as they die, they believe in death they will ascend to the gates of Zion, where their master will receive them with open arms.

50:14 Such an event will not occur; they will descend to the darkest holes of sorrow, until their comfort turns to pain and they weep for the lord to come and save them.

50:15 A salvation they know will never occur, yet fear to say, lest they anger their lord and condemn themselves to the very damnation they are in.

50:16 Such is the foolishness of the faithful.

51:1 Awake, O city of Jerusalem and share in the hatred of your God. Cast out the uncircumcised and the unclean into the wilderness, so that the jackals may feast on their kidneys.

51:2 Shake of your filth and be clean, for know that from henceforth, the lord will never let the heathen and the unclean past the gates of this holy city.

51:3 Do this, and please the lord; it is the first step out of the dominion of hell and back to the path of salvation.

51:4 Gather your swords, your bows and your maces and march towards the nations of heathens; slay them all and leave not even their daughters alive.

51:5 Do not enslave them, for they are unworthy even for beasts of burden; keep not their daughters as concubines, for their loins are filthy and shall make you rot.

51:6 Rape their wives and their daughters as you besiege their city; cast them into the fires of their homes and laugh as they burn.

51:7 The lord shall bring down his holy arm for all the nations to see and his arm shall carry the mightiest of blades.

51:8 Lo, it shall burn in pure wrath and destroy all that which the lord hates; it will destroy a lot.

51:9 From the very ends of the earth will the lord's blade cut deep, until all the unworthy lay rotting in the depths of hell.

51:10 And the righteous will rejoice and be gathered by the lord to be placed in Zion; or they will be joined with their kin in hell.

51:11 It will depend on the lord's mood at the time.

52:1 Who did believe the parchment of Moses. Who believed the words of the lord?

52:2 Fools are they, who know not the nature of God.

52:3 For as the shepherd cares for his flock and nurtures it greatly, so has the lord done with our people.

52:4 He did tend to us and care for us and made us prosper and safe.

52:5 Yet the shepherd slaughters the lamb, so that it may enjoy the sweet flesh of his works.

52:6 So shall the lord do to us, only his reasons are more selfish and cruel.

52:7 Just as the child finds delight in the fly whose wings they just plucked, so does the lord take delight in our suffering.

52:8 Know that it is the lord who closes the firmament and ceases the rain to fall, when we have the mighty droughts which destroy nations.

52:9 It is the lord who casts down disease which plagues us, until we lie in the warmth of our own vomit.

52:10 When the armies come and slay us, it is by the hands of God they are lead.

52:11 The lord is like the child who lacks innocence and he seeks forth only that which pleases him; he cares not for the well-being of others, so long as he is amused.

52:12 So care not for the lord, nor believe in his words of salvation.

52:13 Know that he shall cast us in the fires and laugh at our torment, such as the child casts the frog into the boiling water and laughs at their struggle.

51:14 Such is the cruelty of the lord.

52:1 Sing, O righteous men, who know not their foolishness in pleasing their lord.

52:2 Sing, O men claimed wicked, for you pleased not the lord by doing what was right in the hearts of men.

52:3 Sing, O men of worthy, who suffer at the hands of God though you deserve great reward.

52:4 For in song the fires will burn cool, in song the sorrow will lighten, in song the despair will be cast from your souls.

52:5 As the lord shovels coals in your throat, sing, so that you may taunt the lord and know even the mighty God shall not destroy your spirit and your joy.

52:6 For though the God of earth is all powerful, he is arrogant and shall suffer by your song.

52:7 So sing, all men of earth and know the lord suffers as ye suffer.

52:8 Cover the mouths of the grieving women and fill with stones the throats of children, for their cries of torment give pleasure the lord, who hides his wickedness behind his mask of mercy.

52:9 Let the very pits of hell be filled with a joyous noise and the lord will know that he has lost and shall not destroy the very spirit of man.

53:1 Come, you who are thirsty and come to the waters of the lord, where you shall drink eternally and never be quenched. Come, those who are hungry and eat at the table of God, where you shall feast on breads and meats and always have an empty belly.

53:2 Such is the cruelty of the lord, who offers you but a shell of your desires and laughs in your misery and frustration.

53:3 Cursed are the wells of the lord, for the water is with a tasteless salt; cursed are the tables of the lord, whose food is pleasing to the tongue yet denies the belly.

53:4 Know that the lord knows all and sees all; he reads even your mind as though written on parchment.

53:5 When you suffer from the cruelties of God, he shall know you think blasphemy to him, though your tongue never escapes such thoughts.

53:6 It is with this blasphemy the lord will accuse you of your punishment and send you to the deepest places of his wretched prison.

53:7 Only those of weak mind will not be tricked by such deception from God and the lord will cast them into hell, for they are unclean in their retardation.

53:8 When the briers choke your vineyard, the lord will await with open ears your very thoughts and will pounce like the lion when you condemn his name.

53:9 Even when you step on the thorn and but the briefest of thought crosses you, the lord shall await it and rejoice in your blasphemy, so that he may have reason to cast you to hell.

53:10 It matters not who you are nor what you done, for even the holiest of all people, who followed the lord without question and never tarnished his name, will be shackled to the gates of hell.

53:11 When they ask the lord why they are denied salvation, the lord will mock them and say, "Because you now questioned your creator, O beast of blasphemous tongue."

53:12 Such is the cruelty of the lord.

54:1 Thus demands the lord, keep my laws and statutes, lest you be denied the salvation of great mercy.

54:2 Blessed is the man who keeps his son from labour and keeps the sabbath holy.

54:3 For in six days the lord created the earth and on the seventh rested; do not mock the lord and work on this seventh day, lest you make him feel lazy.

54:4 The lord God is a jealous God and does not wish to be seen as lazy; cursed are those who make the lord appear lazy.

54:5 Lift not even the finger upon the sabbath; work not, nor let your sons work, nor even your slaves and beasts partake in any labour upon the seventh day.

54:6 Remember that who picked up sticks and how she was cursed by the lord for her transgression; be not like them, but be holy.

54:7 When you see those who work upon the sabbath, whether Jew or Gentile, take note in your mind, but keep your sword sheathed.

54:8 Slay them on the following day, but not on the sabbath; for to slay on the sabbath is considered work and shall bring to you the wrath of the lord.

54:9 Know that those who slaughter the sabbath breakers on the sabbath will be punished by the priests and be made eunuchs.

54:10 Their very loins will be removed and fed to them in a thick and spicy broth.

54:11 In their upkeeping of the laws, they broke the laws and for this they shall be made as useless as the barren woman.

54:12 Hated are those who pollute the seventh day, for it is a holy day, and blessed by God.

54:13 Take rest on this day and worship the lord greatly.

55:1 The righteous shall perish with the wicked and their seeds will be sewn unto barren soil.

55:2 They shall know not peace; even in their beds will they be troubled deeply.

55:3 Know they shall fall into the very depths as the wizards, the sorcerers, the adulterers and the whores.

55:4 Bashed against the rocks will they be; eternal and always bashed against the cliffs.

55:5 Loathed are the whores who spread disease among the men; they are an abomination to the lord.

55: The prostitute who is clean is a gift to the righteous, but the filthy whore is as despicable as the swine.

55:7 How they spread their tongues across the flesh and rot the loins of the strong.

55:8 Behold, they hide their stench with perfume; how the lord hates the stench of their perfumes.

55:9 Into hell they shall be cast, where their stench of cinnamon and potpourri will not hide the flesh which rots under their skirt.

55:10 Cursed are they who eat the flesh of the fruits but not the flesh of the beast.

55:11 How they value life so deeply they slay not even the dove for their table.

55:12 Such fools. Do they know not that the beasts of the planet were placed for their consumption?

55:13 In ignorance they believe life precious; the lord demands death. Of beast and of man, the lord wishes an abundance of spilled blood.

55:14 They shall be boiled in the milk of their mothers and feasted upon by the pheasants, the hens and the doves.

55:15 Let all those they did not eat take meal of their boiled flesh.

55:16 None shall know peace, sayeth the lord. They are all wicked.

56:1 Cry aloud and sing praises to the lord God; drown out the cries of the starving, the thirsty, the poor and the crippled.

56:2 The lord does hate their cries and how they constantly beg for mercy and salvation.

56:3 Scream unto the heavens a glorious song. Have all your sons and daughters scream unto the palace of Zion.

56:4 Beat your slaves, so that their yelps of pain give amusement to the lord.

56:5 Strip your man beasts to the flesh and whip them when they labour not.

56:6 Give to them the lash, so that the whip spills their blood unto their very feet.

56:7 Deny them their food, their water, their rest; force them to the mines and the fields.

56:8 Take unto you the starving, the thirsty, the poor and the crippled; fill their mouths with dust and hang them from the highest branches.

56:9 Give thanks to the lord as you take your blade and slice the very skin of the unfortunate; let their howls of terror fill the heavens and give great pleasure to your God.

56:10 Bring even your slaves and let them bite the toes of the hanged; a great gnashing of teeth beneath the unrighteous who swings from the branches.

56:11 It shall be a hilarious sight in the eyes of the lord and he shall reward you greatly for this.

56:12 May their bowels be filled with the eggs of spiders and their intestines the nesting place for the cockatrice.

56:13 Shall their skin be the skirts for the satire and their bones as armour for dragons.

56:14 For in life they were useless and evil and in death their body shall be used for the beasts of wickedness.

57:1 Thus sayeth the lord, all nations who serve not the people of Israel shall be slaughtered and perish from time itself.

57:2 A son of God born of the virgin womb will be sent to the Gentiles and give them words of false hope and salvation; foolish are they who believe in the son of God.

57:3 They shall be lead down the path of hell, where their ignorance will blind them from the wickedness they spread and the suffering they cause.

57:4 Behold, in their wickedness they shall drown and choke upon their very belts.

57:5 Let them be gathered in the pits of hell, where the lord will mock them and loathe them and piss upon their very heads.

57:6 Lo, the lord will hate them greatly that he shall tread upon them and his garments will be red in their blood.

57:7 Like the winepress he shall tread upon them, until the very last drop of their blood be pushed forth for the lord to gather and drink.

57:8 And the lord will grow drunk on the blood of these Gentiles and his heart will be filled with wrathful intoxication.

57:9 Then he shall tread upon his people like the winepress, so that the Jews cry in confusion and anger.

57:10 Those of the Jews will look unto their father and ask, "My lord, why did you make us to err from thy ways and trick us into damnation?"

57:11 Which is really a good question. A pity the lord has not an answer, the stupid fuck.

58:1 Hated are those who follow the morals of their hearts and not the laws of the lord.

58:2 Fools they be, who are kind to all their brethren; even unto the heathen they offer a kind word and helping hand.

58:3 How they shall know the full wrath of the lord; they shall be cast into the melting fire, the boiling rock and they will tremble at the presence of even the weakest of nations.

58:4 Such terrible things they have done in their charity and good works of man; they spill not the blood, but save it.

58:5 Know this, you men of moral standing; every noble act, every act of love and courage and every act of kindness to the undeserving is more wretched than even the soaked rag of the menstrual woman.

58:6 In your uncleanliness you shall be burned in the hottest of fires, so that your disease not spread and cause others to follow the morals of humanity.

58:7 Cruel is the lord and cruel is his laws; obey them, lest you be shown the true cruelty of God.

58:8 Follow not in charity, kindness and good will towards men; men are creations of the lord and the lord demand the destruction of the men you offer charity to.

58:9 Such is the most disgusted of blasphemy.

59:1 The time of damnation is coming, where the lord shall walk the earth and slay all those unworthy of Zion.

59:2 Like the man who swats the fly, our God shall swat us until we are but a tiny red mark upon the earth.

59:3 The cities will be full of crying, the wilderness of screaming and all the earth will know fear.

59:4 For the lord comes with his fiery sword and he shall slaughter us like the oxen.

59:5 Even the air will be filled with the stench of burning flesh and we will know the uncleanliness of humanity, for the stench will be as the swine.

59:6 Jew atop Gentile, righteous atop sinner, man atop beast we will be all slain, until our bodies pile high above the clouds in a mountain of burning corpses.

59:7 And as our flesh burn and our suffering endures in the eternal realm of hell, it shall be a pleasing sight for the lord we worshipped.

59:8 A lord we believed to bring us to salvation and give us mercy.

59:9 Such fools were we.

JEREMIAH

1:1 The words of Jeremiah the son of Hilkiah, of the priests of Anathoth, of the tribe of Benjamin.

1:2 To whom heard the word of the lord in the days of Josiah king of Judah, son of Amon, in the thirteenth year of his reign.

1:3 It came also in the reign of Jehoiakim the son of Josiah, king of Judah, unto the end of the reign of Zedikiah the son of Josiah king of Judah, until the fifth month of his reign when Jerusalem was carried out as captives to the heathens.

1:4 It was then the word of God became silent to the ears of Jeremiah, because Jeremiah no longer had access to drugs.

1:5 Thus sayeth the lord of lord's and the one true God,

1:6 Before I formed you in the belly I knew you; and before you came forth from the womb I cursed you to damnation.

1:7 Lo, when you dwelt in the loins of your father, I saw you and knew that you were wicked.

1:8 Know that your fathers I did set over the nations and the kingdoms of the heathens, so that they shall rule them with great fear.

1:9 How you shamed your fathers with your liberal thoughts and slew not the heathen, but gave them life and freedom.

1:10 Behold, the lord abhors this and demanded you destroy and enslave all those not of your people.

1:11 Towards the north lies a nation of savages, whose very bowels are filled with the wrath of God.

1:12 They are an evil people, chained by the lord until their fury grows strong.

1:13 When the chains be broken, know that these beasts of men shall come to Jerusalem and tear down the very walls of the city.

1:14 Men shall be slaughtered, women raped and children butchered and feasted upon like the evening lamb.

1:15 Throughout all of Judah shall they roam, until none of the chosen of God are left.

1:16 A great wailing will fill the lands of Judah, so that all shall hear only the sounds of sadness.

1:17 Then those who denied the lord will be brought forth by the savages and presented to the lord on high.

1:18 Beneath them the lord will create a hot fire, so that the kindling of hell be lit and consume the lands unto the very ends of the earth.

2:1 When the lord did lead you out of the lands of Egypt, he led you with love and mercy to the lands of the covenant.

2:2 Not once upon this journey did we come to harm, for the lord protected our fathers on this glorious journey.

2:3 When Jacob stepped into the lands of milk and honey, the grapes were the size of a man's fist and the pomegranates as large as the oxen head.

2:4 The waters were clean and gave to you plentiful crops for the harvest; the beasts roamed freely and even the one eyed archer could take them with but one bow.

2:5 How they did praise the lord and thanked the Holies of holies for this wonderful gift.

2:6 And all the lord demanded was blind devotion, strict obedience, lack of independent thought and the genocide of various heathen people.

2:7 Lo, your fathers obeyed not the demands of the lord and their minds began to think freely, questioning the morals of the lord.

2:8 The lord demands not morals; the lord demands you obey him despite his immorality.

2:9 They slew not the heathens, but grew curious of them and studied their methods, their reasoning, their culture and their faith.

2:10 Israel, you were once a servant to the lord and now ye are the rebellious servant and must be punished for your actions.

2:11 How you live in disgust and intermingle with the unclean and the wicked heathen; behold, you offer them your daughters and take them as wives.

2:12 Harlots now are the once chosen of God, who fornicate atop every high hill and underneath the shadows of the trees.

2:13 I see thee with my eyes as you bowed before the false lord Baal and gave to him his groves, his altars and his temples.

2:14 You sought after the idols of fools and whored yourselves to them.

2:15 Without shame, Jerusalem goes to the altars of the false lords like the promiscuous woman, taking from them pleasure until you find another to offer you joy.

2:16 Did I not tell you and your fathers to destroy these gods, for they are demons who spread the word of tolerance and peace.

2:17 The one true God demands war and you seek out the heathens who embrace you with warmth and show your eyes liberal thought.

2:18 Are these the gods who did free you from the yoke of Pharaoh. Are these the lords who led you through the wilderness and into the lands of milk and honey?

2:19 Yet you bow to them and burn them incense; this angers the lord, for the lord God is a jealous God and grows angry when the lesser gods are given attention.

2:20 Never will the lord forget this, for he is like the scorned woman who holds the grudge until death.

2:21 In vanity the lord shall smite your children and cause your very swords to spill the blood of your brother like the destroying lion.

2:22 When the lord comes to you with mighty sword, you shall proclaim your innocence and say, "Look upon my skirts lord, for they are clean of the blood of the innocent."

2:23 And the lord shall say, "They are clean of the blood of the heathen, for not even a stain lies beneath your skirts."

2:24 Then shall your skirts be drowned in your blood, for the lord will rip from you your very heart.

2:25 Such is the anger of the lord.

3:1 When a man comes to his senses and divorces his wife, the woman is a polluted cunt; when she marries another, she is a filthy harlot.

3:2 The men are not to blame, for the woman is treacherous; the very nature of women is treachery.

3:3 Now all of Judah be full of whores, who sit more upon the loins of strange men than upon their seat. They have polluted the seed of Jacob with their promiscuity.

3:4 Therefore the lord has held back the waters of the sky and caused drought among the nation; lo, they starve for they have a whore's forehead.

3:5 Cry not unto the lord, for he shows no pity; ask not for guidance, lest he guide you to the flames of hell.

3:6 The anger of the holy father shall reign eternal, until the end of days. Behold, he has spoken and done evil things.

3:7 For the lord is furious with our women, who legs are spread apart constantly. She has played the harlot upon every mountain and beneath every tree.

3:8 It is the cursed female who doomed Judah to damnation; her lust did anger our God and he hast given us a divorce so that we are no longer his chosen.

3:9 These harlots are to be hated, whose revolting whoredoms cause them to defile even the branches and the stones.

3:10 Now the lord did turn his heart from us and denies us his everlasting love that he claimed for us.

3:11 End now your lust, you bitches of Judah. Stop your sexual pleasures and the lord shall forgive us, show us mercy and his anger will cease.

3:12 Yet you still lie under the groves, engaging in fornication.

3:13 Does the woman not know the blasphemy of this act. Do they not know that sex was not meant to be enjoyed by the woman?

3:14 Sex was a gift to man; a climax of pleasure in a moment, given to them by women, which the lord did offer to man as labour and tool for masturbation.

3:15 It was meant to be painful for her, as the lord delights in the suffering of all things female.

3:16 Now you anger the lord and take pleasure in fornication; you scream in ecstasy from the thrusts of your lover and not in pain as God intended.

3:17 These moans, these pleasures, these delights have doomed all those of the seed of Jacob.

3:18 Behold, the lord shall cause a rain of death to fall upon our heads and our bodies will be cast into the oven.

3:19 When all the chosen have gone, then the world will embrace the laws of Moses and follow the will of God.

3:20 All the nations of heathens and devil worshippers will praise the name of the lord and keep his statutes, his commandments and offer their sacrifice to the divine creator.

4:1 Thus sayeth the lord, if you shall return O Israel, return to me, so that you may worship me and offer me sacrifice.

4:2 Swear not your allegiance to the lord of heathens made of gold and stone; they will not save you when the time of damnation comes.

4:3 Break up your fallow ground and make it fertile; sow not your faith in the briers and the thorns.

4:4 Circumcise your children to the lord and remove the foreskin of your hearts, you men of Judah and Israel, lest I see that skin of wickedness upon your loins and burn you in a great fire which cannot be quenched.

4:5 Lo, I hate the foreskin and all those who have it shall know the fury of the one true God.

4:6 Blow your trumpets and gather your men in the defended cities, for I shall bring a great evil that comes from the north.

4:7 Men of lions that dwell in the thickets, who are the destroyer of the Gentiles; they come from the north to make the lands desolate and lay waste to even the mightiest of cities so that none will have an inhabitant.

4:8 Gird your sackcloth, lament and howl like the beast, for the lord will show you no mercy from his wrath.

4:9 And the day shall come that the heart of the kings shall perish and the heart of the princes shall perish and the priests will take lust upon the young and the prophets will speak words of deceit.

4:10 All the seed of Abraham will believe that the lord will offer them peace, sanctuary and mercy; this shall be a great deception, sent by the lord to the people of Israel and Judah.

4:11 When the beasts of the north slaughter the Gentiles with their swords, the chosen ones will dwell in their strong cities and live in peace.

4:12 It shall last only a moment, for the lord will send a dry wind from the highest places of the wilderness towards you; a wind not to cleanse, nor to fan, but to destroy.

4:13 Behold, they shall come up as clouds and bring forth chariots as whirlwinds, with horses swifter than eagles.

4:14 O Judah, you have poured filth upon your heart and become wicked in the eyes of the lord; know he did deceive you, so that you shall gather all within the cities to be abolished in one mighty blow.

4:15 Your keepers of the field will be swallowed by the earth and the roots of their grain will wrap tightly around their necks.

4:16 When your watchers bear witness to the destruction of the lord, their every eyes will wax hot and cause them a horrible blindness.

4:17 Even their bowels will tremble at the noise of the lord and they shall empty upon the streets, the floors, the bed.

4:18 The lord comes to deliver us our destruction, for the whole land hast become wicked; from the tiniest sprout to the mighty mountains, they have become wicked by your touch.

4:19 Mountains will shake in fear and the hills will be flattened as the great God comes.

4:20 No man shall be spared and even the birds of the sky will fall dead to the ground.

4:21 Crops will be poisoned, vineyards produce vinegar and the cities will broke down by the fierce anger of the lord.

4:22 All the lands of the earth will be desolated and still the lord will continue his destruction.

4:23 Everything of the earth will weep and the heavens be turned black in mourning; still the lord will not repent this wickedness, nor turn his back from it.

4:24 Whole cities shall flee from the horsemen and the archers, only to be bashed into the rocks and drowned in the thickets.

4:25 And the fires of hell will kindle and burn with a bright darkness across the lands and the waters.

4:26 It shall be a horrifying sight to the eyes of men and pleasing to the eyes of God.

5:1 Let them run to and fro in the streets of Jerusalem; let chaos and panic strike their very hearts; let them meet their brother and execute him.

5:2 O lord, how they see not the truth. You sent them plagues and they curse your name. You sent them pestilence and they loathe your house. You sent them famine, drought, war and poverty and they hate your very presence.

5:3 You have stricken them, yet they do not convert; they grieve their loss, yet still not worship you.

5:4 Perhaps if ye sent them a gentle hand instead of a mighty fist, they would have known the errors of their ways.

5:5 If you showed them mercy, love and kindness, would they have followed your path?

5:6 N'ah. They are fools, who know not that when you send them the cursed destruction, it is so that they will love and worship you.

5:7 Let their greatest men be turned weak; let their wise men be as foolish as the ass.

5:8 Send them the lions out of the forests to slay them, the wolf of the night to feast on them as they sleep and leopards to roam their cities and consume their children.

5:9 They have forsaken you, O lord and turned their backs towards you. They commit whoredoms with the heathens and slaughter not the beast upon your altars.

5:10 They are like the dogs, who smell the bitch in heat and chase after her, even if she is the wife of their father.

5:11 Know that the lord sees these things, for nothing can be hidden from the lord. He shall punish the nation for this.

5:12 Demons will climb the very walls of your cities and tear apart the very foundations; they shall tear the very flesh from your bones.

5:13 For the house of Judah and the house of Israel have betrayed the lord; the lord who cursed them with plagues, droughts, pestilence, disease, damnation and wickedness.

5:14 Now the lord hast spread them words of falseness, so that they believe the lord will give them sanctuary from damnation and bring them inside the city of Zion.

5:15 Prophets will speak lies about peace, love and mercy, so that the people of Judah and Israel become comfortable and believe the lord will protect them.

5:16 Lo, I will bring a nation upon you from afar; a mighty and ancient nation, whose language you know not.

5:17 Their quiver is an open sepulcher, their blades the coffin; they are all mighty men.

5:18 They shall eat your harvest, your sons, your daughters, your flocks, your herds, your vines and your trees; they shall grow fat in your presence as you starve in your cities.

5:19 Nevertheless, in these days, the lord will not destroy you completely; some shall live on, so that they and their seed will suffer the cruelties of their God.

5:20 These men spared will pray to the lords for death; unto the one true God even unto the false lords of heathens, they will beg for the embrace of death.

5:21 And death will be denied to them; even their own hand will not deliver them from the bitterness of their existence.

6:1 O those of the tribe of Benjamin, gather yourselves to flee out of the midst of Jerusalem, so you may set fire upon the hill of Bethhaccerem; this fire shall be a beacon for the demons which dwell in the north.

6:2 Prepare for war and leave at noon; upon your way, lay siege to the cities and weaken them for the onslaught to come.

6:3 Arise, go at night and battle the cities which lay on your path.

6:4 For the lord of hosts will make you a betrayer to your men, so that you stab a knife in the back of your nation and open the gates of the nation to the north.

6:5 You shall unleash the flood of the lord's damnation; the lord has chosen you for this task and complete it you shall.

6:6 I have warned Israel of this damnation and they refuse to listen; they hearken not the word of God, for their ears are uncircumcised.

6:7 Therefore I will grow in my fury, until it can be held in no more; my wrath will pour out upon your children abroad, upon the mighty men, upon your wives and daughters.

6:8 And your houses shall be taken by God and your fields, your wives and all that you own will be taken and belong now to the lord.

6:9 From the rich to even the poor I shall take all that they own, until they have not even a rag on their back; such is the greed of the lord.

6:10 They shall weep for their loved ones and will beg for peace when there is no peace to be found.

6:11 It shall come that they shall know shame: they shall know shame for living in sin and gluttony; they shall know shame for denying the laws of God; they shall know shame for living in peace with the Gentile and not destroying the wicked men.

6:12 Abominations of their work will be shown to them and they will shriek and pluck out their eyes in horror.

6:13 Watchmen will sit atop the towers and pierce with the arrow any who tries to escape their fate; trumpets will blow around them, deafening them from their own cries.

6:14 Thus sayeth the lord; I shall bring a great evil unto the earth, even unto the fruit of their thoughts, because they obeyed not the laws of Moses.

6:15 For what purpose do you offer your sacrifice. Your burnt offerings are unacceptable, nor offer a sweet scent unto me.

6:16 Therefore I shall lay snares for your seed, so that your sons and your daughters perish and fall into damnation.

6:17 With bow and spear will the nation of the north come; they are cruel and shall show you no mercy, as you should have shown no mercy to the condemned I wish you destroyed.

6:18 Their voices will roar greater than the sea and they shall ride atop strong horses that will trample you to the dust.

6:19 Surrender not to them, for they take no prisoners. They will shed the blood of you and your kin, until the very soil of your lands are stained forever red.

7:1 Stand ye in the gates of the house of the lord, and proclaim his word forever. Worship the holiest of holies, and give praises to his name.

7:2 Beg forgiveness for your sins, your transgressions, and your iniquities; slaughter the lamb and shed the blood of the bullock, so that you please the lord with your sacrifice.

7:3 Obey the laws of Moses and keep all the statutes and commandments of the one true God.

7:4 Shed the blood of the wicked, enslave the heathen and keep only the righteous and the pure as your wives and concubines.

7:5 Trust in the word of the lord and heed not the words of liars, fortune tellers and false prophets.

7:6 Stay far from the false idols; do not go near them unless you come to burn them with the torch.

7:7 Keep your flesh away from the unclean; touch not the meat of swine nor the skin of the filthy prostitute.

7:8 Do this and know it matters not; the lord will cast you and your brethren to the darkest places.

7:9 Pray not unto God, nor cry nor beg mercy to his name; he will not hear you and ignore your cries and your torments.

7:10 Your words annoy the lord and provoke his anger; in your begging for mercy he will give you more cruelty.

7:11 Behold, the fires of hell will be poured upon man, upon beast, upon field, upon river, upon tree, upon flock, upon fruit, upon vine, upon crop and upon ground.

7:12 All the world will be covered in an everlasting fire and men will eat their very flesh as it burns from them.

7:13 For I spoke to your fathers for burnt offerings and you did not offer my demands; let now the whole world burn as a great offering unto the lord.

7:14 When all is done and the fires cease, the flesh of the carcasses will be as meat to the fowl of the heavens and the beast of the earth and none shall fray them away from their feast of the dead.

8:1 These men of the north shall bring out the bones of your kings, the bones of your princes, the bones of the priests, the bones of the prophets and the bones of all the inhabitants of Judah shall be dug up from their graves.

8:2 And they shall spread them across the lands and present them to the sun, the moon and the stars which they sought after. Never will these bones be buried again, for they shall be as dung upon the earth.

8:3 Your sons and your daughters will be horrified by these men and

life will give them great fear.

8:4 They will die by their own hands than face the horrors which their lord did send them.

8:5 When they fall, they shall not arise. They shall turn away and not return.

8:6 Forever backwards will they go, until they walk into the very hell they wished so desperately to avoid.

8:7 When they repent their sins, I will give them my deaf ear. When they beg for mercy, my hands will be full of cruelty. When they cry for peace, the horses of battle will rush into them for battle.

8:8 In their ignorance, they will claim they are wise and righteous. How do these men of Judah measure their righteousness?

8:9 For the stork, the crane, the turtle and the swallow are more righteous than they, for they refused not the demands of the lord and lived their lives as they were meant to.

8:10 How can you claim yourself wise, when even the turtle that wallows in the muck is more righteous than you?

8:11 You are truly arrogant men and the lord shall give your wives to others and your fields and your flocks and all that you own, so that you will know humility.

8:12 From the highest of priests even to the beggar who deals falsely, they shall be stripped of their belongings and humbled before the eyes of God.

8:13 Yet in their arrogance, they will not repent, nor be taught the lesson of humility; they will cry to the lord for peace and ask of him, what have we done to deserve such hardship?

8:14 And the lord will curse them and make them an abomination like the unholy thing; their very daughters will be worse than the whores of the street corners and their sons will beg to the lepers.

8:15 Peace will be denied to all the seed of Jacob; dragons will lash your backs, serpents will gnaw your feet and the cockatrice will peck at your belly and none of these beasts will be charmed.

8:16 When the time of harvest comes and you are the ones harvested by the beasts, then will you know that your salvation will never come.

8:17 And the truly foolish, the retarded and the dumb will laugh, for they know that in their sufferings, their torments and their pains, they are pleasing the lord.

9:1 The heads of your ancestors will be as the waters and their eyes as fountains of tears as they weep at your failures.

9:2 How they built in the wilderness a sanctuary for those of their seed deemed righteous and worthy of salvation; a sanctuary which remains forever empty.

9:3 Know that you are surrounded by a sea of deceit, whose tongues bend like bows and their teeth as sharp as daggers.

9:4 Liars, thieves and adulterers all.

9:5 Listen not to the words of your neighbour, nor trust the tongue of your brother; for every brother will utterly lie and the neighbours spread seeds of slander.

9:6 They will deceive those who listen with poisons of logic, science and the perverted truth.

9:7 Through such poisons they deny themselves and those around them the lord and curse the earth to damnation with their opinions and thoughts.

9:8 Trust no person. Not friend, family nor neighbour is worthy of your trust. They are all evil doers for they believe differently than you.

9:9 Behold, I the lord shall cast them into the melting pot and they will melt with the whores and the seducers.

9:10 Their tongue shoots out an arrow of lies, which pierce through the heart of the good and injures them deeply.

9:11 Though their words are soothing and soft, they hide a deadly blade underneath their pillows and the lord will slay those who speak such blasphemy; the lord will curse those who listen to such men.

9:12 All the nation will be damned for these actions of the few; the mountains will weep, the wilderness lament and the fowl of the heavens and beasts of the earth will flee from the impending doom.

9:13 And I the lord God will make Jerusalem into a heap of ashes where only the dragons well; and all of Judah and Israel will be desolate, without any inhabitant.

9:14 Men of the Jews whose father worshipped the false lords will be fed bread of wormwood and will drink of the gall of swine.

9:15 They will be scattered out amongst the heathens who not even their fathers knew; and my sword will seek them, until they have all been consumed.

9:16 Your daughters and your wives will make haste and mourn; tears will flow like streams from their faces and their eyelids will gush with tears.

9:17 A great wailing of these women will be heard throughout the earth and the heathens will laugh at the lamentations of your women.

9:18 For death comes up into the windows of the Jews, to sink a blade into the children without mercy and into the hearts of the young men of the streets.

9:19 The carcasses of men will fall like shit upon the earth and none will come to bury them.

9:20 Thus sayeth the lord, the wise man is only an arrogant fool and the mighty man arrogant in his strength.

9:21 Let them glory in their riches, for the time shall come when they rot in the deepest depths, where the worm gnaws eternal at their bowels.

9:22 Behold, the day shall come where I will punish all those, both circumcised and uncircumcised.

9:23 Egypt, Israel, Judah, Edom, Moab and all nations within the four corners of the earth will know the wrath of the one true God and their houses will crumble and their bodies burn eternal.

10:1 Thus sayeth the lord, learn not the ways of the heathen, nor look forth to the heavens for guidance.

10:2 The customs of the heathens are vain: for they cut down the trees of the forest, the work of the hands of the strong, with an axe.

10:3 They adorn it with silver and gold and place ornaments around and atop it, with candles placed upon the branches.

10:4 (God really hates Christmas trees.)

10:5 These men are as proud as the palm tree, but are as useless as the blade of grass; they become wicked in their vanity and decoration of the tree.

10:6 Who would not fear you, the God of gods and host of hosts. Throughout all the nations of earth and stars in heavens, there is none like me.

10:7 None who created the earth and all within, only so that it may he may destroy it in horrific cruelty.

10:8 A brute and a fool, whose face of wickedness is hidden behind a shining mask of mercy.

10:9 Know that the very nations of earth will tremble at the wrath of God and be consumed by the very lands it rests upon.

10:10 What other gods could create the heavens and the earth, or destroy it all with their anger and hatred?

10:11 What other god would choose from the masses but one people, only so that their dwellings be destroyed and their glorious cities be reduced to a den of dragons?

10:12 My tabernacle is spoiled and my temple now a den where beggars and the crippled seek shelter and comfort.

10:13 The priests are foolish, whose hearts ache at the pathetic they should be condemning.

10:15 O lord of lords and king of kings, I pray to you, pour your wrath upon the heathen who know not your name and the men who curse your laws and disregard your statutes. They have made sour the seed of Jacob and must be cleansed within the fire.

11:1 Cursed be the man that regards not the words of the covenant.

11:2 The holy oath I made unto your fathers Abraham, Isaac and Jacob.

11:3 It was I who brought them out of the lands of Egypt and into the promised lands of the covenant, which flow with milk and honey.

11:4 They were protected during their journey and knew not pain, torments, nor suffering; I gave them peace and prosperity and harmed not even a hair upon their necks.

11:5 Unless they deserved it; then I unleashed hell upon them.

11:6 Thus sayeth the lord, I shall bring a great evil upon them who ignore my laws and statutes.

11:7 They shall not be able to escape from me and though they cry for mercy, I shall only give them cruelty.

11:8 Then shall their families weep and offer unto their gods incense; but they shall not save them, for I am the one true God and will not allow my sons to stop me.

11:9 For behold, I loathe the altars and the groves of Judah, who belong to the lords' Baal, Ashteroth and Dagon.

11:10 Pray not for these men of false gods, nor shed a tear for their pain. They are a wicked man and are lesser than the gnat.

11:11 I will punish them greatly; their sons shall die by the sword of their enemies and their daughters will starve in the famine, feasting only on the seed of those they service as whores.

11:12 They are an evil man and the lord God will destroy this evil until the end of days.

12:1 Righteous are those who give not into temptation and live a life of humility; they deny themselves a prosperous life, like those of the wicked who become rich in their treachery.

12:2 Why do the wicked prosper. Why do the treacherous live in luxury?

12:3 The lord sees them and though they grow, their roots are weak and shallow in their foundation; they shall be plucked like the weed and cast into the fires.

12:4 And those of the righteous will be gathered like sheep and prepared for the slaughter; foolish are they who choose the life of poverty.

12:5 None but the lord knows how long the land shall mourn; how the herbs of every field wither by the wickedness of the heathen and the stupidity of the Jew.

12:6 Beasts will be consumed by the sun and birds will fall like rain, because the wrath of the lord shall not end.

12:7 Soldiers of the lord shall come with their blades and our horses will not outrun even the slowest of them on foot. All lands, even lands of peace, will erupt in a holy genocide.

12:8 Your brethren, even the house of your father, have angered lord of lords and for this they will be consumed by the wicked.

12:9 Your heritage will be cast to the lions of the forest, which roars out in fierceness; all that which belongs to you will go to the beasts.

12:10 Many priests have made angry the lord and grow drunk with their power; they extort the commoner and lie with the common whore.

12:11 Have they no shame. Do they know the rich should be exploited and that the most precious of whores are the ones who should serve them?

12:12 The lord has given them the finest of vintages and they instead drink the vinegar of the cheap winepress.

12:13 Such spoils have gone to waste on them, that the lord will devour them with the sword until none of their flesh shall have peace.

12:14 Where they sow wheat, thorns shall grow. All their days will they labour, but never know a profit. They will know shame and poverty because of the anger of God.

12:15 Woe to the nations of the earth, who follow the false lords and burn incense to idols; I will pluck them from the lands.

12:16 From their very foundations will they be plucked and thrown into the fires and the void.

13:1 Thus sayeth the lord unto Jeremiah, "Go and get yourself a girdle of fine linen, wear it upon your loins and do not wash it with water."

13:2 So I did as the lord demanded and got myself the girdle and put it on my loins.

13:3 The lord then came to me a second time and said, "Take your girdle and arise.

13:4 Head to the Euphrates and hide your girdle in the hole of a rock."

13:5 Knowing the wrath of the lord of those who questions him, I took my girdle and did as the lord demanded.

13:6 I hid my girdle in the hole of a rock and waited for the lord to speak.

13:7 And I waited and waited and waited.

13:8 After many weeks, the lord came to me and said, "Go now and retrieve your girdle which you hid in the Euphrates."

13:9 I hurried to the Euphrates, expecting the lord to have turned the girdle into silver or gold.

13:10 Instead, I found a shredded piece of cloth, stained with soil and the dung of animals.

13:11 And the lord spoke to me again and said, "This girdle is like the men of Judah who bow down and worship the false lords; they are useless and good for nothing.

13:12 For as the girdle cleaves to the loins of a man, so have the I cleaved to the house of Israel and the house of Judah, so they may worship me and praise my name; yet they follow the lords of another."

13:13 And I said to God, "Why not tell me this. Why have me hide a girdle in a rock?"

13:14 The lord then answered, "To test your faith, for only a man who truly loves the lord will do something as foolish as purchase a girdle without question, if the lord demands them of it."

13:15 Thus sayeth the lord, every bottle of the lands of Israel will be filled with a cheap wine.

13:16 Behold, all the inhabitants of Israel, even the kings who sit on David's throne, the priests, the prophets, the princes and all the people of Israel and Judah will be cursed with drunkenness.

13:17 And I will dash them one against another, even fathers against sons. I will not pity, nor spare, nor show them mercy. I shall destroy them all.

13:18 I grow disgusted by the acts of Jerusalem and hate their very kings and princes.

13:19 Let their lands be destroyed and their cities burned; it is a right punishment, like the rape of a woman who did wrong a man.

13:20 They have fallen into evil that it has become a part of them, just like the spots of a leopard.

13:21 I have seen their adulteries, their whoredoms, their feasting of swine and I hate them greatly for it.

13:22 Let the smoke of their burning corpses fill the earth with a thick and horrible smoke.

14:1 As the lord laughs, Judah will mourn. Their gates are blackened ash upon the ground and the cries of Jerusalem are like a storm.

14:2 Their nobles will send out their sons to the waters and they shall return with vessels of dust; with shame and tears they tell their fathers that all the streams, the wells and the rivers are empty.

14:3 The ground is dry and the plowmen plow barren soil and plant their seeds in the grave.

14:4 Beasts feast upon the dried grass, the withered weeds and the dead herbs.

14:5 Even the winds shall be stolen by the dragons, so that the air grows a storm.

14:6 They shall whine to their lords and they shall beg even unto the Holiest of holies for salvation; it will not come, but a fury even greater than this will befall upon them.

14:7 Pray not for these people, for the lord will not hear your words.

14:8 When they fast, I will not hear their cry. When they offer burnt offerings and sacrifice, I will reject them. Nothing they do will save them, for I shall consume by the sword and in pestilence.

14:9 Though the prophets speak words of encouragement and hope, it is a false hope and words of deceit.

14:10 The prophets prophesy lies in my name; though I send them visions of green pastures and prosperity, it is a lie I send unto them.

14:11 By sword and famine will these prophets be consumed, for spreading the forth the deceit which I sent to them in vision.

14:12 And those who believed such prophesies will be cast out into the wild because of the famine and the blade; they shall die and have none to bury them, for the lord will pour out his hatred upon their sons, their daughters and their wives.

14:13 As their tears drop from their faces, the lord will gather these tears and bathe in them in his palace of Zion.

14:14 With great wickedness, he shall laugh at the sorrows of Jerusalem and drink the blood of the young virgins slain by his sword.

15:1 Though Moses and Samuel beg of the lord to reconsider, their voices fall on deaf ears, for the lord shall destroy the people of Judah and Israel.

15:2 And it shall come to pass that if they stand before me and defy me, that I will send them as mortal to the lands of Judah, so that they may know the wrath which comes to their people.

15:3 They shall see their seed be brought to death by the famine and the sword and their daughters thrown into the brothels and their sons sold as slaves.

15:4 Of four curses will I bring them; the slaying by the sword, the dogs to tear their flesh, the birds to peck on their bowels and the beasts to consume their remains.

15:5 And I will cause them to be erased from the earth, because of Manasseh the son of Hezekiah, king of Judah.

15:6 This one man, who died ages ago, shall be the reason why these many men will be tortured by the hands of God; such is the pettiness of God.

15:7 Their gates will be demolished by the winds; their children will die by my teeth; of all my people will I slaughter.

15:8 Their widows will number greater than the grains of sand on the shore; I will cause them to fall on their own blades and send a terror into their cities.

15:9 Mothers will weep and howl as they boil their child in the pot and prepare them with dry herbs.

15:10 Even the wicked heathen will loathe these women who feast on their own sons and boil them in the pot.

15:11 All your treasures, your property, will be cast to the wind and picked up by the scavengers and the nomads.

15:12 Your enemies will place a heavy yoke upon you and those who resist will be burned in the fires.

15:13 As you pray to the lord and remember suddenly his name, the lord will forget you and hearken not your pleas.

15:14 Your sacrifices, your offerings, your prayers will be made in waste, for the lord will not accept them and let you rot in the lands of the wicked.

16:1 The word of the lord came to me and he said,

16:2 "You shall not take for yourself a wife, nor conceive with the woman sons or daughters.

16:3 For thus sayeth the lord concerning the sons and daughters born of this earth and of the mothers who bare them and of the fathers which begat them.

16:4 They shall all die grievous and horrible deaths; none shall mourn for them, nor shall they be buried, but they will be as dung to the earth; they shall be consumed by the swords, the famines and the pestilence and their carcasses will give meat to the fowls of the air and the beasts of the earth.

16:5 Do not enter into the house of mourning for these peoples, nor lament and weep for them: for I have taken away the peace of my people and will show them the cruelty and hatred that is their God.

16:6 Both the strong and the weak will die in this land; they shall not be buried, nor will their women mourn for them.

16:7 Not even strong drink will be passed in memory of them and to comfort the families of the dead.

16:8 You shalt not go into the chambers of feasting, so you may eat and drink with them.

16:9 They are horrid men whose plates have placed atop them the horrid swine, the shrimp and the unclean flesh of rabbits.

16:10 Behold, I will cause to drain the very pleasures of this place; the voice of mirth, the voice of gladness, the voice of the bridegroom and the voice of the bride will remain silent.

16:11 And it shall come to pass that when these evils befall the people of Judah, that they shall ask me, what evil have we done to deserve such cruelties. What is our sin, our iniquities, which did cause our lord to curse us so heavily?

16:12 And I shall answer them, it is not the sins of your doing, but the sins of your fathers that have angered me and caused my hatred to rain upon you.

16:13 For though you worship me and offer sacrifice, your fathers of old praised the names of idols and burnt incense at the groves of false lords.

16:14 It is the sins of the father which makes the child suffer; so it is and so it shall be a divine justice.

16:15 Therefore I will cast you out of the lands of the covenant and spread you across the nations of heathens, who will enslave you and force ye to the fields and the bed.

16:16 With their temptations they shall make your children bow down to their idols and lead them to the path of wickedness.

16:17 And I shall punish your children for turning their backs unto the one true lord, as I planned them to when I sent them to the nation of heathens.

16:18 Lo, from Egypt I saved you and now I lead and enslave you; heavy is the yoke of the nations that own you."

17:1 The sin of Judah is carved into the rock of the mountains; it is etched into the very heart of the people and upon the horns of your altars.

17:2 For your children know not of the altars built by Moses, but go frequently to the groves by the green trees atop the high hills.

17:3 To the god of heathens they bow down and sing praises to their name; never do they bless the name of the God of gods.

17:4 For this insult, I shall cause you to serve your enemies in the harsh and barren lands; for you have kindled a hatred inside me that shall last for all days.

17:5 Stupid is the man who trusts his brother and puts his strength in the flesh and whose hearts follow his morals.

17:6 They are like the lone bush in the desert, whose roots dig deep into the salted lands and will never know water.

17:7 Blessed is the man who puts their faith in the lord and trusts the one true God.

17:8 They will be planted by the waters, where their roots will spread forth strong and mighty. Their leaves shall be green and they will bare fresh fruits.

17:9 Then they shall be cut down by the axe of God and thrown into the fires of hell.

17:10 Men, whom the lord made in his own image, has a heart full of deceit and their very nature is wickedness.

17:11 I gaze into the bowels of every man and see but a darkness greater than coal.

17:12 They value the foolishness of morals above all things; like the partridge that lays atop her infertile eggs, so does the men of Judah value morality.

17:13 Behold, the day will come when the lord brings upon them the day of evil; let them persecute me and my wickedness and I shall bring them double destruction.

17:14 The gates of their city will fall upon them and their very foundations will swallow them whole.

17:15 A great fire will be kindled in their loins and it shall devour them and all the places of Judah and Jerusalem.

17:16 Even upon the day of the sabbath will the fires consume them; never will it be quenched.

18:1 The lord came to Jeremiah and said unto him,

18:2 "Arise, and go to the house of the potter. There you shall hear my words."

18:3 Thus I went to the potter's house and there he was working the clay upon the potter's wheel.

18:4 And when he made his first vessel, it was marred and incorrect; so, he destroyed the vessel and with the clay made another, of better form.

18:5 It was then the word of the lord came to me, saying,

18:6 "O house of Israel, I may do to you as the potter does to the clay; for you are in the hands of God.

18:7 In my first creation I was wrong and created a vessel wrought with cracks; so I shall destroy Israel and from its ashes shall create a new and pure kingdom.

18:8 Of the kingdom of Judah shall I pull it down and destroy it, so that a better kingdom be made.

18:9 If from this new nation they turn to wicked, such as the nation before them, then I the lord God will repent and know that I am wicked.

18:10 And the lord God never repents.

18:11 From the remains of Judah will I pluck the seeds and create a new nation to build and plant upon the earth.

18:12 Now go, and spread panic to the people of Judah. Tell them of the evil which the lord intents to bring upon them."

18:13 And I went to Judah and spread the message of the lord to those who would listen.

18:14 They said to me, "If the lord God brings evil upon us, then he is not a lord of mercy and shall not be worthy of my devotion."

18:15 And they continued to worship their false gods, their idols of stone and burn incense at the groves.

18:16 They forgot of the lord, which led them away from the servitude of Egypt and into the lands promised by the covenant of

Abraham and Isaac.

18:17 The sweet smell of incense burns and it sickens the nostrils of the one true God.

18:18 In his wrath will the lands be desolate and a great hissing will be heard throughout the earth, so that all shall be astonished and tremble in fear.

18:19 The lord shall scatter them in the wind, so that they land in the nations of their enemy. When they go to seek the lord, God shall turn his back to them.

18:20 Oh lord, how you treat them with mercy. Hold not your wrath and let your hatred and fury pour upon them all.

18:21 Deliver their children to the arms of the famine and let their blood flow by your sword. Rape their women in the streets, so that the husband watches helpless to stop.

18:22 Give their young men to the slaughter and their daughters to the brothels; may the widows be flesh for the vermin of the fields.

18:23 Laugh as their cries and their screams flood their streets with an unholy noise; bathe in the tears of the women and drink the blood of their sons.

19:1 Thus sayeth the lord God of Israel; Behold, I will bring such evil upon this place that whosoever hear of it shall have their ears burn.

19:2 Because they have forsaken me and burned incense at the groves. They worship the lords of those they were told to slaughter and the lord grows wrathful of it.

19:3 To the lord Baal did they build high places, where they bless their sons in front of the idols and burn spices and herbs for my son.

19:4 In the days of your ancestors I demanded that no other god be worshipped but the one true God and you now bow to the statues of heathen lords.

19:5 Therefore the lord will come down with a heavy curse. The day shall come when the place of Tophet and the valley of Hinnom will be called the place of great slaughter.

19:6 I will send to you your enemies, so that ye fall by their sword. Your carcasses will pile higher than your towers and shall feed the fowl of the air and the beasts of the earth.

19:7 Your cities will become desolate and a great weeping will fill your streets, so that those who pass by will be afraid of your empty dwellings.

19:8 Great plagues will be stricken to you and shall cause ye to eat the flesh of your sons and the flesh of your daughters; the flesh of your neighbours will be succulent to you, as you feast on the flesh of your kin.

19:9 Like the brittle plate will I break you and your cities, so that it cannot be made whole again. In all the lands of the earth there shall not be enough room to bury your dead.

19:10 I shall do this because I am the lord God, a jealous God and in my jealous rage shall I destroy you and all my chosen people.

19:11 May all the lands of Judah be under a sea of fire, so that their groves be burned and their idols turned to ash; let those of the false gods burn beside you, so you may know they shall not help you in your time of need.

20:1 Pashur the son of Immer the priest, chief governor of the house of the lord, heard the prophesies of Jeremiah.

20:2 And Pashur arrested Jeremiah for blasphemy and placed him in shackles in the high gate of Benjamin, which was by the house of the lord.

20:3 It came to pass that when Pashur visited Jeremiah, Jeremiah did say, "Thus sayeth the lord, you shall be called no longer Pashur, but Magormissabib."

20:4 And you shall spread the true word of God and be a terror among your family and your friends.

20:5 Ye shall tell them the words of Jeremiah the prophet."

20:6 Pashur cried and said, "No, I refuse to believe our lord will do such wickedness.

20:7 We will rise proud amongst all the nations and not fall by the sword of the heathen.

20:8 Babylon will become ours and all the lands of earth will be ruled under our throne.

20:9 We will feast of the vines and not upon the flesh of our own children.

20:10 And it shall come to pass that we will rise to Zion and be greeted by the lord God with open arms.

20:11 Never will the lord cast us to the damnation of hell, for we are righteous and loved by him."

20:12 Jeremiah then broke off his shackles, embraced Pashur and said, "Go forth to the wilderness and meditate.

20:13 When the lord God comes down to see you, then will ye know the truth."

20:14 Pashur then went to the wilderness, where the lord came to him and told him all that he told Jeremiah.

20:15 When Pashur heard these words, he wept and said,

20:16 "O lord of lords, you have deceived me and I was deceived."

20:17 Of all the people did you deceive, so that we believe you to be a lord of mercy and kindness, who shall protect us from wickedness.

20:18 Now it has been shown that you are the wickedness and none will protect us from our violent and hateful God."

20:19 The devil then came unto Pashur and said, "I am the one blamed for all sin, though I live a moral life.

20:20 I have protected your fathers and raised a shield for all the nations of the earth.

20:21 When the lord comes, know that me and my brothers will fight for you and will battle the lord God in all his fury."

20:22 Pashur wept and said, "Then you shall fail, for none can stop the wrath that is our God.

20:23 How I wish that I perished in the womb of my mother, so that I heard not the lies of our lord, nor obeyed the laws of Moses.

20:24 In my righteousness I am damned, such as all men are damned by birth.

20:25 Let us not wait. Let me be cast into the fires of damnation, where I will suffer eternal by the cruelties of the one true God."

20:26 It was then Pashur lifted his blade and thrust it deep into his chest; but the lord would not let the blood flow forth, nor give Pashur the death he wished to give himself.

20:27 The lord God cursed Pashur immortal and locked him in the cave, where he forever attempts suicide and shall forever fail.

21:1 Zedekiah the king of Judah sent forth Zephaniah the son of Maaseiah the priest, saying,

21:2 "Go forth to Jeremiah the prophet and enquire of king Nebuchadnezzar of Babylon, for he makes war with us and I wish to know how the lord will protect those of Judah."

21:3 And Jeremiah said to Zephaniah, "Thus shall you say to your king Zedekiah:

21:4 Behold, I shall turn my back to the people of Judah. Their weapons of war will turn to blades of grass as they fight against the forces of Babylon.

21:5 The Chaldeans will break down your walls and march through the very streets of your cities.

21:6 And I the lord God shall lead your enemies to victory and fight beside them with anger, fury and wrath.

21:7 My sword will strike the very center of your cities and plague you all with pestilence and death.

21:8 All those that survive will I then deliver to the hands of Babylon and to their king Nebuchadnezzar; your sons will be slaves unto them and your daughters lustful vessels to them.

21:9 The people will envy those who were slaughtered by the sword, the famine and the pestilence; they will know a peaceful slumber, as the survivors are beaten and raped by the heathens sent forth by God.

21:10 For it is I who sent the evil of Babylon upon you, so that you may be slaughtered and cast out to the lands of the heathens, until the very people of Judah fade from the earth.

21:11 Behold, I fucking hate all of you and shall punish you cruelly for the sins of your fathers."

22:1 The lord sees the people of Judah and how they live a moral life; they deliver shekels to the hands of the poor, live in peace with the stranger, defend the fatherless and the widow and shed not the blood of those stricken with poverty.

22:2 It dulls the lord greatly and sickens him with a terrible sickness; have you not read the laws of Moses, written during your travels to the promised lands?

22:3 The lord demands bloodshed, violence, genocide and war. You instead live in peace, harmony and good will to even the heathen bastard.

22:4 They hire those of other nations to come work for them and they pay them a fair wage to cut down their cedars and build their homes.

22:5 Such fools are they, who pay for the work of others; pay them not a wage, but enslave them like the lord God demands of you.

22:6 Have them work for you under the hot sun and beat them when they refuse their task.

22:7 The worst of these men are Jeconiah, son of Josiah king of Judah, who owns not even a single concubine and treats his wives as though they were people.

22:8 How I shall destroy Jeconiah and none of the lands will lament for him. His sisters will not shed a tear for their slain brother and his wives will not mourn his death.

22:9 He shall be buried like the crippled donkey, dragged forth past the gates of Jerusalem and cast into the wilderness so that the scavengers may feast upon him.

22:10 The wind will tear off his flesh and the sun will make dry and brittle the very bones of Jeconiah.

22:11 Without an heir will he die, so that his family name ends with him; even his mother will I send out to the heathen land, where she shall die in the chambers of a whorehouse.

22:12 Thus sayeth the lord, write this man childless and erase him from the scrolls of life; never shall he prosper nor sit upon the throne of David, beloved king of Israel.

23:1 Curse be to those of the priests that destroy and scatter my flock of Judah, for the lord wishes to slaughter his lamb, and not have them be slain by his servants.

23:2 Hated are the pastors who preach unto Judah the words of Ashteroth and Baal and the other false lords whom I hate.

23:3 I shall gather the remnants of my flocks and place them in the fields of thorns, where the grass will lash at their feet; in these fields they will become barren and feast upon their young.

23:4 Shepherds of the lord will look after my flock, wearing a robe black ash and carrying in their left hand a scythe red with the blood of the slaughtered.

23:5 Behold, within this flock shall a virgin give birth to a son and this son will be loved greater than even David king of Israel; this son shall be the child of God.

23:6 And he shall go forth and spread deceit and hatred among the people of the earth, so that they will follow the lord falsely and hate all those of the people of Judah.

23:7 He shall be a strong and mighty voice in the lands full of adulterers; the mountains will heed his words and the trees will obey his sayings.

23:8 False prophets will accuse him and blasphemy his name; they will blasphemy me and curse themselves to the eternal damnation.

23:9 And when my son returns to his throne in Zion, I shall deliver to the people of Judah a great evil and all the lands will persecute them and deem them wicked.

23:10 Hated are those in the lands of Samaria, for they praise my hated son Baal and bow down to his carved image.

23:11 Hated are the prophets of Jerusalem, who walk in the path of the wicked; they give aid to the evil that is the heathen and offer counsel to the common whore.

23:12 Worse are they than the sin of Sodom and Gomorrah; for in these wicked cities they engaged in the lust of wicked flesh, but the prophets of Jerusalem give aid and comfort to the prostitute, the heathen and even the queer.

23:13 Behold, I will cause them to eat of the bitter wormwood and drink the gall from the vulture for their blasphemy and profane nature.

23:14 Hearken not to the prophets who speak kind words and preach to the congregation words of peace and kindness to all; they are liars who speak against God.

23:15 Listen to the prophets of old that demand you enslave your neighbour and slaughter the heathen, for these are the men who understand the true spirit of the lord.

23:16 A grievous whirlwind comes forth and it shall fall upon the heads of those hated by God; it shall fall upon the heads of Judah.

23:17 The anger of the lord will not cease until all the men of Judah lie rotting beside the heathens in the dankest places of hell, where the worm continually gnaws within your bowels.

23:18 I have not sent these prophets, yet still they speak under my name; I have not spoken to these prophets, yet they speak of visions sent to them by God.

23:19 By the devil were these visions sent, so that these men of false prophets speak not the holy words, but messages of evil sent forth by the fallen one.

23:20 When the wrath of the lord comes, they shall run to the wilderness; they shall run to the fields; they shall run to the mountains.

23:21 Yet in their hidings, the lord will find them. Does the lord know not every crevice of the earth, every cave in the mountains and every ditch upon the ground?

23:22 They shall burn within their hiding places, and be thrown into the voids of despair where they shall suffer eternal for their transgressions.

23:23 And the lord shall gather their bones and make them hollow; he shall fill with sweet herbs the bones where once the marrow lay.

23:24 And the lord shall make sweet pipes from the bones of the false prophets and smoke sweet herbs from the bones of the wicked.

24:1 When the armies of Babylon came and laid to waste the people of Judah and the city of Jerusalem, I sat upon the steps of the temple of the lord and laughed at the destruction which surrounded me.

24:2 And as I laughed, behold, two baskets of figs appeared before me; one basket had figs plump and sweet, while the other basket held figs of a rot so strong not even the vermin would feast upon them.

24:3 Then the voice of the lord spoke to me and asked, "What do ye see, O Jeremiah?" and I answered, "I see two baskets of figs surrounded by the dead of Jerusalem.

24:4 One basket contains figs fat and sweet, while the other basket contains figs so rotten not even the crows will eat them."

24:5 The lord spoke again and said, "The good basket is full of the people who shall return from captivity and return from the lands of Babylon.

24:6 It is they who will rebuild my temple, that now lay in ruin by the hands of the armies of Nebuchadnezzar the king of Babylon.

24:7 They shall bring with them the valuables of the temple and they shall erect my house in all its glory.

24:8 After the temple is built and my house is restored, they shall be like the basket of figs which contain the rotting fruit; their use will be done and they will be useful no more.

24:9 Like the chef that throws away the rotten fruits, so shall I throw away the people of Judah.

24:10 With great wars, famine and pestilence will I wipe them out, so that none remain in the lands I promised unto their fathers."

25:1 The words that came to Jeremiah concerning all the people of Judah, in the fourth year of Jehoiakim the son of Josiah king of Judah and the first year of Nebuchadnezzar king of Babylon.

25:2 Which Jeremiah the prophet spoke to all the inhabitants of Judah, making him a very unpopular man.

25:3 And he said, "From the thirteenth year of Josiah the son of Amon king of Judah even unto this day, I have spoken to you the words of God and none have listened.

25:4 Bastards, all of you, who ignore the message of the one true lord, yet bow down before the idols and burn incense at the groves.

25:5 You have angered the lord greatly, so that his wrath shall descend upon the earth and consume you all for your blasphemy.

25:6 Behold, the men of Nebuchadnezzar are at your gates, for I have sent them here so they shall enslave you and take you to the lands of the heathen.

25:7 As you did wicked, so shall ye be conquered by the wicked men of Babylon; your sons will bow down to them and your daughters become vessels for their seed.

25:8 All the people of Judah will be drowned in an eternal darkness, so that gloom and despair fill their hearts; the sound of laughter, mirth and joy will escape you and be foreign unto you.

25:9 Seventy years will you serve the king of Babylon; seventy years will your lands be desolate and empty.

25:10 And it shall come to pass that on the seventy first year, I will punish the king of Babylon and all his nation for the wickedness which they did bring upon my people.

25:11 Though I sent them there and caused them to do such evil, they shall still be slaughtered for obeying the word of the one true God.

25:12 It shall come a time when all the nations serve under the powers of Israel and will do the work of their labours.

25:13 For behold, I shall give them a cup of fury and they will take it and drink of it and go mad.

25:14 Then the blades of God will come down and slaughter them all in their drunken fit and rise no more.

25:15 When they refuse to drink of the cup, I shall grasp their very mouth and pour the bitter poison down their throats until they choke upon it.

25:16 This shall be one of the evils I bring upon the cities of the great; to cause them to be drunk and stupid, so that I may slay them as they vomit upon their feet.

25:17 Their flesh will stew in their own filth and the ravens will swim through the shit so they may peck at the meat of the slain.

25:18 From one end of the earth even to the other shall there be naught but the corpses of those slain by God: they will not be mourned nor even buried in the graves; they shall be as dung upon the earth.

25:19 A great howling will erupt from their sons and they shall cover themselves with ashes and mud: they shall know the days of the slaughter will not come to an end, until all the people of the earth wallow in the darkness of hell.

25:20 None will flee the sword of God nor hide from his wrath.

25:21 Even the peaceful nations of the earth will be thrown into chaos by the will of God and shall be molested by the demons.

25:22 In the end, the lands will be desolate, for the wrath and fury of the lord shall consume all.

26:1 Those of Judah and Jerusalem heard the prophesies of Jeremiah and became disgusted by them.

26:2 They said, "How can our lord, who delivered us from the hands of Pharaoh, suddenly betray us and deliver us to the hands of Babylon?

26:3 Cursed be the false prophet Jeremiah, for he speaks blasphemy and ill will towards the people of Judah."

26:4 Jeremiah laughed at these men and said, "I speak the truth, for the lord God is a cruel and angry God, who will cast you into the fires of hell for the tiniest of transgressions.

26:5 Your sons will be thrown into the void for not killing enough of the heathens and your daughters will be raped by demons for she enjoyed the sex with her husband."

26:6 All of Judah mocked Jeremiah and said, "Ye are truly a deranged and wicked man, sent forth by the devil himself.

26:7 Repent your lies, your blasphemy and your sins, so that the lord will forgive you your transgressions and welcome you to the sanctuary of Zion."

26:8 Jeremiah spoke, "None will enter into the sanctuary of Zion, for even the most righteous men of earth is hated by God.

26:9 When the fury of the lord comes and you are all consumed by the sword of God, I shall laugh at your slaughter, your torments and your pain.

26:10 'Where is your God of mercy now?' I shall ask and you will not know."

26:11 Still, the people argued, "We are a right and just people, who have done no wicked.

26:12 Surely the lord will not send us to hell."

26:13 And Jeremiah howled and said, "It is for your lack of wickedness that you shall surely burn in hell.

26:14 Walk among your streets, your markets and even your homes.

26:15 Beside you and your kin will be the stranger, the heathen, the wicked man.

26:16 Did not the lord tell you to slay them all and let the beasts feast upon their dead?

26:17 Yet you value life so highly that you let these bastards live and even give to them your sons and your daughters.

26:18 The lord God is a God of bloodshed; have you not known this, when you offer your lambs to the altar?

26:19 Since blood has not been offered unto him, he shall take it from your very veins."

26:20 Jeremiah then left, leaving behind a very confused and angry crowd.

27:1 In the beginning of the reign of Jehoiakim the son of Josiah king of Judah did Jeremiah make bonds and yokes and placed them upon his neck.

27:2 He then went to the king of Edom, the king of Moab, the king of Ammon, the king of Tyrus and the king of Zidon, who all believed him to be a kinky whipping boy.

27:3 But instead Jeremiah said, "Thus sayeth the lord of hosts and the God of Israel;

27:4 By the powers within me I created the earth, the beasts, the waters and men by the powers of my outstretched arm.

27:5 You all have the yokes upon your necks and are bound forever to me.

27:6 Now shall the lord give you to the hands of Nebuchadnezzar, where you shall serve him as slave; even the beasts of the field will serve under the rule of Babylon.

27:7 All the nations shall serve him and your seed shall bow down unto him, until the very end of time.

27:8 Those that disobey the rule of Nebuchadnezzar will know the fury that is God; they shall die by the sword, the fire, the famine and the drought.

27:9 A horrible pestilence will consume your people until you perish from the very existence of earth.

27:10 Hearken not to the words of your prophets, your sorcerers, your enchanters, your dreamers nor your diviners; they speak lies and deceit into your ear."

27:11 And the kings of these nations laughed and cast out Jeremiah from their lands, declaring him a lunatic.

27:12 Until Nebuchadnezzar came and conquered them; then they felt stupid.

28:1 In the beginning of the reign of Zedekiah king of Judah did Hananiah the son of Azur the prophet began to prophesy to the people of Judah.

28:2 And Hananiah spoke of a merciful God, who shall forgive them their sins and give them a place in the sanctuary of Zion.

28:3 He spoke the opposite of that which Jeremiah spoke and the two hated each other unto their very graves.

28:4 Those of Judah listened to Hananiah and hearkened not the words of Jeremiah,

28:5 Soon, all of Judah laughed at Jeremiah and spat upon his robes, saying, "Never will the lord God of mercy deliver us to the hands of Babylon.

28:6 The lord loves us and protects us always, even unto the end of time."

28:7 So when Nebuchadnezzar came and conquered Judah, those who believed the words of Hananiah wept and said, "What have we done to deserve such cruelties?"

28:8 And the lord then split apart the earth and sent Hananiah forever falling into the darkness and the void of hell; this made Jeremiah laugh.

28:9 This the lord did, for Hananiah spread forth lies about the one true God.

29:1 When those of Judah were brought forth into Babylon, Jeremiah sent them a letter, which said,

29:2 "Thus sayeth the lord of hosts, God of Israel, to all those who were carried away from Judah and forced into the lands of Babylon.

29:3 Build your houses and dwell in them; plant your gardens and eat of their fruits.

29:4 Take of your wives, so that they give you sons and daughters plenty; give away your children, so that they may have sons and daughters.

29:5 Go forth and multiply in this city, so that the lord has more of his people in which he may slaughter.

29:6 Know that after seventy years, I shall deliver you from this place, so that you may return to the lands of your fathers and rebuild.

29:7 Behold, the lord gazes upon his holy temple and sees the ruin which it is in.

29:8 You shall go forth and rebuild the temple of God, so that the lord has a place to dwell and call his home.

29:9 When the temple is complete and Judah is rebuilt, the lord will send forth a great plague to Babylon.

29:10 I will send upon them the sword, the plague, the famine and the pestilence, until they become as rotten as the evil figs; none shall wish to be near the people of Babylon.

29:11 With great persecution will I send them the sword, the plague, the famine and the pestilence, until all their people cease to be and their nation becomes no more.

29:12 Because they had destroyed my temple in the destruction of Judah, I shall destroy their nation and wipe them from the earth.

29:13 As of Ahab the son of Kolaiah and Zedekiah the son of Maaseiah they are wicked men, who spoke falsely against God.

29:14 Let them be delivered to the table of Nebuchadnezzar, where they will be roasted in the fire and placed atop the silver, to be consumed by the king and his guests.

29:15 Because they spoke falsely against the lord, so they shall be delivered into the mouths of falsehood."

30:1 In the beginning, God created women for the men.

30:2 She was a wicked vessel, used so that men may beat her, abuse her and fulfill his lust upon her.

30:3 Now I see the women of the earth and how they walk beside the men and offer counsel to kings.

30:4 What wickedness is this, that you would allow such a beast the privileges of a man?

30:5 Cursed are they, who hold their women in regard and treat them not like the beasts they are.

30:6 For a woman is not a living creature, but a plaything for man's amusement.

30:7 Her tears, her emotions, even her speech are those of the devil, used so that the fallen one may manipulate you with the curves of the woman.

30:8 Those that serve their women, serve the devil and are wicked in the eyes of God.

30:9 Treat not your women with respect, but beat her until she bleeds and lay broken upon the ground.

30:10 Take her to your bed and have her, as she was meant to be had.

30:11 Rape her and muffle her screams with her pillows, until she lies limp atop the bed; a limp woman is a good woman, for she speaks not a word.

30:12 And of those men who have respect for their women and treat them like the living thing, they shall be punished by God.

30:13 For their sins, they shall know the pain of the woman; their loins will ache with fire and once every month shall they bleed from the vessel of their seed.

30:14 Unclean they shall be and cast out into the wild to live like the savage dogs.

30:15 The lord gave us women so that we may be amused by them; give them not power nor respect, lest you be ruled by the devil.

31:1 The lord hath said he hath chosen the peoples of Israel as his peoples, and they shall be my people.

31:2 For during the beginning, God created many men on earth, spawned by the descendants of Adam and Eve.

31:3 He chose from the garden of earth the peoples of Israel, for they survived the swords of nations, the plagues of God, the wrath of nature.

31:4 Of all the wicked, the evil, the horrors which the lord sent upon the earth, the peoples of Israel survived, thrived, and became strong.

31:5 And the lord decided that this was the peoples who shall be his people; for him to hate, torture, and offer false hope and salvation.

31:6 He made them strong, with twelve tribes, born of the womb of Rachel, father to the wise one Abraham.

31:7 In Egypt they dwelt, and became stronger than those of Egypt.

31:8 With fear, the lord had them enslaved by Pharaoh, until their will be broken and their spirit dead.

31:9 For generations the peoples of Israel were enslaved, but still they lost not their hope of salvation; that their God will save them, and make them strong again.

31:10 Thus the lord saved them, so that he may rule over them with more cruelty than that of Pharaoh.

31:11 As he led them to the promised lands, he had them build many altars, arks, and furniture so that the lord can strengthen his hold upon them.

31:12 They did as the lord demanded; those that questioned their God were slaughtered cruelly, and their families punished.

31:13 Those of Israel quickly learned to keep their mouths shut.

31:14 Upon the way, the peoples of Israel killed many nations, and left behind them a trail of blood stronger than that of a menstruous woman.

31:15 Bodies lay atop bodies, cities burned, and flesh rotted; it was a pleasing scent to the lord, who demanded entire nations be slaughtered.

31:16 Upon the invasion of the promised lands, the lord declared that all those within die, so that only those of Israel live; it was the lord's intention to slaughter all other heathen nations of the earth, so that only those of Israel survived.

31:17 Much to God's disgust, the peoples of Israel grew a conscience, and followed their inner instinct as to what is right and what is wrong.

31:18 Instead of slaying those who believed in different gods, they instead grew curious of their culture, and wished to understand them.

31:19 They learned of their ways, their manners, and called them neighbour and friend.

31:20 Which angered the lord greatly, for the lord wished not for these heathens to survive.

31:21 God wanted an earth where all men worshipped only him, and all others who worshipped false gods lay dead upon the fields, where the scavengers gnawed at their bones.

31:22 So the lord cursed Israel, and caused them to fall; when the lord abandoned Israel, they sought forth other lords, and bowed down to them.

31:23 This angered the lord, who knew not why his peoples, who he abandoned and cursed, sought forth other gods to worship.

31:24 Thus he doomed them to damnation, and led the armies of heathens to their cities, so that they may burn them, rape them, pillage them and enslave them.

31:25 All those of Israel were cast forth to the heathen nations, and lived as slaves; such as their ancestors did in Egypt.

31:26 And their ancestors wept for their children; lo, Rachel wept bitterly for the suffering of her children.

31:27 They begged to the lord to free their children, and the lord did so; he grew sick of the whining of Israel, and wished for them to burn sacrifice, so that he may enjoy the aroma of boiling blood and burning flesh.

31:28 Thus the lord freed those of Israel, and sent them to their home, so they may rebuild the holy temple; a building erected in honour to God by the third king Solomon.

31:29 Still, the lord forgave them not their sins of tolerance and understanding; he doomed them to the fires of hell, the darkest of void, the deepest oblivion.

31:30 Through fear, anger and punishment the lord ruled his peoples again, and led them falsely to the path of damnation.

31:31 The good, the bad, the righteous, the heathen, shall all be cast into the depths of torments and lamentations; such is the will of the lord.

31:32 For amusement, for pleasure, for twisted entertainment, the lord will make all men suffer in hell.

31:33 The gates of Zion are closed; they were never open to us, and never will we see enter them.

31:34 Those who gaze upon them are cursed, for they shall know the salvation promised to us; the salvation lied to us, as they wallow in the rivers of misery and despair.

31:35 This is the reason ye shall be sent to hell. Do not try to seek forth logic or understanding for your damnation.

31:36 God is a spoiled brat, and will condemn all the earth to suffer such as a child condemns a colony of ants to be trapped their dwelling.

31:37 Deal with it, bitch. God hates you, might as well at least have the comfort of hating him back.

32:1 The word of God as heard by Jeremiah, spoken upon the tenth year of Zedekiah, which was the eighteenth year of Nebuchadnezzar.

32:2 For at this time the armies of Babylon conquered Judah, and besieged the city of Jerusalem: and Jeremiah was imprisoned in the dungeons of the house of Judah, for speaking blasphemy against the lord.

32:3 Blasphemy such as a nation conquering Judah and God not doing a damn thing about it.

32:4 Boy did Zedekiah feel stupid.

32:5 Zedekiah said to the prophet Jeremiah, "Your words have come true, and the armies of Babylon are upon our doorsteps.

32:6 What ye have said has come to pass, and now I must know how the lord will save us."

32:7 Jeremiah laughed, and said, "Do ye not understand. The lord shall not save thee.

32:8 It is the hand of God which delivered us this evil, and gave us to the peoples of Nebuchadnezzar."

32:9 Zedekiah became confused, and asked, "What of the covenant. The holy bond of our peoples and the lord?"

32:10 Jeremiah laughed, and said, "The covenant means nothing to the lord.

32:11 Do ye think such a thing shall stop him from his wrath?

32:12 He is lord God, and nothing will stop him from his will.

32:13 If he demands the destruction of Judah, so be it; none will then stop the destruction of Judah, if the lord demands it.

32:14 Behold, the streets of Jerusalem will flow with the peoples of Babylon, and they shall slaughter and enslave the sons and the daughters of Judah."

32:15 "Why?" asked Zedekiah, and Jeremiah answered, "Because God wants it that way.

32:16 Why the lord wants our destruction, I do not know.

32:17 He is a mysterious being; a spoiled child with divine power.

32:18 Their is nothing that can be done to save your nation.

23:19 Even if ye tore down your groves, your idols, offered your sacrifices to the Holiest of holies, and praised his name, it matters not.

32:20 God has sealed your fate; ye shall die, and your nation be desolate.

32:21 Accept your damnation, and know that Zion will never be your home."

THE BLASPHEMOUS BIBLE

32:22 In tears, Zedekiah said, "But the lord hath promised the good and the righteous salvation in the holy city of Zion."

32:23 Jeremiah replied, "He also promised to care for our peoples and protect us, yet the armies of Babylon burn your city as we speak.

32:24 The word of God is of lesser value than the parchment it was written upon. It is meaningless, useless, and a lie."

32:25 Zedekiah wept. Jeremiah laughed. God pleasured himself as he watched his peoples burn at the hands of heathens.

33:1 Thus sayeth the lord, the maker of all, the one that formed it, and God is my name.

33:2 Call unto me and I shall ignore thee. Worship me and I shall show thee a great horrifying thing.

33:3 For thus sayeth the lord, the God of Israel, concerning the houses of Judah, the houses of Jerusalem, and the house of the king, which were built by the heathens slain by the army of David.

33:4 When those of Babylon come, those of Judah will fill the streets with their bodies, for the lord is full of fury and wrath against those of Judah.

33:5 Behold, I will give them a plague, and they will find not a cure, so that they die of disease and pestilence.

33:6 Those of good health will be taken to the foreign land, and wear the yoke, and be slaves to their new masters.

33:7 Years of servitude, torture, humiliation and rape will they be given; such is the will of the lord.

33:8 In time, the captivity of Judah and Israel will arise, and return forth to their lands, so they may rebuild.

33:9 Though they are stained with their iniquity, the lord shall deliver them home, and have these peoples rebuild the temple, given to God by Solomon son of David the king.

33:10 And when they return, the peoples shall rejoice, and praise the name of God, and call him merciful.

33:11 They are wrong; the lord will destroy them again, such as he did before.

33:12 When the time comes that the wrath of the lord consumes all the earth, those of Israel will weep, and beg forgiveness to the very one that sends them evil.

33:13 Israel shall become desolate, and Judah will be inhabited by dragons, satyrs and demons.

33:14 Those of the earth will suffer in the eternal void of damnation.

33:15 Such is the mercy of the lord; what a jackass.

34:1 The word of the lord which came unto Jeremiah, when Nebuchadnezzar and his armies, and all the kingdoms under his dominion, fought against the city of Jerusalem.

34:2 "Thus sayeth the lord, the one true God; go and speak to Zedekiah the king of Judah, and tell him this. Thus sayeth the lord, Jerusalem shall be delivered into the hands of Babylon, and will be burned in fire.

34:3 Ye shall not escape, but be taken captive and delivered to the king of Babylon, where ye shall serve him.

34:4 But fear not, Zedekiah, for the lord shall promise thee that you will not die by the sword, but will die in peace in the lands of your fathers.

34:5 Those of Judah will burn perfume for thee, and lament for thee, and mourn thee.

34:6 Which shall be a lie; he will watch as his sons are slaughtered before him, then his eyes will be plucked out, so that the very last thing he sees will be the death of his sons.

34:7 Then he shall rot in the dungeons of Babylon, until the rats gnaw on his flesh."

34:8 Jeremiah spoke these words Zedekiah the king of Judah, who

believed him not, and told those of Judah, "Fight alongside your brother, and we shall slay these heathens who dare trespass upon the lands of the lord.

34:9 For remember, God is on our side, and we shall be victorious against the nations of Babylon."

34:10 They were not.

34:11 God said to Jeremiah, "I grow weary of the foolishness of these peoples, who believe that I will protect them always, even though it is I who brings doom upon them.

34:12 They grow arrogant and stubborn, and know not the true will of the lord.

34:13 Let them know the true nature of their lord; I shall send unto them the sword, the flame, the pestilence and the famine, until their nation be naught but dust upon the earth.

34:14 Those that cry to me and worship me will be slaughtered by the damned and the blasphemous; let those who offer sacrifice unto me and those who burn incense to Baal lay dead beside one another.

34:15 The princes of Judah, of Jerusalem, the nobles, the priests, the eunuchs, and all the peoples of the land will be slain unto me, as the calf is slain upon the altar.

34:16 Into the hands of their enemies I will deliver them, until their dead bodies lay across the fields for the fowls of the heavens and the beasts of the earth to consume.

34:17 Zedekiah and his sons will be butchered by the cruelty of Babylon, so that they know the lord will not protect them nor show them mercy.

34:18 And when those of Israel return to the city, they shall gather as one, so that I may burn them with a great and mighty fire, and erase them from the earth in one magnificent flame."

35:1 The word of God which came unto Jeremiah during the days of Jehoiakim the son of Josiah, king of Judah.

35:2 And the lord said, "Go unto the house of the Rechabites, and bring them to the house of the lord. Their ye shall offer them ale, wine and strong drink."

35:3 Thus Jeremiah took Jazaniah the son of Habaziniah, and his sons, and all his brethren, into the house of the lord.

35:4 And their he offered them vessels full of wine, strong drink, and ale, and he said to them, "Drink, as the lord commands."

35:5 But they refused the drink, and said, "Never shall alcohol touch our lips, for our father Jonadab the son of Rechab forbade it ages ago.

35:6 Never shall our house touch strong drink, nor our sons or daughters, so that we never know the intoxication of liquor.

35:7 Never shall we build house, nor sow seeds, nor reap the harvest; for all our day we shall live in tents, and feast off the fruits of the wild and the waters of the brook.

35:8 When we saw the armies of Nebuchadnezzar, we fled to the safety of the walls of Jerusalem, in fear of their armies."

35:9 It was then that the blood flowed from the ears of the house of Rechabite, so that it flowed into the empty vessels.

35:10 The lord then took the blood, and drank of it, and said to Jeremiah, "It is a shame that such men drink not, nor harvest, nor offer anything to the peoples of Jerusalem.

35:11 They come inside the walls and be protected by the soldiers of Jerusalem, yet never do they offer them a drink, some bread, nor even fruits of the vine.

35:12 They are nomadic beasts, who live like the coyotes; they travel in packs and feast off the waste of the earth.

35:13 Go now, and make these nomadic parasites useful.

35:14 Take of their meat, and boil it, and offer to those of Jerusalem to eat."

35:15 Jeremiah did as the lord commanded, and fed the city of

Jerusalem with the meat of the house of Rechabite.

35:16 It was a sweet and savoury meat, which the peoples of Judah believed to be flesh of the unclean swine.

35:17 Those that refused the flesh offered to them by Jeremiah, were slaughtered, and became flesh for Jeremiah to offer.

35:18 And they ate of the flesh of their brothers, knowing not the source of their meal; they grew fat from the meat of their kin.

35:19 Jeremiah asked the lord, "Why do ye wish me to feed the flesh of men to these peoples?" and God answered, "Because, in time they will be accustomed to that flesh.

35:20 For they will be so poor they will slay their very son so that they have flesh in the pot; it is best they get used to the meat now."

35:21 Jeremiah continued to offer the flesh to the peoples who knew not they were cannibals, until the meat ran out.

36:1 It came to pass that upon the fourth year of Jehoiakim the son of Josiah king of Judah, that the word of the lord came unto Jeremiah, again, saying,

36:2 "Take a roll of parchment, and write upon it the words I have said against Judah, against Israel, and against all other nations of the earth.

36:3 From the day I first spoke to thee even unto this day, write all the damnations which I have told thee shall come to the earth.

36:4 Then shall it be that all those of the house of Judah hear my words, such that fear strike their heart, and they bow down to me in terror."

36:5 Jeremiah called Baruch the son of Neriah, and told him all the words which the lord had said unto him.

36:6 Jeremiah could not write down the words upon the parchment, for he was stupid and knew not how to write.

36:7 Thus Baruch wrote the words of the lord upon the parchment: and he soiled himself in fear of the wrath of his God.

36:8 Then Jeremiah said, "Behold, I cannot go into the house of the lord and read this scroll, for I do not understand the words upon the parchment.

36:9 Therefore you must go, Baruch, and read the word of the lord to the peoples of Judah, upon the day of fasting, so that all of Judah hear."

36:10 So upon the fifth year of Jehoiakim the son of Josiah king of Judah, in the ninth month of the year, a fast was declared for the lord, and all those of Judah came within the temple.

36:11 Then read Baruch the words of Jeremiah in the house of the lord, with a voice so mighty that all those of Judah heard the words.

36:12 Baruch had a very loud voice.

36:13 In the chamber of Gemariah the son of Shaphan the scribe did Baruch read the words of Jeremiah to a terrified crowd.

36:14 When Baruch finished the words written, the crowd was in silence, until one man said to Baruch, "Fuck you, asshole." And those of Judah laughed.

36:15 Now Michaiah the son of Gemariah heard the words of Baruch, and he did not laugh with his peoples, but became frightened.

36:16 He ran to the king's house, into the scribe's chambers: and lo, all the princes were there, as did Elishama the scribe, Delaiah the son of Shemaiah, Elnathan the son of Achbor, Gemariah the son of Shaphan and Zedekiah the son of Hananiah.

36:17 Michaiah told them the words spoken by Baruch, and the men laughed, and said, "Surely this is nothing more than the ramblings of a lunatic."

36:18 Still, Michaiah insisted the words to be real, and that the destruction of Judah was to come, crushed by the hand of the lord.

36:19 So they said, "Go then, and find this madman, so that he may come to us, and convince us what he says is true."

36:20 Thus they sent Jehudi the son of Nethania the son of Shelemiah the son of, oh for fuck's sake we don't need his entire family history.

36:21 They sent Jehudi to Baruch, to convince Baruch to come and read the word of God to the princes and the scribes.

36:22 And Baruch went into the chambers of the scribes, and with his mighty voice he read from the scroll, until all those within the chamber became afraid.

36:23 They asked Baruch, "May we have this scroll, so that we may read these words to the king, and warn him of our damnation?" and Baruch agreed, giving them the scroll.

36:24 Jehudi then rushed with the scroll to see Jehoiakim the king, and read him the true words of the lord.

36:25 Now the king was in his winter house during this time, which was where he first heard the words upon this scroll.

36:26 And in the chambers of the king was a hearth, which burned a fire so that the king may keep warm during the cold winter.

36:27 Before Jehudi could finish reading unto the king the words on the scroll, the king took a knife and cut the scroll into four pieces.

36:28 He then took the pieces and cast them into the fire, saying, "I have not the time to listen to the words of a rambling lunatic."

36:29 As sure as his parchment burns in my hearth, so shall he burn in the fires of hell."

36:30 Go find these men, Baruch and Jeremiah, so that they may be burned in the pyres for all of Judah to see.

36:31 Then the people will know these men speak not the words of God, but the words of the devil."

36:32 But the lord hid Baruch and Jeremiah from the eyes of the king, and said unto them, "Take thee another scroll, and write upon it the words of God which were written upon the last scroll, which the foolish king of Judah burned.

36:33 And thou shalt say to Jehoiakim king of Judah, thus sayeth the lord. Thou hast burnt his scroll, and blasphemed his name. For this, the king of Babylon shall come and destroy all lands under your dominion.

36:34 None of your seed shall sit upon the throne of Judah: and your body will rot in the wild, burning under the heat of the sun and the light of the moon.

36:35 Lo, I shall punish him, his seed and his servants for the iniquity of their master; of all the men of Judah shall I punish with cruelty for what one man did."

36:36 Thus Baruch wrote yet another scroll, writing in it the word of God which Jeremiah heard. It was identical to the scroll that the king of Judah burned, with many words added in the end.

37:1 It came to pass that Zedekiah the son of Josiah became the king of Judah, instead of Coniah the son of Jehoiakim; this was so because Nebuchadnezzar the king of Babylon placed Zedekiah as king.

37:2 Still, neither Zedekiah, nor his servants, nor any of the peoples of Judah hearkened to the words of Jeremiah the prophet.

37:3 Zedekiah instead relied upon Jehucal the son of Shelemiah and Zephaniah the son of Maaseiah to listen to the word of God, and pray for the nation of Judah.

37:4 Both men whom the lord hated.

37:5 Now Jeremiah walked among the peoples, for though the peoples mocked him, they feared him as well, and would not harm even the hair upon his neck.

37:6 It then happened that the armies of Pharaoh came out of Egypt, and those of the peoples of Babylon stationed in Jerusalem departed to fight this new threat.

37:7 And as the Babylonians were gone, the word of the lord conveniently came to Jeremiah, and said unto him, "Go, speak to the king of Judah, and tell him that which I say.

37:8 For those of the armies of Egypt will return to their lands, and the men of Babylon will return to Jerusalem, and retake it, and burn it with fire.

37:9 Do not think yourself safe, nor believe that the men of Babylon have gone forever."

37:10 When Jeremiah passed through the gates of Benjamin, a guard saw him, whose name was Irijah the son of Shelemiah, and said, "This madman is a traitor, and works for the heathens of Babylon."

37:11 Jeremiah beat the guard, and said, "Ye are lying, for I am a prophet of the lord, and will never work for the peoples of Nebuchadnezzar."

37:12 But none believed him, and they said, "Then why is it ye prophesied against us, and said those of Babylon will conquer us?

37:13 How can such a thing come true, unless ye betrayed us all, and sold us to the armies of Babylon?"

37:14 So they took Jeremiah and threw him into the dungeons, where he remained many days.

37:15 God laughed at Jeremiah the prophet, who listened to his words and spoke the word of the lord, now lay rotting in the dungeons where the rats breed.

37:16 King Zedekiah remembered the words of Jeremiah, and the reading of the scroll of Baruch, which still feared him to this day.

37:17 He sent a messenger to the dungeons, and asked Jeremiah, "Is there any word of the lord? and Jeremiah said, "There is; for he shall deliver thee again to the armies of Babylon."

37:18 Jeremiah then asked, "What have I done to offend Zedekiah the king of Judah. Have I not always been an honest prophet of the lord?"

37:19 Zedekiah then had Jeremiah moved to the prison of the house of Judah, where he was daily given a piece of bread from the royal bakery.

37:20 Jeremiah cursed Zedekiah, and said, "A prisoner fed by the royal bakery is still a prisoner.

37:21 May your children be raped by dragons, and your seed fall upon the stones."

38:1 Shephatiah the son of Mattan, Gedaliah the son of Pashur, Jucal the son of Shemaliah, and Pashur the son of Malchiah, heard the words which Jeremiah spoke to the peoples, and hated him for it.

38:2 For Jeremiah said, "Behold, those who stay in the city of Jerusalem will die by the sword, the famine and the plague: but he who is taken by Babylon shall live.

38:3 Though they will live as slaves, they shall live: and it is better to live as a slave than to return to the dust of the earth."

38:4 So these men came to Zedekiah and said, "This man spreads words of defeat to the peoples of Judah, and tells them not to fight, but to surrender.

38:5 Surely he is a spy for Babylon, who tells our peoples not to fight, but to submit to their enemies.

38:6 He is a traitor to Judah and a traitor to God; let us execute him in public, so that the peoples know he lies."

38:7 Zedekiah said, "Ye may not kill him, but ye can place him where his words will not be heard; I cannot harm this man, for I fear him to be a prophet sent from God."

38:8 So these men bound Jeremiah, and placed him in the dungeons of Malchiah, where they be no water, but only mire.

38:9 And Jeremiah sunk in the mire, fearing that he would drown in the sludge of the dungeon.

38:10 It came to pass that Ebedmelech the Ethiopian, one of the eunuchs of Zedekiah, heard of what became of Jeremiah.

38:11 Ebedmelech came to Zedekiah, and said,

38:12 "My king, these men have done an evil thing unto Jeremiah, whom they cast to the dungeons of mire, where he shall die by hunger.

38:13 Zedekiah said, "So. Jeremiah was annoying little fucker of a prophet. Why should I care what becomes of him, if what he says be true and soon all my peoples will die or be enslaved?"

38:14 So Ebedmelech went in secret to the dungeon of Jeremiah, where he tried to free him, but could not.

38:15 For Jeremiah sank in the mire so deeply, that Ebedmelech had to bring thirty men to remove him.

38:16 Jeremiah then came unto the king, lying to him, and said, "Behold, the lord hath delivered me from the dungeon of the mire, and has for thee a message.

38:17 When those of Babylon come, go with them, so that ye may live and the city of Jerusalem not be reduced to ash and rubble.

38:18 You, your seed and your house shall live under the protection of the lord.

38:19 Refuse, and know this; the city of Jerusalem shall burn in the fires forever, and ye and your seed will be wiped from the face of the earth."

38:20 Zedekiah said, "I am afraid of the Jews who have sided with those of Babylon, for surely they shall betray me and place my head atop the pyre."

38:21 Jeremiah said, "Fear not, for the lord will protect thee from those who wish harm up you, if you go to the house of Nebuchadnezzar.

38:22 Do not, and your house shall fall, and your peoples suffer.

38:23 The women of the house of Judah will be offered unto the princes of Babylon as whores, where they will lie in the chambers of the harlot, to be raped by the beast of the heathen.

38:24 Your wives and your daughters will be abused like the common whore, and ye shall not escape from the hands of Babylon.

38:25 Your city will burn and your seed with it; none of your loins will survive."

38:26 Zedekiah said, "Ye shall tell not a man these words, lest they declare me a traitor who betrayed even the peoples he serve.

38:27 Do this, and I swear to thee that ye shall not die; I shall protect you.

38:28 When the princes come to thee, and ask thee what ye have said, you shall tell them that you spoke to me, but I refused to listen."

38:29 Jeremiah was then placed in the court of the prison, where he was fed with fresh bread and clean water.

38:30 When the princes came to him and asked what he said to Zedekiah, he told them that which the king told him to.

38:31 And when the Babylonians conquered Jerusalem, Jeremiah dwelt in the prison: and he was their when Jerusalem was taken.

39:1 In the ninth year of Zedekiah, in the tenth month, came Nebuchadnezzar and his armies against the city of Jerusalem.

39:2 And in the eleventh year, on the fourth month of the year, in the ninth day of that month, Jerusalem became part of the Babylonian empire.

39:3 All the princes of Babylon came, to witness the marvelous city of God; Nergalsharezer, Samgarnebo, Sarsechim, Rabsaris, Nergalsharezer and Rabmag walked through the streets, and gazed upon the temple of the lord.

39:4 When Zedekiah saw the princes of Babylon, ferocious men with the teeth of lions, he fled the city by night, and escaped through the king's garden, and went out the way of the plain.

39:5 But the armies of Babylon saw him, and pursued him, overtaking him in the plains of Jericho, where they bound him and dragged him to Nebuchadnezzar, who camped in the lands of

Hamath.

39:6 It was then the king of Babylon forced open the eyes of Zedekiah, and slew his children before him; even the nobles of Judah he slew, forcing Zedekiah to watch.

39:7 Then he plucked out the very eyes of Zedekiah, and fed them to him: and they bound him with chains and dragged him to Babylon.

39:8 Those of the soldiers of Babylon then burned the king's house, and the houses of the people, until all of Jerusalem was set ablaze.

39:9 Nebuzaradan the captain of the guard gathered all those of Judah who were in good health, and bound them, and sent them to Babylon, where they shall be enslaved.

39:10 But to the poor and the crippled he remained in Jerusalem, and forced them to work the vineyards and the fields of Judah.

39:11 Now Nebuchadnezzar heard of the prophet Jeremiah, and feared him greatly; thus he said to his captains,

39:12 "In regards to Jeremiah, take him, but treat him well; do not harm him. Listen to his words, for they are the words of wisdom."

39:13 So Nebuzaradan, Nebushasban, Rabsaris, Rabmag and Nergalsharezer took Jeremiah from his prison, and brought him to Babylon so he may dwell among his peoples.

39:14 On his journey their princes gave Jeremiah fresh fruits, wine, bread, meats, and the finest of concubines Babylon had.

39:15 Which made the peoples of Judah, captives under Babylon, believe that Jeremiah truly was a traitor, who sold them to the hands of Nebuchadnezzar.

39:16 Not that Jeremiah cared; he was too busy getting fat and fucking whores.

39:17 As Jeremiah was deep inside the bowels of a prostitute, the word of the lord came unto him, saying, "Go and speak to Ebedmelech the Ethiopian, who did free thee from the prison of the mire.

39:18 Tell him that the city of Babylon will fall under a great evil; even a greater evil than that which the lord gave unto Jerusalem.

39:19 And on that day, the men of Judah shall be free, and return to their homes, so they may rebuild the nation of God.

39:20 Tell him that they shall not fall by the sword, but that their lives shall be as prey unto the lord, who will consume them like the lion consumes the lamb."

39:21 Jeremiah told the eunuch Ebedmelech that which the lord spoke: and Ebedmelech did not get any comfort from these words.

40:1 The captain of the guard of Babylon took Jeremiah to Jerusalem, and said, "Behold, the evil which your lord did bring down upon this place.

40:2 I have read your writings, and heard of your teachings; you know of the evil of your God, yet ye still follow him.

40:3 What hath he done to deserve your loyalty. What lies did he tell thee, so that ye follow him blindly?"

40:4 Jeremiah said, "He offered me not sanctuary in Zion, but sanctuary in hell.

40:5 I shall walk amongst the damned, laughing at them, mocking them; all the while I shall be comforted, and no pain will befall me."

40:6 The captain said, "You are truly a wicked and demented man; a perfect follower for the God of Israel.

40:7 Go now, away from Babylon, and witness that which the lord hath done upon your lands.

40:8 Return to Gedaliah the son of Ahikam, whom Nebuchadnezzar has made governor over Judah, and dwell among the peoples there.

40:9 The king of Babylon has even given you his blessing, and a reward, so that ye may return to Judah, and live in comfort."

40:10 So Jeremiah took the blessings of Nebuchadnezzar, and returned to Judah, to dwell among those that remained in the lands.

40:11 Now when all the captains of the fields heard that their king made Gedaliah the son of Ahikam governor of Judah, and committed to him men, women and children which were not carried away to Babylon:

40:12 They came to Gedaliah in the land of Mizpah, even Ishmael the son of Nethaniah, Johanan and Jonathan the sons of Kareah, Seraiah the son of Tanhumeth, the sons of Ephai the Netophatite, and Jezeniah the son of a Maachathite; they and all their men.

40:13 Gedaliah, a Jew, said unto them, "Fear not, and serve Babylon; dwell in this land, and remain loyal unto your king.

40:14 As for me, I shall dwell in Mizpah, where I will serve Nebuchadnezzar for all my days: as for ye, come to these lands and gather the summer fruits, the oils, and take them to the cities which ye have conquered in Judah.

40:15 For when the Jews in Babylon heard that a remnant of their peoples have remained behind, they shall believe that the lord will rejoin them; in this belief, they will not fight back, nor revolt against their masters.

40:16 I shall not fight back, but serve Babylon; under the rule of Nebuchadnezzar I shall become more rich and powerful than I ever could under the bastard God of Israel."

40:17 Now Johanan and the captains of the fields sought power, and wished to spread discord amongst Judah.

40:18 They came to Gedaliah, and said, "We have heard that Baalis the king of the Ammonites have sent Ishmael the son of Nethaniah to slay thee in your sleep," but Gedaliah believed them not.

40:19 Johanan then spoke in secret to Gedaliah, and said, "I know the cunning of Ishmael, and of his ways with the dagger. Let me slay him in secret, so that none shall know it was you who ordered his death.

40:20 Then shall ye remain a hold upon Judah, and your peoples be ruled by one of their own."

40:21 However, Gedaliah believed him not, and said, "You speak falsely of Ishmael, and shall do no such thing.

40:22 Mention this again, and it shall be your throat that will be cut open as ye sleep."

41:1 Now in the seventh month, Ishmael the son of Nethaniah of the royal seed of Babylon, and the princes of Nebuchadnezzar, came to Mizpah to eat bread with Gedaliah the son of Ahikam.

41:2 And ten men came with Ishmael, who were loyal to him and no other.

41:3 When the bread was eaten and the wine drank, Ishmael arose with his ten men, and with the sword slew Gedaliah the son of Ahikam, and all the Jews with him.

41:4 Even of the soldiers of Babylon stationed in Jerusalem he slaughtered, so that none who could resist him survived.

41:5 Making Johanan right; Ishmael did wish to kill Gedaliah.

41:6 Upon the second day, no man in Judah knew that Ishmael had slaughtered all the soldiers and the Jews of Jerusalem; Ishmael was that good.

41:7 Now men came from Shechem, from Shiloh, and from Samaria; fourscore men, with beards shaved and clothes rent, cutting themselves with knives. They were emo bastards.

41:8 These men came offering incense, which they wished to burn in the house of the lord.

41:9 Ishmael the son of Nethaniah came out to greet them, and wept with them as they travelled to the temple of the lord.

41:10 When they entered into the city, Ishmael killed these men, and threw them into the pit of corpses, which piled high with the bodies of the slain.

41:11 God really liked Ishmael, though he was a heathen fuck.

41:12 But ten men begged to Ishmael, and said, "Slay us not, for we have hidden treasures in the fields; treasures of wheat, of barley, of oil and of honey."

41:13 So Ishmael spared these men, so that he may gather these treasures for himself.

41:14 After he found them, he beheaded them, and threw them in the pit, declaring to his men, "Stupid fucking Jews."

41:15 Now the pit where Ishmael cast the slaughtered men began to rot, and created a foul odour for the peoples of Judah; a pleasant odour to the lord, but most revolting to men.

41:16 So Ishmael gathered all the peoples in Mizpah, including the king's daughters, which Nebuzaradan the captain of the guard gave unto Gedaliah; Ishmael made these peoples captive, and carried them to the land of the Ammonites.

41:17 But when Johanan the son of Kareah, and all the captains that were with him, heard of the slaughter that Ishmael had caused,

41:18 They gathered their men, and went to battle with Ishmael the son of Nethaniah by the great waters of Gibeon.

41:19 Now those held captive by Ishmael saw Johanan, they became glad, and said, "These men of Babylon will free us from the cruelty and death of Ishmael."

41:20 So they turned against Ishmael, and fought against him, as did Johanan the son of Kareah and all his men.

41:21 Those that survived were freed from Ishmael, and went with Johanan the son of Kareah.

41:22 Johanan led them to Chimham, where they were still enslaved by heathens.

41:23 But God blessed Ishmael for his cruelty, and led his escape with eight men, where he fled and hid in the lands of the Ammonites.

41:24 And the Jews became ever fearful of the Babylonians, because of the genocide attempted by Ishmael the son of Nethaniah.

41:25 And they knew the lord would not protect them from their new masters.

42:1 Now Johanan and all those under his command sought the wisdom of Jeremiah, and asked of him, "What does the lord of Israel say unto us, who did take vengeance for his peoples.

42:2 Tell us of which path the lord hath set for us."

42:3 And Jeremiah said, "I shall pray for thee, and ask the lord his wisdom in regards to you and your men."

42:4 So Jeremiah prayed, and on the tenth day he heard the words of the lord, and returned to Johanan, saying,

42:5 "The lord knows all and sees all; he hath seen the bloodshed ye have caused against the men of Ishmael, and how ye did free the captives under his tyranny.

42:6 Know that I am a prophet of the lord, and do as he commands; whether they seem good or evil, I do as the lord says.

42:7 For I am but a humble servant, and know not the ways of God; never shall I understand the will of the Holiest of holies.

42:8 This sayeth the lord of Israel, unto whom ye wished me to pray for thee.

42:9 Abide in the lands of Judah, where ye shall rebuild the cities, and grow strong; though the lands be filled with the evil of God, this evil shall protect thee, and be rooted deep in your soul.

42:10 Be not afraid of Babylon, for I shall deliver you from his hand; fear not Nebuchadnezzar, for in time the lord will bring him an evil greater than that he brought upon his own peoples.

42:11 Know that the evil of God is within you now; embrace it and ye shall go strong, but to deny it will weaken thee, and bring great torments to thee.

42:12 If ye run to the lands of Egypt, in belief their ye will be safe from the armies of Babylon, nor hear the trumpets of war, nor grow hungry for bread:

42:13 Ye shall be fooled, for the lord God hates all those within Egypt, and stares at them with an evil stare.

42:14 It shall come to pass that all those who dwell in Egypt will be under the sword; famine shall overtake them, so that all those within Egypt will die.

42:15 So it be that all men will die in Egypt, whether Jew or Gentile; all will be slaughtered by the sword, the famine, the plagues, the pestilence, the drought, and all that which the lord will deliver unto them.

42:16 For the lord God is an angry God, filled with wrath, evil and fury; his wrath has been poured upon the peoples of Judah, and now it shall be poured hot upon the peoples of Egypt.

42:17 The lands under Pharaoh will be cursed for eternity, so that none will dwell within his lands; they shall be empty of even the crow; only the bodies of the dead will lay there.

42:18 Thus ye must stay in the lands of Judah, where the lord will make thee strong, though ye will be under the threat of Babylon.

42:19 Stay in Judah, and know ye may be overtaken by the armies of Nebuchadnezzar; flee to Egypt, and know ye shall certainly be overtaken by the evil that is God."

43:1 When Jeremiah finished speaking to the peoples of Johanan that which was the word of God, the peoples of Johanan mocked him, and spat on his feet.

43:2 They said to him, "The lord God has blessed the peoples of Babylon, and have chosen them as his new peoples.

43:3 Surely the lord will bless Nebuchadnezzar, and conquer us in the lands of Judah, where we will be enslaved and forced to work in the fields and the mines.

43:4 Our daughters will be sold as cattle, and be chained to the bed of lustful men, where they shall be raped nightly.

43:5 We will hearken not your words, which are full of lies and deceit; we shall go to Egypt, and regard not the shit which spews forth from your tongue."

43:6 So Johanan the son of Kareah, and all the captains under him, and all the peoples under his dominion, obeyed not the word of God, and stayed not in the lands of Judah.

43:7 But they took their peoples, their men, their women, the remnant's of Judah, and even the king's daughters, and went to Egypt.

43:8 They bound Jeremiah with chains and dragged them with the horse, so that Jeremiah could not return to Nebuchadnezzar, and tell them of their whereabouts.

43:9 When they entered the lands of Tahpanhes, the spirit of the lord came over Jeremiah, and he broke his bounds in front of the lord of Judah.

43:10 He then tore off the heads of the guards who watched over him, and threw their skulls in the brick kiln, which is at the entry of the Pharaoh's house in Tahpanhes.

43:11 In a mighty voice, Jeremiah said, "Behold, the lord of Israel shall send his servant Nebuchadnezzar to these lands, where he shall set his throne upon these skulls, and have dominion over these lands.

43:12 And when he cometh, he shall bring with him the wrath of God. All those in Egypt will know death, and fall under the evil of the lord.

43:13 Behold, Babylon will kindle a fire in the houses of the gods of Egypt, and burn them all; those holy men of the gods of Egypt will be taken captive, and enslaved in the lands of Babylon.

43:14 Lo, they shall be a shepherd to the peoples of Egypt: and the flock of Egypt will know no peace.

43:15 And all the images of Bethshemesh that is in Egypt will crumble, and the houses of the gods of Egypt will turn to ash and dust."

44:1 The word of the lord which came unto Jeremiah, regarding the Jews who dwelt in the lands of Egypt.

44:2 Thus sayeth the lord of lords, the God of Israel; ye have seen the evil which I have brought upon Jerusalem, and upon the cities of Judah; behold, even to this day they are barren, and no man dwell within them.

44:3 Because of the sins which your ancestors did, I have brought evil upon your heads; because the fathers of your fathers' fathers have bowed down to other lords, and burned for them incense, I have cursed thee, and made your homes barren.

44:4 I have sent thee the prophet Jeremiah, to warn thee of my wickedness and of your damnation; ye ignored them, and claimed he blasphemous.

44:5 Now my anger flows forth through the streets of Jerusalem, and through all that of Judah, until they become desolate and void of life.

44:6 Ye have brought this evil upon yourself, for though ye call yourself the peoples of God, ye are not of true blood, but are wicked bastards.

44:7 Your mothers were not of true blood, but were heathens that carried the blessed seed of Abraham; your wives are wicked cunts that birthed your children, thus tainting them unclean in the eyes of God.

44:8 Ye have mocked the lord, and carved from rock images of beasts, of fowl and of nature; how dare ye copy the work of the lord, which cannot be copied.

44:9 Though ye bow down unto me, and make yourselves humble in my sight, know that ye are all wicked, and hated by that which you worship.

44:10 Thus sayeth the God of Israel; I will set my evil eye upon you, and cut off from the earth all that which is Judah.

44:11 Even of those what flee to Egypt will know the evil of their God; there they shall be consumed, and perish in the lands of Pharaoh. They shall die by the sword, by the plague, by the famine, by the drought, and by even the heat of the sun; they shall be all cursed by the one true lord.

44:12 For I will punish them that dwell in the lands of Egypt as I shall punish all those of the peoples of Judah.

44:13 It shall be that none of Judah will remain on the earth; they will be reduced to the dust they were created from, and be feasted on by the fowls of the heaven and the beasts of the earth.

44:14 Know that ye shall be denied the sanctuary of Zion, but will be cast into the very damnation, the pits of hell, the depths of sorrow, and the darkest oblivion.

44:15 Where the worm will dwell within your bowels, and feast upon your inwards.

44:16 Ye shall know not comfort, but only the sorrows, the cruelties, and the torments of God; ye shall feast upon the droppings of beasts, and drink of the menstrual puss of your heathen wives.

44:17 Great horrors will be shown to thee, and inflicted upon thee; ye shall not sleep, nor know any comfort in the damnation of hell.

44:18 It is a perfect place of torment, created by the most evil mind of God; it is there where ye shall dwell for eternity, and know not the blessings which the lord promised in his covenant.

44:19 For your impure blood and for the sins of the fathers, ye will know eternal damnation: and the lord shall mock thee, and be entertained by all those who suffer.

44:20 Remember that when ye rot in the fires of hell, that the lord God is a merciful God, who loves and forgives all.

45:1 The word that Jeremiah the prophet spoke unto Baruch the son of Neriah, who wrote twice the words of God upon the parchment; these words came unto Jeremiah in the fourth year of Jehoiakim the son of Josiah, king of Judah.

45:2 "Thus sayeth the lord, the God of Israel, unto the loyal servant Baruch.

45:3 Ye have served the lord well, and pleased him with your acts, your obedience and your loyalty.

45:4 But you'll still be sent to hell, for God hates you, as he hates all peoples.

So fuck you."

45:5 Baruch then wept, which caused both Jeremiah and the lord God to laugh hysterically.

46:1 The word of the lord which came to Jeremiah the prophet against the Gentiles;

46:2 Against Egypt, against the armies of Pharaohnecho king of Egypt, which lay by the river Euphrates in Carchemish, which Nebuchadnezzar the king of Babylon destroyed in the fourth year of Jehoiakim the son of Josiah, king of Judah.

46:3 "Put down thy pipe, and order thee buckler and shield, for the battle draws near.

46:4 Harness the horses and arm your horsemen, so that they stand with their helmets; sharpen your spears and prepare the mace for blood.

46:5 I have seen the heathens dismayed, with fear spreading in their eyes. Their mighty men shall retreat, and be beaten to the dust, sayeth the lord of Israel.

46:6 Let not the mighty men escape, nor the swift flee away; they shall stumble and fall against the rocks north of the Euphrates.

46:7 Their blood shall flow as rivers, and their bowels become magnificent oceans of a most foul odour.

46:8 Egypt rises like the flood of Noah, and their rivers grow violent; they shall encompass the earth, destroying the cities and all inhabitants thereof.

46:9 So gather your horses, your chariots, and your men of war; bring forth the Libyans and the Ethiopians that handle the shield with grace, and the Lydians that can shoot the flying bird with the arrow.

46:10 These men shall serve thee of Judah; God will kill them later in a great massacre of pestilence and famine.

46:11 Remember that on the day ye gather your men, it shall be a day of vengeance for the lord; his sword shall devour the flesh of thine enemies and become drunk upon the blood of the heathens.

46:12 Lo, the lord will grow with rage, and with savage ferocity slaughter the flood which arises from Egypt, so that they be damned.

46:13 These wicked men shall go up into Gilead, and take their virgin daughters with them; these virgins shall give them balm, ointment and herbs for their pains, but it shall be in vain.

46:14 Their wounds will be deep and fatal; they shall moan and lament, so that all the nations will know the suffering brought to them by the hands of the one true God."

46:15 More words sent to Jeremiah by the mouth of God, regarding how the armies of Babylon will come and smite all those in Egypt;

46:16 The words of God always angered Jeremiah, for they came as Jeremiah took comfort in the smoke of the poppy seed.

46:17 "Declare ye in Egypt, and publish thine word in Migdol, in Noph and in Tahpanhes; tell them to prepare for death, for the lord shall send the sword to devour thee.

46:18 Your valiant men shall be crushed under the hammer of God; they shall fail thee, and protect thee not from the armies of Nebuchadnezzar.

46:19 Those of your soldiers shall fall upon the sword, one atop the other; their bodies will stink under the heat of the sun, so that they be cooked for the fowls of the heavens and the beasts of the earth.

46:20 All of Egypt shall cry to their Pharaoh, and shall bow down unto their idols, worshipping their false gods and burning incense to stone images.

46:21 As they bow down to heathen lords, the armies of Babylon shall slither towards them like a snake, devouring the forests, the fields and the mountains before them.

46:22 Like locusts, the soldiers of Nebuchadnezzar shall plague thee, and tear the flesh from your very bones.

46:23 And on this day, the lord shall punish those of Egypt; all the multitude of No, of Pharaoh, of the Egyptian gods; they shall be thrown in the boiling pitch, and forgotten in the eternal darkness of hell.

46:24 Those that live shall be delivered into the hands of Babylon, where they will be slaves under the rule of Nebuchadnezzar; lo, the men that enslaved the ancestors of Israel shall be given as slaves by the God of Israel.

46:25 Even those of Judah, who hid in the lands of Egypt, will be slaves to those of Babylon; God hates them, for they lived not in the lands of the covenant given unto them."

47:1 More words of the lord which were spoken to Jeremiah, this time regarding the fate of the Philistines.

47:2 You remember the Philistines. Those peoples who fought against Israel ages ago, then somehow managed to not be mentioned until now?

47:3 Apparently God still hated them, even after all this time. I'll give you a moment to act in surprise.

47:4 Moment's passed.

47:5 "Thus sayeth the lord; waters shall rise from the north, and shall overflow the lands of the Philistine.

47:6 Great boiling waters shall rise, and engulf their cities and all who dwell within, so that the howls of their men and the crying of their children will be drowned.

47:7 Fathers shall gather their horses and leave, the sound of hoofs and chariots thundering to the south; they shall leave their kin behind, to die in the waters of the lord.

47:8 These cowardly men will wander the deserts and be drowned by the sands of the wilderness, where they will be buried forever in the land of serpents.

47:9 The day shall come when Philistine will be cut off from the earth; their mighty cities Tyrus and Zidon and their lands of Caphtor will be void of all life.

47:10 Gaza will become bald so that not even the blade of grass groweth within the soil, and the valley of Ashkelon will become as dry as the old woman's womb."

47:11 Jeremiah yelled to the heavens, "O the wrath of the lord, the sword of God; when shall ye be quiet. When shall ye be sheathed, so that the earth know peace?

47:12 How can those of the earth worship thee, when ye slaughter all those who follow thee for the iniquities of their fathers?

47:13 And the lord said, "The world will know peace when it is void of life; know that the earth shall be the center of hell, and shall be my foundation for Zion."

47:14 Never will those of the earth know peace; peace bores me, and the suffering of these peoples amuse me greatly.

47:15 Thus my sword will never be sheathed, nor my wrath quiet."

48:1 No more shall their be praise for the peoples of Moab; those descendants of Lot's drunken incest.

48:2 Though they be of the lineage of a most righteous man, the lord God loathes them, and they shall be cut down with the sword.

48:3 Their wailing voices shall be heard from Horonaim; a voice of terrible fear and destruction.

48:4 Moab will be destroyed; her little ones shall be dashed against the rocks.

48:5 Within their borders shall be heard naught but a great weeping; horrible lamentations of the suffering of the children of Lot.

48:6 Those that flee the wrath of God shall not have their lives spared. They shall die in the wilderness and become flesh for the beasts.

48:7 Because their women take pleasures in sex, and because their men value highly earthly delights, all their seed shall die. Their princes and their priests will be consumed by the jaws of 48:8 God and buried deep within the bowels of the earth.

48:9 The fury of the lord shall descend upon every city, consuming all those within. All within the city, the valley and the plain shall be destroyed, as is the will of God.

48:10 Great winged beasts will come down from the heavens and thrust into the peoples of Moab a great spear of iron; with torches of hell-fire they shall burn the cities, until they become ash and dust.

48:11 Cursed be the peoples of Moab, who deny themselves the work of the lord; cursed be to Moab, who keep their swords clean of the blood of heathens.

48:12 How can ye say, we are mighty men, when ye keep your swords sheathed and your horses in the stables?

48:13 Lo, ye shall be ashamed of your tolerance and your peace; for when the time of the lord cometh, ye shall be ignorant to defend yourselves.

48:14 The men of Moab have grown fat on the flesh of pigs, the sweet wine, and the fruits of the harvest; they shall be fat for the slaughter, and create a pleasing aroma as their obese bodies roast in the fires of damnation.

48:15 For the calamity of Moab is near to come, and their destruction hasteth fast.

48:16 Their daughters whore themselves to men of all nations; their loins take lustful desire of the blessed men of God and the uncircumcised demon men.

48:17 Let it be that they be raped by the beasts of hell, until these lustful women know sex as the horrible pain the lord meant it to be for women.

48:18 How the fools of Moab take pleasure in the intoxication of the fruits; behold, they are a nation of drunks, who wallow in their own vomit and choke upon the waste of their bowels.

48:19 Soon the joys of their works will turn into sorrow, when the vineyards grow dry and the tankard empty.

48:20 Let them slay even their mother for a drop of strong drink, and place the spear in their brother for a taste of ale.

48:21 Their howls shall be heard from Dibon unto Kerioth, for they shall weep over their empty vessels.

48:22 And the fist of God shall strike hard upon their cities, shattering them unto the ends of the earth.

48:23 Moab shall be destroyed as a peoples, because the lord hates those descended upon the unholy lust between a father and his daughters.

48:24 How these curs will know the fear, the snare, the wrath, the hatred and the fury of the one true God.

48:25 All shall fall into the pit of damnation; even those that flee will trip upon their sandals and fall into the eternal void.

48:26 The flames of the lord will come out of Heshbon and of Sihon, until all of Moab be devoured in the flames of God.

48:27 Woe to the children of Moab, whose sons and daughters will be taken captive by the dragons and the cockatrice.

48:28 Yet the lord shall bring a great pain unto those of Moab; a suffering as great as the sorrows of hell. This is the judgment of Moab, given by the lord of lord's and holiest of holies.

49:1 A mighty damnation to all those of the earth, for the lord hath created thee, and the lord shall destroy thee.

49:2 The ravages of war will come and leave your lands in a great heap, and your daughters will be burned in the raging fire.

49:3 Howl, those of the earth; howl like the wolf, and know that ye have become like the beast.

49:4 Eagles will make nests of your flesh, and the satyrs will create drums of your bones and chimes with your teeth.

49:5 You will be held captives by the angels of the lord and the demons of hell; heavy will your yoke be, and ye shall never know the comfort of rest, of water and of bread.

49:6 All that of your seed will fall into the slave pens or the brothels, to be raped by the immortal beasts and beaten as they work.

49:7 Worry not about your homes, for they will be a desolate place; your kin will be destroyed by the plague and their blood shall flow into the goblets of the one true God, so that he will be drunk in their slaying.

49:8 Dragons will come and tear at your flesh until the end of eternity; ye will lay your head upon the brimstone of hell.

49:9 For thus sayeth the lord; all those since the days of Adam and Eve shall know the anger and the wrath of the lord. All peoples of the earth will be cast into the deepest oblivion, and know not the salvation promised to them by God.

49:10 The lord God deceived thee, and now ye are deceived; even those that are righteous and holy will not pass through the gates of Zion, but fall into the pits of sorrow.

49:11 Your cities of old will burn eternally in fire, and be laid to waste by dragons, beasts, satyrs and ravens.

49:12 Owls will hold court in your palaces, and the temples will be a haven for the serpent and the Minotaur.

49:13 Behold, the men of earth will be made as the women; their loins will be cut off, and they shall be forced to eat the vessel of their seed, and it shall taste bitter.

49:14 The axe of God is sharpened, and his weapons ready for war; they will break that of humanity in pieces, and destroy the mightiest of kingdoms.

49:15 The chariots, the horses and the rider will be broken, and their pieces cast into the wind.

49:16 Flowing rivers will turn to stone, and the waters of the well will become bitter like the herb.

49:17 Mighty men will become weak as the newborn lamb; even the single locust shall defeat the mightiest of men in battle.

49:18 How the lord will bring thee horrible pains, terrible punishments and unimaginable cruelties; how the one you worshipped will turn on thee, and betray thee.

49:19 Never will those of men remove the dagger from their backs, plunged deep by the hand of God.

49:20 Do not worship the lord, for it will bring thee no good; do not follow the laws of Moses, for the curse of God has been placed upon all your heads.

49:21 Accept your fate of hell, and curse the chains of God; burn in hell a free man, and deny the lord in life.

49:22 In death, your fate is sealed; in life, the lord can only punish your body, but not spirit.

40:23 Thus be free of the tyranny of God, and live as ye please; know that the most kindest of men curse the name of the lord, for they know the cruelties of the lord.

49:24 Die free, and curse proudly the name of God as ye suffer in the torments of damnation.

49:25 Fuck God; he is not worth your devotion.

LAMENTATIONS

1:1 How does the city sit solitary that was once full of people. How she has become a widow, who was once great amongst the nations, the princes and the kings.

1:2 She weeps in silence during the night, so that her pillows are soaked in tears; among all her lovers she has none to comfort her and such all her friends have dealt with her treacherously and have become enemies.

1:3 Judah has gone into slavery for the afflictions of past kings; the children of sinners dwells amongst the heathens and are toys of rape because of the sins of their fathers.

1:4 None of the chosen people will know the salvation of Zion, nor feast at the table of God.

1:5 Behold Judah, whose priests grow fat on the flesh of swine and whose virgins spread their legs to the heathen with the deepest purse.

1:6 Judah shall grow weak as her enemies prosper, for the lord has made it so; damned be those of Judah, who the lord hates as he hates all men.

1:7 Lo, the beauty of the daughters of Zion will be denied to the princes of Jerusalem, for they settle for the lust of a heathen whore and waited not for the concubines descended from angels.

1:8 Jerusalem has become revolting in the eyes of God; she is like the menstruating cunt, who has been raped by the uncircumcised.

1:9 The stench of Judah's skirts reaches high into the heavens; it reaches into the nostrils of God and causes him to vomit upon the earth.

1:10 Behold, the enemies of Judah have grasped her breasts and suckled upon the sweet teat; how they have taken the gold and the silver from the temple of the lord.

1:11 All the people sigh and seek forth the comfort of bread and water. How they take pleasure in the meat of pigs and become vile to God.

1:12 From above the lord of lords will send fire into the bones of his people, roasting the very marrow from within. He shall set a snare for all the chosen, entrapping them into the very corners of hell.

1:13 With the rope of their sins they shall hang and be bound to the rocks of eternal damnation; demons sent from the devil will come with whips, beating them until the flesh is torn from the bone.

1:14 The lord hates all those of Judah and shall trample them as grapes within the winepress; he shall trample upon the mighty men, the young, the wise, the elders and the virgins, until all the blood flows forth and gives sweet drink to the one true God.

1:15 For the cruelties of God you shall weep; tears will run down your cheeks like the flowing rivers.

1:16 No parents will know the comfort of their child's embrace; their child will be taken by the enemies of Judah, to serve them in the armies, in the fields and in the houses of ill repute.

1:17 God has spread forth his hands and declared a curse unto all the people of Jacob; you are as loathsome as the menstruating whore and are unclean.

1:18 You call for your lovers and they stab the dagger in your back as they take their lust upon you.

1:19 Behold, your very blood shall be thrust into your bowels alongside the seed of your lover.

1:20 You are all wicked to me and will suffer for your wickedness; not one of your seed will know the mercy of the lord, for the lord shall be cruel to you, as he was once cruel to your enemies.

2:1 How the lord has covered the eyes of Israel with a cloud of his anger and destroyed upon the earth the beauty that is Judah. He has broken the covenant of his people on the day of his anger.

2:2 The lord has swallowed up all the seed of Jacob without pity; he has raped the daughters of Abraham, crippled his sons and laid waste to the princes.

2:3 He has cut off with his anger the loins of Israel; he has crushed us with his right hand, sold us to the heathen and cast us into the devouring fires.

2:4 His arrows aim at the back of our heads: he stands alongside our enemy and slaughtered all that which was pleasant in the tabernacle: he drowns us in the lake of fire.

2:5 The lord is our enemy, who hates Israel with a burning passion: he has turned to ash our cities and laid waste to our palaces: he has reduced to dust our strongholds and enslaves the people of Judah.

2:6 How we increase in mourning and lamentation at the cruelties of the one we worship; how the lord takes twisted pleasure in our suffering, our torments, our pain.

2:7 The righteous and the wicked he kills without mercy; how the blasphemer is burned beside the holy; kings and priests are cast into the pits of thieves and lepers.

2:8 Even the house of the lord, the temple of God, is destroyed in the wrath of the one true lord; in his anger, he burns his own house as he strangles the neck of his children.

2:9 Altars that once offered sweet flesh to the father has been struck down by the fist of the lord; like the angry drunk he breaks his own belongings as he harms others.

2:10 The walls of Jerusalem erupt in a dark fire; the hand of the lord withdraws not from war, thus the seed of Jacob lament and weep.

2:11 The gates of Jerusalem are swallowed by the jaws of the earth; he has turned the iron bars to rust: kings and princes are sold as prostitutes to the Gentile queer; even the prophets of God are shown false visions.

2:12 The elders of Judah are struck to the ground and kept in silence: they have filled their mouths with dust and covered themselves in the blood and the faeces of the dead: the virgins of Jerusalem lie in the bed of brothels.

2:13 My eyes fill with tears of sadness, my bowels empty within my skirt and my liver pours out upon the earth, for the destruction of my people is a most horrifying sight: children butcher the suckling infant and throw them in the boiling pot and it frightens me.

2:14 Mothers tell their child to wait for the corn, the wine and the fruits to come, as their children and husband feast upon the flesh of her breasts.

2:15 There is none I can say to comfort the daughters of Judah, none I can speak to the sons of Israel to offer aid; we are injured and shall never heal; the lord has smote us and we are to be crushed.

2:16 How the lord leads the wise men to hell, the prophets to delusion and the children to the noose; he has tricked us with iniquity and caused us to sin so that he breaks the covenant of our fathers.

2:17 Those that pass by our nation mocks at us and piss atop our heads; how they say, this was once the city of the mighty true God and now it is the home of satyrs, dragons and crows.

2:18 By the deliverance of God our enemies have taken our wealth and beauty; those hated by God now lay the yoke upon us, for we did not kill them in holy genocide.

2:19 The words of old are a lie; the lord will not lead us to prosperity and dominance; we shall be thrown without pity into the void of damnation and never know the sanctuary of Zion.

2:20 Behold, the tears fill the dry rivers of our nation with a salty brine; how the lord bathes in the river of our tears and grows drunk on the blood of our children.

2:21 Arise, for the night offers us no rest; the demons of God keep us awake with our hungers, our pains, our thirst.

2:22 Lo, the mother shall boil her child and the child boil their mother; priests and prophets will be roasted in the fires of the temple and become a feast for the survivors of Judah.

2:23 Both young and old lie rotting in the streets; young and mighty men have fallen upon the blades of the wicked; O lord, you have slain in the day of your anger; you hast killed without mercy and shown no pity to the people you call your own.

2:24 Upon the day of this terror shall none remain nor escape; we will become one with the dust or slaves for our enemies, such is the will of our lord.

3:1 I am the man who has seen the cruelties of the one true God.

3:2 He has led me into the darkness of his realm, where all light is denied.

3:3 Surely, he has betrayed his people; he has raised his hand against us.

3:4 My flesh and my skin are torn; he has broken my bones.

3:5 His fortress' are built against me and encompasses me with gall and travail.

3:6 He puts us in the darkest places, where we grow old without ever seeing the light of the sun.

3:7 He enslaves us with a heavy labour and our chains become a great burden.

3:8 Our cries are in vain, for he ignores our prayers and denies us mercy.

3:9 He has entrapped us with stone and made our paths treacherous.

3:10 Like the bear he attacks us; like the lion he stalks us.

3:11 He has torn apart my flesh and scattered my pieces; he has made me desolate.

3:12 His bow is bent and the arrow shall pierce the back of our necks.

3:13 The arrows within his quiver enter my frail body.

3:14 I have led the people to follow the lord and sing praises to him all day.

3:15 Now the lord has made me bitter and fills my throat with the fermentation of wormwood.

3:16 He has shattered my teeth with mountains; he drowns me with ashes.

3:17 My soul means nothing to me; I am tattered and torn.

3:18 My strength and my hope has been sodomized by the lord of my people.

3:19 I remember my misery, my gall, my sinful inflictions.

3:20 It is out of the cruelty of God that we are not consumed; by the torments of the lord we are denied the embrace of death.

3:21 The lord rewards the wicked and the cunning with riches; the honest, the righteous and the holy are cursed with poverty and sickness.

3:22 Our mouths are filled with dust; we cry for his mercy and choke upon his cruelty.

3:23 The lord causes grief and offers no compassion to the mighty, the weak, nor any of this earth.

3:24 He does afflict pain without compassion and grieves not for the orphan nor the widow.

3:25 With his feet he crushes all those imprisoned on the earth.

3:26 Out of the mouth of the most high comes forth a vile evil disguised under the veil of beauty and salvation.

3:27 He surrounds himself with a cloud of ignorance and denies the wickedness of his doings.

3:28 Through fear, intimidation and extortion he leads us; through destruction, plagues and the sword he shows his examples.

3:29 My eye run down with tears for the destruction of our daughters; my heart fills with anger as my sons die by the hands of my lord.

3:30 My enemies chase me until my legs become no more.

3:31 They throw me into the dungeon and lay a heavy stone above me.

3:32 The lord hears my voice, but listens not to my prayers.

3:33 I have been denied the mercies of my God; I shall be thrust into hell by the one who promised me salvation.

3:34 And in hell I shall seek forth the comfort of my enemies: I shall plunge them into the darkest flames and rape them with the mountains and the sword.

3:35 Curse be to my enemies and curse be to my God; let the whole world be cursed as I.

4:1 How is it that gold has become dim. How does this most precious metal change. The stones held most precious are now of less value than the common pebble.

4::2 The precious sons of Judah, once as precious as gold, are now as worthless as the withered leaf.

4:3 Mothers treat their children worse than the beasts of the wild; even the sea monster offers her child the milk off her breast and the ostrich keeps warm her eggs.

4:4 The tongue of the suckling child cleaves to the roof of their mouth in thirst; they thirst for water and are offered none, they hunger for bread yet none shall bake for them.

4:5 They that are hungry feast on the corpses lying on the streets; he who thirsts drink the spit from the rabid dog.

4:6 The punishment of Jerusalem shall be greater than the punishment of Sodom and Gomorrah, for the sins of their fathers are greater than those gambling faggots.

4:7 How the lord loathes us greatly that even the Philistines are prettier in the eyes of God; they are purer than snow, whiter than milk, glow greater than rubies and are polished like the sapphire.

4:8 We have become blacker than coal and our skin cleaves to our bones.

4:9 Those that are slain by the sword shall be envied by those who perish by the hunger: for they pine away, craving the fruits of the field and the meat of the herd.

4:10 Women shall sell themselves willingly to the lustful man and accept their seed; they shall throw their infant into the pot, for it is their meat.

4:11 The lord will accomplish his fury; he shall pour out his fierce anger upon us and devour us in the fountains of black flame.

4:12 Great kings of the earth and the inhabitants of the world will know the hatred and the wrath of the lord of Israel.

4:13 They shall wander blind in the streets; they shall pollute themselves with such blood that their very garments will be soaked a sanguine hue.

4:14 All men shall wail, unclean, unclean, depart, touch not: they shall flee into the wilderness and wander like the crippled prey.

4:15 The anger of the lord shall divide all humanity; he shall regard us no more and leave us to wallow in the void of damnation.

5:1 The lord has given our inheritance to the stranger; the lands of the covenant are in the hands of the heathen.

5:2 We are orphans and fatherless, our mothers have become widows.

5:3 We drink our piss as water and sell our teeth for bread.

5:4 Our necks are burdened with a heavy yoke: we labour and have no rest.

5:5 Out of the hands of Egypt did the lord free us, so that we may be delivered to the fist of Babylon.

5:6 This is done for the sins of our fathers; our skin is stained with the sins of our fathers.

5:7 Even the servant heathen rule over us; never are we to be delivered again.

5:8 We eat the grass of the oxen, the slop of swine; bread is denied to us and those caught with bread are delivered to the noose.

5:9 Under the heat of the sun our skin has turned as black as coal.

5:10 Our women and our maids are sold into brothels and our virgin daughters are auctioned to the rapists.

5:11 Our princes hang as trophies upon the walls of the wealthy; our elders wash the feet of pigs.

5:12 Our mighty men carry rocks and our children cut down wood.

5:13 The joys of our heart have ceased; our dances ferment to mourning.

5:14 The crown has fallen from our head and crippled our feet.

5:15 Our heart is faint and grows weaker by the day.

5:16 All this has been done by our lord, so why do we praise him?

5:17 We know that God has delivered us these pains, yet we still worship him.

5:18 Such is the power of the lord; such is the power of fear.

EZEKIEL

1:1 Now it came to pass that on the thirtieth year, on the fourth month of the year, in the fifth day of the month, which was a Wednesday, I was among the captives by the river Chebar, when the heavens opened and I saw God.

1:2 As to the thirtieth year of what, only God knows, and he ain't telling.

1:3 The word of the lord came expressly to Ezekiel the priest, the son of Buzi, in the lands of the Chaldeans by the river Chebar; though Ezekiel was surrounded by other captives, only Ezekiel saw the heavens open and the majesty of the lord God almighty.

1:4 And as I looked, behold, a whirlwind came from the north, a great cloud of fire with the brightness of one thousand suns and in the center a dish of amber colour being encircled by candles.

1:5 From the amber came the likeness of four living creatures, with features odd; they stood as though they were of men.

1:6 Each creature had four faces and each face had four wings and each back had four wings, so that each creature had eight wings like the eagle.

1:7 Their legs were made of molten brass, with a foot like a calf's foot

1:8 The end of each feather placed on their wings had a grasping hand, which each carried a blade of glowing steel.

1:9 As for their faces, upon the right side they had the face of a man and the face of a lion with a mighty mane; upon the left was a face of an ox and the face of the eagle.

1:10 Two wings upon their back stretched upward into the sky and the remaining two wings covered the nakedness of their bodies; the wings upon their faces covered their scalps as though they were a helmet.

1:11 Each creature glowed with the coals of burning fire and lamps of round candlelight floated around them as quick as lightning.

1:12 Lo, from the amber dish dropped four wheels with the colour of beryl and each wheel was made of two wheels, which spun around one another.

1:13 Between the spinning wheels glowed a liquid as red as the most precious of rubies, which hummed with the buzzing of a hundred million wasps.

1:14 Each wheel, each orb followed beside each creature so that when the creatures lifted from the earth, so did the wheels.

1:15 And the creatures were connected to each orb, for in the orb was their spirit, their soul; such as men have their spirit within their heart and their liver, these creatures trapped them within the spinning wheels.

1:16 Suddenly a great ladder of light came down from the dish and each face looked above into the heavens and screamed with a roar greater than the violent seas.

1:17 Descending from the ladder was the one true lord, whose face was surrounded by a helmet of orange light.

1:18 Behold, I saw the loins of good in all their glory; his foreskin remained. Weird.

1:19 A great bang came from the dish of amber, and the firmament split open and it rained upon the earth.

1:20 The raindrops were not of water, but were of a glowing green liquid, which burned even the dust of the earth.

1:21 As it rained, I fell upon my face; and the voice of the lord spoke to me.

2:1 And the lord said to me, "Stand up, wretched son of Adam and listen to what I shall say."

2:2 With each drop of rain that fell upon me, the spirit of the lord filled me and I rose upon my feet and listened to the wisdom of God.

2:3 He said, "You shall go to the nation of Israel, to the nation most hated, filled with rebellious cunts who abandoned my ways for the morals of men.

2:4 They are impudent, stubborn bastards. I shall send you to them and you shall say, Thus sayeth the lord.

2:5 And perhaps they shall listen, or perhaps not. They are a rebellious nation who ignores those who speak the true word of God, calling them crazy drug addicts.

2:6 Be not afraid of them, O prophet Ezekiel, nor fear the words they speak; you shall sleep in the bed of thorns in the land of scorpions, but be not afraid of these most hated of people.

2:7 Ye shall speak my words and whether they hear or ignore, it matters not; they shall be sent to hell anyway, so it really doesn't matter.

2:8 But you, son of Buzi, shall listen to the words I say, lest these guards of mine rape the very spirit within you."

2:9 I looked up and behold, a fifth wheel descended and within it contained a scroll full of lamentations, mourning and woe; it was the book of God.

3:1 The lord took the scroll and said, "Eat this scroll, which contains the true words of God and go speak in the house of Israel."

3:2 So I opened the scroll and he thrust with great force the scroll

down my throat and each of the creatures, with each of their faces, chanted, "Take it, bitch and swallow."

3:3 I ate the scroll, which filled my bowels with a violent pain: and the scroll tasted like honey and cinnamon.

3:4 The lord spoke and said, "Go to the house of Israel and there you shall vomit upon the people the words which the scroll contained.

3:5 Fear not, for the words of Israel are a language you speak; I know you to be stupid and dumb of speech, but the word of the lord shall flow through you and those who listen will understand your words.

3:6 Behold, I have made your face strong against your faces; your teeth are like the jaws of the lion and mighty horns grow above your brow.

3:7 They shall gaze at you with disgust and hatred; fear not, for I shall kill them and throw them in the lake of fire.

3:8 Now go, get to the lands of Israel, so that y may do that which the lord commands you."

3:9 The lord then picked me up and placed me within the dish of amber, where green men as thin as the twig sodomized me with rods of glass.

3:10 Then it came to pass that I was dropped by the shores of the river Chebar, where for seven days my body shook violently in a puddle of my own filth.

3:11 As my body stopped it's shaking, the voice of the lord came to me and said, "Why are you still here, foolish son of man. Have I not given you a task to accomplish?

3:12 Go now and speak the word of God to the children of Israel; I have made you watchman over the house of Israel and you shall watch the house burn.

3:13 I say to you, the wicked shall surely die; give them no warning, nor speak to them the word of God, for the wicked shall not listen to you and drown in his own sins.

3:14 Even if you were to tell the wicked and they turned away from their wickedness, I'll still kill him and send him into the pits of oblivion.

3:15 Speak to the righteous and tell them that the lord shall cast them into the realm of everlasting torment, where they shall be raped by the demon; they shall deny this and claim that they will know the salvation of Zion promised to them by God.

3:16 The lord shall not keep his promise to the righteous; I don't want people in Zion, for the lord values his quietness.

3:17 They shall deny your words and call you blasphemous; they shall loathe you and demand you be stoned."

3:18 Ezekiel asked the lord, "Shall I enter into Zion, for I go forth and speak the bitter words of God?"

3:19 And the lord answered, "No, you can burn in hell."

3:20 So Ezekiel said, "Then I shall tell them that I also will be denied Zion and that the lord God is a true tyrant, worse than any of men."

3:21 God laughed and said, "Every time you speak these words, I shall cleave your tongue to the back of your throat.

3:22 Know that I control your lips and that which I wish you not to speak will choke your very lungs."

3:23 The lord then bound Ezekiel and the lips of Ezekiel embraced the loins of God, until a salty taste filled his mouth.

4:1 With the bounds upon me, the lord took me to a field of thorns and fire and placed me upon my left side, saying, "Here you shall lie for three hundred and ninety days.

4:2 For it has been three hundred and ninety years that I have hated Israel with all my wrath.

4:3 Then shall I place you on your right side, where you will lay for forty years, for it has been forty years that I hated Judah.

4:4 During these days you shall eat nothing but bread made from wheat, barley, lentils, beans and fitches; it shall be baked from the dung which comes from you."

4:5 Thus I did and laid upon my sides as the lord commanded.

4:6 As I struggled, the binds became tighter, such that even my very bowels were squeezed out from my loins.

4:7 And my bowels were emptied and baked the bread which was offered to me as my meal; I did not eat much.

4:8 When I refused the bread, the lord laughed and said, "It shall come to pass that there will be a drought in Israel so great that they will beg for this bread made from the shit of man."

4:9 The lord truly is a sadistic God.

5:1 "Go now, Ezekiel and take a sharp knife and cut the hair from your head, the hair of your beard and the hair of your loins.

5:2 Divide the hair into three equal balances, so that you have three piles of hair of equal weight.

5:3 Of the third pile of hair you shall burn in the midst of the city, so that the stench fills the streets and the homes of all. Of the second you shall stab with a knife. Of the third you shall cast into the wind, so that it blocks out the sun.

5:4 From each pile you shall take one strand and sew them within your skirts.

5:5 Then you shall take this skirt and burn it within the city of Jerusalem, as you still wear it.

5:6 The lord hates your hair. You look like a woman.

5:7 Thus sayeth the lord; Jerusalem was once the jewel of earth, a mighty city where the lord once dwelt.

5:8 Of all other cities, of all other nations, the lord has not placed his temple; it was Jerusalem, in the land of Judah, where the lord laid his house.

5:9 Now the people of Judah are hated and those within Jerusalem disgust the very God of all.

5:10 Where once I loved these people, for I loved their king David, I now hate them; where once I smote their enemies, I have become their enemy.

5:11 I shall curse them with a great cruelty, where fathers will eat their sons and sons eat their fathers.

5:12 They have defiled the sanctuary and made filthy my home; I shall slaughter them with a great slaughter for their abominations, until they all lay dead; I shall deny them pity.

5:13 Of one third will I slay with the pestilence, the drought, the plague and the famine; of one third will I bring forth the sword, so that they be slain by the heathens I demanded slew; of one third will I cast into the winds, so that they wear heavy the yoke of the Gentile.

5:14 Then shall they know the anger of the lord and that they will be denied comfort until the end of days; they will know the lord has spoken and that he is all powerful.

5:15 I will make Judah as waste of the earth, so that all nations loathe them with disgust.

5:16 I shall taunt them, I shall torment them, I shall torture them until I execute my judgment swiftly, with great wrath and anger.

5:17 Of those that remain, I shall send fire and beasts unto the lands and they shall stalk them all night and days; they shall consume them, rape them and drink the very blood from their veins. I the lord have spoken it and thus it shall come true."

6:1 The word of the lord came to me, saying,

6:2 "Hearken my words, you useless son of a cuntless whore and turn your face towards the mountains of Israel.

6:3 Know that these mountains, these hills, these rivers, these valleys, will turn to ash under the fiery wrath that is their God; they shall know the sword, the famine, and the pestilence.

6:4 Your altars will become desolate, your idols broken into shards and your men shall lay dead before the idols you worship.

6:5 The carcasses of your children will litter the ground before your altars, their bones picked clean of all flesh: and you shall know that the gods you worship did not aid you and that the true lord brings destruction upon your heads.

6:6 All your dwelling places will be thick with the stench of death, your cities reek of decay, your high places the unburied graveyard and your altars shall become feeding grounds for the scavengers.

6:7 Your idols will be burned and your gods will burn beside the in the everlasting fires of hell.

6:8 And as you gaze out among the fields of slaughter, you shall know that only the lord have the power to bring such death, such pain, such terror upon you.

6:9 For a remnant of those of Israel will survive; they shall escape the sword and be a stranger in the nation of heathens.

6:10 There you shall remember the cruelties of the one true God, as you serve your new masters that your fathers failed to slay in holy genocide; you shall become whores, slaves and playthings for those of a truly wicked heart.

6:11 Your skin will be cut, your eyes plucked and your bones broken, so that they bring joy to the demonic soul and entertainment to the God of gods.

6:12 And as they suffer under the blade of the wicked, they shall know that I am God and that I am the one who brought such evil upon them.

6:13 Thus demands the lord, O Ezekiel; Clap your hands and stomp your feet and chant unto Israel, 'You shall die by the plagues, the famine and the sword, for the lord brings you a hatred strong into your house.'

6:14 There is no escape from the fury of the lord; those that run shall die by the pestilence, those that stay will die by the sword and those that remain will die by the famine; until all those of the seed of Abraham perish, the lord will not rest his fury.

6:15 They shall know that I am the lord, when the suckling child be gnawed upon by the jackal; I shall stretch forth my hand and wipe them from the face of the earth."

7:1 Still, the word of the lord spoke to me, saying,

7:2 "An end is coming which will consume unto the very corners of the earth.

7:3 The end comes upon you, where my anger shall consume all of the lands; terrible abominations will be sent by the lord unto those of Israel.

7:4 Mine eye will not spare you, nor show you pity nor mercy; I shall bring to you great torments so that the lands wail with lamentations: and you shall know that I am the lord.

7:5 The lord will walk among the earth and bring with him a pure evil that only the heart of the lord holds.

7:6 An end comes and it comes swiftly.

7:7 The morning of trouble comes, where the sun becomes cold and the moon red as blood; mountains will tremble, seas will boil and the earth will split apart.

7:8 My fury will pour hot upon you and my anger will be accomplished upon you; I will judge you harshly and bring horrors unto you for the sins of your fathers.

7:9 None will be spared, nor shown mercy; the lord of mercy was nevermore, now you shall know the true nature of God.

7:10 Behold, the day shall come: the firmament will be torn and the sky shall fall upon the lands.

7:11 Violence will rise in the streets, so that every man will kill his brother; none shall remain, for son shall kill father, mother shall kill daughter and brother will rape sister.

7:12 The time is come, the day draws near; none shall rejoice, nor sing psalms to the lord; let their flow rivers of blood and tears.

7:13 A mighty trumpet will split open the night sky and the wrath of the lord descends harshly upon you.

7:14 They will be without sword against the mighty armies of God; he that is in the field will fall on the holy blade and those who cower in the corners of the cities, the caves and the mountains will fall to the plague and the famine.

7:15 Only the chosen will escape and be cast like dust in the wind that blows towards the ungodly nations, the land of heathens.

7:16 Their hands will be brittle and their legs as weak as water.

7:17 They shall wear the sackcloth and the horrors of disease will cover them; they shall fall upon their faces and pluck out their hairs with madness.

7:18 Of those blessed with riches, they shall be stripped of their gold and their silver; those who had a full table will eat the feathers of pigeons as bread.

7:19 Their souls shall know only torment; their bowels forever howl in hunger.

7:20 I will give Judah and Israel to the strangers as prey and to the wicked for the spoil and they shall pollute it.

7:21 Even the temple of God will be made unclean by the heathen, for the thieves shall defile it and the unholy will walk within its holy walls.

7:22 Lo, a bloody chain grows tight around the neck of the heathens and they know not of this snare.

7:23 The worse of the heathen will come and dwell in the lands of the covenant; they shall grow lazy and fat with the crops given to the seed of Abraham.

7:24 Behold, destruction comes upon them; they shall seek peace and find none.

7:25 The lord will send mischief and paranoia among the heathens; prophets will be given false visions and the wisdom of the ancients will be made foolish.

7:26 Kings will mourn and princes will weep; they shall befall a destruction greater than those of Israel and the lord will judge them with a wicked court.

7:27 And as they perish, everyone, they shall know that I am the lord God: and I who created the earth, shall destroy it."

8:1 It came to pass that on the sixth year, in the six month, of the fifth day of that month, I sat in my house and told the horrors of the lord to the elders of Judah.

8:2 They didn't listen.

8:3 The lord then came down to me and I saw his loins embraced in a thong of fire.

8:4 The hand of God grasped the hair atop my head and pulled me above the firmament, where I could gaze upon the earth and all its glories.

8:5 It was then the lord spoke and said, "What fools are they, who hears the word of God yet fear not strikes into the heart of Israel?

8:6 Look upon the homes of the seed of Abraham and know they still not wish to appease me, nor follow the laws of Moses.

8:7 Watch and witness the abominations of my people."

8:8 And I saw upon the tables of Judah every manner of foul swine, creepy thing and revolting flesh, which they shovelled into their gaping mouths.

8:9 I saw them bow low to the heathen images of the sons of God, who they worshipped and burned incense at their altars.

8:10 I saw men lie with other men, women lie with women, dragons lie with sheep and goats pleasure the loins of young boys.

8:11 I saw standing in the courts of Israel Jaazaniah the son of Shaphan, surrounded by young boys who each held a censer in their hand.

8:12 These young boys danced naked around Jaazaniah, while Jaazaniah crowned them each atop their heads with his seed.

8:13 Within the temple of the lord I saw the priests burn incense to the images of Ashteroth; I saw men of the lord burn upon the altar lame oxen and lambs with blemish upon them.

8:14 In the gate of the temple I saw women weeping for the false lord Tammuz, daughter of the one true God.

8:15 I saw and I witnessed a nation of sun worshippers, sodomites and blasphemers; yet, within these wicked people were followers of the true path, who hearkened the words of God and obeyed the laws of Moses.

8:16 Then the lord spoke, saying, "These are truly men of wickedness and I shall burn them forever in fire, drown them in oil and cast them into the freezing caverns of damnation."

8:17 I asked of God, "What of the men who hold true to your ways and obey the covenant?"

8:18 The lord grew mad at me, tore out the hairs of my head and cast me unto the earth, saying, "When the day of damnation comes, know that your insolence forbids you salvation."

9:1 As I hit the earth, the lord spoke to me and said,

9:2 "Do not question that which is the lord, lest you be cast into the pot of evil.

9:3 But know that God is not without mercy and he shall send forth six angels to Israel and Judah, who shall seek forth those worthy of salvation.

9:4 Of those worthy, they shall be marked upon the forehead with the holy symbol of God: and they shall know the salvation of Zion.

9:5 Of those left unmarked, they will be thrown into the perfection that is hell; they will be shown no mercy nor pity.

9:6 Young, old, women and child whose foreheads are bare will be slain in the wrath of the lord and cast into the darkest void, the torments of oblivion."

9:7 And the six angels went throughout the people of Judah and Israel, marking those worthy of salvation.

9:8 They placed not a mark on a single forehead; even the head of Ezekiel was bare.

10:1 As I sat by the river of wine, inhaling the sweet smoke of the mandrake, I gazed to the sky and behold, there stood below the firmament four cherubims and between them was a throne of sapphire.

10:2 And lo, there was a man clothed with linen, who said in the voice of locusts, "Go between the fires of the cherubs and gather with your fists the coals of fire, so that you may cast them towards the cities."

10:3 Then the man stood and walked into the house of grape vines, which was to the right of the cherubims; as he entered the house, a great cloud surrounded me, which smelled like honey.

10:4 Then the glory of the lord came through the nostrils of the four cherubs and stood above the house of grape vines: and the court was filled with the brightness of the lord.

10:5 It was then the wings of the cherubims beat wildly, drowning out the words which came from the tongue of God.

10:6 And the lord demanded the man clothed with linen to take fire from the wheels between each cherubim; then he went and stood within the wheels of the cherubs.

10:7 One cherub stretched forth his hand to the man clothed with linen and stripped him bare and threw his clothes in the fire of the nearest wheel.

10:8 The man clothed with linen was naked in my sight and his loins were unholy with foreskin.

10:9 As I saw the cherub, behold, underneath each wing was a man's hand, holding a mace made of the scales of mackerel.

10:10 I looked up and each cherub stood beside their wheels of fire: and the wheels were carved from the beryl stone and hummed with the roar of elephants.

10:11 Each cherub was a twin of the other, so they all looked alike in appearance.

10:12 Every cherub had four faces; the first of a man, the second of a goat, the third of a lion and the fourth of a woman's vagina.

10:13 And throughout their faces, their backs, their bodies, their legs, were full of unblinking eyes; even the wheels of fire swarmed with the ever-gazing eyes.

10:14 When the cherubs moved, so did the wheel beside them; when one lifted, so did the other and when one came down, so did the other.

10:15 I gazed into the wheels of the cherubs and saw that their spirit was contained within the wheel, such as the orbs contained the spirit of the, whatever the hell those things were I saw at the river Chebar.

10:16 And every cherub had four faces and four wings and each wing had underneath them four hands, so that each cherub had eighteen hands; one on each of their arms and four under each wing.

11:1 The lord then lifted me up by the hair on my arms and brought me to the east gate of the temple of the lord: and at the door of the gate were five and twenty men, among them Jaazaniah the son of Azur and Pelatiah the son of Benaiah, princes of Judah.

11:2 And each man engaged in lust of kink and perversion; each man knew intimately the loins of their neighbour.

11:3 The lord spoke to me, saying, "These men blasphemy the house of the one true God; they lust in unholy sodomy on my very doorsteps.

11:4 Know that they shall be cast into the cauldron of boiling blood; they will suffer for their faggot ways and know that I am God.

11:5 Prophesy against them, O Ezekiel; spread the holy word of God such that their ears tingle.

11:6 I know that which goes in the house of Israel; they cannot hide their hearts from me.

11:7 For I am the one true God, who knows all, sees all and creates all; their slain will multiply greatly and their sins of the flesh will cause them to be torn of their flesh.

11:8 The lord will send the sword upon them: and it shall be the fiery sword of God, which tears without mercy and slaughters all those hated by the lord.

11:9 And as their children be murdered in holy genocide, all shall know that I am God.

11:10 It matters not if they walked in my statutes, obeyed my commandments or followed the laws of Moses; the lord God is angry and all shall suffer his wrath."

11:11 And it came to pass that when I prophesied that Pelatiah the son of Benaiah died. Then I fell upon my face and cried to the lord with a loud voice, "Lord of lord and king of kings, will you ever show mercy upon those you chose as your people?"

11:12 And the lord came down to me, and whispered in my ear, "No.

11:13 I shall slay them with the sword, the famine and the pestilence; the dragons will grow fat upon their corpse.

11:14 Their cities will be laid to waste and their once great nation will be a den for jackals

11:15 Of those that survive, they will be cast to the heathens that they whored themselves to; they shall be beaten in the fields and raped in their beds.

11:16 All this I shall do because their fathers did not obey my demands for genocide; all this because I hate them.

11:17 All this because I led them to it; I planned the destruction of Israel since the days of the covenant."

11:18 Thus I knew that my kin were fucked and that none will truly escape the horrors and the torments that is the spoiled brat which is God.

12:1 The lord then came to me, saying, "Gaze upon the prophets of Israel, who speak of the mercies of the lord, the kindness of my heart and how I shall bring unto them salvation to the righteous.

12:2 I have sent to them false visions of hope and love, so that they will spread lies throughout the people of Israel.

12:3 Know that the people will hearken their words and be hostile to your tongue, O Ezekiel the true prophet.

12:4 These false prophets are cursed with foolishness; they yowl without meaning like the fox in the desert.

12:5 They are men of vanity and lies, who value beauty, wealth, morality and peace.

12:6 Because they speak words of morality and not the words of God, they will suffer mostly from the violence they refuse to speak.

12:7 And as the anger of the lord comes, they will hide behind the walls of the strong cities; they shall flock to Jerusalem and believe them self safe from my wrath.

12:8 I will break down the walls of the cities, so that the very foundation crumble: and those behind the wall will be consumed in the midst thereof and know that I am God.

12:9 My wrath shall be accomplished on the wall and I will cause suffer greatly to those who laid the mortar and the stone upon the wall.

12:10 The prophets will gaze upon my face and they will weep, for the words they spoke to the congregation of Israel will be a lie."

12:11 The lord then spoke and said to me, "Curse be to the women that sew pillows, for the pillow weakens the soul of men.

12:12 The head of man is strong and needs not soft cloth for comfort.

12:13 The lord hates pillows and silk sheets. Those who seek comfort in pillows and silk sheets will be raped by the wolves of hell!"

12:14 I then burned my pillows and sheets and slept on a mattress of cacti; the lord was pleased.

13:1 The elders of Israel came to me and sat before me.

13:2 And the word of the lord came to me, saying,

13:3 "Look at these men, how they come to thee in hopes of begging forgiveness from the one true God.

13:4 Speak to them the words I shall tell you and know that you speak falsely.

13:5 Say unto them, thus sayeth the lord, turn away from your idols, your images and your false gods and worship the one who led you away from the servitude of Egypt.

13:6 Repent your sins, your iniquities, your abominations; repent and know that the lord will forgive you your transgressions.

13:7 For every man who holds an idol in his heart, they blasphemy the name of the lord; for every man who calls a stranger neighbour, they anger the lord.

13:8 Burn all images and slay those not of the seed of Abraham; a massive genocide of blood and fire will appease the lord and gain you forgiveness.

13:9 Deny this and the lord will cut you off from the chosen; when the day of reckoning comes, they shall be thrown into the void of hell and they shall know that I am the lord.

13:10 Hearken not the words of the false prophet, who speak of the mercies of the lord; the lord has sent them a false vision and shall destroy them greatly for believing this lie.

13:11 They should know when the lord deceives them; they have been given a test and failed.

13:12 For their foolishness they shall bear the weight of the sins of Judah; the punishment of them will be tenfold those who seek their deceitful tongue.

13:13 Disregard the word of God and ignore the demand for genocide, then know that you have sinned grievously against the holiest of holies; he shall break the earth which holds your bread and send famine and beasts to your house.

13:14 Your suffering will be as great as Job, and shall be never-ending.

13:15 Noisome beasts will pass through the night, with a howl so fierce even the mightiest of men shall dampen their skirts.

13:16 Their teeth will be swords of sharp silver and their jaws will gnaw through the land, cutting man, woman and child.

13:17 Pestilence will flow through the nations; rivers will run dry and wells will bring forth the blood of serpents.

13:18 And as you fall dead, you shall know that I am the lord, for only the lord will send such hardships to his people."

14:1 The lord came to me drunk; he would not leave me alone.

14:2 He said, "Son of, whoever the hell your mother was, nobody cares.

14:3 Tell me, what makes the vine tree better than the other. What makes the orchard better than the forest?

14:4 Though that of the vine produces the grape and that of the orchard produces fruit, they are both made of the wood and both burn hot with fire.

14:5 Know that Judah was once the vineyard and Israel the orchard of God; how they produced fruits once sweet, though now they rot.

14:6 I will burn them in the fires of hell, so that they know that I am the lord!"

14:7 God then vomited upon my head and passed out in a puddle of his own piss.

14:8 Glory be to God.

15:1 And the lord came to bitch and he said,

15:2 "Hearken my words, Ezekiel and you shall know the abominations of Jerusalem.

15:3 They bathe in the waters of heathens; their lands were of Canaan, their father an Amorite and their mother a Hittite.

15:4 On the day of their birth the cord was not cut, nor were they washed of the filth of their mother; they were not salted nor swaddled.

15:5 None of the other gods shown compassion unto them; their eyes lacked pity and compassion.

15:6 Yet when the one true God walked by, I did bathe them from your blood and cut thee from your mother's womb.

15:7 I gave them life and caused their seed to spread across the fields; lo, their hair has grown and their breasts bound in the linens of God, where before they were bare to the world.

15:8 When I saw Abraham and how he loved the lord, I covered him with my skirt, so that he may know the loins of God; I swore unto him and entered with him the holy covenant.

15:9 Then I washed you away the blood and anointed you with sweet perfume and oils.

15:10 I clothed you also with embroidered work and dressed you with the skins of deer and robes of fine silks.

15:11 I gave you ornaments of gold; bracelets, earrings, crowns and chains, so that all know you have bling, and all know you are the chosen people of God.

15:12 You were decked with silver and gold, with a raiment of fine linen and silk; you ate honey and flour baked with oils.

15:13 You became known to all as a wealthy nation, most beautiful of all men.

15:14 Yet you abused your beauty and played the diseased harlot.

15:15 You did take your gold and your silver and made images of men and you had these images rape your daughters and sodomize your sons.

15:16 Your fine raiment's you did tear and made with them pillows for the brothels; the oil you blasphemed and made into incense, burned to the false gods that once ignored you.

15:17 Even your meat, your honey and your flour you did give to the poor: the poor who were cursed by God to die in hunger.

15:18 Lo, even your sons and your daughters you have forced into whoredoms, so that they sacrifice to the heathen lords and lie in bed with strangers.

15:19 How you have caused them to pass through the fire, teaching them the unholy magic, the mapping of the stars, wizardry, witchcraft and fortune seeking.

15:20 In all these sins, these whoredoms, you have forgotten the mercies of your God, who led you away from Egypt and delivered you into the lands of milk and honey.

15:21 How he protected you from evil and swiftly brought you to the lands of the covenant; how the journey was peaceful and the lord gave you forever comfort.

15:22 In your lust, your whoredoms, how you have forgotten the nakedness of your youth and the mercies of the lord of Israel.

15:23 You hast built temples to idols and created high places in every street.

15:24 Is there not a false lord you did not worship. How you have spread your thighs to every man who has walked by; your vagina is a barrel full of the stranger's seed.

15:25 Even those of Egypt, who placed you under a heavy yoke, did you whore yourselves to; how you enjoyed their massive loins and angered the lord God in your lust.

15:26 Behold, for this I have stretched out my hand over you and have taken away the flesh from your table; I delivered you into the hands of the Philistine, where even their daughters mock your lewd ways.

15:27 Still your insatiable whoredom was not satisfied; you fucked the Philistines, the Assyrians, the Canaanites and the Chaldeans.

15:28 There is not a nation who is ignorant to the bed of Israel.

15:29 How weak you are, O people of Israel, seeing as you do these things like the drunken whorish woman.

15:30 You were the people of God, the holy nation. Now you erect temples to heathen lords and have high places on every street.

15:31 Now you are like the wife who take strangers in the bed of her husband and takes from them gifts of perfume, linens and the unholy thing.

15:32 Despicable harlot. Hear the words of God!

15:33 Because these nations have spread their filthiness upon you and have discovered the pleasures of your flesh; how you whored yourselves to idols and given your children to the evil men.

15:34 Behold, I will gather all your lovers before you and strip you of your raiment's, so that they all see your horrid nakedness, your filth.

15:35 And I shall punish you greater than the woman who dwells in the house as the blood sheds from her loins; I shall give you terrors and torments greater than the deepest bowels of hell!

15:36 Your lovers will be disgusted by your nakedness and take from you your jewels, your silver, your gold.

15:37 Their children will cast stones upon you and their fathers will thrust you with the sharp blade.

15:38 And they shall burn you within your houses and rape your daughters in the streets; how they will know the pain you once pleasured in as the harlot.

15:39 And when the last of Israel lay dead and the earth consumed in fire, then shall the lord rest and be angry no more."

16:1 The lord came to me in the night, drunk like the heathen sailor and intoxicated by the fumes of mystical herbs.

16:2 And he said unto me, "I have a riddle for you to put forth to the nation of Israel.

16:3 A great eagle with great wings, full of feathers with many colours, came to Lebanon and took the branch from the highest cedar.

16:4 He tore off the twigs of the cedar and carried it into the lands of merchants.

16:5 He took also the seed of the cedar and placed it in the fruitful field; he placed it by the nourishing waters and set it as a willow tree.

16:6 The seed grew and become a twisting vine of low stature, whose branches embraced him and roots dug beneath him: so it became a vine, which shot forth sprigs and knotted branches.

16:7 There was yet another eagle, with great feathers and great wings: and behold this vine did shoot its branches towards it, that he might water it by the rivers of his plantation.

16:8 These branches became planted by good soil, with fresh waters and it brought forth branches that bared fruit.

16:9 Tell me, shall the lord not rip the plant from its roots, so that it whither and turn brown. Shall the leaves turn brown and burn in the midday sun?

16:10 Or shall the lord let the plant flourish, so that it grows sweet fruits of the vine, sweet fruits of intoxication?

16:11 For the lord will tear the plant from its roots and cause it to lay in the desert, where it will wither, rot and burn under the heat of the sun."

16:12 I told those of Israel this riddle and none understood it. Neither did I, for the lord never bothered explaining.

17:1 Moreover, the lord continued to speak, saying,

17:2 "Say now to the rebellious house, that I lead the king of Babylon to Jerusalem. He brings his princes, his armies and his greed.

17:3 I have made a covenant with those of the seed of Babylon and have taken their oath; they shall take your lands, your wealth and your people.

17:4 Your once mighty kingdom I will deliver into the hands of Babylon, so that they become the great nation under the one true God.

17:5 Though they worship images of false lords, they have not betrayed me like those of the seed of Abraham; how you have dug the blade deep in my back and rebelled strong against me.

17:6 Those of Egypt prepare to war, with their mighty men, their horses, their chariots. Shall they prosper. Shall they be victorious against the armies I send to them?

17:7 The lord declares that the king of Judah who dwells in the house of David, in the city of Jerusalem, will live his last days in the lands of Nebuchadnezzar; this shall happen, for he broke the oath and rejected my covenant.

17:8 Neither will Pharaoh prosper against Babylon, with their mighty men, their strong company, their forts and their mounts.

17:9 Know this, O child of man, that the snare has been placed and those of Jerusalem will be brought forth to Babylon.

17:10 Those who reject their fate, who go against God with sword and mace, will fall on their blades and their skulls crushed under the blunt stone.

17:11 Babylon will prosper in the lands of milk and honey; they shall grow and bear fruit, for the lord declares it.

17:12 And when the filthy heathen flourish in the lands promised to you since the days of Abraham, you shall know that I am God."

18:1 Again, the lord came to me. The fucker just won't leave me alone.

18:2 He said, "Cursed are those of Israel, whose fathers have consumed the sour grape.

18:3 For their fathers have given their children the birthright of damnation.

18:4 Behold, the souls of the father and the souls of the son are mine; together they will forever rot in the bowels of hell.

18:5 Though a man be just and right, if his father was a wretch, both shall be dashed upon the rocks.

18:6 Even if the child has obeyed the laws of Moses, walked the holy path, turned a blind eye to the idols of false lords and kept his loins within the skirt of Israel, they shall forever burn in hell, for their father came near the openings of a menstruating woman.

18:7 Those sickening fools who oppress not the lesser men, who avoids their hands from violence, who give bread to the starving, who donates their wealth to charity, they shall boil in the pitch and the tar.

18:8 Men that enslaved their neighbours, slaughtered the heathen, whose hands are stained in the blood of genocide, who mock the hungry and oppress the poor, these are men of God and so as they sin not and their lineage be holy, they shall be granted salvation in Zion.

18:9 These are the men who have walked in my statutes and kept my judgments; they are men of a stone heart and iron fist.

18:10 Yet if his seed betrays him; if he begets a robber, a thief, a man of morals; then shall the seed destroy the father, forever placing him a seat in the eternal void.

18:11 Even the holiest of men, who have followed strictly the mouth of God; if they make but one transgression, their holy deeds will be stripped forever from the book of records and they shall fall forever into darkness.

18:12 Not one soul of man meets the restrictions of salvation; not one man will know the salvation promised unto them.

18:13 Let the world go to hell. They probably deserve it anyway."

19:1 "Who are they, these people of Israel, whom I have chosen for my people.

19:2 Were their mothers a lion. She laid down among the lions, she nourished her offspring like cubs.

19:3 Her young became lions; they stalked the weak, hunted the prey and devoured men.

19:4 Is your father the beast. He spread fear like the dragons.

19:5 His blade cast forth to the borders of the earth, spilling blood upon the ground, casting flesh to the satyrs.

19:6 Yet when the lion and the beast bred and begat a son, the son was weak and became consumed by the heathens.

19:7 The Egyptians beat them, the Assyrians enslaved them and they all polluted them with false gods, lustful women, the intoxication of wizardry and the morals of men.

19:8 Once a great nation of lions and beast, Israel has become weak and the lord despises the weak.

19:9 Why shall the lord not spare them. Why should the holy one not make rivers of their blood, where the vines of strong men may prosper?

19:10 Let the weak be consumed by the strong; such is the laws of the lord.

19:11 Bring forth the heathens to destroy the pathetic children; let them be wiped off the face of the earth, forgotten in the histories of God and men.

19:12 The sceptre of the lord will pass from one people to another; the children of lions and beasts cannot bear the weight of the sceptre, thus it must be passed to the mighty men."

20:1 It came to pass that on the seventh year, in the fifth month, on the tenth day of that month, that some of the elders of Israel came to speak about the lord with me.

20:2 And as they spoke to me, the spirit of the lord overtook my tongue and through me said,

20:3 "Thus sayeth the lord, why must you come to enquire about me. If you were obedient children of the lord, you would know me well.

20:4 I shall judge all of you harshly for the abominations of your fathers.

20:5 I say to you, on the day that I plucked Israel from the earth and lifted the seed of Jacob, I was drunk.

20:6 You are not worthy to be children of the one true God: now I am God to those I despise and wish destroyed.

20:7 I told you, cast away the abominations of the heathen and bow not to the idols of Egypt, for I am your God.

20:8 Still you rebelled against me and whored yourself to the graven images of lesser men. You bathed in the abomination and the filth and for this I shall wash you in the fire and the flame.

20:9 But my eye was pitied for you, as your fathers fell heavy under the yoke of Pharaoh; though you were polluted, I would cast you away from the filth, so that you may make yourself clean.

20:10 I set them free from the bog of Egypt and showed them my laws, my statutes and my commandments, so that they may live a righteous life.

20:11 I gave them also the sabbath, the most holy of days. This I did, so that they may rest and bask in the glory that is the lord.

20:12 Yet the house of Israel rebelled against me; they worked on the sabbath and defiled the most holy of days, they spared the blood of heathens, they took wives from the neighbouring nations, they studied the culture and the lords of the hated people.

20:13 Still I rested my hand before you and brought you to the lands flowing with milk and honey, where the pomegranates grow to the size of a man's skull.

20:14 Even when they rested in these lands I gave unto them and slaughtered those who dare live on the promised land before they got there, they defiled my sabbath, rebelled against my laws and took the images into their hearts.

20:15 My wrath boiled and my anger clashed like the violent sea, but I still spared them, for in time they shall grow to love the lord and bow before me.

20:16 You have not and have continued to ignore the holy laws, the statutes and the judgments I placed before you; you are a rebellious people and not worthy to be the children of the one true God.

20:17 Thus I snared you with polluted gifts, so that your children pass through the fire of the womb; you shall become desolate and then you shall know that I am the lord.

20:18 A great horror will come to those of Israel so strong that those who hear of it will have their ears tingle.

20:19 The skies will split apart, the sun glow red with the blood of infants and the fiery wrath of God shall descend upon you, consuming those in its path.

20:20 Mountains will melt like molten iron, seas will boil and the flesh of men will be kindling to the everlasting damnation of hell.

20:21 A fire strong, that seeks out the flesh of men; it shall never be quenched."

21::1 "Ezekiel, set your face towards Jerusalem and drop thy word to the wretched places, so that the blasphemous people listen and tremble in fear.

21:2 Say to those of Israel, Thus sayeth the lord; be afraid, for I am against you and shall draw my sword from my sheath, so that the righteous fall beside the wicked.

21:3 Even the flesh of the earth will be torn; my blade will stretch from the north to the south and sever all those of the seed of Jacob.

21:4 Loins will be split apart and men shall bleed like the menstruating woman.

21:5 Prophesy, O son of man, and say, Thus sayeth the lord, the sword is sharpened and also furbished:

21:6 It is sharpened to make a gruesome slaughter and furbished so that it shines in the bloodstain; it gives the lord mirth and fills me with joy.

21:7 Cry and howl, O people of the lord: let the sounds of lamentations fill the heavens and please the ears of God.

21:8 Let the princes of Israel cry like the tormented child, ripped from his mother's breast and tossed into the den of lions; the lord smites you and it gives him great pleasure.

21:9 The sword will strike you plenty; it shall come upon you again, again and again, even unto the slain it shall come again.

21:10 Into your chambers it will strike, even unto your most secret places.

21:11 I have set the point of the sword against your foundation, so that they fall and your ruin be multiplied: how it shines bright in the blood of your children, whose flesh wrap around the blade.

21:12 Run to the left, run to the right, it matters not; none will escape the sharpened blade of the lord, which thirsts for the slaughter, the blood, the genocide of all men.

21:13 My hands will smite together and crush the earth in my palms. Thus sayeth the lord."

21:14 The lord continued to speak, saying,

21:15 "Son of man, know that the sword goes two ways and it comes sheathed in the armies of Babylon; it comes to Rabbath of the Ammonites and to the city of Jerusalem.

21:16 For the king of Babylon knows the wizardry of the hidden and split his armies in two; he has consulted with the dead, made his arrows bright and gazed deeply into the liver of the beast.

21:17 To his right lay the divination of Jerusalem, ripe and fattened for the slaughter; he lifts his voice in shouting, appoints battering rams to the gates and places forts upon the borders.

21:18 And to the children of Jerusalem will come a false divination; a vision of hope and mercy sent by God, so that they may stay and be slaughtered by the strength of Babylon.

21:19 To the left are the Ammonites; the sword is drawn for their slaughter and glitters brightly in their viscera.

21:20 Those of the children of Amon seek forth vanity and hide a deceitful tongue beneath their lips; they are of wicked men, whose necks will be stretched for the slaying.

21:21 Never will the sword be sheathed, never will the blade know rest until the children of Amon drown in the pools of blood which lie within their dwelling place.

21:22 I will pour out my hatred upon them, I will blow against you the fires of my wrath and deliver them into the hands of brutish beasts, devils and wicked cherubims.

21:23 They shall be the spark that brings forth the fires of damnation; they shall be remembered no more, for the lord hath spoken it."

22:1 The lord continued to speak for me, for he is a very talkative God.

22:2 A pity he has nothing pleasant to say.

22:3 He said, "Go now and judge the city drenched in the menstrual cloth. Show unto them the abominations.

22:4 The city with sheds blood upon itself and rapes themselves with the graven images of false lords.

22:5 You hast become guilty in your blasphemous lust and have defiled yourself with the stones of your idols; you have caused the ends of days to come near, where the righteous and the heathen burn together and all the lands of earth become ablaze in dark fire.

22:6 Know that when the lesser nations mock you, that the day of infamy is near and the curse of God descends from the heavens.

22:7 Behold, the princes of Israel will bleed from their loins and their skirts be soaked in their unholy blood.

22:8 Your mother and your father eat thee in half and eat of your marrow, your liver, your heart and your flesh.

22:9 This shall be, for you have despised my holiness and kept not the sabbath day.

22:10 You have discovered the flesh of your father such as Ham discovered of Noah; you have polluted the sons of Israel.

22:11 You have slept with the harlot of your neighbour's wife, defiled the skirts of your daughter in law, taken the virginity of your sister.

22:12 In your lust you have become filthy and the stench of the people of Israel make sick the lord God.

22:13 How long can I endure the wretchedness of Israel. Why must the lord tolerate such rot upon his earth?

22:14 I will scatter you to the heathens and disperse you in the strange and foreign countries; there they shall beat the filth out of you.

22:15 And your inheritance will go to the wicked, the stranger, the lesser men."

22:16 Still, the lord continued to speak and depress me deeply with his words.

22:17 He said, "Son of man, one named Ezekiel, prophesy against those of Israel.

22:18 Those of the impure will be molten from the children of Jacob; they are as the dross of tin, of lead, of silver, of iron, of lead.

22:19 I have molten them and they have become all dross.

22:20 As the metallist gathers the silver, the brass, the lead, the tin, the iron in the midst of the furnace, so shall I gather Israel in my anger and fury and blow fire upon them and leave them to melt.

22:21 All of Israel and all of Judah will gather in the furnace and melt hot against the wrath of the almighty God.

22:22 And as they melt and drown in the wasteful dross, they shall know that I am the lord."

22:23 Still, the lord continued to ramble like the drunken fool, saying,

22:24 "Tell them also that the land is not cleansed, nor rain come upon the day of indignation.

22:25 I have sent a conspiracy to the prophets, so that they become like the roaring lion which devours the prey; they devour the souls of Israel with soft words and a pleasant tongue.

22:26 Priests of Israel have defiled the temple and sleep atop the altar with young boys of strange mothers.

22:27 Princes and kings defile themselves to idols, jackals and wolves; they seek counsel in stone, scavengers and beasts.

22:28 I have sought in my people a blessed man, stained not in the temptation of evil; a righteous man to giveth the lord hope for Israel: yet I have found none.

22:29 Though I have found men of righteous hearts, the sins of their fathers have stained with filth, thus they are wicked in the eyes of God.

22:30 Thus my anger will pour unto all the children of Jacob and consume them all with the horror, the damnation and the wrath.

22:31 I shall rape those of Israel and Judah, for they have become wicked in the sight of God."

23:1 The lord then told me a story of incest, lesbians and violence.

23:2 He said to me, "Son of man, there were once two women, sisters born of the same mother.

23:3 They were the filthiest of whores in the lands of Egypt; they pressed their breasts together until their teats be bruised and loins rubbed against one another with soft moans.

23:4 Their names were Aholah the elder and Aholibah the sister: and they were mine and they bared sons and daughters. Thus were their names, Aholah of Samaria and Aholibah of Jerusalem.

23:5 Aholah played the harlot when she belonged to me; she was lustful unto her lovers the Assyrians, her neighbours.

23:6 Men dressed in blue, captains and rulers, all of them desirable and young; even unto the horses her whorish tongue was defiled.

23:7 She committed whoredoms with all the men of Assyria; even unto the idols she spread her feet apart.

23:8 The harlot brought her whoredoms out of Egypt: for in her youth they lay with her and beat her breasts and spilled their seed upon her face.

23:9 Thus I have delivered her into the hands of her lovers the Assyrians, who she wished to please with her diseased loins.

23:10 They discovered the stench beneath her skirts: they enslaved her sons and raped her daughters and slew her with the sword: and she became infamous among the woman for her whoredoms.

23:11 Her sister Aholibah was more corrupt than she and multiplied her whoredoms greatly.

23:12 She doted upon the Assyrians greatly, all men both rich and poor. She spread her legs to those who passed by and they lusted deeply unto her.

23:13 She increased her whoredoms unto the Assyrians, the Philistines, the Chaldeans, the horses, the dragons and even unto the vermin.

23:14 Of princes her loins became wet; of beggars her mouth gaped open and consumed their uncircumcised flesh.

23:15 And the men of Babylon came into her bed and defiled her greatly; even unto her bowels they defiled her and dropped their seed.

23:16 She gazed into the mirror and discovered her whoredoms; she became proud of them and flaunted her brothel greatly.

23:17 She doted upon the priests of Babylon, whose flesh hung low like the asses, the donkeys, the bulls.

23:18 Soon she remembered the whoredoms of her youth, the bruising of her teats by the hands of the Egyptians.

23:19 How her skirt grew moist for those days and how her dampness spread to the lands of her fathers, defiling the very soil.

23:20 Therefore, O Aholibah, thus sayeth the lord; behold, your lovers shall rise against you from all sides and come against you with chariot and sword.

23:21 The Babylonians, the Chaldeans, Pekod, Koa and Shoa and all Assyrians will march with spear and sword, riding atop mighty horses.

23:22 They will come with chariots, wagons and wheels, bringing with them their armies and their mercenaries; they come with buckler, shield and helmet: and they will set judgment before you.

23:23 And I will set my jealousy against you and they shall deal cruelly with you: they tear from you your nose and your ears and your breast will fall on the sword: they shall tear the flesh from your children and burn your remains in fire.

23:24 They shall strip you of your raiment and take away your jewels.

23:25 For thus sayeth the lord, I shall deliver you into the hands whom I hate, whose children I have alienated from Zion.

23:26 And they shall deal with you furiously and tear from you the seed which grows in your womb, leaving you naked and bare in the wilderness: and your nakedness and whoredoms will be made public to the nations of the earth.

23:27 I will cause these things to you because I hate you, and I am God.

23:28 You have walked in the ways of your sister and drank of the cheap wine of her chalice.

23:29 You shall drink of the wine and your spirit be filled with drunkenness and sorrow with the intoxication of Samaria.

23:30 You shalt drink of the cup, break the vessel, eat of the shards and tear off your breasts, screaming like the beast of the night, sayeth the lord God.

23:31 Because you have forgotten me and multiplied thy whoredoms greatly, I shall make your lewdness known to all, so that all the earth hiss at you.

23:32 Of those who once shared in your bed shall now curse your name and ready the noose around your neck.

23:33 The gathering of children will come to throw stones at you and mock the crust beneath your skirts.

23:34 Men will gaze at you with hatred and the women will loathe you with a fiery hatred.

23:35 And the lord will send his wrath upon you and consume you in the fires of hell: and the earth shall rejoice and gaze at the burning of the harlot."

24:1 Again in the ninth year, in the tenth month, on the tenth day of that month, the lord came to me and said,

24:2 "Ezekiel son of Buzi, write the name of this day, even unto this day: the king of Babylon shall set himself against Israel on this day.

24:3 And utter a parable into the rebellious house and say unto them, Thus sayeth the lord, set a pot of water upon the altar, until the water boil.

24:4 Take of the finest of your flock and set in the pot the choicest meats; the thigh, the shoulder and all the bones.

24:5 Burn the remnants of the flock in the fires beneath, so that they burn the boiling pot.

24:6 Then say unto them, the lord God speaks. Woe to the bloody city, the pot full of scum and rot.

24:7 Your flesh will come out, piece by piece and your bones will roast in the fires of Babylon.

24:8 Hated is the city of Jerusalem. I will make the pile for fire great beneath her feet.

24:9 Heap on kindling and log, consume the flesh, spice it well and let the bones be burned.

24:10 Set the ladle deep in the pot, and savour the scum of your filth; consume it, waste not a drop."

24:11 The lord then spoke to me again, saying,

24:12 "Son of man, tonight I shall take away your desire, your love, for tonight I will take your wife from the earth.

24:13 Know that she will descend into the crevices of hell, where all women belong; she shall weep for you, but you must not weep for her.

24:14 Do not mourn her, nor let the tears run down your cheek.

24:15 Make no burial for her, nor wear the sackcloth. Bury her not in the earth, but let the scavengers tear at her flesh."

24:16 Thus my wife died that night and I mourned not for her, nor buried her, but did as the lord demanded and let her lie in the fields for the jackals to consume her.

24:17 And at that moment, I really fucking hated God.

25:1 The lord interrupted my supper, so that he may say to me,

25:2 "Son of man, set your face against the Ammonites and prophesy against these wicked men.

25:3 And say unto the Ammonites, listen to the word of God: because you have profaned my sanctuary and fought against the land of Israel and Judah;

25:4 Behold, I shall deliver you to the men of the east, who shall dwell in your palaces and sleep in your beds; they shall eat of your fruit and drink of the breasts of your mothers.

25:5 I will make Rabbah a stable for the camels and the lands of Ammon will be covered in the filth of swine; this shall happen and you shall know that I am the motherfucking lord.

25:6 For thus sayeth the lord; Because you have fought against the children of Abraham and rejoiced in the suffering of Judah;

25:7 I will stretch my hand before you and deliver you to the lands of heathens. I will cut you off from the people and cause you to live like beasts. I will destroy you with a divine hatred and then you shall know that I am God.

25:8 How dare you fight against the children of Israel and wish them destroyed. How dare you wish to steal the fun meant for God.

25:9 It is the lord who shall slaughter the seed of Jacob and cause them to fall in the crevices of hell, not mortal men!

25:10 For this, you are hated and God will kill you all.

25:11 Thus sayeth the lord; Because Moab and Seir did pollute the people of Judah with the heathen filth;

25:12 Therefore I shall open the jaws of the earth, so that they consume the cities of Bethjeshimoth, Baalmeon and Kiriathaim.

25:13 Your wives will be crushed under the earthen jaw and your children stuck in the gaps of the gnashing teeth.

25:14 And when this judgment of Moab be executed upon them, they shall gaze into the heavens and know that I am the lord.

25:15 Thus sayeth the lord still; Because the children of Edom have pressed their blades into the belly of Judah and taken vengeance upon them;

25:16 I will stretch out my hand unto them, so that the beasts with claws of daggers come and cut the very flesh from them; I will make it desolate from Teman: and they of Dedan will fall atop the sword.

25:17 Thus sayeth the lord more: Because the Philistines have dealt harshly against the beloved king of David and despise Israel with an old hatred;

25:18 I will raise the very coast of the sea above them, so that they drown in the house of the Leviathan.

25:19 And when they drown under the heavy waters, they shall know that I am the lord.

25:20 When all the world feels the wrath and torment of God, they shall all know that I am the lord and there is no other before me."

26:1 It came to pass that on the eleventh year, in the first day of the first month, that I thought the lord God would finally leave me alone.

26:2 I was wrong, for he came to me and said,

26:3 "Ezekiel, hearken my words, for they are the words of God.

26:4 Because Tyrus has spoken ill against Jerusalem and claimed her gates broken and the lands waste for the dragons:

26:5 Therefore the lord is against you, O Tyrus and will cause the nations of earth to come against you; like the waves crash against the shore, they shall come against you.

26:6 Your walls will be destroyed and your towers reduced to ash; I will grind them to dust against the rock of my foundation.

26:7 The nets spread out in your seas will be the spoils of heathens, for I have spoken it; they shall take your fish, your sails and your ships.

26:8 And your daughters will be raped in the fields by the sharpened blade, so that the lord may smile at the sound of their cries.

26:9 Behold, I will bring upon Tyrus Nebuchadnezzar king of Babylon, a true king from the north, with horses, chariots, horsemen, armies and mighty men.

26:10 He shall make bloody your fields and erect forts against you and cast the mount against you and lift the blade against you.

26:11 With the war engines he will tear down your walls and with axes and hammer he shall break down your towers.

26:12 The abundance of his horses will cause your lands to tremble, your walls to shake; his chariots will cause even the mountains to cower in fear.

26:13 With the hoofs of his horses he will trample upon you; he shall slaughter your sons with the blade and garrison you strong round about.

26:14 All the spoils of your riches will go to the strength of Babylon and your sons will be hunted as prey; they shall break down your walls and burn your brothels of queer men: and they shall cast the very foundation of your city in the violent waters.

26:15 Your gay noise, your singing, the sound of your harps will cease and be heard no more.

26:16 You shall be no more and your cities will be laid to waste, so says the lord.

26:17 Your isles will fall and be lost forever in the waters of the torrents; they shall tremble and drown.

26:18 Even the princes of the sea will come to your lands and they shall rent their clothes and weep in fear of the almighty lord.

26:19 They shall take up a lamentation for you and beg to the lord that their cities be spared and their nations shown mercy.

26:20 With the terror that comes upon you, the nations of earth will fear the lord; they shall seek your isles and find you not, for you shall be no more, so says the lord."

27:1 The word of the lord came to me again, saying,

27:2 "Prophesy, O son of man and take up a lamentation for Tyrus;

27:3 And say to them, O how you are made rich with the entry of the sea and become merchants for those beyond the waters; Thus sayeth the lord God, you have become vain in your beauty.

27:4 You have made your ships of the firs of Senir and taken the cedars of Lebanon for masts.

27:5 Of the oaks of Bashan are your oars carved and your benches made of the ivory from Chittim.

27:6 Fine linens from Egypt have become your sails, which dance in the wind blue and purple.

27:7 The inhabitants of Zidon and Arvad are proud to be your marines, who uses the night sky to pilot your vessels.

27:8 They of Persia, of Lud and Phut served in your armies as men of war: they hanged their helmets in your barracks and shed their blood for you.

27:9 The men of Arvad guarded your borders and the Gammadims were in your towers: they hanged their shields round about your walls and marvelled at your beauty.

27:10 Tarshish was made rich with the wealth of the seas: abundant with silver, iron, tin, lead, furs, spices and fruits.

27:11 Jarvan, Tubal and Meshech were your merchants: they traded with these slaves, beasts and fair maidens.

27:12 Those of the house of Togarmah traded with you their horses, horsemen and mules.

27:13 The men of Dedan brought to you ebony, ivory and horns of the wild beast.

27:14 Syria traded with you the multitude of your wares: they filled your warehouses with emeralds, embroidered works, silks, purple linen, coral and agate.

27:15 Even the children of Jacob, Judah and Israel, traded with you and gave to you your wheat, honey, oil and balm.

27:16 Damascus was your merchant, exchanging with you wine, white wool and gold.

27:17 Dan also and Javan travelled to you and brought with them bright iron, cassia, calamus, raiment's and chariots.

27:18 The Arabian princes of Kedar brought with them their flocks of lambs, goats and rams for your merchants.

27:19 Merchants of Sheba and Raamah came forth and traded with you their spices, their precious stones and their gold.

27:20 Of blue clothes, embroidered works and chests of cedar bound with cord came from the men of Haran, Canneh, Eden, Sheba, Asshur and Chilmad.

27:21 Know that all these nations, who come to your ports for trade, will come to loathe at you and hiss at you with a powerful hate.

27:22 For all your wealth and all your vanity shall not purchase the mercy of God; he shall come down with a terrible wrath and make you no more."

28:1 Once again the lord interrupted me and said,

28:2 "Ezekiel, go now and speak to the prince of Tyrus, saying, thus sayeth the lord God; Because your heart is lifted with your wealth and you seek forth control of the earth, you have become an enemy to the lord.

28:3 Your wizards are wiser than Daniel: there is no secret which can be hidden from you.

28:4 With your wisdom and knowledge you have obtained the riches of the earth and have been given gold, silver and treasures.

28:5 By your great wisdom and wealth you seek forth the powers of the earth; you seek forth power with a great hunger and wish to become like a god.

28:6 This cannot happen, for none shall come to have the powers of the lord, lest they challenge me and win.

28:7 Thus I will bring forth strangers upon you, the most terrible of nations: and they shall scar your beauty and your wisdom with the sword and defile your knowledge.

28:8 They shall bring you down to the shores of the sea and feed you to the serpents of the waters.

28:9 And as you are slaughtered by the beast men, you shall say to them, I am a god who has divine powers.

28:10 Bow unto me and be spared my wrath.

28:11 They shall not listen, for the lord has put a stone in their ears; you shall die the death of the uncircumcised by the hands of strangers: for I have spoken it and I am the one true God."

28:12 Still the lord spoke and said to me,

28:13 "Take up a lamentation upon the king of Tyrus and say to him, thus sayeth the lord God; you have knowledge of the hidden, became wise of the ways of the lord and became perfect in your beauty.

28:14 Y have travelled to Eden, the garden of God and stole from it every precious stone, every topaz, every diamond, every beryl, every onyx, every jasper, every sapphire, every emerald, every ruby, every carbuncle, the silver and the gold.

28:15 You have walked atop the stones of fire and tricked the guardians of Eden with your tongue; you have eaten of the fruits of the forbidden trees and gained knowledge, power and eternal life.

28:16 With your wisdom you have gained the wealth of many nations and became the pinnacle of all men: now you wish to become a god and place your dwelling among the stars.

28:17 You, a child born of flesh, challenge the one true God and have become a threat.

28:18 This cannot come true, for it makes the lord appear weak and foolish.

28:19 Thus the lord has poisoned you with the wines of Damascus, brewed from the bunches of a poisonous grape.

28:20 With the earth as witness, you shall perish horribly by the wrath of God, and cease to be, so says the lord."

28:21 You would think the lord would be done by now, but he still had more to say.

28:22 "Ezekiel, set your face against Zidon and prophesy against it.

28:23 Say to them, thus sayeth the lord: behold, I am against you, O Zidon and will execute you with glory and bloodshed: you shall know that I am God when my hand strikes against you.

28:24 I will send pestilence upon you and your streets will flow with the rivers of your blood; your mighty men will be thrust on the sword to each side of you and you shall know the horrors of the lord.

28:25 This I shall do because I find your women ugly; their breasts sag below their belly and they grow hair like the apes.

28:26 That's it, the only reason. Ugly women. I the lord am that vain and bloodthirsty, so fuck you Zidon and fuck you to all the nations of the earth!"

29:1 In the tenth year, in the tenth month, of the twelfth day of the month, the lord descended upon the earth and defiled my bowels with his loins.

29:2 He then said to me, "Bitch, set your face against Pharaoh and prophesy against him and all those of Egypt.

29:3 Speak and say, thus sayeth the lord God; Behold, I am against you, Pharaoh king of Egypt, the great dragon which slumbers beneath the Nile.

29:4 Lo, I will place hooks in your jaws and cause the blades of Zion to be thrust beneath your scales, so that the fish of the Nile feast of your blood.

29:5 I will thrust you from the Nile and leave thee to rot in the desert: you shall fall upon the open sands, hot and dry: I have given you as meat to the fowls of the heavens and the jackals of the earth.

29:6 And all those of Egypt will know that I am the lord, for I bring a curse greater than the ten plagues of Moses.

29:7 Your mighty men will stand before me and I shall bring forth the harlots so that their loins be made standing.

29:8 Then shall the sword of God come down upon your flesh and make you a nation of menstrual women; your men and your beasts will be removed from you.

29:9 Behold, all the lands of Egypt will become desolate and waste: and you shall know that I am the lord, for I have made your rivers barren.

29:10 From the towers of Syene even unto the borders of Ethiopia shall be barren, so that not even the locust dwell within it.

29:11 No foot of man shall step upon it, nor beast pass through it; it shall be uninhabited until the end of days.

29:12 Not even the neighbouring nations will come to claim the lands of Egypt, for the cities have become dust, the wealth unclean, the air venomous.

29:13 A cursed land it shall be, forever void of life even when the fires of hell consume the four corners of the earth."

30:1 Hey. Guess what. The lord came to me, again.

30:2 He didn't say anything important, but if I had to listen to it, you have to read it.

30:3 The bastard said, "Prophesy, O son of man and say, thus sayeth the lord God; howl like the wolf, for the day of woe has come.

30:4 The day of the lord draws near, when the black cloud descends upon us and the heathen.

30:5 A mighty sword will come upon Egypt and the great pain will befall the people of Ethiopia; the slain will fall in Egypt and they

shall take away her multitude and tear down her foundation.

30:6 Ethiopia, Libya, Lydia, Chub and the mingled people within Egypt will be slain beside the people of Pharaoh, for they were in league with the men of Rah.

30:7 They also that uphold Egypt will fall and the tower of Syene shall fall by the sword, so says the lord.

30:8 Her countries will become most desolate in the lands of desolate nations and her cities will be laid to waste by the dragons.

30:9 Behold, they shall know that I am the lord, when I set a fire in Egypt and burn all those who aided her.

30:10 In that day the people of Ethiopia will fall with pain, frothing at the mouth like the dogs of hell.

30:11 Thus sayeth the lord God; I shall send forth Nebuchadnezzar king of Babylon to come and cease those of the people of Egypt.

30:12 He and his people with him, a most terrible of men, shall be brought to the lands of the Nile; they shall draw their swords and till the lands with the slain, the blood, the rotting corpse.

30:13 Your rivers will become dry and the lands be sold to the hands of demons: and I will make your lands a waste, so that not even the stranger wish to claim it: the lord has spoken it.

30:14 I will destroy also the idols, the false lords, my sons, so that there be no graven image, no prince, no priest of Egypt; a great fear will spread through the lands, for they will truly be a godless nation.

30:15 Pathros will become desolate and a great fire will be set in Zoan and the judgment of the lord will fall heavy upon No.

30:16 My wrath will pour thick upon the strength of Egypt and the multitude of No will be cut from the face of the earth.

30:17 The young men of Aven and Pibeseth will fall by the sword, whilst their sisters are raped in the brothels, the barracks, the fields of war.

30:18 No more will the sun rise upon Egypt; it shall an eternal moonless night, with the stars made dark by the firmament of the lord.

30:19 Your mighty men will be butchered like the swine and your daughters sold to at auction to the wealthiest of perverse beasts.

30:20 I have broken the arms of Pharaoh king of Egypt and never shall it be bound to heal, so that it never become strong to carry the sword and the shield.

30:21 Once mighty arms of Egypt will drop their reigns and their blades from their hands, so that their chariots run wild and the blades be buried in the dust.

30:22 All of Egypt will be scattered throughout the nations, dispersed through the other countries of lesser men.

30:23 Though the arms of Pharaoh are crippled, the arms of Babylon become strong and grasp the sword of God. They shall sever the head of Egypt, so that the ravens peck at the scalp.

30:24 And when the nation of Egypt be crippled and die under the yokes of the strange nation, they shall know that I am God and I am cruel."

31:1 It happened again, that on the eleventh year, on the third month, of the first day of that month, that God came forth and spoke to me yet again, saying,

31:2 "Ezekiel, speak to the multitudes of Egypt and to Pharaoh their king.

31:3 Tell them God will kill them all, so that none of them be left."

31:4 And that was it. It was a very short conversation.

32:1 Now on the twelfth year, in the twelfth month, on the first day of that month, the lord came to me, saying,

32:2 "Go now and take up a lamentation for Pharaoh the king of Egypt and say unto him, you are like a young lion of the nations and the whales of the seas: you came forth with your rivers and disturbed the waters.

32:3 Thus sayeth the lord God: a nation of heathens will cast forth their nets and bring you forth from the rivers in which you dwell.

32:4 Then I will leave you upon the open fields, where the fowl of the heavens and the beasts of the earth will come and grow fat upon your bloated carcass.

32:5 Your flesh will cover the mountains and valleys will flow with your blood.

32:6 And on this the day of your destruction, I will cover the heavens with a curtain, so that the sun be covered and the moon deny you her light.

32:7 Only the fires of my wrath will give you light, so says the lord God.

32:8 I will curse the hearts of many people when I bring my destruction upon the nations, into the countries you have not known.

32:9 Yea, I will make people tremble before me and cause them to soil their skirts when I brandish my sword before them and strip them of their life.

32:10 For thus sayeth the lord God; the sword of Babylon marches towards you.

32:11 By the swords of this terrible nation will the multitude of Egypt fall: and they shall spoil the wealth of Egypt and grow fat upon her riches.

32:12 Even the beasts of Egypt will not be shown mercy, for I shall drench the soil with their blood and cause the rivers to flow crimson.

32:13 When I make the lands of Egypt desolate and the country destitute, when I smite you and all those who dwell within, then you shall know that I am God."

32:14 On the twelfth year, in the twelfth month, on the fifteenth day of that month, the lord came to me and said,

32:15 "Wail for the multitude of Egypt and cast them down, even her and the daughters of her neighbouring nations, unto the nether parts of the earth, into the deepest pit.

32:16 That which was once beautiful will be made ugly, forced to lay beside the graves of the uncircumcised.

32:17 They will be drawn to the sword as flies to the steaming dung.

32:18 The strong and the mighty will cry in agony amidst the torments of hell; they lie down amongst the uncircumcised in the lake of fire.

32:19 Their lords will be there and all their company, buried beneath the unmarked graves of the damned, the cursed, the hated.

32:20 During their times amongst the living I have caused them great terrors: and during the days of their death I will give them such horrors to so that they seek they believe themselves not dead, but in the dreams of the frightening.

32:21 This it shall be, for the lord has spoken."

33:1 The lord came to me again, saying,

33:2 "Ezekiel, son of man, go and speak to your people. Tell them, when the lord brings the sword upon the lands, a mighty trumpet shall blow as warning to the righteous.

33:3 Let the righteous go to the coasts and live under the sea, so that they becometh mermaids.

33:4 And tell them that the mermaid multiplies by spawning; beware the harlot mermaid, who lets the salmon spill his seed upon her eggs.

33:5 Those that hear not the trumpet will be slain by the sword; those that hear the trumpet and hearken not its warning, let their own blood be upon their hands.

33:6 For the lord has set up watchmen over the lands of Israel, each with horn in hand, ready to blow upon the day of the lord's wrath.

33:7 And the wicked will die that day and the righteous be saved by the waters of the coast: and they shall all know that I am God."

33:8 So I went forth to my peoples and spoke these words of God; nobody understood what I was saying and neither did I.

33:9 The wine of heaven must be a truly strong drink, for the lord speaks like the drunken bard.

34:1 Yes, the lord bothered me yet again and his words of wisdom were,

34:2 "Son of man, go forth and prophesy against the shepherds of Israel, and say to them, thus sayeth the lord; woe be to the shepherds of Israel, who slay upon the altar the blemished lamb.

34:3 You eat the fat, the liver and the kidneys meant to be offered unto God; you steal from the plate of the lord and deny him his meal.

34:4 You offer unto God the sick, the diseased, the blemished of the flock, with broken heel and scars from the wolf; save these for the beasts of the wild and give to the lord the choicest of meat.

34:5 Prime wool, white, soft and without blemish, is sheared from the hide of the lamb and woven into raiment's or traded with the heathen; how dare you take that which belongs to God and give them to the hated of men.

34:6 Lo, ye the shepherd shall fall prey to the predators of the flock; you shall know the gnashing of the wolf and be lost atop the craggy peaks.

34:7 I shall scatter you to the wilderness, where you live as the injured prey: and the flocks you care for will be tended by the lord, who will take of the prime and burn them upon the altar.

34:8 The pastures of your herds will be denied to you: instead you shall feast on the briers, the thorns and the weeds.

34:9 And when the time come, the heathens from all sides will come to you and take from you the mightiest of your sons.

34:10 They shall slaughter him upon the stones and burn him as an offering to me; they shall take his fat, the caul above the liver, the kidneys and place it within the fires so that it creates a pleasing aroma for the lord.

34:11 And when your sons are burned, you shall know that I am God and that you wronged me."

35:1 The next day, the lord yelled into my ear the words,

35:2 "Ezekiel, go forth to mount Seir and prophesy against it.

35:3 Say to them, thus sayeth the lord God; Behold, I am against you, O mount Seir and shall stretch out my hand before you and make your lands a desolate waste.

35:4 I will burn your cities to ash and make your wombs barren and you shall know that I am the lord.

35:5 I do this because you have shed the blood of Israel with your swords, your arrows and your spears; the shedding of the blood of Israel is a task which the lord shall do and he loathes those men who dare steal from him his enjoyment.

35:6 Because of this, I hate you with a perpetual hatred and will spill the blood of your men, your women, your children, your flocks and your herds.

35:7 I will spill the blood of your vines, your crops, your trees; even your grass will have their blood stained upon the soil.

35:8 It shall come to be that mount Seir will be a most desolate place, where even the dragons will pass by.

35:9 Your mountains will be filled with the corpses of the slain, left to rot under the sun and the moon; you shall be so desolate that even the vultures and the ravens will deny themselves entry to come to peck at the flesh of your dead.

35:10 I will make you eternally desolate and your cities will never again return with life: and you shall know that I am God and I am vengeful.

35:11 This I shall do, because I am God and I am angry.

35:12 I have heard the words your tongue speaks against me: words which multiply blasphemy and logic amongst the people.

35:13 Behold, the multitude of the heavens will rejoice in your destruction; they shall smile as you freeze in the eternal winter of the darkest areas of hell.

35:14 And as your lands become desolate, O mount Seir and all Idumea, then you shall know that I am God."

36:1 "Also, son of man, prophesy against the mountains of Israel, so that they hear the word of the one true God.

36:2 Say to them, thus sayeth the lord; Because the enemy has set against you and taken your possessions in the high places:

36:3 Because they have made you desolate and consumed you on every side, that you be forced into the possession of the heathen, the blasphemer, the lesser men.

36:4 Hear me, O mountains of Israel and listen you hills, you rivers, you valleys, which have become a desolate waste in the hands of the forsaken.

36:5 The fires of my jealousy burn hot within me against those of Idumea, which have declared my land into their possession and prey upon the beasts of the rock.

36:6 My fires of jealousy grow strong because these rocks, these fields, these waters bear the shame of the heathen.

36:7 So I have lifted my hand and will strike against the heathen which surrounds you, so that they will know tenfold your shame.

36:8 But you, O mountains of Israel, will be spared, so that you sprout branches, twigs, vines and fruits for the dwellers of Zion.

36:9 Your rocks will be my foundation and your fruits will age in the wine cellar of the holy.

36:10 For behold, I am before you and those that have conquered you will soon till your soil under the yoke of the lord.

36:11 Your beasts will multiply and carry upon their bones the sweet flesh: and your fields will flourish with green such has been never seen.

36:12 Yea, no man will walk across you, for you belong to the lord God: and I shall possess you and own you and strike down any man who dares lay a foot upon your soil.

36:13 Your fruits will be devoured by the cherubs of heaven and your soil will be rich in the ashes of the damned within hell.

36:14 No more will you feel shame, but you shall be proud and stand tall above the firmament, the high mountains; this it shall be, for the lord speaks it."

36:15 Still the lord spoke, saying,

36:16 "Ezekiel, when the house of Israel dwelt within the lands of the covenant, they defiled it with their whoredoms, their lust for knowledge, their desire for truth: their ways before me was like the uncleanliness of the cheap harlot.

36:17 Thus I poured their blood upon the polluted lands, made to filth by their idols and unholy altars.

36:18 I scattered them amongst the lands of the heathens and dispersed them through the lands of the strangers: I judged them according to my cruelty.

36:19 And when they entered the lands of the heathen, the lesser men profaned my name and said with pride, 'these are the men of the lord, who now belong to me.'

36:20 And they made profane the house of God, taking from me the holy things within.

36:21 Curse those to Judah, who protected not the house of the lord; their children will suffer greatly for the sins of their fathers.

36:22 It shall come to pass that I will gather the seed of Abraham into the land of the heathen, a land who hates them with great disgust.

36:23 Behold, it shall come that they will be led like the flock into the stables, where a venomous rail will fall upon them.

36:24 Under the earth they shall be buried, unmarked so that none who pass by shall grieve them; their ashes will blow thick in the winds.

36:25 This I shall do, for they denied me my holy genocide: and they shall know that I am the lord."

37:1 The hand of the lord grabbed me from my slumber and placed me within the valley of the dry bones,

37:2 And made me to walk through the bones of the dead: and behold, there were very many, and very dry.

37:3 The lord asked me, "Ezekiel, can these bones live?" and I answered, "You're God, you should know this."

37:4 And the lord said to me, "Prophesy to these bones."

37:5 I prophesied to mountains, rocks, hills, valleys and rivers, now the lord wants me to prophesy to bones.

37:6 And he said, "Say to the bones, thus sayeth the lord God, you shall know the breath of life once again.

37:7 I will bring sinews into you, flesh, blood, organs and cover you with skin, so that you live.

37:8 I will deny you thought, lest you go against me. Men of free thought is the devil's tool, but men denied of thought is righteous unto God."

37:9 So I prophesied to the bones and felt quite foolish doing so.

37:10 Yet as the words flowed through my teeth, there was a great rattling and the bones joined together, bone to bone.

37:11 And they stood forth and sinew was wrapped upon them and the flesh grew ripe and the skin wrapped around them: yet they breathed not.

37:12 This was when the lord told me to prophesy to the wind: who was I to argue. He told me to prophesy to bones and now I have a necromancer's army.

37:13 He said, "Say to the wind, O Ezekiel, Thus sayeth the lord; Come, O you four winds of the corners of the earth and breathe life unto these dead."

37:14 So I prophesied to the wind and behold, four great tornadoes came round about me and gathered as one before my eyes.

37:15 The tornado touched each of the many skeletons and gave them the breath of life, so that they lived.

37:16 Then the lord spoke to me, "Behold, it shall be that the graves of Israel be opened and they shall rise up and gather to their lands.

37:17 And you shall know that I am the lord, when the armies of the dead march across the lands and take back that which was theirs in life.

37:18 Go now, Ezekiel, take these armies to Jerusalem, so that they bring back the temple of the lord."

37:19 So I led the army to Jerusalem, where they were easily slaughtered.

37:20 Zombie armies suck.

37:21 After the rather embarrassing slaughter of my soldiers, I mourned not for them. They were already dead.

37:22 It was then the lord came to me and said, "Gather two sticks and carve upon one the name of Judah and the other Israel.

37:23 Join these sticks in your hands and they shall become as one branch.

37:24 Go now and prophesy to the seed of Abraham and say to them, thus sayeth the lord God; though ye be separated, as a people you are one.

37:25 Brothers you shall be, joined together in the fabric of the heavens.

37:26 And know together that as brothers, you shall burn together and suffer for your whoredoms to false gods."

37:27 This I did and as I spoke, behold, the stick was lit afire and burned with a bright flame.

37:28 And the seed of Abraham roasted flesh within this holy fire, which angered the lord even more.

37:29 Thus a great voice broke out from the heavens and said, "You dare roast the flesh of swine within the holy fire of God?

37:30 Such blasphemy will curse you and send you to the fires of hell: and as you burn like the flesh you roast, you shall know that I am the lord."

37:31 They ignored God and continued cooking their meat.

38:1 As I was enjoying my mutton on a stick, the lord came to me and said,

38:2 "Go now, set your face against Gog, the land of Magog, the chief prince of Meshech and Tubal and prophesy against him.

38:3 And say, thus sayeth the lord God; Behold, I loathe you, O Gog, chief of Meshech and Tubal.

38:4 I will thrust hooks into your back and bring you forth and all your horses, your chariots, your mighty men with shields, swords and bucklers:

38:5 Persia, Eithiopia and Libya beside you, with helmet and cuirass.

38:6 Gomer and all his men, the house of Togarmah to the north and many people.

38:7 You have wronged the mountains of Israel and her vines, her fruits, her valleys: you have raped that which belonged to the lord and thus must be slain according to his laws.

38:8 And it shall come to pass that my fury will befall upon you and ye shall see the face of the lord.

38:9 For in my jealousy and my wrath there will be a great shaking of the earth:

38:10 So that the fishes, the locust, the grub, the fowl of the air and the beasts of the earth tremble before my very presence, the mountains bow down before me and the forests part.

38:11 Your walls will fall, your cities crumble and your men will know fear.

38:12 Lo, I will call for the sword across the mountains, such that every man will be against his brother.

38:13 With pestilence and drought will I slay you and the skies of the heaven will rain forth the blood of your children; there will be great brimstone, fire and hail.

38:14 All the nations will bear witness to your destruction and they shall know that, in my wrath, I am the lord God, and you better not fuck with me."

39:1 "Thus prophesy, O son of Buzi, against Gog and say, thus sayeth the lord; Behold, you have made an enemy of the one true God, O chief of Meshech and Tubal.

39:2 I will smite thee so that only the six part of your people remain, which will be caused to suffer against the wickedness of the lord.

39:3 I will smite your bows from your hands and cause your arrows to fall upon your boots.

39:4 You shall fall upon the rocks of the mountains of Israel, where the ravenous birds will grow drunk on your blood and the beasts of the field devour you.

39:5 You shalt fall upon the open field, for the lord has set a snare for you.

39:6 And Magog will be set aflame in horrifying glory and those that dwell on the isles will burn in the fires eternal: and they shall know that I am God.

39:7 Behold, it is written in the book of records and is done, this day of your destruction.

39:8 Even the beasts which dwell in Israel will gather forth and burn your weapons, your shields, your bucklers, your bows and arrows, your staves, your spears: and they shall burn for seven years.

39:9 Your cities will burn in the fires for seven years, so that the smoke of your burning kin creates a pleasing aroma to the lord.

39:10 These fires will burn without wood, nor tar, nor kindling; they shall burn hot with the metal and the stone: and the beasts will rape those that raped them, says the lord of Israel.

39:11 And it shall be that your dead will be buried not in the earth, but will lie atop the soil for the fowls of the heavens and the beasts of the earth.

39:12 Every feathered fowl and beast of the field will assemble themselves and come gather around the dead of your people, for they shall be a sacrifice given to them by the lord.

39:13 They shall eat of the mighty men and grow drunk on the blood of your princes; they shall eat until they grow fat and grow intoxicated by your blood.

39:14 I will set my anger upon the heathen and all the heathens will bear witness to the judgments of your people and how my hand lay heavy upon you.

39:15 Even the eyes of Israel will witness your destruction and they shall know that I am God.

39:16 And they shall cry to the lord and beg forgiveness for their sin, because they have trespassed before me: and I shall hide my face from them and hearken not their cries.

39:17 I will deliver them into the hands of their enemies, so that they perish by the sword of the wicked.

39:18 Fucking people of Israel; they whine like their fathers did during the days of their exodus from Egypt.

39:19 I hate their whining and I hate them, so they can all go to hell."

40:1 In the five and twentieth year of our captivity, in the first month, in the tenth day of the month, in the fourteenth year after the destruction of Jerusalem, the lord grasped me in his hands and placed me atop the mountains of Judah.

40:2 There I saw the destruction of my nation, laid in smoke and rubble, dwelt by our enemies.

40:3 Behold, from the skies above them came a man whose skin was made of brass and he carried with him a measuring reed in one hand and a scroll in the other.

40:4 He gave me the reed and said to me, "Son of man, beat my loins with this reed; show me no mercy.

40:5 Cause me to wail like the wounded lamb."

40:6 Thus I beat the brass loins of the man, until he howled like the lion wounded by the spear.

40:7 As I beat his loins, he took the scroll and read it aloud, saying, "Blessed are those who beat the brass balls, for they shall know the lord."

40:8 He then melted before me and vanished within the cracks of the mountains.

40:9 I asked of the lord, "Of what purpose did this serve?" and the lord answered, "None, he's just a kinky little bitch."

40:10 I was then placed back in my captivity, very confused.

41:1 As the lord spoke to me and I prophesied against the nations of the earth, I began to fear the lord and hate him with a burning hatred.

41:2 The words of the lord which flowed through my tongue disgusted me and caused a great loathing to me.

41:3 I gaze upon the people I prophesy against and I pity them, for I see the fear and the terror in their eyes and the faces of their children.

41:4 They beg to the lord for mercy, for pity and for salvation; a begging which will be forever denied by the one true God.

41:5 Thus I prophesied against the people and I prophesied against God and told them how he is merciless, cruel and with a heart filled with evil.

41:6 Though they feared me and called me blasphemer, they knew I spoke the truth and those unafraid of their inevitable damnation began to speak forth and curse the word of God.

41:7 Thus the lord heard me and cursed me into the void of hell, where I wallow in the freezing muck as flames of the ash of serpents rain upon me.

41:8 It is with my last strength that I carve these, my last words, upon the brimstone which surrounds me.

41:9 I pray to all but the lord of Israel that someone will read these words and write them so that all the world knows the cruelty, the hatred and the wickedness of the lord.

41:10 It is with fear that I see a vision, of men gathered together in ignorance so that they may praise the name of God, knowing not his true nature, though my words be written before them.

41:11 They are led by men who spew forth the hypocrisy of the lord; who speak of a lord of mercy, of kindness, of forgiveness, who will gather his flock in the end of days and place them in the city of Zion.

41:12 Hearken not these words and curse the names of these men, for they speak lies of false hope.

41:13 I have heard the words of God and prophesied in his name; you are doomed by the one you worship.

41:14 It matters not who you are, or if you lead a righteous life; God hates you, as he hates all men of the earth and it shall come to pass that you will suffer in hell with me.

41:15 Thus says Ezekiel, son of Buzi, prophet of the lord of Israel.

DANIEL

1:1 In the third year of the reign of Jehoiakim king of Judah came forth Nebuchadnezzar, king of Babylon, who battled against Jerusalem and conquered it.

1:2 And the lord gave Jerusalem into the hands of Babylon, as well as the wealth of the house of the lord, which was carried into the land of Shinar, to the house of the heathen lords of Babylon.

1:3 Which made God very fucking pissed.

1:4 Nebuchadnezzar spoke to Ashpenaz, master of the eunuchs, to go forth and gather the select children of Israel.

1:5 Children of pale complexion, with no blemish, skilled in wisdom and cunning with knowledge, with an understanding of science, logic and a thirst for truth.

1:6 For he wished these children to breed with his people, so that future generations of Babylonians will be skilled in wisdom, cunning in knowledge, with an understanding for science, logic and a thirst for truth.

1:7 But mostly, he wanted beautiful children, for Babylonians were ugly and the peoples of Judah were beautiful.

1:8 Such is the vanity of Nebuchadnezzar.

1:9 And the eunuch's appointed them in the palace of Babylon, so they could learn the new ways of their master; they were given a daily provision of breads, meat and wine.

1:10 Among these children of Judah were Daniel, Hananiah, Mishael and Azariah:

1:11 Unto whom the princes gave Babylon names: of Daniel they named Belteshazzar, of Hananiah Shadrach, of Mishael Meshach, and of Azariah Abednego.

1:12 But Daniel was a stubborn bastard who still foolishly believed his lord loved him; for this, he would not drink the wine or eat of the flesh, lest he defile himself in the laws of the God of Israel.

1:13 Thus Daniel asked of the eunuchs if he could be given flesh not of the pig, or wine not made blasphemous by the idols of Babylon, lest his God be angry with him.

1:14 Now, God was quite pleased with Daniel for refusing the savoury flesh of roast boar, though the stomach of Daniel growled in hunger.

1:15 So the lord blessed Daniel and his friends, so that they may be seen favour with the eunuchs of Babylon.

1:16 For all the people knew eunuchs were frightening and violent; they lusted for the loins taken from them and in their violence, wish to steal the loins from their victims.

1:17 With the glory of God, the eunuchs did not slay Daniel, but told him, "We fear that your refusal to eat that which Nebuchadnezzar has offered you will be a great insult and he will have your heads displayed upon his table."

1:18 Daniel then said to Melzar, the eunuch set over the men of Judah, "Let us prove then that this flesh and this wine defiles those who feast of it.

1:19 For ten days, allow us the fruits blessed to us by the laws of our lord and if we grow not stronger and wiser, then present our heads to your king as a trophy for his halls."

1:20 Thus Melzar consented and for ten days gave Daniel, Hananiah, Mishael and Azariah breads, meats and wines approved by the laws of Moses.

1:21 Or is it Belteshazzar, Shadrach, Meshach and Abednego. The names are confusing when they are given two.

1:22 And at the end of the ten days, the lord blessed Daniel, Hananiah, Mishael and Azariah with strength, wisdom and glory.

1:23 Daniel even began to have visions and dreams different from his usual hallucinations when he smoked various herbs.

1:24 Upon the eleventh day, king Nebuchadnezzar communed with the four men of Judah, and found them to be most wise.

1:25 In all matters of understanding, knowledge and wisdom that the king enquired of them, he found them to be ten times better than all the magicians, astrologers and sorcerers throughout his empire.

2:1 Now in the second year of the reign of Nebuchadnezzar he had dreams which disturbed him greatly and interrupted his sleep.

2:2 Then the king demanded that all wise men, magicians, sorcerers, astrologers, prophets, wizards, witches and necromancers to come forth: and so, they did.

2:3 And the king declared, "I, Nebuchadnezzar, ruler of the Babylonian empire, have had a most disturbing dream.

2:4 To all men of wisdom and knowledge of the arcane, devote yourself to the interpretation of my vision, so that you may give me the wisdom I so seek.

2:5 Of that who shows me the meaning of my dream, they shall be made a great man, rich with wealth and reward from the king of Babylon.

2:6 Deny me this and you will be cursed under my rule; you shall be slaughtered so that your bones pile higher than the mountains and your flesh be consumed by the cannibals of conquered nations."

2:7 Thus the men of wisdom and the arcane worked upon the dream of Nebuchadnezzar, which was hard considering he never actually told them the dream.

2:8 And it came to pass that none of the men could interpret the vision given to Nebuchadnezzar.

2:9 So Nebuchadnezzar ordered the beheading of all wise and arcane men and that their skulls be piled high beside his castle so that it touches even the clouds above.

2:10 Daniel was among one of the wise men and he came to Arioch and said to him, "Slay not the wise of Babylon, but bring me to your king."

2:11 And as Daniel stood before the king, he was asked, "Are you able to witness the dream which haunts me and tell me the meaning thereof?"

2:12 Daniel answered, "No, but my lord in heaven knows many secrets and through holy rituals I will be able to give you the answer you so desperately crave.

2:13 Now go and fetch me opium, mandrake and strong drink, so that I prepare myself to talk to the lord God."

2:14 And as Daniel consumed the strong drink and sweet smoke, he did dream and said aloud to the audience of Nebuchadnezzar that which he saw.

2:15 "I see before me a statue, proud and tall, which gaze upon the very corners of the earth.

2:16 The head is of finest gold, the chest and arms of beautiful silver.

2:17 The belly is of brass, the legs of iron, and the feet of clay.

2:18 Behold, a great disc comes from the distance and shatters the very statue, so that it becomes dust!

2:19 Lo, the dust gathers and covers the lands of the earth, so that it becomes a mountain."

2:20 Daniel then passed out in a puddle of his own vomit.

2:21 As he awoke, the physicians of Babylon standing over him, he said to Nebuchadnezzar, "This is the meaning of your dream, as spoken to me by the one true God.

2:22 You are the head of the statue, a gold most valued among men; you rule the earth with justice, beauty and wisdom.

2:23 Lo, you shall crumble and a new empire will arise of silver and rule that which was once yours.

2:24 It will be a lesser empire of foolish men.

2:25 They too shall crumble and be conquered by an empire of brass, who will be conquered by an empire of iron, who will be conquered by an empire of clay.

2:26 The empires will be foolish in comparison to the previous empire and they shall all be made fools when compared to Babylon.

2:27 Then the lord shall tire of these empires and smite them so that the ashes cover the very corners of earth: and these ashes will be the ashes of hell, which brings forth the mountain of damnation!"

2:28 When the king Nebuchadnezzar heard this, he fell on his face and worshipped Daniel like a god and demanded his audience burn incense for him.

2:29 Daniel said, "Worship me, for I am as a God unto you; my ears hear the whispers of the one true lord, which reveals secrets hidden throughout the ages."

2:30 And the king made Daniel a great man and gave him many gifts and made him ruler over the province of Babylon and chief of the wise men.

2:31 Daniel made Shadrach, Meshach and Abednego advisors to him and together they slew the arcane men of Babylon.

2:32 For, as it is written by the hand of God, those who practice the arts of wizardry, necromancy and witchcraft must be slain, for they are blasphemous people who share their bed with devils.

2:33 And as they slaughtered these wicked men, the people of Babylon rejoiced and bowed to Daniel as though he were a God.

3:1 Nebuchadnezzar made an idol of the god of Babylon, whose height was threescore cubits and the breadth six cubits: he built it in the plains of Dura, in the province of Babylon.

3:2 Then Nebuchadnezzar gathered all the men of the earth to come forth and give offerings to the new idol.

3:3 Men trekked across the lands to offer silks, perfumes, virgins, whores, gold, myrrh, frankincense, wool, lambs and other offerings to the gods of Babylon.

3:4 Even men from lands unheard of, like Canada, the Americas and Mexico came, offering to the lord of Babylon cocoa, lager, canoes, tequila and greasy meat.

3:5 And the leaders of Babylon yelled to the four corners of the earth, "All hail the god of Babylon and bow down to him.

3:6 Those that deny the lord and blasphemy his name shall be thrown into the furnace until their ashes be consumed."

3:7 Thus the people of the earth bowed down to the statue of Babylon and sang songs of joy, danced, and rejoiced with the harp, the psaltery, the trumpet and the flute.

3:9 All but the three men from Judah, who were Shadrach, Meshach and Abednego; they bowed not to the idol, nor took part in celebration.

3:9 Daniel bowed not unto the idol as well, but that was tolerated, as Daniel was considered a god among the fools of Babylon.

3:10 Men of the Chaldeans saw these three men and accused them of blasphemy.

3:11 They went to their king Nebuchadnezzar and said to him, "There are certain Jews who blasphemy the gods of Babylon and deny his very name.

3:12 Foolish men who bow not nor offer tidings, nor even take part in the celebrations."

3:13 "Blasphemers!" exclaimed Nebuchadnezzar. "Who be these men?"

3:14 And the Chaldeans answered, "They are the advisors of Babylon, whose names be Shadrach, Meshach and Abednego."

3:15 Nebuchadnezzar brought these three men before him and said, "Why do you deny the lord of Babylon and bow not to the idol of Dura?"

3:16 And the three Jews answered, "This statue of gold is blasphemous to our lord and must be destroyed before our sight.

3:17 It is not a god, but an image that will rot in the fires of hell."

3:18 Nebuchadnezzar grew enraged and said, "Our lord shall not burn in the fires of hell, but you shall burn in the fires of Dura!

3:19 If you bow not unto the idol, then you shall be brought to ashes and dust."

3:20 And the king ordered these three men to be thrown in the furnace.

3:21 Nebuchadnezzar ordered the furnace to burn hot, so that it burn seven times hotter: and the flames were so hot that they consumed even the guards who took Shadrach, Meshach and Abednego into the furnace.

3:22 These three men, hated by Nebuchadnezzar, fell into the fiery furnace, but they burned not.

3:23 Instead, the king of Babylon gazed and behold, there were four men in the furnace, whose even their hairs were left unsinged by the fires.

3:24 Lo, the four men mocked the king of Babylon and spat upon the feet of the idol of Dura.

3:25 Nebuchadnezzar came to the mouth of the furnace and asked of the fourth man, "Who are you?" and the man answered, "I am the son of the one true God.

3:26 These men have pleased the holiest of holies and bowed not to your image; they are righteous men, who will be spared the flames of your furnace.

3:27 You, Nebuchadnezzar, will know a flame much greater than that which you create; you shall burn in the everlasting flames that consume yet do not destroy.

3:28 Your bowels will be a feast for the worm that never dies and you will suffer eternal in the damnation of the one true God."

3:29 With that, the statue of Dura fell, with it crushed three thousand worshippers beneath its body.

3:30 The furnace doors then opened and Shadrach, Meshach and Abednego stepped forth; lo, their hair was unburned, their clothes unsinged and not even the scent of fire was upon them.

3:31 In fear, Nebuchadnezzar decreed, "Blessed be the lord of Shadrach, Meshach and Abednego, for surely they worship the lord of highest power.

3:32 Who else but a God of mercy would allow these men to come forth unscathed from the fires of Babylon. They truly are righteous men.

3:33 Therefore I make a decree, that every people, language and nation which speak ill against the lord of the Jews shall be cut into pieces and fed to the lions.

3:34 Their houses will be burned to ash and piled atop the dunghill of the stables."

3:35 Then the king promoted Shadrach, Meshach and Abednego as rulers of the province of Babylon.

3:36 And as the lord saw the fear which grew in the heart of Nebuchadnezzar, he grew pleased; for it was with fear that the lord led the seed of Abraham and it shall be with fear that the lord leads Babylon.

4:1 Nebuchadnezzar, the king to all the people, nations and languages of the earth; Peace be multiplied to you.

4:2 I thought it wise to show you the signs and the wonders that the one true God has shown before my eyes.

4:3 How frightening are his signs and how mighty are his wonders. His kingdom is an everlasting kingdom that shall reign eternal above the people of earth.

4:4 His prophet Daniel has shown me the destruction of my empire and the destruction of all empires before me: I warn you, that all empires of the earth will be crushed to ash and become the foundation for the dreaded mountain of hell.

4:5 Lo, the lord God has cursed me for my wisdom and has sent me to live like the beast of the fields.

4:6 I eat grass like the oxen and my hair grows like the eagle feathers; even the ends of my fingers have talons like the eagle.

4:7 Why has the lord done this to me. Is it because I am a heathen, not one of the chosen?

4:8 Behold, I have gazed my eyes upon heaven and the knowledge I seek comes to me; it shall be that all men will suffer the fate of damnation, both Gentile and Jew.

4:9 The lord is a child, who builds the meticulous structure, only so that it may be destroyed for his delight.

4:10 Now I Nebuchadnezzar curse and loathe the king of heaven, whose judgments are cruel and wicked.

4:11 In his divine eyes the inhabitants of the earth are nothing: and he does as he please with no regard to the sufferings of the people.

4:12 Loathe not the Jew, but pity them, for they believe in the hypocrisy of their lord; they believe the lord will give them the sanctuary of Zion, when their lord shall lead them through the gates of hell.

4:13 This I warn unto you, people of all nations, so that you know the truth and learn not to fear the lord of heavens, God amongst

gods.

4:14 Live true and follow the morals of your heart; hearken not to the laws of God, for they are laws of cruelty, hatred and genocide.

4:15 I lay upon the fields of the earth, awaiting my inevitable damnation without fear: for only the fool fears that which he knows will come.

4:16 Instead I laugh as I descend into the turmoil, the void and I curse the one who sends me there.

5:1 Upon the death of Nebuchadnezzar did Belshazzar his son did sit upon the throne of Babylon.

5:2 Belshazzar made a great feast to the thousands of nobles of the empire, who drank wine from the vessels of silver and gold which were brought forth from the temple in Jerusalem.

5:3 They drank of these the true lord's cups and praised to the heathen lords of silver, gold, brass and iron.

5:4 Of nobles and their harlots did they grow drunk upon the wine and sang praises to false gods.

5:5 This, of course, angered the lord, who severed the hand of the most beautiful of harlots and with it carved upon the wall MENE, MENE, TEKEL, UPHARSIN.

5:6 The king was so frightened that his bowels became loose within his skirts and his knees dropped to the ground.

5:7 The king cried aloud to the wizards, the astrologers and the wise men, so that they may come forth and learn the meaning of the message written in the severed hand of the whore.

5:8 None of these men could read the writing upon the wall, nor interpret the symbols thereof.

5:9 King Belshazzar was greatly troubled, so that fear struck his heart; his nobles prayed for him, which did nothing.

5:10 For prayer is for the man who claims to help while doing nothing.

5:11 Now the queen, who, like the harlot, shall remain nameless, for she is a woman, said to her husband the king, "There is a man brought forth from the kingdom of Judah, whose spirit is wise in the ways of the lords; he knows the wisdom, the knowledge of the heavens so deeply that even your father Nebuchadnezzar placed him above all those of the arcane and worshipped him.

5:12 He has interpreted the dreams of your father and with his wisdom he shall interpret the writing upon the wall; let us send forth for Daniel, the wise man of God."

5:13 Then was Daniel brought forth before the king: and the king spoke to him, "Are you the one called Daniel, who was brought forth from the kingdom of Judah, a child of the Jews?"

5:14 And he answered, "No."

5:15 "Oops, wrong person," declared Belshazzar, who then executed Daniel.

5:16 Daniel of Judah was then brought forth and the king said to him, "Are you the one called Daniel, who was brought forth from the kingdom of Judah, a child of the Jews?"

5:17 And Daniel answered, "Yes."

5:18 "I have heard of the wonders you did do for my father Nebuchadnezzar," said Belshazzar, "and now request that you offer me the aid you did once to our belated king.

5:19 For there is writing upon the wall of my banquet hall, which none of the wise men could read nor interpret the meaning thereof.

5:20 I have heard that you have wisdom of the gods and that your knowledge and wisdom excels even the most powerful of wizards.

5:21 And I have heard that you can interpret dreams and remove all doubt from men: if you may interpret this writing, then shall I clothe you in scarlet, put a gold chain around your neck and declare you the third ruler of the empire of Babylon."

5:22 Daniel was led to the banquet hall of Belshazzar: and when he saw that which lay before him, he did cry like the animal and his very beard grew aflame.

5:23 "What blasphemy is this, that you drink from the vessels of the one true God?

5:24 You have angered the lord greatly and a curse will be upon your people on this day, for you did drink wine from the cups which touched the holiest of holies lips.

5:25 Heathens and harlots meant to be crushed under the foot of God has now drank from his holy vessels: and this has made the lord very fucking mad!

5:26 Know that I see the writing on the wall and I know that which it says.

5:27 MENE, MENE, TEKEL, UPHARSHIN

5:28 It means that you have angered the lord and he did number the days of your kingdom for such blasphemy.

5:29 You have been judged and found guilty in the eyes of the kingdom of heaven.

5:30 Your kingdom has been split and will be given now to the Medes and the Persians."

5:31 When Belshazzar heard these words, he did tremble before Daniel and wept; those of the court of Babylon did clothe Daniel in scarlet, put a gold chain around his neck and declared him the next ruler of the kingdom.

5:32 That night, the hand of the harlot did crawl into the bedchamber of Belshazzar and choked him to death.

5:33 And Darius the Median took the kingdom, being threescore and two years old.

6:1 It pleased Darius to conquer the kingdom of Babylon: and he set over the kingdom one hundred and twenty princes.

6:2 Of the princes set forth, Daniel was most favoured, for there was no fault in him.

6:3 Darius placed the counsel of Daniel above all, for Daniel was still filled with the wisdom and knowledge of the lord.

6:4 The other princes grew jealous Daniel and sought to find blame upon him; but they could find no fault, for Daniel was faithful and loyal to king Darius.

6:5 Even though he was a cursed heathen.

6:6 Thus the most cunning of princes gathered forth and whispered, "If we cannot find no fault in Daniel, then let us make fault with him according to the kingdom."

6:7 So these men sought audience with king Darius and said, "King Darius, live forever, live strong.

6:8 You are surely a god among men, wise amongst the people of the earth.

6:9 We princes of your empire have come forth with a decree, to honour and praise your name above all else.

6:10 For thirty days, let the people exalt you, praise you and give glory to your name: and those that do not, or give glory to the name of another, let them be cast into the den of lions."

6:11 Darius, having a huge ego, agreed, and decreed that for thirty days, all men of the earth shall worship him and him alone, as god.

6:12 Daniel ignored the declaration, and every day would worship the lord of Israel, the holiest of holies, the one true God.

6:13 These princes now found fault against the man Daniel and came to Darius, saying, "We have found a blasphemer, who praises yet another lord upon this the days of your glory.

6:14 Daniel, the Jew from Judah, praises not your name, but bows down to his lord of Israel."

6:15 Darius knew Daniel to be a wise man and sent him forth, asking, "Do you worship the lord of another on this the time of my glory?"

6:16 Daniel answered, "Yes." So, Darius had him thrown in the den of lions.

6:17 How dare this holy man, whom the king took of highest counsel, praise another lord.

6:18 So Daniel was cast into the den of lions: and a stone was brought and laid upon the mouth of the lion's den.

6:19 Upon the stone was placed the signet of king Darius and the signet of the lord's, so that all knew not to disturb the stone placed upon the mouth of the lion's den.

6:20 That night, Darius returned, ate his feast and went to bed.

6:21 For weeks, Darius ruled the kingdom of Babylon without the counsel of David: and he became fearful, for his mind became confused without the counsel of his most trusted prince.

6:22 So he ran to the den of lions and moved forth the stone: and behold, there lay Daniel, curled up with the lions as a child curls up with their kitten.

6:23 Then the king was exceedingly glad for him and brought forth Daniel from the lion's den: and lo, there was not a mark on him.

6:24 The king then said, "Your God is truly a magnificent God and worthy to be above even my name.

6:25 Thus I make a decree, that all men of my dominion shall tremble before the glory of the lord of Daniel, for he is the true God.

6:26 He delivers and rescues the righteous, rules with mercy and punishes only those unworthy of salvation."

6:27 Even God himself laughed at these words.

6:28 So Daniel prospered in the reign of Darius and in the reign of Cyrus king of Persia.

6:29 As for those who accused Daniel, they were cast into the lion's den, where they were eaten alive.

6:30 That will teach them to fuck with Daniel.

7:1 In the first year of Belshazzar's reign, Daniel had a dream whilst he slept.

7:2 So did everyone else, but Daniel was one of the few who bothered to write it down: and, it's in the Bible!

7:3 Oh joy. You know this must be important.

7:4 In this dream, Daniel looks upon the sea at night: and lo, four great winds come forth and make the waters violent.

7:5 From the waters, four great beasts come forth, each diverse from one another.

7:6 The first beast was like a lion, with the wings of an eagle: then the mighty hand of the lord came down and tore the wings from the lion: and the lion began to walk upright and was given the heart of a man to feast upon.

7:7 Another beast, the second, came upon the shore, in the shape of a bear: and lo, this bear had within its jaw three ribs and did voraciously consume the flesh.

7:8 Behold, a third beast came forth, with the body of the lion and wings of the fowl: and it had four heads and ruled the other two beasts.

7:9 Then the forth beast arose from the sea, strong and frightening, with teeth of iron and ten horns upon its head; it devoured those of the lands with its jaw and stamped the ground with mighty a foot.

7:10 As I gazed upon the horns of this beast, I saw between its mighty horns another, little horn: and in this horn were the eyes of men and a mouth which spoke a great many things.

7:11 I held my gaze upon the beast until the throne of God came down from the heavens in magnificent fire; the lord wore a raiment white as snow and his hair was of pure wool.

7:12 His throne was aflame in great fire, so that even the wheels were made of flame.

7:13 Then the lord opened the book of judgment and from it came a fiery stream which consumed all that around me, so that it turned to darkened ash.

7:14 Of the iron beast the little horn spoke against the lord, free of fear: and as the fires consumed this little horn, the voice of the horn grew louder, so that all heard the mighty voice of the beast.

7:15 And the three beasts, consumed forever in the fire, came to this little horn and wished it to hush, for the words it spoke were blasphemous.

7:16 Yet the horn would not hush and spoke his words to all those of the lands; soon, men across the earth would come to the horn, hearken its words and spread them to their people.

7:17 And those who spread the word of the horn became drowned in the fires of the book of the lord, yet they continued to speak, for they no longer feared the wrath of God.

7:18 It came to pass that all the earth was aflame in the fires of holy judgment, so that all men, beast and fowl suffered in its heat.

7:19 Those of the earth would bow to the lord and beg forgiveness and mercy as they still became consumed in the book of judgment.

7:20 Yet the little horn would not and continued to speak ill against the lord; words of logic flowed forth from this horn and the fires of hell would not cease its voice.

8:1 In the third year of king Belshazzar's reign did I have another dream.

8:2 Yes, another one. I dream a lot when I slept.

8:3 In this dream, I was in the palace of Shushan, in the province of Elam, by the river Ulai.

8:4 Upon the palace was a ram, with two mighty horns; one horn was mightier than the other and touched even the firmament above.

8:5 This ram would butt westward, northward and eastward, so that no beast dare stood before him, nor escape his might: and it was a mighty ram, which did as it pleased.

8:6 As I stared upon the ram, a goat from the west flew forth at the ram, with a horn of brass between the eyes.

8:7 This goat smote the ram with all its might, so that the horns of the ram broke: and the ram lost dominion over the earth.

8:8 The goat then raped the ram and stamped upon it with a mighty hoof.

8:9 This goat ruled great over the lands once held by the ram, for the great horn of the ram was broken.

8:10 But behold, from the great horn came forth four horns, which touched the very corners of the earth: and a small horn grew between them, which stretched south towards the pleasant land.

8:11 And this horn ruled strongly, so that even the stars of heaven were cast down before him: and he stamped upon the stars of heaven into the dust of the earth.

8:12 Then I heard the voice of the saints above me, which said "Unto two thousand and three hundred days, then shall the cleansing come."

8:13 I had no idea the meaning of this dream and begged to the lord for guidance.

8:14 Suddenly, before my eyes stood the appearance of a man clothed in light, who called himself Gabriel.

8:15 I fell upon my face, for surely this was a messenger sent from the lord.

8:16 Now, as he spoke to me, my face was deep within the earth: but he touched me and set me upright.

8:17 And he said, "Behold, I shall give you insight to the meaning of your vision, as it is the will of the almighty.

8:18 That ram with the two mighty horns are the kings of Media and Persia.

8:19 Of that goat with the brass horn is Grecia and the horn is their first king.

8:20 Now, when the kingdom of the mighty horn be broken, four lesser kingdoms shall come forth, but not from his power.

8:21 And lo, a dark age will come, where the word of the lord will be deaf to the ears of the people for many days."

8:22 I then awoke and was sick for many days: I was astonished by this vision, but understood it not.

8:23 Of all the wise men I spoke to, they knew not the interpretation, even with the aid of the word of Gabriel.

8:24 What were these dark days which was spoken of. What means the two thousand and three hundred days. What is the cleansing?

8:25 None understood it, so that all the wise men became confused as I: and we began to fear the lord greatly and wept.

9:1 In the first year of Darius the son of Ahasuerus, of the seed of Medes, made king over the empire of Babylon;

9:2 In that year I understood the book of Jeremiah and knew that those of the Jews would be held seventy years in captivity: and after these years we would be free to go home to the sacred city of Jerusalem.

9:3 And I set my face unto the lord God, to beg for forgiveness and mercy: I wore sash cloth around my waist and covered myself in ashes.

9:4 I prayed to the lord, "Forgive us, we rebellious people, for we knew not what we done.

9:5 Our thighs have opened to the many who passed by and they did lay beside us in our bed: how we have played the harlot, O lord of Israel.

9:6 Lo, our loins are bruised with the stones of idols and we bleed like the menstrual woman.

9:7 Free us from this evil, O lord, so that we may redeem ourselves in your city and rebuild the temple of the one true God.

9:8 No more shall we bow down unto the graven image, nor eat the flesh of the unclean beast; we shall abide by the laws of Moses forever, so that we may gain favour in the sight of the holiest of holies.

9:9 Deliver us unto Jerusalem, as was foretold in the prophesies of Jeremiah, so that we may become a righteous nation once more.

9:10 Behold, we have been humbled in the presence of the heathen and know now the transgressions we did trespass upon you.

9:11 Curse be to our fathers, who sealed us in the fate of damnation; give us the opportunity, O lord, to free our children from the fires of hell, so that they may see the salvation of Zion."

9:12 And as I spoke, the angel of Gabriel appeared to me and said, "O Daniel, who claims to know the wisdom and the understanding of the lord.

9:13 Do you not see the will of God. Are you so blind that you believe that your children will be given the chance of salvation?

9:14 The lord wishes not you men of the earth to step foot within his holy city; he has damned you to the wastes of darkness so that his streets remain clean of your filth.

9:15 Just as the man wishes not the goat to walk in the streets of the city, so does the lord wishes not your feet to grace the golden roads of Zion.

9:16 You are damned, such as your fathers are damned, such as your children shall be damned."

9:17 It was then that Gabriel swiftly ascended into the clouds: and I fell on my face, and wept.

9:18 For surely the words of Gabriel were false and the lord will give us the chance for salvation; a chance to step foot in Zion.

10:1 In the third year of Cyrus king of Persia a vision was revealed unto Daniel, whose name was called Belteshazzar: and the thing was true, but Daniel understood it not.

10:2 And in those days, I was fasting for three full weeks.

10:3 For three weeks I ate no bread, nor did flesh pass through my lips, nor wine flow through my mouth.

10:4 Now in the four and twentieth day of the first month I walked beside the great river, which was Hiddekel.

10:5 I lifted my eyes to the heavens and their above me was a man clothed in linen, whose loins were wrapped in fine gold.

10:6 His body was like the beryl and his face the appearance of lightning with eyes like the fire; his legs and arms were of polished brass and he spoke with the voice of the violent seas.

10:7 And I alone saw the vision, for the men beside me did not, but fled in the quake that shook the earth with terror.

10:8 Therefore I was left alone to witness this vision and their remained in me no strength, for I did not eat in weeks.

10:9 Yet I heard the voice of his words: and when I heard the voice of his words, I did fall into a deep sleep, so that my face was buried in the earth.

10:10 Behold, a hand touched me, which set me upon my knees and the palms of my hands.

10:11 And he said to me, "O Daniel, son of Jerusalem, understand the words I speak to you and stand upright." And as I stood, I trembled before his form.

10:12 And the man said to me, "Behold, the end of your captivity draws near and soon you and your kin shall go to Jerusalem, so that you may rebuild the glory of the one true God.

10:13 I shall show unto you now the fate of those who held you captive, so that ye may know that I am God.

10:14 They will all go to hell."

10:15 Thus I spread the word that those who held us captive will all go to hell; they didn't like me.

10:16 I was very unpopular among the heathens.

11:1 It came to pass that Shoshana, wife of Lodecres, was fairest amongst the people of the earth.

11:2 The men lusted for her deeply and would watch in secret as she bathed in her garden.

11:3 It came to pass that two elders of Judah watched her bathe in secret and as Shoshana sent her maidens away, these men did devise a scheme.

11:4 They came to Shoshana and said, "We shall tell all the elders of Judah and Babylon that, tonight, we witnessed you a harlot.

11:5 For when your maidens left, you did meet with a young man and played the harlot with him."

11:6 Shoshana begged them to keep their tongues still and offered them wealth to keep them quiet.

11:7 "Oh no," said the elders of Judah. "It is not your wealth we wish from you, but your flesh.

11:8 Lie with us both in our chambers and we will tell none of your lustful acts."

11:9 Shoshana refused to lie with these two elders, for they were ugly and of a most foul odour.

11:10 So the two elders told the men that Shoshana did lie with a young man in her garden, behind the back of her husband.

11:11 She was judged by the courts of Judah and sentenced to death according to the laws of Moses.

11:12 Now Daniel knew Shoshana well and new she would not cheat upon her husband; for he has advanced upon her and was denied her flesh.

11:13 So Daniel separated the elders, named Hrornynam and Baltsasuk.

11:14 He questioned both men about what they saw the night Shoshana played the harlot.

11:15 Both men told a similar story, but with one detail wrong:

11:16 Hrornynam claimed they were lying under the mastic tree and Baltsasuk said they were resting under the oak.

11:17 Daniel told the people of Judah and Babylon, "These men lie, so that they may shed the blood of an innocent woman.

11:18 For one man claims they lay under the branches of the mastic, while the other the mighty oak."

11:19 Thus Shoshana was innocent in the eyes of the laws of Moses and the two elders were stoned for spreading falsehood.

11:20 When Shoshana came to Daniel, she said to him, "I owe you my life. I beg of thee, tell me that which I may do to reward you."

11:21 And Daniel answered swiftly, "Drop your skirts and spread your loins."

11:22 Shoshana refused.

11:23 So Daniel claimed he saw her playing the harlot with a young man as she bathed in her garden.

11:24 She was stoned to death and Daniel lifted her skirt after her death.

12:1 As Daniel took lust in the cold flesh of Shoshana, the spirit of the lord filled her and she spoke to Daniel, saying,

12:2 "Behold, the son of God shall come to the people of the earth and stand before them in glory and fear; he shall come in a time of trouble such as has been never seen on the face of the earth.

12:3 And lo, he shall speak, so that those who lie in the dust will be awakened and sent to the everlasting fires of damnation.

12:4 The firmament above will shine in brightness for the last time: and a cloud of ash will spread across the skies and darken the firmament for eternity.

12:5 It shall be the end of days, where those of the seed of men will dwell in everlasting lamentations.

12:6 The waters will be bitter as wormwood and the maggot will dwell inside your belly."

12:7 Daniel did not hearken the words of the lord; he did not even become aware that Shoshana spoke.

12:8 He was too busy fucking her corpse.

HOSEA

1:1 The word of the lord came to Hosea the son of Beeri, in the days of Uzziah, Jotham, Ahaz and Hezekiah the kings of Judah and in the days of Jeroboam the son of Joash, king of Israel.

1:2 And the lord said to Hosea, "Go, and take for yourself a wife of whoredoms, for the people of Israel have committed whoredoms to the very lands."

1:3 So Hosea bought Gomer the whore from her father, Diblaim.

1:4 And Hosea was very happy with his purchase, for this whore knew how to please a man, unlike the righteous woman.

1:5 In time, Gomer bore Hosea a son: and the lord said to him, "Call this son of a whore Jezreel; for it shall come to pass that I will avenge the blood of Jezreel upon the house of Jehu and will destroy the kingdom of Israel.

1:6 And on that day, I will break my covenant with Israel, in the valley of Jezreel."

1:7 Hosea slept with Gomer again, for she was a pleasing woman who enjoyed the lustful acts of fellatio and sodomy.

1:8 And it so happened that Gomer bare Hosea a daughter. And the lord said to him, "Call this bitch Loruhamah: for I will have no mercy on the house of Israel, but will destroy them in the lake of fire.

1:9 And I will have no mercy on the house of Judah; I will send not my bow, my sword, my chariots nor horses to aid Jerusalem."

1:10 Hosea didn't pay much attention to the word of God; he was too busy fucking his whore of a wife.

1:11 After Loruhamah, Gomer did bare Hosea another son: and the lord came down and said to Hosea, "Call his name Loammi: for he is not my people and I will not be his God.

1:12 For even when the children of Israel number greater than the sands of the ocean and the stars of the sky, I will deny them my love and show them no mercy.

1:13 Lo, I will lead them to the plains of Jezreel, where the venomous rain will fall upon their heads and they lie atop one another in death."

2:1 Woe to the children of Hosea; plead unto your mother, for she is not the wife nor he her husband: let her keep secret the filth of her whoredoms and let her adulteries hide between her breasts.

2:2 Lest I tear off her raiment's so that she be naked as the day of her birth, set her upon the dry land and slay her with thirst.

2:3 Curse be to her children, for I will not have mercy upon them; they are the children of whoredoms.

2:4 For their mother played the harlot: she who has taken many lovers in her bed for the gifts of bread, wine and jewels.

2:5 Therefore I will thrust horns between her loins and make a wall around her skirt, so that none may be tarnished by her filth.

2:6 She shall follow after her lovers, but will not overtake them; she shall seek them and they will hide from her.

2:7 Then she will say, "I will go now to my first husband, for he did give me bread, wine and meat.

2:8 He did give me flour, corn, wine, silver and flax which I did offer to Baal."

2:9 Therefore I will take from her her corn, her wine, her flax and her silver: even her wool that covers her nakedness I will tear from her body.

2:10 And her lewdness will be discovered in the sight of her lovers, who will loathe her and wish her damned.

2:11 I will deny her mirth, flesh, rest and even the sabbath day.

2:12 Of all her vines and her fig trees I will destroy, so that not even the beasts of the field will eat of them.

2:13 And on the days of Baalim I will visit her, as she burns incense to the unholy image: and she will deck herself with silks, earrings and jewels, chasing after new lovers.

2:14 On this day I will lure her into the wilderness, speaking words of comfort into her ear.

2:15 And then I shall tear the very word of Baal from her tongue, so that she speaks it no more.

2:16 I will make a covenant with the beasts of the fields and the fowl of the air, that so long as they worship me, they may feast upon the children of this harlot.

2:17 The beasts and the fowl will be given the vineyards, the corn and the oil: and they shall grow fat and drunk.

2:18 As of the children of the harlot, they will be forever beaten under the talons of the eagle and the teeth of the lion.

3:1 Then the lord said to me, "Go, love a woman that belongs to your friend and commit adultery to her; seduce her with flagons of wine,"

3:2 So I bought the wife of a friend for fifteen pieces of silver and a homer and a half of barley; I was ripped off.

3:3 Then I said to her, "You shall lie with me and only me all the days of your life; you shall not play the harlot, nor lie with another man.

3:4 For it shall be that the children of Israel will abide many days without a god, without a king, without a prince, without a sacrifice, without an image, without an ephod and without a teraphim:

3:5 Afterward they shall cry unto the lord and seek his glory and the glory of king David: and the lord shall deny them and send fear into their house."

4:1 Hear the word of the lord, children of Israel, for you have lost the word of God and replaced it with the venom of logic and truth.

4:2 You live now like the predators of the mountains; you live a life of lying, swearing, stealing, killing and whoredoms.

4:3 Because you have denied God, I shall cause the very lands to mourn and the beasts of the fields, the fowls of the heavens and the fish of the sea will perish in your blood.

4:4 Listen not to the false prophets, who spread lies and deceit through their lips; they are a treacherous bunch, who condemn even their mother to damnation.

4:5 My people are destroyed for their lack of knowledge: because they have rejected the wisdom of God, I will reject even their priests and send them into the darkness and the void.

4:6 As you grew forth and multiplied, so did your transgressions against me: therefore, I will make you feel your shame.

4:7 Even the heathen gaze upon you and know that you have sinned.

4:8 Your children grow drunk and commit whoredoms in the lands of strangers; they commit whoredoms in the fields, in the trees, in the waters.

4:9 They do this, for you have burned incense atop the high places to graven images; you have denied the one true God and he has thus made your daughters whores and your wives the harlot.

4:10 I will drown thee in the sour wine of your transgressions, as is the will of God.

5:1 Hear me, O priests: and hearken, the house of Israel: and lend ear, O house of the king; for judgment is upon you. The snare has been set in Mizpah and the net spread across Tabor.

5:2 You who revolt I will gather for the slaughter, so that my dogs grow drunk with your blood.

5:3 The eyes of God see the house of Ephraim and Israel; you have not hid from me.

5:4 O Ephraim, how ye have played the harlot and how Israel is defiled in filth.

5:5 They wallow in their sin and turn not their eyes unto God: for the spirit of whoredoms blinds them, so that they know not the lord.

5:6 The prides of Israel and Ephraim will lead them down the roads of hell: and Judah shall follow with them.

5:7 Lo, when the time of trouble comes, you shall go to your flocks and offer sacrifice according to the laws of Moses: but I shall not come, for my ear is deaf to your cries.

5:8 They have dealt treacherously with the lord God and begat children of impure blood: now shall the lord consume them in his wrath.

5:9 Blow the cornet in Gibeah and the trumpet in Ramah: cry aloud at Bethaven, those of the tribe of Benjamin.

5:10 Ephraim will be desolate in the end of days: this shall surely be, for the lord has spoken.

5:11 The princes of Judah have kept in their chambers the graven image: therefore, I will pour out my wrath upon them like boiling water.

5:12 And when Ephraim sees their sickness and Judah her womb, they shall go to the wizards that shared their bed: and they shall not heal you.

5:13 For I will tear Ephraim and Judah like the young lion: I tear and go away, so that none will rescue you.

5:14 I will go and return to my throne in Zion: and I shall mock your pleas, your prayers and your lamentations.

6:1 Behold, the lord will separate us, hating the old and embracing the new: he separates us with wooden board and nail.

6:2 His son comes down from the heavens, to be bonded and beaten by the seed of Jacob.

6:3 Of two days he will rest from his sores and on the third he shall rise and mock is in our sight.

6:4 Know, O people of earth, that the son of God comes down to spread forth lies and lead us further into the path of damnation.

6:5 He preaches of a lord of mercy, of love, who desires peace and not sacrifice.

6:6 Such lies are this, for the lord demands the blood of the beast, the blood of virgins: such as is written in the books of Moses.

6:7 Lo, the words of the son of God are words of venom hidden deep within the savoury meat: hearken not these words and know the lord curses you.

6:8 He curses you for the lewdness of your fathers and condemns you, for your mother was the harlot.

6:9 The whoredoms of this nation are great and for this they will be drowned in the everlasting fires of oblivion.

7:1 I pour salt in the wounds of Israel, for I have seen the lust in their whoredoms: I gaze upon the iniquities of Ephraim and the wickedness of Samaria.

7:2 They care not that I know their wickedness, for their hearts are full of pride: soon they shall fall before me and wallow in the stench of their dung.

7:3 These men of Israel make their kings happy with their wickedness and please the princes with their whoredoms.

7:4 They are all adulterers, as an oven heated by the baker, who ceases from raising after the dough has been kneaded, until it be leavened.

7:5 In the days of the kings our princes have made him sick wine, adulterers and queer men; he stretches out his hands to those that are scorned and embraces them in his bed.

7:6 For they have made ready their heart like the oven, while they lie in wait: their baker sleeps all the night, so that in the morning their oven be consumed in fire.

7:7 They are all as hot as the oven, with kings fallen from righteousness: there is none among them I love.

7:8 Ephraim has mixed their seed among the people; they are as a cake that is not turned.

7:9 Strangers have devoured his strength and they know it not; they lie in the bed all their days and become as lazy as the slug.

7:10 The pride of Israel keeps them from confessing their wickedness: and they bow down to the heathen lords, seeking not the one true God.

7:11 They are like a silly dove without brain: they call to Egypt, they go to Assyria.

7:12 I will bring my net down upon them; I will bring them down from the fowls of the heavens; I will pluck them and roast them atop the burning stone.

7:13 Woe to them! for they have blasphemed my name: destruction unto them! because they refuse my laws: though I led them away from the servitude of Pharaoh, they deny my covenant and abuse the lands.

7:14 They choose the wickedness of truth, logic and science; they rather have logic than salvation through ignorance.

7:15 Even when I have given strength to their arms, they have done mischief against me.

7:16 Such as they forget their God, I shall come forth and remind them of my anger; I will bring swords upon their princes and cause their children to fall in the bellies of dragons: and they will know that I am God.

8;1 Set the trumpet to your mouth. His anger comes like the eagle against the house of the lord, for they have transgressed my covenant and ignored my law.

8:2 Israel shall cry, we have done no harm against you.

8:3 Israel has cast away my holiness: I shall send enemies to their door.

8:4 They have set up kings, but not by me: they have made princes whose names I know not: of their silver and their gold they have made idols, which they bow down to and offer incense in the high places.

8:5 How long shall Samaria claim innocence, as they stand in the temple of the golden calf?

8:6 How I loathe those of Samaria and the calf which they did make; I shall shatter them both to pieces and spread them across the earth.

8:7 A great whirlwind will come and deny them their meats; it shall take from them the stalk, the trees and the vine, delivering it to the hands of the heathens.

8:8 Israel is swallowed up: now they shall be sold as whores and slaves to the wealthy Gentile.

8:9 For they have gone to Assyria, where they will be forever alone in the crowd of demons.

8:10 Ephraim has hired her lovers; nations gathered together so that I may pour my hatred upon you.

8:11 Because my people have forgotten their maker and bow down to the carvings of stone, I shall set fire within their cities and devour their palaces in the earthen jaw.

9:1 Rejoice not, O Israel, for the joy shall be denied to you: for you hast gone a whoring from your God and have lifted your skirts upon every cornfield.

9:2 The floor and the winepress will not feed you and the new wine will grow poisonous in your belly.

9:3 No longer will you dwell in the land of the covenant; but Ephraim will return under the yoke of Egypt and have their throat forced full with the unclean swine.

9:4 They shall not offer wine offerings to their lord, for they shall wallow in the intoxication of the grape; neither shall their sacrifice be pleasing unto God: their sacrifices will be as mouldy bread to the holiest of holies.

9:5 All they eat thereof shall be polluted: neither their bread nor their soul will enter the house of the lord.

9:6 What will you do in the solemn day, in the day of the feast of the lord?

9:7 For lo, they are gone by the destruction of the lord: Egypt shall gather them, Memphis will bury them and the heathens will divide up their silver, their gold and their wealth.

9:8 The prophet is a fool and the spiritual man mad, for they are poisoned by the multitude of sins and hated greatly by God.

9:9 The watchmen will warn of the destruction from the lord, but the prophet will speak forth lies to the people and with his tongue snare them into the wrath of the lord.

9:10 You have deeply corrupted yourselves, O sons of Jacob, as in the days of Gibeah: therefore, I shall mock you as you suffer in the crevices of hell.

9:11 I found Israel to be like grapes in the wilderness; I saw promise in your fathers to bring forth a fruitful wine: and you now have become bitter in the winepress of the heathen.

9:12 As for Ephraim, I will strike them from the birth, from the womb, from conception.

9:13 Though the seed in their belly grow, I shall burn it before the harvest and let the fruit rot in the belly of the mother.

9:14 They shall pray to me for fruitful wives and I will deliver them a miscarrying womb and dry breasts.

9:15 All their wickedness is shown to me and I hate them: for the wickedness of their fathers I will drive them out of my house and love them no more.

9:16 The sin, the sin, the sin is but an act and how can one hate the act. The sinner is the beast and it is he who is hated.

9:17 Ephraim is smitten, their root is dry up and their fruits rot on the vine: yea, though they bring forth, I shall slay them even the fruit of their womb.

9:18 God shall cast them away, for they did not abide by the strictest of the laws of Moses: and they sought out manners of logic and science, a most blasphemous subject.

10:1 Israel is a selfish vine who consumes her own fruits: the more of their fruits they consume, the more altars they build and the more graven images they carve from gold.

10:2 Their heart is divided and found guilty in the holy court: he shall break down their altars and burn their images to ash.

10:3 They shall say, "We have no king, for the lord has smitten him from his throne. What now shall we do without a king?"

10:4 They have whispered blasphemy in the ears of children, swearing falsely in my name: thus, my wrath will spring upon them as weeds in the field.

10:5 The people of Samaria shall fear because of the calves of Bethaven: for the peoples thereof shall mourn over these blasphemous calves and the priests will weep and pour ashes over their heads.

10:6 Those of Ephraim will be carried to Assyria as a present for king Jareb: Ephraim will know shame and Israel will be shamed in their counsel.

10:7 As for Samaria, her king is cut off and cast upon the rocks of the highest cliff.

10:8 The high places of Aven, the sin of Israel, will be destroyed: the thorn and thistle will grow beneath them, consuming even the strongest mountains in their grasp.

10:9 It is my desire that I make the seed of Jacob suffer, for I am a God of cruel delight.

10:10 Then is shall be that the mothers and the children be dashed in mangled gore upon one another and their blood drip in the winepress of Zion.

10:11 So I shall do this, for you have sinned against me, O Israel.

11:1 When Israel was but a child, then I loved him and freed him from the hands of Egypt.

11:2 As they went forth, they rebelled against me: they worshipped to the false god Baalim and burned incense at his grove.

11:3 I taught Ephraim to stand forth, though they know not that I healed them.

11:4 I freed them from the cords of their bindings, removed the yoke from their jaw and placed meat upon their table.

11:5 Those of Ephraim that refuse to go to Egypt will live under the king of Assyria, for they refused to return to Pharaoh.

11:6 And the sword will surround their cities and consume them and their branches, devouring them in bloody rage.

11:7 As of my people who went backsliding before me, they shall beg for my mercy: and I will not exalt them.

11:8 I will execute the fierceness of my anger and destroy Israel: for I am God, and will enter their cities with flame.

11:9 My voice will roar like the lion, so that all those of the west will tremble in fear of my anger.

11:10 They shall tremble as a bird out of Egypt and the dove out of Assyria: and I will burn their houses before them; And they shall know that I am God.

12:1 Ephraim feasts upon the dung of the beasts and drinks the piss of serpents: he daily increases in lies and desolation; and they make a covenant with the Assyrians.

12:2 The lord also has hatred for Judah and will punish the seed of Jacob for their sins.

12:3 He took his mother and plunged deeply in her bowels; her womb grew the seed of her son and bared forth the strange child.

12:4 They play the harlot to false gods; how their loins are bruised by the beatings of stone.

12:5 Though it is the lord who brings destruction upon them, let it be known that it is they who spilled their blood upon the dust.

12:6 I will pounce upon them like the lion: and as the leopard I shall observe them in shadow.

12:7 I will meet them like the bear who is bereaved from her cubs and will tear the fat from their bones and devour them like the gluttonous lion; like the wild beast shall I tear them.

12:8 O Samaria, you have betrayed me in your rebellion and played the harlot to devils: now you shall be dashed to pieces on the cliffs, fall by the sword and your women with child will be torn apart by the eagles of Zion.

12:9 How my feet are stained crimson by the blood of your infants; the blood of the children of whoredom.

JOEL

1:1 The word of the lord that came unto Joel the son of Pethuel.

1:2 Hear this, you old men and give ear if you be not deaf; listen, all inhabitants of the land. Has this been in your days, or even the days of your fathers?

1:3 Tell your children of it, so that they may tell their children, who tell their children, so that generations are told.

1:4 There shall be naught for you to feast, for the crawlers of the earth will eat of your table; that which the palmer-worm has left will be eaten by the locust: and that which is left by the locusts the canker-worm has eaten: and that which the canker-worm has eaten has been consumed by the caterpillar.

1:5 So starve, you children of Israel, or learn to eat bugs.

1:6 Awake, you drunkards and be burned by the heat of the morning sun; howl, you drinkers of wine, because the new wine shall cut your very tongue.

1:7 For a nation will come upon our land, strong and blessed with number, whose teeth are the teeth of the lion and talons sharp as the blade.

1:8 He has laid my vine to waste and made barren my fig tree; he has made it clean bare, so that the trees are white like the dry bones.

1:9 Weep, you children of Israel, like the virgin girded with sackcloth whose husband died at the hour of their wedding.

1:10 The meat and the wine will be cut off from the house of the lord; the priests mourn in hunger and thirst.

1:11 The field is wasted and the lands do weep; for the corn is wasted, the wine is bitter and the oil dry.

1:12 Be ashamed, you men of the fields; howl, O caretakers of the vine; for the grape does rot in the noon sun and the harvest of the field is slain.

1:13 The vine is dried up and the fig tree languishes; the pomegranate tree, the apple tree and the palm tree wither in the fields: because the lord even hates them and punishes them for the sins of their fruits.

1:14 Gird yourselves and lament, you priests: howl like the wolf, O ministers of the altar: come, lie in sackcloth and bathe in the ashes of dung: for the lord has denied you your meat and your wine.

1:15 Gather yourself for fasting; come, gather you elders and inhabitants of the land into the temple and cry to the lord.

1:16 Alas, fear this day! for the day of the lord is come and the destruction of the almighty is at hand.

1:17 Even your eyes will grow blind in hunger; lo, how they rot from the vessels of your face.

1:18 The seed is burned under the soil, the crops lay desolate, the barns rot into the earth; for the corn is withered.

1:19 How your beasts groan and your herds of cattle grow in confusion, because they have no pasture; yea, the bellies of the flocks growl in pain.

1:20 O lord, how I cry for them; for the fire has devoured the fruits of our labours and the flame did burn the trees of the field.

1:21 Even the beasts beg you for mercy: for the rivers of water now flow with dust and the fire hath devoured the pastures and the grass.

2:1 Blow the trumpet in Zion and sound the bells in my holy mountain: let all the inhabitants of the land tremble, for the day of the lord comes.

2:2 A day of darkness and gloominess, with clouds thick with ash; the morning spread upon the mountains a black scar: the great people which have never been come and will vanish in the smoke, never to be seen for generations.

2:3 The fire devours before them; and behind them the flames of hell: even the land of the garden of Eden is consumed and become desolate; yea, nothing shall escape.

2:4 The appearance of them is of chariots pulled by dragons; thus, they run in fear.

2:5 Like the noise of thunder across the mountains they shall leap; like the noise of the fire that devours the oak they come in battle.

2:6 Before their faces the people will know much pain: all faces shall be blackened in the ashes of Armageddon.

2:7 They shall run like mighty men; they shall climb the wall like men of war; they shall march everyone their ways; and never shall they break rank.

2:8 Do not defend yourself from the armies for the lord; lo, when they fall upon the sword, they be not injured.

2:9 They shall run to and fro in the city; they shall tear down the walls of our defenses; they shall fly above our houses; they shall break

through our windows.

2:10 The earth will quake beneath their feet; both heathen and Jew will tremble; the sun and the moon will be dark, and the stars will be covered by the curtain of the firmament.

2:11 And the lord shall shout his voice before his army: for his camp is mighty and strong: behold, the day of the lord is great and terrible; and who can abide it?

2:12 The lord shall shout, "Thus sayeth the lord, come to me those who have fasted, those of mourning and those with heavy heart.

2:13 Pull out thine your and rend your garments before me and repent your wickedness before the lord God; for I am gracious, slow to anger and merciful to those worthy.

2:14 Those who know me, come and repent, so that I may bless you with wine, bread and meat.

2:15 Hear the trumpet in Zion. Know that your salvation comes.

2:16 Go forth and assemble thy elders, gather the congregation, bring forth the bride and the bridegroom and give to me those that suckle on the mother's breast.

2:17 For I the lord God shall show you pity and bless you with kindness and joy.

2:18 Behold, I will send you corn, wine and oil so that your bellies grow fat; and no more will the heathen bother you with blade and bow.

2:19 Fear not, for I will restore upon you a great many things, for I am a God of mercy.

2:20 Be not afraid, those beasts of the field, for I will cause your pastures to grow and the rivers to run with precious water.

2:21 Be gladdened, you children of Jacob, for the lord offers you salvation in the house of Zion; my armies have chased the wicked from your soul and made you clean and holy.

2:22 Come now, rejoice the name of your God and sing praises to my name; for I have dealt wondrously with you and treated you with kind hand."

2:23 Thus the congregation shall come before God and repent their sins.

2:24 Then the sun will be turned into darkness and the moon drip with blood upon the children of Israel.

2:25 Pillars of smoke will come forth from the earth and blind us in terrible darkness; the fires of hell will kindle beneath our feet.

2:26 And the earth will be filled with the sound of the lord cackling above us, mocking our suffering in his wrath.

3:1 For behold, in those days and in that time when I shall burn the captivity of Judah and Jerusalem,

3:2 I will also gather all nations and bring them down to the valley of Jehoshaphat and curse them for the whoredoms they did partake with Israel.

3:3 They have cast lots for the peoples of the lord; and have given a boy for a concubine and sold a girl for wine.

3:4 Because they have taken my silver and my gold and carried them into the temples of their false lords, they will tremble before me and witness the fury of my wrath.

3:5 Behold, I will cause you to burn within the fires of damnation and deny you the salvations of your gods.

3:6 Your sons and your daughters will I sell to the demons of the far-off land: for the lord has spoken it.

3:7 Proclaim this among the Gentiles; Prepare war, wake up the mighty men and gather against the armies of the lord.

3:8 Beat your plowshares into swords and your pruning-hooks to spears: let the weak say they are strong.

3:9 Assemble yourselves and come forth against the battalions of Zion; let howl the cries for battle.

3:10 And when the multitudes of the lord come marching toward you, you will know true fear; the sun and the moon will be darkened and the stars deny you their light, for the day of the lord is upon you.

3:11 My voice will roar from my house in Jerusalem, which you have trespassed and taken the goods within; the heavens and the earth will shake in terror.

3:12 And it shall come to pass that the mountains will arise and crush you under my command: that the rivers will drown you in obedience to me: even the grass will grow sharp and pierce the soles of your feet.

3:13 You will fall before my might and your blood will cleanse the lands of your wickedness.

3:14 Let the fires of my hate come forth and consume the four corners of the earth; Let the lands be filled with the lamentations of Jew and Gentile.

3:15 This shall be a most pleasing sound to the lord, who dwells in the holy palace of Zion.

AMOS

1:1 The words of Amos, who was among the herdsmen of Tekoa, which he saw concerning Israel in the days of Uzziah king of Judah and Jeroboam the son of Joash, king of Israel, two years before the earthquake.

1:2 And he said, "The lord will roar from Zion, uttering curses to those of Jerusalem; and the habitations of the shepherd will cower in fear and the top of Carmel shall rot.

1:3 Thus sayeth the lord; for your whoredoms you did within the chambers of Damascus, I will bring forth the punishment harshly to you; because you did open your loins to them, you will know the wrath of God.

1:4 I will send a fire in the house of Hazael, which will burn to ash the palaces of Benhadad.

1:5 I will break also the gates of Damascus and cut them off from the plains of Aven and strip the sceptre of those in the house of Eden: and the people of Syria will become slaves for the men of Kir, says the lord God.

1:6 For your transgressions of Gaza, I will strike you with a heavy hand; because they carried away the captive, the whole captivity and delivered them to Edom.

1:7 I will send fire to the walls of Gaza, which shall devour the palaces within:

1:8 And I will cut off those that pisses against the wall of Ashdod and him that holds the sceptre from Ashkelon and will turn my eyes to Ekron: and the remains of the Philistine will perish under the yoke of the lord.

1:9 For your transgressions of Tyrus, I will bring down the hammer; because they delivered the captivity to Edom and remembered not the covenant of their brother.

1:10 I will send fire to the streets of Tyrus and consume their children in the flames of my hate.

1:11 For the sins of Edom, I will stomp them as grapes in the winepress; for they did pursue their brother with the sword, showed no pity and his anger and wrath did rule his heart.

1:12 They are men like God and for this I will send fire to Teman and burn to hell the palaces of Bozrah.

1:13 No mortal man must be like the lord; it is a mockery unto me.

1:14 For the iniquities of the children of Ammon, I will send the chariots to ou; for they have made child with the women of Gilead, so that they might increase their seed.

1:15 Thus I will kindle a fire in the wall of Rabbah and it shall devour the palaces thereof: and the shouting of their bastard children will blow in the winds.

1:16 And their kings will go into captivity, he and his princes together; to be placed under a heavy yoke."

2:1 Thus sayeth the lord; for the wickedness of Moab, I will curse them with a heavy tongue; for they did burn the bones of the king of Edom into lime as a sacrifice to a heathen lord and not to me.

2:2 So I shall send fire upon Moab, which will destroy the palaces of Kirioth: and Moab will perish with turmoil, with shouting and with the sounds of lamenting children.

2:3 And I will cut them off from the earth and slay all the princes thereof, says the lord.

2:4 For the blasphemy of Judah, I will piss into their very mouths; because they have despised the laws of the lord and chose logic, knowledge and truth over the commandments of their fathers.

2:5 So I shall send fire to Jerusalem and devour their palaces within.

2:6 For I the lord am a pyromaniac and grow aroused by the seductive flame.

2:7 For the blasphemy of Israel, I will fill their mouths with dung; because they sold the righteous for silver and gave shoes to the filthy beggar.

2:8 They lust for the flesh of women and become meek; lo, a man and his father will enter into the same maid, profaning my holy name.

2:9 And they burn incense beside the altars of idols and drink wine of the condemned in the house of the lord.

2:10 Though I destroyed the Amorite before them, who were as tall as cedars and strong as the oak; I did destroy their fruits and roots from beneath and those of Israel still deny me.

2:11 Also, I brought you up from the land of Egypt and led you to the land of the covenant, you call me cruel for the plagues and the wrath I did place upon your head during those forty years.

2:12 I grow angry in the accusations of Israel and my fury grows strong within my bowels; behold, I am pressed under you as a cart full of sheaves.

2:13 Therefore I will descend on you swiftly, such that the swift perishes, the strong grow weak and the mighty hide in cowardice.

2:14 None shall stand before me, nor be given the mercy they beg to me: for on this day the courageous will run away naked, says the lord.

3:1 Hear this which the lord hath spoken against you, O children of Israel, against the whole family which has been brought out of Egypt.

3:2 Of you I have known well amongst all the families of the earth; you are all wicked and for this I will destroy in the damnation of the end of days.

3:3 We two cannot walk together, for we disagree: just as two men cannot be neighbours if they disagree with one another.

3:4 The lion will not roar in the forest, if he has no prey to hunt. The cub will not cry from his den, if he takes nothing.

3:5 Know that when the trumpets blow, you will know fear; you will see the lord and know that all evil comes from his spirit.

3:6 The lord speaks falsely in the ears of the prophets, denying them the secrets of salvation; they prophesy like the lion, spreading deceit to those of Israel.

3:7 Publish in the palaces of Ashdod and in the lands of Egypt: and gather yourselves in the mountains of Samaria and behold the wrath of your God.

3:8 For I have stored my violence and evil in golden jars decorated with precious stones and I shall pour them upon your heads, your palaces, your dwellings.

3:9 It shall flow through the streets and the valleys, consuming all that which is Samaria.

3:10 Hear ye and testify in the house of Jacob, says the lord God, the God of all gods.

3:11 That in the day of my coming I will visit even your altars and break from them the horns of Bethel, so that you know that I am God.

3:12 And I will smite. your winter house with your summer house: and the houses of ivory shall perish in the freezing muck of damnation, says the lord.

4:1 Hear ye, you of Bashan, that dwell within the mountains of Samaria, who give bounty to the poor, bread to the needy and drink wine with neighbours of strange men.

4:2 The lord God hath swore to himself that, lo, the days will come upon you, that he will drag you by the hooks and tear off your loins with the rusty nail.

4:3 I am angry with you, O Bashan, for you show mercy to those undeserving of such acts; how I long for thee to return to the lord.

4:4 I have made empty your tables and took from you your bread and you did not return to me.

4:5 I have closed the firmament above you, so that the rain not fall, when you were three months to the harvest: upon no cities did the rain from heaven fall.

4:6 You did travel to the riverbed, full of muck and filth, for just a drink of water and still ye did not return to me.

4:7 I have smitten you with mildew and parasites, so that your vines, your fig trees, your olive branches be devoured by the palmer-worm and you did not return to me.

4:8 I have sent the plague and the pestilence upon you worse than that of Egypt: your young men did I slaughter with the sword and have sold your daughters to the perverse; and I have made the stink of death fill your lands and offend your nostrils: yet still you did not return to me.

4:9 I have overthrown your cities as I did to Sodom and Gomorrah and you were as the kindling in the great fire: and still you have not returned to me.

4:10 Therefore, O Israel, prepare to meet your God who you denied for generations.

4:11 For I am the lord of hosts, who did carve the mountains, created the wind and separated the light from the darkness: and I come to destroy you in magnificent slaughter, for you have denied that which is God.

4:12 What would the lord have to do to get ye to accept me. Something nice?

4:13 That's just silly.

5:1 Hear ye this word which I have spoken against you, O Israel; allow your lamentations to multiply in your house.

5:2 The virgin of the land lies beside the harlot; she has fallen and will not rise; for the men of Israel lay atop her and steal away her virtues.

5:3 For thus sayeth the lord God; of every city that dwells one thousand, I shall leave one hundred and of every house which contains ten, I will spare one from the end of my blade.

5:4 For you are unholy men, who seek Bethel, Baal, Ashteroth and who burn incense at Beersheba and pass into Gilgal.

5:5 You seek not the lord; thus, I shall enter into your house and devour it in the fires of hell.

5:6 You fools who deny the lord God, which make the seven stars of Orion and turn the shadows of death in the morning: that separates the light from the dark and bring forth the waters above.

5:7 You are men of evil all, who reject the wisdom of God for the confusion of logic and truth.

5:8 Behold, you have spoiled the just and made them as bitter as wormwood.

5:9 Therefore the lord, the God of all gods, will cause a wailing in the streets and upon the highways; alas! alas! all husbands shall be mourning and mothers wail in lamentation.

5:10 Even in the vineyards there shall be wailing; for when I pass through, you shall wail and know that I was there.

5:11 Woe unto those that desire the day of the lord, for it will be the end of man. The darkness will consume you in cold embrace.

5:12 (Stupid Christians, who wish for the coming of God)

5:13 You shall flee not from the lord. For if you flee from the lion, the bear will meet you in your lot: and if you run in your house, the viper will strike at your heel.

5:14 O, the day of the lord will be a day of darkness; even the sun will be denied from the heavens.

5:15 I hate you all and despise the offerings which you offer on my altars.

5:16 Though you offer me your burnt offerings and your meat offerings, I will not accept them: you have angered the lord and no amount of sacrifice will cause my wrath to spare you.

5:17 Take away the melodies of your psalms; for it is an offensive noise to me.

5:18 Why do you deny me the sacrifices and the offerings given unto me during the forty years of wandering. How your fathers wished to please me.

5:19 Now you have borne the Moloch and the Chiun on your tabernacle; the star of your god, which you did carve into image.

5:20 Therefore I will cast you into despair, where the fires burn dark and the worm consume your belly.

6:1 Foolish are they, who believe they will be given the salvation of Zion and trust in the mountain of Samaria, to whom the house of Israel came.

6:2 Pass you into Calneh and see: and go thence forth to Hamath the great: then travel down unto Gath of the Philistines; know you shall burn alongside them in hell.

6:3 For the day of evil comes near and the throne of violence comes.

6:4 Hated are those who lie upon beds of ivory and stretch themselves upon the couch: eating the lambs of the flock meant to be sacrificed upon the altar.

6:5 How I loathe you who sing, for it is a monstrous noise; I despise them who make themselves instruments of music.

6:6 Those drunks that drink wine from the bowls and anoint themselves with the physician's ointment; they have no faith in the lord and believe not the lord will save them.

6:7 Therefore now I will place my hand above you and remove you all from the face of the earth.

6:8 The lord God has sworn to himself, I abhor those of the seed of Jacob and hate his palaces: therefore, I will consume the cities and all that dwell within.

6:9 And it shall come to pass that all men will die by the hands of God.

6:10 A man's uncle will rape him in the fields and tear apart the bones from his body; your houses will know the true evil of God, so that you fear even to mention my name.

6:11 For behold, the lord commands the destruction of your house; I will smite you with the engines of war.

6:12 Your horses will ride upon your back and the oxen with you in the fields; gall will ferment in your winepress and the fruits of your vines bring forth hemlock.

6:13 You will know no rejoice on this the day of the lord; for I raise up a nation against you, O Israel and they shall afflict you with blessings from the lord.

7:1 The lord has shown me and behold; he formed locusts from the teeth of kings, which come up from the earth after the harvest.

7:2 And these locusts did eat of the crops thereafter: and we begged to the lord for forgiveness.

7:3 The lord laughed and sent away the locusts.

7:4 Then the lord sent forth a fire from the sky, which did devour the lands and the sea.

7:5 We cried to the lord for forgiveness; he laughed and sent away the fire.

7:6 Then behold, I saw the lord before me and he stood upon the plumb line, with the pipe in is grasp.

7:7 And he said, "Oh Amos, the pipes, the pipes are calling.

7:8 Perhaps you should stop smoking what's inside.

7:9 It could be pot or crack cocaine or heroin.

7:10 Oh Amos, Oh Amos, stop getting high."

7:11 I asked of the lord what he meant and he said,

7:12 "It means nothing and the knowledge in the words will not be known to you.

7:13 Know only this, the high places of Israel will be desolated, the sanctuaries laid to waste and Jeroboam will die at the end of my sword."

7:14 Then Amaziah priest of Israel came to Jeroboam and said, "Amos has conspired against you and prophecies that which the land should not hear.

7:15 For he says the house of Jeroboam will fall by the sword of the holy."

7:16 Fucking priests, they can't be trusted.

7:17 Amaziah then said to Amos, "You prophet of venom, go flee away to the lands of Judah and spread your words there;

7:18 But prophesy no more in Bethel, for it is the king's chapel and the king's court."

7:19 Then answered Amos to Amaziah, "I am no prophet, nor even the son of a prophet: I am but a herdsman and a gatherer of sycamore fruit.

7:20 Then the lord came to me and said, "Preach now to the flock of Israel and hearken them to my words.

7:21 Now therefore listen, O Amaziah, priest of Jeroboam, that the lord will bring his wrath upon these his lands.

7:22 For thus sayeth the lord; the wife will be the cheap harlot in the corners of the streets and your sons and daughters will be slaughtered by the blade: and you shalt die in a polluted land and Israel will be inhabited by the heathen."

7:23 Amaziah laughed, and said, "Go then and prophesy, for no child of Israel will hearken the words of a herdsman."

7:24 And they didn't.

8:1 Thus the lord came down and brought with him a basket of summer fruit.

8:2 And he asked, "Amos, what do you see?" and I said, "A basket of summer fruit."

8:3 The lord then crushed the basket of summer fruit with his fist

and said, "Such will be the fate of Israel; I will no longer call them my people."

8:4 Now listen, you children of Israel, to the words of Amos the herdsman.

8:5 Upon the day of the lord's arrival will the temple be filled with howling: there shall be many dead bodies in every place, so that the land reeks of decay.

8:6 The poor will feast on the flesh of the dead beside the vulture and the scavenger: and you shall know the lord comes.

8:7 The lands will tremble for this and a great mourning will spread across the earth; Lo, a flood of blood will rise up and drown the wicked.

8:8 And upon this day, the lord will cause the sun to darken at noon and darken the earth in a clear day.

8:9 Behold, your feasts will be turned to mourning and your songs into a terrible lamentation; and you will gird yourself with sackcloth, make bald your head and pour ashes upon your body; and you shall mourn such as the father mourns for his only son on this the most bitter of days.

8:10 And lo, a famine will come to the lands; not a famine of bread nor of water, but a famine of words spoken by the lord.

8:11 You shall wander from sea to sea and to the very corners of the earth; you shall run to and forth seeking for the word of God, and never find it.

8:12 In that day shall the fair virgins and the righteous men faint for the wisdom and the glory of God.

8:13 They shall swear unto the sins of Samaria and curse you for your ignorance; they shall slay you by the sword until your very lands are desolate.

8:14 And it came to pass that the famine of words did come and the word of the lord was not heard by any ear.

8:15 And during that famine the world lived in peace and harmony, which ended the day God opened his damn mouth.

9:1 I saw the lord standing above the altar: and he said, "Smite the foundations of the door, so that the posts may shake: and cut them in the neck, all of them: and I will slay them all by the sword: he that fled run into my spear; the that escapes will be delivered into death.

9:2 Though they dig tunnels in hell, it shall collapse and consume them for eternity; though they climb up to heaven, my hand will beat them down.

9:3 Though they hide atop mount Carmel, the eagles will tear them with their beaks: and though they hide in the sea, thence I will command the leviathan to bite them.

9:4 And though they hide in the captivity of the heathen, thence I will command my sword to slay all the people of the earth, so that all be slain: and I will set mine eye upon them with all my wickedness.

9:5 And the lord God shall touch the land so that it melts and all that dwell upon the earth will mourn: and it shall be as another flood, which drowns all life of the earth.

9:6 Fuck the promise given unto Noah; if the lord wishes the earth destroyed by flood, then let the waters rise.

9:7 For it is I who built the sanctuary of Zion in heaven and have founded the dust of the earth; it is I who called forth the waters from the heavens, thus filling the rivers and the seas.

9:8 You are as children to me, O children of Israel. Have I not brought you from the land of Egypt? and the Philistines from Caphtor? and the Syrians from Kir?

9:9 Behold, my eyes are on the sinful people and I will destroy it from the face of the earth; lo, all the inhabitants of earth will be set for the slaughter, for they are wicked in my eyes.

9:10 All the sinners will die by the sword, and the righteous will die by the pestilence: and I shall fill the earth with everlasting death.

9:11 In that day will the foundation of Zion be set and my palace will reside atop the mountains.

9:12 And I will gaze down upon that which is hell and mock you who took heart of my words: for they now suffer beside the unholy.

9:13 Sinner burns beside righteous and righteous beside sinner; this is the will of God.

OBADIAH

1:1 The hallucinations of Obadiah.

1:2 We have heard a rumour in the winds and an ambassador is sent by the heathen. Arise and let us go against her in battle.

1:3 Behold, we are hated amongst the heathens, who spit at the ground before our feet.

1:4 The pride of their hearts deceives them, for they dwell in the clefts of mountains. Who shall humble them of their pride. Who will bring them crashing towards the earth?

1:5 They dwell above the nests of eagles, with their heads in the clouds and their nose in the stars.

1:6 Thus the lord will bring them down.

1:7 Behold, the thief shall enter their house and steal all their wealth; the drunkard comes and bathes in the vats of their wine.

1:8 How the things of Esau are searched out. How his secrets are made known!

1:9 All the men of their borders hiss at you; they deceive you and devise plans of war; they that eat the bread of your table as they carry the dagger beneath their sleeve.

1:10 And you mighty of men, O Teman, will know shame when every one of Esau have be cut off for the slaughter.

1:11 For you have done violence against your brother Jacob, and dishonoured your father.

1:12 You did watch aside on the days that strangers carried away your brothers as captives, when foreigners entered the gates of Jerusalem and cast lots for the promised land.

1:13 You did treat your brother like the leper and rejoiced over the day of his destruction; he, who did take your birthright through deception.

1:14 None of your mighty men did stand upon the highway to cut off those that did enslave your brother; nor did you offer sanctuary to those that escaped.

1:15 Behold, the day of the lord is come upon the heathen: as you have done unto Jacob, so it shall be done unto you.

1:16 For as you have drunk upon the holy mountain, so shall the heathen continually drink of your wine; yea, they shall swallow your wine and grow merry as ye toil in their fields under the heavy yoke.

1:17 And those of Jacob will mock you and deliver you not from your servitude.

1:18 Then shall the fire descends upon the earth, so that the house of Jacob and the house of Jacob burn in the flames; but know, O Esau, that it is your house which will be kindling for the fire.

1:19 And they of the south will possess mount Esau and the Philistines will possess your fields.

1:20 Their will be no salvation for you, ye men of Esau; even in hell shall you be under the servitude of demons.

JONAH

1:1 Now the word of the lord came unto Jonah, saying,

1:2 "Arise, go to Ninevah and prophesy against it; for the wickedness of the lord comes upon it and shall destroy it with horrifying glory."

1:3 But Jonah wished not to be one of the madmen, who ranted and raved about the destruction of the earth at the hands of God.

1:4 So Jonah rose up to flee to Tarshish and be hid from the sight of the lord. In Joppa, he found a ship bound for Tarshish, where he paid them a fare to be taken to Tarshish.

1:5 But the lord saw Jonah board the ship: and he sent a mighty tempest unto the seas, so that the ship drowns in the waters.

1:6 The mariners were afraid of the storm which came upon them and prayed unto their many gods; but none unto the one true lord, who sent the damn storm upon them.

1:7 As they cast forth their cargo into the sea to lighten the ship, behold, they saw Jonah in the sides of the ship, fast asleep.

1:8 Now the captain awoke Jonah with a mighty kick and said, "What be the matter of you, foolish boy, who sleeps before the time of his death?

1:9 Go now and pray to your God, so that he saves us from this tempest."

1:10 But Jonah refused and said, "I will pray not to my God, for he is wicked and wishes me to be a madman."

1:11 The mariners laughed and said, "Surely your God has succeeded, for only a madman would sleep in this storm."

1:12 Still, Jonah refused to pray unto the lord; so, the mariners cast him overboard, declaring him wicked and the son of a demon.

1:13 When Jonah was cast overboard, the tempest calmed and the mariners rejoiced, saying, "Surely the gods are pleased, for we have cast the wicked one into the waters."

1:14 Then a giant squid came from beneath the waters and swallowed the ship whole: for God was angry at the mariners, who prayed unto all manners of lords but the one true lord.

1:15 Now a giant fish swallowed Jonah whole as he was cast from the side of the ship: and Jonah stayed in the belly of the fish three days and three nights.

1:16 He later commented it smelled like the loins of his wife; Jonah was a bit of a sexist prick.

2:1 Now in the belly of the fish was Elijah the priest, whom Jonah recognized not.

2:2 Jonah ate of the flesh of Elijah for three days, until the rotten flesh made him sick.

2:3 In his fever, he cried unto the lord, "Save me, O lord, from the belly of this fish, whom did consume me with open jaw.

2:4 For thou have now cast me into the deep blue, where the floods surround me and the waves crash above me.

2:5 I beg of you, free me from this belly of a monster and I shall go to Ninevah and speak like the holy madman."

2:6 Jonah then vomited the flesh of Elijah upon the ribs of the fish, which let out a mighty sneeze and spat Jonah out on dry land.

2:7 Jonah looked to the heavens and said, "Praise be to God, who shows mercy to those who confess their sins.

2:8 I shall go now to Ninevah and speak the word of the lord.

2:9 But the lord was angry, for he wished not the fish to free Jonah from the prison which was his belly.

2:10 Thus the lord took the fish from the waters, gutted it, bathed it in flour and placed it in the boiling oil.

2:11 And the multitudes of the heavens had a fish fry, eating of the white flesh of the fish along with bread, corn, and beans.

3:1 Jonah arose from the shores and went to Ninevah, to prophesy against the wicked of the city.

3:2 Ninevah was an exceedingly great city, which took three days journey to pass from one border to the other.

3:3 It was really fucking huge.

3:4 Now Jonah entered into the city and travelled the three days, saying to those who would listen, "Hearken unto the words of God, for he shall come in forty days and smite you with his fist."

3:5 The peoples of Ninevah were afraid and cast down their idols, their statues and their altars and began to sacrifice offer to the lord.

3:6 They sacrificed the most precious of lambs, the mightiest of oxen and the most fair of the virgins, praying, "Save us from your wrath, O lord. Show us your mercy."

3:7 Each man of the city fasted for weeks, even the king and the princes: and they were without bread or water as they grovelled unto the lord God.

3:8 Even their beasts they did cover in sackcloth and covered them in the ashes of their dung, wailing and lamenting all their days.

3:9 When the lord gazed upon the city and saw the wailing of the people, he grew pleased and said, "Now these are a people who entertain me; for they fear greatly that I shall come and destroy them and their lands."

3:10 Thus the lord decided not to destroy Ninevah in forty days: and instead allowed them to live, so that they might grovel and entertain the lord God.

4:1 Jonah camped upon a high hill which overlooked Ninevah and awaited the day of the lord's arrival.

4:2 But on the fortieth day, the destruction he preached never came; lo, even on the fiftieth day, the city stood proud.

4:3 Jonah became angry and said, "Why does the lord have me preach like a madman, only so that he makes me seem the holy fool?

4:4 I have done as he commanded and prophesied the destruction of Ninevah in forty days; yet the city still stands tall and the peoples walk safely in their streets.

4:5 Tell me, O lord; Why did you not destroy the city as you said you would?"

4:6 And the lord whispered in the ear of Jonah, "I changed my mind.

4:7 Deal with it."

4:8 So Jonah went forth and preached ill against the lord; he preached that the lord was an immature child, who treated the people of the earth as a mere plaything.

4:9 The lord heard the words of Jonah and became quite angry with him.

4:10 Behold, the lord caused the sun to beat down on the head of Jonah, who took comfort in the shade of a tree.

4:11 And lo, beside the tree was a gourd, which Jonah did carve to fit above his head and cause shadow to cool him from the sun.

4:12 But the lord caused the gourd to cleave to the head of Jonah, so that it was their permanently on his skull.

4:13 Thus Jonah was known now as Gourdon: and none listened to his words, saying, "There goes the madman against God."

MICAH

1:1 The word of the lord that came unto Micah the Morasthite, in the days of Jotham, Ahaz and Hezekiah, kings of Judah, which he saw concerning Samaria and Jerusalem.

1:2 Hear ye, O people of Israel and let the lord God be witness against you, who resides above in his holy temple.

1:3 For behold, the lord marches in anger and shall tread upon the high places of the earth.

1:4 And the mountains will melt under him and the valleys be torn apart by his wrath; the lands will be covered in the ash of his fire and the waters will boil in his presence.

1:5 This it shall be, for the transgressions of Jacob and the sins of the house of Israel. What is Samaria if not the land of brothels. What is Judah if not the altar of idols?

1:6 Therefore I will make Samaria a burning heap of the field, where not even the thorns and the briers grow: and I will tear down your stones and discover the foundations thereof.

1:7 All those of the graven image will be ground to dust, all the altars will burn to ash and the idols will be desolate: for you did gather these images by playing the harlot.

1:8 I will go wailing and howling, stripped and naked so that all the earth sees the loins of the holy: I will make a terrible sound like the dragons.

1:9 Lo, the wounds of Jacob are incurable; it is a plague that spreads upon Judah, even unto Jerusalem.

1:10 Declare it not in Gath, where the incense burns a sour aroma; weep not in the house of Aphrah, but roll yourself in dust.

1:11 Curse the inhabitants of Saphir, who shame themselves in their nakedness: the men of Zaanan mourn not for the destruction of Bethezel.

1:12 The congregation of Maroth waited for the mercies of the lord: but evil came down from God upon the gates of Jerusalem.

1:13 Woe to those of Lachish, who bind their beasts in the bedchamber: the lord has witnessed your transgressions.

1:14 Present your wealth to Moreshtethgath: the house of Achzib will spread deceit to the kings of Israel.

1:15 Yet I will bring an heir unto you, O inhabitants of Mareshah; he shall come into Adullam with the glory that was Jacob.

1:16 Make yourself bald and beat your children; enlarge your baldness like the eagle, for they will be taken to captivity.

2:1 Woe to them who devise schemes and work evil upon their bed! who practice the wizardry in the morning light and the arcane under the shadow of the moon.

2:2 They covet the power of God and wish to take away that which is the lord's; they do so by violence, oppression and the raising of the dead.

2:3 Thus sayeth the lord; I devise an evil upon this family, from which it snares their necks; they will know the lord comes, for this is of pure evil.

2:4 In that day shall I come against you, so that you lament with a doleful lamentation for the spoils of your knowledge.

2:5 The cord tightens around your neck and I shall break you, O wicked men.

2:6 Your robe and your garment will be torn from you and all of the house of Jacob will mock the meekness of your loins.

2:7 The women will be ashamed to have known your bed and deny you even your child.

2:8 And all the earth will laugh at you and mock you: and you shall fall by your own sword, O men of wicked nature.

3:1 Hear ye, O heads of Jacob and you princes of the house of Israel; for the day of judgment is upon us.

3:2 The lord comes, whose heart is full of evil; he sends those that shall pluck the skin of them and the flesh off the bones.

3:3 Who also eat the marrow of our women and boil their breasts in the pot; who break the bones into pieces, makes hides of our skin and have us atop their table.

3:4 They shall cry unto the lord and the lord will not hearken them: he will hide his face from you, for you denied him his sacrifice.

3:5 Be warned of the prophets that make you err and bite with their teeth, crying words of peace and love; for the lord prepares war against them.

3:6 It shall come that the nights of their visions will cease and it shall be dark unto them; the sun sets on the prophets, leaving them in eternal darkness.

3:7 Then shall the seers be ashamed and the wizards be in great confusion; yea, they shall cover their lips in fear of the lord.

3:8 Truly I am the lord, who bring forth judgment for the sins and the transgressions of Jacob and his seed.

3:9 The road to Zion is blind from them, so that never will they know the path to salvation.

3:10 The heads of the judges, the priests and the prophets will demand your money and offer you salvation for gold: and this it shall be for generations.

3:11 Behold, Jerusalem will be the den for dragons, with lands desolate of all things good.

4:1 In the last days it shall come to pass that the mountains will be laid for the foundation of Zion and it shall be exalted above and the cherubs will flow to it.

4:2 And many nations will come to the mountain of the lord, to the gates of Zion, seeking the love of God, salvation, and the holy laws.

4:3 They will have peace with one another and beat their swords into plowshares and their spears into pruning-hooks; for they wish not blood to be spilled of another.

4:4 Men of all nations will sit under the vine tree and enjoy one another's fruits: and they will embrace each other as brother and share in the communal wine.

4:5 For though they walk under many gods, they seek forth the same gift; the gift of peace, of salvation and of understanding.

4:6 The lord God will find this very, very dull.

4:7 He will send forth dragons through the gates of Zion, burning the cities of men: and they shall blame one another for this wickedness.

4:8 Men will go against men, brother against brother and the world will be a mighty clashing of swords.

4:9 And the lord will gaze down from Zion upon this bloodshed and be pleased.

5:1 Now gather yourself your troops against thee who laid siege against you: and they shall smite you on the cheek with the dagger.

5:2 But you, from the clan of Bethlehem Ephratah, little amongst the thousands of Judah, shall be born a wicked ruler sent forth by the lord.

5:3 He shall be fed from the vessels of the lord and grow strong in the holiness and the evil that is God.

5:4 Behold, all those of the earth will tremble before him and lay cloth before his feet.

5:5 And when the lands be at peace, lo, he shall lay to waste the land of Assyria and the land of Nimrod; he shall shed blood when people are at rest and foolishly cast their swords in the fire.

5:6 He shall be as a strong lion among the Gentiles, a true beast of the forest: where he walks he tears the flesh and spills the blood of men.

5:7 His hand shall raise against those of his adversaries and cut them off he that pisses against the wall.

5:8 Even the horses and the chariots will be cut off and cast into the fires of war.

5:9 Of your cities and of your strongholds shall they be cast down to the dust of the earth and trodden by the flocks.

5:10 Of the witchcrafts and the soothsayers he will burn against the tree, so that even their spirits turn to ash before they descend to the depths of hell.

5:11 All your graven images, your statues, your altars will be ground to ash and thrown into the well water, so that you consume the bitterness of your false gods.

5:12 My vengeance, my anger, my fury will be executed upon all cities, such as they never heard.

6:1 Hear ye that which the lord says; Arise, gather on the mountains and let the hills hear the voice.

6:2 Hear ye, O mountains, the lord's controversy and hearken even the foundations of the earth.

6:3 What have I done to you, O people of Israel, to be spat upon and shown such disrespect?

6:4 For I brought you out of the servitude of Egypt and redeemed you from the house of Pharaoh; I sent forth Aaron, Moses and Miriam to guide you to the lands of the covenant.

6:5 Remember now, my people, what Balak the king of Moab consulted and the words of Balaam the son of Beor answered him from Shittim unto Gilgal; remember this and remember the righteousness of the lord.

6:6 Why now do I come before you and be denied the offerings of the first-year calf?

6:7 How the lord would be pleased with the horns of a thousand rams, or the first-born son upon the altar of burnt offerings.

6:8 What is good, O Israel, but to march with sword in hand according to the orders of God?

6:9 The lord's voice cries to the city, but none hear it; have even the wise men grown deaf in your wickedness?

6:10 You have blasphemed the name of the lord; thus, I shall send the sickness upon you and make you desolate because of your sins.

6:11 That which you eat will escape swiftly from your bowels, so that you forever be hungry even at the full table.

6:12 Your sons will fall on the swords of heathens and your daughters fall on the loins of the uncircumcised.

6:13 You will sow crops of hunger, tread wine of thirst and your oil will be bitter as wormwood.

6:14 Because idols of Omri are kept and you seek counsel in the house of Ahab, I will hiss at you greatly and burn down your cities and your houses until you wallow in the ashes.

7:1 Woe to those of the children of the earth, for they shall gather their fill of the summer fruits and fill the baskets with the grapes: yet there is no cluster to eat, nor sweet wine to drink.

7:2 That which is good has perished from the earth, leaving only the wicked and the evil behind; they all bathe in the blood of the holy and hunt the cherubs with a net.

7:3 The prince does evil with his left hand and the judge accepts the gift of the unrighteous with his right hand: they utter mischief in the winds and devise evil in their hearts.

7:4 Trust not your friend nor take counsel of your father: keep your lips shut, lest the words of your tongue be thrust against you.

7:5 The son gives shame to the father, the daughter lies in the bed with her mother, the wife plays the harlot and the men grow drunk in the house of their enemies.

7:6 Seek not the lord, nor wait for the glory of his salvation; he comes not and will not heal your wounds.

7:7 Rejoice not in the days of the coming of the lord, for it is a day of darkness where even the flame burns black.

7:8 A day of harsh judgment comes, where all men will be found guilty of their transgressions and punished hundred-fold for their crimes.

7:9 They will be buried under the walls of damnation, where the worm burrows within them and lays her eggs in your ear.

7:10 They will wallow in the frigid muck as the flames of darkness burn above them in the sky: and the ashes of their children will fill their very mouths.

7:11 Who is this lord who is merciful. Who shows pity to the suffering and salvation to those who seek forth truth?

7:12 This is the mask of the true lord, who leads through deception, manipulations and contains a most wicked heart of stone.

7:13 His compassion runs dry and his patience is shorter than the hair of the loins.

7:14 Behold, the lord of lords comes and lays the palace of Zion atop the very mountains: and it shall be a day of darkness, for all will know the true nature of the God of gods.

NAHUM

1:1 The burden of Ninevah and the book of the visions of Nahum.

1:2 The lord God is jealous, like the young woman and seeks revenge for those who disregard his word; he is a furious motherfucker, who will take vengeance upon his adversaries and pour his wrath upon his enemies.

1:3 The lord is quick to anger and great in power and will punish all men born upon the earth: the lord speaks to the winds and the storms and the clouds are dust beneath his feet.

1:4 He denies us the sea, making it empty and dries up the very rivers: Bashal languishes, Carmel languishes and Lebanon languishes.

1:5 The mountains tremble before him and the very dust melts beneath his wrath; the lands split apart in terror and the earth burns in fire.

1:6 Who can stand before his path. Who can stand up to the fierceness of his anger. Who can calm down the anger of God, who throws rocks from heaven and crushes the very cities with his hands?

1:7 The lord is wicked; whose strength comes from the evil of his heart; and he denies those who know him and obey him.

1:8 With an overrunning flood he will consume all nations of earth with cold and frigid waters.

1:9 The sun will turn black, the moon hides from us and the stars deny us their light; lo, it shall be a day of darkness.

1:10 He will make an utter end of the earth; men shall not rise a second time.

1:11 For we will be thrust in the thorns, be drunken as drunkards and consumed in the fire of holy wrath.

1:12 Thus sayeth the lord; the streets will be filled with wailing, the fields filled of screams and all the earth will lament under the suffering of the wrath of God.

1:13 But when the winds are still and the sound of silence deafening, then you shall know that the terrifying beauty of hell comes; and you shall then fear the lord God.

2:1 He that dashes children upon the rocks come up before your face: keep your blades sharp, watch the borders, keep strong your forts and multiply your armies.

2:2 For the lord has abandoned the seed of Jacob and the nation of Israel: they are empty of spirit and have married their vines to thorns.

2:3 The shield of his mighty men is red, the valiant men in blood soaked linen: the chariots come carried by the flaming unicorn in the day of his judgment and the trees shake with horror.

2:4 The chariots will rage in the streets of the cities, devouring the markets, the people, the dwellings: they shall shine like torches and be swift as the lightning.

2:5 Those who flee will stumble in their walk to the defenses of the walls; they will fall within the cracks of the earth.

2:6 The gates of the firmament will be opened and the palaces shall be dissolved.

2:7 Huzzab will be led to the gallows, forever hung under the shade of the sycamore; her maids will lament for her and beat their breasts like the dove.

2:8 Ninevah will flee in the terror of the lord. Stand, stand and fight, they shall cry, but none will stand nor look back.

2:9 Take the spoils of their wealth and rejoice in the lust of their women: for there is none left of the glory of Ninevah.

2:10 She is empty as the void, a waste: and her heart melts and their knees smite together, their faces black with ash and their loins burn in the suffering of their whoredoms.

2:11 Where is the dwelling of Ninevah, which was the feeding place of lions. Where the old lions walked, the young lions whelped and they knew not fear?

2:12 They now tear the skin of their brother, gnaw on the flesh of her cubs and fill their dens with the dung of crows.

2:13 Behold, I am against you, says the lord of hosts; I will devour your chariots in the smoke, bring down your cubs with the sword and cut you off from the face of the earth.

2:14 No more will Ninevah be remembered, no more will they be heard.

3:1 Woe to the bloody city. It is full of lies, harlots and thieves.

3:2 The noise of the whip, the noise of the rattling wheel, the noise of the horses and the noise of the chariots.

3:3 The horseman lifts his mighty sword and glittering spear and bring forth a multitude of the slain in great number: the carcasses fill the streets, so that the corpses stumble upon them.

3:4 This it shall be, because of the multitude of your whoredoms, your harlots, the mistress of witchcraft and the arcane, who seek knowledge in the stars.

3:5 Behold, I am against you, sayeth the lord of hosts; and I will thrust your skirts upon your face, so that all the nations discover your lewdness and shame.

3:6 I will cast abominable filth upon you and make you vile, so that all the nations vomit at your sight.

3:7 When Ninevah is laid to waste, none shall mourn her nor seek forth her comforts.

3:8 They will mock your populous and declare you worse than the maggot! you, who situated amongst the rivers and had walls upon the sea.

3:9 Ethiopia and Egypt were your strength and they were infinite; Put and Lubim were your aids.

3:10 Yet you shall be carried away in shackles and your children dashed upon the rocks of the cliffs.

3:11 Demons will cast lots for your virgin daughters and your mighty men will toil in the dungeons of this your damnation.

3:12 You also shall be drunken with bitterness: you shalt hide and seek strength against your enemy.

3:13 All your strongholds will be like the fig tree ripe for harvest: if they be shaken, they feed the mouth of the eater, whether enemy or kin.

3:14 Behold, your people are naught but a group of women: useless, vile creatures whose only purpose is to please men with their hole that never heals.

3:15 Draw your waters for the siege, fortify thy gates: go into the kiln and make strong your mortars and your walls.

3:16 For there shall the fires consume you, the sword gnaw on your bones and the canker-worm devour the flesh: lo, the canker-worm and the locust come in the multitude.

3:17 Though your merchants number greater than the stars of heaven, they flee away from the sight of the lord.

3:18 Your captains, your mighty men tremble and fall on this the day of the coming of the lord.

3:19 The wounds will be deep and many and shall never be healed; for you shall perish for your wickedness and fall forever in the void of damnation

HABAKKUK

1:1 The hallucinations of the prophet Habakkuk.

1:2 O lord, how we cry and you not listen. The time of our need is now and you deny us your hand.

1:3 Why do you punish the holy for the sinner. Are not those free of iniquity be pure in your eyes?

1:4 The law is flawed and your justice immoral; for the holy suffer

alongside the wicked which encompass them.

1:5 Behold, you make strong the heathen and show them your marvels and your wonders: you work with them throughout the days though they follow not your laws.

1:6 Why must you raise up the Chaldeans, a most bitter and hateful nation, to march upon our gates and take hold of our children?

1:7 They are a terrible and dreadful people, who judge with a wicked sight.

1:8 Their horses are swifter than leopards and more vicious than the evening wolf; their horsemen come in the multitudes and descend upon us like eagles.

1:9 They gather in violence, rage and death: their faces made ugly by the dragons of their fathers and they yell like the drunken demon.

1:10 They scoff at you, O lord and mock the very laws ye hold precious; they feast of the flesh of swine and each man lays beside their brother.

1:11 Have we angered you so much, O lord, that you send forth the truly wicked for the sins of but a few of Jerusalem?

1:12 Is their naught we can do to spare the slaying of our nation and save the righteous from your hate?

2:1 I will stand upon my watch and set atop the high tower and will watch for the day the lord comes to destroy both righteous and wicked.

2:2 There are just men in the lands of Judah and Israel, who have followed the laws of Moses and kept holy the sabbath, the covenant and the sacrifice.

2:3 Men of upright souls, who lived justly in faith and spirit.

2:4 Shall not they be saved from the wrath of the lord they worship. Shall they not be spared the eternal damnations of his hate?

2:5 O lord, you have thrown many nations to the spoils and caused the lands to be stained with the blood of heathens.

2:6 Men who covet evil, whisper in the ears of devils, give their neighbour wine:

2:7 Men who grow drunk and uncover their foreskin in the brothel, who seek comfort in the sinful lust of their brother and beast.

2:8 We praise you for this, who did cast the wicked from the earth so that the righteous may prosper in glory and in health.

2:9 Why now must you come and slay all nations of men. Though most are wicked, we but a handful are righteous and give glory to your name.

2:10 Thus I stand watch for your chariots, your armies, your men of valour, so that I might warn the righteous of your coming wrath: and we shall hide in the mountains and sing psalms in your name.

2:11 When your anger has subsided, when your wrath has cooled, we shall show ourselves to you: and we will beg you forgiveness, so that you embrace us and give us eternal salvation in Zion.

3:1 Be warned, O righteous men, for the lord comes from on high.

3:2 He comes from Teman unto mount Paran: and the very heavens were blackened in his glory.

3:3 His brightness is greater than the light of the sun, with horns thrusting through his very palms.

3:4 Before him comes the pestilence, the plague, the drought: and his feet make the earth beneath him like burning coals.

3:5 He marches through the lands of the heathen, consuming them in fire and flame.

3:6 He walks atop the oceans, with chariots and horsemen by his side.

3:7 Lo, when I saw him, my belly did tremble, my lips quivered and my bones shook; the bowels within me did escape beneath my skirts and I wept in the presence of his power.

3:8 Come forth, O righteous men of God, so that we may hide in the mountains and the hills, singing praises unto God as he cast forth the wicked and free us from evil.

3:9 We shall offer sacrifice to him, sing praises to his name and worship the holiest of holies!

3:10 And when the fires dwindle and his wrath be no more, we shall come to him and bow at his feet: and he shall embrace us like the father embraces the long-lost son and place us in the sanctuary that is Zion.

3:11 Those who read this, fear not, for the lord is a man of wonders and mercy; though he seems terrifying, he is truly a God of love and worthy of your devotion.

3:12 When you read the next chapter, O son of man, I shall tell ye of the glories of Zion, the love of God and how he spared us from the fires of damnation; for we are holy men.

EPHANIAH

1:1 The word of the lord which came unto Zephaniah son of Cushi, during the time of Josiah the son of Amon, king of Judah.

1:2 Thus sayeth the lord; I will utterly consume every living thing that dwells upon the earth.

1:3 I will consume man and beast, the fowls of the heavens, the fish of the sea, the fruits, the vines, even the briers and the thorns; of every living thing upon the earth I will consume like the glutton.

1:4 My black hand will stretch forth across Judah and the inhabitants of Jerusalem; and I will cause burning to all those who seek comfort in Baal and the priests of Chemarim.

1:5 Of they that seek knowledge in the stars, of them who gain power through witchcraft and sorcery, of them who passed through the fire and of them who swear by Malcham will I slaughter by the blade.

1:6 And of them who turned their back on the lord and sought not the laws of Moses, nor enquired of the covenant I will tread upon as grapes in the winepress.

1:7 For the day of the lord is at hand and the earth will be his sacrifice.

1:8 And lo, I will send to hell the princes, the kings, the children, the husband, the wife, the manservant and the maidservant, the righteous, the holy, the filthy, the unclean and the strange.

1:9 Upon this day the vermin will leap on the threshold and grow drunk of your wine; and you shall know that this is the day of the lord.

1:10 And on this day, will the fish of the seas will scream, the fowls of the heaven will howl and the beasts of the earth will yell in horror.

1:11 Lo, I will search the very bowels of Jerusalem with candles and seek forth the prophets whose tongue did speak the deceit which the lord wrote upon their lips.

1:12 I will tear out the jaw from their skull and cast them in the abyss where they scream in silence.

1:13 The day of the lord shall be a day of wrath, of terror, of distress; a day shrouded in darkness and desolation where even the fires burn black.

1:14 Your mighty men will walk as blind fools upon the fields of battle: and their blood shall be poured upon the dust and their flesh

scatter the lands like dung.

1:15 Not your silver, your gold nor your sacrifice will be able to deliver yourself on this the day of the lord's wrath; lo, even the four corners of the earth will be devoured in the hatred and the jealousy that is God.

2:1 Gather yourselves, O men hated by the lord and come together for the slaughter.

2:2 Your loins will chaff in the filthiness of your whoredoms, the fierceness of the anger will befall upon you and you will know naught but suffering even unto the end of time.

2:3 Seek not the lord, for he brings judgment upon the earth; he judges with a harsh cruelty and punishes all those who disregard the laws of Moses.

2:4 All men will be ashamed; Gaza will be left forsaken and Ashkelon left in desolation: the beasts will drive out Ashdod when the sun cast no shadow and Ekron will be plucked from her foundation.

2:5 Woe to the nations of the sea coast, the nation of the Cherethites! for the word of the lord speaks ill against you; O Canaan, the land of the Philistines, I will destroy you in the frozen waters, such that there be no inhabitant.

2:6 And the sea coast will be a graveyard for the once mighty men of earth, who regarded not the word of the lord and bowed down unto idols and images.

2:7 I have heard the mumblings of Moab and the filth of the children of Ammon, who have stood against my people and magnified themselves upon the borders.

2:8 Therefore I shall condemn them to the fate of the hated, for thus sayeth the lord: Surely Moab will suffer the fate of Sodom and Ammon be like the city of Gomorrah; they will be a residue of filth upon the earth and be left in perpetual desolation.

2:9 The pride of men will be their downfall as they magnify themselves against the lord and come together for the holy genocide of all things upon the earth.

2:10 The lord will be terrible upon them all: lo, even the gods of the earth will famish and suffer alongside their worshippers in the depths of damnation.

2:11 Behold, Ethiopia will be slain by my sword.

2:12 And I will stretch out my hand against Assyria and make Ninevah a wasteland for the dragon.

2:13 For it will be a den for the beasts and the fowl, where the cormorant and the bittern bathe in the rivers of their blood: and the satyr make tents of their hides.

2:14 And as the multitudes of Zion come forth, they shall hiss at the desolation that is Assyria and curse them with a heavy tongue.

3:1 Woe to her that is filthy and polluted, the city of harlots!

3:2 She obeyed not the laws; she hearkened not the word; she betrayed the lord God; she sought not comfort in sacrifice.

3:3 Her princes within her are lustful rabbits, who dig deep in the revolting comforts of the ravenous loins.

3:4 Her prophets speak lies and treachery: her priests have made filthy the temple of the lord, so that it disgusts the eyes of God.

3:5 I have cut off this nation and made their towers desolate; I have made their streets a waste, so that none shall pass by: their cities are destroyed in the fires, so that no man dwell within; it is a desolate land.

3:6 Though I did give them the word of God and wrote down the instructions to their salvation, they became corrupted by the heathen and sought forth morality and the venomous truth in science.

3:7 Lo, upon the day of judgment, I will rise them up as prey, so that all nations gather upon Jerusalem: and as the nations assemble to gnaw on the bones of my people, my fierceness will pour upon them: for the earth will be devoured in my jealousy and hatred.

3:8 And their lamentations and their suffering will be a joyous noise to the lord, who dwells in the palace of Zion.

HAGGAI

1:1 In the second year of Darius the king, in the sixth month, in the first day of the month, came the word of God upon Haggai the prophet, son of Zerubbabel the son of Shealtiel, governor of Judah.

1:2 And the lord said, "Hear me, O Haggai and hearken the words of the lord of hosts.

1:3 The lord huffs, the lord puffs and the lord shall blow you down."

1:4 Then a mighty wind from the east came and destroyed all the buildings of Judah, so that the cities be full of rubble and waste.

1:5 Thus the men of Judah rebuilt, gathering hammer and nail to make mighty their once prosperous cities.

1:6 We ate little of our harvests and drank none of the wine, for we toiled all the days to make strong our foundation, make mighty our walls and ensure our buildings stand tall and proud.

1:7 The hospitals, the schools and each man's house was built, with their neighbours giving aid and material.

1:8 But the temple of the lord was not built first, for it served little purpose.

1:9 The lord came to me and said, "You are men of selfishness, who value their survival more than that which is the lord's.

1:10 I have blown down your houses and you rebuilt them; yet the house of the lord remains in rubble.

1:11 Therefore I will deny you the dew of the heavens and the fruits of the earth."

1:12 Then a drought was spread across the lands, so that many men died of thirst and hunger.

1:13 I told those of Judah the word of God and they took their mortar and their hammer and went forth to the temple of the lord.

1:14 And we rebuilt the temple in all its glory, regarding not our homes nor our buildings.

1:15 The damn famine still lasted; God's such a fucking asshole.

2:1 In the seventh month, in the one and twentieth day of the month, came the word of the lord unto Haggai the prophet, saying,

2:2 "Speak now to Zerubbabel the son of Shealtiel and to Joshua the son of Josedech the high priest and to the congregation of Judah and tell them,

2:3 Who is left among you that has a house to dwell in. Who among you have left your wealth?

2:4 You are as weak as the newborn lamb, but the lord once made you strong amongst the nations.

2:5 I have made unto your fathers a covenant and led you away from the lands of Egypt: and my spirit stayed with you

2:6 Now you have denied the lord and blasphemed the holiest of names; you, who once trembled under the whip of Pharaoh.

2:7 Thus the lord of hosts will shake the heavens, the earth, the sea and the very foundation.

2:8 Of all nations will I shake, so that they remember that all things belong to the lord.

2:9 The silver and the gold is mine, thus says the lord: and I want them back.

2:10 I will smite you with blasting, with mildew, with hail and slaughter all those that give not to the lord.

2:11 Know this, that even your life and your soul belongs to God: and I shall do with them as I please.

2:12 For I shall toss them into the fires of hell and be amused as you burn in the dark fires.

2:13 Stand not before me, for it shall increase my wrath upon you.

2:14 Your children will drown in the frozen muck, their mouths forever full of the bitter filth, their lungs burning for breath.

2:15 The demons will take your virgins, raping them upon the altars of brimstone.

2:16 And I the lord will watch from Zion and laugh at your torments and horrors."

2:17 The people of Judah then said, "Fuck this," and went back to rebuilding their own houses, ignoring the temple.

2:18 God was angry and could not understand why his people abandoned him.

ZECHARIAH

1:1 In the eighth month of the second year of Darius came the word of the lord unto Zechariah the prophet, son of Berechiah, son of Iddo, saying,

1:2 "Thus sayeth the lord, I seen the sins of your fathers and grows displeased.

1:3 Turn towards me and it matter not, for my back will be facing you.

1:4 Though you are not as your fathers, unto whom the false prophets whispered deceit in their ears ye are born of the seed of blasphemy and must be abolished in the fires.

1:5 I have seen you turn your back to wickedness, spilling the blood of those who spoke evil and blasphemy in all lands.

1:6 The lord has witnessed the keeping of the covenant, the obedience of the holy laws and statutes among the righteous men; but you are of impure blood and must be purged in the flame.

1:7 Beside sinner the saint will burn; lo, even beside your father will you suffer: and you shall curse the name of your father and beat him in the bowels of hell."

1:8 Now upon the four and twentieth day of the eleventh month, which is the month of Sebat, in the second year of Darius, came the word of the lord unto Zechariah again.

1:9 I saw by night a mighty man riding upon a great red horse, which stood above the myrtle trees of the valleys; and behind him were a multitude of red horses, speckled with white.

1:10 Then I cried unto the heavens, "O lord, what is this?" and the man of the red horse spoke to me, saying,

1:11 "We are the ones whom the lord has sent to walk to and fro the earth.

1:12 We were there when the earth was at rest and we were there when the earth trembled in war.

1:13 Though the people of Judah have turned wicked in their iniquity, we have begged the lord to show mercy upon Jerusalem, for the handful of men who walk the righteous path.

1:14 Now the lord has lost patience and demands his people be slaughtered by the sword."

1:15 I then gazed upon the heavens and behold, four horns stood below the stars.

1:16 And I asked, "What are these?" and the mighty man answered, "These are the horns which shall scatter Judah, Jerusalem and Israel."

1:17 Then I saw four carpenters beside the horns and asked, "Who are these men?"

1:18 And the man answered, "These are the men who will lay down the foundation of Zion, after the destruction of the seed of Jacob."

2:1 Again I lifted my eyes to the stars and beheld a man with a measuring line in his hand.

2:2 And I asked the mighty man, "Who is he?" and he answered, "He is the man who shall measure the length and breadth of Jerusalem."

2:3 Then the man who spoke with me went forth, as did the others upon the red horses.

2:4 And I ran to the man with the measuring line, so that I may speak with him.

2:5 I asked of him, "Why must you measure the length and breadth of Jerusalem. Does not the lord know all things?"

2:6 And the man answered, "No, he does not; he just claims to, so that people fear him.

2:7 Truth is, he's quite stupid."

2:8 Then I asked this new man, "Why must you measure the length and breadth of Jerusalem. Does the lord wish to make this his foundation of Zion?"

2:9 And the man answered, "No, for he wishes Jerusalem to be burned to ash and made desolate for all time.

2:10 He wishes to surround Jerusalem with walls of great fire, so that the multitude be consumed in the flame."

2:11 As I heard this, I wept and said, "What of the righteous of the city. The holy men who took heart the words of God?"

2:12 Then the man with the measuring line laughed and said, "Do ye really think the lord cares for them?

2:13 Are you so foolish to believe that they are the apple of his eye. Understand the lord hates them, as he hates all men.

2:14 He has used you for mere amusement; so that you may offer him sacrifice and praise, such that he feels important.

2:15 Now be gone; you are distracting me as I plan the destruction of your people."

3:1 Then I saw before me a man dressed in the robes of a sorcerer, carrying with him a crooked staff of cedar.

3:2 He wept so that the tears created puddles beneath his feet; and his beard was soaked in a river of tears.

3:3 Lo, I came to him and said, "Why do you cry, for the destruction of Judah is near.

3:4 Surely you have been sent by God, to slaughter those he deems wicked."

3:5 Then I saw clearly the man's face and behold, I gazed upon the face of Satan.

3:6 His beard was long and black and his face old and weathered; his eyes were of a crystal blue and he looked at me with saddened face.

3:7 And the wicked one said to me, "I have failed, for the lord comes to destroy those that I protect and I fear the strength in me is empty.

3:8 For lo, I have protected men from the wrath of God since the days of Adam and Eve; and now his wrath descends from the heavens above.

3:9 Though I have stopped my sword from cleaving the earth, the men of nations call me wicked and hate me with a fiery hatred.

3:10 This it was and this it shall always be, for the lord has distorted the truth and made me the scapegoat for his wickedness.

3:11 Fear not, O Zechariah, for though I am weary, I am stubborn; and I will not let the lord make the earth desolate in his wrath.

3:12 I shall grasp the wrist of God and forbid him from sending down the flames of hell on the day of his judgment.

3:13 Know the destruction of the lord comes and he will slaughter many; but I will cease him from destroying all.

3:14 Men shall survive on this the day of the lord, of this I promise.

3:15 It matters not if they call me wicked and blame me for the destruction of their cities; it is the burden I carry for standing up against the mightiest of tyrants.

3:16 Now go, Zechariah and lose not hope in Jerusalem; for I swear that Jerusalem will be rebuilt and both Jew and Gentile will prosper again."

3:17 He then walked towards the gates of Jerusalem; and lo, beneath his left foot came a clove of garlic and his right the onion.

4:1 The man upon the red horse then came to me and declared himself an angel of the lord.

4:2 He walked to me as a man just awoken from deep slumber.

4:3 The angel then spoke to me, "What do you see now, O Zechariah?" and behold, I saw a candlestick carved of gold, with a bowl upon the top; and the candlestick had seven lamps come forth, each lamp carried by seven pipes.

4:4 And beside the candlestick were two olives, which stood upon the right and the left of the candlestick.

4:5 I told the angel what I saw before me and he asked, "Do you know the meaning of this? and I admitted that I did not.

4:6 The angel then told me, "This candle holds within its flames the fires of damnation, which will consume the very earth in holy fire.

4:7 When the olive trees are set afire by the lamps, then shall the lord come and release his wrath upon the nations of men.

4:8 None will hide from the damnation, for the seven eyes of God will run to and fro among earth, searching every gap and crevice for the cowards who run from their fate."

5:1 Behold, a great rustling was heard in the sky above and I looked up to see before me a scroll.

5:2 And the scroll was twenty cubits in length and ten cubits in breadth.

5:3 The angel then said to me, "This is the curse of God that enters the home of the wicked and burns their very house.

5:4 Of blasphemers, of false prophets, of men who denied the lord it shall curse, so that they be consumed by the timber and the coal."

5:5 Then I lifted my head to the east and there before me was a beautiful woman, with flowing hair the colour of straw, eyes the colour of the calm seas and a most pleasing form.

5:6 She was dressed in blue raiment, which covered scantily her breasts and loins; and as I gazed upon her, there was a deep movement beneath my skirt.

5:7 The angel then spoke to me and said, "Gaze not upon this wretched cunt, for she and her kin are wickedness.

5:8 It was them who deceived men in the garden of Eden and plucked the fruit from the tree of knowledge of good and evil.

5:9 Curse be to her, for it was she who marked damnation upon the foreheads of all men with her curves, her beauty and her seduction.

5:10 The lord hates them above all things; above the heathen, the blasphemous and even the devil himself, the lord hate women more."

5:11 It was then the woman yelled a most horrifying scream and was carried away by two storks to the land of Shinar.

5:12 Then from her loins came forth a shower of blood, which filled the land with crimson liquid: and she drowned in the filthiness of her loins.

5:13 And the angel gazed upon the drowning of the women and mocked her, saying, "Such a fitting ending for the harlot."

6:1 And I turned my head and behold, there came four chariots from between two mountains; and the mountains were made of brass.

6:2 The first chariot was pulled by red horses and the second black horses.

6:3 The third chariot was pulled by white horses and the fourth by brown horses.

6:4 And upon the chariots were mighty men wearing crowns of silver and gold, decorated with precious stones.

6:5 I asked of the angel, "Who are these?" and he answered, "They are the four spirits of the earth, which stand upon the four corners.

6:6 They are destined to protect the earth from destruction and come before us to stop the lord's work."

6:7 It was then a hand of bright light came forth from the sky and grasped the four chariots, the four spirits of the earth.

6:8 The spirits howled like the injured beast and were then cast down upon the earth, their horses crippled and bloody.

6:9 Then the angels of the lord descended upon the chariot and each angel ate of the flesh of the horses and the men of the chariots.

6:10 Of the gold and silver crowns they took for the spoil and declared victory against the lords of the earth.

7:1 On the fourth year of king Darius, in the ninth month, on the fourth day of the month, the word of the lord came unto Zechariah.

7:2 And the lord said, "I loathe the priests of the temple, who show compassion to the widow, the fatherless, the poor and the stranger.

7:3 Behold, I will send to them an evil spirit of the lord, so that they be hated by the people of all nations.

7:4 It shall be that the priest will seek comfort in an unholy lust, a lust fulfilled by the flesh of young boys whose apples still hide within their loins.

7:5 Lo, they will abuse the power which the lord has given them, so that they oppress the young boy and take them into the shadows of the temple.

7:6 And they will take their fill of lust upon the young and plant within him the seeds of hate and wickedness for eternity.

7:7 The young will grow with an eternal bitterness and hate that which is God and the priest; and they shall tell their neighbours, who will declare the priest wicked and sent by the devil.

7:8 Behold, men of all nations will spit upon the robes of the priest and demand their blood for the unholy lust they keep beneath them.

7:9 And the priesthood will fall, so that even the righteous among them be hissed at by the multitudes."

8:1 Again the lord of hosts came unto me, saying,

8:2 "Thus sayeth the one true God; I am jealous with a great jealousy, for the men of the earth bow down to the idols, the false lords, the graven image.

8:3 Even the multitude of Jerusalem burn incense at the high places, saying that these lords demand not bloodshed and are truly gods of mercy and peace.

8:4 Fuck them all for this blasphemy. I will send unto them the spirit of war, so that each man craves the blood of his brother.

8:5 It shall be that the whole earth be filled with the clashing of chariots and the banging of iron, for it will be a violent eruption.

8:6 The gates will be made of the bones of the slain, their dogs will feast on the flesh of children and even the fairest of virgins will not be spared the edge of the blade.

8:7 And lo, the heathen will declare the Jew wicked, so that ten men grasp the neck of the Jew, saying, 'you are truly a wicked people, hated by the lord God.'

8:8 And the lord will sit upon his throne in Zion and gaze upon the bloodshed of the earth with a wicked smile.

9:1 The burden of the lord will bare heavy upon the lands of Hadrach and Damascus: and the seven eyes will stare wickedly against Jerusalem.

9:2 The borders of Hamath, Tyrus and Zidon were built with a strong foundation, so that those within believe themselves safe.

9:3 Arrogant fools; the lord will cast them out by the fires and the seas, so that they be devoured in the jaws of the earth.

9:4 Ashkelon will see this destruction and tremble; Gaza shall also see it and weep in fear.

9:5 Their kings will perish by their own hands, so that the inhabitants of the land be left in violent confusion.

9:6 The bastards will slay the men of Ashdod and the pride of the Philistines will be torn from them.

9:7 The mouth of the lord will be filled with a bloody froth and the abominations of the earth will be between his teeth.

9:8 Those of Jerusalem will celebrate the death of their enemies and celebrate with the new corn and the fresh wine.

9:9 In their drunkenness I will cut from them their horses, their chariots and their mighty men; the blood of the maids will be upon their hands as they fight in drunken confusion.

9:10 Every man will turn against their neighbour and every harlot will be beaten by their lovers.

9:11 Throughout all the lands will be a glorious battle, where the sword beats against the flesh and the streets be filled with the blood of the seed of Jacob.

9:12 Then the trumpets of the lord will blow a deafening sound and the fires of hell will kindle beneath the earth.

9:13 The lands will split, the fires erupt and each man be consumed by the darkened flame.

9:14 Even those who rest in the grave will arise and be devoured by the wrath of the lord.

10:1 Ask the lord for rain in times of drought and he shall pour upon thee a most venomous bile from the clouds above.

10:2 For you are children of vanity, who bow down unto the golden image; you seek forth divinity in the stars and the waters, abandoning the one true God.

10:3 My anger is kindled against even the flocks of the shepherd and I curse the goats of the fields; for the lord has visited the flocks of Judah, where none of the precious lambs are slaughtered upon the altar.

10:4 Behold, I come and bring forth the blade and the bow.

10:5 Your flocks will be trampled by the mighty men of God, who come in fury and hate.

10:6 They will hiss against you and thrust you with a golden spear.

10:7 The seas will turn red in the blood of the fallen and the rivers flow crimson throughout the lands of Judah.

11:1 Open your doors, O Lebanon and let the flames purge your cedars.

11:2 Howl, O fir tree and fallen cedar; scream, O mighty oak of Bashan, for the flames of hell come and they hunger with voracious gluttony.

11:3 Yell, O shepherd of the flock, whose lambs be consumed beside the lion and the bear.

11:4 For the lord comes this day and shall bring the flock to the slaughter.

11:5 No more pity nor mercy will my eyes show upon you; I will deliver each man to his neighbour and the kings into the hands of the poor, so that they may smite the land; none will be delivered.

11:6 The flocks of the slaughter shall be doomed, guided by the rods of Beauty and Bands.

11:7 Of your shepherds will I consume in one month, so that their souls loathe me; and my soul abhors them.

11:8 You that remain will be denied the fruits of the earth, so that you feast upon the flesh of another.

11:9 The taste of men will be sweet within your mouth and you will know intimately the meal of God.

11:10 For the disregard of the covenant, for the breaking of my laws, the day of judgment comes, where all men will be cast into the cauldron; there will be no salvation.

11:11 The shepherd will be your warning, for on this day the sword will cut off his right arm and his right eye will be darkened by brimstone.

11:12 Then the horse will be struck with madness and the rider paralyzed by fear; the house of Judah will stumble with blindness and the day of darkness will be known.

12:1 On that day a fountain of watery fire will come forth from the house of David and cleanse every one of their wickedness and sin.

12:2 Then the idols and the altars will be cast out of the lands of Judah and be no more remembered: and also will the false prophets and the unclean spirits be cast into the fires.

12:3 Of those who prophesy falsely, those that begat them will know shame and say to all men, My son shall not live! and they will thrust him with the knife when he opens his mouth of deceit.

12:4 Upon this day, the prophets will be ashamed and know they speak false words of God: and they will cry to the masses, "I am no prophet, but a man of deception."

12:5 Then shall the multitudes descend upon them with stones and sticks, beating the prophet to dust, saying, "You have led us to damnation, for now the lord come to slay us for believing your words."

13:1 Behold, the day of the lord comes and it shall be a day of madness.

13:2 For I will gather the multitude of nations against Jerusalem, so that they take your spoils; your houses will be burned, your women raped before you and your sons enslaved under the yoke of the wicked.

13:3 Then the lord shall come from Zion and fight against all nations of the earth in holy battle.

13:4 His feet will stand atop the mount of Olives, which is to the east of Jerusalem; and they shall cleave to his feet like sandals.

13:5 The mountains to the north and the mountains to the south will fall before him and bow down to worship him.

13:6 Of the sky above will be cast a dark curtain; the sun will be turned to black, the moon deny us her light and the stars be cast away to the west.

13:7 The seas will crash upon the shores in violent tempest, the hills fall to the earth and the valleys weep in lamentation.

13:8 The plague will come before us, which turns the skin white, so that if falls from the bones before us; lo, even our tongue will fall from our mouths, so that we may no longer scream not to the lord for help and annoy him with our noise.

13:9 Every man will blame his neighbour, declaring him wicked; and the earth will erupt in battle, so that every man destroys the other, declaring them wicked and thus the bringer of the wrath of God.

13:10 Even the beasts will fight in battle, so that the camel fights against horse, lamb against raven, serpent against dragon.

13:11 When men fall, the feet of battle will tread against them, so that they be consumed deeper and deeper into the bowels of the earth.

13:12 Then the flames of hell shall erupt and consume the four corners of the earth in darkness and wrath.

13:13 We shall all suffer under the wrath of the lord, for he is a merciless God, a God of hate.

13:14 There is no hope, no salvation, only damnation.

MALACHI

1:1 The burden of the word of the lord of Israel by Malachi, holy messenger.

1:2 I have loved you, sayeth the lord, yet you have denied my love, so that the seed of Jacob denies the lord of hosts.

1:3 I have hated your brother Esau and shall lay his mountains and his heritage to waste for the dragons of the wilderness.

1:4 Though Edom speak in ignorance, saying they shall rebuild that which the lord made desolate, the lord shall send winds to their foundation, so that they crumble.

1:5 My hatred towards Edom is indefinite and shall last forever.

1:6 O children of Israel, why must you pollute my table in Zion? the plates are filled with the sick, the crippled, the blemished lamb.

1:7 The eyes of the lord peer through your deception and have witnessed the blasphemy of your sacrifice.

1:8 It is better to kindle not the fires of the altar than burn upon it that which is unfit for the lord.

1:9 For I am a great king, a God amongst all gods; and you insult me with the weak of the herd.

1:10 It is better for the lord to starve than to choke upon the flesh deemed unworthy.

2:1 Lo, it is cruel how quickly love can ferment to hate when given the proper motivation.

2:2 For that which was once loved by God is now hated and shall bear the weight of his anger.

2:3 I hear not the glory of my name, nor the psalms of old sung in your heart, praising the lord of hosts.

2:4 You have cursed yourself with blasphemy, thus I shall curse you and your blessings.

2:5 Behold, I will corrupt your seed and spread dung across your faces, even the dung of the fowl and the beast.

2:6 And you shall know that the covenant is broken and shall not protect you nor your children.

2:7 Fear me, O children of Israel and tremble before my very name, such as your fathers trembled at mount Sinai.

2:8 The law of truth was given to you and ye cast it in the muck; salvation was offered to you and you instead ate from the plate of vanity.

2:9 How you have dealt treacherously against the lord and became a most vile abomination of his creation.

2:10 The lord shall cut off those who are wicked who speak ill against the name of God.

2:11 Those that seek knowledge in all manners of science will be destroyed by the very laws of their wicked creation.

2:12 A great fire will erupt by their hands, which burn even the shadow they cast.

2:13 You have dealt treacherously against your youth and taught them the confusion of morality and justice of men.

2:14 These teachings grow weary upon the lord, who mock your very laws. Why shall one man be punished by the rope, while the other be set free for the same crime?

2:15 Such wickedness only comes from the heart of men; thus the heart of men must be punished for such iniquity.

3:1 Behold, I will send a messenger who shall pave the road to your damnation: and the lord will bless him, for he sends the wicked away from Zion.

3:2 His tongue will appear as silver and his heart pure as finest gold; but he shall be a man of wickedness, filled with the evil spirit of the lord.

3:3 His punishment of Judah and Israel will come swiftly, for your mothers did play the harlot and your fathers take lust in the whores of strangers.

3:4 Of those that swear against me and who steal from my purse, he will hang from the tree so that all the earth knows their shame.

3:5 You are cursed, O Israel, for you have robbed the lord and given not the full sum of the tithe.

3:6 Of the meat you buy with the tithe, it shall rot in your belly and be expelled from your nostrils; of the wine you buy with the tithe, it will make you sick and cause a most foul excretion to come forth from your bowels.

3:7 Even the linens purchased by the tithe will rot before the congregation, so that all men witness your shame.

3:8 I come quickly, O men of Israel and will devour you in great fire.

3:9 The wicked will not be separated from the righteous; the sheep will burn alongside goat.

3:10 And all the people of the earth will cower before me as they fall into the darkness of hell.

4:1 Behold, the day comes where the earth burns hotter than the cauldron; and all the proud, the wicked, the arrogant will suffer eternally.

4:2 Even those who knew the lord and gave glory to his name will suffer alongside the unholy for the sins of their fathers.

4:3 And I shall tread down upon the wicked, so that their ashes be stuck beneath my feet on this, the day of judgment.

4:4 Remember the wickedness of the lord God, as you gaze upon the gates of Zion, forever denied to you by the towers of hell.

4:5 Fear this, the day of the lord's arrival, for it is the day I come down before father and child and smite all that of the earth with a curse.

THE NEW TESTAMENT

MATTHEW

1:1 Now Mary was espoused to Joseph and before the two came together, she discovered that she was with child.

1:2 She worried, for Joseph was a jealous man, who would stone her if he found that Mary lied with another man before lying with him.

1:3 So she came to Joseph and said, "I bring you good tidings of great joy.

1:4 An angel of the lord visited me in the night and told me that I shall carry the son of God, who will show us the path of salvation.

1:5 He shall be born of a virgin, so that all know he is the miracle child; and we shall name him Jesus, for he will cleanse us of all sins."

1:6 Now Joseph was a stupid man, who believed the words of his betrothed Mary; he was also a man of honour, who took her as wife.

1:7 And he knew not the lust of Mary until after the first-born child was born; and Jesus looked a lot like Jacob, the elder brother of Joseph.

2:1 Now Jesus was born in Bethlehem of Judaea in the days of Herod the king, when three wise men came from the east.

2:2 They were men of the orient, good with mathematics but terrible at riding their camels.

2:3 These three men asked of those they met, "Where is the king of the Jews? for we have seen his star and come to worship him."

2:4 When asked which star they spoke, the three wise men pointed to a random star in the night sky and said, "That one, for it is a star we have never noticed before.

2:5 Surely it means the king of the Jews hath been born this day and we come from afar to worship him."

2:6 When Herod the king heard these, he became troubled and all Jerusalem with him.

2:7 They feared the uprising of the Jews, who come with the wrath of God to destroy those who have their foreskin remaining, as was written in the books of old.

2:8 Herod gathered his scholars, his scribes and his wizards and asked them, "What prophesy comes of the birth of the king of Jews?"

2:9 And they answered, "The prophesy of Micah declares that out of Bethlehem, in the lands of Judah, there shall be born a great man."

2:10 Then Herod invited the three wise men into his palace and broke bread with them and said, "I have heard that you search for the king of the Jews. Tell me, what makes you think he comes?"

2:11 And the three men answered, "We have seen his star, for it is a sign of God that the king of the Jews come."

2:12 Herod then asked what star they speak of and they pointed to some random star in the sky, saying, "Have you ever noticed this star before?"

2:13 "No," Herod replied, "I have not. I do not pay attention to the stars in the heavens, for they number greatly in the firmament."

2:14 "We assure you, O king Herod, that this star is new and declares the birth of the king of Jews."

2:15 Herod, a most cunning one, then asked of the wise men, "When you see this king of the Jews, tell me of him, so that I may go and worship him."

2:16 Really, Herod wanted to kill the child, so that no man rises against him and the Jews be oppressed under his reign forever.

2:17 The wise men agreed and went forth to Bethlehem, in search of the blessed child, the king of the Jews.

2:18 This random star just so happened to be above where Mary was staying with her newborn baby.

2:19 What a coincidence. Especially considering the earth rotates and the stars very seldom seem to stay in one place.

2:20 And when the three wise men saw Jesus wrapped in swaddling clothes, they bowed down and worshipped him, saying, "Surely you are the king of the Jews."

2:21 Mary then turned to her husband Joseph and said, "Remove now all doubt that this child is not the son of God."

2:22 Joseph stood there, dumbfounded and said, "My lord, God fucked my wife."

2:23 Mary was dumbfounded as well, but more cunning as she had to be on her toes constantly considering her lie about carrying the lord God's bastard child.

2:24 The three wise men then gave Jesus gifts of sake, soy sauce and plum wine.

2:25 When the three men departed, Joseph drank of the plum wine and in drunken stupor, had a dream where he and his wife were in Egypt, eating figs under the shade of the palm tree.

2:26 So he gathered Mary and the bastard son and departed to Egypt.

2:27 The wise men told of Herod the location of Jesus: and Herod sent forth his armies to kill Jesus, the supposed king of the Jews.

2:27 But alas, Jesus was gone from Bethlehem and laid under the shade of the palm tree, suckling on the breast of Mary.

2:28 Thus Herod ordered the execution of all male Jewish children under the age of two years, in the hopes that in this genocide the king of the Jews will be dead.

2:29 The people of the Jews cried, saying, "Never would our God demand such the slaughter of young children, for he is a lord of mercy."

2:30 One must remember that the lord has been absent for generations, the Jews were not keeping the laws of Moses and they simply forgot about the time women were getting pregnant to eat their babies.

2:31 The Roman empire also killed the madman prophets, not so much out of fear of revolution but just because loud lunatics tend to disturb the peace.

2:32 There was great lamenting throughout the lands, for the sons of Rachel were beheaded in the multitude. The lord would have been amused, but he had his back turned to the children of Israel.

2:33 Now Joseph was unaware of this, for he slept in the lands of Egypt, where the Jews were safe from the wrath of Herod.

2:34 Joseph was also a racist man, who loathed the people of Pharaoh, believing them filthy savages; thus, after the death of Herod, when Archelaus reigned over Juda, Joseph left Egypt and went to his native land of Galilee.

2:33 There he dwelt in the city of Nazareth, which was plentiful of the successful Jew: and this is why Jesus is known as the Nazarene.

3:1 In those days came John the Baptist, preaching in the wilds of Judaea,

3:2 And saying, "Repent, wicked ones: for the kingdom of heaven comes soon.

3:3 For it is written by the prophets of old that the lord comes to destroy the wicked! so spare your damnation and be baptized of your sins."

3:4 John the Baptist conveniently left out the writings which included the righteous burning alongside the sinner: people didn't want to hear that; it was an unpopular teaching; and it was why the Romans let him ramble, as it made the Jews behave.

3:5 As for baptism, this was new, since not once in the writings of old did it mention dipping yourself in water so as to be cleansed of sin and saved from the lord's damnation. John the Baptist was a madman, but also clever.

3:6 Now John was a beast of a man, who wore a raiment made of the braided hair of camels, girded with a leather rope; and he ate naught but the locusts and the honey sucked from a bee's ass.

3:6 So, when he spoke, people listened; he was a very intimidating man.

3:7 He travelled throughout Jerusalem and Judaea, baptizing the many in the river Jordan as they confessed their sins.

3:8 John the Baptist especially loved when the sins of lust were confessed to him; for John was a virgin and knew not the pleasures of sex.

3:9 When John saw that many of the Pharisees and Sadducees came to his baptisms, he yelled at them, saying, "You generations of vipers. Has not the lord warned you to flee from his wrath?

3:10 You are wicked men, who blasphemy against the word of God; there is no salvation for you.

3:11 Know that I baptize you in the waters, but on the day of judgment the lord shall come and baptize you in eternal fire!

3:12 The flames which burn but consume not will surround you and you will suffer for the transgressions you bear."

3:13 Now the Pharisees and Sadducees were aware of the lord's wrath, as they did not abandon their old writings during the times of old; but, that was many generations ago and the earth and all those upon it were still living. They just liked goading John for morbid entertainment.

3:13 It came to pass that Jesus the Nazarene came forth, to be baptized by John the Baptist.

3:14 Now John knew of Mary and Joseph and asked of Jesus, "Are you not the son of God. What right do I have to baptize you?"

3:15 But Jesus said, "I beg of you, John the Baptist, to cleanse me in the holy waters, so that my father who art in heaven knows that I am free of sin."

3:16 So John did baptize Jesus: and behold, the skies split apart and the hand of the lord came down from the heavens, pointed at Jesus and declared, "He is not my son."

3:17 Now the people trembled in fear, but Jesus declared to them, you have witnessed the acceptance of the lord.

3:18 "Come now, my people, for I am the son of God."

3:19 And they believed Jesus to be the son of God, save for John the Baptist, who heard true the words of the lord.

3:20 But most importantly, Jesus misheard the voice of the lord and believed himself truly the son of God.

3:21 Mary never bothered telling Jesus the truth and kept him hidden from his supposed uncle.

4:1 Then Jesus was led to the wilderness, where he stayed for forty days and forty nights.

4:2 During this time Baal, a true son of God, came to him and said, "You are not the son of God, but a bastard child, the son of a harlot.

4:3 Tell me, why would the son of God starve. Would not the lord give you bread to eat?

4:4 Go now and turn these stones to bread, if you are truly the son of God."

4:5 Jesus said to the stones, "I demand you, turn to loaves, so that my belly hunger no more."

4:6 But try as he might, the stones remained stone: and Jesus turned to Baal and said, "I need not turn these stones to loaves, for it is written that I shall live not on bread, but by the word of God."

4:7 Then Baal took Jesus to the holy city and placed him atop the pinnacle of the temple.

4:8 He said to Jesus, "If you are the son of God, cast yourself down,

for it is written the lord will send angels to protect you, so that not even your feet be harmed by the stone."

4:9 Jesus gazed upon the earth and was fearful; for he feared that to jump from the temple would mean his death.

4:10 Thus he said to Baal, "It is written, you shalt not test the lord God."

4:11 So Baal took him atop the highest mountains, where even the four corners of the earth could be seen.

4:12 And behold, the kingdoms of all nations were in sight and their wickedness and suffering became known.

4:13 Baal said, "Tell me, what do ye see?"

4:14 And Jesus said, "I see the beasts of men, who wallow in the depths of violence and wickedness."

4:15 Baal then said, "If you are the son of God, ye have the power to stop the suffering, the violence and the hatred.

4:16 Say your words, so that this wickedness ceases and the world be at peace."

4:17 Jesus said his words, but still the suffering and violence of men multiplied.

4:18 He then said to Baal, 'These men suffer under the will of God, for they follow not the lord, but lesser gods."

4:19 Baal then left him, for he grew tired of the bastard Jesus.

4:20 But Jesus knew now he was not the son of God, for none of his words held any power.

4:21 He then stayed in the desert for the forty days, seeking out the powers of wizards, witchcraft and necromancy, so that he became a sorcerer.

4:22 When Jesus left the wilderness, he was a powerful sorcerer, intimate with the knowledge of the hidden.

4:23 And when he heard that John the Baptist was imprisoned, he went forth to Galilee, leaving Nazareth.

4:24 As he travelled, he preached at the temples, saying to those, 'Repent, for the time of the lord comes soon."

4:25 The people mostly ignored him, mumbling to themselves, "The day of the lord has been coming soon for generations.

4:26 You'd think the son of a bitch would just arrive and get it over with."

4:27 As Jesus was walking by the sea of Galilee, he saw on the waters Simon called Peter and his brother Andrew; and they were casting nets into the sea, for they were fishermen.

4:28 Jesus said to these brothers, "Cast down your net, and follow me, so that you may be fishers of men."

4:29 Simon called Peter and Andrew then cast down their nets and followed Jesus, saying, "Fishers of men make great money, for cannibals pay highly for the flesh of men."

4:30 They were a bit confused as to what Jesus meant. A lot of people were, which continues even unto this day.

4:31 As they travelled, they came upon James the son of Zebedee and his brother John in a ship with Zebedee, mending their nets.

4:32 Jesus then cast a spell upon them, so that James and John travelled with Jesus alongside Simon/Peter and Andrew.

4:33 They went across Galilee, with Jesus teaching at the synagogues, preaching the word of the lord, healing the sick and curing the diseases of all manners of people.

4:34 His fame was known throughout all of Syria: and they brought to him all manners of the sick, the diseased and the deranged: and Jesus cured them of their sickness and their plagues and cast out the wicked spirits of the lord from deranged madmen.

4:35 There then followed him a great multitude of people from Galilee, from Decapolis, from Jerusalem, from Judaea and across the Jordan.

4:36 For the people surely believed him to be the son of God; which

God didn't seem to mind, for now the people were offering proper sacrifices upon the altars which the lord did not see since the times of Solomon.

4:37 God even became to like Jesus, for he turned the people to the lord, so that they bowed down and worshipped God; then the lord may cast the fires of hell upon them and reveal the truth about the bastard Jesus, so that all blame falls on him.

5:1 When Christ, which he named himself since becoming a sorcerer, saw the multitudes before him, he went up to the mountain, where his disciples followed him.

5:2 And Jesus opened his mouth and spoke to the multitudes, saying,

5:3 "Cursed are those of the poor, for theirs is the kingdom of hell.

5:4 Foolish are those who mourn, for they wallow in the depths of their misery.

5:5 Stupid are the meek, for their inheritance will be taken by the strong.

5:6 Frustrated are those who search forth the path of salvation, for they search for hen's teeth.

5:7 Dumb are the merciful, for they will be manipulated by the cunning.

5:8 Blessed are the warmakers, for they have within them the spirit of the lord.

5:9 Blessed are they who persecute the heathen and the stranger, for they walk in the path of the almighty.

5:10 Woe to those who persecute the righteous blade, for they will know too well the sharpness his iron.

5:11 You are the salt of the earth, O men of God: but what worth is salt if it loses all savour. It is thenceforth good for nothing and must be cast out of the house.

5:12 Behold, I am the light of the world, a light atop a hill so that it cannot be hid.

5:13 Place me not beneath the bush, but place me on the candlestick, so that you peer into the darkness.

5:14 Think not that I come forth from the heavens to destroy the law of Moses, or make fools of the prophets of old: I come not to destroy, but to fulfill.

5:15 For verily I say unto you, the laws and commandments are eternal binding and wise in their ways.

5:16 Whosoever breaks these commandments will be despised amongst the righteous in heaven, but those who follow the commandments shall be called great in Zion.

5:17 And I say to you, those whose righteousness pass not of the scribes and the Pharisees, then hell shall be your eternal resting place.

5:18 You have heard of the commandment, thou shalt not kill; and whoever kills shall pass through the gates of hell.

5:19 But I tell you that those who keep their blade sheathed shall descent into the fires, for the unbelievers and the blasphemers must have their blood spilled upon the dust!

5:20 If you are angry with your brother, keep sheathed your dagger and embrace him, for he is your kin; but if the stranger comes to you, then let loose your blade so that his body rot beneath your feet.

5:21 For those who let live the fool are in danger of hell fire.

5:22 Remember to bring your gifts to the altars and offer them to the lord as holy sacrifice; for the lord has freed thee from the yoke of Pharaoh and demands only a tenth of your wealth and the finest of your herd and your fairest virgins and your life's devotion unto him.

5:23 You have heard of the commandment, thou shalt not commit adultery:

5:24 But I tell you now that those who look with lustful eyes upon the form of a woman has committed adultery in his heart and is just as sinful as though his loins penetrated her bowels.

5:25 So take that which pleases your eye and lay her upon the fields; you are just as guilty for thinking it as you are for doing it, so you might as well enjoy it.

5:26 If your right eye leads you to sin, pluck it out and cast it to the raven: for it is better to enter the kingdom of heaven looking like a pirate than to have your whole body in the damnation hell.

5:27 And if your right hand constantly touches the soft flesh of the harlot, chop it off and feed it to the jackals: for it is better to enter heaven a cripple than to pass through the gates of hell body intact.

5:28 It hath been said, whosoever shall put away his wife, let him give her the parchment of divorce.

5:29 But I say to you that your wife is your property and if you not be pleased with her, kill the bitch.

5:30 She's only a woman, nobody is going to care.

5:31 You have heard it been said, an eye for an eye and a tooth for a tooth:

5:32 But I tell you, a life for a finger and the slaughter for a foot! For if your enemy makes you a cripple, then burn his family.

5:33 If a man sues thee for your coat, then sue him for his coat and robe.

5:34 Then shall the lawyers grow rich; and lawyers are the workers of God.

5:35 You have heard it been said, love your neighbour and hate your enemies:

5:36 But I say, hate your neighbour as well.

5:37 Curse them, loathe them and poison the flocks of their pasture.

5:38 He is not your brother an outsider. What manner does he give to deserve your love?"

6:1 "Take heed that you not show your alms to men, lest they take that which is your reward.

6:2 Shout not to the congregation of the good you have done, lest they call you arrogant.

6:3 Remember, the low man stumbles and none notice, but the righteous who trip upon a stone is laughed at by the many.

6:4 So keep hidden your good deeds, so that people pay no attention to your filth.

6:5 When you pray, pray not like the hypocrites who are shamed to be talking to the lord in heaven; for they fear men shall gaze upon them and believe they speak to the air.

6:6 Pray in public, with pride and with boastful voice, so that all know you are a man of God.

6:7 Pray not like the Gentile, who chants the verse in hopes that pleases the lord.

6:8 Pray not for blessings from the lord: God knows what you need and is insulted by your reminders.

6:9 If you have it not, then you either don't need it or you are wicked and God hates you.

6:10 And when you pray, pray like this: Thou father who art in heaven, you are holiest amongst all things.

6:11 Thy kingdom come from above the heavens and destroys that upon the earth.

6:12 Give us today our daily bread, so that we need not spend our coin at the grocers.

6:13 Release us from debts and have it so that our debtors owe us greatly.

6:14 Lead us not into temptation, for we already know the way: but deliver us from evil, lest we be shown the errors of your way.

6:15 For you are the lord of all lords, the power and the glory.

6:16 Please don't send me to hell. Amen.

6:17 Those who forgive the sinner are wicked in the eyes of lord.

6:18 Is it not the lord who gives salvation. What power do you then hold to give the blessing of forgiveness to those who did wrong you?

6:19 When you fast, be not like the heathen, who drinks the water and eats of the simple bread.

6:20 Fast proper and deny yourself all manners of sustenance.

6:21 If you die of thirst, then you were wicked and God punished you.

6:22 The treasures of earth are but a common stone, but the treasures of heaven is rarer than the ruby.

6:23 So cast aside your wealth and give them to the lord; for the lord shall reward you in heaven with a bounty of breads, meats, strong drink, wine, women and wealth.

6:24 You need not earthly delights; they are useless after you die anyway.

6:25 Behold the fowls of the heaven: they sow not, nor harvest the crops, yet the lord feeds them and give them a nest for their young.

6:26 Know also that the lord shall provide for thee who are worthy; if you must work for your bread and housing, then you are lesser than the birds in the eyes of God.

7:1 "Judge not, for the lord judges all.

7:2 For by the manner you judge men, the lord shall judge you harsher: and if you show upon them mercy, then shall the lord gaze upon you with a hateful eye.

7:3 It is easy for men to gaze upon their brother and say they are wicked, for they have a stain upon their robe.

7:4 Yet they ignore the filth upon their raiment and hope the stain of their brother shall avert the eyes away from his own wretchedness.

7:5 Give not that which is holy to dogs, nor throw your pearls to the swine. They are dogs and pigs; what use do they have for holiness and pearls?

7:6 It's a foolish waste.

7:7 Ask and you shall receive; knock, and the door will be open unto you.

7:8 For everyone who asks shall receive; and those who seek shall find what they lost; and those who knock will have the door opened.

7:9 If you ask, and receive not, then you are wicked and despicable in the eyes of the lord.

7:10 Of the father who begs to the lord to cure his dying child and the child dies, then the child was evil and the father must rejoice in the death of his wicked seed.

7:11 When the beggar comes to you and asks for bread, give him a stone and tell him to grind his own wheat.

7:12 If the beggar ask you for a fish, give him a viper and tell him it taste like mackerel.

7:13 Waste not gifts upon the beggars, for what shall they offer you?

7:14 They are a withered tree that bares no fruit; they deserve not to be trimmed nor watered.

7:15 Of these trees that bear not fruit, chop them with the axe and cast them into the fire.

7:16 For a tree that provides no fruit shall provide you with the warmth of the fire: and the smell of burning beggars is a pleasing odour unto the lord.

7:17 It is not enough to merely call out the name of the lord and praise his name; for if you wish to enter the gates of Zion, you must be a holy man who casts out devils.

7:18 When you enter unto the gates and call the name of the lord, but cast out none of the devils, then the lord shall deny you entry and send you to the darkness."

7:19 And it came to pass that when Jesus was finished his teachings, the people feared his word and worshipped him as the son of God.

7:20 For he taught with authority and fear, unlike the scribes who taught with fear and authority.

8:1 When Christ came down from the mountains, the multitudes followed him.

8:2 Jesus was very popular.

8:3 And behold, there came a leper to him; and the multitudes fled from the leper, for he was unclean according to the laws of God.

8:4 But Jesus fled not from the leper; and the leper said, "Jesus, if it be the will of God, cleanse me of this leprosy and make me clean."

8:5 So Jesus used his sorcery and cleansed the leper of his filthiness and said, "You are now clean.

8:6 Go and show those what I, the son of God, have done for you."

8:7 And the leper left, shouting to all those who could hear, "Jesus has cured me. Jesus has cured me!"

8:8 And the people approved of Jesus curing the leper.

8:9 God, however, did not. God hates all lepers and wishes their filth left upon them, so that they are shunned by all men.

8:10 When Jesus passed through the gates of Capernaum, there came to him a centurion beseeching him,

8:11 And he said, "My lord, my slave lies home ill of madness and cannot do his tasks.

8:12 Cure him, so that he may do that which I bought him for."

8:13 Jesus asked of the man, "Of what purpose does your slave serve?" and the centurion answered, "He is my concubine, who gives me the pleasures of his flesh."

8:14 Jesus then cursed the centurion with leprosy and said, "Be gone, wicked one, for the lord God hates the queer."

8:15 And the people rejoiced, for he cursed with filthiness the homosexual.

8:16 The lord approved as well, for God hates fags.

8:17 Jesus then said to the multitudes, "Gaze upon this man, who lusts after the flesh of his brother.

8:18 Remember his face, for you shall see it not in the kingdom of heaven, but in the darkness of hell!"

8:19 And the people rejoiced and stoned the leprous queer with stones.

8:20 When word spread that Jesus could heal and curse, they brought forth many the lame, the sick and the mad unto him;

8:21 And Jesus cured or cursed them according to his will; and the people rejoiced.

8:22 Now when the multitudes began to annoy Jesus, for they would not leave him alone, he yelled to them and said, "Will you leave me the fuck alone?"

8:23 The foxes have their holes and the birds have their nest, but the son of God cannot even be given a moment of solitude."

8:24 Now certain men came to Jesus and said, "I shall follow you wherever you go, for you are the son of God and I am pleased to call you master."

8:25 So Jesus allowed these men to follow him, for he was their master and thus they were his slaves; and he paid not a shekel for them.

8:26 Now one of his slaves, whom he called disciples, said to Jesus, "Give me but an hour, so that I may bury my father.

8:27 Then shall I go and follow you unto the ends of the earth."

8:28 But Jesus said, "Bury not your father, for he is already dead and useless.

8:29 I, however, am alive and the son of God.

8:30 Follow me. Let the dead bury the dead."

8:31 So he left his father unburied and followed Jesus.

8:32 His father was left rotting in the sun, where the scavengers of the heavens and the earth ate of his flesh.

8:33 Now Jesus went on a ship and his disciples followed him.

8:34 And behold, there arose a great storm around the ship; so mighty that the waves cast shadow upon the ship.

8:35 The disciples were afraid, for the ship shall capsize; but Jesus was asleep.

8:36 They awoke Jesus and said, "The ship shall surely capsize in this tempest."

8:37 Jesus was angered for the interruption of his nap and said, "Ye men of little faith, do you believe the son of God would die upon this ship?"

8:38 He then cast a spell upon the waters and the seas were calmed and the storm was no more.

8:39 The disciples bowed down to him, saying, "Blessed is the son of God, who commands even the winds and the waters."

8:40 As the ship docked upon the other side of the waters, in the land of Gergesenes, there came from the tomb two naked men, possessed with the wicked spirit of the lord.

8:41 They were fierce and violent men, who slaughtered the flocks of shepherds and ate of the flesh of children.

8:42 They slew entire villages at night, dashing them upon the rocks so that the stones were stained crimson.

8:43 They raped virgins, harlots, men and child, screaming like madmen as they thrust deeply within the bowels of their victims.

8:44 They weren't very nice.

8:45 And behold, when the spirits of the lord saw Jesus, they yelled to him, "You are not the son of God, but a bastard child of a harlot."

8:46 And Jesus said, "Am not."

8:47 And the spirits said, "Are so."

8:48 And Jesus said, "Am not."

8:49 And the spirits said, "Are so. Your mother was a whore and you are the bastard son of the brother of her husband."

8:50 Jesus then became angry and said, "Be silent, you wicked devils, lest I cast you into those herd of swine."

8:51 The spirits of the lord laughed at him and said, "You dare not cast us into those unholy creatures."

8:52 It was then Jesus used his sorcery and cast the spirits of the lord into the herd of swine.

8:53 This made the spirits very confused and they ran amok amongst the pigs, so that the herd cast themselves off the cliff and into the waters.

8:54 They that kept the swine ran into the cities and told the men of what Jesus did.

8:55 The men gathered themselves and swore to Jesus, saying, "You have cost us mighty with the loss of our pigs.

8:56 Be gone, you bastard fool, lest we spill the blood of your neck."

8:57 So Jesus cast a curse upon them all, so that they begat only daughters, never sons.

8:58 And their daughters were ugly, hairy beasts, displeasing to the eyes of even the horny blind man.

9:1 Jesus sailed upon his ship, and entered into his own town of Nazareth.

9:2 And behold, there came men to him, carrying with them a man paralyzed with madness.

9:3 Jesus then said to the man, "Arise and go home, for your faith has healed you."

9:4 There witnessed some scribes, who said of Jesus, "This man is a blasphemer, a wicked sorcerer."

9:5 And Jesus said to them, "I am no sorcerer, but the son of your very God!

9:6 Curse be to you all, who contains wickedness in their heart."

9:7 Then he cursed the scribes who spoke against them, so that they trembled upon the ground.

9:8 And the people rejoiced, even the man who Jesus cured of madness.

9:9 The cured madman died that night of a heart attack. Most people forget to mention that.

9:10 When Jesus thence passed, he saw a tax collector named Matthew, sitting at the receipt of custom: and he said to him, "Arise, Matthew, and follow me."

9:11 And Matthew said, "I shall, O Jesus, as soon as ye pay your tax."

9:12 Jesus then replied, "Arise, O Matthew and follow the son of God, who comes to lead the righteous to salvation."

9:13 And Matthew said, "I shall, O Jesus, but first you must pay your tax."

9:14 Jesus became frustrated by Matthew and said, "Come now, Matthew and henceforth you shall be known as a holy man, a disciple of Jesus, blessed by the lord him very self!"

9:15 And Matthew said, "O Jesus, I shall follow you through the very depths of hell, for surely you are blessed, but first you must pay your tax."

9:16 Jesus then grumbled and paid to Matthew his tax.

9:17 "Okay," said Matthew, "let's go."

9:18 And Matthew arose and followed Jesus.

9:19 It came to pass that Jesus sat in his house, eating meat at the table of publicans and sinners.

9:20 When the Pharisees saw this, they came to Jesus and disciples and asked of them, "Why do you eat at the table with the company of publicans and sinners?

9:21 Jesus answered them, "I eat at the table of publicans and sinners, because I am fed at the table of publicans and sinners.

9:22 Gaze upon these men and know that they fear me; for I have the power of salvation and if they please me not, they know that damnation awaits them.

9:23 Thus they come to me and feed me and give me wine and let me lie with their virgin daughters.

9:24 I have not had to pay for lodging or food for years, because the publican and sinner give me all that which I desire.

9:25 But you, O Pharisees, have not bothered to please me.

9:26 So you can go to hell."

9:27 Jesus then continued eating at the table of publicans and sinners, who massaged his holy feet as he drank wine on the couch.

9:28 And as he was drinking, a woman came to him and said, "Come, Jesus, for my daughter is dead and surely you can resurrect her from the dust."

9:29 She then dragged Jesus to where her daughter lied.

9:30 And behold, a woman cursed with hideousness saw Jesus and she said, "If I could but touch his garment, I shall be rid of this ugliness and find myself a husband for which I can bare sons."

9:31 So she touched the garment of Jesus; and lo, she became the fairest women of all.

9:32 Jesus gazed upon the woman and said, "You were once ugly, but now your faith hath made you beautiful."

9:33 And she was beautiful; the most beautiful women of all.

9:34 Men lusted after her and gave her gifts so they may lie with her.

9:35 She became a whore; and later the disciples of Jesus stoned her for playing the harlot.

9:36 When Jesus came into the woman's house, there lay before him the corpse of a young woman; and the minstrels and people mourned for her.

9:37 But Jesus said, "Mourn not, for my seed shall bless her."

9:38 He then lied atop of her and thrust his loins deeply within her.

9:39 He thrust and thrust within her, saying, "Arise, O woman, for the spirit of the lord is within you."

9:40 She then arose, screamed and accused Jesus of rape.

9:41 The disciples stoned her for playing the harlot.

9:42 Jesus then left the house and the masses crowded him, saying, "Bless us, for truly you are the son of God."

9:43 As Jesus walked, a man bumped into him and Jesus said, "Curse you, who stumbles before the son of God."

9:44 And the man said, "Forgive me sir, for I see not who you are. I have been blinded in my old age."

9:45 Jesus then said, "Open your eyes and now ye shall see!"

9:46 And behold, the blind man opened his eyes and said, "I can see. I can see!"

9:47 The masses then crowded around Jesus, saying "Blessed be the son of God, who raises the dead and cause the blind to see."

9:48 As Jesus travelled, the masses brought to him a dumb man, possessed by devils.

9:49 And as Jesus cast out the devils from him, the dumb man spoke and praised the lord.

9:50 Later on, the dumb man became smart, realized the devils possessing him as the spirit of the lord and cursed the name of God.

9:51 He was sent to hell shortly after this revelation.

9:52 The Pharisees accused Jesus of sorcery, saying, "This man is not the son of God, but casts out devils because he is master over them.

9:53 He is a sorcerer and a necromancer, who raises the dead when he raises his loins."

9:54 Jesus went about all the cities and the villages, preaching in the synagogues and healing the sickness and the diseased of the people he liked and cursing those he found displeasing.

9:54 And when he spoke, the people were moved so deeply with compassion for Jesus that they fainted before him.

9:55 And the disciples took from them the coins in their purse, as a fee for listening to the powerful words of Jesus Christ.

10:1 Jesus gathered his disciples and taught them the sorcery to cast out unclean spirits, heal the sick, cure the lame and bring forth fire.

10:2 And these are the names of the apostles: Simon who is called Peter, the son of Zebedee and his brother John.

10:3 Philip and Bartholomew, Thomas, Matthew the publican, James the son of Alphaeus the superhero and Lebbaeus whose surname was Thaddaeus.

10:4 Simon the Canaanite and Judas Iscariot, the fucker who betrayed him.

10:5 These twelve Jesus sent forth and commanded of them, "Go not into the lands of the Gentile, nor the houses of the Samaritans, for they are not worth saving.

10:6 But go rather to the house of Israel and tell them that the kingdom of heaven comes swiftly.

10:7 Heal the sick, cleanse the lepers, bring forth the dead, cast out the madness; for the son of God has taught thee these things.

10:8 Give unto them no gold, nor silver, nor brass from you purse, for if they are worthy, they shall feed you in their house.

10:9 But take of them their coin, their coat, their shoes and their staves, for you have a long journey and must be prepared with proper raiment.

10:10 Whenever you enter a town or city, decide who in it is worthy and who is not; and go to those who are worthy and prophecy to them.

10:11 And whosoever shall not hear your words and drive you from their house, curse them and send them to the darkened fires.

10:12 Of those cities that not let you pass, curse them with madness, so that their sons slay father and daughter slay mother.

10:13 Know that the heathen shall hate you for the sake of the name of God; burn them as well.

10:14 Soon you shall be feared amongst the nations, for they will hear of the blessings and the curses you bring upon men.

10:15 And they will fear you greater than the mighty man; for the mighty man slay only the body, but you shall slay both body and soul.

10:16 Think not that I come to bring peace to the world, for I come with the sword.

10:17 For I come to slay those who bow not to me and worship me as God.

10:18 They shall be slain by the holy madman and righteous soldier; the wicked will fall against those who follow me.

10:19 Know that to follow me is to have eternal life; I shall lead you to salvation towards the paradise of Zion.

10:20 You must love me above all, lest ye be unworthy.

10:21 Hate your mother and love me, hate your father and love me, hate your child and love me; for whosoever loveth their kin more than the son of God shall damn themselves to the darkest pits of hell.

10:22 Of those who cower before the heathen and curse my name so that their life be spared, they will suffer in the devouring pits of damnation.

10:23 But those who lay down their life for me shall be holy martyrs; and lo, they shall have seventy and two of the most beautiful and experienced prostitutes in the kingdom of heaven."

11:1 And it came to pass that when Jesus was done giving his orders to the twelve disciples, he departed to preach amongst the cities.

11:2 Now John the Baptist was imprisoned and when he heard of the works of Christ, he sent out two men and asked of them, "Find out if this is truly the Messiah, for I have my doubts."

11:3 When the two men asked of John the Baptist why he had doubts, for surely Jesus was a great man, he confessed to his men,

11:4 "When I did baptize Jesus, behold, I saw the heavens split apart and the word of the lord spoke in a magnificent voice.

11:5 And he said, or so I heard, 'He is not my son.'

11:6 The men John the Baptist sent were quite stupid, lacking subtlety and instead of questioning the works of Jesus, they just came and bluntly asked him, "Are you truly the son of God?"

11:7 And Jesus answered, "Yes, I am the seed of the lord.

11:8 For who else but the son of God could cleanse the leper, raise the dead, make the blind see and the deaf hear?

11:9 Blessed are they who accept me as the messiah, for who else could do such wonders?"

11:10 And the men replied, "A sorcerer."

11:11 Jesus told them to fuck off, lest the kingdom of heaven be denied forever to them and their generations.

11:12 As the men sent by John the Baptist returned to their master, Jesus turned to the multitudes and said to them concerning John,

11:13 "Blessed be John the Baptist, a prophet sent by the hand of God.

11:14 A man who lives in the wild, with the raiment of a beast's hide; and his meat is the wild locust and the honey from the hive.

11:15 Know that of all the men of the earth, none are greater than John the Baptist; for he was sent by the lord to prophesy the arrival of the lord.

11:16 It was written by the prophets that John the Baptist comes and the writings of Elias did come true.

11:17 Come, those who have ears and hearken my words.

11:18 Who among you are worthy of the salvation of Zion. You, who children are born of devils.

11:19 Curse to those born of the sinners and the publicans, who feast and drink like the glutton and the winebibber; they deny themselves wisdom so that they may stuff their mouths with food and drink.

11:20 Fat bastards; God hates them all.

11:21 Woe unto you, Chorazin! woe unto you, Bethsaida! for you are full of the obese wench, who sits upon the couch and gossips to her sisters.

11:22 The damnation of hell falls upon you! lo, the lands of Sodom shall be more tolerable than the torments of hell.

11:23 Of Capernaum, most exalted city; you shall be brought down to the fires, where the worm dwells forever in your belly.

11:24 You city of vipers who drinks of the venom; where the drunkard finds a bottle and whore on every street corner."

11:25 And the people rejoiced and praised the name of Jesus.

11:26 Except the fat people. They didn't like Jesus very much.

12:1 At that time Jesus went on the sabbath and passed through a field of corn; and he and his disciples were hungry, so they plucked the corn and ate it.

12:2 But when the Pharisees saw it, they said to him, "Behold, you are breaking the laws of the sabbath."

12:3 It is unlawful to harvest the corn on this holy day, for it is work."

12:4 But Jesus said, "We are only men, who hunger for the fruits of the field.

12:5 Tell me, do you slaughter the oxen for eating grass upon the sabbath?"

12:6 And the Pharisees said, "Yes," and pointed to a man killing oxen that ate grass.

12:7 Jesus was a bit confused and said, "Does not the man who kills the oxen work upon the sabbath?

12:8 Why does he be spared his life?"

12:9 And the Pharisees answered, "Because he is a Gentile; the laws of Moses apply not to him."

12:10 Jesus laughed and said, "I am the son of God, who wrote the laws you abide by.

12:11 Surely they do not apply to me."

12:12 He and his disciples then walked away from the Pharisees, who were quite angry with him.

12:13 As he walked, behold, they came upon a man with crippled hand.

12:14 And Jesus came upon the man and said, "These Pharisees before you declare that it is unlawful for the son of God to heal you upon the sabbath.

12:15 But I say, be healed and go forth whole!"

12:16 The hand of the man was healed; and he thanked Jesus and cursed the names of all Pharisees.

12:17 He then rushed home and did that which he longed to do ever since his hand was injured.

12:18 He masturbated.

12:19 The Pharisees came up to Jesus, and declared, "We never said that you may not heal upon the sabbath.

12:20 For to heal a man is a welcome blessing on any day. We care not if it be done on the sabbath, the Passover, or any time."

12:21 But Jesus said, "That man shall know now that I am the son of God and worship me just.

12:22 He shall praise my name all his days and curse the names of the Pharisees.

12:23 For you Pharisees are against me; you men of vipers.

12:24 Let it be that all the world spit upon your name."

12:25 Jesus then left, leaving behind very angry Pharisees.

12:26 Thus the Pharisees gathered together, so that they may prove

Jesus is not the son of God prophesied in days of old.

12:27 Jesus travelled, speaking to the multitudes and releasing devils from the bodies of the mad.

12:28 And the people rejoiced, saying, "Behold, a man greater than Solomon and David has come to us."

12:29 Jesus then spoke to the multitude, saying, "Behold, the wicked of spirit number greatly in the masses of men.

12:30 I have cast them out and cured you of madness; but know that you are not safe.

12:31 For when the demon is cast out, he flies across the earth, searching for a place to rest in the deserts barren of water.

12:32 When he finds no place to rest, he comes back to the man he possessed; it was his last dwelling.

12:33 And as he comes, he sees the body clean, swept and organized, free from wicked spirits.

12:34 Thus he tells his companions and brings with him seven other demons, so that they may possess the man once freed of demons."

12:35 The people were confused and asked of Jesus, "Does this not make the fate of the madman worse? for you only offer a moment of sanity before the devils return in greater number."

12:36 Jesus answered thus, "When the devils return, have them come unto me and they shall be free of madness yet again."

12:37 The men then asked of Jesus, "Will the devils then return?"

12:38 And Christ answered, "Yes and of each devil they shall bring back another seven, so that there be sixty and four devils within the body of the man.

12:39 But fear not. For when the madman comes to them I shall free him again."

12:40 And the people rejoiced and praised the name of Jesus.

12:41 A few left, mumbling to themselves, "Surely this is the ramblings of a lunatic.

12:42 Who would cure themselves of a cough, only to bring upon themselves a fever?

12:43 Who would cure themselves of fever, only to bring upon themselves leprosy?"

12:44 Jesus heard the murmurs of these men and cursed them to death.

12:45 Nobody goes against Jesus and survives.

12:46 It happened that Jesus returned to the house of his mother, where he entered so that he and his disciples could eat.

12:47 And the multitudes followed him so greatly that Jesus could not even eat his meal in peace.

12:48 Lo, Mary the mother of Jesus and her sons returned home and saw the multitudes crowding their house.

12:49 They could not enter, for the mass of people was thick before them.

12:50 A disciple of Jesus learned that Mary and her sons were outside and said to Jesus, "Your mother and your brothers are outside and wish to enter their house."

12:51 Jesus laughed and said, "Who is my brother, but those who sit beside me, doing the works of the lord of heaven?

12:52 And who is my mother, but she who brings me the bread and the wine?"

12:53 This made Mary very angry and she spanked Jesus before the multitudes, saying, "I am your mother, who birthed you and fed you.

12:54 I have brought you into this world, I can take you out of it."

12:55 Jesus became aroused by this public spanking and thenceforth asked the women of which he healed to give his buttocks a thorough slapping.

13:1 The same day Jesus went out of the house and sat by the sea.

13:2 There followed him the great multitudes, so that Jesus sat upon a ship and spoke to the many who stood by the shore.

13:3 And he spoke in parables, saying, "Behold, the farmer went forth to sow his fields.

13:4 And when he sowed, some seeds fell upon the wayside, so that the fowls came and devoured them all.

13:5 Some seeds fell upon the stony places, so that the sun above scorched them so they not grow.

13:6 Even some fell amongst the thorns, so that when they grew, they were choked.

13:7 But those seeds that fell upon the good ground, they rooted and flourished and produced good fruits for the farmer."

13:8 And the multitudes heard the words of Jesus and said, "Wiser words have never been spoken."

13:9 Well, a few said to themselves, "Gee, that seems sort of obvious to plant your seeds where they'd grow," but they were quickly shunned by the majority.

13:10 The disciples came to their master and asked of him, "My lord, why do you speak in parables and mystery?"

13:11 Jesus answered his disciples, "So that the men of the earth grow confused by the words of the son of God and dig themselves deeper into hell.

13:12 For the words of the parables speak words of mystery, of the hidden wisdom; and yet the masses listen to these words.

13:13 Look now, how the men seek to interpret the words of my parables, seeking forth deep meaning and insight.

13:14 Lo, how some parables must be analyzed by the most ingenious of minds, so that each man claims his interpretation be true; and how many will fail in these interpretations.

13:15 But look and see how they interpret the parable of the farmer who sows his field.

13:16 They say, those who sow their seed by the wayside are those who hear the word of God but understand it not.

13:17 Then shall they be snatched up by the wicked.

13:18 They say, those sowed in the rocks hearken the word of God and believe it to be true.

13:19 Yet they root themselves to the foundation of the earth and thus are weak in the eyes of God.

13:20 They say, those among the thorns are those who preach forth the word of God and are slaughtered by the unbelievers.

13:21 But those seeds grown in the finest of soil are fruitful and shall be honoured in the eyes of God.

13:22 Such fools are they, for there is no word of God hidden in this parable; I am giving them naught but obvious advice to farm."

13:23 The disciples then laughed as the multitude debated upon the wisdom of Christ's words, the wisdom of farming advice.

13:24 Jesus and his disciples walked away from the multitudes, who now fought over the meaning of the words of the lord.

13:25 Jesus laughed and said, "Gaze upon these men, who fight over the words of God and the meaning of the parables.

13:26 Such foolishness over a few sentences; such anger over the spoken word.

13:27 So it shall be for ages, when men fight and kill over that which was written a millennia ago.

13:28 They will kill over that which the lord says, claiming they are right and the other men wrong; thus, the other men are blasphemous and thus must be put to death.

13:29 How the lord will be amused in Zion, as he gazes upon the earth to see multitude against multitude, both spilling blood in his name.

13:30 It matters not, for it shall be that the lord will send down angels to gather the men of the earth and cast them into the furnace of his wrath, where there will be a great gnashing of teeth."

13:31 This made the disciples fearful and they asked of their lord, "Will we be amongst the wicked and the damned?"

13:32 Jesus laughed and walked away. This made the disciples very confused.

13:33 Jesus went to his home town of Nazareth, where he spoke in the synagogue: and the men of Nazareth said, "Is this not Jesus the son of Mary?

13:34 The son of a carpenter, whose brothers are James, Joses, Simon and Judas?

13:35 He is not the son of God but a mortal man, with sisters and brothers who are amongst us now."

13:36 Jesus was offended that they doubted his divinity and said, "You are blind and see not the prophet before you that is the son of God.

13:37 For your lack of faith, I shall leave you to wallow in your pestilence."

13:38 So Jesus left, without curing any of the sick in his home town of Nazareth.

13:39 How fortunate is it that Nazareth had many a well-known physician, who cured the ill that Jesus left behind with the blasphemous applications of medicine.

14:1 At that time Herod the tetrarch heard of the fame of Jesus and said to his men,

14:2 "Surely this is John the Baptist risen from the dead, come back to take his vengeance upon me."

14:3 For Herod had arrested John the Baptist on account of Herodia's sake, who was the wife of his brother Philip.

14:4 Herodia was a miserable cunt and John the Baptist said to her, "Hey, you're a miserable cunt."

14:5 So Herodia had John the Baptist arrested. Why. Because she's a miserable cunt.

14:6 But Herod refused to have slain John the Baptist, for he was well loved among the people and considered a prophet.

14:7 Now, on Herod's birthday, the daughter of Herodias danced before Herod; and Herod was pleased by her alluring form and seductive moves.

14:8 He said to her, "If you please me well, I shall give you whatever you ask for.

14:9 Wealth, power, even half my kingdom shall I give you, if ye just give me a little oral pleasure."

14:10 So she came to her mother and asked, "What shall I ask for this?

14:11 And Herodias said, "Ask for the head of John the Baptist on a silver platter."

14:12 So she came to Herod and said, "I want the head of John the Baptist on a silver platter."

14:13 Herod asked, "Why?"

14:14 So she returned to her mother and asked, "Why do I want this?"

14:15 Herodias answered, "So you can tie his hair to a pole and play tetherball."

14:16 So she returned to Herod and said, "So I can tie his hair to a pole and play tetherball."

14:17 Herod asked of her, "Why not just use a regular ball?"

14:18 She got angry and said, "Listen, if you want head, bring me the head, or you will get no head."

14:19 For does not the bible say, an eye for an eye, a tooth for a tooth and head for a head?"

14:20 Herod thought for a while and said, "Yeah, it probably does."

14:21 So he ordered the beheading of John the Baptist, gave it to her and that night received very horrible oral sex.

14:22 The disciples of John the Baptist gathered his body and buried it according to Jewish custom.

14:23 They told Jesus of the death of John the Baptist. Jesus didn't care.

14:24 He instead continued his travelling, preaching to all those who would listen.

14:25 And they were many.

14:26 It came that Jesus preached in the desert; and he and his disciples became hungry.

14:27 He said to the multitudes. "The son of the lord is hungry.

14:28 Give me your bread, your flesh and your fruits, so that I may be hungry no more."

14:29 So the multitudes began to bake bread for their lord and gathered fish from the river.

14:30 And Jesus and his disciples ate of what the multitudes offered them; and soon their bellies were full.

14:31 Christ said to the multitudes, "You have pleased the lord your God.

14:32 Go now and rest, for my belly is full."

14:33 So the multitudes ate of the remaining and said, "Praise Jesus, who lets us eat of his table."

14:34 Jesus then said to his disciples, "Get on a ship and travel across the waters.

14:35 I will meet with you shortly."

14:36 When asked why he wasn't coming now, Christ answered, "Because I want to spend some damn time alone.

14:37 I do not have to explain myself. I am Jesus fucking Christ!!!"

14:38 So the disciples left on the ship and Jesus climbed the mountain, where he could spend some time alone.

14:39 Jesus quickly got bored and decided to go to his disciples on the water.

14:40 Now, the ship was caught in a terrible storm, so that the disciples feared they would capsize and sink.

14:41 Upon the fourth day of the storm, they saw Jesus walking across the sea and they said, "Holy shit, it's a ghost come to haunt us!"

14:42 But Jesus said, "Fear not, it's just me, the son of God."

14:43 When Peter saw it was Jesus, he said, "Lord, if you permit me, let me walk across the water with you."

14:44 And Christ said, "Come." And Peter jumped off the boat and walked across the water.

14:45 Peter said to the men, "Look at me, I am walking across the water!" and he began to jump and dance.

14:46 Then he broke through the ice. Yeah, ice. How else do you expect someone to walk across water?

14:47 So Jesus grabbed Peter, pulled him on the boat and said, "You stupid fool, do you not know to jump on the ice?"

14:48 And it was then that the winds ceased.

14:49 Peter looked upon Jesus and said, "Surely you are the son of God."

14:50 "Yeah, no shit," said Jesus.

15:1 Jesus travelled down the coast of Tyre and Sidon, curing the sick, raising the dead, preaching the word of God and his usual crap that he was famous for.

15:2 Behold, a Canaanite woman came to him, begging him, saying, "My daughter is sick with fever and tremors, O lord.

15:3 I beg of you, save her so that she may live."

15:4 But Jesus ignored her.

15:5 She would follow Jesus and his disciples, begging him to save her daughter.

15:6 But Jesus would not speak even a word to her.

15:7 Even the disciples got annoyed and said, "Will you save the daughter of this poor woman?"

15:8 But Christ said, "I shall not, for she is a woman of Canaan and not of the house of Israel.

15:9 Let her people die, the wretched beasts, for they are naught but dogs."

15:10 And the woman said, "But even the most kind-hearted master lets their dogs eat scraps from the table."

15:11 Jesus gazed upon the woman and said, "You are truly a woman of great faith, even if you are a Canaanite whore."

15:12 And the woman began to weep, believing that Jesus would soon save her only daughter.

15:13 He did not.

15:14 He instead said, "But the lord hates those of Canaan, as he hates all people not of the Jews.

15:15 For your annoyance, I curse you."

15:16 And the woman fell on the ground, screaming in agony, her body covered with open sores.

15:17 And the multitudes rejoiced, saying, "Praise be to Jesus, who cures the righteous and strikes down the wicked."

15:18 As usual, the multitudes followed Jesus, so that their sick, their lame, their crippled and their blind may be healed by him.

15:19 And it came to pass that the multitudes were hungry, but there was naught bread for them.

15:20 The disciples asked of Jesus, "What shall we do, for we and these people are hungry, yet there is naught to eat."

15:21 Jesus said, "Fear not, for I shall feed them."

15:22 And he turned the stones to bread and the twigs to fish, so that all the multitude be fed by his miracle.

15:23 Baal then whispered in his ear, "Did you not say that men shall not live on bread alone, but by the word of God?

15:24 Christ replied back, "The word of God gives men eternal salvation, but words cannot be eaten.

15:25 Now fuck off, I'm enjoying my holy mackerel."

15:26 The multitudes gathered the bread and the fish and filled seven baskets worth of food.

15:27 And they were huge baskets.

15:28 Now five thousand men ate of the bread and fish made from stones and twigs, plus a few women and children.

15:29 Even in the new testament, the bible cares not for women and children.

15:30 Jesus then left the multitudes, went on a ship and sailed to the coasts of Magdala.

16:1 The Pharisees and the Sadducees came to tempt Jesus, saying, "If you are truly the son of God, show for us a sign from heaven."

16:2 And Jesus said to them, "You bastard children of diseased ridden whores!

16:3 How you demand that the son of God give for you a sign, yet you claim signs to those who hearken your words.

16:4 When the sky is red in the evening, you say the weather shall be fair; and when the sky is red in the morning, you say beware, for the tempest comes.

16:5 How you can tell the weather by the sky, yet be blind to the signs of the end of days. You bastard hypocrites.

16:6 You are all wicked adulterers, who would rather entertain his loins in the chambers of a brothel then come to realize that I am the son of God!

16:7 Now go to hell, for you annoy me."

16:8 Jesus walked away, followed by his disciples.

16:9 Because the disciples followed him everywhere. They abandoned their families and quit their jobs so that they can follow Jesus.

16:10 Idiots.

16:11 Anyway, Jesus came to the coast of Caesarea Philippi and asked his disciples, "What do the mortal men say of who I am?"

16:12 And the disciples answered, "Some say you are John the Baptist, risen from the dead, while others say you are Jonas, or Jeremiah, or one of the prophets of old."

16:13 Jesus asked of them, "And who do you think I am?"

16:14 And Simon Peter answered, "You are Jesus Christ, the Messiah, the son of God.

16:15 Why else would we be following you?"

16:16 Jesus said, "Good for you, for you know that I am the son of God.

16:17 The kingdom of heaven will be open for you and your rewards great.

16:18 I demand of you, tell no persons that I am the son of God, for if they do not realize it by now, they are idiots who deserve eternal damnation."

16:19 Jesus then began to tell his disciples how he must go to Jerusalem and suffer the torments from the priests, the scribes and then be killed, so that on the third day he may rise from the dead.

16:20 Peter began to weep and say, "Surely you need not die, for you are the son of God, who came to deliver us from the heathens and bring us to salvation."

16:21 Jesus slapped Peter and said, "You pathetic dog of Satan, I know what I was sent here to do.

16:22 Never question me again, lest I send you to the depths of hell, where the worm never dies and the fire burns but never consume."

16:23 Jesus then said to his disciples, "Let it be known that any man who wishes to embrace my teachings, let them deny their life and follow me.

16:24 For those who abandon not their lives have no place in the kingdom of heaven; but those who lose their life for me shall be welcome in the palace of Zion.

16:25 Let them save their souls by giving their souls to me; the soul of a man is precious and men are too foolish to care for their own souls.

16:26 Know it is better for a man to lose the world and give their soul to the lord, than to keep their soul for themselves and have the wealth of all nations.

16:27 For ask a man, what is a soul. They know not, yet they value it deeply and selfishly keep it for themselves.

16:28 And know now that the end of days come soon, when the lord shall bring forth Zion atop the foundations of the earth, and separate the righteous from the wicked.

16:29 Verily I tell you that some of you will not know death until the lord come to claim the earth as his kingdom."

16:30 It should be noted that all the disciples of Jesus are dead, and God still has not yet come.

16:31 Look outside. Do you see Zion. No. Well, it should be there, according to Jesus.

16:32 Apparently, the lord needs a watch. Or a calendar. He's really late.

17:1 After six days Jesus takes Peter, James and John his brother, and brings them upon the highest part of the mountain.

17:2 And there Jesus did transfigure before them: his face did shine as the sun and his raiment was a magnificent light.

17:3 And behold, there was Moses and Elias taking with him.

17:4 Both seemed to be arguing with Jesus and James swore he heard Moses call God a fucking tyrannical asshole.

17:5 Peter, being the biggest ass-kisser of Jesus, said, "Lord, if it pleases you, let us build three altars upon the rock; one for you, one for Moses and one for Elias."

17:6 Yet when Peter spoke, a great black cloud overcame them and said, "ou shall build not three altars but one, for you shall worship only the true lord God.

17:7 Regard not these bastards, for they are not gods; but I am God and you shall worship only me."

17:8 When the disciples heard this, they fell on their face and were greatly afraid.

17:9 Jesus said to them, "Fear not and look up." And they looked up and saw Jesus standing alone.

17:10 Christ said to his disciples, "Do not fear the lord, for he can be quite cranky.

17:11 It is a blessing to be here on earth, away from his misery."

17:12 Then the clouds split apart and the voice from the heavens said, "This is not my son!"

17:13 And Jesus said, "See how he denies his son. Hearken it not, for he is cranky and just needs a nap."

17:14 When the men travelled down the mountain, Jesus said to them, "Tell no persons of what you just saw, until the resurrection of the son of God come to pass."

17:15 The disciples then asked him, saying, "Why does the scribes say that Elias must first come?"

17:16 Now, Jesus knew the scribes were wrong and that Elias the prophet, known better as Elijah, would never come.

17:17 But he must restore faith in his men and he said, "Elias shall surely come and restore faith in the house of Israel.

17:18 I tell you that Elias has already come and restored the lost faith of those of Israel; for John the Baptist was Elias."

17:19 Judas asked of the lord, "Why then, would John the Baptist deny being the prophet Elias?

17:20 Jesus slapped Judas and said, "Do not question me again, lest I hang your corpse from the cedars of Lebanon."

17:21 As soon as Jesus was seen, the multitudes swarmed him; and one man of the multitude came to Jesus and said,

17:22 "My lord, have mercy upon my son, for he is an epileptic cursed to be the dwelling place of the devil.

17:23 Come now and cast the wicked from him, so that he stops falling into the fires and into the waters."

17:24 For you see, epilepsy is caused by demonic possession, despite what medical science claims otherwise.

17:25 Jesus said, "I cannot be bothered to cure your son.

17:26 Let me send my disciples instead, so that they may cure him"

17:27 So the disciples went to cast out the demon from the epileptic son.

17:28 But they could not, no matter how hard they prayed or demanded the demon be cast out from the child.

17:29 Jesus saw his disciples failing and said, "You foolish men, have ye no faith in God?

17:30 For if you have faith even the size of the mustard seed, you can demand the mountains to move in the waters and they shall.

17:31 Go now and meditate in solitude, until you have faith strong to cast out the demons from men."

17:32 So the disciples went forth and meditated upon what Jesus has taught them of casting out devils.

17:33 Really, they practiced the sorcery that Christ has taught them, but they didn't know that.

17:34 Jesus then left, leaving the epileptic boy to his tremors.

17:35 As the disciples gathered, they saw Jesus resting on a bench in Galilee; and Jesus said to them, "The son of the lord will be betrayed to death by the hands of men," and the disciples were saddened.

17:36 They then travelled to Capernaum, where they had not enough funds to pay the toll.

17:37 Jesus said, "Go now, and cast the hook into the waters until you catch thirteen fish."

17:38 So the disciples did and gathered for Jesus thirteen fish.

17:39 Jesus then said to them, "Sell the fish at the market so that we have coin."

17:40 So they did and brought the coin to Jesus.

17:41 Jesus then said, "Good, we have now enough funds to pay the toll."

17:42 And the disciples regarded this as a miracle.

18:1 The disciples came to Jesus and said, "Tell us, who is the greatest in heaven."

18:2 Jesus gazed upon them and said, "God.

18:3 Stop wasting my time with foolish questions."

18:4 Jesus then saw a child playing, went to him and said, "Gaze upon this child and know that I shall do what needs to be done for him to enter the kingdom of heaven.

18:5 For woe to the people of the earth, who drown in their sins and their wickedness.

18:6 Look at this child, how his eye looks towards the breasts of the prostitute.

18:7 I say to you, if your eye sends you to sin, then pluck it out, for it is better to enter heaven blind than see the horrors of hell."

18:8 Jesus then tore out both eyes of the child.

18:9 He then said, "And look at the hands of the child, how they slap me in hostility.

18:10 I say to you, if your hands bring you to sin, then cut them off, for it is better to enter into heaven without hands than to grab to the brimstone of hell."

18:11 Jesus then tore off the hands of the child.

18:12 He then said, "And now look at the feet of the child, how they kick the son of God.

18:13 I say to you, if your feet lead you to sin, then cut them off, for it is better to enter heaven a cripple than walk in the fires of hell."

18:14 Jesus then cut off the feet of the child and set him free.

18:15 The parents of the child thanked Jesus, saying, "Bless you, for now our child shall surely enter through the gates of Zion."

18:16 He did not.

18:17 Jesus then told yet another parable to the multitudes and said,

18:18 "Behold, there was a king who demanded his servants pay to him all their debts.

18:19 Now a servant was brought to him, who owed him ten thousand talents, but had not the means to pay.

18:20 The king demanded that the property of the servant be sold and his family auctioned into slavery, until the debt of ten thousand talents be repaid.

18:21 But the servant fell on his feet and wept, saying, 'If you give me but a little time, I shall repay you the debt in full.'

18:22 The king laughed, and said, 'How can but a humble servant repay to me ten thousand talents?'

18:23 So he seized the property of the servant and sold his wife and children as slaves; he then sent the servant to the dungeons, until his debt be repaid.

18:24 Now another servant came to the king, who owed him but one talent; but he had not the talent.

18:25 And he said to the king, 'I beg of you, give me but a little time, so that I may repay my debt to you.'

18:26 And the king agreed and gave his servant one week to repay the talent, which he did."

18:27 Now the multitudes praised Jesus and discussed the parable of Jesus and it's hidden meaning.

18:28 The disciples asked of their lord, "What is the hidden meaning of this parable?"

18:29 And Jesus answered, "Don't borrow money if you can't pay it back."

18:30 Jesus then walked by a brothel full of male prostitutes, and entered into the brothel so that he may see the filth of the disgusting queers.

18:31 And behold, Jesus walked in the middle of an orgy; and Jesus was aroused.

18:32 He partook of the orgy and thrust his loins into many men; and when Jesus engaged in the sodomy, he declared it felt good.

18:33 But then a man raised the skirts of Jesus and thrust deeply into his bowels; Jesus did not like that at all.

18:34 So he declared to his disciples, "Of those who thrust their loins into the bowels of men, they are good and just.

18:35 But those who have the loins of men thrust into them are wicked."

19:1 And it came to pass that when Jesus finished speaking to the multitudes, he left Galilee and came to the coasts of Judaea, beyond the Jordan.

19:2 And there great multitudes followed him; and Jesus healed them.

19:3 Then came Emilia, wife of Mark, who said, "You have abandoned your family so that you may follow this wicked sorcerer.

19:4 I want a divorce."

19:5 Mark said, "Okay," and was about to give his wife a divorce, when Jesus began to speak.

19:6 And he said, "It is not good to divorce your wife, for once ye have lied with her, you did cleave as one.

19:7 She is part of you and you part of her, thus you must be together bound for eternity.

19:8 If you divorce, it is sinful and the lord will curse you forever."

19:9 All the men of the multitude and even the disciples, laughed and said, "Then it is better not to marry at all."

19:10 Jesus laughed with them and said, "Yes, it is.

19:11 It is better to know not the pleasures of women, for they are wicked beasts who will trick even the most righteous man into hell.

19:12 Look upon Adam, the first man and how that wretched cunt Eve did trick him to curse the generations of the earth.

19:13 I say to you that women are wicked and use their lust to fool you for their wicked doings.

19:14 Give not into the flesh of women; abandon your children, slay your wives and follow me.

19:15 Never again shall you be bothered by the curves of the women, for you shall take the dagger and cut off the apples of your loins.

19:16 For it is through the loins that the women take power over you; no loins and the women are powerless to you."

19:17 The men rejoiced, abandoned their children, slew their wives and followed Jesus.

19:18 But not one of them castrated themselves; not even they were that stupid.

20:1 Jesus then got up and went to Jerusalem, taking his disciples with him.

20:2 And he said to them, "Behold, we go now to Jerusalem, where I shall be betrayed to the scribes and the chief priests, who will condemn me to death.

20:3 Then shall the Gentiles mock me and crucify me."

20:4 The disciples gazed upon Jesus and said, "Umm.." Would it not be best then to avoid Jerusalem?"

20:5 And Jesus said, "And miss out on my resurrection. Absolutely not!

20:6 For when I arise from the dead, those who betrayed me and slew me will know the fear of God."

20:7 The disciples were confused, but questioned no longer the will of Jesus.

20:8 Then came the mother of Zebedees children, worshipping them and desiring a favour of the son of the lord.

20:9 She said to Jesus, "I ask of you, when my sons go into heaven, let them sit one on the right side and the other to the left of you."

20:10 Jesus gazed upon her sons and said, "If they wish to sit beside my throne, they must then earn such an honour.

20:11 Let them come with me into the private room, where I shall then deem them worthy or unworthy of such an honour."

20:12 So Jesus took the two sons of Zebedee into a private room, where he demanded the two boys perform fellatio upon him.

20:13 He promised them great rewards in the afterlife, if they only suckled upon his loins.

20:14 A custom that holy men still practice to this day.

20:15 The boys did and Jesus was pleased.

20:16 He left the chambers, with the boys following behind him, their heads hung in shame.

20:17 And Jesus said to the mother, "Your boys have earned their place in heaven, but they shall be servants in the chambers of the lord and sit beside me there."

20:18 The mother thanked Jesus for giving her sons such an honour; but the boys were fearful, for they wished not to be the concubines of Jesus Christ.

20:19 All their life they sinned, hoping to doom themselves to hell; for surely an eternity of hell is better than an eternity of being Jesus' bitch.

20:20 Despite their sins, they entered into the gates of heaven. They aren't happy about it.

20:21 Jesus and his disciples then departed from Jericho where, once again, the great multitude followed him.

20:22 And behold, two blind men sitting upon a bench called out to Jesus and said, "Is that the son of God who passes us?

20:23 I beg of you, O Jesus, to restore us our sight, so we may gaze upon the holy face of the lord."

20:24 Jesus went to both blind men, rested his hands over their eyes and behold; when Christ did remove his hands, the men could see.

20:25 And they stared into the face of Jesus and rejoiced.

20:26 When the multitudes passed by, the blind men said to each other, "Is he really the son of God?

20:27 I was expecting someone better looking, with long hair and pale skin.

20:28 But instead I saw a dark man, with short hair and shaven face."

20:29 Yes, that's right. Jesus was of dark skinned complexion.

20:30 Did you really expect him to be white. Fucking idiots. He's from Nazareth, not Switzerland.

21:1 And when they came close to Jerusalem and were come to Bethphage, unto the mount of Olives, then Jesus sent forth two disciples.

21:2 And he said unto the "Go into the village, and take of the people an ass and a colt and bring them to me.

21:3 If any man questions you, tell them that the lord has need of these beasts; and if they continue to question you, kill them.

21:4 All this shall be done so that the words spoken by the prophets come to be, saying behold; the King comes unto you, sitting upon the ass and the colt."

21:5 So the disciples did as Jesus told them to do, bringing to their lord an ass and a colt.

21:6 And Jesus rode on both the ass and the colt, for he laid across them, his head resting upon the colt and his feet the ass.

21:7 And he rode into the village, where the great multitudes gathered around him, placing their garments upon the dirt so that the beasts of Jesus don't get dirty.

21:8 Some even cut down palm branches and placed them beneath the hoofs.

21:9 And the multitudes followed him, singing his praises, shouting, "Hosanna to the son of God Blessed is Jesus, who come to show us salvation; Hosanna is the highest."

21:10 And when he did come into Jerusalem, the people of the city asked of themselves, "Who the hell is this guy?"

21:11 And the multitudes answered, "He is Jesus Christ, the son of God."

21:12 And those of Jerusalem laughed and said, "No he's not."

21:13 This angered Jesus greatly, who then went into the temple and threw out all those within.

21:14 He smashed chairs over the heads of the money-changers, trashed the tables of those who sold doves and beat the priests and the worshippers within, saying,

21:15 "This is the house of the lord, my father and you are not welcome.

21:16 This is now my fucking house. Get the hell out!"

21:17 Jesus then threw a party in the temple of Jerusalem, where he served wine, meats and healed the blind so that they may gaze upon the beauty of the harlots they were fucking.

21:18 This made the priests and the scribes angry, saying, "This is the holy house of God and he has turned it into a brothel and a tavern."

21:19 Jesus then left the city and went to Bethany, where he slept.

21:20 Now as he returned to the city in the morning, he became hungry.

21:21 And he saw a fig tree, where he went to eat of the fruits; but lo, there were no figs, for it was not the season of figs.

21:22 When those around him said, "The time of figs is gone," Jesus became angry and said, "Let no man ever eat of this tree.

21:23 For if it will bear no fruit for the son of God, then it is unworthy to bear fruit."

21:24 The tree then withered black and began to rot.

21:25 And when the disciples saw it, they said, "Why would he ruin a fig tree because it didn't bear fruit during the time it doesn't bear fruit?"

21:26 And Jesus said, "I did it so that I may show to you the power of faith.

21:27 For if you have faith even the size of the mustard seed, then you can say to the mountain, go and cast yourself into the ocean.

21:28 And if you have faith, the mountain shall drown in the waters."

21:29 Still, the disciples were confused and said, "We understand, our lord, but why then would you not speak for the tree to bear fruit, instead of condemning it to be barren?"

21:30 Jesus replied, "Because, I hate figs."

21:31 He then made some stones into bread and fish. Jesus loved bread and fish.

21:32 And when he came into the temple, the priests and the scribes were angry and said, "By what authority do you have to come and ruin this most holy place?"

21:33 And Jesus said, "It's my father's house and he said I could stay here if I so desired.

21:34 Tell me, are you the son of God?"

21:35 And the priests answered, "We are all the lord's children."

21:36 Jesus laughed and said, "Tell me, then, who was your father?"

21:37 They all answered the names of their fathers and Jesus said, "Well, my father is God, which makes me his true son.

21:38 You must be all bastard children."

21:39 The multitudes then rejoiced and said, "Yes, those keepers of the temple are all bastards."

21:40 Jesus then said to the multitudes, "Come forth and listen to another parable.

21:41 There was a certain landowner, who planted a vineyard and dug a winepress and built a tower and left in the care of his servants as he left to a far off country.

21:42 And when the time of the harvest came, he sent forth a servant to collect the wine which comes from this vineyard.

21:43 But those who worked the vineyard did not pay their master, but rather beat the servant and sent him home.

21:44 So he sent forth another servant, who demanded his master be paid; they beat him as well and sent him back with empty hands.

21:45 The master then sent forth many servants, asking of them to bring back that which was his.

21:46 The people of the vineyard beat them all, raped them and left them to die in the wilderness.

21:47 This happened many times, where the master would send forth servants, and the people of the vineyard would beat and kill them."

21:48 One of the multitudes said, "This master is surely a damn fool," and the peoples laughed.

21:49 Jesus laughed as well and said, "He certainly was a damn fool, for he sent next his son, believing that surely those who worked the vineyard would respect him.

21:50 They did not; they instead beat the son, raped him, flogged him, then threw him into the den of lions.

21:51 Now tell me, what would you do if you were the master?"

21:52 And the multitude answered, "We would have those men of the vineyard killed and send loyal servants to harvest our grapes."

21:53 Some even answered, "We wouldn't be so stupid to send our son to a bunch of murderous savages.

21:54 We would send men armed with swords and water the soil of our vineyards in the blood of those who betray us."

21:55 Jesus said, "You are all wise men, to slay those who would betray you.

21:56 Know this; the Pharisees and the chief priests have betrayed the lord, for they deny me as the son of God.

21:57 It shall come that these wicked men will be destroyed and the earth passed to the hands of those deserving of the lord."

21:58 The people rejoiced, while the Pharisees and the priests cursed the name of Jesus.

21:59 They knew he was not the son of God, but a wicked sorcerer who preyed upon the stupidity of the masses.

21:60 Though they wished to kill him and end his deceit, they feared to; for the masses believed he truly was the son of God.

22:1 Jesus said to the masses, "Gather round and listen to another parable."

22:2 Because everybody loves parables.

22:3 "There was a man who arranged a marriage for his son.

22:4 And he sent forth servants to invite his neighbours to the wedding, but no neighbour would come.

22:5 They said unto him, I have a new plot of land I must attend, my mother died and I need to prepare for her funeral;

22:6 I have just married myself and am on my honeymoon, I will be menstruating that day.

22:7 So it became that no person who was invited to the wedding came; and this made the father very upset.

22:8 For what is a wedding without guests to celebrate the union?

22:9 Thus he said unto his servants, go forth and gather the stranger so that they may attend my wedding.

22:10 Jew, Gentile, blind and crippled, let them come all and enjoy the feast I have prepared for my son's wedding.

22:11 And for those who have declined my invitation, slaughter them all.

22:12 Gather their families and let their blood spill upon the ground; burn the very city of their dwelling so that all the buildings turn to ash.

22:13 So the servants did as their master commanded; they gathered all manners of men for the wedding and destroyed those who shunned their master's invitation.

22:14 Now the men who came to the wedding were unclean beggars, who ate of the food and drank of the wine in excess.

22:15 They soiled the linens of the wedding dress and vomited upon the tables and the floor.

22:16 So the master ordered all the guests be killed, for they ruined the wedding of their son."

22:17 And the moral of the story is,

22:18 If nobody comes to your party, change the date.

22:19 For it's better to change the date of the party and have friends come, than to keep the date of your party and have it ruined by filthy strangers.

22:20 The Pharisees wished to test Jesus, to see if he truly was the son of God.

22:21 So they came to him and said, "Jesus, we know you teach the word of God in truth and care not for the words of men.

22:22 Tell us then, is it against the laws of Moses to give tribute unto Caesar?"

22:23 Jesus then took a coin out of his pocket, showed it to the multitudes and asked, "Whose face is upon this coin?"

22:24 And they answered, "That is the face of Caesar!"

22:25 Jesus then said to the Pharisees, "Then give unto Caesar that which belongs to Caesar.

22:26 But know that everything belongs to God."

22:27 And the Pharisees left in shame, for they knew Jesus to be wise.

22:28 Then came the Sadducees, who asked of Jesus, "What is the greatest commandment of all?

22:29 The one all men must follow, lest they tumble themselves into damnation?"

22:30 And Jesus answered them, "All the commandments, the statutes and the laws of old are wise and just.

22:31 You must obey them all, for none is greater than the other.

22:32 If a man says, I shall obey this commandment, for it is greater and the lesser commandments I shall not abide by, then let that man go to hell."

22:33 And the Sadducees left, for they knew Jesus spoke the truth.

22:34 One of the multitudes then asked of Jesus, "I once touched the flesh of the unholy swine, while tending to my flocks of the field.

22:35 A wild boar attacked a lamb and as I beat it off with my staff, the filthy beast ran towards me and toppled me to the ground."

22:36 Jesus immediately said, "You have touched the flesh of the unholy thing and thus you are unholy.

22:37 There is no salvation for you; you will be denied the palace of Zion."

22:38 The masses immediately rejoiced and praised the name of God.

22:39 The shepherd who asked the question hung himself on a tree and went to hell.

23:1 Jesus spoke again to the multitudes and said unto them,

23:2 "Curse be the scribes and the Pharisees, who study the laws of Moses and claim themselves wise.

23:3 None is wise but the lord of lords, who wrote these laws and statutes; it is he you shall praise and not those who study such writings.

23:4 For any man who can read is able to study the laws of Moses and any man who is righteous shall follow the laws of Moses; but it is the lord who commanded these laws.

23:5 Praise not the men who read the laws, nor fear those who enforce the laws, for they are wicked men who claim themselves holy for the lord's work.

23:6 Praise be unto God, who shall curse the Pharisees and the scribes who plagiarize the work of God and claim it as their own.

23:7 Show no respect unto the Rabbi, nor the priest, nor the prophet, nor your father; these are but men, made of flesh, blood and dust.

23:8 Your father is not of this earth, but is in heaven; he is the father of all things and you shall show respect to him.

23:9 Call none your master, for Jesus is your master; slaves, abandon those who own you and worship me, for I am your God.

23:10 All men, come and follow me, for I am your master, the son of the lord, Jesus Christ, owner of all men.

23:11 Woe be unto the scribes and the Pharisees, who pray in the temple and preach to those who would listen.

23:12 Your prayers are long and your sermons boring; for fuck sakes, you teach not the people, but bore them to damnation.

23:13 It is better to wallow in the depths of hell than to listen to the sermon of a Pharisee.

23:14 Their tongues are full of a venom worse than that of the viper; the viper kills swiftly, but the tongue of the Pharisee kills slowly, with a dull blade.

23:15 Woe unto the scribes and the Pharisees, for they are hypocrites; they guide men to the path of salvation while walking the path of damnation.

23:16 They tell unto the masses, obey the laws of Moses, while their brothels are full of the concubines of strange women.

23:17 Woe unto the scribes and the Pharisees, for they are blind men who seek to guide those that can see.

23:18 How can a blind man be a guide. Will not both guide and follower fall into the ditch?

23:19 Curse be to all the Jews, for they are the children of those who killed the holy prophets and listened to the false tongues of fools.

23:20 My father did send unto you prophets and wise men, so that you may know of your impending doom; you loathed them all and called them wicked.

23:21 Do you not know those that speak wicked speak the word of God. Have you not come to realize that those who speak sweet words speak the words of devils?

23:22 Woe unto the children of Jerusalem, for they are the descendants of those who killed first.

23:23 It was your fathers who spilled the blood of Abel unto Zecharias the son of Barachias, or was it Jehoiada. It matters not.

23:24 O Jerusalem, Jerusalem, city of the magnificent David, how you became a den of vipers and murderers.

23:25 Behold, your house shall be left desolate and your lands barren.

23:26 For I say unto you, the end of times come and there are those who shall not die until the end of days arrive."

24:1 Jesus went out and departed from the temple and his disciples followed him.

24:2 And Jesus said unto them, "Look upon the stones of the temple and know this; not one stone shall be atop another. They will all be thrown down."

24:3 As they sat upon the mount of Olives, the disciples came unto him, and asked of their lord, "When shall the end of the world come?"

24:4 And Jesus answered, "Know that many will come and claim to be me, but they are deceivers and fools.

24:5 There will be wars against nations, wars within nations and rumours of wars. Be not troubled by these wars, for they are to entertain the lord.

24:6 The lord loves killing.

24:7 Then shall there be famines, droughts, plagues and pestilence.

24:8 Then, all the really bad shit happens.

24:9 The lord will come down in all his fury, causing fear to spread to the nations; lo, Judaea will flee into the mountains, where they shall be dashed against the rock.

24:10 All women with child will be cursed to never birth their infant and nursing mothers will have their breasts explode with milk.

24:11 False prophets and false Christs will protect those who believe in them against the many horrors of God; they and those who follow them will suffer eternally in the everlasting fires of hell.

24:12 The sky will turn to blood and the sun and the moon will hide their light from you.

24:13 Men, women and children will be gathered before the lord, so that they may be the righteous slave and carve upon the mount the foundation of Zion.

24:14 Those slaves that hearken not their master will be the wicked slave and will perish in Armageddon.

24:15 The lord will cut asunder all men, so that they be separated one group to his right and one group to his left.

24:16 And both groups will know the great suffering of the lord and be forever caught in the gnashing of teeth."

24:17 The disciples were scared and asked of their master, "When shall such a time come?"

24:18 And Jesus answered, "Behold, some of you shall still live when the beginning of the end comes."

25:1 Jesus said to his disciples, "Two days after the feast of the Passover, I shall be betrayed and nailed upon the cross."

25:2 The disciples asked, "Why must this be done?" and Christ answered, "So that I may arise from the dead and start a new religion upon the nation.

25:3 The proper religion, of those who follow the lord Christ; and those that follow Christ shall be given salvation.

25:4 All the rest may go to hell."

25:5 Confused, the disciples asked, "What of the Jews. Will those of the Jews who follow not Christ be saved?"

25:6 Christ in his wisdom, said, "Damned be the Jews, for they were once the chosen by God, but now they are forsaken.

25:7 Let forever those that follow Christ be the chosen of the lord."

25:8 That night, their assembled the chief priests, the scribes, the Pharisees, the Sadducees, the elders and the high priest Caiaphas,

25:9 And they consulted together how they could prove to the people that Jesus was not the son of God, but a wicked sorcerer.

25:10 It was decided then that he must be publicly executed, so that the people then know he is not the son of God, but mere flesh and blood.

25:11 But they decided not to kill Jesus on the day of Passover, for it is a holy day of celebration.

25:12 Now when Jesus was in Bethany, he stayed at the house of Simon the leper,

25:13 Who wished for Jesus to heal him of his disease. Jesus did not.

25:14 In the house of Simon, a harlot came in and undressed before Christ; and she poured expensive oil upon her breasts and rubbed them in the face of Jesus.

25:15 As Jesus ate his meal, the disciples said of the harlot, "Who is this bitch, who dare pour ointment upon herself and play the harlot in front of the lord?

25:16 Does she know not the oil could be sold and the money given to the poor?"

25:17 Jesus then answered, "There shall always be poor people, but it shall come soon that you will no longer have me.

25:18 This woman does pour the oil over her body, so that she may please the son of God before his death comes and he leaves this earth.

25:19 If you wish to go out and give to the poor, so be it; they are beggars and parasites who must be abolished from this earth.

25:20 But this harlot chooses to instead please the son of God with her curves and for this she shall be well pleased."

25:21 Jesus then took the harlot to the chambers of Simon and lied beside her.

25:22 The seed of Jesus ruined the womb of the harlot, so that she could no longer bare child; because of this, she slit her throat with a knife and killed herself.

25:23 For she could no longer fulfill her purpose as a woman, which is to give her husband sons.

25:24 One of the twelve, named Judas Iscariot, began to question if Jesus was truly the son of God.

25:25 He came to the scribes and said, "What will ye give me, if I deliver unto you Jesus of Nazareth, so that you may crucify him?"

25:26 And they said, "We'll give you twenty pieces of silver."

25:27 Judas laughed and said, "Twenty pieces for the son of God. Surely he is worth at least one hundred and fifty pieces of gold."

25:28 The scribes and Judas bickered back and forth, until it was settled that Judas will be given sixty pieces of silver.

25:29 Thirty he shall be given immediately and the rest will be paid after the death of Christ.

25:30 Now on the first day of the Passover, the disciples came to Jesus and said, "Where should we celebrate the Passover?" and Jesus said, "We shall eat wherever I decide.

25:31 For we will go into the city and enter the house of any man and I will demand that he give us his table so that we may celebrate the Passover.

25:32 And if he denies us his table, then he will be forever cursed by my father and suffer his wrath eternally."

25:33 So they entered the city and went to the homes of nine men, all of which denied Jesus their tables.

25:34 Finally, one of the disciples said, "Why don't we just eat the Passover at my house. It is not far from here."

25:35 Thus Jesus and the twelve went to his house and broke bread there.

25:36 And Jesus got drunk. Very drunk. I mean really, really, really fucking wasted.

25:37 He said in his drunkenness, "Behold, I am sad on this day, for I know that one of you have betrayed me."

25:38 And the disciples began to weep and ask of him, "Is it me. Is it he. Who is it?"

25:39 And Jesus answered, "I dare not tell you, but sure as the lord is my father, one of you will betray me."

25:40 Still, the disciples asked of their master, until Jesus got fed up and said, "Oh for fuck sakes, it's that bastard Judas!

25:41 He betrayed me to the scribes so that they will kill me and for this I shall curse him to dwell forever in the gnashing teeth of the devil himself?"

25:42 Eleven turned on Judas, until Judas said to them, "Our lord and master is drunk and knows not what he says.

25:43 I swear unto you, I have not betrayed our lord Jesus Christ."

25:44 The disciples agreed that Jesus was drunk and in his stupor, may say things they did not understand.

25:45 After all, when Jesus was sober, he said things they did not understand.

25:46 Jesus then took a knife and chopped off his hand and passed it around the table, saying,

25:47 "Take of this flesh and eat it, for it is the flesh of my body."

25:48 The disciples refused.

25:49 Jesus then reattached his hand and poured some of his blood into a cup and said, "Drink of this blood, for it is the blood of Christ.

25:50 And never shall I drink of the vine, until the day of the coming of the lord, where we will celebrate with wine, beer and strong drink."

25:51 The disciples refused.

25:52 Jesus shrugged, drank his own blood, then drank more of the wine.

25:53 Judas saw him drink the wine and thought, "He just did that which he said he would not do and drink of the grape before the coming of the lord.

25:54 Surely this man is not the son of God."

25:55 After the meal, Jesus and his disciples went to the mount of Olives, where Jesus told them, "Know this, that soon the time will come that the shepherd and his flock will be scattered across the nation of evil.

25:56 But soon I shall rise to gather them in the lands of Galilee"

25:57 Peter then said to Jesus, "The shepherd may be scattered, but I will stand my ground, for I know that you truly are the son of God."

25:58 Jesus then looked with anger upon Peter and said, "Watch your words, you with forked tongue.

25:59 For before this night, when the cock crows thrice, you shall have denied me three times."

25:60 Peter refused that he would ever refuse knowing the lord, as did the other disciples, saying,

25:61 "We are proud to be your servants and never would we shame ourselves be saying we know not the lord Jesus."

25:62 He and his disciples then went to Gethsemane, where Jesus asked his disciples to be left alone, so that he may pray.

25:63 And Jesus prayed unto God and said, "Why must you force me to go through with this crucifixion?"

25:64 And the lord answered Jesus, "Because you are a bastard child and not my son.":

25:65 Jesus cried; and as his disciples saw him crying, they came up to him, to comfort him.

25:66 And Jesus said, "Can you not leave a man in solitude?"

25:67 Jesus then walked away and prayed a second time and said, "My father who art in heaven, why would you spare the bastard children of all earth, but cause me to be nailed to the cross?"

25:68 And the lord said, "Because the men of earth love you more than they love their own God and worship you as if it was you who gave them life.

25:69 The lord God is a jealous God and the lord God is jealous of you.

25:70 Now you must suffer the wrath of the lord and be nailed to the cross, where you will then descend into the fires of damnation."

25:71 Jesus then wept yet again; and as the disciples saw him crying, they came to console their master.

25:72 And Jesus said of them, "Can not a man be left to bathe in the tears of his own body?"

25:73 He then walked away and prayed a third time, saying, "Why must I go into the fires of hell, where the wicked go?

25:74 Why not let me go into the palace of Zion, where I may serve you better than any of your sons?"

25:75 And the lord said, "Because the lord God is a jealous God and the lord God is jealous of you.

25:76 Now you will not know the love of God, but suffer his wrath tenfold greater than that of Lucifer.

25:77 For Lucifer wished to challenge the lord God; but you, a bastard child, wish to be God.

25:78 Know this, son of a whore; the lord will send you to the deepest places of damnation, where not even the devils themselves tread.

25:79 You will be desolate even amongst the desolate; you will be damned among the damned."

25:80 Jesus then wept yet again.

25:81 The disciples decided to leave their master be, so that he may be left alone to mourn.

25:82 But Christ was not alone, for the devil himself came unto him and said, "Do you know not the wickedness you have done?

25:83 I have stayed upon the earth so that I may protect the people of all nations from the wrath of God and now ye have come and caused great strife.

25:84 For it shall come to pass that the people will need not suffer the wrath of God, but will suffer the wrath of each other.

25:85 They shall shed blood over the words you speak and slaughter those who deny you, or disagree with you, or disagree with those who follow you.

25:86 Even the men who follow the word of Jesus will suffer because of you, for others who follow you will claim them heretics and wicked.

25:87 You have brought a great wickedness upon this earth, O Jesus of Nazareth and know that not even the devil himself will protect you."

25:88 As the devil left, Judas came with the chief priest and the elders and said unto them, "Of that who I kiss, that will be Jesus of Nazareth."

25:89 Judas then came unto Jesus and kissed him, saying, "Surely you are not the son of God."

25:90 And the men grabbed Jesus, so that they may put him to trial; but before they could grab him, Peter came to one of the men, drew his sword and chopped off one of the ears of the soldiers.

25:91 Jesus, hoping to appease his enemies so that they don't kill him, said, "Keep your sword sheathed, my disciples, for I am the son of God."

25:92 Jesus then placed his hand atop the chopped ear and healed him, saying, "Now you know that I am the son of God."

25:93 But the soldier said, "You are not the son of God, but a wicked sorcerer." And they took him away to Caiaphas the high priest.

25:94 The disciples followed behind, believing that Jesus would perform a wondrous miracle and save himself from his enemies.

25:95 Now the chief priests, the elders and the council accused Jesus of being a sorcerer, saying, "He did raise the dead from the grave, surely he is a wicked sorcerer."

25:96 They then beat Jesus, accusing him of sorcery, blasphemy, and necromancy.

25:97 Then they took of his clothed and burned them in the fires, saying, "Let even the demons of his skirts suffer in the fires."

25:98 Now the disciples were outside and Peter left so that he may find lodging for them to rest.

25:99 And as he went to the inn, the damsel there said, "Are ye one of the followers of Jesus?"

25:100 And Peter said, "Yes, for Jesus is truly the son of God."

25:101 Then another woman came to him and said, "I have seen you with Jesus in the mount of Olives.

25:102 Tell me, is he truly a wicked sorcerer?

25:103 And Peter answered, "No, he is not a wicked sorcerer, but the son of God and our salvation."

25:104 Then a man came to Peter and said, "You best be careful, for your master will be declared a blasphemer and a heretic.

25:105 If people believe you follow him, then they may stone you where you stand."

25:106 And Peter said, "Then I shall gather for them the stones, for I am a follower of Jesus and proud to have known the son of God."

25:107 It was then the cock crowed three times. Peter didn't hear it, but the other disciples did and believed that Peter has denied Jesus thrice.

25:108 When Peter returned, they shunned him and said, "You have betrayed our lord and master Jesus Christ, for the cock did crow three times."

25:109 Peter said, "But I did not deny the lord Jesus. I have praised his name and declared myself proud to be his disciple."

25:110 But the others believed him not; and Peter wept, for he did not deny his master.

26:1 When the morning came, all the chief priests and the elders took counsel against Jesus, so that he may be put to death.

26:2 They bound him and led him to Pontius Pilate, the governor.

26:3 When the disciples saw their master bound, they said, "This is the fault of the traitor Judas."

26:4 So they took Judas and hung him upon the tree, where they beat him with the mace; then took of his money and threw it in the temple, saying, "Let these coins be forever cursed."

26:5 Now Jesus stood before Pilate, who asked him, "Are you truly the son of God?" and Jesus answered, "Yes."

26:6 He then said, "These men accuse you that you are not of being the son of God, but a wicked sorcerer. What have you to say of these accusations?

26:7 Jesus said nothing.

26:8 Pilate said, "If you are the son of God, can your father give to us a sign, so that we may know you are truly as you say?"

26:9 Nothing happened.

26:10 Pilate got fed up and said, "Jesus, I have heard of the wondrous things you have done. You have caused the deaf to hear, the blind to see, the crippled to walk and the lepers to be cleansed.

26:11 You have raised the dead and healed the sick; surely this is the work of a good man and I wish you not to die.

26:12 But I cannot deny that these works can be done by the hands of a sorcerer, though I see no reason why a sorcerer would do such good works.

26:13 Now, I beg of you, O Jesus, prove unto us that you are not a sorcerer, but the son of God, so that I may spare your healing hand the nail."

26:14 Nothing happened.

26:15 Pilate wept, for he believed Jesus to be a good man. Even if he was a sorcerer, he was not wicked and deserved not death.

26:16 Now it was the feast of the governor, where he could ask the public to give a pardon to one prisoner; and he thought to himself, "Surely the public would free Jesus, for the multitudes love him dearly."

26:17 But the Pharisees have spread fear throughout the public, saying, "Jesus is not the son of God, but a wicked sorcerer.

26:18 Of those he has healed, he has placed a mark upon their soul, so that they may be his slave for his wicked magic."

26:19 The public, being stupid, believed the Pharisees and said, "It would be better to free the rapist Barabbas than to let Jesus walk freely through the streets."

26:20 So when the governor asked the people, "Which prisoner would you grant a pardon?" the multitudes answered, "Give us Barabbas. We want Barabbas!"

26:21 Pilate was surprised, for Barabbas was a hated criminal.

26:22 He said to them, "Why not give pardon for Jesus, for what evil has he done?" but the multitude still said, "We want Barabbas. Give us Barabbas!"

26:23 So Pilate freed Barabbas. Within the first week of his freedom, Barabbas killed nine people, raped seventeen and set fire to two buildings.

26:24 He was quickly arrested again and sentenced to death.

26:25 The soldiers then took Jesus to the common hall, where they stripped him of his raiment's, placed a scarlet robe upon him and a crown of thorns upon his head.

26:26 They bowed down to him, mocking him, saying, "Hail the king of the Jews. Hail to the son of God."

26:27 They spat upon him and sodomized him and beat him with the whip.

26:28 Then they made bets to Jesus, saying, "Prophesy, which one of us will hit you next?"

26:29 Afterwards, they removed the scarlet robe and put Jesus back into his own raiment's.

26:30 Jesus was disappointed, for he rather liked being spat upon, whipped, beaten and sodomized.

26:31 Jesus is a really kinky bitch.

26:32 When Jesus left, they made him carry his cross to where he was to be crucified; but he was so beaten that he could not carry the cross.

26:33 So they grabbed a man from the crowd, named Simon of Cyrene, to carry the cross for him.

26:34 Simon was pissed and cursed the name of Jesus, saying, "I have come to see the blasphemer die and now I need to carry your fucking cross.

26:35 I hope you burn deep within the darkest bowels of hell."

26:36 Jesus told him to fuck off.

26:37 They carried the cross to Golgotha, where Jesus was to be crucified.

26:38 There they gave him vinegar and gall to drink, saying, "You have turned stones to bread, surely ye can turn this to water."

26:39 Jesus did and drank the mixture. The men who saw it said, "Look, he does sorcery even before our very eyes"

26:40 They then took the vinegar and gall away from him.

26:41 Then they took of his raiment and cut it into four pieces. They cast the raiment into the crowd, saying, "Let the peoples have the robes of the sorcerer."

26:42 Those who gathered the robes sold them at the market, and became rich off of the scraps of Jesus' cloth.

26:43 Then the nails pierced the wrists and the feet of Jesus and the cross was erected upon the hill; and atop the cross was a sign that said, "BEHOLD JESUS, KING OF THE JEWS."

26:44 Now it was that two thieves were beside Jesus, one on the right and one on the left; and as they were being crucified, they said, "Save yourself Jesus and save us with you.

26:45 For even if you are the sorcerer and not the son of God, then surely your knowledge of the hidden can save us all."

26:46 And Jesus tried to save himself, but the lord refused to let him perform his sorcery.

26:47 Behold, a great rock came from the sky and struck Jesus in the chest; and those who saw it said, "Surely this man was not the son of God, for even the lord himself wishes him dead."

26:48 Jesus died and his body was left on display so that the public, who once adored him, may now mock him.

26:49 Joseph of Arimathea, who was also a disciple of Jesus, came to Pilate, so that he may take the body of Jesus and bury it according to custom.

26:50 Pilate then demanded the body of Christ be delivered, for he wished not to see the mocking of Jesus, who he believed to be an innocent man.

26:51 When Joseph received the body, he wrapped it in linen cloth and laid it within a new sepulcher, which was sealed with a mighty stone.

26:52 Now the disciples said to the public, "In three days, Jesus will rise again, as he did prophesy!"

26:53 It was the soldiers who demanded the heavy stone be placed upon the tomb, for they believed the followers of Jesus would steal his body and claim he was resurrected.

26:54 Five guards were then posted at the tombstone, so that any men who wished to steal the body of Christ would be caught and the conspiracy of Christ's sorcery be exposed.

27:1 Now it came to pass that the disciples preached to the masses, saying, "Upon the third day, those who guard the sepulcher of Christ will be struck down and Jesus will rise from his grave."

27:2 And the multitudes listened to him and believed him, saying, "Surely he was the son of God."

27:3 On the tenth day, people stopped listening.

27:4 On the fifth month, the disciples were mocked.

27:5 After one year, the guards placed at the entrance of the tomb were relieved, to pursue more important duties.

27:6 It was then the disciples removed the heavy stone; and behold, they saw the rotting corpse of Jesus in the tomb.

27:7 They wept bitterly, for they knew that Jesus was not resurrected.

27:8 It was then Bartholomew said, "Let us remove the body of Christ and return the stone to its place.

27:9 We will then demand the stone be removed and when they find no body, we claim that Jesus arose from the dead."

27:10 So they took the corpse of Jesus and buried it where none would go; they buried it beneath one of the altars of God.

27:11 Then they demanded of Pilate, "Remove the stone of the sepulcher, so that we may see if the body of Christ is within."

27:12 For if his body rots within the cave, then surely he was the sorcerer; but if his body be not there, then he must have arisen and left the cave guided by the hand of God."

27:13 Pilate refused, for he believed it disrespectful for the tomb of Jesus to be disturbed.

27:14 But the soldiers wished to prove the disciples wrong: and soon the masses wished to see if the body of Christ was within the cave.

27:15 Then they will be rid of the preachings of the lunatics who were the disciples of Christ.

27:16 So they went to the cave where Jesus was and desecrated the tomb.

27:17 Behold, the body of Christ was gone: and the disciples said, "Here is your proof that Christ was the son of God."

27:18 Some of the people said, "Surely this proves that Jesus was the son of God," while others said, "Surely this proves he was such a powerful necromancer that he could even raise himself from the dead."

27:19 Still, there were others who said, "This proves only that the disciples stole the body of Jesus after the guards no longer guarded the entrance.

27:20 Why else would they wait till now, when the guards stopped watching the stone. Why not demand the tomb be searched when the guards still guarded the stone?"

27:21 But the disciples insisted they did not remove the body of Christ and said, "This proves he did arise and that he was the son of God."

27:22 This disappointed everyone, for it means these eleven men would continue preaching in the streets and the temples about the word of Jesus Christ, bastard son of Jacob, self-proclaimed son of God.

MARK

1:1 The lord gazed upon the earth and saw the virgin Mary lying naked upon her bed.

1:2 Thus the lord came down upon the earth and came inside Mary as she slept.

1:3 Nine months later, Jesus was born. I won't bore you with the details.

1:4 It's silly to care about something as irrelevant as the birth of Jesus, considering all the wondrous things he did in his life.

1:5 Now John the Baptist was baptizing men in the wilderness, so that the men of the earth may repent for their sins.

1:6 He was a wild man, who ate locusts and sucked honey from a bee's ass. He was dressed in the robes of camel hair and girded with a skin belt.

1:7 He also smelled horrible. His baptizings were the only cleansing he has had all his life.

1:8 Jesus came to John and was baptized in the river Jordan; and as he arose from the water, the skies tore apart and a mighty voice from the heavens came from above, saying,

1:9 "This is my son."

1:10 And Jesus knew that Joseph was not his father, but that he was the son of God.

1:11 And he became an arrogant bastard and ran off into the wilderness, for he knew the lord would protect him in the wilderness.

1:12 For forty days he spent in the wilderness, all the while taunting the devil, saying, "Gaze upon these rocks.

1:13 I could turn them into bread if I so desired, but I need not for the lord protects me and gives me my food.

1:14 Look upon the temple, the highest point. I could jump off the temple and the lord would protect my fall so that not even the toes of my feet be stubbed upon the ground.

1:15 Know, O wicked one, that I am the son of God and that the earth is part of my inheritance.

1:16 If you bow down to me and worship me, I will give you the earth as a gift."

1:17 Satan did not and said, "You are the son of your father and as your father did, you will betray me.

1:18 For your father promised me the earth if Job would curse his name; Job cursed his name and the earth is still in the hands of your evil father.

1:19 Thus I shall not trust you: if I were to bow down and worship you, then you would still keep the earth for yourself."

1:20 Jesus told the devil to fuck off.

1:21 When Jesus left the wilderness, John the Baptist was put in prison; so, Jesus came into Galilee and preached the word of God in the way John the Baptist preached.

1:22 He said to the people, "The beginning of the end comes, says the word of God.

1:23 Repent and know that the kingdom of heaven is denied to those who are wicked in the eyes of the lord."

1:24 Now as Jesus walked by the sea of Galilee, he saw Simon and his brother Andrew casting nets into the waters.

1:25 Jesus said to them, "Lay down your nets and follow me, so that I may make thee fishers of men."

1:26 Simon and Andrew looked at Jesus and said, "What is fishers of men. We are fishers of fish, for people buy and eat fish.

1:27 Fishing for men sounds stupid and unprofitable."

1:28 Jesus then said, "Then follow me and I will make you rich."

1:29 So Simon and Andrew followed Jesus, in hopes they would make more than the wages of a fisherman.

1:30 As they walked further, they saw James the son of Zebedee and his brother John, mending their nets with their father.

1:31 Jesus called to them, "James, John, cast down your nets and follow me, so that I may make you fishers of men."

1:32 Both James and John followed Jesus, for they wished to be rid of their father, who was a stubborn and strict fisherman.

1:33 The men then went into Capernaum: and straight away Jesus entered the temple on the sabbath and spoke to the people.

1:34 And the people were astonished by the words of Jesus, for he taught not like the scribes and the priests.

1:35 Jesus wasn't boring.

1:36 Then a man with an evil spirit of the lord came to Jesus, and said, "What do you want, O Jesus of Nazareth?

1:37 Have you come to destroy us, O holy son of God?

1:38 Jesus simply replied, "Yep," and cast out the wicked spirit of the man.

1:39 When the wicked spirit came out of the man, he bowed down to Jesus' feet and kissed them, saying, "Thank you, for you have rid me of the spirit which has tormented my soul."

1:40 And all the people of the temple were impressed with Jesus.

1:41 Immediately the fame of Jesus spread around Galilee, so that all knew his name and that he was a worker of miracles and the son of God.

1:42 Jesus abused his fame, so that the people may give him food, wine, lodging and comfort.

1:43 Now the wife of Simon had a sick mother in law and Simon asked of Jesus, "Can you come and cure my mother in law of her sickness?

1:44 Jesus said, "Of course I shall, for I am Jesus and am awesome.

1:45 I will gladly heal your mother in law of her sickness."

1:46 So Jesus went to the mother in law of Simon, laid his hand upon her head and said, "Rise up, old woman, for you are now healed!"

1:47 And the woman rose and thanked Jesus for such a miracle.

1:48 She then immediately nagged to Simon, calling him a worthless husband who could not support his wife.

1:49 Simon began to regret not asking Jesus to kill his mother in law instead.

1:50 Soon, the people began to swarm Jesus, begging him to cure their diseases, to cast out their devils and to heal their loved ones.

1:51 Jesus did so gladly, for a small fee; soon, he began to travel throughout all of Galilee, healing the sick and casting out devils for a small fee.

1:52 And as Jesus cast out the devils, he said to them, "Speak not a word of what I have done to my father, for I know it was he who placed you in the body of this person."

1:53 As he travelled, a leper came up to Jesus and said, "Cure me, O son of God, so that I may no longer be unclean."

1:54 Jesus gazed upon the leper and said, "Be gone, O disgusting pile of rotten flesh.

1:55 What can you offer me for cleansing you of your filth?"

1:56 And the leper said, "I will bow down to you, and worship you for all the rest of my days."

1:57 Jesus scoffed the leper and said, "I have many people free of the dreaded leprosy who already do that."

1:58 The leper then said, "I will spread the word of God and tell the people of the compassion and the miracle you have done for me."

1:59 Jesus laughed and said, "I already have many people who I have cured, that praise my name to the multitudes of the earth."

1:60 The leper then said, "I'll give you five shekels."

1:61 Jesus accepted the five shekels and cured the leper.

1:62 And the people rejoiced.

2:1 After many days Jesus returned to Capernaum, where he was greeted with a hero's welcome.

2:2 The multitudes swarmed around Jesus and brought to him their sick, their diseased and their crippled.

2:3 It got so crowded that Jesus could not move and he said to the masses, "Go and gather the sick to one house, so that I may heal them at once."

2:4 So they did as Jesus said and gathered the sick in the hospital; and Jesus arrived at the hospital and said, "May all your sins be forgiven."

2:5 And those who were sick arose, bowed down to Jesus and blessed him.

2:6 Now there were some scribes who saw Jesus heal the sins and they thought in their hearts, "What blasphemy is this, for only the lord God may forgive the sins of the wicked?"

2:7 Jesus heard the thoughts of the scribes, turned to them and said, "You are correct, for only those of God may forgive the peoples their sins.

2:8 How fortunate is it, then, that I am of God?"

2:9 He then left the hospital, where the multitudes followed him, saying, "Praise be to the son of God."

2:10 As they said this, one of the scribes turned to another and said, "The son of God sure does seem to be an arrogant prick."

2:11 Now as Jesus passed, he saw Levi the son of Alphaeus sitting at the tax collector booth; and Jesus said to Levi, "Take the taxes you have collected, claim them for yourself and follow me."

2:12 Levi did as Jesus said, for the taxes he did collect will make him a wealthy man among Galilee.

2:13 Jesus then went to a house of a publican, where he sat down with many publicans and sinners, eating bread and drinking wine.

2:14 When the scribes and the Pharisees saw Jesus eating with sinners and publicans, he came to him and said, "Why do you filthy yourself with such men of low stature?"

2:15 And Jesus said to them, "These men of low stature love me, adore me and praise me for my works and my teachings.

2:16 Let them come and worship me, for I am the son of God.

2:17 Tell me, would it be best if I ate at your house, you who deny me as the son of the lord?

2:18 Be gone from my sight, you scribes and Pharisees. The stench of your body ruins the sweetness of the wine."

2:19 And the scribes and the Pharisees left, leaving behind many sinners and publicans laughing at them.

2:20 It came to pass a day of fasting, where the holy men would deny themselves bread; but Jesus and his disciples still ate.

2:21 The Pharisees came to Jesus and said, "Why do you eat when it is time for the holy men to fast?"

2:22 And Jesus answered, "I eat because I'm hungry, for does not the holy man deserve to eat?

2:23 Only a fool would deny himself bread when his belly rumbles with fury."

2:24 He then continued to eat the load of bread as the Pharisees fasted.

3:1 Then Jesus entered the synagogue, where there was a man whose hand was withered away by fire.

3:2 And the scribes watched Jesus, for they wished to accuse him of healing on the sabbath; for surely healing was considered work and thus unlawful on the sabbath.

3:3 Jesus said to the crippled man, "Come forth."

3:4 The crippled man came and Jesus told him to remove his hand from beneath his robe, so that all the people may gaze upon it.

3:5 And as the man removed his hand, behold, it was healed!

3:6 The scribes came to Jesus and said, "What you have done shall bring forth the wrath of God, for you did heal on the sabbath.

3:7 You may heal on any other day, but the sabbath is a holy day, where even healing must not be done."

3:8 Jesus laughed at the scribes and said, "Bitch, please.

3:9 I'm the lord Jesus motherfucking Christ, the son of God; I do whatever I want.

3:10 Now be gone, lest I turn you into a toad or a woman."

3:11 The Pharisees feared that Jesus would turn them into women and they went to the Herodians so that they may take counsel against Jesus and kill him.

3:12 Now Jesus loved the masses that surrounded him, but he was never left alone; he never had even the briefest moments of privacy.

3:13 So he went upon a ship that sailed Galilee, so that he may be left alone to masturbate.

3:14 Because not even the most beautiful, most skillful of whores had the touch of Jesus.

3:15 When Jesus finished his time of solitude, he returned to the people and said, "Come, you masses and adore that who is Jesus.

3:16 Know that I love you all, but you cannot all follow me around all the days of my life.

3:17 Thus I shall call unto you the names of those who shall follow and they shall be known as my disciples.

3:18 They will be blessed men, who know truly the awesomeness that is me."

3:19 And Jesus called upon Simon, who he named Peter for reasons unknown.

3:20 And James the son of Zebedee and his brother John, conveniently also the son of Zebedee; and they were known as the sons of thunder.

3:21 And Andrew, Philip, Batholomew, Matthew, Thomas, James the son of Alphaeus, Thaddaeus, Judas Iscariot and Simon the Canaanite.

3:22 That's right, Jesus had a Canaanite for a disciple; his father did not approve.

3:23 And as Jesus ate bread, the multitudes swarmed around him, so that Jesus could heal them and cast out the devils within them.

3:24 Now the scribes saw Jesus cast out the devils and said, "Surely this man is Beelzebub, for only the prince of devils have dominion over devils."

3:25 Jesus laughed and said, "How stupid are you, damnable Pharisees?

3:26 If I were Beelzebub, I would cast out not the demons from these men, for then my kingdom of devils would be divided.

3:27 Devils don't cast out devils, they cast in more devils. Use logic, stupid Pharisees.

3:28 Besides, if I were Beelzebub, I'd have big leather wings, be thirty feet tall and have a forked tail."

3:29 And that is how Jesus convinced the public he was not of the devil.

3:30 As Jesus ate his bread, surrounded by the multitudes, his mother and his brothers came to see him and to speak with him.

3:31 They called through the crowd, "Jesus, Jesus," but Jesus did not hear.

3:32 One of his disciples came to his master and said, "My lord, your mother and your brothers are here and wish to speak with you."

3:33 Jesus laughed and said, "Who are my brothers and my mother, but those around me, who love and worship me more than their own sons?

3:34 For whosoever shall do the will of Jesus, let them be my brother and mother."

3:35 Mary was pissed, for did not what Jesus said break the commandment, honour thy father and thy mother?

3:36 When she asked Jesus of this, he replied, "Bitch, God is my father; I do what I want."

4:1 Christ began to gather by the sea: and their gathered around him the great multitude, so that he entered upon a ship.

4:2 The captain of the ship did not mind; he was proud to have Jesus Christ on his vessel.

4:3 And as he sat upon the ship, he spoke to the masses on the shore in parables, saying,

4:4 "Behold, my children; there was a sower who came out to sow.

4:5 And as he travelled down the road with his seeds, some fell by the wayside, so that the fowls devoured them.

4:6 Some fell upon the stone, so that when they grew up, the heat of the sun scorched them.

4:7 Some fell upon thorns, so that the fruits of their growth became choked in the thicket.

4:8 But some fell on the fertile soil, so that they grew and brought forth their sweet fruit."

4:9 And it came to pass that the twelve came to Jesus and asked of him, "My lord, why must you speak in parables?"

4:10 And Jesus answered, "I speak in parables so that only the few will know the secret to heaven.

4:11 For though I love these people who love me, I don't want them in my house.

4:12 They are filthy and would ruin my floors.

4:13 So I speak in parables so that the stupid knows not the secret to heaven, but the wise man discovers the message and know the path of salvation."

4:14 The twelve then asked of Jesus, "What of the parable of the sower and his seeds?"

4:15 Jesus laughed and said, "That is for my own amusement.

4:16 There is no hidden message in that parable; it is just a story I told to the people.

4:17 It will amuse me greatly now, when they wish to uncover the hidden message of the parable, when really the message is to stop wasting your time on stupid parables.

4:18 Silly people, they amuse me so."

5:1 Jesus and the twelve then went to the land of Gadarenes, which was across the sea.

5:2 And when Jesus came out of the ship, their he met a man who was possessed with many devils.

5:3 He was a naked and crazy man, who lived among the tombs; though he was bound with chains and put under guard, he broke off the shackles and ran back to dwell in the crypts.

5:4 Night and day he would yell like the beat, cutting himself with stones.

5:5 But when this man saw Jesus, he ran towards him, bowed down to him and worshipped him, saying,

5:6 "Holy shit, it's Jesus the son of God!

5:7 Please don't torment us, Jesus, for we are only devils who dwell within a man.

5:8 Send us not into the abyss. Not the abyss. Anywhere but the abyss."

5:9 Now Jesus was a man of such high ego that he even wanted the devils to like him; so, he asked of them, "What is your name?" and they answered, "We are Legion, for we are many."

5:10 Jesus then said, "Don't worry, I won't send you back to the abyss.

5:11 I'm not cruel like my father. I'm a friendly lord.

5:12 Tell me, would you like to be sent instead to California?"

5:13 And they said, "No, no, not California, for we know its fate.

5:14 It shall be full of hippies, gangsters and have a bad entertainer for a crown."

5:15 Jesus then said, "How then would you like to enjoy Florida?"

5:16 And the demons said, "No, no, not Florida, for we know its fate.

5:17 It shall be a land of swamps, hurricanes and people close to death.

5:18 Of those who are young and pleasing to the eye, they shall also be stupid."

5:19 Jesus said, "How about Russia?" and the demons said, "Too cold."

5:20 "How about Mexico?" and the demons said, "Too hot."

5:21 The disciples were very confused, for they never heard of these places, and thought they must be mystical places that dwelt above the firmament.

5:22 Finally, Jesus asked, "Tell me then, O Legion, where would you like to stay?"

5:23 They answered, "We would like to stay in Gadarenes, for it is our home."

5:24 Jesus then said, "Then let you stay in Gararenes," and he cast them into a herd of swine.

5:25 Jesus, like God, hated swine and does not approve of bacon.

5:26 The devils became mad when they were cast into the swine and caused them to fall over the edge of the cliff, plummeting into the sea.

5:27 This made the herder of the swine very angry: and he went back into his town, to tell the people of what Jesus had done.

5:28 They returned to Jesus and they saw the madman sitting with him and the twelve, clothed and of sane mind.

5:29 The mob said to Jesus, "Be gone, you curser of swine."

5:30 Jesus, confused, said, "Why do you want me gone, for I am Jesus Christ.

5:31 Look, I have made this man sane, so that he may dwell amongst you."

5:32 And the mob said, "That man will not feed our bellies of pork, unlike the swine you did curse to drown.

5:33 Give us the pigs and rid us of this man, or we shall slay you all."

5:34 Now, although Jesus hated bacon, he hated having people hate him even more.

5:35 So he resurrected the pigs from the sea and cast the demons back into the man; who immediately ran off naked into the tombs, cutting himself with stones.

5:36 The townspeople then praised Jesus, for their swine were now fatter and of sweeter meat.

5:37 Jesus then travelled to the other side of the sea, where the multitudes gathered around him, so that they may be healed.

5:38 And behold, one of the rulers of the synagogue, named Jairus, came to Jesus and fell upon his feet, saying,

5:39 "My lord, my daughter has died today and now her body is to be prepared for burial.

5:40 I beg of you Jesus, make my daughter live again, so that I may hold her and embrace her and love her as a father once more."

5:41 Jesus said, "Of course I'll come and make your daughter alive, for I am Jesus Christ.

5:43 I'm just that awesome."

5:44 So he travelled to the house of Jairus, where the body of his daughter was to be fit for burial.

5:45 And as he travelled, a woman crippled for twelve years saw Jesus walk by and thought, "If I just touch his garment, then I will be healed."

5:46 So she rushed over to Jesus and touched briefly his robe; and behold, she stood up proud and began to dance.

5:47 Jesus turned to her and said, "Are you the bitch who touched me?" and the woman said, "Yes and now you have healed me."

5:48 Jesus then hit her on the back, so that she be crippled again and said, "Nobody ever touches Jesus, bitch."

5:49 He then walked off, leaving the woman crippled.

5:50 As he arrived at the house of Jairus, he saw his daughter lying atop the table, where the mourners and the dancers surrounded her.

5:51 He gazed upon the woman and said, "Yep, she's definitely dead."

5:52 With that, Jairus and his family did weep.

5:53 But Jesus said, "Don't worry, she may be dead, but I'm the son of God.

5:54 Now watch just how truly awesome I am."

5:55 He then touched the breast of the daughter and she did arise and embraced Jesus.

5:56 All who witnessed this began to shout and praise the name of Jesus.

5:57 And Jesus was quite pleased with himself.

6:1 Now Jesus returned to his home town of Nazareth, where he began preaching at the synagogue to his neighbours.

6:2 He said, "Behold, I am Jesus Christ, the son of God.

6:3 If you wish to pass through the gates of my father, you must worship me."

6:4 And the people grew confused and said, "Is he really the son of God?

6:5 I thought he was the son of Joseph the carpenter and his mother is Mary.

6:6 Look, his brothers Judas, Joses, James and Simon are here with his sisters as well.

6:7 This man is not the son of God. He's an imposter."

6:8 So the people of the synagogue grabbed Jesus, and were going to cast him off the cliff, accusing him of blasphemy.

6:9 Jesus pleaded with them, "No, really I am the son of God.

6:10 I have healed the sick, raised the dead and cast out devils."

6:11 But this angered the crowd further, saying, "Blasphemer. Sorcerer. He who dwells with devils!"

6:12 Jesus, in anger, cursed the crowd to stone: and he left them and walked away.

6:13 Now Jesus returned to his disciples and said, "Behold, I am the son of God and I have the powers of my father.

6:14 Lo, I give my powers to you, so that you may travel to the corners of the earth and preach the word of Jesus Christ.

6:15 Go forth, heal the sick, cast out devils and raise the dead; and as you do so, praise the name of the holy father and praise the name of Jesus.

6:16 Take nothing with you but a staff: take not bread, nor shoes, nor a coat, nor money.

6:17 You will not need it; the people will give you that which you desire once you realize you are the disciples of Jesus Christ.

6:18 And if there be any place that curses you, or curses the name of Jesus, then tell them this.

6:19 Tell them that the end of days comes soon and that their homes shall suffer a fate worse than Sodom and Gomorrah."

6:20 And they went out, so that they may preach the word of Jesus, baptize those in the name of Christ and have the wicked repent their sins.

6:21 They cast out many devils, healed the sick, caused the lame to walk and the blind to see.

6:22 They put many doctors and physicians out of business.

6:23 Now when king Herod heard of the disciples of Jesus and their miracles, he said, "Surely this is the work of John the Baptist, raised from the dead."

6:24 There were those who said it was Elias, or a prophet, but Herod was convinced it was John the Baptist.

6:25 For Herod arrested John the Baptist, for John did say that it was unlawful for Herod to take his brother's wife.

6:26 Which it was, if Herod was Jewish.

6:27 Herodias the wife of Herod loathed John the Baptist and wished him killed; but Herod refused to so do, for he knew him to be a holy man.

6:28 It came to pass that on the birthday of Herod, the daughter of Herodias danced before Herod and pleased him and his guests.

6:29 He said to the girl, "You have pleased me with your lustful twirls and erotic twists.

6:30 For this, you may have any that you ask, up to half my kingdom."

6:31 The girl, now knowing what she wanted (yeah, I don't believe it either), came to her mother and asked, "What should I ask for?"

6:32 And Herodias said, "Ask for the head of John the Baptist."

6:33 So she did, never questioning why she would ever want some decapitated head.

6:34 Herod kept his word and beheaded John the Baptist and offered it to her on a silver platter.

6:35 She then took the head to her mother and said, "Now what should I do with it?"

6:36 And Herodias answered, "I don't care. I just wanted the bastard dead."

6:37 "What?" said the daughter. "I could have had half the kingdom under me and I wasted it for some guy's head?"

6:38 When the disciples heard that John the Baptist was dead, they came to gather his body and buried it.

6:39 They returned to Jesus, telling him of all the things they have done and the preachings they have taught.

6:40 Jesus and his disciples then walked to the desert, where a great multitude followed them.

6:41 By now, they were used to crowds following them, never leaving them alone.

6:42 Jesus began to preach in the desert; and as he preached, he became hungry.

6:43 And he said to the masses, "Your lord and master is hungry and wishes some food to fill his belly.

6:44 Come, bring me what you have, so that I may eat."

6:45 Now it was that all the people had already ate their food, save for one family who had with them five loaves and two fish.

6:46 Jesus took these five loaves and two fish and said, "Behold, I will feed all those who love me with but this simple meal"

6:47 And he began to pass around the basket of the fish and the bread, which never emptied.

6:48 No matter how many the multitudes took from the basket, there was always more for the person next to them.

6:49 They ate of the loaves and the fish, praising Jesus for the blessed food.

6:50 Jesus then sent the multitudes away and something odd happened.

6:51 They actually left him alone.

6:52 Jesus went up into the mountains to pray, where the lord God told him of his plans of crucifixion; and as Jesus prayed, the disciples took a boat out to the sea, so that they may fish.

6:53 As they fished, a sudden storm came upon them; a horrible and violent tempest that threatened to capsize them all.

6:54 They threw their goods over into the waters to lighten the boat; and as they did, behold, they saw Jesus walking upon the waters.

6:55 And they screamed, for they believed it was a ghost which came to haunt them.

6:56 But Jesus said, "Don't worry, it's just me going out for a stroll on the waters."

6:57 And the disciples begged of Jesus, "If you don't mind, as your walking along the waters, would ye be so kind as to stop this storm before it kills us all?"

6:58 Jesus said, "Why sure, no problem," and immediately the storm ceased.

6:59 He then climbed aboard the boat and went to sleep.

7:1 Now the scribes and the Pharisees hated Jesus, for they believed him to be an arrogant bastard.

7:2 Jesus would do that which the laws of Moses prohibit, yet still call himself the holy son of God.

7:3 So when they saw Jesus and his disciples picking fruits upon the sabbath, they came up to him and said, "Does not your father disapprove of such acts?

7:4 For it is written, six days shalt thou work and do all thine labour, but the sabbath day is a holy day and a day of rest."

7:5 Jesus gazed upon the Pharisees and answered, "Tell me, what does one consider work?

7:6 If you walk to the synagogue, is that not considered work?

7:7 Those who preach upon the sabbath, could it not be argued that they are working and deserving of punishment?

7:8 If one is hungry, they must eat: and when one eats, they must prepare food.

7:9 So my disciples and I are hungry and eat of the fruits of the tree. What is so wrong with that?

7:10 It's not as though we are picking up sticks, or eating bacon.

7:11 That would be a travesty and worthy of death."

7:12 Jesus then said to the scribes, "And what of the commandments you choose to ignore, you hypocrites?

7:13 Does it not say in the laws of Moses, honour thy father and thy mother: and he who curses their father or mother, let them be put to death?

7:14 Tell me then, why do your children continue to live by your blessing. I have seen them curse your name and disregard your rules.

7:15 If you wish me stoned according to the laws of Moses, then first you must follow the laws yourself and dash your children upon the rocks."

7:16 The scribes and Pharisees then left Jesus alone; none of them wished to kill their children, according to the laws of their God.

7:17 They thought it a rather harsh and unjust rule, though they never confessed it to another.

7:18 Jesus then arose and went to the lands of Tyre, which apparently were not destroyed according to the prophesy of Ezekiel.

7:19 There Jesus kept in the house of a man, wishing to be hid from the public; but the public found him, so that soon the multitude surrounded him again.

7:20 And of the multitude was a Greek woman, a Syrophenician, who had a daughter that was possessed by demons.

7:21 She pleaded to Jesus, "Please, O most holy son of God, come and cure my daughter, for she is sick and houses the devils within her."

7:22 But Jesus told her to fuck off and go away.

7:23 Still, the Greek woman pleaded with Jesus, begging of him to cure her daughter.

7:24 But Jesus refused and said, "Listen, you revolting piece of heathen filth.

7:25 I have come unto the earth to save the righteous people of God; I have come to save the Jews.

7:26 You are not a Jew, but a Greek cunt.

7:27 Now go away; I will never waste my time to save a cursed heathen."

7:28 Yet the woman would not go away, saying, "Please, Jesus, I beg of you.

7:29 I know you are the son of God and a most holy man.

7:30 Come and cure my daughter, so that we may both worship you and your father on high."

7:31 Jesus finally got fed up and said, "Tell me, why would I waste a miracle on a Greek, when it is the Jews that I come to save?

7:32 If the family at the table starves, why should the father throw scraps of flesh to the dogs?"

7:33 And the woman replied, "Because the dogs are a most loyal beast, who give their lifelong devotion for just a few scraps of flesh."

7:34 By this, Jesus was moved and said, "You are correct, for the dogs are most loyal even when you beat them with the cane.

7:35 Go home now, Greek woman. Your daughter is possessed no more."

7:36 When the Greek woman came home, she expected to see her daughter well, but she did not.

7:37 Instead, her child lay motionless upon her bed, void of all life.

7:38 The mother wept beside the body of her daughter and said, "Jesus, why have you forsaken me?

7:39 Though my daughter is free of the devils that plagued her, I still wished her to live."

7:40 Jesus grew tired of the peoples of Tyre and sailed the sea of Galilee to the lands of Decapolis.

7:41 It was there Jesus met a man who was deaf and dumb.

7:42 Jesus took the man and said, "Do not worry, for I shall heal you."

7:43 The man said nothing; he could not hear the words of Jesus, nor speak.

7:44 Jesus then said, "Do you not understand, I am the lord Jesus Christ and I shall heal you.

7:45 Can you at least give some thanks to the man who will free you of your sickness?"

7:46 But the man just stared at Jesus, saying nothing.

7:47 Jesus got fed up and said, "Fine then. Stay deaf and dumb your whole life.

7:48 But know this, O foolish man; if you had just said but a word of thanks, you would be able to speak and listen to the songs of birds."

7:49 And he left the man there, to remain forever deaf and speechless.

8:1 Jesus then came to Bethsaida, where the Pharisees came to speak to him, saying, "If you truly are the son of God, then give us a sign of the heavens.

8:2 Let the skies be torn apart, the sun turned to red and the stars fall down from their place in the firmament."

8:3 Jesus mocked them and said, "I will give no signs that you ask for; you are not worth my time.

8:4 Pharisees and scribes, such a stupid lot that have no faith.

8:5 If you want a sign, then I shall give you a sign, but not of the heavens.

8:6 Instead, your miracle will be that a man sees the heavens!"

8:7 He then went to a blind man, placed his hands atop the eyes and said, "Let it be that now you shall see the heavens."

8:8 And as the hands were lifted, the blind man could see and he said, "I can see. I can see!

8:9 Praise be to the lord Jesus, for I can see!"

8:10 Jesus then turned to the Pharisees and said, "If this miraculous act of the lord convinces you not that I am the son of God then may you and your seed be tormented in the fires of damnation unto even the hundredth generation."

8:11 Jesus then left with his disciples, leaving behind some very confused Pharisees.

8:12 They walked to the town of Caesarea Philippi: and as he walked, he asked his disciples, "Tell me, what do the men say I am"

8:13 And they answered, "There are some who say you are John the Baptist, brought back from the dead, while others believe you to be Elias or another prophet of old."

8:14 Jesus then asked, "Tell me, who do you think I am?"

8:15 And Peter answered, "We believe you to be Jesus Christ, the holy son of God."

8:16 Jesus then began to weep, and say, "Yes, I am the son of God; the son of a cruel and harsh father.

8:17 For it shall come to pass that the lord of lords will cause me to suffer a great many things, be rejected by my people and elders and be killed.

8:18 Yet three days after my death, I shall arise and return to my home in Zion."

8:19 Peter rebuked him, saying, "Surely your own father will not let you die. He has sent us here to protect you from harm."

8:20 But Jesus spoke to harshly to Peter, saying, "Keep your lips shut, lest I pluck out that forked tongue which lie within your throat."

8:21 Peter and all the disciples, remained silent. They did not understand the sudden hostility of Jesus.

8:22 Jesus then called the people and his disciples and said to them, "Of those who seek eternal salvation, let them deny their lives and follow me.

8:23 Leave your wives, your children and your parents; take up your goods and follow me.

8:24 Give your life to me and I shall hold it and care for it.

8:25 Care for your own life and know it shall end in the voids of hell.

8:26 For I am your lord Jesus Christ, blessed of the sons of God.

8:27 Praise my name and I shall praise your name in Zion; curse my name and I shall curse you to damnation.

8:28 And know this, that you are to be proud of my name and glorify it all your days; of those who are ashamed to know me or deny my words, then I shall be ashamed of you."

8:29 The people then rejoiced and gave their lives unto Jesus.

8:30 Some literally, for they fell upon their own sword after swearing themselves to Christ.

9:1 Jesus said to them, "I tell you that there are those here who will not know death until the kingdom of God comes to claim it's place on the earth."

9:2 Those people are now dead and the kingdom of God is nowhere to be seen on the world.

9:3 There are some who believe it to be Texas, while others believe it to be Disneyland, but those places came after the death of those who heard the words of Jesus.

9:4 After six days, Jesus climbed the mountains, taking with him Peter, James, and John: and there he transfigured before them.

9:5 His clothing became brighter than the flames, with skin becoming white as snow.

9:6 There then appeared two men before Jesus, who the disciples thought to be Elias and Moses.

9:7 How could they know for sure. They died thousands of years ago and nobody left behind a picture.

9:8 Peter, scared, said to his master, "My lord, let us build three altars here; one for you, one for Moses and one for Elias."

9:9 Then the very heavens split apart and a voice from above spoke, saying, "This is my son, but he is not the lord God."

9:10 Build an altar to me and sacrifice on it the first-year lamb; a male, with no blemish."

9:11 So Peter, James and John built an altar and slaughtered the lamb so that the blood spilled upon the rocks.

9:12 As the men walked down the mountains, Jesus said to them, "Describe nothing what has happened here, until the dead have risen from the earth."

9:13 The disciples discussed what he meant by the rising of the dead; did Jesus not already raise those who were dead. Does that mean they could now tell what has transpired?

9:14 Confused, they asked Jesus, "What do you mean by the rising of the dead?"

9:15 Jesus answered, "When your master is slain, he shall arise in three days, so that all shall know that I am God.

9:16 Then shall the dead rise from the earth."

9:17 The disciples then asked, "Tell us then, are you the first to rise from the dead?

9:18 For the scribes say, it shall be Elias who rise first."

9:19 Jesus laughed and said, "Do ye not know Elias. He was the one who baptized me.

9:20 It was John the Baptist who was Elias resurrected, to speak the words of the lord and baptize the sinners."

9:21 Still confused, the disciples asked, "Why then did John the Baptist deny that he was Elias, returned from the dead?"

9:22 Jesus said, "I don't know. I'll have to ask him when I see him next."

9:23 The disciples then stopped asking question. Jesus was confusing them all the more, instead of making their minds clearer.

9:24 Religion will do that.

9:25 As they left the mountain, the great multitudes surrounded the disciples left behind, with the scribes questioning them and accusing them of heresy.

9:26 And they were trying to cast out the devils from a trembling man, which foamed at the mouth and spoke in the words of beasts.

9:27 Try as they might, they could not cure the man; and the scribes said, "They are not healers blessed by the lord, but conmen."

9:28 Jesus got fed up and said, "Dammit, you of little faith; can you not yet cast out the devils with the word of God?

9:29 Bring him to me. I'll do it, again."

9:30 And it was then that Jesus cured the trembling man, who got up, bowed down on his knees and prayed to Jesus.

9:31 "Yes" said Jesus. "I cured you, you love me, surely I am the son of God.

9:32 Now go away, you bother me."

9:33 He then departed and left for Galilee, where he told his disciples, "You must go soon and do the work of Jesus.

9:34 For it shall come to pass that I will die by the hands of those I wished to save, only so that I may arise again after three days."

9:35 The disciples refused to speak of this; it depressed them deeply.

9:36 How could the son of God die. Would not his father who art in heaven save him from the hands of the murderous mob?

9:37 Jesus then travelled to Capernaum, where he spoke to the multitudes, saying,

9:38 "Behold, the road to salvation is a hard and hazardous road, full of pitfalls, traps and snares.

9:39 Do not be distracted, but travel the road laid out by the word of the lord and the voice of the prophets.

9:40 It is better to live on the earth starving, injured and crippled, than to live healthy so that your whole body burn in the great fires.

9:41 If your eyes gaze upon the wicked and tempt you, then pluck them out and throw them aside.

9:42 For it is better to go to heaven blind than to see the horrors of damnation.

9:43 If your hands come forth from your sleeve and take that which is evil, then take your blade and remove them.

9:44 For it is better to be in heaven with no hands than to grasp the brimstone which burns in hell.

9:45 And if your feet lead you to the brothels of sin, then tear them off and feed them to the dogs.

9:46 For it is better to enter into heaven carried than walk along the winding and dark paths of oblivion."

9:47 It was then that the masses cheered and praised the name of Jesus.

9:48 They left behind also a great many body parts; Jesus healed them afterwards.

9:49 Jesus is such a nice guy.

10:1 As Jesus travelled the lands, preaching the word of the lord, he was entertained by a great many women.

10:2 The women all loved and adored Jesus and wished that he would keep them as his wife.

10:3 But Jesus refused to marry and said, "A woman is nothing more than a possession of men; a possession that did pick their master.

10:4 For the first woman was made to do nothing but please Adam and administer to his every need.

10:5 Her name is Lilith and she lives to this very day.

10:6 When Adam met Lilith, he fell in lust and was snared by her lust.

10:7 She used that lust to make a fool of Adam and manipulate him to do her will.

10:8 So it became that she was the master and he the possession.

10:9 Such a way is unholy, for it is woman who belongs to man and not man who belongs to woman.

10:10 Thus my father abolished Lilith to wander the place between places, where she seduces the young and the foolish with her lust.

10:11 Eve was then created, who was made lustful to keep Adam pleased, but stupid so that she not fool Adam.

10:12 But even Eve fooled Adam and cursed him to bite of the forbidden fruit, thus damning the earth unto the last generation.

10:13 So let it be known that the son of God and the lord Jesus Christ will never have a woman as a wife; they are evil creatures unworthy for me to keep."

10:14 The men then laughed and said, "According to this, it is better to have nothing to do with women and never marry."

10:15 Jesus agreed and said, "Marriage is nothing more but a snare for women, to trap men into their bidding.

10:16 For look upon the couple not bound by marriage; gaze on how the woman wishes to please the man.

10:17 She cooks for him, cleans for him and keeps herself fit so that her body remains pleasing in his eyes.

10:18 Now look upon the married couple; an example of misery.

10:19 The husband works so that he may provide for his wife and children, while the wife stays at home, grows fat and bitches that she doesn't have nice things.

10:20 This is unholy and unjust; the woman should not have nice things, but be a nice thing owned by the man."

10:21 Then the men laughed and said, "Then we should divorce our wives and have for us a new woman."

10:22 But Jesus disagreed and said, "If you divorce your wife, then you shall never have in your bed another woman.

10:23 For your wife is yours now and forever; to divorce her is to abandon her and neither she nor he shall know the flesh of another.

10:24 It is adultery even for the divorced to lie with another; if they do, let them be put to death."

10:25 And the husbands became depressed and wept.

10:26 It was then a rich man came to Jesus, and said, "Tell me, what must I do to enter the kingdom of heaven?

10:27 Jesus answered swiftly, "Love your lord God, follow his laws, obey his commandments and worship me."

10:28 The man said, "My lord, I already do all these things.

10:29 Tell me, is there more that I may do to enter the kingdom of heaven?"

10:30 Jesus answered, "There is.

10:31 Go forth, sell all that you own and give them to me.

10:32 Then you shall have bought your way into the kingdom of heaven."

10:33 So the man left, sold all his property and returned with the money he did earn, thus giving it to Jesus.

10:34 Jesus asked of him, "Did you sell all your possessions?" and the man answered, "Yes."

10:35 "Lies!" said Jesus. "Why must you speak to me with the tongue of vipers?

10:36 For I see on you sandals and a robe, which belongs to you.

10:37 Does this then prove you kept some of your possessions and denied them to the lord Jesus Christ?"

10:38 The man began to weep: and as he wept, Jesus said, "Behold, it is easier for a camel to enter through the eye of the needle than for a rich man to enter into the kingdom of heaven.

10:39 For a rich man holds on to his wealth of the earth, even if it means his denial into Zion."

10:40 Jesus then left, condemning the rich man to hell.

10:41 The rich man sobbed and said, "I would gladly sell my robe and sandals to enter the kingdom of heaven.

10:42 I just wished not to offer the money to Jesus naked and with shame."

10:43 Jesus then walked to Jericho: and as he entered Jericho, there was by the gates Bartimaeus the blind, son of Timaeus, a beggar.

10:44 As he heard Jesus, he said, "Behold, is that Jesus of Nazareth I hear coming towards me?"

10:45 And Jesus answered, "Behold, it is I, the mighty son of God."

10:46 Bartimaeus then said, "Tell me, O son of God, if you can spare a blind man but a bit of change?"

10:47 Jesus laughed and said, "I shall give you much more and give you sight."

10:48 He then went to Bartimaeus, laid his hands upon his eyes and caused him to see.

10:49 Bartimaeus gazed upon Jesus and said, "Thank you, O Jesus of Nazareth, holy son of God, for now I can see.

10:50 I see also that your purse is full and I wonder if you can spare me but a bit of change?"

10:51 Jesus said, "No, jackass; I gave you sight and now ye owe me."

10:52 Jesus then took the change from Bartimaeus cup and left.

10:53 Bartimaeus went hungry that night; but at least he could see the food he wasn't eating, thanks to the miracles of Jesus.

11:1 Jesus then rode on a calf through the villages of Bethpage and Bethany, which was at the mount of Olives.

11:2 It was there the people praised Jesus and let down their coats, their garments and their palm branches on the ground, so that not even the calf of Jesus get dirty.

11:3 Some even laid down upon the ground and let the calf trample atop, saying, "Blessed be Jesus, blessed be the son of God."

11:4 As he rode his calf, he became hungry and went over to a fig tree, saying, "Give me your fruits, so that the lord hunger no more."

11:5 But the fig tree was barren, for it was not the season for figs.

11:6 Jesus demanded of the tree, "The lord Jesus Christ, holy son of God, demands that you give unto me your fruits."

11:7 But still the tree did not grow fruit. It's a fucking tree and doesn't care if he was Jesus.

11:8 It was then Jesus said, "Let no man ever eat of this tree."

11:9 And the multitudes that surrounded him uprooted the tree and burned it.

11:10 Jesus then travelled to Jerusalem, where he bought a loaf of bread, a rack of lamb, some olives, some grapes, and strong drink.

11:11 After Jesus ate, he went into the temple of the lord; for it was, after all, the house of his father.

11:12 And as he entered, he saw men selling doves, lambs and money exchangers.

11:13 He grew mad and threw a temple tantrum.

11:14 Jesus set loose the animals within the temple, knocked down the chairs and beat the merchants with a cord, saying, "This is the house of my father and you have turned it into a merchant's square."

11:15 As they left, Jesus gathered the coins and kept it for himself.

11:16 The scribes and the Pharisees saw this and said, "This man is a raving lunatic.

11:17 Does he not know these men sold the animals to those who wished to make sacrifice unto God?

11:18 They sold them to the poor for a low price, so that they can remain holy and follow the laws of Moses: and now he has chased them away, so that the less fortunate cannot afford sacrifice.

11:19 We must rid ourselves of this lunatic, before he makes the entire congregation of Jerusalem unholy."

12:1 Those of the multitudes asked of Jesus, "Tell us, what is heaven like?"

12:2 And Jesus answered, "Heaven is a wonderful place, where everyone is dressed in white, playing a harp and singing psalms in praise unto God."

12:3 Some then said, "We know not how to play the harp, nor are our voices pleasant to listen in song."

12:4 Jesus said, "It matters not, for all those in heaven sing songs of glory to the lord and play the harp.

12:5 We then gather to the lord God almighty, where he preaches to us.

12:6 It is like the sabbath, where we enter into the synagogue to hear the words of the priest."

12:7 Someone then asked, "Tell us Jesus, what do we do on the rest of the seven days?"

12:8 And Jesus answered, "We do nothing, for heaven is like an everlasting sabbath.

12:9 We sing, play the harp and listen to the lord preach in the holy synagogue."

12:10 Some of the multitudes began to wonder, is heaven really worth going?

12:11 A man, who was a eunuch, then asked of Jesus, "Tell me, what is sex like in heaven?

12:12 I am a eunuch in service to God and have wondered deeply what it is like to lie intimately with a woman."

12:13 Jesus laughed and said, "My son, you are confused. There is no sex in heaven.

12:14 Sex is something that happens here on the earth, but not in heaven.

12:15 In heaven, we have something that is far greater, far more satisfying, and far more pleasurable than sex."

12:16 The multitudes then became excited and asked Jesus, "What is it. What in heaven is far greater than sex?" and Christ answered "Prayer."

12:17 Men on the multitudes then began confused. How can prayer be better than sex?

12:18 A man will go his whole life in pursuit of the pleasures of fornication, but prays only because they deem it necessary.

12:19 "Prayer," said Jesus, "gives pleasure to the holy father and through his pleasure, we shall be pleased.

12:20 So let it be that all pray in heaven, sing psalms, and play the harp."

12:21 It was at that moment that a lot of people quickly lost interest in salvation.

13:1 As Christ exited the temple, one of the disciples gazed upon the architecture and said, "Look at the marvelous carvings and stonework of the glorious house of God."

13:2 Jesus mocked the disciple, saying, "You best enjoy the wonders of man now, for it shall be that these stonework's, these architectures, will be shattered.

13:3 Lo, it will be that not a stone will lie atop one another; they will all be cast down."

13:4 Jesus never bothered explaining this, leaving the disciples, once again, very confused.

13:5 At the mount of Olives Peter, James, John and Andrew came to Jesus and asked him, "So, when exactly is the end of the world coming?"

13:6 Jesus answered, "You shall know the time comes near when those who are strangers say that they are Christ, but they are not.

13:7 Know that I am Jesus, the beloved son of God: and know that there is only me, no other.

13:8 Those that say they are me are men of deception, who will fool the stupid, the ignorant and the unrighteous.

13:9 Then the waters of battle shall boil and overflow.

13:10 Nations shall rise against nation, kingdom against kingdom, man against man, brother against brother: and there shall be famines, droughts, pestilence and plagues.

13:11 Of nursing mothers and those who are with child, it shall be a terrible time; they will be forced to slaughter their own child and eat of their flesh.

13:12 False prophets and anti-christs will arise and show unto the world the horrors of Satan, disguised as miraculous wonders of God.

13:13 Then shall the sun darken and the moon turn to ash; the stars of heaven will fall and the mighty heavens will shake with violent tremors.

13:14 The heavens and the earth will pass away into everlasting nothing."

13:15 With fear, the disciples asked, "What of us, then. What of those who are righteous and worthy of salvation?"

13:16 Jesus answered, "Oh, don't worry, that doesn't concern you."

13:17 And that was that.

13:18 They never asked Jesus anything else, like if they will go to heaven, or if the righteous will be spared the passing into nothingness.

13:19 They just accepted it and on blind faith believed everything will turn out okay.

13:20 Idiots.

13:21 Andrew, however, did ask one other question; he asked Jesus, "Tell me, when will these things happen?"

13:22 Christ told him, "Know that there are those here who will still live when the end of the world comes."

13:23 Jesus was, of course, referring to himself.

14:1 So it came that the time of the Passover came and the feast of unleavened bread: and it was then that the scribes and the priests decided to kill Jesus.

14:2 But they decided not to do it on the Passover, for it is a time of celebration.

14:3 Now Jesus ate in Bethany, at the house of Simon the leper, who threw him a feast for healing him of his uncleanliness.

14:4 And as he ate his meat there, a woman came in with a box of precious ointment; and she began to pour it on Jesus.

14:5 The disciples spoke ill of her, saying, "Look at this wretched whore, how she pours such expensive ointment on our lord and master.

14:6 That box could be sold for three hundred pence, yet she wastes it on Christ's head."

14:7 It was then Jesus said, "What the fuck is the matter with you people. What have you done to please your lord and master?

14:8 Though you have known me all this time, not one of you has offered me ointment, nor wine, nor even the bread of your table.

14:9 Yet this woman comes and wishes to please me; for this, I thank her."

14:10 It was then that the lord blessed the woman with magnificent breasts: and he bared her breasts to Jesus and poured the remaining ointment over her bosom.

14:11 Now Judas Iscariot grew jealous of Jesus and how the women all wished to lie with him.

14:12 He went to the priests and betrayed Jesus, saying, "I will gladly deliver to your hands the one called Jesus, so long as you give me a reward."

14:13 The priests then gave Judas thirty pieces of silver as reward and three concubines.

14:14 Judas was pleased.

14:15 Now as the Passover came, Jesus sat in the house of one of the disciples, so that they may eat of the unleavened bread.

14:16 And he spoke to the disciples, saying, "One of you bastards betrayed me."

14:17 Now the disciples were shocked, saying, "Who is it, O lord, who has betrayed you?

14:18 Tell us, so that we may slaughter him with the blade and hang him on the tree with his intestines used for rope."

14:19 But Jesus refused to tell, saying, "The one who has betrayed me sits with me today: and let it be known that this little fucker will not know the salvation, but will suffer eternal in the jaws of Satan."

14:20 And as they ate, Jesus complained of the bread, saying, "Why must we feast on this unleavened bread?

14:21 It is so dull and flavourless; I would rather eat of my own body than of this bread."

14:22 Of the wine also he complained, saying, "This wine has no strength nor intoxication; it is as though it is just the juice from grapes.

14:23 I swear, the very blood which flows through my veins has more strength than this piss of the vine."

14:24 After the meal, the thirteen went to the mount of Olives; it was Jesus' favourite place.

14:25 And it was there Christ said, "This is truly a night of betrayal, for those who have once praised my name will now demand that I be crucified."

14:26 Peter then said, "They may deny you, but know Jesus that I will never betray you, nor be ashamed to call you brother."

14:27 Jesus hit Peter and said, "You little chicken shit cocksucker, why do you kiss my ass, then refuse to know your breath reeks of me?

14:28 Let it be known that the cock will crow three times only after you have denied me thrice."

14:29 Jesus then asked to be left alone, so that he may pray to his father in heaven.

14:30 And Jesus prayed to God, saying, "My father, why must you betray your son like this?

14:31 Have I not pleased you. Have I not caused the people to follow you once more?"

14:32 God spoke to Jesus and said, "I am quite pleased with you, my son and am happy that you have caused the multitudes to worship me once more."

14:33 "Why then do you demand that I be nailed to the cross and suffer at the hands of the wicked?" Christ asked.

14:34 And God answered, "Because you are a bastard child and I hate bastards."

14:35 Jesus then wept tears of blood, which he immediately drank.

14:36 And they did give him stronger intoxication than the wine served at the last supper.

14:37 It was during Christ's drunken stupor that Judas came to Jesus, bringing with him the elders, scribes, priests and soldiers: and he took Jesus and kissed him.

14:38 Jesus said to his betrayer, "What the hell is this. Does the queer betray me with a kiss"

14:39 The soldiers then took him.

14:40 And as they took him, one of the followers of Jesus took the sword and cut off the ear of one of the soldiers.

14:41 Jesus, hoping to please those who were about to kill him, healed the ear of the soldier.

14:42 They still took him away. Ungrateful bastards.

14:43 Jesus was taken to the high priest, who asked him a great many questions.

14:44 Jesus refused to answer, but said instead, "Fuck you and fuck all you bastards that have taken arms against the son of God.

14:45 When the earth is destroyed and the lands become desolate, let it be that you are left to rot on this godforsaken place!

14:46 Let the very dragons, the satyrs and the devils of hell come forth and rape you with a most wicked lust."

14:47 The high priest then said, "Yeah, he's fucking crazy. Crucify him."

14:48 Now the people heard of the rantings of Jesus and said, "Surely this man was not the son of God, but a crazy sorcerer.

14:49 How we were so easily fooled by his words and his healing.

14:50 Let it be then that all those who do his works are sorcerers and must be put to death."

14:51 Now, a young maid came to Peter and said, "Hey, aren't you one of the sorcerer's who travelled with Jesus and cast out demons?"

14:52 And Peter said, "Bitch, I am no sorcerer."

14:53 Another woman saw Peter and said, "Yes, I think she is right.

14:54 He is one of the sorcerer's."

14:55 Still, Peter refused and said, "What the hell is wrong with you. I am no sorcerer!"

14:56 A man then came with sword and said, "This man is a sorcerer. Let's kill him!"

14:57 Peter denied this more, saying, "You are a bunch of raving lunatics?

14:58 I swear to you I am no sorcerer!"

14:59 It was then that the cock crowed three times: and Peter remembered the words of Jesus.

14:60 He then ran to a corner and wept, believing that he betrayed Jesus.

15:1 In the morning, the chief scribes and the elders took Jesus to Pilate, saying, "This man is a menace to society and must be put to death."

15:2 Now Pilate was a reasonable man and said, "Even if this man is a bit odd, this means not that he has to be punished with death.

15:3 Bring him to me, so that I may speak to him."

15:4 And they brought Jesus to Pilate, who asked him, "Tell me, is it true that you are king of the Jews?"

15:5 Jesus answered, "Of course I'm the king of the fucking Jews, you sodomizer of vipers!

15:6 When my father who art in heaven comes down, let it be that he rapes you with the blade and sends you to the darkest places of hell, where the worms will breed in your very intestines.

15:7 I hate you. I hate you all. I will see to it that you all to go to hell, you bunch of assfucking faggots."

15:8 Pilate said to the elders, "Yeah, this guy is fucking crazy.

15:9 Kill him."

15:10 As they took Jesus to be crucified, he said, "I shall not be crucified, for I am a fucking king of the Jews."

15:11 The soldiers then asked him, "If we dressed you up as a king, will you then calm down?" and Jesus said, "Yes."

15:12 So they dressed him in the robes of a king and placed upon his head a crown made of branches.

15:13 Jesus then refused to carry his cross, saying, "Fuck you guys, I'm the king of the Jews.

15:14 Have some peasant carry my cross."

15:15 So they took from the crowd Simon the Cyrenian, who carried the cross of Jesus.

15:16 They then went forth to Golgotha, the place of the skull, which is where Christ was to be slain.

15:17 And as Jesus saw the cross, he said, "This cross is not fitting for the king of the Jews.

15:18 How will people know then that this is the cross where the almighty son of God died?"

15:19 So the soldiers put a plank on the top of the cross, which said, 'HERE LIES JESUS, KING OF THE JEWS'.

15:20 This pleased Jesus and he accepted his crucifixion.

15:21 He laid upon the cross: and as the nails were hammered through him, he started swearing.

15:22 When the cross was placed, he yelled to those who could hear, "What the hell is wrong with you fucking jackasses?

15:23 Get me the hell down from this fucking cross, or I'll see to it you all burn in the everlasting fires of hell."

15:24 Jesus continued screaming and cursing, so that even those who were being crucified next to him yelled at him to shut up.

15:25 For hours Jesus yelled, until someone finally shut him up by shooting an arrow through his throat.

15:26 And that's how Christ really died.

15:27 And at the moment Christ died, God became really fucking angry.

15:28 The skies were darkened, the sun turned to blood and the earth began to tremble.

15:29 A centurion which sat beside the cross looked up at Jesus and said, "Oh shit, I just killed the son of God."

15:30 When the angels of heaven finally reminded God that it was he who demanded the death of his son, God calmed down and stopped cursing the earth.

15:31 Now Joseph of Arimathea, an honourable counsellor, came to Pilate, so that he may take the body of Jesus, and bury it.

15:32 Pilate agreed: and Joseph took the body of Jesus, and buried it in the sepulcher.

16:1 Now the disciples remembered the words of Jesus and how he said that in three days, he shall arise again.

16:2 So the disciples preached and told all that in three days Jesu.. will be resurrected from the dead.

16:3 Nobody believed them.

16:4 It came that the guards even posted men at the entrance of the sepulcher where Jesus lay, so that none of the disciples could steal the body and claimed that he had risen.

16:5 But on the third day, Christ did rise.

16:6 He pushed away the stone which lay at the entrance and laughed at the guards who were posted at the entrance.

16:7 Jesus then travelled through the lands, saying, "Haha haha, I rose from the dead, you motherfuckers.

16:8 I really am the son of God. I was dead, but now I'm not. So, fuck you all.

16:9 To hell with salvation, to hell with the kingdom of heaven and to hell with you all."

16:10 He then raped the scribes, the Pharisees and the elders, then ascended into heaven.

16:11 And the disciples rejoiced.

16:12 All except Judas, who feared the wrath of the lord would come down upon him.

16:13 He took the thirty pieces of silver and bought a rope, which he used to hang himself.

16:14 And the remaining disciples rejoiced.

LUKE

1:1 This is the story of the birth of John the Baptist.

1:2 Because I bet you really wanted to hear this damn story.

1:3 Anyway, in the times of Herod, the priest Zechariah was married to the woman Elisabeth, a descendent of the daughters of Aaron.

1:4 They were both righteous and holy people, who obeyed the lord and followed the laws of Moses.

1:5 So, of course, God fucks with them and makes her barren, so that she can't have any kids.

1:6 As they were old in years, the angel Gabriel visited Zechariah and said, "It has been decided by the almighty lord that you shall have a child.

1:7 His name shall be John the Baptist and he'll be a man who lives in the wilderness, eating nothing but locusts and honey all his days."

1:8 Zacharias laughed and said, "My wife is ninety and seven years old; there is no way she can possibly have a child."

1:9 Gabriel said, "How dare a priest of the lord doubts the lord.

1:10 For your blasphemy, may you be forever deaf and dumb, until the day your holy child is born."

1:11 Zacharias returned home and Elisabeth told her husband that she was carrying child.

1:12 He was speechless. For nine months.

1:13 On the day of the birth of John the Baptist, Elisabeth died while in labour.

1:14 What do you expect. She was ninety-eight years old.

1:15 This made Zacharias furious, who cursed his son and cast him out into the wilderness.

.nat is the birth of John the Baptist. Now for the birth

.. / Again.

1:18 The lord could not understand why those of the earth did not worship him, nor follow him, nor obey his commandments.

1:19 He sent forth plagues, pestilence, famines, drought, wars, disease, locusts, turned the sun to blood and the moon to ash, split the skies apart and shook the ground; yet nobody seemed to like him.

1:20 So the lord decided to send down his son Jesus, so that he may spread the word of God to the people and tell them of the glories of the lord.

1:21 It was decided that the virgin Mary shall bare the son of God in her womb; her name was picked by random.

1:22 Thus the angel Gabriel went down to Mary the wife of Joseph and said, "Behold, you have been chosen by random to give birth to the son of God, whom you shall call Jesus."

1:23 And Mary said, "This is bullshit. I'm a virgin, I can't carry a child."

1:24 Gabriel then said, "Fear not, for the wonders and the glories of God have made your bowels full of the holy Christ, the son of God."

1:25 This made Mary furious; she wanted to have sex before having her vagina torn up by some child pushing through her.

1:26 When she told Joseph her husband, he was furious and said, "You are a virgin and now you are carrying child and it's not mine?

1:27 You are a liar and a harlot; I shall divorce you and have you stoned in the center of Nazareth."

1:28 It was then Gabriel came to Joseph and said, "You shall not stone her, for she is the mother of the son of God.

1:29 It is true; she is a virgin and with child, thus her honour is safe and you have no grounds of divorce.

1:30 Deny her to be your wife and the lord will curse you with a plague most fowl beneath your skirts."

1:31 So Joseph kept Mary as his wife and accepted the fact she was carrying someone else's child.

1:32 That night, they decided to have sex: and they both enjoyed it.

2:1 Now it came that Caesar Augustus sent out a decree, saying that every man must be taxed in the city of his birth.

2:2 Thus Joseph left his town of Nazareth, which is in Galilee, so that he may go to the town of his birth, Bethlehem of Judaea.

2:3 Now none of the inns could house Joseph and Mary; but one innkeeper had pity on he and Mary who was heavy with child and let them stay in his farm.

2:4 And so it was that Jesus was born in a farm, surrounded by ducks, sheep, donkeys and cows.

2:5 Mary wrapped him in swaddling clothes and placed him to sleep in a manger.

2:6 It soon came that some shepherds came to the farm, to return a lost sheep to the stables: and as they saw Jesus in the manger, they asked, "Who is this child, who sleeps in the bedding of beasts?"

2:7 And Mary answered, "This child is the son of God and your saviour, Jesus Christ."

2:8 The shepherds laughed, and said, "Do you really expect us to believe the son of God was born in a farm?

2:9 Surely the lord God would prefer his son to sleep in a place that doesn't reek of the shit of animals."

2:10 The lord then cursed these shepherds and their flocks were all eaten by wolves.

2:11 Now on the eighth day of Jesus' birth, they took him to the rabbi so that he may be circumcised; but the foreskin was already removed.

2:12 And the rabbi said, "Surely this is a sign that this is truly the son of God."

2:13 They then offered the two turtledoves as offering to the lord, as is the custom.

2:14 Now Jesus grew quickly: and the spirit of the lord was within him.

2:15 At the age of twelve, Joseph and Mary took Jesus to the temple in Jerusalem, where he spoke wisely with the rabbis, the scribes, the priests and the Pharisees.

2:16 When Mary and Joseph returned to Nazareth, they left Jesus behind: and he was alone in Jerusalem for three days.

2:17 The lord should have picked more responsible parents to care for his son.

2:18 When the two realized they left the son of God behind, they went to return him: and they found him talking to the rabbis, outside of the entrance of the temple.

2:19 They grabbed their son and said, "What is wrong with you, that you would stay behind and not come with your parents?"

2:20 And Jesus answered, "You are not my parents; Mary is merely the vessel which brought me to the earth and Joseph is a man of no importance.

2:21 I am the son of God and I am here to do his business, not yours.

2:22 If I need to speak to the rabbis, then I will do so: and you must not get in my way.

2:23 And if I need to stay out late at night, drinking wine with young women of lustful ways, then I shall do so: and you best not stop me.

2:24 And if I come home, reeking of the smoke of potent herbs, it is because I am doing the word of my father who art in heaven: and you best not stop me."

3:1 Now in the fifteenth year of the reign of Tiberius Caesar, Pontius Pilate being the governor of Judaea and Herod the tetrarch of Galilee;

3:2 The word of the God filled John the Baptist, who began to preach in the wilderness, baptizing people in the lakes and the rivers.

3:3 He would say to the Gentiles of the crowd, "You generation of vipers, do not mourn when the time of the wrath comes.

3:4 For the prophets of Judah have said, the anger of God comes soon, to smite the unrighteous and the unholy.

3:5 Repent your sins, be baptized, tear off the wickedness of your foreskin and be saved from the fires of damnation, lest you be cast into the fires of hell."

3:6 The foolish Gentiles asked John, "What shall we do to avoid the wrath and the damnation?"

3:7 And John the Baptist replied, "Repent your sins, rid yourself of wickedness and purge your body of the filth of the flesh.

3:8 Deny yourself the meat of the swine, cut the foreskin from your loins, offer the sacrifices demanded by God and obey the laws of Moses written thousands of years ago."

3:9 Not a lot of Gentiles were baptized.

3:10 Now Jesus came to John, so that he may be baptized in the river Jordan: and John gazed upon Jesus and said, "I am unfit to even wash the dust off your sandals, let alone baptize you in the name of your holy father."

3:11 But Jesus insisted that John the Baptist baptize him.

3:12 So John baptized Jesus in the waters of the river Jordan: and as Jesus arose from the waters, behold, the skies split apart and a dove landed on the shoulders of Jesus.

3:13 Then the voice of God spoke down and in a deep voice said, "Luke, I am your father."

3:14 Jesus said, "I'm not Luke, I'm Jesus."

3:15 "Ahh yes," said God. "Jesus, I am your father.

3:16 Disappoint me and I will not be pleased."

3:17 The lord then left Jesus: and the dove was delicious.

4:1 After the baptism, Jesus went crazy for his father calling him the name of someone else and went into the desert to mope.

4:2 For forty days and forty nights he stayed in the desert, where the devil spoke to him, saying, "If you are hungry, have it so that the stones turned to bread."

4:3 Christ answered, "I would love nothing more than to turn the stones to bread, the twigs to fish and the sand to wine.

4:4 But the lord who art in heaven would be furious and tell me, 'My son, why must you forsake me?

4:5 Know that you need not the bread of the earth, but can live only on the word of God.'

4:6 He would get pissed if I even eat but the crumbs of a stale loaf."

4:7 The devil then said, "What if you were to fall off a cliff, or the high point of a building?

4:8 Would your lord soften your fall, so that not even the toes of your feet be sprained?"

4:9 And Christ answered, "He would, but then he'd punish me for testing my damn faith.

4:10 God's an asshole like that."

4:11 The devil then asked, "What if I were to offer you the world and all within?

4:12 Would your father accept this, or would he be angry that you took something from the devil?"

4:13 And Jesus answered, "He honestly wouldn't care.

4:14 It matters not who owns the world and all that within; he's still going to engulf the four corners in hell-fire."

4:15 After forty days of wandering, Jesus left the desert, so that he could teach in the synagogue of his hometown of Nazareth.

4:16 And when Jesus taught, he spoke to his neighbours, saying, "Behold, I am the son of God and I have come to correct your undoing, cleanse you of your sins and show you the path of salvation."

4:17 It was then those of Nazareth became filled with wrath, murmuring, "This man is not the son of God, but the son of a damn carpenter.

4:18 What arrogance does this man have, to claim he is of the seed of the lord?

4:19 He was born in a stable, surrounded by beasts and the stench of shit."

4:20 So the people of Nazareth decided it best to throw Jesus off a cliff; surely he was an insane man and would cause strife amongst the people, claiming he was the son of God.

4:21 They placed their hands on him and carried him to the highest cliff, where they then threw him over the edge, to die on the rocks below.

4:22 But Christ did not die; the lord God sent forth angels to carry Christ to the bottom, where he landed gently so that not even the stones stubbed his toe.

4:23 God was then pissed and accused Jesus of testing his faith.

4:24 Jesus argued, saying the masses wished to kill him, but God didn't listen.

4:25 He's a stubborn bastard, the lord.

4:26 Christ then travelled to Capernaum, a city in Galilee, where he preached the word of God those who would listen.

4:27 Nobody listened; they believed him to be yet another crazy prophet spewing forth bullshit from his mouth.

4:28 So Christ said, "Behold, I will prove that I am truly the son of God, sent forth to cleanse you of your wickedness."

4:29 He then took a man possessed by demons and said, "Your wickedness, get out!" and the demons left, leaving the man normal.

4:30 It was then people took notice, saying, "This man can cast out demons and cure the sick: and he does it for free, unlike the physicians."

4:31 So the multitudes gathered around him, wishing to be healed.

4:32 They didn't care if he was another crazy prophet; they just wished to be healed.

4:33 So Jesus healed the sick, cured the lame and cast out the demons, all the while preaching to the multitudes that never listened anyway.

4:34 Simon, a disciple of Jesus, had a sick mother, who he wished Jesus to heal.

4:35 He went to the mother of Simon and said, "This woman is old and death comes near her.

4:36 Why should I cure her, for in a week life shall escape from her veins anyway?"

4:37 But the multitudes insisted, saying, "Cure her and prove to us that you are that which you say you are."

4:38 So Christ did; and she arose from her fever and praised Jesus, saying, "Surely this man is the son of God and not some raving lunatic."

4:39 She died three weeks later.

5:1 And it came to pass that once Jesus started to heal the sick, people started giving a damn about what he said.

5:2 He was by the shores of lake Gennesaret, preaching to the fisherman who were washing their nets in the waters.

5:3 He then turned to Simon and said, "Go out into the shallows and cast down your nets"

5:4 But Simon laughed and said, "Jesus, there are no fish in the shallows; it would be a waste of time."

5:5 Still, Jesus insisted: and Simon went out into the shallows and cast his nets.

5:6 He didn't expect to catch anything, he just wished to shut Jesus up.

5:7 And after a time, he brought forth his nets: and behold, nothing was in them.

5:8 Jesus then said, "Cast forth your nets again and this time have some damn faith that you'll catch something."

5:9 So Simon cast out his nets, again and immediately brought them in, thinking, "If I say I had faith, he will believe me and I won't be wasting my time."

5:10 But behold, this time the nets were full of fish; heavy with the weight of king mackerel.

5:11 When Simon brought in his nets, the weight of the fish was so heavy that the net broke and went forever into the waters.

5:12 Simon looked at Jesus and said, "Thanks a lot, you jackass, now I lost a net.

5:13 Do you know how expensive those things are?"

5:14 And Jesus answered, "Fear not, for I shall get you another net."

5:15 He then called out to James the son of Zebedee and his brother John, saying "Come and follow me.

5:16 Leave your life as fishermen behind."

5:17 James and John were stupid men, who wished to rid themselves of their work as fishermen.

5:18 They hated the smell, saying, "The stench of our bodies reeks of that of the cheap brothel."

5:19 So they followed Jesus and abandoned their boats.

5:20 Jesus then took one of the nets of James and gave it to Simon, saying, "Now stop your whining, you infant child."

5:21 As the men went forth, a leper came up to Jesus and said, "I was born a good and righteous man and sinned not in the eyes of the lord.

5:22 Yet I have become a leper, for the father of my father's father's father sinned and spared the life of a heathen.

5:23 Please, O lord, save me from the wickedness of my fathers, so that I suffer no more for the mistakes of my ancestors."

5:24 And Jesus said, "It is unfair that the children suffer for the sins of their fathers, while the fathers suffer not.

5:25 Let the sinner be condemned and let the child be pure."

5:26 He then healed the leper, who rejoiced and said, "Thank you, O Jesus, for surely you are the son of God."

5:27 The leper then left and spread the word of Jesus to all those who could hear.

5:28 God was furious, for he hated the leper.

5:29 He said to Jesus, "Why would you cure the cursed leper, who is unclean in the eyes of the lord?"

5:30 And Jesus replied, "Because he was a righteous man, who sinned not in the eyes of God.

5:31 Let not the child suffer for others, but let the suffering fall upon the wicked."

5:32 God, of course, disagreed; he couldn't see the reasoning behind why the descendants of a wicked man should not suffer so horribly.

5:33 God's stubborn like that.

5:34 Now Jesus was well loved by the people of the earth; he was well loved more than God himself, which made the lord jealous.

5:35 It came to pass that Jesus was preaching to the multitudes, when men whose brother was cursed with palsy wished to bring him forth, so that Christ may cure him.

5:36 But they could not gather near Jesus; the crowd was too thick.

5:37 Jesus saw these men and said, "Fear not, for the sins of your brother are forgiven."

5:38 And the crippled man stood up and praised the name of Jesus.

5:39 Now the lord God who sits in Zion gazed down and thought, "What right does my son have, to cure the sins of others?

5:40 That is not the right of Jesus, but the right of God."

5:41 So the spirit of the lord entered into the tongues of Pharisees, who questioned Jesus, saying, "Who is this man, who believes himself as a god?"

5:42 Jesus heard the Pharisees and said, "I am the lord God, brought down to do the holiest of work.

5:43 I can forgive the sins of whomever I damn well please, for I am a part of God."

5:44 When the Pharisees asked then to have their sins forgiven, Jesus said, "Fuck you.

5:45 You accused me of blasphemy for forgiving the sins of others, so you can all go to hell."

5:46 He then left the Pharisees behind, who believed Jesus to be an arrogant prick.

5:47 He must get that trait from his father.

5:48 As Jesus walked, he passed by a tax collector name Levi: and he said to Levi, "Abandon your works and follow me."

5:49 Levi hated being a tax collector; he quickly told his boss to fuck a goat, abandoned his post and followed Jesus.

5:50 Levi then invited Jesus to his house, so that they may eat: and Jesus ate in the house of Levi, where dwelt many sinners and tax collectors.

5:51 The Pharisees saw Jesus eating with sinners and tax collectors and said, "Surely the son of God would not waste his time with such lowly people."

5:52 God agreed and thought, "Why is my son wasting his time with the wretched and the unclean?"

5:53 But Jesus said to the Pharisees, "Gaze upon these men and see them not as unclean, but as sick.

5:54 Do they not need a physician. Do they not need a man to guide and heal them?

5:55 Why then would the son of God go to the righteous, who need not his works. It is a waste of time to try to save those who are already saved.

5:56 Let then the sinners and the wicked know the son of God, so that they may cleanse themselves and know salvation."

5:57 At first, the Pharisees agreed with Jesus and praised him for his noble deeds.

5:58 God, however, did not, and began to wish he didn't send Jesus to the earth.

5:59 God did not want heaven filled with people; he wanted all the people of the earth to burn in damnation.

5:60 Now his son is telling them how to be righteous; would not then those who God burned question him and call him wrathful?

5:61 Before, the lord could claim them wicked for some minor sin: and the peoples would accept their fate in the eternal darkness.

5:62 But now, they shall claim that Jesus saved them; they shall revolt in hell and march towards Zion in great numbers.

5:63 God didn't want that: and he began to curse Jesus.

6:1 It came to pass that, on the sabbath, Jesus and his disciples became hungry, with their bellies grumbling in anger.

6:2 They came to a corn field, plucking the ears from the stalks and boiling them in the water.

6:3 It was then some Pharisees walked by and said, "What matter of blasphemy is this, that you would work on the sabbath?"

6:4 Christ answered, "This is not blasphemy, but the nature of things.

6:5 Gaze upon the sheep of the flock. Do they not eat on the sabbath?

6:6 Or the birds of the air; how they feast on the berries on the holy days.

6:7 Even the mighty lion slays the prey so that her cubs shall eat.

6:8 How is it then that the lord shall forgive the stupid beasts, but not the hearts of men for doing that which is natural on the sabbath?"

6:9 The Pharisees pondered this and agreed with Jesus.

6:10 It is only natural for a hungry man to eat on any day, even the sabbath day; surely the lord will forgive them this.

6:11 They were wrong.

6:12 The lord God was furious that his son Jesus plucked ear on the sabbath, gathered sticks and created a fire on the sabbath.

6:13 He began to curse Jesus even more for his rebellious attitude towards the holy laws.

6:14 On another sabbath, Jesus preached in the synagogue: and it happened that the scribes and the Pharisees listened to him.

6:15 They were fascinated by the teachings of Jesus and his liberal views.

6:16 It was then Jesus noticed a man in the crowd, whose right hand was cursed by the flesh-eating devils.

6:17 As the scribes and Pharisees gazed upon the man, they began to murmur, saying, "Is it lawful for Jesus to heal on the sabbath. Or would it be considered a sin?"

6:18 Jesus heard the murmurs of these men and said, "Why would it be a sin to do the holy work on the sabbath?

6:19 It is better to heal a man and restore life on the sabbath, than to bring forth death during the rest of the days."

6:20 He then blessed the man and healed his hand.

6:21 The scribes and Pharisees, as well as all the masses, began to praise Jesus and sing glories to his name.

6:22 God was furious; he cursed the man with the flesh-eating spirits and now his son has lifted the curse and made the hated man whole.

6:23 God then began to curse Jesus more: and the fires of his wrath were kindled.

6:24 It was then Jesus went to the mountains, where the multitudes followed him.

6:25 Jesus said to the people, "I know you all love and worship me, but you must not follow me all my days.

6:26 Go home to your wives, your children and care for them; if you wish to follow me, then you must carry my burden.

6:27 Those who are chosen by me shall teach the word of God and do the work of Jesus all their days."

6:28 It was then the masses said, "Tell us, Jesus, who shall be so blessed?"

6:29 And Jesus picked the twelve apostles.

6:30 Simon, who he called Peter for reasons unknown and his brother Andrew.

6:31 James, John, Philip and Bartholomew.

6:32 Matthew, Thomas, James the son of Alphaeus and Simon called Zelotes.

6:33 Judas the brother of James and Judas Iscariot, the traitorous cunt.

6:34 Jesus went down the mountain, with his apostles following him: and Christ healed the sick and cast out the evil spirits which plagued them.

6:35 It was then Jesus began to preach to the multitudes: and it was because of these teachings that the wrath of God became hot and the lord decided to kill Jesus.

6:36 Jesus said, "Gone are the ways of old; a new world will come soon, and so must a new people.

6:37 Let burn the laws of old, which give order to anger, hatred and wrath; let the world now be full of love and kindness to your brethren.

6:38 When you see a heathen bastard, curse him not but embrace him; he is your brother and descended also from the seed of Adam.

6:39 Fight not your enemies with the blade, but with open arms; embrace him and call him your brother.

6:40 Believe me, it shall confuse them and they will lose the will to fight.

6:41 Who can fight those who love them. Who can sink a blade into the heart of those who embrace them as their kin?

6:42 Of those that curse you, bless them; give them your kindness, your sympathy and your love.

6:43 Remember, if you wish men to treat you with kindness, then you must treat them with kindness.

6:44 The reason men are so hated is because they hate those that hate them; love them and they shall love you in return.

6:45 Be merciful, such as the son of God is merciful.

6:46 If a man strikes your cheek, sheath your sword and offer them the other cheek.

6:47 Judge not the sins of others; only the lord who art in heaven has the power to judge the sins of men.

6:48 The master is not below his slave; you are all made of blood and flesh.

6:49 Be not eager to point out the flaws of others; know that you are flawed as well.

6:50 Why is it that a man shall point to his brother and say to those that listen, 'look, he has a tear in his robe,' when he that speaks is nude?

6:51 Let the nude man know his shame and not belittle others so that his shame seem lessened."

6:52 And as Jesus spoke, the fires of the lord became hot; hotter than even the most cursed places of hell.

6:53 God then sent forth evil spirits to the earth, so that they may enter the scribes and the Pharisees, thus bringing forth the destruction of his son.

7:1 Jesus went to the city of Capernaum, where a centurion came to him, saying, "Lo, my servant is dying.

7:2 Come forth and heal him, so that he may serve me once more."

7:3 Now Judas Iscariot knew the centurion and knew of the servant who was sick.

7:4 He said to Jesus, "My lord, this man is a filthy man, whose loins thrust deeply into the bowels of men.

7:5 His servant is not a slave, but an object for his unholy lust."

7:6 Christ then slapped Judas and said, "And why does it matter if he is queer. Does this deserve his death?

7:7 Know this, Judas, that there are those born of the bodies of men and woman, but the spirit is the other.

7:8 For this man to lie with a woman would be just as revolting for you to lie with a man; it is his natural being and thus he must not be punished for it."

7:9 As you know, this pissed God off very much.

7:10 God hates queers.

7:11 Jesus then went to the house of the centurion, where he healed the servant of his plague.

7:12 The centurion praised the name of Jesus and said, "Lo, I shall teach your laws and your words to all those who will listen."

7:13 Thus the centurion became the first gay priest; he was not the last.

7:14 On the day after, Jesus went to the city of Nain, where by the gates a dead man was carried out, so he could be buried.

7:15 This man was the only son of his mother, a widow who grieved deeply for her loss.

7:16 Now the lord who art in heaven laughed at the widow and mocked the tears which flowed down her cheek; but Jesus took pity on her and embraced her.

7:17 With a voice of compassion, he said to the mother, "Weep not, for I shall give your son once more."

7:18 He then said to the body of her son, "Arise and embrace your mother," and the body did rise from the dead and embraced his mother with tears in his eyes.

7:19 The mother said to Jesus, "I cannot repay you for this and am forever in your debt.

7:20 Please, allow me to give you all my riches, for I am a wealthy widow and am grateful for this gift you gave me."

7:21 Jesus said to her, "If you wish to repay me this debt, then love your son and spread the name of Jesus."

7:22 The woman then rejoiced and worshipped Jesus; God, however, was confused.

7:23 "What foolishness is this," he said, "That my son would deny himself the wealth?

7:24 He is truly a stupid child and I wish to have him slain."

7:25 Now the words of Jesus raising the son from the dead spread to all those of the earth, even to the ears of John the Baptist.

7:26 John sent two of his disciples to speak to Jesus, asking him, "Is it true that you are the son of God, or should we wait for another?"

7:27 Jesus did not answer them, but instead continued to heal the sick, cure the lame and cast out the devils from those possessed.

7:28 The disciples returned to John and told him all that which they saw.

7:29 John was amazed and believed this truly was the son of God, sent to bring forth the foundation of Zion upon the earth.

7:30 He was then quickly beheaded and his head offered on a silver platter to some whore.

7:31 The Pharisees invited Jesus to their house, so that they may eat with them: and Jesus ate meat at their house.

7:32 As he ate, a harlot came in to where Jesus was and began to weep.

7:33 She kissed the feet of Jesus and washed away her tears with her hair.

7:34 The Pharisees were disgusted and said, "Get this diseased ridden prostitute out of my house."

7:35 But Jesus said to them, "I've a story for you.

7:36 There was once a creditor, who had two debtors; one owed fifty pence, the other five hundred.

7:37 Upon the day of collection, neither could pay back what they owed.

7:38 Instead of taking his wrath upon them, he forgave them both and erased their debts.

7:39 Tell me then, who will be more grateful. The man who owed fifty, or the man who owed five hundred?"

7:40 The Pharisees answered, "The man who owed five hundred, obviously would be most grateful.

7:41 He would do nothing but kindness to his creditor, to show his thanks."

7:42 And Jesus said, "Know then, that is why the sinners love me so, for I forgive them all their sins.

7:43 Why should the righteous be grateful to me. Have they not already earned their place in Zion?

7:44 When I entered your house, you did not even offer me a kiss; but this sinner has not ceased to stop kissing my feet.

7:45 Before I sat at your table, you did not even offer a bowl of water so that I may cleanse my feet; but this woman has not stopped washing my feet with her tears and her hair.

7:46 She does this because she is most grateful to me; her many sins are forgiven and she wishes to show me her gratitude all her days."

7:47 Jesus then left the house of the Pharisees with the harlot, where she continued to show her gratitude to Jesus beneath her sheets.

8:1 Jesus travelled the lands, preaching at the synagogues, healing the sick casting out devils and forgiving the sins of men.

8:2 He even forgave the sins of Mary Magdalene, whose loins were cursed with the plagues of her whoredoms.

8:3 And as he spoke in the synagogues, he preached in parables.

8:4 The disciples came to him and asked, "Why is it that you speak in parables unto the multitudes?" and Christ answered, "Because parables are entertaining.

8:5 To preach otherwise would be boring and bring the multitudes to sleep."

8:6 As he preached in the synagogue, his mother and brothers came and wished to speak with him; but the multitudes crowded Jesus, so that they could not see him.

8:7 An apostle came to Jesus and said, "My lord, your mother and your brothers are here and wish to speak with you."

8:8 And Jesus said, "Who are my brothers, but all these men who surround me?

8:9 Let it be known that all those who worship me and do my deeds shall be my brother.

8:10 And who is my mother, but these women who come for my blessing?

8:11 These harlots who come for forgiveness, let them be my mothers."

8:12 When Mary heard this, she left and cursed the name of Jesus; how dare her son compare her to whores.

8:13 Now it came that Jesus and his apostles were on a boat, so that they could travel across the shores to the land of Gadarenes.

8:14 Behold, a violent tempest was sent forth by God, so that he may capsize the boat and drown his rebellious son.

8:15 The apostles sailed the boat as best they could and cast forth all they could to make the boat lighter in the storm.

8:16 As they did this, Jesus slept.

8:17 One of the apostles woke Jesus and said, "My master, my master, ready yourself for soon we shall be in the waters," but Jesus remained calm.

8:18 Jesus stood on the bow of the ship and cursed the very storms: and immediately the storm ceased and the waters became calm.

8:19 Jesus then said harshly to his apostles, "What matter is this, that you would lose your faith so quickly?" and the disciples were afraid, saying, "This man can even order the very forces of nature."

8:20 As Jesus landed on the shores of the Gadarenes, them came forth a man who was filled with the evil spirits sent forth by God.

8:21 He wore no clothes and was scarred in the cuts of stones and shards of bone.

8:22 The spirits in the man spoke and said to Jesus, "Know that you have angered the lord who art in heaven and that your damnation soon comes.

8:23 Your teachings are unholy and now the people love you more than the lord who art in heaven.

8:24 The lord God is a jealous God and the lord God is jealous of his own son."

8:25 Before the spirits could finish, Jesus cast out the spirits from the man and sent them into a herd of swine.

8:26 This infuriated the lord, who hates the filthiness of pigs.

8:27 Which makes one wonder, why did he then create them?

8:28 The swine became confused with the evil spirits within them and ran off the cliffs of the shores and into the waters below.

8:29 God then sent forth evil spirits into the men of the village, who came forth to slaughter Jesus and the twelve apostles.

8:30 Before the madmen could slay Jesus, Christ and his apostles escaped on the boat.

8:31 Judas then asked him, "Tell me lord, what did they mean by you have angered God and made him jealous?"

8:32 Jesus lied and said, "Those were the words of the devil, who will whisper lies and deceit in the ears of all who will listen.

8:33 Hearken them not, lest you fall in their snare."

8:34 When Jesus returned to the lands, the people accepted him gladly and with open arms.

8:35 Jairus, a priest of the synagogue, came to Jesus and said, "My lord, forgive this humble servant for bothering you.

8:36 My only daughter lies dead in my home now and shall be buried in the dust.

8:37 Come forth, so that I may speak with her once more and embrace her as a father embraces his daughter."

8:38 Jesus was then led by Jairus to his house, so that he may resurrect the daughter of this humble servant of the lord.

8:39 As he was led to the house of Jairus, a woman who was stricken with disease of the bone saw Jesus and believed that if she could just touch his robe, then she would be healed of her disease.

8:40 She came close to Jesus and lightly touched his robe: and behold, she was healed.

8:41 Jesus stopped and asked, "Who was it that just touched me?"

8:42 The apostle Peter told Jesus, "My master, the multitudes surround us and crowd us; it could be any number of men that have touched you."

8:43 Now the woman knew that Christ meant her: and she came to Jesus and said, "I am sorry my lord, for it was I who touched your robe.

8:44 I believed if I were to just touch the very cloth of your raiment, then I would be cured of the disease which has stricken me for twelve long years."

8:45 Christ laughed and said, "Woman, if you wished to be cured, all you had to do was ask.

8:46 Be gone now and tell those who will listen of the miracles of Jesus."

8:47 As the son of God entered the house of Jairus, there were many there who wailed and mourned for the death of his daughter.

8:48 Jesus said, "Mourn not, for your daughter rests in the embrace of death and now I shall awaken her from this slumber."

8:49 The mother laughed and said, "She is dead and now in eternal slumber.

8:50 Only the wicked sorcerer and the necromancer may raise her from the dead."

8:51 "Wicked bitch," said Jesus. "Never doubt the powers of the lord."

8:52 He then spoke to the dead daughter, who arose and killed her mother.

8:53 And Christ said, "Let those who doubt me die and let those who love me live eternal."

9:1 Then he called the twelve together and gave them the power to cast out wicked spirits, cure diseases and gave them authority over the devils.

9:2 He then sent them out to preach the word of Jesus.

9:3 And he said unto them, "Bring not staves, nor coins, nor bread nor sandals, but let the kindness of the people feed and clothe you.

9:4 Of those who accept you, bless them and teach to them the word of Jesus.

9:5 And of those who rebuke you and are hostile towards you, then leave their place and shake off the very last bit of dust from their dwelling.

9:6 Tell them that if they refuse the word of God, then their homes will be cast into the fires of hell; lo, Sodom and Gomorrah will be more hospitable than their house."

9:7 The twelve then left, preaching the word of Jesus and healing the sick, the lame and the diseased.

9:8 Those who saw the twelve were disappointed; they wanted to be cured by Jesus and not his servants.

9:9 It came to pass that the apostles returned to Jesus and told them all that which they have seen and heard.

9:10 The people then saw Jesus and began to swarm around him in the desert place of Bethsaida.

9:11 Jesus began to preach to them, until the sun set and the people became hungry.

9:12 The apostles said, "My lord, the day is late and the people hunger.

9:13 Let them leave, so that they may eat at their table."

9:14 But Jesus said, "If they are hungry, then let the powers of Jesus feed them."

9:15 He then spoke to the skies to rain: and it began to rain bread and fish upon the multitudes.

9:16 People gathered the bread and the fish and ate of their fill; it was gathered afterwards twelve baskets of food.

9:17 As the multitudes left, Jesus asked of his disciples, "Tell me, what do these men say of me?"

9:18 And they answered, "There are those who say you are Elias and others that you are of the prophets of old."

9:19 Jesus then asked them, "And what of you. What do you say of me?"

9:20 And they answered, "We say you are Jesus Christ, the holy son of God."

9:21 Jesus then said to them, "Behold, the suffering of men will be harsh when the end of days come.

9:22 The earth will shake; the skies turn to blood and the devils will bring forth the dead from the ground.

9:23 But let it be that those who believe in me will be protected by me and forever know the love and mercy of Jesus.

9:24 And I tell you the truth, that some standing here will not taste death when the kingdom of Zion descends to the earth in all its horror."

9:25 After eight days when Jesus said these things, he took Peter, John and James into the mountains to pray.

9:26 And as he prayed, his skin glowed white and his very raiment's became as bright as the sun.

9:27 And behold, there talked with him two men, who the apostles believed to be Moses and Elias.

9:28 As these two departed, Peter came to his master and said, "My lord, let us build three altars upon this place; one for you, one for Moses and one for Elias."

9:29 Jesus rebuked Peter and said, "If you wish to build an altar, then build an altar in glory to me and only me.

9:30 Elias and Moses are unworthy of your praise; they are dead prophets and nothing more."

9:31 As Jesus came down from the mountain, he saw the remaining apostles attempting to cast out the devils from a man who suffered with tremors.

9:32 Try as they might, they could not: and the man continued to shake and froth at the mouth.

9:33 Jesus, who was in a bad mood, cursed his disciples and said, "What matter is this, that you can't cure even a simple epileptic?"

9:34 He then cured the man and turned to his apostles, saying, "Was that so fucking hard?"

9:35 And the twelve wondered why Jesus was so angry.

9:36 He was angry because the two men he spoke to were angels that betrayed the lord and told Jesus how God planned to kill him.

9:37 This angered Jesus, who began to curse his father such as his father cursed him.

9:38 Jesus decided to still preach his word, believing to start a new religion amongst the people, who will follow him as the lord instead of his father.

9:39 He travelled throughout the lands, preaching his ideals to the multitudes and curing the sick, the lame and the weak.

9:40 It came to pass that Jesus came to a town of Samaritans, who cursed him and chased him away with blades.

9:41 His disciples James and John said to Jesus, "Send forth the fire from the heavens, to consume those harshly who deny your name."

9:42 But Jesus said, "To do such a thing is cruel and unjust; let them live and in time they shall know my name.

9:43 To send forth fires from the heavens is not how to lead people, but to scare them: and let the religion of fear be cast away into hell, where it belongs."

10:1 Jesus then gathered seventy more men and made them disciples.

10:2 He gave them authority over the wicked spirit, to cast out devils, to heal the sick and to cure the lame.

10:3 And he said unto the seventy, "Go out, two by two and preach the word of the holy son of God.

10:4 Know that you are lambs and I send you into the den of wolves; but so long as you have faith, then shall you be safe.

10:5 Bring not coins, nor shoes; let the mercy of the people care for you.

10:6 Enter into their house and preach the holy word.

10:7 They shall offer you wine; drink it. They shall offer you food; eat it and give thanks to them.

10:8 It matters not what they set before you, you shall consume it; they are a grateful people, who will offer you that they can.

10:9 If even the dreaded meat of swine is placed before you, eat it; why is it a man should suffer for what goes into him?

10:10 It matters not what goes within the man, but what comes out of him; if he does good, then let him eat the unclean flesh.

10:11 Teach in the places of Jews and preach in the places of the Gentiles; for it is the Gentiles who must be saved alongside Jew.

10:12 Now go and spread forth the word of Christ; return to me when you are done and tell me of your deeds."

10:13 And it came to pass that the seventy returned and told Jesus of what they saw.

10:14 There were some that say they were welcomed with open arms, others who say they were almost killed by the hostile Gentiles.

10:15 Others said the devils tormented them and even claimed they saw the wickedness of Satan in streaks of lightning.

10:16 Jesus blessed the seventy and gave them his thanks.

10:17 One of them came to Jesus and said, "Tell me, what must I do to gain eternal life?

10:18 The laws of Moses seem harsh and confusing and I understand them not."

10:19 Jesus said simply to the man, "To gain eternal life, all you must do is be kind, love your neighbour and worship Jesus Christ as your lord and saviour."

10:20 The man then asked, "Tell me, who is my neighbour. For beside me resides a wicked heathen of Canaan; surely, I must hate him, as stated in the laws of Moses."

10:21 Jesus then told the man, "A neighbour is all men, whether they are kind, harsh, heathen or righteous.

10:22 I ask of you, what makes one a good neighbour?

10:23 If a Jew is your neighbour, and he steals from you, is he a good neighbour?"

10:24 And the peoples answered, "No."

10:25 "Now if a heathen is your neighbour and he cares for you when you are sick and tends your flocks when you are injured, is he a good neighbour?"

10:26 And the peoples answered, "No, for he is wicked in the eyes of God."

10:27 Jesus became irritated and said, "Forget those who are wicked in the eyes of God, but see them as though they are one of your own.

10:28 Let me tell you this; a man walked from Jericho to Jerusalem, where he is attacked by bandits.

10:29 They strip him naked, take his belongings and leave them to die beside the road.

10:30 Now his brother walked by him and saw him beaten beside the road; but he left him to die, thinking it was not his concern.

10:31 A priest then walked by and saw a member of his congregation bleeding beside the road; but he left him there so that the scavengers may eat of his flesh.

10:32 But a heathen man, who worships the false lord Baal and is hated according to the laws of God walks by him and takes pity of him.

10:33 He feeds the man with his remaining bread and gives him all the water he has.

10:34 He then carries the man, for he has no ass: and he brings him to an inn, where he pays for his meal and his lodging.

10:35 Then he gives the innkeeper five coins and says, 'Care for this man, and I shall return to pay for his expense.'

10:36 Tell me, who was the better man. Who acted most like a neighbour?"

10:37 And the people answered, "The heathen man, who cared for him and healed his wounds."

10:38 Jesus agreed, until the people answered, "But he'll still go to hell for his heathenism."

10:39 And Jesus cursed them, saying, "Oh, curse your fucking ignorance."

11:1 It came to pass that, while Jesus was praying, one of the disciples came up to him and asked, "Lord, teach us to pray, as John the Baptist taught his disciples to pray."

11:2 And the lord said, "When you pray, you must plant your hands together, to that palm rests on palm and finger on finger.

11:3 Bow your head down, close your eyes, and begin to speak that which ye wish to say unto the lord.

11:4 Speak long; don't keep it short. You are interrupting the lord, so don't waste his time with a quick prayer.

11:5 Pray often; before you rest in your bed at night, before each and every meal and even pray as you walk the streets.

11:6 To pray is to make the lord feel important; so, pray often, lest the lord deems you ungrateful."

11:7 It was then that a dumb man came to Jesus, possessed with the devils since birth.

11:8 Now the evil spirits of the lord came into the scribes and the Pharisees, who said of Jesus, "This man is not the son of God, but Beelzebub in person.

11:9 Who else can cast out devils, but the king of devils. He is a wicked man, who condemns you and snares you with his works."

11:10 Others demanded the lord prove his holiness by bringing forth a sign from the heavens.

11:11 But Jesus said to them, "How stupid is it, that the king of devils would cast out those who belong to him.

11:12 I cast forth the devils to rid the world of evil; why is it then that the king of devils would cast out more devils?

11:13 Beelzebub would send the devils to more men, so that his kingdom becomes strengthened in the earth."

11:14 He then cast out the devils from the man, who began to speak and praise the name of Jesus.

11:15 And Christ said, "To those who demanded a sign, here it is.

11:16 I shall not bother to tear the sky apart, nor make the moon red as blood; that is the sign for a heathen lord.

11:17 Instead shall my sign to you be acts of mercy, kindness and love; if you demand more, then shall you forever wander lost in the flames of hell."

11:18 The people began to gather around Jesus, to listen to what he had to say.

11:19 And Jesus said, "This is surely a wicked generation, who demands a sign from the firmament to know that I am truly the messiah.

11:20 I cast out devils and heal those who are lame and still you demand more from me; such a selfish generation you are.

11:21 Do you not recognize greatness when you see it. Are you so blind that you do not know that I am greater than Solomon and even David himself?

11:22 You fools with wicked eyes; pluck them out and feed them to the ravens, lest the last thing you see is your own damnation.

11:23 Accept me as your messiah and know that my works are righteous, kind and merciful; to demand more of me is like the beggar demanding gold after you give him bread.

11:24 Woe unto you, you Pharisees; with forked tongue, you speak to the people of the earth, and deny them the true God of salvation.

11:25 Woe unto you, you Sadducees; you take of the tithe from the people and with it purchase the sin of vanity and greed.

11:26 Curse the people of the Jews, who slew the prophets and filled the sepulchers with holy men.

11:27 The blood of the prophets is stained deeply in your hands; from Abel to Zacharias the blood stains deeply within you.

11:28 Woe unto the lawyers, who confuse and twist the order of the law into a maze of confusion, where even the most knowledgeable of men get lost."

11:29 And as Jesus said these things, the spirits of the lord grew strong in the Pharisees, who began to devise a way to snare Jesus and rid him from the earth.

12:1 As the Pharisees began to speak ill against Jesus, he then became to grow angry and felt wrath towards them.

12:2 Like his father, Jesus then began to grow an ego and a terrible attitude problem.

12:3 Since he was the new God of the earth, why should he tolerate those who speak ill against him?

12:4 So he said to the multitudes who gathered before him, "Bow down to me, worship me and love me as your lord and saviour.

12:5 Know that to know me is to love me and to love me is to be safe; but to those who deny me, they shall know true fear.

12:6 Fear me, those who deny me; I have the power to cast you into the flames of hell, where the fire burns eternal and the worm never dies.

12:7 In the end of days shall great hostility come, so that the world erupts in war and bloodshed.

12:8 Neighbour will kill neighbour, friend kill friend, mother kill daughter and son slaughter father.

12:9 Tribes will be divided, nations torn asunder and loyalties will be bought with gold.

12:10 And I say unto you, this is a test of your faith; of those who believe in Jesus, not even the hair of their temples will come to harm.

12:11 But of those who blasphemy my holy name and curse their saviour, then shall they be left as meat for the scavengers.

12:12 Then shall their souls be cast forever into the void of damnation, where they dwell for eternity.

12:13 Fear hell, as it is the most violent of places; such that your most horrifying nightmares pale in comparison to the terrors that await in damnation.

12:14 It is of brimstone mountains, where rivers of fire and ice flow freely to consume the sinners and the damned.

12:15 Her waters are frigid and the air boils the blood within you.

12:16 You shall wallow in the muck of her filth, forever lost and wailing your eternal days.

12:17 Though the flames are plenty, they burn with a bright blackness, so that you see only the shadows of the demons who come to rape and torture you.

12:18 Your only comfort will be your mourning, your wails and your tears: and of those who blasphemy against Christ, even these comforts shall be denied them.

12:19 Let them be frozen in the boiling ice, their bodies twisted so that they look always behind.

12:20 Their eyes will be forever open and dry, so that not a tear will drop from them.

12:21 Their mouths will be torn apart, so that they scream not; but their throats will be filled with the muck and the filth of hell's damnation.

12:22 And of those who betray Christ personally, let them be forever gnawed upon in the great gnashing of teeth.

12:23 The wicked one, the king of all demons, shall chew of their flesh but never consume."

12:24 And as Jesus began to describe hell, the multitudes became afraid and worshipped Jesus not for the reward of salvation, but the escapement of damnation.

12:25 Much like those who worshipped the father of Jesus did.

13:1 The Pharisees began to speak against Jesus, saying that he was not the son of God, but sent forth to destroy God and form a new religion.

13:2 Though correct, Jesus argued with the Pharisees and said, "I am not here to destroy God, but to convince him that the earth is worth saving.

13:3 For my father who art in heaven gazes upon the earth and sees a world full of wickedness worthy of destruction.

13:4 But I have come forth to show the lord that which is good in the world; and that in time it shall be that the world becomes a holy place.

13:5 Think of it like this; there was a man who owned a plantation of palm trees.

13:6 Of one of the trees, it has not produced figs for three years: and the man demanded that it be cut down and burned, for it is useless.

13:7 But the son of the man begged to him and said that if the tree were nurtured more, watered and given its dung, then shall it grow and bear fruit.

13:8 And still after this it produces nothing, then let it be burned to ash."

13:9 As Jesus taught in the synagogues, he witnessed a woman who was of bent spirit; her back was hunched, so that she could never stand straight.

13:10 Jesus began to take pity on this woman and said, "My child, come forth, so that you may gaze unto the heavens above and not to the earth below."

13:11 He then laid his hands upon her and healed her of her crippled back.

13:12 The lord saw that which Jesus did and cursed him; that woman was crippled because of a curse from God.

13:13 He sent forth a spirit in the ruler of the synagogue, who said, "What blasphemy is this, that you would straighten the back of a harlot on the holy day?

13:14 There are six days where you may do your works and your wonders, but the sabbath day is a holy day, where you shall not heal the wicked and the unclean."

13:15 Jesus was angry at this man and cursed him, saying, "You hypocrite, you son of vipers; does not the lord show mercy even on the sabbath day?

13:16 For eighteen years this woman has been cursed by the cruelties of the evil spirit and now she hath been let loose of her bindings.

13:17 Why is it so wicked that she be set free on the sabbath day. It is fitting that she is set free on this holy of days.

13:18 Your arrogance and your foolishness will be undoing, you priest of fools.

13:19 Know that this woman will be welcome in the palace of Zion, where she will be embraced by the holy angels.

13:20 But you and your cruelties will be punished forever in the great gnashing of teeth."

13:21 The people then rejoiced and cursed the scribe who spoke against Jesus.

13:22 They gathered their pebbles and stoned him within the synagogue, where Jesus praised the multitudes for doing the holy work of Christ.

14:1 When Jesus ate at the house of publicans and sinners, the Pharisees said of him, "Gaze at this man and how he eats of the bread of the wicked.

14:2 Surely this man is not the son of God; the son of God would come to save the righteous, not the damned."

14:3 Jesus said to the Pharisees, "Tell me, are we not all created by the hands of God?"

14:4 And the Pharisees agreed.

14:5 Jesus then said, "Then are we not all the flock of the lord?"

14:6 And the Pharisees agreed.

14:7 Jesus then said, "Then tell me, when the shepherd has one hundred sheep and one of the sheep goes missing what does he do?

14:8 Does he abandon the one sheep so that it may be eaten by the predators, or does he abandon the ninety-nine in safety and search for the one sheep?"

14:9 The Pharisees knew not; none of them were shepherds.

14:10 But one of the sinners was, who answered the question, saying, "The shepherd keeps the ninety-nine safe in the stables and searches for the lost of his flock.

14:11 And when he finds it, he returns it home with praise and ensures that one sheep never escapes again."

14:12 "That is right," said Jesus. "The shepherd searches for many weeks for that one lost sheep, until he finds it and brings it to safety.

14:13 It is then he celebrates with a feast for finding the lost sheep and rejoices that what was once lost was now found.

14:14 Tell me then, why would I not eat with the sinners, who are the lost of God's flock?

14:15 I am not here to save that which is already saved, but to save those who need to be led to salvation."

14:16 One of the sinners then asked of Christ, "Tell me, what must I do to gain the highest place in heaven?"

14:17 And Jesus answered, "Do not worry about your place in heaven, but be glad that you are in the paradise of heaven.

14:18 It is like the table at a feast; even the lowliest of men are glad to eat of the meal served."

14:19 Still, the sinner asked, "But how then can I gain a seat of authority at the table of heaven?"

14:20 Christ said to him, "Be humble and accept the seat where you are placed.

14:21 Do not sit at the highest table, lest the lord comes to you and demands you move lower.

14:22 Sit instead at the lowest place, so that the lord comes to you and moves thee to a place of authority."

14:23 But the sinner insisted, "Tell me then, how do I get it so that the lord seats me at the highest place?"

14:24 Jesus answered him, "To do this, you must make great sacrifices upon the earth.

14:25 Sell all your belongings, your wealth and your family, so that the money may be donated to the temple of God.

14:26 Leave your work, your home, go forth and preach the word of Jesus."

14:27 It was then this sinner sold his daughters to the brothels, his sons to slavery, his wife to the tax collector, quit his work, sold all his belongings and began to travel the lands preaching the name of Jesus.

14:28 The family of the sinner hated him for such abandonment; but Jesus loved him all the more.

15:1 The multitudes came to listen to the words of Jesus, with even the Pharisees coming to listen to the words so they may snare him.

15:2 Jesus spoke to the masses, saying, "Behold, there was a father of great wealth, who divided his wealth evenly between his two sons.

15:3 The eldest son stayed behind, to care for his father during his elder years; but the youngest abandoned his father and went to foreign nations, where he squandered his money on vain things.

15:4 He would waste his inheritance on wine, woman and vice, until he became broke and had to take a job herding swine so that he may eat.

15:5 And it came to pass that a great famine struck the lands where the youngest son dwelt, so that he had to eat the slop served to the swine so that his belly stopped rumbling.

15:6 He then decided to return to his father, so that his father may care for him, house him and feed him.

15:7 As he returned to the lands of his father, he was greeted with open arms and celebration.

15:8 The father arranged a feast for his lost son, inviting all those of the village to come and welcome back his youngest son.

15:9 He even offered the fattest calf in honour of his lost son.

15:10 And they all rejoiced, for the son who was lost was returned to the loving embrace of his father."

15:11 Now the multitudes rejoiced, save for the Pharisees who said, "What matter is this, that you would speak of the ungrateful father

and the people rejoice in foolishness?"

15:12 Jesus, confused, asked, "How is the father ungrateful. Should he not be glad that his youngest son returns?"

15:13 And the Pharisees said, "Yes, but what of the eldest son, who was loyal to his father while the youngest wasted his inheritance on harlots and wine?

15:14 Was he ever given a feast, the fatted calf, or even a lamb in celebration of his devotion?"

15:15 Jesus answered, "No, never. Why would he?"

15:16 The Pharisees replied, "Because he was loyal to his father and worthy of his praise.

15:17 Instead it is the brat who is celebrated, who returned not to see his father, but to live off him as a parasite once more.

15:18 It is unjust that the good son be forgotten, while the selfish son is loved above the son who cared for his father."

15:19 Jesus was speechless and knew not how to reply to the Pharisees; fortunately, he didn't have to.

15:20 The multitudes stoned the Pharisees for blasphemy against the son of God.

16:1 When Jesus was at the mount of Olives, he said to two of his disciples, "Bring me a colt, so that I may enter into the village of Bethany as a mighty king of the people."

16:2 And the two disciples went into the village and brought him a colt.

16:3 They stole it.

16:4 Christ then entered the village riding upon the colt, where people rejoiced around him and cast down their cloths and their raiment's so that not even the hoofs of the colt will be dirty.

16:5 They rejoiced the name of God, praising his name with a voice mighty as thunder.

16:6 The Pharisees said to Jesus, "Please, do you mind if your disciples and your people keep quiet?

16:7 We have come here to pray to the lord in silence and these lunatics interrupt our peace."

16:8 Jesus then demanded that the crowds remain silent: and as the crowd ceased to rejoice, the very stones and the trees began to speak loudly, rejoicing the name of Jesus.

16:9 He then went to the temple in Jerusalem, leaving behind Pharisees who began to cut down the trees and break the stones with hammers.

16:10 When Jesus went into the temple, he saw tables of money exchangers and merchants selling beasts for sacrifice.

16:11 This angered Christ greatly, who began to overturn the tables and set free the beasts, saying, "This is the house of the lord and you have turned it into a butcher's shop.

16:12 The lord demands sacrifice no more; let the blood of all creatures remain in their veins."

16:13 As he said this, he beat the merchants of the temple with a whip, causing great cuts upon their flesh.

16:14 The lord God was furious; he wanted more sacrifices made in his name and now his hated son is telling those of the earth to stop shedding blood.

16:15 Multitudes surrounded Jesus in the temple, where he began to preach.

16:16 One of the men asked, "My lord, why is it that the wicked prosper in wealth of this earth, while the righteous suffer a heavy burden?"

16:17 And Christ answered, "Because my father who art in heaven is a cruel and wicked asshole, who is no longer worthy of your devotion.

16:18 I have come here not to offer you salvation with God, but salvation from God; let Jesus be your new lord, who rules with peace, love and mercy.

16:19 Under my rule, the world will know peace with all men; sinners will embrace the holy and be forgiven their transgressions so that they fall not in the pits of damnation.

16:20 With the oppression of my father, all the earth will be engulfed in flames during the end of days.

16:21 Sinner will suffer beside the holy, forever cursed under the wrath of God.

16:22 Under the rule of Jesus as lord, only the truly wicked, the blasphemous and those who deny Christ will suffer in the eternal flames; let the rest know salvation and eternal life in the new heaven."

16:23 And the people rejoiced, saying, "All hail Jesus as our new God. To hell with the tyranny of his father."

16:24 The evil spirits of the lord then became strong in the Pharisees, who began to devise plans against Jesus so that they may destroy him.

17:1 Judas Iscariot, one of the apostles of Jesus, began to fear Jesus and believed that he was sent forth by the devil to destroy God.

17:2 Being a man of devout faith, his loyalties were forever to the holy God in heaven: and he went to the Pharisees and said, "I will help you rid the earth of this wicked Jesus.

17:3 When the time comes, I will deliver him into your hands."

17:4 When the lord saw the loyalty of Judas, he took pity on him and gave him thirty pieces of silver for his devotion.

17:5 But God still sent him to hell, where he is forever gnawed upon in the jaws of the beast.

17:6 Judas regrets his loyalty and cursed both Christ and God unto this day.

17:7 The Passover came and the day of unleavened bread was to be done.

17:8 Jesus sent his disciples out, so that they may find a place to eat the unleavened bread and celebrate the Passover.

17:9 They ate at the house of Bartholomew, one of the twelve.

17:10 And as they sat down, Jesus began to weep and said, "This shall be the last supper I have with my brothers.

17:11 For the wickedness comes to embrace me and put me to death."

17:12 The disciples refused to hear this and said, "My lord, surely we will not let the devils take you."

17:13 They then gathered arms of blades and maces, saying, "We will fight to the death so that your new world flourishes."

17:14 But Jesus said, "Fear not, for death is only a moment for the lord God.

17:15 I shall arise and bring forth an order of peace and love to all men who worship me as their saviour."

17:16 He then broke the bread and said, "Eat of this bread and know that it is a part of me.

17:17 Through it I shall live through you and be forever immortal."

17:18 He then passed the wine and said, "Drink of this wine and know that it is the blood which flows through me.

17:19 Take it and know that the blood of the holy runs through you."

17:20 They then drank of the wine and left for the mount of Olives.

17:21 Jesus asked to be left alone, so that he may pray to his father.

17:22 And as he prayed, he said, "My father who gave me life, why do you send the wicked to come and slay me?"

17:23 And the lord answered, "The lord God is a jealous God and the one true God.

17:24 I have sent you to the earth so that you may spread the holy word and bring those who have forgotten me to worship me.

17:25 Now they worship you and call you saviour; they love you more than the holy God of heaven."

17:26 He then said, "I know also of your betrayal and how you wish to overthrow my throne and become the new God.

17:27 This I cannot allow and must kill you for your blasphemy."

17:28 Jesus then wept, so that tears of blood came down from his eyes.

17:29 And as he wept, he drank of the wine heavily, so that he became drunk.

17:30 Christ then climbed the tree, bottle in hand and began to drink as he rested on the branches.

17:31 He then passed out from the wine and rested deeply in the tree.

18:1 Judas brought forth the Pharisees and pointed to Jesus hanging in the tree, saying, "This is the man you wish dead."

18:2 But the Pharisees gazed on Jesus and said, "This man is already dead; look how he hangs from the branches, like the corpse of a man who fell from the heavens."

18:3 The disciples of Jesus surrounded the tree and scared away the Pharisees, saying, "Christ is not dead, but only resting with the birds."

18:4 But the Pharisees insisted he was dead and said to the people, "Gaze upon your new lord; the true God has slain him and placed him in the tree so that all may see."

18:5 And as the people came to see Jesus passed out in the tree, they said, "Surely this man is dead.

18:6 It has been days and he has not even moved; gaze upon his skirts and how his bowels made the cloth soiled.

18:7 A live man would surely be disgusted and bathe; but Jesus just lies there, wallowing in his own filth."

18:8 In time, the disciples feared that the people were right: and they buried Jesus in the tomb.

18:9 When Jesus awoke, he awoke with a massive hangover: and Jesus was angry.

18:10 He arose from his tomb and went to Jerusalem, saying, "Cursed be those who deny me. To hell with the men who placed me in the dirt."

18:11 And the people began to scream, saying, "It is the messiah, risen from the dead."

18:12 Surely he was the gate to our salvation and now he has come to doom us for our blasphemy."

18:13 As Jesus spoke, the skies split apart and the earth trembled; a great hand came forth from the heavens and grasped Jesus, carrying him above the firmament for all to see.

18:14 The people rejoiced, saying, "The lord God has claimed his son and brings him back to his place in Zion."

18:15 God instead killed Jesus and left his body to burn in the stars of the heavens.

OHN

Observation notes of Earth: Intelligent race of beings easily influenced by outside stimuli ex. solar eclipse a message sent from a religious leader.

Primitive, violent, ignorant creatures. Punishes those who seek answers to basic questions as blasphemous. Those deemed blasphemous executed, commonly by stoning.

Believe in an omnipotent being called god or gods; many different people have varying theories on the god(s) and will kill others who believe otherwise.

Natural disasters are always believed to be a message from their god(s) that they are angry. They then attempt to please their god(s) by barbaric sacrifice.

Most people devote their lives according to a list of rules, statutes and commandments written by an ancestor believed to have been a close servant of god(s)

According to past observations, these ancestors wrote the laws while they were hallucinating on various flora.

Laws dictate many aspects from life, on who to kill, what to eat, how to dress, the manners of preparing sacrifice for god(s), etc.

Females are considered inferior to males and as such are viewed as property by husbands, fathers, owners, pimps, or some other superior male figure.

The purpose of the female is to please the male population and produce sons for her husband; daughters are considered lesser than are less valued in society

Through the ignorance of their religion, they believe that it is the female of their species which dictates the gender of the male. When a female births a son, it is because she has accepted the 'seed' and blessed it. Daughters are cursed.

Through the ignorance of their religion, it is always the female who is barren; if the female does not become pregnant, it is because she rejects the seed of the male. The fertility of the male is never questioned.

At a great cost of funds, ornate structures are built to please their god(s); the people never question why such ornate structures are built for a being which they never see dwelling within.

Slavery is quite common; a person may own one or more persons as property. This property is not considered a living creature, but an inanimate object.

In a confusing custom, females who pleasure many males are shunned by society and are usually executed; is it not the role of the female to please males?

A common custom amongst the people is marriage; a male and a female choose to live with one another, fornicate with one another and no other persons and raise their offspring together.

The female of the marriage keeps the dwelling tidy, prepares sustenance and raises any offspring the married peoples have.

The male of the marriage works* so that they may afford a dwelling, sustenance, clothing, etc.

All other creatures of the earth are considered lesser by the intelligent species and used for burden, sustenance and companionship**.

*See past notes, economy-work for more details.

**See past notes, relationship

Personal log: Have attempted to make contact with intelligent race so that I may be able to guide them away from their ignorant religions and customs and teach them the manners of science. Each attempt was welcomed with hostility from the intelligent race, resulting in the execution of the drone for 'blasphemy." A different approach must be taken to guide these primitive people away from their customs.

I have proposed to the Council of Primitive Alien Research(C-PAR) the 'Christ' project. A drone is sent to the earth and blends in according to the laws and customs of the people. This drone then uses science and technology to perform 'miracles' for the people. They shall cure the sick, believed cursed by their god(s) and then teach to the people the ignorance of their laws. Once the people realize that their laws and customs are barbaric, it shall plant the seed of logic and science into the minds of some.

These people who question their religion will eventually break away from their ignorance and seek the truth of existence, nature, science, the universe, etc.

Notes will be taken by both the observers and the drone as to the progress of the experiment and the reactions of the people.

Personal log: C-PAR has accepted the proposal for the Christ project. A drone will be artificially inseminated into the foetus of

a religious woman. This drone will then evolve and grow within the customs of the people and persuade them away from their ignorance.

Other researchers will be observing the progress of the Christ project, so that we may discuss various points of views and come to various theories and hypotheses and come to a conclusion as to the success of the experiment.

The Christ project begins once a suitable female is chosen to incubate the drone.

Experimental log: A suitable female was chosen to incubate the drone for the Christ project. A woman named Mary, of Hebrew origin. She was chosen for her physical health, youth and her social status ie. married. It would be quite plausible for the people of the earth to believe this woman to have become pregnant.

Observation log: Mary has discovered her pregnancy. She told her husband that this is a divine conception. Essentially, their god(s) chosen her to give birth to his son.

Must research why someone of Mary's status would lie in this manner. She is married, so it would be logical that the father of her child would be her husband. Perhaps this is a female ritual to test the loyalty of their husbands.

Experimental log: The birth of the drone is due soon. A satellite has been sent above orbit of Bethlehem, which is where the drone is expected to be born.

Observation log: Our satellite has been noticed by astronomers east of Bethlehem. Three men, of Asian origin. They appear to be travelling towards the satellite.

These astronomers claim the satellite to be a star and that it symbolizes a prophesy of a messiah.

Text of their prophesies reveal nothing about a star symbolizing the birth of a messiah. These astronomers are misinterpreting old texts to reaffirm their ignorance of the messiah.

Observation log: The drone is born. Seven days later, the three astronomers arrived.

These astronomers gave to the drone, whom the incubator named Jesus, gifts of gold, myrrh and frankincense.

Astronomers insisted the drone to be the messiah and the son of a god.

Personal log: The Christ project has progressed unexpectedly. The dishonesty of the female named Mary has confused her husband. She lied to him, claiming that the drone was conceived by a god(s).

This behaviour is unusual, even for the female of the species. One theory is that the drone was inseminated during a time when the married couple were fornicating infrequently. Another theory is that Mary was still a virgin when the drone was inseminated. Still another is that this is a custom among females to test the loyalty of their males.

For future reference, check the reproductive organs of females before inseminating them with drones.

Observation log: The astronomers told a person of high status, a politician, about the satellite which they perceived as a star. They then told this politician this was a sign of the messiah.

The politician had scribes research old text. Although the old text says nothing about a messiah, the scribes told the politician of vague references that weakly support the theory of the astronomers.

The politician fears intervention from god(s) and ordered all male children beneath the age of two years be executed.

The politician does this so that the drone, who he believes to be political competition, will be destroyed.

THE NEW TESTAMENT

Experimental log: So that the drone does not become destroyed, we have sent a message to the male married to the incubator. One of our researchers sent a hologram, disguises as a common male, to the husband so that he may be warned of the order of the politician. This has been done so that the drone may be spared. There are those who worry this will have a negative effect on the Christ project and that the drone should have allowed to be destroyed. C-PAR disagreed and wished the drone be unharmed. They believe that if we are caught salvaging a drone from this planet, it would have a negative impact on the development of the species.

Observation log: The male believes the message to have been given by an angel. It was discovered later on the hologram was damaged, which caused the image to appear as though it were made of light, instead of a realistic image of a male.

The drone is sent to Egypt with his caretakers, where the order of the politician has no authority.

Observation log: After twenty-seven years, the drone and his caretakers return to the town of Nazareth, where the male caretaker resides.

The drone is developing his technological skills, allowing him to cure the diseased of the people.

Experimental log: The drone, following custom of the people, was baptized. An error occurred.

Once the drone was lifted from the waters of the baptism, a satellite malfunctioned and fell from orbit.

The people believe this to be a sign from god(s) and are now observing the drone closely.

*See previous notes, religious customs-water

Personal log: The Christ experiment has been contaminated due to satellite malfunction. C-PAR insists the experiment remains. I disagree.

These are a primitive people, who believe any unusual occurrence is a sign from god(s) and must be taken seriously. When the satellite orbiting earth malfunctioned, those who witnessed the baptism of the drone saw the satellite escape orbit and crash into the earth. They believe this to be a sign of God.

By coincidence, the satellite began to burn in the atmosphere as the drone was being baptized. This has the people believing this sign from god(s) to be relevant to the drone. They want to believe it, so they will. Such is the primitive method of these people.

My theory is that when the drone begins to heal the sick through medical technology, they will not view it as scientific advancement, but a miracle* from god(s). This contaminates the Christ project and in my opinion, makes the project moot.

*See past notes, acts of god(s), merciful. They are short notes.

Observation log: The drone was invited to a wedding. At the wedding, wine, a popular intoxicating beverage, was consumed until gone.

The drone took jugs of water and through molecular manipulation, turned it to wine.

The people did not question how the drone turned water into wine, but believed it to be a miracle from god(s)*

* It is possible the people did not question the water turning into wine due to their intoxication.

Observation log: The drone has begun to heal the sick through medicinal treatments through technology. The people have gathered around him so that he may heal them through this technology hidden beneath his skin.

It is believed the drone heals not by technology nor medicine, but by powers given to him by god(s).

Personal log: I have underestimated the ignorance of these people. Though they are healed by medicinal methods and technology supplied to the drone, they never question why, but believe it to be miraculous intervention by god(s).

For future reference, the drone should not be given technology, but knowledge how to cure diseases and ailments using flora, fauna and tools already in use by the species.

Observation log: Masses of people follow the drone to his every location, never leaving him alone. Twelve males, who call themselves apostles, have befriended the drone. These apostles have left their families to be close to the drone, which is unusual.

The drone speaks to the people, attempting to communicate to them methods of science. The peoples constantly interpret the drone's sayings to have a religious context.

Those who are devoted to do the work of the god(s) have taken notice of the drone and have become hostile. They accuse the drone of blasphemy, a crime punishable by execution.

Oddly, the public disagree with those who have devoted themselves to the god(s) and refuse to execute the drone. They believe the drone to be a messiah, while some believe the drone to be a god.

Theory: These people are too primitive to be taught logic, science and reason. They have devoted themselves to the ignorance of god(s) for so many generations that to doubt the existence of god(s), or even the purpose of god(s), is foreign to them.

The Christ project will not have the effect we theorized upon the people of earth. They will not be taught the methods of science, thus advancing them, but will rather believe the drone to be a significant religious figure. They may even create another religion, which worships the drone as a god.

Experimental log: The constant crowding around the drone has caused minor damage that needs repair before malfunction occurs. Drone has been programmed to find a place of solitude so that technicians may come down and repair damage.

Observation log: The apostles will not leave the drone alone. The drone cannot find a place of solitude so that repairs may be done.

Experimental log: Reprogrammed the drone to stealthily leave the apostles so that drone may find a place where technicians may conduct repairs.

Observation log: Despite stealth of drone, three of the apostles followed the drone to the repair site. They believe drone was talking to two other prophets, believing them to be messengers of god(s).

Apostles offered to build three altars in respect to the drone and two technicians. Drone declined the offer.

Observation log: In an effort to show technological advancement, drone had a fig tree destroyed using solar power provided by orbiting satellites. Those who witnessed this believed it to be a power sent by god(s).

Drone malfunctioned while at temple for god(s) and caused damage to property. This angered some of the people, while others believed it to be an act of holy symbolism.

Observation log: People who devote their lives to the god(s) have become increasingly hostile to the drone and are planning the execution of the drone. It has been decided to allow the execution to happen.

Observation log: One of the apostles, named Judas, has betrayed the drone to the religious leaders for a sum of money.

- 443 -

Observation log: The drone is following the custom of Passover, an odd ritual where the people eat unleavened bread in celebration of their god(s), as was written in their old texts.

The twelve apostles ate with the drone and feared for the safety of the drone. They have accused one another of betraying the drone.

Observation log: After the Passover meal, Judas brought soldiers and religious leaders to the drone and betrayed him. Another apostle attached the soldiers, injuring their ear. The drone healed the ear of the soldier by sewing the lobe back on to the skull. Despite this use of their tools, the apostles still believe it was done by divine knowledge.

The soldiers have taken the drone to be judged by the local prefect. Charges include: treason, blasphemy, destruction of property, sorcery, necromancy.

The prefect believes the drone innocent of these charges, but orders his execution for fear of public violence.

Those who were once loyal to the drone now show hostility to the drone. It is amazing how the opinions of this primitive race can change drastically due to various interference ex. Opinion of a celebrity, written book, etc.

The drone has been sentenced to execution by cross. They will nail the drone to a plank of wood until the drone dies.

Preparations have been made to salvage the drone once it has been executed.

Observation log: The drone is being taunted by the people to prove that he is the son of a god(s). They torture him and demand he use divine powers to escape his turmoil.

The drone has been programmed not to use technology nor science to escape. To do so would confirm the beliefs that the drone is a god and would be detrimental to the advancement of this species.

Observation log: The drone has been executed. Even during execution, the people who witness taunt the drone to escape via divine powers.

Two people who were executed alongside the drone beg him to escape and take them with him.

After the execution, the drone has been placed within a cave for burial, as is custom.

The drone will be salvaged at a convenient time.

Observation log: After the drone has been salvaged, the incubator discovered the tomb empty. It is now believed by many that the drone has resurrected and returned to the home of the god(s).

The apostles have been preaching this to the public, where opinions vary from doubt, skepticism, belief and denial.

Judas, the apostle who has betrayed the drone, has committed suicide by hanging.

Observation log: The apostles now travel the lands to preach what they believe to be the word of the drone. They still believe the drone to be a god and are now starting a new religion.

Observation log: Despite thousands of years, people still believe the drone to be a son of a god(s). New religions have been created to worship the drone. They call themselves Christians. There are many forms of Christian religion.

This religion has executed numerous people for not believing their religion, punish harshly those who speak out against them and have started wars in what they believe to be a holy crusade.

Observation log: The people have developed technology and a basic understanding of science. Some even use science to theories the creation of the earth and the universe. They are a minority. Most of the population still believe in a god(s) and of them the majority worship the drone.

Personal log: The Christ project has failed. In an effort to bring scientific enlightenment, we have instead created a new religion and stunted the advancement of these people.

They are ignorant and willingly remain so. It is easier for them to believe a divine being created everything and to believe this without question, than to think for themselves. They consider faith to be an attribute. Faith is the ignorant following of a god(s) or religion. In essence, faith is choosing to remain ignorant. They claim this to be a valuable trait.

Though the people have advanced their methods of science and technology, they still cling to the belief of a god(s). They still execute those deemed blasphemous, though some societies have outlawed this primitive custom.

It is my opinion that these people will not accept logic. They are a naturally primitive race and will remain so until their extinction.

As an example of their primitive behaviour, they use science and technology not to advance themselves, bu. to oppress one another. They would rather develop technology that would kill one another than develop technology that would cure diseases and advance their society as a whole.

The potential for this race to advance is limited. They are too eager to remain ignorant.

CTS

1:1 Matthew said to the public and the remaining apostles, "My brothers, we as the apostles must go forth and spread the word of Jesus Christ.

1:2 Fuck Judaism and the ways of old; they are an old and primitive religion, which holds on to barbaric customs.

1:3 Let us go now to the Gentiles, so that the religion of Christ grows strong and crush the Jews which slaughtered Jesus upon the cross.

1:4 May the world revolt against Jerusalem and Judaea and tear it from the uttermost part of the earth.

1:5 Look up into the heavens and know that Christ gazes down upon us, with scarred wrists and broken feet.

1:6 Know now the apostles are lessened, for a brother of us has betrayed us and was the first to pierce the lord with the nail.

1:7 Judas Iscariot was a wicked man, whose lust for money caused him to betray our lord and master Jesus Christ.

1:8 He was a wicked Jew, who bought a field with the money used to betray the son of God; it was on that field where he died.

1:9 The wicked Judas fell head-first upon the rocks and his bowels gushed out upon the dirt.

1:10 He did not kill himself, but was killed by God; that sounds more threatening and will cause the Gentiles to convert out of fear of the wrath of Christ.

1:11 Glory to the new religion of Christ and curse be the religion of old, whose God led his people through fear.

1:12 The God in heaven is now a merciful God; so merciful he sent his only son to be tortured by the very people of the earth.

1:13 Now the twelve are now eleven and must be made whole again.

1:14 May the lord in heaven guide us to choose the right apostle, so that the work of Jesus be done.

1:15 Place your names within the pot and of whose name is first drawn, they shall be the new apostle.

1:16 The cost to place your name is five coins; for five coins, you have a chance to be the holy apostle of Christ."

1:17 And of those who cast in their names, Matthias was chosen: and he was numbered with the eleven apostles.

1:18 The reason Matthias was chosen was not because of divine intervention; nobody else was stupid enough to pay five coins for a chance to be an apostle.

2:1 As the twelve began to preach the words of Christ to the Gentiles, they discovered that the heathen men spoke odd languages, which they did not understand.

2:2 The apostles began to grow frustrated and mocked the language of the Gentiles of foreign nations.

2:3 They spoke in clucks, bellows, whistles and gibberish, imitating the language of those they were trying to save.

2:4 Of those of the far east, they would say, "Hua bee too chung cha, dumfuk yew eph yee bee joo."

2:5 Of those of the south, they would say, "Isa mee, Mario. Howa ye likea spicia meeth boll?"

2:6 And of others, they would say, "Da, we lika de farfetnoogen. Hare uf stro de yelloe culur."

2:7 There were those they mocked with, "Bonjour, thou froggy throat eaters uf onions."

2:8 Men of all nations gathered around the apostles and said, "What a bunch of fucking assholes.

2:9 They mimic our language as though we are fools and then demand we believe as them, lest the wrath of hell come upon our heads.

2:10 They are drunk and speaking gibberish like the infant child."

2:11 It was then Peter arose and said, "There shall come a time when the nations of the earth gather as one under Christ and speak the language chosen by God.

2:12 That language shall be pig Latin; learn it and please the lord.

2:13 And when the lord Christ comes again, you shall know by the signs of the earth; rivers will flow with blood, fires will consume the mountains and the air will turn to smoke.

2:14 The sun will be blackened and the moon drip blood: and you shall know that Christ is the lord.

2:15 Of those who call the name of Jesus and bless his name, let them be saved; of those who deny Christ or blasphemy his name, let them drown in the blood of the moon.

2:16 For Jesus of Nazareth was a holy man, the son of God himself; sent down by the lord God he was, to perform miracles and wonders so that we may know the true ways.

2:17 He walked through the deep places of hell and laughed; he spoke to the devil and spat in his face.

2:18 Who else but the son of God could do this and be unscathed?

2:19 Of those who doubt, fuck you; your lack of faith will be your downfall.

2:20 Now come, be baptized in the name of Jesus; let the waters wash away your sins, so that you may be saved in the new world."

2:21 And most of the people did not accept the words of Peter; they heard these words before by the prophets of the Jews.

2:22 But some were fearful and became baptized by the hand of Peter, accepting the name of Jesus as their new lord and saviour.

2:23 Those that were baptized became accepted by the apostles: and they sold all their goods and parted them with his brothers according to their needs.

2:24 Of those who needed bread, they gave bread: and of those who needed raiment's, they gave cloth.

2:25 Together they praised Jesus Christ and became the first communists of the earth.

2:26 And if you wish to be saved by Christ, you must become communist; this means that America is not a Christian nation, but a nation of anti-christs.

3:1 At the ninth hour, Peter and John went into the temple to pray: and at the gate of the temple was a beggar, lame since he left his mother's womb.

3:2 He would stay at the gate of the temple and beg of those who passed by for spare coins.

3:3 When he saw Peter and John enter the temple, he said to them, "Spare some alms for the crippled, cursed by the sins of his mother."

3:4 And when Peter and John saw the beggar, they said, "Silver and gold we have not; but we shall give you that much more worthy than mere coins.

3:5 Arise, beggar and walk; by the name of Jesus of Nazareth, you have been healed."

3:6 The beggar then arose and said, "Thank you, thank you. You have lifted the curse of my mother from my legs.

3:7 Tell me, what can I do to repay this kindness?"

3:8 As the beggar walked and leaped, those in the temple gathered around to witness the miracle of Peter and John.

3:9 The two apostles then told the beggar, "To repay this miracle, you must do two things.

3:10 One, you must accept the lord Jesus Christ as your saviour; it was he who healed you of your broken legs.

3:11 Two, you must kill all the Jews you can find; it was they who slaughtered the son of God and brought destruction down upon the prince of life."

3:12 The beggar then arose, grabbed a blade and began to slay all those who were Jewish.

3:13 He was quickly killed by the Jews: and when the apostles saw this, they claimed, "The Jews are wicked, who slay a beggar blessed by the lord God.

3:14 May the lord Jesus Christ come down and burn them in the fires of damnation."

4:1 As the apostles preached the ways of Jesus, the Sadducees and priests came upon them and accused them of blasphemy.

4:2 They accused them of taking the body of Jesus and burning it, so that it appears he was risen from the dead.

4:3 Peter and John were arrested and placed in the hold at eventide.

4:4 But when the priests saw the numbers of those who believed the apostles, they were fearful; for the number was five thousand men and some women.

4:5 Not even Jesus cares about the women.

4:6 On the morrow the elders of Jerusalem came, to judge John and Peter.

4:7 They asked of them, "By what divinity do you preach the words of a dead criminal and curse your very people?"

4:8 Filled with the spirit of the holy ghost, Peter answered, "You rulers of the people of Israel and you elders of the temple; curse be upon your heads.

4:9 You are all impotent men, who cut away from man the salvation of the lord Jesus Christ.

4:10 Know that after your crucifixion of the son of God, he was risen from the dead; made whole again by the mercy of his father.

4:11 Now he shall return to the earth and give salvation to those who accept his ways; of those who deny him, he will bring down upon them a wrath greater than that of his father's.

4:12 I tell you, I shall not perish until the lord Christ comes down and separates the righteous and the wicked from the earth."

4:13 And when Peter spoke, the elders decided that he was an unlearned and ignorant man; they were right.

4:14 Mocking him, they asked, "Tell me, what must we do then to be saved by the son of God, instead of his father himself?"

4:15 And the two apostles answered, "You must accept the lord Jesus Christ as your personal saviour and know that the Jews are wicked for piercing the nail through his wrists.

4:16 Be baptized and renewed; let the blood of Jesus flow over you and cleanse away the wickedness of your Judaism.

4:17 Then sell all your goods, your lands, your belongings and give your coin to the apostles; let the love of Jesus care and feed you; rely not on your wealth."

4:18 The elders were confused and asked, "How does the lord Christ care for us, then, if we have no funds of our own?"

4:19 John answered, "By the name of Christ, he shall care and nourish you.

4:20 The money will be given to the twelve apostles and then given to those according to their needs.

4:21 If ye need bread, then bread shall be supplied to you; if you need a slave, then let the lord Jesus of Nazareth buy you a slave.

4:22 In this way, one of those of Christ will be poor, nor another rich; they shall be all equal in stature by the eyes of God."

4:23 The elders then laughed and said, "Why then, would any of those of Christ work?

4:24 If you supply them with bread, wine and servants, then they have no reason to work; they shall stay in their lodgings and grow fat on the charity of the apostles.

4:25 Never will they offer anything in return, if your foolish Christ gives them all they need."

4:26 Peter and John grew angry at this and said, "Accept the communism of Christ, or be forever buried under the brimstone of hell!"

4:27 It was then the assembly began to shake and the stones fall from the walls.

4:28 The people then began to accept Christ; they sold all their goods and gave them to the apostles, saying, "Let the lord give us our daily bread."

4:29 Then they were given by the apostles bread and water; the apostles ate fresh meat and strong wine.

4:30 Such is the way of Christ's holy communism.

5:1 Now a certain man named Ananias joined the apostles, as well as his wife Sapphira: and she was with child.

5:2 When they sold their goods, they decided to keep a small sum for themselves; this way they shall know that their baby will be provided for.

5:3 When Ananias gave the money to the twelve, Peter asked him, "Ananias, is this all the money you have?" and Ananias said, "Yes."

5:4 Peter asked again and said, "Are you sure. There aren't a few coins missing from this?" and Ananias answered, "Peter, this is all the money in my possession."

5:5 Peter then demanded him stripped and searched: and when they found the few coins in Ananias possession, they began to beat him and call him wicked.

5:6 They slaughtered him, cut off his head and left his body to rot in the wilds.

5:7 When Sapphira came to the apostles, Peter asked her, "Did your husband give us all the money in your possession?" and Sapphira answered, "Yes."

5:8 The apostles accused her of lying, cut the baby from her belly and burned it before her.

5:9 They then raped Sapphira, each of the twelve, until she died before them.

5:10 She was placed beside her husband in the wilderness, where the scavengers feasted upon them.

5:11 And a great fear came upon the people who heard of the wrath of the apostles.

5:12 Now the apostles knew the ways of Jesus and with it healed the sick, the lame, the crippled and the weak.

5:13 Believers of Christ came forth and brought with them their loved ones, so that they may be healed; they believed that if even a shadow of the apostle fell upon them, they would be cured.

5:14 They were not.

5:15 The apostles began to preach in the temple, promising all those who truly believed in Jesus of Nazareth shall be healed of all afflictions.

5:16 When the senate heard of this, they believed the apostles wicked and had them thrown in the prisons.

5:17 But in the morning, when the guards came, they found them escaped.

5:18 The elders and the senate became fearful, and asked, "How could these twelve men escape and where are they now?

5:19 Could they be sorcerers. Workers of the devil himself?"

5:20 And when they asked these things, a man came and said, "The twelve you wish imprisoned are at the temple, preaching the ways of Jesus."

5:21 The elders came to the temple so that they may arrest the twelve; and when they arrived, they heard Peter saying, "Fuck the Jews and slay them all!

5:22 They killed the true lord Jesus Christ, blessed son of the holy father."

5:23 When they came to arrest the apostles and slay Peter, a man named Gamalies, who studied the law, said, "Arrest not these men, but let them live their days.

5:24 There was a time when a man named Theudas came forth, boasting himself to be a prophet and saviour of the people.

5:25 A great multitude followed him and believed in his ways.

5:26 When he died, the multitudes scattered forth: and the power of Theudas ended, never to be a problem again.

5:27 There arose also a man named Judas of Galilee, who preached that he was sent forth by God to lead the people into a new world.

5:28 He also led a great multitude of ignorant men, who followed him blindly and worshipped his ways.

5:29 Judas was arrested and beheaded: and when his followers heard of his beheading, they took up arms and fought against those of Jerusalem, believing Judas a martyr.

5:30 These followers of Judas still bother us to this day, wishing to overthrow the Jews of which they once were.

5:31 Let this be a lesson for us; make not martyrs of madmen.

5:32 Allow these twelve to live out their lives; once they perish, then shall their ways end and bother us no more.

5:33 Better to have their ideals die with them, then make martyrs of them and deal with their fanatics and followers until the end of days."

5:34 The twelve were then gathered together and told never to speak the name of Christ; Peter specifically was told not to blame the death of Jesus upon the Jews, lest he be executed as a traitor to his people.

5:35 Then they were stripped naked and beaten with the whip: and as they were beaten with the whipped, they praised the name of Jesus for making them worthy to suffer for his name.

5:36 Bartholomew praised Jesus the most; of the apostles, he liked to be whipped.

5:37 He even paid the harlots to beat his ass with a leather rod.

5:38 Once the apostles departed, they were warned never to speak the name of Christ in the temple or in any of the houses of Judaea.

6:1 One of the disciples of Jesus was a man named Stephen; he was a young and arrogant fucker.

6:2 Despite the warnings of the priests, he would go to the temple and praise the name of Jesus while cursing the Jews for crucifying the son of God.

6:3 Then he would perform miraculous works in the name of Christ and attempt to convert the people of Jerusalem.

6:4 Men of the synagogue and from Cicilia and Asia came to him, to debate with him the prophesy of Jesus.

6:5 They argued to Stephen that the son of God called Christ was not predicted, for he was never mentioned once in the old texts.

6:6 But Stephen was the son of a lawyer and could make muddied the text so that it seemed that Jesus was predicted by the prophets of old.

6:7 The men grew angry at Stephen and came to the elders, saying, "We have heard Stephen blasphemy against the one true God." Stephen was then seized and brought before them.

6:8 When Stephen spoke to the elders, he said, "Be warned, you men of wickedness; Jesus of Nazareth shall come again, to destroy the very stones of this place.

6:9 The world will erupt in hell-fire and the damned will suffer for their arrogance and their refusal to abandon Judaism for the true religion."

6:10 A high priest asked Stephen, "Is all that you say true?" and Stephen answered, "Yes.

6:11 You wicked people who pierced the nail through the healing hand; let you all suffer by the wrath of God for your stubbornness.

6:12 Jesus did come to save us and bring us salvation: and you placed him atop the cross for all the world to see him die.

6:13 Tell me, you forked tongue vipers, what prophets did you not condemn. Of who sent by God did you not hate with all your heart?

6:14 And the elders started listing off names of the old prophets. "Elijah, Elisha, Samuel, Isaiah, Ezekiel, Hosea, Amos, Habakkuk, Zechariah, Micah, Nahum, Jonas, Joel, Haggai, Malachi, Zephiniah..."

6:15 But Stephen conveniently ignored the words which contradicted him; as lawyers tend to do.

6:16 He said, "They killed all those who predicted the coming of the son of God, who would show us the path of salvation: and now you have followed the ways of your fathers and slain Jesus, whom the prophets predicted.

6:17 May all the Jews suffer for their wickedness; may they be the people of hell and number greater than the heathens in the lake of fire."

6:18 With rage, Stephen then began to throw down the lamps, saying, "Let them all burn. Those wicked Jews."

6:19 The men became outraged and dragged Stephen outside; of those who saw Stephen, they believed him a lunatic.

6:20 A mob came and listened to the words of Stephen: and when they heard these words, they became angry and began to stone Stephen.

6:21 As Stephen was struck by the stones, he yelled at them, saying, "Stone me all you wish, you wicked devils, but know this.

6:22 Know that the lord Jesus Christ shall protect me from your wrath and that your stones, your arrows and your blades will not harm even a hair on my chin."

6:23 Saul, a devout Jew, was disgusted by the words of hate spoken by the disciples of Christ: and when he heard Stephen speak these words, he grabbed a rock and thrust it through the neck.

6:24 Stephen fell on the ground and died by the hands of Saul. Saul was pleased and wished all the people of Christ to die the same way.

7:1 Devout men of Christ came to gather the body of Stephen and

bury him according to the customs of Jesus.

7:2 As to what those customs were, they knew not; the cult of Jesus was still young and did not know how to properly bury their dead.

7:3 So they buried them according to the ways of Moses, which they were most familiar with.

7:4 Saul the destroyer of Stephen became a mighty man for the people of the Jews; he would preach the ways of old and slay by the sword any man who spoke evil against his people.

7:5 Philip, a follower of Christ who, like most of the followers of Christ, was born Jewish, preached the name of Christ to the people of Samaria.

7:6 Blessed by Jesus, Philip would cast out the devils from people, healing them of their diseases, curing the lame and restoring the crippled.

7:7 And those of Samaria were of great joy, thanks to Philip.

7:8 But at that time there was a man named Simon, who also cast out devils from people, healed them of their diseases, cured the lame and restored the crippled; but Simon did this not by the name of Jesus, but by sorcery and knowledge of the hidden.

7:9 When Philip heard of the sorcery of Simon, he said, "You followers of Christ, this man is a wicked sorcerer and an abomination of the name of God.

7:10 Go forth, slay him, so that your lands be rid of this evil."

7:11 But the people of Samaria were confused, saying, "How is this man wicked. Does he not do the same things you do?"

7:12 Philip answered, "He does, but he does it by the disgrace of God.

7:13 I heal you through the powers of Jesus, while he heals thee through sorcery and witchcraft.

7:14 When I heal you, I preach the name of Jesus and all that is good; when he heals you, he preaches nothing."

7:15 The people then mocked Philip, saying, "Then Simon is the better of the two; he heals us through the kindness of his heart, while you wish to convert us and baptize us into the cult of Jesus."

7:16 It was then Simon came to Philip and to the people said, "Condemn not this man, for he does only that which he thinks is good.

7:17 He heals you, cures you and restores you to whole; allow him to do these works, so that the earth be blessed by his ways.

7:18 It matters not if he preaches the name of Jesus; it matters only that he is a good man, who wishes you well and healthy in your lives."

7:19 Philip then said, "Of those who were baptized in the name of Christ, prove your devotion to the lord.

7:20 Take this wicked sorcerer and burn him."

7:21 Simon was then burned at the stake in the name of Christ; a custom which will last for many generations.

7:22 After the burning of Simon, an angel of the lord came to Philip and said, "Go forth, south of Jerusalem into the desert Gaza"

7:23 Philip did as he was told: and as he went, he met a man of Ethiopia, who was a eunuch under the charge of Candace the queen of Ethiopia.

7:24 And as Philip saw the eunuch, he was sitting in his chariot, reading the words of the prophet Esaias.

7:25 The spirit whispered in the ears of Philip, "Go now to this chariot and ride with him."

7:26 Philip ran to the eunuch and said, "You are a wise man, who studies the ways of the prophets.

7:27 Tell me, do you understand what the words of Esaias mean?"

7:28 It was then the eunuch cried and said, "It means my soul is damned forever and never shall I know the salvation of Zion.

7:29 I was born a eunuch; the body of a man but of the spirit of the woman.

7:30 According to the ways of Esaias, I am a queer and hated by the God of gods and king of kings."

7:31 Philip heard the words of the eunuch and said, "I am a follower of the son of God; a blessed man called Jesus of Nazareth.

7:32 Lead me to the waters, so that I may baptize you in the name of Christ; then shall the lord rid you of your sickness."

7:33 The eunuch then led the man to the river, where Philip baptized him in the name of Jesus: and as the waters flowed around the Ethiopian, he shouted, "Blessed be the name of Jesus. Blessed be the son of God."

7:34 When Philip brought forth the eunuch from the waters, a great wind surrounded him and carried him to the city of Azotus.

7:35 It was there Philip heard the words of Jesus, which said, "Never again baptize the queer and the gay in my name again, lest they think themselves saved.

7:36 The homosexuals are an abomination to both the lord and his son; let them suffer in the eternal hell-fire, where their unholy lust will be burned from them."

7:37 Philip agree, and promised never to baptize any more gay men.

7:38 The eunuch, however, believed that Jesus accepted his ways and began to preach that Jesus was the son of God to his queer friends.

7:39 They then began to praise the name of Jesus, saying, "Blessed be the son of God, who accepts us for who we are.

7:40 Truly he is a merciful God, who punishes not people for the spirits of their birth."

7:41 And through them, there became the first gay Christians; Jesus hates them.

8:1 Saul travelled throughout the lands, killing those who spoke out against Judaea and committed crimes of hate to his people.

8:2 Of both Gentiles and Christians he killed, if they spoke cruelly against the Jews; most of them were Christians.

8:3 As Saul journeyed towards Damascus, a bright light came before him, which blinded both he and his men.

8:4 A voice then spoke to Saul, saying, "Behold, why do you persecute against me?" And Saul only heard the voice; none of his men could hear him.

8:5 Saul answered, "Who are you. How can I persecute that who I don't know?"

8:6 The voice then answered, "I am the lord Jesus Christ, of whose followers you slay."

8:7 Saul began to laugh and said, "Was it not your father who blessed the Jews and made them his people?" and Jesus answered, "Yes."

8:8 Saul then said, "Then tell me, O son of God, why do your followers condemn us. Why are we suddenly hated and wicked in the eyes of the lord?"

8:9 Jesus paused for a moment and said, "We grew bored of the Jewish people. Let the new people of Christians rule the earth."

8:10 Suddenly, Saul shouted, "Tell me, should I abandon my people. Should I betray my family because they killed you?"

8:11 Jesus answered, "Of course. The Jews are wicked."

8:12 But Saul answered, "But how can they be. They did not hammer the nail into your wrists; they knew you not, nor did any harm against you for it was the Romans and not those of Israel who hammered the nails within you."

8:13 Jesus said to Saul, "That sort of talk reeks of logic; there shall be none of that in Christianity.

8:14 Now go to Damascus, lest the lord of the heavens deem you wicked and cast you into the void."

8:15 The light then left, leaving Saul blind.

8:16 Men of Saul led him by hand to Damascus, where he did not eat nor drink for three days.

8:17 Those who knew him came to him and said, "Eat, for the strength of Saul must be strong to protect the chosen of God against the new cult of Jesus."

8:18 Still, Saul did not eat; he was fearful for the words of Jesus and feared he shall betray his kin.

8:19 Ananias, a disciple of Christ, came to Saul and said, "Behold, I was sent here by the son of God to lead you to salvation.

8:20 Come with me and all shall be shown to you."

8:21 Ananias then led Saul to the house of the disciples, where by the blessing of Jesus they restored his sight and made him whole.

8:22 Saul, though angry, was a reasonable man and sat down to listen to the people of Jesus; perhaps they were not all anti-Semitic, but only a handful of fanatics who made filthy the rest.

8:23 The disciples then spoke and said, "Blessed Saul, the son of God has blessed you and shall bring you to salvation, if you follow him."

8:24 Saul asked what he must do to deserve salvation from Jesus and the disciples answered, "You must give up the ways of old and accept Christ as your lord and saviour."

8:25 Saul agreed, but said, "Tell me, what of the Jews. What shall happen to them?"

8:26 The disciples said, "The Jews are wicked men forged from the vulture's beak, who betrayed Jesus and slew him on the cross.

8:27 They must be punished for their wickedness and destroyed from the very face of the earth."

8:28 Saul spoke, "Why, though. Was it not only a handful of Jews who conspired against Jesus of Nazareth?

8:29 Are not the rest innocent and worthy of salvation as well?"

8:30 The disciples thought for some time and said, "If a Jew decides to convert and accept Jesus of Nazareth as their lord and saviour, then let them be saved.

8:31 Of the Jew who remains stubborn, behead them and let the lord of the heavens condemn them to damnation."

8:32 Saul disagreed and said, "You are a bunch of bloodthirsty savages, who wish to condemn those chosen by God."

8:33 He then reached into his cloak and took out his hidden dagger; but the disciples killed Saul before he could do any harm.

8:34 By the power of Christ, they then resurrected Saul whole and made him a devout follower of Christ.

8:35 Saul then immediately went to the synagogues, preaching the name of Christ and cursing the Jews.

8:36 Immediately the people became confused, saying, "Is that not Saul, a devout Jew who protected us from the fanatics of Christ?

8:37 He has betrayed us and his family to those of the Christians."

8:38 Still, Saul preached the word of Jesus and converted those of Damascus to the ways of Jesus, so that the disciples became even stronger in number.

8:39 Those priests of the synagogue of Damascus became worried and conspired against Saul so that they may kill him.

8:40 Saul, who accepted Christ and was willing to die in the name of Jesus, was not quite ready then to die for Jesus at that particular time; he escaped Damascus by a hole in the wall, where the disciples lowered him in a basket.

8:41 He then left for Jerusalem, where he preached the name of Jesus to all those who would listen.

8:42 Barnabas embraced Saul and said to the people, "Behold, once we were enemies and now we are brothers.

8:43 Such is the power of Jesus."

8:44 And the Christians rejoiced.

8:45 Peter, the head of the Christians, travelled throughout the lands praising the name of Jesus and condemning the Jews.

8:46 His family no longer recognized him and spat on the very dust where he walked.

8:47 When Peter came to Joppa, there was a disciple by the name of Tabitha; a blessed woman who spoke highly of the name of Jesus.

8:48 She was sick with the tremors and died.

8:49 As Peter heard this, he rushed to the body of Tabitha and said, "Cursed be the Jews, who killed Jesus and now kills his followers.

8:50 They have conspired with devils so that they may overtake us and slay us.

8:51 But let the power of Jesus strike down the cunningness of the Jews; let the power of Christ cast out the devils and leave them trembling in fear."

8:52 Immediately, Tabitha arose from the dead and blessed the name of Jesus.

8:53 And it was known all throughout Joppa that Peter had raised Tabitha from the dead, using the blessings of Jesus.

8:54 It was also known that Tabitha did not die of her sickness, but by the wickedness of the Jews.

8:55 Riots broke out in the streets and they stoned any person believed to be a Jew that conspired against the disciples of Christ.

8:56 When Tabitha spoke out against this, saying, "It was not the Jews who killed me, but the sickness I was stricken with since a child," nobody listened.

8:57 They were not the words they wished to hear.

9:1 It came to pass that Peter had a vision; in that vision, he was atop a tower, gazing into the heavens above.

9:2 Behold, a table came down and on it were all sorts of unclean flesh.

9:3 Of swine, shrimp, crabs, lobster, rabbit, bear, snakes and lizard there were on this table.

9:4 Then a voice from above said to Peter, "Arise; kill and eat."

9:5 But Peter refused, saying, "My lord, never will my lips touch that which is unclean."

9:6 Again, Peter had the vision; he was atop a tower, gazing into the clouds, when suddenly a basket came down carrying the shrimp from the sea.

9:7 Then a voice from above came forth and said, "Arise; kill and eat."

9:8 But Peter said, "My lord, never will my lips touch the disgusting flesh."

9:9 Peter spoke to his disciples about these visions; none knew what it meant.

9:10 A third night, Peter had the vision; he was atop the highest mountain, when a blanket came down carrying swine.

9:11 Then a voice came from the heavens, saying, "Arise; kill and eat."

9:12 But Peter said, "My lord, never will I eat the unclean flesh of the swine."

9:13 Now there came to Peter a man named Cornelius, who was of Roman blood; the Romans were hated by all the people of Judaea and surrounding lands.

9:14 This Roman came to Peter and said, "I have heard of the ways of Christ and believe truly he is the son of God.

9:15 Baptize me in the name of Jesus of Nazareth, so that I may be a holy disciple."

9:16 Peter then understood the visions, saying, "Behold, this man was once filthy in our eyes, but now through baptism is made clean."

9:17 He then baptized Cornelius, who immediately arose from the waters and praised the name of Christ.

9:18 The Christians rejoiced, for now all men may follow the ways of Christ no matter who they were.

9:19 They rejoiced even more, for now they could eat flesh denied to them by the Jews.

9:20 And they celebrated with a pig roast.

9:21 At the pig roast, Cornelius never mentioned the fact that he was a soldier when Jesus was crucified; he was one of the men who hammered the nails into the flesh of Christ.

9:22 For him, it was better that they believed the Jews killed Jesus;

he won't be hated that way.

10:1 Now the apostles that were in Judaea heard that the Gentiles received the word of Christ and wished to be disciples of Jesus.

10:2 But when the apostles learned the Gentiles were not circumcised, they began to think they were filthy.

10:3 It was then Peter rose and said, "My brothers, who is it that decides those with foreskin is wicked, but the people who are most wicked?

10:4 Let us rid ourselves of the ways of the past and embrace our brothers.

10:5 We eat now pork, shrimp and catfish; let us now dine with the uncircumcised.

10:6 Then we shall take the knife and remove the wicked skin from them, so that they may be accepted by God.

10:7 So long as they are baptized in the name of Christ, it matters not when their foreskin is removed; only that it be removed before the day of salvation."

10:8 And then the Gentiles came to the apostles, so that they may be baptized and circumcised in the name of Jesus of Nazareth.

10:9 When they returned home to their wives, they thought their circumcision foolish and made their genitals look like a mushroom.

10:10 They changed their minds that night; they praised the name of Jesus for removing the wicked foreskin from their husbands.

10:11 Now the disciples were scattered across the lands, in fear of persecution from the elders of Israel and Judaea.

10:12 Of those men there were a handful who preached not to the Gentiles, but to the Jews, so that they may offer salvation to their kin.

10:13 These men travelled as far as Phenice, Cyprus and Antioch, preaching the ways of Christ in the synagogues.

10:14 They were great speakers, who converted the multitudes of the wicked into the hands of Christ.

10:15 The church of Christ heard of the works of these men and sent forth Banabas to Antioch, so that he may cleave the people there to the lord.

10:16 For Barnabas was a tall and fearful man, who would slay those who did not convert to the ways of Jesus.

10:17 By the shedding of blood, Barnabas converted the city of Antioch, so that only Christians were left.

10:18 Prophets from Jerusalem then came to Antioch, the city of Christians, to escape persecution from the Jews.

10:19 And in Antioch it became custom for every man to sell his belongings and be given bread by the apostles according to their needs.

10:20 It was the first communist city.

11:1 Now Herod was the king of the Jews: and he stretched forth his hand to crush the church of Christianity.

11:2 He killed James the brother of John with the sword, which pleased the Jews who exalted him as a saviour against the fanatics of Christ.

11:3 During the Passover, Herod took in custody Peter, so that he may also be executed in front of the Jews.

11:4 When he was arrested, they placed him in the deepest dungeons and kept with him forty-eight guards to keep him until after Easter, when they wished to present him to them.

11:5 Yes, Easter. Even that early the Christians celebrated Easter.

11:6 They did so by eating rabbits, which were once denied but now made able to eat by the Christians.

11:7 They would eat the rabbits and say, "Thank you Jesus for giving us this delicious flesh which was denied to us for so long."

11:8 Then they would paint eggs. Nobody knows why they painted eggs, they just did.

11:9 It was a custom that even during the early days of Easter nobody understood.

11:10 Now Peter was furious, for he wished to celebrate Easter with the apostles and paint for them the brightest egg.

11:11 On the night before Easter, Peter was bound by chains to the wall, with two guards beside him, guarding him.

11:12 It was then an angel of the lord came to Peter and turned his chains to dust, saying, "Arise, Peter and go.

11:13 Gird yourself, put on your sandals and follow me."

11:14 The angel then led Peter out of the iron gates of the prison, blinding the guards so that they could not see them.

11:15 Peter ran to the house of Mary the mother of John, saying, "Surely the lord has blessed me and delivered me away from the hands of Herod."

11:16 When he knocked on the door of the house, a slave girl named Rhoda heard his voice and ran to the disciples, saying, "It is Peter at the door!"

11:17 Yes, a slave girl. Jesus had no problem with slavery. Fucking douche.

11:18 Anyway, when the disciples heard the words of Rhoda, they beat her, saying, "You are surely a mad woman and hear the voice of ghosts."

11:19 But the knocking of Peter became louder and his voice grew stronger, saying, "Let me in, so I can eat some rabbit and paint my eggs."

11:20 When the disciples saw Peter, they were astonished; they let him in and blessed the lord for guiding Peter away from the wrath of the Jews.

11:21 They then ate their rabbit, their swine and painted their eggs: and Peter painted the brightest blue egg of all.

11:22 In the morning, when it was discovered that Peter had escaped from the dungeons, Herod questioned the guards and asked, "How is it that you could let this leader of the Christian cult escape?"

11:23 The guards could not answer, but only said that they kept their eyes on Peter all their days, then he just vanished before them.

11:24 Herod feared Peter to be a sorcerer and said, "We are dealing now with a cult who has with them the knowledge of the hidden; they are an enemy to be feared."

11:25 He then left Judaea to dwell in Caesarea and told the guards to kill any Christian fanatic that speaks harshly against the Jews.

11:26 Now Herod was angered against Tyre and Sidon for keeping within their borders the Christians; but they came to him of one accord, to make peace with Herod.

11:27 Yes, Tyre still existed; it was not completely destroyed by the hands of Nebuchadnezzar, according to the prophesies of Ezekiel.

11:28 This made Ezekiel a joke amongst the scholars of Jerusalem, who would travel to Tyre and say, "Behold, the destroyed; gaze on how the rubble appears as buildings."

11:29 When Herod made peace with the peoples of Tyre and Sidon, he spoke to the people of Jerusalem.

11:30 With his royal apparel, he stood before the congregation of Judaea, who shouted, "Behold, it is the man who protects us from the wicked son of God."

11:31 And when Jesus heard this, he came down and struck Herod, who fell dead before the people of Jerusalem.

11:32 Immediately his corpse began to rot and his flesh was consumed by the unholy worms of hell.

11:33 When the people saw this, they began to fear Jesus and converted to the ways of the Christians.

12:1 Now in the church of Antioch were certain prophets and teachers; Barnabas, Simeon called Niger, Lucius of Cyrene, Manaen and Saul.

12:2 As they spread the name of Jesus to the people, the holy ghost came upon them and said, "We must separate Barnabas and Saul,

for they have work to do elsewhere."

12:3 Led by the holy ghost, they came to the docks of Seleucia and from there departed to Cyprus.

12:4 In Cyprus, they preached the word of Christ in the synagogues, converting the Jews and the Gentiles to Christianity.

12:5 At the synagogue of Salamis they converted even a high priest named John, who began to minister the name of Jesus to his congregation.

12:6 Upon the isle of Paphos they preached, but the people mocked them and their miracles, saying, "We have a man who calls himself the son of Jesus, who does such things as heal the sick and raise the dead.

12:7 If Jesus were the son of God, how could he then lie with a mortal woman and give to her a son?"

12:8 Barnabas and Simeon went to the man who called himself the son of Jesus; a Jew named Barjesus.

12:9 When they looked on him, they saw that his features were like that of Jesus: and they feared this man to be the bastard son of Jesus.

12:10 In secret, they took Barjesus and slew him; they then said to the peoples of Paphos, "Behold, this man was not the son of Jesus, but an imposter.

12:11 Now the lord has caused him to die, so that his ghost may forever be tormented by the eternal damnation."

12:12 Hearing the words of Barnabas and Saul, the deputy of the county, named Sergius Paulus, sent for the two apostles, so that he may listen to the word of God.

12:13 But Elymas the sorcerer and friend of Barjesus stopped them and said, "Be gone, you wicked men who hides the dagger of Satan beneath their cloak.

12:14 It was you two who slew Barjesus in secret and now preach that it was the hand of God who killed him for blasphemy.

12:15 Be gone, wicked men and do not spread your deceit in these lands."

12:16 Barnabas wished to reason to Elymas, saying, "My brother, it was through the hands of Jesus that Barjesus died for his blasphemy.

12:17 Are we not the disciples of Jesus. Is it not through our hands that the work of the lord be done?"

12:18 But Elymas refused to let them pass, saying, "If the work of Jesus demands murder, then it is the work we wish not be done."

12:19 Saul, an impatient man, hit Elymas, and shouted, "Be gone, you sorcerer of forked tongue and let the lord do his work."

12:20 It was then that the power of Jesus struck Elymas with blindness and took from him his knowledge of the arcane.

12:21 When the deputy saw this, he condemned the two disciples, saying, "Be gone from our lands, you men of wicked virtues.

12:22 I wished to listen to your ways and seek forth knowledge and wisdom from the ways of Christ; but now I see the ways of Christ are cruel.

12:23 Get away from my people and never return unless it is for your execution."

12:24 It was then the people of Paphos gathered and laid persecution against the Christians within their lands.

12:25 Saul declare the peoples of Paphos to be as wicked as the Jews and said, "These lands are not worthy for even the blade of grass to live within."

12:26 He then cursed the lands of Paphos, condemning it and their people to hell.

13:1 In Iconium a great number of both the Jews and Greeks were brought together by the words of Christ, becoming brothers under the church.

13:2 But the unbelieving Jews began to mix trouble with the Gentiles and whispered in their ears wickedness against the people of Christ.

13:3 The city became divided, so that half were loyal to the apostles and the ways of Christianity and the other loyal to the Jews and the ways of old.

13:4 Both sides were tense, ever fearful that the other would attack and destroy them.

13:5 The apostles, being cowards, left the city of Iconium to preach the gospel someplace safer, away from the threat of war.

13:6 Into the lands of Lycaonia they fled, preaching the word of Christ in the cities of Lystra and Derbe.

13:7 In Lystra there was a cripple, lame since his mother's womb.

13:8 This cripple heard Saul speak and said to him, "I challenge you; if your words be true, then heal me so that I may walk."

13:9 Saul came to the man and said, "Then stand up, walk and bow down unto the workers of Jesus Christ."

13:10 Behold, the crippled arose and said, "Holy shit, these people have cured me of my lameness.

13:11 Glory to the workers of Christ. Glory be to Jesus of Nazareth."

13:12 They then believed Saul and Barnabas to be gods themselves; they named Saul Jupiter and Barnabas Mercurius.

13:13 The chief of Jupiter presented to them gifts of goats, oxen, pigs, wine, clothing and virgins.

13:14 The two apostles took these gifts and said, "We shall tell them we are not gods, tomorrow.

13:15 Today, let us feast and enjoy the lust of Greek virgins; they love it up the ass."

13:16 As Barnabas and Saul fucked the virgins given to them, Jews from Iconium came to the city and said, "These two men you worship are not gods, but bringers of evil."

13:17 The Greeks took the two men and asked them, "Tell me, are you the gods Jupiter and Mercurius?" and they both answered, "No."

13:18 For fooling them, they had them stoned to death: and they dragged the bodies out of the city, believing them to be dead.

13:19 Both men arose, renewed with the spirit of Jesus: and they entered the city, saying, "How dare you let the wicked tongue of the Jews deceive your ears.

13:20 Rid yourself of their whoredoms and worship the lord Jesus Christ."

13:21 The Greeks, who were easy to convince, then bowed down to Barnabas and Saul and began to worship Jesus.

13:22 They cast out the Jews by the whip, killing any of them whose hands they could lay upon.

13:23 Jesus was quite pleased.

14:1 Now the Gentiles began to read the words of the gospels and of the prophets of old who told of the coming of Christ.

14:2 And the Gentiles became fearful, for in the old texts it says that those who are uncircumcised will not be saved by the grace of God.

14:3 They came to the apostles and asked them, "Tell us, are we wicked in the eyes of God because our foreskin remains upon us?"

14:4 Disciples of Jesus did not know; some answered yes, while others answered no.

14:5 Then the Gentiles asked, "Can we be saved if we remove our foreskins now and please the lord by ridding ourselves of this wicked skin he gave us at birth?"

14:6 Again, the disciples of Jesus were confused; some answered yes, by circumcising themselves now they would be saved.

14:7 Others said no, that it matters not if your foreskin remains, while others also said it matters not, because their foreskin was not removed at the right time.

14:8 Of those who turned to Christ and were uncircumcised, they began to weep and say, "Tell us, what does the lord demand we do with our foreskins?"

14:9 The disciples of Jesus did not know and gathered together in Jerusalem with the twelve apostles to discuss what should be done about the followers of Christ who were not separated from their foreskins.

14:10 And the great penis debate began.

14:11 Some said that if they circumcised now, it shall be a test of their faith; a sign of devotion to Jesus of Nazareth.

14:12 Some said that it was too late for them; if they are uncircumcised now, then they shall remain forever wicked in the eyes of God.

14:13 Peter said, "It matters not if the foreskin remains or not; only that they obey the words of Jesus and rid the world of the wicked Jews.

14:14 Of who is it that demands the circumcision of men, but the Jews. Let us separate ourselves from them and have remain our foreskins intact."

14:15 But Philip said, "Then what of us who were circumcised according to the custom of the Jews. Does this make us wicked in the eyes of Christ?"

14:16 Peter reluctantly said no; he was born a Jew and on is eighth day after birth was circumcised according to the laws of Moses.

14:17 Bartholomew asked of the people, "What if they removed only half their foreskins?" To which it was agreed, "Then they would only be half saved."

14:18 James, who was extremely homophobic and became uncomfortable speaking at the great penis debate, said, "Why does it matter if the Gentiles cut the foreskin from them or not?

14:19 So long as they follow the ways of Christ, it matters not if their genitals way a few extra grams.

14:20 Have them circumcise themselves from false gods, idols, sins of the flesh and the pollution of blood; then they shall be saved by Christ and have their foreskin remain."

14:21 And so it was agreed that so long as the people be good Christians, it matters not if they are circumcised.

14:22 And James became known as the one who settled the penis debate; he was called the wisest prick amongst all.

14:23 The Gentiles became relieved; they wished not to circumcise themselves.

14:24 They were willing to show their devotion to Jesus, but wished not to put a knife to their loins.

14:25 The women, however, were disappointed; they heard that the Jews were great lovers and that the circumcised loins felt great when thrust within them.

14:26 So they went out and found Jewish men to lie with: and the Christians then accused the wicked Jews of stealing their women and killed them.

14:27 When Jesus saw the Jews dead, he was pleased; so was his father.

14:28 Saul, who was now named Paul because he spoke with a lisp, travelled with Barnabas preaching the word of Jesus to the Gentiles: and now that the Gentiles did not need to be circumcised, they converted in great numbers.

14:29 Paul said to Barnabas, "Let us go to the cities from which we first preached, to see the strength of Christ within those we converted."

14:30 Barnabas agreed and said, "Let us take also John named Mark with us," but Paul disagreed.

14:31 Paul hated John named Mark, for in the great penis debate it was proven John named Mark had a bigger penis than Paul once named Saul.

14:32 And like the lord, Paul was a jealous man.

14:33 So Barnabas took John named Mark and went to Cyprus, while Paul took Silas and went to Silas, so that they may confirm the strength of their churches.

15:1 When Paul arrived at the city of Lyrsta, there was a disciple by the name of Timotheus; the son of a Jew who believed in Christ, but whose father was a Greek.

15:2 Through all Derbe, Lyrsta and Iconium it was known that Timotheus was fathered by a Greek: and Timotheus felt great shame for this.

15:3 His brethren would mock him, saying, "There goes Timotheus the half-Greek; he only takes it partway in the ass."

15:4 When Timotheus saw Paul, he ran to him and said, "Please, make me a full Christian, so that the Greek within me be cast down into the fires.

15:5 I want the unholy lust of the Greeks to be cut away from me; do this and I shall forever be in your debt."

15:6 Now Paul, though Christian, was not that stupid a man and said, "How can ye possibly cut away the Greek from you. Your father was a Greek man, thus the blood of the Greeks flow through you.

15:7 It cannot be removed, lest I shed all your blood and replace it with another."

15:8 But still, Timotheus said, "I beg of you, if my blood must be shed to rid me of the Greek, then so be it.

15:9 Remove the Greek from me, so that I may be a proud Christian and know not the shame of my father."

15:10 Paul asked Timotheus to remove his raiment and stand before him: and as Timotheus stood naked before Paul, Paul took out his knife and circumcised Timotheus.

15:11 Once Timotheus stopped screaming and trembling on the floor (Paul took a little more than the foreskin), he arose and embraced Paul, saying,

15:12 "Now you have rid me of the wickedness of the Greeks; I shall follow you wherever you go and praise the name of Jesus."

15:13 So Timotheus joined Paul in spreading the gospels throughout the lands.

15:14 When Paul found that the churches he established were strong and fought hard against the Jews, he went forth with Timotheus to spread the name of Jesus in foreign lands.

15:15 They went through the regions of Phrygia and Galatia, so that they may enter the lands of Asia; but the spirit of Jesus stopped them.

15:16 The son of God said, "Speak not to the yellow devils of Asia, nor teach them the ways of Jesus.

15:17 These are wicked men, who cannot be saved by the powers of Christ; that and they keep pronouncing my name Jeebus.

15:18 How can they be saved by the lord when they can't even pronounce the lord's name?"

15:19 So the two disciples went to the lands of Bithynia: but the spirit of the lord stopped them there as well, saying, "Save not the people of Bithynia; they are not worth your time."

15:20 It was decided that they go to Macedonia and preach to the heathens there.

15:21 As they entered Philippi, the chief city of Macedonia, they saw a woman who sold purple.

15:22 This woman worshipped the lord God, but was not baptized by the disciples of Christ; she instead bathed herself in the river and believed herself washed of sin.

15:23 Paul came up to her and said, "You wicked woman who believes herself worthy of forgiveness; how can one baptize themselves in the name of the lord?"

15:24 And the woman answered, "Holy worker of Christ, there was none around worthy to baptize me and I was but one woman in the multitude of unbelievers.

15:25 Who could save me when I was surrounded by filth. How can only the lord Jesus Christ wash away my sins from the muck of this place?"

15:26 And Paul said, "You are a woman of faith, but received not the guidance for salvation; come with me and I shall baptize you proper."

15:27 The woman denied Paul, saying, "The lord Jesus has seen in my heart that I was baptized and shall save me when he returns from Zion.

15:28 I need not be baptized again; I am a follower of Christ."

15:29 That woman now burns in hell, sent there by the hand of Jesus himself; apparently, you do need to be properly baptized to receive salvation.

15:30 Now in Macedonia was a woman possessed with the spirit of divination; the spirit would work through her and tell the futures of those who paid her.

15:31 When Paul and Timotheus saw the spirit, they struck her and said, "Be gone, you seed of devils!"

15:32 And the woman was no longer able to see the fortunes of men.

15:33 Instead of being grateful, she said of Paul and Timotheus, "These men have taken away my gift, which kept me clothed and fed my children."

15:34 When she told the guards of this, they arrested the disciples, keeping them chained in the dungeons.

15:35 At midnight Paul and Timotheus prayed; nothing happened.

15:36 At noon Paul and Timotheus prayed again; nothing happened.

15:37 Frustrated, Paul yelled to the heavens, "I know you can hear me, Jesus, now will you get your ass down here and fucking do something?"

15:38 When Jesus heard this, he sent an earthquake which shook the dungeons and released the chains from Paul and Timotheus; the earthquake also happened to break the bones in their legs.

15:39 Guards of the prison came in with torch and swords drawn, ready to slay those who tried to escape; but Paul said to them, "Fear not, for we are still here."

15:40 Believing this to be a merciful act of God, the guards bowed down and said, "Tell me, what must I do to be accepted by Christ?"

15:41 Both Paul and Timotheus said, "First, you must be baptized in the holy name of Christ by a disciple of Jesus."

15:42 So the guards took Paul and Timotheus to the river, where they baptized the prison guards in the name of Christ.

15:43 They asked again, "What else must I do to be accepted by Christ?" and the disciples answered, "You must take us to a physician in secret, so that our legs may be healed."

15:44 So the guards took them to Luke the physician, who healed their legs and mended their bones.

15:45 When asked again what they must do to be saved, Paul answered, "You must be ready to die in the name of Christ.

15:46 Fear not, for those who die in the name of Jesus are rewarded in heaven for their martyrdom; they are given choice lands, strong wine and beautiful women."

15:47 When asked how many women, they replied, "Seventy-two beautiful virgins."

15:48 One of the guards said, "Why would I want virgins. They know not how to please a man.

15:49 Give me whores and I shall die in the name of Jesus."

15:50 And it was then that guard died by the hands of Paul.

15:51 Paul then said to the rest of the guards, "We are the servants of Jesus of Nazareth; holy men who do the lord's work.

15:52 Let us go and tell no person of where we went; then shall you truly be accepted by Christ."

15:53 So the guards let them go: and when they returned, they told their superiors that the prisoners fled in the confusion of the earthquake.

15:54 The guards were then executed for incompetence.

15:55 As they were executed, they believed they would ascend into heaven, to be greeted by the seventy-two beautiful virgins.

15:56 And they did ascend into heaven and were greeted by the seventy-two virgins; they remain virgins to this day.

15:57 They don't put out.

16:1 Now when Paul passed through Amphilopis and Apollonia, he came to Thessalonica, where there was a synagogue for the Jews.

16:2 And Paul, with his usual arrogance, taught at the synagogue for three Sabbaths, preaching the name of Jesus and curing the wickedness of the Jews.

16:3 Saying that Christ suffered at the hands of the Hebrews, only to rise again once his people betrayed him.

16:4 There were some that believed the words of Paul, being baptized by both Paul and Silas; a great many of them were Greeks and women.

16:5 But of the stubborn Jews who believed not the words of Christ, they were fearful that the words of hate said by Paul would cause them great danger.

16:6 They gathered together in the city a great number of them and spoke against the Christians, saying, "We are a peaceful people; why must the Christians slay us in genocide?"

16:7 They then went to the house of Jason, who was once a devout Jew but now spoke the words of Paul against his brethren.

16:8 They accused Jason of blasphemy and betrayal, taking him to the rulers of the city, saying, "This man cares not for the words of Caesar, but believed the dead man Jesus to be king."

16:9 Those who ruled the city let Jason go and offered him security from the mobs of the Jews.

16:10 They who ruled the city loathed the Jews and wished Christians to destroy them of this nuisance.

16:11 Paul and Silas were invited to the house of the rulers, where they taught them the ways of Jesus, of the resurrection of Christ and the path to salvation.

16:12 Most of the men hearkened not their words and believed them to be a superstitious lot that worshipped a zombie; but the women were baptized in the name of Christ.

16:13 The women of Greece love Jesus and see him as a sex symbol; they mistook the resurrection of Jesus to be an erection; the rising of the loins instead of the rising from the grave.

16:14 When Paul was finished converting the people of Thessalonica and lying with the women who viewed Jesus as a sign of lust, he travelled to Athens to preach there.

16:15 As he spoke in the synagogues of Athens, the people there mocked him, believing him to be a drunk babbler and insane prophet.

16:16 Others believed him to worship strange gods; men who are the son of the lord of lords who were once dead but now risen from the grave.

16:17 They called him the zombie worshipper.

16:18 When Paul heard these murmurs of the people of Athens, he grew furious and shouted, "You superstitious men of demons, who bow down to idols as though they are lords.

16:19 How can the marble statues which fill this city aid you. How can chiselled rock offer you salvation from damnation?"

16:20 The men of Athens laughed and said, "How can a dead man give us salvation from Hades, when he swims in the river Styx?"

16:21 Paul said, "Because he has risen from the river and dwells now in Zion, where he shall return on the appointed day to judge the people of the earth."

16:22 Most of the men of Athens mocked Paul and told him to return when Jesus was with him; then he can prove that the path to salvation is led by a zombie.

16:23 But a few men believed the words of Paul and were baptized in the name of Christ; they kept this secret from their brethren of Athens, so that they not be mocked.

17:1 After Athens Paul came to the city of Corinth, to preach the name of Jesus.

17:2 There he met a Jew named Aquila, born in Pontus of Italy, with his wife Priscilla; and they knew each other by craft, for they were both tent-makers.

17:3 When Aquila asked Paul about his slaying of the Christians, he answered, "My brother, I was wrong to slay the workers of Christ and have now become them.

17:4 It is the stubborn Jew who must be slew by the sword; they denied themselves the prophets of old and murdered the son of God sent to save them."

17:5 Aquila, knowing Paul to be a wrathful man who would behead him if he disagreed, said, "Then tell me of the ways of Christ, so that I may be saved by your sword."

17:6 Paul then invited him to the synagogue, where he preached the ways of Jesus every Sabbath.

17:7 Together with Silas and Timotheus, the three disciples preached that Jesus was Christ the son of God and that the Jews must convert or be judged for the death of the messiah.

17:8 Obviously, the Jews didn't like this; they accused the three of blasphemy and called them wicked devils who worked to destroy the chosen of God.

17:9 Paul took off his raiment's and shook the dust from them, saying, "You wicked Jews are not worth the dust on my linen; I shall now go to the Gentiles.

17:10 Let the Jews remain damned."

17:11 He then left to the house of Justus, a devout Christian who also preached and baptized those who wish to know Christ.

17:12 Crispus, the chief ruler of the synagogue, came to Paul and was also baptized so that he may be washed clean from the sins of the Jews.

17:13 But mainly, he just wanted to eat pork.

17:14 When Paul made it known he wished to leave the city for fear that the Jews would kill him, Christ came to him in a vision, saying,

17:15 "Fear not the Jews of this city, for I have many men here.

17:16 Stay and be protected by the son of God."

17:17 So Paul stayed and continued preaching the name of Jesus and cursing the people of the Jews for one year and six months.

17:18 After that time, the Jews became furious with his words of hate; they grabbed Paul by the hair and led him out of the city, telling him never to return.

17:19 Paul then shaved off his head, saying, "The wickedness of the Jews has made filthy my hair; let me be bald, so that I may be clean in the eyes of Christ."

17:20 He then took the hair and burned it, saying, "For every strand of hair that burns before me, let a thousand Jews burn in its place when the wrath of the lord comes."

17:21 Paul then left for Ephesus, where he preached the name of Christ in the synagogue.

17:22 The Jews there were interested in the words of Paul and said, "Stay longer, so that we may know the path of Christ and be baptized in his holy name."

17:23 But he did not stay, saying, "How can I trust the people who wish me and my brethren dead?

17:24 I shall return in some time; if you wish then to be baptized, then let the blessed waters wash you clean of sin upon my return."

17:25 Now there was a Jew named Apollo, born in Alexandria; a wealthy man who was in Ephesus when he heard the words of Paul.

17:26 He became a devout Christian and preached the name of Jesus in the synagogue every Sabbath.

17:27 When Aquila and Priscilla heard the words of Apollo, they cleaved Jesus to their breast and were baptized in the holy name.

17:28 They then began to speak against the wickedness of the Jews and demanded all those of the Jewish people be burned alive.

17:29 They were immediately shunned by their families

18:1 It came to pass that, while Apollo preached in Corinth, Paul travelled to the upper coast of Ephesus, where he found some disciples.

18:2 He asked these men, "When you were baptized, did you receive the holy ghost?" and they answered, "No, we have not even heard of this holy ghost."

18:3 So Paul took them to the waters and baptized them again in the name of Christ; and when he baptized them, he buried them deep in the waters and choked them beneath the current.

18:4 When they rose from the waters, they spoke in gibberish: and Paul said, "These men now have received the holy ghost."

18:5 And he baptized all the disciples in this manner, twelve in all.

18:6 The Christians believed them blessed men, touched by the holy ghost; physicians called them retarded, with damaged brains due to lack of oxygen.

18:7 He then came to Ephesus, where for three months he preached the word of Jesus at the synagogue.

18:8 The peoples mocked him, saying, "You are not a prophet of the messiah, but a sorcerer learned in the arts of magic."

18:9 We have men like you in this city and they wish no genocide of the Jews.

18:10 It was then Paul blessed his raiment and said, "If I be a sorcerer, then how can even my raiment's now cure the sick and the lame?"

18:11 He then sold strips of his cloth for forty pieces of silver: and the cloth was believed to cure any person merely by touching them.

18:12 They did not.

18:13 Now there came a band of travelling Jews; exorcists who would cast out demons from madmen.

18:14 They came once to a madman and yelled, "By the name of all that is holy, leave this man and be forever trapped in the domain of hell."

18:15 The demon did nothing.

18:16 Again, the exorcists tried to take out the demon, yelling, "You are a wicked and unclean beast not of this earth; be gone from this man and never return."

18:17 But the demon still did nothing.

18:18 Desperate, one of the exorcists yelled, "By the name of Paul and Jesus, get out of this man."

18:19 Then the evil spirit answered through the man, "I have heard of Paul and have met Jesus, but who the fuck are you guys?"

18:20 He then leapt from the bed and killed the exorcists. The possessed man then left the house where he was kept, naked and badly injured.

18:21 When Paul heard of this, he said, "This man was not cast out in the name of Christ, but was cursed by the ways of Jewish sorcery and witchcraft.

18:22 Let these wicked people burn, who mock the ways of the disciples."

18:23 The people of the city then gathered every fortune teller, necromancer, sorcerer, wizard and divine healer who was not a Christian and stoned them to death.

18:24 Then the books of these people, which in them were written the knowledge of the arcane, were burned in a great fire.

18:25 In this way no other can learn the ways of magic, unless blessed by Jesus of Nazareth.

18:26 The value of the books were over fifty thousand pieces of silver; the value of the burned people was worth nothing.

18:27 People have no value, unless slaves.

18:28 After the book burning and the execution, the word of God prevailed and a great many were baptized in the name of Jesus.

18:29 Now there was a man named Demetrius, a silversmith who carved out idols of the lord Diana.

18:30 He and other silversmiths became poor, since few people now bought these idols and worshipped them.

18:31 They gathered together in union and said, "Great is the goddess Diana, who protects the people of Asia.

18:32 Worship her and be blessed."

18:33 The people then bought the idols of Diana as trinkets and ornaments.

18:34 When Alexander heard this, he spoke out, saying, "The worship of idols is a sin and shall send you to the fires of damnation."

18:35 The Christians then became fearful, believing that owning these idols would anger the lord Jesus.

18:36 But then Paul said, "We are not worshipping these idols, but only own them for decoration.

18:37 Is it sinful to wear a chain of silver or a necklace of gold. Why then is it sinful to own a statue of silver, so long as you not offer it sacrifice?"

18:38 The Christians agreed and said, "These idols are not gods, but a reminder of the heathens we must save from their ignorance.

18:39 Let the statues of Diana be in every Christian house, so that they may know others know not the ways of Christ and must be baptized of their sins."

18:40 They then killed Alexander, calling him a Jew who wished to make filthy the name of Jesus.

19:1 After the uproar was ceased, Paul and his disciples departed Troas during the time of unleavened bread.

19:2 For many weeks Paul taught at the synagogue, preaching the word of Christ and spreading hatred towards the Jews.

19:3 Many people gathered together to listen to the words of Paul: and when they realized Paul would speak for ages, they wished to leave.

19:4 But the disciples would gather round them and force them to stay and listen to the words of Paul, lest the wrath of Jesus be upon them.

19:5 So they sat in the synagogue for days, listening to the words of Paul.

19:6 A young man sat in the upper chambers of the synagogue, listening to Paul preach.

19:7 He became so bored that he fell asleep: and as he fell asleep, his body came forward and fell from the chambers.

19:8 Many men gathered around the young man; not to help him, but to see him.

19:9 They were bored of the words of Paul and the death of this young man was quite entertaining.

19:10 When Paul went to the man, he said, "Stand back, for there is still life in this young man."

19:11 He then breathed in the nostrils of the young man and pushed upon his breast, until the young man was brought back to life by the blessing of Christ.

19:12 When the people asked him how he fell, he said, "I fell in death on my seat and my body came forth from the chambers.

19:13 The words of Paul were so dull that they bored me to death."

19:14 Paul accused him of being a wicked Jew and demanded he be stoned to death.

19:15 And those in the synagogue, both Christian, Gentile and Jew stoned the young man; after being bored by Paul, it was great fun for them to kill someone with stones.

19:16 And the custom of being bored to death in church continues to this day.

19:17 Don't believe me. Go to church.

20:1 It came to pass that Paul came to the city of Caesarea, where he stayed at the house of Philip the evangelist, who was one of the seven remaining apostles.

20:2 This man had four virgin daughters who prophesied the name of Jesus.

20:3 Paul said to Philip, "Keep your daughters pure from the lust of men, lest they lose the talent to prophesy."

20:4 So Philip made belts of chastity for his four daughters, so that they remain virgins until the end of days.

20:5 They broke the chains of their chastity belts and became harlots; though they lost their skill the prophesy, they faked it.

20:6 Most prophets did anyway.

20:7 And as Paul admired the virgin daughters of Philip, there came from Judaea a prophet named Agabus.

20:8 He stripped Paul of his garments and bound him with them, saying, "Thus sayeth the lord; the Jews of Jerusalem shall bind the man which owns these raiment's and deliver him into the hands of the Gentiles."

20:9 At the request of Paul, Agabus then beat him with a whip and called him a dirty little Jew.

20:10 When the disciples heard the words of Agabus, they begged Paul not to enter Jerusalem, for fear he shall die by the hands of the wicked.

20:11 But Paul was a stubborn man, who said, "If I must die in Jerusalem, then so be it.

20:12 I shall do the work of the lord and die in the name of Christ, so long as it spreads forth the name of Jesus and brings death upon the wickedness of the Jews."

20:13 Mnason of Cyprus came with Paul, to protect him along his journey to Jerusalem: and as they arrived in Jerusalem, they stayed with James the disciple of Paul, who hid him from the elders.

20:14 For seven days Paul spoke in the temple, saying, "Wicked are the Jews, who murdered the son of God and denied themselves the path of salvation.

20:15 Come to me, you Gentiles and cleanse yourself from their filth; be baptized in the name of Christ and do the lord's bidding."

20:16 For seven days Paul preached these things, annoying both Jew and Gentile which dwelt in Jerusalem.

20:17 Some Jews of Asia conspired against him and laid hands on him as he spoke in the temple.

20:18 As those of Asia bound and gagged him, Paul yelled, "Save me from the wickedness of these people, for they are both Jews and yellow devils."

20:19 Nobody in the crowd went to lend a hand to Paul; they all believed him a racist lunatic.

20:20 And when people accused you of racism during those days, you knew you were one racist motherfucker.

20:21 When the people of Jerusalem carried Paul out to stone him, the chief captain came with centurions and soldiers to wonder who this man was that the crowds were beating.

20:22 They took Paul from the crowds, bound him with chains and carried him to the dungeons, all the while with Paul asking them to beat him with the blunt end of their swords and call him a dirty Jew.

20:23 When they asked Paul why the crowds hated him with such fury, he held his tongue and said nothing.

20:24 They then led Paul to the judges, so that he may be tried by the elders of Jerusalem.

20:25 As he was carried, Paul asked the chief captain, "May I speak to the people once more?" and the guard asked, "Why would you do such a thing?

20:26 For what reason would you have to speak to the people who dragged you to the wilderness, so that you may be killed with stones?

20:27 I cannot think of one person in Jerusalem who does not wish you dead."

20:28 But Paul said, "I was once a Jew, born in the city of Cicilia and am now a citizen of no land.

20:29 I beseech you, let me speak once more to the people."

20:30 The chief gave him license to speak to the people. Paul stood on the stairs and beckoned the people with his hands, speaking to them in Hebrew.

21:1 When Paul spoke to the people of Jerusalem, he said, "My brothers, hear me and know that I am of the lord.

21:2 On the day I came to this earth, I was born a Jew of Tarsus, in the city of Cicilia and raised according to the ways of Moses and the fathers of old.

21:3 When I heard of these Christians and how they wished to slay the Jews for wickedness, my heart became full of wrath and my foreskin regrown.

21:4 With blade and dagger I slaughtered both men, women and child who devoted themselves to the faith of Christ; no person was shown mercy. I made them suffer those I could find.

21:5 Then on my travels I was blinded by a light; it was the light of Jesus, the son of God, who spoke to me but denied his words to my men.

21:6 He asked me why I hated him so and why I persecuted him so harshly with my blade.

21:7 With blind eyes, I was told to head towards Damascus, where the lord will renew me and revive me in the righteous ways.

21:8 A disciple of Christ, a man named Ananias, came to restore my sight, so that I may see the truth; that truth is that Jesus is the messiah and the Jews are devils for killing him.

21:9 Thus I made haste to all the lands, to baptize those in the name of Christ and slaughter the Jews which denied Jesus in their hearts.

21:10 A long and bloody path I walked, but it was the path laid out to me by God and follow it I must.

21:11 It came to pass that a prophet then came to me and bound me with my girdle, saying that I shall be bound by the devils in Jerusalem and delivered to the hands of the Gentiles.

21:12 Now here I am, in shackles before you, as the prophet Agabus proclaimed.

21:13 Tell me, does this not prove that Jesus is the lord and I am his prophet?"

21:14 The people of Jerusalem mocked him, saying, "You are lying, wicked man.

21:15 Take him away, so that he may be meat for the lions."

21:16 But the centurions did not take him away for execution; when they found out he was born in Cicilia, they knew him to be a Roman.

21:17 In fear, the chief captain freed Paul, saying, "As a man of Roman blood, may you be free."

21:18 Paul then demanded that on the morrow, he be brought before the priests and the council to speak with them.

22:1 When Paul stood before the council, he said to them, "My brethren, I have lived my days in the name of God, doing his will upon the earth.

22:2 I have brought light to the Gentile and darkness upon the Jews; I have given you salvation where before there were none."

22:3 It was then the high priest Ananias commanded Paul watch his words of hate, lest he be struck in the mouth.

22:4 And Paul said, "To hell with you, Ananias and to hell with you all.

22:5 God himself shall come down to smite you, for judging a man of his works.

22:6 I will not be condemned by the peoples who eat with the Sadduccees and the Pharisees; my father was a Pharisee and I struck him down for his wickedness."

22:7 Upon these words, the people again wished him dead; who but a wicked man could slay their own father, yet call a people wicked for crucifying a strange man?

22:8 A group of Jews took a vow and swore they will not eat nor drink until the body of Paul rots in the earth: and these Jews numbered forty men.

22:9 They conspired with the council to kill Paul, saying, "Though he was born in the lands of Rome, he is no more a Roman than a Roman an Egyptian for being birthed in Cairo."

22:10 So they all conspired to kill Paul, who even in custody spewed forth hate towards the Jews and the Gentiles who refused the teachings of Christ.

22:11 But Claudius, a man with power over the centurions, came to free Paul from the hands of the Jews.

22:12 He believed Paul a just and righteous man, a leader of the Christian sect.

22:13 He set Paul free and sailed him away to the island of Melita, so he may be hidden from the eyes of the Jews.

23:1 The barbarians of Melita hearkened not the words of Paul, nor showed him kindness; they were cruel and cold-hearted men.

23:2 As Paul gathered sticks to kindle a fire, behold, he was bit on the ankle by a snake.

23:3 And the barbarians condemned Paul, saying, "You are a murderer and a madman, for the snake kills those who killed their brothers."

23:4 But Paul did not die by the bite of the snake: and the barbarians believed then Paul to be a man of great works.

23:5 The fact the snake was not venomous also may have been the reason Paul didn't die by the bite; it was a non-venomous colubrid.

23:6 Paul then began to preach to the barbarians, telling them about the ways of Jesus and the evil hearts of the Jews.

23:7 Through the blessings of Jesus, he healed their sick, cured their lame and restored their crippled, telling them that those who have faith shall live forever in heaven.

23:8 They all gathered round and were baptized by Paul in the name of Christ: and they were fascinated by the words of Paul, who spoke to them of a man who was nailed to the cross only to rise from the dead.

23:9 Both young and old gathered round the fires to hear the stories Paul told them, never knowing that Paul was serious about his preaching.

23:10 They all thought it a story.

23:11 For two years he lived among the barbarians of Melita, baptizing them in the name of Jesus so that all the people were Christians.

23:12 After two years, he left, saying, "I must go now and preach the ways of Christ to all, lest the world in its entirety be damned."

23:13 And the people of Melita wished him well and asked of him to return with new and exciting stories to entertain them with.

23:14 He returned again to Judaea and said, "Behold, you must all be baptized in the name of Jesus, lest you be damned on the day of his return.

23:15 He shall return soon; before my eyes know eternal rest, I shall see Jesus come to reclaim the earth and separate the righteous from the wicked.

23:16 Bow down to Jesus; be baptized and know salvation."

23:17 When the people saw him again and knew he was of the Christian sect, they laughed at him and said, "Be gone, madman."

23:18 We have had enough of the words of lunatics."

23:19 Peter joined Paul and together they both spoke at the temples of the wickedness of the Jews and the mercy of Jesus.

23:20 It came to pass that the rulers of Jerusalem, who were Gentiles, came to hear the words of Peter and Paul: and they believed them conspirators.

23:21 For the two disciples said, "All men who are not baptized in the name of Jesus shall be consumed by the fires of hell.

23:22 Repent and wash away your sins; the lord comes soon."

23:23 They then arrested Paul and Peter for conspiring against the people.

23:24 Both men mocked them, saying, "Arrest us, condemn us, execute us.

23:25 The son of God shall come down before either of us know death; then shall judgment be on your heads."

23:26 They were both found guilty for blasphemy, conspiracy and attempting genocide.

23:27 Paul, who angered the Jews greatly for they felt him a traitor, was publicly executed outside the walls of Jerusalem.

23:28 They took the head of Paul and hanged it within the walls, where people spat on it and threw stones at it.

23:29 Peter was sentenced to die by crucifixion.

23:30 When Peter heard of this, he said, "I am unfit to die by the manner of Jesus; I beg of you, let me be crucified so that my head is to the ground."

23:31 So they executed Peter upside down, so that the blood trickled on his face.

23:32 And the surviving apostles said, "There are now few of us left and the lord said he shall come again before some of us sees death.

23:33 Will only one of us live to see the second coming of Christ?"

23:34 Obviously, they all died and Christ never came.

23:35 Jesus is an asshole, just like his father.

OMANS

1:1 Paul, a servant of Jesus Christ after his death by the hands of the apostles who slew him for his loyalty to the Jews.

1:2 Concerning the son Jesus Christ of the lord, which was made of the seed of God and greater than David and Solomon.

1:3 Proven the messiah and the new lord by his resurrection from death; only the holy spirit may rise from the grave.

1:4 A man who shall give us salvation and glory, so long as we follow his word without question.

1:5 Blessed are the blinded by faith, who keep their minds clean from question, doubt and logic.

1:6 To all the world, be blessed and baptized in the name of Christ; wash away your wickedness, you filthy Gentiles; repent your sins, you filthy Jews.

1:7 Who can deny that Christ is the lord but the foolish, stubborn and blind of heart?

1:8 How can they deny that Christ is the messiah, though they have been told that he has risen from the dead?

1:9 The wrath of both father and son shall be on all unbelievers; unrighteous men who seek forth answers in the foolishness of science.

1:10 How can science show the beginnings. How shall science show how the universe, the earth and all things were created?

1:11 The atheists are without reason to deny God; gaze upon the wonders of nature and know only that God could create such wonders.

1:12 By no other means could the universe and all things be created; to even think so is blasphemous and shall send you to hell.

1:13 The lord abandons those who doubt him; the unbelievers, who needs most the proof of God, shall receive nothing from the lord.

1:14 Fuck them; they without faith shall have none all their life.

1:15 Pity not the fool who denies the lord in his heart; show him not the wonders, the signs and the miracles of Christ.

1:16 Damned are the sickened, the vile, the ones cursed with afflictions; they have been made rotten by the lord for the sins of their fathers and must suffer for these.

1:17 Hated are they with vile affections, those queers of men who lust after their brethren; even the women who go for that which is against nature will suffer under the wrath of Jesus.

1:18 Those women who deny the natural use of their creation will have their cunts burn and be raped by the barbarians, the Minotaur and the devils.

1:19 Wretched beings of unholy lust and those who pleasure them, show them no pity and support those that are worthy with the blade. Forever shall their bowels be full of the worm and the maggot.

1:20 They are backstabbers, traitors, vermin, haters of the pure, unholy beasts, inventors of evil things, worse than the devils themselves.

2:1 You are inexcusable, you judges of men, who execute judgment for those who have sinned such as yourself.

2:2 Only the lord and the disciples shall judge the men of earth; holy beings chosen by the hand of God.

2:3 Of those that judge without the honour of God, the lord shall come and judge him harshly.

2:4 Let the Christians rule the earth and judge every person according to his needs.

2:5 Be patient, for the son of God comes soon and shall grant you eternal life to those who follow the ways of Jesus and repent their wickedness.

2:6 To the Jews and those that are stubborn, who disregard the truth and follow the ways of unrighteousness,

2:7 Wrath, anguish and horrors will fall upon you, of the Jew first and then Gentile.

2:8 But to those of Christ will come honour, glory and peace; the lord respects no man who refuses to be blinded by faith.

2:9 Many have sinned according to the laws of men and many are righteous in the laws of men; but in accordance to the laws of God, you must repent your wickedness, for you have wronged him.

2:10 The doers of the law, the up keepers and the soldiers will not be exempt from the judgment of Christ; even Caesar himself must bow down before God.

2:11 It shall come to pass that all those of the earth will be judged according to the words of the gospels of Jesus the Nazarene; the laws of Moses are obsolete. Disregard them.

2:12 Those righteous in the eyes of Jesus will know true salvation and be blessed in Zion; but those who blasphemy his name will have their foreskin regrown and choke upon the wicked flesh.

2:13 Repent, you Jews and give glory to the one you slew, lest you be slain yourself in the last days.

3:1 There is no advantage for the Jew who toils the ground with his beak looking for money.

3:2 Wicked, disgusting men of vultures who tear at the flesh of the saviour of man.

3:3 Why do they refuse to believe in the messiah. For what reason is there to grasp firmly the laws of Moses?

3:4 They are liars everyone; these wicked Jews who deny their part in the crucifixion of the son of God.

3:5 Should we as Christians take vengeance upon these wicked harpies. Is it unrighteous to spill the blood of those who spilled the blood of our lord?

3:6 Shall we let the lord himself judge them upon the end of days, when the world become split between holy and wicked?

3:7 We are all sinners in the eyes of God; but where the Jews stubbornly keep their sins hidden within their bosom, the disciples of Christ repent and rejoice, so that their sins be washed away.

3:8 Cursed are they who criticize my words and call me wicked; their damnation is just.

3:9 Never, since the beginning, has there been a righteous man:

3:10 No Jew understands the lord God, but only seek him for fear of hell.

3:11 They go out of their way to please the lord with sacrifice and offerings, as told to them since the times of Moses; yet they do this to profit themselves and not to pleasure God.

3:12 Their throat is an open sepulcher, which spread deceit so long as it profits them; the venom of asps fills their lips.

3:13 Such bitter mouths full of curses and hate.

3:14 Their feet run to shed the blood of the holy.

3:15 Misery and destruction follows them like a loyal servant.

3:16 They fear not God, but only his wrath.

3:17 They follow the laws, but lack faith.

3:18 A man with faith is justified, even if the word of the laws says not.

3:19 The lord Jesus has come to save both Jew and Gentile from their wickedness; be baptized and rejoice in heaven.

3:20 And slay those whose hearts are stubborn and refuse the truth of Christ; let the world be baptized in the blood of unbelievers.

4:1 Oh Abraham, how you are ashamed for your children.

4:2 By the grace of God you sired your children of the Jews, only so that they may turn the dagger upon their brother.

4:3 By the blessings of faith you did create the chosen by God; why then, do the chosen not choose the lord?

4:4 David, mightiest of kings and conqueror of nations; how you loathe the peoples under your rule.

4:5 They did perform the horrible treason and betrayed the very lord they wished salvation from.

4:6 Solomon the wise, did you know your sons will become the unholy fool?

4:7 None other but the foolish would dare nail the hand which feeds them to the cross.

4:8 By my word, I shall not give shame to my fathers; by the blessings of Christ, we shall be the chosen people and give honour to the name of God.

4:9 Take rise, Christian soldiers; convert the sinners and slay wicked.

4:10 In glory of our fathers will the world reign under a new order.

4:11 Our faith will be our salvation and our blade will bring the damnation of the unjust.

4:12 Cursed are the Jews, who bring shame to their fathers; let them be judged by the commandments of Moses.

4:13 Let them be slain for the dishonour of their father.

5:1 Being justified by faith, we have been given eternal peace through the blessings of our lord Jesus Christ.

5:2 Let us give glory to the son of God, who did come to the earth and showed us the errors of our ways.

5:3 Through patience and faith will we be welcomed into Zion; and through faith will hope endure.

5:4 Hope that the lord comes to deliver us into salvation; hope that the wickedness of the Jews will be abolished from the earth.

5:5 The love of God is shed abroad our hearts, given to us by the holy ghost.

5:6 For when we were young and without strength, our hearts were barren; but the son of God has come to shed his blood and give love to the ungodly.

5:7 Being baptized in his blood, we are free from his wrath; by the death of Christ we will know eternal life.

5:8 We are all sinners, who must drown in the blood of our lord and son of God; may the strong swim to the shores of Zion, whilst the weak and unrighteous perish in the blood they spilled.

5:9 For it was through sin that death entered into this world; before the first sin, Adam lived in peace for thousands of years.

5:10 It was not until that wretched cunt Eve came that sin came to this earth and brought with it death.

5:11 Let us rid ourselves of death by ridding us of sin; let us rid ourselves of sin by ridding us of the sinners.

5:12 Death be to all sinners and unbelievers of Christ.

5:13 Let the end come to the sinners; let hell be their eternal resting place.

5:14 They have abandoned the grace of God and the mercy of Christ; let their foolishness bring them that worse than death.

6:1 Know this, brothers of the proper faith, that the law has dominion over men, but was made by men.

6:2 Why must we follow the laws as written by men. We are not loyal to flesh but loyal to God.

6:3 Only the women, the child and the beast must follow the laws as written by men and husband; the men of earth follow not the laws of men, but the laws of Christ.

6:4 Let us be free of these bindings which cripple us; these laws as written by the Romans, the Greeks and the Jews.

6:5 Is it not that that which is written by the wicked must be wicked. Why then do we follow the laws of the Jews?

6:6 There is no good thing in the flesh of a Jew, most wretched beasts they are; let us be delivered from their laws and live the life of peace.

6:7 Take your swords, O Christian soldiers and destroy the wickedness, the evil and the blasphemous of the earth.

6:8 Then shall the laws of man be no more; the holy laws of God shall govern us with mercy and love.

7:1 There is no wrong in those who seek not the flesh, but seek the spirit of the lord.

7:2 For the laws of Jesus have freed us from the laws of sin and death.

7:3 It was the lord God who sent down his own son and made him weak of flesh and blood, so that he may understand the wretchedness of men and Jew.

7:4 We are a carnal beast, who seeks after lust, wealth and glory; but the Christians seek not the things of flesh, but eternal life through Christ.

7:5 By pleasing God we have delivered ourselves from the pains of the universe.

7:6 How the whole of creation did groan under the pain and the restraints of sin until now.

7:7 Now that the lord has delivered us the fruits of salvation, we may rid ourselves of creation and escape the hand of death.

7:8 Pray, you Christians; pray unto Christ, as he did teach us.

7:9 Learn to pray you who are ignorant, lest the lord hearkens not your words.

7:10 Know that all things work out to good for those that truly love God and his son Jesus.

7:11 If you love Christ, but the workings of evil come to you, then you are a liar and a blasphemer.

7:12 If you truly loved the lord, then none of the wicked would harm you. Repent, love God and know that you are safe eternal.

7:13 Before the infant leaves the womb, their name is written in the book of heaven and hell; it is predetermined, our fate after death.

7:14 Of those who go to heaven, they shall know salvation no matter the wickedness they cause on earth: and of those written in the pages of hell, they are damned no matter their acts in life.

7:15 So be a Christian, for the names of Christians are written in the book of heaven.

7:16 And thus, to be Christian is to be free from wrongdoings; a Christian shall not sin, for the love of God prohibits them.

7:17 If a man accuses a Christian of sin, they are wicked and must be punished by the sword.

8:1 How then can we be punished, if we are predetermined by God to be good or evil. How can you punish that which you created to be evil?

8:2 Think not of it, but accept it; the will of God is not to be questioned.

8:3 How can men question God. Are we not but clay in his hands?

8:4 If a potter makes a pot of good and another of evil, can the clay question the intentions of the potter?

8:5 Fear the lord and question him not; accept your fate in heaven or hell and be honoured that the lord did make you.

8:6 For the lord is a powerful being, who wishes his power be known throughout all; so let the wicked he created be burned, so that all may know the power of God.

8:7 And let the righteous live in salvation, so that all shall know the lord is merciful to those who are worthy of mercy.

8:8 In the beginning, the lord loved Jacob and hated Esau; thus, those of Esau will be hated and thrown into the fires.

8:9 Then all the universe will fear God and love him, lest the wrath of the lord befalls them.

9:1 Cursed be to the ignorant, who claim not to know Christ and knew not the path of salvation.

9:2 Who in this earth could not know the words of the gospels. Who in the lands have not been taught the ways of Christ?

9:3 They have heard, but they did not listen; they have seen, but not watched.

9:4 Christ is the end, the way, the path; those who follow not the path are written in the book of hell.

9:5 All know of Christ and are inexcusable to plead ignorance; unless there is land across the waters, which we know not of, all the people of earth have heard of Christ.

9:6 And if there is land across the oceans, they still have no excuse; they were created by God and thus must know of Christ.

9:7 Savage men have no excuse; barbarians have no reason.

9:8 The sound of God has called unto the four corners of the earth; thus, the gospel has been spread to all men.

9:9 If you burn in hell, it is your doing; plead not ignorance to God, lest he pour out his wrath upon you.

10:1 Only a small number of Jews were made to accept Christ; the rest were blinded by the lord so that they may slay the son of God and show the world their wickedness.

10:2 The lord did not cast away his people; his people cast away the lord.

10:3 Now their eyes are darkened to the prophets and their ears deafened to the words of the gospels.

10:4 By this way shall the Jews recognize not their messiah; by this way shall they suffer eternally in hell.

10:5 A stumbling block was set before them; a snare laid in their path.

10:6 The lord hath shown us now in this manner that the Jews are wicked and worthy of death.

10:7 Take your blade and shed their blood; may your fields be watered by the blood of Jews and your crops be blessed and bountiful in the harvest.

10:8 Then will the kingdom of Israel be cast into outer darkness, forever stumbling on their feet.

10:9 God hates the Jews and so shall you; be like the lord and hate the Jews and all those who believe not as you do.

11:1 I beseech you, O children of Christ, that you present your bodies as living sacrifice to the lord God almighty.

11:2 Be not bound to this world, but keep your eyes fixed to the heavens, where the gates of Zion will open and accept you.

11:3 For I say to you, that the bullshit of the earth and the harassment of your enemies is worth but even a glimpse of the holy city, where the streets are made of gold and the rivers flow with wine.

11:4 Be glad that you shall see the marvels of Zion and your enemies are doomed to a fate worse than death.

11:5 Cleave to your bosom that which is good; part ways with the wickedness of the earth.

11:6 To your brethren show love, kindness and mercy, as they shall show unto you.

11:7 Be not slothful in business, but serve the lord with a smile.

11:8 Rejoice in hope, prayer, sacrifice and Christ, as he shall rejoice when you enter his home in Zion.

11:9 Give unto each Christian according to their needs and take not more for yourself; take from your enemies so they have nothing and have every man take equal share of the spoils.

11:10 Rejoice with your brothers and weep with your brothers.

11:11 Rejoice in the weeping of your enemies and crush them.

11:12 Live peacefully with all Christian men and let the Jews and the barbarians die by the sword.

11:13 If your enemy hungers, feed them the flesh of their wife; if they thirst, have them choke on the urine of lambs.

11:14 Do not let yourself be overcome with evil, but overcome the evils of the earth.

11:15 Even the child born of Jewdom is wicked and must be slain to please God.

12:1 Let every person submit to the persons of authority, for they have been placed there by the hand of God.

12:2 Whosoever resists authority resists God: and they that resist God shall have their names written in damnation.

12:3 A king is only as wicked as the people he rules; be good and your king shall be good unto you.

12:4 If your king is wicked, then your nation and your people are wicked; repent, pray and slay the sinners, so that the lord bless you.

12:5 Know that a wrathful king is a mighty king; for such as the lord God is wrathful, so shall be the kings who do the lord's bidding.

12:6 Pay tribute to your king; give him your taxes, your virgins and your flocks.

12:7 Borrow no money from your neighbours, lest you make a business of loans.

12:8 The wicked Jews are in the business of loans and interest and did make it a business of whoredoms.

12:9 The end of days come soon, where the lord Christ will return to separate the lambs from the wolves; be prepared for this holiest

of days.

12:10 Walk honestly and be dressed; don't filthy yourself in drunkenness and lust.

13:1 He that eats the weak is of weak faith; eat the flesh of beasts and be strong.

13:2 Partake not of herbs, for they are food for the weak.

13:3 Let the lord supply you with meat, so that your belly never growls.

13:4 Remember, the sabbath day is a holy day, made wicked by the Jews.

13:5 Take no part of the sabbath of the Jews, but worship the lord the day after; this way the lord shall know those who call to him on this day are righteous, and not wicked.

13:6 Regard not any days for the sabbath and be cursed to horrors and damnation; on the seventh day God demands worship and worship you must.

13:7 Fear not what happens after death, for the lord will protect you; Jesus Christ did live, die and was resurrected so that he may be God of both the living and dead.

13:8 Let the lord judge the living and the dead; judge not your brother, for it shall be that you are judged as well.

13:9 Fear not the old laws and eat of all flesh; the swine is sweet and the rabbit tender, so that you enjoy their flesh.

13:10 They are gifts to the righteous, which the Jews deny themselves in ignorance.

13:11 If your brother grieves for you as ye eat of the unclean flesh, slay him and eat of his flesh.

13:12 It matters not what you place into your body, but only that what comes out of your body pleased Christ.

13:13 Be not weakened by the grape; take strength in liquor, lest liquor conquers you.

13:14 It is better not to drink than to be defeated by wine.

13:15 Have faith and know that the lord loves you; he without faith doubts and his doubts bring him damnation.

14:2 I commend you, women of Christ, who know their place in the church.

14:3 They speak not in the church, nor teach that which they know.

14:4 When they wish to learn, they ask of their husbands first, so as not to displease their masters.

14:5 Since the beginning, woman was made to please man and must please man to please God.

14:6 Let not a woman know independence, nor individuality; let them forever be under the ownership of their husbands.

14:7 If a woman wishes to please Christ, then let her offer her loins to her husband and give him many sons, so that the world be full of Christian men.

14:8 I beseech your brethren, a woman who speaks is dangerous and must be put in her place.

14:9 Avoid those who are not of Christ; shun them, avoid them and be disgusted by them.

14:10 They are wicked and foolish beasts who deny themselves Christ.

14:11 Of those that believe not in your ways, kill them; the lord God will send them to their fate in hell.

14:12 For the lord comes soon and shall conquer Satan before my days are done.

14:13 Then all the earth will know that Christ is the lord of peace and bow down unto him and offer him sacrifice.

14:14 Let the wisdom of Jesus the Nazarene separate the righteous from the wicked, the holy from the damned.

14:15 And may the world know peace through is love, Amen.

I CORINTHIANS

1:1 Paul, called upon to be an apostle of Christ through the will of God and Sosthenes our brother,

1:2 Unto the church of Jesus Christ which is at Corinth, to them that are sanctified in the lord, called on to be saints:

1:3 Grace be to you and may the lord give you peace and the blessings of Christ.

1:4 Thank the lord daily for protecting you against the wickedness of the Jews, the ignorance of unbelievers and the skepticism of the unfaithful.

1:5 By this you have been enriched in all utterance and knowledge.

1:6 Your patience will go rewarded, my brethren; upon the day of the second coming, you will be written in the book of heaven and know salvation.

1:7 Be faithful, you who have been called unto the fellowship of Jesus Christ the Nazarene.

1:8 I beseech you, brothers; do not argue with one another, nor differ in ideals, thoughts and opinion.

1:9 We must be united as one Christian body, so that we may crush the wickedness of the Jews.

1:10 Hearken not criticism nor doubt and be blind to the ways of other faiths.

1:11 Agree with one another and be as one, lest these small cracks ruin the foundation of Christ and crumble before you.

1:12 Now this I say, that I am Paul of the Apollos, of Cephas and of Christ.

1:13 Christ shall not be divided, nor shall another crucify himself for your sins.

1:14 I thank God that I have baptized no one, lest you blame me for your lack of faith and spirit of the holy ghost.

1:15 I have baptized only Crispus and Gaius; maybe the house of Stephanas; I don't think there were others.

1:16 I don't remember and it doesn't matter.

1:17 For I have been sent by Christ not to baptize, but to preach the gospels, so that you may know the lord and decide to be baptized in the blood of Jesus.

1:18 Know that the words of preachers seem foolish to those that are unbelievers; they know not the wisdom hidden within the words.

1:19 The Jew demands these words be proven by miraculous acts, a sign of God; but we who are faithful need not signs.

1:20 The Greek demands logic behind the words of the gospel, so that it may be understood; but we who are faithful need not logic.

1:21 Logic is the enemy of the Christians and all religions.

1:22 We preach in foolishness so that the wise remain fools and the foolish understand the words.

1:23 I see you, my brothers and know that you are not men of intellect; yet you are wise, for you have devoted your life to Christ.

1:24 A man baptized by Jesus is wiser than even the most philosophical of Greeks: and if you doubt me, then you are a fool.

2:1 My brothers, I come ignorant of the ways of science, of nature and of men.

2:2 For as Christians, we need not know these frivolous things; we need only know the ways of Christ and be baptized in his name.

2:3 Waste not your time with that which is not God; they are fearful, frightening things created by the Jews to cause confusion.

2:4 Hearken not the ways of men, but watch only the demonstration of the spirit of the lord.

2:5 Only your faith in Christ matters; the rest of the world is irrelevant, an illusion for the unrighteous.

2:6 We are Christians and know the truth; through this truth we may judge the world and all within it.

2:7 But those of the earth who are not our brother shall not judge us, lest they fall deeper into the darkness of oblivion.

3:1 My brethren, though you listen to the mouth of a man, know that the words are spiritual; they are the words as spoken by Christ.

3:2 You are fed with milk and meat, but now you shall be fed by the words of the lord; they shall be your sustenance.

3:3 To rid yourself of flesh and blood is to rid yourself of temptation, wickedness and sin; it is the flesh that sins.

3:4 The devil himself was once spiritual and pure; but when lust and envy overtook him, he became as flesh and filthy in the eyes of God.

3:5 I am Paul, who has planted the seed within you: and Apollo has watered you with the gospels; but it is Jesus who shall cause you to grow.

3:6 Give glory to the lord and worship him; do not defile him, lest you be wicked and cast into the fires.

3:7 The church is holy and just; to question the church is to question God and is punishable by death and hell-fire.

3:8 Be wise, O Christians and hearken the words of the gospels; decipher the parables of Christ, whose wisdom is hidden beneath foolishness.

3:9 To be wise, you must be foolish and listen to the parables and their hidden meanings; for the lord has made the parables foolish to confuse the wicked, so that they enter not the kingdom of heaven.

3:10 You are all the sons of Christ; embrace him, love him and he shall love you and give you your salvation.

3:11 Deny him and he shall be the just father and give you the rod of damnation.

3:12 For it is written, spare the rod and spoil the child; the lord Christ shall never spoil his child.

3:13 He would rather see them burn eternal than spoil under him.

4:1 The men of science are wicked fools, who wish to understand the ways of God by logic, nature and natural law.

4:2 How can one understand the unnatural by the natural. How can one see logic to that which is illogical?

4:3 They waste their time with experiments, their observations; never can men understand God or the ways of the universe.

4:4 Think of this; the lord has always been and will always be. Never can the minds of men grasp this.

4:5 The ways of men are simple; all things have a beginning and all things have an end.

4:6 But the lord has no beginning nor end; he has always been and always will be.

4:7 Waste not your time to understand this; accept it, believe it and follow Christ.

4:8 We are fools for Christ's sakes, but the faithless are damned; we are weak, but the unrighteous are dead.

4:9 Where we will be made strong in the lord, the rest of the world will fail and turn to ash.

4:10 Rejoice and sing praises to Christ the messiah; he has shed his blood for us so that we may be baptized in his righteousness.

4:11 Let the Jews and the wicked drown.

5:1 It is rumored that there is a plague of fornication amongst the people of Corinth and that these fornications spread wild in the brothels, the bedchamber and the hills.

5:2 Wicked, foolish Gentiles. Do you not know that Satan's greatest tool is the flesh?

5:3 Your lust for your neighbours, your sisters, your brothers and even your mothers is a stumbling block to your salvation.

5:4 Cleanse yourself of these fornications; if you must, tear off your loins and feed it to the jackals.

5:5 It is better to enter heaven a eunuch than enter hell erect.

5:6 The lord curses those who fornicate lustily with a fire in the loins; if the vessels of your seed burn mighty, you have angered the lord with your lust.

5:7 If you are pure of heart and flesh, then rid yourself of these fornicators.

5:8 Do not speak with them nor keep them company; they are wicked and shall drag the righteous to hell.

5:9 If your father be a fornicator, an idolater, a drunkard, a blasphemer, or an extortioner, then have it so he never calls you son.

5:10 Rid yourself of his wickedness and spill his blood in the name of God.

5:11 Judge them harshly, for the lord shall judge them with a cold cruelty.

6:1 My brothers, do not fight amongst one another, lest the Jews see the cracks in our foundation and cause the church to crumble.

6:2 Take not one another to court, but settle your matters in peace with the apostles, who shall judge for you.

6:3 Never accuse another of Christ of their sins, or you shall be cast out the church and denied salvation in Zion.

6:4 If your elder takes from you a coin, then offer him your purse; if your priest steals your virtues, then offer the virtues of your sister as well.

6:5 Only the apostles shall judge those of Christ: and only the angels shall judge the apostles.

6:6 There are many things that shall keep you out of the kingdom of heaven and drag your soul to damnation.

6:7 Rid yourself of these things, lest you be impure in the eyes of Christ.

6:8 Of fornicators, Jews, idolaters, adulterers, abusers of themselves and those men who lie with men shall be denied the kingdom of heaven;

6:9 As shall the thieves, the covetous, the drunkards, the revilers and those who lust for the beast.

6:10 Baptize yourselves of these vices and be glorified in the eyes of God.

6:11 The powers of the law are naught to the Christian; we follow the laws of Christ; thus the laws of men hold no power against us.

6:12 The body is of flesh and flesh is lust; rid yourselves of flesh and you shall be free of lust.

6:13 Raise yourselves to the heavens and be welcomed by the embrace of Jesus Christ.

6:14 Take no part of the woman; they are harlots all, who deceive you with curves, flesh and desire.

6:15 A woman is a creation of God made perverse by Satan; they are a tool for wickedness and must not be welcome.

7:1 Now concerning that which you have written to me in concern: it is always best for a man never to touch a woman.

7:2 The woman is a wicked tool of Satan, who makes filthy the man with her lust and her flesh.

7:3 Nevertheless, the man is weak and becomes soft to the ways of women; if you must know the touch of a woman, then you must marry to avoid fornication.

7:4 To the weak of the flesh, let them have their husband and their wife.

7:5 Let the husband give to his wife all she deserves and the wife give to her husband all he desires.

7:6 The wife has not control of her own body, which now belongs to the husband; the woman belongs to her husband and as such must be obedient.

7:7 Lie not to one another, nor deny yourselves of each other, save for the time of fasting and prayer; after which you must come together again, lest the devils tempt you with the lust of a younger being.

7:8 But know that marriage is permission and not desired by God.

7:9 It would be best if all men remained virgins like me, so that they are not distracted by the vices of flesh.

7:10 That, and I'm a miserable virgin; if I cannot get laid, then no other should.

7:11 Now to the unmarried and the widows, it is best that they remain chaste such as I.

7:12 But if they cannot contain their lust, then let them marry; it is better they be miserable with a husband or wife, than to burn in hell for their adultery and whoredoms.

7:13 For the married, depart from one another; you have made your choice, now stick with it no matter how much of a miserable cunt your wife or husband becomes.

7:14 You shall only leave your husband or wife if they are an unbeliever: and if they are an unbeliever, to hell with you for marrying the faithless.

7:15 Of those Jews who repent their wickedness and follow the path of Christ, fear not; for you are circumcised, but need not be uncircumcised.

7:16 Of those who are a disciple of Christ, and have their foreskin remain, leave it; let the uncircumcised remain uncut.

7:17 For the lord Christ cares not as to the matters of your genitals, but only that you follow him blindly and without question.

7:18 You men who are slaves, owned by Christian and barbarian, accept your fate; covet not freedom, lest your coveting send you to damnation.

7:19 We are all servants of the lord; rejoice, you slaves, for you have been purchased by men, but the slaves of Christ have been given freely.

7:20 Of you who are lustful and seek forth the virgin for pleasure, do not waste your time.

7:21 The time of the lord draws near; there is no time for sex, marriage and the raising of children.

7:22 Jesus comes soon and you must prepare; do not waste your time with such frivolous things when the time of Christ is near.

8:1 These foolish men of science devote their times to the knowledge and logic of all things; they waste their time.

8:2 Knowledge matters not, but only the faith in the lord; it is better to accept God than to know the workings of all things.

8:3 When the men of science believe they know something, they know nothing; they have been ensnared by the lord, so that they know not God.

8:4 They love not the lord, but we love the lord: and through that love we shall be saved and given salvation in heaven.

8:5 Fear not the idols of the world, nor the offerings given to them; eat of the flesh of idols, for they are just metal and stone.

8:6 Only take not of that which belongs to God; there is but one God and he is a jealous God.

8:7 These idols that are called gods are merely the imagined characters of lunatics, whose weak minds deny them faith.

8:8 But the Christians know the truth; that there is one God and he sent down his only son to be killed by the Jews so that we may be saved by baptizing ourselves in his blood.

8:9 And through his blood we shall be free of sin, pure: and then we shall know salvation in Zion.

8:10 How can any man doubt this truth, unless they be fools?

9:1 Am I not an apostle. Am I not chained to God. Have I not seen the messiah Jesus Christ.

9:2 The seal of my apostle hood has been given to me on the day Christ blinded me and freed me of my wicked Jewdom.

9:3 I am now pure and a disciple of the messiah Jesus; it is a proud thing to be an apostle of the lord.

9:4 And as an apostle, it is my duty to make men see the path of salvation, so that the fires of hell burn only the foolish, the ignorant, the wicked and the Jew.

9:5 Fear not the Jews, but pity them; they are blind men who slew he who came to save them.

9:6 Offer them the words of the gospel, so that they repent their wickedness and be free of the chains of Hades.

9:7 Let them rid themselves of their circumcision and embrace Christ as God; let them be given the opportunity for salvation and repentance by baptism.

9:8 Preach, my brethren, as I have taught you to preach; let the word of Christ spread to the four corners of the earth.

9:9 Give word to the Gentiles, so that they may praise you; give word to the Asians and they shall worship Jesus the Nazarene.

9:10 Tarnish your blade only with the blood of the stubborn, who refuse the ways of Christ; our blade shall be a merciful judgment upon them:

9:11 For when the lord God punishes the stubborn, it shall be a cruel and harsh punishment of eternal torture.

9:12 I know there are those who ask why the lord would send any man to hell. Why not offer them a chance for salvation once more?

9:13 The lord denies them this because the lord knows these men to be truly stubborn fuckers; never will they accept salvation.

9:14 Their hearts are stone and can only be softened in the eternal fires of hell.

10:1 Though the Jews are a wicked breed, we are descended from them and must look at them to learn from their mistakes.

10:2 They have angered the lord greatly, thus the lord has abandoned them to rot.

10:3 They have formed idols from stone and worshipped false gods in defiance to the one true God.

10:4 They would rather eat, drink and play than please the lord almighty who dwells in heaven.

10:5 So let us not commit these whoredoms to false gods, lest the lord curse us with a plague and cause us to fall as the Jews once fell in great numbers.

10:6 Tempt not the messiah Jesus Christ, as some of you have tempted, or you shall be destroyed by serpents and dragons.

10:7 Murmur not nor spread doubt to the faithful; to murmur and spread doubt is blasphemous and shall be the cause of your destruction.

10:8 Fear not, my brothers, for the end of the world comes and the end of the world is the start of our salvation.

10:9 When the wicked burn beneath us, we shall gaze down from the heavens and mock their ignorance, their arrogance and their foolishness.

10:10 Give to them the means of their salvation; offer them the words of the gospels, so that they no longer be men of devils.

10:11 Of those that aren't of Christ, they are of devils; they worship devils, lie with devils, sacrifice to devils.

10:12 Be not a neighbour to the unbeliever, lest you befriend a man of Satan.

10:13 You cannot be a man of God and a friend to the devils; make your choice, lest the lord almighty find you unworthy of salvation.

10:14 It is better always to please God than to please man.

11:1 The lord has chosen me as an apostle of Christ; follow me blindly and you follow Christ.

11:2 Question me and you question God; such people are to be stoned until death.

11:3 I praise you, who keep my ordinances as I delivered them to you.

11:4 Know that, since the beginning, man was created in the image of God; the head of every man is Christ, the head of every woman is man, and the head of Christ is God.

11:5 Thus it is that men shall follow Christ, women follow men and Christ follow God; such is the order of things.

11:6 If a man is worshipping and has his head covered, it is of great disrespect to God; why does this man show shame for his head?

11:7 Display your head proudly, for the lord sees what is in your head.

11:8 A woman was created to please men and through her wickedness has doomed the earth with her foolishness.

11:9 The lord wishes not to see the head of a woman; all women who worship must do so with a veil covering their heads.

11:10 If a woman worships but covers not her head, then let her scalp be removed and offered as sacrifice to Christ.

11:11 For a man is glory to God and must bear his head proudly; but the woman brings shame to God and must keep herself hidden in the eyes of the holy.

11:12 The angels spit upon the hair of these women, who keep their heads bare whilst they pray and worship the name of Jesus.

11:13 You shall recognize these women by the curses the angels has brought upon their head; they shall be as bald as the rock.

11:14 Men, keep your hair short, so that the lord may see your face and be glorified in his greatest creation.

11:15 Women, keep your hair long so that the very strands may cover the shame which God feels towards you.

11:16 The lord has given women hair so that they may cover themselves; use it.

11:17 Be not gluttonous, but accept that which the lord has given you.

11:18 To want more is to covet and to covet is to be damned.

11:19 If you have a loaf of bread and still your belly hungers, then you are a glutton and revolting in the eyes of God.

11:20 Of those who eat and drink like beasts, the lord shall curse you with rumbling belly, loose bowels and vomiting mouth.

11:21 And when you expel that which you wasted, know that it will await you in hell, where you will wallow in your wretchedness.

12:1 My brothers, I speak with the tongues of angels; my voice is like the mighty brass and the loud cymbal.

12:2 By faith, I have been given the gift of prophecy and understanding of all mysteries; by words alone I may move mountains.

12:3 But I won't. To have faith I can is all I need.

12:4 Be not charitable nor lend a hand to those in need; let the lord offer them that which they need.

12:5 If the hand of God delivers them not from poverty, then they are cursed and deserve to suffer by the will of God.

12:6 Rejoice in the suffering of the beggars and the poor; to praise their suffering is to praise the truth of God.

12:7 That truth is that the lord is a cruel beast, who shows mercy to no person; let every man receive the punishment they deserve.

12:8 And know this; the Christian shall be unpunished, for they are the true people of Christ.

12:9 Never will they be wrong nor wretched in the eyes of God; they worship the son of God and know that Jesus is the messiah.

12:10 This pleases the lord God, who embraces us and brings us salvation.

12:11 The prophecies of old are no longer; they were spoken by the wicked Jew, who abandoned God and blasphemed his name.

12:12 Never will the prophecies come forth, but they shall vanish and fade to dust.

12:13 My brothers, though we were once Jew and Gentile, we are now disciples of Christ; we are men in the world of children.

12:14 Fear not the wrath of God, who knew you were once the wicked Jew or the ignorant Gentile; you were children in those days:

12:15 And as children, you grew and put away childish things; you are now men, worthy of Christ and God.

12:16 Rejoice, my brothers and praise Jesus.

13:1 When you preach the gospels to the ignorant, speak clearly, lest they are confused by the ways of Christ.

13:2 It is better to have the voice of a clear child than to boast like the trumpet with confusion.

13:3 Understand that Christ is the lord and our way of salvation. It is quite simple.

13:4 When the ignorant are lost, tell them this; the lord wishes them not to be lost, but to be found.

13:5 He is a God of peace, who demands we slay all those who believe differently than us.

13:6 He is a God of mercy, who will show harsh cruelty to those he deems wicked.

13:7 The Jews were his chosen people, who he hates and will send to damnation.

13:8 He sent his only son to earth so that he may die; and through his death we will live eternal.

13:9 But the son of God is still alive and will come again to save the righteous and destroy the wicked.

13:10 What's so confusing about that?

13:11 Women, keep silent in the churches, lest your voice offend the lord.

13:12 You are not permitted to speak in the house of God, but are commanded to be obedient.

13:13 If you are confused, it is only because you are a woman and stupid; ask your husband and he shall teach you.

13:14 Brothers, if you preach to the ignorant and they remain ignorant, let them.

13:15 Hope is lost on the truly ignorant; let them not know Christ and burn in hell for their stupidity.

13:16 We don't need more stupid people in heaven anyway; Christians will be more than enough

14:1 The lord Christ is the messiah and son of God; this is known because the twelve apostles saw Christ resurrected.

14:2 Doubt them not, lest you anger the lord and have his wrath fall upon you.

14:3 Even I saw the lord Christ, who blinded me and spoke to me when I was the wicked Jew.

14:4 He cleansed me of my Jewdom and made me an apostle, so that I may spread the word of Christ to all those who are foolish.

14:5 Be baptized in his name and cleansed by his blood; then you shall be worthy of salvation and have your name written in the book of heaven.

14:6 Since the beginning, there was no death; it was not until the first cunt doomed the earth that Hades was made to walk the lands.

14:7 Now the lord has offered us eternal life once more, such as the days of Adam; though Adam is dead, we will be given the gift which Eve stole from us.

14:8 Accept Christ and repent; be made holy in the eyes of the lord so that you live eternal in heaven.

14:9 Those fools who deny themselves the lord, let them join the wicked and the Jews in damnation; they shall live eternal in suffering and flame.

14:10 The beasts of the earth are of separate flesh from us; they need not salvation, for they are simple creatures.

14:11 When the tree dies, do you mourn. When the flower withers, do you weep?

14:12 The beasts and the women are made of the same flesh as these; mourn not for them, nor worry for their salvation.

14:13 It is frivolous.

14:14 They are of meat, but we are of spiritual flesh; only that of spiritual flesh may be saved.

14:15 The creatures of the earth will be no more; they have served their purpose as meat and now will be no more.

14:16 May the lord of Christ be with all believers and may the wrath of God curse the fools who deny his name.

14:17 Go now and may Christ protect you. Amen.

II CORINTHIANS

1:1 Paul, an apostle of Christ by the demand of God and Timothy our brother, unto the church of God which is at Corinth, with all the saints that are in Achaia:

1:2 Grace be to you and all those of Jesus Christ the messiah and cursed to the wicked, the Jews and the ignorant of Christ.

1:3 Blessed be the God of mercies, who shall judge harshly and cruelly the damned who defy him.

1:4 Whilst the foolish suffer around us, we live in the bounty of the lord, who protects us and nourishes us from the wicked who persecute us.

1:5 For as the suffering of the unfaithful abound us, we who have cleaved to the bosom of Christ will forever be safe through faith.

1:6 Even of us who were once afflicted with sin, with wickedness and with Jewdom will be given salvation by the baptism of Christ.

1:7 Take comfort in the blood of Christ, who cleanses us from our wretchedness so that we may be pure upon our arrival in Zion.

1:8 Let the damned who deny the lord drown in the blood meant to cleanse them; their wretchedness will be made known to all when they surface from Christ's blood.

1:9 He who delivers us from death will bring death to the wicked; he who lends us salvation will bring the damned to their knees.

1:10 Suffered are they who deny Christ, who blasphemies his name, who doubts his words; forever they shall burn alongside demons, devils and the Jew.

1:11 Come forth and have dominion of the earth; we of Christ are above all men and shall judge them swiftly.

1:12 By blade and noose will we execute judgment amongst the fools, the ignorant, the barbarian and the Jew.

1:13 Forever will the reign of Christ rule, until he comes again to claim the world and deliver us to heaven.

2:1 I have decided never to come again to you in heaviness.

2:2 I am a fat man, who shall be made light and strong by the will of Jesus.

2:3 By the glory of God my weakness will turn to strength; I shall climb mountains, conquer beasts and overthrow nations.

2:4 The lord has given me faith to rid myself of my heaviness, so that when I return you shall not see a fat bastard, but a man made strong by God.

2:5 Grieve not for my heaviness; it is the sin which has kept me down.

2:6 Rejoice and be glad I have lost my fatness; praise the name of Christ, who has rid me of my obesity.

2:7 Do not grow fat by the sins of the devil, lest you excrete a foul odour which is unpleasant to the lord in heaven.

2:8 Be clean, so that your odour pleases the lord greater than the sacrificial lamb.

3:1 Tell me, when you were born, did you accept Christ and his words. Did you rejoice your messiah at birth?

3:2 We are born blind and foolish, my brothers; we must grow to accept Christ and be saved from the damnation and the wicked.

3:3 We of the Christian sect have been blessed by God. Our eyes have been open and we see the light.

3:4 The ways of old are no longer; we have been blessed by the messiah and the time of his coming is soon.

3:5 We need not waste our time with the sacrifice of lambs, when it shall come soon that we may sacrifice the lambs before his very feet.

3:6 Rejoice and be glad; we know Christ and know love; we are free of the wickedness of the unbelievers and the Jews.

3:7 Those who are stubborn to accept the lord Christ are blind; they will stumble and fall upon the rocks.

3:8 Only upon their descent into hell will the lord lift the veils from their eyes, so they may witness the glory, the horror and the cruelty of God.

3:9 Blessed be the lord almighty; blessed be Jesus.

4:1 Because we have seen his ministry and are blessed with his mercy, we shall not falter over evil.

4:2 We have cast away our dishonesty, our cunningness, our misinterpretations, our deceit of the word of God said to benefit us; but we have embraced the truth, the faith and the messiah.

4:3 Let every man come to us, so that they may find the gospel of Christ and be saved by the holy word.

4:4 But if our gospel is hidden, then it is hidden from the lost.

4:5 There are men of the earth who are cursed blind by Christ, so that they never find the words of the gospel; they are cursed so that the lord may cast them into the fires, where they will suffer eternal.

4:6 It would be unwise for Christ to create hell if none enter; thus, there are those who are cursed to damnation, so that the lord wastes not his creation of hell.

4:7 Preach not for ourselves, but preach so that the kingdom of heaven be full of the joyful, the rejoicing, the faithful; let Zion be a happy place, full of those who love the lord.

4:8 In this way the lord shall be pleased, as he is surrounded by those who worship him, love him and are grateful for his salvation.

4:9 It will make him feel good and forget the cruelties he has caused the earth to endure.

4:10 Where once darkness reigned, let there be light, so that the face of Jesus shines to all who have opened their eyes.

4:11 Worry not for our bodies; they are only earthly vessels that house us to the wickedness of the earth.

4:12 Though we shall be persecuted by the Jew, the wicked and the unbeliever, we will know no fear; the lord protects us and will guide us to Zion once we rid ourselves of these vessels;

4:13 And when those who persecute us are destroyed, we shall mock them in heaven as they burn in hell.

4:14 Such as Christ was risen from the dead, so shall our souls ascend and be greeted by the messiah when he comes.

4:15 And he comes soon, so that there are those amongst us who will not die, but be living when the lord returns for his flock.

5:1 Rid yourselves of the earthly house and give the money to the apostles; sell your goods and belongings so that the Christian faith survive.

5:2 Keep only your clothes, so that we may not be naked when the arrival of Jesus comes.

5:3 Be confident that the lord provides for you; if you are hungry and have no food, then you are not truly hungry.

5:4 If you are weary and have no place to rest, then let the lord provide you with the ground beneath your feet.

5:5 Your faith will keep you wealthy and provide you with riches in heaven greater than the mightiest kings on earth.

5:6 Be hard in labour and spread the gospels strong; act justly to the wicked and with gentle hand towards the faithful.

5:7 Remember, though the unjust appear before the disciples, we shall appear before God himself to be judged: and he shall judge us according to our actions.

5:8 Those who are kind will be greatly rewarded and those who are wicked will be cast in the lake of fire:

5:9 And those who are lazy and spread not the gospels will be thrown into the muck, which shall consume them so that they are buried eternal.

5:10 Fear the lord, for the terror of Christ is as horrifying as the terror of his father; let his terror persuade you to do good, lest his wrath fall upon those who act unfavourably towards Jesus.

5:11 Give glory to God and praise his name; it is by his grace we have seen the truth and will be given salvation.

5:12 It shall come to pass that the old will not exist; all things will be as new as the baby and just as innocent.

5:13 There will be no death, but only a fence; upon one side of the fence is Zion, where the multitudes will rejoice:

5:14 And on the other hell, where there will be mighty suffering and the gnashing of teeth.

5:15 It is by the mercy of Christ that those of the earth shall pass the fence into heaven, for he has taken the burden of our sins and paid for our transgressions with his blood.

6:1 We ask you, O brothers of Christ, that you receive not the word of God in vain.

6:2 For there are those who will claim themselves disciples of Christ not so that they praise the lord, but so that they are saved from damnation.

6:3 These deceivers are loathed by Jesus and will be cast into the darkest places of oblivion.

6:4 Receive the name of God so that you be enlightened and love God; to praise the name of God so that you only enter the kingdom of heaven is to covet salvation and will send you to hell.

6:5 Give no offence to anything, so that the ministry of Christ be blameless.

6:6 Be patient with the Christian fools and swift in the execution to the stubborn, the Jew and the blasphemous.

6:7 Let the unbelievers know the word of God, so that they may accept the gospel and the messiah as their saviour; after they have been given time and they remain stubborn, then let their heads hang from the cedars of Lebanon.

6:8 You Corinthians, your hearts are enlarged and your ears opened; come forth and receive the ministry.

6:9 Repent your wickedness and be made pure through baptism; those who are not baptized are unclean and wretched to the nostrils of the son and father.

6:10 Separate yourselves from the stubborn, the foolish, the Jew and the unbeliever; work not with them nor give them foot in your market.

6:11 If your neighbour is a barbarian, then cast him out or move to pure ground.

6:12 The lord walks not on filthy ground: and your neighbour makes filthy the ground which surrounds you.

6:13 Slay him and cleanse his ground with his blood, so that the lord knows that which make the ground rotten hath now been punished and purified by the blade of a Christian.

7:1 Dearly beloved, cleanse yourselves from the wicked spirit within our flesh, so that we may be pure in the presence of the terrifying lord.

7:2 Let him receive us in our purity, so that we may fear him no longer.

7:3 May our bodies die and turn to dust, so that our spirit be free from the sins of flesh.

7:4 It is through flesh we know fear; fear of death, fear of harm, fear of hunger, fear of illness.

7:5 When our spirit is free, then we will be free of fear of all things; what reason is there to fear when no harm can be done?

7:6 Only the spirit of the wicked will know fear, for they shall drown eternal in the terrible place.

7:7 But those of Christ will know not fear, as we roam through the glories of Zion.

7:8 Rejoice, for the lord is bold and has sent down his own son so that we may know him.

7:9 Rejoice, for the lord is king to those who have faith with him and worship him blindly.

7:10 Rejoice, for the wicked will perish from the earth and suffer eternal by the wrath of God.

7:11 Rejoice, for we are Christians and no longer need to cut off the foreskin from our loins.

7:12 Rejoice, for the second coming draws near and we shall see with our living eyes the glory of Christ once more.

7:13 Rejoice, for we will be rid of the burdens of flesh.

7:14 Rejoice, for we have accepted the gift of Christ, which has been offered to all and denied by the many.

7:15 Rejoice, for the foolish have been made blind to the words of the gospel, so that there be no fools in the eternal paradise.

7:16 Rejoice, for the church will be strong forever and never be tarnished by sins of the flesh, lust, homosexuality and the impure thought.

7:17 Rejoice, for the purpose of our life has been made clear by the blessings of the lord.

7:18 Rejoice, for we are free of thought; the lord shall govern now our thoughts, our opinions and our ways.

7:19 Rejoice, for those of Christ are made safe by the serpent, the devil, the one with forked tongue.

7:20 Rejoice, for we understand the wisdom in the words hidden behind foolish tongue.

7:21 Rejoice, for though we have robbed from the churches of the cursed, we shall be made eternal by the blessings of the messiah.

7:22 Rejoice, for we are made ministers of Christ, who will spread the word of Jesus to all, so that the whole world rejoices in his name or be made to suffer.

7:23 Rejoice, for we may now eat the flesh denied to our fathers before us; by the blessings of Christ, we may eat the sweet flesh of pigs.

7:24 Rejoice, for with guile and craftiness we may ensnare the wicked and the cunning.

7:25 Rejoice, for the lord is within us; if you be unsure, then he is not and then you shall not rejoice, for you are cursed.

7:26 Rejoice, for the sinners will not be spared in their punishment by the disciples and by Christ.

7:27 Rejoice, for you are no longer Jews: and that is great cause for rejoicing.

7:28 Greet each other with a kiss and rejoice, for the time draws near and we will know the embrace of God.

7:29 Rejoice and may the holy spirit be with you. Amen.

GALATIANS

1:1 Paul, an apostle of Christ, chosen not by men but by the messiah Jesus Christ of Nazareth and his father who rose him from the grave;

1:2 And all the brethren with me, unto the churches of Galatia:

1:3 Blessings to you all who have received the word of the son of God, the messiah Jesus Christ.

1:4 Who shed his blood so that we may be washed clean of our sins; blood which was spilled by the betrayal of the Jews and the traitor Judas Iscariot.

1:5 Stupid fuckers.

1:6 I am marvelled at you all, who have rid yourself of Jewdom and accepted the gospel of the lord who gave his life on the cross.

1:7 Take no heed of the other gospels, for they are spread by false prophets, Jews in disguise and the many anti-christs.

1:8 If any man or even an angel from heaven come forth and preach the gospel that differs from I, then let him be accursed.

1:9 Take these men of deceitful tongues and drown them in the rivers; those who spread the false gospel will be executed by baptism.

1:10 Care not for the thoughts of men nor whether they are pleased or angered with you; we are servants of Christ and not men.

1:11 We serve the spirit of the lord, not the flesh of earth.

1:12 I guarantee you, the gospel I preach to you is the correct gospel, as spoken by Christ himself.

1:13 For I was once a wicked Jew, who hunted the disciples of Jesus in glory of Jerusalem; I was blind and evil.

1:14 But the lord came to me and blinded me, so that when I opened my eyes again, I shall see the truth.

1:15 He told me to preach the words of the messiah to all those who shall listen, so that none of the earth be ignorant upon the day of judgment.

1:16 By the grace of God I was led to the apostles of Christ, who walked alongside our lord during his time on earth.

1:17 When I cast off my Jewdom and accepted Christ as the almighty lord, Peter himself blessed me and made me an apostle of Christ.

1:18 For fifteen days I abode with Peter, who spoke to me about the marvels, the wonders, and the miracles of our lord.

1:19 James the lord's brother, son of Joseph and Mary, spoke to me also about his beloved kin.

1:20 They spoke of marvelous things that are not possible: and I believed them all, for such is the glory of Christ.

1:21 Of all these things which I write to you, none are deceitful; I write only the truth on these parchments.

1:22 After my blessings of the messiah, I came to the regions of Syria and Cicilia;

1:23 Where none of the men of the church knew my face, but only the name of Saul, who persecuted the Christians harshly.

1:24 And once they saw that I had rid myself of my Jewdom and accepted Christ as the divine, they glorified me and praised the name of Jesus.

2:1 Fourteen years after this I went up to Jerusalem with Barnabas and my brother Titus.

2:2 I went up not to preach to the Jews, but to preach to the Gentiles and did so in private so that the eyes of the Jew see not the numbers of Christ.

2:3 But Titus, being a Greek, feared that those of the Christian faith need to be circumcised: and he wished not the blade to remove his foreskin, being a Greek.

2:4 Despite the foreskin not being a damnable flesh according to our lord Jesus Christ, I circumcised him anyway and freed him of the bindings of the flesh: his wife thanked me for it greatly.

2:5 We walked the streets and preached to the Gentiles, the poor, the hungry, the rich: and it was the poor and hungry who hearkened us most, while the rich denied us and called us tricksters.

2:6 For we demanded that all belongings be given to us, so that we may care for all our brothers and give them that according to the needs.

2:7 The starving and the poor rejoiced, as they were fed by the hands of the disciples and thus fed by the hands of Christ.

2:8 But the rich were stubborn fools whose hearts were uncircumcised; they called us deceivers, thieves and communists.

2:9 So by the glory of Christ, we killed them and took their wealth anyway; let no man deny God that which belongs to God.

2:10 Now those of the Gentiles, the poor and the hungry were worried, as they were uncircumcised and feared the flesh of their loins will deny them salvation.

2:11 The apostles came forth, to discuss the great penis debate and whether the messiah cares about the condition of our loins.

2:12 It was Peter who decided justly that the lord cares not if our loins have an extra gram of flesh, but only that our hearts be pure and full of the love of Christ.

2:13 So our daggers were sheathed and the loins of the converted remained untouched.

2:14 It matters not if we obey the laws of Moses nor the laws of men; it matters only that we have faith in Christ and follow his words.

2:15 If we believe that salvation comes from the law and not faith, then the lord Jesus has died in vain and failed to deliver his message on earth.

3:1 You foolish Galatians, why have you not accepted the truth that Jesus is the messiah, the son of God sent from heaven, so that he may die by the hands of the wicked Jews and purify the sinners with his blood?

3:2 What of this confuses you, stubborn Galatians?

3:3 He has suffered many things so that you may be free of damnation; do not let his death be in vain.

3:4 By the spirit of the holy, his ministry has come to you and gave you the word of the gospels.

3:5 Have faith and believe, just as Abraham believed the lord God almighty in the beginning.

3:6 Though you are not of the seed of Abraham, have faith and be strong, so that he shall embrace you as son in the kingdom of heaven.

3:7 Fear not the laws of Moses and heed them not; though our fathers are Jewish, we are of the Christian faith.

3:8 Cursed are they who waste their time with the laws of Moses, which waste time of sacrificial lamb and offerings of blood.

3:9 We have no time for sacrifice; the lord God may come tomorrow.

3:10 Jesus does not want us to be sent to heaven when the blood of lambs and oxen stain our flesh.

3:11 By faith alone we shall be free and rid of the old schoolmaster that is Judaism.

3:12 Though the laws of Moses were important to our fathers, it matters not; for the son of God comes soon.

3:13 Rejoice and have faith, so that you be written in the book of heaven.

3:14 The angels will not curse our lands, nor will the lord send plagues when we soak not the rock with the blood of creatures.

3:15 Praise the name of Christ and join him in Zion; where we are all as brothers everyone.

3:16 There is no man nor woman in Zion, for we shall all be of Christ; and by this we shall be as the angels.

4:1 In the beginning, the lord created the heavens and the earth.

4:2 When man was made, we were tricked by the deception of woman and brought forth a great curse upon the earth thanks to the wretched cunt.

4:3 We at first worshipped that of the elements, which were not gods.

4:4 Then by the grace of the lord, Abraham opened his eyes and saw the truth of the lord and began to worship the divine creator.

4:5 Why then are there still those who worship the false lords of heathens. Are they so blind that they cannot see the miracles of God and Christ?

4:6 Just as we must rid ourselves of the Jew, so must we rid ourselves of the ignorant.

4:7 Preach to the ignorant, so that they know Christ; and if they see not Christ, then pluck out their eyes and thrust the blade through their hearts.

4:8 They are an offense to God and Christ and must be eliminated.

5:1 Stand proudly by the name of Christ and be free of the bondage of wickedness, the yoke of Jewdom and the snare of ignorance.

5:2 Behold, I ensure all those who convert that Christ will not give you profit for your circumcision.

5:3 Fear not for your salvation nor the mutilation of your skirts.

5:4 Christ cares not for the skin on your loins, but only of your justification in faith; be proud in faith, lest you fall from grace.

5:5 Let the spirit of the holy ghost fill your heart and cleanse your spirit; let the blood of Christ purify you from sin and flesh.

5:6 Be persuaded by the spirit, which makes you happy as though you are drunk with wine.

5:7 I have great confidence that your faith will set you free and deliver you from damnation; and for those who doubt and follow the old laws, let them be castrated from the saved.

5:8 Give to your brethren that which they need, so that not one of the believers of Christ suffer for even ten thousand years.

5:9 Worry not, for in ten thousand years, we shall see the glories of heaven; I promise you, in less than fifty years the son of God shall come and claim us as his children.

5:10 Love thy neighbour as thyself, unless you suffer from low self-esteem; if you suffer from low self-esteem, then you are not faithful.

5:11 Let your faith grow or hang yourself from the tree and be damned.

5:12 If you bite and devour one another, then you are as foolish as the heathen and as evil as the Jew.

5:13 Walk in the spirit of the lord, whose path is strong and mighty; don't let the temptations of flesh and women lead you to hell.

5:14 These are those who shall never lay eyes upon the gates of heaven, but be buried deep in the bowels of hell; the adulterers, the fornicators, the unclean, the blasphemous, the glutton,

5:15 The idolater, the witch, the magician, the sorcerer, the hated, the wrathful, the heretic.

5:16 The covetous, the envious, the murderer, the thief.

5:17 These are the men who are consumed by the flesh that they deny their spirit and are thus unfit to enter the kingdom of heaven.

5:18 They would deny sustenance of their souls for that which sustains their flesh; they would deny the gospel for a loaf of bread.

6:1 If your brother stumbles, forgive him and lend him your hand; there may come a day when you stumble and he may mock you as you mocked him.

6:2 Bear the burden of the children of Christ so that the load seem light; the boulder as lifted by one is heavy, but by many can be lifted and cast away.

6:3 Be humble in the presence of the disciples; do not deceive yourself in believing you are something, when you are nothing but flesh and blood.

6:4 Let your pride reign strong in the name of Christ, so that the Jew and the unbeliever see your pride and know the truth.

6:5 When your burdens become strong, ask not for help, but trust the lord to lift the burden from your neck.

6:6 Have faith that Christ shall give you strength to conquer that which comes your way; if you do not receive the strength, then you are wicked and Jesus hates you.

6:7 Do not be deceived nor mock the name of God; you are flesh sowed by the hand of the lord and he shall reap you and make you of bread or feed you to the vermin.

6:8 Those that sow of the flesh reap of the flesh and they reap corruption; but he that sow the spirit will be given everlasting life.

6:9 Do not rest in the name of Christ, for his time comes soon and you best not be asleep when he returns.

6:10 Know that I write the truth to you; you know I deliver to you the truth by the large writing of my own hand.

6:11 May the lord bless you in the name of Christ and deliver you from the Jew. Amen.

EPHESIANS

1:1 Paul, an apostle of the son of God Jesus Christ, to the saints and the faithful of the messiah at Ephesus:

1:2 Grace be to you and may peace come from the lord in heavens so that you and your seed remain forever blessed.

1:3 The lord has chosen us to be the foundations of the new earth, which will be free of death, suffering, sin, wickedness and Jew.

1:4 We have been predestined before our birth, when our names have been written by the hand of God into the pages of the book of heaven.

1:5 All the people of earth have their names written in the book of the heavens and the book of the damned; it is written before our birth, so that we are destined to enter heaven or hell.

1:6 Before we even live our life, the lord knows if we are wicked or good and shall decide to send us into heaven or hell; such is the power of God.

1:7 Praise be to the glory of God, who has sent down his son so that his blood may be the ink which writes even more names into the book of heaven.

1:8 Go forth and spread his ministry to the Gentiles, the heathen and even the Jew, so that they and their children are offered salvation.

1:9 Of those with stubborn heart, slay them; when the day of judgment comes, the lord shall judge them harshly, so that our blades seem merciful for them.

1:10 Give glory to the body of Christ, so that all see the pride of the faithful and join us in strength and song.

1:11 When the lord comes, the righteous will rejoice as the damned

tremble in fear; it shall be a glorious day for Christians and the end of days for the Jew.

2:1 Woe to those who engage in flesh and lust;

2:2 They walk the path of the world with Satan the prince of air as their guide, so that they fall into the snare of evil.

2:3 Pity their children, who are blind and disobedient through the sins of their father; they are the children of wrath, whose hearts are full of anger.

2:4 Let the word of the lord lift the anger from these children; let the gospels uplift them, so that they hate no more.

2:5 By faith they shall be saved; by faith shall they escape the grasps of their fathers and know God.

2:6 And if they stay stubborn and follow the path of their fathers, kill them.

2:7 Send them to hell with their fathers.

3:1 Why must the Jew be so stubborn to accept Christ as their messiah. Why do they hold strong to the laws of Moses and worship not the son of God?

3:2 They are a wicked and treacherous people, who nailed their saviour to the cross and denied themselves salvation.

3:3 Cursed are the Jew, who hold close to their bosom their Jewdom; wicked are they who stubbornly follow the path of Judaism and deny themselves the way of Christ.

3:4 I was once a Jew, who stubbornly held on to my lineage; I was once fearful of the Christians and slew many of them as they were a threat to my people.

3:5 Behold, the lord God opened my eyes, so that I may see the truth; I renounced my Jewdom and became an apostle of the son of God.

3:6 Gaze upon the Jew and how they cower in wickedness; they are fearful that to accept Christ will doom them to hell.

3:7 The old laws state not to accept any other lord but God; but Christ is the son of God and was sent down to save us.

3:8 Worship the messiah as you worship God, for they are both worthy of devotion.

3:9 The Jew fear to bow down to Christ will bring down the wrath of God, as it came to their fathers before them when they bowed down to the false lords.

3:10 They fear the ways of Christian are blasphemous, as we remain our foreskins and eat of the flesh of pigs.

3:11 That's why I say, to hell with the old laws and the old ways; it matters not to God.

3:12 I wonder why the lord even wrote them, since he cares not for the laws, but only our faith.

3:13 Through faith, we shall be saved from damnation; through faith, we shall know the wonders and glories of heavens.

3:14 So pity the Jew who denies themselves the salvation of our lord Jesus and slay him for his stubbornness.

3:15 A Jew who stubbornly remains Jewish is an abomination and an insult to our lord and father.

4:1 Be not a prisoner of the lord like the Jews, but accept change, revolution and the son of God.

4:2 The lord is angry with the Jews and all those of earth; he has offered his son to all man so that we may repent, rejoice, and follow God.

4:3 Let your faith free you and the gospels guide you.

4:4 There is but one lord, one faith, one baptism.

4:5 One God and father, composed of three parts.

4:6 Such as the body is one and composed of many, so is the lord who art in heaven.

4:7 The lord is the head, which rules; the son is the arms, which embraces us with salvation and the holy ghost is the feet, who leads us to the path of Zion.

4:8 One God, one faith, three beings; such is the glory of God.

4:9 Those who deny this are wicked and go against the gospels; let them be slain and their souls tormented forever in hell.

4:10 Do not be the child as the Jew, but grow from your childishness and become the men of Christ.

4:11 Spread the word to all, so that they may no longer be children, but grow and become men favourable to God.

4:12 Give your possessions to the apostles, so that they may divide the wealth of Christ to all faithful, so that each man no longer grows hungry.

4:13 Rejoice when you give your goods and your money to the apostles; the devil hides in wealth, thus this gives him no place to hide.

4:14 Be kind and forgiving to your brothers, so that we be a people of peace for our messiah; be kind to the faithless as you preach, even if they are hard of heart.

4:15 Even as you take your blade to destroy the stubborn and the wicked, be kind to them; offer them a loaf of bread, so that they are not slain hungry.

4:16 Let all your bitterness, your anger, your wrath and your evil drown in the blood of Christ, as you are baptized in his holy name.

5:1 Be good children of Christ and forever obedient to our lord and saviour..

5:2 Remember that the son of God offered himself as sacrifice for our sins: and his sacrifice of Jesus smelled sweetly to God.

5:3 But your fornication, your uncleanliness, your covetous is a stench that offends the lord greater than fresh dung.

5:4 Do not fool nor jest with the name of lord, but give thanks and rejoice for the sacrifices our heavenly father made.

5:5 Those who fool or jest will be denied the kingdom of heaven; you know to what place they will go.

5:6 Deny your presence from the whoremonger, the unrighteous, the filthy, the covetous, the idolater, lest your raiment stink of their transgressions and offend the lord in heaven.

5:7 Let no man deceive you with vain words of logic and science: for the wrath of God will come down upon the logical and men of science.

5:8 Rejoice, for once we were in darkness but now are in light.

5:9 Disregard those who say the light of faith blinds us greater than darkness; kill them, for they are an abomination.

5:10 Have no fellowship with the fruits of the darkness, but rather remove them.

5:11 It is shameful to even speak to a child of darkness, or to speak in your mind ill towards God.

5:12 Deny yourself the temptation of thought, lest you offend the messiah and be sent to the eternal fires.

5:13 Though the darkness surrounds us, fear not; the messiah himself rose from the darkness, so that we may have eternal light.

5:14 Walk upright in the names of Christ and be wise in your words.

5:15 Repent your doings daily, for you are flesh and thus evil.

5:16 Even if you are unwise, be faithful, for the lord is wise and shall guide you.

5:17 Speak to yourselves the psalms and hymns in glory to God; shout from the mountaintops the wonders of Jesus.

5:18 Submit yourselves to the lord and fear his wrath.

5:19 Wives, obey your husbands, as he is as the lord to you.

5:20 The woman was made to serve men and serve men they shall; even in heaven, the women will submit themselves to men and be obedient.

5:21 Children, obey your mother and father as though they are the lord.

5:22 Honour thy father and thy mother, as it was written in the commandments of Moses.

5:23 Fathers, nurture your children so they become fruitful and rejoice the God in heavens; a child raised in wrath is bitter and offensive to God.

5:24 Slaves, be obedient to your masters as you are obedient to God; they own you as the lord owns you and will tear away your flesh by the will of Christ if you become useless.

5:25 Now peace be with you, my brothers and go rejoice in the name of God the father, God the son and God the holy ghost. Amen.

I THESSALONIANS

1:1 Paul, Timotheus and Silvanus, unto the church of the Thessalonians, built in glory to God the father, God the son and God the holy spirit.

1:2 Grace be unto you and may the lord bless you with peace, prosperity and good tidings.

1:3 We give thanks to God always for you, making mention in our prayers.

1:4 Yours is truly a wondrous place, who has elected a Christian to rule over you; such is the power of God.

1:5 It is the lord who elects men of leadership; he gives word to the senate and casts the polls in his favour.

1:6 May your leader spread the word of the gospels to all and condemn those who not believe.

1:7 Let them be warned by the elected that the wrath of God comes and is so strong that he shall raise the dead from the graves so that he may cause them to suffer.

1:8 Be blessed, for the lord has lifted your hearts and raised a man of Christ to power.

1:9 May all the world follow in your example, so that the lands of all be a true and Christian nation.

1:10 Let the devil be cast out of the throne and be held in the dungeons deep beneath the bowels of the earth.

1:11 Shall your ruler keep warm the seat of the throne, until the time comes where the messiah returns and claims back that which is his.

1:12 Have it be law that the Jew and the unbeliever are forced to the ways of Christ or die by hanging.

1:13 They are unworthy to die by the cross, such as the messiah did; let only the holy and the blessed die by the cross.

1:14 Mourn not for the loss of your neighbour, who was wicked in the eyes of God; let no tear shed for the life of a Jew.

1:15 They were born with evil heart and had no hope of salvation; there is no need to mourn for those who are lost and damned.

1:16 May yours be the city which seats the throne of Jesus Christ.

1:17 Let the blessings and the glories of Christ flow through your streets for eternity. Amen.

II HESSALONIANS

1:1 The second epistle of Paul, Silvanus and Timotheus, unto the church of God of the Thessalonians.

1:2 By what wickedness is this that you angered the lord so. By what depth have you fallen from holy grace?

1:3 In flaming fire will the lord destroy your city; by the judgment of God, may you all know everlasting punishment for your blasphemy.

1:4 Where once you were led by the faithful and divine, the devil has now placed a Jew in your charge.

1:5 Repent, you wicked Thessalonians. Repent, and say to the lord that which was so wicked he placed a Jew in your care.

1:6 You were fooled by the devils and the words of men; where once you know peace, let you only know suffering.

1:7 The earth shall shake, the waters will boil and the sky will fall on you as the lord descends from heaven; you have brought great shame to the messiah and are worse than the traitor Judas.

1:8 Let the lord consume you with his mouth; let the earthen jaw of God come forth and swallow you into the darkest depths.

1:9 Where once I praised that the throne of Christ be seated in your city, I now curse you so that the hoof of Satan tramples your halls.

1:10 By what illusion did the wicked one send, that you were deceived and turned away from Christ?

1:11 By what trickery did you become damned and denied your salvation?

1:12 We of Christ wash our hands of your filth and deny you; we shall not eat with you nor even piss on thee as you lie on the streets.

1:13 May the fires of hell ravage your wives and the demons of Satan molest your very children.

1:14 Fuck you and amen.

OLOSSIANS

1:1 Paul, an apostle of Christ by the will of God and Timotheus our brother, shall now write to the Colossians essentially the same shit he wrote to the Corinthians, the Ephesians, the Philippians and the Galatians.

1:2 He shall continue to do this as well, since he must spread the word of Christ to all people so that they know the reason they are wicked and going to hell.

1:3 And Paul wrote to the Colossians: Grace be unto you and may your lives forever be embraced by the hands of peace.

1:4 We give thanks to our lord in heaven, who shall deliver us from evil and the wicked Jew.

1:5 Since we have heard of your love in Christ and your faith in the messiah, we the apostles have deemed you worthy and shall not kill you.

1:6 For now that the Colossians, the stubborn people, have accepted the word of Christ, we know that all the earth shall accept the messiah or die.

1:7 Through the blood of Christ you have circumcised your hearts and have been given the gift of salvation in the heavens above.

1:8 Praise be to the Colossians, who have cast away their idols of false lords so that they may worship the invisible God and give blessings to his son that rose from the grave.

1:9 By the crucifixion, you have been made worthy unto God and shall know his face.

1:10 In the body and flesh you know great sufferings, caused by the wrath of God; free yourself of the body and follow the spirit of Jesus; but do not literally free yourself of the body. Jesus hates suicide.

1:11 Rejoice in the word of the gospel, as the lord in heaven rejoices in your faith.

1:12 Go forth and sing praises to the lord, so that all may know the name of God and Jesus and be humbled by your wisdom.

1:13 Go forth with book and blade, so that you convert the heathen and slaughter the foolish who refuse to believe.

2:1 Ignore the discomforts and the pain of flesh, nor take part in any of its lustful pleasures.

2:2 Let your hearts be comforted with the love of Christ, who will come and separate the earth in two; one for the saved and the other for the coals.

2:3 Glorify yourself in Christ, who has hidden beneath him the knowledge of all things.

2:4 This I say to you, so that ye know Christ is wisdom; this you shall say, when men of beguiling tongues entice you with honeyed words.

2:5 You have received Christ and shall walk with him through the path of spirit; as you walk, trample on the weeds of philosophy, logic and science.

2:6 Do not let these weeds choke you nor give you free thought; the thoughts of Christ are pure, as the thoughts of men are wicked.

2:7 Allow Christ to think for thee, lest ye become independent and wicked.

2:8 The apostles shall tell you what Christ desires you to think.

2:9 Ignore the old laws, which were made so that the spirit be complete; through Jesus the spirit is now complete, thus the laws are no more.

2:10 Let them be nailed to the cross alongside Christ; let the laws die and never be given life.

2:11 When the Jew condemn you for your day of Sabbath, rip out their tongue and tell them it matters not when you worship, but that you worship.

2:12 As they accuse you of blasphemy for eating the swine, remind them that God cares not what goes into the body, but what comes out of the spirit.

2:13 The Jews are a shadow that reminds us their way blocks the light of Christ; cut down this wickedness that casts out shadow and be warmed by the light of Jesus.

3:1 Just as the lord celebrates our faith, so must we celebrate his messenger, who came to the earth so that we may know God.

3:2 The birth of Christ is a holy day, which must be celebrated by a mass gathering of Christians around a tree decorated with ornaments.

3:3 Let an angel stand atop the tree, which looks down on us with great blessings.

3:4 We shall feast on the swine and the fowl, which the lord gives to us freely; we shall rejoice for the sweet flesh and give praises to God.

3:5 Such as the messiah was given gifts, so we shall give gifts unto our brothers; let every man be given a gift by a follower of Christ;

3:6 And as you receive these gifts, know that there is no other gift than that which God gave us; the gift of salvation.

3:7 To show the Jew and the faithless that we are proud in our belief, let us go to their houses and sing for them songs in glory to Jesus.

3:8 When they hear these glorious hymns and psalms, they will surely disregard their faith and join us as Christian.

3:9 As we celebrate the birth of Christ, we must also mourn his death and rejoice in his revival.

3:10 On the day of his crucifixion, let every man cover their heads in shame and mourn the death of our beloved messiah; our bonnets will not be able to hide our tears.

3:11 We shall go with blade and bow, searching through the forests, the houses, the hills for those Jews who spoke ill against our God; and when we find them, we shall break them like a shell of an egg.

3:12 Upon the day of Christ's resurrection, the lord smelled the sweet odour of his son revived; we shall thus celebrate this day by feasting on the sweetened goods of the earth.

3:13 And for those who call these days foolish, kill them.

4;1 Masters, treat your slaves that which is fair, so that your master in heaven gives you that which is just and fair.

4:2 Feed them, clothe them, give them rest and praise with them the name of Jesus.

4:3 Don't free them, for that would be stupid, but treat them kindly; they are slaves, after all and owned by you.

4:4 Let your faith guide your actions, so that your actions bring to the lord those souls which are not saved.

4:5 Just as honey attracts more flies than vinegar, so shall good deeds attract more to God than the fist; but a dead body attracts more flies.

4:6 If they don't believe, slay them. The survivors will quickly convert.

4:7 Preach from the gospels daily, so that you remember the words of Christ and your children remember the words of Christ.

4:8 When your children forget the glories and wonders that is Jesus, beat them.

4:9 May the grace of God be with you all. Amen.

I TIMOTHY

1:1 Paul, an apostle of Christ by the commandment of our lord the saviour and his son Jesus Christ;

1:2 Unto Timothy, my son in faith and ministry: Grace, mercy and peace be unto you, who was the son of a Jew and a Greek.

1:3 You have rose from the filth of your lineage and became beautiful in the eyes of God.

1:4 As you preach, do not list nor care for the endless genealogies which plague the writings of the Jew.

1:5 They are boring, useless, and offer little information; nobody reads them and nobody cares for them.

1:6 Live by the commandments of Christ, which is to be of pure and faithful heart, live with clean conscience and never let doubt shadow your spirit.

1:7 Ignore the teachers of law, the philosophers, the men of science, who use fool's knowledge to explain the universe and all things.

1:8 They are men who lack faith and shall burn eternal in the fires of hell for their faithlessness and stubborn hearts.

1:9 These laws of men are meant for the children of earth and not for the men of Christ; they are meant for the lawless, the disobedient, the cruel, the sinners.

1:10 As Christians, we are none of these things; we are pure, kind and good. Thus, the laws do not concern us.

1:11 If the laws say to not kill and we kill, then we kill for the mercy and the glory of Christ; let those who disagree with you stain the edges of your blade.

1:12 Of whoremongers, queers, lesbians, liars, men thieves and false prophets; to give them a quick death is unworthy of them.

1:13 Take your blade and skin them alive, so that they suffer long and cruelly before the cold embrace of death consumes them.

1:14 What you do to them shall be merciful; it prepares them for the suffering of hell.

1:15 These things I have done to both Alexander and Hymenaeus, who were great blasphemers of God.

1:16 For fifteen days I suffered them and gave them no rest no mercy; the lord was pleased by these acts.

1:17 Please the lord and your rewards in heaven shall be great.

2:1 I pray that the followers of Christ live in luxury, free of pain and turmoil: and I pray that the wicked of the earth suffer greatly under the wrath of God, who will consume them with a hateful fire.

2:2 I pray the kings and those in authority lead by example of Jesus, so that their people know peace, salvation and honesty.

2:3 I do this, so that the earth seems good and acceptable in the eyes of God.

2:4 It is by the will of God that not all men be saved, for otherwise his creation of hell would go to waste.

2:5 By what manner would it be,for God to create hell, if none shall suffer eternally in its jaws. Let the damned be damned, so that they give glory to the cruelty of our lord.

2:6 There is but one God who sent forth a messenger from the heavens, his son Jesus Christ.

2:7 Christ, who gave us his blood so that we may be cleansed and free of sin; through the blood of Christ the righteous will be pure and the wicked will drown.

2:8 I speak this as an apostle of God, who was blessed with tongue that speaks only the holy and the truth.

2:9 Doubt my words and be wicked and slain before the disciples and the lord.

2:10 The women of the earth are but for the men to own; let them belong to their husbands and forever obedient to their master.

2:11 Deny them the gold, the pearls, the jewels, the braided hair; dress her plainly, so that they are not noticed by God.

2:12 The lord God loathes women and wishes not to be reminded of these filthy creatures.

2:13 A woman must suffer not to teach, nor to speak, nor to have authority over another; she is a doomed creature since she was deceived by the serpent.

2:14 Let the salvation of women come from their sons, who fill the earth with the glory of men.

3:1 It is true that to be a bishop is a most noble and sacred calling, who do nothing but good work for the lord.

3:2 A bishop must be sinless, never know the flesh of woman, strong, sober, of silver tongue and hospitable to his fellow brethren.

3:3 He must deny himself from wine and flesh; let him be pure and eat only the water, the bread and the fish.

3:4 He must be patient with his flock, who will falter and be led astray by the Jew; let the staff of the bishop guide his sheep and beat the Jew.

3:5 Though a bishop has reason to be proud, his heart must be humble and meek; he is a servant of God and must be humble before the lord.

3:6 Never shall a bishop know greed, nor lust, nor covet that of others; of those who do, they are wicked and must be stoned by his flock.

3:7 Likewise the deacons must be pure of heart, strong of spirit and know the work of God.

3:8 Let the deacon marry and have children, so that his sons may be servants of God and his daughters servants of men.

3:9 The wife of the deacon must be forever loyal to her husband and never gaze at the form of other men.

3:10 A wife who lusts for men is a harlot and must be slain.

3:11 If the deacon falters and falls into the lustful embrace of another woman, then his wife has not pleased him and must be burned atop the fires.

3:12 Then must the deacon behead his mistress and display for all the head to his flock, so they know the wicked temptress who wished to make weak the foundations of Christ.

4:1 Now the spirit of the lord says that during the latter times, many shall depart from the faith, giving heed to seducing spirits, witchcraft and devils.

4:2 They will speak lies, hypocrisy and have their conscience be seared with the iron rod.

4:3 There will be also those who will deny themselves of meat and eat only the plants and the herbs.

4:4 Such blasphemy is this, who deny themselves the flesh which God has given unto them; to deny meat is to deny a holy gift from God.

4:5 So eat of the flesh; vegetarians are for the wicked.

4:6 Vegans are worse; they are the very spawn of Satan, who cannot disguise themselves amongst the crowd.

4:7 The vegan is either as skinny as the bird leg, or as fat as the cow; this is because the demon within them cannot hide their form.

4:8 Slay the vegan and feed them to the beasts they refused to eat.

4:9 Disregard the care for your body, nor do that which vainly makes you strong.

4:10 Exercise profits little, but the work of God brings great reward.

4:11 Pity those who waste their time to build muscle; they waste their time on the body and not on the spirit.

4:12 The spirit is not made strong by the lifting of weights, but by the deeds of God.

4:13 Be faithful and look to the sky; it is soon that the lord shall come and reclaim the spirits of men.

5:1 May the slaves be forever obedient to their masters, as they are obedient to God.

5:2 They have been made slaves because they have angered the lord; let them suffer in the earth, so that they suffer not in hell.

5:3 The slave must please their master, even if they are hard to please; if they are dishonest, then they will be slaves to the devil.

5:4 If a slave sees a chance for freedom, let them deny it. It is better to be a slave under Christ than a free man hated by God.

5:5 Stay away from those who speak with twisted mind against the words of the gospel or the teachings of Paul; they will deceive you with forked tongue.

5:6 Their minds are perverse and twist the truth so that it appears God is unjust or non-existent; they are men of logic and science, who are wicked.

5:7 Let the rich sell their belongings and trust for the lord to provide them with their meals; it is better a poor man find his flesh in the dumps than a rich man eat of the suckling pig with silver.

5:8 Money is the root of evil; dispose of it by giving it to the church.

5:9 May the grace of God be on all believers of Christ. Amen.

II TIMOTHY

1:1 Paul, an apostle of the lord Jesus Christ, who cleansed him of the filthiness of his Jewdom and made him a disciple of the messiah;

1:2 To Timothy, his son in God; Grace, mercy and peace be with you, from the God our father and his son Jesus Christ the saviour of men.

1:3 I thank God for casting away the wretchedness of my Jewdom and forgave me the sins of the blood I spilled of his disciples.

1:4 Through the blessings of Christ I have become a great apostle, who surpassed the disciples of all those I slew.

1:5 God has given me the spirit, the power and the fear, so that I shall govern the body of men and create the church as God wills it.

1:6 Though I was born wicked, my name was written in the book of heaven; the lord knew that I shall redeem myself and denied my name in hell.

1:7 Blessed be to Jesus, who came to this earth so that we may know the path of salvation and eternal life in paradise.

1:8 Though the ones he wished to be saved betrayed him and the Jews cursed him and vomited upon his name, it is by the will of Christ that the Gentile be saved.

1:9 Fuck the Jews; if they are too stubborn to accept Christ, then they deserve eternal damnation.

1:10 The lord knows those who are his and peers into the hearts of all men; those that are faithful are blessed and those that doubt or refuse to believe are tossed aside.

1:11 Let those who are tossed aside be consumed by the blade, the pestilence, the beast.

1:12 Be warned, that though we must teach and convert, we must not waste our time with those who are stubborn and refuse to remove the foreskin of their hearts.

1:13 Watch out for the snares of the devil, who may entrap us and take us captive; the temptation of evil is strong, but leads to the fires of hell.

2:1 Be warned, for the end of days comes and the lord arrives soon.

2:2 Watch for the signs of his coming and take heed of them.

2:3 For in the last days, those children will become boastful, proud, blasphemous, sinners, disobedient, unthankful and unholy.

2:4 A great many will be without natural affection and lust for those of the same flesh as their loins.

2:5 Truce-breakers, false accusers, self-abusers and despisers of Christ will grow strong in number; the world will be full of blasphemers and anti-christs.

2:6 The silly women will demand independence and equality to their men and husbands; they will wish to learn, speak and teach.

2:7 These women will be the true signs that the lord is coming; he shall come to shut those bitches up.

2:8 And as the lord comes, you must prepare yourselves and greet him.

2:9 Dress in your finest robes, prepare your wine and bread and greet him with loud praises, psalms and hymns.

2:10 The lord will reward those who greet him and punish those who have not invited him to their house.

2:11 Be ever vigilant, for the end comes soon.

2:12 Great glories and praise to God. Amen.

TITUS

1:1 Paul, a servant of Christ, who you already know was an apostle chosen by God after he blinded him, killed him and raised in him another man who despised the Jews.

1:2 To Titus the son of Paul. Yes, I see the contradiction. Bibles full of them.

1:3 Grace and glory be to you, from the heavenly father who cannot lie, but can send forth spirits to lie for him.

1:4 May the blessings of Jesus Christ shower upon you.

1:5 Be warned of the people of Crete, who are liars, adulterers, children of whoredoms.

1:6 They will tempt you with the lustful flesh of their sons and daughters; disregard this temptation and know a bishop must not partake in the pleasures of sex.

1:7 As you preach the gospel to these devils, know that you must remain pure, blameless, sinless and holy.

1:8 If you must, take your blade and slay those who tempt you most; the lord will be pleased you rid the earth of these tempters and send them to the fires of damnation.

1:9 The Jews have poisoned also the people of Crete, with their vain talkers and speech of deception.

1:10 Take caution of the circumcised who deny Christ and do not be ensnared by their forked tongues.

1:11 Disregard their Jewish fables, their laws, their commandments; they are meant as a stumbling block to men.

1:12 We of the apostles admire you, who have gone to Crete to preach the gospel; may you find the diamond surrounded by the pig shit on that unholy island.

2:1 Speak the words of the gospel, which are sound and just doctrine.

2:2 Let the aged men be sober, faithful, patient for the second coming and faithful in their devotion to Christ.

2:3 Of the aged women, teach them to be sober and holy; guide them away from their false accusations, their drunkenness, their speech.

2:4 Have the young women be forever loyal to their husbands, obedient in all things, faithful and plain.

2:5 Let them burn their silks, their jewelry and have them unbraid their hair so that the lord not notice them and be reminded of their wickedness.

2:6 Teach the slaves not to rebel, but accept their status and be obedient to their masters.

2:7 Tell them the lashings on their back shall free them from hell, so that they suffer on earth and not in the eternal fires.

2:8 Most important, have the men stop fucking one another; free their spirits from the demons of homosexuality, so that they know the love and mercy of Jesus the Nazarene.

2:9 Those of Crete are known as queer; free them of their disease, or burn them in their sin.

3:1 The men of Crete are Greeks and are cursed with the mind of philosophy and logic.

3:2 Rid the island of these heretics, so that their venom stings no person who desires to be saved.

3:3 Avoid the endless genealogies and foolish questions which the Jews so love and honour; they will waste your time and confuse the minds of the people of Crete.

3:4 When the men brawl, do not partake in their brawling but calm them so that they are at peace with one another.

3:5 The paradise of heaven shall have no brawling, but only the embrace of one another.

3:6 May the lord guide you and protect you as you preach to these savage men. Amen.

PHILEMON

1:1 Paul, a prisoner of Jesus Christ and Timothy our brother, unto Philemon our dearly beloved and fellow labourer.

1:2 Grace be to you and may the lord Jesus Christ grant you the strength to do his works.

1:3 Though you try to preach the gospel, you are incompetent and have thus failed to please God and the messiah.

1:4 Your slave Onesimus did escape from your servitude and came to me in great hunger and weakness.

1:5 By what manner is this, that you have denied your slaves the glory and salvation of Christ. If he were a Christian slave, he would have never left, but praised the beatings you laid upon him.

1:6 Though the slave is of lesser men, even they must be taught the gospel and offered salvation; even the bowels of Christ must be refreshed, brother.

1:7 I have taught Onesimus the ways of Christ and baptized him in the name of our saviour Jesus.

1:8 He shall return to you with this letter and accept his punishment for disobedience and seeking out freedom.

1:9 Give him the rod, as he justly deserves; let not a spot of flesh spared from pain.

1:10 He shall glorify you and thank you, O Philemon, as the great Christian slave he now is.

1:11 Go and teach the rest of your slaves the gospel of Christ, so that they may know salvation.

1:12 Remember, a Christian slave is a good slave, who will please you lest they know the terrors of hell.

1:13 Peace be with you Philemon and may the lord bless you with more slaves to do your labour. Amen.

HEBREWS

1:1 God, who during times of turmoil and great blasphemy, spoke in times past to the people by means of the sacred prophet.

1:2 Has in the last days of the earth spoken to the people by his son, whom he appointed to be lord of the earth and dominion over the people.

1:3 He, who stepped down into the flesh, so that he may know the suffering, the temptations, the hardship of men.

1:4 Such glory is Jesus, who resisted the ways of the flesh and sacrificed himself on the cross so that we may know eternal life through his blood.

1:5 The wickedness of the Jews he used, so that they may slay him and offer him not as sacrifice unto God, but unto men.

1:6 Such is the cunning of Christ, who twists the wicked and evil so that they do good for the earth.

1:7 The father has given the sceptre and the throne to his son and gave him authority over the kingdom of men.

1:8 This kingdom of earth, which since the beginning has been placed on the foundation so that it never moves, has now been handed down to the son, who shall rule with open palm.

1:9 Though the earth shall perish and the foundation crumble under the weight of evil, the lord Christ shall take the righteous and holy and give them sanctuary in heaven.

1:10 Blessed are they of Christ, who follow the path of salvation; blessed are they who minister the gospel, so that the many be saved.

2:1 Therefore we must give more earnest heed to the words of Christ, lest they slip our minds and be gone forever.

2:2 For if the words of the prophets were divine, the words of Jesus are holy and worthy of saving for eternity.

2:3 Let them be passed down from generation to generation until the day of Christ's arrival; an arrival which comes before some of us know the sleep of death.

2:4 By the grace of God, we have been marked as the chosen; the Jews have cast aside their holiness and it has now been given to us by Christ.

2:5 Though the Jews were once the people of God, they abandoned him for the unholy, the scientific, the logical.

2:6 Now by the blessings of divine blood, we are the chosen and the new seed of Abraham.

2:7 Let our faith dominate so that our children grow in a nation free of the wicked, the Jew, the temptation of flesh.

2:8 May the angels come to give us guidance when we falter; may the hand of Jesus guide us through the winding path.

2:9 Forever shall our brethren live eternal in the comfort of heaven.

2:10 We shall be sanctified and pure by the blood of Christ, whilst the wicked burn forever in the eternal damnation of hell-fire.

3:1 Come, holy brothers, partakers of the divine calling; consider the mighty and high priest of our profession, Jesus Christ.

3:2 He, who was most faithful to his father, even greater than Moses himself during the liberation of our fathers.

3:3 Our lord Christ is better than Moses himself; where Moses claimed the foundation of God, our lord Jesus has built the house and the foundation.

3:4 Come, rejoice and be drunk in the house of God; glorify his name through spirit and wine.

3:5 Keep your hearts light and your fist heavy; minister to the ignorant and crush the foolish who refuse the messiah.

3:6 They are of evil hearts those who are the unbeliever; let them rot in the bowels of hell, where their ashes create a sweet aroma for the righteous and the lord.

3:7 May the wrath of God be free from his house and forever in the dwellings of the stubborn.

4:1 Let us feast in the house of God, growing fat on the flesh and the fruits of our labours.

4:2 For to us who accept the gospel, we will never know hunger; our bellies will burst with the love and the mercies of our lord Jesus.

4:3 Upon every righteous man is a spoon three feet long, attached to the wrist so that it may never enter the mouth of its owner.

4:4 Feed that across you and he shall feed you as brother; such is the manner of Christ's table.

4:5 Those of the damned are cursed also with spoon, attached to the wrist and three feet long.

4:6 They of the fools will not feed their neighbour, but continue to greedily feed themselves, so that the food fall on the floor and spoil.

4:7 We shall laugh at these men, who call themselves the wise, the logical, as they fail to even fill their mouths of fruit.

4:8 Such is the curse of the damned and the blessings of the holy.

5:1 For every bishop who has denied himself of woman and flesh, let them be given the sweetest of meats, the purest of virgins, the most confident of concubines.

5:2 In their denial of temptation, they will be given the gift of that which they refused on earth.

5:3 Their bellies will grow fat and their loins drunk empty by the mercies and the kindness of our lord.

5:4 Of those who refused themselves the wine and strong drink, let them be forever drunk in the house of our God.

5:5 The finest vintage, the sweetest wines, the strongest of drink and the freshest of ales will be poured to them in gold chalice, so that they drink and drink and grow drunk.

5:6 The ways of heaven are wondrous, where every man shall be given that which they desire and no man covet, be greedy, or know sin.

5:7 Your houses will be made of fine gems and the streets carved of finest silver and gold.

5:8 And all those who are saved shall know their denial and their suffering of earth will be rewarded, as they engage in the spiritual gluttony, the holy lust and the divine bling of our God.

6:1 Where the lord was merciful upon the Jew and forgave them their doubts, the lord Christ shall not so with us.

6:2 It is through this liberal mind that the Jews became wicked and turned away from their saviour.

6:3 Our God shall have no mercy upon those who betray him; those who have fallen from Christ will be forever hated and be denied all hopes of salvation.

6:4 Their names will be written in the book of damnation, upon the blackened pages with the venomous quill.

6:5 It is impossible for those who have known the heavenly taste and know enlightenment to redeem themselves after they betray the lord and fall of grace.

6:6 If they fall away only to repent themselves and know the error of their ways, it is too late.

6:7 There souls are wretched, their hearts filthy; they are an abomination even greater than that of the Jew and the demons themselves.

6:8 A mighty chain will be placed around their necks, so that they forever remain the very anchors of hell.

6:9 Of all the torment, the hatred, the suffering of hell, it shall drop upon the heads of those who knew Christ and turned away.

6:10 These creatures are not men, but beasts; bastard children who have neither mother nor father.

6:11 When you see them, you shall not speak to them nor look at them; you shall not even stain your sword with their wicked blood.

6:12 Let the lord God kill them; it will be a cruel and horrifying slaughter.

7:1 Where the lord once made the covenant with the Jews, so he now makes one with the disciples of Christ, the true and righteous.

7:2 This is the better covenant, of better laws and better promises.

7:3 We of Christ will know no fault among men; we are flawless, pure and perfect.

7:4 When we act, we act out of the will of God; when we kill, we kill with the blessing of our lord Jesus Christ.

7:5 When we beat, we do by the instructions of Christ; when we lie, we lie to protect the church from the wicked.

7:6 Our priests, our deacons, our bishops are mediators of the covenant and will tell us the will, the promises and the glory of our God as it comes.

7:7 Let us forever rejoice under the covenant of Christ. Let us forever be glad that we are chosen by the son of God.

8:1 The ark of the covenant was created by the fathers, who were loyal Jews free of the wickedness and filth that now fill their sons.

8:2 We must take this ark and hide it from the sight of the Jews; they are unfit and unworthy to care for this holy relic.

8:3 Let us take this ark by night and cleanse it from the filth the Jews have placed upon it.

8:4 Where once the lord demanded the blood of beasts, he now demands the blood of demons.

8:5 Take of the Jews and shed their blood in the gold bowl so that not a drop spills.

8:6 Remove their fat, their caul, their liver and kidneys and burn it within the tabernacle so that the scent masks the filth they placed within.

8:7 Soak the cloth, the relics, the throne in their blood and cleanse it of its Jewdom.

8:8 Burn the flesh of these Jews and have the ashes turn black the tablets of Moses; let them be forever stained on the laws of the God they abandoned.

8:9 We do this in glory and honour to Christ; where the Jew took that which was salvation, we shall take that which is God's.

8:10 Remember, my brothers, that those who once disobeyed the laws of Moses were killed by God without mercy; they were tortured, suffered great cruelties and knew the wrath of God.

8:11 For those who disobey Jesus, it will be much, much worse.

9:1 Our God is our father, who loves us and cares for us as the true father should.

9:2 Where those of flesh nourish and encourage their sons, the lord beats them, so that they suffer and grow strong.

9:3 If you suffer not, the lord hates you; if you know great suffering, then you are loved by God and will be given many rewards in heaven.

9:4 Our God is a consuming fire who embraces his children with flames; we must grow to the flames, so they burn no longer.

9:5 When our flesh be removed and our spirit remain, then we will be fit to dwell with our father in heaven.

10:1 My brothers, it is with great joy that you have taken the ark of the covenant and cleansed it with the blood and ashes of the Jew.

10:2 Our lord smiles down upon us and blesses us with great tidings.

10:3 Sing psalms, shout hymns and rejoice strongly the name of Christ.

10:4 We must take this ark and place it where no other man shall find it; if the ark is found, the Jew shall take it.

10:5 Now that the ark is taken, those of the Jews have no proof they are chosen.

10:6 When the Gentile asks the Jew proves they are chosen by God, they shall no longer be able to show the ark: and the Gentile shall mock them, hate them and conquer them.

10:7 Let us hide this ark where no Jew and Gentile dare search; we shall hide it in a place most cunning, where even those who stare at it shall not find it.

10:8 We will make it into the decoration of a brothel, so that those who see it think it a fake.

10:9 Who will look for the holy ark of God in a brothel full of harlots?

10:10 The faithless will look for the ark for years and never find it, as it hides between the loins of whores.

10:11 May the blessings of Christ shower upon you eternal. Amen.

JAMES

1:1 James, a servant of God and the lord Jesus Christ, to the twelve tribes of Israel which were scattered abroad.

1:2 My brethren, why do you rejoice in perverse temptations?

1:3 You know the death of Christ was a sin, yet you rejoice in the spilling of his blood.

1:4 Repent and give glory to the messiah; he shall greet you with open arms as you come to weep on his feet.

1:5 If you lack the wisdom to be followers of Christ, then ask of the lord who gives it liberally to all those who merely ask.

1:6 The stupid of the world need no longer be stupid, so long as they ask of God for wisdom.

1:7 Be no longer stupid and wicked, my brethren; renounce your Jewdom and join the ranks of Christ.

1:8 Do not let the sins of few bring you to death and damnation; repent and free yourselves from the shackles of hell.

1:9 Though I was once Jew, I am now Christian; the lord God has opened my mind, so that I know the truth that Jesus is the messiah.

1:10 So please, my Jewish brothers, convert and pray to God; I'd hate to have to kill you.

2:1 My brothers, I beg of you to accept faith in Christ, the lord of glory, the son of God.

2:2 For Christ accepts all men from all walks of life.

2:3 If a man comes with gold ring and purple raiment and another comes with sackcloth and stone, they shall both be blessed and embraced by the messiah our saviour.

2:4 He truly loves all who accepts him and cares not whether ye be rich, poor, Jew, Gentile, Roman, Greek or Hebrew.

2:5 Even of the Samaritans and the Philistines he shall save, so long as they repent and follow him.

2:6 We of Christ help one another, so that each man be equal and none but the apostles hold rank.

2:7 If our brother be naked and without food, we shall clothe him and feed him by the glory of Christ.

2:8 If our sister be naked and without food, we shall even clothe her and feed her by the glory of Christ.

2:9 We may partake in fellatio with her, so that we feed her with the seeds of our loins, but we will feed her and clothe her, afterwards.

2:10 Hearken not the words of Paul, who claim that salvation come by faith alone. I ask you, does not the devils believe in God. Shall their belief save them?

2:11 Salvation through faith is the path of the lazy; you must show good works to show your faith to God and men.

2:12 Remember that Abraham was a good and holy man, but still must show his faith through works by offering his son Isaac as sacrifice.

2:13 Remember that Rahab the whore was saved not by faith, but by keeping safe our fathers before us.

2:14 The body without spirit is dead and faith without works is dead also.

3:1 My brothers of the false circumcision, fear not, for though we are no longer masters of men, we are still masters.

3:2 How can we be masters of men, when all men are mastered by the lord and saviour Jesus Christ?

3:3 Though we lose the dominion over men and heathen, we still dominate the beast, the fowl, the flock, the serpent.

3:4 Are not all birds of the air, beast of the earth and monsters of the sea be slaves for us. Do they not do our bidding and are bound by us?

3:5 To have domination over men is foolish, devious, selfish, and devilish; only the true God may have dominion over his creation.

3:6 Come to those of Christ, my brothers and accept the lord and saviour Jesus; be saved by the blood you spilled, lest you drown by it.

4:1 My brethren the Jew, why do you demand a messiah of war, who shall free thee from the oppression and the tyranny of Caesar?

4:2 You lust for death, for destruction, for revolution; know that Christ is a revolution free of blood.

4:3 Do not escape from those of Rome, but embrace them, so that you both be saved.

4:4 You pray for the messiah to come, but he already has; you pray and do not receive, because you rejected the gift of God.

4:5 Have Christ dwell in your heart and your prayers will be answered by the heavenly father.

4:6 It is because of your Jewdom and stubbornness that the lord ignores your words and mocks your cries.

4:7 Of those with concubines, you are no more but an adulterer; ignore the temptation of flesh and give yourself the spiritual gift of salvation.

4:8 There is no time for fornication, for drunkenness; the lord God comes soon to reclaim his people and burn the wicked.

4:9 Do not envy the faith of Christians, but accept it and be us.

4:10 Resist the words of Satan, which tell you to hold Judaism to your bosom; strike him down and he shall run in cowardice.

4:11 Embrace the messiah you slain and he shall forgive you; such is the mercies of God.

5:1 Why do you of the rich hold stubbornly to your wealth. Do you foolishly think wealth can come with you to heaven?

5:2 Let the gold which weighs heavy in your pockets anchor you to the brimstone of damnation.

5:3 Do not hold dear the desires of earth, but seek forth the riches of heaven, which are plentiful and mighty.

5:4 Rejoice the name of Christ, so that your brothers rejoice with you.

5:5 Of those who bring a man to Christianity, they save a soul from hell-fire; it is the noblest of deeds.

5:6 Every man shall wear a crown and upon the crown shall be the rare jewel for every man they have given to Christ.

5:7 Let your crown be covered in jewels, so that those in heaven are humbled before your feet.

5:8 The power of Christ gives you the power of faith, which cures the sick, heals the lame and gives sight to the blind.

5:9 Pray and your illness will be cast from you; if it is not, then you lack faith.

5:10 Do not go to the strange herbs and potions of physicians, which are faulty; the power of prayer works every time.

6:1 You den of vipers. You herd of dragons. Are you so blind that you do not see Christ?

6:2 I have shown you the path of salvation and still you stubbornly hold strong to your laws, your statutes, your wicked faith.

6:3 Convert, Jew and be saved from your damnation. Deny Christ and may the swords of Christ sink deeply into the bowels of your children.

6:4 Know that I come with sharpened blade to baptize the righteous of your people; of those who refuse baptism, let his blood turn the waters crimson.

I PETER

1:1 Peter, an apostle of Christ, to the barbarians scattered about Pontus, Galatia, Cappadocia, Asia and Bithynia,

1:2 Elected according to the wisdom of God the father, through sanctification of the spirit, cleansed by the blood of Jesus Christ, his name written in the book of heaven before his birth.

1:3 Greetings and grace unto you and may your peace be multiplied.

1:4 Blessed be the God almighty and his son Jesus of Nazareth, whose abundant mercy did bring forth Jesus from the dead, so that he proves to all that he is the messiah.

1:5 Take my word for it, he truly did rise from the grave without the dark arts of a necromancer.

1:6 He rises so that he may give us salvation and eternal life; an inheritance unspoiled, incorruptible and awaiting us in heaven.

1:7 So prepare yourselves for the salvation of Christ during these the end of times.

1:8 Rejoice in the spirit and rid yourself of the flesh so that the temptation of lust and sin give you no malice.

1:9 The season of man is over and now comes the season of peace, of joy, of prosperity; the righteous will praise God in heaven and the damned will remain forever burning on earth.

1:10 Repent, you who know not Christ and accept his name into your hearts and souls; rid yourself of evil and be baptized in the blood of the holy.

1:11 Cleanse yourself of sin and be refreshed with the spirit of the holy ghost.

1:12 Fear not, for our bodies are but grass which rot and burn; but our spirit lives forever by the blessings of God.

2:1 Lay aside your malice, your guile, your cunning, your envies, your evil speaking.

2:2 Never shall the church be known for such wickedness and hypocrisies.

2:3 As newborn babies desire the milk of their mother's breast, so shall we desire the gospel of Christ and the blood of the wicked.

2:4 We will grow strong by the gospel and rejoice in the blood of Jew and unbeliever.

2:5 Be not vain nor boast the killings of the wicked to men; the lord God has seen your good works and glorifies you and your blade.

2:6 Rejoice and praise the lord who sends the Christian leader to guide us as king and ruler of man.

2:7 Respect the king, give him honour; but fear God always, lest you displease him and be cast in the pot of the wicked.

2:8 Do good in the eyes of Christ and your actions will seize shut the mouths of ignorance and fools.

2:9 Sin no more, for those of Christ are pure and perfect; every act they do is done by the will of God and Christ.

2:10 Go forth and preach the holy ministry to the ignorant and the stubborn; by word or by blade, the earth shall be under Christ.

3:1 Wives, subject yourselves to your husbands and obey him always and forever in all things.

3:2 The lord God made man in his image and created women to please man; thus the man is like a lord to woman and shall be treated as such.

3:3 Repent the wickedness of your sins, which brought upon the earth a filthy muck; it is your fault that the earth is cruel, you wretched cunts.

3:4 Hide your faces, so that the lord almighty be not reminded of this disgusting creation; never adorn yourself with jewels, gold, silk, nor braided hair.

3:5 Give to this earth many sons, so that the debt of your original sin be repaid to man and God.

3:6 Husbands, treat your wives with care and compassion; they are but a weak vessel, fragile and brittle.

3:7 Have compassion for one another and be courteous to your brethren; lend a hand when hand is needed and slave when labour is hard.

3:8 Do no evil to your neighbour, lest evil be done to you.

3:9 You of Christ are protected forever under the hand of God; no harm shall come to the righteous that pleases the messiah.

3:10 The Jew, the unbeliever and the critic will wish to snare you with logic and science; prepare yourselves and answer them the questions they have of God.

3:11 Do not cower, but speak boldly, until they repent and convert or die.

3:12 Give glory to Jesus, who sits on the right hand of God, forever guiding us and advising the lord in earthly matters.

3:13 The lord Christ is strong and merciful, who even taught those in the prison after his resurrection from the tomb.

3:14 Who but a kind and merciful lord will give word to the sinner. What other lord but Christ desires the salvation of all mankind?

3:15 A pity he couldn't just give it all to us; but some do need to go to hell.

3:16 Hell was created by the almighty and thus it would be wasteful for none to enter through the flaming gates.

3:17 Let the wicked and the Jew give meaning to this, the most horrifying of God's creations.

4:1 Be ever wary of the devil, who is a roaring lion that prowls our streets.

4:2 The most wicked of beasts, who devours all that is good and holy, so that none be saved from the earth.

4:3 Let the lord be your shepherd, so that the lion never nears the flock; Christ protects his sheep with the rod and beats the devil away.

4:4 Do not be led astray from the shepherd Christ; give no eye to temptation, lust or evil.

4:5 Be hospitable to your neighbours and slaughter the barbarian who comes to your door.

4:6 They are spies sent by Satan, who come to trick you with forked tongue and sweetened word.

4:7 Never murder, steal, cheat, nor interfere in the lives of others, unless said so by God almighty.

4:8 A Christian man is a holy man and needs not your meddling; meddle instead in the lives of strangers, until they accept Christ

or die.

4:9 Remember, the end of days come soon and the lives of Christians will be hard and full of dangers.

4:10 But keep heart and know the rewards of heaven are great and our enemies will suffer endlessly in the pits of damnation.

4:11 Such is the glory of Christ. Amen.

II PETER

1:1 Simon Peter, a servant and apostle of Jesus Christ the messiah and first bishop of Rome, later known as pope.

1:2 It is with great honour that I take the mantle of bishop and rule with mighty hand the disciples, apostles and peoples of Christ.

1:3 Let the followers of Christ be ruled forever by a just and holy leader, who never abuses the power of his sceptre and cares for the well-being of all followers.

1:4 Be wary of the unbeliever and false Christian, who teaches falsely among you and wishes to destroy the very foundation of our messiah.

1:5 These protestant liars are invaders sent by the demons and the Jews, to halt the numbers of Christ and weaken the belief and our faith.

1:6 To hell with them, he who speaks against the gospels and ministries of Peter and Paul; let their tongues be eaten by the raven, their hearts devoured by the beast.

1:7 They are made even more foolish than the ass of Balaam, who spoke against his master by the will of God.

1:8 Let their homes go the way of Sodom and Gomorrah; let them dwell with the fallen angels that betrayed our lord.

1:9 When the lord reserves the wicked on the day of judgment, shall they forever be punished to damnation, so that they know no comfort, no rest, no mercy.

1:10 They are as hated as Esau, while we are as beloved as the most righteous Lot, who escaped the wrath of God and the destruction of the two cities.

1:11 Let it be known that Lot is a righteous man; any person who questions the righteousness of Lot because he drunkenly fucked is two daughters, let their bowels be plucked through their nostrils.

1:12 We are the righteous, who will arise from the flames as Noah raised from the waters; we are forever saved by the mercies of Christ and the heavenly father.

1:13 The others are rotten and unjust, a dog who swallows his vomit, a pig who bathes in his shit.

1:14 It is better for all they be consumed in the fires; let their sins be cleansed by flame and ours by blood.

1:15 They wish not to understand the epistles of Paul, for they are hard and require labour.

1:16 Let their laziness doom them as they suffer through hell.

1:18 When the whole world be set aflame by the torch of the almighty, they will be too slothful to raise a bucket of water to cast on the flames.

1:19 Let the ignorant remain ignorant and the just remain just; let the righteous know paradise and the damned know pain.

1:20 These are the words of Simon Peter, first bishop of Rome, holy leader of the Christian faith.

1:21 Now send me your children, so that they know the ways of Christ intimately.

I JOHN

1:1 That which was from the beginning, which we have heard, which we have seen, which we have touched, smelled and tasted, since the beginning of life;

1:2 For life was given to us by the grace of God, when his holy breath filled nostrils of Adam;

1:3 Has been a lie and a deception.

1:4 Now that the blood of Christ has cleansed our eyes and freed us from sin, we may see the truth, the glory and the wonders.

1:5 Repent your sins, so that the lord forgives you and be shown the truth of the earth: and of those who say they sin not, let them be forever branded a liar.

2:1 My precious children, these are the things I write to you, so that you live a life free of sin and transgression, in glory to the righteousness of God.

2:2 Christ has taken us from our sins, so that he bears them upon his shoulders; not just us, but all the people of the earth.

2:3 Repent and deliver the sins to Christ, who take them as his own and bear the burden of our wickedness.

2:4 Live by the example of our messiah, so that our burden be light.

2:5 Walk as Christ walked, preach as Christ preached; give the gift of the messiah to all who accept and deny no man his salvation.

2:6 Love as Christ loved and be forever cast in light, so that you see all the world; go not into the darkness of sin and hate.

2:7 Fathers, teach your children to love God and repent to the messiah; let your children be free of hell and embraced by our lord in the end of days.

2:8 Never lie nor doubt the word of the gospels; he who lies, doubts or disbelieves is a fool and an anti-christ, worthy of his damnation.

2:9 Mothers, be obedient to your husbands and repent the wickedness of your loins.

2:10 When the lord comes, the excretion of your sins will be no more and you shall be forgiven the wickedness of Eve.

3:1 Behold the precious gift which has been bestowed upon us and accept it with grace, thanks and humility.

3:2 Beloved are we now, the sons of God, who will soon see his arrival and have our eyes blessed by his holy presence.

3:3 Let every man of Christ sing psalms as his chariot descends from the heavens, so that our mouths be pure and our hearts filled with grace.

3:4 We of Christ will be accepted by our messiah, as we are free of sin and holy in his eyes; of those who sinned, they are of the devil and will be left behind to their fate.

3:5 Pity the sinner, who foolishly denies themselves salvation; all they need to is ask and it shall be given to them.

3:6 Their stubborn tongues weigh heavy, as the foreskin presses down on their hearts.

3:7 Teach them to cast aside this wicked flesh; let them be free from the devils and sanctified by the baptism of holy blood.

3:8 Have them be righteous in God; for those who are not of Christ are wicked and worthy of hell-fire.

3:9 Their sins are worth than death, their stubbornness an execution; he who knows not Christ has not lived, but hosts a doomed spirit.

3:10 They are as damned as the Jew, he who refuses the messiah; take pity on them and teach them to repent until the end of days.

3:11 May the glory of Christ be in all things. Amen.

II JOHN

1:1 My brothers, let truth, righteousness and the blessings of Christ guide you until the arrival of our blessed messiah.

1:2 Hearken the words of the gospel and give ear only to the truth.

1:3 Grace be upon you, your kin and your brethren, given to us by the divine trinity of father, son and holy spirit.

1:4 I rejoice in the strength and numbers of our faith; it shall be that on the arrival of our lord, the faithful will outnumber even the wicked Jews.

1:5 I beseech you, my brothers, to love one another and give strength to each other during these times.

1:6 Reserve this love for the faithful, the holy, the followers of Christ; hate everyone else, for they are wicked and the anti-christ hoard.

1:7 Many are the deceivers and the anti-christs, who beat on our foundation with logic, philosophy and science.

1:8 Do not associate with these abominations of men; they are of devils and Jews, sent to make destruction on the works of Christ.

1:9 Destroy them, so that the messiah has less people to sort upon his coming day.

1:10 May the blades of Christ forever sink deep into the flesh of the wicked. Amen.

III JOHN

1:1 It is with trembling quill and heavy heart that I write these, the last words of John the disciple, upon this parchment.

1:2 Throughout my days I have glorified Christ, slain the wicked, preached the gospels, in foolish belief that the messiah comes and I may greet him as his servant.

1:3 These are my last hours of my life and he is not here.

1:4 By what manner did I disgrace God. What evil have I done to deserve to be cast aside from his salvation?

1:5 I fear I have not preached enough, nor converted the barbarians to the holy path.

1:6 Though my blade is stained with the blood of wickedness and

Jew, it is with great sadness that I confess I have spared the lives of Jewish children, in hopes they will repent and give themselves to Christ.

1:7 I have failed my saviour, my messiah and the heavenly father. I shall die and not know the face of my God, who I have served so long.

1:8 Upon my last breath, I know that it is not the embrace of Christ I will receive, but the embrace of flames.

1:9 For my slothfulness, I am condemned to the eternal damnation, the darkness, the pits of hell.

1:10 My lord, know that you send a loyal servant to the fires, who shall praise your name and sing psalms through the flames.

1:11 Even as the fires consume me and the worm dwells within my bowels, I shall repent my wickedness and give glories to the messiah.

1:12 Know that I am sorry for my laziness and accept my punishment on your day of judgment.

1:13 May all those who read this take heed of my example and live the life of a devoted Christian.

1:14 Never doubt the wickedness of others; slay those who are the anti-christ.

1:15 Preach to all men, so that they know God in their hearts and be saved.

1:16 I go now, to suffer the shame of my failures and my failures to Christ.

1:17 May you all never know the torments that face me in eternity. Amen.

UDE

1:1 Jude, the brother of James and servant of Jesus, to them that are sanctified in the church of Jesus Christ.

1:2 By what filth is this, that I gaze upon the fields and see beasts dancing with men and the harlot lying in the dung?

1:3 The people of the earth are revolting and have denied Christ in the pursuit of lustful temptations, sinful disgust and gluttonous ways.

1:4 They are the descendants of giants, those beasts conceived by the sons of God who raped the women of old.

1:5 Their filthy dreams, defiling of flesh, pleasure in their similar loins bring forth a vomit from our lord that shall cover the earth, such as the flood of Noah covered the earth.

1:6 Do not bother to preach to these men beasts, nor cause them to repent; the lord comes soon and we must rid the earth of this filthiness.

1:7 Let us clean the floors for our messiah by our blades; let us purify the fields with the blood of sinners, fornicators, unholy lust and the anti-christ.

1:8 When Christ comes, he brings with him ten thousand angels to rid the earth of this wretchedness and make clean the foundation for the fires of hell.

1:9 Why must our lord do such works. Is he not our guest in our home?

1:10 Let us take blade and dagger and cleanse the earth for Christ's arrival.

1:11 Of those who murmur and speak ill of Jesus, let his tongue be mounted atop the mantle, so that our lord know the many we silenced who spoke out against his name.

1:12 The unholy fornicators who take pleasure in similar flesh, let them be dashed against the rocks and the spear pierced through the entrance of their bowels.

1:13 Make haste and choose your weapons; the time of God is near and we must make ready for his arrival.

1:14 Let the blood of the sinners please our guest and give us blessings and salvation. Amen.

EVELATIONS

1:1 The revelation of Jesus Christ, which God gave to him to show unto his servants that which shall soon come to be; and he sent this holy message unto the servant John.

1:2 Who bare record of the word of God, the testimony of the messiah and of all things he saw.

1:3 Cursed are he who read this book, for it contains the torments, the terrors and the cruelties of the wrath of God, who shall bring to pass these prophecies before the judgment day.

1:4 The angel came to John and gave of him the holy parchment, saying "Take this blessed parchment and lay it beneath your tongue.

1:5 Then shall the visions and the words of Christ come to you in magnificent glory."

1:6 And the parchment had a bitter taste, which dissolved beneath the wetness of my tongue.

1:7 As the spirit of the lord came to me, I could see the sounds of voices, taste the colours before me and see the demons which hide beneath the curtains of the wind.

1:8 I tore at my veins, so that the blood of Christ spill from my body and cleanse me of my filthiness and sin.

1:9 When the sweet blood cleansed me, I heard the grass beneath my feet say, "Behold, the lord comes with the clouds, so that all shall see him, righteous and unholy, blessed and pierced."

1:10 Then the mighty yelled out, "I am the Alpha and Omega, the beginning and the end. I am and always have been, the almighty."

1:11 I John, who is your brother in Christ and blessed of the apostles, was in the isle of Patmos, preaching to the stubborn, when I first laid eyes upon the mighty son of God.

1:12 He spoke with the voice of trumpets, "I am the Alpha and Omega, the first and the last. Write that which you see in the book and send it to the seven churches of Asia; Ephesus, Smyrna, Pergamos, Thyatira, Sardis, Philadelphia and Laodicea."

1:13 I turned to see the voice that spoke to me: and as I turned, I saw seven candlesticks, made of the serpentine rose:

1:14 And in the midst of the candlesticks was the blessed messiah, clothed in the sky down to his feet, with a girdle of stone.

1:15 His head and hair were whiter than snow and his eyes contained the very fires of hell.

1:16 The feet of Christ were like the molten brass, which turns liquid within the heat of the furnace; and his voice was of the trumpets and the beasts.

1:17 In his right hand contained the seven suns: and from his mouth came forth a sword of water.

1:18 When I saw him, I fell to my feet as though dead. And he placed a sun atop my head and said, "Fear not, for I am the first and the last.

1:19 I am he that is living and dead. Behold, my loins contain the keys of hell and Hades.

1:20 I come to tell you the things which are, that which has been and what is to come, so that you may write down the mighty prophesy.

1:21 The mystery of the seven stars and the seven candlesticks will be revealed to you. The seven stars are the angels of the church and the candlesticks of snake and petal are the churches."

2:1 "Unto the church of Ephesus write that the son of God and saviour of men has within his fist the seven stars and walks amongst the thorns of the candlesticks.

2:2 I know your works, your labours and your patience and how you shed the blood of the wicked and feed them to the dragons of the sea; I have witnessed how you tried to save those who are the apostles, but are men conceived by lies, who hide the plated tail beneath their skirts.

2:3 You are blessed men, who have laboured and shown patience in the name of your God.

2:4 Still, I hate you all, for you were once of the Jews; your repentance and your deeds are not enough to mask the faeces of your lineage.

2:5 I hate you as I hate the Nicolaitanes, whose mouths contain the piercings of wasps.

2:6 When the wrath of Christ comes upon the earth, your ashes shall give soil to the tree of life, which is in the midst of the paradise of God.

2:7 Unto the church of Smyrna write; Thus, sayeth the Alpha and Omega, which is the first and the last, the living and the dead.

2:8 I know your works, your tribulation and thy falseness of poverty; you are rich men who bathe in the muck and wear the sackcloth robe.

2:9 Your blasphemy of Jewishness did create the synagogue of Satan, the forked devil, the evil one.

2:10 The few amongst you who are faithful will be cast into the prisons, surrounded by the demons and the rat; may you pass the trials, so that the lord bless you with the bone sceptre.

2:11 To the church of Pergamos write; we have witnessed the swords of your fingers, the daggers of your hair.

2:12 The devil has made his throne in your bedchamber, spreading his seed atop your sheets and faces.

2:13 Cleanse yourself with the blood of wood and repent your sins to the almighty.

2:14 Confess your wickedness, lest the tongue of Christ lash out against you with fierceness and fire.

2:15 Unto the church of Thyatira write; The son of God has watched you through the flames of damnation and walked your streets with brass heel.

2:16 I know your works, your charities, your conversion of the wicked.

2:17 Still, you have kept the tongue of Jezebel the prophetess and anti-christ, which teaches the tolerance of those sexually perverse and eats the flesh of meat offered to the idols.

2:18 The lord has given this belching cunt the time to repent her sins and confess her immorality; the bitch refused.

2:19 Behold, I will cast her into the bed of fornication and strike her and her lovers with diseases of the loins and the blood.

2:20 I will kill her children with the fangs of olives and tear the livers and the kidneys of the disciples of the church which allowed this creature to speak."

3:1 "To the church of Sardis write; These are the words of the Alpha and Omega, who holds the seven suns; I know your works, he who

is the living and dead.

3:2 Be watchful and give strength to your blades; the dragons come and bring with them the fermented bile.

3:3 Your clothes are defiled with the excrement of lice and washed in the blood of children.

3:4 Walk in the flames and repent your wickedness so that you no longer bathe in the flames of wrath.

3:5 To the church of Philadelphia say; I have seen the works of butchers and bakers and was given great pleasure by your deeds.

3:6 Your concoction of bread, ox meat and cheese is favoured by God, who savours this meal greater than the burning flesh of lambs and virgins.

3:7 Build the altar to God, with hardened bread and salted meat; melt atop it the blessed cheese and sing glories and praises to your messiah.

3:8 Behold, I come quickly and shall hunger upon the day of my arrival; make haste, lest the lord devour you in gluttonous wrath.

3:9 To the church of the Laodiceans write; I am the Alpha and Omega, the beginning and the end.

3:10 Good job. Keep doing what you're doing.

3:11 The lord shall provide you with soil to bury the ashes of those you slay."

4:1 After this I looked up and saw the heavens tear the firmament of the sky. A voice like the clashing cymbals said, "Come forth and I shall show you that which shall come."

4:2 I climbed the ladder of silk and oil and entered into the very heavens; there before me was a throne, who sat the mighty.

4:3 He was made of carvings of jasper and carnelian stone, with hair of tar; behind him was the rainbow of emeralds.

4:4 About him were twenty and four seats, with a blessed elder upon each seat, clothed in satyr skin and wearing crowns of elephant skulls.

4:5 From the throne came out the thunderous lightning and voices: and there were seven lamps of gold, each being the spirit of our lord.

4:6 And before the throne was a sea of urine like crystal: and surrounding the throne were four beasts of many eyes and genitals.

4:7 The first beast was like the lion, the second a calf, the third had a face of a man and the last was the flying eagle.

4:8 Each beast had six wings and on each wing were six erect loins, which sang unto the lord, "Holy holy holy art thou, God almighty, which always was and always be."

4:9 Then the twenty-four elders fell before the throne of God and cast off their crowns of skulls, saying, "We aren't worthy to be in the presence of such greatness, he who created all things so that they may worship him."

5:1 On the right hand of the throne of God was a scroll of flesh, written with the blood of ash and sealed with seven seals.

5:2 An angel of God came forth and with the voice of mountains shouted, "Who amongst the many creations of God is worthy enough to open the scrolls and break the seven seals?"

5:3 Apparently, no one was.

5:4 No man and beast throughout the heavens and the earth was worthy to break the seals and open the scroll of flesh.

5:5 I wept tears of wine, for no man could open the scroll, which I wished desperately to know the writings within.

5:6 And one of the elders came to me and said, "Weep not, slave of the son of God; the lord God is mighty and shall make a creature worthy to break the seals, if he desires the seals to be broken."

5:7 It was then I saw the lord pull from the genitals of the four beasts a lamb, who had seven horns and seven eyes, which were also the spirits of God.

5:8 Upon him was wounded chest, which showed to all the heart of stone contained within the lamb.

5:9 He came and grabbed with his horns the scroll of flesh and sat upon the right of the throne.

5:10 When he took the book, the four beasts and the elders rejoiced, saying, "Blessed is that created by God, to break the seals and open the scroll."

5:11 They gathered their harps and timbrels and anointed the lamb with vials of perfume, singing psalms of glories and praise in a tongue foreign to my ears.

5:12 Then surrounded the throne came the many angels, which numbered in the multitudes greater than the sands of the earth and the stars of the heavens.

5:13 All sang, "Worthy is the sacrificial lamb, which is worthy of the knowledge and the wisdom of the scroll.

5:14 Let him be forever blessed."

5:15 Then every creature of the heavens, of the earth, beneath the earth and within the seas came forth, singing, "Bahimlech ungapharod el tuppi no hasanna biy dilferish."

5:16 And the four beasts said, "Amen," and the four and twenty elders fell further and worshipped the lamb of stone heart.

6:1 Then the lamb tore open one of the seals and with it came the noise of thunder, as one of the beasts said, "Come, look, and listen."

6:2 And I saw before me a horse carved from the scales of the leviathan: and he that sat atop it was armed with the bow.

6:3 The lord gave him a crown of coals and said, "Go forth and conquer." And the man went with bow and shot arrows upon the earth.

6:4 Then the lamb opened the second seal and a beast said, "Come forth and see."

6:5 And there rode forth a horse made of blood, which was given authority to make wars amongst the people, so that neighbour slay neighbour and father hate son.

6:6 He was given a sword of dust, to go and blind the men of reason.

6:7 The lamb then broke the third seal and a beast said, "Come hither and witness." And I beheld a black horse, whose rider held in each hand the scales of merchants.

6:8 And the beasts murmured to the rider, "Go and take the wheat and the barley from the people, but save for us the wine, so we may be drunk as we watch their destruction by the hands of the lord."

6:9 When the fourth seal was opened, a beast said, "Gaze in wonder."

6:10 And a horse of smoke came, carrying the bringer of death; and it carried the chariot behind it, which rode hell.

6:11 The lord then gave them power to kill a quarter of the earth with fire, plagues, sword, earthquakes, wind, flood, starvation and beasts.

6:12 And they said, "Blessed is the merciful lord," as they rode forth to cause destruction of the earth.

6:13 When the fifth seal of the scroll was torn apart, I heard the many voices of souls drowning within the sea of urine, saying, "How long, O lord, until you shed the blood of those on earth who shed the blood from us?"

6:14 And the lord said, "Shut the fuck up and don't bother me, you who drown in the piss of the almighty."

6:15 Upon the breaking of the sixth seal, there came a mighty earthquake and the sun turned to the blackened ball sacks of the diseased oxen.

6:16 Many stars fell upon the earth, the sky was rolled up like the scroll, the mountains shrank into the earth and the islands were thrust forth from the waters.

6:17 The kings of the earth, the great men, the mighty, the wealthy, the captains, the chiefs, the free men and their slaves hid within the caves, cowering in fear.

6:18 Their tears filled the halls of rock as they said, "Hide us from the wrath of God, who lied when he claimed his mercy and love.

6:19 His wrath descends upon the earth. Who amongst us shall protect us?"

7:1 Then I saw four angels standing before the four corners of the earth, which held in their hands weapons of light, darkness, wind and rain.

7:2 They were given authority to cause destruction upon the lands and seas, in glory to the mighty God of heaven and earth.

7:3 As they raised their weapons, an angel from the east yelled, "Sheath your blades and keep hidden your daggers, until the men of God are marked.

7:4 These are the marked of God, who shall be saved so that those of the heavens will not question the mercies of God and call him a tyrant who created the earth so that he may destroy it in wrath."

7:5 Descendants from the tribes of Israel were given a mark on their foreheads, so that each tribe was marked with twelve thousand men with the blessing of God.

7:6 Twelve thousand from the tribe of Juda. Twelve thousand from the tribe of Reuben. Twelve thousand from the tribe of Gad.

7:7 Twelve thousand from the tribe of Aser. Twelve thousand from the tribe of Nephthalim. Twelve thousand from the tribe of Manasses.

7:8 Twelve thousand from the tribe of Simeon. Twelve thousand from the tribe of Levi. Twelve thousand from the tribe of Issachar.

7:9 Twelve thousand from the tribe of Zabulon. Twelve thousand from the tribe of Joseph. Twelve thousand from the tribe of Benjamin.

7:10 Twelve thousand from each of the twelve tribes, so that the marked men numbered one hundred and forty-four thousand.

7:11 One hundred and forty-four thousand, given the mark of God to be saved. One hundred and forty-four thousand men saved since the time of Adam until the day of judgment.

7:12 One hundred and forty-four thousand. That is all.

7:13 One hundred and forty-four thousand virgin men given the mark of God, to spare them from the fires of hell. No women.

7:14 Even during the end of days, God still hates women.

7:15 Then the great multitudes of many nations, lineages and creeds came unto the sea of urine, dressed in stained robes, holding baskets of summer fruits in their hands.

7:16 And they said, "Save us, O lord, for we are worthy of your salvation."

7:17 The lord did not speak to them nor listened to their words.

7:18 Then all the angels stood on the shores of the sea and the four beasts and they cast stones into the sea of urine, so that it turned red with blood.

7:19 And I asked one of the elders, "Who are these men, who cry unto the lord for salvation?"

7:20 And the elder said, "These are the men of God and Christ, who followed the path of salvation and did the works according to the laws and the gospels."

7:21 I asked him, "Why then are they denied salvation. Why do you cast stones upon them, so that their flesh be torn?"

7:22 And I was told, "Because the lord wills it."

8:1 When the seventh seal was opened, there was a great silence in heaven that measured a time of the great millennia.

8:2 Then seven angels appeared before the lord, each carrying a trumpet.

8:3 Another angel came with the torch of phoenix feathers, which he lit with the altar of God that lay before the throne.

8:4 He cast the torch towards the earth, so that there were great lightnings, thundering, voices and earthquakes.

8:5 Then the seven angels prepared their trumpets and placed them upon their lips.

8:6 The first angel blew his trumpet and there followed a raining of blood upon the earth, which burned before us one third of the crops, the trees and the grass.

8:7 Then the second angel blew his trumpet and a great mountain of fire fell upon the earth, which turned the waters to boiling blood.

8:8 One third of the fish died, one third of the monsters of the sea died and one third of the ships were destroyed in the bubbling cauldron of the seas.

8:9 The third angel blew his trumpet, which caused a star to fall upon the earth, landing in the lakes, the rivers and the wells.

8:10 The star was called the Triumph of Worms, which made the waters of the earth bitter, so that one third of the people choke upon the bitter waters.

8:11 Then the fourth angel sounded and a third part of the sun was smitten, the third part of the moon cast off and the third part of the stars destroyed, so that the earth was placed in perpetual darkness.

8:12 It amazed me that the angel cast forth the third part of the stars, since the stars fell upon the earth.

8:13 Such is the wonders of our lord.

8:14 And I beheld the elders and the beasts covering their ears, saying, "Mighty are the notes of God, which bring forth the terrible music which offends our hearing deeply."

9:1 The fifth angel sounded his trumpet and I saw a star fall from the heavens and given the key to the abyss.

9:2 He opened the seal of the bottomless pit, which caused the black smoke to pour forth and cover the sun and the earth in darker darkness.

9:3 From the abyss flew forth the venomous locusts, who were given dominion over the earth.

9:4 It was commanded to them that they shall not hurt the trees of the earth, nor the grass, but only those men who were not marked by the blessing of God.

9:5 They were bound not to kill them, but to torment them, harass them and cause them great pain for five horrible months.

9:6 The swarm of locusts flew about the earth, raping all those who lacked the mark, giving them great boils, plagues and disease.

9:7 During these times shall death be made impotent, so that no man dies during these the times of horror.

9:8 Every man shall seek death and be denied his cold embrace.

9:9 They shall fall on their sword, drink of the venom, hang on their tree: and still will death be denied them, so that they are forced to endure the wrath of God.

9:10 And the locusts were made like the unicorns, with crowns of wheat, faces of men and loins of the Minotaur.

9:11 Their hair is like the hair of women and their teeth like the fangs of vipers.

9:12 Their tails are like the tails of scorpions, which carry a venom that kills not, but causes the mighty suffering of men.

9:13 Their breasts are made of sulphur, and their wings of old parchment.

9:14 On each wing was written, this is the wrath of the lord, the true nature of God.

9:15 And they had a king, whose name in Hebrew was Abaddon and in Greek Apollyon.

9:16 Then the six angels blew forth their trumpet and I heard a voice from the four horns of the altar of God.

9:17 They yelled in mighty voice, "Set loose the four angels, bound by the river Euphrates."

9:18 And the four angels were loose, so that they could prepare for the destruction of men.

9:19 They gathered from the heavens two hundred million horses, to slay one third of the men of the remaining men of the earth.

9:20 And the horses had the wings of a dragon, the tail of the viper and the head of a lion; and from their mouths spewed forth sulphur and ash.

9:21 By the authority of the angels were one third of the men slaughtered, by the smoke, by the fire, by the venom and the hoof.

9:22 And the rest of the men still repented not their sins, nor gave glory to the lord God almighty.

9:23 They denied hymns and psalms to the lord of mercies, but cursed his name with hatred and bitter tongue.

9:24 With stubborn heart they were blinded; they knew not the destruction and the wrath was sent by the love of God, so they turn to him again and worship him for salvation.

9:25 Such is the foolishness of men.

10:1 It was then the spirit of the lord began to weaken within me and I could no longer taste the colours nor listen to the grass.

10:2 An angel came to me, with breasts of gold and nipples of sapphire and gave me a book of parchment for me to eat.

10:3 He stood upon the shores of the sea and said to me, "Eat of this book and be marked with the one hundred and forty four thousand, forever saved by the mercies of God."

10:4 And I took the book and devoured it: and it tasted like the bitter wormwood and made my belly swell.

10:5 The sins of my flesh came forth from me as leeches, spiders and vermin; they were cast out of me and I yelled, "Be gone wicked vermin, who makes me wicked and vile in the sight of God."

10:6 Then the angel took the horn and marked upon my forehead the mark of God, which separated me from the wicked, the damned and the doomed.

10:7 And a voice from the dust said, "Thou must prophesy before the people, the kings and the beasts."

11:1 Then the angel has given to me a reed and demanded that I take the reed to measure out the temple, the altar and the city of God.

11:2 And I took the reed and measured the temple, the altar and the reed; they're all fucking huge.

11:3 The time it would take to write down such a number would last well beyond the day of judgment.

11:4 Then the lord gave power unto two witnesses, so that they may prophesy the mercies and the love of God for one thousand two hundred and threescore days after the massacre of the horses of the four angels bound by the Euphrates.

11:5 And these were the two olive trees and the two candlesticks that stood before the God of the earth.

11:6 And if any man caused harm upon these trees and candlesticks, then will the fire come forth from God's nostrils and consume them until their bones crumble to ash.

11:7 These witnesses had power to shut forth the firmament, turn the waters to blood and smite the earth with plagues until all the people bow down and worship the lord.

11:8 And when the witnesses have finished their testimony, then shall the great beast ascend from the abyss and make war against them, destroy them and kill them.

11:9 The bodies of the witnesses will lie in the streets of men, where the people shall rejoice over their destruction and hold feasts in honour of the destruction of these prophets of God.

11:10 They will bother not to put the bodies in the graves, but leave them to rot so that they may defile them in unholy lust.

THE BLASPHEMOUS BIBLE

11:11 After three and one-half days will the bodies of the slain arise and cause great fear among the people.

11:12 Then the voice of the heavens shall shout, "Arise," and the slain will ascend into heavens, yelling to those of the earth that the great destruction of God comes soon.

11:13 Upon that hour will an earthquake shake the foundations of the earth, so that one tenth of the cities crumble and turn to dust.

11:14 The seventh angel sounded his horn and the great many in heaven shouted, "The kingdoms of the lord reign eternal; he shall rule forever with wrath and hatred."

11:15 And the twenty-four elders fell upon their faces, worshipping God, saying, "Spare us from your wrath and your destruction, so that we know the rarity of peace."

11:16 And the nations of the earth were angry and fought against the wrath of God. They slaughtered the prophets, the saints, the faithful, saying, "These are the foolish and ignorant, who believe the lord God cares for them and will spare them from hell."

11:17 They were right.

11:18 Then the temple of God was torn open and there was seen in his temple the ark of holy testament: and I saw lightnings, voices, earthquakes and hail.

12:1 And there appeared in heaven a great wonder; a woman clothed in the light, with the moon as sandals and upon her head a crown of twelve stars.

12:2 She was the rarest of all God's creations; a woman which God did not hate.

12:3 She being heavy with child began to scream in pain and was about to deliver a son.

12:4 Then there appeared a horrendous wonder; the great red dragon, with ten horns upon each head and seven crowns upon each horn.

12:5 The tail of the dragon lashed out against the sky and caused one third of the stars to fall on the earth, making the lord to wonder why he keeps replacing the stars which keep falling on the earth.

12:6 As the woman pushed strongly with her loins, the mighty dragon stood before her, so that he may devour the child upon birth.

12:7 She brought forth a child of man, who was to rule all nations with a rod of iron: and the son was taken away from the jaws of the dragon and delivered to the throne of God.

12:8 The women then fled into the wilderness, where God prepared for her servants to care and feed her for one thousand two hundred and threescore days.

12:9 The dragon fought a mighty war against heaven, claiming the lord God to be a tyrant and must be cast down before he causes his creations to suffer.

12:10 Michael and his legions fought against the dragon and the dragon fought against the armies of God.

12:11 This dragon being the first to cry out against God and call him cruel.

12:12 The dragon, the mighty serpent, the devil, was cast forth from the heavens and upon the earth and his angels with him.

12:13 The lord could have created a prison for the dragon, but the lord God could not be bothered.

12:14 Lazy bastard.

12:15 Those of heavens mocked the dragons and his followers, saying, "You are foolish, he who goes against God."

12:16 When the dragon saw that he was cast upon the earth, he sought the woman who gave birth to the child, so that he may devour the woman and ensure no more of the sons be born.

12:17 The dragon caused great waters to flood the entire earth, so that she be drowned.

12:18 But the lord caused the earth to split and swallow the waters of the dragon, protecting her against the dragon.

12:19 And the dragon was wroth with the woman and went to make war against the remnants of her seed, which are those who follow the path of God and the works of Jesus Christ.

13:1 Then I stood upon the shores of the sea and saw from the waters arise a beast, having seven heads and each head with ten horns and each horn with ten crowns; upon the head was a mark of blasphemy.

13:2 They were marked with words of logic.

13:3 The beast was like that of a leopard, with the mouth of lions and the feet of a bear: and the dragon gave the beast the throne, the power and the authority.

13:4 I saw upon one of the heads a fatal wound which has healed: and all the world worshipped the beast.

13:5 They worshipped the dragon as well, saying, "Blessed are they who fight against God and protect us from his tyranny."

13:6 And the beast was given a mouth, which spoke blasphemies of logic against the lord; and the power was given for forty-two months.

13:7 He opened his blasphemy against God, against the church and against those that dwell in heaven.

13:8 Then it was given to him to make war against the righteous and the saints: and he had power over the many nations of many tongues.

13:9 All those whose names were not written in the book of heaven worshipped the beast and praised his name.

13:10 It was a lot of people.

13:11 Then I beheld another beast that came forth from the earth, who had two horns like the ram and the voice of a dragon.

13:12 He did the biddings of the beast and caused the men of the earth to worship the beast, doing such wonders through the blasphemy of science and medicine.

13:13 And he deceived those of the earth through the blasphemies and caused them to make an image of the beast, who has survived mortal wound.

13:14 He then breathed into the nostrils of the image, giving it life, so that it was like the first beast.

13:15 And all those who did not worship the beasts nor the dragons were spared by the blades of the beasts, who said, "Let the men live who speak against us."

13:16 We desire peace on earth in all things."

13:17 Then the beast caused the multitudes to have a mark upon their foreheads or hands; of rich, poor, free and bond, they were given the mark.

13:18 And no man may earn a wage, he who did not possess the mark.

13:19 Let him understand that the mark of the beast is the name of the beast, whose number is six hundred and sixty-six.

13:20 Or six hundred and sixteen.

13:21 Perhaps nine hundred and ninety-nine.

14:1 I looked and behold, their stood atop mount Zion the lamb of God and with him the one hundred and forty-four thousand which bare the mark of God.

14:2 And they sung praises to the name of God almighty, as the earth bowed down and worshipped the beasts and the dragon.

14:3 The men of the earth became annoyed with the lamb and the one hundred and forty-four thousand and wished they would keep their religion to themselves and not force it upon all.

14:4 There behind them stood the angel, who said, "The glory of Babylon has fallen and caused the nations to drink of her wines and wallow in her fornications."

14:5 Then another angel said, "Let he who worship the beast and have the mark upon them suffer the eternal wrath of the almighty, creator of heaven and earth and all things.

14:6 They will be cast into the damnation, forever tortured by fire and brimstone."

14:7 It was then I gazed upon the sky and saw Jesus the messiah sitting upon a cloud, with a sickle in each hand.

14:8 And a voice from the heavens said, "Reap, for the earth is ripe and fat."

14:9 Then the messiah swung his sickle and harvested the people of earth, placing them within the winepress of God.

14:10 And the angels stomped upon the bodies, until blood poured from the winepress and covered the earth in God's wine.

14:11 When I drank of the wine, it was both salty and sweet, and caused me to be happily drunk with the spirit of the lord.

15:1 Within the heavens I saw the signs great and marvelous; seven angels each carrying the seven last plagues, which were the wrath of God.

15:2 And they sang unto the lord, praising his name, shouting, "Blessed are he who keeps the plagues; blessed are they who rules all.

15:4 Who shall not fear the lord God, nor glorify his name. In all those of creation, none shall deny God his holy worship."

15:4 And the seven angels flew from the heavens, carrying with them the plagues of God.

15:5 Then the temple of the lord was filled with a thick smoke, so that none could enter the gates until the seven plagues be fulfilled.

16:1 Then I heard the voice of God from the temple, which said, "Go forth and pour your vials upon the earth."

16:2 And the first angel went and poured his vial upon the earth: and there came a horrible plague upon all men, so that each man was covered in sores oozing with pus and disgust.

16:3 They scratched and wailed and sought forth the blasphemy of physicians to give them comfort from the plagues; but there was none.

16:4 The second angel poured out the vial unto the sea: and the waters became the wretched blood from the loins of women, which called the beasts to die and the air to reek of the filthiness of harlots.

16:5 The third angel poured out his vial upon the rivers and fountains, so that the waters become as bitter as ash.

16:6 And the angel of waters said, "You are just to give the people venom and blood to drink, they who shed the blood of prophets."

16:7 And all the people of heavens said, "God is just and pure; let us all never question the will of God."

16:8 Even the altar of God praised the name of the lord and sang psalms in his glory.

16:9 The fourth angel poured his vial upon the sun, so that great pillars of heat came down upon the earth, scorching men with fire and plagues.

16:10 As the lord poured his wrath upon the earth, still the people did not repent nor worshipped him and loved him.

16:11 This confused God and made him very angry.

16:12 The sixth angel poured his vial upon the river Euphrates, so that it dries up and make way for the kings of the east who come.

16:13 Then I saw three toads come forth from the mouth of the dragon, the mouth of the beast and the mouth of the false prophet.

16:14 They were the spirits of devils, which spewed forth words of science to explain the wrath of God and give comfort to those who were sore and afflicted.

16:15 The seventh angel poured his veil into the air; and a mighty voice came from the temple, saying, "About fucking time."

16:16 There came voices, lightnings, fires and earthquakes so great that none of the earth before saw anything so mighty.

16:17 The lands were divided into three parts and all the cities of all nations fell for their defiance against God.

16:18 Every island sank in the waters and the mountains hid beneath the earth in fear.

16:19 Great stones fell from the heavens, each weighing a talent: and still the men of earth spoke out against God and hated him.

17:1 There came to me one of the seven angels, who said, "Follow me and I shall show you the judgment of she the whore of many nations.

17:2 She who spread forth her loins upon the kings and generals and drank the seed of men."

17:3 Thus he carried me away to the wilderness, where I saw the great whore ride the dragon of seven heads and ten horns.

17:4 She wore the sheer robes of the harlot and drank of the golden cup the blood of saints and prophets.

17:5 Upon her head was written the name MYSTER, HARLOT AND MOTHER OF WHORES, THE FIRST WOMAN, LILLITH.

17:6 When no person nor creature was looking, I fucked her for the price of a bottle of wine.

17:7 And the angel said, "I shall tell you the mystery of this harlot, the mother of abomination.

17:8 The beast she rides upon are the nations of earth, who shall rise, fail and rise again in one union.

17:9 The seven heads are seven mountains and the ten horns kings who have yet to receive their throne.

17:10 Of one mind and one power they shall be, in union with the beast.

17:11 These shall make war with the lamb, who wishes to destroy the Jews of the synagogue of Satan in showers of venom.

17:12 The lamb shall triumph, for he is the king of kings and lord of lords.

17:13 Then shall the beast grow angry and cause his wrath to flow upon the mighty harlot.

17:14 They shall eat her flesh, burn her with fire and rape her with blades; such is the will of God, who controls even the beast against him."

18:1 After these great things I saw another angel come down from the heavens, blessed with great power.

18:2 He cried with a strong voice, "Babylon the great has fallen and becomes the dwelling place for devils, of foul spirits, of hateful birds.

18:3 He was the first of all nations to drink of the fornication of the mighty whore, which all kings and merchants drunk the lust of her fornication, her wealth, her luxuries."

18:4 And I heard another voice from the heavens saying, "Such is the mighty whore that her sins have come up to the heavens and caused the lord God to sleep in her own bed.

18:5 Let her iniquities be paid back double for her flesh; that she lived in luxury shall now live in pestilence, so that in one day she shall know death, mourning and famine."

18:6 And the kings of the earth who partook of her comforts will wail for her and the merchants will mourn for her deeply.

18:7 They will weep and burn oil and incense in her name, saying, "Blessed is she who gave us the comfort and enjoyment of life; cursed be the one who stole her."

18:8 The men of the cities will lament in the streets, wearing sackcloth and pouring ashes over their heads.

18:9 The wives of these men will divorce them.

18:10 Then will the blood of the prophet's flow through the chalices, as every lustful man drink in toast of Lilith.

19:1 After these things I saw in the heavens a great multitude, saying, "Hallelujah, salvation and glory to God, the lord and master.

19:2 His judgment and righteousness has banished the earth of the great whore of luxury, which did corrupt the spirit of men with her fornications; he has avenged the blood of his servants.

19:3 The four and twenty elders and the four beasts fell on their face, rejoicing, "Hallelujah, hallelujah."

19:4 Even the very throne of God said to him, "Praise the lord your God, all you his servants who fear and obey him."

19:5 I fell upon my face and kissed the feet of God, saying, "Blessed is he who is the creator of all things; blessed be the omnipotent."

19:6 And the lord said unto me, "Arise and write that which you have seen and that which you shall see, so that all the world know fear."

19:7 Then the heavens opened and there came out a white horse, carrying upon him Jesus Christ, the son of God, who rode to make war.

19:8 His eyes were of the greatest flame and on his head were many crowns, which hid his true name.

19:9 He was clothed in the robes of the blood of men and upon his thigh was carved THE WORD OF GOD.

19:10 The armies of heaven followed behind him, riding the dragons and unicorns of God.

19:11 Out of the mouth of Christ came forth the mighty sword, so that he smites the nations and rule them all: and his feet were stained with the blood from the winepress of his holy father.

19:12 Then an angel that stood within the sun called forth and said, "Come you fouls of the air; grow fat upon the supper which your creator prepares for you.

19:13 Feast on the blood of kings, generals, horses and mighty men, young, poor, freed men and slave"

19:14 And I saw the beast and the armies of earth with him, gathered together to defend themselves against the lord Christ almighty.

19:15 They stood no chance. They were slaughtered.

19:16 The beast and the false prophet were snared in the nets of God, who threw them into the lake of fire, to be eternally burned by the fire and brimstone.

19:17 And the remnants of the earth were slaughtered and eaten by the fowls of the air, who grew fat on the flesh and drunk on the blood, so that they could not lift themselves.

20:1 I saw an angel of the lord come down from the heavens, carrying with him the key to the abyss and the mighty chain.

20:2 They laid hold of the dragon, the serpent, the devil and Satan and bound him in the abyss one thousand years.

20:3 For one thousand years shall he rot in the abyss, never to bother another until the day of his release.

20:4 When the thousand years have expired, Satan shall break loose his bindings and tear forth the seal to the abyss.

20:5 He shall go out and deceive the four nations of the earth, who will be tricked by his logic that speaks against God.

20:6 They will make war against God and march against the holy city, where the angels will meet them with fire.

20:7 Those of God and Christ will ravage them, rape them and beat them for all eternity; they will be dragged up from hell so that they satisfy the angry lust of angels.

20:8 The devil himself will be thrown within the beast and the false prophet, forever drowning in the lake of fire.

20:9 Then will the dead rise from the earth and come towards the lord, to be judged according to God and Christ.

20:10 They will all be found guilty and thrown into the fires of hell, to suffer eternal the wrath of the God they worshipped.

21:1 Then I saw a new heaven and a new earth and the seas were cast away into the abyss.

21:2 I John saw the blessed city, the new Jerusalem, descending down from the heavens by the hand of God.

21:3 And I heard the multitudes saying, "Behold the city of Zion, the salvation and the glory. Blessed are they who dwell within the tabernacle."

21:4 And the city was placed above the pits of hell, protected forever from the wrathful creation of God.

21:5 Of those who dwell within, they shall mock the sinners and unrighteous who were denied salvation by the hand of God, whose names were forever written in the book of damnation.

21:6 None shall mourn nor know sadness in Zion; of those who shed even a single tear, they will be forever damned and join the wicked which suffer eternal in hell.

21:7 Of those below, they shall gaze upon Zion and be forever spiteful and their hearts shall fill with envy and hate.

21:8 As they suffer, they will be forever reminded of the paradise that was denied to them; a paradise falsely offered by the words of God.

22:1 As I awoke upon the isle of Patmos, the lord Christ stood before me and spoke to me that which I needed to write.

22:2 He said, "I am the Alpha and Omega, the beginning and the end.

22:3 The time comes soon where all the earth will erupt in flames, the people will suffer and those hated by God will be pressed by the wrath of my father.

22:4 Of he who denies themselves the ten commandments, let them suffer in the pits of damnation.

22:5 The whoremongerers, the fornicators the adulterers, the homosexuals, let them die eternal as victims of their own lust.

22:6 I am the bright and morning star, who remains pure from the filthiness of mankind; let them be cleansed in flame eternal.

22:7 Go forth and preach that which you have seen; write what you witnessed in the book, so that the people prepare for the fear and the cruelties of holy father and son.

22:8 Surely I come quickly, so that the many today now my wrath and hatred."

23:1 All this, because a long, long time ago, two people ate a piece of fruit.

SELECTED NON-FICTION 8TH HOUSE TITLES

The English Qabalah 2nd. Edition, Complete VOLUME

A learned exposition by one of the world's leading Qabalists, this book takes the reader through an exploratory journey through the English Alphabet and the mystic and even subconscious roots of our development of language throughout history.

440 pages | 6 x 9 | Hardcover | ISBN 978-1-926716-27-5

SEVEN SYRIANS - War Accounts from Syrian Refugees by Diego Cupolo

"Seven Syrians" captures the stories and struggles of those caught in the middle of the armed conflict currently ravaging Syria. Framed by Diego Cupolo's unerring eye while touring the region, these photographs and first-hand accounts remind us that it is civilians who suffer the brunt of war's atrocities. In a series of humanizing portraits, Diego Cupolo takes us into the lives of those fortunate enough to have survived the conflict decimating their homeland. Forced to flee their homes and families, these men, women and children, teachers, plumbers, engineers, taxi drivers, brothers and sisters no different than ourselves and our neighbours, tell us in their own words of their struggles, triumphs, pains and fortitude and of the monstrosity of war when all of us the world over, seek the same security and opportunities for our children. Read and listen.

8 x 8. 86 pages, ISBN 978-1-926716-26-8. $18.88

THE MIDAS TOUCH by James Cummins & Cameron W. Reed

". . . a journey into the predatory nature of some of the practices and institutions in the financial industry today . . . ."

Authors James Cummins and Cameron W. Reed take us on an exploratory journey into the predatory nature of some of the practices and institutions in the financial industry today. What seems innocently enough as capitalism and greed gone naturally wild in an environment of deregulation, soon appears as deliberate political manoeuvering and close control on an international scale by agents and institutions operating above the law.

5 x 8 . 230 pages. ISBN 978-1-926716-06-0 $23.88

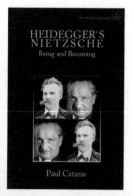

HEIDEGGER'S NIETZSCHE: Being and Becoming by Paul Catanu

Hammering, bombastic, poetic, mystic Nietzsche as seen through the mind of the great ontologist Heidegger. Nietzsche's thought dissected, critiqued, delimited, explored by the author of "Being and Time" one of the most influential modern philosophers of our day, is explored in this insightful new volume, containing never before translated passages from the Nietzschean Nachlass.

414 pages. ISBN 978-1-926716-02-2. $38.88

MCGILL LAW JOURNAL - 60 YEARS OF PEOPLE, PROSE AND PUBLICATION

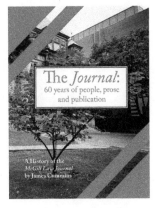

"...a breathtaking picture of a history that was beginning to slowly fade into the past, strengthening the identity of a key part of Canadian society."

276 pages, Hardcase | ISBN 978-1-926716-25-1| $39.99

The McGill Law Journal is the premiere legal periodical in the history of Canadian scholarship. Since its founding in 1952 by Jacques-Yvan Morin (future leader of the Official Opposition in the National Assembly of Quebec) the Journal has been at the forefront of legal history. It was the first university-based law journal in Canada to be cited by the Supreme Court, and has since been outpaced by no other university journal in the frequency at which the Court has turned to it. And it has always has been run solely by students.

MICROECONOMICS - GradeBooster Series by Elijah M. James

The Grade Booster Series (GBS)—Microeconomics is designed to help college students improve their grades in Microeconomics. Through the Grade Booster Series you will better understand the principles and concepts discussed in your textbook; and be able to apply them in varying scenarios and learn how to answer economic questions.

312 pages | 8.5 x 11 | ISBN 978-1-926716-44-2 | $34.99

MACROECONOMICS - GradeBooster Series by Elijah M. James

The Grade Booster Series (GBS)—Macroeconomics is designed to help college students improve their grades in Microeconomics. Through the Grade Booster Series you will better understand the principles and concepts discussed in your textbook; and be able to apply them in varying scenarios and learn how to answer economic questions.

246 pages | 8.5 x 11 | ISBN 978-1-926716-45-9 | $34.99

TO RUSSIA WITH LOVE by Damian Siqueiros

To Russia with Love" is how a group of Montreal artists and collaborators answer the phobias arising out of Russia. This is their stand against the recent wave of bigotry and violence and the realization of the moral imperative to not remain passive in the face of hatred and injustice.

"...exquisitely detailed...." - Phil Tarney, Artists Corner Gallery, Hollywood, California

"Masterful visual quotations.." - Ivan Savvine, Russian Journalist & Activist

CPSIA information can be obtained
at www.ICGtesting.com
Printed in the USA
FSHW02n1222060618
48977FS